The Norton Reader

EIGHTH EDITION

W. W. NORTON & COMPANY, INC.
also publishes

THE NORTON ANTHOLOGY OF AMERICAN LITERATURE
edited by Nina Baym et al.

THE NORTON ANTHOLOGY OF CONTEMPORARY FICTION
edited by R. V. Cassill

THE NORTON ANTHOLOGY OF ENGLISH LITERATURE
edited by M. H. Abrams et al.

THE NORTON ANTHOLOGY OF LITERATURE BY WOMEN
edited by Sandra M. Gilbert and Susan Gubar

THE NORTON ANTHOLOGY OF MODERN POETRY
edited by Richard Ellmann and Robert O'Clair

THE NORTON ANTHOLOGY OF POETRY
edited by Arthur M. Eastman et al.

THE NORTON ANTHOLOGY OF SHORT FICTION
edited by R. V. Cassill

THE NORTON ANTHOLOGY OF WORLD MASTERPIECES
edited by Maynard Mack et al.

THE NORTON FACSIMILE OF
THE FIRST FOLIO OF SHAKESPEARE
prepared by Charlton Hinman

THE NORTON INTRODUCTION TO LITERATURE
edited by Carl E. Bain, Jerome Beaty, and J. Paul Hunter

and the

NORTON CRITICAL EDITIONS

The Norton Reader

An Anthology of Expository Prose

EIGHTH EDITION

Arthur M. Eastman, General Editor
VIRGINIA POLYTECHNIC INSTITUTE AND STATE UNIVERSITY

Caesar R. Blake
UNIVERSITY OF TORONTO

Hubert M. English, Jr.
UNIVERSITY OF MICHIGAN

Joan E. Hartman
COLLEGE OF STATEN ISLAND,
CITY UNIVERSITY OF NEW YORK

Alan B. Howes
UNIVERSITY OF MICHIGAN

Robert T. Lenaghan
UNIVERSITY OF MICHIGAN

Leo F. McNamara
UNIVERSITY OF MICHIGAN

Linda H. Peterson
YALE UNIVERSITY

James Rosier
UNIVERSITY OF PENNSYLVANIA

W · W · NORTON & COMPANY · *New York* · *London*

The text of this book is composed in Electra.
Composition by Com Com.
Manufacturing by R. R. Donnelley.
Book design by Antonina Krass.

Library of Congress Cataloging-in-Publication Data

The Norton reader: an anthology of expository prose / Arthur M.
   Eastman, general editor : [contributers] Caesar R. Blake . . . [et
   al.].—8th ed.
      p.   cm.
   Includes bibliographical references and index.
   1. College readers. I. Eastman, Arthur M. 1918–   . II. Blake,
   Caesar R. (Caesar Robert), 1925–
   PE1122.N68   1992   91-40367
   808.88′8   dc20

ISBN 0-393-96194-X

W. W. Norton & Company, Inc., 500 Fifth Avenue, New York, N.Y. 10110
W. W. Norton & Company, Ltd., 10 Coptic Street, London WC1A 1PU

2 3 4 5 6 7 8 9 0

Contents

PEOPLE, PLACES

HUMAN NATURE

EDUCATION

LANGUAGE AND COMMUNICATION

AN ALBUM OF STYLES

SIGNS OF THE TIMES

NATURE AND THE ENVIRONMENT

ETHICS

PROSE FORMS: APOTHEGMS

HISTORY

POLITICS AND GOVERNMENT

SCIENCE

LITERATURE AND THE ARTS

PROSE FORMS: PARABLES

PHILOSOPHY AND RELIGION

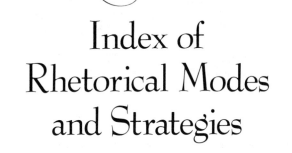

Index of
Rhetorical Modes
and Strategies

RHETORICAL MODES

DESCRIPTION

EXPOSITION

RHETORICAL STRATEGIES

TITLE, AND OPENING AND CLOSING PARAGRAPHS

Preface

Since much of what usually appears in our Preface has moved in this eighth edition to the section entitled "To Students: Reading and Writing with *The Norton Reader*," these few pages will deal primarily with matters of history.

In the early sixties the seven original editors, all at the University of Michigan, all male (for such the English Department then predominantly was), almost all members of the Freshman English Committee, became dissatisfied with the crop of new readers available and thought that they might put together an improvement. (This is not to say that there had not earlier been excellent readers—by Keast, for example, or Locke, Gibson, and Arms, or Thompson, or Martin and Ohmann.)

Basically, they agreed, they would include works from the past as well as the present, foreign as well as native, long as well as short, light as well as serious, and in addition, those kinds of literature—journals, letters, characters, apothegms, parables—that are first cousins, in the family of the expository, to the essay and the article. They lacked, however, any scheme or program, any set of thematic or rhetorical headings by which to guide their selections. Excellence would be their pillar of smoke by day, of fire by night.

If that sounds presumptuous, as the editors soon discovered, it was, for about excellence, as Lord Chesterfield remarked to his wayward son (who tended to say "one man's meat is another man's poison") "tastes differ." The method of selection the editors agreed on was for each to make a certain number of nominations (say ten), to have these reviewed by a second editor, then by a third. More times than not, however, one or both of the reviewing editors disagreed with the nominator. Further, after the initial batch of nominations, each editor had to offer a second batch, this time to be reviewed by two editors who had had nothing to do with that editor's earlier submissions. The point, of course, was to avoid "sweetheart" arrangements—X approving Y's choices if Y approved X's. The result of this process, which has continued through all subsequent editions, was three files. The first contained nominations that had received the approval of both reviewers; the second those that both reviewers had rejected; and the third, those on which the reviewers had divided or about which both had registered uncertainty. The nominations that had achieved full approval were "in." Those with double-negative reviews were "out." Those in-between were reviewed by the General Editor, checked against approved essays to avoid substantial duplications, checked against the needs of the thematic groups that seemed to be forming, and then taken in or thrown out.

With each new edition voices from the field influenced editorial judgment. As Doctor Johnson said, "that book is good in vain that is not read," and when Freshman English instructors reported that they had not read or certainly had not assigned certain pieces, those pieces joined the formerly rejected. Further, voices from the field, from the first edition to this, have made valuable suggestions for additional selections, as have the good people at Norton, all of which have received careful consideration and many of which have been gratefully accepted.

So much for history. What is new in this edition? Briefly, the contributions of a new editor, Linda H. Peterson, director of Yale's Bass Writing Program; Joan Hartman's opening essay, "To Students: Reading and Writing with *The Norton Reader,*" which is lean and clear in style and eminently sane; a timely new section, "Nature and the Environment" including essays by such gifted writers as Aldo Leopold, Gretel Ehrlich, and Edward Abbey; a yet fuller selection of women, minority, and Canadian voices; a broader offering of multiple selections by the same authors; and, belatedly but usefully, new opening source notes putting individual essays in a context expanded upon in the appendix of author biographies.

For many contributions and much support we thank our users, and these especially: Maureen G. Andrews, Northern Michigan University; Andrew J. Angyal, Elon College; Joan Baum, City University of New York-York College; Samuel I. Bellman, California State Polytechnic University-Pomona; Gail Berkeley, Reed College; Louise C. Berry, University of Tennessee; Blair F. Bigelow, Suffolk University; Edwin Block, Marquette University; W. Dale Brown, Calvin College; Ingrid Brunner, Lehigh County Community College; Donna M. Campbell, State University of New York at Buffalo; Roger D. Carlstrom, Yukima Valley Community College; S. L. Chalghian, Macomb Community College; Paul Cohen, Southwest Texas State University; Marianne Cooley, University of Houston; Fred D. Crawford, Central Michigan University; E. T. A. Davidson, State University of New York at Oneonta; Naomi Diamond, Ryerson Polytechnic Institute; Louise Dibble, Suffolk Community College; Wilfred O. Dietrich, Blinn College; Mary Alice Dillman, Ohio Wesleyan University; Ann Elsdon, Dawson College; Kristina Faber, Shippensburg University of Pennsylvania; Susan Fellows, Palo-

mar Community College; Frank Fennell, Loyola University; James Fe-
tler, Foothill College; Terry Fleenor, Bakersfield College; Carol Franks,
Portland State University; Peggy L. Garrett, Kutatown University; Paula
Gillespie, Marquette University; Marshall Gilliland, University of Sas-
katchewan; Elizabeth Goodenough, Claremont McKenna College;
Katherine Gotteschalk, Cornell University; John K. Hanes, Duquesne
University; Richard E. Hansen, Mary Washington College; Joan C.
Haug, Sacramento City College; Eugene Hill, Mount Holyoke College;
Charles Hofmiller, University of Bridgeport; Patricia J. Howard, Baylor
University; Frank Hubbard, Marquette University; Kenneth Johnson,
Florida International University; Wendy L. Johnston, De Anza College;
Susan King, Biola University; Joyce Kinkead, Utah State University;
Neil Kortenaar, University of Toronto-Erindale College; Frank E.
LaRosa, San Diego City College; Lorraine Levin, Long Beach City
College-Pacific Coast Campus; Leo Manglaviti, Marywood College;
Margaret Masson, Calvin College; Charlotte C. Morse, Virginia Com-
monwealth University; Gary Nagy, Long Beach City College; Lee Nich-
olson, Modesto Junior College; Avise Nissen, George Washington Uni-
versity; Frank Novak, Pepperdine University; Eric Nye, University of
Wyoming; Robert M. O'Neil, California State University-Fresno; Scott
Orme, Spokane Community College; Celia Orona, San Diego Mesa
College; Linda Palmer, California State University-Sacramento; Sheri L.
Phillabaum, St. Leo College; Albert J. Rivers, Marquette University;
Stephen Robitaille, Santa Fe Community College; G. Arthur Ross,
Fraser Valley College; Abba Rubin, Vanderbilt University; Richard H.
Rupp, Appalachian State University; Dennis Rygiel, Auburn University;
Robert A. Schmegler, University of Rhode Island; Ronald A. Sharp,
Kenyon College; M.P.A. Sheaffer, Millersville University of Pennsyl-
vania; William K. Siebenschuh, Case Western Reserve University;
Joyce Smoot, Virginia Polytechnic Institute and State University; Sam
Solecki, University of Toronto; Bill M. Stiffler, Harford Community
College; Joe Taylor, St. Leo College; Susan D. Tilka, Southwest Texas
State University; George Y. Trail, University of Houston; John R. Va-
lone, Sacramento City College; Rhonda Wauhkonen, University of
Ottowa; Elizabeth Winston, University of Tampa; Ronald Zollweg,
Mohawk Valley Community College

—Arthur M. Eastman

To Students: Reading and Writing with *The Norton Reader*

This is the eighth edition of *The Norton Reader;* its first edition goes back to 1965. The editors have put together a selection of essays on a range of subjects, some familiar, others more specialized. You'll find the first kind in sections like "Personal Report," "People, Places," and "Signs of the Times," the second in sections like "Science," "Literature and the Arts," and "Philosophy and Religion." Some of these sections go back to the first edition: "Personal Report" opened the first as it still does the eighth. Others have come and gone: in this edition, for example, we've dropped a section called "Mind"—transferring some of its essays to "Human Nature"—and added a section called "Nature and the Environment." Some essays have appeared in all eight editions of *The Norton Reader*: E. B. White's "Once More to the Lake," for example, and Jonathan Swift's "A Modest Proposal." Others—about one-third—are new to this edition. You'll find some of the essays long, some short; some formal, some informal; some calculatedly challenging, some simpler.

The editors—now nine of us—search widely in order to include a range of material and a range of authors. Although most of the essays are contemporary, some are older; although most of them are written in English, a few are translated from other languages. You'll hear in them male and female voices; American, British, and Canadian voices; African-American, Asian-American, American Indian, and Spanish-American voices. What the essays have in common is excellence: at least three editors, without actually defining good writing to ourselves or for each other, have agreed on the inclusion of each essay. We find their subjects important, timely, timeless, engaging. We find their authors, sometimes well known, sometimes less well known, speaking with authority and, often, seeing with a distinctive angle of vision. We find their writing convincing and clear, their style lean when elaboration is not required and adequate to complexity. The essays are not invariably simple to read: they originally appeared in publications read by informed and educated general readers.

The editors have provided a large number of essays, more than any instructor will assign during a semester: this time the regular edition contains 207; the shorter, 121. The organization, by kinds of writing and kinds of subjects, is loose. We know that there are many kinds of college writing courses; we know that instructors link reading and writing in a variety of ways. Our aim in *The Norton Reader* is to accommodate all or most of them. In consequence, we limit our editorial presence. You'll find, after some but not all of the essays, questions addressed to you as readers and others addressed to you as writers. We intend them to focus your reading of the essays: questions addressed to readers ask about the essays' content, meaning, and argument; questions addressed to writers ask about their authors' strategies—how they present their content and how they make their meanings clear. In the questions addressed to you as writers there's also at least one follow-up writing assignment—out of the many assignments that are possible. We leave it to your instructors to direct you through the essays, to decide which ones to assign and how to use them.

READING

We hope that, in addition to following your instructors' assignments, you'll also follow your own interests. But we don't count on it. Putting essays in a textbook, even one called a "reader," makes reading them seem artificial. They were written for and read by readers who read them naturally: because they wanted to know—or know more—about their subjects, because they knew—or knew of—their authors, or because the essays, appearing in publications they ordinarily read, tempted them to launch into unfamiliar subjects written about by authors they had never heard of. Outside the classroom, readers bring their own interests and motives to reading; inside the classroom, you are left to generate your own in response to assignments.

As editors, we've tried to make available some of the choices available to the original readers of these essays. Information about them appears in two places. A footnote at the beginning of each essay tells when and where it first appeared and, if it began as a talk, when and where it was delivered and to whom. Maya Angelou's "Graduation," for example, is a chapter from her autobiography, *I Know Why the Caged Bird Sings*, published in 1969; Scott Russell Sanders' "Looking at Women" was published in a journal called the *Georgia Review* in 1989; Francis Bacon's "Of Revenge" was published in a collection of his essays called, simply, *Essays*, in 1625; Chief Seattle's "Address" (which is translated), was delivered in response to a treaty offered to his people in 1854; Frances FitzGerald's "Rewriting American History" comes from her *America Revised*, published in *The New Yorker* and then as a book in 1979. We don't, however, explain the differences between the *Georgia Review* and *The New Yorker*; the first, a noncommercial journal published three times a year by the University of Georgia, has fewer and presumably more select and self-selected readers than *The New Yorker*, a commercial magazine published weekly. If more information about context helps situate you in relation to what you are reading, ask your instructors. As editors, we could swamp a smaller number of essays with additional information about their contexts, but we prefer to include more essays and keep contextual information spare.

A section called "Authors" at the end of *The Norton Reader* provides biographical and bibliographical information about the authors whose essays we include. Outside the classroom, we may know something about the authors we read before we read them or we may encounter them as unknowns. We may choose to let them speak for themselves, to see what we can discover about them as they do. Sometimes knowing who they are and where their voices come from helps us to hear them and to grasp what they say—and sometimes it doesn't. Putting biographical information at the end provides, in a textbook, something like the choices ordinary readers have as to how much knowledge about authors to bring to their reading.

An index listing essays by title and by author also appears at the end of *The Norton Reader*. It's of course useful for locating essays; it's also useful for identifying multiple essays by the same author. This edition includes multiple selections by eighteen authors, among them, for example, Joan Didion, Gretel Ehrlich, Stephen Jay Gould, and George Orwell. When you enjoy your encounter with particular authors, it's worth looking in the index to see if we've included additional essays by them; following an author provides motives for reading such as ordinary readers have.

In addition to information about contexts and authors, we also provide, in footnotes, explanations of material in the essays themselves. Our rules for annotation go something like this: (1) *Don't* define words, except foreign words, that appear in desk dictionaries. You can go to yours or, often more sensibly, guess from context. If an unfamiliar word is central to the meaning of an essay, the author is likely to define it.

(2) *Do* provide information about people, places, works, theories, and unfamiliar things. For example, for Maya Angelou's "Graduation," we explain Gabriel Prosser, Nat Turner, and Harriet Tubman (but not Abraham Lincoln and Christopher Columbus); Stamps (it's not immediately clear that it's an Arkansas town); and the poem "Invictus." For Frances FitzGerald's "Rewriting American History," we explain socialist realism and American nuclear bomb tests in the Pacific. We don't always agree among ourselves on what needs annotation or how much information constitutes an explanation. (In this we're not unique: all annotators make assumptions about the information readers they don't fully know bring to their reading.) Our experience in the classroom helps us estimate the annotation you need. But you can be sure that we'll fail in some places and affront you in others by explaining what you find obvious. When we fail, ask your instructors for help; when we affront you, take our efforts as well intentioned. Again, rather than swamping a smaller number of essays with annotation, we keep it spare.

Our last rule for notes is the trickiest. (3) Explain, don't interpret—that is, provide information but leave readers to decide how authors frame and engage the material we explain and how it contributes to their meanings. Francis Bacon's "Of Revenge," for example, ends: "Public revenges are for the most part fortunate; as that for the death of Caesar; for the death of Pertinax; for the death of Henry the third of France; and many more. But in private revenges it is not so. Nay rather, vindictive persons live the life of witches; who as they are mischievous, so end they infortunate." We explain Pertinax and Henry III (but not Caesar). You sensibly could guess, without annotation, that all three were, first, public persons and, second, assassinated. We give dates—Pertinax assassinated in 193, Henry III in 1589—but leave you to consider what Bacon's illustrations, ranging over time, contribute to his meaning. We also leave you to work out what made these revenges "for the most part fortunate," because Bacon himself, with his terse, elliptical style, demands that you do. He contrasts these public revenges with private revenges that are "not so," that is, not for the most part fortunate, and then points out the consequences for the assassins themselves, who end unfortunately. To work out the meanings engaged by Bacon's illustrations is to interpret rather than to explain. Working out meanings is the work of readers and, in the classroom, of communities of readers and instructors.

Finally, of course, we include the authors' own notes, distinguishing theirs from ours by adding their names in square brackets. In general, authors' notes are infrequent: extensive notes indicate academic writers addressing other academics within their disciplines rather than nonacademic writers addressing general readers. This edition of *The Norton Reader* includes a report published in a scientific journal, "Handgun

Regulations, Crime, Assaults, and Homicide: A Tale of Two Cities," from the *New England Journal of Medicine,* which has extensive notes. Scientific reports accessible to general readers are not easy to find. This one stands in useful contrast to the essays by Stephen Jay Gould that we also include: he's a scientist who writes for general readers, who popularizes science. Among the differences between the handgun report and Gould's essays is the presence (or the absence) of authors' notes.

Assignments in *The Norton Reader* will motivate you to "read" but won't make you readers, that is, persons who bring to what they read their own interests and who are ready to engage in the activity of making meaning out of words encountered on a page. Reading is a solitary enterprise and making meaning somewhat mysterious. Watch yourself as you do it. Try to notice what happens when you succeed and when you fail, for failure is as instructive as success. Ordinarily you are the sole judge of both. Short-answer tests elicit only your superficial comprehension. Writing about what you read, in essay examinations or papers, tests your comprehension of large structures. But sentence to sentence, paragraph to paragraph, your comprehension is manifest only to you. Mark up your texts as a record: where do you deal confidently with meaning and where tentatively and where do you drift away, either willfully or inadvertently? And what can you learn about yourselves as readers through this kind of marking?

Because assigned reading is shared reading, class discussion can move the making of meaning from a solitary to a social enterprise. The classroom provides a community of readers and opportunities to demystify reading. What interests and motives do we, students and instructors alike, bring to texts? What strategies do we employ when we read? Are there other, more useful ones? What meanings are common to us, what meanings individual? What is responsive and responsible reading? When do individual meanings become irresponsible, and how do we decide? These are questions that concern writers as well as readers: making meaning by writing is the flip side of making it by reading. In neither enterprise is meaning passed from hand to hand like nickels, dimes, and quarters.

WRITING

Making meaning by writing is less mysterious than making it by reading. Most instructors of writing, however they choose to link reading and writing, emphasize what's called process. Process refers to working in stages on multiple drafts; product refers to final drafts. Multiple drafts provide evidence for what we do and how we do it. Student writers seldom have time to proceed through as many drafts as do professional writers and experienced writers. But learning to distribute the time you have over several drafts rather than one will turn out to be the most efficient use of it.

Experienced writers know they can't do everything at once: assemble material, assess its usefulness, disperse it in sections, paragraphs, and sentences, and write it out in well-formed sentences. Student writers, however, often expect to produce a finished single draft. If that's what you expect of yourself, then a writing course is a good place to change your expectations and cultivate more sensible and profitable practices. When you try to produce a finished single draft, you are likely to thin out your evidence and disperse it in simple ways; lock yourself into structures you can't change even if, in the course of writing, you discover new meanings; and write lumpy sentences that need to be reformed. In addition, single-draft writing, when you're aiming for something reasonably thoughtful and deserving of a respectable grade, is harder than multiple-draft writing and no quicker.

The process experienced writers go through when they write is something like this. They start with freewriting, brainstorming, listing, or whatever other heuristic devices—that is, means of discovering what to write—that they have learned work for them. They try out what they have to say in rough drafts. As they shape their material they find what it means and what they want it to mean; as they find what it means and what they want it to mean they figure out how to shape it—shape and meaning are reciprocal. Large and small are also reciprocal: they work back and forth among complete drafts and smaller units—sections and paragraphs in longer drafts, paragraphs in shorter. As shape and meaning come together, they refine still smaller units, that is, sentences, phrases, and even words.

Then, when they have a draft that in some sense satisfies them, they turn themselves around. Having written for themselves and made their own meaning, they attend to writing for others, to transmitting what they mean. They try to distance themselves from themselves and from their draft by putting it aside for a time, if they can, and by imagining themselves as readers other than themselves bringing to what they've written other interests, other motives. Writing for oneself takes commitment: we have to turn off the censor that inhibits our writing and embarrasses us with what we have written. Writing for others takes skepticism: we have to turn the censor back on—or find a reader or readers who will dramatize for us the experience of making meaning from our draft and help us to see how we have been understood and misunderstood.

This is the rough sequence of tasks experienced writers perform in overlapping stages. They revise at all stages and their revisions are substantial. What inexperienced writers call revision—tinkering with surface features by rewording, pruning, and correcting—they call editing and proofreading. These tasks they do at the end, when they are ready to stop revising and prepare what they call a final draft; if larger elements of a draft need repair, it's too soon to work on smaller elements.

To distance yourself from your own drafts or to respond to someone else's, individually and in groups, think about a hierarchy of questions.

1. When you write in response to an assignment, ask, "Did I do what I was told to do?" When you write on a subject you choose yourself, ask, "Did I do what I promised to do in the introduction?" In the second instance, you can revise your introduction to make a promise you keep: experienced writers expect to revise their introductions radically as their drafts take shape. In the first instance, you'll have to decide whether or not what you have written is a reasonable substitute for the assignment and, if it is, how to introduce it honestly.

2. Then ask, "Is the material I have included appropriate? Have I included enough, and have I interpreted it fairly and adequately?" Appropriateness is more or less straightforward. Inclusiveness is problematic. Ordinarily, experienced writers are more inclusive than student writers. You may find the essays in *The Norton Reader* dense and overspecific; your instructors, on the other hand, may find your essays skimpy and underspecific. Experienced writers thicken their writing with particulars to transmit their meanings and engage readers' recognition, understanding, and imagination. Because they are more in control of their writing than student writers, they are able to be more inclusive, to sustain multiple examples and illustrations.

Responsible writers want to interpret material fairly; slanted interpretation is the stock-in-trade of advertisers and hucksters. Interpreting material fairly means maintaining its emphases and distorting its inflections as little as possible. In general, experienced writers interpret adequately and student writers underinterpret. One way of assessing adequacy is looking at quotations. How many are there? (Experienced writers ordinarily use fewer than student writers.) How necessary are they? (Experienced writers paraphrase more than they quote.) How well are they integrated? (Experienced writers introduce quotations by explaining who is speaking, where the voice is coming from, and what to listen for; they finish off quotations by linking them to what follows.)

3. Then ask, "Is the material well deployed?" Writing involves putting readers in possession of interrelated material in a temporal order: readers read from start to finish. Sometimes material explained near the end might better be explained near the beginning; sometimes material explained near the beginning might better be postponed. When paragraphs follow each other, transitional words like *therefore* may not be necessary; when they don't, missing connections can't be supplied by *therefore*.

4. Then ask, "At the sentence level, which sentences unfold unprob-
lematically and which sentences make readers stumble?" Readers who
can identify what makes them stumble as they read your writing can
teach you more about well-formed sentences than any set of rules for
forming them.

Writing, unlike reading, is both a solitary and a social enterprise: while
we compose and revise by ourselves, we eventually put our drafts into
circulation. A writing classroom, at best, introduces social dimensions
into the process, as students put less-than-final drafts into circulation and
receive responses to them. It provides a community of readers to read
each other's writing as well as the writing of professional and experienced writers in a text such as *The Norton Reader*. Honing one's skills
as a reader on professional writing is good training: it will help you to
respond to the writing of less-experienced writers, others' writing and
your own.

The Norton Reader

EIGHTH EDITION

Personal Report

Dylan Thomas

MEMORIES OF CHRISTMAS

One Christmas was so much like another, in those years, around the sea-town corner now and out of all sound except the distant speaking of the voices I sometimes hear a moment before sleep, that I can never remember whether it snowed for six days and six nights when I was twelve or whether it snowed for twelve days and twelve nights when I was six; or whether the ice broke and the skating grocer vanished like a snowman through a white trap-door on that same Christmas Day that the mince-pies finished Uncle Arnold and we tobogganed down the seaward hill, all the afternoon, on the best tea-tray, and Mrs. Griffiths complained, and we threw a snowball at her niece, and my hands burned so, with the heat and the cold, when I held them in front of the fire, that I cried for twenty minutes and then had some jelly.

All the Christmases roll down the hill towards the Welsh-speaking sea, like a snowball growing whiter and bigger and rounder, like a cold and headlong moon bundling down the sky that was our street; and they stop at the rim of the ice-edged, fish-freezing waves, and I plunge my hands in the snow and bring out whatever I can find; holly or robins or pudding, squabbles and carols and oranges and tin whistles, and the fire in the front room, and bang go the crackers, and holy, holy, holy, ring the bells, and the glass bells shaking on the tree, and Mother Goose, and Struwelpeter[1]—oh! the baby-burning flames and the clacking scissor-man!—Billy Bunter[2] and Black Beauty, Little Women and boys who

From *Quite Early One Morning* (1954).

1. The title character of *Struwelpeter (Slovenly Peter)*, or *Merry Tales and Funny Pictures*, a children's book originally in German, by Dr. Heinrich Hoffmann, containing gaily grim admonitory narratives in verse about little Pauline, for example, who played with matches and got burned up; or the little boy who sucked his thumbs until the tall scissorman cut them off.
2. The humorous fat boy in Frank Richards' tales of English school life.

have three helpings, Alice and Mrs. Potter's badgers,[3] penknives, teddy-bears—named after a Mr. Theodore Bear, their inventor, or father, who died recently in the United States—mouth-organs, tin-soldiers, and blancmange, and Auntie Bessie playing "Pop Goes the Weasel" and "Nuts in May" and "Oranges and Lemons" on the untuned piano in the parlor all through the thimble-hiding musical-chairing blind-man's-buffing party at the end of the never-to-be-forgotten day at the end of the unremembered year.

In goes my hand into that wool-white bell-tongued ball of holidays resting at the margin of the carol-singing sea, and out come Mrs. Prothero and the firemen.

It was on the afternoon of the day of Christmas Eve, and I was in Mrs. Prothero's garden, waiting for cats, with her son Jim. It was snowing. It was always snowing at Christmas; December, in my memory, is white as Lapland, though there were no reindeers. But there were cats. Patient, cold, and callous, our hands wrapped in socks, we waited to snowball the cats. Sleek and long as jaguars and terrible-whiskered, spitting and snarling they would slink and sidle over the white back-garden walls, and the lynx-eyed hunters, Jim and I, fur-capped and moccasined trappers from Hudson's Bay off Eversley Road, would hurl our deadly snowballs at the green of their eyes. The wise cats never appeared. We were so still, Eskimo-footed arctic marksmen in the muffling silence of the eternal snows—eternal, ever since Wednesday—that we never heard Mrs. Prothero's first cry from her igloo at the bottom of the garden. Or, if we heard it at all, it was, to us, like the far-off challenge of our enemy and prey, the neighbor's Polar Cat. But soon the voice grew louder. "Fire!" cried Mrs. Prothero, and she beat the dinner-gong. And we ran down the garden, with the snowballs in our arms, towards the house, and smoke, indeed, was pouring out of the dining-room, and the gong was bombilating, and Mrs. Prothero was announcing ruin like a town-crier in Pompeii. This was better than all the cats in Wales standing on the wall in a row. We bounded into the house, laden with snowballs, and stopped at the open door of the smoke-filled room. Something was burning all right; perhaps it was Mr. Prothero, who always slept there after midday dinner with a newspaper over his face; but he was standing in the middle of the room, saying "A fine Christmas!" and smacking at the smoke with a slipper.

"Call the fire-brigade," cried Mrs. Prothero as she beat the gong.

"They won't be there," said Mr. Prothero, "it's Christmas."

There was no fire to be seen, only clouds of smoke and Mr. Prothero standing in the middle of them, waving his slipper as though he were conducting.

"Do something," he said.

3. Beatrix Potter, creator of *Peter Rabbit* and other animal tales for children, among them *The Tale of Mr. Tod*, a badger.

And we threw all our snowballs into the smoke—I think we missed Mr. Prothero—and ran out of the house to the telephone-box.

"Let's call the police as well," Jim said.   10

"And the ambulance."

"And Ernie Jenkins, he likes fires."

But we only called the fire-brigade, and soon the fire-engine came and three tall men in helmets brought a hose into the house and Mr. Prothero got out just in time before they turned it on. Nobody could have had a noisier Christmas Eve. And when the firemen turned off the hose and were standing in the wet and smoky room, Jim's aunt, Miss Prothero, came downstairs and peered in at them. Jim and I waited, very quietly, to hear what she would say to them. She said the right thing, always. She looked at the three tall firemen in their shining helmets, standing among the smoke and cinders and dissolving snowballs, and she said: "Would you like something to read?"

Now out of that bright white snowball of Christmas gone comes the stocking, the stocking of stockings, that hung at the foot of the bed with the arm of a golliwog dangling over the top and small bells ringing in the toes. There was a company, gallant and scarlet but never nice to taste though I always tried when very young, of belted and busbied and musketed lead soldiers so soon to lose their heads and legs in the wars on the kitchen table after the tea-things, the mince-pies, and the cakes that I helped to make by stoning the raisins and eating them, had been cleared away; and a bag of moist and many-colored jelly-babies and a folded flag and a false nose and a tram-conductor's cap and a machine that punched tickets and rang a bell; never a catapult; once, by a mistake that no one could explain, a little hatchet; and a rubber buffalo, or it may have been a horse, with a yellow head and haphazard legs; and a celluloid duck that made, when you pressed it, a most unducklike noise, a mewing moo that an ambitious cat might make who wishes to be a cow; and a painting-book in which I could make the grass, the trees, the sea, and the animals any color I pleased: and still the dazzling sky-blue sheep are grazing in the red field under a flight of rainbow-beaked and pea-green birds.

Christmas morning was always over before you could say Jack Frost.   15
And look! suddenly the pudding was burning! Bang the gong and call the fire-brigade and the book-loving firemen! Someone found the silver three-penny-bit with a currant on it; and the someone was always Uncle Arnold. The motto in my cracker read:

> Let's all have fun this Christmas Day,
> Let's play and sing and shout hooray!

and the grown-ups turned their eyes towards the ceiling, and Auntie Bessie, who had already been frightened, twice, by a clockwork mouse, whimpered at the sideboard and had some elderberry wine. And someone put a glass bowl full of nuts on the littered table, and my uncle said, as he said once every year: "I've got a shoe-nut here. Fetch me a shoehorn to open it, boy."

And dinner was ended.

And I remember that on the afternoon of Christmas Day, when the others sat around the fire and told each other that this was nothing, no, nothing, to the great snowbound and turkey-proud yule-log-crackling holly-berry-bedizined and kissing-under-the-mistletoe Christmas when *they* were children, I would go out, school-capped and gloved and mufflered, with my bright new boots squeaking, into the white world on to the seaward hill, to call on Jim and Dan and Jack and to walk with them through the silent snowscape of our town.

We went padding through the streets, leaving huge deep footprints in the snow, on the hidden pavements.

"I bet people'll think there's been hippoes."

"What would you do if you saw a hippo coming down Terrace Road?"

"I'd go like this, bang! I'd throw him over the railings and roll him down the hill and then I'd tickle him under the ear and he'd wag his tail . . ."

"What would you do if you saw *two* hippoes . . .?"

Iron-flanked and bellowing he-hippoes clanked and blundered and battered through the scudding snow towards us as we passed by Mr. Daniel's house.

"Let's post Mr. Daniel a snowball through his letter box."

"Let's write things in the snow."

"Let's write 'Mr. Daniel looks like a spaniel' all over his lawn."

"Look," Jack said, "I'm eating snow-pie."

"What's it taste like?"

"Like snow-pie," Jack said.

Or we walked on the white shore.

"Can the fishes see it's snowing?"

"They think it's the sky falling down."

The silent one-clouded heavens drifted on to the sea.

"All the old dogs have gone."

Dogs of a hundred mingled makes yapped in the summer at the sea-rim and yelped at the trespassing mountains of the waves.

"I bet St. Bernards would like it now."

And we were snowblind travelers lost on the north hills, and the great dewlapped dogs, with brandy-flasks round their necks, ambled and shambled up to us, baying "Excelsior."[4]

4. "Higher"—recalling Henry Wadsworth Longfellow's poem "Excelsior," in which a traveler who has adopted that word as his motto perishes while climbing a dangerous, snowy mountain trail, and is found by monks of Saint Bernard and their "faithful hound."

We returned home through the desolate poor sea-facing streets where only a few children fumbled with bare red fingers in the thick wheel-rutted snow and catcalled after us, their voices fading away, as we trudged uphill, into the cries of the dock-birds and the hooters of ships out in the white and whirling bay.

Bring out the tall tales now that we told by the fire as we roasted chestnuts and the gaslight bubbled low. Ghosts with their heads under their arms trailed their chains and said "whooo" like owls in the long nights when I dared not look over my shoulder; wild beasts lurked in the cubby-hole under the stairs where the gas-meter ticked. "Once upon a time," Jim said, "there were three boys, just like us, who got lost in the dark in the snow, near Bethesda Chapel, and this is what happened to them . . ." It was the most dreadful happening I had ever heard.

And I remember that we went singing carols once, a night or two before Christmas Eve, when there wasn't the shaving of a moon to light the secret, white-flying streets. At the end of a long road was a drive that led to a large house, and we stumbled up the darkness of the drive that night, each one of us afraid, each one holding a stone in his hand in case, and all of us too brave to say a word. The wind made through the drive-trees noises as of old and unpleasant and maybe web-footed men wheezing in caves. We reached the black bulk of the house. 40

"What shall we give them?" Dan whispered.

" 'Hark the Herald'? 'Christmas comes but Once a Year' ?"

"No," Jack said: "We'll sing 'Good King Wenceslas.' I'll count three."

One, two, three, and we began to sing, our voices high and seemingly distant in the snow-felted darkness round the house that was occupied by nobody we knew. We stood close together, near the dark door.

> Good King Wenceslas looked out
> On the Feast of Stephen.

And then a small, dry voice, like the voice of someone who has not spoken for a long time, suddenly joined our singing: a small, dry voice from the other side of the door: a small, dry voice through the keyhole. And when we stopped running we were outside *our* house; the front room was lovely and bright; the gramophone was playing; we saw the red and white balloons hanging from the gas-bracket; uncles and aunts sat by the fire; I thought I smelt our supper being fried in the kitchen. Everything was good again, and Christmas shone through all the familiar town. 45

"Perhaps it was a ghost," Jim said.

"Perhaps it was trolls," Dan said, who was always reading.

"Let's go in and see if there's any jelly left," Jack said. And we did that.

Margaret Laurence

WHERE THE WORLD BEGAN

A strange place it was, that place where the world began. A place of incredible happenings, splendors and revelations, despairs like multitudinous pits of isolated hells. A place of shadow-spookiness, inhabited by the unknowable dead. A place of jubilation and of mourning, horrible and beautiful.

It was, in fact, a small prairie town.

Because that settlement and that land were my first and for many years my only real knowledge of this planet, in some profound way they remain my world, my way of viewing. My eyes were formed there. Towns like ours, set in a sea of land, have been described thousands of times as dull, bleak, flat, uninteresting. I have had it said to me that the railway trip across Canada is spectacular, except for the prairies, when it would be desirable to go to sleep for several days, until the ordeal is over. I am always unable to argue this point effectively. All I can say is—well, you really have to live there to know that country. The town of my childhood could be called bizarre, agonizingly repressive or cruel at times, and the land in which it grew could be called harsh in the violence of its seasonal changes. But never merely flat or uninteresting. Never dull.

In winter, we used to hitch rides on the back of the milk sleigh, our moccasins squeaking and slithering on the hard rutted snow of the roads, our hands in ice-bubbled mitts hanging onto the box edge of the sleigh for dear life, while Bert grinned at us through his great frosted mustache and shouted the horse into speed, daring us to stay put. Those mornings, rising, there would be the perpetual fascination of the frost feathers on windows, the ferns and flowers and eerie faces traced there during the night by unseen artists of the wind. Evenings, coming back from skating, the sky would be black but not dark, for you could see a cold glitter of stars from one side of the earth's rim to the other. And then the sometime astonishment when you saw the Northern Lights flaring across the sky, like the scrawled signature of God. After a blizzard, when the snowplow hadn't yet got through, school would be closed for the day, the assumption being that the town's young could not possibly flounder through five feet of snow in the pursuit of education. We would then gaily don snowshoes and flounder for miles out into the white dazzling deserts, in pursuit of a different kind of knowing. If you came back too

First published in *Maclean's* (Dec. 1972).

close to night, through the woods at the foot of the town hill, the thin black branches of poplar and chokecherry now meringued with frost, sometimes you heard coyotes. Or maybe the banshee wolf-voices were really only inside your head.

Summers were scorching, and when no rain came and the wheat became bleached and dried before it headed, the faces of farmers and townsfolk would not smile much, and you took for granted, because it never seemed to have been any different, the frequent knocking at the back door and the young men standing there, mumbling or thrusting defiantly their requests for a drink of water and a sandwich if you could spare it. They were riding the freights, and you never knew where they had come from, or where they might end up, if anywhere. The Drought and Depression were like evil deities which had been there always. You understood and did not understand.

Yet the outside world had its continuing marvels. The poplar bluffs and the small river were filled and surrounded with a zillion different grasses, stones, and weed flowers. The meadowlarks sang undaunted from the twanging telephone wires along the gravel highway. Once we found an old flat-bottomed scow, and launched her, poling along the shallow brown waters, mending her with wodges of hastily chewed Spearmint, grounding her among the tangles of yellow marsh marigolds that grew succulently along the banks of the shrunken river, while the sun made our skins smell dusty-warm.

My best friend lived in an apartment above some stores on Main Street (its real name was Mountain Avenue, goodness knows why), an elegant apartment with royal-blue velvet curtains. The back roof, scarcely sloping at all, was corrugated tin, of a furnace-like warmth on a July afternoon, and we would sit there drinking lemonade and looking across the back lane at the Fire Hall. Sometimes our vigil would be rewarded. Oh joy! Somebody's house burning down! We had an almost-perfect callousness in some ways. Then the wooden tower's bronze bell would clonk and toll like a thousand speeded funerals in a time of plague, and in a few minutes the team of giant black horses would cannon forth, pulling the fire wagon like some scarlet chariot of the Goths, while the firemen clung with one hand, adjusting their helmets as they went.

The oddities of the place were endless. An elderly lady used to serve, as her afternoon tea offering to other ladies, soda biscuits spread with peanut butter and topped with a whole marshmallow. Some considered this slightly eccentric, when compared with chopped egg sandwiches, and admittedly talked about her behind her back, but no one ever refused these delicacies or indicated to her that they thought she had slipped a cog. Another lady dyed her hair a bright and cheery orange, by strangers often mistaken at twenty paces for a feather hat. My own beloved stepmother wore a silver fox neckpiece, a whole pelt, *with the embalmed head still on.* My Ontario Irish grandfather said, "sparrow grass," a more interesting term than asparagus. The town dump was known as "the nuisance grounds," a phrase fraught with weird connotations, as though the effluvia of our lives was beneath contempt but at the same time was subtly threatening to the determined and sometimes hysterical propriety of our ways.

Some oddities were, as idiom had it, "funny ha ha"; others were "funny peculiar." Some were not so very funny at all. An old man lived, deranged, in a shack in the valley. Perhaps he wasn't even all that old, but to us he seemed a wild Methuselah figure, shambling among the underbrush and the tall couchgrass, muttering indecipherable curses or blessings, a prophet who had forgotten his prophecies. Everyone in town knew him, but no one knew him. He lived among us as though only occasionally and momentarily visible. The kids called him Andy Gump,[1] and feared him. Some sought to prove their bravery by tormenting him. They were the medieval bear baiters, and he the lumbering bewildered bear, half blind, only rarely turning to snarl. Everything is to be found in a town like mine. Belsen,[2] writ small but with the same ink.

All of us cast stones in one shape or another. In grade school, among the vulnerable and violet girls we were, the feared and despised were those few older girls from what was charmingly termed "the wrong side of the tracks." Tough in talk and tougher in muscle, they were said to be whores already. And may have been, that being about the only profession readily available to them.

The dead lived in that place, too. Not only the grandparents who had, in local parlance, "passed on" and who gloomed, bearded or bonneted, from the sepia photographs in old albums, but also the uncles, forever eighteen or nineteen, whose names were carved on the granite family stones in the cemetery, but whose bones lay in France.[3] My own young mother lay in that graveyard, beside other dead of our kin, and when I was ten, my father, too, only forty, left the living town for the dead dwelling on the hill.

When I was eighteen, I couldn't wait to get out of that town, away from the prairies. I did not know then that I would carry the land and town all my life within my skull, that they would form the mainspring and source of the writing I was to do, wherever and however far away I might live.

This was my territory in the time of my youth, and in a sense my life since then has been an attempt to look at it, to come to terms with it. Stultifying to the mind it certainly could be, and sometimes was, but not to the imagination. It was many things, but it was never dull.

1. Chinless character in a comic strip popular in the 1920s and 1930s.
2. The Nazi concentration camp Bergen-Belsen.
3. That is, who had been killed in World War I. The Canadian war dead were buried in Canadian cemeteries in northeastern France and Belgium.

The same, I now see, could be said for Canada in general. Why on earth did generations of Canadians pretend to believe this country dull? We knew perfectly well it wasn't. Yet for so long we did not proclaim what we knew. If our upsurge of so-called nationalism seems odd or irrelevant to outsiders, and even to some of our own people (*what's all the fuss about?*), they might try to understand that for many years we valued ourselves insufficiently, living as we did under the huge shadows of those two dominating figures, Uncle Sam and Britannia. We have only just begun to value ourselves, our land, our abilities. We have only just begun to recognize our legends and to give shape to our myths.

There are, God knows, enough aspects to deplore about this country. 15 When I see the killing of our lakes and rivers with industrial wastes, I feel rage and despair. When I see our industries and natural resources increasingly taken over by America, I feel an overwhelming discouragement, especially as I cannot simply say "damn Yankees." It should never be forgotten that it is we ourselves who have sold such a large amount of our birthright for a mess of plastic Progress. When I saw the War Measures Act being invoked in 1970,[4] I lost forever the vestigial remains of the naïve wish-belief that repression could not happen here, or would not. And yet, of course, I had known all along in the deepest and often hidden caves of the heart that anything can happen anywhere, for the seeds of both man's freedom and his captivity are found everywhere, even in the microcosm of a prairie town. But in raging against our injustices, our stupidities, I do so *as family*, as I did, and still do in writing, about those aspects of my town which I hated and which are always in some ways aspects of myself.

The land still draws me more than other lands. I have lived in Africa and in England, but splendid as both can be, they do not have the power to move me in the same way as, for example, that part of southern Ontario where I spent four months last summer in a cedar cabin beside a river. "Scratch a Canadian, and you find a phony pioneer," I used to say to myself in warning. But all the same it is true, I think, that we are not yet totally alienated from physical earth, and let us only pray we do not become so. I once thought that my lifelong fear and mistrust of cities made me a kind of old-fashioned freak; now I see it differently.

The cabin has a long window across its front western wall, and sitting at the oak table there in the mornings, I used to look out at the river and at the tall trees beyond, green-gold in the early light. The river was

---

4. By Prime Minister Pierre Elliott Trudeau, citing an "apprehended insurrection" in the wake of terrorist kidnapings by the separatist FLQ (Front de Libération du Québec). Under the provisions of this act, the armed forces took over many police functions, and certain civil liberties—notably habeas corpus—were suspended so that suspected terrorists could be held in jail without being charged.

bronze; the sun caught it strangely, reflecting upon its surface the near-shore sand ripples underneath. Suddenly, the crescenting of a fish, gone before the eye could clearly give image to it. The old man next door said these leaping fish were carp. Himself, he preferred muskie, for he was a real fisherman and the muskie gave him a fight. The wind most often blew from the south, and the river flowed toward the south, so when the water was wind-riffled, and the current was strong, the river seemed to be flowing both ways. I liked this, and interpreted it as an omen, a natural symbol.

A few years ago, when I was back in Winnipeg, I gave a talk at my old college. It was open to the public, and afterward a very old man came up to me and asked me if my maiden name had been Wemyss. I said yes, thinking he might have known my father or my grandfather. But no. "When I was a young lad," he said, "I once worked for your great-grandfather, Robert Wemyss, when he had the sheep ranch at Raeburn." I think that was a moment when I realized all over again something of great importance to me. My long-ago families came from Scotland and Ireland, but in a sense that no longer mattered so much. My true roots were here.

I am not very patriotic, in the usual meaning of that word. I cannot say "My country right or wrong" in any political, social or literary context. But one thing is inalterable, for better or worse, for life.

This is where my world began. A world which includes the ancestors—both my own and other people's ancestors who become mine. A world which formed me, and continues to do so, even while I found it in some of its aspects, and continue to do so. A world which gave me my own lifework to do, because it was here that I learned the sight of my own particular eyes.

Wallace Stegner

THE TOWN DUMP

The town dump of Whitemud, Saskatchewan, could only have been a few years old when I knew it, for the village was born in 1913 and I left there in 1919. But I remember the dump better than I remember most things in that town, better than I remember most of the people. I spent more time with it, for one thing; it has more poetry and excitement in it than people did.

It lay in the southeast corner of town, in a section that was always full

From *Wolf Willow* (1959).

of adventure for me. Just there the Whitemud River left the hills, bent a little south, and started its long traverse across the prairie and international boundary to join the Milk. For all I knew, it might have been on its way to join the Alph:[1] simply, before my eyes, it disappeared into strangeness and wonder.

Also, where it passed below the dumpground, it ran through willowed bottoms that were a favorite campsite for passing teamsters, gypsies, sometimes Indians. The very straw scattered around those camps, the ashes of those strangers' campfires, the manure of their teams and saddle horses, were hot with adventurous possibilities.

It was as an extension, a living suburb, as it were, of the dumpground that we most valued those camps. We scoured them for artifacts of their migrant tenants as if they had been archaeological sites full of the secrets of ancient civilizations. I remember toting around for weeks the broken cheek strap of a bridle. Somehow or other its buckle looked as if it had been fashioned in a far place, a place where they were accustomed to flatten the tongues of buckles for reasons that could only be exciting, and where they made a habit of plating the silver with some valuable alloy, probably silver. In places where the silver was worn away the buckle underneath shone dull yellow: probably gold.

It seemed that excitement liked that end of town better than our end. Once old Mrs. Gustafson, deeply religious and a little raddled in the head, went over there with a buckboard full of trash, and as she was driving home along the river she looked and saw a spent catfish, washed in from Cypress Lake or some other part of the watershed, floating on the yellow water. He was two feet long, his whiskers hung down, his fins and tail were limp. He was a kind of fish that no one had seen in the Whitemud in the three or four years of the town's life, and a kind that none of us children had ever seen anywhere. Mrs. Gustafson had never seen one like him either; she perceived at once that he was the devil, and she whipped up the team and reported him at Hoffman's elevator.

We could hear her screeching as we legged it for the river to see for ourselves. Sure enough, there he was. He looked very tired, and he made no great effort to get away as we pushed out a half-sunken rowboat from below the flume, submerged it under him, and brought him ashore. When he died three days later we experimentally fed him to two half-wild cats, but they seemed to suffer no ill effects.

At that same end of town the irrigation flume crossed the river. It always seemed to me giddily high when I hung my chin over its plank edge and looked down, but it probably walked no more than twenty feet above the water on its spidery legs. Ordinarily in summer it carried about six or eight inches of smooth water, and under the glassy hurrying of the

5

1. The imaginary, mysterious river of Samuel Taylor Coleridge's poem "Kubla Khan."

little boxed stream the planks were coated with deep sun-warmed moss as slick as frogs' eggs. A boy could sit in the flume with the water walling up against his back, and grab a cross brace above him, and pull, shooting himself sledlike ahead until he could reach the next brace for another pull and another slide, and so on across the river in four scoots.

After ten minutes in the flume he would come out wearing a dozen or more limber black leeches, and could sit in the green shade where darning needles flashed blue, and dragonflies hummed and darted and stopped, and skaters dimpled slack and eddy with their delicate transitory footprints, and there stretch the leeches out one by one while their sucking ends clung and clung, until at last, stretched far out, they let go with a tiny wet *puk* and snapped together like rubber bands. The smell of the river and the flume and the clay cutbanks and the bars of that part of the river was the smell of wolf willow.

But nothing in that end of town was as good as the dumpground that scattered along a little runoff coulee dipping down toward the river from the south bench. Through a historical process that went back, probably, to the roots of community sanitation and distaste for eyesores, but that in law dated from the Unincorporated Towns Ordinance of the territorial government, passed in 1888, the dump was one of the very first community enterprises, almost our town's first institution.

More than that, it contained relics of every individual who had ever lived there, and of every phase of the town's history.

The bedsprings on which the town's first child was begotten might be there; the skeleton of a boy's pet colt; two or three volumes of Shakespeare bought in haste and error from a peddler, later loaned in carelessness, soaked with water and chemicals in a house fire, and finally thrown out to flap their stained eloquence in the prairie wind.

Broken dishes, rusty tinware, spoons that had been used to mix paint; once a box of percussion caps, sign and symbol of the carelessness that most of those people felt about all matters of personal or public safety. We put them on the railroad tracks and were anonymously denounced in the *Enterprise*. There were also old iron, old brass, for which we hunted assiduously, by night conning junkmen's catalogues and the pages of the *Enterprise* to find how much wartime value there might be in the geared insides of clocks or in a pound of tea lead[2] carefully wrapped in a ball whose weight astonished and delighted us. Sometimes the unimaginable outside world reached in and laid a finger on us. I recall that, aged no more than seven, I wrote a St. Louis junk house asking if they preferred their tea lead and tinfoil wrapped in balls, or whether they would rather have it pressed flat in sheets, and I got back

2. An alloy used for lining the chests in which tea was stored and transported.

a typewritten letter in a window envelope instructing me that they would be happy to have it in any way that was convenient for me. They added that they valued my business and were mine very truly. Dazed, I carried that windowed grandeur around in my pocket until I wore it out, and for months I saved the letter as a souvenir of the wondering time when something strange and distinguished had singled me out.

We hunted old bottles in the dump, bottles caked with dirt and filth, half buried, full of cobwebs, and we washed them out at the horse trough by the elevator, putting in a handful of shot along with the water to knock the dirt loose; and when we had shaken them until our arms were tired, we hauled them off in somebody's coaster wagon and turned them in at Bill Anderson's pool hall, where the smell of lemon pop was so sweet on the dark pool-hall air that I am sometimes awakened by it in the night, even yet.

Smashed wheels of wagons and buggies, tangles of rusty barbed wire, the collapsed perambulator that the French wife of one of the town's doctors had once pushed proudly up the planked sidewalks and along the ditchbank paths. A welter of foul-smelling feathers and coyote-scattered carrion which was all that remained of somebody's dream of a chicken ranch. The chickens had all got some mysterious pip at the same time, and died as one, and the dream lay out there with the rest of the town's history to rustle to the empty sky on the border of the hills.

There was melted glass in curious forms, and the half-melted office safe left from the burning of Bill Day's Hotel. On very lucky days we might find a piece of the lead casing that had enclosed the wires of the town's first telephone system. The casing was just the right size for rings, and so soft that it could be whittled with a jackknife. It was a material that might have made artists of us. If we had been Indians of fifty years before, that bright soft metal would have enlisted our maximum patience and craft and come out as ring and metal and amulet inscribed with the symbols of our observed world. Perhaps there were too many ready-made alternatives in the local drug, hardware, and general stores; perhaps our feeble artistic response was a measure of the insufficiency of the challenge we felt. In any case I do not remember that we did any more with the metal than to shape it into crude seal rings with our initials or pierced hearts carved in them; and these, though they served a purpose in juvenile courtship, stopped something short of art.

The dump held very little wood, for in that country anything burnable got burned. But it had plenty of old iron, furniture, papers, mattresses that were the delight of field mice, and jugs and demijohns that were sometimes their bane, for they crawled into the necks and drowned in the rain water or redeye that was inside.

If the history of our town was not exactly written, it was at least

15

hinted, in the dump. I think I had a pretty sound notion even at eight or nine of how significant was that first institution of our forming Canadian civilization. For rummaging through its foul purlieus I had several times been surprised and shocked to find relics of my own life tossed out there to rot or blow away.

The volumes of Shakespeare belonged to a set that my father had bought before I was born. It had been carried through successive moves from town to town in the Dakotas, and from Dakota to Seattle, and from Seattle to Bellingham, and Bellingham to Redmond, and from Redmond back to Iowa, and from there to Saskatchewan. Then, stained in a stranger's house fire, these volumes had suffered from a house-cleaning impulse and been thrown away for me to stumble upon in the dump. One of the Cratchet girls had borrowed them, a hatchet-faced, thin, eager, transplanted Cockney girl with a frenzy, almost a hysteria, for reading. And yet somehow, through her hands, they found the dump, to become a symbol of how much was lost, how much thrown aside, how much carelessly or of necessity given up, in the making of a new country. We had so few books that I was familiar with them all, had handled them, looked at their pictures, perhaps even read them. They were the lares and penates, part of the skimpy impedimenta of household gods we had brought with us into Latium.[3] Finding those three thrown away was a little like finding my own name on a gravestone.

And yet not the blow that something else was, something that impressed me even more with the dump's close reflection of the town's intimate life. The colt whose picked skeleton lay out there was mine. He had been incurably crippled when dogs chased our mare, Daisy, the morning after she foaled. I had labored for months to make him well; had fed him by hand, curried him, exercised him, adjusted the iron braces that I had talked my father into having made. And I had not known that he would have to be destroyed. One weekend I turned him over to the foreman of one of the ranches, presumably so that he could be cared for. A few days later I found his skinned body, with the braces still on his crippled front legs, lying on the dump.

Not even that, I think, cured me of going there, though our parents all forbade us on pain of cholera or worse to do so. The place fascinated us, as it should have. For this was the kitchen midden of all the civilization we knew; it gave us the most tantalizing glimpses into our lives as well as into those of the neighbors. It gave us an aesthetic distance from which to know ourselves.

The dump was our poetry and our history. We took it home with us

20

---

3. The region of Italy settled by the Trojans after their defeat by the Greeks in the Trojan War. Later, in Roman families, the lares and penates were the ancestral household gods; they came to embody the continuity of the family.

by the wagonload, bringing back into town the things the town had used and thrown away. Some little part of what we gathered, mainly bottles, we managed to bring back to usefulness, but most of our gleanings we left lying around barn or attic or cellar until in some renewed fury of spring cleanup our families carted them off to the dump again, to be rescued and briefly treasured by some other boy with schemes for making them useful. Occasionally something we really valued with a passion was snatched from us in horror and returned at once. That happened to the mounted head of a white mountain goat, somebody's trophy from old times and the far Rocky Mountains, that I brought home one day in transports of delight. My mother took one look and discovered that his beard was full of moths.

I remember that goat; I regret him yet. Poetry is seldom useful, but always memorable. I think I learned more from the town dump than I learned from school: more about people, more about how life is lived, not elsewhere but here, not in other times but now. If I were a sociologist anxious to study in detail the life of any community, I would go very early to its refuse piles. For a community may be as well judged by what it throws away—what it has to throw away and what it chooses to—as by any other evidence. For whole civilizations we have sometimes no more of the poetry and little more of the history than this.

THE READER

1. *Is Stegner's description of the dump and its surroundings vivid? Where does his writing directly appeal to the senses, and which senses are called into play?*

2. *Why does Stegner say (p. 14) that finding the three volumes of Shakespeare in the dump was "a little like finding my own name on a gravestone"? What is the purpose and effect of his allusion to Virgil's* Aeneid *in the sentence just before that?*

3. *Through what particular details does Stegner portray the dump as a record of his childhood? How is it shown to be also a record of the brief history of the town? In what respects does it more widely reflect and suggest European and American history and culture and, ultimately, the ancient past, the foundations of civilization?*

THE WRITER

1. *Stegner begins his reminiscence of the town dump by saying that it had "poetry and excitement" in it. In what ways does he seek to convey those qualities to the reader?*

2. *In his second paragraph, Stegner speaks of the Alph, the "sacred river"*

of Coleridge's poem "Kubla Khan." Why? How does allusion to that
poem help him convey the strangeness and wonder he then felt?
3. In paragraphs 5–8, Stegner departs, as he had departed to a lesser
  degree in the two preceding paragraphs, from his description of the
  dump. Explain how that departure is justified and whether the writing
  there is appropriate to the essay as a whole.
4. Write an essay in which you deduce things about a person or a family
  from a room. You might use your room or an attic or a basement.

Zora Neale Hurston

HOW IT FEELS TO BE COLORED ME

I am colored but I offer nothing in the way of extenuating circumstances except the fact that I am the only Negro in the United States
whose grandfather on the mother's side was *not* an Indian chief.

I remember the very day that I became colored. Up to my thirteenth
year I lived in the little Negro town of Eatonville, Florida. It is exclusively a colored town. The only white people I knew passed through the
town going to or coming from Orlando. The native whites rode dusty
horses, the Northern tourists chugged down the sandy village road in
automobiles. The town knew the Southerners and never stopped cane
chewing[1] when they passed. But the Northerners were something else
again. They were peered at cautiously from behind curtains by the timid.
The more venturesome would come out on the porch to watch them go
past and got just as much pleasure out of the tourists as the tourists got
out of the village.

The front porch might seem a daring place for the rest of the town,
but it was a gallery seat for me. My favorite place was atop the gate-post.
Proscenium box for a born first-nighter. Not only did I enjoy the show,
but I didn't mind the actors knowing that I liked it. I usually spoke to
them in passing. I'd wave at them and when they returned my salute,
I would say something like this: "Howdy-do-well-I-thank-you-where-you-
goin'?" Usually automobile or the horse paused at this, and after a queer
exchange of compliments, I would probably "go a piece of the way" with
them, as we say in farthest Florida. If one of my family happened to

Originally published in *The World Tomorrow* (Vol. 11, May 1928); reprinted in *I Love
Myself When I'm Laughing* (1975), a collection of Hurston's writings edited by Alice
Walker.

1. Chewing sugar cane.

come to the front in time to see me, of course negotiations would be rudely broken off. But even so, it is clear that I was the first "welcome-to-our-state" Floridian, and I hope the Miami Chamber of Commerce will please take notice.

During this period, white people differed from colored to me only in that they rode through town and never lived there. They liked to hear me "speak pieces" and sing and wanted to see me dance the parse-me-la, and gave me generously of their small silver for doing these things, which seemed strange to me for I wanted to do them so much that I needed bribing to stop. Only they didn't know it. The colored people gave no dimes. They deplored any joyful tendencies in me, but I was their Zora nevertheless. I belonged to them, to the nearby hotels, to the county— everybody's Zora.

But changes came in the family when I was thirteen, and I was sent   5
to school in Jacksonville. I left Eatonville, the town of the oleanders, [2] as Zora. When I disembarked from the river-boat at Jacksonville, she was no more. It seemed that I had suffered a sea change. I was not Zora of Orange County any more, I was now a little colored girl. I found it out in certain ways. In my heart as well as in the mirror, I became a fast brown—warranted not to rub nor run.

But I am not tragically colored. There is no great sorrow dammed up in my soul, nor lurking behind my eyes. I do not mind at all. I do not belong to the sobbing school of Negrohood who hold that nature some- how has given them a lowdown dirty deal and whose feelings are all hurt about it. Even in the helter-skelter skirmish that is my life, I have seen that the world is to the strong regardless of a little pigmentation more or less. No, I do not weep at the world—I am too busy sharpening my oyster knife. [3]

Someone is always at my elbow reminding me that I am the grand- daughter of slaves. It fails to register depression with me. Slavery is sixty years in the past. The operation was successful and the patient is doing well, thank you. The terrible struggle [4] that made me an American out of a potential slave said "On the line!" The Reconstruction said "Get set!"; and the generation before said "Go!" I am off to a flying start and I must not halt in the stretch to look behind and weep. Slavery is the price I paid for civilization, and the choice was not with me. It is a bully adventure and worth all that I have paid through my ancestors for it. No one on earth ever had a greater chance for glory. The world to be won and nothing to be lost. It is thrilling to think—to know that for any

2. Fragrant tropical flowers.
3. Cf. the popular expression "The world is my oyster."
4. I.e., the Civil War. The Reconstruction was the period immediately following the war; one of its better effects was that north- ern educators came south to teach newly freed slaves.

act of mine, I shall get twice as much praise or twice as much blame. It is quite exciting to hold the center of the national stage, with the spectators not knowing whether to laugh or to weep.

The position of my white neighbor is much more difficult. No brown specter pulls up a chair beside me when I sit down to eat. No dark ghost thrusts its leg against mine in bed. The game of keeping what one has is never so exciting as the game of getting.

I do not always feel colored. Even now I often achieve the unconscious Zora of Eatonville before the Hegira.[5] I feel most colored when I am thrown against a sharp white background.

For instance at Barnard.[6] "Beside the waters of the Hudson" I feel my race. Among the thousand white persons, I am a dark rock surged upon, and overswept, but through it all, I remain myself. When covered by the waters, I am; and the ebb but reveals me again.

Sometimes it is the other way around. A white person is set down in our midst, but the contrast is just as sharp for me. For instance, when I sit in the drafty basement that is The New World Cabaret with a white person, my color comes. We enter chatting about any little nothing that we have in common and are seated by the jazz waiters. In the abrupt way that jazz orchestras have, this one plunges into a number. It loses no time in circumlocutions, but gets right down to business. It constricts the thorax and splits the heart with its tempo and narcotic harmonies. This orchestra grows rambunctious, rears on its hind legs and attacks the tonal veil with primitive fury, rending it, clawing it until it breaks through to the jungle beyond. I follow those heathen—follow them exultingly. I dance wildly inside myself; I yell within, I whoop; I shake my assegai[7] above my head, I hurl it true to the mark *yeeeeooww!* I am in the jungle and living in the jungle way. My face is painted red and yellow and my body is painted blue. My pulse is throbbing like a war drum. I want to slaughter something—give paid, give death to what, I do not know. But the piece ends. The men of the orchestra wipe their lips and rest their fingers. I creep back slowly to the veneer we call civilization with the last tone and find the white friend sitting motionless in his seat, smoking calmly.

"Good music they have here," he remarks, drumming the table with his fingertips.

Music. The great blobs of purple and red emotion have not touched him. He has only heard what I felt. He is far away and I see him but dimly across the ocean and the continent that have fallen between us. He is so pale with his whiteness then and I am *so* colored.

5. I.e., a journey undertaken away from a dangerous situation into a more highly desirable one (literally, the flight of Mohammed from Mecca in A.D. 622).

6. American women's college in New York City, near the Hudson River (cf. the psalmist's "by the waters of Babylon").

7. South African hunting spear.

At certain times I have no race, I am *me*. When I set my hat at a certain angle and saunter down Seventh Avenue, Harlem City, feeling as snooty as the lions in front of the Forty-Second Street Library, for instance. So far as my feelings are concerned, Peggy Hopkins Joyce[8] on the Boule Mich with her gorgeous raiment, stately carriage, knees knocking together in a most aristocratic manner, has nothing on me. The cosmic Zora emerges. I belong to no race nor time. I am the eternal feminine with its string of beads.

I have no separate feeling about being an American citizen and colored. I am merely a fragment of the Great Soul that surges within the boundaries. My country, right or wrong.

Sometimes, I feel discriminated against, but it does not make me angry. It merely astonishes me. How *can* any deny themselves the pleasure of my company? It's beyond me.

But in the main, I feel like a brown bag of miscellany propped against a wall. Against a wall in company with other bags, white, red and yellow. Pour out the contents, and there is discovered a jumble of small things priceless and worthless. A first-water diamond, an empty spool, bits of broken glass, lengths of string, a key to a door long since crumbled away, a rusty knife-blade, old shoes saved for a road that never was and never will be, a nail bent under the weight of things too heavy for any nail, a dried flower or two still a little fragrant. In your hand is the brown bag. On the ground before you is the jumble it held—so much like the jumble in the bags, could they be emptied, that all might be dumped in a single heap and the bags refilled without altering the content of any greatly. A bit of colored glass more or less would not matter. Perhaps that is how the Great Stuffer of Bags filled them in the first place—who knows?

8. Peggy Hopkins Joyce, American beauty and fashion-setter of the twenties; the Boule Mich is the Boulevard Saint-Michel, a fashionable Parisian street.

Maya Angelou

GRADUATION

The children in Stamps[1] trembled visibly with anticipation. Some adults were excited too, but to be certain the whole young population had come down with graduation epidemic. Large classes were graduating from both the grammar school and the high school. Even those who were years removed from their own day of glorious release were anxious

From *I Know Why the Caged Bird Sings* (1970).

1. A town in Arkansas.

to help with preparations as a kind of dry run. The junior students who were moving into the vacating classes' chairs were tradition-bound to show their talents for leadership and management. They strutted through the school and around the campus exerting pressure on the lower grades. Their authority was so new that occasionally if they pressed a little too hard it had to be overlooked. After all, next term was coming, and it never hurt a sixth grader to have a play sister in the eighth grade, or a tenth-year student to be able to call a twelfth grader Bubba. So all was endured in a spirit of shared understanding. But the graduating classes themselves were the nobility. Like travelers with exotic destinations on their minds, the graduates were remarkably forgetful. They came to school without their books, or tablets or even pencils. Volunteers fell over themselves to secure replacements for the missing equipment. When accepted, the willing workers might or might not be thanked, and it was of no importance to the pregraduation rites. Even teachers were respectful of the now quiet and aging seniors, and tended to speak to them, if not as equals, as beings only slightly lower than themselves. After tests were returned and grades given, the student body, which acted like an extended family, knew who did well, who excelled, and what piteous ones had failed.

Unlike the white high school, Lafayette County Training School distinguished itself by having neither lawn, nor hedges, nor tennis court, nor climbing ivy. Its two buildings (main classrooms, the grade school and home economics) were set on a dirt hill with no fence to limit either its boundaries or those of bordering farms. There was a large expanse to the left of the school which was used alternately as a baseball diamond or basketball court. Rusty hoops on swaying poles represented the permanent recreational equipment, although bats and balls could be borrowed from the P.E. teacher if the borrower was qualified and if the diamond wasn't occupied.

Over this rocky area relieved by a few shady tall persimmon trees the graduating class walked. The girls often held hands and no longer bothered to speak to the lower students. There was a sadness about them, as if this old world was not their home and they were bound for higher ground. The boys, on the other hand, had become more friendly, more outgoing. A decided change from the closed attitude they projected while studying for finals. Now they seemed not ready to give up the old school, the familiar paths and classrooms. Only a small percentage would be continuing on to college—one of the South's A & M (agricultural and mechanical) schools, which trained Negro youths to be carpenters, farmers, handymen, masons, maids, cooks and baby nurses. Their future rode heavily on their shoulders, and blinded them to the collective joy that had pervaded the lives of the boys and girls in the grammar school graduating class.

Parents who could afford it had ordered new shoes and readymade clothes for themselves from Sears and Roebuck or Montgomery Ward. They also engaged the best seamstresses to make the floating graduating dresses and to cut down secondhand pants which would be pressed to a military slickness for the important event.

Oh, it was important, all right. Whitefolks would attend the ceremony, and two or three would speak of God and home, and the Southern way of life, and Mrs. Parsons, the principal's wife, would play the graduation march while the lower-grade graduates paraded down the aisles and took their seats below the platform. The high school seniors would wait in empty classrooms to make their dramatic entrance.

In the Store I was the person of the moment. The birthday girl. The center. Bailey[2] had graduated the year before, although to do so he had had to forfeit all pleasures to make up for his time lost in Baton Rouge.

My class was wearing butter-yellow piqué dresses, and Momma launched out on mine. She smocked the yoke into tiny crisscrossing puckers, then shirred the rest of the bodice. Her dark fingers ducked in and out of the lemony cloth as she embroidered raised daisies around the hem. Before she considered herself finished she had added a crocheted cuff on the puff sleeves, and a pointy crocheted collar.

I was going to be lovely. A walking model of all the various styles of fine hand sewing and it didn't worry me that I was only twelve years old and merely graduating from the eighth grade. Besides, many teachers in Arkansas Negro schools had only that diploma and were licensed to impart wisdom.

The days had become longer and more noticeable. The faded beige of former times had been replaced with strong and sure colors. I began to see my classmates' clothes, their skin tones, and the dust that waved off pussy willows. Clouds that lazed across the sky were objects of great concern to me. Their shiftier shapes might have held a message that in my new happiness and with a little bit of time I'd soon decipher. During that period I looked at the arch of heaven so religiously my neck kept a steady ache. I had taken to smiling more often, and my jaws hurt from the unaccustomed activity. Between the two physical sore spots, I suppose I could have been uncomfortable, but that was not the case. As a member of the winning team (the graduating class of 1940) I had outdistanced unpleasant sensations by miles. I was headed for the freedom of open fields.

Youth and social approval allied themselves with me and we trammeled memories of slights and insults. The wind of our swift passage remodeled my features. Lost tears were pounded to mud and then to

_____

2. The author's brother.

dust. Years of withdrawal were brushed aside and left behind, as hanging ropes of parasitic moss.

My work alone had awarded me a top place and I was going to be one of the first called in the graduating ceremonies. On the classroom black-board, as well as on the bulletin board in the auditorium, there were blue stars and white stars and red stars. No absences, no tardinesses, and my academic work was among the best of the year. I could say the preamble to the Constitution even faster than Bailey. We timed ourselves often: "We the people of the United States in order to form a more perfect union . . ." I had memorized the Presidents of the United States from Washington to Roosevelt in chronological as well as alphabetical order.

My hair pleased me too. Gradually the black mass had lengthened and thickened, so that it kept at last to its braided pattern, and I didn't have to yank my scalp off when I tried to comb it.

Louise and I had rehearsed the exercises until we tired out ourselves. Henry Reed was class valedictorian. He was a small, very black boy with hooded eyes, a long, broad nose and an oddly shaped head. I had admired him for years because each term he and I vied for the best grades in our class. Most often he bested me, but instead of being disappointed I was pleased that we shared top places between us. Like many Southern Black children, he lived with his grandmother, who was as strict as Momma and as kind as she knew how to be. He was courte-ous, respectful and soft-spoken to elders, but on the playground he chose to play the roughest games. I admired him. Anyone, I reckoned, suffi-ciently afraid or sufficiently dull could be polite. But to be able to operate at a top level with both adults and children was admirable.

His valedictory speech was entitled "To Be or Not to Be." The rigid tenth-grade teacher had helped him write it. He'd been working on the dramatic stresses for months.

The weeks until graduation were filled with heady activities. A group of small children were to be presented in a play about buttercups and daisies and bunny rabbits. They could be heard throughout the building practicing their hops and their little songs that sounded like silver bells. The older girls (nongraduates, of course) were assigned the task of making refreshments for the night's festivities. A tangy scent of ginger, cinnamon, nutmeg and chocolate wafted around the home economics building as the budding cooks made samples for themselves and their teachers.

In every corner of the workshop, axes and saws split fresh timber as the woodshop boys made sets and stage scenery. Only the graduates were left out of the general bustle. We were free to sit in the library at the back of the building or look in quite detachedly, naturally, on the measures being taken for our event.

Even the minister preached on graduation the Sunday before. His subject was, "Let your light so shine that men will see your good works and praise your Father, Who is in Heaven." Although the sermon was purported to be addressed to us, he used the occasion to speak to backsliders, gamblers and general ne'er-do-wells. But since he had called our names at the beginning of the service we were mollified.

Among Negroes the tradition was to give presents to children going only from one grade to another. How much more important this was when the person was graduating at the top of the class. Uncle Willie and Momma had sent away for a Mickey Mouse watch like Bailey's. Louise gave me four embroidered handkerchiefs. (I gave her crocheted doilies.) Mrs. Sneed, the minister's wife, made me an undershirt to wear for graduation, and nearly every customer gave me a nickel or maybe even a dime with the instruction "Keep on moving to higher ground," or some such encouragement.

Amazingly the great day finally dawned and I was out of bed before I knew it. I threw open the back door to see it more clearly, but Momma said, "Sister, come away from that door and put your robe on."

I hoped the memory of that morning would never leave me. Sunlight was itself young, and the day had none of the insistence maturity would bring it in a few hours. In my robe and barefoot in the backyard, under cover of going to see about my new beans, I gave myself up to the gentle warmth and thanked God that no matter what evil I had done in my life He had allowed me to live to see this day. Somewhere in my fatalism I had expected to die, accidentally, and never have the chance to walk up the stairs in the auditorium and gracefully receive my hard-earned diploma. Out of God's merciful bosom I had won reprieve.

Bailey came out in his robe and gave me a box wrapped in Christmas paper. He said he had saved his money for months to pay for it. It felt like a box of chocolates, but I knew Bailey wouldn't save money to buy candy when we had all we could want under our noses.

He was as proud of the gift as I. It was a soft-leather-bound copy of a collection of poems by Edgar Allan Poe, or, as Bailey and I called him, "Eap." I turned to "Annabel Lee" and we walked up and down the garden rows, the cool dirt between our toes, reciting the beautifully sad lines.

Momma made a Sunday breakfast although it was only Friday. After we finished the blessing, I opened my eyes to find the watch on my plate. It was a dream of a day. Everything went smoothly and to my credit. I didn't have to be reminded or scolded for anything. Near evening I was too jittery to attend to chores, so Bailey volunteered to do all before his bath.

Days before, we had made a sign for the Store, and as we turned out the lights Momma hung the cardboard over the doorknob. It read clearly: CLOSED. GRADUATION.

My dress fitted perfectly and everyone said that I looked like a sunbeam in it. On the hill, going toward the school, Bailey walked behind with Uncle Willie, who muttered, "Go on, Ju." He wanted him to walk ahead with us because it embarrassed him to have to walk so slowly. Bailey said he'd let the ladies walk together, and the men would bring up the rear. We all laughed, nicely.

Little children dashed by out of the dark like fireflies. Their crepe-paper dresses and butterfly wings were not made for running and we heard more than one rip, dryly, and the regretful "uh uh" that followed.

The school blazed without gaiety. The windows seemed cold and unfriendly from the lower hill. A sense of ill-fated timing crept over me, and if Momma hadn't reached for my hand I would have drifted back to Bailey and Uncle Willie, and possibly beyond. She made a few slow jokes about my feet getting cold, and tugged me along to the now-strange building.

Around the front steps, assurance came back. There were my fellow "greats," the graduating class. Hair brushed back, legs oiled, new dresses and pressed pleats, fresh pocket handkerchiefs and little handbags, all homesewn. Oh, we were up to snuff, all right. I joined my comrades and didn't even see my family go in to find seats in the crowded auditorium.

The school band struck up a march and all classes filed in as had been rehearsed. We stood in front of our seats, as assigned, and on a signal from the choir director, we sat. No sooner had this been accomplished than the band started to play the national anthem. We rose again and sang the song, after which we recited the pledge of allegiance. We remained standing for a brief minute before the choir director and the principal signaled to us, rather desperately I thought, to take our seats. The command was so unusual that our carefully rehearsed and smooth-running machine was thrown off. For a full minute we fumbled for our chairs and bumped into each other awkwardly. Habits change or solidify under pressure, so in our state of nervous tension we had been ready to follow our usual assembly pattern: the American national anthem, then the pledge of allegiance, then the song every Black person I knew called the Negro National Anthem. All done in the same key, with the same passion and most often standing on the same foot.

Finding my seat at last, I was overcome with a presentiment of worse things to come. Something unrehearsed, unplanned, was going to happen, and we were going to be made to look bad. I distinctly remember being explicit in the choice of pronoun. It was "we," the graduating class, the unit, that concerned me then.

The principal welcomed "parents and friends" and asked the Baptist minister to lead us in prayer. His invocation was brief and punchy, and for a second I thought we were getting on the high road to right action. When the principal came back to the dais, however, his voice had changed. Sounds always affected me profoundly and the principal's voice was one of my favorites. During assembly it melted and lowed weakly into the audience. It had not been in my plan to listen to him, but my curiosity was piqued and I straightened up to give him my attention.

He was talking about Booker T. Washington, our "late great leader," who said we can be as close as the fingers on the hand, etc. . . . Then he said a few vague things about friendship and the friendship of kindly people to those less fortunate than themselves. With that his voice nearly faded, thin, away. Like a river diminishing to a stream and then to a trickle. But he cleared his throat and said, "Our speaker tonight, who is also our friend, came from Texarkana to deliver the commencement address, but due to the irregularity of the train schedule, he's going to, as they say, 'speak and run.' " He said that we understood and wanted the man to know that we were most grateful for the time he was able to give us and then something about how we were willing always to adjust to another's program, and without more ado—"I give you Mr. Edward Donleavy."

Not one but two white men came through the door off-stage. The shorter one walked to the speaker's platform, and the tall one moved to the center seat and sat down. But that was our principal's seat, and already occupied. The dislodged gentleman bounced around for a long breath or two before the Baptist minister gave him his chair, then with more dignity than the situation deserved, the minister walked off the stage.

Donleavy looked at the audience once (on reflection, I'm sure that he wanted only to reassure himself that we were really there), adjusted his glasses and began to read from a sheaf of papers.

He was glad "to be here and to see the work going on just as it was in the other schools."

At the first "Amen" from the audience I willed the offender to immediate death by choking on the word. But Amens and Yes, sir's began to fall around the room like rain through a ragged umbrella.

He told us of the wonderful changes we children in Stamps had in store. The Central School (naturally, the white school was Central) had already been granted improvements that would be in use in the fall. A well-known artist was coming from Little Rock to teach art to them. They were going to have the newest microscopes and chemistry equipment for their laboratory. Mr. Donleavy didn't leave us long in the dark over who made these improvements available to Central High. Nor were we to be ignored in the general betterment scheme he had in mind.

He said that he had pointed out to people at a very high level that one of the first-line football tacklers at Arkansas Agricultural and Mechanical College had graduated from good old Lafayette County Train-

35

ing School. Here fewer Amen's were heard. Those few that did break through lay dully in the air with the heaviness of habit.

He went on to praise us. He went on to say how he had bragged that "one of the best basketball players at Fisk sank his first ball right here at Lafayette County Training School."

40   The white kids were going to have a chance to become Galileos and Madame Curies and Edisons and Gauguins, and our boys (the girls weren't even in on it) would try to be Jesse Owenses and Joe Louises.

Owens and the Brown Bomber were great heroes in our world, but what school official in the white-goddom of Little Rock had the right to decide that those two men must be our only heroes? Who decided that for Henry Reed to become a scientist he had to work like George Washington Carver, as a bootblack, to buy a lousy microscope? Bailey was obviously always going to be too small to be an athlete, so which concrete angel glued to what country seat had decided that if my brother wanted to become a lawyer he had to first pay penance for his skin by picking cotton and hoeing corn and studying correspondence books at night for twenty years?

The man's dead words fell like bricks around the auditorium and too many settled in my belly. Constrained by hard-learned manners I couldn't look behind me, but to my left and right the proud graduating class of 1940 had dropped their heads. Every girl in my row had found something new to do with her handkerchief. Some folded the tiny squares into love knots, some into triangles, but most were wadding them, then pressing them flat on their yellow laps.

On the dais, the ancient tragedy was being replayed. Professor Parsons sat, a sculptor's reject, rigid. His large, heavy body seemed devoid of will or willingness, and his eyes said he was no longer with us. The other teachers examined the flag (which was draped stage right) or their notes, or the windows which opened on our now-famous playing diamond.

Graduation, the hush-hush magic time of frills and gifts and congratulations and diplomas, was finished for me before my name was called. The accomplishment was nothing. The meticulous maps, drawn in three colors of ink, learning and spelling decasyllabic words, memorizing the whole of *The Rape of Lucrece* [3]—it was for nothing. Donleavy had exposed us.

45   We were maids and farmers, handymen and washerwomen, and anything higher that we aspired to was farcical and presumptuous.

Then I wished that Gabriel Prosser and Nat Turner [4] had killed all whitefolks in their beds and that Abraham Lincoln had been assassinated before the signing of the Emancipation Proclamation, and that

---

3. A narrative poem of 1,855 lines, by Shakespeare.

4. Leaders of Virginia slave rebellions in 1800 and 1831 respectively.

Harriet Tubman[5] had been killed by that blow on her head and Christopher Columbus had drowned in the *Santa Maria*.

It was awful to be a Negro and have no control over my life. It was brutal to be young and already trained to sit quietly and listen to charges brought against my color with no chance of defense. We should all be dead. I thought I should like to see us all dead, one on top of the other. A pyramid of flesh with the whitefolks on the bottom, as the broad base, then the Indians with their silly tomahawks and teepees and wigwams and treaties, the Negroes with their mops and recipes and cotton sacks and spirituals sticking out of their mouths. The Dutch children should all stumble in their wooden shoes and break their necks. The French should choke to death on the Louisiana Purchase (1803) while silkworms ate all the Chinese with their stupid pigtails. As a species, we were an abomination. All of us.

Donleavy was running for election, and assured our parents that if he won we could count on having the only colored paved playing field in that part of Arkansas. Also—he never looked up to acknowledge the grunts of acceptance—also, we were bound to get some new equipment for the home economics building and the workshop.

He finished, and since there was no need to give any more than the most perfunctory thank-you's, he nodded to the men on the stage, and the tall white man who was never introduced joined him at the door. They left with the attitude that now they were off to something really important. (The graduation ceremonies at Lafayette County Training School had been a mere preliminary.)

The ugliness they left was palpable. An uninvited guest who wouldn't leave. The choir was summoned and sang a modern arrangement of "Onward, Christian Soldiers," with new words pertaining to graduates seeking their place in the world. But it didn't work. Elouise, the daughter of the Baptist minister, recited "Invictus,"[6] and I could have cried at the impertinence of "I am the master of my fate, I am the captain of my soul."

My name had lost its ring of familiarity and I had to be nudged to go and receive my diploma. All my preparations had fled. I neither marched up to the stage like a conquering Amazon, nor did I look in the audience for Bailey's nod of approval. Marguerite Johnson, I heard the name again, my honors were read, there were noises in the audience of appreciation, and I took my place on the stage as rehearsed.

I thought about colors I hated: ecru, puce, lavender, beige and black.

There was shuffling and rustling around me, then Henry Reed was

50

5. Nineteenth-century black abolitionist, a "conductor" on the Underground Railroad.
6. An inspirational poem by the nineteenth-century poet William Ernest Henley, once very popular for occasions such as this one.

giving his valedictory address, "To Be or Not to Be." Hadn't he heard
the whitefolks? We couldn't *be*, so the question was a waste of time.
Henry's voice came out clear and strong. I feared to look at him. Hadn't
he got the message? There was no "nobler in the mind" for Negroes
because the world didn't think we had minds, and they let us know it.
"Outrageous fortune"? Now, that was a joke. When the ceremony was
over I had to tell Henry Reed some things. That is, if I still cared. Not
"rub," Henry, "erase." "Ah, there's the erase." Us.

Henry had been a good student in elocution. His voice rose on tides
of promise and fell on waves of warnings. The English teacher had
helped him to create a sermon winging through Hamlet's soliloquy. To
be a man, a doer, a builder, a leader, or to be a tool, an unfunny joke,
a crusher of funky toadstools. I marveled that Henry could go through
with the speech as if we had a choice.

I had been listening and silently rebutting each sentence with my eyes
closed; then there was a hush, which in an audience warns that something unplanned is happening. I looked up and saw Henry Reed, the
conservative, the proper, the A student, turn his back to the audience
and turn to us (the proud graduating class of 1940) and sing, nearly
speaking,

> "Lift ev'ry voice and sing
> Till earth and heaven ring
> Ring with the harmonies of Liberty . . ."

It was the poem written by James Weldon Johnson. It was the music
composed by J. Rosamond Johnson. It was the Negro national anthem.
Out of habit we were singing it.

Our mothers and fathers stood in the dark hall and joined the hymn
of encouragement. A kindergarten teacher led the small children onto
the stage and the buttercups and daisies and bunny rabbits marked time
and tried to follow:

> "Stony the road we trod
> Bitter the chastening rod
> Felt in the days when hope, unborn, had died.
> Yet with a steady beat
> Have not our weary feet
> Come to the place for which our fathers sighed?"

Each child I knew had learned that song with his ABC's and along
with "Jesus Loves Me This I Know." But I personally had never heard
it before. Never heard the words, despite the thousands of times I had
sung them. Never thought they had anything to do with me.

On the other hand, the words of Patrick Henry had made such an
impression on me that I had been able to stretch myself tall and trem-

bling and say, "I know not what course others may take, but as for me, give me liberty or give me death."

And now I heard, really for the first time:

> "We have come over a way that with tears
> has been watered,
> We have come, treading our path through
> the blood of the slaughtered."

While echoes of the song shivered in the air, Henry Reed bowed his head, said "Thank you," and returned to his place in the line. The tears that slipped down many faces were not wiped away in shame.

60

We were on top again. As always, again. We survived. The depths had been icy and dark, but now a bright sun spoke to our souls. I was no longer simply a member of the proud graduating class of 1940; I was a proud member of the wonderful, beautiful Negro race.

Oh, Black known and unknown poets, how often have your auctioned pains sustained us? Who will compute the lonely nights made less lonely by your songs, or the empty pots made less tragic by your tales?

If we were a people much given to revealing secrets, we might raise monuments and sacrifice to the memories of our poets, but slavery cured us of that weakness. It may be enough, however, to have it said that we survive in exact relationship to the dedication of our poets (include preachers, musicians and blues singers).

Bruno Bettelheim

A VICTIM

Many students of discrimination are aware that the victim often reacts in ways as undesirable as the action of the aggressor. Less attention is paid to this because it is easier to excuse a defendant than an offender, and because they assume that once the aggression stops the victim's reactions will stop too. But I doubt if this is of real service to the persecuted. His main interest is that the persecution cease. But that is less apt to happen if he lacks a real understanding of the phenomenon of persecution, in which victim and persecutor are inseparably interlocked.

Let me illustrate with the following example: in the winter of 1938 a Polish Jew murdered the German attaché in Paris, vom Rath. The Gestapo used the event to step up anti-Semitic actions, and in the camp

From *The Informed Heart: Autonomy in a Mass Age* (1960).

new hardships were inflicted on Jewish prisoners. One of these was an
order barring them from the medical clinic unless the need for treatment had originated in work accident.

Nearly all prisoners suffered from frostbite which often led to gan-
grene and then amputation. Whether or not a Jewish prisoner was
admitted to the clinic to prevent such a fate depended on the whim of
an SS private. On reaching the clinic entrance, the prisoner explained
the nature of his ailment to the SS man, who then decided if he should
get treatment or not.

I too suffered from frostbite. At first I was discouraged from trying
to get medical care by the fate of Jewish prisoners whose attempts had
ended up in no treatment, only abuse. Finally things got worse and I
was afraid that waiting longer would mean amputation. So I decided to
make the effort.

When I got to the clinic, there were many prisoners lined up as usual,
a score of them Jews suffering from severe frostbite. The main topic of
discussion was one's chances of being admitted to the clinic. Most Jews
had planned their procedure in detail. Some thought it best to stress
their service in the German army during World War I: wounds received
or decorations won. Others planned to stress the severity of their frostbite. A few decided it was best to tell some "tall story," such as that an
SS officer had ordered them to report at the clinic.

Most of them seemed convinced that the SS man on duty would not
see through their schemes. Eventually they asked me about my plans.
Having no definite ones, I said I would go by the way the SS man dealt
with other Jewish prisoners who had frostbite like me, and proceed
accordingly. I doubted how wise it was to follow a preconceived plan,
because it was hard to anticipate the reactions of a person you didn't
know.

The prisoners reacted as they had at other times when I had voiced
similar ideas on how to deal with the SS. They insisted that one SS man
was like another, all equally vicious and stupid. As usual, any frustration
was immediately discharged against the person who caused it, or was
nearest at hand. So in abusive terms they accused me of not wanting
to share my plan with them, or of intending to use one of theirs; it
angered them that I was ready to meet the enemy unprepared.

No Jewish prisoner ahead of me in the line was admitted to the clinic.
The more a prisoner pleaded, the more annoyed and violent the SS
became. Expressions of pain amused him; stories of previous services
rendered to Germany outraged him. He proudly remarked that *he* could
not be taken in by Jews, that fortunately the time had passed when Jews
could reach their goal by lamentations.

When my turn came he asked me in a screeching voice if I knew that
work accidents were the only reason for admitting Jews to the clinic, and

if I came because of such an accident. I replied that I knew the rules, but that I couldn't work unless my hands were freed of the dead flesh. Since prisoners were not allowed to have knives, I asked to have the dead flesh cut away. I tried to be matter-of-fact, avoiding pleading, deference, or arrogance. He replied: "If that's all you want, I'll tear the flesh off myself." And he started to pull at the festering skin. Because it did not come off as easily as he may have expected, or for some other reason, he waved me into the clinic.

Inside, he gave me a malevolent look and pushed me into the treat- 10
ment room. There he told the prisoner orderly to attend to the wound. While this was being done, the guard watched me closely for signs of pain but I was able to suppress them. As soon as the cutting was over, I started to leave. He showed surprise and asked why I didn't wait for further treatment. I said I had gotten the service I asked for, at which he told the orderly to make an exception and treat my hand. After I had left the room, he called me back and gave me a card entitling me to further treatment, and admittance to the clinic without inspection at the entrance.

* * *

Because my behavior did not correspond to what he expected of Jewish prisoners on the basis of his projection, he could not use his prepared defenses against being touched by the prisoner's plight. Since I did not act as the dangerous Jew was expected to, I did not activate the anxieties that went with his stereotype. Still he did not altogether trust me, so he continued to watch while I received treatment.

Throughout these dealings, the SS felt uneasy with me, though he did not unload on me the annoyance his uneasiness aroused. Perhaps he watched me closely because he expected that sooner or later I would slip up and behave the way his projected image of the Jew was expected to act. This would have meant that his delusional creation had become real.

Joan Didion

ON GOING HOME

I am home for my daughter's first birthday. By "home" I do not mean the house in Los Angeles where my husband and I and the baby live, but the place where my family is, in the Central Valley of California. It is a vital although troublesome distinction. My husband likes my family but is uneasy in their house, because once there I fall into their

From *Slouching towards Bethlehem* (1966).

ways, which are difficult, oblique, deliberately inarticulate, not my husband's ways. We live in dusty houses ("D-U-S-T," he once wrote with
his finger on surfaces all over the house, but no one noticed it) filled with
mementos quite without value to him (what could the Canton dessert
plates mean to him? how could he have known about the assay scales,
why should he care if he did know?), and we appear to talk exclusively
about people we know who have been committed to mental hospitals,
about people we know who have been booked on drunk-driving charges,
and about property, particularly about property, land, price per acre and
C-2 zoning and assessments and freeway access. My brother does not
understand my husband's inability to perceive the advantage in the
rather common real-estate transaction known as "sale-leaseback," and
my husband in turn does not understand why so many of the people he
hears about in my father's house have recently been committed to
mental hospitals or booked on drunk-driving charges. Nor does he understand that when we talk about sale-leasebacks and right-of-way condemnations we are talking in code about the things we like best, the yellow
fields and the cottonwoods and the rivers rising and falling and the
mountain roads closing when the heavy snow comes in. We miss each
other's points, have another drink and regard the fire. My brother refers
to my husband, in his presence, as "Joan's husband." Marriage is the
classic betrayal.

Or perhaps it is not any more. Sometimes I think that those of us who
are now in our thirties were born into the last generation to carry the
burden of "home," to find in family life the source of all tension and
drama. I had by all objective accounts a "normal" and a "happy" family
situation, and yet I was almost thirty years old before I could talk to my
family on the telephone without crying after I had hung up. We did not
fight. Nothing was wrong. And yet some nameless anxiety colored the
emotional charges between me and the place that I came from. The
question of whether or not you could go home again was a very real part
of the sentimental and largely literary baggage with which we left home
in the fifties; I suspect that it is irrelevant to the children born of the
fragmentation after World War II. A few weeks ago in a San Francisco
bar I saw a pretty young girl on crystal take off her clothes and dance
for the cash prize in an "amateur-topless" contest. There was no particular sense of moment about this, none of the effect of romantic degradation, of "dark journey," for which my generation strived so assiduously.
What sense could that girl possibly make of, say, *Long Day's Journey
into Night?*[1] Who is beside the point?

That I am trapped in this particular irrelevancy is never more appar-

---

1. A powerful domestic tragedy by the modern American playwright Eugene O'Neill,
based on his early life.

ent to me than when I am home. Paralyzed by the neurotic lassitude engendered by meeting one's past at every turn, around every corner, inside every cupboard, I go aimlessly from room to room. I decide to meet it head-on and clean out a drawer, and I spread the contents on the bed. A bathing suit I wore the summer I was seventeen. A letter of rejection from *The Nation*, an aerial photograph of the site for a shopping center my father did not build in 1954. Three teacups hand-painted with cabbage roses and signed "E.M.," my grandmother's initials. There is no final solution for letters of rejection from *The Nation* and teacups hand-painted in 1900. Nor is there any answer to snapshots of one's grandfather as a young man on skis, surveying around Donner Pass in the year 1910. I smooth out the snapshot and look into his face, and do and do not see my own. I close the drawer, and have another cup of coffee with my mother. We get along very well, veterans of a guerrilla war we never understood.

Days pass. I see no one. I come to dread my husband's evening call, not only because he is full of news of what by now seems to me our remote life in Los Angeles, people he has seen, letters which require attention, but because he asks what I have been doing, suggests uneasily that I get out, drive to San Francisco or Berkeley. Instead I drive across the river to a family graveyard. It has been vandalized since my last visit and the monuments are broken, overturned in the dry grass. Because I once saw a rattlesnake in the grass I stay in the car and listen to a country-and-Western station. Later I drive with my father to a ranch he has in the foothills. The man who runs his cattle on it asks us to the roundup, a week from Sunday, and although I know that I will be in Los Angeles I say, in the oblique way my family talks, that I will come. Once home I mention the broken monuments in the graveyard. My mother shrugs.

I go to visit my great-aunts. A few of them think now that I am my cousin, or their daughter who died young. We recall an anecdote about a relative last seen in 1948, and they ask if I still like living in New York City. I have lived in Los Angeles for three years, but I say that I do. The baby is offered a horehound drop, and I am slipped a dollar bill "to buy a treat." Questions trail off, answers are abandoned, the baby plays with the dust motes in a shaft of afternoon sun.

It is time for the baby's birthday party: a white cake, strawberry-marshmallow ice cream, a bottle of champagne saved from another party. In the evening, after she has gone to sleep, I kneel beside the crib and touch her face, where it is pressed against the slats, with mine. She is an open and trusting child, unprepared for and unaccustomed to the ambushes of family life, and perhaps it is just as well that I can offer her little of that life. I would like to give her more. I would like to promise her that she will grow up with a sense of her cousins and of rivers and of her great-grandmother's teacups, would like to pledge her a picnic on a river with fried chicken and her hair uncombed, would like to give her *home* for her birthday, but we live differently now and I can promise her nothing like that. I give her a xylophone and a sundress from Madeira, and promise to tell her a funny story.

THE READER

1. *Does the author take a single attitude or several toward "home"? Try to specify the attitude or attitudes.*
2. *What does the author mean by "the ambushes of family life" (p. 33)?*
3. *Explain whether the essay gives you any clues as to why so much of the talk at home is "about people we know who have been committed to mental hospitals, about people we know who have been booked on drunk-driving charges, and about property" (p. 32)?*
4. *In her concluding sentence, the author tells us she gives as birthday gifts to her daughter "a xylophone and a sundress from Madeira." Are these appropriate? Why or why not? Explain why she would like to give other gifts.*
5. *In "On Keeping a Notebook," Didion says that it is good to keep in touch with the people we used to be (p. 72). Is her account of this visit an effort to do that? Are there recalled phrases and observations in "On Going Home" like those she quotes from her notebooks, or does the different argument change the character of the phrases and observations she recalls?*

THE WRITER

1. *The author speaks of herself at home as "paralyzed by the neurotic lassitude engendered by meeting one's past at every turn" (p. 33). What details in the essay help explain that feeling?*
2. *If you have read or seen the play, explain the appropriateness of the author's reference (p. 32) to O'Neill's* Long Day's Journey into Night.
3. *Didion speaks of family life as "the source of all tension and drama." Point to details in the essay that illustrate that view. What kinds of details about her family might she have considered but rejected because they didn't advance that view or, indeed, contradicted it?*
4. *Write an essay about a trip you have made back to your home or back to a place you were once familiar with.*

Joyce Maynard

FOUR GENERATIONS

My mother called last week to tell me that my grandmother is dying. She has refused an operation that would postpone, but not prevent, her death from pancreatic cancer. She can't eat, she has been hemorrhaging, and she has severe jaundice. "I always prided myself on being different," she told my mother. "Now I *am* different. I'm yellow."

My mother, telling me this news, began to cry. So I became the mother for a moment, reminding her, reasonably, that my grandmother is eighty-seven, she's had a full life, she has all her faculties, and no one who knows her could wish that she live long enough to lose them. Lately my mother has been finding notes in my grandmother's drawers at the nursing home, reminding her, "Joyce's husband's name is Steve. Their daughter is Audrey." In the last few years she hadn't had the strength to cook or garden, and she's begun to say she's had enough of living.

My grandmother was born in Russia, in 1892—the oldest daughter in a large and prosperous Jewish family. But the prosperity didn't last. She tells stories of the pogroms and the cossacks who raped her when she was twelve. Soon after that, her family emigrated to Canada, where she met my grandfather.

Their children were the center of their life. The story I loved best, as a child, was of my grandfather opening every box of Cracker Jack in the general store he ran, in search of the particular tin toy my mother coveted. Though they never had much money, my grandmother saw to it that her daughter had elocution lessons and piano lessons, and assured her that she would go to college.

But while she was at college, my mother met my father, who was blue-eyed and blond-haired and not Jewish. When my father sent love letters to my mother, my grandmother would open and hide them, and when my mother told her parents she was going to marry this man, my grandmother said if that happened, it would kill her.

Not likely, of course. My grandmother is a woman who used to crack Brazil nuts open with her teeth, a woman who once lifted a car off the ground, when there was an accident and it had to be moved. She has been representing her death as imminent ever since I've known her— twenty-five years—and has discussed, at length, the distribution of her possessions and her lamb coat. Every time we said goodbye, after our

5

Originally appeared in the *New York Times* "Hers" column (Apr. 12, 1979).

annual visit to Winnipeg, she'd weep and say she'd never see us again. But in the meantime, while every other relative of her generation, and a good many of the younger ones, has died (nursed usually by her), she has kept making knishes, shopping for bargains, tending the healthiest plants I've ever seen.

After my grandfather died, my grandmother lived, more than ever, through her children. When she came to visit, I would hide my diary. She couldn't understand any desire for privacy. She couldn't bear it if my mother left the house without her.

This possessiveness is what made my mother furious (and then guilt-ridden that she felt that way, when of course she owed so much to her mother). So I harbored the resentment that my mother—the dutiful daughter—would not allow herself. I—who had always performed specially well for my grandmother, danced and sung for her, presented her with kisses and good report cards—stopped writing to her, ceased to visit.

But when I heard that she was dying, I realized I wanted to go to Winnipeg to see her one more time. Mostly to make my mother happy, I told myself (certain patterns being hard to break). But also, I was offering up one more particularly fine accomplishment: my own dark-eyed, dark-skinned, dark-haired daughter, whom my grandmother had never met.

10   I put on my daughter's best dress for our visit to Winnipeg, the way the best dresses were always put on me, and I filled my pockets with animal crackers, in case Audrey started to cry. I scrubbed her face mercilessly. On the elevator going up to her room, I realized how much I was sweating.

Grandma was lying flat with an IV tube in her arm and her eyes shut, but she opened them when I leaned over to kiss her. "It's Fredelle's daughter, Joyce," I yelled, because she doesn't hear well anymore, but I could see that no explanation was necessary. "You came," she said. "You brought the baby."

Audrey is just one, but she has seen enough of the world to know that people in beds are not meant to be so still and yellow, and she looked frightened. I had never wanted, more, for her to smile.

Then Grandma waved at her—the same kind of slow, finger-flexing wave a baby makes—and Audrey waved back. I spread her toys out on my grandmother's bed and sat her down. There she stayed, most of the afternoon, playing and humming and sipping on her bottle, taking a nap at one point, leaning against my grandmother's leg. When I cranked her Snoopy guitar, Audrey stood up on the bed and danced. Grandma wouldn't talk much anymore, though every once in a while she would say how sorry she was that she wasn't having a better day. "I'm not always like this," she said.

Mostly she just watched Audrey. Sometimes Audrey would get off the bed, inspect the get-well cards, totter down the hall. "Where is she?" Grandma kept asking. "Who's looking after her?" I had the feeling, even then, that if I'd said, "Audrey's lighting matches," Grandma would have shot up to rescue her.

We were flying home that night, and I had dreaded telling her, remembering all those other tearful partings. But in the end, I was the one who cried. She had said she was ready to die. But as I leaned over to stroke her forehead, what she said was, "I wish I had your hair" and "I wish I was well." 15

On the plane flying home, with Audrey in my arms, I thought about mothers and daughters, and the four generations of the family that I know most intimately. Every one of those mothers loves and needs her daughter more than her daughter will love or need her some day, and we are, each of us, the only person on earth who is quite so consumingly interested in our child.

Sometimes I kiss and hug Audrey so much she starts crying—which is, in effect, what my grandmother was doing to my mother, all her life. And what makes my mother grieve right now, I think, is not simply that her mother will die in a day or two, but that, once her mother dies, there will never again be someone to love her in quite such an unreserved, unquestioning way. No one else who believes that, fifty years ago, she could have put Shirley Temple out of a job, no one else who remembers the moment of her birth. She will only be a mother, then, not a daughter anymore.

Audrey and I have stopped over for a night in Toronto, where my mother lives. Tomorrow she will go to a safe-deposit box at the bank and take out the receipt for my grandmother's burial plot. Then she will fly back to Winnipeg, where, for the first time in anybody's memory, there was waist-high snow on April Fool's Day. But tonight she is feeding me, as she always does when I come, and I am eating more than I do anywhere else. I admire the wedding china (once my grandmother's) that my mother has set on the table. She says (the way Grandma used to say to her, of the lamb coat), "Some day it will be yours."

THE READER

1. *What difference does it make to this essay that the last paragraph is in the present tense?*

2. *This is a short narrative essay about four generations of women in a family. It also touches on topics appropriate to a more impersonal analysis. What are some of these, and how are they treated here?*

3. *Compare this essay with the one by Joyce Maynard's mother, Fredelle*

(p. 38). Are their conclusions similar? This is certainly the shorter of the two. Are there other differences?

THE WRITER

1. *This essay has a thesis sentence. Where is it? What difference does its placement make?*
2. *This essay and Fredelle Maynard's "And Therefore I Have Sailed the Seas . . ." (p. 38) tell you about five generations of women in this family. On the basis of what you are told, write a sketch for a family history. What in that sketch would also be useful for a more general social history?*

Fredelle Maynard

AND THEREFORE I HAVE SAILED THE SEAS . . .

I know just when it came to me, the realization that I was growing old. There had been intimations earlier, like the time a shoe-store clerk called out to a fellow worker, "Would you help the lady with the glasses?" There was the unpleasant incident when I jumped into a taxicab at Los Angeles airport for a ride that proved to be about a hundred yards. The driver, a sullen late-adolescent, announced, "Five dollars." "For that?" I said, handing him three. He flung open the cab door. "Old lady, *you* mean." But that was vengeance, not justice.

The decisive moment came some years ago, in my mid-fifties. It is not irrelevant to this story that I was on my way home from an exhilarating conference, wearing what my daughters call my author suit, looking and feeling smart. In the airport lounge, where Boston passengers waited for a late plane, two individuals caught my attention. One was a charming young woman in a loose gauzy gown, ankle length, with flowing cornsilk hair and bare feet—Rossetti or Burne-Jones crossed with late sixties flower child.[1] A little girl, just learning to walk, alternately nestled in her lap or staggered about the room. The other notable passenger, almost certainly European, was a middle-aged man who might have stepped out of the pages of *Town and Country*—impeccably groomed, wearing on

From *The Tree of Life* (1988).

1. Dante Gabriel Rossetti (1828–82) and Sir Edward Coley Burne-Jones (1833–98), English painters of the pre-Raphaelite school, whose works often depicted a romanticized medieval world.

this steamy day a soft grey Borsalino felt, creamy silk shirt with French cuffs and gold cufflinks, supple Italian shoes. Not handsome but what the French call a *joli laid.* [2]

Once on the plane—open seating—the young woman settled herself and her baby in a bulkhead seat and began to spread out her gear. Diaper bag, bottle, doll, cracker snacks. The elegant European sat immediately behind these two; I took a seat across the aisle. As the young woman stood to place her bag in the overhead rack, the man jumped up. "Please let me help you." She looked surprised, shook her head, stowed the bag and sat down again without a backward look. Minutes later, the toddler came weaving down the aisle, gumming a cookie. The man reached out with winning smile and took one grubby paw in his own beautifully manicured hand. The little girl squawked and the mother turned, gathering her child up as if to protect against imminent abduction. The man bowed to her back. As the plane neared its destination, he made one further attempt, tapping her shoulder. "Would you allow me to assist with your baggage when we reach Boston?" The young woman turned and stared. It was not a rejecting stare, the kind that would have acknowledged, while refusing, a romantic advance. It was merely incredulous. (Why on earth is this old fellow bothering me?) "My husband is meeting us," she said. In some embarrassment now—several passengers obviously listening in—the man looked about with a shrug which assured us all he was only trying to help. For the first time our eyes met. I smiled. I suppose my look might have translated as "You know what young women are like" with overtones of "Well, aren't you an attractive man!" I certainly didn't intend it to be flirtatious. The European stared—(Why on earth . . .)—and in that moment I knew I was no longer young.

"And therefore I have sailed the seas and come / To the holy city of Byzantium." [3] I like the place I am now. Observing women my age who dye their hair or undergo cosmetic surgery, I am honestly amazed. How—after what they must by now have endured—how can they imagine that female power resides in a rag or a bone or a hank of hair? "Brightness falls from the air; / Queens have died young and fair; / Dust hath closed Helen's eye . . ." but the spirit endures. [4] I am old enough now to have known loss and pain, rejection and failure, grief and devastation. I have learned the difficulty and necessity of change. I have reordered my priorities. At twenty I wanted a man handsome, charming, witty, sophisticated, artistic—and a good dancer. Now the man I choose must be responsible, compassionate, honest, independent, generous-hearted . . . and must love women. That I now *choose* is an important

2. A French idiom for someone who is at once ugly and pretty.
3. From "Sailing to Byzantium" (1927) by William Butler Yeats.
4. From "A Litany in Time of Plague" (1592) by Thomas Nashe.

difference. Literally and metaphorically, I do not wait for the phone to ring.

When I look for origins of my later-life confidence, I see that it comes, not from years of achievements, but from the way I am treated by those closest to me. This is not a simple matter of being "loved." My parents surely loved me. My husband may have done so. My daughters, growing up, offered the love born of need. What has changed my feeling about myself, and so my life, has come partly from friends but mostly from being with a man who from the first respected me more than I could then respect myself. Days after our meeting, Sydney Bacon, still an eccentric stranger, said, "Have you any idea how often you say *'Sure'*?" and then, startlingly, "I don't know where your boundaries are. You seem prepared to accept invasion at any point." Fiercely protective of his own boundaries, he showed me how to protect mine. "Who is Sheila?" I asked one day, picking up a birthday card from his desk. "Why do you ask?" he countered. When I said, "Idle curiosity," he said, "There is no such thing as idle curiosity," and then, with finality, returning the card to its envelope: "Sheila is the person who sent me the card." When we traveled together, he would never allow me to put *my* things into *his* suitcase. "But you've got lots of room," I'd protest, gesturing towards my bulging luggage. "If you can't manage, throw something out—or buy another suitcase," he said. Not unkind, just firm, the door marked PRIVATE. The first time I asked, "Do you love me?" he said, "You know the Tantric[5] definition of love: *I recognize and respect your essence.*"

The physical changes of aging—some seem to happen overnight—come as a shock. Sometimes I feel I am traveling in disguise, a young girl inexplicably trapped in that body I glimpse as I pass reflecting windows. Grey hair, thickened middle, round where one hopes for flat and flat where one hopes for round. . . . Recent acquaintances, seeing a studio portrait of me at twenty, ripe against a background of leaves and flowers, ask, "Who's that?" I have become accustomed, though not resigned, to the camera's current images of someone with jowls and lines. (The worst comes when a well-meaning friend says, "Here's a great picture of you!")

These are the inevitable losses of age, to be borne as well as possible with Hemingway-style courage, grace under pressure. It is certainly true, however, that some losses are gains. Vanity no longer stands in the way of comfort and good sense. Was that really me, the girl who wore waist cinchers so tightly laced that I could not have swallowed a marshmallow? Who, like Cinderella's sisters, squeezed her feet into agonizingly tight shoes and teetered about on three-inch heels hoping to attract the

5. From the mystical writings of the Tantric school of Buddhism.

prince? Once I wore corselets and nylons in the hottest weather. It has been decades now since I owned a girdle; I go bare-legged and sandaled or barefoot all summer. I have accepted the fact that I will never be thin—that, regardless of diets, certain unwelcome redistributions of flesh have occurred. I would have liked a different figure. But I have, after decades of dissatisfaction, come to terms with my face. Young, I sighed for this one's eyes and that one's perfect nose. At sixty-past, I look in the mirror and, without vanity, am on the whole pleased with what I see. I have made this face. It is mine.

Along with youthful vanity, I am losing—have perhaps finally lost— the vision of life as competition. Looking back at my growing years, I can't remember a time when I didn't think it important to be best. This may be typical for a child of first-generation immigrants; certainly I observed, when I left my parents' insular world, that WASP friends did not run so hard. In our family, I longed to be best loved, never guessing how costly success would be. By the age of three, I had become self-consciously good, working for those moments when my mother would say to my older sister, "Look at Freidele![6] She never gives me any trouble." At five I discovered school and a new, grander arena where I might be best at reading, best in composition, best in behavior. I rejoiced the day the school nurse weighed all the second graders. "I'm over-weight!" I reported happily to my mother. "I'm more overweight than anybody in the room!" Being first in class, most admired elocutionist, teacher's pet (chosen to distribute ink and clap blackboard erasers)—for years I saw these as worthy goals, prizes to lay at my parents' feet.

Graduating from Harvard with a Ph.D., Phi Beta Kappa, provided a satisfactory close to academic competition; I mailed the diploma to my parents, another trophy of the hunt. Married the following year, I became once more a runner, toe poised at the starting line for the homemaker marathon. *Get ready, get set. . . .* With no hope, in a New England town, of entering the "best family" race, already determined by birth and old money, I set my own terms for social success. I would be best hostess. Had prizes been given, during those early married years, for complication of menu and multiplicity of occasion, I would have taken all the blue ribbons. I gave parties when people arrived in Dur-ham[7] and when they left; I entertained groups of ten, twenty, thirty at dinners where every ingredient had been tormented into a new shape or flavor. Preparing for a party, I pored over cookbooks in search of novelty. Should I purée the green beans with nutmeg and mace, or sauté them with onions and almonds? I made seven-layer tortes and ratatouille involving separate preparation of a dozen different vegetables. I prided

6. The Jewish diminutive of the Anglicized "Fredelle."

7. Durham, New Hampshire, Maynard's New England home.

myself on the range and absolute originality of my hors d'oeuvres, serving the first chocolate-covered ants ever offered at a Durham soirée. I once prefaced a dinner with thirteen appetizers, six hot and seven cold.

10   At the age I am now, I look back at the run farther, faster period of my life with astonishment. Partly the difference is a matter of my having less energy. But mostly it's a shift in perspective. The notion of life as open competition has come to seem absurd. There will always be women more popular and more accomplished, who give better parties, write better books. This realization comes not as defeat but as blessed relief. At last I can forget about coming first in class. I take time now to read, reflect, sew, garden, walk, talk with friends, play with my grandchildren.

My daughters, grown, continue to mystify, delight, amaze. Rona, the straggly plump schoolgirl, has become an exquisite woman whose closets and drawers, once a scandal, are far tidier than mine. As a child, she seemed uncoordinated, physically lethargic; today, she runs before breakfast and works out on an exercise bike. Joyce, our problem eater who dreaded mealtimes and subsisted largely on a diet of popcorn and fried chicken wings, is a superb cook and hostess. Growing up in rural New Hampshire, she longed for the brighter lights and prospects of cities; today she lives happily in rural New Hampshire with a pond, a meadow, a wood, and an orchard of her own. These things I could not have foreseen. Still, I can look at two poised, competent women and recognize my babies. Rona was a remote, almost regal infant. The reticent cool remains; it no longer feels hostile. Joyce, a cuddly baby, was all confidence and energy; she has carried those qualities into adult life. Both daughters smile at my writing and lecturing about child care. *"You* a parenting expert?" one said, not without affection. *"You* will tell other people how to raise their children?" It's true I was a most imperfect mother—overprotective, overambitious, overinvolved. But when I consider Rona and Joyce—as mothers, as writers, as unique individuals—I think I must have done something right. I cherish the memory of Rona in a fury of adolescent rebellion, shouting as she slammed the door: "I'll say one thing for you. You gave me the strength to fight you!"

Given my experience, the pure pleasure of grandparenting has taken me by surprise. I was never the kind of parent who asks, "When are you going to make me a grandma?", could not have imagined myself wearing a charm bracelet with dangling grandchild silhouettes. When Rona announced her pregnancy, I felt not rapture but dismay. So young, newly married, still a student—and the world waiting to be explored. What did she need a baby for? The actual child produced no swift instinctive rush of tenderness. I remember looking down at the rosy fragrant newborn, a blue-eyed stranger, and thinking, "I have no room for him in my life." As it happened, I had to make room. A year later, Benjamin and his mother came to visit me. After my own recent divorce,

I saw an active small boy as one more complication. He rushed about the rooms, imperiling Mexican pottery. He scribbled on the walls. He woke early and stayed up late. He *needed*—Pampers, drives to day care, comfort, toast. Gradually, that need became less irritant than bond, but a bond quite different from what I had experienced in mothering. My daughters for years had seemed flesh of my flesh, an extension of my being; their pain was mine. This first grandchild made possible a love almost wholly free from narcissism. I love Benjamin—as I have come to love Joyce's children, Audrey, Charlie, Willie—with a passion born of the blood tie but also, purely, for the person he is.

Benjamin has never called me Grandma. He was a year or so—just beginning to talk, having trouble with his Gs—when I walked into the kitchen where he sat banging on his high-chair tray. At the sound of my footsteps, he stopped banging, grinned, held out his arms to be picked up and said, *"Das. Das."* And Das I have remained. Das is a personality different both from Fredelle Maynard and from Rona and Joyce's mother. She is freer, less dogmatic, less intrusive. She makes fewer demands. She is more generous, eager to give whatever will be useful without looking for returns. Above all, she pays attention.

At fourteen, Benjamin is taller than I. He speaks Computer while I, hopelessly mired in the Neanderthal simplicities of typewriter and ball-point pen, don't know a modem from a floppy disk. It has been years now since I could beat him, or even hold my own, in a game of Big Boggle. (I am not so reckless as to try chess.) But still, when he comes to my house for the weekly sleepover, he reaches for the colored plastic drinking glasses I bought when he was in nursery school. Scarcely a detail has changed in our long-established rituals. I hug him; he manages to not quite evade the embrace. He heads first for the kitchen, opens the fridge and leans on the door taking stock. He pours himself a glass of ginger ale and we talk—not a connected conversation, just bits and pieces. Anything really important will emerge later if at all. "Is there soup? Can I have it at 4:30—and supper at 6?" Then he's off. He fits in his braces retainer, stretches out on the couch, reads, does his home-work, watches television. Sometimes he invites me to watch a program with him; sometimes he's up for a board game. If he finds a pretext to come into the room where I'm working, I try to help him towards the conversational opening he needs. That's when I might hear that he's unhappy at the new school. Very, very occasionally now, he'll ask me to read him a story. I never have to ask, "Which book?" This silent guarded boy, a Dungeons and Dragons devotee, a fan of Stephen King, wants once again the stories we have read together since he was a small child: "Clever Gretchen," "The Little Mermaid," "The Ugly Duck-ling."

With Audrey, Joyce's eight-year old, the relationship is qualitatively very different. She's a girl, after all, a girl who shares something of my temperament and most of my interests. But one element in the pattern seems to me absolutely the same. For both Audrey and Benjamin, my house is safe territory—like goal in a children's game, a place where you can't be tagged, you're home free. What happens here—again like a children's game—is ritual, ordered, exactly as it has always been. Audrey still brings to my house the Mexican wax dolls I gave her on her first overnight visit years ago. They're sadly deteriorated, short on fingers and feet. She doesn't really play with them any more but they're part of the scene. I always have Lipton's chicken noodle soup on hand. It's no longer her favorite, but she likes knowing it's there.

I read once, in a book called *The Vital Connection*, [8] that no matter what they do or don't do, grandparents affect the emotional well-being of their grandchildren simply because they exist. I understand that. My own grandparents were not, from a child's point of view, ideal. (Too old, too strange.) But they *mattered*. The only surviving pair, my father's parents, were separated from me by experience, culture and, most definitively, language. They spoke not a word of English; I knew very little Yiddish—not enough, certainly, to follow Zaida's [9] discourses on the nature of the universe. What I remember, though, is how hard I tried. "Can there be a watch without a watchmaker?" he would ask. "A world without God?" Though theological-philosophical argument had never much interested me, I hung on my grandfather's words. This gentle old man in yarmulka [1] and rusty caftan, bent reverently over the Talmud, [2] was my father's father. He had known my father as a little boy, a young man, and had himself once been a young man, a lover. My grandfather was living history—spirit of the *shtetl*, survivor of the Tsar's pogroms, evidence of Diaspora. [3] I wanted his secrets, and my grandmother's, but had to settle for Russian tea sweetened with *veranya*, cherry jam, and thin dry poppyseed cookies tasting of flour. Brought to alien Winnipeg by their grown sons, my grandparents knew nothing of the world beyond their curtains. When I wore fashionable toeless shoes, my grandmother wept and pressed a crumpled dollar bill into my hand. When I acquired a bicycle, my grandfather said, "Now we need a radio," an apparent *non sequitur* [4] later elucidated by my father. "Zaida's afraid you might get hurt on the bike. He thinks if anything happened to you, the news would be flashed on the air at once." Since in all my years of visiting, my grandparents and I never had anything approaching a real

8. *The Vital Connection* (1985) by Arthur Kornhaber and Kenneth L. Woodward.
9. Yiddish for grandfather or wise old man.
1. Skullcap worn by male Orthodox Jews.
2. The text of Jewish law and teachings.
3. Experiences of Jewish culture: *shtetls* were the Jewish villages of Eastern Europe, Tsar's pogroms refers to the government's massacres of Jews under the Russian Tsars, Diaspora refers to the scattering of Jews in the Gentile world.
4. An illogical inference.

conversation, it is perhaps true that they did not know me. Yet I felt loved. Precisely because our chief communication was nonverbal, their tender affection had a special quality, unconnected with character or achievement. My grandparents loved my *being*.

So I think now that this purity of feeling—you are, therefore I love—is a grandparent's most precious gift. Parents love, of course, but in complicated ways, the love so often shot through with need, ambition, exasperation, anger, disappointment, pride. To the parent, a child represents a second chance at being a perfect person. Inevitably, there's pressure on the child to go farther, achieve more. To a grandparent, the child represents a second chance at being a perfect *parent*. The result, at least in my experience, is uniquely liberating. I wanted my daughters to be successful writers and—successfully, but at some cost—pushed them towards that goal. I want my grandchildren to be happy. If Benjamin were to prove a computer genius I would be gratified, no doubt. But if he were to become a chef or a bicycle mechanic (possibilities suggested by his interests, not mine), I would be equally pleased so long as he enjoyed his work and did it well.

On Parents' Night, I used to appear at school like a horse trainer at the racetrack. How is my entry doing—compared with the others, compared with previous performance? What could we do to improve distance and speed? I thought of this when I had occasion, once again, to line up at the teacher's desk. Benjamin was spending a week with me during his parents' absence; I was attending Parents' Night on their behalf. In the high-school auditorium, mothers and fathers milled about or stood in line to get the latest report on their children. Waiting, I remembered all the times I had performed this ritual, the usual reward being a tribute to my daughters' good behavior and brains. As I moved up the line I caught familiar drifting murmurs: "She's doing beautifully." "Great improvement." "We really enjoy him." As my turn arrived and I identified myself to each teacher, the smiles faded. Benjamin was a very bright boy, no question. Likable. Academically a disaster. He came to class without his textbook, paid no attention, clowned, distracted classmates, failed to hand in homework, appeared indifferent to either encouragement or reproof.

Had I received such a report on my children, I would, I fear, have first questioned the teacher's capacity. How could she have failed to stimulate or appreciate my brilliant daughters? Then I would have gone raging home. *Do you realize your whole future is at stake? What has come over you? If you don't pick up those grades, there'll be no movies, no trips to Boston, no new guitar.* And finally, *How can you do this to me?* To me. My children were my representatives in the world; their failure would be mine. As Benjamin's grandmother, I felt none of these things. I saw his teachers as allies, not adversaries. Riding home on the bus, I was overwhelmed with anxiety and grief. What I had heard revealed not a bad boy or an indolent one, but a troubled child. How could I have wished to reprove, or to punish? The important thing was to help.

20   Mostly, as a grandparent, I keep a sense of perspective. This child is not me, not mine. I have no right to impose on him my wants, my expectations.

When I was a young mother, I knew all about the dangers of spoiling a child. Picking up a crying baby, allowing just one more turn on the swing, giving cookies to a child who hadn't finished his spinach—in effect, giving children what they wanted—all that was spoiling, and led to No Good End. Spoiled children became difficult, demanding adults. So I made, and tried to keep, a lot of rules. I ran a tight ship.

Over the years, I've changed my mind about the dangers of giving children, within reason, what they want. I think truly "spoiled" individuals, selfish and self-absorbed, are those whose needs, in childhood, were never met. And in any case, spoiling seems to me a grandparent's prerogative. With Benjamin, Audrey, Charlie and Willie I run a loose ship. I let Audrey spend an entire day in nightgown and bathrobe if she feels like taking things easy. I allow Benjamin to glut on raw cookie dough and TV. I have on occasion shared my bed with *three* grandchildren (all wiggly, one damp) to settle a squabble over *whose turn.* When Charlie scatters blocks over the living-room floor I can say, "I'll pick them up tomorrow." I have been known to agree with a tired child that it's too late for toothbrushing. And none of this matters, or will corrupt their characters, because the children draw no conclusions from what goes on in Grandma's house to what's permissible in the real world. My house is Liberty Hall, Queen for a Day, Name Your Tune. [5]

My eagerness to give my grandchildren time has, I suppose, a melancholy undernote. I won't always be here for them. As a young mother, I felt immortal. Right into my thirties and forties, the age at which I began to lose people dear to me, I would say, *"If* I die," not "When I die." I still feel immortal in flashes—when crocuses push through the frozen earth, when Audrey hugs, giggles and whispers all at once. But mostly I'm very aware of the fact that I don't have forever with these flowers, my children's children. I want, in whatever time we have together, to give them strength for the road ahead, tell them what I know. I show Audrey how to roll pie crust and how to root a new African violet from one furry leaf. I teach Benjamin to operate the sewing machine. When Joyce's Charlie asks, "Why did God let the airplane crash and kill people?" I take that very seriously; I try to explain. I want to pass on skills that have served me well, along with a sense of who I am, that

5. Places where dreams come true: Liberty Hall is any place where you do as you like, "Queen for a Day" and "Name [That] Tune" are television game shows with dazzling prizes for the winner.

being a part of who *they* are. I tell my grandchildren stories about their parents and my parents, and about my own unimaginable childhood in a world without television. When Audrey asks, "What's Jewish?" I try to explain in terms meaningful to eight-year olds—about Jewish food, Jewish holidays, about the wineglass ground underfoot at a Jewish wedding and the solemn bar mitzvah processions, following the Torah in its tasseled, filigreed silver case, that celebrates a Jewish male's coming of age.

When I think of my hopes for my grandchildren, what comes to me is a film called *The Triumph of Job*. [6] Set in wartime Hungary, it tells the story of an elderly Jewish couple whose children, all seven of them, died at birth. Now, in the shadow of death, the old man determines to realize a lifelong dream. He will "raise a man for the Lord." The couple adopts a child—Christian, since only a Christian can inherit their small substance, survive the coming catastrophe. In their brief time together—it's perhaps a year, a year during which love grows painfully, powerfully, between these grandparent figures and their wild child—Job and his wife prepare the boy for survival. This you must remember, this you must do. One day the father begins, "When you are alone—" and the child bursts out, "I don't want to be alone, I want to be with you." "The old cannot always remain with the young," Job says gently. "So now you must learn to be alone."

I thought of that film the day Audrey and I walked along the Toronto lakefront, eating ice cream and popcorn simultaneously, planning the next adventure. Out of nowhere, Audrey said, "Grandma, I wish you could always be just the way you are now." Startling at the adult prescience in that wish, looking at Audrey with her wild-honey-colored skin and huge dark Yemenite eyes, I thought of a scene in *The Triumph of Job*. With the Germans on the march, their fatal trucks advancing, the old woman packs a chest of linens and silver for the child who will be left behind. Then she lights the candles; it is Sabbath eve. "Dear God," she prays, "only let me live to bake his wedding bread."

Time. Ay, there's the rub. Between the desire and the reality falls the shadow. I have never feared death, because death is not real on my pulses. But the recognition that time is finite—that has come. I remember when I was in my forties, an elderly friend brought flowers for my garden saying, "So you'll think of me when I'm gone." As we walked to her car, a new one, she gestured. "This will be our last car." I wondered then at her serene acceptance. Wouldn't there always be another car, another visit? Mrs. Phillips is long gone now; her Canterbury bells blow about my yard, seeded everywhere, and I think of her and I think of my own ending. I feel a sense of waste, also some

6. *The [Revolt] of Job* (1986) directed by Imre Gyongyossy.

outrage, that life won't go on forever—just when I'm getting the hang of it.

One day recently, when I was summering in New Hampshire, a real-estate agent called. "Do you own property in Durham?" "Yes," I said, proprietary. "I'm standing on it right now." "Would you be interested in selling?" the voice asked. I was surprised at my irrational rage. Selling *my house?* Someone else swinging on my porch, picking my crimson tulips, cutting down the lilac? Obliterating the pencil marks that show my children's heights as they grew? Obliterating *me?* I put down the phone trembling.

These days, when I glance at obituaries (a recent interest), I see that most of the departed are my age or younger. Cancer, heart, after long illness. . . . On annual trips to New Hampshire, I see old people who were once members of our kindergarten car pool. My parents have died, the love of my youth has died. I am at the top of the tree, beyond the fruiting branches. But I am still here, still looking skyward.

THE READER

1. This essay was written by a woman who is a child psychologist and a grandmother. Select passages in which one or the other voice or role dominates. How do the two work together in this essay?

2. Define narcissism (p. 43). How close does Joyce Maynard come to this topic in "Four Generations" (p. 35)? What is her attitude toward it?

3. Maynard credits the change in her feelings about herself to a man who respected her, but she devotes most of her essay to her family, especially her grandchildren. Is this inconsistent?

THE WRITER

1. Why did Maynard begin with two opening anecdotes? What might have been her strategy as a writer?

2. This essay and Joyce Maynard's "Four Generations" (p. 35) tell you about five generations in their family. On the basis of what you are told, write a sketch for a family history. What in that sketch would also be useful for a more general social history of American families over the past century?

3. Taking the facts from the grandmother's account, and perhaps their interpretation as well, invent a journal entry from a grandchild's point of view about a visit to her house.

Loren Eiseley

THE BROWN WASPS

There is a corner in the waiting room of one of the great Eastern stations where women never sit. It is always in the shadow and overhung by rows of lockers. It is, however, always frequented—not so much by genuine travelers as by the dying. It is here that a certain element of the abandoned poor seeks a refuge out of the weather, clinging for a few hours longer to the city that has fathered them. In a precisely similar manner I have seen, on a sunny day in midwinter, a few old brown wasps creep slowly over an abandoned wasp nest in a thicket. Numbed and forgetful and frost-blackened, the hum of the spring hive still resounded faintly in their sodden tissues. Then the temperature would fall and they would drop away into the white oblivion of the snow. Here in the station it is in no way different save that the city is busy in its snows. But the old ones cling to their seats as though these were symbolic and could not be given up. Now and then they sleep, their gray old heads resting with painful awkwardness on the backs of the benches.

Also they are not at rest. For an hour they may sleep in the gasping exhaustion of the ill-nourished and aged who have to walk in the night. Then a policeman comes by on his round and nudges them upright.

"You can't sleep here," he growls.

A strange ritual then begins. An old man is difficult to waken. After a muttered conversation the policeman presses a coin into his hand and passes fiercely along the benches prodding and gesturing toward the door. In his wake, like birds rising and settling behind the passage of a farmer through a cornfield, the men totter up, move a few paces and subside once more upon the benches.

One man, after a slight, apologetic lurch, does not move at all. Tubercularly thin, he sleeps on steadily. The policeman does not look back. To him, too, this has become a ritual. He will not have to notice it again officially for another hour.

Once in a while one of the sleepers will not awake. Like the brown wasps, he will have had his wish to die in the great droning center of the hive rather than in some lonely room. It is not so bad here with the shuffle of footsteps and the knowledge that there are others who share the bad luck of the world. There are also the whistles and the sounds of everyone, everyone in the world, starting on journeys. Amidst so many journeys somebody is bound to come out all right. Somebody.

5

From *The Night Country* (1971).

Maybe it was on a like thought that the brown wasps fell away from the old paper nest in the thicket. You hold till the last, even if it is only to a public seat in a railroad station. You want your place in the hive more than you want a room or a place where the aged can be eased gently out of the way. It is the place that matters, the place at the heart of things. It is life that you want, that bruises your gray old head with the hard chairs; a man has a right to his place.

But sometimes the place is lost in the years behind us. Or sometimes it is a thing of air, a kind of vaporous distortion above a heap of rubble. We cling to a time and place because without them man is lost, not only man but life. This is why the voices, real or unreal, which speak from the floating trumpets at spiritualist seances are so unnerving. They are voices out of nowhere whose only reality lies in their ability to stir the memory of a living person with some fragment of the past. Before the medium's cabinet both the dead and the living revolve endlessly about an episode, a place, an event that has already been engulfed by time.

This feeling runs deep in life; it brings stray cats running over endless miles, and birds homing from the ends of the earth. It is as though all living creatures, and particularly the more intelligent, can survive only by fixing or transforming a bit of time into space or by securing a bit of space with its objects immortalized and made permanent in time. For example, I once saw, on a flower pot in my own living room, the efforts of a field mouse to build a remembered field. I have lived to see this episode repeated in a thousand guises, and since I have spent a large portion of my life in the shade of a nonexistent tree, I think I am entitled to speak for the field mouse.

10   One day as I cut across the field which at that time extended on one side of our suburban shopping center, I found a giant slug feeding from a runnel of pink ice cream in an abandoned Dixie cup. I could see his eyes telescope and protrude in a kind of dim, uncertain ecstasy as his dark body bunched and elongated in the curve of the cup. Then, as I stood there at the edge of the concrete, contemplating the slug, I began to realize it was like standing on a shore where a different type of life creeps up and fumbles tentatively among the rocks and sea wrack. It knows its place and will only creep so far until something changes. Little by little as I stood there I began to see more of this shore that surrounds the place of man. I looked with sudden care and attention at things I had been running over thoughtlessly for years. I even waded out a short way into the grass and the wild-rose thickets to see more. A huge black-belted bee went droning by and there were some indistinct scurryings in the underbrush.

Then I came to a sign which informed me that this field was to be the site of a new Wanamaker suburban store. Thousands of obscure lives were about to perish, the spores of puffballs would go smoking off to new fields, and the bodies of little white-footed mice would be crunched under the inexorable wheels of the bulldozers. Life disappears or modifies its appearances so fast that everything takes on an aspect of illusion—a momentary fizzing and boiling with smoke rings, like pouring dissident chemicals into a retort. Here man was advancing, but in a few years his plaster and bricks would be disappearing once more into the insatiable maw of the clover. Being of an archaeological cast of mind, I thought of this fact with an obscure sense of satisfaction and waded back through the rose thickets to the concrete parking lot. As I did so, a mouse scurried ahead of me, frightened of my steps if not of that ominous Wanamaker sign. I saw him vanish in the general direction of my apartment house, his little body quivering with fear in the great open sun on the blazing concrete. Blinded and confused, he was running straight away from his field. In another week scores would follow him.

I forgot the episode then and went home to the quiet of my living room. It was not until a week later, letting myself into the apartment, that I realized I had a visitor. I am fond of plants and had several ferns standing on the floor in pots to avoid the noon glare by the south window.

As I snapped on the light and glanced carelessly around the room, I saw a little heap of earth on the carpet and a scrabble of pebbles that had been kicked merrily over the edge of one of the flower pots. To my astonishment I discovered a full-fledged burrow delving downward among the fern roots. I waited silently. The creature who had made the burrow did not appear. I remembered the wild field then, and the flight of the mice. No house mouse, no *Mus domesticus*, had kicked up this little heap of earth or sought refuge under a fern root in a flower pot. I thought of the desperate little creature I had seen fleeing from the wild-rose thicket. Through intricacies of pipes and attics, he, or one of his fellows, had climbed to this high green solitary room. I could visualize what had occurred. He had an image in his head, a world of seed pods and quiet, of green sheltering leaves in the dim light among the weed stems. It was the only world he knew and it was gone.

Somehow in his flight he had found his way to this room with drawn shades where no one would come till nightfall. And here he had smelled green leaves and run quickly up the flower pot to dabble his paws in common earth. He had even struggled half the afternoon to carry his burrow deeper and had failed. I examined the hole, but no whiskered twitching face appeared. He was gone. I gathered up the earth and refilled the burrow. I did not expect to find traces of him again.

Yet for three nights thereafter I came home to the darkened room and my ferns to find the dirt kicked gaily about the rug and the burrow reopened, though I was never able to catch the field mouse within it. I dropped a little food about the mouth of the burrow, but it was never

15

touched. I looked under beds or sat reading with one ear cocked for rustlings in the ferns. It was all in vain; I never saw him. Probably he ended in a trap in some other tenant's room.

But before he disappeared I had come to look hopefully for his evening burrow. About my ferns there had begun to linger the insubstantial vapor of an autumn field, the distilled essence, as it were, of a mouse brain in exile from its home. It was a small dream, like our dreams, carried a long and weary journey along pipes and through spider webs, past holes over which loomed the shadows of waiting cats, and finally, desperately, into this room where he had played in the shuttered daylight for an hour among the green ferns on the floor. Every day these invisible dreams pass us on the street, or rise from beneath our feet, or look out upon us from beneath a bush.

Some years ago the old elevated railway in Philadelphia was torn down and replaced by a subway system. This ancient El with its barnlike stations containing nut-vending machines and scattered food scraps had, for generations, been the favorite feeding ground of flocks of pigeons, generally one flock to a station along the route of the El. Hundreds of pigeons were dependent upon the system. They flapped in and out of its stanchions and steel work or gathered in watchful little audiences about the feet of anyone who rattled the peanut-vending machines. They even watched people who jingled change in their hands, and prospected for food under the feet of the crowds who gathered between trains. Probably very few among the waiting people who tossed a crumb to an eager pigeon realized that this El was like a food-bearing river, and that the life which haunted its banks was dependent upon the running of the trains with their human freight.

I saw the river stop.

The time came when the underground tubes were ready; the traffic was transferred to a realm unreachable by pigeons. It was like a great river subsiding suddenly into desert sands. For a day, for two days, pigeons continued to circle over the El or stand close to the red vending machines. They were patient birds, and surely this great river which had flowed through the lives of unnumbered generations was merely suffering from some momentary drought.

They listened for the familiar vibrations that had always heralded an approaching train; they flapped hopefully about the head of an occasional workman walking along the steel runways. They passed from one empty station to another, all the while growing hungrier. Finally they flew away.

I thought I had seen the last of them about the El, but there was a revival and it provided a curious instance of the memory of living things for a way of life or a locality that has long been cherished. Some weeks after the El was abandoned workmen began to tear it down. I went to work every morning by one particular station, and the time came when the demolition crews reached this spot. Acetylene torches showered passersby with sparks, pneumatic drills hammered at the base of the structure, and a blind man who, like the pigeons, had clung with his cup to a stairway leading to the change booth, was forced to give up his place.

It was then, strangely, momentarily, one morning that I witnessed the return of a little band of the familiar pigeons. I even recognized one or two members of the flock that had lived around this particular station before they were dispersed into the streets. They flew bravely in and out among the sparks and the hammers and the shouting workmen. They had returned—and they had returned because the hubbub of the wreckers had convinced them that the river was about to flow once more. For several hours they flapped in and out through the empty windows, nodding their heads and watching the fall of girders with attentive little eyes. By the following morning the station was reduced to some burned-off stanchions in the street. My bird friends had gone. It was plain, however, that they retained a memory for an insubstantial structure now compounded of air and time. Even the blind man clung to it. Someone had provided him with a chair, and he sat at the same corner staring sightlessly at an invisible stairway where, so far as he was concerned, the crowds were still ascending to the trains.

I have said my life has been passed in the shade of a nonexistent tree, so that such sights do not offend me. Prematurely I am one of the brown wasps and I often sit with them in the great droning hive of the station, dreaming sometimes of a certain tree. It was planted sixty years ago by a boy with a bucket and a toy spade in a little Nebraska town. That boy was myself. It was a cottonwood sapling and the boy remembered it because of some words spoken by his father and because everyone died or moved away who was supposed to wait and grow old under its shade. The boy was passed from hand to hand, but the tree for some intangible reason had taken root in his mind. It was under its branches that he sheltered; it was from this tree that his memories, which are my memories, led away into the world.

After sixty years the mood of the brown wasps grows heavier upon one. During a long inward struggle I thought it would do me good to go and look upon that actual tree. I found a rational excuse in which to clothe this madness. I purchased a ticket and at the end of two thousand miles I walked another mile to an address that was still the same. The house had not been altered.

I came close to the white picket fence and reluctantly, with great effort, looked down the long vista of the yard. There was nothing there to see. For sixty years that cottonwood had been growing in my mind. Season by season its seeds had been floating farther on the hot prairie winds. We had planted it lovingly there, my father and I, because he had a great hunger for soil and live things growing, and because none of these things had long been ours to protect. We had planted the little sapling and watered it faithfully, and I remembered that I had run out with my small bucket to drench its roots the day we moved away. And all the years since it had been growing in my mind, a huge tree that somehow stood for my father and the love I bore him. I took a grasp on the picket fence and forced myself to look again.

A boy with the hard bird eye of youth pedaled a tricycle slowly up beside me.

"What'cha lookin' at?" he asked curiously.

"A tree," I said.

"What for?" he said.

30 "It isn't there," I said, to myself mostly, and began to walk away at a pace just slow enough not to seem to be running.

"What isn't there?" the boy asked. I didn't answer. It was obvious I was attached by a thread to a thing that had never been there, or certainly not for long. Something that had to be held in the air, or sustained in the mind, because it was part of my orientation in the universe and I could not survive without it. There was more than an animal's attachment to a place. There was something else, the attachment of the spirit to a grouping of events in time; it was part of our mortality.

So I had come home at last, driven by a memory in the brain as surely as the field mouse who had delved long ago into my flower pot or the pigeons flying forever amidst the rattle of nut-vending machines. These, the burrow under the greenery in my living room and the red-bellied bowls of peanuts now hovering in midair in the minds of pigeons, were all part of an elusive world that existed nowhere and yet everywhere. I looked once at the real world about me while the persistent boy pedaled at my heels.

It was without meaning, though my feet took a remembered path. In sixty years the house and street had rotted out of my mind. But the tree, the tree that no longer was, that had perished in its first season, bloomed on in my individual mind, unblemished as my father's words. "We'll plant a tree here, son, and we're not going to move any more. And when you're an old, old man you can sit under it and think how we planted it here, you and me, together."

I began to outpace the boy on the tricycle.

35 "Do you live here, Mister?" he shouted after me suspiciously. I took a firm grasp on airy nothing—to be precise, on the bole of a great tree. "I do," I said. I spoke for myself, one field mouse, and several pigeons. We were all out of touch but somehow permanent. It was the world that had changed.

THE READER

1. *Eiseley writes of old men in train stations, brown wasps, a field mouse, pigeons near the El, and his own return to his boyhood home in Nebraska. What do these matters have in common? Can you state the essay's theme?*

2. *In "Once More to the Lake" (p. 55), White describes his return to a lake he had known years earlier. What reflections arise in his mind on this occasion? Are they similar to, or different from, Eiseley's thoughts upon returning to his Nebraska home and the nonexistent tree?*

3. *Would Eiseley agree with Thoreau's remarks in "Observation" (p. 204)? If so, in what particular ways would he agree?*

THE WRITER

1. *Some psychologists study animal behavior in order to learn about human behavior, but many of them write about animals in a very different fashion. Do you think that Eiseley's way of relating the behavior of animals to human behavior makes sense? If you are studying psychology, it might be interesting to compare a selection from your textbook with this essay.*

2. *Eiseley's essay contains sentences like "We cling to a time and place because without them man is lost, not only man but life" (p. 50) and "A boy with the hard bird eye of youth pedaled a tricycle slowly up beside me" (p. 54). What is the difference between these two kinds of sentences? Can you show how Eiseley manages to connect one kind with the other?*

3. *Write an essay comparing the theme or purpose of "The Brown Wasps" with that of Lorenz's "The Taming of the Shrew" (p. 588). Does Lorenz take a similar approach to his subject? Consider also the manner of the writing: how would you characterize it in each instance?*

E. B. White

ONCE MORE TO THE LAKE

One summer, along about 1904, my father rented a camp on a lake in Maine and took us all there for the month of August. We all got ringworm from some kittens and had to rub Pond's Extract on our arms

Originally appeared in "One Man's Meat," White's column for *Harper's Magazine* (Oct. 1941).

and legs night and morning, and my father rolled over in a canoe with all his clothes on; but outside of that the vacation was a success and from then on none of us ever thought there was any place in the world like that lake in Maine. We returned summer after summer—always on August 1st for one month. I have since become a salt-water man, but sometimes in summer there are days when the restlessness of the tides and the fearful cold of the sea water and the incessant wind which blows across the afternoon and into the evening make me wish for the placidity of a lake in the woods. A few weeks ago this feeling got so strong I bought myself a couple of bass hooks and a spinner and returned to the lake where we used to go, for a week's fishing and to revisit old haunts.

I took along my son, who had never had any fresh water up his nose and who had seen lily pads only from train windows. On the journey over to the lake I began to wonder what it would be like. I wondered how time would have marred this unique, this holy spot—the coves and streams, the hills that the sun set behind, the camps and the paths behind the camps. I was sure the tarred road would have found it out and I wondered in what other ways it would be desolated. It is strange how much you can remember about places like that once you allow your mind to return into the grooves which lead back. You remember one thing, and that suddenly reminds you of another thing. I guess I remembered clearest of all the early mornings, when the lake was cool and motionless, remembered how the bedroom smelled of the lumber it was made of and of the wet woods whose scent entered through the screen. The partitions in the camp were thin and did not extend clear to the top of the rooms, and as I was always the first up I would dress softly so as not to wake the others, and sneak out into the sweet outdoors and start out in the canoe, keeping close along the shore in the long shadows of the pines. I remembered being very careful never to rub my paddle against the gunwale for fear of disturbing the stillness of the cathedral.

The lake had never been what you would call a wild lake. There were cottages sprinkled around the shores, and it was in farming country although the shores of the lake were quite heavily wooded. Some of the cottages were owned by nearby farmers, and you would live at the shore and eat your meals at the farmhouse. That's what our family did. But although it wasn't wild, it was a fairly large and undisturbed lake and there were places in it which, to a child at least, seemed infinitely remote and primeval.

I was right about the tar: it led to within half a mile of the shore. But when I got back there, with my boy, and we settled into a camp near a farmhouse and into the kind of summertime I had known, I could tell that it was going to be pretty much the same as it had been before—I knew it, lying in bed the first morning, smelling the bedroom, and hearing the boy sneak quietly out and go off along the shore in a boat.

I began to sustain the illusion that he was I, and therefore, by simple transposition, that I was my father. This sensation persisted, kept cropping up all the time we were there. It was not an entirely new feeling, but in this setting it grew much stronger. I seemed to be living a dual existence. I would be in the middle of some simple act, I would be picking up a bait box or laying down a table fork, or I would be saying something, and suddenly it would be not I but my father who was saying the words or making the gesture. It gave me a creepy sensation.

We went fishing the first morning. I felt the same damp moss covering the worms in the bait can, and saw the dragonfly alight on the tip of my rod as it hovered a few inches from the surface of the water. It was the arrival of this fly that convinced me beyond any doubt that everything was as it always had been, that the years were a mirage and there had been no years. The small waves were the same, chucking the rowboat under the chin as we fished at anchor, and the boat was the same boat, the same color green and the ribs broken in the same places, and under the floor-boards the same fresh-water leavings and débris— the dead helgramite,[1] the wisps of moss, the rusty discarded fishhook, the dried blood from yesterday's catch. We stared silently at the tips of our rods, at the dragonflies that came and went. I lowered the tip of mine into the water, tentatively, pensively dislodging the fly, which darted two feet away, poised, darted two feet back, and came to rest again a little farther up the rod. There had been no years between the ducking of this dragonfly and the other one—the one that was part of memory. I looked at the boy, who was silently watching his fly, and it was my hands that held his rod, my eyes watching. I felt dizzy and didn't know which rod I was at the end of.

We caught two bass, hauling them in briskly as though they were mackerel, pulling them over the side of the boat in a businesslike manner without any landing net, and stunning them with a blow on the back of the head. When we got back for a swim before lunch, the lake was exactly where we had left it, the same number of inches from the dock, and there was only the merest suggestion of a breeze. This seemed an utterly enchanted sea, this lake you could leave to its own devices for a few hours and come back to, and find that it had not stirred, this constant and trustworthy body of water. In the shallows, the dark, water-soaked sticks and twigs, smooth and old, were undulating in clusters on the bottom against the clean ribbed sand, and the track of the mussel was plain. A school of minnows swam by, each minnow with its small individual shadow, doubling the attendance, so clear and sharp in the sunlight. Some of the other campers were in swimming, along the shore, one of them with a cake of soap, and the water felt thin and clear

1. The nymph of the mayfly, used as bait.

and unsubstantial. Over the years there had been this person with the cake of soap, this cultist, and here he was. There had been no years.

Up to the farmhouse to dinner through the teeming, dusty field, the road under our sneakers was only a two-track road. The middle track was missing, the one with the marks of the hooves and the splotches of dried, flaky manure. There had always been three tracks to choose from in choosing which track to walk in; now the choice was narrowed down to two. For a moment I missed terribly the middle alternative. But the way led past the tennis court, and something about the way it lay there in the sun reassured me; the tape had loosened along the backline, the alleys were green with plantains and other weeds, and the net (installed in June and removed in September) sagged in the dry noon, and the whole place steamed with midday heat and hunger and emptiness. There was a choice of pie for dessert, and one was blueberry and one was apple, and the waitresses were the same country girls, there having been no passage of time, only the illusion of it as in a dropped curtain— the waitresses were still fifteen; their hair had been washed, that was the only difference—they had been to the movies and seen the pretty girls with the clean hair.

Summertime, oh summertime, pattern of life indelible, the fade-proof lake, the woods unshatterable, the pasture with the sweetfern and the juniper forever and ever, summer without end; this was the background, and the life along the shore was the design, the cottagers with their innocent and tranquil design, their tiny docks with the flagpole and the American flag floating against the white clouds in the blue sky, the little paths over the roots of the trees leading from camp to camp and the paths leading back to the outhouses and the can of lime for sprinkling, and at the souvenir counters at the store the miniature birch-bark canoes and the post cards that showed things looking a little better than they looked. This was the American family at play, escaping the city heat, wondering whether the newcomers in the camp at the head of the cove were "common" or "nice," wondering whether it was true that the people who drove up for Sunday dinner at the farmhouse were turned away because there wasn't enough chicken.

It seemed to me, as I kept remembering all this, that those times and those summers had been infinitely precious and worth saving. There had been jollity and peace and goodness. The arriving (at the beginning of August) had been so big a business in itself, at the railway station the farm wagon drawn up, the first smell of the pine-laden air, the first glimpse of the smiling farmer, and the great importance of the trunks and your father's enormous authority in such matters, and the feel of the wagon under you for the long ten-mile haul, and at the top of the last long hill catching the first view of the lake after eleven months of not seeing this cherished body of water. The shouts and cries of the other campers when they saw you, and the trunks to be unpacked, to give up their rich burden. (Arriving was less exciting nowadays, when you sneaked up in your car and parked it under a tree near the camp and took out the bags and in five minutes it was all over, no fuss, no loud wonderful fuss about trunks.)

Peace and goodness and jollity. The only thing that was wrong now, really, was the sound of the place, an unfamiliar nervous sound of the outboard motors. This was the note that jarred, the one thing that would sometimes break the illusion and set the years moving. In those other summertimes all motors were inboard; and when they were at a little distance, the noise they made was a sedative, an ingredient of summer sleep. They were one-cylinder and two-cylinder engines, and some were make-and-break and some were jump-spark, [2] but they all made a sleepy sound across the lake. The one-lungers throbbed and fluttered, and the twin-cylinder ones purred and purred, and that was a quiet sound too. But now the campers all had outboards. In the daytime, in the hot mornings, these motors made a petulant, irritable sound; at night, in the still evening when the afterglow lit the water, they whined about one's ears like mosquitoes. My boy loved our rented outboard, and his great desire was to achieve singlehanded mastery over it, and authority, and he soon learned the trick of choking it a little (but not too much), and the adjustment of the needle valve. Watching him I would remember the things you could do with the old one-cylinder engine with the heavy flywheel, how you could have it eating out of your hand if you got really close to it spiritually. Motor boats in those days didn't have clutches, and you would make a landing by shutting off the motor at the proper time and coasting in with a dead rudder. But there was a way of reversing them, if you learned the trick, by cutting the switch and putting it on again exactly on the final dying revolution of the flywheel, so that it would kick back against compression and begin reversing. Approaching a dock in a strong following breeze, it was difficult to slow up sufficiently by the ordinary coasting method, and if a boy felt he had complete mastery over his motor, he was tempted to keep it running beyond its time and then reverse it a few feet from the dock. It took a cool nerve, because if you threw the switch a twentieth of a second too soon you would catch the flywheel when it still had speed enough to go up past center, and the boat would leap ahead, charging bull-fashion at the dock.

We had a good week at the camp. The bass were biting well and the sun shone endlessly, day after day. We would be tired at night and lie down in the accumulated heat of the little bedrooms after the long hot day and the breeze would stir almost imperceptibly outside and the smell of the swamp drift in through the rusty screens. Sleep would come easily

10

---

2. Methods of ignition timing.

and in the morning the red squirrel would be on the roof, tapping out his gay routine. I kept remembering everything, lying in bed in the mornings—the small steamboat that had a long rounded stern like the lip of a Ubangi, and how quietly she ran on the moonlight sails, when the older boys played their mandolins and the girls sang and we ate doughnuts dipped in sugar, and how sweet the music was on the water in the shining night, and what it had felt like to think about girls then. After breakfast we would go up to the store and the things were in the same place—the minnows in a bottle, the plugs and spinners disarranged and pawed over by the youngsters from the boys' camp, the fig newtons and the Beeman's gum. Outside, the road was tarred and cars stood in front of the store. Inside, all was just as it had always been, except there was more Coca-Cola and not so much Moxie and root beer and birch beer and sarsaparilla. We would walk out with a bottle of pop apiece and sometimes the pop would backfire up our noses and hurt. We explored the streams, quietly, where the turtles slid off the sunny logs and dug their way into the soft bottom; and we lay on the town wharf and fed worms to the tame bass. Everywhere we went I had trouble making out which was I, the one walking at my side, the one walking in my pants.

One afternoon while we were there at that lake a thunderstorm came up. It was like the revival of an old melodrama that I had seen long ago with childish awe. The second-act climax of the drama of the electrical disturbance over a lake in America had not changed in any important respect. This was the big scene, still the big scene. The whole thing was so familiar, the first feeling of oppression and heat and a general air around camp of not wanting to go very far away. In midafternoon (it was all the same) a curious darkening of the sky, and a lull in everything that had made life tick; and then the way the boats suddenly swung the other way at their moorings with the coming of a breeze out of the new quarter, and the premonitory rumble. Then the kettle drum, then the snare, then the bass drum and cymbals, then crackling light against the dark, and the gods grinning and licking their chops in the hills. Afterward the calm, the rain steadily rustling in the calm lake, the return of light and hope and spirits, and the campers running out in joy and relief to go swimming in the rain, their bright cries perpetuating the deathless joke about how they were getting simply drenched, and the children screaming with delight at the new sensation of bathing in the rain, and the joke about getting drenched linking the generations in a strong indestructible chain. And the comedian who waded in carrying an umbrella.

When the others went swimming my son said he was going in too. He pulled his dripping trunks from the line where they had hung all through the shower, and wrung them out. Languidly, and with no thought of going in, I watched him, his hard little body, skinny and bare, saw him wince slightly as he pulled up around his vitals the small, soggy, icy garment. As he buckled the swollen belt suddenly my groin felt the chill of death.

THE READER

1. White had not been back to the lake for many years. What bearing has this fact on the experience the essay describes?
2. How do the differences between boats of the past and boats of today relate to or support the point of the essay?
3. What is the meaning of White's last sentence? What relation has it to the sentence just preceding? How has White prepared us for this ending?
4. Read White's "Some Remarks on Humor" (p. 1132). Is he writing humor in "Once More to the Lake"?

THE WRITER

1. What has guided White in his selection of the details he gives about the trip? Why, for example, does he talk about the road, the dragonfly, the bather with the cake of soap?
2. In "On Keeping a Notebook," Didion says that it is good to keep in touch with the people we used to be (p. 72). Is that what White is doing here?
3. Write an account of an experience, real or imagined, in which you return to a place you haven't seen for a while. Think about what point you wish to make through your narrative.

Anatole Broyard

INTOXICATED BY MY ILLNESS

So much of a writer's life consists of assumed suffering, rhetorical suffering, that I felt something like relief, even elation, when the doctor told me that I had cancer of the prostate. Suddenly there was in the air a rich sense of crisis, real crisis, yet one that also contained echoes of ideas like the crisis of language, the crisis of literature, or of personality. It seemed to me that my existence, whatever I thought, felt or did, had taken on a kind of meter, as in poetry, or in taxis.

When you learn that your life is threatened, you can turn toward this knowledge or away from it. I turned toward it. It was not a choice, but

Originally appeared in the *New York Times Magazine* (Nov. 12, 1989).

an automatic shifting of gears, a tacit agreement between my body and my brain. I thought that time had tapped me on the shoulder, that I had been given a real deadline at last. It wasn't that I believed the cancer was going to kill me, even though it had spread beyond the prostate—it could probably be controlled, either by radiation or hormonal manipulation. No, what struck me was the startled awareness that one day something, whatever it might be, was going to interrupt my leisurely progress. It sounds trite, yet I can only say that I realized for the first time that I don't have forever.

Time was no longer innocuous, nothing was casual any more. I understood that living itself had a deadline. Like the book I had been working on—how sheepish I would feel if I couldn't finish it. I had promised it to myself and to my friends. Though I wouldn't say this out loud, I had promised it to the world. All writers privately think this way.

When my friends heard I had cancer, they found me surprisingly cheerful and talked about my courage. But it has nothing to do with courage, at least not for me. As far as I can tell, it's a question of desire. I'm filled with desire—to live, to write, to do everything. Desire itself is a kind of immortality. While I've always had trouble concentrating, I now feel as concentrated as a diamond, or a microchip.

5   I remember a time in the 1950s when I tried to talk a friend of mine named Jules out of committing suicide. He had already made one attempt and when I went to see him he said "Give me a good reason to go on living." He was 30 years old.

I saw what I had to do. I started to sell life to him, like a real estate agent. Just look at the world, I said. How can you not be curious about it? The streets, the houses, the trees, the shops, the people, the movement and the stillness. Look at the women, so appealing, each in her own way. Think of all the things you can do with them, the places you can go together. Think of books, paintings, music. Think of your friends.

While I was talking I wondered, am I telling Jules the truth? He didn't think so, because he put his head in the oven a week later. As for me, I don't know whether I believed what I said or not, because I just went on behaving like everybody else. But I believe it now. When my wife made me a hamburger the other day I thought it was the most fabulous hamburger in the history of the world.

With this illness one of my recurrent dreams has finally come true. Several times in the past I've dreamed that I had committed a crime—or perhaps I was only accused of a crime, it's not clear. When brought to trial I refused to have a lawyer—I got up instead and made an impassioned speech in my own defense. This speech was so moving that I could feel myself tingling with it. It was inconceivable that the jury would not acquit me—only each time I woke before the verdict. Now cancer is the crime I may or may not have committed and the eloquence of being alive, the fervor of the survivor, is my best defense.

The way my friends have rallied around me is wonderful. They remind me of a flock of birds rising from a body of water into the sunset. If that image seems a bit extravagant, or tinged with satire, it's because I can't help thinking there's something comical about my friends' behavior, all these witty men suddenly saying pious, inspirational things.

They are not intoxicated as I am by my illness, but sobered. Since I refused to, they've taken on the responsibility of being serious. They appear abashed, or chagrined, in their sobriety. Stripped of their playfulness these pals of mine seem plainer, homelier—even older. It's as if they had all gone bald overnight.

Yet one of the effects of their fussing over me is that I feel vivid, multicolored, sharply drawn. On the other hand—and this is ungrateful—I remain outside of their solicitude, their love and best wishes. I'm isolated from them by the grandiose conviction that I am the healthy person and they are the sick ones. Like an existential hero, I have been cured by the truth while they still suffer the nausea of the uninitiated.

I've had eight-inch needles thrust into my belly where I could feel them tickling my metaphysics. I've worn Pampers. I've been licked by the flames and my sense of self has been singed. Sartre[1] was right: you have to live each moment as if you're prepared to die.

Now at last I understand the conditional nature of the human condition. Yet, unlike Kierkegaard[2] and Sartre, I'm not interested in the irony of my position. Cancer cures you of irony. Perhaps my irony was all in my prostate. A dangerous illness fills you with adrenaline and makes you feel very smart. I can afford now, I said to myself, to draw conclusions. All those grand generalizations toward which I have been building for so many years are finally taking shape. As I look back at how I used to be, it seems to me that an intellectual is a person who thinks that the classical cliché's don't apply to him, that he is immune to homely truths. I know better now. I see everything with a summarizing eye. Nature is a terrific editor.

In the first stages of my illness, I couldn't sleep, urinate or defecate—the word ordeal comes to mind. Then when my doctor changed all this and everything worked again, what a voluptuous pleasure it was. With a cry of joy I realized how marvelous it is simply to function. My body, which in the last decade or two had become a familiar, no longer thrilling old flame, was reborn as a brand-new infatuation.

I realize of course that this elation I feel is just a phase, just a rush of consciousness, a splash of perspective, a hot flash of ontological

1. Jean-Paul Sartre (1905–80), French philosopher, dramatist, novelist, and critic.
2. Søren Aabye Kierkegaard (1813–55), Danish philosopher who, a rebel against secure bourgeois morality, proposed a system based on faith, knowledge, thought, and reality that was revived in the twentieth century by German philosophers Heidegger and Jaspers and furthered by Sartre and other members of the French existential movement.

alertness. But I'll take it, I'll use it. I'll use everything I can while I wait for the next phase. Illness is primarily a drama and it should be possible to enjoy it as well as to suffer it. I see now why the romantics were so fond of illness—the sick man sees everything as metaphor. In this phase I'm infatuated with my cancer. It stinks of revelation.

As I look ahead, I feel like a man who has awakened from a long afternoon nap to find the evening stretched out before me. I'm reminded of D'Annunzio,[3] the Italian poet, who said to a duchess he had just met at a party in Paris, "Come, we will have a profound evening." Why not? I see the balance of my life—everything comes in images now—as a beautiful paisley shawl thrown over a grand piano.

Why a paisley shawl, precisely? Why a grand piano? I have no idea. That's the way the situation presents itself to me. I have to take my imagery along with my medicine.

3. Gabriel D'Annunzio (1836–1938), whose work, with no apparent concern for morality, conscience, or thought, expresses that the well-exercised pleasures of the senses alone give meaning to life.

Prose Forms: Journals

Occasionally one catches oneself having said something aloud, obviously with no concern to be heard, even by oneself. And all of us have overheard, perhaps while walking, a solitary person muttering or laughing softly or exclaiming abruptly. Something floats up from the world within, forces itself to be expressed, takes no real account of the time or the place, and certainly intends no conscious communication.

With more self-consciousness, and yet without a specific audience, one sometimes speaks out at something that has momentarily filled attention from the world without. A sharp play at the ball game, the twist of a political speech, an old photograph—something from the outer world impresses the mind, stimulates it, focuses certain of its memories and values, interests and needs. Thus stimulated, one may wish to share an experience with another, to inform or amuse that person, to rouse him or her to action or persuade someone to a certain belief. Often, though, the person experiencing may want most to talk to himself or herself, to give a public shape in words to thoughts and feelings but for the sake of a kind of private dialogue. Communication to another may be an ultimate desire, but the immediate motive is to articulate the experience for oneself.

To articulate, to shape the experience in language for one's own sake, one may keep a journal. Literally a day-book, the journal enables one to write down something about the experiences of a day which for a great variety of reasons may have been especially memorable or impressive. The journal entry may be merely a few words to call to mind a thing done, a person seen, a menu enjoyed at a dinner party. It may be concerned at length with a political crisis in the community, or a personal crisis in the home. It may even as noble as it was with some pious people in the past who used the journal to keep a record of their consciences, a periodic reckoning of their moral and spiritual accounts. In its most public aspect, the idea of a journal calls to mind the newspaper or the record of proceedings like the U.S. Congressional Record *and the* Canadian Hansard. *In its most closely private form, the journal becomes the diary.*

65

To keep a journal is to hold onto experiences through writing. But to get it down on paper begins another adventure. For the journalist has to focus on what he or she has experienced, and to be able to say what, in fact, the experience is. What of it is new? What of it is remarkable because of associations in the memory it stirs up? Is this like anything I—or others—have experienced before? Is it a good or a bad thing to have happened? And why, specifically? The questions multiply themselves quickly, and as the journalist seeks to answer the appropriate ones, he or she begins to know what is being contemplated. As one tries to find the words that best represent this discovery, the experience becomes even more clear in its shape and meaning. We can imagine Emerson going to the ballet, being absorbed in the spectacle, thinking casually of this or that association the dancer and the movements suggest. When he writes about the experience in his journal, a good many questions, judgments, and speculations get tied up with the spectacle, and it is this complex of event and this total relation to it that becomes the experience he records. The simple facts of time, place, people, and actions drop down into one's consciousness and set in motion ideas and feelings which give those facts their real meaning to oneself.

Once this consciousness of events is formulated in words, the journalist has it, not only in the sense of understanding what has been seen or felt or thought, but also in the sense of having it there to contemplate long after the event itself. When we read a carefully kept journal covering a long period and varied experiences, we have the pleasure of a small world re-created for us in the consciousness of one who experienced it. Even more, we feel the continuity, the wholeness, of the writer. Something of the same feeling is there for the person who kept the journal: a whole world of events preserved in the form of their experienced reality, and with it the persistent self in the midst of that world. That world and that self are always accessible on the page and ultimately, therefore, usably real.

Beyond the value of the journal as record, there is the instructive value of the habit of mind and hand journal keeping can assure. One begins to attend more carefully to what happens to and around oneself. One learns the resources of language as a means of representing what one sees, and gains skill and certainty in doing justice to experience and to one's own consciousness. And the journal represents a discipline. It brings together an individual and a complex environment in a relation that teaches the individual something of himself or herself, something of the world, and something of the meaning of their relation. There is scarcely a moment in life when one is not poised for the lesson. When it comes with the promise of special force, there is the almost irresistible temptation to catch the impulse, give it form, make it permanent, assert its meaning. And so one commits oneself to language. To have given up one's experience to words is to have begun marking out the limits and potential of its meaning. In the journal that meaning is developed and clarified to oneself primarily. When the whole intention of the development and the clarification is the consideration of another reader, the method of the journal redirects itself to become that of the essay.

Joan Didion: ON KEEPING A NOTEBOOK

" 'That woman Estelle,' " the note reads, " 'is partly the reason why George Sharp and I are separated today.' *Dirty crepe-de-Chine wrapper, hotel bar, Wilmington RR, 9:45 a.m. August Monday morning.*"

Since the note is in my notebook, it presumably has some meaning to me. I study it for a long while. At first I have only the most general notion of what I was doing on an August Monday morning in the bar of the hotel across from the Pennsylvania Railroad station in Wilmington, Delaware (waiting for a train? missing one? 1960? 1961? why Wilmington?), but I do remember being there. The woman in the dirty crepe-de-Chine wrapper had come down from her room for a beer, and the bartender had heard before the reason why George Sharp and she were separated today. "Sure," he said, and went on mopping the floor. "You told me." At the other end of the bar is a girl. She is talking, pointedly, not to the man beside her but to a cat lying in the triangle of sunlight cast through the open door. She is wearing a plaid silk dress from Peck & Peck, and the hem is coming down.

Here is what it is: the girl has been on the Eastern Shore, and now she is going back to the city, leaving the man beside her, and all she can see ahead are the viscous summer sidewalks and the 3 a.m. long-distance calls that will make her lie awake and then sleep drugged through all the steaming mornings left in August (1960? 1961?). Because she must go directly from the train to lunch in New York, she wishes that she had a safety pin for the hem of the plaid silk dress, and she also wishes that she could forget about the hem and the lunch and stay in the cool bar that smells of disinfectant and malt and make friends with the woman in the crepe-de-Chine wrapper. She is afflicted by a little self-pity, and she wants to compare Estelles. That is what that was all about.

Why did I write it down? In order to remember, of course, but exactly what was it I wanted to remember? How much of it actually happened? Did any of it? Why do I keep a notebook at all? It is easy to deceive oneself on all those scores. The impulse to write things down is a peculiarly compulsive one, inexplicable to those who do not share it, useful only accidentally, only secondarily, in the way that any compulsion tries to justify itself. I suppose that it begins or does not begin in the cradle. Although I have felt compelled to write things down since I was five years old, I doubt that my daughter ever will, for she is a singularly blessed and accepting child, delighted with life exactly as life presents itself to her, unafraid to go to sleep and unafraid to wake up.

From *Slouching towards Bethlehem* (1969).

Keepers of private notebooks are a different breed altogether, lonely and resistant rearrangers of things, anxious malcontents, children afflicted apparently at birth with some presentiment of loss.

My first notebook was a Big Five tablet, given to me by my mother with the sensible suggestion that I stop whining and learn to amuse myself by writing down my thoughts. She returned the tablet to me a few years ago; the first entry is an account of a woman who believed herself to be freezing to death in the Arctic night, only to find, when day broke, that she had stumbled onto the Sahara Desert, where she would die of the heat before lunch. I have no idea what turn of a five-year-old's mind could have prompted so insistently "ironic" and exotic a story, but it does reveal a certain predilection for the extreme which has dogged me into adult life; perhaps if I were analytically inclined I would find it a truer story than any I might have told about Donald Johnson's birthday party or the day my cousin Brenda put Kitty Litter in the aquarium.

So the point of my keeping a notebook has never been, nor is it now, to have an accurate factual record of what I have been doing or thinking. That would be a different impulse entirely, an instinct for reality which I sometimes envy but do not possess. At no point have I ever been able successfully to keep a diary; my approach to daily life ranges from the grossly negligent to the merely absent, and on those few occasions when I have tried dutifully to record a day's events, boredom has so overcome me that the results are mysterious at best. What is this business about "shopping, typing piece, dinner with E, depressed"? Shopping for what? Typing what piece? Who is E? Was this "E" depressed, or was I depressed? Who cares?

In fact I have abandoned altogether that kind of pointless entry; instead I tell what some would call lies. "That's simply not true," the members of my family frequently tell me when they come up against my memory of a shared event. "The party was *not* for you, the spider was *not* a black widow, *it wasn't that way at all.*" Very likely they are right, for not only have I always had trouble distinguishing between what happened and what merely might have happened, but I remain unconvinced that the distinction, for my purposes, matters. The cracked crab that I recall having for lunch the day my father came home from Detroit in 1945 must certainly be embroidery, worked into the day's pattern to lend verisimilitude; I was ten years old and would not now remember the cracked crab. The day's events did not turn on cracked crab. And yet it is precisely that fictitious crab that makes me see the afternoon all over again, a home movie run all too often, the father bearing gifts, the child weeping, an exercise in family love and guilt. Or that is what it was to me. Similarly, perhaps it never did snow that August in Vermont; perhaps there never were flurries in the night wind, and maybe no one else felt the ground hardening and summer already dead even as we pretended to bask in it, but that was how it felt to me, and it might as well have snowed, could have snowed, did snow.

How it felt to me: that is getting closer to the truth about a notebook. I sometimes delude myself about why I keep a notebook, imagine that some thrifty virtue derives from preserving everything observed. See enough and write it down, I tell myself, and then some morning when the world seems drained of wonder, some day when I am only going through the motions of doing what I am supposed to do, which is write—on that bankrupt morning I will simply open my notebook and there it will all be, a forgotten account with accumulated interest, paid passage back to the world out there: dialogue overheard in hotels and elevators and at the hatcheck counter in Pavillon (one middle-aged man shows his hat check to another and says, "That's my old football number"); impressions of Bettina Aptheker and Benjamin Sonnenberg and Teddy ("Mr. Acapulco") Stauffer; careful *aperçus* about tennis bums and failed fashion models and Greek shipping heiresses, one of whom taught me a significant lesson (a lesson I could have learned from F. Scott Fitzgerald, but perhaps we all must meet the very rich for ourselves) by asking, when I arrived to interview her in her orchid-filled sitting room on the second day of a paralyzing New York blizzard, whether it was snowing outside.

I imagine, in other words, that the notebook is about other people. But of course it is not. I have no real business with what one stranger said to another at the hat-check counter in Pavillon; in fact I suspect that the line "That's my old football number" touched not my own imagination at all, but merely some memory of something once read, probably "The Eighty-Yard Run." Nor is my concern with a woman in a dirty crepe-de-Chine wrapper in a Wilmington bar. My stake is always, of course, in the unmentioned girl in the plaid silk dress. *Remember what it was to be me:* that is always the point.

It is a difficult point to admit. We are brought up in the ethic that others, any others, all others, are by definition more interesting than ourselves; taught to be diffident, just this side of self-effacing. ("You're the least important person in the room and don't forget it," Jessica Mitford's governess would hiss in her ear on the advent of any social occasion; I copied that into my notebook because it is only recently that I have been able to enter a room without hearing some such phrase in my inner ear.) Only the very young and the very old may recount their dreams at breakfast, dwell upon self, interrupt with memories of beach picnics and favorite Liberty lawn dresses and the rainbow trout in a creek near Colorado Springs. The rest of us are expected, rightly, to affect absorption in other people's favorite dresses, other people's trout.

And so we do. But our notebooks give us away, for however dutifully we record what we see around us, the common denominator of all we see is always, transparently, shamelessly, the implacable "I." We are not talking here about the kind of notebook that is patently for public consumption, a structural conceit for binding together a series of graceful *pensées*; [1] we are talking about something private, about bits of the mind's string too short to use, an indiscriminate and erratic assemblage with meaning only for its maker.

And sometimes even the maker has difficulty with the meaning. There does not seem to be, for example, any point in my knowing for the rest of my life that, during 1964, 720 tons of soot fell on every square mile of New York City, yet there it is in my notebook, labeled "FACT." Nor do I really need to remember that Ambrose Bierce liked to spell Leland Stanford's [2] name "£eland $tanford" or that "smart women almost alwayswear black in Cuba," a fashion hint without much potential for practical application. And does not the relevance of these notes seem marginal at best?:

> In the basement museum of the Inyo County Courthouse in Independence, California, sign pinned to a mandarin coat: "This MANDARIN COAT was often worn by Mrs. Minnie S. Brooks when giving lectures on her TEAPOT COLLECTION."
> Redhead getting out of car in front of Beverly Wilshire Hotel, chinchilla stole, Vuitton bags with tags reading:
> > MRS LOU FOX
> > HOTEL SAHARA
> > VEGAS

Well, perhaps not entirely marginal. As a matter of fact, Mrs. Minnie S. Brooks and her MANDARIN COAT pull me back into my own childhood, for although I never knew Mrs. Brooks and did not visit Inyo County until I was thirty, I grew up in just such a world, in houses cluttered with Indian relics and bits of gold ore and ambergris and the souvenirs my Aunt Mercy Farnsworth brought back from the Orient. It is a long way from that world to Mrs. Lou Fox's world, where we all live now, and is it not just as well to remember that? Might not Mrs. Minnie S. Brooks help me to remember what I am? Might not Mrs. Lou Fox help me to remember what I am not?

1. Thoughts, reflections.   2. A nineteenth-century American millionaire.

But sometimes the point is harder to discern. What exactly did I have in mind when I noted down that it cost the father of someone I know $650 a month to light the place on the Hudson in which he lived before the Crash?[3] What use was I planning to make of this line by Jimmy Hoffa: "I may have my faults, but being wrong ain't one of them"? And although I think it interesting to know where the girls who travel with the Syndicate have their hair done when they find themselves on the West Coast, will I ever make suitable use of it? Might I not be better off just passing it on to John O'Hara? What is a recipe for sauerkraut doing in my notebook? What kind of magpie keeps this notebook? *"He was born the night the Titanic went down."* That seems a nice enough line, and I even recall who said it, but is it not really a better line in life than it could ever be in fiction?

But of course that is exactly it: not that I should ever use the line, but that I should remember the woman who said it and the afternoon I heard it. We were on her terrace by the sea, and we were finishing the wine left from lunch, trying to get what sun there was, a California winter sun. The woman whose husband was born the night the *Titanic* went down wanted to rent her house, wanted to go back to her children in Paris. I remember wishing that I could afford the house, which cost $1,000 a month. "Someday you will," she said lazily. "Someday it all comes." There in the sun on her terrace it seemed easy to believe in someday, but later I had a low-grade afternoon hangover and ran over a black snake on the way to the supermarket and was flooded with inexplicable fear when I heard the checkout clerk explaining to the man ahead of me why she was finally divorcing her husband. "He left me no choice," she said over and over as she punched the register. "He has a little seven-month-old baby by her, he left me no choice." I would like to believe that my dread then was for the human condition, but of course it was for me, because I wanted a baby and did not then have one and because I wanted to own the house that cost $1,000 a month to rent and because I had a hangover.

It all comes back. Perhaps it is difficult to see the value in having one's self back in that kind of mood, but I do see it; I think we are well advised to keep on nodding terms with the people we used to be whether we find them attractive company or not. Otherwise they turn up unannounced and surprise us, come hammering on the mind's door at 4 a.m. of a bad night and demand to know who deserted them, who betrayed them, who is going to make amends. We forget all too soon the things we thought we could never forget. We forget the loves and the betrayals alike, forget what we whispered and what we screamed, forget who we were. I have already lost touch with a couple of people I used to be; one of them, a seventeen-year-old, presents little threat, although it would be of some interest to me to know again what it feels like to sit on a river levee drinking vodka-and-orange-juice and listening to Les Paul and Mary Ford and their echoes sing "How High the Moon" on the car radio. (You see I still have the scenes, but I no longer perceive myself among those present, no longer could even improvise the dialogue.) The other one, a twenty-three-year-old, bothers me more. She was always a good deal of trouble, and I suspect she will reappear when I least want to see her, skirts too long, shy to the point of aggravation, always the injured party, full of recriminations and little hurts and stories I do not want to hear again, at once saddening me and angering me with her vulnerability and ignorance, an apparition all the more insistent for being so long banished.

It is a good idea, then, to keep in touch, and I suppose that keeping in touch is what notebooks are all about. And we are all on our own when it comes to keeping those lines open to ourselves: your notebook will never help me, nor mine you. *"So what's new in the whiskey business?"* What could that possibly mean to you? To me it means a blonde in a Pucci bathing suit sitting with a couple of fat men by the pool at the Beverly Hills Hotel. Another man approaches, and they all regard one another in silence for a while. "So what's new in the whiskey business?" one of the fat men finally says by way of welcome, and the blonde stands up, arches one foot and dips it in the pool, looking all the while at the cabaña where Baby Pignatari is talking on the telephone. That is all there is to that, except that several years later I saw the blonde coming out of Saks Fifth Avenue in New York with her California complexion and a voluminous mink coat. In the harsh wind that day she looked old and irrevocably tired to me, and even the skins in the mink coat were not worked the way they were doing them that year, not the way she would have wanted them done, and there is the point of the story. For a while after that I did not like to look in the mirror, and my eyes would skim the newspapers and pick out only the deaths, the cancer victims, the premature coronaries, the suicides, and I stopped riding the Lexington Avenue IRT[4] because I noticed for the first time that all the strangers I had seen for years—the man with the seeing-eye dog, the spinster who read the classified pages every day, the fat girl who always got off with me at Grand Central—looked older than they once had.

It all comes back. Even that recipe for sauerkraut: even that brings it back. I was on Fire Island when I first made that sauerkraut, and it was raining, and we drank a lot of bourbon and ate the sauerkraut and went to bed at ten, and I listened to the rain and the Atlantic and felt safe. I made the sauerkraut again last night and it did not make me feel any safer, but that is, as they say, another story.

4. A New York City subway line; one of its stops is the Grand Central railway terminal.

THE READER

1. What distinction does Didion make between a diary and a notebook?
2. What uses does a notebook have for Didion?
3. Didion says she uses her notebook to "tell what some would call lies" (p. 69). Why does she do this? Would some people call these things truths? Why?
4. What does Didion imply is the difference between a notebook and a diary?
5. Is the visit Didion describes in "On Going Home" (p. 31) an effort to keep in touch with the people we used to be (p. 72)? One test would be to check "On Going Home" for phrases and observations like those she quotes from her notebooks. Are there any?

THE WRITER

1. Didion says that "we are brought up in the ethic that others . . . are by definition more interesting than ourselves." Explain whether she believes this can be harmful to one's development as a writer.
2. Didion says, "How it felt to me: that is getting closer to the truth about a notebook." What writing strategies does she use to convey "how it felt"?
3. Try keeping a notebook for a week, jotting down the sort of things that Didion does. At the end of the week, take one or two of your entries and expand on them, as Didion does with the entries on Mrs. Minnie S. Brooks and Mrs. Lou Fox.
4. References to her notebooks give you a lot of biographical detail about Didion's life, as does her essay "On Going Home" (p. 31). Restricting yourself to that information, sketch out as much of her biography as you can and then write a paragraph of that biography.

Ralph Waldo Emerson: FROM JOURNAL

I like to have a man's knowledge comprehend more than one class of topics, one row of shelves. I like a man who likes to see a fine barn as well as a good tragedy. [1828]

The Religion that is afraid of science dishonors God and commits suicide. [1831]

The things taught in colleges and schools are not an education, but the means of education. [1831]

Don't tell me to get ready to die. I know not what shall be. The only preparation I can make is by fulfilling my present duties. This is the everlasting life. [1832]

My aunt [Mary Moody Emerson] had an eye that went through and through you like a needle. "She was endowed," she said, "with the fatal gift of penetration." She disgusted everybody because she knew them too well. [1832]

I am sure of this, that by going much alone a man will get more of a noble courage in thought and word than from all the wisdom that is in books. [1833]

I fretted the other night at the hotel at the stranger who broke into my chamber after midnight, claiming to share it. But after his lamp had smoked the chamber full and I had turned round to the wall in despair, the man blew out his lamp, knelt down at his bedside, and made in low whisper a long earnest prayer. Then was the relation entirely changed between us. I fretted no more, but respected and liked him. [1835]

I believe I shall some time cease to be an individual, that the eternal tendency of the soul is to become Universal, to animate the last extremities of organization. [1837]

It is very hard to be simple enough to be good. [1837]

A man must have aunts and cousins, must buy carrots and turnips, must have barn and woodshed, must go to market and to the blacksmith's shop, must saunter and sleep and be inferior and silly. [1838]

How sad a spectacle, so frequent nowadays, to see a young man after ten years of college education come out, ready for his voyage of life—and to see that the entire ship is made of rotten timber, of rotten, honeycombed, traditional timber without so much as an inch of new plank in the hull. [1839]

A sleeping child gives me the impression of a traveler in a very far country. [1840]

In reading these letters of M.M.E. I acknowledge (with surprise that I could ever forget it) the debt of myself and my brothers to that old religion which, in those years, still dwelt like a Sabbath peace in the country population of New England, which taught privation, self-denial, and sorrow. A man was born, not for prosperity, but to suffer for the benefit of others, like the noble rock-maple tree which all around the villages bleeds for the service of man.[1] Not praise, not men's acceptance

1. The sap of the rock or sugar maple is collected and made into maple syrup.

of our doing, but the Spirit's holy errand through us, absorbed the thought. How dignified is this! how all that is called talents and worth in Paris and in Washington dwindles before it! [1841]

All writing is by the grace of God. People do not deserve to have good writing, they are so pleased with bad. In these sentences that you show me, I can find no beauty, for I see death in every clause and every word. There is a fossil or a mummy character which pervades this book. The best sepulchers, the vastest catacombs, Thebes and Cairo, Pyramids, are sepulchers to me. I like gardens and nurseries. Give me initiative, spermatic, prophesying, man-making words. [1841]

15   When summer opens, I see how fast it matures, and fear it will be short; but after the heats of July and August, I am reconciled, like one who has had his swing, to the cool of autumn. So will it be with the coming of death. [1846]

In England every man you meet is some man's son; in America, he may be some man's father. [1848]

Every poem must be made up of lines that are poems. [1848]

Love is necessary to the righting the estate of woman in this world. Otherwise nature itself seems to be in conspiracy against her dignity and welfare; for the cultivated, high-thoughted, beauty-loving, saintly woman finds herself unconsciously desired for her sex, and even enhancing the appetite of her savage pursuers by these fine ornaments she has piously laid on herself. She finds with indignation that she is herself a snare, and was made such. I do not wonder at her occasional protest, violent protest against nature, in fleeing to nunneries, and taking black veils. Love rights all this deep wrong. [1848]

Natural Aristocracy. It is a vulgar error to suppose that a gentleman must be ready to fight. The utmost that can be demanded of the gentleman is that he be incapable of a lie. There is a man who has good sense, is well informed, well-read, obliging, cultivated, capable, and has an absolute devotion to truth. He always means what he says, and says what he means, however courteously. You may spit upon him—nothing could induce him to spit upon you—no praises, and no possessions, no compulsion of public opinion. You may kick him—he will think it the kick of a brute—but he is not a brute, and will not kick you in return. But neither your knife and pistol, nor your gifts and courting will ever make the smallest impression on his vote or word; for he is the truth's man, and will speak and act the truth until he dies. [1849]

Love is temporary and ends with marriage. Marriage is the perfection   20
which love aimed at, ignorant of what it sought. Marriage is a good
known only to the parties—a relation of perfect understanding, aid,
contentment, possession of themselves and of the world—which dwarfs
love to green fruit. [1850]

I found when I had finished my new lecture that it was a very good
house, only the architect had unfortunately omitted the stairs. [1851]

This filthy enactment [The Fugitive Slave Law[2]] was made in the
nineteenth century, by people who could read and write. I will not obey
it, by God. [1851]

Henry [Thoreau] is military. He seemed stubborn and implacable;
always manly and wise, but rarely sweet. One would say that, as Webster
could never speak without an antagonist, so Henry does not feel himself
except in opposition. He wants a fallacy to expose, a blunder to pillory,
requires a little sense of victory, a roll of the drums, to call his powers
into full exercise. [1853]

Shall we judge the country by the majority or by the minority? Certainly, by the minority. The mass are animal, in state of pupilage, and
nearer the chimpanzee. [1854]

All the thoughts of a turtle are turtle. [1854]   25

Resources or feats. I like people who can do things. When Edward
and I struggled in vain to drag our big calf into the barn, the Irish girl
put her finger into the calf's mouth, and led her in directly. [1862]

George Francis Train said in a public speech in New York, "Slavery
is a divine institution." "So is hell," exclaimed an old man in the crowd.
[1862]

You complain that the Negroes are a base class. Who makes and keeps
the Jew or the Negro base, who but you, who exclude them from the
rights which others enjoy? [1867]

2. A law enacted in 1850 to compel the arrest of runaway slaves and their return to their
owners.

Henry David Thoreau: FROM JOURNAL

As the least drop of wine tinges the whole goblet, so the least particle of truth colors our whole life. It is never isolated, or simply added as treasure to our stock. When any real progress is made, we unlearn and learn anew what we thought we knew before. [1837]

Not by constraint or severity shall you have access to true wisdom, but by abandonment, and childlike mirthfulness. If you would know aught, be gay before it. [1840]

It is the man determines what is said, not the words. If a mean person uses a wise maxim, I bethink me how it can be interpreted so as to commend itself to his meanness; but if a wise man makes a common-place remark, I consider what wider construction it will admit. [1840]

Nothing goes by luck in composition. It allows of no tricks. The best you can write will be the best you are. Every sentence is the result of a long probation. The author's character is read from title-page to end. Of this he never corrects the proofs. We read it as the essential character of a handwriting without regard to the flourishes. And so of the rest of our actions; it runs as straight as a ruled line through them all, no matter how many curvets about it. Our whole life is taxed for the least thing well done: it is its net result. How we eat, drink, sleep, and use our desultory hours, now in these indifferent days, with no eye to observe and no occasion [to] excite us, determines our authority and capacity for the time to come. [1841]

5   What does education often do? It makes a straight-cut ditch of a free, meandering brook. [1850]

All perception of truth is the detection of an analogy; we reason from our hands to our head. [1851]

To set down such choice experiences that my own writings may inspire me and at last I may make wholes of parts. Certainly it is a distinct profession to rescue from oblivion and to fix the sentiments and thoughts which visit all men more or less generally, that the contemplation of the unfinished picture may suggest its harmonious completion. Associate reverently and as much as you can with your loftiest thoughts. Each thought that is welcomed and recorded is a nest egg, by the side of which more will be laid. Thoughts accidentally thrown together become a frame in which more may be developed and exhibited. Perhaps this is the main value of a habit of writing, of keeping a journal— that so we remember our best hours and stimulate ourselves. My

thoughts are my company. They have a certain individuality and separate existence, aye, personality. Having by chance recorded a few discon-
nected thoughts and then brought them into juxtaposition, they suggest
a whole new field in which it was possible to labor and to think. Thought
begat thought. [1852]

It is pardonable when we spurn the proprieties, even the sanctities,
making them stepping-stones to something higher. [1858]

There is always some accident in the best things, whether thoughts
or expressions or deeds. The memorable thought, the happy expression,
the admirable deed are only partly ours. The thought came to us because
we were in a fit mood; also we were unconscious and did not know that
we had said or done a good thing. We must walk consciously only part
way toward our goal, and then leap in the dark to our success. What we
do best or most perfectly is what we have most thoroughly learned by
the longest practice, and at length it falls from us without our notice,
as a leaf from a tree. It is the *last* time we shall do it—our unconscious
leavings. [1859]

The expression "a *liberal* education" originally meant one worthy of   10
freemen. Such is education simply in a true and broad sense. But education ordinarily so called—the learning of trades and professions which
is designed to enable men to earn their living, or to fit them for a
particular station in life—is *servile*. [1859]

Walt Whitman: ABRAHAM LINCOLN

August 12th. —I see the President almost every day, as I happen to
live where he passes to or from his lodgings out of town. He never sleeps
at the White House during the hot season, but has quarters at a healthy
location some three miles north of the city, the Soldiers' home, a United
States military establishment. I saw him this morning about 8½ coming
in to business, riding on Vermont avenue, near L street. He always has
a company of twenty-five or thirty cavalry, with sabres drawn and held
upright over their shoulders. They say this guard was against his personal
wish, but he let his counselors have their way. The party makes no great
show in uniform or horses. Mr Lincoln on the saddle generally rides a
good-sized, easy-going gray horse, is dress'd in plain black, somewhat
rusty and dusty, wears a black stiff hat, and looks about as ordinary in

Published in 1882.

attire, &c., as the commonest man. A lieutenant, with yellow straps, rides at his left, and following behind, two by two, come the cavalry men, in their yellow-striped jackets. They are generally going at a slow trot, as that is the pace set them by the one they wait upon. The sabres and accoutrements clank, and the entirely unornamental *cortège* as it trots towards Lafayette square arouses no sensation, only some curious stranger stops and gazes. I see very plainly ABRAHAM LINCOLN's dark brown face, with the deep-cut lines, the eyes, always to me witha deep latent sadness in the expression. We have got so that we exchange bows, and very cordial ones. Sometimes the President goes and comes in an open barouche. The cavalry always accompany him, with drawn sabres. Often I notice as he goes out evenings—and sometimes in the morning, when he returns early—he turns off and halts at the large and handsome residence of the Secretary of War, on K street, and holds conference there. If in his barouche, I can see from my window he does not alight, but sits in his vehicle, and Mr. Stanton comes out to attend him. Sometimes one of his sons, a boy of ten or twelve, accompanies him, riding at his right on a pony. Earlier in the summer I occasionally saw the President and his wife, toward the latter part of the afternoon, out in a barouche, on a pleasure ride through the city. Mrs. Lincoln was dress'd in complete black, with a long crape veil. The equipage is of the plainest kind, only two horses, and they nothing extra. They pass'd me once very close, and I saw the President in the face fully, as they were moving slowly, and his look, though abstracted, happen'd to be directed steadily in my eye. He bow'd and smiled, but far beneath his smile I noticed well the expression I have alluded to. None of the artists or pictures has caught the deep, though subtle and indirect expression of this man's face. There is something else there. One of the great portrait painters of two or three centuries ago is needed.

The Inauguration

March 4. —The President very quietly rode down to the capitol in his own carriage, by himself, on a sharp trot, about noon, either because he wish'd to be on hand to sign bills, or to get rid of marching in line with the absurd procession, the muslin temple of liberty, and pasteboard monitor. I saw him on his return, at three o'clock, after the performance was over. He was in his plain two-horse barouche, and look'd very much worn and tired; the lines, indeed, of vast responsibilities, intricate ques-tions, and demands of life and death, cut deeper than ever upon his dark brown face; yet all the old goodness, tenderness, sadness, and canny shrewdness, underneath the furrows. (I never see that man without feeling that he is one to become personally attach'd to, for his combina-tion of purest, heartiest tenderness, and native western form of manli-ness.) By his side sat his little boy, of ten years. There were no soldiers, only a lot of civilians on horseback, with huge yellow scarfs over their shoulders, riding around the carriage. (At the inauguration four years ago, he rode down and back again surrounded by a dense mass of arm'd cavalrymen eight deep, with drawn sabres; and there were sharpshooters station'd at every corner on the route.) I ought to make mention of the closing levee[1] of Saturday night last. Never before was such a compact jam in front of the White House—all the grounds fill'd, and away out to the spacious sidewalks. I was there, as I took anotion to go—was in the rush inside with the crowd—surged along the passage-ways, the blue and other rooms, and through the great east room. Crowds of country people, some very funny. Fine music from the Marine band, off in a side place. I saw Mr. Lincoln, drest all in black, with white kid gloves and a claw-hammer coat, receiving, as in duty bound, shaking hands, looking very disconsolate, and as if he would give anything to be somewhere else.

Death of President Lincoln

April 16, '65.—I find in my notes of the time, this passage on the death of Abraham Lincoln: He leaves for America's history and biography, so far, not only its most dramatic reminiscence—he leaves, in my opinion, the greatest, best, most characteristic, artistic, moral personality. Not but that he had faults, and show'd them in the Presidency; but honesty, goodness, shrewdness, conscience, and (a new virtue, unknown to other lands, and hardly yet really known here, but the foundation andtie of all, as the future will grandly develop,) UNIONISM, in its truest and amplest sense, form'd the hard-pan of his character. These he seal'd with his life. The tragic splendor of his death, purging, illuminating all, throws round his form, his head, an aureole that will remain and will grow brighter through time, while history lives, and love of country lasts. By many has this Union been help'd; but if one name, one man, must be pick'd out, he, most of all, is the conservator of it, to the future. He was assassinated—but the Union is not assassinated—*çaira!*[2] One falls, and another falls. The soldier drops, sinks like a wave—but the ranks of the ocean eternally press on. Death does its work, obliterates a hundred, a thousand—President, general, captain, private—butthe Nation is immortal.

No Good Portrait of Lincoln

Probably the reader has seen physiognomies (often old farmers, sea-captains, and such) that, behind thier homeliness, or even ugliness, held superior points so subtle, yet so palpable, making the real life of their faces almost as impossible to depict as a wild perfume or fruit-taste, or

1. An occasion of statefor the receiving of
visits, ceremonial greetings, and interviews.
2. It goes on; it succeeds.

a passionate tone of the living voice—and such was Lincoln's face, the peculiar color, the lines of it, the eyes, mouth, expression. Of technical beauty it had nothing—but to the eye of a great artist it furnished a rare study, a feast and fascination. The current portraits are all failures—most of them caricatures.

May Sarton: FROM JOURNAL OF A SOLITUDE

September 17th. Cracking open the inner world again, writing even a couple of pages, threw me back into depression, not made easier by the weather, two gloomy days of darkness and rain. I was attacked by a storm of tears, those tears that appear to be related to frustration, to buried anger, and come upon me without warning. I woke yesterday so depressed that I did not get up till after eight.

I drove to Brattleboro[1] to read poems at the new Unitarian church there in a state of dread and exhaustion. How to summon the vitality needed? I had made an arrangement of religious poems, going back to early books and forward into the new book not yet published. I suppose it went all right—at least it was not a disaster—but I felt (perhaps I am wrong) that the kind, intelligent people gathered in a big room looking out on pine trees did not really want to think about God. His absence (many of the poems speak of that) or His presence. Both are too frightening.

On the way back I stopped to see Perley Cole, my dear old friend, who is dying, separated from his wife, and has just been moved from a Dickensian nursing home into what seems like a far better one. He grows more transparent every day, a skeleton or nearly. Clasping his hand, I fear to break a bone. Yet the only real communication between us now (he is very deaf) is a handclasp. I want to lift him in my arms and hold him like a baby. He is dying a terribly lonely death. Each time I see him he says, "It is rough" or "I did not think it would end like this."

Everywhere I look about this place I see his handiwork: the three small trees by a granite boulder that he pruned and trimmed so they pivot the whole meadow; the new shady border he dug out for me one of the last days he worked here; the pruned-out stone wall between my field and the church. The second field where he cut brush twice a year and cleared out to the stone wall is growing back to wilderness now.

From *Journal of a Solitude* (1970–1971), published in 1973.

1. Brattleboro, Vermont.

What is done here has to be done over and over and needs the dogged strength of a man like Perley. I could have never managed it alone. We cherished this piece of land together, and fought together to bring it to some semblance of order and beauty.

I like to think that this last effort of Perley's had a certain ease about it, a game compared to the hard work of his farming years, and a game where his expert knowledge and skill could be well used. How he enjoyed teasing me about my ignorance!

While he scythed and trimmed, I struggled in somewhat the same way at my desk here, and we were each aware of the companionship. We each looked forward to noon, when I could stop for the day and he sat on a high stool in the kitchen, drank a glass or two of sherry with me, said, "Court's in session!" and then told me some tall tale he had been cogitating all morning.

It was a strange relationship, for he knew next to nothing about my life, really; yet below all the talk we recognized each other as the same kind. He enjoyed my anger as much as I enjoyed his. Perhaps that was part of it. Deep down there was understanding, not of the facts of our lives so much as of our essential natures. Even now in his hard, lonely end he has immense dignity. But I wish there were some way to make it easier. I leave him with bitter resentment against the circumstances of this death. "I know. But I did not approve. And I am not resigned."

In the mail a letter from a twelve-year-old child, enclosing poems, her mother having pushed her to ask my opinion. The child does really look at things, and I can write something helpful, I think. But it is troubling how many people expect applause, recognition, when they have not even begun to learn an art or a craft. Instant success is the order of the day; "I want it *now!*" I wonder whether this is not part of our corruption by machines. Machines do things very quickly and outside the natural rhythm of life, and we are indignant if a car doesn't start at the first try. So the few things that we still do, such as cooking (though there are TV dinners!), knitting, gardening, anything at all that cannot be hurried, have a very particular value.

September 18th. The value of solitude—one of its values—is, of course, that there is nothing to *cushion* against attacks from within, just as there is nothing to help balance at times of particular stress or depression. A few moments of desultory conversation with dear Arnold Miner, when he comes to take the trash, may calm an inner storm. But the storm, painful as it is, might have had some truth in it. So sometimes one has simply to endure a period of depression for what it may hold of illumination if one can live through it, attentive to what it exposes or demands.

The reasons for depression are not so interesting as the way one handles it, simply to stay alive. This morning I woke at four and lay awake for an hour or so in a bad state. It is raining again. I got up finally and went about the daily chores, waiting for the sense of doom to lift—and what did it was watering the house plants. Suddenly joy came back because I was fulfilling a simple need, a living one. Dusting never has this effect (and that may be why I am such a poor housekeeper!), but feeding the cats when they are hungry, giving Punch clean water, makes me suddenly feel calm and happy.

10   Whatever peace I know rests in the natural world, in feeling myself a part of it, even in a small way. Maybe the gaiety of the Warner family, their wisdom, comes from this, that they work close to nature all the time. As simple as that? But it is not simple. Their life requires patient understanding, imagination, the power to endure constant adversity— the weather, for example! To go with, not against the elements, an inexhaustible vitality summoned back each day to do the same tasks, to feed the animals, clean out barns and pens, keep that complex world alive.

October 6th. A day when I am expecting someone for lunch is quite unlike ordinary days. There is a reason to make the flowers look beautiful all over the house, and I know that Anne Woodson, who is coming today, will notice them, for she sees this house in a way that few of my friends do, perhaps because she has lived here without me, has lived her way into the place by pruning and weeding, and once even tidying the linen cupboard!

It is a mellow day, very gentle. The ash has lost its leaves and when I went out to get the mail and stopped to look up at it, I rejoiced to think that soon everything here will be honed down to structure. It is all a rich farewell now to leaves, to color. I think of the trees and how simply they let go, let fall the riches of a season, how without grief (it seems) they can let go and go deep into their roots for renewal and sleep. Eliot's statement comes back to me these days:

> Teach us to care and not to care
> Teach us to sit still. [2]

It is there in Mahler's *Der Abschied,* which I play again every autumn (Bruno Walter with Kathleen Ferrier). [3] But in Mahler it is a cry of loss, a long lyrical cry just *before* letting go, at least until those last long

2. From T. S. Eliot's *Ash Wednesday* (1930), lines 38–39.
3. A famous record of Mahler's song "The Farewell," evocative of the coming of winter and death. Mahler died before it could be performed, and the premiere was conducted by his disciple Bruno Walter. Kathleen Ferrier was to die within a few years of recording the song.

phrases that suggest peace, renunciation. But I think of it as the golden leaves and the brilliant small red maple that shone transparent against the shimmer of the lake yesterday when I went over to have a picnic with Helen Milbank.

Does anything in nature despair except man? An animal with a foot caught in a trap does not seem to despair. It is too busy trying to survive. It is all closed in, to a kind of still, intense waiting. Is this a key? Keep busy with survival. Imitate the trees. Learn to lose in order to recover, and remember that nothing stays the same for long, not even pain, psychic pain. Sit it out. Let it all pass. Let it go.

Yesterday I weeded out violets from the iris bed. The iris was being choked by thick bunches of roots, so much like fruit under the earth. I found one single very fragrant violet and some small autumn crocuses. Now, after an hour's work as the light failed and I drank in the damp smell of earth, it looks orderly again.

October 9th. Has it really happened at last? I feel released from the rack, set free, in touch with the deep source that is only *good,* where poetry lives. We have waited long this year for the glory, but suddenly the big maple is all gold and the beeches yellow with a touch of green that makes the yellow even more intense. There are still nasturtiums to be picked, and now I must get seriously to work to get the remaining bulbs in.

It has been stupidly difficult to let go, but that is what has been needed. I had allowed myself to get overanxious, clutching at what seemed sure to pass, and clutching is the surest way to murder love, as if it were a kitten, not to be squeezed so hard, or a flower to fade in a tight hand. Letting go, I have come back yesterday and today to a sense of my life here in all its riches, depth, freedom for soulmaking.

It's a real break-through. I have not written in sonnet form for a long time, but at every major crisis in my life when I reach a point of clarification, where pain is transcended by the quality of the experience itself, sonnets come. Whole lines run through my head and I cannot *stop* writing until whatever it is gets said.

Found three huge mushrooms when I went out before breakfast to fill the bird feeder. So far only jays come, but the word will get around.

October 11th. The joke is on me. I filled this weekend with friends so that I would not go down into depression, not knowing that I should have turned the corner and be writing poems. It is the climactic moment of autumn, but already I feel like Sleeping Beauty as the carpet of leaves on the front lawn gets thicker and thicker. The avenue of beeches as I drive up the winding road along the brook is glorious beyond words, wall on wall of transparent gold. Laurie Armstrong came for roast beef Sunday dinner. Then I went out for two hours late in the afternoon and put in a hundred tulips. In itself that would not be a big job, but everywhere I have to clear space for them, weed, divide perennials, rescue iris that is being choked by violets. I really get to weeding only in spring and autumn, so I am working through a jungle now. Doing it I feel strenuously happy and at peace. At the end of the afternoon on a gray day, the light is sad and one feels the chill, but the bitter smell of earth is a tonic.

I can hardly believe that relief from the anguish of these past months is here to stay, but so far it does feel like a true change of mood—or rather, a change of *being* where I can stand alone. So much of my life here is precarious. I cannot always believe even in my work. But I have come in these last days to feel again the validity of my struggle here, that it is meaningful whether I ever "succeed" as a writer or not, and that even its failures, failures of nerve, failures due to a difficult temperament, can be meaningful. It is an age where more and more human beings are caught up in lives where fewer and fewer inward decisions can be made, where fewer and fewer real choices exist. The fact that a middle-aged, single woman, without any vestige of family left, lives in this house in a silent village and is responsible only to her own soul means something. The fact that she is a writer and can tell where she is and what it is like on the pilgrimage inward can be of comfort. It is comforting to know there are lighthouse keepers on rocky islands along the coast. Sometimes, when I have been for a walk after dark and see my house lighted up, looking so alive, I feel that my presence here is worth all the Hell.

I have time to think. That is the great, the greatest luxury. I have time to be. Therefore my responsibility is huge. To use time well and to be all that I can in whatever years are left to me. This does not dismay. The dismay comes when I lose the sense of my life as connected (as if by an aerial) to many, many other lives whom I do not even know and cannot ever know. The signals go out and come in all the time.

Why is it that poetry always seems to me so much more a true work of the soul than prose? I never feel elated after writing a page of prose, though I have written good things on concentrated will, and at least in a novel the imagination is fully engaged. Perhaps it is that prose is earned and poetry given. Both can be revised almost indefinitely. I do not mean to say that I do not work at poetry. When I am really inspired I can put a poem through a hundred drafts and keep my excitement. But this sustained battle is possible only when I am in a state of grace, when the deep channels are open, and when they are, when I am both profoundly stirred and balanced, then poetry comes as a gift from powers beyond my will.

I have often imagined that if I were in solitary confinement for an indefinite time and knew that no one would ever read what I wrote, I would still write poetry, but I would not write novels. Why? Perhaps because the poem is primarily a dialogue with the self and the novel a dialogue with others. They come from entirely different modes of being. I suppose I have written novels to find out what I *thought* about something and poems to find out what I *felt* about something.

January 7th. I have worked all morning—and it is now afternoon—to try to make by sheer art and craft an ending to the first stanza of a lyric that shot through my head intact. I should not feel so pressed for time, but I do, and I suppose I always shall. Yeats[4] speaks of spending a week on one stanza. The danger, of course, is overmanipulation, when one finds oneself manipulating *words*, not images or concepts. My problem was to make a transition viable between lovers in a snowstorm and the whiteness of a huge amaryllis I look at across the hall in the cosy room—seven huge flowers that make constant silent hosannas as I sit here.

In a period of happy and fruitful isolation such as this, any interruption, any intrusion of the social, any obligation breaks the thread on my loom, breaks the pattern. Two nights ago I was called at the last minute to attend the caucus of Town Meeting . . . and it threw me. But at least the companionship gave me one insight: a neighbor told me she had been in a small car accident and had managed to persuade the local paper to ignore her true age (as it appears on her license) and to print her age as thirty-nine! I was really astonished by this confidence. I am proud of being fifty-eight, and still alive and kicking, in love, more creative, balanced, and potent than I have ever been. I mind certain physical deteriorations, but not *really.* And not at all when I look at the marvelous photograph that Bill sent me of Isak Dinesen[5] just before she died. For after all we make our faces as we go along, and who when young could ever look as she does? The ineffable sweetness of the smile, the total acceptance and joy one receives from it, life, death, everything taken in and, as it were, savored—and let go.

Wrinkles here and there seem unimportant compared to *Gestalt* of the whole person I have become in this past year. Somewhere in *The Poet and the Donkey* Andy speaks for me when he says, "Do not deprive me of my age. I have earned it."

My neighbor's wish to be known forever as thirty-nine years old made me think again of what K said in her letter about the people in their

25

4. William Butler Yeats (1865–1939), Irish poet and dramatist.
5. Modern Danish short-story writer who despite painful illness in her later years continued writing until her death at seventy-seven.

thirties mourning their lost youth because we have given them no ethos that makes maturity appear an asset. Yet we have many examples before us. It looks as if T. S. Eliot came into a fully consummated happy marriage only when he was seventy. Yeats married when he was fifty or over. I am coming into the most fulfilled love of my life now. But for some reason Americans are terrified of the very idea of passionate love going on past middle age. Are they afraid of being alive? Do they want to be dead, i.e., *safe?* For of course one is never safe when in love. Growth is demanding and may seem dangerous, for there is loss as well as gain in growth. But why go on living if one has ceased to grow? And what more demanding atmosphere for growth than love in any form, than any relationship which can call out and requires of us our most secret and deepest selves?

My neighbor who wishes to remain thirty-nine indefinitely does so out of anxiety—she is afraid she will no longer be "attractive" if people know her age. But if one wants mature relationships, one will look for them among one's peers. I cannot imagine being in love with someone much younger than I because I have looked on love as an *éducation sentimentale.* About love I have little to learn from the young.

30   *January 8th.* Yesterday was a strange, hurried, uncentered day; yet I did not have to go out, the sun shone. Today I feel centered and time is a friend instead of the old enemy. It was zero this morning. I have a fire burning in my study, yellow roses and mimosa on my desk. There is an atmosphere of festival, of release, in the house. We are one, the house and I, and I am happy to be alone—time to think, time to be. This kind of open-ended time is the only luxury that really counts and I feel stupendously rich to have it. And for the moment I have a sense of fulfillment both about my life and about my work that I have rarely experienced until this year, or perhaps until these last weeks. I look to my left and the transparent blue sky behind a flame-colored cyclamen, lifting about thirty winged flowers to the light, makes an impression of stained glass, light-flooded. I have put the vast heap of unanswered letters into a box at my feet, so I don't see them. And now I am going to make one more try to get that poem right. The last line is still the problem.

Woody Allen: SELECTIONS FROM THE ALLEN NOTEBOOKS

Following are excerpts from the hitherto secret, private journal of Woody Allen, which will be published posthumously or after his death, whichever comes first.

Getting through the night is becoming harder and harder. Last evening, I had the uneasy feeling that some men were trying to break into my room to shampoo me. But why? I kept imagining I saw shadowy forms, and at 3 A.M. the underwear I had draped over a chair resembled the Kaiser on roller skates. When I finally did fall asleep, I had that same hideous nightmare in which a woodchuck is trying to claim my prize at a raffle. Despair.

I believe my consumption has grown worse. Also my asthma. The wheezing comes and goes, and I get dizzy more and more frequently. I have taken to violent choking and fainting. My room is damp and I have perpetual chills and palpitations of the heart. I noticed, too, that I am out of napkins. Will it never stop?

Idea for a story: A man awakens to find his parrot has been made Secretary of Agriculture. He is consumed with jealousy and shoots himself, but unfortunately the gun is the type with a little flag that pops out, with the word "Bang" on it. The flag pokes his eye out, and he lives—a chastened human being who, for the first time, enjoys the simple pleasures of life, like farming or sitting on an air hose.

Thought: Why does man kill? He kills for food. And not only food: frequently there must be a beverage.

Should I marry W.? Not if she won't tell me the other letters in her name. And what about her career? How can I ask a woman of her beauty to give up the Roller Derby? Decisions . . .

Once again I tried committing suicide—this time by wetting my nose and inserting it into the light socket. Unfortunately, there was a short in the wiring, and I merely caromed off the icebox. Still obsessed by thoughts of death, I brood constantly. I keep wondering if there is an afterlife, and if there is will they be able to break a twenty?

I ran into my brother today at a funeral. We had not seen one another

Published in 1972.

for fifteen years, but as usual he produced a pig bladder from his pocket and began hitting me on the head with it. Time has helped me understand him better. I finally realize his remark that I am "some loathsome vermin fit only for extermination" was said more out of compassion than anger. Let's face it: he was always much brighter than me—wittier, more cultured, better educated. Why he is still working at McDonald's is a mystery.

Idea for story: Some beavers take over Carnegie Hall and perform *Wozzeck*. [1] (Strong theme. What will be the structure?)

Good Lord, why am I so guilty? Is it because I hated my father? Probably it was the veal-parmigian' incident. Well, what *was* it doing in his wallet? If I had listened to him, I would be blocking hats for a living. I can hear him now: "To block hats—that is everything." I remember his reaction when I told him I wanted to write. "The only writing you'll do is in collaboration with an owl." I still have no idea what he meant. What a sad man! When my first play, *A Cyst for Gus,* was produced at the Lyceum, he attended opening night in tails and a gas mask.

10   Today I saw a red-and-yellow sunset and thought, How insignificant I am! Of course, I thought that yesterday, too, and it rained. I was overcome with self-loathing and contemplated suicide again—this time by inhaling next to an insurance salesman.

Short story: A man awakens in the morning and finds himself transformed into his own arch supports (This idea can work on many levels. Psychologically, it is the quintessence of Kruger, Freud's disciple who discovered sexuality in bacon.)

How wrong Emily Dickinson was! Hope is not "the thing with feathers." The thing with feathers has turned out to be my nephew. I must take him to a specialist in Zurich.

I have decided to break off my engagement with W. She doesn't understand my writing, and said last night that my *Critique of Metaphysical Reality* reminded her of *Airport.* We quarreled, and she brought up the subject of children again, but I convinced her they would be too young.

Do I believe in God? I did until Mother's accident. She fell on some

1. A lurid and dissonant opera by the modern composer Alban Berg. Carnegie Hall is a famous concert hall in New York City.

meat loaf, and it penetrated her spleen. She lay in a coma for months, unable to do anything but sing "Granada" to an imaginary herring. Why was this woman in the prime of life so afflicted—because in her youth she dared to defy convention and got married with a brown paper bag on her head? And how can I believe in God when just last week I got my tongue caught in the roller of an electric typewriter? I am plagued by doubts. What if everything is an illusion and nothing exists? In that case, I definitely overpaid for my carpet. If only God would give me some clear sign! Like making a large deposit in my name at a Swiss bank.

Had coffee with Melnick today. He talked to me about his idea of having all government officials dress like hens. 15

Play idea: A character based on my father, but without quite so prominent a big toe. He is sent to the Sorbonne[2] to study the harmonica. In the end, he dies, never realizing his one dream—to sit up to his waist in gravy. (I see a brilliant second-act curtain, where two midgets come upon a severed head in a shipment of volleyballs.)

While taking my noon walk today, I had more morbid thoughts. What *is* it about death that bothers me so much? Probably the hours. Melnick says the soul is immortal and lives on after the body drops away, but if my soul exists without my body I am convinced all my clothes will be too loose-fitting. Oh, well . . .

Did not have to break off with W. after all, for as luck would have it, she ran off to Finland with a professional circus geek. All for the best, I suppose, although I had another of those attacks where I start coughing out of my ears.

Last night, I burned all my plays and poetry. Ironically as I was burning my masterpiece, *Dark Penguin,* the room caught fire, and I am now the object of a lawsuit by some men named Pinchunk and Schlosser. Kierkegaard was right.

2. The University of Paris.

Ned Rorem: FROM THE NANTUCKET DIARY OF NED ROREM, 1973–1985

Conversation is neither an art nor a graceful fashion for English-speaking peoples. Americans mean what they say though they sometimes struggle to say what they mean. The French do finally say what they mean though they seldom mean literally what they say. Despite their indirection, their metaphor and irony, the French are succinct; Americans, despite their one-track-mindedness, their clumsy longing for a bull's-eye, are convoluted. This dogma is French but I am American.

Vagaries of English. Verb, *to put*, i.e., *to place*, and problems for the French both in sense and in pronunciation:

> To put out (as extinguish a fire)
> To put out (as outdoors: the cat)
> To be put out (annoyed)
> To put out for (deliver the goods, usually sex)
> To put up (to house)
> To put up (to bottle or can)
> To put up with (tolerate)
> To put up on (place on the shelf)
> To feel put upon (feel used)
> To put over (to deceive; to put one over on)
> To put over . . . a deal
> To put under . . . under a counter

Every professional musician receives daily requests for his time, his money, or the use of his name on a letterhead. These are mostly consigned to the wastebasket. But I've allowed myself to get depressed by the solicitation of something called "Artists to End Hunger" and its pious lay-notion of art. As a Quaker I'm hardly immune to the world's wrongs, but this bunch's propaganda is naive and crass. It's naive to accept hunger as an abstraction (whose hunger? where?) that can be assuaged by "art." Hunger isn't eased by concerts, but by planting crops, planning birth control, meeting of nations. Music doesn't change people, but the sight of suffering might. It's crass to use hunger as a promotional device: to construe the personal elation of pianist Ilana Vered—whoever she may be—as a service to humanity. Rather than a glossy photo of her, why not one of emaciated children? Throughout the prospectus is talk of "creating opportunities for artists," "media publi-

Published in 1987.

cizing," "seeking government support" for musicians, but no mention of how the proposed program will benefit the hungry.

Like a fool I sent these reactions to the "Artists to End Hunger" board along with the wish for my name not to be linked to their self-serving organization. They answered, stating that my "points stimulated much thought. . . . We discovered that our Purpose and Intended Results were not as clear as we had thought," plus goobledegook about "will" and "commitment," and enclosing a letter ("Dear Ned") from a Marguerite Chandler who begins, "As a fellow Quaker and as a member of the board of 'Artists to End Hunger,' I feel moved to speak to you," following with long pieties which shift the meaning of "hunger" to suit her purposes. Again like a fool I answered:

"To speak of 'hunger of the human spirit' is to use the word metaphorically. It may be that 'majestic music,' as you so sentimentally put it, feeds the spirit, but your group's policy is presumably to feed the body. I will not be convinced that an Indian child, numb from lack of food, can be 'nourished' by Beethoven; nor will I listen to a person who asserts the contrary unless that person has literally starved. To draw no distinction between music and bread, and to claim that a starving human is eased by one as by the other, is cruel.

"You inadvertently insult me when speaking of 'we who are the appreciators of art.' I am a practitioner, not a mere appreciator, as you should have known before soliciting me. Meanwhile, to contend that the aim, and thus the financial profits, of art should be toward ending misery is to invent rules for your convenience. But taking your contention as solid: why should an artist donate financial gains *as well as his art* to the poor? Most artists themselves are poor; nor has their art ever in its history existed for purposes of financial gain, or even been profitable compared to the works of munitions makers or, indeed, to Quaker businessmen. Don't talk to artists about 'impoverishment of the human spirit.' Talk instead about nuclear disarmament. And don't talk about 'the *really* poor' until you yourself have physically starved.

Sincerely . . ."

Shrink all this to half a page.

What's the purpose of art?

Well, I don't know the purpose. But the function (and there's a difference) is to satisfy that indefinable area within us that can't be satisfied by the senses, or at least by the *grosser* senses: taste, touch, and smell. It's indefinable precisely because, were it defined, it wouldn't need to be. Art is its own definition. Are words then art? Tough question. Poetry, yes. But is a novel art—or is it high art?

The nauseating conclusion of the "Artists to End Hunger" people is that art is necessarily ennobling. Now, there is no example, ever, of its being ennobling, and few artists are themselves noble—whatever noble is.

The Quaker woman writes of the starving Somalians who nevertheless retain "great dignity and courage" and she asks herself "Who are the *really* poor?"—meaning us affluent pigs. One wonders how she'd react to starving people who were not, in her eyes, dignified. Do they get demerits?

But the *purpose* of art?

JH[1] says: to make money.

15　　　　Composers who teach: The supposition, that because we know how we can show how, is at best risky. (Does the goose know how it lays the golden egg?) The supposition has been visibly risky for centuries, yet Broadway angels still sink billions into flops, nothing into hits, and great art seems a lottery. Still, Boston University proposes to accord me $60,000 yearly to instruct young composers.

If I "knew how," would I tell? Why not bottle it and sell it and make a mint? Or is there room for another me? Teaching the "art" of composition (unlike the *crafts* of orchestration or counterpoint or ditchdigging) can come only after the fact. Pupils must first produce something that the teacher may criticize.

What can I do? I can smell a rat. And I can intuit who I think the pupil thinks he is and help to clear the debris between himself and his self. A piece results from the taking of your material and stretching and shrinking it, heating and cooling it, weaving and unraveling it, enriching and depleting it, and this according to both textbook and instinct. But if the material itself is second-rate, how can I make it first-rate, even for myself?

1. James Holmes, Rorem's live-in companion.

People, Places

Thomas Jefferson

GEORGE WASHINGTON

I think I knew General Washington intimately and thoroughly; and were I called on to delineate his character, it should be in terms like these.

His mind was great and powerful, without being of the very first order; his penetration strong, though not so acute as that of a Newton, Bacon, or Locke; and as far as he saw, no judgment was ever sounder. It was slow in operation, being little aided by invention or imagination, but sure in conclusion. Hence the common remark of his officers, of the advantage he derived from councils of war, where hearing all suggestions, he selected whatever was best; and certainly no general ever planned his battles more judiciously. But if deranged during the course of the action, if any member of his plan was dislocated by sudden circumstances, he was slow in re-adjustment. The consequence was, that he often failed in the field, and rarely against an enemy in station, as at Boston and York. He was incapable of fear, meeting personal dangers with the calmest unconcern. Perhaps the strongest feature in his character was prudence, never acting until every circumstance, every consideration, was maturely weighed; refraining if he saw a doubt, but, when once decided, going through with his purpose, whatever obstacles opposed. His integrity was most pure, his justice the most inflexible I have ever known, no motives of interest or consanguinity, of friendship or hatred, being able to bias his decision. He was, indeed, in every sense of the words, a wise, a good, and a great man. His temper was naturally irritable and high toned; but reflection and resolution had obtained a firm and habitual ascendency over it. If ever, however, it broke its bonds, he was most tremendous in his

From a letter written in 1814 to a Doctor Jones, who was writing a history and wanted to know about Washington's role in the Federalist-Republican controversy.

wrath. In his expenses he was honorable, but exact; liberal in contributions to whatever promised utility; but frowning and unyielding on all visionary projects, and all unworthy calls on his charity. His heart was not warm in its affections; but he exactly calculated every man's value, and gave him a solid esteem proportioned to it. His person, you know, was fine, his stature exactly what one would wish, his deportment easy, erect and noble; the best horseman of his age, and the most graceful figure that could be seen on horseback. Although in the circle of his friends, where he might be unreserved with safety, he took a free share in conversation, his colloquial talents were not above mediocrity, possessing neither copiousness of ideas, nor fluency of words. In public, when called on for a sudden opinion, he was unready, short and embarrassed. Yet he wrote readily, rather diffusely, in an easy and correct style. This he had acquired by conversation with the world, for his education was merely reading, writing and common arithmetic, to which he added surveying at a later day. His time was employed in action chiefly, reading little, and that only in agriculture and English history. His correspondence became necessarily extensive, and, with journalizing his agricultural proceedings, occupied most of his leisure hours within doors. On the whole, his character was, in its mass, perfect, in nothing bad, in few points indifferent; and it may truly be said, that never did nature and fortune combine more perfectly to make a man great, and to place him in the same constellation with whatever worthies have merited from man an everlasting remembrance. For his was the singular destiny and merit, of leading the armies of his country successfully through an arduous war, for the establishment of its independence; of conducting its councils through the birth of a government, new in its forms and principles, until it had settled down into a quiet and orderly train; and of scrupulously obeying the laws through the whole of his career, civil and military, of which the history of the world furnishes no other example.

    * * * I am satisfied, the great body of republicans think of him as I do. We were, indeed, dissatisfied with him on his ratification of the British treaty. But this was short lived. We knew his honesty, the wiles with which he was encompassed, and that age had already begun to relax the firmness of his purposes; and I am convinced he is more deeply seated in the love and gratitude of the republicans, than in the Pharisaical homage of the federal monarchists.[1] For he was no monarchist from preference of his judgment. The soundness of that gave him correct views of the rights of man, and his severe justice devoted

---

1. Jefferson here compares those who sought to make the new United States a kingdom, with Washington as king, to the biblical Pharisees, the haughty sect of ancient Israel.

him to them. He has often declared to me that he considered our new Constitution as an experiment on the practicability of republican government, and with what dose of liberty man could be trusted for his own good; that he was determined the experiment should have a fair trial, and would lose the last drop of his blood in support of it. And these declarations he repeated to me the oftener and more pointedly, because he knew my suspicions of Colonel Hamilton's views,[2] and probably had heard from him the same declarations which I had, to wit, "that the British constitution, with its unequal representation, corruption and other existing abuses, was the most perfect government which had ever been established on earth, and that a reformation of those abuses would make it an impracticable government." I do believe that General Washington had not a firm confidence in the durability of our government. He was naturally distrustful of men, and inclined to gloomy apprehensions; and I was ever persuaded that a belief that we must at length end in something like a British constitution, had some weight in his adoption of the ceremonies of levees,[3] birthdays, pompous meetings with Congress, and other forms of the same character, calculated to prepare us gradually for a change which he believed possible, and to let it come on with as little shock as might be to the public mind.

These are my opinions of General Washington which I would vouch at the judgment seat of God, having been formed on an acquaintance of thirty years. I served with him in the Virginia legislature from 1769 to the Revolutionary war, and again, a short time in Congress, until he left us to take command of the army. During the war and after it we corresponded occasionally, and in the four years of my continuance in the office of Secretary of State, our intercourse was daily, confidential and cordial. After I retired from that office, great and malignant pains were taken by our federal monarchists, and not entirely without effect, to make him view me as a theorist, holding French principles of government,[4] which would lead infallibly to licentiousness and anarchy. And to this he listened the more easily, from my known disapprobation of the British treaty. I never saw him afterwards, or these malignant insinuations should have been dissipated before his just judgment, as mists before the sun. I felt on his death, with my countrymen, that "verily a great man hath fallen this day in Israel."

2. Alexander Hamilton (1755–1804) advocated a strong central federal government, led by the "wealthy, good, and wise." His views were opposed by the relatively more democratic views of Jefferson.
3. Morning receptions held by a head of state to enable him to attend to public affairs while rising and dressing. The form was characteristic of European monarchs.
4. Radical political views advanced by extreme democrats in the course of the French Revolution.

THE READER

1. *What, in Jefferson's view, are Washington's outstanding virtues? What are Washington's greatest defects? What is Jefferson's overall judgment of the character of Washington? Does this portrait of Washington agree with what you have been taught and have learned about the man?*

2. *From what he writes about Washington, can you infer those qualities of character that Jefferson most admires? If so, do you agree?*

3. *Do we learn anything from Jefferson's portrait about what Washington looked like? About his family life? About his hobbies? About his religion? If not, are these important omissions in the characterization of a person in public life?*

THE WRITER

1. *What does Jefferson produce by including in his portrait certain defects or shortcomings of Washington?*

2. *Is Jefferson's characterization of Washington persuasive? What kinds of authority (explicit and implicit) does this piece set forth for the correctness of its view?*

3. *Write in the manner of Jefferson a characterization of an important figure in public life today. Consider whether this manner enables you to bring out what you think is essential truth, and whether the attempt brings to light any special problems concerning either the task itself or public life today.*

Nathaniel Hawthorne

ABRAHAM LINCOLN

Of course, there was one other personage, in the class of statesmen, whom I should have been truly mortified to leave Washington without seeing; since (temporarily, at least, and by force of circumstances) he was the man of men. But a private grief had built up a barrier about him, impeding the customary free intercourse of Americans with their chief magistrate; so that I might have come away without a glimpse of his very remarkable physiognomy, save for a semi-official opportunity of which I was glad to take advantage. The fact is, we were invited to annex ourselves, as supernumeraries, to a deputation that was about to wait

One of a series of sketches published in the *Atlantic Monthly*, "Abraham Lincoln" appeared in 1862.

upon the President, from a Massachusetts whip factory, with a present of a splendid whip.

Our immediate party consisted only of four or five (including Major Ben Perley Poore,[1] with his note-book and pencil), but we were joined by several other persons, who seemed to have been lounging about the precincts of the White House, under the spacious porch, or within the hall, and who swarmed in with us to take the chances of a presentation. Nine o'clock had been appointed as the time for receiving the deputation, and we were punctual to the moment; but not so the President, who sent us word that he was eating his breakfast, and would come as soon as he could. His appetite, we were glad to think, must have been a pretty fair one; for we waited about half an hour in one of the antechambers, and then were ushered into a reception-room, in one corner of which sat the Secretaries of War and of the Treasury, expecting, like ourselves, the termination of the Presidential breakfast. During this interval there were several new additions to our group, one or two of whom were in a working-garb, so that we formed a very miscellaneous collection of people, mostly unknown to each other, and without any common sponsor, but all with an equal right to look our head servant in the face.

By and by there was a little stir on the staircase and in the passageway, and in lounged a tall, loose-jointed figure, of an exaggerated Yankee port and demeanor, whom (as being about the homeliest man I ever saw, yet by no means repulsive or disagreeable) it was impossible not to recognize as Uncle Abe.

Unquestionably, Western man though he be, and Kentuckian by birth, President Lincoln is the essential representative of all Yankees, and the veritable specimen, physically, of what the world seems determined to regard as our characteristic qualities. It is the strangest and yet the fittest thing in the jumble of human vicissitudes, that he, out of so many millions, unlooked for, unselected by any intelligible process that could be based upon his genuine qualities, unknown to those who chose him, and unsuspected of what endowments may adapt him for his tremendous responsibility, should have found the way open for him to fling his lank personality into the chair of state—where, I presume, it was his first impulse to throw his legs on the council-table, and tell the Cabinet Ministers a story. There is no describing his lengthy awkwardness, nor the uncouthness of his movement; and yet it seemed as if I had been in the habit of seeing him daily, and had shaken hands with him a thousand times in some village street; so true was he to the aspect of the pattern American, though with a certain extravagance which, possibly, I exaggerated still further by the delighted eagerness with

1. American journalist and biographer.

which I took it in. If put to guess his calling and livelihood, I should have taken him for a country school-master as soon as anything else. He was dressed in a rusty black frock coat and pantaloons, unbrushed, and worn so faithfully that the suit had adapted itself to the curves and angularities of his figure, and had grown to be an outer skin of the man. His hair was black, still unmixed with gray, stiff, somewhat bushy, and had apparently been acquainted with neither brush nor comb that morning, after the disarrangement of the pillow; and as to a nightcap, Uncle Abe probably knows nothing of such effeminacies. His complexion is dark and sallow, betokening, I fear, a insalubrious atmosphere around the White House; he has thick black eyebrows and an impending brow; his nose is large, and the lines about his mouth are very strongly defined.

5   The whole physiognomy is as coarse a one as you would meet anywhere in the length and breadth of the States; but, withal, it is redeemed, illuminated, softened, and brightened by a kindly though serious look out of his eyes, and an expression of homely sagacity, that seems weighted with rich results of village experience. A great deal of native sense; no bookish cultivation, no refinement; honest at heart, and thoroughly so, and yet, in some sort, sly—at least, endowed with a sort of tact and wisdom that are akin to craft, and would impel him, I think, to take an antagonist in flank, rather than to make a bull-run at him right in front. But, on the whole, I like this sallow, queer, sagacious visage, with the homely human sympathies that warmed it; and, for my small share in the matter, would as lief have Uncle Abe for a ruler as any man whom it would have been practicable to put in his place.

Immediately on his entrance the President accosted our member of Congress, who had us in charge, and, with a comical twist of his face, made some jocular remark about the length of his breakfast. He then greeted us all round, not waiting for an introduction, but shaking and squeezing everybody's hand with the utmost cordiality, whether the individual's name was announced to him or not. His manner towards us was wholly without pretence, but yet had a kind of natural dignity, quite sufficient to keep the forwardest of us from clapping him on the shoulder and asking him for a story. A mutual acquaintance being established, our leader took the whip out of its case, and began to read the address of presentation. The whip was an exceedingly long one, its handle wrought in ivory (by some artist in the Massachusetts State Prison, I believe), and ornamented with a medallion of the President, and other equally beautiful devices; and along its whole length there was a succession of golden bands and ferrules. The address was shorter than the whip, but equally well made, consisting chiefly of an explanatory description of these artistic designs, and closing with a hint that the gift was a suggestive and emblematic one, and that the President would recognize the use to which such an instrument should be put.

This suggestion gave Uncle Abe rather a delicate task in his reply, because, slight as the matter seemed, it apparently called for some declaration, or intimation, or faint foreshadowing of policy in reference to the conduct of the war, and the final treatment of the Rebels. But the President's Yankee aptness and not-to-be-caughtness stood him in good stead, and he jerked or wiggled himself out of the dilemma with an uncouth dexterity that was entirely in character; although, without his gesticulation of eye and mouth—and especially the flourish of the whip, with which he imagined himself touching up a pair of fat horses—I doubt whether his words would be worth recording, even if I could remember them. The gist of the reply was, that he accepted the whip as an emblem of peace, not punishment; and, this great affair over, we retired out of the presence in high good humor, only regretting that we could not have seen the President sit down and fold up his legs (which is said to be a most extraordinary spectacle), or have heard him tell one of those delectable stories for which he is so celebrated. A good many of them are afloat upon the common talk of Washington, and are certainly the aptest, pithiest, and funniest little things imaginable; though, to be sure, they smack of the frontier freedom, and would not always bear repetition in a drawing-room, or on the immaculate page of the *Atlantic*. [2]

Good Heavens! what liberties have I been taking with one of the potentates of the earth, and the man on whose conduct more important consequences depend than on that of any other historical personage of the century! But with whom is an American citizen entitled to take a liberty, if not with his own chief magistrate? However, lest the above allusions to President Lincoln's little peculiarities (already well known to the country and to the world) should be misinterpreted, I deem it proper to say a word or two in regard to him, of unfeigned respect and measurable confidence. He is evidently a man of keen faculties, and, what is still more to the purpose, of powerful character. As to his integrity, the people have that intuition of it which is never deceived. Before he actually entered upon his great office, and for a considerable time afterwards, there is no reason to suppose that he adequately estimated the gigantic task about to be imposed on him, or, at least, had any distinct idea how it was to be managed; and I presume there may

2. This passage was one of those omitted from the article as originally published, and the following note was appended to explain the omission, which had been indicated by a line of points:

"We are compelled to omit two or three pages, in which the author describes the interview, and gives his idea of the personal appearance and deportment of the President. The sketch appears to have been written in a benign spirit, and perhaps conveys a not inaccurate impression of its august subject; but it lacks *reverence*, and it pains us to see a gentleman of ripe age, and who has spent years under the corrective influence of foreign institutions, falling into the characteristic and most ominous fault of Young America."

have been more than one veteran politician who proposed to himself to take the power out of President Lincoln's hands into his own, leaving our honest friend only the public responsibility for the good or ill success of the career. The extremely imperfect development of his statesmanly qualities, at that period, may have justified such designs. But the President is teachable by events, and has now spent a year in a very arduous course of education; he has a flexible mind, capable of much expansion, and convertible towards far loftier studies and activities than those of his early life; and if he came to Washington a backwoods humorist, he has already transformed himself into as good a statesman (to speak moderately) as his prime minister.[3]

3. Presumably the secretary of state, William H. Seward.

THE READER

1. *In one sentence, summarize Hawthorne's attitude toward Lincoln in the first seven paragraphs.*
2. *In his final paragraph, Hawthorne seeks to prevent misunderstanding by stressing his respect for and confidence in Lincoln. Is there anything in the paragraph that runs counter to that expression? To what effect?*

THE WRITER

1. *What is the basic pattern of the opening sentence of the fifth paragraph? Find other examples of this pattern. What is their total impact on Hawthorne's description?*
2. *Write a paragraph of description of someone you know, using the same pattern for the entire paragraph that you discovered for Hawthorne's sentence in the previous question.*
3. *In the footnote to the seventh paragraph, the editor of the* Atlantic Monthly *explains his omission of the first seven paragraphs. On the evidence of this statement, what sort of person does the editor seem to be? Is there anything in the omitted paragraphs that would tend to justify his decision as editor? Is the full description superior to the last paragraph printed alone? Explain.*
4. *Describe someone you know who has a strong personality that has contrasting characteristics.*

David McCullough

THE UNEXPECTED MRS. STOWE[1]

She had been brought up to make herself useful. And always it suited her.

As a child she had been known as Hattie. She had been cheerful but shy, prone to fantasies, playful, and quite pretty. After she became famous, she would describe herself this way: "To begin, then, I am a little bit of a woman,—somewhat more than forty, about as thin and dry as a pinch of snuff; never very much to look at in my best days, and looking like a used-up article now." She wasn't altogether serious when she wrote that, but the description was the one people would remember.

She was born in Litchfield, Connecticut—in a plain frame house that still stands—in 1811, when Lincoln was two years old and when Dolley Madison was in the White House. She was the seventh of the nine children Roxana Foote bore Lyman Beecher before being gathered to her reward, and she was such a worker, even when very small, that her preacher father liked to say he would gladly have given a hundred dollars if she could have been born a boy.

As a child she had found most of his sermons about as intelligible as Choctaw, she wrote later, and never would she be at peace with his religion. But she loved him, and for all his gloomy talk of sin and damnation it is not hard to understand why. He was a powerful, assertive figure who had an almost fiendish zest for life—for hunting and fishing with his sons, for listening to all music, and for playing the violin, which he did badly. But could he only play what he heard inside him, he told them all, he could be another Paganini.[2] Best of all he loved to go out and "snare souls," as he said. In a corner of the cellar he kept a pile of sand, and if his day was not enough to use him up, and stormy weather kept him from outdoor exercise, down he would go, shovel in hand, to sling sand about.

Sunday mornings he would come bounding along through the sunshine, late again for that appointed hour when weekly he brought down Calvinist thunder upon the heads of upright Litchfield people. He had a special wrath for drunkards and Unitarians, and he believed passionately in the Second Coming. But something in him made him shy away

5

First published in *American Heritage* (Aug. 1973).

1. The title refers to Harriet Beecher Stowe (1811–96), American novelist whose book *Uncle Tom's Cabin* aided the abolitionist movement against slavery.
2. Nicolò Paganini, Italian violinist and superb virtuoso in technical achievement.

from the strictest tenet of his creed—total predestination—and its logic. Once when he had agreed to exchange pulpits with another pastor, he was told that the arrangement had been preordained. "Is that so?" he said. "Then I won't do it!" and he didn't.

The happiest times in her childhood, Hattie would write later, were the days spent away from him, visiting an Aunt Harriet in Nutplains, Connecticut, in a house filled with books and pictures gathered by a seafaring uncle and a wonderful old Tory[3] grandmother, who in private still said Episcopal prayers for the king and queen.

At twelve Hattie often wandered off from the noisy parsonage to lie on a green hillside and gaze straight into a solid blue sky and dream of Byron. One month she read *Ivanhoe* seven times.

In 1832, when Hattie had turned twenty-one, Lyman Beecher answered the call to become the first president of the Lane Theological Seminary in Cincinnati. He packed up his children and a new wife and set off for what he called "the majestic West." A New Jerusalem was to be established on the banks of the Ohio. The family spirits were lifted; and crossing the Alleghenies, they all sang "Jubilee." A Philadelphia journal likened the exodus of the Reverend Mr. Beecher and his family to the migration of Jacob and his sons.

The following summer the Lane Theological Seminary's first (and at that time, only) professor, Calvin Ellis Stowe, a Biblical scholar and Bowdoin graduate, traveled west in the Beecher's wake. For all his learning and devotion to the Almighty, Stowe was a very homely and peculiar worker in the vineyard.

He was accompanied by a beautiful young bride, Eliza, who soon became Hattie Beecher's best friend in Cincinnati but died not very long afterward. Apparently it was a shared grief over Eliza that brought Hattie and Calvin Stowe together. Years later, with some of the proceeds from *Uncle Tom's Cabin,* they would commission an artist to do a portrait of Eliza, and every year thereafter, on Eliza's birthday, the two of them would sit before the portrait and reminisce about Eliza's virtues.

The wedding took place in early January, 1836. What exactly she saw in him is a little hard to say. The night before the ceremony, trying to describe her emotions in a letter to a school friend, she confessed she felt "nothing at all." But Lord Byron had not appeared in Cincinnati. At twenty-four she may have felt she was getting on.

Calvin was thirty-three, but he seemed as old as her father. He was fluent in Greek, Latin, Hebrew, French, Italian, German; he was an authority on education; he knew the Bible better than her father. Also, it is recorded, he had a grand sense of humor. But he was as fat and

---

3. A member of the conservative British political party or, in the United States, a British loyalist who opposed American independence.

forgetful and fussy as an old woman. In the midst of a crisis, as she would soon discover, he had a bad habit of taking to his bed, and he had absolutely no "faculty," that Yankee virtue she defined simply as being the opposite of shiftlessness.

He also had an eye for pretty women, as he admitted to Hattie, and a taste for spirits, but these proclivities, it seems, never got him into any particular trouble.

But there was more. Calvin, from his boyhood until his dying day, was haunted by phantoms. They visited him most any time, but favored dusk. They appeared quite effortlessly out of the woodwork, the floor, or the furniture. There was a regular cast of characters, Calvin said, as real and familiar to him as anyone else he knew. Among his favorites were a giant Indian woman and a dark dwarf who between them carried a huge bull fiddle. There was a troupe of old Puritans from his native Natick, all shadowy and dark blue in color, and one "very pleasant-looking human face" he called Harvey. They performed music for Calvin Stowe, and somehow or other they talked to him without making any sound at all, or so he said. He had no reluctance about discussing the subject, and there is no indication that any of his circle thought the less of him for it.

Still, the marriage proved difficult soon enough. Hattie became pregnant almost immediately, and just about then Calvin was asked by the state of Ohio to go to Prussia to study educational systems there. Professing a profound fear of the salt sea, he told her he would never see her again in this life. She insisted that he go, and had twin daughters while he was away. There was a third child two years later, then another, and two more later on. A professor's wages were never enough, even when old Lyman could pay Calvin in full, which was seldom. Hattie's health began to fail. "She lived overmuch in her emotions," one son would explain years later.

"It is a dark, sloppy, rainy, muddy disagreeable day," she wrote once to Calvin when he was in Detroit attending a church convention. ". . . I am sick of the smell of sour milk, and sour meat, and sour everything, and then the clothes *will* not dry, and no wet thing does, and everything smells moldy; and altogether I feel as if I never wanted to eat again."

She began going off on visits to relatives, leaving Calvin and the children behind. The visits grew longer. She went to the White Mountains, then to Brattleboro, Vermont, to try the water cure. The expenses were met by gifts from distant admirers of the family: the Stowes felt that the Lord had a hand in it. Hattie stayed on for nearly a year at Brattleboro, living on brown bread and milk, enduring the interminable sitz baths of one Dr. Wesselhoeft, and writing home exuberant letters about moonlight snowball fights. And no sooner did she return to the

15

cluttered house in Cincinnati than the professor hauled himself off to Brattleboro, there to stay even longer than she had. When a cholera epidemic broke out in Cincinnati and more than a hundred people a day were dying, she wrote to tell him to stay right where he was. She would manage.

In all they were separated a total of three years and more, and their letters back and forth speak of strong, troubled feelings. The hulking, clumsy Stowe, bearded, nearsighted, complained that she never folded his newspaper properly and that her letters of late were too uninteresting for him to read aloud to his friends. She in turn would run on about her own miseries. The house depressed her, she worried about money, she hated the climate in Cincinnati. She thought too much about death.

But she also told him, "There are a thousand favorite subjects on which I could talk with you better than anyone else. If you were not already my dearly loved husband I should certainly fall in love with you."

And Calvin would write to her when she was visiting her sister in Hartford, "And now my dear wife, I want you to come home as quick as you can. The fact is I cannot live without you and if we were not so prodigious poor I would come for you at once. There is no woman like you in this wide world."

In this same letter Calvin proclaimed to her—and apparently he was the first to do so—"My dear, you must be a literary woman. It is so written in the book of fate." He advised her to make all her plans accordingly, as though she had little else to do. "Get a good stock of health and brush up your mind," he declared. And he told her to drop her middle initial, *E* (for Elizabeth), from her name. "It only encumbers it and interferes with the flow and euphony." Instead: "Write yourself fully and always Harriet Beecher Stowe, which is a name euphonious, flowing, and full of meaning."

She had already written quite a little—temperance tracts, articles on keeping the Sabbath, New England "sketches," for which she drew heavily on Calvin's seemingly inexhaustible fund of childhood reminiscences. Once she had done an article about a slave. She had been selling these pieces to *Godey's Lady's Book* and one or two other magazines. She got two dollars a page on the average, which was more profitable than taking in boarders, she decided. But no one in the family, other than Calvin, had taken her writing very seriously.

She worked at the kitchen table, confusion all around, a baby in a clothes basket at her feet. She couldn't spell very well, and her punctuation would always be a puzzle for her publishers. She dreamed, she said in a letter to Calvin, of a place to work without "the constant falling of soot and coal dust on everything in the room."

Then in July of 1849 she was writing to tell him that their infant son

Charley was dead of cholera. The summer before she had nearly died of it herself, with her father praying over her all through one terrible, sweltering night, the room alive with mosquitoes. She had been unable to do a thing for the child, she told Calvin. For almost a week she watched him die, with no way to help, she said, no way even to ease his suffering.

Calvin returned to her very soon after that, determined to leave   25
Cincinnati for good. He had accepted a professorship at Bowdoin College, in Brunswick, Maine, and before he could settle up his affairs in Cincinnati, he characteristically sent Harriet and three of the children off to Maine ahead of him.

She left Cincinnati in the early spring of 1850, a shabby little figure, perfectly erect, perhaps no more than five feet tall, nearly forty, and pregnant once again. She boarded a riverboat at the foot of town, saying farewell with no misgivings. She was going home, she felt.

She was also heading for a sudden and colossal notoriety of a kind never known by any American woman before, and very few since; but of that she had no notion whatever. Nor did she or anyone else alive have any idea how important those seventeen years in Cincinnati had been to her and, as things turned out, to the whole course of American history.

She sailed up the Ohio to Pittsburgh, where she changed to a canal-boat. Already she was feeling so good she got out and walked the towpath between locks. At Johnstown the boat and all its passengers were hoisted up and over the Allegheny Mountains by that thrilling mechanical contrivance of the nineteenth century, the Portage Railroad. East of the mountains she went by rail to New York and there crossed by ferry to Brooklyn to see her younger brother, Henry Ward, pastor of Plymouth Church. As children they had sometimes been taken for twins, only Henry Ward had been thick of speech and considered the slow one. Now she took note of his obvious success, and they went out for a drive in a spotless six-hundred-dollar carriage, a recent gift from his parishioners.

In a few days she went on to Hartford, still looking after the children and all their baggage. Her spirits were soaring. At Hartford she stayed with her sisters Mary and Isabella; in Boston with her brother Edward, who was growing ever more militant over the slavery issue. All the Beechers were growing more militant over one thing or another. For Isabella it was women's rights; for the brilliant Catherine, education; for Charles, freedom from theological authority. From Boston, Harriet took the Bath Steamer to Maine, sailing headlong into a northeaster.

On the day they were scheduled to arrive at Brunswick, one story goes,   30
the president of Bowdoin sent a professor named Smith down to greet

the new faculty wife, but Smith returned disappointed, saying she must have been delayed. Nobody got off the boat, he said, except an old Irish woman and her brats.

Brunswick offered precious few of the eastern civilities Mrs. Stowe had longed for, and the house Calvin had taken in advance turned out to be deserted, dreary, and damp, to use her words. She went straight to work, refinishing floors, putting up wallpaper—the pioneer again. When Calvin wrote from Cincinnati to say he was sick and plainly dying and that she and theirs would soon be plunged into everlasting debt, she read the letter with humor and stuffed it into the stove.

Calvin showed up before summer, her baby was born, she rested two weeks. When winter came, there were holes in her shoes, and the house was so cold during one long storm that the children had trouble sitting still long enough to eat their meals. They were living on $1,700 a year. It was during the following spring that she began *Uncle Tom's Cabin*.

People are still trying to interpret the book and to explain just how and why she came to write it. At first she said she really didn't write it at all. She said the book come to her in visions and all she did was write down what she saw. When someone reproached her for letting Little Eva die, she answered, "Why, I could not help it. I felt as badly as anyone could! It was like a death in my own family and it affected me so deeply that I could not write a word for two weeks after her death." Years later she stated categorically, "God wrote it." And a great many of her readers were quite willing to let it go at that.

The truth is, the subject of the book had been all around her for a very long time. Old Lyman had been able to make Litchfield farmers weep when he preached on slavery. In Cincinnati she had opened her own Sunday school to black children, and the Lane Seminary had been a hotbed of abolitionist fervor. The Underground Railroad,[4] she later claimed, went directly through her Cincinnati house, which was a bit of an exaggeration; but on one occasion Calvin and her brother Charles did indeed help a black woman and her child elude a slave hunter. The only time she was in an actual slave state, during a visit across the Ohio River in Kentucky, she made no show of emotion about it. But stories she heard from the Negro women she knew in Cincinnati moved her enormously, particularly those told by a gentle person named Eliza Buck, who helped her with housework and whose children, Harriet Stowe discovered with incredulity, had all been fathered by the woman's former master in Kentucky. "You know, Mrs. Stowe," she had said, "slave women cannot help themselves."

Eliza Buck told her of lashings and of Negro families split up and

---

4. A secret network for transporting slaves to freedom prior to and during the Civil War.

"sold down the river." Once on an Ohio River wharf Mrs. Stowe had
seen with her own eyes a husband and wife torn apart by a slave trader.

By the time she came east to Maine, Henry Ward was using his
Brooklyn pulpit to raise money to buy children out of slavery. In Boston
she and Edward had talked long and emotionally about the Fugitive
Slave Bill, then being debated in Congress, which made it a federal
crime to harbor or assist the escaped "property" of a slave master. Her
duty was plain. There was, she said, a standard higher than an act of
Congress.

She did some research in Boston and corresponded with Frederick
Douglass[5] on certain details. But for all that, the book would be written
more out of something within her, something she knew herself about
bondage and the craving for liberation, than from any documentary
sources or personal investigation of Negro slavery in the South. Indeed
she really knew very little about Negro slavery in the South. Her critics
would be vicious with her for this, of course, and she would go so far
as to write a whole second book in defense of her sources. But *Uncle
Tom's Cabin* could never be accounted for that way.

There is probably something to the story that she began the book as
a result of a letter from Edward's wife. "Hattie," wrote her sister-in-law
from Boston, "if I could use the pen as you can, I would write something
that will make this whole nation feel what an accursed thing slavery is."
To which Hattie answered, "As long as the baby sleeps with me nights,
I can't do much at anything, but I will do it at last. I will write that thing
if I live."

The story appeared first as a serial in the *National Era,* an antislavery
paper, beginning in June, 1851. It took her a year to write it all, and
apparently she did Uncle Tom's death scene first and at a single sitting,
writing on brown wrapping paper when her writing paper ran out. The
finished story was brought out in book form by the publisher, John P.
Jewett, in two volumes on March 20, 1852, a month before the serialized
version ended.

Calvin thought the book had little importance. He wept over it, but
he wept over most of the things she wrote. Her publisher warned that
her subject was unpopular and said she took too long to tell her story.
On the advice of a friend who had not read the manuscript, she decided
to take a 10 percent royalty on every copy sold instead of a fifty-fifty
division of profit or losses, as had also been offered to her.

She herself expected to make no money from it; she thought it
inadequate and was sure her friends would be disappointed with her.
Within a week after publication ten thousand copies had been sold. The

40

5. Frederick Douglass (1818–95), a black American abolitionist, orator, and writer who
described his experiences as a slave in *Narrative of the Life of Frederick Douglass.*

publisher had three power presses running twenty-four hours a day. In a year sales in the United States came to more than three hundred thousand. The book made publishing history right from the start. In England, where Mrs. Stowe had no copyright and therefore received no royalties, sales were even more stupendous. A million and a half copies were sold in about a year's time. The book appeared in thirty-seven different languages. "It is no longer permissible to those who can read not to have read it," wrote George Sand from France, who said Mrs. Stowe had no talent, only genius, and called her a saint.

The book had a strange power over almost everyone who read it then, and for all its Victorian mannerisms and frequent patches of sentimentality much of it still does. Its characters have a vitality of a kind comparable to the most memorable figures in literature. There is a sweep and power to the narrative, and there are scenes that once read are not forgotten. The book is also rather different from what most people imagine, largely because it was eventually eclipsed by the stage version, which Mrs. Stowe had nothing to do with (and from which she never received a cent) and which was probably performed more often than any play in the language, evolving after a few years into something between circus and minstrel show. (One successful road company advertised ". . . a pack of genuine bloodhounds; two Toppsies; Two Marks, Eva and her Pony 'Prince'; African Mandolin Players; 'Tinker' the famous Trick Donkey.") In the book, for example, no bloodhounds chase Eliza and her baby across the ice.

What the book did at the time was to bring slavery out into the open and show it for what it was, in human terms. No writer had done that before. Slavery had been argued over in the abstract, preached against as a moral issue, its evils whispered about in polite company. But the book made people at that time *feel* what slavery was all about. ("The soul of eloquence is feeling," old Lyman had written.)

Moreover, Harriet Stowe had made a black man her hero, and she took his race seriously, and no American writer had done that before.

The fundamental fault, she fervently held, was with the system. Every white American was guilty, the Northerner no less than the slaveholder, especially the churchgoing kind, *her* kind. Simon Legree, it should perhaps always be remembered, was a Vermonter.

That Uncle Tom would one day be used as a term of derision ("A Negro who is held to be humiliatingly subservient or deferential to whites," according to the *American Heritage Dictionary*) she would have found impossible to fathom, and heartbreaking. For her he was something very close to a black Christ. He is the one character in all her book who lives, quite literally, by the Christian ideal. And if one has doubts that she could see black as beautiful or that she saw emancipation for the black man as a chance for full manhood and dignity, there is her description of Eliza's husband, George Harris, as straight-backed, confident, "his face settled and resolute." When George and his family, having escaped into Ohio, are cornered by slave hunters, Mrs. Stowe writes a scene in which George is fully prepared to kill his tormentors and to die himself rather than permit his wife and son to be taken back into slavery. ". . . I am a free man, standing on God's free soil," George yells from the rock ledge to which he has retreated, "and my wife and my child I claim as mine. . . . We have arms to defend ourselves and we mean to do it. You can come up if you like; but the first one of you that comes within the range of our bullets is a dead man, and the next, and the next, and so on till the last."

She seems to have been everywhere at once after the book was published—Hartford, New Haven, Brooklyn, Boston. Almost immediately the South began boiling with indignation. She was a radical, it was said. All the Beechers were radicals. She began receiving threatening letters from the South, and once Calvin unwrapped a small parcel addressed to her to find a human ear that had been severed from the head of a black slave. Calvin grew more and more distraught. They decided it was time to move again, now to Andover, Massachusetts, to take up a previously offered teaching job at the seminary there.

Then they were sailing to England, where huge crowds waited for her at railroad stations, hymns were composed in her honor, children came up to her carriage with flowers. She went about in a gray cloak carrying a paint box. She was a tireless tourist. And she worried. "The power of fictitious writing, for good as well as evil is a thing which ought most seriously to be reflected on. No one can fail to see that in our day it is becoming a very great agency."

When war came, everyone told her it was her war, and she thought so too. In South Carolina, as the war commenced, the wife of a plantation owner wrote in her diary that naturally slavery had to go, but added, "Yes, how I envy those saintly Yankee women, in their clean cool New England homes, writing to make their fortunes and shame us."

Harriet Stowe never saw the Civil War as anything but a war to end slavery, and all her old Beecher pacifist principles went right out the window. "Better, a thousand times better, open, manly, energetic war, than cowardly and treacherous peace," she proclaimed. Her oldest son, Frederick, put on a uniform and went off to fight. Impatient with Lincoln for not announcing emancipation right away, she went down to Washington when he finally proclaimed that the slaves would be free, and was received privately in the White House. The scene is part of our folklore. "So this is the little woman who made this big war," Lincoln is supposed to have said as he shook her hand.

50

She was sitting in the gallery at the Boston Music Hall, attending a concert, on January 1, 1863, the day the Emancipation Proclamation became effective. When an announcement of the historic event was made from the stage, somebody called out that she was in the gallery. In an instant the audience was on its feet cheering while she stood and bowed, her bonnet awry.

After the war she kept on writing. In fact, as is sometimes overlooked, that is what Harriet Beecher Stowe was, a writer, and one of the most industrious we have ever had. Unwittingly she had written the abolition-ist manifesto, although she did not consider herself an abolitionist. She agreed with her father that abolitionists "were like men who would burn down their houses to get rid of the rats." She was not a crusader pure and simple. She never considered herself an extremist, and she seldom took an extreme position on any issue. She was a reformer, and there was an evangelical undercurrent to just about everything she wrote. But writing was her work, her way to make herself useful.

Her life was about half over when she wrote *Uncle Tom's Cabin*, but for thirty years more she wrote almost a book a year on the average, plus innumerable essays, poems, children's stories, and magazine articles, many of which she did under the pseudonym Christopher Crowfield. Perhaps her most artful novel, *The Minister's Wooing*, ran to fifty printings, and a magazine article, "The True Story of Lady Byron's Life," which appeared in the *Atlantic Monthly* in 1869, caused more furor than anything published in America since *Uncle Tom's Cabin*.

During a second visit to England she had become fast friends with the widow of Lord Byron,[6] who confided the terrible secret that the great Byron had committed incest with his half sister and that a child had been born as a result. Mrs. Stowe kept the secret for thirteen years, but when Byron's former mistress, Countess Guiccioli, published her memoirs and portrayed Lady Byron as a self-righteous tyrant who would drive any mortal male to excesses, Harriet Stowe decided it was time to strike a blow in her friend's behalf, Lady Byron by this time having been dead for nearly a decade. So she told the whole story.

All kinds of accusations were hurled at her, some quite unpleasant. She rode out the storm, however, and again, as with *Uncle Tom*, she wrote a book to justify what she had written. But her standing with the American public would never be the same.

She could write in all kinds of places, under every kind of condition. She was always bothered by deadlines, and it seems she was always in need of money. The royalties poured in, but the more she had the more

6. George Gordon Lord Byron (1788– 1824), English romantic poet who created, in his life and his works, the persona of a passionate, defiant young man doomed by some mysterious, unnamable sin.

she spent—on a huge Gothic villa in Hartford that was all gables and turrets and was never finished completely; on a cotton plantation in Florida where she intended to provide Negroes with a program of work and education; and later, when that failed, on an orange and lemon grove at Mandarin, Florida, "where the world is not," she said, and where she hoped her unfortunate son Frederick might find himself.

Frederick had trouble staying sober. His problem had started before the war, but at Gettysburg he had been hit in the head by a shell fragment, and, his mother would always believe, he had never been himself again. "After that," one of her grandsons would write, "he not only was made drunk by the slightest amount of alcohol but he could not resist taking it."

Calvin grew enormously fat, ever more distant, and of even less use than before when it came to the everyday details of life. Moreover, Harriet found fame increasingly difficult. She had become a national institution. Her correspondence alone would have drained a less vigorous spirit.

Tragedy struck repeatedly. In 1857, upon returning from Europe, she learned that her son Henry, a student at Dartmouth, had drowned while swimming in the Connecticut River. In 1870 Frederick, unable to endure his mother's Florida experiment any longer, wrote her a touching apology and went to sea, shipping around the Horn. It is known that he got as far as San Francisco, but after that he disappeared and was never heard from again. She would go to her grave with every confidence that he would return one day.

But it was the Brooklyn scandal that hurt her worst of all, she said. In November of 1872 a New York paper reported that her beloved brother Henry Ward, by then the most popular preacher in America, had been carrying on an adulterous affair with one of his parishioners. His enemies swept in for the kill. For all the Beechers gossip was agonizing. A sensational trial resulted, the husband bringing suit against Beecher for alienation of his wife's affections. It dragged on for six months and was the talk of the country. Whether Beecher was guilty or innocent was never proved one way or the other. He denied everything, the jury was unable to agree on a verdict, and as far as his sister was concerned his character was never even in question.

The whole story was a slanderous fabrication, she said, and she stood by him through the entire grisly, drawn-out business, as did all the Beechers except Isabella Beecher Hooker, who was only a half sister, it was noted, and was regarded by many as just a little unbalanced. (Isabella, who called herself *the* inspired one," wanted to take charge of a service at Plymouth Church herself and "as one commissioned from

60

on high" declare her brother's guilt from his own pulpit. Years later,
when he was dying, she even tried to force her way into his house to
get a deathbed confession.)

But it would be mistaken to suggest that Harriet's life became increasingly burdensome. Quite the contrary. As time passed she seems to have
grown ever more liberated from her past. She drew further and further
from the shadow of her harsh Calvinist heritage, eventually rejecting it
altogether. She had long since discarded the doctrine of original sin.
Neither man nor nature was necessarily corrupt, she now held. Hers was
a faith of love and Christian charity. She had a seemingly limitless love
for the whole human family. Years before, Catherine, her spinster sister,
had been the first of the Beechers to rebel against the traditional faith
when a young man she was engaged to marry, a gifted Yale professor
of philosophy, was lost at sea and Catherine had had to face the terrible
Calvinist conclusion that the young man was consigned to eternal damnation because he had never repented. In time all of Lyman Beecher's
offspring would desert the faith. Henry Ward would even go so far as
to preach that there is no hell.

For Harriet, Calvinism was repugnant, a "glacial" doctrine, although
she admired enormously the fervor it had given the Puritan colonists of
her native New England and the solid purpose and coherence of the
communities they established. Like many of her time she sorely lamented the decline of Christian faith in the land. It was the root of the
breakdown of the old order, she believed. Mostly, it seems, she admired
the backbone the old religion gave people. "They who had faced eternal
ruin with an unflinching gaze," she wrote, "were not likely to shrink
before the comparatively trivial losses and gains of any mere earthly
conflict." If she herself could not accept the articles of the Puritan faith,
she seemed to wish everybody else would. And once from Florida she
wrote: ". . . never did we have a more delicious spring. I never knew such
altogether perfect weather. It is enough to make a saint out of the
toughest old Calvinist that ever set his face as a flint. How do you think
New England theology would have fared, if our fathers had landed here
instead of on Plymouth Rock?"

Like numerous other literary figures of the day she tried spiritualism
and claimed that her son Henry had returned from somewhere beyond
to pluck a guitar string for her. She became an Episcopalian, and she
developed an open fondness for such things as Europe (Paris and Italy
especially), Rubens, elegant society, and Florida, in particular Florida
(". . . this wild, wonderful, bright, and vivid growth, that is all new,
strange and unknown by name to me . . ."). The theater and dancing
were no longer viewed as sinful. She rejected the idea that "there was
something radically corrupt and wicked in the body and in the physical

system." She took a little claret now on occasion. An account of a visit to Portsmouth, New Hampshire, suggests that once at least she may have taken a little too much claret.

She was asked to give readings, to go on the lyceum, as the contemporary lecture circuit was called, like Robert Ingersoll, P. T. Barnum,[7] and the feminists. She needed the money, so at age sixty-one, having never made a public speech before, she embarked on a new career with its endless train rides, bad food, and dreary hotels. She was very shy at first and not much good at it. But she got over that and in time became quite accomplished. "Her performance could hardly be called a reading," reported the Pittsburgh *Gazette*, "it was recitative and she seldom glanced at the book. Her voice betrayed the veritable Yankee twang. . . . Her voice is low, just tinged in the slightest with huskiness, but is quite musical. In manner she was vivacious and gave life to many of the pages, more by suggestive action than by utterances. . . . She seemed perfectly possessed on the stage, and read with easy grace. . . ."

She found she could move her audiences to great emotional heights, but to laughter especially. And she loved the life. Her health picked up. "I never sleep better than after a long day's ride," she wrote.

Her appearance never changed much. She put on no new airs. Nothing, in fact, good or bad, seemed capable of changing that plain, earnest, often whimsical manner. She acquired a number of new friendships that meant a great deal to her, with Oliver Wendell Holmes and Mark Twain particularly. Henry Drummond, the noted Scottish religious writer, wrote, after a visit to Hartford: "Next door to Twain I found Mrs. Harriet Beecher Stowe, a wonderfully agile old lady, as fresh as a squirrel still, but with the face and air of a lion." And he concluded: "I have not been so taken with any one on this side of the Atlantic."

Her affections for Calvin seem to have grown stronger, if anything. He had become absorbed in Semitic studies, let his beard grow, and took to wearing a skullcap. She began calling him "My Old Rabbi." His apparitions took up more and more of his time, and for a while he was having nightly encounters with the Devil, who came on horseback, Calvin said. But otherwise his mind stayed quick and clear until the end, and she found him exceedingly good company.

In their last years they seem also to have had few financial worries. Among other things a book of his, *The Origin and History of the Books of the Bible,* had a surprisingly large sale. And their affairs in general were being capably managed by their twin daughters, Eliza and Harriet, maiden ladies who apparently had considerable "faculty."

Calvin died peacefully enough, with Harriet at his bedside, on August

7. Robert Ingersoll (1833–99), American lawyer and orator known as "the Great Agnostic"; Phineas T. Barnum (1810–91), American circus entrepreneur.

6, 1886. She lived on for another ten years, slipping off ever so gradually into a gentle senility.

In a letter to Oliver Wendell Holmes[8] she wrote: "I make no mental effort of any sort; my brain is tired out. It was a woman's brain and not a man's, and finally from sheer fatigue and exhaustion in the march and strife of life it gave out before the end was reached. And now I rest me, like a moored boat, rising and falling on the water, with loosened cordage and flapping sail."

She was eighty-two. She spent hours looking at picture books, bothering no one, or went out gathering flowers, "a tiny withered figure in a garden hat," as one writer described her. On occasion she took long walks beside the river, an Irish nurse generally keeping her company. Sometimes, Mark Twain would recall, she "would slip up behind a person who was deep in dreams and musings and fetch a war whoop that would jump that person out of his clothes."

And every now and then, during moments of astonishing clarity, she would talk again about *Uncle Tom's Cabin*, the book that had just "come" to her in visions. Once, years earlier, when she was having trouble writing, she had said: "If there had been a grand preparatory blast of trumpets or had it been announced that Mrs. Stowe would do this or that, I think it likely I could not have written; but nobody expected anything . . . and so I wrote freely."

She died near midnight on July 1, 1896.

8. Oliver Wendell Holmes (1809–94), physician, author, and Harvard professor who represented the ideal of the New England intellectual.

Virginia Woolf

ELLEN TERRY[1]

When she came on to the stage as Lady Cicely in *Captain Brassbound's Conversion*,[2] the stage collapsed like a house of cards and all the limelights were extinguished. When she spoke it was as if someone drew a bow over a ripe, richly seasoned 'cello; it grated, it glowed, and it growled. Then she stopped speaking. She put on her glasses. She gazed

From *The Moment and Other Essays* (1947).

1. Ellen Alice Terry (1847–1928) came from a famous Victorian family of actors and actresses. She made her stage debut in 1856 at the age of nine and celebrated her fiftieth anniversary on the stage in 1906, the year she starred in *Captain Brassbound's Conversion*.

2. A play by George Bernard Shaw (1856–1950), written with Terry in mind for the female lead as Lady Cicely.

intently at the back of a settee. She had forgotten her part. But did it matter? Speaking or silent, she was Lady Cicely—or was it Ellen Terry? At any rate, she filled the stage and all the other actors were put out, as electric lights are put out in the sun.

Yet this pause when she forgot what Lady Cicely said next was significant. It was a sign not that she was losing her memory and past her prime, as some said. It was a sign that Lady Cicely was not a part that suited her. Her son, Gordon Craig, insists that she only forgot her part when there was something uncongenial in the words, when some speck of grit had got into the marvelous machine of her genius. When the part was congenial, when she was Shakespeare's Portia, Desdemona, Ophelia, every word, every comma was consumed. Even her eyelashes acted. Her body lost its weight. Her son, a mere boy, could lift her in his arms. "I am not myself," she said. "Something comes upon me. . . . I am always-in-the-air, light and bodiless." We, who can only remember her as Lady Cicely on the little stage at the Court Theatre, only remember what, compared with her Ophelia or her Portia, was as a picture postcard compared with the great Velasquez[3] in the gallery.

It is the fate of actors to leave only picture postcards behind them. Every night when the curtain goes down the beautiful colored canvas is rubbed out. What remains is at best only a wavering, insubstantial phantom—a verbal life on the lips of the living. Ellen Terry was well aware of it. She tried herself, overcome by the greatness of Irving[4] as Hamlet and indignant at the caricatures of his detractors, to describe what she remembered. It was in vain. She dropped her pen in despair. "Oh God, that I were a writer!" she cried. "Surely a *writer* could not string words together about Henry Irving's Hamlet and say *nothing, nothing.*" It never struck her, humble as she was, and obsessed by her lack of book learning, that she was, among other things, a writer. It never occurred to her when she wrote her autobiography, or scribbled page after page to Bernard Shaw late at night, dead tired after a rehearsal, that she was "writing." The words in her beautiful rapid hand bubbled off her pen. With dashes and notes of exclamation she tried to give them the very tone and stress of the spoken word. It is true, she could not build a house with words, one room opening out of another, and a staircase connecting the whole. But whatever she took up became in her warm, sensitive grasp a tool. If it was a rolling-pin, she made perfect pastry. If it was a carving knife, perfect slices fell from the leg of mutton. If it were a pen, words peeled off, some broken, some suspended in midair, but all far more expressive than the tappings of the professional typewriter.

With her pen then at odds and ends of time she has painted a

3. Diego Rodriquez de Silva y Velasquez (1599–1660), Spanish painter known for his powerful, larger-than-life portraits.

4. Henry Irving (1838–1905), English tragedian who performed with Terry and first actor to be knighted.

self-portrait. It is not an Academy portrait, glazed, framed, complete. It is rather a bundle of loose leaves upon each of which she has dashed off a sketch for a portrait—here a nose, here an arm, here a foot, and there a mere scribble in the margin. The sketches done in different moods, from different angles, sometimes contradict each other. The nose cannot belong to the eyes; the arm is out of all proportion to the foot. It is difficult to assemble them. And there are blank pages, too. Some very important features are left out. There was a self she did not know, a gap she could not fill. Did she not take Walt Whitman's words for a motto? "Why, even I myself, I often think, know little or nothing of my real life. Only a few hints—a few diffused faint clues and indirections. . . . I seek . . . to trace out here."

Nevertheless, the first sketch is definite enough. It is the sketch of her childhood. She was born to the stage. The stage was her cradle, her nursery. When other little girls were being taught sums and pothooks she was being cuffed and buffeted into the practice of her profession. Her ears were boxed, her muscles suppled. All day she was hard at work on the boards. Late at night when other children were safe in bed she was stumbling along the dark streets wrapped in her father's cloak. And the dark street with its curtained windows was nothing but a sham to that little professional actress, and the rough and tumble life on the boards was her home, her reality. "It's all such sham there," she wrote—meaning by "there" what she called "life lived in houses"—"sham—cold—hard—pretending. It's not sham here in our theater—here all is real, warm and kind—we live a lovely spiritual life here."

That is the first sketch. But turn to the next page. The child born to the stage has become a wife. She is married at sixteen to an elderly famous painter. [5] The theater has gone; its lights are out and in its place is a quiet studio in a garden. In its place is a world full of pictures and "gentle artistic people with quiet voices and elegant manners." She sits mum in her corner while the famous elderly people talk over her head in quiet voices. She is content to wash her husband's brushes; to sit to him; to play her simple tunes on the piano to him while he paints. In the evening she wanders over the Downs with the great poet, Tennyson. "I was in Heaven," she wrote. "I never had one single pang of regret for the theater." If only it could have lasted! But somehow—here a blank page intervenes—she was an incongruous element in that quiet studio. She was too young, too vigorous, too vital, perhaps. At any rate, the marriage was a failure.

5. The English painter G. F. Watts (1817–1904) was forty-four when he married Terry, perhaps not "elderly" but more than twice her age.

And so, skipping a page or two, we come to the next sketch. She is a mother now. Two adorable children claim all her devotion. She is living in the depths of the country, in the heart of domesticity. She is up at six. She scrubs, she cooks, she sews. She teaches the children. She harnesses the pony. She fetches the milk. And again she is perfectly happy. To live with children in a cottage, driving her little cart about the lanes, going to church on Sunday in blue and white cotton—that is the ideal life! She asks no more than that it shall go on like that for ever and ever. But one day the wheel comes off the pony cart. Huntsmen in pink leap over the hedge. One of them dismounts and offers help. He looks at the girl in a blue frock and exclaims: "Good God! It's Nelly!" She looks at the huntsman in pink and cries, "Charles Reade!"[6] And so, all in a jiffy, back she goes to the stage, and to forty pounds a week. For—that is the reason she gives—the bailiffs are in the house. She must make money.

At this point a very blank page confronts us. There is a gulf which we can only cross at a venture. Two sketches face each other; Ellen Terry in blue cotton among the hens; Ellen Terry robed and crowned as Lady Macbeth on the stage of the Lyceum. The two sketches are contradictory yet they are both of the same woman. She hates the stage; yet she adores it. She worships her children; yet she forsakes them. She would like to live for ever among pigs and ducks in the open air; yet she spends the rest of her life among actors and actresses in the limelight. Her own attempt to explain the discrepancy is hardly convincing. "I have always been more woman than artist," she says. Irving put the theater first. "He had none of what I may call my bourgeois qualities—the love of being in love, the love of a home, the dislike of solitude." She tries to persuade us that she was an ordinary woman enough; a better hand at pastry than most; an adept at keeping house; with an eye for color, a taste for furniture, and a positive passion for washing children's heads. If she went back to the stage it was because—well, what else could she do when the bailiffs were in the house?

This is the little sketch that she offers us to fill in the gap between the two Ellen Terrys—Ellen the mother, and Ellen the actress. But here we remember her warning: "Why, even I myself know little or nothing of my real life." There was something in her that she did not understand; something that came surging up from the depths and swept her away in its clutches. The voice she heard in the lane was not the voice of Charles Reade; nor was it the voice of the bailiffs. It was the voice of her genius; the urgent call of something that she could not define, could

---

6. Charles Reade (1814–84), English novelist and playwright who convinced Terry to return to the stage in 1874 and act in his drama *The Wandering Heir*.

not suppress, and must obey. So she left her children and followed the voice back to the stage, back to the Lyceum, back to a long life of incessant toil, anguish, and glory.

But, having gazed at the full-length portrait of Ellen Terry as Sargent[7] painted her, robed and crowned as Lady Macbeth, turn to the next page. It is done from another angle. Pen in hand, she is seated at her desk. A volume of Shakespeare lies before her. It is open at *Cymbeline,* and she is making careful notes in the margin. The part of Imogen presents great problems. She is, she says, "on the rack" about her interpretation. Perhaps Bernard Shaw can throw light upon the question? A letter from the brilliant young critic of the *Saturday Review* lies beside Shakespeare. She has never met him, but for years they have written to each other, intimately, ardently, disputatiously, some of the best letters in the language. He says the most outrageous things. He compares dear Henry to an ogre, and Ellen to a captive chained in his cage. But Ellen Terry is quite capable of holding her own against Bernard Shaw. She scolds him, laughs at him, fondles him, and contradicts him. She has a curious sympathy for the advanced views that Henry Irving abominated. But what suggestions has the brilliant critic to make about Imogen? None apparently that she has not already thought for herself. She is as close and critical a student of Shakespeare as he is. She has studied every line, weighed the meaning of every word; experimented with every gesture. Each of those golden moments when she becomes bodiless, not herself, is the result of months of minute and careful study. "Art," she quotes, "needs that which we can give her, I assure you." In fact this mutable woman, all instinct, sympathy, and sensation, is as painstaking a student and as careful of the dignity of her art as Flaubert[8] himself.

But once more the expression on that serious face changes. She works like a slave—none harder. But she is quick to tell Mr. Shaw that she does not work with her brain only. She is not in the least clever. Indeed, she is happy she tells him, *"not to be clever."* She stresses the point with a jab of her pen. "You clever people," as she calls him and his friends, miss so much, mar so much. As for education, she never had a day's schooling in her life. As far as she can see, but the problem baffles her, the main spring of her art is imagination. Visit mad-houses, if you like; take notes; observe; study endlessly. But first, imagine. And so she takes her part away from the books out into the woods. Rambling down grassy rides, she lives her part until she is it. If a word jars or grates, she must rethink it, rewrite it. Then when every phrase is her own, and every

7. John Singer Sargent (1856–1925), American painter who lived and worked mostly in London.

8. Gustave Flaubert (1821–80), French novelist.

gesture spontaneous, out she comes onto the stage and is Imogen, Ophelia, Desdemona.

But is she, even when the great moments are on her, a great actress? She doubts it. "I cared more for love and life," she says. Her face, too, has been no help to her. She cannot sustain emotion. Certainly she is not a great tragic actress. Now and again, perhaps, she has acted some comic part to perfection. But even while she analyses herself, as one artist to another, the sun slants upon an old kitchen chair. "Thank the Lord for my eyes!" she exclaims. What a world of joy her eyes have brought her! Gazing at the old "rush-bottomed, sturdy-legged, and wavy-backed" chair, the stage is gone, the limelights are out, the famous actress is forgotten.

Which, then, of all these women is the real Ellen Terry? How are we to put the scattered sketches together? Is she mother, wife, cook, critic, actress, or should she have been, after all, a painter? Each part seems the right part until she throws it aside and plays another. Something of Ellen Terry it seems overflowed every part and remained unacted. Shakespeare could not fit her; not Ibsen; nor Shaw. The stage could not hold her; nor the nursery. But there is, after all, a greater dramatist than Shakespeare, Ibsen, or Shaw. There is Nature. Hers is so vast a stage, and so innumerable a company of actors, that for the most part she fobs them off with a tag or two. They come on and they go off without breaking the ranks. But now and again Nature creates a new part, an original part. The actors who act that part always defy our attempts to name them. They will not act the stock parts—they forget the words, they improvise others of their own. But when they come on, the stage falls like a pack of cards and the limelights are extinguished. That was Ellen Terry's fate—to act a new part. And thus while other actors are remembered because they were Hamlet, Phèdre, or Cleopatra, Ellen Terry is remembered because she was Ellen Terry.

THE READER

1. *Woolf evidently wants to persuade her readers that Ellen Terry was an extraordinary woman, yet she offers little or no objective evidence of the kind we might expect—Terry's accomplishments, her honors, critical opinions of her acting, the testimony of those who knew her, etc. What does Woolf do instead to try to convince us?*

2. *On p. 117 Woolf invites us to compare "a picture postcard" with "the great Velasquez in the gallery." What is her point?*

3. *What is Woolf saying about Ellen Terry's writing in "The nose cannot belong to the eyes; the arm is out of all proportion to the foot. It is difficult to assemble them" (p. 118)?*

THE WRITER

1. *Much of this essay takes the form of descriptions of actual photographs and imagined drawings. Write a brief essay conveying the quality of a certain experience or period in your own life through this same visual technique.*
2. *It would be easier to write an intimate sketch of someone you know well personally as opposed to someone you don't know (as Woolf did not know Ellen Terry). In the latter case, what resources would you have to rely on and what could you do to make the sketch personal? Try writing such a sketch.*

Daniel Mark Epstein

THE CASE OF HARRY HOUDINI

When my grandfather was a boy he saw the wild-haired magician escape from a riveted boiler. He would remember that image as long as he lived, and how Harry Houdini, the rabbi's son, defeated the German Imperial Police at the beginning of the twentieth century. Hearing those tales and others even more incredible, sixty years after the magician's death we cannot help but wonder: What did the historical Houdini *really* do? And how on earth did he do it?

The newspaper accounts are voluminous, and consistent. The mere cataloguing of Houdini's escapes soon grows tedious, which they were not, to be sure, in the flesh. But quickly: the police stripped him naked and searched him thoroughly before binding his wrists and ankles with five pairs of irons. Then they would slam him into a cell and turn the key of a three-bond burglar-proof lock. He escaped, hundreds of times, from the most secure prisons in the world. He hung upside down in a straitjacket from the tallest buildings in America, and escaped in full view of the populace. He was chained hand and foot and nailed into a packing case weighted with lead; the packing case was dropped from a tugboat into New York's East River and ninety seconds later Houdini surfaced. The packing case was hauled up intact, with the manacles inside, still fastened. He was sealed into a paper bag and got out without disturbing the seal. He was sewn into a huge football, into the belly of a whale, and escaped. In California he was buried six feet underground, and clawed his way out. He did this, he did that. These are facts that cannot be exaggerated, for they were conceived as exaggerations. We

Originally appeared in *The New Criterion* (Oct. 1986).

know he did these things because his actions were more public than the proceedings of Congress, and most of them he performed over and over, so no one would miss the point.

How did he do such things? For all rational people who are curious, sixty years after the magician's death, there is good news and bad news. The good news is that we know how the vast majority of Houdini's tricks were done, and the explanations are as fascinating as the mystery was. Much of our knowledge comes from the magician's writings, for Houdini kept ahead of his imitators by exposing his cast-off tricks. We have additional information from technicians and theater historians. No magician will reveal Houdini's secrets—their code forbids it. But so much controversy has arisen concerning his powers—so much conjecture they may have been supernatural—that extraordinary measures have been taken to assure us Houdini was a *mortal* genius. Many secrets have leaked out, and others have been discovered from examining the props. So at last we know more about Houdini's technique than any other magician's.

The disturbing news is that, sixty years after his last performance, some of his more spectacular escapes remain unexplained. And while magicians such as Doug Henning are bound not to expose their colleagues, they are free to admit what mystifies them. They know how Houdini walked through the brick wall at Hammerstein's Roof Garden, in 1914, but they do not know how he made the elephant disappear in 1918. This trick he performed only for a few months in New York. And when people asked him why he did not continue he told them that Teddy Roosevelt, a great hunter, had begged him to stop before he exhausted the world's supply of pachyderms.

But before we grapple with the mysteries, let us begin with what we can understand. Let us begin with my grandfather's favorite story, the case of Harry Houdini versus the German Police. Houdini's first tour of Europe depended upon the good will and cooperation of the law. When he arrived in London in 1900 the twenty-six-year-old magician did not have a single booking. His news clippings eventually inspired an English agent, who had Houdini manacled to a pillar in Scotland Yard. Seeing that Houdini was securely fastened, Superintendent Melville of the Criminal Investigation Department said he would return in a couple of hours, when the escapist had worn himself out. By the time Melville got to the door the magician was free to open it for him.

The publicity surrounding his escape from the most prestigious police force in the world opened up many another door for the young magician. Booked at the Alhambra Theater in London, he performed his "Challenge" handcuff act, which had made him famous on the vaudeville circuit. After some card tricks and standard illusions, Houdini would stand before the proscenium and challenge the world to restrain him

5

with ropes, straitjackets, handcuffs, whatever they could bring on, from lockshops, prisons, and museums. A single failure might have ruined him. There is no evidence that he ever failed, though in several cases he nearly died from the effort required to escape from sadistic shackles. The "Challenge" act filled the Alhambra Theater for two months. Houdini might have stayed there if Germany had not already booked him; the Germans could hardly wait to get a look at Houdini.

As he had done in America and England, Houdini began his tour of Germany with a visit to police headquarters. The Dresden officers were not enthusiastic, yet they could hardly refuse the magician's invitation to lock him up. That might suggest a crisis of confidence. And like their colleagues the world over, the Dresden police viewed Houdini's news clippings as so much paper in the balance with their locks and chains. Of course the Dresden police had no more success than those of Kansas City, or San Francisco, or Scotland Yard. Their manacles were paper to him. The police chief reluctantly signed the certificate Houdini demanded, but the newspapers gave him little coverage.

So on his opening night at Dresden's Central Theatre, Houdini arranged to be fettered in the leg irons and manacles of the Mathildegasse Prison. Some of the locks weighed forty pounds. The audience, packed to the walls, went wild over his escape, and the fact that he spoke their language further endeared him. If anything could have held him captive it would have been the adoring burghers of Dresden, who mobbed the theater for weeks. The manager wanted to buy out Houdini's contract with the Wintergarten of Berlin, so as to hold him over in Dresden, but the people of Berlin could not wait to see the magician.

Houdini arrived in Berlin in October of 1900. The first thing he did was march into the police station, strip stark naked, and challenge the jailors. They could not hold him. This time Count von Windheim, the highest ranking policeman in Germany, signed the certificate of Houdini's escape. The Wintergarten was overrun. The management appealed to the theater of Houdini's next engagement, in Vienna, so they might hold him over an extra month in Berlin. The Viennese finally yielded, demanding an indemnity equal to Houdini's salary for one month. When the magician, at long last, opened at the Olympic Theater in Paris, in December of 1901, he was the highest paid foreign entertainer in French history.

But meanwhile there was big trouble brewing in Germany. It seems the police there had little sense of humor about Houdini's peculiar gifts, and the Jew had quickly exhausted what little there was. In Dortmund he escaped from the irons that had bound Glowisky, a notorious murderer, beheaded three days before. At Hanover the police chief, Count von Schwerin, plotted to disgrace Houdini, challenging him to escape from a special straitjacket reinforced with thick leather. Houdini agonized for one and a half hours while von Schwerin looked on, his jubilant smile melting in wonder, then rage, as the magician worked himself free.

The cumulative anger of the German police went public in July of 1901. Inspector Werner Graff witnessed Houdini's escape from all the manacles at the Cologne police station and vowed to end the humiliation. It was not a simple matter of pride. Graff, along with von Schwerin and other officials, feared Houdini was weakening their authority and inviting jailbreaks, if not other kinds of antisocial behavior. So Graff wrote a letter to Cologne's newspaper, the *Rheinische Zeitung.* The letter stated that Houdini had escaped from simple restraints at the police headquarters, by trickery; but his publicity boasted he could escape from restraints *of any kind.* Such a claim, Graff wrote, was a lie, and Houdini ought to be prosecuted for fraud.

Though he knew the letter was nonsense the magician could not ignore it, for it was dangerous nonsense. If the police began calling him a fraud in every town he visited, Houdini would lose his audience. So he demanded that Graff apologize and the newspaper publish a retraction: Graff refused, and other German dailies reprinted his letter. Should Harry Houdini sue the German policeman for libel? Consider the circumstances. Germany, even in 1901, was one of the most authoritarian states in the world. Houdini was an American, a Jew who embarrassed the police. A libel case against Graff would turn upon the magician's claim that he could escape from *any* restraint, and the courtroom would become an international theater. There a German judge and jury would try his skill, and, should they find it wanting, Houdini would be washed up, exiled to play beer halls and dime museums. Only an artist with colossal pride and total confidence in his methods would act as Houdini did. He hired the most prominent trial lawyer in Cologne, and ordered him to sue Werner Graff and the Imperial Police of Germany for criminal libel.

There was standing room only in the Cologne *Schöffengericht.* The judge allowed Werner Graff to seek out the most stubborn locks and chains he could find, and tangle Houdini in them, in full view of everyone. Here was a hitch, for Houdini did not wish to show the crowd his technique. He asked the judge to clear the courtroom, and in the ensuing turmoil the magician released himself so quickly no one knew how he had done it. The *Schöffengericht* fined the astonished policeman and ordered a public apology. So Graff's lawyer appealed the case.

Two months later Graff was better prepared. In the *Strafkammer,* or court of appeals, he presented thirty letters from legal authorities declaring that the escape artist could not justify his advertisements. And Graff had a shiny new pair of handcuffs. The premier locksmith of Germany had engineered the cuffs especially for the occasion. Werner Graff explained to the judge that the lock, once closed, could never be opened, even with its own key. Let Houdini try to get out of these.

This time the court permitted Houdini to work in privacy, and a guard led the magician to an adjacent chamber. Everyone else settled down for a long wait, in a chatter of anticipation. They were interrupted four minutes later by the entrance of Houdini, who tossed the manacles on the judge's bench. So the *Strafkammer* upheld the lower court's decision, as did the *Oberlandesgericht* in a "paper" appeal. The court fined Werner Graff thirty marks and ordered him to pay for the trials as well as a published apology. Houdini's next poster showed him in evening dress, his hands manacled, standing before the judge, jurors, and a battery of mustachioed policemen. Looking down on the scene is a bust of the Kaiser against a crimson background, and a scroll that reads: "The Imperial Police of Cologne slandered Harry Houdini . . . were compelled to advertise 'An Honorary Apology' and pay costs of the trials. By command of Kaiser Wilhelm II, Emperor of Germany."

Now this is surely a wondrous tale, like something out of the Arabian Nights, and it will seem no less wonderful when we understand the technique that made it come true. In 1901, when Houdini took on the Imperial Police, he was not whistling in the dark. By the time he left America at the end of the nineteenth century he had dissected every kind of lock he could find in the New World, and whatever he could import from the old one. Arriving in London Houdini could write that there were only a few kinds of British handcuffs, "seven or eight at the utmost," and these were some of the simplest he had ever seen. He searched the markets, antique shops, and locksmiths, buying up all the European locks he could find so he could dismantle and study them.

Then during his Berlin engagement he worked up to ten hours a day at Mueller's locksmith on the Mittelstrasse, studying restraints. He was the Bobby Fischer of locks. With a chessmaster's foresight Houdini devised a set of picks to release every lock in existence, as well as *any he could imagine.* Such tireless ingenuity produced the incandescent light bulb and the atom bomb. Houdini's creation of a theatrical metaphor made a comparable impact on the human spirit. He had a message which he delivered so forcefully it goes without mentioning in theater courses: humankind cannot be held in chains. The European middle class had reached an impressionable age, and the meaning of Houdini's theater was not lost upon them. Nor was he mistaken by the aristocracy, who stayed away in droves. The spectacle of this American Jew bursting from chains by dint of ingenuity did not amuse the rich. They wanted desperately to demythologize him.

It was not about to happen in the German courtroom. When Werner Graff snapped the "new" handcuffs on Houdini, they were not strange to the magician. He had already invented them, so to speak, as well as the pick to open them, and the pick was in his pocket. Only a locksmith whose knowledge surpassed Houdini's could stop him; diligent study assured him that, as of 1901, there could be no such locksmith on the face of the earth.

What else can we understand about the methods of Harry Houdini, born Ehrich Weiss? We know he was a superbly conditioned athlete who did not smoke or take a drop of alcohol. His straitjacket escapes he performed in full view of the world so they could see it was by main force and flexibility that he freed himself. He may or may not have been able to dislocate his shoulders at will—he said he could, and it seems no more marvelous than certain other skills he demonstrated. Friends reported that his toes could untie knots most of us could not manage with our fingers. And routinely the magician would hold his breath for as long as four minutes to work underwater escapes. To cheapen the supernatural claims of the fakir Rahman Bey, Houdini remained underwater in an iron box for ninety minutes, as against the Egyptian's sixty. Examining Houdini, a physician testified that the fifty-year-old wizard had halved his blood pressure while doubling his pulse. Of course, more wonderful than any of these skills was the courage allowing him to employ them, in predicaments where any normal person would panic.

These things are known about Houdini. The same tireless ingenuity, when applied to locks and jails, packing cases and riveted boilers; the same athletic prowess, when applied at the bottom of the East River, or while dangling from a rope attached to the cornice of the Sun Building in Baltimore—these talents account for the vast majority of Houdini's exploits. As we have mentioned, theater historians, notably Raymund Fitzsimons in his *Death and the Magician*, have carefully exposed Houdini's ingenuity, knowing that nothing can tarnish the miracle of the man's existence. Their accounts are technical and we need not dwell on them, except to say they *mostly* support Houdini's oath that his effects were achieved by natural, or mechanical means. The Houdini problem arises from certain outrageous effects no one has ever been able to explain, though capable technicians have been trying for more than sixty years.

Let us briefly recall those effects. We have mentioned the Disappearing Elephant. On January 7, 1918, Houdini had a ten-thousand-pound elephant led onto the bright stage of the Hippodrome in New York City. A trainer marched the elephant around a cabinet large enough for an elephant, proving there was space behind. There was no trapdoor in the floor of the Hippodrome, and the elephant could not fly. Houdini ushered the pachyderm into the cabinet and closed the curtains. Then he opened them, and where the elephant had stood there was nothing but empty space. Houdini went on with his program, which might have been making the Hippodrome disappear, for all the audience knew. A reporter for the *Brooklyn Eagle* noted: "The program says that the elephant vanished into thin air. The trick is performed fifteen feet from the backdrop and the cabinet is slightly elevated. That explanation is as good as any." After Houdini stopped making elephants disappear, nineteen weeks later, the trick would never be precisely duplicated.

That is the single "conventional" illusion of Houdini's repertoire that remains unexplained. He was not the greatest illusionist of his time, though he was among them. His expertise was the "escape" act, that specialty of magic furthest removed from theater, for its challenges are quite real and sometimes beyond the magician's control. It was the escapes, as his wife later wrote, that were truly dangerous, and Houdini privately admitted some anxieties about them. Give a wizard twenty years to build a cabinet which snuffs an elephant, and you will applaud his cleverness if he succeeds, in the controlled environment of his theater. But surrender the same man, stark naked, to the Russian police, who stake their honor upon detaining him in a convict van, and you may well suspect the intercession of angels should he get out.

And that is exactly what Houdini did, in one of the strangest and most celebrated escapes of his career. Strange, because it was Houdini's habit to escape only from barred jail cells where the locks were within easy reach, and then only after inspection, so he might hide picks in crannies, or excuse himself if he foresaw failure. But the Siberian Transport Cell made his blood boil. On May 11, 1903, the chief of the Russian secret police searched the naked Houdini inside and out. The revolt of 1905 was in its planning stages and the Imperial Police were understandably touchy. The magician's wrists were padlocked and his ankles fettered before the police locked him into the *carette*. Mounted on a wagon, the zinc-lined steel cell stood in the prison courtyard in view of chief Lebedoeff, his staff, and a number of civilians. Twenty-eight minutes later Houdini was walking around the courtyard, stretching. Nobody saw him get out, but he was out. The police ran to the door of the *carette*. The door was still locked and the shackles lay on the floor of the undamaged van. The police were so furious they would not sign the certificate of escape, but so many people had witnessed the event that the news was soon being shouted all over Moscow. Doug Henning has written: "It remains one of his escapes about which the real method is pure conjecture."

In the Houdini Museum at Niagara Falls, Canada, you may view the famous Mirror Handcuffs. If you are a scholar you can inspect them. In March of 1904 the London *Daily Mirror* discovered a blacksmith who had been working for five years to build a set of handcuffs no mortal man could pick. Examining the cuffs, the best locksmiths in London agreed they had never seen such an ingenious mechanism. The newspaper challenged Houdini to escape from them. On March 17, before a house of four thousand in the London Hippodrome, a journalist fastened the cuffs on Houdini's wrists and turned the key six times. The magician retired to his cabinet onstage, and the band struck up a march. He did not emerge for twenty minutes. When he did, it was to hold the lock up to the light. Remember that most "Challenge" handcuffs were regulation, and familiar to Houdini. He studied the lock in the light, and then went back into the cabinet, as the band played a waltz.

Ten minutes later Houdini stuck his head out, asking if he could have a cushion to kneel on. He was denied. After almost an hour Houdini came out of the cabinet again, obviously worn out, and his audience groaned. He wanted the handcuffs to be unlocked for a moment so he could take off his coat, as he was sweating profusely. The journalist denied the request, since Houdini had never before seen the handcuffs unlocked, and that might give him an advantage. Whereupon Houdini, in full view of the four thousand, extracted a penknife from his pocket and opened it with his teeth. Turning the coat inside out over his head, he shredded it loose with the penknife, and returned to the cabinet. Someone called out that Houdini had been handcuffed for more than an hour. As the band played on, the journalists of the London *Daily Mirror* could taste the greatest scoop of the twentieth century. But ten minutes later there was a cry from the cabinet and Houdini leapt out of it, free, waving the handcuffs high in the air. While the crowd roared, several men from the audience carried Houdini on their shoulders around the theater. He was crying as if his heart would break.

For all his other talents Houdini was a notoriously wooden actor, and we may assume the rare tears were altogether real, the product of an uncounterfeitable emotion. It is as if the man himself had been over-whelmed by his escape. Eighty years of technological progress have shed no light upon it. We know how Houdini got out of other handcuffs, but not these. As far as anyone can tell, the Mirror Handcuffs remain as the blacksmith described them—a set of handcuffs no mortal man could pick. One is tempted to dismiss the whole affair as mass hypnosis.

In the same Canadian museum you may view the Chinese Water Torture Cell, in which the magician was hung upside down, in water, his ankles padlocked to the riveted roof. His escape from this cell was the crowning achievement of his stage career, and though he performed it on tour during the last ten years of his life, no one has the slightest notion how he did it. The gifted Doug Henning revived the act in 1975, on television. But he would be the first to tell you his was *not* Houdini's version, but his own, and he would not do it onstage before a live audience seven nights a week, with matinees on Wednesday and Saturday, because the trick would be unspeakably dangerous even if he could perform it there. When Houdini died he willed the contraption to his

25

brother Hardeen, a fine magician in his own right. But Hardeen would not get in it either, and the instructions were to be burned upon his death. Again, as with the Vanishing Elephant, we are reviewing a stage illusion under controlled conditions, and may bow to a master's technical superiority, without fretting that he has used supernatural powers.

But the Mirror Handcuffs and the Siberian Van Escape are troublesome, as are certain of Houdini's escapes from reinforced straitjackets, and packing cases underwater. So is the fact that he was buried six feet underground, and clawed his way out. He only tried it once, and nearly died in the struggle, but the feat was attested, and you do not need a degree in physics to know it is as preposterous as rising from the dead. The weight of the earth is so crushing you could not lift it in the open air. Try doing this with no oxygen. The maestro himself misjudged the weight, and, realizing his folly, tried to signal his crew when the grave was not yet full. They could not hear him and kept right on shoveling as fast as they could, so as not to keep him waiting. Then they stood back, to watch. A while later they saw his bleeding hands appear above the ground.

If we find Houdini's record unsettling, imagine what our grandparents must have thought of him. They knew almost nothing of his technique. Where we remain troubled by a few of his illusions and escapes, our ancestors were horrified by most of them. The European journalists thought he was some kind of hobgoblin, a shapeshifter who could crawl through keyholes, or dematerialize and reappear at will. One can hardly blame them. Despite his constant reassurances that his effects were technical, and natural, the practical-minded layman could not believe it, and even fellow magicians were disturbed by his behavior.

30   So we come to the central issue in the case of Harry Houdini. It is an issue he carefully avoided in public, while studying it diligently in private. To wit: Can a magician, by the ultimate perfection of a technique, generate a force which, at critical moments, will achieve a supernatural result? Houdini's writings show this was the abiding concern of his intellectual life. It is, of course, the essential mystery of classical magic since before the Babylonians. Yet it remained a private and professional concern until Houdini's career forced it upon the public.

With the same determination that opened the world's locks, Houdini searched for an answer. His own technique was so highly evolved that its practice might have satisfied him, but his curiosity was unquenchable. He amassed the world's largest collection of books pertaining to magic and the occult, and no less a scholar than Edmund Wilson honored Houdini's authority. The son of a rabbi, Houdini pursued his studies with rabbinic thoroughness. And, from the beginning of his career, he sought out the living legends of magic and badgered them in retirement, sometimes with tragicomic results.

As far back as 1895 it seemed to Houdini something peculiar was going on when he performed the Metamorphosis with his wife Bess. You have probably seen this classic illusion. Two friends of mine once acted it in my living room, as a birthday present. When the Houdinis performed the Metamorphosis, Bess whould handcuff Harry, tie him in a sack, and lock him in a trunk. She would draw a curtain hiding the trunk and then it would open, showing Houdini free upon the stage. Where was Bess? Inside the trunk, inside the sack, handcuffed—there was Bess. The method of this trick is only mysterious if you cannot pay for it. But the Houdinis' *timing* of the Metamorphosis got very mysterious indeed. They polished the act until it happened in less than three seconds— three rather blurred seconds in their own minds, to be sure. Believe me, you cannot get *in*to the trunk in less than three seconds. So when the Houdinis had done the trick they were often as stunned as their audience. It seemed a sure case of technique unleashing a supernatural force. Perplexed, Houdini planned to interview Hermann the Great, the pre-eminent conjuror in America in 1895, and ask Hermann what was up. But Hermann died as Houdini was about to ask him the question.

And Houdini shadowed the marvelous Harry Kellar, cross-examining him, and Alexander Heimburger, and the decrepit Ira Davenport, who had been a medium as well as a magician. But the great magicians flatly denied the psychic possibility, and Davenport would not answer to Houdini's satisfaction. In 1903 he discovered that Wiljalba Frikell, a seemingly mythic wizard of the nineteenth century, was still alive, in retirement near Dresden. When the ancient mage would not acknowledge his letters, Houdini grew convinced Wiljalba Frikell was the man to answer his question. He took the train to Dresden and knocked on Frikell's door. His wife sent Houdini away. On the road in Germany and Russia, Houdini continued to send letters and gifts to Frikell. And at last, six months after he had been turned away from Frikell's door, the reclusive magician agreed to see him.

Houdini rang the doorbell at 2:00 P.M. on October 8, 1903, the exact hour of his appointment. The door swung open. An hour earlier Wiljalba Frikell had dressed in his best suit, and laid out his scrapbooks, programs, and medals for Houdini to view. Houdini excitedly followed Frikell's wife into the room where the master sat surrounded by the mementos of his glorious career. But he would not be answering any of the questions that buzzed in Houdini's brain. The old man was stone dead.

Throughout his life Houdini categorically denied that any of his effects were achieved by supernatural means. He crusaded against mediums, clairvoyants, and all who claimed psychic power, advertising that

35

he would reproduce any of their manifestations by mechanical means. In the face of spiritualists who accused *him* of being a physical medium, he protested that all his escapes and illusions were tricks. He was probably telling the truth, as he understood it. But Rabbi Drachman, who spoke at Houdini's funeral, and had been in a position to receive confidences, said: "Houdini possessed a wondrous power that he never understood, and which he never revealed to anyone in life."

Houdini was not Solomon; he was a vaudeville specialist. If he ever experienced a psychic power it surely humbled his understanding. And to admit such a power, in his position, would have been a monumental stupidity. Why? If for no other reason, Talmudic law forbids the performance of miracles, and Houdini was the obedient son of Rabbi Weiss. Also, in case he should forget the Jewish law, it is strictly against the magician's code to claim a supernatural power, for reasons impossible to ignore. Mediums made such claims, at their own risk. Two of the more famous mediums of the nineteenth century, Ira and William Davenport, achieved manifestations similar to Houdini's. Audiences in Liverpool, Leeds, and Paris rioted, stormed the stage, and ran the mediums out of town, crying their performances were an outrage against God and a danger to man. Whether or not the acts were supernatural is beside the point—billing them as such was bad business, and hazardous to life and limb. Yet the Davenports were no more than a sideshow, compared to Houdini. The man was blinding. There had not been such a public display of apparent miracles in nearly two thousand years. Had the Jew so much as hinted his powers were spiritual he might have expected no better treatment than the renegade Hebrew of Nazareth.

Houdini was the self-proclaimed avatar of nothing but good old American know-how, and that is how he wished to be remembered. His wife of thirty years, Beatrice Houdini (known as "Bess"), was loyal to him in this, as in all other things. Pestered for revelations about Houdini's magic long after his death, the widow swore by her husband's account. But against her best intentions, Bess clouded the issue by saying just a little more than was necessary. It was in a letter to Sir Arthur Conan Doyle, who had been a close friend of hers and Houdini's.

The friendship was an odd one. The author of Sherlock Holmes believed in Spiritualism, and championed the séance with all the fervor with which Houdini opposed it. There were two great mysteries in Doyle's life: the powers of Sherlock Holmes and Harry Houdini. Doyle knew the Houdinis intimately, and nothing the magician said could shake Sir Arthur's conviction that certain of Houdini's escapes were supernatural. Doyle never stopped trying to get Houdini to confess. In 1922 it was more than a personal issue. The séance had become big business in America, with millions of bereaved relatives paying to communicate with their dear departed. Spiritualism was a home-grown, persuasive religious movement, a bizarre reaction to American science and pragmatism. The great critic Edmund Wilson, who admired Houdini and understood his gifts, recognized that the magician had appeared at a critical moment in the history of Spiritualism. Houdini was the only man living who had the authority, and the competence, to expose the predatory mediums, and his success was decisive.

Yet Houdini's lecture-demonstrations, and exposures of false mediums, only fueled Doyle's suspicions that his friend was the real thing, a physical medium. In all fairness, Sir Arthur Conan Doyle was a credulous old gentleman, who knew nothing of Houdini's techniques. But his instinct was sound. Two months after Houdini died, Sir Arthur wrote to Bess in despair of ever learning the truth from the magician's lips, and she wrote Doyle a long letter. What concerns us here are a few sentences which, coming from the woman who shared his life and work, and maintained her loyalty to Houdini alive and dead, we must regard as altogether startling.

> I will never be offended by anything you say for him or about him, but that he possessed psychic powers—he never knew it. As I told Lady Doyle often he would get a difficult lock, I stood by the cabinet and I would hear him say, "This is beyond me," and after many minutes when the audience became restless I nervously would say "Harry, if there is anything in this belief in Spiritism,—why don't you call on them to assist you," and before many minutes had passed Houdini had mastered the lock.
>
> We never attributed this to psychic help. We just knew that that particular instrument was the one to open that lock, and so did all his tricks.

The tone of this letter penned so soon after her husband's death is somber throughout, painfully sincere. This was not a subject for levity, this being the central issue in the life of Harry Houdini. So what on earth is Bess trying to tell Sir Arthur when she testifies to the invocation of spirits in one sentence, and repudiates psychic help in the next? What kind of double-talk is this, when the widow refers to the summoning of spiritual aid as "that particular instrument," as if a spirit were no different from any other skeleton key? It sounds like sheer euphemism; it sounds like the Houdinis' lifetime of work had uncovered a power so terrifying they would not admit it to each other, let alone the world. Would that Albert Einstein had been so discreet in 1905.

So what if Harry Houdini, once in a while, "spirited" himself out of a Siberian Van, or a pair of Mirror Handcuffs, or a packing case at the bottom of the East River? It is perhaps no more remarkable than that an American Jew won a verdict against the German Police for criminal libel in 1901, or reversed a religious movement in America in 1922.

Houdini died in Detroit on Halloween in 1926, of acute appendicitis. He was born in Budapest on March 24, 1874, but told the world he was born in Appleton, Wisconsin on April 6. Not until after World War II did Americans discover that their greatest magician was an alien. Houdini's work was no more miraculous than his life. His life was no more miraculous than the opening and closing of a flower.

THE READER

1. Do you find the figure of Houdini appealing, attractive, as Epstein presents him? What do you take to be the outstanding qualities of his character?
2. How important to this account of Houdini is the fact that he was a Jew? What are some of the implications here of that fact? What might Epstein be saying (even if unexpressed) in his account of the confrontations between Houdini and the German police?
3. What, according to Epstein, was the message to mankind of Houdini's career? What details in the essay exemplify that message?

THE WRITER

1. At several points in his account of Houdini, Epstein creates an effect of suspense. How does he manage that effect? What purposes does it serve?
2. Epstein's account of Houdini leaves some unanswered questions. What are they? Why are they unanswered? Would it be a better account if there were no questions left unanswered? Do you see any connection between the fact of unanswered questions and the theme of the essay?

Virginia Woolf

MY FATHER: LESLIE STEPHEN

By the time that his children were growing up, the great days of my father's life were over. His feats on the river and on the mountains had been won before they were born. Relics of them were to be found lying about the house—the silver cup on the study mantelpiece; the rusty alpenstocks that leaned against the bookcase in the corner; and to the end of his days he would speak of great climbers and explorers with a

First published in the *London Times* (Nov. 28, 1932) as "Leslie Stephen, the Philosopher at Home: A Daughter's Memories."

peculiar mixture of admiration and envy. But his own years of activity were over, and my father had to content himself with pottering about the Swiss valleys or taking a stroll across the Cornish moors.

That to potter and to stroll meant more on his lips than on other people's is becoming obvious now that some of his friends have given their own version of those expeditions. He would start off after breakfast alone, or with one companion. Shortly after dinner he would return. If the walk had been successful, he would have out his great map and commemorate a new short cut in red ink. And he was quite capable, it appears, of striding all day across the moors without speaking more than a word or two to his companion. By that time, too, he had written the *History of English Thought in the Eighteenth Century,* which is said by some to be his masterpiece; and the *Science of Ethics*—the book which interested him most; and *The Playground of Europe,* in which is to be found "The Sunset on Mont Blanc"—in his opinion the best thing he ever wrote. He still wrote daily and methodically, though never for long at a time.

In London he wrote in the large room with three long windows at the top of the house. He wrote lying almost recumbent in a low rocking chair which he tipped to and fro as he wrote, like a cradle, and as he wrote he smoked a short clay pipe, and he scattered books round him in a circle. The thud of a book dropped on the floor could be heard in the room beneath. And often as he mounted the stairs to his study with his firm, regular tread he would burst, not into song, for he was entirely unmusical, but into a strange rhythmical chant, for verse of all kinds, both "utter trash," as he called it, and the most sublime words of Milton and Wordsworth, stuck in his memory, and the act of walking or climbing seemed to inspire him to recite whichever it was that came uppermost or suited his mood.

But it was his dexterity with his fingers that delighted his children before they could potter along the lanes at his heels or read his books. He would twist a sheet of paper beneath a pair of scissors and out would drop an elephant, a stag, or a monkey, with trunks, horns, and tails delicately and exactly formed. Or, taking a pencil, he would draw beast after beast—an art that he practiced almost unconsciously as he read, so that the flyleaves of his books swarm with owls and donkeys as if to illustrate the "Oh, you ass!" or "Conceited dunce" that he was wont to scribble impatiently in the margin. Such brief comments, in which one may find the germ of the more temperate statements of his essays, recall some of the characteristics of his talk. He could be very silent, as his friends have testified. But his remarks, made suddenly in a low voice between the puffs of his pipe, were extremely effective. Sometimes with one word—but his one word was accompanied by a gesture of the hand—he would dispose of the tissue of exaggerations which his own sobriety seemed to provoke. "There are 40,000,000 unmarried women in London alone!" Lady Ritchie once informed him. "Oh, Annie, Annie!" my father exclaimed in tones of horrified but affectionate rebuke. But Lady Ritchie, as if she enjoyed being rebuked, would pile it up even higher next time she came.

The stories he told to amuse his children of adventures in the Alps— but accidents only happened, he would explain, if you were so foolish as to disobey your guides—or of those long walks, after one of which, from Cambridge to London on a hot day, "I drank, I am sorry to say, rather more than was good for me," were told very briefly, but with a curious power to impress the scene. The things that he did not say were always there in the background. So, too, though he seldom told anecdotes, and his memory for facts was bad, when he described a person— and he had known many people, both famous and obscure—he would convey exactly what he thought of him in two or three words. And what he thought might be the opposite of what other people thought. He had a way of upsetting established reputations and disregarding conventional values that could be disconcerting, and sometimes perhaps wounding, though no one was more respectful of any feeling that seemed to him genuine. But when, suddenly opening his bright blue eyes and rousing himself from what had seemed complete abstraction, he gave his opinion, it was difficult to disregard it. It was a habit, especially when deafness made him unaware that this opinion could be heard, that had its inconveniences.

"I am the most easily bored of men," he wrote, truthfully as usual; and when, as was inevitable in a large family, some visitor threatened to stay not merely for tea but also for dinner, my father would express his anguish at first by twisting and untwisting a certain lock of hair. Then he would burst out, half to himself, half to the powers above, but quite audibly, "Why can't he go? Why can't he go?" Yet such is the charm of simplicity—and did he not say, also truthfully, that "bores are the salt of the earth"?—that the bores seldom went, or, if they did, forgave him and came again.

Too much, perhaps, has been said of his silence; too much stress has been laid upon his reserve. He loved clear thinking; he hated sentimentality and gush; but this by no means meant that he was cold and unemotional, perpetually critical and condemnatory in daily life. On the contrary, it was his power of feeling strongly and of expressing his feeling with vigor that made him sometimes so alarming as a companion. A lady, for instance, complained of the wet summer that was spoiling her tour in Cornwall. But to my father, though he never called himself a democrat, the rain meant that the corn was being laid; some poor man was being ruined; and the energy with which he expressed his sympathy—not with the lady—left her discomfited. He had something of the same respect for farmers and fishermen that he had for climbers and explorers. So, too, he talked little of patriotism, but during the South African War—and all wars were hateful to him—he lay awake thinking that he heard the guns on the battlefield. Again, neither his reason nor his cold common sense helped to convince him that a child could be late for dinner without having been maimed or killed in an accident. And not all his mathematics together with a bank balance which he insisted must be ample in the extreme could persuade him, when it came to signing a check, that the whole family was not "shooting Niagara to ruin,"[1] as he put it. The pictures that he would draw of old age and the bankruptcy court, of ruined men of letters who have to support large families in small houses at Wimbledon (he owned a very small house at Wimbledon), might have convinced those who complain of his under-statements that hyperbole was well within his reach had he chosen.

Yet the unreasonable mood was superficial, as the rapidity with which it vanished would prove. The checkbook was shut; Wimbledon and the workhouse were forgotten. Some thought of a humorous kind made him chuckle. Taking his hat and his stick, calling for his dog and his daughter, he would stride off into Kensington Gardens, where he had walked as a little boy, where his brother Fitzjames and he had made beautiful bows to young Queen Victoria and she had swept them a curtsy; and so, round the Serpentine, to Hyde Park Corner, where he had once saluted the great Duke himself; and so home. He was not then in the least "alarming"; he was very simple, very confiding; and his silence, though one might last unbroken from the Round Pond to the Marble Arch, was curiously full of meaning, as if he were thinking half aloud, about poetry and philosophy and people he had known.

He himself was the most abstemious of men. He smoked a pipe perpetually, but never a cigar. He wore his clothes until they were too shabby to be tolerable; and he held old-fashioned and rather puritani-cal views as to the vice of luxury and the sin of idleness. The relations between parents and children today have a freedom that would have been impossible with my father. He expected a certain standard of behavior, even of ceremony, in family life. Yet if freedom means the right to think one's own thoughts and to follow one's own pursuits, then no one respected and indeed insisted upon freedom more com-pletely than he did. His sons, with the exception of the Army and Navy, should follow whatever professions they chose; his daughters, though he cared little enough for the higher education of women, should have the same liberty. If at one moment he rebuked a daughter sharply for smoking a cigarette—smoking was not in his opinion a nice habit in the other sex—she had only to ask him if she might become

1. The reference is to going over Niagara Falls in a boat.

a painter, and he assured her that so long as she took her work seriously he would give her all the help he could. He had no special love for painting; but he kept his word. Freedom of that sort was worth thousands of cigarettes.

It was the same with the perhaps more difficult problem of literature. Even today there may be parents who would doubt the wisdom of allowing a girl of fifteen the free run of a large and quite unexpurgated library. But my father allowed it. There were certain facts—very briefly, very shyly he referred to them. Yet "Read what you like," he said, and all his books, "mangy and worthless," as he called them, but certainly they were many and various, were to be had without asking. To read what one liked because one liked it, never to pretend to admire what one did not—that was his only lesson in the art of reading. To write in the fewest possible words, as clearly as possible, exactly what one meant—that was his only lesson in the art of writing. All the rest must be learned for oneself. Yet a child must have been childish in the extreme not to feel that such was the teaching of a man of great learning and wide experience, though he would never impose his own views or parade his own knowledge. For, as his tailor remarked when he saw my father walk past his shop up Bond Street, "There goes a gentleman that wears good clothes without knowing it."

In those last years, grown solitary and very deaf, he would sometimes call himself a failure as a writer; he had been "jack of all trades, and master of none." But whether he failed or succeeded as a writer, it is permissible to believe that he left a distinct impression of himself on the minds of his friends. Meredith[2] saw him as "Phoebus Apollo turned fasting friar" in his earlier days; Thomas Hardy, years later, looked at the "spare and desolate figure" of the Schreckhorn[3] and thought of

> him,
> Who scaled its horn with ventured life and limb,
> Drawn on by vague imaginings, maybe,
> Of semblance to his personality
> In its quaint glooms, keen lights, and rugged trim.

But the praise he would have valued most, for though he was an agnostic nobody believed more profoundly in the worth of human relationships, was Meredith's tribute after his death: "He was the one man to my knowledge worthy to have married your mother." And Lowell,[4] when he called him "L.S., the most lovable of men," has best described the quality that makes him, after all these years, unforgettable.

2. George Meredith (1828–1909), English novelist and poet.
3. One of the peaks in the Swiss Alps.

4. James Russell Lowell, nineteenth-century American poet, essayist, and editor.

THE READER

1. *What are the basic qualities Woolf admires, as revealed in this selection?*

2. *Would you like to have been Leslie Stephen's son or daughter? Why, or why not?*

3. *In some of her other work, Woolf shows a deep and sensitive concern for women's experience and awareness. Do you find a feminist awareness here? In what way?*

4. *In her novel* To the Lighthouse, *Woolf creates the fictional character of Mr. Ramsay from recollections of her father. Compare the characterization in her essay with this passage from the novel: "What he said was true. It was always true. He was incapable of untruth; never tampered with a fact; never altered a disagreeable word to suit the pleasure or convenience of any mortal being, least of all of his own children, who, sprung from his loins, should be aware from childhood that life is difficult; facts uncompromising; and the passage to that fabled land where our brightest hopes are extinguished, our frail barks founder in darkness (here Mr. Ramsay would straighten his back and narrow his little blue eyes upon the horizon), one that needs, above all, courage, truth, and the power to endure." (*To the Lighthouse, Harcourt, Brace & World, 1927; © 1955 Leonard Woolf, pp. 10–11.)*

THE WRITER

1. *Giving praise can be a difficult rhetorical and social undertaking. How does Woolf avoid the pitfalls or try to? Compare Lessing's "My Father" (p. 140) to this selection. Does Lessing take similar risks?*

2. *What are the main currents of the Stephens' family life as revealed here? Because any such description must be selective, what does Woolf leave out? Do the omissions detract from her essay? If you think so, say why.*

3. *If you didn't know that Leslie Stephen was Woolf's father, could you deduce that fact from the way she writes about him? Why, or why not?*

4. *Write a sketch about a father, real or fictional, adopting a tone similar to Woolf's in this sketch.*

Doris Lessing

MY FATHER

We use our parents like recurring dreams, to be entered into when needed; they are always there for love or for hate; but it occurs to me that I was not always there for my father. I've written about him before, but novels, stories, don't have to be "true." Writing this article is difficult because it has to be "true." I knew him when his best years were over.

There are photographs of him. The largest is of an officer in the 1914–18 war. A new uniform—buttoned, badged, strapped, tabbed—confines a handsome, dark young man who holds himself stiffly to confront what he certainly thought of as his duty. His eyes are steady, serious, and responsible, and show no signs of what he became later. A photograph at sixteen is of a dark, introspective youth with the same intent eyes. But it is his mouth you notice—a heavily-jutting upper lip contradicts the rest of a regular face. His moustache was to hide it: "Had to do something—a damned fleshy mouth. Always made me uncomfortable, that mouth of mine."

Earlier a baby (eyes already alert) appears in a lace waterfall that cascades from the pillowy bosom of a fat, plain woman to her feet. It is the face of a head cook. "Lord, but my mother was a practical female—almost as bad as you!" as he used to say, or throw at my mother in moments of exasperation. Beside her stands, or droops, arms dangling, his father, the source of the dark, arresting eyes, but otherwise masked by a long beard.

The birth certificate says: Born 3rd August, 1886, Walton Villa, Creffield Road, S. Mary at the Wall, R.S.D. Name, Alfred Cook. Name and surname of Father: Alfred Cook Tayler. Name and maiden name of Mother: Caroline May Batley. Rank or Profession: Bank Clerk. Colchester, Essex.

They were very poor. Clothes and boots were a problem. They "made their own amusements." Books were mostly the Bible and *The Pilgrim's Progress.* [1] Every Saturday night they bathed in a hipbath in front of the kitchen fire. No servants. Church three times on Sundays. "Lord, when I think of those Sundays! I dreaded them all week, like a nightmare coming at you full tilt and no escape." But he rabbited

First published in the London *Sunday Telegraph* (Sept. 1, 1963).

1. An allegory of Christian's progress toward heaven through a world filled with tempters, by the seventeenth-century writer John Bunyan.

with ferrets along the lanes and fields, bird-nested, stole fruit, picked nuts and mushrooms, paid visits to the blacksmith and the mill and rode a farmer's carthorse.

They ate economically, but when he got diabetes in his forties and subsisted on lean meat and lettuce leaves, he remembered suet puddings, treacle puddings, raisin and currant puddings, steak and kidney puddings, bread and butter pudding, "batter cooked in the gravy with the meat," potato cake, plum cake, butter cake, porridge with treacle, fruit tarts and pies, brawn, pig's trotters and pig's cheek and home-smoked ham and sausages. And "lashings of fresh butter and cream and eggs." He wondered if this diet had produced the diabetes, but said it was worth it.

There was an elder brother described by my father as: "Too damned clever by half. One of those quick, clever brains. Now I've always had a slow brain, but I get there in the end, damn it!"

The brothers went to a local school and the elder did well, but my father was beaten for being slow. They both became bank clerks in, I think, the Westminster Bank, and one must have found it congenial, for he became a manager, the "rich brother," who had cars and even a yacht. But my father did not like it, though he was conscientious. For instance, he changed his writing, letter by letter, because a senior criticised it. I never saw his unregenerate hand, but the one he created was elegant, spiky, careful. Did this mean he created a new personality for himself, hiding one he did not like, as he hid his "damned fleshy mouth"? I don't know.

Nor do I know when he left home to live in Luton, or why. He found family life too narrow? A safe guess—he found everything too narrow. His mother was too down-to-earth? He had to get away from his clever elder brother?

Being a young man in Luton was the best part of his life. It ended in 1914, so he had a decade of happiness. His reminiscences of it were all of pleasure, the delight of physical movement, of dancing in particular. All his girls were "a beautiful dancer, light as a feather." He played billiards and ping-pong (both for his country); he swam, boated, played cricket and football,[2] went to picnics and horse races, sang at musical evenings. One family of a mother and two daughters treated him "like a son only better. I didn't know whether I was in love with the mother or the daughters, but oh I did love going there; we had such good times." He was engaged to one daughter, then, for a time, to the other. An engagement was broken off because she was rude to a waiter. "I could not marry a woman who allowed herself to insult someone who was defenceless." He used to say to my wryly smiling mother: "Just as well

10

2. Soccer.

I didn't marry either of *them;* they would never have stuck it out the way you have, old girl."

Just before he died he told me he had dreamed he was standing in a kitchen on a very high mountain holding X in his arms. "Ah, yes, that's what I've missed in my life. Now don't you let yourself be cheated out of life by the old dears. They take all the colour out of everything if you let them."

But in that decade—"I'd walk 10, 15 miles to a dance two or three times a week and think nothing of it. Then I'd dance every dance and walk home again over the fields. Sometimes it was moonlight, but I liked the snow best, all crisp and fresh. I loved walking back and getting into my digs[3] just as the sun was rising. My little dog was so happy to see me, and I'd feed her, and make myself porridge and tea, then I'd wash and shave and go off to work."

The boy who was beaten at school, who went too much to church, who carried the fear of poverty all his life, but who nevertheless was filled with the memories of country pleasures; the young bank clerk who worked such long hours for so little money, but who danced, sang, played, flirted—this naturally vigorous, sensuous being was killed in 1914, 1915, 1916. I think the best of my father died in that war, that his spirit was crippled by it. The people I've met, particularly the women, who knew him young, speak of his high spirits, his energy, his enjoyment of life. Also of his kindness, his compassion and—a word that keeps recurring—his wisdom. "Even when he was just a boy he understood things that you'd think even an old man would find it easy to condemn." I do not think these people would have easily recognised the ill, irritable, abstracted, hypochondriac man I knew.

He "joined up" as an ordinary soldier out of a characteristically quirky scruple: it wasn't right to enjoy officers' privileges when the Tommies[4] had such a bad time. But he could not stick the communal latrines, the obligatory drinking, the collective visits to brothels, the jokes about girls. So next time he was offered a commission he took it.

His childhood and young man's memories, kept fluid, were added to, grew, as living memories do. But his war memories were congealed in stories that he told again and again, with the same words and gestures, in stereotyped phrases. They were anonymous, general, as if they had come out of a communal war memoir. He met a German in no-man's-land, but both slowly lowered their rifles and smiled and walked away. The Tommies were the salt of the earth, the British fighting men the best in the world. He had never known such comradeship. A certain brutal officer was shot in a sortie by his men, but the other officers, recognising rough justice, said nothing. He had known men intimately

15

3. Lodgings.   4. Foot soldiers.

who saw the Angels at Mons.[5] He wished he could force all the generals on both sides into the trenches for just one day, to see what the common soldiers endured—*that* would have ended the war at once.

There was an undercurrent of memories, dreams, and emotions much deeper, more personal. This dark region in him, fate-ruled, where nothing was true but horror, was expressed inarticulately, in brief, bitter exclamations or phrases of rage, incredulity, betrayal. The men who went to fight in that war believed it when they said it was to end war. My father believed it. And he was never able to reconcile his belief in his country with his anger at the cynicism of its leaders. And the anger, the sense of betrayal, strengthened as he grew old and ill.

But in 1914 he was naïve, the German atrocities in Belgium inflamed him, and he enlisted out of idealism, although he knew he would have a hard time. He knew because a fortuneteller told him. (He could be described as uncritically superstitious or as psychically gifted.) He would be in great danger twice, yet not die—he was being protected by a famous soldier who was his ancestor. "And sure enough, later I heard from the Little Aunties that the church records showed we were descended the backstairs way from the Duke of Wellington, or was it Marlborough? Damn it, I forget. But one of them would be beside me all through the war, she said." (He was romantic, not only about this solicitous ghost, but also about being a descendant of the Huguenots, on the strength of the "e" in Tayler; and about "the wild blood" in his veins from a great uncle who, sent unjustly to prison for smuggling, came out of a ten-year sentence and earned it, very efficiently, along the coasts of Cornwall until he died.)

The luckiest thing that ever happened to my father, he said, was getting his leg shattered by shrapnel ten days before Passchendaele.[6] His whole company was killed. He knew he was going to be wounded because of the fortuneteller, who had said he would know. "I did not understand what she meant, but both times in the trenches, first when my appendix burst and I nearly died, and then just before Passchendaele, I felt for some days as if a thick, black velvet pall was settled over me. I can't tell you what it was like. Oh, it was awful, awful, and the second time it was so bad I wrote to the old people and told them I was going to be killed."

His leg was cut off at mid-thigh, he was shell-shocked, he was very ill for many months, with a prolonged depression afterwards. "You should always remember that sometimes people are all seething underneath. You don't know what terrible things people have to fight against. You should look at a person's eyes, that's how you tell. . . . When I was like

5. An apparition that appeared during a World War I battle.
6. A prolonged and futile battle of World War I, in which British and Commonwealth forces sustained massive casualties.

that, after I lost my leg, I went to a nice doctor man and said I was going mad, but he said, don't worry, everyone locks up things like that. You don't know—horrible, horrible, awful things. I was afraid of myself, of what I used to dream. I wasn't myself at all."

In the Royal Free Hospital was my mother, Sister McVeagh. He married his nurse which, as they both said often enough (though in different tones of voice), was just as well. That was 1919. He could not face being a bank clerk in England, he said, not after the trenches. Besides, England was too narrow and conventional. Besides, the civilians did not know what the soldiers had suffered, they didn't want to know, and now it wasn't done even to remember "The Great Unmentionable." He went off to the Imperial Bank of Persia, in which country I was born.

The house was beautiful, with great stone-floored high-ceilinged rooms whose windows showed ranges of snow-streaked mountains. The gardens were full of roses, jasmine, pomegranates, walnuts. Kermanshah he spoke of with liking, but soon they went to Teheran, populous with "Embassy people," and my gregarious mother created a lively social life about which he was irritable even in recollection.

Irritableness—that note was first struck here, about Persia. He did not like, he said, "the graft and the corruption." But here it is time to try and describe something difficult—how a man's good qualities can also be his bad ones, or if not bad, a danger to him.

My father was honourable—he always knew exactly what that word meant. He had integrity. His "one does not do that sort of thing," his "no, it is *not* right," sounded throughout my childhood and were final for all of us. I am sure it was true he wanted to leave Persia because of "the corruption." But it was also because he was already unconsciously longing for something freer, because as a bank official he could not let go into the dream-logged personality that was waiting for him. And later in Rhodesia, too, what was best in him was also what prevented him from shaking away the shadows: it was always in the name of honesty or decency that he refused to take this step or that out of the slow decay of the family's fortunes.

In 1925 there was leave from Persia. That year in London there was an Empire Exhibition, and on the Southern Rhodesian stand some very fine maize cobs and a poster saying that fortunes could be made on maize at 25/-[7] a bag. So on an impulse, turning his back forever on England, washing his hands of the corruption of the East, my father collected all his capital, £800, I think, while my mother packed curtains from Liberty's, clothes from Harrods, visiting cards, a piano, Persian rugs, a governess and two small children.

Soon, there was my father in a cigar-shaped house of thatch and mud

7. Twenty-five shillings. A shilling was then worth about twenty-five cents.

on the top of a kopje[8] that overlooked in all directions a great system
of mountains, rivers, valleys, while overhead the sky arched from horizon
to empty horizon. This was a couple of hundred miles south from the
Zambesi, a hundred or so west from Mozambique, in the district of
Banket, so called because certain of its reefs were of the same formation
as those called *banket* on the Rand. Lomagundi—gold country, tobacco
country, maize country—wild, almost empty. (The Africans had been
turned off it into reserves.) Our neighbours were four, five, seven miles
off. In front of the house . . . no neighbours, nothing; no farms, just wild
bush with two rivers but no fences to the mountains seven miles away.
And beyond these mountains and bush again to the Portuguese border,[9]
over which "our boys" used to escape when wanted by the police for pass
or other offences.

And then? There was bad luck. For instance, the price of maize
dropped from 25/- to 9/- a bag. The seasons were bad, prices bad, crops
failed. This was the sort of thing that made it impossible for him ever
to "get off the farm," which, he agreed with my mother, was what he
most wanted to do.

It was an absurd country, he said. A man could "own" a farm for years
that was totally mortgaged to the Government and run from the Land
Bank, meanwhile employing half-a-hundred Africans at 12/- a month
and none of them knew how to do a day's work. Why, two farm
labourers from Europe could do in a day what twenty of these ignorant
black savages would take a week to do. (Yet he was proud that he had
a name as a just employer, that he gave "a square deal.") Things got
worse. A fortuneteller had told him that her heart ached when she saw
the misery ahead for my father: this was the misery.

But it was my mother who suffered. After a period of neurotic illness,
which was a protest against her situation, she became brave and resourceful. But she never saw that her husband was not living in a real
world, that he had made a captive of her common sense. We were always
about to "get off the farm." A miracle would do it—a sweepstake, a
goldmine, a legacy. And then? What a question! We would go to
England where life would be normal with people coming in for musical
evenings and nice supper parties at the Trocadero after a show. Poor
woman, for the twenty years we were on the farm, she waited for when
life would begin for her and for her children, for she never understood
that what was a calamity for her was for them a blessing.

Meanwhile my father sank towards his death (at 61). Everything
changed in him. He had been a dandy and fastidious, now he hated to
change out of shabby khaki. He had been sociable, now he was misan-

8. Small hill. The term is South African
Dutch.

9. That is, the border of Mozambique, then
a Portuguese possession.

thropic. His body's disorders—soon diabetes and all kinds of stomach ailments—dominated him. He was brave about his wooden leg, and even went down mine shafts and climbed trees with it, but he walked clumsily and it irked him badly. He greyed fast, and slept more in the day, but would be awake half the night pondering about. . . .

30   It could be gold divining. For ten years he experimented on private theories to do with the attractions and repulsions of metals. His whole soul went into it but his theories were wrong or he was *unlucky*—after all, if he had found a mine he would have had to leave the farm. It could be the relation between the minerals of the earth and of the moon; his decision to make infusions of all the plants on the farm and drink them himself in the interests of science; the criminal folly of the British Government in not realising that the Germans and the Russians were conspiring as Anti-Christ to . . . the inevitability of war because no one would listen to Churchill, but it would be all right because God (by then he was a British Israelite[1]) had destined Britain to rule the world; a prophecy said 10 million dead would surround Jerusalem—how would the corpses be cleared away?; people who wished to abolish flogging should be flogged; the natives understood nothing but a good beating; hanging must not be abolished because the Old Testament said "an eye for an eye and a tooth for a tooth. . . ."

Yet, as this side of him darkened, so that it seemed all his thoughts were of violence, illness, war, still no one dared to make an unkind comment in his presence or to gossip. Criticism of people, particularly of women, made him more and more uncomfortable till at last he burst out with: "It's all very well, but no one has the right to say that about another person."

In Africa, when the sun goes down, the stars spring up, all of them in their expected places, glittering and moving. In the rainy season, the sky flashed and thundered. In the dry season, the great dark hollow of night was lit by veld fires: the mountains burned through September and October in chains of red fire. Every night my father took out his chair to watch the sky and the mountains, smoking, silent, a thin shabby fly-away figure under the stars. "Makes you think—there are so many worlds up there, wouldn't really matter if we did blow ourselves up— plenty more where we came from."

The Second World War, so long foreseen by him, was a bad time. His son was in the Navy and in danger, and his daughter a sorrow to him. He became very ill. More and more often it was necessary to drive him into Salisbury with him in a coma, or in danger of one, on the back seat. My mother moved him into a pretty little suburban house in town

1. A reference to the contention that the English-speaking peoples are the descendants of the "ten tribes" of Israel, deported by Sargon of Assyria on the fall of Samaria in 721 B.C.

near the hospitals, where he took to his bed and a couple of years later died. For the most part he was unconscious under drugs. When awake he talked obsessively (a tongue licking a nagging sore place) about "the old war." Or he remembered his youth. "I've been dreaming—Lord, to see those horses come lickety-split down the course with their necks stretched out and the sun on their coats and everyone shouting. . . . I've been dreaming how I walked along the river in the mist as the sun was rising. . . . Lord, lord, lord, what a time that was, what good times we all had then, before the old war."

THE READER

1. Find facts about Lessing's father that are repeated or referred to more than once. Why does she repeat them?
2. Lessing says that it was difficult for her to write about her father because she "knew him when his best years were over." What other things about those "best years" might she have wanted to know that she apparently didn't?

THE WRITER

1. Lessing says that "writing this article is difficult because it has to be 'true.'" Why does she put quotation marks around "true"? Why would it be more difficult to write something that has to be "true" than, as she says, stories that "don't have to be 'true'"? How has she tried to make this sketch "true"? How well do you think she has succeeded?
2. If a stranger were writing about Lessing's father but had the same facts available, might the account differ in any ways? Explain.
3. If you wrote a sketch of a father after reading Woolf's "My Father: Leslie Stephen" (p. 134), write another sketch about the same or a different father, adopting a tone similar to Lessing's.

Annie Dillard

TERWILLIGER BUNTS ONE

One Sunday afternoon Mother wandered through our kitchen, where Father was making a sandwich and listening to the ball game. The Pirates were playing the New York Giants at Forbes Field. In those days, the Giants had a utility infielder named Wayne Terwilliger. Just as

From Part Two of *An American Childhood* (1987).

Mother passed through, the radio announcer cried—with undue drama—"Terwilliger bunts one!"

"Terwilliger bunts one?" Mother cried back, stopped short. She turned. "Is that English?"

"The player's name is Terwilliger," Father said. "He bunted."

"That's marvelous," Mother said. " 'Terwilliger bunts one.' No wonder you listen to baseball. 'Terwilliger bunts one.' "

For the next seven or eight years, Mother made this surprising string of syllables her own. Testing a microphone, she repeated, "Terwilliger bunts one"; testing a pen or a typewriter, she wrote it. If, as happened surprisingly often in the course of various improvised gags, she pretended to whisper something else in my ear, she actually whispered, "Terwilliger bunts one." Whenever someone used a French phrase, or a Latin one, she answered solemnly, "Terwilliger bunts one." If Mother had had, like Andrew Carnegie, the opportunity to cook up a motto for a coat of arms, hers would have read simply and tellingly, "Terwilliger bunts one." (Carnegie's was "Death to Privilege.")

She served us with other words and phrases. On a Florida trip, she repeated tremulously, "That . . . is a royal poinciana." I don't remember the tree; I remember the thrill in her voice. She pronounced it carefully, and spelled it. She also liked to say "portulaca."

The drama of the words "Tamiami Trail" stirred her, we learned on the same Florida trip. People built Tampa on one coast, and they built Miami on another. Then—the height of visionary ambition and folly—they piled a slow, tremendous road through the terrible Everglades to connect them. To build the road, men stood sunk in muck to their armpits. They fought off cottonmouth moccasins and six-foot alligators. They slept in boats, wet. They blasted muck with dynamite, cut jungle with machetes; they laid logs, dragged drilling machines, hauled dredges, heaped limestone. The road took fourteen years to build up by the shovelful, a Panama Canal in reverse, and cost hundreds of lives from tropical, mosquito-carried diseases. Then, capping it all, some genius thought of the word Tamiami: they called the road from Tampa to Miami, this very road under our spinning wheels, the Tamiami Trail. Some called it Alligator Alley. Anyone could drive over this road without a thought.

Hearing this, moved, I thought all the suffering of road building was worth it (it wasn't my suffering), now that we had this new thing to hang these new words on—Alligator Alley for those who liked things cute, and, for connoisseurs like Mother, for lovers of the human drama in all its boldness and terror, the Tamiami Trail.

Back home, Mother cut clips from reels of talk, as it were, and played them back at leisure. She noticed that many Pittsburghers confuse "leave" and "let." One kind relative brightened our morning by mentioning why she'd brought her son to visit: "He wanted to come with me, so I left him." Mother filled in Amy and me on locutions we missed. "I can't do it on Friday," her pretty sister told a crowded dinner party, "because Friday's the day I lay in the stores."

(All unconsciously, though, we ourselves used some pure Pittsburg- 10 hisms. We said "tele pole," pronounced "telly pole," for that splintery sidewalk post I loved to climb. We said "slippy"—the sidewalks are "slippy." We said, "That's all the farther I could go." And we said, as Pittsburghers do say, "This glass needs washed," or "The dog needs walked"—a usage our father eschewed; he knew it was not standard English, nor even comprehensible English, but he never let on.)

"Spell 'poinsettia,'" Mother would throw out at me, smiling with pleasure. "Spell 'sherbet.'" The idea was not to make us whizzes, but, quite the contrary, to remind us—and I, especially, needed reminding— that we didn't know it all just yet.

"There's a deer standing in the front hall," she told me one quiet evening in the country.

"Really?"

"No. I just wanted to tell you something once without your saying, 'I know.'"

Supermarkets in the middle 1950s began luring, or bothering, custom- 15 ers by giving out Top Value Stamps or Green Stamps. When, shopping with Mother, we got to the head of the checkout line, the checker, always a young man, asked, "Save stamps?"

"No," Mother replied genially, week after week, "I build model airplanes." I believe she originated this line. It took me years to deter- mine where the joke lay.

Anyone who met her verbal challenges she adored. She had surgery on one of her eyes. On the operating table, just before she conked out, she appealed feelingly to the surgeon, saying, as she had been planning to say for weeks, "Will I be able to play the piano?" "Not on me," the surgeon said. "You won't pull that old one on me."

It was, indeed, an old one. The surgeon was supposed to answer, "Yes, my dear, brave woman, you will be able to play the piano after this operation," to which Mother intended to reply, "Oh, good, I've always wanted to play the piano." This pat scenario bored her; she loved having it interrupted. It must have galled her that usually her acquaintances were so predictably unalert; it must have galled her that, for the length of her life, she could surprise everyone so continually, so easily, when she had been the same all along. At any rate, she loved anyone who, as she put it, saw it coming, and called her on it.

She regarded the instructions on bureaucratic forms as straight lines. "Do you advocate the overthrow of the United States government by force or violence?" After some thought she wrote, "Force." She re-garded children, even babies, as straight men. When Molly learned to crawl, Mother delighted in buying her gowns with drawstrings at the bottom, like Swee'pea's,[1] because, as she explained energetically, you could easily step on the drawstring without the baby's noticing, so that she crawled and crawled and crawled and never got anywhere except into a small ball at the gown's top.

20   When we children were young, she mothered us tenderly and depend-ably; as we got older, she resumed her career of anarchism. She collared us into her gags. If she answered the phone on a wrong number, she told the caller, "Just a minute," and dragged the receiver to Amy or me, saying, "Here, take this, your name is Cecile," or, worse, just, "It's for you." You had to think on your feet. But did you want to perform well as Cecile, or did you want to take pity on the wretched caller?

During a family trip to the Highland Park Zoo, Mother and I were alone for a minute. She approached a young couple holding hands on a bench by the seals, and addressed the young man in dripping tones: "Where have you been? Still got those baby-blue eyes; always did slay me. And this"—a swift nod at the dumbstruck young woman, who had removed her hand from the man's—"must be the one you were telling me about. She's not so bad, really, as you used to make out. But listen, you know how I miss you, you know where to reach me, same old place. And there's Ann over there—see how she's grown? See the blue eyes?"

And off she sashayed, taking me firmly by the hand, and leading us around briskly past the monkey house and away. She cocked an ear back, and both of us heard the desperate man begin, in a high-pitched wail, "I swear, I never saw her before in my life. . . ."

On a long, sloping beach by the ocean, she lay stretched out sunning with Father and friends, until the conversation gradually grew tedious, when without forethought she gave a little push with her heel and rolled away. People were stunned. She rolled deadpan and apparently effort-lessly, arms and legs extended and tidy, down the beach to the distant water's edge, where she lay at ease just as she had been, but half in the surf, and well out of earshot.

She dearly loved to fluster people by throwing out a game's rules at whim—when she was getting bored, losing in a dull sort of way, and when everybody else was taking it too seriously. If you turned your back, she moved the checkers around on the board. When you got them all straightened out, she denied she'd touched them; the next time you turned your back, she lined them up on the rug or hid them under your chair. In a betting rummy game called Michigan, she routinely played

1. The infant in the comic strip "Popeye" by Elzie Crisler Segar.

out of turn, or called out a card she didn't hold, or counted backward, simply to amuse herself by causing an uproar and watching the rest of us do double takes and have fits. (Much later, when serious suitors came to call, Mother subjected them to this fast card game as a trial by ordeal; she used it as an intelligence test and a measure of spirit. If the poor man could stay a round without breaking down or running out, he got to marry one of us, if he still wanted to.)

She excelled at bridge, playing fast and boldly, but when the stakes were low and the hands dull, she bid slams for the devilment of it, or raised her opponents' suit to bug them, or showed her hand, or tossed her cards in a handful behind her back in a characteristic swift motion accompanied by a vibrantly innocent look. It drove our stolid father crazy. The hand was over before it began, and the guests were appalled. How do you score it, who deals now, what do you do with a crazy person who is having so much fun? Or they were down seven, and the guests were appalled. "Pam!" "Dammit, Pam!" He groaned. What ails such people? What on earth possesses them? He rubbed his face.

She was an unstoppable force; she never let go. When we moved across town, she persuaded the U.S. Post Office to let her keep her old address—forever—because she'd had stationery printed. I don't know how she did it. Every new post office worker, over decades, needed to learn that although the Doaks' mail is addressed to here, it is delivered to there.

Mother's energy and intelligence suited her for a greater role in a larger arena—mayor of New York, say—than the one she had. She followed American politics closely; she had been known to vote for Democrats. She saw how things should be run, but she had nothing to run but our household. Even there, small minds bugged her; she was smarter than the people who designed the things she had to use all day for the length of her life.

"Look," she said. "Whoever designed this corkscrew never used one. Why would anyone sell it without trying it out?" So she invented a better one. She showed me a drawing of it. The spirit of American enterprise never faded in Mother. If capitalizing and tooling up had been as interesting as theorizing and thinking up, she would have fired up a new factory every week, and chaired several hundred corporations.

"It grieves me," she would say, "it grieves my heart," that the company that made one superior product packaged it poorly, or took the wrong tack in its advertising. She knew, as she held the thing mournfully in her two hands, that she'd never find another. She was right. We children wholly sympathized, and so did Father; what could she do, what could anyone do, about it? She was Samson in chains.[2] She paced.

25

---

2. The Israelite champion against the Philistines to whom he was betrayed by Delilah (see Judges xiv–xvi).

30   She didn't like the taste of stamps so she didn't lick stamps; she licked the corner of the envelope instead. She glued sandpaper to the sides of kitchen drawers, and under kitchen cabinets, so she always had a handy place to strike a match. She designed, and hounded workmen to build against all norms, doubly wide kitchen counters and elevated bathroom sinks. To splint a finger, she stuck it in a lightweight cigar tube. Conversely, to protect a pack of cigarettes, she carried it in a Band-Aid box. She drew plans for an over-the-finger toothbrush for babies, an oven rack that slid up and down, and—the family favorite—Lendalarm. Lendalarm was a beeper you attached to books (or tools) you loaned friends. After ten days, the beeper sounded. Only the rightful owner could silence it.

She repeatedly reminded us of P. T. Barnum's dictum: You could sell anything to anybody if you marketed it right. The adman who thought of making Americans believe they needed underarm deodorant was a visionary. So, too, was the hero who made a success of a new product, Ivory soap. The executives were horrified, Mother told me, that a cake of this stuff floated. Soap wasn't supposed to float. Anyone would be able to tell it was mostly whipped-up air. Then some inspired adman made a leap: Advertise that it floats. Flaunt it. The rest is history.

She respected the rare few who broke through to new ways. "Look," she'd say, "here's an intelligent apron." She called upon us to admire intelligent control knobs and intelligent pan handles, intelligent andirons and picture frames and knife sharpeners. She questioned everything, every pair of scissors, every knitting needle, gardening glove, tape dispenser. Hers was a restless mental vigor that just about ignited the dumb household objects with its force.

Torpid conformity was a kind of sin; it was stupidity itself, the mighty stream against which Mother would never cease to struggle. If you held no minority opinions, or if you failed to risk total ostracism for them daily, the world would be a better place without you.

Always I heard Mother's emotional voice asking Amy and me the same few questions: Is that your own idea? Or somebody else's? "*Giant* is a good movie," I pronounced to the family at dinner. "Oh, really?" Mother warmed to these occasions. She all but rolled up her sleeves. She knew I hadn't seen it. "Is that your considered opinion?"

35   She herself held many unpopular, even fantastic, positions. She was scathingly sarcastic about the McCarthy hearings[3] while they took

3. The televised hearings in 1954 [the army accused Wisconsin Senator Joseph R. McCarthy (1908–57) of improperly seeking preferential treatment for a former colleague then in the service; Senator McCarthy, widely known as a communist-hunter, accused the army of covering up certain espionage action] led to the senator's loss of public favor and contributed to his "condemnation" by the Senate in December 1954.

place, right on our living-room television; she frantically opposed Father's wait-and-see calm. "We don't know enough about it," he said. "I do," she said. "I know all I need to know."

She asserted, against all opposition, that people who lived in trailer parks were not bad but simply poor, and had as much right to settle on beautiful land, such as rural Ligonier, Pennsylvania, as did the oldest of families in the finest of hidden houses. Therefore, the people who owned trailer parks, and sought zoning changes to permit trailer parks, needed our help. Her profound belief that the country-club pool sweeper was a person, and that the department-store saleslady, the bus driver, telephone operator, and housepainter were people, and even in groups the steelworkers who carried pickets and the Christmas shoppers who clogged intersections were people—this was a conviction common enough in democratic Pittsburgh, but not altogether common among our friends' parents, or even, perhaps, among our parents' friends.

Opposition emboldened Mother, and she would take on anybody on any issue—the chairman of the board, at a cocktail party, on the current strike; she would fly at him in a flurry of passion, as a songbird selflessly attacks a big hawk.

"Eisenhower's going to win," I announced after school. She lowered her magazine and looked me in the eyes: "How do you know?" I was doomed. It was fatal to say, "Everyone says so." We all knew well what happened. "Do you consult this Everyone before you make your decisions? What if Everyone decided to round up all the Jews?" Mother knew there was no danger of cowing me. She simply tried to keep us all awake. And in fact it was always clear to Amy and me, and to Molly when she grew old enough to listen, that if our classmates came to cruelty, just as much as if the neighborhood or the nation came to madness, we were expected to take, and would be each separately capable of taking, a stand.

Margaret Mead

HOME AND TRAVEL

For many people moving is one kind of thing and travel is something very different. Travel means going away from home and staying away from home; it is an antidote to the humdrum activities of everyday life, a prelude to a holiday one is entitled to enjoy after months of dullness. Moving means breaking up a home, sadly or joyfully breaking with the

From Mead's memoir, *Blackberry Winter* (1972).

past; a happy venture or a hardship, something to be endured with good or ill grace.

For me, moving and staying at home, traveling and arriving, are all of a piece. The world is full of homes in which I have lived for a day, a month, a year, or much longer. How much I care about a home is not measured by the length of time I have lived there. One night in a room with a leaping fire may mean more to me than many months in a room without a fireplace, a room in which my life has been paced less excitingly.

From the time I can first remember, I knew that we had not always lived where we were living then—in Hammonton, New Jersey, where we had moved so that Mother could work on her doctoral thesis. I knew that I had spent my first summer at a resort called Lavallette, a place I did not visit again until I was seventeen, there to have the only authentic attack of homesickness I have ever had, brought on by the sound of the pounding surf. I knew also that we had lived on St. Marks Square, Philadelphia, because the next winter we lived near St. Marks Square and still knew people who lived there.

Every winter we went to live in or near Philadelphia so that Father would not have to travel too far or stay in the city on the nights that he lectured at the University. From the time I was seven years old, we went somewhere for the summer, too. So we moved four times a year, because for the fall and spring we returned to the house in Hammonton.

5   All the other houses were strange—houses that had to be made our own as quickly as possible so that they no longer would be strange. This did not mean that they were frightening, but only that we had to learn about every nook and corner, for otherwise it was hard to play hide-and-go-seek. As soon as we arrived, I ran ahead to find a room for myself as far away as possible from everyone else, preferably at the top of the house where I would always be warned by footsteps that someone was coming. After that, until we were settled in, I was busy exploring, making my own the new domain. Later, when I was about fourteen, I was in charge of unpacking, getting beds made, food in the icebox, and the lamps filled and lit before nightfall.

The next step was to explore the neighborhood. I had to find out what other children lived nearby and whether there were woods, wild flowers, tangles, or jungles—any hidden spot that could be turned into a miniature primeval forest where life could be quickly shaped to an imaginary world.

In Hammonton we had five whole acres, a good part of which was second-growth bush, studded with blueberries, which the little Italian children who were our neighbors picked and sold back to us. In Lansdowne and Swarthmore there were bits of woodlot. But in Philadelphia there was nothing, only stone walls of different heights on which to walk.

Nothing, except for the winter when we lived at the edge of the park near the zoo.

However far away we moved and however often, we always came home again to Hammonton and the familiar and loved things that were too fragile to take with us—although Mother was very permissive about allowing us to carry along all the objects each of us wanted. In Hammonton there was the same blueberry thicket in which to wander along old paths and make new ones, the same surrey, which we hired from the livery stable, and the same door which was never opened—a second door on the front porch which was used only on one occasion, on the night the neighbors pounded on it to tell us that our chimney had caught fire.

There was the great tree from which a hornets' nest blew down in a storm. I had been dancing in the wind when it blew down and, still dancing, plunged my hands into it. I can still remember the wind but not the stings with which I was said to have been covered. There were the tall evergreen arborvitae that divided the lawn into little squares, where Grandma played games with us until one day she put her hand to her heart and then she did not play running games anymore. And outside the mock-orange hedge we once found faeces, and Mother said, in a tone of disgust close to horror, that they were human faeces.

There was the well with a pump that we used to prime with hot water, until one day my five-year-old brother and a desperado friend a year younger threw everything detachable down the well, and then it was never used again. There was an old dinghy in which we grew flowers until the boys tore it up. And once, when the barn had been reshingled and the old shingles had been piled in the barn for the winter, the two little boys threw all of them out. Grandma said it just showed how two children, each one quite good by himself, could get into mischief. You never could tell, when you put two children together, what the outcome would be. This enlarged my picture of what boys were like.

It was contrapuntal to an engraving in a homemade copper frame that stood on the mantelpiece. This showed a pair of children, a little girl diligently sewing a fine seam and a boy, beautiful and remote, simply sitting and looking out at the world. Long years later, the same picture provided the central image in a bitter little verse of feminine protest that I wrote when Edward Sapir [1] told me I would do better to stay at home and have children than to go off to the South Seas to study adolescent girls:

> Measure your thread and cut it
> To suit your little seam,
> Stitch the garment tightly, tightly,
> And leave no room for dream.

1. A well-known anthropologist and linguistics scholar.

. . .

Head down, be not caught looking
Where the restless wild geese fly.

There were treasures on Mother's dressing table, too—a Wedgwood
pin dish, a little porcelain Mary and her lamb, the pale green, flowered
top of a rose bowl that had broken, and Mother's silver-backed comb
and brush and mirror. All these things held meaning for me. Each
was—and still is—capable of evoking a rush of memories.

Taken altogether, the things that mattered a great deal to me when
I was a child are very few when I compare them to the overloaded
tables and overcrowded shelves through which children today have to
thread their way. Only if they are very fortunate will they be able to
weave together into memories the ill-assorted mass of gadgets, toys,
and easily forgotten objects, objects without a past or a future, and
piles of snapshots that will be replaced by new, brightly colored snapshots next year.

The difficulty, it seems to me, is not—as so many older people claim—
that in the past life was simpler and there were fewer things, and so
people were somehow better, as well as more frugal. It is, rather, that
today's children have to find new ways of anchoring the changing moments of their lives, and they have to try to do this with very little help
from their elders, who grew up in an extraordinarily different world.
How many of the young people who are rebelling against the tyranny
of things, who want to strip their lives down to the contents of a
rucksack, can remember and name the things that lay on their mother's
dressing table or can describe every toy and book they had as a child?

15   It has been found that when desperate, unhappy youngsters are preparing to break away from a disordered, drug-ridden commune in which
they have been living for months, they first gather together in one spot
their few possessions and introduce a semblance of order among them.
The need to define who you are by the place in which you live remains
intact, even when that place is defined by a single object, like the small
blue vase that used to mean home to one of my friends, the daughter
of a widowed trained nurse who continually moved from one place to
another. The Bushmen of the Kalahari Desert often build no walls when
they camp in the desert. They simply hollow out a small space in the
sand. But then they bend a slender sapling into an arch to make a
doorway, an entrance to a dwelling as sacrosanct from invasion as the
walled estates of the wealthy are or as Makati, in Manila, is, where
watchmen guard the rich against the poor.

I realized how few things are needed to make a "home" when I took
my seven-year-old daughter on her first sea voyage. The ship—the *Marine Jumper*, an unrenovated troopship with iron decks—was crowded

with over a thousand students. They were bunked below where the troops had slept, while Cathy and I shared one cabin with six other members of the staff. Cathy climbed into her upper berth, opened the little packages that had been given to her as going-away presents, and arranged them in a circle around her. Then she leaned over the side of the berth and said, "Now I am ready to see the ship."

Home, I learned, can be anywhere you make it. Home is also the place to which you come back again and again. The really poignant parting is the parting that may be forever. It is this sense that every sailing may be a point of no return that haunts the peoples of the Pacific islands. On the very day I arrived in Samoa, people began to ask, "When will you leave?" When I replied, "In a year," they sighed, "Alas, *talofai*"— our love to you—with the sadness of a thousand partings in their voices. Their islands were peopled by voyagers who set off on a short known journey and whose canoes were blown hundreds of miles off course. But even when a fishing canoe goes out there is a chance that it will upset on the dangerous reef and that someone will be drowned. The smallest journey may be forever.

I have seen something similar on the seacoast of Portugal, where every year for four hundred years fishermen set out in their frail boats for the fishing banks across the treacherous Atlantic and no one could tell when—or whether—they would return. Portugal is still a widow's walk. The old women, dressed in black, still seem to be looking out to sea for the men who disappeared into the distance and an unknown fate.

In all my years of field work, each place where I have lived has become home. Each small object I have brought with me, each arrangement on a shelf of tin cans holding beads or salt for trade or crayons for the children to draw with becomes the mark of home. When it is dismantled on the last morning—a morning that is marked by the greed of those who have little and hope for a share of whatever is left behind, as well as by the grief of feeling that someone is leaving forever—on that morning, I weep. I, too, know that this departure, unlike my forays from home as a child, is likely to be forever.

THE READER

1. *What is Mead's implied definition of home?*

2. *In Frost's poem "The Death of the Hired Man," a husband and a wife give two different definitions of home. The husband says: "Home is the place where, when you have to go there, / They have to take you in." The wife replies: "I should have called it / Something you some-how haven't to [i.e., don't have to] deserve." Explain which of these definitions you think comes closer to Mead's definition of home.*

3. *Mead had a long career as an anthropologist studying people of other,*

*more primitive cultures. In this essay, is she looking at her own culture
in ways that are similar to those she might adopt in looking at another
culture? Explain.*

4. *Mead recounts an incident in which she was told it would be better
   if she stayed at home and had children, rather than going to the South
   Seas. Explain in what ways the poem she wrote is a reply.*
5. *Read Thomas' "Memories of Christmas" (p. 1) and White's "Once
   More to the Lake" (p. 55). In each case, explain whether the place
   described helps to "define" the author.*

THE WRITER

1. *Write about an object that has symbolic or nostalgic importance for
   you.*
2. *Describe the floor plan of the first home you can remember living in.
   What incidents do you associate with particular parts of the home?*
3. *Mead speaks of "the need to define who you are by the place in which
   you live." Write an essay explaining the extent to which the place in
   which you live can define who you are. What things can it tell about
   you? What things can't it tell about you?*
4. *Read Didion's "On Going Home" (p. 31). Then write a brief essay
   comparing and contrasting Didion's implied definition of home with
   Mead's.*

N. Scott Momaday
THE WAY TO RAINY MOUNTAIN

A single knoll rises out of the plain in Oklahoma, north and west of
the Wichita Range. For my people, the Kiowas, it is an old landmark,
and they gave it the name Rainy Mountain. The hardest weather in the
world is there. Winter brings blizzards, hot tornadic winds arise in the
spring, and in summer the prairie is an anvil's edge. The grass turns
brittle and brown, and it cracks beneath your feet. There are green belts
along the rivers and creeks, linear groves of hickory and pecan, willow
and witch hazel. At a distance in July or August the steaming foliage
seems almost to writhe in fire. Great green and yellow grasshoppers are
everywhere in the tall grass, popping up like corn to sting the flesh, and
tortoises crawl about on the red earth, going nowhere in the plenty of
time. Loneliness is an aspect of the land. All things in the plain are

From *The Way to Rainy Mountain* (1969).

isolate; there is no confusion of objects in the eye, but *one* hill or *one* tree or *one* man. To look upon that landscape in the early morning, with the sun at your back, is to lose the sense of proportion. Your imagination comes to life, and this, you think, is where Creation was begun.

I returned to Rainy Mountain in July. My grandmother had died in the spring, and I wanted to be at her grave. She had lived to be very old and at last infirm. Her only living daughter was with her when she died, and I was told that in death her face was that of a child.

I like to think of her as a child. When she was born, the Kiowas were living the last great moment of their history. For more than a hundred years they had controlled the open range from the Smoky Hill River to the Red, from the headwaters of the Canadian to the fork of the Arkansas and Cimarron. In alliance with the Comanches, they had ruled the whole of the southern Plains. War was their sacred business, and they were among the finest horsemen the world has ever known. But warfare for the Kiowas was preeminently a matter of disposition rather than of survival, and they never understood the grim, unrelenting advance of the U.S. Cavalry. When at last, divided and ill-provisioned, they were driven onto the Staked Plains in the cold rains of autumn, they fell into panic. In Palo Duro Canyon they abandoned their crucial stores to pillage and had nothing then but their lives. In order to save themselves, they surrendered to the soldiers at Fort Sill and were imprisoned in the old stone corral that now stands as a military museum. My grandmother was spared the humiliation of those high gray walls by eight or ten years, but she must have known from birth the affliction of defeat, the dark brooding of old warriors.

Her name was Aho, and she belonged to the last culture to evolve in North America. Her forebears came down from the high country in western Montana nearly three centuries ago. They were a mountain people, a mysterious tribe of hunters whose language has never been positively classified in any major group. In the late seventeenth century they began a long migration to the south and east. It was a journey toward the dawn, and it led to a golden age. Along the way the Kiowas were befriended by the Crows, who gave them the culture and religion of the Plains. They acquired horses, and their ancient nomadic spirit was suddenly free of the ground. They acquired Tai-me, the sacred Sun Dance doll, from that moment the object and symbol of their worship, and so shared in the divinity of the sun. Not least, they acquired the sense of destiny, therefore courage and pride. When they entered upon the southern Plains they had been transformed. No longer were they slaves to the simple necessity of survival; they were a lordly and dangerous society of fighters and thieves, hunters and priests of the sun. According to their origin myth, they entered the world through a hollow log. From one point of view, their migration was the fruit of an old prophecy, for indeed they emerged from a sunless world.

5　　Although my grandmother lived out her long life in the shadow of Rainy Mountain, the immense landscape of the continental interior lay like memory in her blood. She could tell of the Crows, whom she had never seen, and of the Black Hills, where she had never been. I wanted to see in reality what she had seen more perfectly in the mind's eye, and traveled fifteen hundred miles to begin my pilgrimage.

Yellowstone, it seemed to me, was the top of the world, a region of deep lakes and dark timber, canyons and waterfalls. But, beautiful as it is, one might have the sense of confinement there. The skyline in all directions is close at hand, the high wall of the woods and deep cleavages of shade. There is a perfect freedom in the mountains, but it belongs to the eagle and the elk, the badger and the bear. The Kiowas reckoned their stature by the distance they could see, and they were bent and blind in the wilderness.

Descending eastward, the highland meadows are a stairway to the plain. In July the inland slope of the Rockies is luxuriant with flax and buckwheat, stonecrop and larkspur. The earth unfolds and the limit of the land recedes. Clusters of trees, and animals grazing far in the distance, cause the vision to reach away and wonder to build upon the mind. The sun follows a longer course in the day, and the sky is immense beyond all comparison. The great billowing clouds that sail upon it are the shadows that move upon the grain like water, dividing light. Farther down, in the land of the Crows and Blackfeet, the plain is yellow. Sweet clover takes hold of the hills and bends upon itself to cover and seal the soil. There the Kiowas paused on their way; they had come to the place where they must change their lives. The sun is at home on the plains. Precisely there does it have the certain character of a god. When the Kiowas came to the land of the Crows, they could see the dark lees of the hills at dawn across the Bighorn River, the profusion of light on the grain shelves, the oldest deity ranging after the solstices. Not yet would they veer southward to the caldron of the land that lay below; they must wean their blood from the northern winter and hold the mountains a while longer in their view. They bore Tai-me in procession to the east.

A dark mist lay over the Black Hills, and the land was like iron. At the top of a ridge I caught sight of Devil's Tower upthrust against the gray sky as if in the birth of time the core of the earth had broken through its crust and the motion of the world was begun. There are things in nature that engender an awful quiet in the heart of man; Devil's Tower is one of them. Two centuries ago, because they could not do otherwise, the Kiowas made a legend at the base of the rock. My grandmother said:

> Eight children were there at play, seven sisters and their brother. Suddenly the boy was struck dumb; he trembled and began to run upon his hands and feet. His fingers became claws, and his body was covered with fur. Directly there was a bear where the boy had been. The sisters were terrified; they ran, and the bear after them. They came to the stump of a great tree, and the tree spoke to them. It bade them climb upon it, and as they did so it began to rise into the air. The bear came to kill them, but they were just beyond its reach. It reared against the tree and scored the bark all around with its claws. The seven sisters were borne into the sky, and they became the stars of the Big Dipper.

From that moment, and so long as the legend lives, the Kiowas have kinsmen in the night sky. Whatever they were in the mountains, they could be no more. However tenuous their well-being, however much they had suffered and would suffer again, they had found a way out of the wilderness.

My grandmother had a reverence for the sun, a holy regard that now is all but gone out of mankind. There was a wariness in her, and an ancient awe. She was a Christian in her later years, but she had come a long way about, and she never forgot her birthright. As a child she had been to the Sun Dances; she had taken part in those annual rites, and by them she had learned the restoration of her people in the presence of Tai-me. She was about seven when the last Kiowa Sun Dance was held in 1887 on the Washita River above Rainy Mountain Creek. The buffalo were gone. In order to consummate the ancient sacrifice—to impale the head of a buffalo bull upon the medicine tree—a delegation of old men journeyed into Texas, there to beg and barter for an animal from the Goodnight herd. She was ten when the Kiowas came together for the last time as a living Sun Dance culture. They could find no buffalo; they had to hang an old hide from the sacred tree. Before the dance could begin, a company of soldiers rode out from Fort Sill under orders to disperse the tribe. Forbidden without cause the essential act of their faith, having seen the wild herds slaughtered and left to rot upon the ground, the Kiowas backed away forever from the medicine tree. That was July 20, 1890, at the great bend of the Washita. My grandmother was there. Without bitterness, and for as long as she lived, she bore a vision of deicide.

Now that I can have her only in memory, I see my grandmother in the several postures that were peculiar to her: standing at the wood stove on a winter morning and turning meat in a great iron skillet; sitting at the south window, bent above her beadwork, and afterwards, when her

10

vision failed, looking down for a long time into the fold of her hands; going out upon a cane, very slowly as she did when the weight of age came upon her; praying. I remember her most often at prayer. She made long, rambling prayers out of suffering and hope, having seen many things. I was never sure that I had the right to hear, so exclusive where they of all mere custom and company. The last time I saw her she prayed standing by the side of her bed at night, naked to the waist, the light of a kerosene lamp moving upon her dark skin. Her long, black hair, always drawn and braided in the day, lay upon her shoulders and against her breasts like a shawl. I do not speak Kiowa, and I never understood her prayers, but there was something inherently sad in the sound, some merest hesitation upon the syllables of sorrow. She began in a high and descending pitch, exhausting her breath to silence; then again and again—and always the same intensity of effort, of something that is, and is not, like urgency in the human voice. Transported so in the dancing light among the shadows of her room, she seemed beyond the reach of time. But that was illusion; I think I knew then that I should not see her again.

Houses are like sentinels in the plain, old keepers of the weather watch. There, in a very little while, wood takes on the appearance of great age. All colors wear soon away in the wind and rain, and then the wood is burned gray and the grain appears and the nails turn red with rust. The windowpanes are black and opaque; you imagine there is nothing within, and indeed there are many ghosts, bones given up to the land. They stand here and there against the sky, and you approach them for a longer time than you expect. They belong in the distance; it is their domain.

Once there was a lot of sound in my grandmother's house, a lot of coming and going, feasting and talk. The summers there were full of excitement and reunion. The Kiowas are a summer people; they abide the cold and keep to themselves, but when the season turns and the land becomes warm and vital they cannot hold still; an old love of going returns upon them. The aged visitors who came to my grandmother's house when I was a child were made of lean and leather, and they bore themselves upright. They wore great black hats and bright ample shirts that shook in the wind. They rubbed fat upon their hair and wound their braids with strips of colored cloth. Some of them painted their faces and carried the scars of old and cherished enmities. They were an old council of warlords, come to remind and be reminded of who they were. Their wives and daughters served them well. The women might indulge themselves; gossip was at once the mark and compensation of their servitude. They made loud and elaborate talk among themselves, full of jest and gesture, fright and false alarm. They went abroad in fringed and flowered shawls, bright beadwork and German silver. They were at home in the kitchen, and they prepared meals that were banquets.

There were frequent prayer meetings, and great nocturnal feasts. When I was a child I played with my cousins outside, where the lamplight fell upon the ground and the singing of the old people rose up around us and carried away into the darkness. There were a lot of good things to eat, a lot of laughter and surprise. And afterwards, when the quiet returned, I lay down with my grandmother and could hear the frogs away by the river and feel the motion of the air.

Now there is a funeral silence in the rooms, the endless wake of some final word. The walls have closed in upon my grandmother's house. When I returned to it in mourning, I saw for the first time in my life how small it was. It was late at night, and there was a white moon, nearly full. I sat for a long time on the stone steps by the kitchen door. From there I could see out across the land; I could see the long row of trees by the creek, the low light upon the rolling plains, and the stars of the Big Dipper. Once I looked at the moon and caught sight of a strange thing. A cricket had perched upon the handrail, only a few inches away from me. My line of vision was such that the creature filled the moon like a fossil. It had gone there, I thought, to live and die, for there, of all places, was its small definition made whole and eternal. A warm wind rose up and purled like the longing within me.

The next morning I awoke at dawn and went out on the dirt road to Rainy Mountain. It was already hot, and the grasshoppers began to fill the air. Still, it was early in the morning, and the birds sang out of the shadows. The long yellow grass on the mountain shone in the bright light, and a scissortail hied above the land. There, where it ought to be, at the end of a long and legendary way, was my grandmother's grave. Here and there on the dark stones were ancestral names. Looking back once, I saw the mountain and came away. 15

Gretel Ehrlich

THE SOLACE OF OPEN SPACES

It's May and I've just awakened from a nap, curled against sagebrush the way my dog taught me to sleep—sheltered from wind. A front is pulling the huge sky over me, and from the dark a hailstone has hit me on the head. I'm trailing a band of two thousand sheep across a stretch

From *The Solace of Open Spaces* (1985).

of Wyoming badlands, a fifty-mile trip that takes five days because sheep shade up in hot sun and won't budge until it's cool. Bunched together now, and excited into a run by the storm, they drift across dry land, tumbling into draws[1] like water and surge out again onto the rugged, choppy plateaus that are the building blocks of this state.

The name Wyoming comes from an Indian word meaning "at the great plains," but the plains are really valleys, great arid valleys, sixteen hundred square miles, with the horizon bending up on all sides into mountain ranges. This gives the vastness a sheltering look.

Winter lasts six months here. Prevailing winds spill snowdrifts to the east, and new storms from the northwest replenish them. This white bulk is sometimes dizzying, even nauseating, to look at. At twenty, thirty, and forty degrees below zero, not only does your car not work, but neither do your mind and body. The landscape hardens into a dungeon of space. During the winter, while I was riding to find a new calf, my jeans froze to the saddle, and in the silence that such cold creates I felt like the first person on earth, or the last.

Today the sun is out—only a few clouds billowing. In the east, where the sheep have started off without me, the benchland tilts up in a series of eroded red-earthed mesas, planed flat on top by a million years of water; behind them, a bold line of muscular scarps rears up ten thousand feet to become the Big Horn Mountains. A tidal pattern is engraved into the ground, as if left by the sea that once covered this state. Canyons curve down like galaxies to meet the oncoming rush of flat land.

5   To live and work in this kind of open country, with its hundred-mile views, is to lose the distinction between background and foreground. When I asked an older ranch hand to describe Wyoming's openness, he said, "It's all a bunch of nothing—wind and rattlesnakes—and so much of it you can't tell where you're going or where you've been and it don't make much difference." John, a sheepman I know, is tall and handsome and has an explosive temperament. He has a perfect intuition about people and sheep. They call him "Highpockets," because he's so long-legged; his graceful stride matches the distances he has to cover. He says, "Open space hasn't affected me at all. It's all the people moving in on it." The huge ranch he was born on takes up much of one county and spreads into another state; to put 100,000 miles on his pickup in three years and never leave home is not unusual. A friend of mine has an aunt who ranched on Powder River and didn't go off her place for eleven years. When her husband died, she quickly moved to town, bought a car, and drove around the States to see what she'd been missing.

Most people tell me they've simply driven through Wyoming, as if

1. A land basin that water drains into or through.

there were nothing to stop for. Or else they've skied in Jackson Hole, a place Wyomingites acknowledge uncomfortably because its green beauty and chic affluence are mismatched with the rest of the state. Most of Wyoming has a "lean-to" look. Instead of big, roomy barns and Victorian houses, there are dugouts, low sheds, log cabins, sheep camps, and fence lines that look like driftwood blown haphazardly into place. People here still feel pride because they live in such a harsh place, part of the glamorous cowboy past, and they are determined not to be the victims of a mining-dominated future.

Most characteristic of the state's landscape is what a developer euphemistically describes as "indigenous growth right up to your front door"—a reference to waterless stands of salt sage, snakes, jack rabbits, deerflies, red dust, a brief respite of wildflowers, dry washes, and no trees. In the Great Plains the vistas look like music, like Kyries[2] of grass, but Wyoming seems to be the doing of a mad architect—tumbled and twisted, ribboned with faded, deathbed colors, thrust up and pulled down as if the place had been startled out of a deep sleep and thrown into a pure light.

I came here four years ago. I had not planned to stay, but I couldn't make myself leave. John, the sheepman, put me to work immediately. It was spring, and shearing time. For fourteen days of fourteen hours each, we moved thousands of sheep through sorting corrals to be sheared, branded, and deloused. I suspect that my original motive for coming here was to "lose myself" in new and unpopulated territory. Instead of producing the numbness I thought I wanted, life on the sheep ranch woke me up. The vitality of the people I was working with flushed out what had become a hallucinatory rawness inside me. I threw away my clothes and bought new ones; I cut my hair. The arid country was a clean slate. Its absolute indifference steadied me.

Sagebrush covers 58,000 square miles of Wyoming. The biggest city has a population of fifty thousand, and there are only five settlements that could be called cities in the whole state. The rest are towns, scattered across the expanse with as much as sixty miles between them, their populations two thousand, fifty, or ten. They are fugitive-looking, perched on a barren, windblown bench, or tagged onto a river or a railroad, or laid out straight in a farming valley with implement stores and a block-long Mormon church. In the eastern part of the state, which slides down into the Great Plains, the new mining settlements are boomtowns, trailer cities, metal knots on flat land.

Despite the desolate look, there's a coziness to living in this state.   10

---

2. A musical setting of the Kyrie eleison (Greek, meaning "Lord have mercy"), as the first movement of a Mass.

There are so few people (only 470,000) that ranchers who buy and sell cattle know one another statewide; the kids who choose to go to college usually go to the state's one university, in Laramie; hired hands work their way around Wyoming in a lifetime of hirings and firings. And despite the physical separation, people stay in touch, often driving two or three hours to another ranch for dinner.

Seventy-five years ago, when travel was by buckboard or horseback, cowboys who were temporarily out of work rode the grub line—drifting from ranch to ranch, mending fences or milking cows, and receiving in exchange a bed and meals. Gossip and messages traveled this slow circuit with them, creating an intimacy between ranchers who were three and four weeks' ride apart. One old-time couple I know, whose turn-of-the-century homestead was used by an outlaw gang as a relay station for stolen horses, recall that if you were traveling, desperado or not, any lighted ranch house was a welcome sign. Even now, for someone who lives in a remote spot, arriving at a ranch or coming to town for supplies is cause for celebration. To emerge from isolation can be disorienting. Everything looks bright, new, vivid. After I had been herding sheep for only three days, the sound of the camp tender's pickup flustered me. Longing for human company, I felt a foolish grin take over my face; yet I had to resist an urgent temptation to run and hide.

Things happen suddenly in Wyoming, the change of seasons and weather; for people, the violent swings in and out of isolation. But good-naturedness is concomitant with severity. Friendliness is a tradition. Strangers passing on the road wave hello. A common sight is two pickups stopped side by side far out on a range, on a dirt track winding through the sage. The drivers will share a cigarette, uncap their thermos bottles, and pass a battered cup, steaming with coffee, between windows. These meetings summon up the details of several generations, because, in Wyoming, private histories are largely public knowledge.

Because ranch work is a physical and, these days, economic strain, being "at home on the range" is a matter of vigor, self-reliance, and common sense. A person's life is not a series of dramatic events for which he or she is applauded or exiled but a slow accumulation of days, seasons, years, fleshed out by the generational weight of one's family and anchored by a land-bound sense of place.

In most parts of Wyoming, the human population is visibly outnumbered by the animal. Not far from my town of fifty, I rode into a narrow valley and startled a herd of two hundred elk. Eagles look like small people as they eat car-killed deer by the road. Antelope, moving in small, graceful bands, travel at sixty miles an hour, their mouths open as if drinking in the space.

The solitude in which westerners live makes them quiet. They telegraph thoughts and feelings by the way they tilt their heads and listen; pulling their Stetsons into a steep dive over their eyes, or pigeon-toeing one boot over the other, they lean against a fence with a fat wedge of Copenhagen beneath their lower lips and take in the whole scene. These detached looks of quiet amusement are sometimes cynical, but they can also come from a dry-eyed humility as lucid as the air is clear.

Conversation goes on in what sounds like a private code; a few phrases simply a complex of meanings. Asking directions, you get a curious list of details. While trailing sheep I was told to "ride up to that kinda upturned rock, follow the pink wash, turn left at the dump, and then you'll see the water hole." One friend told his wife on roundup to "turn at the salt lick and the dead cow," which turned out to be a scattering of bones and no salt lick at all.

Sentence structure is shortened to the skin and bones of a thought. Descriptive words are dropped, even verbs; a cowboy looking over a corral full of horses will say to a wrangler, "Which one needs rode?" People hold back their thoughts in what seems to be a dumbfounded silence, then erupt with an excoriating perceptive remark. Language, so compressed, becomes metaphorical. A rancher ended a relationship with one remark: "You're a bad check," meaning bouncing in and out was intolerable, and even coming back would be no good.

What's behind this laconic style is shyness. There is no vocabulary for the subject of feelings. It's not a hangdog shyness, or anything coy— always there's a robust spirit in evidence behind the restraint, as if the earth-dredging wind that pulls across Wyoming had carried its people's voices away but everything else in them had shouldered confidently into the breeze.

I've spent hours riding to sheep camp at dawn in a pickup when nothing was said; eaten meals in the cookhouse when the only words spoken were a mumbled "Thank you, ma'am" at the end of dinner. The silence is profound. Instead of talking, we seem to share one eye. Keenly observed, the world is transformed. The landscape is engorged with detail, every movement on it chillingly sharp. The air between people is charged. Days unfold, bathed in their own music. Nights become hallucinatory; dreams, prescient.

Spring weather is capricious and mean. It snows, then blisters with heat. There have been tornadoes. They lay their elephant trunks out in the sage until they find houses, then slurp everything up and leave. I've noticed that melting snowbanks hiss and rot, viperous, then drip into calm pools where ducklings hatch and livestock, being trailed to summer range, drink. With the ice cover gone, rivers churn a milkshake brown, taking culverts and small bridges with them. Water in such an arid place (the average annual rainfall where I live is less than eight inches) is like blood. It festoons drab land with green veins; a line of cottonwoods following a stream; a strip of alfalfa; and, on ditch banks, wild asparagus growing.

I've moved to a small cattle ranch owned by friends. It's at the foot of the Big Horn Mountains. A few weeks ago, I helped them deliver a calf who was stuck halfway out of his mother's body. By the time he was freed, we could see a heartbeat, but he was straining against a swollen tongue for air. Mary and I held him upside down by his back feet, while Stan, on his hands and knees in the blood, gave the calf mouth-to-mouth resuscitation. I have a vague memory of being pneumonia-choked as a child, my mother giving me her air, which may account for my romance with this wind-swept state.

If anything is endemic to Wyoming, it is wind. This big room of space is swept out daily, leaving a bone yard of fossils, agates, and carcasses in every stage of decay. Though it was water that initially shaped the state, wind is the meticulous gardener, raising dust and pruning the sage.

I try to imagine a world in which I could ride my horse across uncharted land. There is no wilderness left; wildness, yes, but true wilderness has been gone on this continent since the time of Lewis and Clark's overland journey.

Two hundred years ago, the Crow, Shoshone, Arapaho, Cheyenne, and Sioux roamed the intermountain West, orchestrating their movements according to hunger, season, and warfare. Once they acquired horses, they traversed the spines of all the Big Wyoming ranges—the Absarokas, the Wind Rivers, the Tetons, the Big Horns—and wintered on the unprotected plains that fan out from them. Space was life. The world was their home.

What was life-giving to Native Americans was often nightmarish to sodbusters who had arrived encumbered with families and ethnic pasts to be transplanted in nearly uninhabitable land. The great distances, the shortage of water and trees, and the loneliness created unexpected hardships for them. In her book *O Pioneers!*, Willa Cather gives a settler's version of the bleak landscape:

> The little town behind them had vanished as if it had never been, had fallen behind the swell of the prairie, and the stern frozen country received them into its bosom. The homesteads were few and far apart; here and there a windmill gaunt against the sky, a sod house crouching in a hollow.

The emptiness of the West was for others a geography of possibility. Men and women who amassed great chunks of land and struggled to preserve unfenced empires were, despite their self-serving motives, unwitting geographers. They understood the lay of the land. But by the 1850s the Oregon and Mormon trails sported bumper-to-bumper traffic.

Wealthy landowners, many of them aristocratic absentee landlords, known as remittance men because they were paid to come West and get out of their families' hair, overstocked the range with more than a million head of cattle. By 1885 the feed and water were desperately short, and the winter of 1886 laid out the gaunt bodies of dead animals so closely together that when the thaw came, one rancher from Kaycee claimed to have walked on cowhide all the way to Crazy Woman Creek, twenty miles away.

Territorial Wyoming was a boy's world. The land was generous with everything but water. At first there was room enough, food enough, for everyone. And, as with all beginnings, an expansive mood set in. The young cowboys, drifters, shopkeepers, schoolteachers, were heroic, lawless, generous, rowdy, and tenacious. The individualism and optimism generated during those times have endured.

John Tisdale rode north with the trail herds from Texas. He was a college-educated man with enough money to buy a small outfit near the Powder River. While driving home from the town of Buffalo with a buckboard full of Christmas toys for his family and a winter's supply of food, he was shot in the back by an agent of the cattle barons who resented the encroachment of small-time stockmen like him. The wealthy cattlemen tried to control all the public grazing land by restricting membership in the Wyoming Stock Growers Association, as if it were a country club. They ostracized from roundups and brandings cowboys and ranchers who were not members, then denounced them as rustlers. Tisdale's death, the second such cold-blooded murder, kicked off the Johnson County cattle war, which was no simple good-guy-bad-guy shoot-out but a complicated class struggle between landed gentry and less affluent settlers—a shocking reminder that the West was not an egalitarian sanctuary after all.

Fencing ultimately enforced boundaries, but barbed wire abrogated space. It was stretched across the beautiful valleys, into the mountains, over desert badlands, through buffalo grass. The "anything is possible" fever—the lure of any new place—was constricted. The integrity of the land as a geographical body, and the freedom to ride anywhere on it, were lost.

I punched cows[3] with a young man named Martin, who is the great-grandson of John Tisdale. His inheritance is not the open land that Tisdale knew and prematurely lost but a rage against restraint.

Wyoming tips down as you head northeast; the highest ground—the Laramie Plains—is on the Colorado border. Up where I live, the Big Horn River leaks into difficult, arid terrain. In the basin where it's

30

3. Herded cattle.

dammed, sandhill cranes gather and, with delicate legwork, slice through the stilled water. I was driving by with a rancher one morning when he commented that cranes are "old-fashioned." When I asked why, he said, "Because they mate for life." Then he looked at me with a twinkle in his eyes, as if to say he really did believe in such things but also understood why we break our own rules.

In all this open space, values crystalize quickly. People are strong on scruples but tenderhearted about quirky behavior. A friend and I found one ranch hand, who's "not quite right in the head," sitting in front of the badly decayed carcass of a cow, shaking his finger and saying, "Now, I don't want you to do this ever again!" When I asked what was wrong with him, I was told, "He's goofier than hell, just like the rest of us." Perhaps because the West is historically new, conventional morality is still felt to be less important than rock-bottom truths. Though there's always a lot of teasing and sparring, people are blunt with one another, sometimes even cruel, believing honesty is stronger medicine than sympathy, which may console but often conceals.

The formality that goes hand in hand with the rowdiness is known as the Western Code. It's a list of practical do's and don'ts, faithfully observed. A friend, Cliff, who runs a trapline in the winter, cut off half his foot while chopping a hole in the ice. Alone, he dragged himself to his pickup and headed for town, stopping to open the ranch gate as he left, and getting out to close it again, thus losing, in his observance of rules, precious time and blood. Later, he commented, "How would it look, them having to come to the hospital to tell me their cows had gotten out?"

Accustomed to emergencies, my friends doctor each other from the vet's bag with relish. When one old-timer suffered a heart attack in hunting camp, his partner quickly stirred up a brew of red horse liniment and hot water and made the half-conscious victim drink it, then tied him onto a horse and led him twenty miles to town. He regained consciousness and lived.

35   The roominess of the state has affected political attitudes as well. Ranchers keep up with world politics and the convulsions of the economy but are basically isolationists. Being used to running their own small empires of land and livestock, they're suspicious of big government. It's a "don't fence me in" holdover from a century ago. They still want the elbow room their grandfathers had, so they're strongly conservative, but with a populist twist.

Summer is the season when we get our "cowboy tans"—on the lower parts of our faces and on three fourths of our arms. Excessive heat, in the nineties and higher, sends us outside with the mosquitoes. In winter we're tucked inside our houses, and the white wasteland outside appears to be expanding, but in summer all the greenery abridges space. Summer is a go-ahead season. Every living thing is off the block and in the race: battalions of bugs in flight and biting; bats swinging around my log cabin as if the bases were loaded and someone had hit a home run. Some of summer's high-speed growth is ominous: larkspur, death camas, and green greasewood can kill sheep—an ironic idea, dying in this desert from eating what is too verdant. With sixteen hours of daylight, farmers and ranchers irrigate feverishly. There are first, second, and third cuttings of hay, some crews averaging only four hours of sleep a night for weeks. And, like the cowboys who in summer ride the night rodeo circuit, nighthawks make daredevil dives at dusk with an eerie whirring sound like a plane going down on the shimmering horizon.

In the town where I live, they've had to board up the dance-hall windows because there have been so many fights. There's so little to do except work that people wind up in a state of idle agitation that becomes fatalistic, as if there were nothing to be done about all this untapped energy. So the dark side to the grandeur of these spaces is the small-mindedness that seals people in. Men become hermits; women go mad. Cabin fever explodes into suicides, or into grudges and lifelong family feuds. Two sisters in my area inherited a ranch but found they couldn't get along. They fenced the place in half. When one's cows got out and mixed with the other's, the women went at each other with shovels. They ended up in the same hospital room but never spoke a word to each other for the rest of their lives.

After the brief lushness of summer, the sun moves south. The range grass is brown. Livestock is trailed back down from the mountains. Water holes begin to frost over at night. Last fall Martin asked me to accompany him on a pack trip. With five horses, we followed a river into the mountains behind the tiny Wyoming town of Meeteetse. Groves of aspen, red and orange, gave off a light that made us look toasted. Our hunting camp was so high that clouds skidded across our foreheads, then slowed to sail out across the warm valleys. Except for a bull moose who wandered into our camp and mistook our black gelding for a rival, we shot at nothing.

One of our evening entertainments was to watch the night sky. My dog, a dingo bred to herd sheep, also came on the trip. He is so used to the silence and empty skies that when an airplane flies over he always looks up and eyes the distant intruder quizzically. The sky, lately, seems to be much more crowded than it used to be. Satellites make their silent passes in the dark with great regularity. We counted eighteen in one hour's viewing. How odd to think that while they circumnavigated the planet, Martin and I had moved only six miles into our local wilderness and had seen no other human for the two weeks we stayed there.

40   At night, by moonlight, the land is whittled to slivers—a ridge, a river, a strip of grassland stretching to the mountains, then the huge sky. One morning a full moon was setting in the west just as the sun was rising. I felt precariously balanced between the two as I loped across a meadow. For a moment, I could believe that the stars, which were still visible, work like cooper's bands, holding together everything above Wyoming.

Space has a spiritual equivalent and can heal what is divided and burdensome in us. My grandchildren will probably use space shuttles for a honeymoon trip or to recover from heart attacks, but closer to home we might also learn how to carry space inside ourselves in the effortless way we carry our skins. Space represents sanity, not a life purified, dull, or "spaced out" but one that might accommodate intelligently any idea or situation.

From the clayey soil of northern Wyoming is mined bentonite, which is used as a filler in candy, gum, and lipstick. We Americans are great on fillers, as if what we have, what we are, is not enough. We have a cultural tendency toward denial, but, being affluent, we strangle ourselves with what we can buy. We have only to look at the houses we build to see how we build *against* space, the way we drink against pain and loneliness. We fill up space as if it were a pie shell, with things whose opacity further obstructs our ability to see what is already there.

Human Nature

Jerome S. Bruner

FREUD AND THE IMAGE OF MAN

By the dawn of the sixth century before Christ, the Greek physicist-philosophers had formulated a bold conception of the physical world as a unitary material phenomenon. The Ionians had set forth a conception of matter as fundamental substance, transformation of which accounted for the myriad forms and substances of the physical world. Anaximander was subtle enough to recognize that matter must be viewed as a generalized substance, free of any particular sensuous properties. Air, iron, water or bone were only elaborated forms, derived from a more general stuff. Since that time, the phenomena of the physical world have been conceived as continuous and monistic, as governed by the common laws of matter. The view was a bold one, bold in the sense of running counter to the immediate testimony of the senses. It has served as an axiomatic basis of physics for more than two millennia. The bold view eventually became the obvious view, and it gave shape to our common understanding of the physical world. Even the alchemists rested their case upon this doctrine of material continuity and, indeed, had they known about neutron bombardment, they might even have hit upon the proper philosopher's stone.

The good fortune of the physicist—and these matters are always relative, for the material monism of physics may have impeded nineteenth-century thinking and delayed insights into the nature of complementarity in modern physical theory—this early good fortune or happy insight has no counterpart in the sciences of man. Lawful continuity between man and the animal kingdom, between dreams and unreason on one side and waking rationality on the other, between madness and sanity, between consciousness and unconsciousness, between the mind of the child and the adult mind, between primitive and civilized man—each of these has been a cherished discontinuity pre-

First published in the *Partisan Review* (Vol. 23, No. 3, 1956).

served in doctrinal canons. There were voices in each generation, to be sure, urging the exploration of continuities. Anaximander had a passing good approximation to a theory of evolution based on natural selection; Cornelius Agrippa offered a plausible theory of the continuity of mental health and disease in terms of bottled-up sexuality. But Anaximander did not prevail against Greek conceptions of man's creation nor did Cornelius Agrippa against the demonopathy of the *Malleus Maleficarum.* [1] Neither in establishing the continuity between the varied states of man nor in pursuing the continuity between man and animal was there conspicuous success until the nineteenth century.

I need not insist upon the social, ethical, and political significance of an age's image of man, for it is patent that the view one takes of man affects profoundly one's standard of dignity and the humanly possible. And it is in the light of such a standard that we establish our laws, set our aspirations for learning, and judge the fitness of men's acts. Those who govern, then, must perforce be jealous guardians of man's ideas about man, for the structure of government rests upon an uneasy consensus about human nature and human wants. Since the idea of man is of the order of *res publica,* [2] it is an idea not subject to change without public debate. Nor is it simply a matter of public concern. For man as individual has a deep and emotional investment in his image of himself. If we have learned anything in the last half-century of psychology, it is that man has powerful and exquisite capacities for defending himself against violation of his cherished self-image. This is not to say that Western man has not persistently asked: "What is man that thou art mindful of him?" It is only that the question, when pressed, brings us to the edge of anxiety where inquiry is no longer free.

Two figures stand out massively as the architects of our present-day conception of man: Darwin and Freud. Freud's was the more daring, the more revolutionary, and in a deep sense, the more poetic insight. But Freud is inconceivable without Darwin. It is both timely and perhaps historically just to center our inquiry on Freud's contribution to the modern image of man. Darwin I shall treat as a necessary condition for Freud and for his success, recognizing, of course, that this is a form of psychological license. Not only is it the centenary of Freud's birth; it is also a year in which the current of popular thought expressed in commemoration of the date quickens one's awareness of Freud's impact on our times.

5   Rear-guard fundamentalism did not require a Darwin to slay it in an age of technology. He helped, but this contribution was trivial in comparison with another. What Darwin had done was to propose a set of

---

1. *The Hammer for Evil Doers,* a notorious medieval book about demons and witch-   craft.

2. The state.

principles unified around the conception that all organic species had their origins and took their form from a common set of circumstances— the requirements of biological survival. All living creatures were on a common footing. When the post-Darwin era of exaggeration had passed and religious literalism had abated into a new nominalism, what remained was a broad, orderly, and unitary conception of organic nature, a vast continuity from the monocellular protozoans to man. Biology had at last found its unifying principle in the doctrine of evolution. Man was not unique but the inheritor of an organic legacy.

As the summit of an evolutionary process, man could still view himself with smug satisfaction, indeed proclaim that God or Nature had shown a persistent wisdom in its effort to produce a final, perfect product. It remained for Freud to present the image of man as the unfinished product of nature: struggling against unreason, impelled by driving inner vicissitudes and urges that had to be contained if man were to live in society, host alike to seeds of madness and majesty, never fully free from an infancy anything but innocent. What Freud was proposing was that man at his best and man at his worst is subject to a common set of explanations: that good and evil grow from a common process.

Freud was strangely yet appropriately fitted for his role as architect of a new conception of man. We must pause to examine his qualifications, for the image of man that he created was in no small measure founded on his painfully achieved image of himself and of his times. We are concerned not so much with his psychodynamics, as with the intellectual traditions he embodies. A child of his century's materialism, he was wedded to the determinism and the classical physicalism of nineteenth-century physiology so boldly represented by Helmholtz. Indeed, the young Freud's devotion to the exploration of anatomical structures was a measure of the strength of this inheritance. But at the same time, as both Lionel Trilling and W. H. Auden have recognized with much sensitivity, there was a deep current of romanticism in Freud—a sense of the role of impulse, of the drama of life, of the power of symbolism, of ways of knowing that were more poetic than rational in spirit, of the poet's cultural alienation. It was perhaps this romantic's sense of drama that led to his gullibility about parental seduction and to his generous susceptibility to the fallacy of the dramatic instance.

Freud also embodies two traditions almost as antithetical as romanticism and nineteenth-century scientism. He was profoundly a Jew, not in a doctrinal sense but in his conception of morality, in his love of the skeptical play of reason, in his distrust of illusion, in the form of his prophetic talent, even in his conception of mature eroticism. His prophetic talent was antithetic to a Utopianism either of innocence or of social control. Nor did it lead to a counsel of renunciation. Free oneself of illusion, of neurotic infantilism, and "the soft voice of intellect" would prevail. Wisdom for Freud was neither doctrine nor formula, but the achievement of maturity. The patient who is cured is the one who is now free enough of neurosis to decide intelligently about his own destiny. As for his conception of mature love, it has always seemed to me that its blend of tenderness and sensuality combined the uxorious imagery of the Chassidic tradition[3] and the sensual quality of the Song of Songs. And might it not have been Freud rather than a commentator of the Haftorahs[4] who said, "In children, it was taught, God gives humanity a chance to make good its mistakes." For the mordern trend of permissiveness toward children is surely a feature of the Freudian legacy.

But for all the Hebraic quality, Freud is also in the classical tradition—combining the Stoics and the great Greek dramatists. For Freud as for the Stoics, there is no possibility of man disobeying the laws of nature. And yet, it is in this lawfulness that for him the human drama inheres. His love for Greek drama and his use of it in his formulation are patent. The sense of the human tragedy, the inevitable working out of the human plight—these are the hallmarks of Freud's case histories. When Freud, the tragic dramatist, becomes a therapist, it is not to intervene as a directive authority. The therapist enters the drama of the patient's life, makes possible a play within a play, the transference, and when the patient has "worked through" and understood the drama, he has achieved the wisdom necessary for freedom. Again, like the Stoics, it is in the recognition of one's own nature and in the acceptance of the laws that govern it that the good life is to be found.

10   Freud's contribution lies in the continuities of which he made us aware. The first of these is the continuity of organic lawfulness. Accident in human affairs was no more to be brooked as "explanation" than accident in nature. The basis for accepting such an "obvious" proposition had, of course, been well prepared by a burgeoning nineteenth-century scientific naturalism. It remained for Freud to extend naturalistic explanation to the heart of human affairs. The *Psychopathology of Everyday Life* is not one of Freud's deeper works, but "the Freudian slip" has contributed more to the common acceptance of lawfulness in human behavior than perhaps any of the more rigorous and academic formulations from Wundt to the present day. The forgotten lunch engagement, the slip of the tongue, the barked shin could no longer be dismissed as accident. Why Freud should have succeeded where the novelists, philosophers, and academic psychologists had failed we will consider in a moment.

3. Or Hasidic; the reference is to a Jewish sect devoted to mystical rather than secular study.

4. Writings of the Old Testament Prophets.

Freud's extension of Darwinian doctrine beyond Haeckel's theorem that ontogeny recapitulates phylogeny[5] is another contribution to continuity. It is the conception that in the human mind, the primitive, infantile, and archaic exist side-by-side with the civilized and evolved.

> Where animals are concerned we hold the view that the most highly developed have arisen from the lowest. . . . In the realm of mind, on the other hand, the primitive type is so commonly preserved alongside the transformations which have developed out of it that it is superfluous to give instances in proof of it. When this happens, it is usually the result of a bifurcation in development. One quantitative part of an attitude or an impulse has survived unchanged while another has undergone further development. This brings us very close to the more general problem of conservation in the mind. . . . Since the time when we recognized the error of supposing that ordinary forgetting signified destruction or annihilation of the memory-trace, we have been inclined to the opposite view that nothing once formed in the mind could ever perish, that everything survives in some way or other, and is capable under certain conditions of being brought to light again . . . (Freud, *Civilization and Its Discontents*, pp. 14–15).

What has now come to be common sense is that in everyman there is the potentiality for criminality, and that these are neither accidents nor visitations of degeneracy, but products of a delicate balance of forces that, under different circumstances, might have produced normality or even saintliness. Good and evil, in short, grow from a common root.

Freud's genius was in his resolution of polarities. The distinction of child and adult was one such. It did not suffice to reiterate that the child was father to the man. The theory of infantile sexuality and the stages of psychosexual development were an effort to fill the gap, the latter clumsy, the former elegant. Though the alleged progression of sexual expression from the oral, to the anal, to the phallic, and finally to the genital has not found a secure place either in common sense or in general psychology, the developmental continuity of sexuality has been recognized by both. Common sense honors the continuity in the baby-books and in the permissiveness with which young parents of today resolve their doubts. And the research of Beach and others has shown the profound effects of infantile experience on adult sexual behavior—even in lower organisms.

If today people are reluctant to report their dreams with the innocence once attached to such recitals, it is again because Freud brought into common question the discontinuity between the rational purposefulness of waking life and the seemingly irrational purposelessness of

5. That is, the evolution of the fetus into an independent organism parallels the evolutionary development of that species.

fantasy and dream. While the crude symbolism of Freud's early efforts at dream interpretation has come increasingly to be abandoned—that telephone poles and tunnels have an invariant sexual reference—the conception of the dream as representing disguised wishes and fears has become common coin. And Freud's recognition of deep unconscious processes in the creative act, let it also be said, has gone far toward enriching our understanding of the kinship between the artist, the humanist, and the man of science.

Finally, it is our heritage from Freud that the all-or-none distinction between mental illness and mental health has been replaced by a more humane conception of the continuity of these states. The view that neurosis is a severe reaction to human trouble is as revolutionary in its implications for social practice as it is daring in formulation. The "bad seed" theories, the nosologies of the nineteenth century, the demonologies and doctrines of divine punishment—none of these provided a basis for compassion toward human suffering comparable to that of our time.

One may argue, at last, that Freud's sense of the continuity of human conditions, of the likeness of the human plight, has made possible a deeper sense of the brotherhood of man. It has in any case tempered the spirit of punitiveness toward what once we took as evil and what we now see as sick. We have not yet resolved the dilemma posed by these two ways of viewing. Its resolution is one of the great moral challenges of our age.

Why, after such initial resistance, were Freud's views so phenomenally successful in transforming common conceptions of man?

One reason we have already considered: the readiness of the Western world to accept a naturalistic explanation of organic phenomena and, concurrently, to be readier for such explanation in the mental sphere. There had been at least four centuries of uninterrupted scientific progress, recently capped by a theory of evolution that brought man into continuity with the rest of the animal kingdom. The rise of naturalism as a way of understanding nature and man witnessed a corresponding decline in the explanatory aspirations of religion. By the close of the nineteenth century, religion, to use Morton White's phrase, "too often agreed to accept the role of a non-scientific spiritual grab-bag, or an ideological know-nothing." The elucidation of the human plight had been abandoned by religion and not yet adopted by science.

It was the inspired imagery, the proto-theory of Freud that was to fill the gap. Its success in transforming the common conception of man was not simply its recourse to the "cause-and-effect" discourse of science. Rather it is Freud's imagery, I think, that provides the clue to this ideological power. It is an imagery of necessity, one that combines the dramatic, the tragic, and the scientific views of necessity. It is here that

Freud's intellectual heritage matters so deeply. Freud's is a theory or a proto-theory peopled with actors. The characters are from life: the blind, energic, pleasure-seeking id; the priggish and punitive super-ego; the ego, battling for its being by diverting the energy of the others to its own use. The drama has an economy and a terseness. The ego develops canny mechanisms for dealing with the threat of id impulses: denial, projection,[6] and the rest. Balances are struck between the actors, and in the balance is character and neurosis. Freud was using the dramatic technique of decomposition, the play whose actors are parts of a single life. It is a technique that he himself had recognized in fantasies and dreams, one he honored in "The Poet and the Daydream."

The imagery of the theory, moreover, has an immediate resonance with the dialectic of experience. True, it is not the stuff of superficial conscious experience. But it fits the human plight, its conflictedness, its private torment, its impulsiveness, its secret and frightening urges, its tragic quality.

Concerning its scientific imagery, it is marked by the necessity of the classical mechanics. At times the imagery is hydraulic: suppress this stream of impulses, and perforce it breaks out in a displacement elsewhere. The system is a closed and mechanical one. At times it is electrical, as when cathexes are formed and withdrawn like electrical charges. The way of thought fitted well the common-sense physics of its age.

Finally, the image of man presented was thoroughly secular; its ideal type was the mature man free of infantile neuroticism, capable of finding his own way. This freedom from both Utopianism and asceticism has earned Freud the contempt of ideological totalitarians of the Right and the Left. But the image has found a ready home in the rising, liberal intellectual middle class. For them, the Freudian ideal type has become a rallying point in the struggle against spiritual regimentation.

I have said virtually nothing about Freud's equation of sexuality and impulse. It was surely and still is a stimulus to resistance. But to say that Freud's success lay in forcing a reluctant Victorian world to accept the importance of sexuality is as empty as hailing Darwin for his victory over fundamentalism. Each had a far more profound effect.

Can Freud's contribution to the common understanding of man in the twentieth century be likened to the impact of such great physical and biological theories as Newtonian physics and Darwin's conception of evolution? The question is an empty one. Freud's mode of thought is not a theory in the conventional sense, it is a metaphor, an analogy, a way of conceiving man, a drama. I would propose that Anaximander is the proper parallel: his view of the connectedness of physical nature

20

---

6. The attribution to others of one's own feelings.

was also an analogy—and a powerful one. Freud is the ground from which theory will grow, and he has prepared the twentieth century to nurture the growth. But far more important, he has provided an image of man that has made him comprehensible without at the same time making him contemptible.

Benjamin Franklin

THE CONVENIENCE OF BEING "REASONABLE"

I believe I have omitted mentioning that, in my first voyage from Boston, being becalmed off Block Island, our people set about catching cod, and hauled up a great many. Hitherto I had stuck to my resolution of not eating animal food, and on this occasion I considered, with my master Tryon,[1] the taking every fish as a kind of unprovoked murder, since none of them had, or ever could do us any injury that might justify the slaughter. All this seemed very reasonable. But I had formerly been a great lover of fish, and, when this came hot out of the frying-pan, it smelled admirably well. I balanced some time between principle and inclination, till I recollected that, when the fish were opened, I saw smaller fish taken out of their stomachs; then thought I, "if you eat one another, I don't see why we mayn't eat you." So I dined upon cod very heartily, and continued to eat with other people, returning only now and then occasionally to a vegetable diet. So convenient a thing it is to be a *reasonable creature*, since it enables one to find or make a reason for everything one has a mind to do.

From the first part of *The Autobiography* (1791), written in the summer of 1771.

1. "When about 16 years of age, I happened to meet with a book written by one [Thomas] Tryon [*The Way to Health, Wealth, and Happiness*, 1682] recommending a vegetable diet. I determined to go into it. * * * My refusing to eat flesh occasioned an inconveniency, and I was frequently chid for my singularity" [Franklin, *The Autobiography*].

William Golding

THINKING AS A HOBBY

While I was still a boy, I came to the conclusion that there were three grades of thinking; and since I was later to claim thinking as my hobby, I came to an even stranger conclusion—namely, that I myself could not think at all.

I must have been an unsatisfactory child for grownups to deal with. I remember how incomprehensible they appeared to me at first, but not, of course, how I appeared to them. It was the headmaster of my grammar school who first brought the subject of thinking before me—though neither in the way, nor with the result he intended. He had some statuettes in his study. They stood on a high cupboard behind his desk. One was a lady wearing nothing but a bath towel. She seemed frozen in an eternal panic lest the bath towel slip down any farther; and since she had no arms, she was in an unfortunate position to pull the towel up again. Next to her, crouched the statuette of a leopard, ready to spring down at the top drawer of a filing cabinet labeled A-AH. My innocence interpreted this as the victim's last, despairing cry. Beyond the leopard was a naked, muscular gentleman, who sat, looking down, with his chin on his fist and his elbow on his knee. He seemed utterly miserable.

Some time later, I learned about these statuettes. The headmaster had placed them where they would face delinquent children, because they symbolized to him the whole of life. The naked lady was the Venus of Milo. She was Love. She was not worried about the towel. She was just busy being beautiful. The leopard was Nature, and he was being natural. The naked, muscular gentleman was not miserable. He was Rodin's Thinker, an image of pure thought. It is easy to buy small plaster models of what you think life is like.

I had better explain that I was a frequent visitor to the headmaster's study, because of the latest thing I had done or left undone. As we now say, I was not integrated. I was, if anything, disintegrated; and I was puzzled. Grownups never made sense. Whenever I found myself in a penal position before the headmaster's desk, with the statuettes glimmering whitely above him, I would sink my head, clasp my hands behind my back and writhe one shoe over the other.

The headmaster would look opaquely at me through flashing spectacles.

First published in *Holiday Magazine* (Aug. 1961).

5

"What are we going to do with you?"

Well, what *were* they going to do with me? I would writhe my shoe some more and stare down at the worn rug.

"Look up, boy! Can't you look up?"

Then I would look up at the cupboard, where the naked lady was frozen in her panic and the muscular gentleman contemplated the hindquarters of the leopard in endless gloom. I had nothing to say to the headmaster. His spectacles caught the light so that you could see nothing human behind them. There was no possibility of communication.

"Don't you ever think at all?"

No, I didn't think, wasn't thinking, couldn't think—I was simply waiting in anguish for the interview to stop.

"Then you'd better learn—hadn't you?"

On one occasion the headmaster leaped to his feet, reached up and plonked Rodin's masterpiece on the desk before me.

"That's what a man looks like when he's really thinking."

I surveyed the gentleman without interest or comprehension.

"Go back to your class."

Clearly there was something missing in me. Nature had endowed the rest of the human race with a sixth sense and left me out. This must be so, I mused, on my way back to the class, since whether I had broken a window, or failed to remember Boyle's Law, or been late for school, my teachers produced me one, adult answer: "Why can't you think?"

As I saw the case, I had broken the window because I had tried to hit Jack Arney with a cricket ball and missed him; I could not remember Boyle's Law because I had never bothered to learn it; and I was late for school because I preferred looking over the bridge into the river. In fact, I was wicked. Were my teachers, perhaps, so good that they could not understand the depths of my depravity? Were they clear, untormented people who could direct their every action by this mysterious business of thinking? The whole thing was incomprehensible. In my earlier years, I found even the statuette of the Thinker confusing. I did not believe any of my teachers were naked, ever. Like someone born deaf, but bitterly determined to find out about sound, I watched my teachers to find out about thought.

There was Mr. Houghton. He was always telling me to think. With a modest satisfaction, he would tell me that he had thought a bit himself. Then why did he spend so much time drinking? Or was there more sense in drinking than there appeared to be? But if not, and if drinking were in fact ruinous to health—and Mr. Houghton was ruined, there was no doubt about that—why was he always talking about the clean life and the virtues of fresh air? He would spread his arms wide with the action of a man who habitually spent his time striding along mountain ridges.

"Open air does me good, boys—I know it!"   20

Sometimes, exalted by his own oratory, he would leap from his desk and hustle us outside into a hideous wind.

"Now, boys! Deep breaths! Feel it right down inside you—huge draughts of God's good air!"

He would stand before us, rejoicing in his perfect health, an open-air man. He would put his hands on his waist and take a tremendous breath. You could hear the wind, trapped in the cavern of his chest and struggling with all the unnatural impediments. His body would reel with shock and his ruined face go white at the unaccustomed visitation. He would stagger back to his desk and collapse there, useless for the rest of the morning.

Mr. Houghton was given to high-minded monologues about the good life, sexless and full of duty. Yet in the middle of one of these monologues, if a girl passed the window, tapping along on her neat little feet, he would interrupt his discourse, his neck would turn of itself and he would watch her out of sight. In this instance, he seemed to me ruled not by thought but by an invisible and irresistible spring in his nape.

His neck was an object of great interest to me. Normally it bulged a   25
bit over his collar. But Mr. Houghton had fought in the First World War alongside both Americans and French, and had come—by who knows what illogic?—to a settled detestation of both countries. If either country happened to be prominent in current affairs, no argument could make Mr. Houghton think well of it. He would bang the desk, his neck would bulge still further and go red. "You can say what you like," he would cry, "but I've thought about this—and I know what I think!"

Mr. Houghton thought with his neck.

There was Miss Parsons. She assured us that her dearest wish was our welfare, but I knew even then, with the mysterious clairvoyance of childhood, that what she wanted most was the husband she never got. There was Mr. Hands—and so on.

I have dealt at length with my teachers because this was my introduction to the nature of what is commonly called thought. Through them I discovered that thought is often full of unconscious prejudice, ignorance and hypocrisy. It will lecture on disinterested purity while its neck is being remorselessly twisted toward a skirt. Technically, it is about as proficient as most businessmen's golf, as honest as most politicians' intentions, or—to come near my own preoccupation—as coherent as most books that get written. It is what I came to call grade-three thinking, though more properly, it is feeling, rather than thought.

True, often there is a kind of innocence in prejudices, but in those days I viewed grade-three thinking with an intolerant contempt and an incautious mockery. I delighted to confront a pious lady who hated the Germans with the proposition that we should love our enemies. She taught me a great truth in dealing with grade-three thinkers; because of her, I no longer dismiss lightly a mental process which for nine-tenths of the population is the nearest they will ever get to thought. They have immense solidarity. We had better respect them, for we are outnumbered and surrounded. A crowd of grade-three thinkers, all shouting the same thing, all warming their hands at the fire of their own prejudices, will not thank you for pointing out the contradictions in their beliefs. Man is a gregarious animal, and enjoys agreement as cows will graze all the same way on the side of a hill.

30   Grade-two thinking is the detection of contradictions. I reached grade two when I trapped the poor, pious lady. Grade-two thinkers do not stampede easily, though often they fall into the other fault and lap behind. Grade-two thinking is a withdrawal, with eyes and ears open. It became my hobby and brought satisfaction and loneliness in either hand. For grade-two thinking destroys without having the power to create. It set me watching the crowds cheering His Majesty and King and asking myself what all the fuss was about, without giving me anything positive to put in the place of that heady patriotism. But there were compensations. To hear people justify their habit of hunting foxes and tearing them to pieces by claiming that the foxes liked it. To hear our Prime Minister talk about the great benefit we conferred on India by jailing people like Pandit Nehru and Gandhi. To hear American politicians talk about peace in one sentence and refuse to join the League of Nations in the next. Yes, there were moments of delight.

But I was growing toward adolescence and had to admit that Mr. Houghton was not the only one with an irresistible spring in his neck. I, too, felt the compulsive hand of nature and began to find that pointing out contradiction could be costly as well as fun. There was Ruth, for example, a serious and attractive girl. I was an atheist at the time. Grade-two thinking is a menace to religion and knocks down sects like skittles. I put myself in a position to be converted by her with an hypocrisy worthy of grade three. She was a Methodist—or at least, her parents were, and Ruth had to follow suit. But, alas, instead of relying on the Holy Spirit to convert me, Ruth was foolish enough to open her pretty mouth in argument. She claimed that the Bible (King James Version) was literally inspired. I countered by saying that the Catholics believed in the literal inspiration of Saint Jerome's *Vulgate*,[1] and the two books were different. Argument flagged.

At last she remarked that there were an awful lot of Methodists, and they couldn't be wrong, could they—not all those millions? That was too easy, said I restively (for the nearer you were to Ruth, the nicer she

1. The Latin Bible as revised in the fourth century A.D. by Jerome and used thereafter as the authoritative text for Roman Catholic ritual.

was to be near to) since there were more Roman Catholics than Methodists anyway; and they couldn't be wrong, could they—not all those hundreds of millions? An awful flicker of doubt appeared in her eyes. I slid my arm around her waist and murmured breathlessly that if we were counting heads, the Buddhists were the boys for my money. But Ruth had *really* wanted to do me good, because I was so nice. She fled. The combination of my arm and those countless Buddhists was too much for her.

That night her father visited my father and left, red-cheeked and indignant. I was given the third degree to find out what had happened. It was lucky we were both of us only fourteen. I lost Ruth and gained an undeserved reputation as a potential libertine.

So grade-two thinking could be dangerous. It was in this knowledge, at the age of fifteen, that I remember making a comment from the heights of grade two, on the limitations of grade three. One evening I found myself alone in the school hall, preparing it for a party. The door of the headmaster's study was open. I went in. The headmaster had ceased to thump Rodin's Thinker down on the desk as an example to the young. Perhaps he had not found any more candidates, but the statuettes were still there, glimmering and gathering dust on top of the cupboard. I stood on a chair and rearranged them. I stood Venus in her bath towel on the filing cabinet, so that now the top drawer caught its breath in a gasp of sexy excitement. "A-ah!" The portentous Thinker I placed on the edge of the cupboard so that he looked down at the bath towel and waited for it to slip.

Grade-two thinking, though it filled life with fun and excitement, did not make for content. To find out the deficiencies of our elders bolsters the young ego but does not make for personal security. I found that grade two was not only the power to point out contradictions. It took the swimmer some distance from the shore and left him there, out of his depth. I decided that Pontius Pilate was a typical grade-two thinker. "What is truth?" he said, a very common grade-two thought, but one that is used always as the end of an argument instead of the beginning. There is still a higher grade of thought which says, "What is truth?" and sets out to find it.

But these grade-one thinkers were few and far between. They did not visit my grammar school in the flesh though they were there in books. I aspired to them, partly because I was ambitious and partly because I now saw my hobby as an unsatisfactory thing if it went no further. If you set out to climb a mountain, however high you climb, you have failed if you cannot reach the top.

I *did* meet an undeniably grade-one thinker in my first year at Oxford. I was looking over a small bridge in Magdalen Deer Park, and a tiny mustached and hatted figure came and stood by my side. He was a

German who had just fled from the Nazis to Oxford as a temporary refuge. His name was Einstein.

But Professor Einstein knew no English at that time and I knew only two words of German. I beamed at him, trying wordlessly to convey by my bearing all the affection and respect that the English felt for him. It is possible—and I have to make the admission—that I felt here were two grade-one thinkers standing side by side; yet I doubt if my face conveyed more than a formless awe. I would have given my Greek and Latin and French and a good slice of my English for enough German to communicate. But we were divided; he was as inscrutable as my headmaster. For perhaps five minutes we stood together on the bridge, undeniable grade-one thinker and breathless aspirant. With true greatness, Professor Einstein realized that my contact was better than none. He pointed to a trout wavering in midstream.

He spoke: *"Fisch."*

40   My brain reeled. Here I was, mingling with the great, and yet helpless as the veriest grade-three thinker. Desperately I sought for some sign by which I might convey that I, too, revered pure reason. I nodded vehemently. In a brilliant flash I used up half of my German vocabulary.

"Fisch. Ja Ja."

For perhaps another five minutes we stood side by side. Then Professor Einstein, his whole figure still conveying good will and amiability, drifted away out of sight.

I, too, would be a grade-one thinker. I was irreverent at the best of times. Political and religious systems, social customs, loyalties and traditions, they all came tumbling down like so many rotten apples off a tree. This was a fine hobby and a sensible substitute for cricket, since you could play it all the year round. I came up in the end with what must always remain the justification for grade-one thinking, its sign, seal and charter. I devised a coherent system for living. It was a moral system, which was wholly logical. Of course, as I readily admitted, conversion of the world to my way of thinking might be difficult, since my system did away with a number of trifles, such as big business, centralized government, armies, marriage. . . .

It was Ruth all over again. I had some very good friends who stood by me, and still do. But my acquaintances vanished, taking the girls with them. Young women seemed oddly contented with the world as it was. They valued the meaningless ceremony with a ring. Young men, while willing to concede the chaining sordidness of marriage, were hesitant about abandoning the organizations which they hoped would give them a career. A young man on the first rung of the Royal Navy, while perfectly agreeable to doing away with big business and marriage, got as rednecked as Mr. Houghton when I proposed a world without any battleships in it.

Had the game gone too far? Was it a game any longer? In those 45
prewar days, I stood to lose a great deal, for the sake of a hobby.

Now you are expecting me to describe how I saw the folly of my ways
and came back to the warm nest, where prejudices are so often called
loyalties, where pointless actions are hallowed into custom by repetition,
where we are content to say we think when all we do is feel.

But you would be wrong. I dropped my hobby and turned professional.

If I were to go back to the headmaster's study and find the dusty
statuettes still there, I would arrange them differently. I would dust
Venus and put her aside, for I have come to love her and know her for
the fair thing she is. But I would put the Thinker, sunk in his desperate
thought, where there were shadows before him—and at his back, I
would put the leopard, crouched and ready to spring.

THE READER

1. It has been said: "Third-rate thinkers think like everybody else because
   everybody else thinks the same way. Second-rate thinkers think differently from everybody else because everybody else thinks the same way.
   First-rate thinkers think." Does this saying correspond to Golding's
   message? Would you modify it in any way in light of what he writes?
2. What are the special attractions and what are the penalties of grade-
   three thinking? Grade-two? Grade-one?
3. Are Golding's three categories all-encompassing? If so, how? If not,
   what additional ones would you add?
4. Are Golding's categories useful for assessing the value of a person's
   statements? Choose several selections in this book, and examine them
   by Golding's implied criteria.

THE WRITER

1. Why does Golding, at the end of his essay, return to the three statuettes? Have the statuettes anything to do with the three kinds of
   thinking described in the essay? Why would Golding rearrange the
   statuettes as he does in the final paragraph?
2. Why does Golding include the anecdote about Einstein? Does it have
   any bearing upon his account of the three categories of thinking?
3. One would not usually consider thinking a "hobby." Why does Golding do so? Write an essay on something else not usually considered
   a hobby, using the title "————as a Hobby."
4. Golding is the author of Lord of the Flies. If you have read that novel,
   write an essay attempting to relate his depiction of characters and
   events to the three categories of thinking.

Desmond Morris

TERRITORIAL BEHAVIOR

A territory is a defended space. In the broadest sense, there are three kinds of human territory: tribal, family and personal.

It is rare for people to be driven to physical fighting in defense of these "owned" spaces, but fight they will, if pushed to the limit. The invading army encroaching on national territory, the gang moving into a rival district, the trespasser climbing into an orchard, the burglar breaking into a house, the bully pushing to the front of a queue, the driver trying to steal a parking space, all of these intruders are liable to be met with resistance varying from the vigorous to the savagely violent. Even if the law is on the side of the intruder, the urge to protect a territory may be so strong that otherwise peaceful citizens abandon all their usual controls and inhibitions. Attempts to evict families from their homes, no matter how socially valid the reasons, can lead to siege conditions reminiscent of the defense of a medieval fortress.

The fact that these upheavals are so rare is a measure of the success of Territorial Signals as a sytem of dispute prevention. It is sometimes cynically stated that "all property is theft," but in reality it is the opposite. Property, as owned space which is *displayed* as owned space, is a special kind of sharing system which reduces fighting much more than it causes it. Man is a co-operative species, but he is also competitive, and his struggle for dominance has to be structured in some way if chaos is to be avoided. The establishment of territorial rights is one such structure. It limits dominance geographically. I am dominant in my territory and you are dominant in yours. In other words, dominance is shared out spatially, and we all have some. Even if I am weak and unintelligent and you can dominate me when we meet on neutral ground, I can still enjoy a thoroughly dominant role as soon as I retreat to my private base. Be it ever so humble, there is no place like a home territory.

Of course, I can still be intimidated by a particularly dominant individual who enters my home base, but his encroachment will be dangerous for him and he will think twice about it, because he will know that here my urge to resist will be dramatically magnified and my usual subservience banished. Insulted at the heart of my own territory, I may easily explode into battle—either symbolic or real—with a result that may be damaging to both of us.

From *Manwatching: A Field Guide to Human Behavior* (1977).

In order for this to work, each territory has to be plainly advertised   5
as such. Just as a dog cocks its leg to deposit its personal scent on the
trees in its locality, so the human animal cocks its leg symbolically all
over his home base. But because we are predominantly visual animals
we employ mostly visual signals, and it is worth asking how we do this
at the three levels: tribal, family, and personal.

First: the Tribal Territory. We evolved as tribal animals, living in
comparatively small groups, probably of less than a hundred, and we
existed like that for millions of years. It is our basic social unit, a group
in which everyone knows everyone else. Essentially, the tribal territory
consisted of a home base surrounded by extended hunting grounds. Any
neighboring tribe intruding on our social space would be repelled and
driven away. As these early tribes swelled into agricultural supertribes,
and eventually into industrial nations, their territorial defense systems
became increasingly elaborate. The tiny, ancient home base of the
hunting tribe became the great capital city, the primitive warpaint
became the flags, emblems, uniforms, and regalia of the specialized
military, and the war-chants became national anthems, marching songs,
and bugle calls. Territorial boundary-lines hardened into fixed borders,
often conspicuously patrolled and punctuated with defensive structures—forts and lookout posts, checkpoints and great walls, and, today,
customs barriers.

Today each nation flies its own flag, a symbolic embodiment of its
territorial status. But patriotism is not enough. The ancient tribal hunter
lurking inside each citizen finds himself unsatisfied by membership in
such a vast conglomeration of individuals, most of whom are totally
unknown to him personally. He does his best to feel that he shares a
common territorial defense with them all, but the scale of the operation
has become inhuman. It is hard to feel a sense of belonging with a tribe
of fifty million or more. His answer is to form sub-groups, nearer to his
ancient pattern, smaller, and more personally known to him—the local
club, the teenage gang, the union, the specialist society, the sports
association, the political party, the college fraternity, the social clique,
the protest group, and the rest. Rare indeed is the individual who does
not belong to at least one of these splinter groups, and take from it a
sense of tribal allegiance and brotherhood. Typical of all these groups
is the development of Territorial Signals—badges, costumes, headquarters, banners, slogans, and all the other displays of group identity. This
is where the action is, in terms of tribal territorialism, and only when
a major war breaks out does the emphasis shift upwards to the higher
group level of the nations.

Each of these modern pseudo-tribes sets up its own special kind of
home base. In extreme cases non-members are totally excluded, in others
they are allowed in as visitors with limited rights and under a control

system of special rules. In many ways they are like miniature nations, with their own flags and emblems and their own border guards. The exclusive club has its own "customs barrier": the doorman who checks your "passport" (your membership card) and prevents strangers from passing in unchallenged. There is a government: the club committee; and often special displays of the tribal elders: the photographs or portraits of previous officials on the walls. At the heart of the specialized territories there is a powerful feeling of security and importance, a sense of shared defense against the outside world. Much of the club chatter, both serious and joking, directs itself against the rottenness of everything outside the club boundaries—in that "other world" beyond the protected portals.

In social organizations which embody a strong class system, such as military units and large business concerns, there are many territorial rules, often unspoken, which interfere with the official hierarchy. High-status individuals, such as officers or managers, could in theory enter any of the regions occupied by the lower levels in the peck order, but they limit this power in a striking way. An officer seldom enters a sergeant's mess or a barrack room unless it is for a formal inspection. He respects those regions as alien territories even though he has the power to go there by virtue of his dominant role. And in businesses, part of the appeal of unions, over and above their obvious functions, is that with their officials, headquarters, and meetings they add a sense of territorial power for the staff workers. It is almost as if each military organization and business concern consists of two warring tribes: the officers versus the other ranks, and the management versus the workers. Each has its special home base within the system, and the territorial defense pattern thrusts itself into what, on the surface, is a pure social hierarchy. Negotiations between managements and unions are tribal battles fought out over the neutral ground of a boardroom table, and are as much concerned with territorial display as they are with resolving problems of wages and conditions. Indeed, if one side gives in too quickly and accepts the other's demands, the victors feel strangely cheated and deeply suspicious that it may be a trick. What they are missing is the protracted sequence of ritual and counter-ritual that keeps alive their group territorial identity.

10   Likewise, many of the hostile displays of sports fans and teenage gangs are primarily concerned with displaying their group image to rival fan-clubs and gangs. Except in rare cases, they do not attack one another's headquarters, drive out the occupants, and reduce them to a submissive, subordinate condition. It is enough to have scuffles on the borderlands between the two rival territories. This is particularly clear at football matches, where the fan-club headquarters becomes temporarily shifted from the club-house to a section of the stands, and where minor fighting

breaks out at the unofficial boundary line between the massed groups of rival supporters. Newspaper reports play up the few accidents and injuries which do occur on such occasions, but when these are studied in relation to the total numbers of displaying fans involved it is clear that the serious incidents represent only a tiny fraction of the overall group behavior. For every actual punch or kick there are a thousand war-cries, war dances, chants, and gestures.

Second: the Family Territory. Essentially, the family is a breeding unit and the family territory is a breeding ground. At the center of this space, there is the nest—the bedroom—where, tucked up in bed, we feel at our most territorially secure. In a typical house the bedroom is upstairs, where a safe nest should be. This puts it farther away from the entrance hall, the area where contact is made, intermittently, with the outside world. The less private reception rooms, where intruders are allowed access, are the next line of defense. Beyond them, outside the walls of the building, there is often a symbolic remnant of the ancient feeding grounds—a garden. Its symbolism often extends to the plants and animals it contains, which cease to be nutritional and become merely decorative—flowers and pets. But like a true territorial space it has a conspicuously displayed boundary-line, the garden fence, wall, or railings. Often no more than a token barrier, this is the outer territorial demarcation, separating the private world for the family from the public world beyond. To cross it puts any visitor or intruder at an immediate disadvantage. As he crosses the threshold, his dominance wanes, slightly but unmistakably. He is entering an area where he senses that he must ask permission to do simple things that he would consider a right elsewhere. Without lifting a finger, the territorial owners exert their dominance. This is done by all the hundreds of small ownership "markers" they have deposited on their family territory: the ornaments, the "possessed" objects positioned in the rooms and on the walls; the furnishings, the furniture, the colors, the patterns, all owner-chosen and all making this particular home base unique to them.

It is one of the tragedies of modern architecture that there has been a standardization of these vital territorial living units. One of the most important aspects of a home is that it should be similar to other homes only in a general way, and that in detail it should have many differences, making it a *particular* home. Unfortunately, it is cheaper to build a row of houses, or a block of flats, so that all the family living-units are identical, but the territorial urge rebels against this trend and house-owners struggle as best they can to make their mark on their mass-produced properties. They do this with garden-design, with front-door colors, with curtain patterns, with wallpaper and all the other decorative elements that together create a unique and different family environment. Only when they have completed this nest-building do they feel truly "at home" and secure.

When they venture forth as a family unit they repeat the process in a minor way. On a day-trip to the seaside, they load the car with personal belongings and it becomes their temporary, portable territory. Arriving at the beach they stake out a small territorial claim, marking it with rugs, towels, baskets, and other belongings to which they can return from their seaboard wanderings. Even if they all leave it at once to bathe, it retains a characteristic territorial quality and other family groups arriving will recognize this by setting up their own "home" bases at a respectful distance. Only when the whole beach has filled up with these marked spaces will newcomers start to position themselves in such a way that the inter-base distance becomes reduced. Forced to pitch between several existing beach territories they will feel a momentary sensation of intrusion, and the established "owners" will feel a similar sensation of invasion, even though they are not being directly inconvenienced.

The same territorial scene is being played out in parks and fields and on riverbanks, wherever family groups gather in their clustered units. But if rivalry for spaces creates mild feelings of hostility, it is true to say that, without the territorial system of sharing and space-limited dominance, there would be chaotic disorder.

15   Third: the Personal Space. If a man enters a waiting-room and sits at one end of a long row of empty chairs, it is possible to predict where the next man to enter will seat himself. He will not sit next to the first man, nor will he sit at the far end, right away from him. He will choose a position about halfway between these two points. The next man to enter will take the largest gap left, and sit roughly in the middle of that, and so on, until eventually the latest newcomer will be forced to select a seat that places him right next to one of the already seated men. Similar patterns can be observed in cinemas, public urinals, airplanes, trains, and buses. This is a reflection of the fact that we all carry with us, everywhere we go, a portable territory called a Personal Space. If people move inside this space, we feel threatened. If they keep too far outside it, we feel rejected. The result is a subtle series of spatial adjustments, usually operating quite unconsciously and producing ideal compromises as far as this is possible. If a situation becomes too crowded, then we adjust our reactions accordingly and allow our personal space to shrink. Jammed into an elevator, a rush-hour compartment, or a packed room, we give up altogether and allow body-to-body contact, but when we relinquish our Personal Space in this way, we adopt certain special techniques. In essence, what we do is to convert these other bodies into "nonpersons." We studiously ignore them, and they us. We try not to face them if we can possibly avoid it. We wipe all expressiveness from our faces, letting them go blank. We may look up at the

ceiling or down at the floor, and we reduce body movements to a minimum. Packed together like sardines in a tin, we stand dumbly still, sending out as few social signals as possible.

Even if the crowding is less severe, we still tend to cut down our social interactions in the presence of large numbers. Careful observations of children in play groups revealed that if they are high-density groupings there is less social interaction between the individual children, even though there is theoretically more opportunity for such contacts. At the same time, the high-density groups show a higher frequency of aggressive and destructive behavior patterns in their play. Personal Space— "elbow room"—is a vital commodity for the human animal, and one that cannot be ignored without risking serious trouble.

Of course, we all enjoy the excitement of being in a crowd, and this reaction cannot be ignored. But there are crowds and crowds. It is pleasant enough to be in a "spectator crowd," but not so appealing to find yourself in the middle of a rush-hour crush. The difference between the two is that the spectator crowd is all facing in the same direction and concentrating on a distant point of interest. Attending a theater, there are twinges of rising hostility toward the stranger who sits down immediately in front of you or the one who squeezes into the seat next to you. The shared armrest can become a polite, but distinct, territorial boundary-dispute region. However, as soon as the show begins, these invasions of Personal Space are forgotten and the attention is focused beyond the small space where the crowding is taking place. Now, each member of the audience feels himself spatially related, not to his cramped neighbors, but to the actor on the stage, and this distance is, if anything, too great. In the rush-hour crowd, by contrast, each member of the pushing throng is competing with his neighbors all the time. There is no escape to a spatial relation with a distant actor, only the pushing, shoving bodies all around.

Those of us who have to spend a great deal of time in crowded conditions become gradually better able to adjust, but no one can ever become completely immune to invasions of Personal Space. This is because they remain forever associated with either powerful hostile or equally powerful loving feelings. All through our childhood we will have been held to be loved and held to be hurt, and anyone who invades our Personal Space when we are adults is, in effect, threatening to extend his behavior into one of these two highly charged areas of human interaction. Even if his motives are clearly neither hostile nor sexual, we still find it hard to suppress our reactions to his close approach. Unfortunately, different countries have different ideas about exactly how close is close. It is easy enough to test your own "space reaction": when you are talking to someone in the street or in any open space, reach out with your arm and see where the nearest point on his body comes. If you hail from western Europe, you will find that he is at roughly fingertip distance from you. In other words, as you reach out, your fingertips will just about make contact with his shoulder. If you come from eastern Europe you will find you are standing at "wrist distance." If you come from the Mediterranean region you will find that you are much closer to your companion, at little more than "elbow distance."

Trouble begins when a member of one of these cultures meets and talks to one from another. Say a British diplomat meets an Italian or an Arab diplomat at an embassy function. They start talking in a friendly way, but soon the fingertips man begins to feel uneasy. Without knowing quite why, he starts to back away gently from his companion. The companion edges forward again. Each tries in his way to set up a Personal Space relationship that suits his own background. But it is impossible to do. Every time the Mediterranean diplomat advances to a distance that feels comfortable for him, the British diplomat feels threatened. Every time the Briton moves back, the other feels rejected. Attempts to adjust this situation often lead to a talking pair shifting slowly across a room, and many an embassy reception is dotted with western-European fingertip-distance men pinned against the walls by eager elbow-distance men. Until such differences are fully understood and allowances made, these minor differences in "body territories" will continue to act as an alienation factor which may interfere in a subtle way with diplomatic harmony and other forms of international transaction.

20   If there are distance problems when engaged in conversation, then there are clearly going to be even bigger difficulties where people must work privately in a shared space. Close proximity of others, pressing against the invisible boundaries of our personal body-territory, makes it difficult to concentrate on nonsocial matters. Flat-mates, students sharing a study, sailors in the cramped quarters of a ship, and office staff in crowded work-places, all have to face this problem. They solve it by "cocooning." They use a variety of devices to shut themselves off from the others present. The best possible cocoon, of course, is a small private room—a den, a private office, a study, or a studio—which physically obscures the presence of other nearby territory-owners. This is the ideal situation for non-social work, but the space-sharers cannot enjoy this luxury. Their cocooning must be symbolic. They may, in certain cases, be able to erect small physical barriers, such as screens and partitions, which give substance to their invisible Personal Space boundaries, but when this cannot be done, other means must be sought. One of these is the "favored object." Each space-sharer develops a preference, repeatedly expressed until it becomes a fixed pattern, for a particular chair, or table, or alcove. Others come to respect this, and friction is reduced. This sytem is often formally arranged (this is my desk, that is yours), but

even where it is not, favored places soon develop. Professor Smith has a favorite chair in the library. It is not formally his, but he always uses it and others avoid it. Seats around a mess-room table, or a boardroom table, become almost personal property for specific individuals. Even in the home, father has his favorite chair for reading the newspaper or watching television. Another device is the blinkers-posture. Just as a horse that over-reacts to other horses and the distractions of the noisy race-course is given a pair of blinkers to shield its eyes, so people studying privately in a public place put on pseudo-blinkers in the form of shielding hands. Resting their elbows on the table, they sit with their hands screening their eyes from the scene on either side.

A third method of reinforcing the body-territory is to use personal markers. Books, papers, and other personal belongings are scattered around the favored site to render it more privately owned in the eyes of companions. Spreading out one's belongings is a well-known trick in public-transport situations, where a traveler tries to give the impression that seats next to him are taken. In many contexts carefully arranged personal markers can act as an effective territorial display, even in the absence of the territory owner. Experiments in a library revealed that placing a pile of magazines on the table in one seating position successfully reserved that place for an average of 77 minutes. If a sports-jacket was added, draped over the chair, then the "reservation effect" lasted for over two hours.

In these ways, we strengthen the defenses of our Personal Spaces, keeping out intruders with the minimum of open hostility. As with all territorial behavior, the object is to defend space with signals rather than with fists and at all three levels—the tribal, the family, and the personal—it is a remarkably efficient system of space-sharing. It does not always seem so, because newspapers and newscasts inevitably magnify the exceptions and dwell on those cases where the signals have failed and wars have broken out, gangs have fought, neighboring families have feuded, or colleagues have clashed, but for every territorial signal that has failed, there are millions of others that have not. They do not rate a mention in the news, but they nevertheless constitute a dominant feature of human society—the society of a remarkably territorial animal.

THE READER

1. *Morris predicts people's behavior when they are selecting seats (p. 192). Does observation confirm his prediction? Does the balancing of threat and rejection seem like a good explanation?*
2. *Is racism territorial?*
3. *Although he clearly recognizes that territorial behavior can lead to trouble, Morris speaks approvingly of it as "a remarkably efficient*

system of space-sharing." If you wanted to challenge his argument, where would you start—his definitions, his evidence, his conclusions?

THE WRITER

1. *The essay is obviously organized to discuss territorial behavior on three levels. Does it progress from level to level? Is there any repetition? To what degree is each level an independent subessay?*
2. *Describe tribal subdivision in a large social unit like a high school or college. What are the Territorial Signals?*

Jacob Bronowski

THE REACH OF IMAGINATION

For three thousand years, poets have been enchanted and moved and perplexed by the power of their own imagination. In a short and summary essay I can hope at most to lift one small corner of that mystery; and yet it is a critical corner. I shall ask, What goes on in the mind when we imagine? You will hear from me that one answer to this question is fairly specific: which is to say, that we can describe the working of the imagination. And when we describe it as I shall do, it becomes plain that imagination is a specifically *human* gift. To imagine is the characteristic act, not of the poet's mind, or the painter's, or the scientist's, but of the mind of man.

My stress here on the word *human* implies that there is a clear difference in this between the actions of men and those of other animals. Let me then start with a classical experiment with animals and children which Walter Hunter thought out in Chicago about 1910. That was the time when scientists were agog with the success of Ivan Pavlov in forming and changing the reflex actions of dogs, which Pavlov had first announced in 1903. Pavlov had been given a Nobel prize the next year, in 1904; although in fairness I should say that the award did not cite his work on the conditioned reflex, but on the digestive gland.

Hunter duly trained some dogs and other animals on Pavlov's lines. They were taught that when a light came on over one of three tunnels out of their cage, that tunnel would be open; they could escape down it, and were rewarded with food if they did. But once he had fixed that conditioned reflex, Hunter added to it a deeper idea: he gave the mechanical experiment a new dimension, literally—the dimension of time.

From *Proceedings of the American Academy of Arts and Letters and National Institute of Arts and Letters* (2nd ser., No. 17, 1967).

Now he no longer let the dog go to the lighted tunnel at once; instead, he put out the light, and then kept the dog waiting a little while before he let him go. In this way Hunter timed how long an animal can remember where he has last seen the signal light to his escape route.

The results were and are staggering. A dog or a rat forgets which one of three tunnels has been lit up within a matter of seconds—in Hunter's experiment, ten seconds at most. If you want such an animal to do much better than this, you must make the task much simpler: you must face him with only two tunnels to choose from. Even so, the best that Hunter could do was to have a dog remember for five minutes which one of two tunnels had been lit up.

I am not quoting these times as if they were exact and universal: they surely are not. Hunter's experiment, more than fifty years old now, had many faults of detail. For example, there were too few animals, they were oddly picked, and they did not all behave consistently. It may be unfair to test a dog for what he *saw*, when he commonly follows his nose rather than his eyes. It may be unfair to test any animal in the unnatural setting of a laboratory cage. And there are higher animals, such as chimpanzees and other primates, which certainly have longer memories than the animals that Hunter tried.

Yet when all these provisos have been made (and met, by more modern experiments) the facts are still startling and characteristic. An animal cannot recall a signal from the past for even a short fraction of the time that a man can—for even a short fraction of the time that a child can. Hunter made comparable tests with six-year-old children, and found, of course, that they were incomparably better than the best of his animals. There is a striking and basic difference between a man's ability to imagine something that he saw or experienced, and an animal's failure.

Animals make up for this by other and extraordinary gifts. The salmon and the carrier pigeon can find their way home as we cannot: they have, as it were, a practical memory that man cannot match. But their actions always depend on some form of habit: on instinct or on learning, which reproduce by rote a train of known responses. They do not depend, as human memory does, on calling to mind the recollection of absent things.

Where is it that the animal falls short? We get a clue to the answer, I think, when Hunter tells us how the animals in his experiment tried to fix their recollection. They most often pointed themselves at the light before it went out, as some gun dogs point rigidly at the game they scent—and get the name *pointer* from the posture. The animal makes ready to act by building the signal into its action. There is a primitive imagery in its stance, it seems to me; it is as if the animal were trying to fix the light on its mind by fixing it in its body. And indeed, how else

can a dog mark and (as it were) name one of three tunnels, when he has
no such words as *left* and *right*, and no such numbers as *one, two, three?*
The directed gesture of attention and readiness is perhaps the only
symbolic device that the dog commands to hold on to the past, and
thereby to guide himself into the future.

I used the verb *to imagine* a moment ago, and now I have some
ground for giving it a meaning. *To imagine* means to make images and
to move them about inside one's head in new arrangements. When you
and I recall the past, we imagine it in this direct and homely sense. The
tool that puts the human mind ahead of the animal is imagery. For us,
memory does not demand the preoccupation that it demands in animals,
and it lasts immensely longer, because we fix it in images or other
substitute symbols. With the same symbolic vocabulary we spell out the
future—not one but many futures, which we weigh one against another.

10   I am using the word *image* in a wide meaning, which does not restrict
it to the mind's eye as a visual organ. An image in my usage is what
Charles Peirce called a *sign*, without regard for its sensory quality. Peirce
distinguished between different forms of signs, but there is no reason to
make his distinction here, for the imagination works equally with them
all, and that is why I call them all images.

Indeed, the most important images for human beings are simply
words, which are abstract symbols. Animals do not have words, in our
sense: there is no specific center for language in the brain of any animal,
as there is in the human being. In this respect at least we know that the
human imagination depends on a configuration in the brain that has
only evolved in the last one or two million years. In the same period,
evolution has greatly enlarged the front lobes in the human brain, which
govern the sense of the past and the future; and it is a fair guess that
they are probably the seat of our other images. (Part of the evidence for
this guess is that damage to the front lobes in primates reduces them
to the state of Hunter's animals.) If the guess turns out to be right, we
shall know why man has come to look like a highbrow or an egghead:
because otherwise there would not be room in his head for his imagination.

The images play out for us events which are not present to our senses,
and thereby guard the past and create the future—a future that does not
yet exist, and may never come to exist in that form. By contrast, the lack
of symbolic ideas, or their rudimentary poverty, cuts off an animal from
the past and the future alike, and imprisons him in the present. Of all
the distinctions between man and animal, the characteristic gift which
makes us human is the power to work with symbolic images: the gift of
imagination.

This is really a remarkable finding. When Philip Sidney in 1580
defended poets (and all unconventional thinkers) from the Puritan

charge that they were liars, he said that a maker must imagine things that are not. Halfway between Sidney and us, William Blake said, "What is now proved was once only imagined." About the same time, in 1796, Samuel Taylor Coleridge for the first time distinguished between the passive fancy and the active imagination, "the living Power and prime Agent of all human Perception." Now we see that they were right, and precisely right: the human gift is the gift of imagination—and that is not just a literary phrase.

Nor is it just a literary gift; it is, I repeat, characteristically human. Almost everything that we do that is worth doing is done in the first place in the mind's eye. The richness of human life is that we have many lives; we live the events that do not happen (and some that cannot) as vividly as those that do; and if thereby we die a thousand deaths, that is the price we pay for living a thousand lives. (A cat, of course, has only nine.) Literature is alive to us because we live its images, but so is any play of the mind—so is chess: the lines of play that we foresee and try in our heads and dismiss are as much a part of the game as the moves that we make. John Keats said that the unheard melodies are sweeter, and all chess players sadly recall that the combinations that they planned and which never came to be played were the best.

I make this point to remind you, insistently, that imagination is the manipulation of images in one's head; and that the rational manipulation belongs to that, as well as the literary and artistic manipulation. When a child begins to play games with things that stand for other things, with chairs or chessmen, he enters the gateway to reason and imagination together. For the human reason discovers new relations between things not by deduction, but by that unpredictable blend of speculation and insight that scientists call induction, which—like other forms of imagination—cannot be formalized. We see it at work when Walter Hunter inquires into a child's memory, as much as when Blake and Coleridge do. Only a restless and original mind would have asked Hunter's questions and could have conceived his experiments, in a science that was dominated by Pavlov's reflex arcs and was heading toward the behaviorism of John Watson.[1]

Let me find a spectacular example for you from history. What is the most famous experiment that you had described to you as a child? I will hazard that it is the experiment that Galileo is said to have made in Sidney's age, in Pisa about 1590, by dropping two unequal balls from the Leaning Tower. There, we say, is a man in the modern mold, a man after our own hearts: he insisted on questioning the authority of Aristotle and St. Thomas Aquinas, and seeing with his own eyes whether (as they

15

1. Watson, a forerunner of B. F. Skinner, argued that all human behavior consists of conditioned reflexes in response to environmental stimuli.

said) the heavy ball would reach the ground before the light one. Seeing is believing.

Yet seeing is also imagining. Galileo did challenge the authority of Aristotle, and he did look at his mechanics. But the eye that Galileo used was the mind's eye. He did not drop balls from the Leaning Tower of Pisa—and if he had, he would have got a very doubtful answer. Instead, Galileo made an imaginary experiment in his head, which I will describe as he did years later in the book he wrote after the Holy Office silenced him: the *Discorsi . . . intorno a due nuove scienze,*[2] which was smuggled out to be printed in the Netherlands in 1638.

Suppose, said Galileo, that you drop two unequal balls from the tower at the same time. And suppose that Aristotle is right—suppose that the heavy ball falls faster, so that it steadily gains on the light ball, and hits the ground first. Very well. Now imagine the same experiment done again, with only one difference: this time the two unequal balls are joined by a string between them. The heavy ball will again move ahead, but now the light ball holds it back and acts as a drag or brake. So the light ball will be speeded up and the heavy ball will be slowed down; they must reach the ground together because they are tied together, but they cannot reach the ground as quickly as the heavy ball alone. Yet the string between them has turned the two balls into a single mass which is heavier than either ball—and surely (according to Aristotle) this mass should therefore move faster than either ball? Galileo's imaginary experiment has uncovered a contradiction; he says trenchantly, "You see how, from your assumption that a heavier body falls more rapidly than a lighter one, I infer that a (still) heavier body falls more slowly." There is only one way out of the contradiction: the heavy ball and the light ball must fall at the same rate, so that they go on falling at the same rate when they are tied together.

This argument is not conclusive, for nature might be more subtle (when the two balls are joined) than Galileo has allowed. And yet it is something more important: it is suggestive, it is stimulating, it opens a new view—in a word, it is imaginative. It cannot be settled without an actual experiment, because nothing that we imagine can become knowledge until we have translated it into, and backed it by, real experience. The test of imagination is experience. But then, that is as true of literature and the arts as it is of science. In science, the imaginary experiment is tested by confronting it with physical experience; and in literature, the imaginative conception is tested by confronting it with human experience. The superficial speculation in science is dismissed because it is found to falsify nature; and the shallow work of art is

2. *Treatise . . . on Two New Sciences.* In 1630, after publishing his heretical theory that the earth moves around the sun, Galileo was forced by the Inquisition to recant it under threat of torture.

discarded because it is found to be untrue to our own nature. So when Ella Wheeler Wilcox died in 1919, more people were reading her verses than Shakespeare's; yet in a few years her work was dead. It had been buried by its poverty of emotion and its trivialness of thought: which is to say that it had been proved to be as false to the nature of man as, say, Jean Baptiste Lamarck and Trofim Lysenko[3] were false to the nature of inheritance. The strength of the imagination, its enriching power and excitement, lies in its interplay with reality—physical and emotional.

I doubt if there is much to choose here between science and the arts: the imagination is not much more free, and not much less free, in one than in the other. All great scientists have used their imagination freely, and let it ride them to outrageous conclusions without crying "Halt!" Albert Einstein fiddled with imaginary experiments from boyhood, and was wonderfully ignorant of the facts that they were supposed to bear on. When he wrote the first of his beautiful papers on the random movement of atoms, he did not know that the Brownian motion which it predicted could be seen in any laboratory. He was sixteen when he invented the paradox that he resolved ten years later, in 1905, in the theory of relativity, and it bulked much larger in his mind than the experiment of Albert Michelson and Edward Morley[4] which had upset every other physicist since 1881. All his life Einstein loved to make up teasing puzzles like Galileo's, about falling lifts and the detection of gravity; and they carry the nub of the problems of general relativity on which he was working.

Indeed, it could not be otherwise. The power that man has over nature and himself, and that a dog lacks, lies in his command of imaginary experience. He alone has the symbols which fix the past and play with the future, possible and impossible. In the Renaissance, the symbolism of memory was thought to be mystical, and devices that were invented as mnemonics (by Giordano Bruno, for example, and by Robert Fludd) were interpreted as magic signs. The symbol is the tool which gives man his power, and it is the same tool whether the symbols are images or words, mathematical signs or mesons. And the symbols have a reach and a roundness that goes beyond their literal and practical

20

3. Lamarck (1744–1829), French biologist who held that characteristics acquired by experience were biologically transmittable. Lysenko (1898–1976), Russian biologist who has held that hereditary properties of organisms could be changed by manipulating the environment.
4. Physicists had believed space to be filled with an ether which made possible the propagation of light and magnetism; the Michelson-Morley experiment proved this untrue. Einstein, an outsider, always claimed not to have heard of the experiment until after he published his special theory of relativity, which not only accounted for the Michelson-Morley findings but resolved such paradoxes as the impossibility of distinguishing qualitatively between gravity and the pull caused by acceleration of an elevator, or lift.

meaning. They are the rich concepts under which the mind gathers many particulars into one name, and many instances into one general induction. When a man says *left* and *right,* he is outdistancing the dog not only in looking for a light; he is setting in train all the shifts of meaning, the overtones and the ambiguities, between *gauche* and *adroit* and *dexterous,* between *sinister* and the sense of right. When a man counts *one, two, three,* he is not only doing mathematics; he is on the path to the mysticism of numbers in Pythagoras and Vitruvius and Kepler, to the Trinity and the signs of the Zodiac.

I have described imagination as the ability to make images and to move them about inside one's head in new arrangements. This is the faculty that is specifically human, and it is the common root from which science and literature both spring and grow and flourish together. For they do flourish (and languish) together; the great ages of science are the great ages of all the arts, because in them powerful minds have taken fire from one another, breathless and higgledy-piggledy, without asking too nicely whether they ought to tie their imagination to falling balls or a haunted island. Galileo and Shakespeare, who were born in the same year, grew into greatness in the same age; when Galileo was looking through his telescope at the moon, Shakespeare was writing *The Tempest* and all Europe was in ferment, from Johannes Kepler to Peter Paul Rubens, and from the first table of logarithms by John Napier to the Authorized Version of the Bible.

Let me end with a last and spirited example of the common inspiration of literature and science, because it is as much alive today as it was three hundred years ago. What I have in mind is man's ageless fantasy, to fly to the moon. I do not display this to you as a high scientific enterprise; on the contrary, I think we have more important discoveries to make here on earth than wait for us, beckoning, at the horned surface of the moon. Yet I cannot belittle the fascination which that ice-blue journey has had for the imagination of men, long before it drew us to our television screens to watch the tumbling astronauts. Plutarch and Lucian, Ariosto and Ben Jonson wrote about it, before the days of Jules Verne and H. G. Wells and science fiction. The seventeenth century was heady with new dreams and fables about voyages to the moon. Kepler wrote one full of deep scientific ideas, which (alas) simply got his mother accused of witchcraft. In England, Francis Godwin wrote a wild and splendid work, *The Man in the Moone,* and the astronomer John Wilkins wrote a wild and learned one, *The Discovery of a New World.* They did not draw a line between science and fancy; for example, they all tried to guess just where in the journey the earth's gravity would stop. Only Kepler understood that gravity has no boundary, and put a law to it—which happened to be the wrong law.

All this was a few years before Isaac Newton was born, and it was all in his head that day in 1666 when he sat in his mother's garden, a young man of twenty-three, and thought about the reach of gravity. This was how he came to conceive his brilliant image, that the moon is like a ball which has been thrown so hard that it falls exactly as fast as the horizon, all the way round the earth. The image will do for any satellite, and Newton modestly calculated how long therefore an astronaut would take to fall round the earth once. He made it ninety minutes, and we have all seen now that he was right; but Newton had no way to check that. Instead he went on to calculate how long in that case the distant moon would take to round the earth, if indeed it behaves like a thrown ball that falls in the earth's gravity, and if gravity obeyed a law of inverse squares. He found that the answer would be twenty-eight days.

In that telling figure, the imagination that day chimed with nature, and made a harmony. We shall hear an echo of that harmony on the day when we land on the moon, because it will be not a technical but an imaginative triumph, that reaches back to the beginning of modern science and literature both. All great acts of imagination are like this, in the arts and in science, and convince us because they fill out reality with a deeper sense of rightness. We start with the simplest vocabulary of images, with *left* and *right* and *one, two, three,* and before we know how it happened the words and the numbers have conspired to make a match with nature: we catch in them the pattern of mind and matter as one.

25

THE READER

1. *How does the Hunter experiment provide Bronowski with the ground for defining the imagination?*
2. *On p. 198, Bronowski attributes the imagination to a "configuration" in the brain. Configuration seems vague here. What else shows uncertainty about exactly what happens in the brain? Does this uncertainty compromise the argument of this essay?*

THE WRITER

1. *Bronowski discusses the work of Galileo and Newton in the middle and at the end of his essay. What use does he make of their work? Does it justify placing them in the central and final positions?*
2. *What function is given to the mind by the title metaphor of reaching (later extended to symbols on p. 198)? What words does Bronowski use to indicate the objects reached for? What is the significance of his selecting these words?*
3. *Bronowski says that "seeing is also imagining." Write a brief essay exploring that assertion.*

Henry David Thoreau

OBSERVATION

There is no such thing as pure *objective* observation. Your observation, to be interesting, *i.e.* to be significant, must be *subjective*. The sum of what the writer of whatever class has to report is simply some human experience, whether he be poet or philosopher or man of science. The man of most science is the man most alive, whose life is the greatest event. Senses that take cognizance of outward things merely are of no avail. It matters not where or how far you travel—the farther commonly the worse—but how much alive you are. If it is possible to conceive of an event outside to humanity, it is not of the slightest significance, though it were the explosion of a planet. Every important worker will report what life there is in him. It makes no odds into what seeming deserts the poet is born. Though all his neighbors pronounce it a Sahara, it will be a paradise to him; for the desert which we see is the result of the barrenness of our experience. No mere willful activity whatever, whether in writing verses or collecting statistics, will produce true poetry or science. If you are really a sick man, it is indeed to be regretted, for you cannot accomplish so much as if you were well. All that a man has to say or do that can possibly concern mankind, is in some shape or other to tell the story of his love—to sing, and, if he is fortunate and keeps alive, he will be forever in love. This alone is to be alive to the extremities. It is a pity that this divine creature should ever suffer from cold feet; a still greater pity that the coldness so often reaches to his heart. I look over the report of the doings of a scientific association and am surprised that there is so little life to be reported; I am put off with a parcel of dry technical terms. Anything living is easily and naturally expressed in popular language. I cannot help suspecting that the life of these learned professors has been almost as inhuman and wooden as a rain-gauge or self-registering magnetic machine. They communicate no fact which rises to the temperature of bloodheat. It doesn't all amount to one rhyme.

Entry for May 6, 1854 from Thoreau's *Journal* (1837–59).

M. F. K. Fisher

MOMENT OF WISDOM

Tears do come occasionally into one's eyes, and they are more often than not a good thing. At least they are salty and, no matter what invisible wound they seep from, they purge and seal the tissues. But when they roll out and down the cheeks it is a different thing, and more amazing to one unaccustomed to such an outward and visible sign of an inward cleansing. Quick tears can sting and tease the eyeballs and their lids into suffusion and then a new clarity. The brimming and, perhaps fortunately, rarer kind, however, leaves things pale and thinned out, so that even a gross face takes on a procelain-like quality, and—in my own case—there is a sensation of great fragility or weariness of the bones and spirit.

I have had the experience of such tears very few times. Perhaps it is a good idea to mention one or two of them, if for no other reason than to remind myself that such a pure moment may never come again.

When I was twelve years old, my family was slowly installing itself about a mile down Painter Avenue outside Whittier, California, the thriving little Quaker town where I grew up, on an orange ranch with shaggy, neglected gardens and a long row of half-wild roses along the narrow county road. Our house sat far back in the tangle, with perhaps two hundred yards of gravel driveway leading in toward it.

There was a wide screened porch across the front of the house, looking into the tangle. It was the heart of the place. We sat there long into the cool evenings of summer, talking softly. Even in winter, we were there for lunch on bright days, and in the afternoon drinking tea or beer. In one corner, there was always a good pile of wood for the hearth fire in the living room, and four wide doors led into that room. They were open most of the time, although the fire burned day and night, brightly or merely a gentle token, all the decades we lived on the Ranch.

My grandmother had her own small apartment in the house, as seemed natural and part of the way to coexist, and wandering missionaries and other men of her own cut of cloth often came down the road to see her and discuss convocations and get money and other help. They left books of earnest import and dubious literary worth, like one printed in symbols for the young or illiterate, with Jehovah an eye surrounded by shooting beams of forked fire. Grandmother's friends, of whom I remember not a single one, usually stayed for a meal. Mother was often absent from such unannounced confrontations, prey to almost ritual attacks of what were referred to as "sick headaches," but my father always carved at his seat, head of the table. Grandmother, of course, was there. Father left early, and we children went up to bed, conditioned to complete lack of interest in the murmur of respectful manly voices and our grandmother's clear-cut Victorian guidance of the churchly talk below us. That was the pattern the first months at the Ranch, before the old lady died, and I am sure we ate amply and well, and with good manners, and we accepted sober men in dusty black suits as part of being alive.

When we moved down Painter Avenue into what was then real country, I was near intoxication from the flowers growing everywhere— the scraggly roses lining the road, all viciously thorned as they reverted to wildness, and poppies and lupine in the ditches and still between the rows of orange trees (soon to disappear as their seeds got plowed too deeply into the profitable soil), and exotic bulbs springing up hit or miss in our neglected gardens. I rooted around in all of it like a virgin piglet snuffling for truffles. My mother gave me free rein to keep the house filled with my own interpretations of the word "posy." It was a fine season in life.

One day, I came inside, very dusty and hot, with a basket of roses and weeds of beauty. The house seemed mine, airy and empty, full of shade. Perhaps everyone was in Whittier, marketing. I leaned my forehead against the screening of the front porch and breathed the wonderful dry air of temporary freedom, and off from the county road and onto our long narrow driveway came a small man, smaller than I, dressed in the crumpled hot black I recognized at once as the Cloth and carrying a small valise.

I wiped at my sweaty face and went to the screen door, to be polite to another of my grandmother's visitors. I wished I had stayed out, anywhere at all, being that age and so on, and aware of rebellion's new pricks.

He was indeed tiny, and frail in a way I had never noticed before in anyone. (I think this new awareness and what happened later came from the fact that I was alone in the family house and felt for the moment like a stranger made up of Grandmother and my parents and maybe God—that eye, Jehovah, but with no lightning.) He would not come in. I asked him if he would like some cool water, but he said no. His voice was thin. He asked to see Mother Holbrook, and when I told her she had died a few days before he did not seem at all bothered, and neither was I, except that he might be.

He asked if I would like to buy a Bible. I said no, we had many of them. His hands were too shaky and weak to open his satchel, but when I asked him again to come in, and started to open the door to go out to help him, he told me in such a firm way to leave him alone that I did. I did not reason about it, for it seemed to be an agreement between us.

He picked up his dusty satchel, said goodbye in a very gentle voice, and walked back down the long driveway to the county road and then south, thinking God knows what hopeless thoughts. A little past our gate, he stopped to pick one of the dusty roses. I leaned my head against the screening of our porch and was astounded and mystified to feel slow fat quiet tears roll from my unblinking eyes and down my cheeks.

I could not believe it was happening. Where did they spring from, so fully formed, so unexpectedly? Where had they been waiting, all my long life as a child? What had just happened to me, to make me cry without volition, without a sound or a sob?

In a kind of justification of what I thought was a weakness, for I had been schooled to consider all tears as such, I thought, If I could have given him something of mine . . . If I were rich, I would buy him a new black suit. . . . If I had next week's allowance and had not spent this week's on three Cherry Flips . . . If I could have given him some cool water or my love . . .

But the tiny old man, dry as a ditch weed, was past all that, as I came to learn long after my first passionate protest—past or beyond.

The first of such tears as mine that dusty day, which are perhaps rightly called the tears of new wisdom, are the most startling to one's supposed equanimity. Later, they have a different taste. Perhaps they seem more bitter because they are recognizable. But they are always as unpredictable. Once, I was lying with my head back, listening to a long program of radio music from New York, with Toscanini[1] drawing fine blood from his gang. I was hardly conscious of the sound—with my mind, anyway—and when it ended, my two ears, which I had never thought of as cup-like, were so full of silent tears that as I sat up they drenched and darkened my whole front with little gouts of brine. I felt amazed, beyond my embarrassment in a group of near-friends, for the music I had heard was not the kind I thought I liked, and the salty water had rolled down from my half-closed eyes like October rain, with no sting to it but perhaps promising a good winter.

Such things are, I repeat to myself, fortunately rare, for they are too mysterious to accept with equanimity. I prefer not to dig too much into their comings, but it is sure that they cannot be evoked or foretold. If anger has a part in them, it is latent, indirect—not an incentive. The

15

1. Arturo Toscanini (1867–1957), internationally esteemed Italian conductor. From 1926 to 1936 he conducted the New York Philharmonic Orchestra; in 1937 the NBC Symphony Orchestra was formed for him, and he conducted it until his retirement in 1954.

helpless weeping and sobbing and retching that sweeps over somebody
who inadvertently hears Churchill's voice rallying Englishmen to protect their shores, or Roosevelt telling people not to be afraid of fear, or
a civil-rights chieftain saying politely that there is such a thing as democracy—those violent physical reactions are proof of one's being alive and
aware. But the slow, large tears that spill from the eye, flowing like
unblown rain according to the laws of gravity and desolation—these are
the real tears, I think. They are the ones that have been simmered,
boiled, sieved, filtered past all anger and into the realm of acceptive
serenity.

There is a story about a dog and an ape that came to love each other.
The dog finally died, trying to keep the ape from returning to the jungle
where he should have been all along and where none but another ape
could follow. And one becomes the dog, the ape, no matter how clumsily
the story is told. One is the hapless lover.

I am all of them. I feel again the hot dusty screening on my forehead
as I watch the little man walk slowly out to the road and turn down past
the ditches and stop for a moment by a scraggly rosebush. If I could only
give him something, I think. If I could tell him something true.

It was a beginning for me, as the tears popped out so richly and ran
down, without a sigh or cry. I could see clearly through them, with no
blurring, and they did not sting. This last is perhaps the most astonishing
and fearsome part, past denial of any such encounter with wisdom, or
whatever it is.

Isaac Asimov

THE EUREKA PHENOMENON

In the old days, when I was writing a great deal of fiction, there would
come, once in a while, moments when I was stymied. Suddenly, I would
find I had written myself into a hole and could see no way out. To take
care of that, I developed a technique which invariably worked.

It was simply this—I went to the movies. Not just any movie. I had
to pick a movie which was loaded with action but which made no
demands on the intellect. As I watched, I did my best to avoid any
conscious thinking concerning my problem, and when I came out of the
movie I knew exactly what I would have to do to put the story back on
the track.

From *The Left Hand of the Electron* (1972).

It never failed.

In fact, when I was working on my doctoral dissertation, too many years ago, I suddenly came across a flaw in my logic that I had not noticed before and that knocked out everything I had done. In utter panic, I made my way to a Bob Hope movie—and came out with the necessary change in point of view.

It is my belief, you see, that thinking is a double phenomenon like breathing.   5

You can control breathing by deliberate voluntary action: you can breathe deeply and quickly, or you can hold your breath altogether, regardless of the body's needs at the time. This, however, doesn't work well for very long. Your chest muscles grow tired, your body clamors for more oxygen, or less, and you relax. The automatic involuntary control of breathing takes over, adjusts it to the body's needs and unless you have some respiratory disorder, you can forget about the whole thing.

Well, you can think by deliberate voluntary action, too, and I don't think it is much more efficient on the whole than voluntary breath control is. You can deliberately force your mind through channels of deductions and associations in search of a solution to some problem and before long you have dug mental furrows for yourself and find yourself circling round and round the same limited pathways. If those pathways yield no solution, no amount of further conscious thought will help.

On the other hand, if you let go, then the thinking process comes under automatic involuntary control and is more apt to take new pathways and make erratic associations you would not think of consciously. The solution will then come while you *think* you are *not* thinking.

The trouble is, though, that conscious thought involves no muscular action and so there is no sensation of physical weariness that would force you to quit. What's more, the panic of necessity tends to force you to go on uselessly, with each added bit of useless effort adding to the panic in a vicious cycle.

It is my feeling that it helps to relax, deliberately, by subjecting your   10
mind to material complicated enough to occupy the voluntary faculty of thought, but superficial enough not to engage the deeper involuntary one. In my case, it is an action movie; in your case, it might be something else.

I suspect it is the involuntary faculty of thought that gives rise to what we call "a flash of intuition," something that I imagine must be merely the result of unnoticed thinking.

Perhaps the most famous flash of intuition in the history of science took place in the city of Syracuse in third-century B.C. Sicily. Bear with me and I will tell you the story—

About 250 B.C., the city of Syracuse was experiencing a kind of

Golden Age. It was under the protection of the rising power of Rome, but it retained a king of its own and considerable self-government; it was prosperous; and it had a flourishing intellectual life.

The king was Hieron II, and he had commissioned a new golden crown from a goldsmith, to whom he had given an ingot of gold as raw material. Hieron, being a practical man, had carefully weighed the ingot and then weighed the crown he received back. The two weights were precisely equal. Good deal!

But then he sat and thought for a while. Suppose the goldsmith had subtracted a little bit of the gold, not too much, and had substituted an equal weight of the considerably less valuable copper. The resulting alloy would still have the appearance of pure gold, but the goldsmith would be plus a quantity of gold over and above his fee. He would be buying gold with copper, so to speak, and Hieron would be neatly cheated.

Hieron didn't like the thought of being cheated any more than you or I would, but he didn't know how to find out for sure if he had been. He could scarcely punish the goldsmith on mere suspicion. What to do?

Fortunately, Hieron had an advantage few rulers in the history of the world could boast. He had a relative of considerable talent. The relative was named Archimedes and he probably had the greatest intellect the world was to see prior to the birth of Newton.

Archimedes was called in and was posed the problem. He had to determine whether the crown Hieron showed him was pure gold, or was gold to which a small but significant quantity of copper had been added.

If we were to reconstruct Archimedes' reasoning, it might go as follows. Gold was the densest known substance (at that time). Its density in modern terms is 19.3 grams per cubic centimeter. This means that a given weight of gold takes up less volume than the same weight of anything else! In fact, a given weight of pure gold takes up less volume than the same weight of *any* kind of impure gold.

The density of copper is 8.92 grams per cubic centimeter, just about half that of gold. If we consider 100 grams of pure gold, for instance, it is easy to calculate it to have a volume of 5.18 cubic centimeters. But suppose that 100 grams of what looked like pure gold was really only 90 grams of gold and 10 grams of copper. The 90 grams of gold would have a volume of 4.66 cubic centimeters, while the 10 grams of copper would have a volume of 1.12 cubic centimeters; for a total value of 5.78 cubic centimeters.

The difference between 5.18 cubic centimeters and 5.78 cubic centimeters is quite a noticeable one, and would instantly tell if the crown were of pure gold, or if it contained 10 per cent copper (with the missing 10 per cent of gold tucked neatly in the goldsmith's strongbox).

All one had to do, then, was measure the volume of the crown and compare it with the volume of the same weight of pure gold.

The mathematics of the time made it easy to measure the volume of many simple shapes: a cube, a sphere, a cone, a cylinder, any flattened object of simple regular shape and known thickness, and so on.

We can imagine Archimedes saying, "All that is necessary, sire, is to pound that crown flat, shape it into a square of uniform thickness, and then I can have the answer for you in a moment."

Whereupon Hieron must certainly have snatched the crown away and   25
said, "No such thing. I can do that much without you; I've studied the principles of mathematics, too. This crown is a highly satisfactory work of art and I won't have it damaged. Just calculate its volume without in any way altering it."

But Greek mathematics had no way of determining the volume of anything with a shape as irregular as the crown, since integral calculus had not yet been invented (and wouldn't be for two thousand years, almost). Archimedes would have had to say, "There is no known way, sire, to carry through a non-destructive determination of volume."

"Then think of one," said Hieron testily.

And Archimedes must have set about thinking of one, and gotten nowhere. Nobody knows how long he thought, or how hard, or what hypotheses he considered and discarded, or any of the details.

What we do know is that, worn out with thinking, Archimedes decided to visit the public baths and relax. I think we are quite safe in saying that Archimedes had no intention of taking his problem to the baths with him. It would be ridiculous to imagine he would, for the public baths of a Greek metropolis weren't intended for that sort of thing.

The Greek baths were a place for relaxation. Half the social aristoc-   30
racy of the town would be there and there was a great deal more to do than wash. One steamed one's self, got a massage, exercised, and engaged in general socializing. We can be sure that Archimedes intended to forget the stupid crown for a while.

One can envisage him engaging in light talk, discussing the latest news from Alexandria and Carthage, the latest scandals in town, the latest funny jokes at the expense of the country-squire Romans—and then he lowered himself into a nice hot bath which some bumbling attendant had filled too full.

The water in the bath slopped over as Archimedes got in. Did Archimedes notice that at once, or did he sigh, sink back, and paddle his feet awhile before noting the water-slop. I guess the latter. But, whether soon or late, he noticed, and that one fact, added to all the chains of reasoning his brain had been working on during the period of relaxation when it was unhampered by the comparative stupidities (even in Archimedes) of voluntary thought, gave Archimedes his answer in one blinding flash of insight.

Jumping out of the bath, he proceeded to run home at top speed through the streets of Syracuse. He did *not* bother to put on his clothes. The thought of Archimedes running naked through Syracuse has titillated dozens of generations of youngsters who have heard this story, but I must explain that the ancient Greeks were quite lighthearted in their attitude toward nudity. They thought no more of seeing a naked man on the streets of Syracuse, than we would on the Broadway stage.

And as he ran, Archimedes shouted over and over, "I've got it! I've got it!" Of course, knowing no English, he was compelled to shout it in Greek, so it came out, *"Eureka! Eureka!"*

35   Archimedes' solution was so simple that anyone could understand it—once Archimedes explained it.

If an object that is not affected by water in any way, is immersed in water, it is bound to displace an amount of water equal to its own volume, since two objects cannot occupy the same space at the same time.

Suppose, then, you had a vessel large enough to hold the crown and suppose it had a small overflow spout set into the middle of its side. And suppose further that the vessel was filled with water exactly to the spout, so that if the water level were raised a bit higher, however slightly, some would overflow.

Next, suppose that you carefully lower the crown into the water. The water level would rise by an amount equal to the volume of the crown, and that volume of water would pour out the overflow and be caught in a small vessel. Next, a lump of gold, known to be pure and exactly equal in weight to the crown, is also immersed in the water and again the level rises and the overflow is caught in a second vessel.

If the crown were pure gold, the overflow would be exactly the same in each case, and the volume of water caught in the two small vessels would be equal. If, however, the crown were of alloy, it would produce a larger overflow than the pure gold would and this would be easily noticeable.

40   What's more, the crown would in no way be harmed, defaced, or even as much as scratched. More important, Archimedes had discovered the "principle of buoyancy."

And was the crown pure gold? I've heard that it turned out to be alloy and that the goldsmith was executed, but I wouldn't swear to it.

How often does this "Eureka phenomenon" happen? How often is there this flash of deep insight during a moment of relaxation, this triumphant cry of "I've got it! I've got it!" which must surely be a moment of the purest ecstasy this sorry world can afford?

I wish there were some way we could tell. I suspect that in the history of science it happens *often;* I suspect that very few significant discoveries are made by the pure technique of voluntary thought; I suspect that voluntary thought may possibly prepare the ground (if even that), but that the final touch, the real inspiration, comes when thinking is under involuntary control.

But the world is in a conspiracy to hide the fact. Scientists are wedded to reason, to the meticulous working out of consequences from assumptions to the careful organization of experiments designed to check those consequences. If a certain line of experiments ends nowhere, it is omitted from the final report. If an inspired guess turns out to be correct, it is *not* reported as an inspired guess. Instead, a solid line of voluntary thought is invented after the fact to lead up to the thought, and that is what is inserted in the final report.

The result is that anyone reading scientific papers would swear that *nothing* took place but voluntary thought maintaining a steady clumping stride from origin to destination, and that just can't be true.

It's such a shame. Not only does it deprive science of much of its glamour (how much of the dramatic story in Watson's *Double Helix* do you suppose got into the final reports announcing the great discovery of the structure of DNA?[1]), but it hands over the important process of "insight," "inspiration," "revelation" to the mystic.

The scientist actually becomes ashamed of having what we might call a revelation, as though to have one is to betray reason—when actually what we call revelation in a man who has devoted his life to reasoned thought, is after all merely reasoned thought that is not under voluntary control.

Only once in a while in modern times do we ever get a glimpse into the workings of involuntary reasoning, and when we do, it is always fascinating. Consider, for instance, the case of Friedrich August Kekule von Stradonitz.

In Kekule's time, a century and a quarter ago, a subject of great interest to chemists was the structure of organic molecules (those associated with living tissue). Inorganic molecules were generally simple in the sense that they were made up of few atoms. Water molecules, for instance, are made up of two atoms of hydrogen and one of oxygen (H_2O). Molecules of ordinary salt are made up of one atom of sodium and one of chlorine ($NaCl$), and so on.

Organic molecules, on the other hand, often contained a large number of atoms. Ethyl alcohol molecules have two carbon atoms, six hydrogen atoms, and an oxygen atom (C_2H_6O); the molecule of ordinary cane sugar is $C_{12}H_{22}O_{11}$, and other molecules are even more complex.

Then, too, it is sufficient, in the case of inorganic molecules generally,

45

50

1. I'll tell you, in case you're curious. None! [Asimov's note]. How Francis Crick and James Watson discovered the molecular structure of this vital substance is told in Watson's autobiographical book, *The Double Helix*.

merely to know the kinds and numbers of atoms in the molecule; in organic molecules, more is necessary. Thus, dimethyl ether has the formula C_2H_6O, just as ethyl alcohol does, and yet the two are quite different in properties. Apparently, the atoms are arranged differently within the molecules—but how to determine the arrangements?

In 1852, an English chemist, Edward Frankland, had noticed that the atoms of a particular element tended to combine with a fixed number of other atoms. This combining number was called "valence." Kekule in 1858 reduced this notion to a system. The carbon atom, he decided (on the basis of plenty of chemical evidence) had a valence of four; the hydrogen atom, a valence of one; and the oxygen atom, a valence of two (and so on).

Why not represent the atoms as their symbols plus a number of attached dashes, that number being equal to the valence. Such atoms could then be put together as though they were so many Tinker Toy units and "structural formulas" could be built up.

It was possible to reason out that the structural formula of ethyl alcohol was

$$
\begin{array}{cc}
\text{H} & \text{H} \\
| & | \\
\text{H}-\text{C}-\text{C}-\text{O}-\text{H,} \\
| & | \\
\text{H} & \text{H}
\end{array}
$$

while that of dimethyl ether was

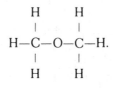

In each case, there were two carbon atoms, each with four dashes attached; six hydrogen atoms, each with one dash attached; and an oxygen atom with two dashes attached. The molecules were built up of the same components, but in different arrangements.

Kekule's theory worked beautifully. It has been immensely deepened and elaborated since his day, but you can still find structures very much like Kekule's Tinker Toy formulas in any modern chemical textbook. They represent oversimplifications of the true situation, but they remain extremely useful in practice even so.

The Kekule structures were applied to many organic molecules in the years after 1858 and the similarities and contrasts in the structures neatly

55

matched similarities and contrasts in properties. The key to the rationalization of organic chemistry had, it seemed, been found.

Yet there was one disturbing fact. The well-known chemical benzene wouldn't fit. It was known to have a molecule made up of equal numbers of carbon and hydrogen atoms. Its molecular weight was known to be 78 and a single carbon-hydrogen combination had a weight of 13. Therefore, the benzene molecule had to contain six carbon-hydrogen combinations and its formula had to be C_6H_6.

But that meant trouble. By the Kekule formulas, the hydrocarbons (molecules made up of carbon and hydrogen atoms only) could easily be envisioned as chains of carbon atoms with hydrogen atoms attached. If all the valences of the carbon atoms were filled with hydrogen atoms, as in "hexane," whose molecule looks like this—

$$
\begin{array}{cccccc}
H & H & H & H & H & H \\
| & | & | & | & | & | \\
H-C-C-C-C-C-C-H \\
| & | & | & | & | & | \\
H & H & H & H & H & H
\end{array}
$$

the compound is said to be saturated. Such saturated hydrocarbons were found to have very little tendency to react with other substances.

If some of the valences were not filled, unused bonds were added to those connecting the carbon atoms. Double bonds were formed as in "hexene"—

60

$$
\begin{array}{cccccc}
H & H & H & H & H & H \\
| & | & | & | & | & | \\
H-C-C-C=C-C-C-H \\
| & | & & & | & | \\
H & H & & & H & H
\end{array}
$$

Hexene is unsaturated, for that double bond has a tendency to open up and add other atoms. Hexene is chemically active.

When six carbons are present in a molecule, it takes fourteen hydrogen atoms to occupy all the valence bonds and make it inert—as in hexane. In hexene, on the other hand, there are only twelve hydrogens. If there were still fewer hydrogen atoms, there would be more than one double bond; there might even be triple bonds, and the compound would be still more active than hexene.

Yet benzene, which is C_6H_6 and has eight fewer hydrogen atoms than hexane, is *less* active than hexene, which has only two fewer hydrogen atoms than hexane. In fact, benzene is even less active than hexane itself. The six hydrogen atoms in the benzene molecule seem to satisfy the six carbon atoms to a greater extent than do the fourteen hydrogen atoms in hexane.

For heaven's sake, why?

This might seem unimportant. The Kekule formulas were so beautifully suitable in the case of so many compounds that one might simply dismiss benzene as an exception to the general rule.

65   Science, however, is not English grammar. You can't just categorize something as an exception. If the exception doesn't fit into the general system, then the general system must be wrong.

Or, take the more positive approach. An exception can often be made to fit into a general system, provided the general system is broadened. Such broadening generally represents a great advance and for this reason, exceptions ought to be paid great attention.

For some seven years, Kekule faced the problem of benzene and tried to puzzle out how a chain of six carbon atoms could be completely satisfied with as few as six hydrogen atoms in benzene and yet be left unsatisfied with twelve hydrogen atoms in hexene.

Nothing came to him!

And then one day in 1865 (he tells the story himself) he was in Ghent, Belgium, and in order to get to some destination, he boarded a public bus. He was tired and, undoubtedly, the droning beat of the horses' hooves on the cobblestones, lulled him. He fell into a comatose half-sleep.

70   In that sleep, he seemed to see a vision of atoms attaching themselves to each other in chains that moved about. (Why not? It was the sort of thing that constantly occupied his waking thoughts.) But then one chain twisted in such a way that head and tail joined, forming a ring—and Kekule woke with a start.

To himself, he must surely have shouted "Eureka," for indeed he had it. The six carbon atoms of benzene formed a ring and not a chain, so that the structural formula looked like this:

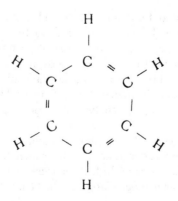

To be sure, there were still three double bonds, so you might think the molecule had to be very active—but now there was a difference. Atoms in a ring might be expected to have different properties from those in a chain and double bonds in one case might not have the properties of those in the other. At least, chemists could work on that assumption and see if it involved them in contradictions.

It didn't. The assumption worked excellently well. It turned out that organic molecules could be divided into two groups: aromatic and aliphatic. The former had the benzene ring (or certain other similar rings) as part of the structure and the latter did not. Allowing for different properties within each group, the Kekule structures worked very well.

For nearly seventy years, Kekule's vision held good in the hard field of actual chemical techniques, guiding the chemist through the jungle of reactions that led to the synthesis of more and more molecules. Then, in 1932, Linus Pauling applied quantum mechanics to chemical structure with sufficient subtlety to explain just why the benzene ring was so special and what had proven correct in practice proved correct in theory as well.

Other cases? Certainly.   75

In 1764, the Scottish engineer James Watt was working as an instrument maker for the University of Glasgow. The university gave him a model of a Newcomen steam engine, which didn't work well, and asked him to fix it. Watt fixed it without trouble, but even when it worked perfectly, it didn't work well. It was far too inefficient and consumed incredible quantities of fuel. Was there a way to improve that?

Thought didn't help; but a peaceful, relaxed walk on a Sunday afternoon did. Watt returned with the key notion in mind of using two separate chambers, one for steam only and one for cold water only, so that the same chamber did not have to be constantly cooled and reheated to the infinite waste of fuel.

The Irish mathematician William Rowan Hamilton worked up a theory of "quaternions" in 1843 but couldn't complete that theory until he grasped the fact that there were conditions under which $p \times q$ was *not* equal to $q \times p$. The necessary thought came to him in a flash one time when he was walking to town with his wife.

The German physiologist Otto Loewi was working on the mechanism of nerve action, in particular, on the chemicals produced by nerve endings. He awoke at 3 A.M. one night in 1921 with a perfectly clear notion of the type of experiment he would have to run to settle a key point that was puzzling him. He wrote it down and went back to sleep. When he woke in the morning, he found he couldn't remember what his inspiration had been. He remembered he had written it down, but he couldn't read his writing.

The next night, he woke again at 3 A.M. with the clear thought once   80 more in mind. This time, he didn't fool around. He got up, dressed himself, went straight to the laboratory and began work. By 5 A.M. he had proved his point and the consequences of his findings became important enough in later years so that in 1936 he received a share in the Nobel prize in medicine and physiology.

How very often this sort of thing must happen, and what a shame that scientists are so devoted to their belief in conscious thought that they so consistently obscure the actual methods by which they obtain their results.

THE READER

1. *Does Asimov argue that science ought to abandon reasoned thought in favor of intuition?*
2. *Is cultivation of "the Eureka phenomenon" encouraged in any of the science courses you may have taken or are now taking? Why, or why not?*
3. *In "The Reach of Imagination" (p. 196), Bronowski discusses imagination and science. Are there points on which Asimov and Bronowski would seem to be in agreement concerning science?*

THE WRITER

1. *What does Asimov find wrong about scientific reports as they are customarily written? Do you agree? If scientific writing were not strictly reasonable, wouldn't there be a danger of misrepresenting science?*
2. *Have you ever experienced anything like "the Eureka phenomenon" Asimov describes? If so, write an account of what happened. Tell what your feelings were when the phenomenon occurred. Did you ever report the discovery in just that way to any one else (to a teacher, for example)? If so, what was the other person's response?*

Paul Theroux

BEING A MAN

There is a pathetic sentence in the chapter "Fetishism" in Dr. Norman Cameron's book *Personality Development and Psychopathology*. It goes, "Fetishists are nearly always men; and their commonest fetish is a woman's shoe." I cannot read that sentence without thinking that it is just one more awful thing about being a man—and perhaps it is an important thing to know about us.

I have always disliked being a man. The whole idea of manhood in America is pitiful, in my opinion. This version of masculinity is a little like having to wear an ill-fitting coat for one's entire life (by contrast, I imagine femininity to be an oppressive sense of nakedness). Even the expression "Be a man!" strikes me as insulting and abusive. It means: Be stupid, be unfeeling, obedient, soldierly and stop thinking. Man means "manly"—how can one think about men without considering the terrible ambition of manliness? And yet it is part of every man's life. It is a hideous and crippling lie; it not only insists on difference and connives at superiority, it is also by its very nature destructive—emotionally damaging and socially harmful.

The youth who is subverted, as most are, into believing in the masculine ideal is effectively separated from women and he spends the rest of his life finding women a riddle and a nuisance. Of course, there is a female version of this male affliction. It begins with mothers encouraging little girls to say (to other adults) "Do you like my new dress?" In a sense, little girls are traditionally urged to please adults with a kind of coquettishness, while boys are enjoined to behave like monkeys toward each other. The nine-year-old coquette proceeds to become womanish in a subtle power game in which she learns to be sexually indispensable, socially decorative and always alert to a man's sense of inadequacy.

Femininity—being lady-like—implies needing a man as witness and seducer; but masculinity celebrates the exclusive company of men. That is why it is so grotesque; and that is also why there is no manliness without inadequacy—because it denies men the natural friendship of women.

It is very hard to imagine any concept of manliness that does not belittle women, and it begins very early. At an age when I wanted to meet girls—let's say the treacherous years of thirteen to sixteen—I was told to take up a sport, get more fresh air, join the Boy Scouts, and I

5

From *Sunrise with Seamonsters* (1985).

was urged not to read so much. It was the 1950s and if you asked too many questions about sex you were sent to camp—boy's camp, of course: the nightmare. Nothing is more unnatural or prison-like than a boy's camp, but if it were not for them we would have no Elks' Lodges, no pool rooms, no boxing matches, no Marines.

And perhaps no sports as we know them. Everyone is aware of how few in number are the athletes who behave like gentlemen. Just as high school basketball teaches you how to be a poor loser, the manly attitude toward sports seems to be little more than a recipe for creating bad marriages, social misfits, moral degenerates, sadists, latent rapists and just plain louts. I regard high school sports as a drug far worse than marijuana, and it is the reason that the average tennis champion, say, is a pathetic oaf.

Any objective study would find the quest for manliness essentially right-wing, puritanical, cowardly, neurotic and fueled largely by a fear of women. It is also certainly philistine. There is no book-hater like a Little League coach. But indeed all the creative arts are obnoxious to the manly ideal, because at their best the arts are pursued by uncompetitive and essentially solitary people. It makes it very hard for a creative youngster, for any boy who expresses the desire to be alone seems to be saying that there is something wrong with him.

It ought to be clear by now that I have something of an objection to the way we turn boys into men. It does not surprise me that when the President of the United States has his customary weekend off he dresses like a cowboy—it is both a measure of his insecurity and his willingness to please. In many ways, American culture does little more for a man than prepare him for modeling clothes in the L. L. Bean[1] catalog. I take this as a personal insult because for many years I found it impossible to admit to myself that I wanted to be a writer. It was my guilty secret, because being a writer was incompatible with being a man.

There are people who might deny this, but that is because the American writer, typically, has been so at pains to prove his manliness that we have come to see literariness and manliness as mingled qualities. But first there was a fear that writing was not a manly profession—indeed, not a profession at all. (The paradox in American letters is that it has always been easier for a woman to write and for a man to be published.) Growing up, I had thought of sports as wasteful and humiliating, and the idea of manliness was a bore. My wanting to become a writer was not a flight from that oppressive role-playing, but I quickly saw that it was at odds with it. Everything in stereotyped manliness goes against the life of the mind. The Hemingway personality is too tedious to go into

1. A mail-order and retail store in Freeport, Maine, known for rugged sporting clothes and camping gear.

here, and in any case his exertions are well known, but certainly it was
not until this aberrant behavior was examined by feminists in the 1960s
that any male writer dared question the pugnacity in Hemingway's
fiction. All the bullfighting and arm wrestling and elephant shooting
diminished Hemingway as a writer, but it is consistent with a prevailing
attitude in American writing: one cannot be a male writer without first
proving that one is a man.

It is normal in America for a man to be dismissive or even somewhat   10
apologetic about being a writer. Various factors make it easier. There
is a heartiness about journalism that makes it acceptable—journalism is
the manliest form of American writing and, therefore, the profession the
most independent-minded women seek (yes, it is an illusion, but that is
my point). Fiction-writing is equated with a kind of dispirited failure and
is only manly when it produces wealth—money is masculinity. So is
drinking. Being a drunkard is another assertion, if misplaced, of manliness. The American male writer is traditionally proud of his heavy
drinking. But we are also a very literal-minded people. A man proves his
manhood in America in old-fashioned ways. He kills lions, like Hemingway; or he hunts ducks, like Nathanael West; or he makes pronouncements like, "A man should carry enough knife to defend himself with,"
as James Jones once said to a *Life* interviewer. Or he says he can drink
you under the table. But even tiny drunken William Faulkner loved to
mount a horse and go fox hunting, and Jack Kerouac roistered up and
down Manhattan in a lumberjack shirt (and spent every night of *The
Subterraneans* with his mother in Queens). And we are familiar with the
lengths to which Norman Mailer is prepared, in his endearing way, to
prove that he is just as much a monster as the next man.[2]

When the novelist John Irving was revealed as a wrestler, people took
him to be a very serious writer; and even a bubble reputation like Eric
(Love Story) Segal's was enhanced by the news that he ran the marathon
in a respectable time. How surprised we would be if Joyce Carol Oates
were revealed as a sumo wrestler or Joan Didion active in pumping iron.
"Lives in New York City with her three children" is the typical woman
writer's biographical note, for just as the male writer must prove he has
achieved a sort of muscular manhood, the woman writer—or rather her
publicists—must prove her motherhood.

There would be no point in saying any of this if it were not generally
accepted that to be a man is somehow—even now in feminist-influenced
America—a privilege. It is on the contrary an unmerciful and punishing
burden. Being a man is bad enough; being manly is appalling (in this
sense, women's lib has done much more for men than for women). It

2. The writers named in this paragraph and
the next are twentieth-century Americans
whose personal lives may be seen as conforming (or not conforming, in the cases of
Oates and Didion) to stereotypical ideas of
masculinity.

is the sinister silliness of men's fashions, and a clubby attitude in the arts. It is the subversion of good students. It is the so-called Dress Code of the Ritz-Carlton Hotel in Boston, and it is the institutionalized cheating in college sports. It is the most primitive insecurity.

And this is also why men often object to feminism but are afraid to explain why: of course women have a justified grievance, but most men believe—and with reason—that their lives are just as bad.

THE READER

1. *What, according to Theroux, are the problems with "being a man"? Is he right?*
2. *Are there any places in his essay where Theroux seems to expect disagreement with his statements and might almost be said to invite disagreement? Give examples, and explain why you perceive him as expecting or inviting disagreement.*
3. *Theroux asserts that men in America aren't expected to be writers and Keller (p. 1020) asserts that women aren't expected to be scientists. To what degree do they see the same kind of thinking behind these expectations?*

THE WRITER

1. *Theroux takes a very personal approach to his topic. Is he in any way objective? How does he establish his authority in the essay? Does he persuade you that he knows what he is talking about? If so, how?*
2. *Indicate any places where Theroux uses hyperbolic language. What is his purpose in doing so? Is he ever outrageous in his assertions? If so, why?*
3. *Write an essay called "Being a Student," using whatever forceful means you can command to persuade your reader that being a student constitutes a definite hardship. Advance, if you wish, any possible remedies.*

Scott Russell Sanders

LOOKING AT WOMEN

On that sizzling July afternoon, the girl who crossed at the stoplight in front of our car looked, as my mother would say, as though she had been poured into her pink shorts. The girl's matching pink halter bared

First published in *Georgia Review* (Spring 1989).

her stomach and clung to her nubbin breasts, leaving little to the imagination, as my mother would also say. Until that moment, it had never made any difference to me how much or little a girl's clothing revealed, for my imagination had been entirely devoted to other mysteries. I was eleven. The girl was about fourteen, the age of my buddy Norman who lounged in the back seat with me. Staring after her, Norman elbowed me in the ribs and murmured, "Check out that chassis."

His mother glared around from the driver's seat. "Hush your mouth."

"I was talking about that sweet Chevy," said Norman, pointing out a souped-up jalopy at the curb.

"I know what you were talking about," his mother snapped.

No doubt she did know, since mothers could read minds, but at first I did not have a clue. Chassis? I knew what it meant for a car, an airplane, a radio, or even a cannon to have a chassis. But could a girl have one as well? I glanced after the retreating figure, and suddenly noticed with a sympathetic twitching in my belly the way her long raven ponytail swayed in rhythm to her walk and the way her fanny jostled in those pink shorts. In July's dazzle of sun, her swinging legs and arms beamed at me a semaphore I could almost read.

As the light turned green and our car pulled away, Norman's mother cast one more scowl at her son in the rearview mirror, saying, "Just think how it makes her feel to have you two boys gawking at her."

How? I wondered.

"Makes her feel like hot stuff," said Norman, owner of a bold mouth.

"If you don't get your mind out of the gutter, you're going to wind up in the state reformatory," said his mother.

Norman gave a snort. I sank into the seat, and tried to figure out what power had sprung from that sashaying girl to zap me in the belly.

Only after much puzzling did it dawn on me that I must finally have drifted into the force-field of sex, as a space traveler who has lived all his years in free fall might rocket for the first time within gravitational reach of a star. Even as a bashful eleven-year-old I knew the word *sex*, of course, and I could paste that name across my image of the tantalizing girl. But a label for a mystery no more explains a mystery than the word *gravity* explains gravity. As I grew a beard and my taste shifted from girls to women, I acquired a more cagey language for speaking of desire, I picked up disarming theories. First by hearsay and then by experiment, I learned the delicious details of making babies. I came to appreciate the urgency for propagation that litters the road with maple seeds and drives salmon up waterfalls and yokes the newest crop of boys to the newest crop of girls. Books in their killjoy wisdom taught me that all the valentines and violins, the waltzes and glances, the long fever and ache of romance, were merely embellishments on biology's instructions that we multiply our kind. And yet, the fraction of desire that actually leads to procreation is so vanishingly small as to seem irrelevant. In his lifetime a man sways to a million longings, only a few of which, or perhaps none at all, ever lead to the fathering of children. Now, thirty years away from that July afternoon, firmly married, twice a father, I am still humming from the power unleashed by the girl in pink shorts, still wondering how it made her feel to have two boys gawk at her, still puzzling over how to dwell in the force-field of desire.

How should a man look at women? It is a peculiarly and perhaps neurotically human question. Billy goats do not fret over how they should look at nanny goats. They look or don't look, as seasons and hormones dictate, and feel what they feel without benefit of theory. There is more billy goat in most men than we care to admit. None of us, however, is pure goat. To live utterly as an animal would make the business of sex far tidier but also drearier. If we tried, like Rousseau,[1] to peel off the layers of civilization and imagine our way back to some pristine man and woman who have not yet been corrupted by hand-me-down notions of sexuality, my hunch is that we would find, in our speculative state of nature, that men regarded women with appalling simplicity. In any case, unlike goats, we dwell in history. What attracts our eyes and rouses our blood is only partly instinctual. Other forces contend in us as well: the voices of books and religions, the images of art and film and advertising, the entire chorus of culture. Norman's telling me to relish the sight of females and his mother's telling me to keep my eyes to myself are only two of the many voices quarreling in my head.

If there were a rule book for sex, it would be longer than the one for baseball (that byzantine sport), more intricate and obscure than tax instructions from the Internal Revenue Service. What I present here are a few images and reflections that cling, for me, to this one item in such a compendium of rules: How should a man look at women?

Well before I was to see any women naked in the flesh, I saw a bevy of them naked in photographs, hung in a gallery around the bed of my freshman roommate at college. A *Playboy* subscriber, he would pluck the centerfold from its staples each month and tape another airbrushed lovely to the wall. The gallery was in place when I moved in, and for an instant before I realized what I was looking at, all that expanse of skin reminded me of a meat locker back in Newton Falls, Ohio. I never quite shook that first impression, even after I had inspected the pinups at my

---

1. Jean Jacques Rousseau (1712–78), Swiss-born French philosopher, author, political theorist, and composer. His closeness to nature, individualism, rebellion against the established social and political order, and glorification of the emotions made him the father of French romanticism.

leisure on subsequent days. Every curve of buttock and breast was news to me, an innocent kid from the Puritan back roads. Today you would be hard pressed to find a college freshman as ignorant as I was of female anatomy, if only because teenagers now routinely watch movies at home that would have been shown, during my teen years, exclusively on the fly-speckled screens of honky-tonk cinemas or in the basement of the Kinsey Institute.[2] I studied those alien shapes on the wall with a curiosity that was not wholly sexual, a curiosity tinged with the wonder that astronomers must have felt when they pored over the early photographs of the far side of the moon.

The paper women seemed to gaze back at me, enticing or mocking, yet even in my adolescent dither I was troubled by the phony stare, for I knew this was no true exchange of looks. Those mascaraed eyes were not fixed on me but on a camera. What the models felt as they posed I could only guess—perhaps the boredom of any numbskull job, perhaps the weight of dollar bills, perhaps the sweltering lights of fame, perhaps a tingle of the power that launched a thousand ships.

Whatever their motives, these women had chosen to put themselves on display. For the instant of the photograph, they had become their bodies, as a prizefighter does in the moment of landing a punch, as a weightlifter does in the moment of hoisting a barbell, as a ballerina does in the whirl of a pirouette, as we all do in the crisis of making love or dying. Men, ogling such photographs, are supposed to feel that where so much surface is revealed there can be no depths. Yet I never doubted that behind the makeup and the plump curves and the two dimensions of the image there was an inwardness, a feeling self as mysterious as my own. In fact, during moments when I should have been studying French or thermodynamics, I would glance at my roommate's wall and invent mythical lives for those goddesses. The lives I made up were adolescent ones, to be sure; but so was mine. Without that saving aura of inwardness, these women in the glossy photographs would have become merely another category of objects for sale, alongside the sports cars and stereo systems and liquors advertised in the same pages. If not extinguished, however, their humanity was severly reduced. And if by simplifying themselves they had lost some human essence, then by gaping at them I had shared in the theft.

What did that gaping take from me? How did it affect my way of seeing other women, those who would never dream of lying nude on a fake tiger rug before the million-faceted eye of a camera? The bodies in the photographs were implausibly smooth and slick and inflated, like balloon caricatures that might be floated overhead in a parade. Free of

2. Indiana University's Institute for Sex Research, directed, beginning in 1942, by American biologist Alfred Charles Kinsey (1894–1956).

sweat and scars and imperfections, sensual without being fertile, tempting yet impregnable, they were Platonic ideals of the female form,
divorced from time and the fluster of living, excused from the perplexities of mind. No actual woman could rival their insipid perfection.

The swains who gathered to admire my roommate's gallery discussed
the pinups in the same tones and in much the same language as the
farmers back home in Ohio used for assessing cows. The relevant parts
of male or female bodies are quickly named—and, the *Kamasutra* [3] and
Marquis de Sade [4] notwithstanding, the number of ways in which those
parts can be stimulated or conjoined is touchingly small—so these studly
conversations were more tedious than chitchat about the weather. I
would lie on my bunk pondering calculus or Aeschylus and unwillingly
hear the same few nouns and fewer verbs issuing from one mouth after
another, and I would feel smugly superior. Here I was, improving my
mind, while theirs wallowed in the notorious gutter. Eventually the
swains would depart, leaving me in peace, and from the intellectual
heights of my bunk I would glance across at those photographs—and
yield to the gravity of lust. Idiot flesh! How stupid that a counterfeit
stare and artful curves, printed in millions of copies on glossy paper,
could arouse me. But there it was, not the first proof of my body's
automatism and not the last.

Nothing in men is more machinelike than the flipping of sexual
switches. I have never been able to read with a straight face the claims
made by D. H. Lawrence and lesser pundits that the penis is a god, a
lurking dragon. It more nearly resembles a railroad crossing signal, which
stirs into life at intervals to announce, "Here comes a train." Or, if the
penis must be likened to an animal, let it be an ill-trained circus dog,
sitting up and playing dead and heeling whenever it takes a notion,
oblivious of the trainer's commands. Meanwhile, heart, lungs, blood
vessels, pupils, and eyelids all assert their independence like the members of a rebellious troupe. Reason stands helpless at the center of the
ring, cracking its whip.

20   While he was president, Jimmy Carter raised a brouhaha by confessing in a *Playboy* interview, of all shady places, that he occasionally felt
lust in his heart for women. What man hasn't, aside from those who feel
lust in their hearts for other men? The commentators flung their stones
anyway. Naughty, naughty, they chirped. Wicked Jimmy. Perhaps Mr.
Carter could derive some consolation from psychologist Allen Wheelis,
who blames male appetite on biology: "We have been selected for

3. *Kamasutra* (first century?), a detailed account of the art and technique of Indian
erotics by the sage Vātsyāyana.
4. Marquis de Sade (1740–1814), French
author whose works, because of their pornographic and blasphemous subject matter
led, in his lifetime, to repeated imprisonment and have been denied official publication by the French courts as recently as
1957.

desiring. Nothing could have convinced us by argument that it would be worthwhile to chase endlessly and insatiably after women, but something has transformed us from within, a plasmid has invaded our DNA, has twisted our nature so that now this is exactly what we *want* to do." Certainly, by Darwinian logic, those males who were most avid in their pursuit of females were also the most likely to pass on their genes. Consoling it may be, yet it is finally no solution to blame biology. "I am extremely sexual in my desires: I carry them everywhere and at all times," William Carlos Williams[5] tells us on the opening page of his autobiography. "I think that from that arises the drive which empowers us all. Given that drive, a man does with it what his mind directs. In the manner in which he directs that power lies his secret." Whatever the contents of my DNA, however potent the influence of my ancestors, I still must direct that rebellious power. I still must live with the consequences of my looking and my longing.

Aloof on their blankets like goddesses on clouds, the pinups did not belong to my funky world. I was invisible to them, and they were immune to my gaze. Not so the women who passed me on the street, sat near me in classes, shared a table with me in the cafeteria: it was risky to stare at them. They could gaze back, and sometimes did, with looks both puzzling and exciting. It only complicated matters for me to realize that so many of these strangers had taken precautions that men should notice them. The girl in matching pink halter and shorts who set me humming in my eleventh year might only have wanted to keep cool in the sizzle of July. But these alluring college femmes had deeper designs. Perfume, eye shadow, uplift bras (about which I learned in the Sears catalog), curled hair, stockings, jewelry, lipstick, lace—what were these if not hooks thrown out into male waters?

I recall being mystified in particular by spike heels. They looked painful to me, and dangerous. Danger may have been the point, since the spikes would have made good weapons—they were affectionately known, after all, as stilettos. Or danger may have been the point in another sense, because a woman teetering along on such heels is tipsy, vulnerable, broadcasting her need for support. And who better than a man to prop her up, some guy who clomps around in brogans wide enough for the cornerstones of flying buttresses? (For years after college, I felt certain that spike heels had been forever banned, like bustles and foot-binding, but lately they have come back in fashion, and once more one encounters women teetering along on knife points.)

Back in those days of my awakening to women, I was also baffled by lingerie. I do not mean underwear, the proletariat of clothing, and I do

5. William Carlos Williams (1883–1963), American poet and physician.

not mean foundation garments, pale and sensible. I mean what the woman who lives in the house behind ours—owner of a shop called "Bare Essentials"—refers to as "intimate apparel." Those two words announce that her merchandise is both sexy and expensive. These flimsy items cost more per ounce than truffles, more than frankincense and myrrh. They are put-ons whose only purpose is in being taken off. I have a friend who used to attend the men's-only nights at Bare Essentials, during which he would invariably buy a slinky outfit or two, by way of proving his serious purpose, outfits that wound up in the attic because his wife would not be caught dead in them. Most of the customers at the shop are women, however, as the models are women, and the owner is a woman. What should one make of that? During my college days I knew about intimate apparel only by rumor, not being that intimate with anyone who would have tricked herself out in such finery, but I could see the spike heels and other female trappings everywhere I turned. Why, I wondered then and wonder still, do so many women decorate themselves like dolls? And does that mean they wish to be viewed as dolls?

On this question as on many others, Simone de Beauvoir[6] has clarified matters for me, writing in *The Second Sex:* "The 'feminine' woman in making herself prey tries to reduce man, also, to her carnal passivity; she occupies herself in catching him in her trap, in enchaining him by means of the desires she arouses in him in submissively making herself a thing." Those women who transform themselves into dolls, in other words, do so because that is the most potent identity available to them. "It must be admitted," Beauvoir concedes, "that the males find in woman more complicity than the oppressor usually finds in the oppressed. And in bad faith they take authorization from this to declare that she has *desired* the destiny they have imposed on her."

25   *Complicity, oppressor, bad faith:* such terms yank us into a moral realm unknown to goats. While I am saddled with enough male guilt to believe three-quarters of Beauvoir's claim, I still doubt that men are so entirely to blame for the turning of women into sexual dolls. I believe human history is more collaborative than her argument would suggest. It seems unlikely to me that one-half the species could have "imposed" a destiny on the other half, unless that other half were far more craven than the females I have known. Some women have expressed their own skepticism on this point. Thus Joan Didion: "That many women are victims of condescension and exploitation and sex-role stereotyping was scarcely news, but neither was it news that other women are not: nobody

6. Simone de Beauvoir (1908–86), French novelist and essayist who served as one of the most articulate exponents of existentialism. *Le Deuxième Sexe* (1949; trans- lated as *The Second Sex*, 1953), a thorough analysis of women's status in society, became a classic of feminist literature.

forces women to buy the package." Beauvoir herself recognized that many members of her sex refuse to buy the "feminine" package: "The emancipated woman, on the contrary, wants to be active, a taker, and refuses the passivity man means to impose on her."

Since my college years, back in the murky 1960s, emancipated women have been discouraging their unemancipated sisters from making spectacles of themselves. Don't paint your face like a clown's or drape your body like a mannequin's, they say. Don't bounce on the sidelines in skimpy outfits, screaming your fool head off, while men compete in the limelight for victories. Don't present yourself to the world as a fluff pastry, delicate and edible. Don't waddle across the stage in a bathing suit in hopes of being named Miss This or That.

A great many women still ignore the exhortations. Wherever a crown for beauty is to be handed out, many still line up to stake their claims. Recently, Miss Indiana Persimmon Festival was quoted in our newspaper about the burdens of possessing the sort of looks that snag men's eyes. "Most of the time I enjoy having guys stare at me," she said, "but every once in a while it makes me feel like a piece of meat." The news photograph showed a cheerleader's perky face, heavily made-up, with starched hair teased into a blond cumulus. She put me in mind not of meat but of a plastic figurine, something you might buy from a booth outside a shrine. Nobody should ever be seen as meat, mere juicy stuff to satisfy an appetite. Better to appear as a plastic figurine, which is not meant for eating, and which is a gesture, however crude, toward art. Joyce described the aesthetic response as a contemplation of form without the impulse to action. Perhaps that is what Miss Indiana Persimmon Festival wishes to inspire in those who look at her, perhaps that is what many women who paint and primp themselves desire: to withdraw from the touch of hands and dwell in the eye alone, to achieve the status of art.

By turning herself (or allowing herself to be turned into) a work of art, does a woman truly escape men's proprietary stare? Not often, says the British critic John Berger. Summarizing the treatment of women in Western painting, he concludes that—with a few notable exceptions, such as works by Rubens and Rembrandt—the woman on canvas is a passive object displayed for the pleasure of the male viewer, especially for the owner of the painting, who is, by extension, owner of the woman herself. Berger concludes: "Men look at women. Women watch themselves being looked at. This determines not only most relations between men and women but also the relation of women to themselves. The surveyor of woman in herself is male: the surveyed female. Thus she turns herself into an object—and most particularly an object of vision: a sight."

That sweeping claim, like the one quoted earlier from Beauvoir, also

seems to me about three-quarters truth and one-quarter exaggeration. I
know men who outdo the peacock for show, and I know women who
are so fully possessed of themselves that they do not give a hang whether
anybody notices them or not. The flamboyant gentlemen portrayed by
Van Dyck are no less aware of being *seen* than are the languid ladies
portrayed by Ingres. With or without clothes, both gentlemen and ladies
may conceive of themselves as objects of vision, targets of envy or
admiration or desire. Where they differ is in their potential for action:
the men are caught in the midst of a decisive gesture or on the verge
of making one; the women wait like fuel for someone else to strike a
match.

30   I am not sure the abstract nudes favored in modern art are much of
an advance over the inert and voluptuous ones of the old school. Think
of two famous examples: Duchamp's *Nude Descending a Staircase*
(1912), where the faceless woman has blurred into a waterfall of jagged
shards, or Picasso's *Les Demoiselles d'Avignon* (1907), where the five
angular damsels have been hammered as flat as cookie sheets and fitted
with African masks. Neither painting invites us to behold a woman, but
instead to behold what Picasso or Duchamp can make of one.

The naked women in Rubens, far from being passive, are gleefully
active, exuberant, their sumptuous pink bodies like rainclouds or plump
nebulae. "His nudes are the first ones that ever made me feel happy
about my own body," a woman friend told me in one of the Rubens
galleries of the Prado Museum. I do not imagine any pinup or store-
window mannequin or bathing-suited Miss Whatsit could have made
her feel that way. The naked women in Rembrandt, emerging from the
bath or rising from bed, are so private, so cherished in the painter's gaze,
that we as viewers see them not as sexual playthings but as loved persons.
A man would do well to emulate that gaze.

I have never thought of myself as a sight. How much that has to do
with being male and how much with having grown up on the back roads
where money was scarce and eyes were few, I cannot say. As a boy, apart
from combing my hair when I was compelled to and regretting the
patches on my jeans (only the poor wore patches), I took no trouble over
my appearance. It never occurred to me that anybody outside my family,
least of all a girl, would look at me twice. As a young man, when young
women did occasionally glance my way, without any prospect of appearing handsome I tried at least to avoid appearing odd. A standard haircut
and the cheapest versions of the standard clothes were camouflage
enough. Now as a middle-aged man I have achieved once more that
boyhood condition of invisibility, with less hair to comb and fewer
patches to humble me.

Many women clearly pass through the world aspiring to invisibility.

Many others just as clearly aspire to be conspicuous. Women need not make spectacles of themselves in order to draw the attention of men. Indeed, for my taste, the less paint and fewer bangles the better. I am as helpless in the presence of subtle lures as a male moth catching a whiff of pheromones. I am a sucker for hair ribbons, a scarf at the throat, toes leaking from sandals, teeth bared in a smile. By contrast, I have always been more amused than attracted by the enameled exhibitionists whom our biblical mothers would identify as brazen hussies or painted Jezebels or, in the extreme cases, as whores of Babylon.

To encounter female exhibitionists in their full glory and variety, you need to go to a city. I never encountered ogling as a full-blown sport until I visited Rome, where bands of Italian men joined with gusto in appraising the charms of every passing female, and the passing females vied with one another in demonstrating their charms. In our own cities the most notorious bands of oglers tend to be construction gangs or street crews, men who spend much of their day leaning on the handles of shovels or pausing between bursts of riveting guns, their eyes tracing the curves of passersby. The first time my wife and kids and I drove into Boston we followed the signs to Chinatown, only to discover that Chinatown's miserably congested main street was undergoing repairs. That street also proved to be the city's home for X-rated cinemas and girlie shows and skin shops. LIVE SEX ACTS ON STAGE. PEEP SHOWS. PRIVATE BOOTHS. Caught in a traffic jam, we spent an hour listening to jackhammers and wolf whistles as we crept through the few blocks of pleasure palaces, my son and daughter with their noses hanging out the windows, my wife and I steaming. Lighted marquees peppered by burnt-out bulbs announced the titles of sleazy flicks; life-size posters of naked women flanked the doorways of clubs: leggy strippers in miniskirts, the originals for some of the posters, smoked on the curb between numbers.

After we had finally emerged from the zone of eros, eight-year-old Jesse inquired, "What was *that* place all about?"

"Sex for sale," my wife Ruth explained.

That might carry us some way toward a definition of pornography: making flesh into a commodity, flaunting it like any other merchandise, divorcing bodies from selves. By this reckoning, there is a pornographic dimension to much advertising, where a charge of sex is added to products ranging from cars to shaving cream. In fact, the calculated imagery of advertising may be more harmful than the blatant imagery of the pleasure palaces, that frank raunchiness which Kate Millett refers to as the "truthful explicitness of pornography." One can leave the X-rated zone of the city, but one cannot escape the sticky reach of commerce, which summons girls to the high calling of cosmetic glamor, fashion, and sexual display, while it summons boys to the panting chase.

35

You can recognize pornography, according to D. H. Lawrence, "by the insult it offers, invariably, to sex, and to the human spirit." He should know, Millet argues in *Sexual Politics*, for in her view Lawrence himself was a purveyor of patriarchal and often sadistic pornography. I think she is correct about the worst of Lawrence, and that she identifies a misogynist streak in his work; but she ignores his career-long struggle to achieve a more public, tolerant vision of sexuality as an exchange between equals. Besides, his novels and stories all bear within themselves their own critiques. George Steiner reminds us that "the list of writers who have had the genius to enlarge our actual compass of sexual awareness, who have given the erotic play of the mind a novel focus, an area of recognition previously unknown or fallow, is very small." Lawrence belongs on that brief list. The chief insult to the human spirit is to deny it, to claim that we are merely conglomerations of molecules, to pretend that we exist purely as bundles of appetites or as food for the appetites of others.

Men commit that insult toward women out of ignorance, but also out of dread. Allen Wheelis again: "Men gather in pornographic shows, not to stimulate desire, as they may think, but to diminish fear. It is the nature of the show to reduce the woman, discard her individuality, her soul, make her into an object, thereby enabling the man to handle her with greater safety, to use her as a toy. . . . As women move increasingly toward equality, the felt danger to men increases, leading to an increase in pornography and, since there are some men whose fears cannot even so be stilled, to an increase also in violence against women."

Make her into an object: all the hurtful ways for men to look at women are variations on this betrayal. "Thus she turns herself into an object," writes Berger. A woman's ultimate degradation is in "submissively making herself a thing," writes Beauvoir. To be turned into an object— whether by the brush of a painter or the lens of a photographer or the eye of a voyeur, whether by hunger or poverty or enslavement, by mugging or rape, bullets or bombs, by hatred, racism, car crashes, fires, or falls—is for each of us the deepest dread; and to reduce another person to an object is the primal wrong.

Caught in the vortex of desire, we have to struggle to recall the wholeness of persons, including ourselves. Beauvoir speaks of the temptation we all occasionally feel to give up the struggle for a self and lapse into the inertia of an object: "Along with the ethical urge of each individual to affirm his subjective existence, there is also the temptation to forgo liberty and become a thing." A woman in particular, given so much encouragement to lapse into thinghood, "is often very well pleased with her role as the *Other.*"

Yet one need not forgo liberty and become a thing, without a center or a self, in order to become the Other. In our mutual strangeness, men and women can be doorways one for another, openings into the creative mystery that we share by virtue of our existence in the flesh. "To be sensual," James Baldwin writes, "is to respect and rejoice in the force of life, of life itself, and to be *present* in all that one does, from the effort of loving to the breaking of bread." The effort of loving is reciprocal, not only in act but in desire, an *I* addressing a *Thou*, a meeting in that vivid presence. The distance a man stares across at a woman, or a woman at a man, is a gulf in the soul, out of which a voice cries, *Leap, leap.* One day all men may cease to look on themselves as prototypically human and on women as lesser miracles; women may cease to feel themselves the targets for desire; men and women both may come to realize that we are all mere flickerings in the universal fire; and then none of us, male or female, need give up humanity in order to become the *Other.*

Ever since I gawked at the girl in pink shorts, I have dwelt knowingly in the force-field of sex. Knowingly or not, it is where we all dwell. Like the masses of planets and stars, our bodies curve the space around us. We radiate signals constantly, radio sources that never go off the air. We cannot help being centers of attraction and repulsion for one another. That is not all we are by a long shot, nor all we are capable of feeling, and yet, even after our much-needed revolution in sexual consciousness, the power of eros will still turn our heads and hearts. In a world without beauty pageants, there will still be beauty, however its definition may have changed. As long as men have eyes, they will gaze with yearning and confusion at women.

When I return to the street with the ancient legacy of longing coiled in my DNA, and the residues from a thousand generations of patriarchs silting my brain, I encounter women whose presence strikes me like a slap of wind in the face. I must prepare a gaze that is worthy of their splendor.

THE READER

1. *What question does Sanders pose in this essay? Does he answer it?*
2. *In what ways or to what extent does your experience of either looking at women or of being looked at correspond with the account Sanders gives of his?*
3. *Sanders asserts that to be turned into an object is for all of us "the deepest dread." Do you agree?*

THE WRITER

1. *By what means and to what effect does Sanders present himself in this essay? What does that presentation have to do with the nature and purpose of his essay?*

234

2. *Several times in the course of his essay Sanders introduces quotations from other writers. What stance does he take toward the assertions made in the several quotations? How is that stance related to the attitude he takes toward his essay's main topic?*
3. *Why and how does Sanders relate sexuality to art and to commerce?*
4. *Following Sanders' advice, take any available relevant advertisement and write a brief essay in analysis of the specific assumptions underlying the display.*

Oliver Sacks

REBECCA

Rebecca was no child when she was referred to our clinic. She was nineteen, but, as her grandmother said, "just like a child in some ways." She could not find her way around the block, she could not confidently open a door with a key (she could never "see" how the key went, and never seemed to learn). She had left/right confusion, she sometimes put on her clothes the wrong way—inside out, back-to-front, without appearing to notice, or, if she noticed, without being able to get them right. She might spend hours jamming a hand or foot into the wrong glove or shoe—she seemed, as her grandmother said, to have "no sense of space." She was clumsy and ill-coordinated in all her movements—a "klutz," one report said, a "motor moron" another (although when she danced, all her clumsiness disappeared).

Rebecca had a partial cleft palate, which caused a whistling in her speech; short, stumpy fingers, with blunt, deformed nails; and a high, degenerative myopia requiring very thick spectacles—all stigmata of the same congenital condition which had caused her cerebral and mental defects. She was painfully shy and withdrawn, feeling that she was, and had always been, a "figure of fun."

But she was capable of warm, deep, even passionate attachments. She had a deep love for her grandmother, who had brought her up since she was three (when she was orphaned by the death of both parents). She was very fond of nature, and, if she was taken to the city parks and botanic gardens, spent many happy hours there. She was very fond too of stories, though she never learned to read (despite assiduous, and even frantic, attempts), and would implore her grandmother or others to read to her. "She has a hunger for stories," her grandmother said; and fortu-

Chapter 21 of *The Man Who Mistook His Wife for a Hat and Other Clinical Tales* (1970).

nately her grandmother loved reading stories and had a fine reading voice which kept Rebecca entranced. And not just stories—poetry too. This seemed a deep need or hunger in Rebecca—a necessary form of nourishment, of reality, for her mind. Nature was beautiful, but mute. It was not enough. She needed the world represented to her in verbal images, in language, and seemed to have little difficulty following the metaphors and symbols of even quite deep poems, in striking contrast to her incapacity with simple propositions and instructions. The language of feeling, of the concrete, of image and symbol formed a world she loved and, to a remarkable extent, could enter. Though conceptually (and "propositionally") inept, she was at home with poetic language, and was herself, in a stumbling, touching way, a sort of "primitive," natural poet. Metaphors, figures of speech, rather striking similitudes, would come naturally to her, though unpredictably, as sudden poetic ejaculations or allusions. Her grandmother was devout, in a quiet way, and this also was true of Rebecca: she loved the lighting of the Shabbath candles, the benisons and orisons[1] which thread the Jewish day; she loved going to the synagogue, where she too was loved (and seen as a child of God, a sort of innocent, a holy fool); and she fully understood the liturgy, the chants, the prayers, rites and symbols of which the Orthodox service consists. All this was possible for her, accessible to her, loved by her, despite gross perceptual and spatiotemporal problems, and gross impairments in every schematic capacity—she could not count change, the simplest calculations defeated her, she could never learn to read or write, and she would average 60 or less in IQ tests (though doing notably better on the verbal than the performance parts of the test).

Thus she was a "moron," a "fool," a "booby," or had so appeared, and so been called, throughout her whole life, but one with an unexpected, strangely moving, poetic power. Superficially she *was* a mass of handicaps and incapacities, with the intense frustrations and anxieties attendant on these; at this level she was, and felt herself to be, a mental cripple—beneath the effortless skills, the happy capacities, of others; but at some deeper level there was no sense of handicap or incapacity, but a feeling of calm and completeness, of being fully alive, of being a soul, deep and high, and equal to all others. Intellectually, then, Rebecca felt a cripple; spiritually she felt herself a full and complete being.

When I first saw her—clumsy, uncouth, all-of-a-fumble—I saw her merely, or wholly, as a casualty, a broken creature, whose neurological impairments I could pick out and dissect with precision: a multitude of

5

1. Shabbath candles, among Sephardic Jews and in the State of Israel, Shabbath (also Shabbat and Shabat) is the Sabbath, the day of holiness and rest observed from sunset on Friday to nightfall of the following day. In Jewish homes, the woman of the house lights white Sabbath candles before sunset on Friday evening. Benisons and orisons, blessings and prayers.

apraxias and agnosias,[2] a mass of sensorimotor impairments and breakdowns, limitations of intellectual schemata and concepts similar (by Piaget's[3] criteria) to those of a child of eight. A poor thing, I said to myself, with perhaps a "splinter skill," a freak gift, of speech; a mere mosaic of higher cortical functions, Piagetian schemata—most impaired.

The next time I saw her, it was all very different. I didn't have her in a test situation, "evaluating" her in a clinic. I wandered outside, it was a lovely spring day, with a few minutes in hand before the clinic started, and there I saw Rebecca sitting on a bench, gazing at the April foliage quietly, with obvious delight. Her posture had none of the clumsiness which had so impressed me before. Sitting there, in a light dress, her face calm and slightly smiling, she suddenly brought to mind one of Chekov's[4] young women—Irene, Anya, Sonya, Nina—seen against the backdrop of a Chekovian cherry orchard. She could have been any young woman enjoying a beautiful spring day. This was my human, as opposed to my neurological, vision.

As I approached, she heard my footsteps and turned, gave me a broad smile, and wordlessly gestured. "Look at the world," she seemed to say. "How beautiful it is." And then there came out, in Jacksonian spurts,[5] odd, sudden, poetic ejaculations: "spring," "birth," "growing," "stirring," "coming to life," "seasons," "everything in its time." I found myself thinking of Ecclesiastes: "To everything there is a season, and a time to every purpose under the heaven. A time to be born, and a time to die; a time to plant, and a time. . . ."[6] This was what Rebecca, in her disjointed fashion, was ejaculating—a vision of seasons, of times, like that of the Preacher. "She is an idiot Ecclesiastes," I said to myself. And in this phrase, my two visions of her—as idiot and as symbolist—met, collided and fused. She had done appallingly in the testing—which, in a sense, was designed, like all neurological and psychological testing, not merely to uncover, to bring out deficits, but to decompose her into functions and deficits. She had come apart, horribly, in formal testing, but now she was mysteriously "together" and composed.

Why was she so decomposed before, how could she be so recomposed now? I had the strongest feeling of two wholly different modes of thought, or of organization, or of being. The first schematic—pattern-seeing, problem-solving—this is what had been tested, and where she

2. *Apraxias* and *agnosias*, terms describing inabilities to recognize familiar objects.
3. Jean Piaget (1896–1980), Swiss psychologist, pioneer student of cognitive development through childhood.
4. Anton Pavlovich Chekov (1860–1904), Russian playwright and short-story writer.
5. The spurts are "words or phrases uttered under stress of emotion when they cannot be spoken voluntarily." (*The Oxford Companion of the Mind*, ed. R. L. Gregory, 1987). John Hughlings Jackson (1835–1911), the father of British neurology, was a student of aphasia, or the impairment of the power to use words.
6. Ecclesiastes iii.

had been found so defective, so disastrously wanting. But the tests had given no inkling of anything *but* the deficits, anything, so to speak, *beyond* her deficits.

They had given me no hint of her positive powers, her ability to perceive the real world—the world of nature, and perhaps of the imagination—as a coherent, intelligible, poetic whole: her ability to see this, think this, and (when she could) live this; they had given me no intimation of her inner world, which clearly *was* composed and coherent, and approached as something other than a set of problems or tasks.

But what was the composing principle which could allow her composure (clearly it was something other than schematic)? I found myself thinking of her fondness for tales, for narrative composition and coherence. Is it possible, I wondered, that this being before me—at once a charming girl, and a moron, a cognitive mishap—can *use* a narrative (or dramatic) mode to compose and integrate a coherent world, in place of the schematic mode, which, in her, is so defective that it simply doesn't work? And as I thought, I remembered her dancing, and how this could organize her otherwise ill-knit and clumsy movements.

Our tests, our approaches, I thought, as I watched her on the bench—enjoying not just a simple but a sacred view of nature—our approach, our "evaluations," are ridiculously inadequate. They only show us deficits, they do not show us powers; they only show us puzzles and schemata, when we need to see music, narrative, play, a being conducting itself spontaneously in its own natural way.

Rebecca, I felt, was complete and intact as "narrative" being, in conditoins which allowed her to organize herself in a narrative way; and this was something very important to know, for it allowed one to see her, and her potential, in a quite different fashion from that imposed by the schematic mode.

It was perhaps fortunate that I chanced to see Rebecca in her so-different modes—so damaged and incorrigible in the one, so full of promise and potential in the other—and that she was one of the first patients I saw in our clinic. For what I saw in her, what she showed me, I now saw in them all.

As I continued to see her, she seemed to deepen. Or perhaps she revealed, or I came to respect, her depths more and more. They were not wholly happy depths—no depths ever are—but they were predominantly happy for the greater part of the year.

Then, in November, her grandmother died, and the light, the joy, she had expressed in April now turned into the deepest grief and darkness. She was devastated, but conducted herself with great dignity. Dignity, ethical depth, was added at this time, to form a grave and lasting counterpoint to the light, lyrical self I had especially seen before.

I called on her as soon as I heard the news, and she received me, with great dignity, but frozen with grief, in her small room in the now empty house. Her speech was again ejaculated, "Jacksonian," in brief utterances of grief and lamentation. "Why did she have to go?" she cried; and added, "I'm crying for me, not for her." Then, after an interval, "Grannie's all right. She's gone to her Long Home." Long Home! Was this her own symbol, or an unconscious memory of, or allusion to, Ecclesiastes? "I'm so cold," she cried, huddling into herself. "It's not outside, it's winter inside. Cold as death," she added. "She was a part of me. Part of me died with her."

She was complete in her mourning—tragic and complete—there was absolutely no sense of her being then a "mental defective." After half an hour, she unfroze, regained some of her warmth and animation, said: "It is winter. I feel dead. But I know the spring will come again."

The work of grief was slow, but successful, as Rebecca, even when most stricken, anticipated. It was greatly helped by a sympathetic and supportive great aunt, a sister of her Grannie, who now moved into the house. It was greatly helped by the synagogue, and the religious community, above all by the rites of "sitting shiva,"[7] and the special status accorded her as the bereaved one, the chief mourner. It was helped too perhaps by her speaking freely to me. And it was helped also, interestingly, by *dreams,* which she related with animation, and which clearly marked *stages* in the grief-work (see Peters 1983).[8]

As I remember her, like Nina, in the April sun, so I remember her, etched with tragic clearness, in the dark November of that year, standing in a bleak cemetery in Queens, saying the Kaddish[9] over her grandmother's grave. Prayers and Bible stories had always appealed to her, going with the happy, the lyrical, the "blessing" side of her life. Now, in the funeral prayers, in the 103rd Psalm, and above all in the Kaddish, she found the right and only words for her comfort and lamentation.

20   During the intervening months (between my first seeing her, in April, and her grandmother's death that November) Rebecca—like all our "clients" (an odious word then becoming fashionable, supposedly less degrading than "patients"), was pressed into a variety of workshops and classes, as part of our Developmental and Cognitive Drive (these too were "in" terms at the time).

It didn't work with Rebecca, it didn't work with most of them. It was not, I came to think, the right thing to do, because what we did was to drive them full-tilt upon their limitations, as had already been done, futilely, and often to the point of cruelty, throughout their lives.

---

7. The Jewish tradition of sitting on chairs of less than normal height (or even sitting on the floor or ground) during the seven days of mourning (shiva) following the burial of a near relative.

8. L. R. Peters, "The Role of Dreams in the Life of a Mentally Retarded Individual," *Ethos* (1983, pp. 49–65) [Sacks' note].

9. A prayer praising God, recited by mourners after the death of a near relative.

We paid far too much attention to the defects of our patients, as Rebecca was the first to tell me, and far too little to what was intact or preserved. To use another piece of jargon, we were far too concerned with "defectology," and far too little with "narratology," the neglected and needed science of the concrete.

Rebecca made clear, by concrete illustrations, by her own self, the two wholly different, wholly separate, forms of thought and mind, "paradigmatic" and "narrative" (in Bruner's[1] terminology). And though equally natural and native to the expanding human mind, the narrative comes first, has spiritual priority. Very young children love and demand stories, and can understand complex matters presented as stories, when their powers of comprehending general concepts, paradigms, are almost nonexistent. It is this narrative or symbolic power which gives *a sense of the world*—a concrete reality in the imaginative form of symbol and story—when abstract thought can provide nothing at all. A child follows the Bible before he follows Euclid.[2] Not because the Bible is simpler (the reverse might be said), but because it is cast in a symbolic and narrative mode.

And in this way, Rebecca, at nineteen, was still, as her grandmother said, "just like a child." Like a child, but not a child, because she was adult. (The term "retarded" suggests a persisting child, the term "mentally defective" a defective adult; both terms, both concepts, combine deep truth and falsity.)

With Rebecca—and with other defectives allowed, or encouraged in, a personal development—the emotional and narrative and symbolic powers can develop strongly and exuberantly, and may produce (as in Rebecca) a sort of natural poet—or (as in José)[3] a sort of natural artist—while the paradigmatic or conceptual powers, manifestly feeble from the start, grind very slowly and painfully along, and are only capable of a very limited and stunted development.

Rebecca realized this fully—as she had shown it to me so clearly, right from the very first day I saw her, when she spoke of her clumsiness, and of how her ill-composed and ill-organized movements became well-organized, composed and fluent, with music; and when she *showed* me how she herself was composed by a natural scene, a scene with an organic, aesthetic and dramatic unity and sense.

Rather suddenly, after her grandmother's death, she became clear and decisive. "I want no more classes, no more workshops," she said. "They do nothing for me. They do nothing to bring me together." And then, with that power for the apt model or metaphor I so admired, and which

25

1. Jerome Bruner (1915–90), American psychologist and educator.
2. Euclid (fl 300 B.C.), Greek mathematician who lived and taught at Alexandria.

His *Elements* in thirteen books became the basis of modern geometry.
3. José, an "autist artist," central figure in another chapter of Sacks' book.

was so well developed in her despite her low IQ, she looked down at the office carpet and said:

"I'm like a sort of living carpet. I need a pattern, a design, like you have on that carpet. I come apart, I unravel, unless there's a design." I looked down at the carpet, as Rebecca said this, and found myself thinking of Sherrington's[4] famous image, comparing the brain/mind to an "enchanted loom," weaving patterns ever-dissolving, but always with meaning. I thought: can one have a raw carpet without a design? Could one have the design without the carpet (but this seemed like the smile without the Cheshire cat[5])? A "living" carpet, as Rebecca was, had to have both—and she especially, with her lack of schematic structure (the warp and woof, the *knit*, of the carpet, so to speak), might indeed unravel without a design (the scenic or narrative structure of the carpet).

"I must have meaning," she went on. "The classes, the odd jobs have no meaning. . . . What I really love," she added wistfully, "is the theater."

We removed Rebecca from the workshop she hated, and managed to enroll her in a special theater group. She loved this—it composed her; she did amazingly well: she became a complete person, poised, fluent, with style, in each role. And now if one sees Rebecca on stage, for theater and the theater group soon became her life, one would never even guess that she was mentally defective.

Postscript

The power of music, narrative and drama is of the greatest practical and theoretical importance. One may see this even in the case of idiots, with IQs below 20 and the extremest motor incompetence and bewilderment. Their uncouth movements may disappear in a moment with music and dancing—suddenly, with music, they know how to move. We see how the retarded, unable to perform fairly simple tasks involving perhaps four or five movements or procedures in sequence, can do these perfectly if they work to music—the sequence of movements they cannot hold as schemes being perfectly holdable as music, i.e., embedded in music. The same may be seen, very dramatically, in patients with severe frontal lobe damage and apraxia—an inability to *do* things, to retain the simplest motor sequences and programs, even to walk, despite perfectly preserved intelligence in all other ways. This procedural defect, or motor idiocy, as one might call it, which completely defeats any ordinary system of rehabilitative instruction, vanishes at once if music

4. Sir Charles Scott Sherrington (1857–1952), English physiologist.
5. In Lewis Carroll's *Alice's Adventures in* *Wonderland* (1865), a creature that has the ability to vanish at will, its grin being the last thing to go.

is the instructor. All this, no doubt, is the rationale, or one of the rationales, of work songs.

What we see, fundamentally, is the power of music to organize—and to do this efficaciously (as well as joyfully!), when abstract or schematic forms of organizations fail. Indeed, it is especially dramatic, as one would expect, precisely when no other form of organization will work. Thus music, or any other form of narrative, is essential when working with the retarded or apraxic—schooling or therapy for them must be centred on music or something equivalent. And in drama there is still more—there is the power of *rôle* to give organization, to confer, while it lasts, an entire personality. The capacity to perform, to play, to *be,* seems to be a "given" in human life, in a way which has nothing to do with intellectual differences. One sees this with infants, one sees it with the senile, and one sees it, most poignantly, with the Rebeccas of this world.

THE READER

1. *Sacks describes what he calls two wholly different modes of thought, or of organization, or of being: the "schematic" and the "narrative." How do they differ? What are the specific characteristics of each, as he describes them?*
2. *What relationship is Sacks suggesting between the worlds of nature, of story, of music, of theater, when he observes that Rebecca has composure in all these?*
3. *In the following poem, Richard Snyder describes a child with Down's syndrome. In what particular ways are this child and Rebecca alike?*

    "A Mongoloid Child Handling Shells on the Beach"

    She turns them over in her slow hands,
    as did the sea sending them to her;
    broken bits from the mazarine maze,
    they are the calmest things on this sand.

    The unbroken children splash and shout,
    rough as surf, gay as their nesting towels.
    But she plays soberly with the sea's
    small change and hums back to it its slow vowels.

THE WRITER

1. *What is Sacks' attitude toward Rebecca? What details in his description does Sacks use to convey these attitudes?*
2. *At the beginning of his essay Sacks gives us an account of two meetings with Rebecca. How do they contrast? What consequences does he draw from this contrast? Is this an effective way to begin this particular essay? If so, explain.*

3. *Write a brief essay on the scene described in Snyder's poem, above, showing how it might be characterized in the two modes Sacks calls "schematic" and "narrative."*

Malcolm Cowley

THE VIEW FROM 80

Even before he or she is 80, the aging person may undergo another identity crisis like that of adolescence. Perhaps there had also been a middle-aged crisis, the male or the female menopause, but for the rest of adult life he had taken himself for granted, with his capabilities and failings. Now, when he looks in the mirror, he asks himself, "Is this really me?"—or he avoids the mirror out of distress at what it reveals, those bags and wrinkles. In his new makeup he is called upon to play a new role in a play that must be improvised. André Gide, that long-lived man of letters, wrote in his journal, "My heart has remained so young that I have the continual feeling of playing a part, the part of the 70-year-old that I certainly am; and the infirmities and weaknesses that remind me of my age act like a prompter, reminding me of my lines when I tend to stray. Then, like the good actor I want to be, I go back into my role, and I pride myself on playing it well."

In his new role the old person will find that he is tempted by new vices, that he receives new compensations (not so widely known), and that he may possibly achieve new virtues. Chief among these is the heroic or merely obstinate refusal to surrender in the face of time. One admires the ships that go down with all flags flying and the captain on the bridge.

Among the vices of age are avarice, untidiness, and vanity, which last takes the form of a craving to be loved or simply admired. Avarice is the worst of those three. Why do so many old persons, men and women alike, insist on hoarding money when they have no prospect of using it and even when they have no heirs? They eat the cheapest food, buy no clothes, and live in a single room when they could afford better lodging. It may be that they regard money as a form of power; there is a comfort in watching it accumulate while other powers are dwindling away. How often we read of an old person found dead in a hovel, on a mattress partly stuffed with bankbooks and stock certificates! The bankbook syndrome, we call it in our family, which has never succumbed.

Untidiness we call the Langley Collyer syndrome. To explain, Langley

From *The View from 80* (1980).

Collyer was a former concert pianist who lived alone with his 70-year-old brother in a brownstone house on upper Fifth Avenue. The once fashionable neighborhood had become part of Harlem. Homer, the brother, had been an admiralty lawyer, but was now blind and partly paralyzed; Langley played for him and fed him on buns and oranges, which he thought would restore Homer's sight. He never threw away a daily paper because Homer, he said, might want to read them all. He saved other things as well and the house became filled with rubbish from roof to basement. The halls were lined on both sides with bundled newspapers, leaving narrow passageways in which Langley had devised booby traps to catch intruders.

On March 21, 1947, some unnamed person telephoned the police to report that there was a dead body in the Collyer house. The police broke down the front door and found the hall impassable, then they hoisted a ladder to a second-story window. Behind it Homer was lying on the floor in a bathrobe; he had starved to death. Langley had disappeared. After some delay, the police broke into the basement, chopped a hole in the roof, and began throwing junk out of the house, top and bottom. It was 18 days before they found Langley's body, gnawed by rats. Caught in one of his own booby traps, he had died in a hallway just outside Homer's door. By that time the police had collected, and the Department of Sanitation had hauled away, 120 tons of rubbish, including besides the newspapers, 14 grand pianos and the parts of a dismantled Model T Ford.

Why do so many old people accumulate junk, not on the scale of Langley Collyer, but still in a dismaying fashion? Their tables are piled high with it, their bureau drawers are stuffed with it, their closet rods bend with the weight of clothes not worn for years. I suppose that the piling up is partly from lethargy and partly from the feeling that everything once useful, including their own bodies, should be preserved. Others, though not so many, have such a fear of becoming Langley Collyers that they strive to be painfully neat. Every tool they own is in its place, though it will never be used again; every scrap of paper is filed away in alphabetical order. At last their immoderate neatness becomes another vice of age, if a milder one.

The vanity of older people is an easier weakness to explain, and to condone. With less to look forward to, they yearn for recognition of what they have been: the reigning beauty, the athlete, the soldier, the scholar. It is the beauties who have the hardest time. A portrait of themselves at twenty hangs on the wall, and they try to resemble it by making an extravagant use of creams, powders, and dyes. Being young at heart, they think they are merely revealing their essential persons. The athletes find shelves for their silver trophies, which are polished once a year. Perhaps a letter sweater lies wrapped in a bureau drawer. I remember one evening when a no-longer athlete had guests for dinner and tried to find his sweater. "Oh, that old thing," his wife said. "The moths got into it and I threw it away." The athlete sulked and his guests went home early.

Often the yearning to be recognized appears in conversation as an innocent boast. Thus, a distinguished physician, retired at 94, remarks casually that a disease was named after him. A former judge bursts into chuckles as he repeats bright things that he said on the bench. Aging scholars complain in letters (or one of them does), "As I approach 70 I'm becoming avid of honors, and such things—medals, honorary degrees, etc.—are only passed around among academics on a *quid pro quo* basis (one hood capping another)." Or they say querulously, "Bill Underwood has ten honorary doctorates and I have only three. Why didn't they elect me to . . . ?" and they mention the name of some learned society. That search for honors is a harmless passion, though it may lead to jealousies and deformations of character, as with Robert Frost in his later years. Still, honors cost little. Why shouldn't the very old have more than their share of them?

To be admired and praised, especially by the young, is an autumnal pleasure enjoyed by the lucky ones (who are not always the most deserving). "What is more charming," Cicero observes in his famous essay *De Senectute*, [1] "than an old age surrounded by the enthusiasm of youth!
. . . Attentions which seem trivial and conventional are marks of honor—the morning call, being sought after, precedence, having people rise for you, being escorted to and from the forum. . . . What pleasures of the body can be compared to the prerogatives of influence?" But there are also pleasures of the body, or the mind, that are enjoyed by a greater number of older persons.

10   Those pleasures include some that younger people find hard to appreciate. One of them is simply sitting still, like a snake on a sun-warmed stone, with a delicious feeling of indolence that was seldom attained in earlier years. A leaf flutters down; a cloud moves by inches across the horizon. At such moments the older person, completely relaxed, has become a part of nature—and a living part, with blood coursing through his veins. The future does not exist for him. He thinks, if he thinks at all, that life for younger persons is still a battle royal of each against each, but that now he has nothing more to win or lose. He is not so much above as outside the battle, as if he had assumed the uniform of some small neutral country, perhaps Liechtenstein or Andorra. From a distance he notes that some of the combatants, men or women, are jostling ahead—but why do they fight so hard when the most they can hope for

1. *On Old Age.*

is a longer obituary? He can watch the scrounging and gouging, he can hear the shouts of exultation, the moans of the gravely wounded, and meanwhile he feels secure; nobody will attack him from ambush.

Age has other physical compensations besides the nirvana of dozing in the sun. A few of the simplest needs become a pleasure to satisfy. When an old woman in a nursing home was asked what she really liked to do, she answered in one word: "Eat." She might have been speaking for many of her fellows. Meals in a nursing home, however badly cooked, serve as climactic moments of the day. The physical essence of the pensioners is being renewed at an appointed hour; now they can go back to meditating or to watching TV while looking forward to the next meal. They can also look forward to sleep, which has become a definite pleasure, not the mere interruption it once had been.

Here I am thinking of old persons under nursing care. Others ferociously guard their independence, and some of them suffer less than one might expect from being lonely and impoverished. They can be rejoiced by visits and meetings, but they also have company inside their heads. Some of them are busiest when their hands are still. What passes through the minds of many is a stream of persons, images, phrases, and familiar tunes. For some that stream has continued since childhood, but now it is deeper; it is their present and their past combined. At times they conduct silent dialogues with a vanished friend, and these are less tiring—often more rewarding—than spoken conversations. If inner resources are lacking, old persons living alone may seek comfort and a kind of companionship in the bottle. I should judge from the gossip of various neighborhoods that the outer suburbs from Boston to San Diego are full of secretly alcoholic widows. One of those widows, an old friend, was moved from her apartment into a retirement home. She left behind her a closet in which the floor was covered wall to wall with whiskey bottles. "Oh, those empty bottles!" she explained. "They were left by a former tenant."

Not whiskey or cooking sherry but simply giving up is the greatest temptation of age. It is something different from a stoical acceptance of infirmities, which is something to be admired. At 63, when he first recognized that his powers were failing, Emerson wrote one of his best poems, "Terminus":

> It is time to be old,
> To take in sail:—
> The god of bounds,
> Who sets to seas a shore,
> Came to me in his fatal rounds,
> And said: "No more!
> No farther shoot
> Thy broad ambitious branches, and thy root.

Fancy departs: no more invent;
Contract thy firmament
To compass of a tent."

Emerson lived in good health to the age of 79. Within his narrowed
firmament, he continued working until his memory failed; then he
consented to having younger editors and collaborators. The givers-up see
no reason for working. Sometimes they lie in bed all day when moving
about would still be possible, if difficult. I had a friend, a distinguished
poet, who surrendered in that fashion. The doctors tried to stir him to
action, but he refused to leave his room. Another friend, once a successful artist, stopped painting when his eyes began to fail. His doctor made
the mistake of telling him that he suffered from a fatal disease. He then
lost interest in everything except the splendid Rolls-Royce, acquired in
his prosperous days, that stood in the garage. Daily he wiped the dust
from its hood. He couldn't drive it on the road any longer, but he used
to sit in the driver's seat, start the motor, then back the Rolls out of the
garage and drive it in again, back twenty feet and forward twenty feet;
that was his only distraction.

15   I haven't the right to blame those who surrender, not being able to
put myself inside their minds or bodies. Often they must have compelling reasons, physical or moral. Not only do they suffer from a variety
of ailments, but also they are made to feel that they no longer have a
function in the community. Their families and neighbors don't ask them
for advice, don't really listen when they speak, don't call on them for
efforts. One notes that there are not a few recoveries from apparent
senility when that situation changes. If it doesn't change, old persons
may decide that efforts are useless. I sympathize with their problems,
but the men and women I envy are those who accept old age as a series
of challenges.

For such persons, every new infirmity is an enemy to be outwitted,
an obstacle to be overcome by force of will. They enjoy each little victory
over themselves, and sometimes they win a major success. Renoir was
one of them. He continued painting, and magnificently, for years after
he was crippled by arthritis; the brush had to be strapped to his arm.
"You don't need your hand to paint," he said. Goya was another of the
unvanquished. At 72 he retired as an official painter of the Spanish court
and decided to work only for himself. His later years were those of the
famous "black paintings" in which he let his imagination run (and also
of the lithographs, then a new technique). At 78 he escaped a reign of
terror in Spain by fleeing to Bordeaux. He was deaf and his eyes were
failing; in order to work he had to wear several pairs of spectacles, one
over another, and then use a magnifying glass; but he was producing
splendid work in a totally new style. At 80 he drew an ancient man

propped on two sticks, with a mass of white hair and beard hiding his face and with the inscription "I am still learning."

Giovanni Papini said when he was nearly blind, "I prefer martyrdom to imbecility." After writing sixty books, including his famous *Life of Christ,* he was at work on two huge projects when he was stricken with a form of muscular atrophy. He lost the use of his left leg, then of his fingers, so that he couldn't hold a pen. The two big books, though never to be finished, moved forward slowly by dictation; that in itself was a triumph. Toward the end, when his voice had become incomprehensible, he spelled out a word, tapping on the table to indicate letters of the alphabet. One hopes never to be faced with the need for such heroic measures.

"Eighty years old!" the great Catholic poet Paul Claudel wrote in his journal. "No eyes left, no ears, no teeth, no legs, no wind! And when all is said and done, how astonishingly well one does without them!"

Lewis Thomas

THE LONG HABIT

We continue to share with our remotest ancestors the most tangled and evasive attitudes about death, despite the great distance we have come to understanding some of the profound aspects of biology. We have as much distaste for talking about personal death as for thinking about it; it is an indelicacy, like talking in mixed company about venereal disease or abortion in the old days. Death on a grand scale does not bother us in the same special way: we can sit around a dinner table and discuss war, involving 60 million volatilized human deaths, as though we were talking about bad weather; we can watch abrupt bloody death every day, in color, on films and television, without blinking back a tear. It is when the numbers of dead are very small, and very close, that we begin to think in scurrying circles. At the very center of the problem is the naked cold deadness of one's own self, the only reality in nature of which we can have absolute certainty, and it is unmentionable, unthinkable. We may be even less willing to face the issue at first hand than our predecessors because of a secret new hope that maybe it will go away. We like to think, hiding the thought, that with all the marvelous ways in which we seem now to lead nature around by the nose, perhaps we

First published in the *New England Journal of Medicine* (Apr. 13, 1972); reprinted in Thomas' essay collection *The Lives of the Cell* (1974).

can avoid the central problem if we just become, next year, say, a bit smarter.

"The long habit of living," said Thomas Browne, "indisposeth us to dying." These days, the habit has become an addiction: we are hooked on living, the tenacity of its grip on us, and ours on it, grows in intensity. We cannot think of giving it up, even when living loses its zest—even when we have lost the zest for zest.

We have come a long way in our technologic capacity to put death off, and it is imaginable that we might learn to stall it for even longer periods, perhaps matching the life-spans of the Abkhasian Russians, who are said to go on, springily, for a century and a half. If we can rid ourselves of some of our chronic, degenerative diseases, and cancer, strokes and coronaries, we might go on and on. It sounds attractive and reasonable, but it is no certainty. If we became free of disease, we would make a much better run of it for the last decade or so, but might still terminate on about the same schedule as now. We may be like the genetically different lines of mice, or like Hayflick's different tissue-culture lines, programmed to die after a predetermined number of days clocked by their genomes. If this is the way it is, some of us will continue to wear out and come unhinged in the sixth decade, and some much later, depending on genetic timetables.

If we ever do achieve freedom from most of today's diseases, or even complete freedom from disease, we will perhaps terminate by drying out and blowing away on a light breeze, but we will still die.

Most of my friends do not like this way of looking at it. They prefer to take it for granted that we only die because we get sick, with one lethal ailment or another, and if we did not have our diseases we might go on indefinitely. Even biologists choose to think this about themselves, despite the evidences of the absolute inevitability of death that surround their professional lives. Everything dies, all around, trees, plankton, lichens, mice, whales, flies, mitochondria. In the simplest creatures it is sometimes difficult to see it as death, since the strands of replicating DNA they leave behind are more conspicuously the living parts of themselves than with us (not that it is fundamentally any different, but it seems so). Flies do not develop a ward round[1] of diseases that carry them off, one by one. They simply age, and die, like flies.

We hanker to go on, even in the face of plain evidence that long, long lives are not necessarily pleasurable in the kind of society we have arranged thus far. We will be lucky if we can postpone the search for new technologies for a while, until we have discovered some satisfactory

1. That is, the variety of ailments a doctor sees during his circuit among the patients in a hospital ward.

things to do with the extra time. Something will surely have to be found to take the place of sitting on the porch reexamining one's watch.

Perhaps we would not be so anxious to prolong life if we did not detest so much the sickness of withdrawal. It is astonishing how little information we have about this universal process, with all the other dazzling advances in biology. It is almost as though we wanted not to know about it. Even if we could imagine the act of death in isolation, without any preliminary stage of being struck down by disease, we would be fearful of it.

There are signs that medicine may be taking a new interest in the process, partly from interest, partly from an embarrassed realization that we have not been handling this aspect of disease with as much skill as physicians once displayed, back in the days before they became convinced that disease was their solitary and sometimes defeatable enemy. It used to be the hardest and most important of all the services of a good doctor to be on hand at the time of death, and to provide comfort, usually in the home. Now it is done in hospitals, in secrecy (one of the reasons for the increased fear of death these days may be that so many people are totally unfamiliar with it; they never actually see it happen in real life). Some of our technology permits us to deny its existence, and we maintain flickers of life for long stretches in one community of cells or another, as though we were keeping a flag flying. Death is not a sudden all-at-once affair; cells go down in sequence, one by one. You can, if you like, recover great numbers of them many hours after the lights have gone out, and grow them out in cultures. It takes hours, even days, before the irreversible word finally gets around to all the provinces.

We may be about to rediscover that dying is not such a bad thing to do after all. Sir William Osler took this view; he disapproved of people who spoke of the agony of death, maintaining that there was no such thing.

In a 19th-century memoir about an expedition in Africa, there is a   10
story about an explorer who was caught by a lion, crushed across the chest in the animal's great jaws, and saved in the instant by a lucky shot from a friend. Later, he remembered the episode in clear detail. He was so amazed by the extraordinary sense of peace and calm, and total painlessness, associated with his partial experience of being killed, that he constructed a theory that all creatures are provided with a protective physiologic mechanism, switched on at the verge of death, carrying them through in a haze of tranquility.

I have seen agony in death only once, in a patient with rabies, who remained acutely aware of every stage in the process of his own disintegration over a 24-hour period, right up to his final moment. It was as though, in the special neuropathology of rabies, the switch had been prevented from turning.

We will be having new opportunities to learn more about the physiology of death at first hand, from the increasing numbers of cardiac patients who have been through the whole process and then back again. Judging from what has been found out thus far, from the first generation of people resuscitated from cardiac standstill (already termed the Lazarus syndrome), Osler seems to have been right. Those who remember parts or all of their episodes do not recall any fear, or anguish. Several people who remained conscious throughout, while appearing to have been quite dead, could only describe a remarkable sensation of detachment. One man underwent coronary occlusion with cessation of the heart and dropped for all practical purposes dead in front of a hospital, and within a few minutes his heart had been restarted by electrodes and he breathed his way back into life. According to his account, the strangest thing was that there were so many people around him, moving so urgently, handling his body with such excitement, while all his awareness was of quietude.

In a recent study of the reaction to dying in patients with obstructive disease of the lungs, it was concluded that the process was considerably more shattering for the professional observers than the observed. Most of the patients appeared to be preparing themselves with equanimity for death, as though intuitively familiar with the business. One elderly woman reported that the only painful and distressing part of the process was in being interrupted; on several occasions she was provided with conventional therapeutic measures to maintain oxygenation or restore fluids and electrolytes, and each time she found the experience of coming back harrowing, she deeply resented the interference with her dying.

I find myself surprised by the thought that dying is an all-right thing to do, but perhaps it should not surprise. It is, after all, the most ancient and fundamental of biologic functions, with its mechanisms worked out with the same attention to detail, the same provision for the advantage of the organism, the same abundance of genetic information for guidance through the stages, that we have long since become accustomed to finding in all the crucial acts of living.

15   Very well. But even so, if the transformation is a co-ordinated, integrated physiologic process in its initial, local stages, there is still that permanent vanishing of consciousness to be accounted for. Are we to be stuck forever with this problem? Where on earth does it go? Is it simply stopped dead in its tracks, lost in humus, wasted? Considering the tendency of nature to find uses for complex and intricate mechanisms, this seems to me unnatural. I prefer to think of it as somehow separated off at the filaments of its attachment, and then drawn like an

easy breath back into the membrane of its origin, a fresh memory for a biospherical nervous system, but I have no data on the matter.

This is for another science, another day. It may turn out, as some scientists suggest, that we are forever precluded from investigating consciousness, by a sort of indeterminacy principle that stipulates that the very act of looking will make it twitch and blur out of sight. It this is true, we will never learn. I envy some of my friends who are convinced about telepathy; oddly enough, it is my European scientist acquaintances who believe it most freely and take it most lightly. All their aunts have received Communications, and there they sit, with proof of the motility of consciousness at their fingertips, and the making of a new science. It is discouraging to have had the wrong aunts, and never the ghost of a message.

THE READER

1. *"They simply age, and die, like flies" (p. 248). What makes this sentence, which concludes the opening section of this brief essay, effective? What does Thomas establish in this opening section? What does he consider in the next section, which constitutes the bulk of his essay? What is the logic that connects the two, and what is the basic assumption underlying the second section?*

2. *What does this essay have in common with Thomas "On Magic in Medicine" (p. 483)? Is Thomas ever "unscientific"? Can you infer from these two essays his estimate of science—what it can do and what it can't do?*

THE WRITER

1. *In paragraph 14, Thomas considers the subject of death anew. What is his perspective here? How does the next paragraph set the limits on that perspective? Explain the metaphor with which he ends the next paragraph.*

2. *Write a brief account of a hypothetical society that has a different attitude toward death from ours. What attitudes about other things would follow from a different attitude toward death?*

Elisabeth Kübler-Ross

ON THE FEAR OF DEATH

*Let me not pray to be sheltered from
dangers but to be fearless in facing
them.*
*Let me not beg for the stilling of
my pain but for the heart to conquer it.*
*Let me not look for allies in life's
battlefield but to my own strength.*
*Let me not crave in anxious fear to
be saved but hope for the patience to
win my freedom.*
*Grant me that I may not be a
coward, feeling your mercy in my
success alone; but let me find the grasp
of your hand in my failure.*

RABINDRANATH TAGORE,
Fruit-Gathering

Epidemics have taken a great toll of lives in past generations. Death in infancy and early childhood was frequent and there were few families who didn't lose a member of the family at an early age. Medicine has changed greatly in the last decades. Widespread vaccinations have practically eradicated many illnesses, at least in western Europe and the United States. The use of chemotherapy, especially the antibiotics, has contributed to an ever decreasing number of fatalities in infectious diseases. Better child care and education has effected a low morbidity and mortality among children. The many diseases that have taken an impressive toll among the young and middle-aged have been conquered. The number of old people is on the rise, and with this fact come the number of people with malignancies and chronic diseases associated more with old age.

Pediatricians have less work with acute and life-threatening situations as they have an ever increasing number of patients with psychosomatic disturbances and adjustment and behavior problems. Physicians have more people in their waiting rooms with emotional problems than they have ever had before, but they also have more elderly patients who not only try to live with their decreased physical abilities and limitations but who also face loneliness and isolation with all its pains and anguish. The

From *On Death and Dying* (1969).

majority of these people are not seen by a psychiatrist. Their needs have to be elicited and gratified by other professional people, for instance, chaplains and social workers. It is for them that I am trying to outline the changes that have taken place in the last few decades, changes that are ultimately responsible for the increased fear of death, the rising number of emotional problems, and the greater need for understanding of and coping with the problems of death and dying.

When we look back in time and study old cultures and people, we are impressed that death has always been distasteful to man and will proba- bly always be. From a psychiatrist's point of view this is very understand- able and can perhaps best be explained by our basic knowledge that, in our unconscious, death is never possible in regard to ourselves. It is inconceivable for our unconscious to imagine an actual ending of our own life here on earth, and if this life of ours has to end, the ending is always attributed to a malicious intervention from the outside by some- one else. In simple terms, in our unconscious mind we can only be killed; it is inconceivable to die of a natural cause or of old age. Therefore death in itself is associated with a bad act, a frightening happening, something that in itself calls for retribution and punishment.

One is wise to remember these fundamental facts as they are essential in understanding some of the most important, otherwise unintelligible communications of our patients.

The second fact that we have to comprehend is that in our uncon- scious mind we cannot distinguish between a wish and a deed. We are all aware of some of our illogical dreams in which two completely opposite statements can exist side by side—very acceptable in our dreams but unthinkable and illogical in our wakening state. Just as our unconscious mind cannot differentiate betwee the wish to kill somebody in anger and the act of having done so, the young child is unable to make this distinction. The child who angrily wishes his mother to drop dead for not having gratified his needs will be traumatized greatly by the actual death of his mother—even if this event is not linked closely in time with his destructive wishes. He will always take part or the whole blame for the loss of his mother. He will always say to himself—rarely to others—"I did it, I am responsible, I was bad, therefore Mommy left me." It is well to remember that the child will react in the same manner if he loses a parent by divorce, separation, or desertion. Death is often seen by a child as an impermanent thing and has therefore little distinc- tion from a divorce in which he may have an opportunity to see a parent again.

Many a parent will remember remarks of their children such as, "I will bury my doggy now and next spring when the flowers come up again, he will get up." Maybe it was the same wish that motivated the ancient

Egyptians to supply their dead with food and goods to keep them happy and the old American Indians to bury their relatives with their belongings.

When we grow older and begin to realize that our omnipotence is really not so omnipotent, that our strongest wishes are not powerful enough to make the impossible possible, the fear that we have contributed to the death of a loved one diminishes—and with it the guilt. The fear remains diminished, however, only so long as it is not challenged too strongly. Its vestiges can be seen daily in hospital corridors and in people associated with the bereaved.

A husband and wife may have been fighting for years, but when the partner dies, the survivor will pull his hair, whine and cry louder and beat his chest in regret, fear and anguish, and will hence fear his own death more than before, still believing in the law of talion—an eye for an eye, a tooth for a tooth—"I am responsible for her death, I will have to die a pitiful death in retribution."

Maybe this knowledge will help us understand many of the old customs and rituals which have lasted over the centuries and whose purpose is to diminish the anger of the gods or the people as the case may be, thus decreasing the anticipated punishment. I am thinking of the ashes, the torn clothes, the veil, the *Klage Weiber* [1] of the old days—they are all means to ask you to take pity on them, the mourners, and are expressions of sorrow, grief, and shame. If someone grieves, beats his chest, tears his hair, or refuses to eat, it is an attempt at self-punishment to avoid or reduce the anticipated punishment for the blame that he takes on the death of a loved one.

This grief, shame, and guilt are not very far removed from feelings of anger and rage. The process of grief always includes some qualities of anger. Since none of us likes to admit anger at a deceased person, these emotions are often disguised or repressed and prolong the period of grief or show up in other ways. It is well to remember that it is not up to us to judge such feelings as bad or shameful but to understand their true meaning and origin as something very human. In order to illustrate this I will again use the example of the child—and the child in us. The five-year-old who loses his mother is both blaming himself for her disappearance and being angry at her for having deserted him and for no longer gratifying his needs. The dead person then turns into something the child loves and wants very much but also hates with equal intensity for this severe deprivation.

The ancient Hebrews regarded the body of a dead person as something unclean and not to be touched. The early American Indians talked about the evil spirits and shot arrows in the air to drive the spirits away.

1. Wailing wives.

Many other cultures have rituals to take care of the "bad" dead person, and they all originate in this feeling of anger which still exists in all of us, though we dislike admitting it. The tradition of the tombstone may originate in this wish to keep the bad spirits deep down in the ground, and the pebbles that many mourners put on the grave are left-over symbols of the same wish. Though we call the firing of guns at military funerals a last salute, it is the same symbolic ritual as the Indian used when he shot his spears and arrows into the skies.

I give these examples to emphasize that man has not basically changed. Death is still a fearful, frightening happening, and the fear of death is a universal fear even if we think we have mastered it on many levels.

What has changed is our way of coping and dealing with death and dying and our dying patients.

Having been raised in a country in Europe where science is not so advanced, where modern techniques have just started to find their way into medicine, and where people still live as they did in this country half a century ago, I may have had an opportunity to study a part of the evolution of mankind in a shorter period.

I remember as a child the death of a farmer. He fell from a tree and was not expected to live. He asked simply to die at home, a wish that was granted without questioning. He called his daughters into the bedroom and spoke with each one of them alone for a few moments. He arranged his affairs quietly, though he was in great pain, and distributed his belongings and his land, none of which was to be split until his wife should follow him in death. He also asked each of his children to share in the work, duties, and tasks that he had carried on until the time of the accident. He asked his friends to visit him once more, to bid goodbye to them. Although I was a small child at the time, he did not exclude me or my siblings. We were allowed to share in the preparations of the family just as we were permitted to grieve with them until he died. When he did die, he was left at home, in his own beloved home which he had built, and among his friends and neighbors who went to take a last look at him where he lay in the midst of flowers in the place he had lived in and loved so much. In that country today there is still no make-believe slumber room, no embalming, no false makeup to pretend sleep. Only the signs of very disfiguring illnesses are covered up with bandages and only infectious cases are removed from the home prior to the burial.

Why do I describe such "old-fashioned" customs? I think they are an indication of our acceptance of a fatal outcome, and they help the dying patient as well as his family to accept the loss of a loved one. If a patient is allowed to terminate his life in the familiar and beloved environment, it requires less adjustment for him. His own family knows him well

15

enough to replace a sedative with a glass of his favorite wine; or the smell of a home-cooked soup may give him the appetite to sip a few spoons of fluid which, I think is still more enjoyable than an infusion. I will not minimize the need for sedatives and infusions and realize full well from my own experience as a country doctor that they are sometimes life-saving and often unavoidable. But I also know that patience and familiar people and foods could replace many a bottle of intravenous fluids given for the simple reason that it fulfills the physiological need without involving too many people and/or individual nursing care.

The fact that children are allowed to stay at home where a fatality has stricken and are included in the talk, discussions, and fears gives them the feeling that they are not alone in the grief and gives them the comfort of shared responsibility and shared mourning. It prepares them gradually and helps them view death as part of life, an experience which may help them grow and mature.

This is in great contrast to a society in which death is viewed as taboo, discussion of it is regarded as morbid, and children are excluded with the presumption and pretext that it would be "too much" for them. They are then sent off to relatives, often accompanied with some uncon-vincing lies of "Mother has gone on a long trip" or other unbelievable stories. The child senses that something is wrong, and his distrust in adults will only multiply if other relatives add new variations of the story, avoid his questions or suspicions, shower him with gifts as a meager substitute for a loss he is not permitted to deal with. Sooner or later the child will become aware of the changed family situation and, depending on the age and personality of the child, will have an unresolved grief and regard this incident as a frightening, mysterious, in any case very trau-matic experience with untrustworthy grownups, which he has no way to cope with.

It is equally unwise to tell a little child who lost her brother that God loved little boys so much that he took little Johnny to heaven. When this little girl grew up to be a woman she never solved her anger at God, which resulted in a psychotic depression when she lost her own little son three decades later.

20   We would think that our great emancipation, our knowledge of sci-ence and of man, has given us better ways and means to prepare our-selves and our families for this inevitable happening. Instead the days are gone when a man was allowed to die in peace and dignity in his own home.

The more we are making advancements in science, the more we seem to fear and deny the reality of death. How is this possible?

We use euphemisms, we make the dead look as if they were asleep, we ship the children off to protect them from the anxiety and turmoil around the house if the patient is fortunate enough to die at home, we don't allow children to visit their dying parents in the hospitals, we have long and controversial discussions about whether patients should be told the truth—a question that rarely arises when the dying person is tended by the family physician who has known him from delivery to death and who knows the weaknesses and strengths of each member of the family.

I think there are many reasons for this flight away from facing death calmly. One of the most important facts is that dying nowadays is more gruesome in many ways, namely, more lonely, mechanical, and dehumanized; at times it is even difficult to determine technically when the time of death has occurred.

Dying becomes lonely and impersonal because the patient is often taken out of his familiar environment and rushed to an emergency room. Whoever has been very sick and has required rest and comfort especially may recall his experience of being put on a stretcher and enduring the noise of the ambulance siren and hectic rush until the hospital gates open. Only those who have lived through this may appreciate the discomfort and cold necessity of such transportation which is only the beginning of a long order—hard to endure when you are well, difficult to express in words when noise, light, pumps, and voices are all too much to put up with. It may well be that we might consider more the patient under the sheets and blankets and perhaps stop our well-meant efficiency and rush in order to hold the patient's hand, to smile, or to listen to a question. I include the trip to the hospital as the first episode in dying, as it is for many. I am putting it exaggeratedly in contrast to the sick man who is left at home—not to say that lives should not be saved if they can be saved by a hospitalization but to keep the focus on the patient's experience, his needs and his reactions.

When a patient is severely ill, he is often treated like a person with no right to an opinion. It is often someone else who makes the decision if and when and where a patient should be hospitalized. It would take so little to remember that the sick person too has feelings, has wishes and opinions, and has—most important of all—the right to be heard.

Well, our presumed patient has now reached the emergency room. He will be surrounded by busy nurses, orderlies, interns, residents, a lab technician perhaps who will take some blood, an electrocardiogram technician who takes the cardiogram. He may be moved to X-ray and he will overhear opinions of his condition and discussions and questions to members of the family. He slowly but surely is beginning to be treated like a thing. He is no longer a person. Decisions are made often without his opinion. If he tries to rebel he will be sedated and after hours of waiting and wondering whether he has the strength, he will be wheeled

25

into the operating room or intensive treatment unit and become an object of great concern and great financial investment.

He may cry for rest, peace, and dignity, but he will get infusions, transfusions, a heart machine, or tracheotomy[2] if necessary. He may want one single person to stop for one single minute so that he can ask one single question—but he will get a dozen people around the clock, all busily preoccupied with his heart rate, pulse, electrocardiogram or pulmonary functions, his secretions or excretions but not with him as a human being. He may wish to fight it all but it is going to be a useless fight since all this is done in the fight for his life, and if they can save his life they can consider the person afterwards. Those who consider the person first may lose precious time to save his life! At least this seems to be the rationale or justification behind all this—or is it? Is the reason for this increasingly mechanical, depersonalized approach our own defensiveness? Is this approach our own way to cope with and repress the anxieties that a terminally or critically ill patient evokes in us? Is our concentration on equipment, on blood pressure our desperate attempt to deny the impending death which is so frightening and discomforting to us that we displace all our knowledge onto machines, since they are less close to us than the suffering face of another human being which would remind us once more of our lack of omnipotence, our own limits and failures, and last but not least perhaps our own mortality?

Maybe the question has to be raised: Are we becoming less human or more human? * * * [I]t is clear that whatever the answer may be, the patient is suffering more—not physically, perhaps, but emotionally. And his needs have not changed over the centuries, only our ability to gratify them.

2. The surgical opening of a passage through the neck into the trachea.

THE READER

1. *Thomas, in "The Long Habit" (p. 247), also speaks of dying. To what extent is he in harmony with Kübler-Ross? What differences do you find? What is the special contribution of each author?*

2. *To speak of rights, as Kübler-Ross does in the last pages of her essay, is to raise the question of where they come from. For example, the Declaration of Independence (p. 928) implies that the rights it asserts come from God. From what source would you expect Kübler-Ross to derive the rights she speaks of?*

3. *Kübler-Ross doubts the rationale for efficiency in medical care but, at the same time, recognizes the lifesaving results of this efficiency. There is obviously a dilemma here. What are the extreme opposite positions that define the dilemma? What is the best intermediate or compromise position?*

THE WRITER

1. *How is Kübler-Ross' essay organized? What difference does it make that she postpones presenting generalizations about her subject until late in her discussion?*
2. *Kübler-Ross opens her discussion with a quotation. Read Shakespeare's Sonnet 73 and Hopkins' "Spring and Fall: To a Young Child" (below). Would these poems be appropriate for introducing her essay? Why, or why not?*

73

That time of year thou mayst in me behold
When yellow leaves, or none, or few, do hang
Upon those boughs which shake against the cold,
Bare ruined choirs, where late the sweet birds sang.
In me thou see'st the twilight of such day
As after sunset fadeth in the west;
Which by and by black night doth take away,
Death's second self, that seals up all in rest.
In me thou see'st the glowing of such fire,
That on the ashes of his youth doth lie,
As the deathbed whereon it must expire,
Consumed with that which it was nourished by.
This thou perceiv'st, which makes thy love more strong,
To love that well which thou must leave ere long.

—William Shakespeare

SPRING AND FALL

TO A YOUNG CHILD

Margaret, are you grieving
Over Goldengrove unleaving?
Leaves, like the things of man, you
With your fresh thoughts care for, can you?
Ah! as the heart grows older
It will come to such sights colder
By and by, nor spare a sigh
Though worlds of wanwood leafmeal lie;
And yet you *will* weep and know why.
Now no matter, child, the name:
Sorrow's springs are the same.
Nor mouth had, no nor mind, expressed
What heart heard of, ghost [soul] guessed:
It is the blight man was born for,
It is Margaret you mourn for.

—Gerard Manley Hopkins

3. *Write a brief comparison between Thomas and Kübler-Ross along the lines suggested above (question 1, "The Reader").*

Stephen Jay Gould

OUR ALLOTTED LIFETIMES

Meeting with Henry Ford in E. L. Doctorow's *Ragtime*, J. P. Morgan praises the assembly line as a faithful translation of nature's wisdom:

> Has it occurred to you that your assembly line is not merely a stroke of industrial genius but a projection of organic truth? After all, the interchangeability of parts is a rule of nature. . . . All mammals reproduce in the same way and share the same designs of self-nourishment, with digestive and circulatory systems that are recognizably the same, and they enjoy the same senses. . . . Shared design is what allows taxonomists to classify mammals as mammals.

An imperious tycoon should not be met with equivocation; nonetheless, I can only reply "yes, and no" to Morgan's pronouncement. Morgan was wrong if he thought that large mammals are geometric replicas of small ones. Elephants have relatively smaller brains and thicker legs than mice, and these differences record a general rule of mammalian design, not the idiosyncracies of particular animals.

Morgan was right in arguing that large animals are essentially similar to small members of their group. The similarity, however, does not lie in a constant shape. The basic laws of geometry dictate that animals must change their shape in order to perform the same function at different sizes. I remind readers of the classical example, first discussed by Galileo in 1638: the strength of an animal's leg is a function of its cross-sectional area (length × length); the weight that the leg must support varies as the animal's volume (length × length × length). If a mammal did not alter the relative thickness of its legs as it got larger, it would soon collapse since body weight would increase much faster than the supporting strength of limbs. Instead, large mammals have relatively thicker leg bones than small mammals. To remain the same in function, animals must change their form.

The study of these changes in form is called "scaling theory." Scaling theory has uncovered a remarkable regularity of changing shape over the 25-millionfold range of mammalian weight from shrew to blue whale. If we plot brain weight versus body weight for all mammals on the

First published in *Natural History* (Vol. 86, No. 7, 1977).

so-called mouse-to-elephant (or shrew-to-whale) curve, very few species deviate far from a single line expressing the general rule: brain weight increases only two-thirds as fast as body weight as we move from small to large mammals. (We share with bottle-nosed dolphins the honor of greatest deviance from the curve.)

We can often predict these regularities from the physical behavior of objects. The heart, for example, is a pump. Since all mammalian hearts are similar in function, small hearts will pump considerably faster than large ones (imagine how much faster you could work a finger-sized toy bellows than the giant model that fuels a blacksmith's large forge). On the mouse-to-elephant curve for mammals, the length of a heartbeat increases between one-fourth and one-third as fast as body weight as we move from small to large mammals. The generality of this conclusion has just been affirmed in an interesting study by J. E. Carrel and R. D. Heathcote on the scaling of heart rate in spiders. They used a cool laser beam to illuminate the hearts of resting spiders and drew a crab spider-to-tarantula curve for eighteen species spanning nearly a thousandfold range of body weight. Again, scaling is very regular with heart rate increasing four-tenths as fast as body weight (or .409 times as fast, to be exact).

We may extend this conclusion for hearts to a very general statement about the pace of life in small versus large animals. Small animals tick through life far more rapidly than large ones—their hearts work more quickly, they breathe more frequently, their pulse beats much faster. Most importantly, metabolic rate, the so-called fire of life, scales only three-fourths as fast as body weight in mammals. Large mammals generate much less heat per unit of body weight to keep themselves going. Tiny shrews move frentically, eating nearly all their waking lives to keep their metabolic fire burning at its maximal rate among mammals; blue whales glide majestically, their hearts beating the slowest rhythm among active, warmblooded creatures.

If we consider the scaling of lifetime among mammals, an intriguing synthesis of these disparate data seems to suggest itself. We have all had enough experience with mammalian pets of various sizes to understand that small mammals tend to live for a shorter time than large ones. In fact, the scaling of mammalian lifetime follows a regular curve at about the same rate as heartbeat and breath time—between one-fourth and one-third as fast as body weight as we move from small to large animals. (Again, *Homo sapiens* emerges as a very peculiar animal. We live far longer than a mammal of our body size should. I have argued elsewhere that humans evolved by a process called "neoteny"—the retention of shapes and growth rates that characterize juvenile stages of our primate ancestors. I also believe that neoteny is responsible for our elevated longevity. Compared with other mammals, all stages of human life—

from juvenile features to adulthood—arise "too late." We are born as helpless embryos after a long gestation; we mature late after an extended childhood; we die, if fortune be kind, at ages otherwise reached only by the very largest warmblooded creatures.)

Usually, we pity the pet mouse or gerbil that lived its full span of a year or two at most. How brief its life, while we endure for the better part of a century. As the main theme of this column, I want to argue that such pity is misplaced (our personal grief, of course, is quite another matter; with this, science does not deal). J. P. Morgan of *Ragtime* was right—small and large mammals are essentially similar. Their lifetimes are scaled to their life's pace, and all endure for approximately the same amount of biological time. Small mammals tick fast, burn rapidly, and live for a short time; large ones live long at a stately pace. Measured by their own internal clocks, mammals of different sizes tend to live for the same amount of time.

Yet we are prevented from grasping this important and comforting concept by a deeply ingrained habit of Western thought. We are trained from earliest memory to regard absolute Newtonian time as the single valid measuring stick in a rational and objective world. We impose our kitchen clock, ticking equably, upon all things. We marvel at the quickness of a mouse, express boredom at the torpor of a hippopotamus. Yet each is living at the appropriate pace of its own biological clock.

I do not wish to deny the importance of absolute, astronomical time to organisms. Animals must measure it to lead successful lives. Deer must know when to regrow their antlers, birds when to migrate. Animals track the day–night cycle with their circadian rhythms; jet lag is the price we pay for moving much faster than nature intended. Bamboos can somehow count 120 years before flowering again.

But absolute time is not the appropriate measuring stick for all biological phenomena. Consider the song of the humpback whale. These magnificent animals sing with such volume that their sounds travel through water for thousands of miles, perhaps even around the world, as their leading student Roger S. Payne has suggested. E. O. Wilson has described the awesome effect of these vocalizations: "The notes are eerie yet beautiful to the human ear. Deep basso groans and almost inaudibly high soprano squeaks alternate with repetitive squeals that suddenly rise or fall in pitch." We do not know the function of these songs. Perhaps they enable whales to find each other and to stay together during their annual transoceanic migrations.

Each whale has its own characteristic song; the highly complex patterns are repeated over and over again with great faithfulness. No scientific fact that I have learned in the last decade struck me with more force than Payne's report that the length of some songs may extend for more than half an hour. I have never been able to memorize the five-minute first Kyrie of the B-minor Mass[1] (and not for want of trying); how could a whale sing for thirty minutes and then repeat itself accurately? Of what possible use is a thirty-minute repeat cycle—far too long for a human to recognize: we would never grasp it as a single song (without Payne's recording machinery and much study after the fact). But then I remembered the whale's metabolic rate, the enormously slow pace of its life compared with ours. What do we know about a whale's perception of thirty minutes? A humpback may scale the world to its own metabolic rate: its half-hour song may be our minute waltz.[2] From any point of view, the song is spectacular; it is the most elaborate single display so far discovered in any animal. I merely urge the whale's point of view as an appropriate perspective.

We can provide some numerical precision to support the claim that all mammals, on average, live for the same amount of biological time. In a method developed by W. R. Stahl, B. Gunther, and E. Guerra in the late 1950s and early 1960s, we search the mouse-to-elephant equations for biological properties that scale at the same rate against body weight. For example, Gunther and Guerra give the following equations for mammalian breath time and heartbeat time versus body weight.

$$\text{breath time} = .0000470 \text{ body}^{0.28}$$
$$\text{heartbeat time} = .0000119 \text{ body}^{0.28}$$

(Nonmathematical readers need not be overwhelmed by the formalism. The equations simply mean that both breath time and heartbeat time increase about .28 times as fast as body weight as we move from small to large mammals.) If we divide the two equations, body weight cancels out because it is raised to the same power.

$$\frac{\text{breath time}}{\text{heartbeat time}} = \frac{.0000470 \; \text{body}^{0.28}}{.0000119 \; \text{body}^{0.28}} = 4.0$$

This says that the ratio of breath time to heartbeat time is 4.0 in mammals of any body size. In other words, all mammals, whatever their size, breathe once for each four heartbeats. Small animals breathe and beat their hearts faster than large animals, but both breath and heart slow up at the same relative rate as mammals get larger.

Lifetime also scales at the same rate to body weight (.28 times as fast as we move from small to large mammals). This means that the ratio of both breath time and heartbeat time to lifetime is also constant

15

1. By Johann Sebastian Bach; the movement is woven together from many independent musical lines.

2. The reference is to the "Minute Waltz," by Frédéric Chopin, which is not only brief but fast-moving.

over the whole range of mammalian size. When we perform an exercise similar to that above, we find that all mammals, regardless of their size, tend to breathe about 200 million times during their lives (their hearts, therefore, beat about 800 million times). Small mammals breathe fast, but live for a short time. Measured by the sensible internal clocks of their own hearts or the rhythm of their own breathing, all mammals live about the same time. (Astute readers, having counted their breaths, may have calculated that they should have died long ago. But *Homo sapiens* is a markedly deviant mammal in more ways than braininess alone. We live about three times as long as mammals of our body size "should," but we breathe at the "right" rate and thus live to breathe about three times as much as an average mammal of our body size.)

The mayfly lives but a day as an adult. It may, for all I know, experience that day as we live a lifetime. Yet all is not relative in our world, and such a short glimpse of it must invite distortion in interpreting events ticking on longer scales. In a brilliant metaphor, the pre-Darwinian evolutionist Robert Chambers spoke of a mayfly watching the metamorphosis of a tadpole into a frog (from *Vestiges of the Natural History of Creation*, 1844):

> Suppose that an ephemeron [a mayfly], hovering over a pool for its one April day of life, were capable of observing the fry of the frog in the waters below. In its aged afternoon, having seen no change upon them for such a long time, it would be little qualified to conceive that the external branchiae [gills] of these creatures were to decay, and be replaced by internal lungs, that feet were to be developed, the tail erased, and the animal then to become a denizen of the land.

Human consciousness arose but a minute before midnight on the geologic clock. Yet we mayflies, ignorant perhaps of the messages buried in earth's long history, try to bend an ancient world to our purposes. Let us hope that we are still in the morning of our April day.

THE READER

1. *What relationships does Gould show among mammals? Which of these relationships hold between human beings and other mammals?*
2. *What contrast does Gould make between astronomical time and biological time? Which is more important for human beings?*
3. *In his concluding paragraph Gould speaks to us as "we mayflies." In what sense is the term appropriate to human beings at this point?*

THE WRITER

1. *What is Gould's thesis in this essay? Where does the thesis become manifest? How has Gould prepared the reader for the thesis?*
2. *For what purpose does Gould use the song of the blue whale?*
3. *In his final paragraph Gould seems to invite his reader to reflect on geologic time and the place of human beings in it. Write an essay, reflecting on human experience that this invitation leads you to.*

Education

Eudora Welty

CLAMOROUS TO LEARN

From the first I was clamorous to learn—I wanted to know and begged to be told not so much what, or how, or why, or where, as when. How soon?

> Pear tree by the garden gate,
> How much longer must I wait?

This rhyme from one of my nursery books was the one that spoke for me. But I lived not at all unhappily in this craving, for my wild curiosity was in large part suspense, which carries its own secret pleasure. And so one of the godmothers of fiction was already bending over me.

When I was five years old, I knew the alphabet, I'd been vaccinated (for smallpox), and I could read. So my mother walked across the street to Jefferson Davis Grammar School[1] and asked the principal if she would allow me to enter the first grade after Christmas.

"Oh, all right," Said Miss Duling. "Probably the best thing you could do with her."

Miss Duling, a lifelong subscriber to perfection, was a figure of authority, the most whole-souled I have ever come to know. She was a dedicated schoolteacher who denied herself all she might have done or whatever other way she might have lived (this possibility was the last that could have occurred to us, her subjects in school). I believe she came of well-off people, well-educated, in Kentucky, and certainly old photographs show she was a beautiful, high-spirited-looking young lady—and came down to Jackson to its new grammar school that was going begging for a principal. She must have earned next to nothing; Mississippi then

From a set of three lectures delivered at Harvard University in April 1983, to inaugurate the William E. Massey lecture series; later published as *One Writer's Beginnings* (1985).

1. Named after the president of the Confederate States of America (1861–65) and located in Jackson, Mississippi.

as now was the nation's lowest-ranking state economically, and our legislature has always shown a painfully loud reluctance to give money to public education. That challenge *brought* her.

In the long run she came into touch, as teacher or principal. with three generations of Jacksonians. My parents had not, but everybody else's parents had gone to school to her. She'd taught most of our leaders somewhere along the line. When she wanted something done—some civic oversight corrected, some injustice made right overnight, or even a tree spared that the fool telephone people were about to cut down— she telephoned the mayor, or the chief of police, or the president of the power company, or the head doctor at the hospital, or the judge in charge of a case, or whoever, and calling them by their first names, *told* them. It is impossible to imagine her meeting with anything less than compliance. The ringing of her brass bell from their days at Davis School would still be in their ears. She also proposed a spelling match between the fourth grade at Davis School and the Mississippi Legislature, who went through with it; and that told the Legislature.

Her standards were very high and of course inflexible, her authority was total; why *wouldn't* this carry with it a brass bell that could be heard ringing for a block in all directions? That bell belonged to the figure of Miss Duling as though it grew directly out of her right arm, as wings grew out of an angel or a tail out of the devil. When we entered, marching, into her school, by strictest teaching, surveillance, and order we learned grammar, arithmetic, spelling, reading, writing, and geography; and she, not the teachers, I believe, wrote out the examinations: need I tell you, they were "hard."

She's not the only teacher who has influenced me, but Miss Duling, in some fictional shape or form, has stridden into a larger part of my work than I'd realized until now. She emerges in my perhaps inordinate number of schoolteacher characters. I loved those characters in the writing. But I did not, in life, love Miss Duling. I was afraid of her high-arched bony nose, her eyebrows lifted in half-circles above her hooded, brilliant eyes, and of the Kentucky R's in her speech, and the long steps she took in her hightop shoes. I did nothing but fear her bearing-down authority, and did not connect this (as of course we were meant to) with our own need or desire to learn, perhaps because I already had this wish, and did not need to be driven.

She was impervious to lies or foolish excuses or the insufferable plea of not knowing any better. She wasn't going to have any frills, either, at Davis School. When a new governor moved into the mansion, he sent his daughter to Davis School; her name was Lady Rachel Conner. Miss Duling at once called the governor to the telephone and told him, "She'll be plain Rachel here."

Miss Duling dressed as plainly as a Pilgrim on a Thanksgiving poster we made in the schoolroom, in a longish black-and-white checked ging-ham dress, a bright thick wool sweater the red of a railroad lantern—she'd knitted it herself—black stockings and her narrow elegant feet in black hightop shoes with heels you could hear coming, rhythmical as a parade drum down the hall. Her silky black curly hair was drawn back out of curl, fastened by high combs, and knotted behind. She carried her spectacles on a gold chain hung around her neck. Her gaze was in general sweeping, then suddenly at the point of concentration upon you. With a swing of her bell that took her whole right arm and shoulder, she rang it, militant and impartial, from the head of the front steps of Davis School when it was time for us all to line up, girls on one side, boys on the other. We were to march past her into the school building, while the fourth-grader she nabbed played time on the piano, mostly to a tune we could have skipped to, but we didn't skip into Davis School.

10   Little recess (open-air exercises) and big recess (lunch-boxes from home opened and eaten on the grass, on the girls' side and the boys' side of the yard) and dismissal were also regulated by Miss Duling's bell. The bell was also used to catch us off guard with fire drill.

It was examinations that drove my wits away, as all emergencies do. Being expected to measure up was paralyzing. I failed to make 100 on my spelling exam because I missed one word and that word was "uncle." Mother, as I knew she would, took it personally. "You couldn't spell *uncle?* When you've got those five perfectly splendid uncles in West Virginia? What would *they* say to that?"

It was never that Mother wanted me to beat my classmates in grades; what she wanted was for me to have my answers right. It was unclouded perfection I was up against.

My father was much more tolerant of possible error. He only said, as he steeply and impeccably sharpened my pencils on examination morn-ing, "Now just keep remembering: the examinations were made out for the *average* student to pass. That's the majority. And if the majority can pass, think how much better *you* can do."

I looked to my mother, who had her own opinions about the majority. My father wished to treat it with respect, she didn't. I'd been born left-handed, but the habit was broken when I entered the first grade in Davis School. My father had insisted. He pointed out that everything in life had been made for the convenience of right-handed people, because they were the majority, and he often used "what the majority wants" as a criterion for what was for the best. My mother said she could not promise him, could not promise him at all, that I wouldn't stutter as a consequence. Mother had been born left-handed too; her family consisted of five left-handed brothers, a left-handed mother, and a father who could write with both hands at the same time, also backwards and forwards and upside down, different words with each hand. She had

been broken of it when she was young, and she said she used to stutter.
"But you still stutter," I'd remind her, only to hear her say loftily, 15
"You should have heard me when I was your age."

In my childhood days, a great deal of stock was put, in general, in the
value of doing well in school. Both daily newspapers in Jackson saw the
honor roll as news and published the lists, and the grades, of all the honor
students. The city fathers gave the children who made the honor roll
free season tickets to the baseball games down at the grandstand. We
all attended and all worshiped some player on the Jackson Senators: I
offered up my 100's in arithmetic and spelling, reading and writing,
attendance and, yes, deportment—I must have been a prig!—to Red
McDermott, the third baseman. And our happiness matched that of
knowing Miss Duling was on her summer vacation, far, far away in
Kentucky.

Every school week, visiting teachers came on their days for special
lessons. On Mondays, the singing teacher blew into the room fresh from
the early outdoors, singing in her high soprano "How do you do?" to
do-mi-sol-do,[2] and we responded in chorus from our desks, "I'm ve-ry
well" to do-sol-mi-do. Miss Johnson taught us rounds—"Row row row
your boat gently down the stream"—and "Little Sir Echo," with half
the room singing the words and the other half being the echo, a competition. She was from the North, and she was the one who wanted us all
to stop the Christmas carols and see snow. The snow falling that morning outside the window was the first most of us had ever seen, and Miss
Johnson threw up the window and held out wide her own black cape
and caught flakes on it and ran, as fast as she could go, up and down
the aisles to show us the real thing before it melted.

Thursday was Miss Eyrich and Miss Eyrich was Thursday. She came
to give us physical training. She wasted no time on nonsense. Without
greeting, we were marched straight outside and summarily divided into
teams (no choosing sides), put on the mark, and ordered to get set for
a relay race. Miss Eyrich cracked out "Go!" Dread rose in my throat.
My head swam. Here was my turn, nearly upon me. (Wait, have I been
touched—was that slap the touch? Go on! Do I go on without our
passing a word? What word? Now am I racing too fast to turn around?
Now I'm nearly home, but where is the hand waiting for mine to touch?
Am I too late? Have I lost the whole race for our side?) I lost the relay
race for our side before I started, through living ahead of myself, dread-
ing to make my start, feeling too late prematurely, and standing transfixed by emergency, trying to think of a password. Thursdays still can
make me hear Miss Eyrich's voice. "On your mark—get set—GO!"

2. Syllables indicating the first, third, fifth, and eighth tones of the scale.

Very composedly and very slowly, the art teacher, who visited each room on Fridays, paced the aisle and looked down over your shoulder at what you were drawing for her. This was Miss Ascher. Coming from behind you, her deep, resonant voice reached you without being a word at all, but a sort of purr. It was much the sound given out by our family doctor when he read the thermometer and found you were running a slight fever: "Um-hm. Um-hm." Both alike, they let you go right ahead with it.

20   The school toilets were in the boys' and girls' respective basements. After Miss Duling had rung to dismiss school, a friend and I were making our plans for Saturday from adjoining cubicles. "Can you come spend the day with me?" I called out, and she called back, "I might could."

"Who—said—MIGHT—COULD?" It sounded like "Fe Fi Fo Fum!"

We both were petrified, for we knew whose deep measured words those were that came from just outside our doors. That was the voice of Mrs. McWillie, who taught the other fourth grade across the hall from ours. She was not even our teacher, but a very heavy, stern lady who dressed entirely in widow's weeds with a pleated black shirtwaist with a high net collar and velvet ribbon, and a black skirt to her ankles, with black circles under her eyes and a mournful, Presbyterian expression. We children took her to be a hundred years old. We held still.

"You might as well tell me, " continued Mrs. McWillie. "I'm going to plant myself right here and wait till you come out. Then I'll see who it was I heard saying 'MIGHT-COULD.' "

If Elizabeth wouldn't go out, of course I wouldn't either. We knew her to be a teacher who would not flinch from standing there in the basement all afternoon, perhaps even all day Saturday. So we surrendered and came out. I priggishly hoped Elizabeth would clear it up which child it was—it wasn't me.

25   "So it's you." She regarded us as a brace, made no distinction: whoever didn't say it was guilty by association. "If I ever catch you down here one more time saying 'MIGHT-COULD,' I'm going to carry it to Miss Duling. You'll be kept in every day for a week! I hope you're both sufficiently ashamed of yourselves?" Saying "might-could" was bad, but saying it in the basement made bad grammar a sin. I knew Presbyterians believed that you could go to Hell.

Mrs. McWillie never scared us into grammar, of course. It was my first-year Latin teacher in high school who made me discover I'd fallen in love with it. It took Latin to thrust me into bona fide alliance with words in their true meaning. Learning Latin (once I was free of Caesar) fed my love for words upon words, words in continuation and modification, and the beautiful, sober, accretion of a sentence. I could see the achieved sentence finally standing there, as real, intact, and built to stay as the Mississippi State Capitol at the top of my street, where I could walk through it on my way to school and hear underfoot the echo of its marble floor, and over me the bell of its rotunda.

On winter's rainy days, the schoolrooms would grow so dark that sometimes you couldn't see the figures on the blackboard. At that point, Mrs. McWillie, that stern fourth-grade teacher, would let her children close their books, and she would move, broad in widow's weeds like darkness itself, to the window and by what light there was she would stand and read aloud "The King of the Golden River."[3] But I was excluded—in the other fourth grade, across the hall. Miss Louella Varnado, my teacher, didn't copy Mrs. McWillie; we had a spelling match: you could spell in the dark. I did not then suspect that there was any other way I could learn the story of "The King of the Golden River" than to have been assigned in the beginning to Mrs. McWillie's cowering fourth grade, then wait for her to treat you to it on the rainy day of her choice. I only now realize how much the treat depended, too, on there not having been money enough to put electric lights in Davis School. John Ruskin had to come in through courtesy of darkness. When in time I found the story in a book and read it to myself, it didn't seem to live up to my longings for a story with that name; as indeed, how could it?

3. A fantasy for children by the English author John Ruskin (1819–1900).

John Holt

HOW TEACHERS MAKE CHILDREN HATE READING

When I was teaching English at the Colorado Rocky Mountain School, I used to ask my students the kinds of questions that English teachers usually ask about reading assignments—questions designed to bring out the points that *I* had decided *they* should know. They, on their part, would try to get me to give them hints and clues as to what I wanted. It was a game of wits. I never gave my students an opportunity to say what they really thought about a book.

I gave vocabulary drills and quizzes too. I told my students that every time they came upon a word in their book they did not understand, they were to look it up in the dictionary. I even devised special kinds of

From *The Under-Achieving School* (1967). Originally appeared in *Redbook* (Nov. 1967).

vocabulary tests, allowing them to use their books to see how the words were used. But looking back, I realize that these tests, along with many of my methods, were foolish.

My sister was the first person who made me question my conventional ideas about teaching English. She had a son in the seventh grade in a fairly good public school. His teacher had asked the class to read Cooper's *The Deerslayer.* The choice was bad enough in itself; whether looking at man or nature, Cooper was superficial, inaccurate and sentimental, and his writing is ponderous and ornate. But to make matters worse, this teacher had decided to give the book the microscope and x-ray treatment. He made the students look up and memorize not only the definitions but the derivations of every big word that came along— and there were plenty. Every chapter was followed by close questioning and testing to make sure the students "understood" everything.

Being then, as I said, conventional, I began to defend the teacher, who was a good friend of mine, against my sister's criticisms. The argument soon grew hot. What was wrong with making sure that children understood everything they read? My sister answered that until this year her boy had always loved reading, and had read a lot on his own; now he had stopped. (He was not really to start again for many years.)

5
Still I persisted. If children didn't look up the words they didn't know, how would they ever learn them? My sister said, "Don't be silly! when you were little you had a huge vocabulary, and were always reading very grown-up books. When did you ever look up a word in a dictionary?"

She had me. I don't know that we had a dictionary at home; if we did, I didn't use it. I don't use one today. In my life I doubt that I have looked up as many as fifty words, perhaps not even half that.

Since then I have talked about this with a number of teachers. More than once I have said, "According to tests, educated and literate people like you have a vocabulary of about twenty-five thousand words. How many of these did you learn by looking them up in a dictionary?" They usually are startled. Few claim to have looked up even as many as a thousand. How did they learn the rest?

They learned them just as they learned to talk—by meeting words over and over again, in different contexts, until they saw how they fitted.

Unfortunately, we English teachers are easily hung up on this matter of understanding. Why should children understand everything they read? Why should anyone? Does anyone? I don't, and I never did. I was always reading books that teachers would have said were "too hard" for me, books full of words I didn't know. That's how I got to be a good reader. When about ten, I read all the D'Artagnan stories and loved them. It didn't trouble me in the least that I didn't know why France was at war with England or who was quarreling with whom in the

French court or why the Musketeers should always be at odds with Cardinal Richelieu's men. I didn't even know who the Cardinal was, except that he was a dangerous and powerful man that my friends had to watch out for. This was all I needed to know.

Having said this, I will now say that I think a big, unabridged dictionary is a fine thing to have in any home or classroom. No book is more fun to browse around in—*if* you're not made to. Children, depending on their age, will find many pleasant and interesting things to do with a big dictionary. They can look up funny-sounding words, which they like, or words that nobody else in the class has ever heard of, which they like, or long words, which they like, or forbidden words, which they like best of all. At a certain age, and particularly with a little encouragement from parents or teachers, they may become very interested in where words came from and when they came into the language and how their meanings have changed over the years. But exploring for the fun of it is very different from looking up words out of your reading because you're going to get into trouble with your teacher if you don't.

While teaching fifth grade two years or so after the argument with my sister, I began to think again about reading. The children in my class were supposed to fill out a card—just the title and author and a one-sentence summary—for every book they read. I was not running a competition to see which child could read the most books, a competition that almost always leads to cheating. I just wanted to know what the children were reading. After a while it became clear that many of these very bright kids, from highly literate and even literary backgrounds, read very few books and deeply disliked reading. Why should this be?

At this time I was coming to realize, as I described in my book *How Children Fail,* that for most children school was a place of danger, and their main business in school was staying out of danger as much as possible. I now began to see also that books were among the most dangerous things in school.

From the very beginning of school we make books and reading a constant source of possible failure and public humiliation. When children are little we make them read aloud, before the teacher and other children, so that we can be sure they "know" all the words they are reading. This means that when they don't know a word, they are going to make a mistake, right in front of everyone. Instantly they are made to realize that they have done something wrong. Perhaps some of the other children will begin to wave their hands and say, "Ooooh! O-o-o-oh!" Perhaps they will just giggle, or nudge each other, or make a face. Perhaps the teacher will say, "Are you sure?" or ask someone else what he thinks. Or perhaps, if the teacher is kindly, she will just smile a sweet, sad smile—often one of the most painful punishments a child can suffer in school. In any case, the child who has made the mistake knows he has made it, and feels foolish, stupid, and ashamed, just as any of us would in his shoes.

Before long many children associate books and reading with mistakes, real or feared, and penalties and humiliation. This may not seem sensible, but it is natural. Mark Twain once said that a cat that sat on a hot stove lid would never sit on one again—but it would never sit on a cold one either. As true of children as of cats. If they, so to speak, sit on a hot book a few times, if books cause them humiliation and pain, they are likely to decide that the safest thing to do is to leave all books alone.

After having taught fifth-grade classes for four years I felt quite sure of this theory. In my next class were many children who had had great trouble with schoolwork, particularly reading. I decided to try at all costs to rid them of their fear and dislike of books, and to get them to read oftener and more adventurously.

One day soon after school had started, I said to them, "Now I'm going to say something about reading that you have probably never heard a teacher say before. I would like you to read a lot of books this year, but I want you to read them only for pleasure. I am not going to ask you questions to find out whether you understand the books or not. If you understand enough of a book to enjoy it and want to go on reading it, that's enough for me. Also I'm not going to ask you what words mean.

"Finally," I said, "I don't want you to feel that just because you start a book, you have to finish it. Give an author thirty or forty pages or so to get his story going. Then if you don't like the characters and don't care what happens to them, close the book, put it away, and get another. I don't care whether the books are easy or hard, short or long, as long as you enjoy them. Furthermore I'm putting all this in a letter to your parents, so they won't feel they have to quiz and heckle you about books at home."

The children sat stunned and silent. Was this a teacher talking? One girl, who had just come to us from a school where she had had a very hard time, and who proved to be one of the most interesting, lively, and intelligent children I have ever known, looked at me steadily for a long time after I had finished. Then, still looking at me, she said slowly and solemnly, "Mr. Holt, do you really mean that?" I said just as solemnly, "I mean every word of it."

Apparently she decided to believe me. The first book she read was Dr. Seuss's *How the Grinch Stole Christmas,* not a hard book even for most third graders. For a while she read a number of books on this level. Perhaps she was clearing up some confusion about reading that her teachers, in their hurry to get her up to "grade level," had never given her enough time to clear up. After she had been in the class six weeks or so and we had become good friends, I very tentatively suggested that, since she was a skillful rider and loved horses, she might like to read *National Velvet.* I made my sell as soft as possible, saying only that it was about a girl who loved and rode horses, and that if she didn't like it, she could put it back. She tried it, and though she must have found it quite a bit harder than what she had been reading, finished it and liked it very much.

During the spring she really astonished me, however. One day, in one of our many free periods, she was reading at her desk. From a glimpse of the illustrations I thought I knew what the book was. I said to myself, "It can't be," and went to take a closer look. Sure enough, she was reading *Moby Dick,* in the edition with woodcuts by Rockwell Kent. When I came close to her desk she looked up. I said, "Are you really reading that?" She said she was. I said, "Do you like it?" She said, "Oh, yes, it's neat!" I said, "Don't you find parts of it rather heavy going?" She answered "Oh, sure, but I just skip over those parts and go on to the next good part."

This is exactly what reading should be and in school so seldom is—an exciting, joyous adventure. Find something, dive into it, take the good parts, skip the bad parts, get what you can out of it, go on to something else. How different is our mean-spirited, picky insistence that every child get every last little scrap of "understanding" that can be dug out of a book.

For teachers who really enjoy doing it, and will do it with gusto, reading aloud is a very good idea. I have found that not just fifth graders but even ninth and eleventh graders enjoy it. Jack London's "To Build a Fire" is a good read-aloud story. So are ghost stories, and "August Heat," by W. F. Harvey, and "The Monkey's Paw," by W. W. Jacobs, are among the best. Shirley Jackson's "The Lottery" is sure-fire, and will raise all kinds of questions for discussion and argument. Because of a TV program they had seen and that excited them, I once started reading my fifth graders William Golding's *Lord of the Flies,* thinking to read only a few chapters, but they made me read it to the end.

In my early fifth-grade classes the children usually were of high IQ, came from literate backgrounds and were generally felt to be succeeding in school. Yet it was astonishingly hard for most of those children to express themselves in speech or in writing. I have known a number of five-year-olds who were considerably more articulate than most of the fifth graders I have known in school. Asked to speak, my fifth graders were covered with embarrassment; many refused altogether. Asked to write, they would sit for minutes on end, staring at the paper. It was hard for most of them to get down a half page of writing, even on what seemed to be interesting topics or topics they chose themselves.

In desperation I hit on a device that I named the Composition Derby. I divided the class into teams, and told them that when I said, "Go," they were to start writing something. It could be about anything they wanted, but it had to be about something—they couldn't just write "dog dog dog dog" on the paper. It could be true stories, descriptions of people or places or events, wishes, made-up stories, dreams—anything they liked. Spelling didn't count, so they didn't have to worry about it. When I said, "Stop," they were to stop and count up the words they had written. The team that wrote the most words would win the derby.

25   It was a success in many ways and for many reasons. The first surprise was that the two children who consistently wrote the most words were two of the least successful students in the class. They were bright, but they had always had a very hard time in school. Both were very bad spellers, and worrying about this had slowed down their writing without improving their spelling. When they were free of this worry and could let themselves go, they found hidden and unsuspected talents.

One of the two, a very driven and anxious little boy, used to write long adventures, or misadventures, in which I was the central character— "The Day Mr. Holt Went to Jail," "The Day Mr. Holt Fell Into the Hole," "The Day Mr. Holt Got Run Over," and so on. These were very funny, and the class enjoyed hearing me read them aloud. One day I asked the class to write a derby on a topic I would give them. They groaned; they liked picking their own. "Wait till you hear it," I said. "It's 'The Day the School Burned Down.'"

With a shout of approval and joy they went to work, and wrote furiously for 20 minutes or more, laughing and chuckling as they wrote. The papers were all much alike; in them the children danced around the burning building, throwing in books and driving me and the other teachers back in when we tried to escape.

In our first derby the class wrote an average of about ten words a minute; after a few months their average was over 20. Some of the slower writers tripled their output. Even the slowest, one of whom was the best student in the class, were writing 15 words a minute. More important, almost all the children enjoyed the derbies and wrote interesting things.

Some time later I learned that Professor S. I. Hayakawa, teaching freshman English, had invented a better technique. Every day in class he asked his students to write without stopping for about half an hour. They could write on whatever topic or topics they chose, but the important thing was not to stop. If they ran dry, they were to copy their last sentence over and over again until new ideas came. Usually they came before the sentence had been copied once. I use this idea in my own classes, and call this kind of paper a Non-Stop. Sometimes I ask students to write a Non-Stop on an assigned topic, more often on anything they choose. Once in a while I ask them to count up how many words they have written, though I rarely ask them to tell me; it is for their own information. Sometimes these papers are to be handed in; often they are what I call private papers, for the students' eyes alone.

The private paper has proved very useful. In the first place, in any English class—certainly any large English class—if the amount the students write is limited by what the teacher can find time to correct, or even to read, the students will not write nearly enough. The only remedy is to have them write a great deal that the teacher does not read. In the second place, students writing for themselves will write about many things that they would never write on a paper to be handed in, once they have learned (sometimes it takes a while) that the teacher means what he says about the papers' being private. This is important, not just because it enables them to get things off their chest, but also because they are most likely to write well, and to pay attention to how they write, when they are writing about something important to them.

Some English teachers, when they first hear about private papers, object that students do not benefit from writing papers unless the papers are corrected. I disagree for several reasons. First, most students, particularly poor students, do not read the corrections on their papers; it is boring, even painful. Second, even when they do read these corrections, they do not get much help from them, do not build the teacher's suggestions into their writing. This is true even when they really believe the teacher knows what he is talking about.

Third, and most important, we learn to write by writing, not by reading other people's ideas about writing. What most students need above all else is practice in writing, and particularly in writing about things that matter to them, so that they will begin to feel the satisfaction that comes from getting important thoughts down in words and will care about stating these thoughts forcefully and clearly.

Teachers of English—or, as some schools say (ugh!), Language Arts— spend a lot of time and effort on spelling. Most of it is wasted; it does little good, and often more harm than good. We should ask ourselves, "How do good spellers spell? What do they do when they are not sure which spelling of a word is right?" I have asked this of a number of good spellers. Their answer never varies. They do not rush for a dictionary or rack their brains trying to remember some rules. They write down the word both ways, or several ways, look at them and pick the one that looks best. Usually they are right.

Good spellers know what words look like and even, in their writing muscles, feel like. They have a good set of word images in their minds, and are willing to trust these images. The things we do to "teach" spelling to children do little to develop these skills or talents, and much to destroy them or prevent them from developing.

The first and worst thing we do is to make children anxious about spelling. We treat a misspelled word like a crime and penalize the misspeller severely; many teachers talk of making children develop a "spelling conscience," and fail otherwise excellent papers because of a few spelling mistakes. This is self-defeating. When we are anxious, we don't perceive clearly or remember what we once perceived. Everyone knows how hard it is to recall even simple things when under emotional pressure; the harder we rack our brains, the less easy it is to find what we are looking for. If we are anxious enough, we will not trust the messages that memory sends us. Many children spell badly because although their first hunches about how to spell a word may be correct, they are afraid to trust them. I have often seen on children's papers a word correctly spelled, then crossed out and misspelled.

There are some tricks that might help children get sharper word images. Some teachers may be using them. One is the trick of air writing; that is, of "writing" a word in the air with a finger and "seeing" the image so formed. I did this quite a bit with fifth graders, using either the air or the top of a desk, on which their fingers left no mark. Many of them were tremendously excited by this. I can still hear them saying, "There's nothing there, but I can see it!" It seemed like black magic. I remember that when I was little I loved to write in the air. It was effortless, voluptuous, satisfying, and it was fun to see the word appear in the air. I used to write "Money Money Money," not so much because I didn't have any as because I liked the way it felt, particularly that *y* at the end, with its swooping tail.

Another thing to help sharpen children's image-making machinery is taking very quick looks at words—or other things. The conventional machine for doing this is the tachistoscope. But these are expensive, so expensive that most children can have few chances to use them, if any at all. With some three-by-five and four-by-eight file cards you can get the same effect. On the little cards you put the words or the pictures that the child is going to look at. You hold the larger card over the card to be read, uncover it for a split second with a quick wrist motion, then cover it up again. Thus you have a tachistoscope that costs one cent and that any child can work by himself.

Once when substituting in a first-grade class, I thought that the children, who were just beginning to read and write, might enjoy some of the kind of free, nonstop writing that my fifth graders had. One day about 40 minutes before lunch, I asked them all to take pencil and paper and start writing about anything they wanted to. They seemed to like the idea, but right away one child said anxiously, "Suppose we can't spell a word."

"Don't worry about it," I said. "Just spell it the best way you can."

A heavy silence settled on the room. All I could see were still pencils and anxious faces. This was clearly not the right approach. So I said, "All right, I'll tell you what we'll do. Any time you want to know how to spell a word, tell me and I'll write it on the board."

They breathed a sigh of relief and went to work. Soon requests for words were coming fast; as soon as I wrote one, someone asked me another. By lunchtime, when most of the children were still busily writing, the board was full. What was interesting was that most of the words they had asked for were much longer and more complicated than anything in their reading books or workbooks. Freed from worry about spelling, they were willing to use the most difficult and interesting words that they knew.

The words were still on the board when we began school next day. Before I began to erase them, I said to the children, "Listen, everyone. I have to erase these words, but before I do, just out of curiosity, I'd like to see if you remember some of them."

The result was surprising. I had expected that the child who had asked for and used a word might remember it, but I did not think many others would. But many of the children still knew many of the words. How had they learned them? I suppose each time I wrote a word on the board a number of children had looked up, relaxed yet curious, just to see what the word looked like, and these images and the sound of my voice saying the word had stuck in their minds until the next day. This, it seems to me, is how children may best learn to write and spell.

What can a parent do if a school, or a teacher, is spoiling the language for a child by teaching it in some tired way? First, try to get them to change, or at least let them know that you are eager for change. Talk to other parents; push some of these ideas in the PTA; talk to the English department at the school; talk to the child's own teacher. Many teachers and schools want to know what the parents want.

If the school or teacher cannot be persuaded, then what? Perhaps all you can do is try not to let your child become too bored or discouraged or worried by what is happening in school. Help him meet the school's demands, foolish though they may seem, and try to provide more interesting alternatives at home—plenty of books and conversation, and a serious and respectful audience when a child wants to talk. Nothing that ever happened to me in English classes at school was as helpful to me as the long conversations I used to have every summer with my uncle, who made me feel that the difference in our ages was not important and that he was really interested in what I had to say.

At the end of her freshman year in college a girl I know wrote home to her mother, "Hooray! Hooray! Just think—I never have to take English any more!" But this girl had always been an excellent English student, had always loved books, writing, ideas. It seems unnecessary and foolish and wrong that English teachers should so often take what should be the most flexible, exciting, and creative of all school courses and make it into something that most children can hardly wait to see the last of. Let's hope that we can and soon will begin to do much better.

45

THE READER

1. *What are the major indictments Holt makes against conventional teaching methods? What alternatives does he propose?*
2. *Booth discusses various metaphors (including man as machine and man as animal) that underline different theories of education ("Is There Any Knowledge That a Man Must Have?," p. 337). How would Holt respond to these metaphors? If Holt were to construct a metaphor of his own, what might it be?*
3. *Is the kind of teaching that Holt describes likely to lead to students' having the knowledge that Booth believes essential?*

THE WRITER

1. *Here are two accounts of a young boy's going to school, the second a summary or précis of the first. Determine what has been removed from the original in the summary. Then write a short comparison of original and summary from Holt's educational point of view, as it can be inferred from his essay.*

> His days were rich in formal experience. Wearing overalls and an old sweater (the accepted uniform of the private seminary), he sallied forth at morn accompanied by a nurse or a parent and walked (or was pulled) two blocks to a corner where the school bus made a flag stop. This flashy vehicle was as punctual as death: seeing us waiting at the cold curb, it would sweep to a halt, open its mouth, suck the boy in, and spring away with an angry growl. It was a good deal like a train picking up a bag of mail. At school the scholar was worked on for six or seven hours by half a dozen teachers and a nurse, and was revived on orange juice in midmorning. In a cinder court he played games supervised by an athletic instructor, and in a cafeteria he ate lunch worked out by a dietitian.
>
> —E. B. White, "Education"

> His days followed a set routine. He wore overalls and an old sweater, as everyone else did in his school. In the morning, a parent or nurse walked the two blocks with him to the corner where he met the school bus. The bus was always on time. During the six or seven hours of the school day, he had six teachers. The school also employed a nurse and a dietitian. Games were supervised. The children ate in the cafeteria. Orange juice was served during the morning session.
>
> —End-of-year examinations in English for college-bound students, grades 9–12, Commission on English

2. *Holt uses some unconventional methods to teach students to read and to enjoy reading. Write about a teacher whose methods brought a subject or an idea to life for you. What are the qualities that distinguish a good teacher?*

Caroline Bird

COLLEGE IS A WASTE OF TIME AND MONEY

A great majority of our nine million college students are not in school because they want to be or because they want to learn. They are there because it has become the thing to do or because college is a pleasant place to be; because it's the only way they can get parents or taxpayers to support them without working at a job they don't like; because Mother wanted them to go, or some other reason entirely irrelevant to the course of studies for which college is supposedly organized.

As I crisscross the United States lecturing on college campuses, I am dismayed to find that professors and administrators, when pressed for a candid opinion, estimate that no more than 25 percent of their students are turned on by classwork. For the rest, college is at best a social center or aging vat, and at worst a young folks' home or even a prison that keeps them out of the mainstream of economic life for a few more years.

The premise—which I no longer accept—that college is the best place for all high-school graduates grew out of a noble American ideal. Just as the United States was the first nation to aspire to teach every small child to read and write, so, during the 1950s, we became the first and only great nation to aspire to higher education for all. During the '60s we damned the expense and built great state university systems as fast as we could. And adults—parents, employers, high-school counselors—began to push, shove and cajole youngsters to "get an education."

It became a mammoth industry, with taxpayers footing more than half the bill. By 1970, colleges and universities were spending more than 30 billion dollars annually. But still only half our highschool graduates were going on. According to estimates made by the economist Fritz Machlup, if we had been educating every young person until age 22 in that year of 1970, the bill for higher education would have reached 47.5 billion dollars, 12.5 billion more than the total corporate profits for the year.

Figures such as these have begun to make higher education for all look financially prohibitive, particularly now when colleges are squeezed by the pressures of inflation and a drop-off in the growth of their traditional market.

Predictable demography has caught up with the university empire builders. Now that the record crop of postwar babies has graduated from college, the rate of growth of the student population has begun to

From *The Case Against College* (1975).

decline. To keep their mammoth plants financially solvent, many institutions have begun to use hard-sell, Madison-Avenue techniques to attract students. They sell college like soap, promoting features they think students want: innovative programs, an environment conducive to meaningful personal relationships, and a curriculum so free that it doesn't sound like college at all.

Pleasing the customers is something new for college administrators. Colleges have always known that most students don't like to study, and that at least part of the time they are ambivalent about college, but before the student riots of the 1960s educators never thought it either right or necessary to pay any attention to student feelings. But when students rebelling against the Vietnam war and the draft discovered they could disrupt a campus completely, administrators had to act on some student complaints. Few understood that the protests had tapped the basic discontent with college itself, a discontent that did not go away when the riots subsided.

Today students protest individually rather than in concert. They turn inward and withdraw from active participation. They drop out to travel to India or to feed themselves on subsistence farms. Some refuse to go to college at all. Most, of course, have neither the funds nor the self-confidence for constructive articulation of their discontent. They simply hang around college unhappily and reluctantly.

All across the country, I have been overwhelmed by the prevailing sadness on American campuses. Too many young people speak little, and then only in drowned voices. Sometimes the mood surfaces as diffidence, wariness, or coolness, but whatever its form, it looks like a defense mechanism, and that rings a bell. This is the way it used to be with women, and just as society had systematically damaged women by insisting that their proper place was in the home, so we may be systematically damaging 18-year-olds by insisting that their proper place is in college.

Campus watchers everywhere know what I mean when I say students are sad, but they don't agree on the reason for it. During the Vietnam war some ascribed the sadness to the draft; now others blame affluence, or say it has something to do with permissive upbringing.

Not satisfied with any of these explanations, I looked for some answers with the journalistic tools of my trade—scholarly studies, economic analyses, the historical record, the opinions of the especially knowledgeable, conversations with parents, professors, college administrators, and employers, all of whom spoke as alumni too. Mostly I learned from my interviews with hundreds of young people on and off campuses all over the country.

My unnerving conclusion is that students are sad because they are not needed. Somewhere between the nursery and the employment office, they become unwanted adults. No one has anything in particular against them. But no one knows what to do with them either. We already have too many people in the world of the 1970s, and there is no room for so many newly minted 18-year-olds. So we temporarily get them out of the way by sending them to college where in fact only a few belong.

To make it more palatable, we fool ourselves into believing that we are sending them there for their own best interests, and that it's good for them, like spinach. Some, of course, learn to like it, but most wind up preferring green peas.

Educators admit as much. Nevitt Sanford, distinguished student of higher education, says students feel they are "capitulating to a kind of voluntary servitude." Some of them talk about their time in college as if it were a sentence to be served. I listened to a 1970 Mount Holyoke graduate: "For two years I was really interested in science, but in my junior and senior years I just kept saying, 'I've done two years; I'm going to finish'. When I got out I made up my mind that I wasn't going to school anymore because so many of my courses had been bullshit."

But bad as it is, college is often preferable to a far worse fate. It is better than the drudgery of an uninspiring nine-to-five job, and better than doing nothing when no jobs are available. For some young people, it is a graceful way to get away from home and become independent without losing the financial support of their parents. And sometimes it is the only alternative to an intolerable home situation.

It is difficult to assess how many students are in college reluctantly. The conservative Carnegie Commission estimates from 5 to 30 percent. Sol Linowitz, who was once chairman of a special committee on campus tension of the American Council on Education, found that "a significant number were not happy with their college experience because they felt they were there only in order to get the 'ticket to the big show' rather than to spend the years as productively as they otherwise could."

Older alumni will identify with Richard Baloga, a policeman's son, who stayed in school even though he "hated it" because he thought it would do him some good. But fewer students each year feel this way. Daniel Yankelovich has surveyed undergraduate attitudes for a number of years, and reported in 1971 that 74 percent thought education was "very important." But just two years earlier, 80 percent thought so.

The doubters don't mind speaking up. Leon Lefkowitz, chairman of the department of social studies at Central High School in Valley Stream, New York, interviewed 300 college students at random, and reports that 200 of them didn't think that the education they were getting was worth the effort. "In two years I'll pick up a diploma," said one student, "and I can honestly say it was a waste of my father's bread."

Nowadays, says one sociologist, you don't have to have a reason for going to college; it's an institution. His definition of an institution is an arrangement everyone accepts without question; the burden of proof is

15

not on why you go, but why anyone thinks there might be a reason for not going. The implication is that an 18-year-old is too young and confused to know what he wants to do, and that he should listen to those who know best and go to college.

I don't agree. I believe that college has to be judged not on what other people think is good for students, but on how good it feels to the students themselves.

I believe that people have an inside view of what's good for them. If a child doesn't want to go to school some morning, better let him stay at home, at least until you find out why. Maybe he knows something you don't. It's the same with college. If high-school graduates don't want to go, or if they don't want to go right away, they may perceive more clearly than their elders that college is not for them. It is no longer obvious that adolescents are best off studying a core curriculum that was constructed when all educated men could agree on what made them educated, or that professors, advisors, or parents can be of any particular help to young people in choosing a major or a career. High-school graduates see college graduates driving cabs, and decide it's not worth going. College students find no intellectual stimulation in their studies and drop out.

If students believe that college isn't necessarily good for them, you can't expect them to stay on for the general good of mankind. They don't go to school to beat the Russians to Jupiter, improve the national defense, increase the GNP, or create a new market for the arts—to mention some of the benefits taxpayers are supposed to get for supporting higher education.

Nor should we expect to bring about social equality by putting all young people through four years of academic rigor. At best, it's a roundabout and expensive way to narrow the gap between the highest and lowest in our society anyway. At worst, it is unconsciously elitist. Equalizing opportunity through universal higher education subjects the whole population to the intellectual mode natural only to a few. It violates the fundamental egalitarian principle of respect for the differences between people.

Of course, most parents aren't thinking of the "higher" good at all. They send their children to college because they are convinced young people benefit financially from those four years of higher education. But if money is the only goal, college is the dumbest investment you can make. I say this because a young banker in Poughkeepsie, New York, Stephen G. Necel, used a computer to compare college as an investment with other investments available in 1974 and college did not come out on top.

For the sake of argument, the two of us invented a young man whose rich uncle gave him, in cold cash, the cost of a four-year education at any college he chose, but the young man didn't have to spend the money on college. After bales of computer paper, we had our mythical student write to his uncle: "Since you said I could spend the money foolishly if I wished, I am going to blow it all on Princeton."

The much respected financial columnnist Sylvia Porter echoed the common assumption when she said last year, "A college education is among the very best investments you can make in your entire life." But the truth is not quite so rosy, even if we assume that the Census Bureau is correct when it says that as of 1972, a man who completed four years of college would expect to earn $199,000 more between the ages of 22 and 64 than a man who had only a high-school diploma.

If a 1972 Princeton-bound high-school graduate had put the $34,181 that his four years of college would have cost him into a savings bank at 7.5 percent interest compounded daily, he would have had at age 64 a total of $1,129,200, or $528,200 more than the earnings of a male college graduate, and more than five times as much as the $199,000 extra the more educated man could expect to earn between 22 and 64.

The big advantage of getting your college money in cash now is that you can invest it in something that has a higher return than a diploma. For instance, a Princeton-bound high-school graduate of 1972 who liked fooling around with cars could have banked his $34,181, and gone to work at the local garage at close to $1,000 more per year than the average high-school graduate. Meanwhile, as he was learning to be an expert auto mechanic, his money would be ticking away in the bank. When he became 28, he would have earned $7,199 less on his job from age 22 to 28 than his college-educated friend, but he would have had $73,113 in his passbook—enough to buy out his boss, go into the used-car business, or acquire his own new-car dealership. If successful in business, he could expect to make more than the average college graduate. And if he had the brains to get into Princeton, he would be just as likely to make money without the four years spent on campus. Unfortunately, few college-bound high-school graduates get the opportunity to bank such a large sum of money, and then wait for it to make them rich. And few parents are sophisticated enough to understand that in financial returns alone, their children would be better off with the money than with the education.

Rates of return and dollar signs on education are fascinating brain teasers, but obviously there is a certain unreality to the game. Quite aside from the noneconomic benefits of college, and these should loom larger once the dollars are cleared away, there are grave difficulties in assigning a dollar value to college at all.

In fact there is no real evidence that the higher income of college graduates is due to college. College may simply attract people who are slated to earn more money anyway; those with higher IQs, better family

30

backgrounds, a more enterprising temperament. No one who has wrestled with the problem is prepared to attribute all of the higher income to the impact of college itself.

Christopher Jencks, author of *Inequality*, a book that assesses the effect of family and schooling in America, believes that education in general accounts for less than half of the difference in income in the American population. "The biggest single source of income differences," writes Jencks, "seems to be the fact that men from high-status families have higher incomes than men from low-status families even when they enter the same occupations, have the same amount of education, and have the same test scores."

Jacob Mincer of the National Bureau of Economic Research and Columbia University states flatly that of "20 to 30 percent of students at any level, the additional schooling has been a waste, at least in terms of earnings." College fails to work its income-raising magic for almost a third of those who go. More than half of those people in 1972 who earned $15,000 or more reached that comfortable bracket without the benefit of a college diploma. Jencks says that financial success in the U.S. depends a good deal on luck, and the most sophisticated regression analyses have yet to demonstrate otherwise.

But most of today's students don't go to college to earn more money anyway. In 1968, when jobs were easy to get, Daniel Yankelovich made his first nationwide survey of students. Sixty-five percent of them said they "would welcome less emphasis on money." By 1973, when jobs were scarce, that figure jumped to 80 percent.

The young are not alone. Americans today are all looking less to the pay of a job than to the work itself. They want "interesting" work that permits them "to make a contribution," express themselves" and "use their special abilities," and they think college will help them find it.

Jerry Darring of Indianapolis knows what it is to make a dollar. He worked with his father in the family plumbing business, on the line at Chevrolet, and in the Chrysler foundry. He quit these jobs to enter Wright State University in Dayton, Ohio, because "in a job like that a person only has time to work, and after that he's so tired that he can't do anything else but come home and go to sleep."

Jerry came to college to find work "helping people." And he is perfectly willing to spend the dollars he earns at dull, well-paid work to prepare for lower-paid work that offers the reward of service to others.

Jerry's case is not unusual. No one works for money alone. In order to deal with the nonmonetary rewards of work, economists have coined the concept of "psychic income" which according to one economic dictionary means "income that is reckoned in terms of pleasure, satisfaction, or general feelings of euphoria."

Psychic income is primarily what college students mean when they talk about getting a good job. During the most affluent years of the late 1960s and early 1970s college students told their placement officers that they wanted to be researchers, college professors, artists, city planners, social workers, poets, book publishers, archeologists, ballet dancers, or authors.

The psychic income of these and other occupations popular with students is so high that these jobs can be filled without offering high salaries. According to one study, 93 percent of urban university professors would choose the same vocation again if they had the chance, compared with only 16 percent of unskilled auto workers. Even though the monetary gap between college professor and auto worker is now surprisingly small, the difference in psychic income is enormous.

But colleges fail to warn students that jobs of these kinds are hard to come by, even for qualified applicants, and they rarely accept the responsibility of helping students choose a career that will lead to a job. When a young person says he is interested in helping people, his counselor tells him to become a psychologist. But jobs in psychology are scarce. The Department of Labor, for instance, estimates there will be 4,300 new jobs for psychologists in 1975 while colleges are expected to turn out 58,430 B.A.s in psychology that year.

Of 30 psych majors who reported back to Vassar what they were doing a year after graduation in 1972, only five had jobs in which they could possibly use their courses in psychology, and two of these were working for Vassar.

The outlook isn't much better for students majoring in other psychic-pay disciplines: sociology, English, journalism, anthropology, forestry, education. Whatever college graduates want to do, most of them are going to wind up doing what there is to do.

John Shingleton, director of placement at Michigan State University, accuses the academic community of outright hypocrisy. "Educators have never said, 'Go to college and get a good job,' but this has been implied, and now students expect it. . . . If we care what happens to students after college, then let's get involved with what should be one of the basic purposes of education: career preparation."

In the 1970s, some of the more practical professors began to see that jobs for graduates meant jobs for professors too. Meanwhile, students themselves reacted to the shrinking job market, and a "new vocational-ism" exploded on campus. The press welcomed the change as a return to the ethic of achievement and service. Students were still idealistic, the reporters wrote, but they now saw that they could best make the world better by healing the sick as physicians or righting individual wrongs as lawyers.

But there are no guarantees in these professions either. The American Enterprise Institute estimated in 1971 that there would be more than the target ratio of 100 doctors for every 100,000 people in the population by 1980. And the odds are little better for would-be lawyers. Law schools are already graduating twice as many new lawyers every year as the Department of Labor thinks will be needed, and the oversupply is growing every year.

And it's not at all apparent that what is actually learned in a "professional" education is necessary for success. Teachers, engineers and others I talked to said they find that on the job they rarely use what they learned in school. In order to see how well college prepared engineers and scientists for actual paid work in their fields, The Carnegie Commission queried all the employees with degrees in these fields in two large firms. Only one in five said the work they were doing bore a "very close relationship" to their college studies, while almost a third saw "very little relationship at all." An overwhelming majority could think of many people who were doing their same work, but had majored in different fields.

Majors in nontechnical fields report even less relationship between their studies and their jobs. Charles Lawrence, a communications major in college and now the producer of "Kennedy & Co.," the Chicago morning television show, says, "You have to learn all that stuff and you never use it again. I learned my job doing it." Others employed as architects, nurses, teachers and other members of the so-called learned professions report the same thing.

Most college administrators admit that they don't prepare their graduates for the job market. "I just wish I had the guts to tell parents that when you get out of this place you aren't prepared to do anything," the academic head of a famous liberal-arts college told us. Fortunately, for him, most people believe that you don't have to defend a liberal-arts education on those grounds. A liberal-arts education is supposed to provide you with a value system, a standard, a set of ideas, not a job. "Like Christianity, the liberal arts are seldom practiced and would probably be hated by the majority of the populace if they were," said one defender.

The analogy is apt. The fact is, of course, that the liberal arts are a religion in every sense of that term. When people talk about them, their language becomes elevated, metaphorical, extravagant, theoretical and reverent. And faith in personal salvation by the liberal arts is professed in a creed intoned on ceremonial occasions such as commencements.

50   If the liberal arts are a religious faith, the professors are its priests. But disseminating ideas in a four-year college curriculum is slow and most expensive. If you want to learn about Milton, Camus, or even Margaret Mead you can find them in paperback books, the public library, and even on television.

And when most people talk about the value of a college education, they are not talking about great books. When at Harvard commencement, the president welcomes the new graduates into "the fellowship of educated men and women," what he could be saying is, "Here is a piece of paper that is a passport to jobs, power and instant prestige." As Glenn Bassett, a personnel specialist at G.E. says, "In some parts of G.E., a college degree appears completely irrelevant to selection to, say, a manager's job. In most, however, it is a ticket of admission."

But now that we have doubled the number of young people attending college, a diploma cannot guarantee even that. The most charitable conclusion we can reach is that college probably has very little, if any, effect on people and things at all. Today, the false premises are easy to see:

First, college doesn't make people intelligent, ambitious, happy, or liberal. It's the other way around. Intelligent, ambitious, happy, liberal people are attracted to higher education in the first place.

Second, college can't claim much credit for the learning experiences that really change students while they are there. Jobs, friends, history, and most of all the sheer passage of time, have as big an impact as anything even indirectly related to the campus.

Third, colleges have changed so radically that a freshman entering in   55
the fall of 1974 can't be sure to gain even the limited value research studies assigned to colleges in the '60s. The sheer size of undergraduate campuses of the 1970s makes college even less stimulating now than it was 10 years ago. Today even motivated students are disappointed with their college courses and professors.

Finally, a college diploma no longer opens as many vocational doors. Employers are beginning to realize that when they pay extra for someone with a diploma, they are paying only for an empty credential. The fact is that most of the work for which employers now expect college training is now or has been capably done in the past by people without higher educations.

College, then, may be a good place for those few young people who are really drawn to academic work, who would rather read than eat, but it has become too expensive, in money, time, and intellectual effort to serve as a holding pen for large numbers of our young. We ought to make it possible for those reluctant, unhappy students to find alternative ways of growing up, and more realistic preparation for the years ahead.

James Thurber

UNIVERSITY DAYS

I passed all the other courses that I took at my university, but I could never pass botany. This was because all botany students had to spend several hours a week in a laboratory looking through a microscope at plant cells, and I could never see through a microscope. I never once saw a cell through a microscope. This used to enrage my instructor. He would wander around the laboratory pleased with the progress all the students were making in drawing the involved and, so I am told, interesting structure of flower cells, until he came to me. I would just be standing there. "I can't see anything," I would say. He would begin patiently enough, explaining how anybody can see through a microscope, but he would always end up in a fury, claiming that I could *too* see through a microscope but just pretended that I couldn't. "It takes away from the beauty of flowers anyway," I used to tell him. "We are not concerned with beauty in this course," he would say. "We are concerned solely with what I may call the *mechanics* of flars." "Well," I'd say, "I can't see anything." "Try it just once again," he'd say, and I would put my eye to the microscope and see nothing at all, except now and again a nebulous milky substance—a phenomenon of maladjustment. You were supposed to see a vivid, restless clockwork of sharply defined plant cells. "I see what looks like a lot of milk," I would tell him. This, he claimed, was the result of my not having adjusted the microscope properly, so he would readjust it for me, or rather, for himself. And I would look again and see milk.

I finally took a deferred pass, as they called it, and waited a year and tried again. (You had to pass one of the biological sciences or you couldn't graduate.) The professor had come back from vacation brown as a berry, bright-eyed, and eager to explain cell-structure again to his classes. "Well," he said to me, cheerily, when we met in the first laboratory hour of the semester, "we're going to see cells this time, aren't we?" "Yes, sir," I said. Students to right of me and to left of me and in front of me were seeing cells; what's more, they were quietly drawing pictures of them in their notebooks. Of course, I didn't see anything.

"We'll try it," the professor said to me, grimly, "with every adjustment of the microscope known to man. As God is my witness, I'll arrange this glass so that you see cells through it or I'll give up teaching. In twenty-two years of botany, I—" He cut off abruptly for he was

From *My Life and Hard Times* (1933).

beginning to quiver all over, like Lionel Barrymore,[1] and he genuinely wished to hold onto his temper; his scenes with me had taken a great deal out of him.

So we tried it with every adjustment of the microscope known to man. With only one of them did I see anything but blackness or the familiar lacteal opacity, and that time I saw, to my pleasure and amazement, a variegated constellation of flecks, specks, and dots. These I hastily drew. The instructor, noting my activity, came back from an adjoining desk, a smile on his lips and his eyebrows high in hope. He looked at my cell drawing. "What's that?" he demanded, with a hint of a squeal in his voice. "That's what I saw," I said. "You didn't, you didn't, you *didn't!*" he screamed, losing control of his temper instantly, and he bent over and squinted into the microscope. His head snapped up. "That's your eye!" he shouted. "You've fixed the lens so that it reflects! You've drawn your eye!"

Another course that I didn't like, but somehow managed to pass, was economics. I went to that class straight from the botany class, which didn't help me any in understanding either subject. I used to get them mixed up. But not as mixed up as another student in my economics class who came there direct from a physics laboratory. He was a tackle on the football team, named Bolenciecwcz. At that time Ohio State University had one of the best football teams in the country, and Bolenciecwcz was one of its outstanding stars. In order to be eligible to play it was necessary for him to keep up in his studies, a very difficult matter, for while he was not dumber than an ox he was not any smarter. Most of his professors were lenient and helped him along. None gave him more hints in answering questions or asked him simpler ones than the economics professor, a thin, timid man named Bassum. One day when we were on the subject of transportation and distribution, it came Bolenciecwcz's turn to answer a question. "Name one means of transportation," the professor said to him. No light came into the big tackle's eyes. "Just any means of transportation," said the professor. Bolenciecwcz sat staring at him. "That is," pursued the professor, "any medium, agency, or method of going from one place to another." Bolenciecwcz had the look of a man who is being led into a trap. "You may choose among steam, horse-drawn, or electrically propelled vehicles," said the instructor. "I might suggest the one which we commonly take in making long journeys across land." There was a profound silence in which everybody stirred uneasily, including Bolenciecwcz and Mr. Bassum. Mr. Bassum abruptly broke this silence in an amazing manner. "Choo-choo-choo," he said, in a low voice, and turned instantly scarlet. He glanced appealingly around the

5

1. Lionel Barrymore (1878–1954), famed American actor, especially noted for elderly roles.

room. All of us, of course, shared Mr. Bassum's desire that Bolenciecwcz should stay abreast of the class in economics, for the Illinois game, one of the hardest and most important of the season, was only a week off. "Toot, toot, too-toooooot!" some student with a deep voice moaned, and we all looked encouragingly at Bolenciecwcz. Somebody else gave a fine imitation of a locomotive letting off steam. Mr. Bassum himself rounded off the little show. "Ding, dong, ding, dong," he said, hopefully. Bolenciecwcz was staring at the floor now, trying to think, his great brow furrowed, his huge hands rubbing together, his face red.

"How did you come to college this year, Mr. Bolenciecwcz?" asked the professor. "*Chuffa* chuffa, *chuffa* chuffa."

"M'father sent me," said the football player.

"What on?" asked Bassum.

"I git an 'lowance," said the tackle, in a low, husky voice, obviously embarrassed.

10   "No, no," said Bassum. "Name a means of transportation. What did you *ride* here on?"

"Train," said Bolenciecwcz.

"Quite right," said the professor. "Now, Mr. Nugent, will you tell us—"

If I went through anguish in botany and economics—for different reasons—gymnasium work was even worse. I don't even like to think about it. They wouldn't let you play games or join in the exercises with your glasses on and I couldn't see with mine off. I bumped into professors, horizontal bars, agricultural students, and swinging iron rings. Not being able to see, I could take it but I couldn't dish it out. Also, in order to pass gymnasium (and you had to pass it to graduate) you had to learn to swim if you didn't know how. I didn't like the swimming pool, I didn't like swimming, and I didn't like the swimming instructor, and after all these years I still don't. I never swam but I passed my gym work anyway, by having another student give my gymnasium number (978) and swim across the pool in my place. He was a quiet, amiable blond youth, number 473, and he would have seen through a microscope for me if we could have got away with it, but we couldn't get away with it. Another thing I didn't like about gymnasium work was that they made you strip the day you registered. It is impossible for me to be happy when I am stripped and being asked a lot of questions. Still, I did better than a lanky agricultural student who was cross-examined just before I was. They asked each student what college he was in—that is, whether Arts, Engineering, Commerce, or Agriculture. "What college are you in?" the instructor snapped at the youth in front of me. "Ohio State University," he said promptly.

It wasn't that agricultural student but it was another a whole lot like him who decided to take up journalism, possibly on the ground that when farming went to hell he could fall back on newspaper work. He didn't realize, of course, that that would be very much like falling back full-length on a kit of carpenter's tools. Haskins didn't seem cut out for journalism, being too embarrassed to talk to anybody and unable to use a typewriter, but the editor of the college paper assigned him to the cow barns, the sheep house, the horse pavilion, and the animal husbandry department generally. This was a genuinely big "beat," for it took up five times as much ground and got ten times as great a legislative appropriation as the College of Liberal Arts. The agricultural student knew animals, but nevertheless his stories were dull and colorlessly written. He took all afternoon on each of them, on account of having to hunt for each letter on the typewriter. Once in a while he had to ask somebody to help him hunt. "C" and "L," in particular, were hard letters for him to find. His editor finally got pretty much annoyed at the farmer-journalist because his pieces were so uninteresting. "See here, Haskins," he snapped at him one day, "why is it we never have anything hot from you on the horse pavilion? Here we have two hundred head of horses on this campus—more than any other university in the Western Conference[2] except Purdue—and yet you never get any real low-down on them. Now shoot over to the horse barns and dig up something lively." Haskins shambled out and came back in about an hour; he said he had something. "Well, start it off snappily," said the editor. "Something people will read." Haskins set to work and in a couple of hours brought a sheet of typewritten paper to the desk; it was a two-hundred-word story about some disease that had broken out among the horses. Its opening sentence was simple but arresting. It read: "Who has noticed the sores on the tops of the horses in the animal husbandry building?"

Ohio State was a land grant university and therefore two years of military drill was compulsory. We drilled with old Springfield rifles and studied the tactics of the Civil War even though the World War was going on at the time. At 11 o'clock each morning thousands of freshmen and sophomores used to deploy over the campus, moodily creeping up on the old chemistry building. It was good training for the kind of warfare that was waged at Shiloh[3] but it had no connection with what was going on in Europe. Some people used to think there was German money behind it, but they didn't dare say so or they would have been thrown in jail as German spies. It was a period of muddy thought and marked, I believe, the decline of higher education in the Middle West.

As a soldier I was never any good at all. Most of the cadets were glumly indifferent soldiers, but I was no good at all. Once General

15

2. The Big Ten.   Union victory.
3. In southwestern Tennessee, site of 1862

Littlefield, who was commandant of the cadet corps, popped up in front of me during regimental drill and snapped, "You are the main trouble with this university!" I think he meant that my type was the main trouble with the university but he may have meant me individually. I was mediocre at drill, certainly—that is, until my senior year. By that time I had drilled longer than anybody else in the Western Conference, having failed at military at the end of each preceding year so that I had to do it all over again. I was the only senior still in uniform. The uniform which, when new, had made me look like an interurban railway conductor, now that it had become faded and too tight made me look like Bert Williams in his bellboy act.[4] This had a definitely bad effect on my morale. Even so, I had become by sheer practice little short of wonderful at squad maneuvers.

One day General Littlefield picked our company out of the whole regiment and tried to get it mixed up by putting it through one movement after another as fast as we could execute them: squads right, squads left, squads on right into line, squads right about, squads left front into line, etc. In about three minutes one hundred and nine men were marching in one direction and I was marching away from them at an angle of forty degrees, all alone. "Company, halt!" shouted General Littlefield. "That man is the only man who has it right!" I was made a corporal for my achievement.

The next day General Littlefield summoned me to his office. He was swatting flies when I went in. I was silent and he was silent too, for a long time. I don't think he remembered me or why he had sent for me, but he didn't want to admit it. He swatted some more flies, keeping his eyes on them narrowly before he let go with the swatter. "Button up your coat!" he snapped. Looking back on it now I can see that he meant me although he was looking at a fly, but I just stood there. Another fly came to rest on a paper in front of the general and began rubbing its hind legs together. The general lifted the swatter cautiously. I moved restlessly and the fly flew away. "You startled him!" barked General Littlefield, looking at me severely. I said I was sorry. "That won't help the situation!" snapped the General, with cold military logic. I didn't see what I could do except offer to chase some more flies toward his desk, but I didn't say anything. He stared out the window at the faraway figures of co-eds crossing the campus toward the library. Finally, he told me I could go. So I went. He either didn't know which cadet I was or else he forgot what he wanted to see me about. It may have been that he wished to apologize for having called me the main trouble with the university; or maybe he had decided to compliment me on my brilliant drilling of the day before and then at the last minute decided not to. I don't know. I don't think about it much any more.

4. Popular vaudeville comedian.

THE READER

1. On the basis of this essay, what do you think Thurber's definition or description of an ideal college education would be?

2. In "Examsmanship and the Liberal Arts" (p. 318), Perry distinguishes between two kinds of knowledge: "cow" and "bull." Read or review the Perry essay, and then determine, judging by Thurber's essay, which kind of knowledge seems to have been in greater demand at Thurber's university.

3. In "Some Remarks on Humor" (p. 1132), White says about humorists: "Humorists fatten on trouble. . . . You find them wrestling with foreign languages, fighting folding ironing boards and swollen drain-pipes, suffering the terrible discomfort of tight boots. . . . They pour out their sorrows profitably, in a form that is not quite fiction nor quite fact either. Beneath the sparkling surface of these dilemmas flows the strong tide of human woe." Discuss the validity of White's assertion, and test it by applying it to Thurber's essay.

THE WRITER

1. Why did Thurber pick these particular incidents of his college career to write about? What do they have in common?

2. Take one of the incidents in the essay, and analyze how Thurber describes it. What do you think he may have added to or subtracted from what actually happened? Take a similar incident (real or imagined), and, in a brief essay, try to treat it the way Thurber treats his incidents.

Adrienne Rich

TAKING WOMEN STUDENTS SERIOUSLY

I see my function here today as one of trying to create a context, delineate a background, against which we might talk about women as students and students as women. I would like to speak for awhile about this background, and then I hope that we can have, not so much a question period, as a raising of concerns, a sharing of questions for which we as yet may have no answers, an opening of conversations which will go on and on.

The talk that follows was addressed to teachers of women. . . . It was given for the New Jersey College and University Coalition on Women's Education, May 9, 1978 [Rich's note].

When I went to teach at Douglass, a women's college, [1] it was with a particular background which I would like briefly to describe to you. I had graduated from an all-girls' school in the 1940s, where the head and the majority of the faculty were independent, unmarried women. One or two held doctorates, but had been forced by the Depression (and by the fact that they were women) to take secondary school teaching jobs. These women cared a great deal about the life of the mind, and they gave a great deal of time and energy—beyond any limit of teaching hours—to those of us who showed special intellectual interest or ability. We were taken to libraries, art museums, lectures at neighboring colleges, set to work on extra research projects, given extra French or Latin reading. Although we sometimes felt "pushed" by them, we held those women in a kind of respect which even then we dimly perceived was not generally accorded to women in the world at large. They were vital individuals, defined not by their relationships but by their personalities; and although under the pressure of the culture we were all certain we wanted to get married, their lives did not appear empty or dreary to us. In a kind of cognitive dissonance, we knew they were "old maids" and therefore supposed to be bitter and lonely; yet we saw them vigorously involved with life. But despite their existence as alternate models of women, the *content* of the education they gave us in no way prepared us to survive as women in a world organized by and for men.

From that school, I went on to Radcliffe, congratulating myself that now I would have great men as my teachers. From 1947 to 1951, when I graduated, I never saw a single woman on a lecture platform, or in front of a class, except when a woman graduate student gave a paper on a special topic. The "great men" talked of other "great men," of the nature of Man, the history of Mankind, the future of Man; and never again was I to experience, from a teacher, the kind of prodding, the insistence that my best could be even better, that I had known in high school. Women students were simply not taken very seriously. Harvard's message to women was an elite mystification: we were, of course, part of Mankind; we were special, achieving women, or we would not have been there; but of course our real goal was to marry—if possible, a Harvard graduate.

In the late sixties, I began teaching at the City College of New York—a crowded, public, urban, multiracial institution as far removed from Harvard as possible. I went there to teach writing in the SEEK Program, [2] which predated Open Admissions and which was then a kind of model for programs designed to open up higher education to poor,

---

1. Part of Rutgers University in New Jersey.
2. SEEK is an acronym for "Search for Education, Elevation, and Knowledge"; the instructors in the program included not only college teachers but also creative artists and writers.

black, and Third World students. Although during the next few years we were to see the original concept of SEEK diluted, then violently attacked and betrayed, it was for a short time an extraordinary and intense teaching and learning environment. The characteristics of this environment were a deep commitment on the part of teachers to the minds of their students; a constant, active effort to create or discover the conditions for learning, and to educate ourselves to meet the needs of the new college population; a philosophical attitude based on open discussion of racism, oppression, and the politics of literature and language; and a belief that learning in the classroom could not be isolated from the student's experience as a member of an urban minority group in white America. Here are some of the kinds of questions we, as teachers of writing, found ourselves asking:

(1) What has been the student's experience of education in the inadequate, often abusively racist public school system, which rewards passivity and treats a questioning attitude or independent mind as a behavior problem? What has been her or his experience in a society that consistently undermines the selfhood of the poor and the nonwhite? How can such a student gain that sense of self which is necessary for active participation in education? What does all this mean for us as teachers?

(2) How do we go about teaching a canon of literature which has consistently excluded or depreciated nonwhite experience?

(3) How can we connect the process of learning to write well with the student's own reality, and not simply teach her/him how to write acceptable lies in standard English?

When I went to teach at Douglass College in 1976, and in teaching women's writing workshops elsewhere, I came to perceive stunning parallels to the questions I had first encountered in teaching the so-called disadvantaged students at City. But in this instance, and against the specific background of the women's movement, the questions framed themselves like this:

(1) What has been the student's experience of education in schools which reward female passivity, indoctrinate girls and boys in stereotypic sex roles, and do not take the female mind seriously? How does a woman gain a sense of her *self* in a system—in this case, patriarchal capitalism—which devalues work done by women, denies the importance and uniqueness of female experience, and is physically violent toward women? What does this mean for a woman teacher?

(2) How do we, as women, teach women students a canon of litera-

ture which has consistently excluded or depreciated female experience, and which often expresses hostility to women and validates violence against us?

(3) How can we teach women to move beyond the desire for male
approval and getting "good grades" and seek and write their own
truths that the culture has distorted or made taboo? (For women,
of course, language itself is exclusive: I want to say more about
this further on.)

In teaching women, we have two choices: to lend our weight to the
forces that indoctrinate women to passivity, self-depreciation, and a
sense of powerlessness, in which case the issue of "taking women students seriously" is a moot one; or to consider what we have to work
against, as well as with, in ourselves, in our students, in the content of
the curriculum, in the structure of the institution, in the society at large.
And this means, first of all, taking ourselves seriously: Recognizing that
central responsibility of a woman to herself, without which we remain
always the Other, the defined, the object, the victim; believing that
there is a unique quality of validation, affirmation, challenge, support,
that one woman can offer another. Believing in the value and significance of women's experience, traditions, perceptions. Thinking of ourselves seriously, not as one of the boys, not as neuters, or androgynes,
but *as women*.

Suppose we were to ask ourselves, simply: What does a woman need
to know? Does she not, as a self-conscious, self-defining human being,
need a knowledge of her own history, her much-politicized biology, an
awareness of the creative work of women of the past, the skills and crafts
and techniques and powers exercised by women in different times and
cultures, a knowledge of women's rebellions and organized movements
against our oppression and how they have been routed or diminished?
Without such knowledge women live and have lived without context,
vulnerable to the projections of male fantasy, male prescriptions for us,
estranged from our own experience because our education has not reflected or echoed it. I would suggest that not biology, but ignorance of
our selves, has been the key to our powerlessness.

But the university curriculum, the high-school curriculum, do not
provide this kind of knowledge for women, the knowledge of Woman-
kind, whose experience has been so profoundly different from that of
Mankind. Only in the precariously budgeted, much-condescended-to
area of women's studies is such knowledge available to women students.
Only there can they learn about the lives and work of women other than
the few select women who are included in the "mainstream" texts,
usually misrepresented even when they do appear. Some students, at

some institutions, manage to take a majority of courses in women's studies, but the message from on high is that this is self-indulgence, soft-core education: the "real" learning is the study of Mankind.

If there is any misleading concept, it is that of "coeducation": that because women and men are sitting in the same classrooms, hearing the same lectures, reading the same books, performing the same laboratory experiments, they are receiving an equal education. They are not, first because the content of education itself validates men even as it invalidates women. Its very message is that men have been the shapers and thinkers of the world, and that this is only natural. The bias of higher education, including the so-called sciences, is white and male, racist and sexist; and this bias is expressed in both subtle and blatant ways. I have mentioned already the exclusiveness of grammar itself: "The student should test himself on the above questions"; "The poet is representative. He stands among partial men for the complete man." Despite a few half-hearted departures from custom, what the linguist Wendy Martyna has named "He-Man" grammar prevails throughout the culture. The efforts of feminists to reveal the profound ontological implications of sexist grammar are routinely ridiculed by academicians and journalists, including the professedly liberal *Times* columnist, Tom Wicker, and the professed humanist, Jacques Barzun. Sexist grammar burns into the brains of little girls and young women a message that the male is the norm, the standard, the central figure beside which we are the deviants, the marginal, the dependent variables. It lays the foundation for androcentric thinking, and leaves men safe in their solipsistic tunnel-vision.

Women and men do not receive an equal education because outside the classroom women are perceived not as sovereign beings but as prey. The growing incidence of rape on and off the campus may or may not be fed by the proliferations of pornographic magazines and X-rated films available to young males in fraternities and student unions; but it is certainly occurring in a context of widespread images of sexual violence against women, on billboards and in so-called high art. More subtle, more daily than rape is the verbal abuse experienced by the woman student on many campuses—Rutgers for example—where, traversing a street lined with fraternity houses, she must run a gauntlet of male commentary and verbal assault. The undermining of self, of a woman's sense of her right to occupy space and walk freely in the world, is deeply relevant to education. The capacity to think independently, to take intellectual risks, to assert ourselves mentally, is inseparable from our physical way of being in the world, our feelings of personal integrity. If it is dangerous for me to walk home late of an evening from the library, *because I am a woman and can be raped,* how self-possessed, how exuberant can I feel as I sit working in that library? how much of my

10

working energy is drained by the subliminal knowledge that, as a woman, I test my physical right to exist each time I go out alone? Of this knowledge, Susan Griffin has written:

> . . . more than rape itself, the fear of rape permeates our lives. And what does one do from day to day, with *this* experience, which says, without words and directly to the heart, *your existence, your experience, may end at any moment.* Your experience may end, and the best defense against this is not to be, to deny being in the body, as a self, to . . . avert your gaze, make yourself, as a presence in the world, less felt.[3]

Finally, rape of the mind. Women students are more and more often now reporting sexual overtures by male professors—one part of our overall growing consciousness of sexual harassment in the workplace. At Yale a legal suit has been brought against the university by a group of women demanding an explicit policy against sexual advances toward female students by male professors. Most young women experience a profound mixture of humiliation and intellectual self-doubt over seductive gestures by men who have the power to award grades, open doors to grants and graduate school, or extend special knowledge and training. Even if turned aside, such gestures constitute mental rape, destructive to a woman's ego. They are acts of domination, as despicable as the molestation of the daughter by the father.

But long before entering college the woman student has experienced her alien identity in a world which misnames her, turns her to its own uses, denying her the resources she needs to become self-affirming, self-defined. The nuclear family teaches her that relationships are more important than selfhood or work; that "whether the phone rings for you, and how often," having the right clothes, doing the dishes, take precedence over study or solitude; that too much intelligence or intensity may make her unmarriageable; that marriage and children—service to others—are, finally, the points on which her life will be judged a success or a failure. In high school, the polarization between feminine attractiveness and independent intelligence comes to an absolute. Meanwhile, the culture resounds with messages. During Solar Energy Week in New York I saw young women wearing "ecology" T-shirts with the legend: CLEAN, CHEAP AND AVAILABLE; a reminder of the 1960s antiwar button which read: CHICKS SAY YES TO MEN WHO SAY NO. Department store windows feature female mannequins in chains, pinned to the wall with legs spread, smiling in positions of torture. Feminists are depicted in the media as "shrill," "strident," "puritanical," or "humorless," and the lesbian choice—the choice of the woman-identified woman—as pathological or sinister. The young woman sitting in the philosophy classroom,

---

3. Rich is quoting (as her note to the passage says) from the manuscript of Griffin's *Rape: The Power of Consciousness* (New York, 1979).

the political science lecture, is already gripped by tensions between her nascent sense of self-worth, and the battering force of messages like these.

Look at a classroom: look at the many kinds of women's faces, postures, expressions. Listen to the women's voices. Listen to the silences, the unasked questions, the blanks. Listen to the small, soft voices, often courageously trying to speak up, voices of women taught early that tones of confidence, challenge, anger, or assertiveness, are strident and unfeminine. Listen to the voices of the women and the voices of the men; observe the space men allow themselves, physically and verbally, the male assumption that people will listen, even when the majority of the group is female. Look at the faces of the silent, and of those who speak. Listen to a woman groping for language in which to express what is on her mind, sensing that the terms of academic discourse are not her language, trying to cut down her thought to the dimensions of a discourse not intended for her *(for it is not fitting that a woman speak in public);* or reading her paper aloud at breakneck speed, throwing her words away, deprecating her own work by a reflex prejudgment: *I do not deserve to take up time and space.*

As women teachers, we can either deny the importance of this context in which women students think, write, read, study, project their own futures; or try to work with it. We can either teach passively, accepting these conditions, or actively, helping our students identify and resist them.

One important thing we can do is *discuss* the context. And this need not happen only in a women's studies course; it can happen anywhere. We can refuse to accept passive, obedient learning and insist upon critical thinking. We can become harder on our women students, giving them the kinds of "cultural prodding" that men receive, but on different terms and in a different style. Most young women need to have their intellectual lives, their work, legitimized against the claims of family, relationships, the old message that a woman is always available for service to others. We need to keep our standards very high, not to accept a woman's preconceived sense of her limitations; we need to be hard to please, while supportive of risk-taking, because self-respect often comes only when exacting standards have been met. At a time when adult literacy is generally low, we need to demand more, not less, of women, both for the sake of their futures as thinking beings, and because historically women have always had to be better than men to do half as well. A romantic sloppiness, an inspired lack of rigor, a self-indulgent incoherence, are symptoms of female self-depreciation. We should help our women students to look very critically at such symptoms, and to understand where they are rooted.

Nor does this mean we should be training women students to "think

15

like men." Men in general think badly: in disjuncture from their personal lives, claiming objectivity where the most irrational passions seethe, losing, as Virginia Woolf[4] observed, their senses in the pursuit of professionalism. It is not easy to think like a woman in a man's world, in the world of the professions; yet the capacity to do that is a strength which we can try to help our students develop. To think like a woman in a man's world means thinking critically, refusing to accept the givens, making connections between facts and ideas which men have left unconnected. It means remembering that every mind resides in a body; remaining accountable to the female bodies in which we live; constantly retesting given hypotheses against lived experience. It means a constant critique of language, for as Wittgenstein[5] (no feminist) observed, "The limits of my language are the limits of my world." And it means that most difficult thing of all: listening and watching in art and literature, in the social sciences, in all the descriptions we are given of the world, for the silences, the absences, the nameless, the unspoken, the encoded—for there we will find the true knowledge of women. And in breaking those silences, naming our selves, uncovering the hidden, making ourselves present, we begin to define a reality which resonates to *us*, which affirms *our* being, which allows the woman teacher and the woman student alike to take ourselves, and each other, seriously: meaning, to begin taking charge of our lives.

4. Woolf (1882–1941), prominent British novelist, essayist, and feminist.
5. Ludwig Josef Johann Wittgenstein (1889–1951), Austrian-born British philosopher.

Dorothy Gies McGuigan

TO BE A WOMAN AND A SCHOLAR

On a Saturday morning in June exactly three hundred years ago this year, the first woman in the world to receive a doctoral degree mounted a pulpit in the cathedral of Padua to be examined in Aristotelian dialectics.

Her name was Elena Lucrezia Cornaro Piscopia. She was thirty-two years old, single, daughter of one of the wealthiest families in Venice. Precociously brilliant, she had begun to study Aristotle at the age of seven. Her father had backed her studies and supplied the best of tutors; by the time she enrolled in the University of Padua, she knew not only Latin and Greek, French, English, and Spanish, but also Hebrew, Arabic, and Chaldaic.

From *Changing Family, Changing Workplace: New Research* (1980).

News of the unique phenomenon of a woman scholar had drawn such throngs to witness her doctoral trial that it had to be moved from the hall of the University of Padua into the cathedral. Elena had first applied to take her doctorate in theology, but the Chancellor of the university's Theological Faculty, Cardinal Gregorio Barbarigo, Bishop of Padua, had refused indignantly. "Never," he replied. "Woman is made for motherhood, not for learning." He wrote later of the incident, "I talked with a French cardinal about it and he broke out in laughter." Reluctantly Barbarigo agreed that she be allowed to take the doctoral examination in philosophy. A modest, deeply religious young woman, Elena Cornaro had quailed before the prospect of the public examination; it was her proud, ambitious father who had insisted. A half hour before the solemn program began, Elena expressed such anguish and reluctance that her confessor had to speak very sternly to persuade her to go through with it. Her examiners were not lenient because of her sex, for the prestige of the university was at stake. But Elena's replies—in Latin, of course— were so brilliant that the judges declared the doctorate in philosophy was "hardly an honor for so towering an intellect." The doctoral ring was placed on Elena's finger, the ermine cape of teacher laid about her shoulders, and the laurel crown of poet placed on her dark curly head. The entire assembly rose and chanted a Te Deum.[1]

What was it like to be a gifted woman, an Elena Cornaro, three hundred years ago? What happened to a bright woman in the past who wanted to study another culture, examine the roots of a language, master the intricacies of higher mathematics, write a book—or prevent or cure a terrible disease?

To begin with, for a woman to acquire anything that amounted to real learning, she needed four basics.   5

She needed to survive. In the seventeenth century women's life expectancy had risen only to thirty-two; not until 1750 did it begin to rise appreciably and reach, in mid-nineteenth century, age forty-two. A woman ambitious for learning would do well to choose a life of celibacy, not only to avoid the hazards of childbirth but because there was no room for a scholar's life within the confines of marriage and childbearing. Elena Cornaro had taken a vow of chastity at the age of eleven, turned down proposals of marriage to become an oblate of the Benedictine Order.

Secondly, to aspire to learning a woman needed basic literacy; she had to be one of the fortunate few who learned at least to read and write. Although literacy studies in earlier centuries are still very incomplete and comparative data on men's and women's literacy are meager, it appears that before 1650 a bare 10 percent of women in the city of London could sign their names. What is most striking about this particular study is that

---

1. Festival hymn of rejoicing and praise of God.

when men are divided by occupation—with clergy and the professions at the top, 100 percent literate, and male laborers at the bottom of the scale, about 15 percent literate—women as a group fell below even unskilled male laborers in their rate of literacy. By about 1700 half the women in London could sign their names; in the provinces women's literacy remained much lower.

The third fundamental a woman needed if she aspired to learning was, of course, an economic base. It was best to be born, like Elena Cornaro, to a family of wealth who owned a well-stocked library and could afford private tutors. For girls of poor families the chance of learning the bare minimum of reading and writing was small. Even such endowed charity schools as Christ's Hospital in London were attended mostly by boys; poor girls in charity schools were apt to have their literacy skills slighted in favor of catechism, needlework, knitting, and lace-making in preparation for a life in domestic service.

The fourth fundamental a woman scholar needed was simply a very tough skin, for she was a deviant in a society where the learned woman, far from being valued, was likely to hear herself preached against in the pulpit and made fun of on the public stage. Elena Cornaro was fortunate to have been born in Italy where an array of learned women had flourished during the Renaissance and where the woman scholar seems to have found a more hospitable ambiance than in the northern countries.

10   In eighteenth-century England the gifted writer Lady Mary Wortley Montagu, writing in 1753 about proposed plans for a little granddaughter's education, admonished her daughter with some bitterness "to conceal whatever Learning [the child] attains, with as much solicitude as she would hide crookedness or lameness."

In post-Renaissance Europe two overriding fears dominated thinking on women's education: the fear that learning would unfit women for their social role, defined as service to husband and children and obedience to the church; and, a corollary of the first, that open access to education would endanger women's sexual purity. For while humanist philosophy taught that education led to virtue, writers on education were at once conflicted when they applied the premise to women. Nearly all, beginning with the influential sixteenth-century Juan Luis Vives, opted for restricting women's learning. Only a few radical thinkers—some men, such as Richard Mulcaster in Tudor England and the extraordinary Poullain de la Barre in seventeenth-century France, some women, like the feisty Bathsua Makin and revolutionary Mary Wollstonecraft—spoke out for the full development of women's intellectual potential.

In any case, since institutions of higher learning were designed for young men entering the professions—the church, the law, government service—from which women were excluded, they were excluded too from the universities that prepared for them. And, just as importantly, they were excluded from the grammar or preparatory schools, whose curriculum was based on Latin, the code language of the male intellectual elite. Since most scholarly texts were written in Latin, ignorance of that language prevented women from reading scholarly literature in most fields—which only gradually and belatedly became available in translation.

Richard Hyrde, a tutor in the household of Sir Thomas More and himself a defender of learning in women, cited the common opinion:

> . . . that the frail kind of women, being inclined of their own courage unto vice, and mutable at every newelty [sic], if they should have skill in many things that must be written in the Latin and Greek tongue . . . it would of likelihood both inflame their stomachs a great deal the more to that vice, that men say they be too much given unto of their own nature already and instruct them also with more subtility and conveyance, to set forward and accomplish their froward intent and purpose.

And yet, despite all the hurdles, some bright women did manage to make a mark as scholars and writers. Sometimes girls listened in on their brothers' tutored lessons. A fortunate few, like Elena Cornaro, had parents willing and able to educate daughters equally with sons. The daughters of Sir Thomas More, of the Earl of Arundel, and of Sir Anthony Cooke in Tudor England were given excellent educations. Arundel's daughter, Lady Joanna Lumley, produced the earliest known English translation of a Greek drama.

But by far the largest number of women scholars in the past were almost totally self-educated. Through sheer intellectual curiosity, self-discipline, often grinding hard work, they taught themselves what they wanted to know. Such self-teaching may well be the only truly joyous form of learning. Yet it has its drawbacks: it may also be haphazard and superficial. Without access to laboratory, lecture, and dissecting table, it was all but impossible for women to train themselves in higher mathematics, for instance, in science, in anatomy.

Mary Wollstonecraft wrote in 1792 that most women who have acted like rational creatures or shown any vigor of intellect have accidentally been allowed "to run wild," and running wild in the family library was the usual way intellectually ambitious women educated themselves. Such a self-taught scholar was Elizabeth Tanfield, Viscountess Cary, who as a girl in Elizabethan England, taught herself French, Spanish, Italian, Latin, and added Hebrew "with very little teaching." Her unsympathetic mother refused to allow her candles to read at night, so Elizabeth bribed the servants, and by her wedding day—she was married at fifteen—she had run up a candle debt of a hundred pounds. She wrote numerous translations, poetry—most of which she destroyed—and at least one play, *Mariam, the Faire Queen of Jewry.*

Very often the critical phase of women's intellectual development took place at a different period in their lives from the normal time of men's greatest development. Gifted women often came to a period of intellectual crisis and of intense self-teaching during adulthood.

When Christine de Pisane, daughter of the Italian astrologer and physician at the court of Charles V of France, found herself widowed at twenty-five with three children to support, she turned to writing—certainly one of the first, if not the first, woman in Europe to support herself through a literary career. But Christine found her education wholly inadequate, and at the age of thirty-four she laid down a complete course of study for herself, teaching herself Latin, history, philosophy, literature. She used her pen later on to urge better educational opportunities for women, to defend her sex from the charges of such misogynistic writers as Jean de Meung.[2] In her book, *The City of Ladies,* Christine imagined talented women building a town for themselves where they could lead peaceful and creative lives—an existence impossible, she considered, in fifteenth-century France.

Like Christine de Pisane, the Dutch scholar Anna van Schurman of Utrecht, a contemporary of Elena Cornaro, found her early education superficial and unsatisfying. Like most upper middle class girls of the seventeenth century, Anna, precocious though she was, had been taught chiefly to sing nicely, to play musical instruments, to carve portraits in boxwood and wax, to do needlework and tapestry and cut paperwork. At the age of twenty-eight, frustrated by the lack of intellectual stimulation in her life, Anna turned her brilliant mind to serious studies, became one of the finest Latinists of her day, learned Hebrew, Syriac, Chaldaic, wrote an Ethiopian grammar that was the marvel of Dutch scholars, carried on an international correspondence—in Latin, of course—with all the leading scholars of continental Europe. When a professor of theology at Leyden wrote that women were barred from equality with men "by the sacred laws of nature," Anna wrote a Latin treatise in reply in 1641, defending the intellectual capacity of women and urging, as Christine de Pisane had, much greater educational opportunities. Her work was widely translated and made Anna van Schurman a model for women scholars all over Europe.

In France, during the lifetime of Anna van Schurman, a group of bright, intellectually malnourished women—most of them convent-educated—developed one of the most ingenious devices for women's lifelong learning. Bored with the dearth of cultivated conversation at the French court, the Marquise de Rambouillet, Mlle de Scudéry, Mme de Lafayette, and a host of others opened their town houses in Paris, invited men and women of talent and taste to hone their wits and talk of science and philosophy, literature and language, love and friendship. The salon

2. Medieval French author of the satirical antifeminist portion of the influential poem *The Romance of the Rose.*

has been described as "an informal university for women." Not only did it contribute to adult women's education, but it shaped standards of speaking and writing for generations in France and profoundly influenced French culture as a whole.

An offshoot of the salons were the special lecture courses offered by eminent scholars in chemistry, etymology and other subjects—lectures largely attended by women. Fontenelle wrote his popular book on astronomy, *The Plurality of Worlds,* specifically for a female readership, and Descartes declared he had written his *Discourse on Method* in French rather than Latin so that women too would be able to read it.

There was, rather quickly, a backlash. Molière's satires on learned women did much to discredit the ladies who presided at salons—and who might at times be given to a bit of overelegance in speech and manner. When Abbé Fénélon wrote his influential treatise, *On the Education of Girls,* in 1686—just eight years after Elena Cornaro had won her doctorate—he mentioned neither Elena Cornaro nor Anna van Schurman nor Christine de Pisane. He inveighed against the pernicious effect of the salons. Declaring that "A woman's intellect is normally more feeble and her curiosity greater than those of men, it is undesirable to set her to studies which may turn her head. A girl," admonished that worthy French cleric, "must learn to obey without respite, to hold her peace and allow others to do the talking. Everything is lost if she obstinately tries to be clever and to get a distaste for domestic duties. The virtuous woman spins, confines herself to her home, keeps quiet, believes and obeys."

So much for the encouragement of women scholars in late seventeenth century France.

Across the Channel in England in the second half of the seventeenth century, bright ambitious women were studying not only the classics and languages but learning to use the newly perfected telescope and microscope, and to write on scientific subjects. Margaret Cavendish, Duchess of Newcastle, a remarkable woman with a wide-ranging mind and imagination, wrote not only biography, autobiography, and romance, but also popular science—she called it "natural philosophy"—directed especially to women readers. The versatile and talented writer Aphra Behn—the first woman in England to make her living by her pen—translated Fontenelle's *Plurality of Worlds* into English in 1688. In the preface she declared she would have preferred to write an original work on astronomy but had "neither health nor leisure" for such a project; it was, in fact, the year before her death and she was already ailing. But she defended the Copernican system vigorously against the recent attack by a Jesuit priest, did not hesitate to criticize the author, Fontenelle, and to correct an error in the text on the height of the earth's atmosphere.

But the learned lady in England as in France found herself criticized from the pulpit and satirized on the stage. Margaret Cavendish was

25

dubbed "Mad Madge of Newcastle." Jonathan Swift poked fun at Mary
Astell for her proposal to found a women's college. Thomas Wright in
The Female Virtuosos, the anonymous authors of *The Humours of
Oxford* and *Female Wits,* Shadwell, Congreve, and others lampooned
the would-be woman scholar. The shy poet, Anne, countess of Winchilsea, who had only reluctantly identified herself as author of a published
volume of verse, was cruelly pilloried by Pope and Gay in their play
Three Hours after Marriage. And Aphra Behn, author of a phenomenal
array of plays, poems, novels, and translations, could read this published
verse about herself and her work at about the same time she was translating Fontenelle:

> Yet hackney writers, when their verse did fail
> To get 'em brandy, bread and cheese, and ale,
> Their wants by prostitution were supplied;
> Show but a tester [sixpence] you might up and ride;
> For punk and poetess agree so pat
> You cannot well be this, and not be that.

So if one asks what it was like to be a gifted woman, to aspire to
learning at the time of Elena Cornaro, the answer must be that it was
a difficult and demanding choice, requiring not merely intellectual gifts
but extraordinary physical and mental stamina, and only a rare few
women succeeded in becoming contributing scholars and writers. All the
usual scholarly careers were closed to women, so than even for women
who succeeded in educating themselves to the level of their male colleagues, the opportunities to support themselves were meager.

In a day when it was considered impermissible for a woman to speak
in public, it was also considered inappropriate and unfeminine to draw
attention to herself by publishing a work under her own name. Many—
perhaps most—women scholars and writers—from Anne, Countess of
Winchilsea, Lady Mary Wortley Montagu down to Fanny Burney and
Jane Austen—published their works at first either anonymously or pseudonymously. Nor was Elizabeth Tanfield the only woman scholar who
destroyed her own writings before they were published.

And what of Elena Cornaro's life after she won her doctorate in 1678?
During the six years she lived after that event, she divided her time
between scholarly pursuits and service to the poor, sick and needy.
Baroque Italy paid honor to its unique woman scholar. Certainly Elena
Cornaro aroused no antagonisms, but rather filled with discretion the
approved nunlike role designated for the woman in Catholic countries
who chose not to marry. Scholars and statesmen from several countries
made a point of visiting her in Padua, and she was invited to join fellow
scholars in the Academy of Ricovrati in Padua. When she died of
tuberculosis in 1684 at the age of thirty-eight—a disease that was in a

measure responsible for her eminence, for she had been sent to Padua partly to escape the damp air of Venice—her funeral attracted a greater throng than her doctoral examination. A delegation of distinguished university faculty accompanied the procession through the streets of Padua, and on her coffin were heaped books in the languages she had mastered and the sciences she had studied. She was buried in the Chapel of St. Luke among the Benedictine monks, having carefully instructed her maid to sew her robe together at the hem so that even in death her modesty would be preserved.

Of her writings very little has survived. She had arranged to have her correspondence and many of her manuscripts destroyed before she died, and the remainder of her writings were disseminated as souvenirs among family and friends.

After Elena Cornaro's death a half century passed before a second woman, again Italian, Laura Maria Catherina Bassi, was awarded a doctorate at the University of Bologna. Not until 150 years later did American universities admit women for degrees, and two centuries passed before Oxford and Cambridge conferred degrees on women. Only in our own decade, in 1970, did the Catholic Church finally award the degree of Doctor of Theology that had been denied Elena Cornaro to two women: one to the sixteenth century Spanish saint, Teresa of Avila, the other to fourteenth century St. Catherine of Siena, who had in fact never learned to read and write. One hopes that in some academic elysium those two saintly ladies are proudly showing off their belated scholarly credentials.

THE READER

1. *What obstacles stood in the way of the woman seeking learning in Elena Cornaro's time and what "four basics" did she need to overcome them? Which of these obstacles do women still encounter? Are there any new difficulties today?*
2. *Estimates of literacy in the past, McGuigan notes, were made on the basis of signatures. How would we estimate literacy today? What, beyond signing one's name, constitutes literacy?*

THE WRITER

1. *Characterize McGuigan's tone: restrained? objective? angry? amused? outraged? other? Why do you think McGuigan adopts this tone? Would a different tone have been more appropriate to her subject and purpose?*
2. *Why does McGuigan begin her essay with a description of the day Elena Cornaro received her doctoral degree? Describe another opening*

she might have used. What would have been the effect of this alternate opening?

3. *What do you imagine were Elena Cornaro's thoughts and feelings in the hour before her public examination for the doctorate? Write an essay exploring this question. You might like to try placing yourself in her position and writing from her point of view.*

William Zinsser

COLLEGE PRESSURES

Dear Carlos: I desperately need a dean's excuse for my chem midterm which will begin in about 1 hour. All I can say is that I totally blew it this week. I've fallen incredibly, inconceivably behind.

Carlos: Help! I'm anxious to hear from you. I'll be in my room and won't leave it until I hear from you. Tomorrow is the last day for . . .

Carlos: I left town because I started bugging out again. I stayed up all night to finish a take-home make-up exam & am typing it to hand in on the 10th. It was due on the 5th. P.S. I'm going to the dentist. Pain is pretty bad.

Carlos: Probably by Friday I'll be able to get back to my studies. Right now I'm going to take a long walk. This whole thing has taken a lot out of me.

Carlos: I'm really up the proverbial creek. The problem is I really *bombed* the history final. Since I need that course for my major I . . .

Carlos: Here follows a tale of woe. I went home this weekend, had to help my Mom, & caught a fever so didn't have much time to study. My professor . . .

Carlos: Aargh! Trouble. Nothing original but everything's piling up at once. To be brief, my job interview . . .

Hey Carlos, good news! I've got mononucleosis.

Who are these wretched supplicants, scribbling notes so laden with anxiety, seeking such miracles of postponement and balm? They are men and women who belong to Branford College, one of the twelve residential colleges at Yale University, and the messages are just a few of the hundreds that they left for their dean, Carlos Hortas—often slipped under his door at 4 A.M.—last year.

But students like the ones who wrote those notes can also be found on campuses from coast to coast—especially in New England and at many other private colleges across the country that have high academic

First appeared in *Blair and Ketchum's Country Journal* (Vol. 6, No. 4, Apr. 1979).

standards and highly motivated students. Nobody could doubt that the notes are real. In their urgency and their gallows humor they are authentic voices of a generation that is panicky to succeed.

My own connection with the message writers is that I am master of Branford College. I live in its Gothic quadrangle and know the students well. (We have 485 of them.) I am privy to their hopes and fears—and also to their stereo music and their piercing cries in the dead of night ("Does anybody *ca-a-are* ?"). If they went to Carlos to ask how to get through tomorrow, they come to me to ask how to get through the rest of their lives.

Mainly I try to remind them that the road ahead is a long one and that it will have more unexpected turns than they think. There will be plenty of time to change jobs, change careers, change whole attitudes and approaches. They don't want to hear such liberating news. They want a map—right now—that they can follow unswervingly to career security, financial security. Social Security and, presumably, a prepaid grave.

What I wish for all students is some release from the clammy grip of   5
the future. I wish them a chance to savor each segment of their education as an experience in itself and not as a grim preparation for the next step. I wish them the right to experiment, to trip and fall, to learn that defeat is as instructive as victory and is not the end of the world.

My wish, of course, is naïve. One of the few rights that America does not proclaim is the right to fail. Achievement is the national god, venerated in our media—the million-dollar athlete, the wealthy executive—and glorified in our praise of possessions. In the presence of such a potent state religion, the young are growing up old.

I see four kinds of pressure working on college students today: economic pressure, parental pressure, peer pressure, and self-induced pressure. It is easy to look around for villains—to blame the colleges for charging too much money, the professors for assigning too much work, the parents for pushing their children too far, the students for driving themselves too hard. But there are no villains; only victims.

"In the late 1960s," one dean told me, "the typical question that I got from students was 'Why is there so much suffering in the world?' or 'How can I make a contribution?' Today it's 'Do you think it would look better for getting into law school if I did a double major in history and political science, or just majored in one of them?' " Many other deans confirmed this pattern. One said: "They're trying to find an edge—the intangible something that will look better on paper if two students are about equal."

Note the emphasis on looking better. The transcript has become a sacred document, the passport to security. How one appears on paper is more important than how one appears in person. *A* is for Admirable and *B* is for Borderline, even though, in Yale's official system of grading, *A* means "excellent" and *B* means "very good." Today, looking very good is no longer good enough, especially for students who hope to go on to law school or medical school. They know that entrance into the better schools will be an entrance into the better law firms and better medical practices where they will make a lot of money. They also know that the odds are harsh, Yale Law School, for instance, matriculates 170 students from an applicant pool of 3,700; Harvard enrolls 550 from a pool of 7,000.

10   It's all very well for those of us who write letters of recommendation for our students to stress the qualities of humanity that will make them good lawyers or doctors. And it's nice to think that admission officers are really reading our letters and looking for the extra dimension of commitment or concern. Still, it would be hard for a student not to visualize these officers shuffling so many transcripts studded with *A* s that they regard a *B* as positively shameful.

The pressure is almost as heavy on students who just want to graduate and get a job. Long gone are the days of the "gentleman's C," when students journeyed through college with a certain relaxation, sampling a wide variety of courses—music, art, philosophy, classics, anthropology, poetry, religion—that would send them out as liberally educated men and women. If I were an employer I would rather employ graduates who have this range and curiosity than those who narrowly pursued safe subjects and high grades. I know countless students whose inquiring minds exhilarate me. I like to hear the play of their ideas. I don't know if they are getting *A* s or *C* s, and I don't care. I also like them as people. The country needs them, and they will find satisfying jobs. I tell them to relax. They can't.

Nor can I blame them. They live in a brutal economy. Tuition, room, and board at most private colleges now comes to at least $7,000, not counting books and fees. This might seem to suggest that the colleges are getting rich. But they are equally battered by inflation. Tuition covers only 60 percent of what it costs to educate a student, and ordinarily the remainder comes from what colleges receive in endowments, grants, and gifts. Now the remainder keeps being swallowed by the cruel costs—higher every year—of just opening the doors. Heating oil is up. Insurance is up. Postage is up. Health-premium costs are up. Everything is up. Deficits are up. We are witnessing in America the creation of a brotherhood of paupers—colleges, parents, and students, joined by the common bond of debt.

Today it is not unusual for a student, even if he works part time at college and full time during the summer, to accrue $5,000 in loans after four years—loans that he must start to repay within one year after graduation. Exhorted at commencement to go forth into the world, he is already behind as he goes forth. How could he not feel under pressure throughout college to prepare for this day of reckoning? I have used "he," incidentally, only for brevity. Women at Yale are under no less pressure to justify their expensive education to themselves, their parents, and society. In fact, they are probably under more pressure. For although they leave college superbly equipped to bring fresh leadership to traditionally male jobs, society hasn't yet caught up with this fact.

Along with economic pressure goes parental pressure. Inevitably, the two are deeply intertwined.

I see many students taking pre-medical courses with joyless tenacity.   15
They go off to their labs as if they were going to the dentist. It saddens me because I know them in other corners of their life as cheerful people.

"Do you want to go to medical school?" I ask them.

"I guess so," they say, without conviction, or "Not really."

"Then why are you going?"

"Well, my parents want me to be a doctor. They're paying all this money and . . ."

Poor students, poor parents. They are caught in one of the oldest webs   20
of love and duty and guilt. The parents mean well; they are trying to steer their sons and daughters toward a secure future. But the sons and daughters want to major in history or classics or philosophy—subjects with no "practical" value. Where's the payoff on the humanities? It's not easy to persuade such loving parents that the humanities do indeed pay off. The intellectual faculties developed by studying subjects like history and classics—an ability to synthesize and relate, to weigh cause and effect, to see events in perspective—are just the faculties that make creative leaders in business or almost any general field. Still, many fathers would rather put their money on courses that point toward a specific profession—courses that are pre-law, pre-medical, pre-business, or, as I sometimes heard it put, "pre-rich."

But the pressure on students is severe. They are truly torn. One part of them feels obligated to fulfill their parents' expectations; after all, their parents are older and presumably wiser. Another part tells them that the expectations that are right for their parents are not right for them.

I know a student who wants to be an artist. She is very obviously an artist and will be a good one—she has already had several modest local exhibits. Meanwhile she is growing as a well-rounded person and taking humanistic subjects that will enrich the inner resources out of which her art will grow. But her father is strongly opposed. He thinks that an artist is a "dumb" thing to be. The student vacillates and tries to please everybody. She keeps up with her art somewhat furtively and takes some of the "dumb" courses her father wants her to take—at least they are dumb courses for her. She is a free spirit on a campus of tense students—no small achievement in itself—and she deserves to follow her muse.

Peer pressure and self-induced pressure are also intertwined, and they begin almost at the beginning of freshman year.

"I had a freshman student I'll call Linda," one dean told me, "who came in and said she was under terrible pressure because her roommate, Barbara, was much brighter and studied all the time. I couldn't tell her that Barbara had come in two hours earlier to say the same thing about Linda."

The story is almost funny—except that it's not. It's symptomatic of all the pressures put together. When every student thinks every other student is working harder and doing better, the only solution is to study harder still. I see students going off to the library every night after dinner and coming back when it closes at midnight. I wish they would sometimes forget about their peers and go to a movie. I hear the clacking of typewriters in the hours before dawn. I see the tension in their eyes when exams are approaching and papers are due: "*Will I get everything done?*"

Probably they won't. They will get sick. They will get "blocked." They will sleep. They will oversleep. They will bug out. *Hey Carlos, help!*

Part of the problem is that they do more than they are expected to do. A professor will assign five-page papers. Several students will start writing ten-page papers to impress him. Then more students will write ten-page papers, and a few will raise the ante to fifteen. Pity the poor student who is still just doing the assignment.

Once you have twenty or thirty percent of the student population deliberately overexerting," one dean points out, "it's bad for everybody. When a teacher gets more and more effort from his class, the student who is doing normal work can be perceived as not doing well. The tactic works, psychologically."

Why can't the professor just cut back and not accept longer papers? He can, and he probably will. But by then the term will be half over and the damage done. Grade fever is highly contagious and not easily reversed. Besides, the professor's main concern is with his course. He knows his students only in relation to the course and doesn't know that they are also overexerting in their other courses. Nor is it really his business. He didn't sign up for dealing with the student as a whole person and with all the emotional baggage the student brought along from home. That's what deans, masters, chaplains, and psychiatrists are for.

To some extent this is nothing new: a certain number of professors have always been self-contained islands of scholarship and shyness, more comfortable with books than with people. But the new pauperism has widened the gap still further, for professors who actually like to spend time with students don't have as much time to spend. They also are overexerting. If they are young, they are busy trying to publish in order not to perish, hanging by their finger nails onto a shrinking profession. If they are old and tenured, they are buried under the duties of administering departments—as departmental chairmen or members of committees—that have been thinned out by the budgetary axe.

Ultimately it will be the students' own business to break the circles in which they are trapped. They are too young to be prisoners of their parents' dreams and their classmates' fears. They must be jolted into believing in themselves as unique men and women who have the power to shape their own future.

"Violence is being done to the undergraduate experience," says Carlos Hortas. "College should be open-ended: at the end it should open many, many roads. Instead, students are choosing their goal in advance, and their choices narrow as they go along. It's almost as if they think that the country has been codified in the type of jobs that exist—that they've got to fit into certain slots. Therefore, fit into the best-paying slot.

"They ought to take chances. Not taking chances will lead to a life of colorless mediocrity. They'll be comfortable. But something in the spirit will be missing."

I have painted too drab a portrait of today's students, making them seem a solemn lot. That is only half of their story; if they were so dreary I wouldn't so thoroughly enjoy their company. The other half is that they are easy to like. They are quick to laugh and to offer friendship. They are not introverts. They are unusually kind and are more considerate of one another than any student generation I have known.

Nor are they so obsessed with their studies that they avoid sports and extracurricular activities. On the contrary, they juggle their crowded hours to play on a variety of teams, perform with musical and dramatic groups, and write for campus publications. But this in turn is one more cause of anxiety. There are too many choices. Academically, they have 1,300 courses to select from; outside class they have to decide how much spare time they can spare and how to spend it.

This means that they engage in fewer extracurricular pursuits than their predecessors did. If they want to row on the crew and play in the symphony they will eliminate one; in the '60s they would have done both. They also tend to choose activities that are self-limiting. Drama, for instance, is flourishing in all twelve of Yale's residential colleges as it never has before. Students hurl themselves into these productions—as actors, directors, carpenters, and technicians—with a dedication to create the best possible play, knowing that the day will come when the run will end and they can get back to their studies.

They also can't afford to be the willing slave of organizations like the

35

Yale Daily News. Last spring at the one-hundredth anniversary banquet of that paper—whose past chairmen include such once and future kings as Potter Stewart, Kingman Brewster, and William F. Buckley, Jr.— much was made of the fact that the editorial staff used to be small and totally committed and that "newsies" routinely worked fifty hours a week. In effect they belonged to a club; Newsies is how they defined themselves at Yale. Today's student will write one or two articles a week, when he can, and he defines himself as a student. I've never heard the word Newsie except at the banquet.

If I have described the modern undergraduate primarily as a driven creature who is largely ignoring the blithe spirit inside who keeps trying to come out and play, it's because that's where the crunch is, not only at Yale but throughout American education. It's why I think we should all be worried about the values that are nurturing a generation so fearful of risk and so goal-obsessed at such an early age.

I tell students that there is no one "right" way to get ahead—that each of them is a different person, starting from a different point and bound for a different destination. I tell them that change is a tonic and that all the slots are not codified nor the frontiers closed. One of my ways of telling them is to invite men and women who have achieved success outside the academic world to come and talk informally with my students during the year. They are heads of companies or ad agencies, editors of magazines, politicians, public officials, television magnates, labor leaders, business executives, Broadway producers, artists, writers, economists, photographers, scientists, historians—a mixed bag of achievers.

40   I ask them to say a few words about how they got started. The students assume that they started in their present profession and knew all along that it was what they wanted to do. Luckily for me, most of them got into their field by a circuitous route, to their surprise, after many detours. The students are startled. They can hardly conceive of a career that was not pre-planned. They can hardly imagine allowing the hand of God or chance to nudge them down some unforeseen trail.

THE READER

1. *On p. 311, Zinsser names four kinds of pressure on college students. Are there others? Are they equally strong? What counterpressures exist? What would be necessary for a state of equilibrium? Would those changes or that state be desirable?*

2. *In his fifth paragraph, Zinsser says he wishes "for all students . . . some release from the clammy grip of the future" so that they could both "savor each segment of their education" and "learn that defeat is as*

instructive as victory." Are these two compatible? Which is more important, savoring each segment of one's education or learning from defeat? How would a college program designed to fulfill either or both of these two functions differ from that of the average college or from the one you are pursuing?

THE WRITER

1. By beginning with quotations from student notes to the counseling dean, Zinsser seeks to establish the problem of college pressures as a concrete personal reality; then he seeks to generalize, using those personal statements to represent also the situation of other students at other colleges. Does this plan work? What makes the statements sound authentic or inauthentic?

2. In describing the four kinds of pressure, Zinsser has to make transitions. One of these [*"Along with economic pressure . . . " (p. 313)*] is loose. Could it be tightened? Should it be? What about the others? What are the logical relations among the four kinds of pressure?

3. On p. 316, Zinsser refers to *"the blithe spirit"* inside the *"driven"* college student. Gaylin, in *"What You See Is the Real You" (p. 675)*, rejects such analyses. Which view do you find more persuasive? Why?

4. In the New York Times for *May 14, 1970*, Fred Hechinger reported an apparent increase in cheating by college students and pointed out that, historically, cheating occurs when grades are used to determine success in competition for economic and social rewards. He then concluded that some people are wondering if this process is not damaging the colleges, if *"the economic and political system is improperly exploiting the educational system."* By making *"system"* the subject of the clause, he avoided having to say who in particular is responsible for the problem. Write an essay in which you show who is responsible, or show that the problem doesn't exist at present or isn't important, or redefine the problem to lead to different conclusions.

5. Write an essay on one of these topics:
   a) The Value of Failure
   b) The Necessity for Pressures
   c) Ways to Eliminate Pressures
   d) An Alternative to Grading
   Then write a paragraph rebutting the point of view in your essay. Which seems more effective to you? Why?

William G. Perry, Jr.

EXAMSMANSHIP AND THE LIBERAL ARTS: A STUDY IN EDUCATIONAL EPISTEMOLOGY

"But sir, I don't think I really deserve it, it was mostly bull, really."
This disclaimer from a student whose examination we have awarded a
straight "A" is wondrously depressing. Alfred North Whitehead invented its only possible rejoinder: "Yes sir, what you wrote is nonsense,
utter nonsense. But ah! Sir! It's the right *kind* of nonsense!"

Bull, in this university,[1] is customarily a source of laughter, or a
problem in ethics. I shall step a little out of fashion to use the subject
as a take-off point for a study in comparative epistemology. The phenomenon of bull, in all the honor and opprobrium with which it is
regarded by students and faculty, says something, I think, about our
theories of knowledge. So too, the grades which we assign on examinations communicate to students what these theories may be.

We do not have to be out-and-out logical-positivists[2] to suppose that
we have something to learn about "what we think knowledge is"
by having a good look at "what we do when we go about measuring
it." We know the straight "A" examination when we see it, of course,
and we have reason to hope that the student will understand why his
work receives our recognition. He doesn't always. And those who
receive lesser honor? Perhaps an understanding of certain anomalies in our customs of grading good bull will explain the students' confusion.

I must beg patience, then, both of the reader's humor and of his
morals. Not that I ask him to suspend his sense of humor but that I shall
ask him to go beyond it. In a great university the picture of a bright
student attempting to outwit his professor while his professor takes pride
in not being outwitted is certainly ridiculous. I shall report just such a
scene, for its implications bear upon my point. Its comedy need not
present a serious obstacle to thought.

As for the ethics of bull, I must ask for a suspension of judgment. I
wish that students could suspend theirs. Unlike humor, moral commitment is hard to think beyond. Too early a moral judgment is precisely

From *Examining in Harvard College: A Collection of Essays (1964)*.

1. Harvard.
2. *Members of a contemporary school of
philosophy which sees philosophy as an activity rather than a body of knowledge, and*
*concerns itself not with abstract notions of
what a thing is but with empirical observation of what it does.*

what stands between many able students and a liberal education. The stunning realization that the Harvard Faculty will often accept, as evidence of knowledge, the cerebrations of a student who has little data at his disposal, confronts every student with an ethical dilemma. For some it forms an academic focus for what used to be thought of as "adolescent disillusion." It is irrelevant that rumor inflates the phenomenon to mythical proportions. The students know that beneath the myth there remains a solid and haunting reality. The moral "bind" consequent on this awareness appears most poignantly in serious students who are reluctant to concede the competitive advantage to the bullster and who yet feel a deep personal shame when, having succumbed to "temptation," they themselves receive a high grade for work they consider "dishonest."

I have spent many hours with students caught in this unwelcome bitterness. These hours lend an urgency to my theme. I have found that students have been able to come to terms with the ethical problem, to the extent that it is real, only after a refined study of the true nature of bull and its relation to "knowledge." I shall submit grounds for my suspicion that we can be found guilty of sharing the students' confusion of moral and epistemological issues.

I

I present as my "premise," then, an amoral *fabliau.* Its hero-villain is the Abominable Mr. Metzger '47. Since I celebrate his virtuosity, I regret giving him a pseudonym, but the peculiar style of his bravado requires me to honor also his modesty. Bull in pure form is rare; there is usually some contamination by data. The community has reason to be grateful to Mr. Metzger for having created an instance of laboratory purity, free from any adulteration by matter. The more credit is due him, I think, because his act was free from premeditation, deliberation, or hope of personal gain.

Mr. Metzger stood one rainy November day in the lobby of Memorial Hall. A junior, concentrating in mathematics, he was fond of diverting himself by taking part in the drama, a penchant which may have had some influence on the events of the next hour. He was waiting to take part in a rehearsal in Sanders Theatre, but, as sometimes happens, no other players appeared. Perhaps the rehearsal had been canceled without his knowledge? He decided to wait another five minutes.

Students, meanwhile, were filing into the Great Hall opposite, and taking seats at the testing tables. Spying a friend crossing the lobby toward the Great Hall's door, Metzger greeted him and extended appropriate condolences. He inquired, too, what course his friend was being tested in. "Oh, Soc. Sci. something-or-other." "What's it all about?"

asked Metzger, and this, as Homer remarked of Patroclus, was the beginning of evil for him.

10   "It's about Modern Perspectives on Man and Society and All That," said his friend. "Pretty interesting, really."

"Always wanted to take a course like that," said Metzger. "Any good reading?"

"Yeah, great. There's this book"—his friend did not have time to finish.

"Take your seats please" said a stern voice beside them. The idle conversation had somehow taken the two friends to one of the tables in the Great Hall. Both students automatically obeyed; the proctor put blue-books before them; another proctor presented them with copies of the printed hour-test.

Mr. Metzger remembered afterwards a brief misgiving that was suddenly overwhelmed by a surge of curiosity and puckish glee. He wrote "George Smith" on the blue book, opened it, and addressed the first question.

15   I must pause to exonerate the Management. The Faculty has a rule that no student may attend an examination in a course in which he is not enrolled. To the wisdom of this rule the outcome of this deplorable story stands witness. The Registrar, charged with the enforcement of the rule, has developed an organization with procedures which are certainly the finest to be devised. In November, however, class rosters are still shaky, and on this particular day another student, named Smith, was absent. As for the culprit, we can reduce his guilt no further than to suppose that he was ignorant of the rule, or, in the face of the momentous challenge before him, forgetful.

We need not be distracted by Metzger's performance on the "objective" or "spot" questions on the test. His D on these sections can be explained by those versed in the theory of probability. Our interest focuses on the quality of his essay. It appears that when Metzger's friend picked up his own blue book a few days later, he found himself in company with a large proportion of his section in having received on the essay a C+. When he quietly picked up "George Smith's" blue book to return it to Metzger, he observed that the grade for the essay was A. In the margin was a note in the section man's hand. It read "Excellent work. Could you have pinned these observations down a bit more closely? Compare . . . in . . . pp. . . ."

Such news could hardly be kept quiet. There was a leak, and the whole scandal broke on the front page of Tuesday's *Crimson*. With the press Metzger was modest, as becomes a hero. He said that there had been nothing to it at all, really. The essay question had offered a choice of two books, Margaret Mead's *And Keep Your Powder Dry* or Geoffrey Gorer's *The American People*. Metzger reported that having read neither of them, he had chosen the second "because the title gave me some notion as to what the book might be about." On the test, two critical comments were offered on each book, one favorable, one unfavorable. The students were asked to "discuss." Metzger conceded that he had played safe in throwing his lot with the more laudatory of the two comments, "but I did not forget to be balanced."

I do not have Mr. Metzger's essay before me except in vivid memory. As I recall, he took his first cue from the name Geoffrey, and committed his strategy to the premise that Gorer was born into an "Anglo-Saxon" culture, probably English, but certainly "English speaking." Having heard that Margaret Mead was a social anthropologist, he inferred that Gorer was the same. He then entered upon his essay, centering his inquiry upon what he supposed might be the problems inherent in an anthropologist's observation of a culture which was his own, or nearly his own. Drawing in part from memories of table-talk on cultural relativity[3] and in part from creative logic, he rang changes on the relation of observer to observed, and assessed the kind and degree of objectivity which might accrue to an observer through training as an anthropologist. He concluded that the book in question did in fact contribute a considerable range of " 'objective', and even 'fresh'," insights into the nature of our culture. "At the same time," he warned, "these observations must be understood within the context of their generation by a person only partly freed from his embeddedness in the culture he is observing, and limited in his capacity to transcend those particular tendencies and biases which he has himself developed as a personality in his interraction with this culture since his birth. In this sense the book portrays as much the character of Geoffrey Gorer as it analyzes that of the American people." It is my regrettable duty to report that at this moment of triumph Mr. Metzger was carried away by the temptations of parody and added, "We are thus much the richer."

In any case, this was the essay for which Metzger received his honor grade and his public acclaim. He was now, of course, in serious trouble with the authorities.

I shall leave him for the moment to the mercy of the Administrative Board of Harvard College and turn the reader's attention to the section man who ascribed the grade. He was in much worse trouble. All the consternation in his immediate area of the Faculty and all the glee in other areas fell upon his unprotected head. I shall now undertake his defense.

I do so not simply because I was acquainted with him and feel a respect for his intelligence; I believe in the justice of his grade! Well, perhaps "justice" is the wrong word in a situation so manifestly absurd. This is more a case in "equity." That is, the grade is equitable if we

20

3. "An important part of Harvard's educa-   note]. The houses are residences for upper-
tion takes place during meals in the   classmen.
Houses." An Official Publication [Perry's

accept other aspects of the situation which are equally absurd. My proposition is this: if we accept as valid those C grades which were accorded students who, like Metzger's friend, demonstrated a thorough familiarity with the details of the book without relating their critique to the methodological problems of social anthropology, then "George Smith" deserved not only the same, but better.

The reader may protest that the C's given to students who showed evidence only of diligence were indeed not valid and that both these students and "George Smith" should have received E's. To give the diligent E is of course not in accord with custom. I shall take up this matter later. For now, were I to allow the protest, I could only restate my thesis: that "George Smith's" E would, in a college of liberal arts, be properly a "better" E.

At this point I need a short-hand. It is a curious fact that there is no academic slang for the presentation of evidence of diligence alone. "Parroting" won't do; it is possible to "parrot" bull. I must beg the reader's pardon, and, for reasons almost too obvious to bear, suggest "cow."

Stated as nouns, the concepts look simple enough:

> cow (pure): data, however relevant, without relevancies.
> bull (pure): relevancies, however relevant, without data.

25   The reader can see all too clearly where this simplicity would lead. I can assure him that I would not have imposed on him this way were I aiming to say that knowledge in this university is definable as some neuter compromise between cow and bull, some infertile hermaphrodite. This is precisely what many diligent students seem to believe: that what they must learn to do is to "find the right mean" between "amounts" of detail and "amounts" of generalities. Of course this is not the point at all. The problem is not quantitative, nor does its solution lie on a continuum between the particular and the general. Cow and bull are not poles of a single dimension. A clear notion of what they really are is essential to my inquiry, and for heuristic purposes I wish to observe them further in the celibate state.

When the pure concepts are translated into verbs, their complexities become apparent in the assumptions and purposes of the students as they write:

> To cow (v. intrans.) or the act of cowing:
>   To list data (or perform operations) without awareness of, or comment upon, the contexts, frames of reference, or points of observation which determine the origin, nature, and meaning of the data (or procedures). To write on the assumption that "a fact is a fact." To present evidence of hard work as a substitute for understanding, without any intent to deceive.

To bull (*v. intrans.*) or the act of bulling:

To discourse upon the contexts, frames of reference and points of observation which would determine the origin, nature, and meaning of data if one had any. To present evidence of an understanding of form in the hope that the reader may be deceived into supposing a familiarity with content.

At the level of conscious intent, it is evident that cowing is more moral, or less immoral, than bulling. To speculate about unconscious intent would be either an injustice or a needless elaboration of my theme. It is enough that the impression left by cow is one of earnestness, diligence, and painful naiveté. The grader may feel disappointment or even irritation, but these feelings are usually balanced by pity, compassion, and a reluctance to hit a man when he's both down and moral. He may feel some challenge to his teaching, but none whatever to his one-ups-manship. He writes in the margin: "See me."

We are now in a position to understand the anomaly of custom: As instructors, we always assign bull an E, *when we detect it;* whereas we usually give cow a C, *even though it is always obvious.*

After all, we did not ask to be confronted with a choice between morals and understanding (or did we?). We evince a charming humanity, I think, in our decision to grade in favor of morals and pathos. "I simply *can't* give this student an E after he has *worked* so hard." At the same time we tacitly express our respect for the bullster's strength. We recognize a colleague. If he knows so well how to dish it out, we can be sure that he can also take it.

Of course it is just possible that we carry with us, perhaps from our own school-days, an assumption that if a student is willing to work hard and collect "good hard facts" he can always be taught to understand their relevance, whereas a student who has caught onto the forms of relevance without working at all is a lost scholar. 30

But this is not in accord with our experience.

It is not in accord either, as far as I can see, with the stated values of a liberal education. If a liberal education should teach students "how to think," not only in their own fields but in fields outside their own—that is, to understand "how the other fellow orders knowledge," then bulling, even in its purest form, expresses an important part of what a pluralist university holds dear, surely a more important part than the collecting of "facts that are facts" which schoolboys learn to do. Here then, good bull appears not as ignorance at all but as an aspect of knowledge. It is both relevant and "true." In a university setting good bull is therefore of more value than "facts," which, without a frame of reference, are not even "true" at all.

Perhaps this value accounts for the final anomaly: as instructors, we are inclined to reward bull highly, *where we do not detect its intent,* to the consternation of the bullster's acquaintances. And often we do not examine the matter too closely. After a long evening of reading blue books full of cow, the sudden meeting with a student who at least understands the problems of one's field provides a lift like a draught of refreshing wine, and a strong disposition toward trust.

This was, then, the sense of confidence that came to our unfortunate section man as he read "George Smith's" sympathetic considerations.

II

35   In my own years of watching over students' shoulders as they work, I have come to believe that this feeling of trust has a firmer basis than the confidence generated by evidence of diligence alone. I believe that the theory of a liberal education holds. Students who have dared to understand man's real relation to his knowledge have shown themselves to be in a strong position to learn content rapidly and meaningfully, and to retain it. I have learned to be less concerned about the education of a student who has come to understand the nature of man's knowledge, even though he has not yet committed himself to hard work, than I am about the education of the student who, after one or two terms at Harvard, is working desperately hard and still believes that collected "facts" constitute knowledge. The latter, when I try to explain to him, too often understands me to be saying that he "doesn't *put in enough generalities.*" Surely he has "put in *enough* facts."

I have come to see such quantitative statements as expressions of an entire, coherent epistemology. In grammar school the student is taught that Columbus discovered America in 1492. The *more* such items he gets "right" on a given test the more he is credited with "knowing." From years of this sort of thing it is not unnatural to develop the conviction that knowledge consists of the accretion of hard facts by hard work.

The student learns that the more facts and procedures he can get "right" in a given course, the better will be his grade. The more courses he takes, the more subjects he has "had," the more credits he accumulates, the more diplomas he will get, until, after graduate school, he will emerge with his doctorate, a member of the community of scholars.

The foundation of this entire life is the proposition that a fact is a fact. The necessary correlate of this proposition is that a fact is either right or wrong. This implies that the standard against which the rightness or wrongness of a fact may be judged exists *someplace*—perhaps graven upon a tablet in a Platonic world[4] outside and above *this* cave of tears. In grammar school it is evident that the tablets which enshrine

4. That is, a world of ideal forms, of which this world is but the distorted image. See Plato's "The Allegory of the Cave," p. 1153.

the spelling of a word or the answer to an arithmetic problem are visible to my teacher who need only compare my offerings to it. In high school I observe that my English teachers disagree. This can only mean that the tablets in such matters as the goodness of a poem are distant and obscured by clouds. They surely exist. The pleasing of befuddled English teachers degenerates into assessing their prejudices, a game in which I have no protection against my competitors more glib of tongue. I respect only my science teachers, authorities who *really know.* Later I learn from them that "this is only what we think *now.*" But eventually, surely. . . . Into this epistemology of education, apparently shared by teachers in such terms as "credits," "semester hours" and "years of French" the student may invest his ideals, his drive, his competitiveness, his safety, his self-esteem, and even his love.

College raises other questions: by whose calendar is it proper to say that Columbus discovered America in 1492? How, when and by whom was the year 1 established in this calendar? What of other calendars? In view of the evidence for Leif Ericson's previous visit (and the American Indians), what historical ethnocentrism is suggested by the use of the word "discover" in this sentence? As for Leif Ericson, in accord with what assumptions do you order the evidence?

These questions and their answers are not "more" knowledge. They are devastation. I do not need to elaborate upon the epistemology, or rather epistemologies, they imply. A fact has become at last "an observation or an operation performed in a frame of reference." A liberal education is founded in an awareness of frame of reference even in the most immediate and empirical examination of data. Its acquirement involves relinquishing hope of absolutes and of the protection they afford against doubt and the glib-tongued competitor. It demands an ever widening sophistication about systems of thought and observation. It leads, not away from, but *through* the arts of gamesmanship to a new trust. 40

This trust is in the value and integrity of systems, their varied character, and the way their apparently incompatible metaphors enlighten, from complementary facets, the particulars of human experience. As one student said to me: "I used to be cynical about intellectual games. Now I want to know them thoroughly. You see I came to realize that it was only when I knew the rules of the game cold that I could tell whether what I was saying was tripe."

We too often think of the bullster as cynical. He can be, and not always in a light-hearted way. We have failed to observe that there can lie behind cow the potential of a deeper and more dangerous despair. The moralism of sheer work and obedience can be an ethic that, unwilling to face a despair of its ends, glorifies its means. The implicit refusal to consider the relativity of both ends and means leaves the operator in an unconsidered proprietary absolutism. History bears witness that in the pinches this moral superiority has no recourse to negotiation, only to force.

A liberal education proposes that man's hope lies elsewhere: in the negotiability that can arise from an understanding of the integrity of systems and of their origins in man's address to his universe. The prerequisite is the courage to accept such a definition of knowledge. From then on, of course, there is nothing incompatible between such an epistemology and hard work. Rather the contrary.

I can now at last let bull and cow get together. The reader knows best how a productive wedding is arranged in his own field. This is the nuptial he celebrates with a straight A on examinations. The masculine context must embrace the feminine particular, though itself "born of woman." Such a union is knowledge itself, and it alone can generate new contexts and new data which can unite in their turn to form new knowledge.

45　　　In this happy setting we can congratulate in particular the Natural Sciences, long thought to be barren ground to the bullster. I have indeed drawn my examples of bull from the Social Sciences, and by analogy from the Humanities. Essay-writing in these fields has long been thought to nurture the art of bull to its prime. I feel, however, that the Natural Sciences have no reason to feel slighted. It is perhaps no accident that Metzger was a mathematician. As part of my researches for this paper, furthermore, a student of considerable talent has recently honored me with an impressive analysis of the art of amassing "partial credits" on examinations in advanced physics. Though beyond me in some respects, his presentation confirmed my impression that instructors of Physics frequently honor on examinations operations structurally similar to those requisite in a good essay.

The very qualities that make the Natural Sciences fields of delight for the eager gamesman have been essential to their marvelous fertility.

III

As priests of these mysteries, how can we make our rites more precisely expressive? The student who merely cows robs himself, without knowing it, of his education and his soul. The student who only bulls robs himself, as he knows full well, of the joys of inductive discovery—that is, of engagement. The introduction of frames of reference in the new curricula of Mathematics and Physics in the schools is a hopeful experiment. We do not know yet how much of these potent revelations the very young can stand, but I suspect they may rejoice in them more than we have supposed. I can't believe they have never wondered about Leif Ericson and that word "discovered," or even about 1492. They have simply been too wise to inquire.

Increasingly in recent years better students in the better high schools and preparatory schools *are* being allowed to inquire. In fact they appear to be receiving both encouragement and training in their inquiry. I have the evidence before me.

Each year for the past five years all freshmen entering Harvard and Radcliffe have been asked in freshman week to "grade" two essays answering an examination question in History. They are then asked to give their reasons for their grades. One essay, filled with dates, is 99% cow. The other, with hardly a date in it, is a good essay, easily mistaken for bull. The "official" grades of these essays are, for the first (alas!) C+ "because he has worked so hard," and for the second (soundly, I think) B+. Each year a larger majority of freshmen evaluate these essays as would the majority of the faculty, and for the faculty's reasons, and each year a smaller minority give the higher honor to the essay offering data alone. Most interesting, a larger number of students each year, while not overrating the second essay, award the first the straight E appropriate to it in a college of liberal arts.

For us who must grade such students in a university, these develop- 50 ments imply a new urgency, did we not feel it already. Through our grades we describe for the students, in the showdown, what we believe about the nature of knowledge. The subtleties of bull are not peripheral to our academic concerns. That they penetrate to the center of our care is evident in our feelings when a student whose good work we have awarded a high grade reveals to us that he does not feel he deserves it. Whether he disqualifies himself because "there's too much bull in it," or worse because "I really don't think I've worked that hard," he presents a serious educational problem. Many students feel this sleaziness; only a few reveal it to us.

We can hardly allow a mistaken sense of fraudulence to undermine our students' achievements. We must lead students beyond their concept of bull so that they may honor relevancies that are really relevant. We can willingly acknowledge that, in lieu of the date 1492, a consideration of calendars and of the word "discovered," may well be offered with intent to deceive. We must insist that this does not make such considerations intrinsically immoral, and that, contrariwise, the date 1492 may be no substitute for them. Most of all, we must convey the impression that we grade understanding qua understanding. To be convincing, I suppose we must concede to ourselves in advance that a bright student's understanding is understanding even if he achieved it by osmosis rather than by hard work in our course.

These are delicate matters. As for cow, its complexities are not what need concern us. Unlike good bull, it does not represent partial knowledge at all. It belongs to a different theory of knowledge entirely. In our theories of knowledge it represents total ignorance, or worse yet, a knowledge downright inimical to understanding. I even go so far as to propose that we award no more C's for cow. To do so is rarely, I feel, the act of mercy it seems. Mercy lies in clarity.

The reader may be afflicted by a lingering curiosity about the fate of Mr. Metzger. I hasten to reassure him. The Administrative Board of Harvard College, whatever its satanic reputations, is a benign body. Its members, to be sure, were on the spot. They delighted in Metzger's exploit, but they were responsible to the Faculty's rule. The hero stood in danger of probation. The debate was painful. Suddenly one member, of a refined legalistic sensibility, observed that the rule applied specifically to "examinations" and that the occasion had been simply an hour-test. Mr. Metzger was merely "admonished."

THE READER

1. Perry speaks several times of "good bull." Explain what "bad bull" would be in Perry's view, and give an example of it.
2. Perry points out the essential inaccuracy of such a supposedly simple statement of fact as "Columbus discovered America in 1492." Analyze one or two other such commonly accepted statements of fact in the same way Perry does.
3. Perry says that the ideal is "a productive wedding" between bull and cow. Find another essay in this book that you think represents such a "productive wedding," and explain how the author has brought that wedding about.

THE WRITER

1. Near the beginning of his essay, Perry says that he must "beg patience . . . both of the reader's humor and of his morals" (p. 318). Why does he find this necessary, and what assumptions does he make about his readers?
2. What tone does Perry adopt in his essay? Explain how the indicated words in these phrases contribute to Perry's creation of a tone appropriate to his thesis: (1) "the stunning realization that the Harvard Faculty will often accept, as evidence of knowledge, the cerebrations of a student who has little data at his disposal"; (2) "the peculiar style of his bravado requires me to honor also his modesty"; (3) "Bull in pure form is rare; there is usually some contamination by data"; (4) "some neuter compromise between cow and bull, some infertile hermaphrodite." Find and comment on other examples that help to define the tone of the essay.
3. In "Education by Poetry" (p. 1091), Frost talks about the importance of metaphor in a liberal education. Write an essay relating Frost's remarks about metaphor to Perry's remarks about the place of bull and cow in a liberal education.

Lewis Thomas

HUMANITIES AND SCIENCE

Lord Kelvin was one of the great British physicists of the late nine-teenth century, an extraordinarily influential figure in his time, and in some ways a paradigm of conventional, established scientific leadership. He did a lot of good and useful things, but once or twice he, like Homer, nodded. The instances are worth recalling today, for we have nodders among our scientific eminences still, from time to time, needing to have their elbows shaken.

On one occasion, Kelvin made a speech on the overarching impor-tance of numbers. He maintained that no observation of nature was worth paying serious attention to unless it could be stated in precisely quantitative terms. The numbers were the final and only test, not only of truth but about meaning as well. He said, "When you can measure what you are speaking about, and express it in numbers, you know something about it. But when you cannot—your knowledge is of a meagre and unsatisfactory kind."

But, as at least one subsequent event showed, Kelvin may have had things exactly the wrong way round. The task of converting observations into numbers is the hardest of all, the last task rather than the first thing to be done, and it can be done only when you have learned, beforehand, a great deal about the observations themselves. You can, to be sure, achieve a very deep understanding of nature by quantitative measure-ment, but you must know what you are talking about before you can begin applying the numbers for making predictions. In Kelvin's case, the problem at hand was the age of the earth and solar sytem. Using what was then known about the sources of energy and the loss of energy from the physics of that day, he calculated that neither the earth nor the sun were [sic] older than several hundred million years. This caused a consid-erable stir in biological and geological circles, especially among the evolutionists. Darwin himself was distressed by the numbers; the time was much too short for the theory of evolution. Kelvin's figures were described by Darwin as one of his "sorest troubles."

T. H. Huxley had long been aware of the risks involved in premature extrapolations from mathematical treatment of biological problems. He said, in an 1869 speech to the Geological Society concerning numbers, "This seems to be one of the many cases in which the admitted accuracy of mathematical processes is allowed to throw a wholly inadmissible appearance of authority over the results obtained by them. . . . As the

From *Late Night Thoughts on Listening to Mahler's Ninth Symphony* (1983).

329

grandest mill in the world will not extract wheat flour from peascods, so pages of formulas will not get a definite result out of loose data."

The trouble was that the world of physics had not moved fast enough to allow for Kelvin's assumptions. Nuclear fusion and fission had not yet been dreamed of, and the true age of the earth could not even be guessed from the data in hand. It was not yet the time for mathematics in this subject.

There have been other examples, since those days, of the folly of using numbers and calculations uncritically. Kelvin's own strong conviction that science could not be genuine science without measuring things was catching. People in other fields of endeavor, hankering to turn their disciplines into exact sciences, beset by what has since been called "physics envy," set about converting whatever they knew into numbers and thence into equations with predictive pretensions. We have it with us still, in economics, sociology, psychology, history, even, I fear, in English-literature criticism and linguistics, and it frequently works, when it works at all, with indifferent success. The risks of untoward social consequences in work of this kind are considerable. It is as important—and as hard—to learn *when* to use mathematics as *how* to use it, and this matter should remain high on the agenda of consideration for education in the social and behavioral sciences.

Of course, Kelvin's difficulty with the age of the earth was an exceptional, almost isolated instance of failure in quantitative measurement in nineteenth-century physics. The instruments devised for approaching nature by way of physics became increasingly precise and powerful, carrying the field through electromagnetic theory, triumph after triumph, and setting the stage for the great revolution of twentieth-century physics. There is no doubt about it: measurement works when the instruments work, and when you have a fairly clear idea of what it is that is being measured, and when you know what to do with the numbers when they tumble out. The system for gaining information and comprehension about nature works so well, indeed, that it carries another hazard: the risk of convincing yourself that you know everything.

Kelvin himself fell into this trap toward the end of the century. (I don't mean to keep picking on Kelvin, who was a very great scientist; it is just that he happened to say a couple of things I find useful for this discussion.) He stated, in a summary of the achievements of nineteenth-century physics, that it was an almost completed science; virtually everything that needed knowing about the material universe had been learned; there were still a few anomalies and inconsistencies in electromagnetic theory, a few loose ends to be tidied up, but this would be done within the next several years. Physics, in these terms, was not a field any longer likely to attract, as it previously had, the brightest and most imaginative young brains. The most interesting part of the work had already been done. Then, within the next decade, came radiation, Planck, the quantum, Einstein, Rutherford, Bohr, and all the rest—quantum mechanics—and the whole field turned over and became a brand-new sort of human endeavor, still now, in the view of many physicists, almost a full century later, a field only at its beginnings.

But even today, despite the amazements that are turning up in physics each year, despite the jumps taken from the smallest parts of nature—particle physics—to the largest of all—the cosmos itself—the impression of science that the public gains is rather like the impression left in the nineteenth-century public mind by Kelvin. Science, in this view, is first of all a matter of simply getting all the numbers together. The numbers are sitting out there in nature, waiting to be found, sorted and totted up. If only they had enough robots and enough computers, the scientists could go off to the beach and wait for their papers to be written for them. Second of all, what we know about nature today is pretty much the whole story: we are very nearly home and dry. From here on, it is largely a problem of tying up loose ends, tidying nature up, getting the files in order. The only real surprises for the future—and it is about those that the public is becoming more concerned and apprehensive—are the technological applications that the scientists may be cooking up from today's knowledge.

I suggest that the scientific community is to blame. If there are disagreements between the world of the humanities and the scientific enterprise as to the place and importance of science in a liberal-arts education, and the role of science in twentieth-century culture, I believe that the scientists are themselves responsible for a general misunderstanding of what they are really up to.

Over the past half century, we have been teaching the sciences as though they were the same academic collection of cut-and-dried subjects as always, and—here is what has really gone wrong—as though they would always be the same. The teaching of today's biology, for example, is pretty much the same kind of exercise as the teaching of Latin was when I was in high school long ago. First of all, the fundamentals, the underlying laws, the essential grammar, and then the reading of texts. Once mastered, that is that: Latin is Latin and forever after will be Latin. And biology is precisely biology, a vast array of hard facts to be learned as fundamentals, followed by a reading of the texts.

Moreover, we have been teaching science as though its facts were somehow superior to the facts in all other scholarly disciplines, more fundamental, more solid, less subject to subjectivism, immutable. English literature is not just one way of thinking, it is all sorts of ways. Poetry is a moving target. The facts that underlie art, architecture, and music are not really hard facts, and you can change them any way you like by arguing about them, but science is treated as an altogether

10

different kind of learning: an unambiguous, unalterable, and endlessly useful display of data needing only to be packaged and installed somewhere in one's temporal lobe in order to achieve a full understanding of the natural world.

And it is, of course, not like this at all. In real life, every field of science that I can think of is incomplete, and most of them—whatever the record of accomplishment over the past two hundred years—are still in the earliest stage of their starting point. In the fields I know best, among the life sciences, it is required that the most expert and sophisticated minds be capable of changing those minds, often with a great lurch, every few years. In some branches of biology the mind-changing is occurring with accelerating velocities. The next week's issue of any scientific journal can turn a whole field upside down, shaking out any number of immutable ideas and installing new bodies of dogma, and this is happening all the time. It is an almost everyday event in physics, in chemistry, in materials research, in neurobiology, in genetics, in immunology. The hard facts tend to soften overnight, melt away, and vanish under the pressure of new hard facts, and the interpretations of what appear to be the most solid aspects of nature are subject to change, now more than at any other time in history. The conclusions reached in science are always, when looked at closely, far more provisional and tentative than are most of the assumptions arrived at by our colleagues in the humanities.

The running battle now in progress between the sociobiologists and the antisociobiologists is a marvel for students to behold, close up. To observe, in open-mouthed astonishment, the polarized extremes, one group of highly intelligent, beautifully trained, knowledgeable, and imaginative scientists maintaining that all sorts of behavior, animal and human, are governed exclusively by genes, and another group of equally talented scientists saying precisely the opposite and asserting that all behavior is set and determined by the environment, or by culture, and both sides brawling in the pages of periodicals such as *The New York Review of Books*, is an educational experience that no college student should be allowed to miss. The essential lesson to be learned has nothing to do with the relative validity of the facts underlying the argument, it is the argument itself that is the education: we do not yet know enough to settle such questions.

15   It is true that any given moment there is the appearance of satisfaction, even self-satisfaction, within every scientific discipline. On any Tuesday morning, if asked, a good working scientist will gladly tell you that the affairs of the field are nicely in order, that things are finally looking clear and making sense, and all is well. But come back again, on another Tuesday, and he may let you know that the roof has just fallen in on his life's work, that all the old ideas—last week's ideas in some

cases—are no longer good ideas, that something strange has happened.

It is the very strangeness of nature that makes science engrossing. That ought to be at the center of science teaching. There are more than seven-times-seven types of ambiguity in science, awaiting analysis. The poetry of Wallace Stevens is crystal-clear alongside the genetic code.

I prefer to turn things around in order to make precisely the opposite case. Science, especially twentieth-century science, has provided us with a glimpse of something we never really knew before, the revelation of human ignorance. We have been used to the belief, down one century after another, that we more or less comprehend everything bar one or two mysteries like the mental processes of our gods. Every age, not just the eighteenth century, regarded itself as the Age of Reason, and we have never lacked for explanations of the world and its ways. Now, we are being brought up short, and this has been the work of science. We have a wilderness of mystery to make our way through in the centuries ahead, and we will need science for this but not science alone. Science will, in its own time, produce the data and some of the meaning in the data, but never the full meaning. For getting a full grasp, for perceiving real significance when significance is at hand, we shall need minds at work from all sorts of brains outside the fields of science, most of all the brains of poets, of course, but also those of artists, musicians, philosophers, historians, writers in general.

It is primarily because of this need that I would press for changes in the way science is taught. There is a need to teach the young people who will be doing the science themselves, but this will always be a small minority among us. There is a deeper need to teach science to those who will be needed for thinking about it, and this means pretty nearly everyone else, in hopes that a few of these people—a much smaller minority than the scientific community and probably a lot harder to find—will, in the thinking, be able to imagine new levels of meaning that are likely to be lost on the rest of us.

In addition, it is time to develop a new group of professional thinkers, perhaps a somewhat larger group than the working scientists, who can create a discipline of scientific criticism. We have had good luck so far in the emergence of a few people ranking as philosophers of science and historians and journalists of science, and I hope more of these will be coming along, but we have not yet seen a Ruskin or a Leavis or an Edmund Wilson. Science needs critics of this sort, but the public at large needs them more urgently.

I suggest that the introductory courses in science, at all levels from grade school through college, be radically revised. Leave the fundamentals, the so-called basics, aside for a while, and concentrate the attention of all students on the things that are *not* known. You cannot possibly teach quantum mechanics without mathematics, to be sure, but you can

20

describe the strangeness of the world opened up by quantum theory. Let it be known, early on, that there are deep mysteries, and profound paradoxes, revealed in their distant outlines, by the quantum. Let it be known that these can be appraoched more closely, and puzzled over, once the language of mathematics has been sufficiently mastered.

Teach at the outset, before any of the fundamentals, the still imponderable puzzles of cosmology. Let it be known, as clearly as possible, by the youngest minds, that there are some things going on in the universe that lie beyond comprehension, and make it plain how little is known.

Do not teach that biology is a useful and perhaps profitable science; that can come later. Teach instead that there are structures squirming inside all our cells, providing all the energy for living, that are essentially foreign creatures, brought in for symbiotic living a billion or so years ago, the lineal descendants of bacteria. Teach that we do not have the ghost of an idea how they got there, where they came from, or how they evolved to their present structure and function. The details of oxidative phosphorylation[1] and photosynthesis can come later.

Teach ecology early on. Let it be understood that the earth's life is a system of interliving, interdependent creatures, and that we do not understand at all how it works. The earth's environment, from the range of atmospheric gases to the chemical constituents of the sea, has been held in an almost unbelievably improbable state of regulated balance since life began, and the regulation of stability and balance is accomplished solely by the life itself, like the internal environment of an immense organism, and we do not know how *that* one works, even less what it means. Teach that.

Go easy, I suggest, on the promises sometimes freely offered by science. Technology relies and depends on science these days, more than ever before, but technology is nothing like the first justification for doing research, nor is it necessarily an essential product to be expected from science. Public decisions about what to have in the way of technology are totally different problems from decisions about science, and the two enterprises should not be tangled together. The central task of science is to arrive, stage by stage, at a clearer comprehension of nature, but this does not mean, as it is sometimes claimed to mean, a search for mastery over nature. Science may provide us, one day, with a better understanding of ourselves, but never, I hope, with a set of technologies for doing something or other to improve ourselves. I am made nervous by assertions that human consciousness will someday be unraveled by research, laid out for close scrutiny like the workings of a computer, and then, *and then!* I hope with some fervor that we can learn a lot more than we now know about the human mind, and I see no reason why this

---

1. "A vital process of intracellular respiration" (*American Heritage Dictionary*).

strange puzzle should remain forever and entirely beyond us. But I would be deeply disturbed by any prospect that we might use the new knowledge in order to begin doing something about it, to improve it, say. This is a different matter from searching for information to use against schizophrenia or dementia, where we are badly in need of technologies, indeed likely one day to be sunk without them. But the ordinary, every-day, more or less normal human mind is too marvelous an instrument ever to be tampered with by anyone, science or no science.

The education of humanists cannot be regarded as complete, or even adequate, without exposure in some depth to where things stand in the various branches of science, and particularly, as I have said, in the areas of our ignorance. This does not mean that I know how to go about doing it, nor am I unaware of the difficulties involved. Physics professors, most of them, look with revulsion on assignments to teach their subject to poets. Biologists, caught up by the enchantment of their new power, armed with flawless instruments to tell the nucleotide sequences of the entire human genome, nearly matching the physicists in the precision of their measurements of living processes, will resist the prospect of broad survey courses; each biology professor will demand that any student in his path must master every fine detail within that professor's research program. The liberal-arts faculties, for their part, will continue to view the scientists with suspicion and apprehension. "What do the scientists want?" asked a Cambridge professor in Francis Cornford's wonderful *Microcosmographia Academica.* "Everything that's going," was the quick answer. That was back in 1912, and universities haven't much changed.

25

The worst thing that has happened to science education is that the great fun has gone out of it. A very large number of good students look at it as slogging work to be got through on the way to medical school. Others look closely at the premedical students themselves, embattled and bleeding for grades and class standing, and are turned off. Very few see science as the high adventure it really is, the wildest of all explorations ever undertaken by human beings, the chance to catch close views of things never seen before, the shrewdest maneuver for discovering how the world works. Instead, they become baffled early on, and they are misled into thinking that bafflement is simply the result of not having learned all the facts. They are not told, as they should be told, that everyone else—from the professor in his endowed chair down to the platoons of postdoctoral students in the laboratory all night—is baffled as well. Every important scientific advance that has come in looking like an answer has turned, sooner or later—usually sooner—into a question. And the game is just beginning.

An appreciation of what is happening in science today, and of how great a distance lies ahead for exploring, ought to be one of the rewards of a liberal-arts education. It ought to be a good in itself, not something to be acquired on the way to a professional career but part of the cast of thought needed for getting into the kind of century that is now just down the road. Part of the intellectual equipment of an educated person, however his or her time is to be spent, ought to be a feel for the queernesses of nature, the inexplicable things.

And maybe, just maybe, a new set of courses dealing systematically with ignorance in science might take hold. The scientists might discover in it a new and subversive technique for catching the attention of students driven by curiosity, delighted and surprised to learn that science is exactly as Bush described it: an "endless frontier." The humanists, for their part, might take considerable satisfaction watching their scientific colleagues confess openly to not knowing everything about everything. And the poets, on whose shoulders the future rests, might, late nights, thinking things over, begin to see some meanings that elude the rest of us. It is worth a try.

THE READER

1. *What does Thomas believe that scientists "are really up to"?*
2. *What, in Thomas' view, is the relationship between science and technology? The differences? Why is it important that science and technology be distinguished?*
3. *Does Thomas imply that there are often things wrong about the way the humanities are usually taught? Have you been taught that English literature is "one way of thinking," or have you been taught to regard poetry as a "moving target" (p. 331)?*

THE WRITER

1. *Thomas' essay implies that science and the humanities have more in common than is customarily supposed. What details in the discussion lead to that implication?*
2. *Write a brief essay supporting or denying Thomas' assertion that "the conclusions reached in science are always . . . far more provisional and tentative than are most of the assumptions arrived at . . . in the humanities."*
3. *Thomas suggests that "a new set of courses dealing systematically with ignorance in science might take hold." Write a brief description of one such course. Then compare it with some courses it might replace, coming to some conclusion as to which might be more valuable for you.*
4. *Write a definition of "the scientific method," as you take that term to be commonly understood. Then write a critique of that definition as Thomas' view might suggest.*

5. *Here Thomas is dealing with a subject that is sweeping and important and in "Notes on Punctuation" (p. 395) with one that is restricted and minor. Describe the personality Thomas presents to you here and then the one he presents in "Notes on Puctuation." Are they similar? Different? Do they overlap? Is his analysis in "On Magic in Medicine" (p. 483) consistent with this personality or these personalities?*

6. *In "About Symbol," Dillard says: "All our knowledge is partial and approximate; if we are to know electrons and chimpanzees less than perfectly, and call it good enough, we may as well understand phenomena like love and death, or art and freedom, imperfectly also" (p. 1064). Write a brief essay comparing Dillard's idea with Thomas' assertion that conclusions in science are "far more provisional and tentative than are most of the assumptions . . . in the humanities."*

Wayne C. Booth

IS THERE ANY KNOWLEDGE THAT A MAN *MUST* HAVE?[1]

Everyone lives on the assumption that a great deal of knowledge is not worth bothering about; though we all know that what looks trivial in one man's hands may turn out to be earth-shaking in another's, we simply cannot know very much, compared with what might be known, and we must therefore choose. What is shocking is not the act of choice which we all commit openly but the claim that some choices are wrong.

From *The Knowledge Most Worth Having* (1967).

1. Some years after the following essay was first reprinted, I began to receive complaints from women who were angered by my use of "man" in the title and throughout the essay. At first I assumed that the readers were over-reacting, because I had certainly never intended to exclude women from my subject.

Once I had reread the essay carefully, however, I discovered, with some shock, that the women had a right to complain. Though I had been thinking of both men and women as I wrote, I had simply failed to consider how my language would strike female readers, consciously or unconsciously, or how it might encourage males to see themselves as the real center of all thought about education. My excuse now is only that I wrote before the feminist critique of language had got well under way, and that I was an author who badly needed that critique.

One result of my shock was another talk to undergraduates, "Is There Any Knowledge That a *Woman* Must Have?" now available in *The Vocation of a Teacher* (1988). In it I don't take back any of the suggestions I make here, but I go beyond them to consider what special educational problems are faced by any woman who lives in a male-dominated society like ours [Booth's note].

Especially shocking is the claim implied by my title: There is some knowledge that a man *must* have.

There clearly is no such thing, if by knowledge we mean mere acquaintance with this or that thing, fact, concept, literary work, or scientific law. When C. P. Snow and F. R. Leavis exchanged blows on whether knowledge of Shakespeare is more important than knowledge of the second law of thermodynamics, they were both, it seemed to me, much too ready to assume as indispensable what a great many wise and good men have quite obviously got along without. And it is not only nonprofessionals who can survive in happy ignorance of this or that bit of lore. I suspect that many successful scientists (in biology, say) have lost whatever hold they might once have had on the second law; I know that a great many literary scholars survive and even flourish without knowing certain "indispensable" classics. We all get along without vast loads of learning that other men take as necessary marks of an educated man. If we once begin to "reason the need" we will find, like Lear, that "our basest beggars/Are in the poorest thing superfluous." Indeed, we can survive, in a manner of speaking, even in the modern world, with little more than the bare literacy necessary to tell the "off" buttons from the "on."

Herbert Spencer would remind us at this point that we are interpreting *need* as if it were entirely a question of private survival. Though he talks about what a man must know to stay alive, he is more interested, in his defense of science, in what a *society* must know to survive: "Is there any knowledge that *man* must have?"—not a man; but *man*. This question is put to us much more acutely in our time than it was in Spencer's, and it is by no means as easy to argue now as it was then that the knowledge needed for man's survival is scientific knowledge. The threats of atomic annihilation, of engulfing population growth, of depleted air, water, and food must obviously be met, if man is to survive, and in meeting them man will, it is true, need more and more scientific knowledge; but it is not at all clear that more and more scientific knowledge will by itself suffice. Even so, a modern Herbert Spencer might well argue that a conference like this one, with its emphasis on the individual and his cognitive needs, is simply repeating the mistakes of the classical tradition. The knowledge most worth having would be, from his point of view, that of how to pull mankind through the next century or so without absolute self-destruction. The precise proportions of different kinds of knowledge—physical, biological, political, ethical, psychological, historical, or whatever—would be different from those prescribed in Spencer's essay, but the nature of the search would be precisely the same.

We can admit the relevance of this emphasis on social utility and at the same time argue that our business here is with other matters entirely.

If the only knowledge a man *must* have is how to cross the street without getting knocked down—or, in other words, how to navigate the centuries without blowing himself up—then we may as well close the conference and go home. We may as well also roll up the college and mail it to a research institute, because almost any place that is not cluttered up with notions of liberal education will be able to discover and transmit practical bits of survival-lore better than we can. Our problem of survival is a rather different one, thrust at us as soon as we change our title slightly once again to "Is there any knowledge (other than the knowledge for survival) that a man must have?" That slight shift opens a new perspective on the problem, because the question of what it is to be a man, of what it is to be fully human, is the question at the heart of liberal education.

To be human, to be human, to be fully human. What does it mean?   5
What is required? Immediately, we start feeling nervous again. Is the speaker suggesting that some of us are not fully human *yet?* Here come those hierarchies again. Surely in our pluralistic society we can admit an unlimited number of legitimate ways to be a man, without prescribing some outmoded aristocratic code!

Who—or what—is the creature we would educate? Our answer will determine our answers to educational questions, and it is therefore, I think, worth far more vigorous effort than it usually receives. I find it convenient, and only slightly unfair, to classify the educational talk I encounter these days under four notions of man, three of them metaphorical, only one literal. Though nobody's position, I suppose, fits my types neatly, some educators talk as if they were programming machines, some talk as if they were conditioning rats, some talk as if they were training ants to take a position in the anthill, and some—precious few—talk as if they thought of themselves as men dealing with men.

One traditional division of the human soul, you will remember, was into three parts: the vegetable, the animal, and the rational. Nobody, so far as I know, has devised an educational program treating students as vegetables, though one runs into the analogy used negatively in academic sermons from time to time. Similarly, no one ever really says that men are ants, though there is a marvelous passage in Kwame Nkrumah's autobiography in which he meditates longingly on the order and pure functionality of an anthill.[2] Educators do talk of men as machines or as animals, but of course they always point out that men are much more complicated than any other known animals or machines. My point here is not so much to attack any one of these metaphors—dangerous as I

---

2. Nkrumah was the first premier of the African republic of Ghana; he was ultimately deposed in a coup and went to live in China.

think they are—but to describe briefly what answers to our question each of them might suggest.

Ever since Descartes, La Mettrie,[3] and others explicitly called a man a machine, the metaphor has been a dominant one in educational thinking. Some have thought of man as a very complex machine, needing very elaborate programming; others have thought of him as a very simple machine, requiring little more than a systematic pattern of stimuli to produce foretellable responses. I heard a psychologist recently repeat the old behaviorist claim (first made by John B. Watson, I believe) that if you would give him complete control over any normal child's life from birth, he could turn that child into a great musician or a great mathematician or a great poet—you name it and he could produce it. On being pressed, the professor admitted that this claim was only "in theory," because we don't yet have the necessary knowledge. When I pushed further by asking why he was so confident in advance of experimental proof, it became clear that his faith in the fundamental metaphor of man as a programmable machine was unshakable.

When the notion of man as machine was first advanced, the machine was a very simple collection of pulleys and billiard balls and levers. Such original simplicities have been badly battered by our growing awareness both of how complex real machines can be and of how much more complex man is than any known machine. Modern notions of stimulus-response patterns are immeasurably more complicated than anything Descartes imagined, because we are now aware of the fantastic variety of stimuli that the man-machine is subject to and of the even more fantastic complexity of the responding circuits.

But whether the machine is simple or complex, the educational task for those who think of man under this metaphor is to program the mechanism so that it will produce the results that we have foreordained. We do not simply fill the little pitchers, like Mr. Gradgrind in Dickens' *Hard Times;*[4] we are much too sophisticated to want only undigested "pour-back," as he might have called his product. But we still program the information channels so that the proper if-loops and do-loops will be followed and the right feedback produced. The "programming" can be done by human teachers, of course, and not only by machines; but it is not surprising that those whose thinking is dominated by this metaphor tend to discover that machines are better teachers than men. The more ambitious programmers do not hesitate to claim that they can teach both thought and creativity in this way. But I have yet to see a program that can deal effectively with any subject that cannot be

10

---

3. René Descartes (1596–1650), French philosopher and mathematician; Julian Offray de La Mettrie (1709–51), French physician and philosopher.

4. Thomas Gradgrind thought of his students as "little pitchers . . . who were to be filled so full of facts."

reduced to simple yes and no answers, that is, to answers that are known in advance by the programmer and can thus be fixed for all time.

We can assume that subtler machines will be invented that can engage in simulated dialogue with the pupil, and perhaps even recognize when a particularly bright pupil has discovered something new that refutes the program. But even the subtlest teaching machine imaginable will still be subject, one must assume, to a final limitation: it can teach only what a machine can "learn." For those who believe that man is literally nothing but a very complicated machine, this is not in fact a limitation; machines will ultimately be able to duplicate all mental processes, thus "learning" everything learnable, and they will be able in consequence to teach everything.

I doubt this claim for many reasons, and I am glad to find the testimony of Norbert Wiener, the first and best known cyberneticist, to the effect that there will always remain a radical gap between computers and the human mind. But "ultimately" is a long way off, and I am not so much concerned with whether ultimately man's mind will closely resemble some ultimately inventable machine as I am with the effects, here and now, of thinking about men under the analogy with machines of today. Let me simply close this section with an illustration of how the mechanistic model can permeate our thought in destructive ways. Ask yourselves what picture of creature-to-be-educated emerges from this professor of teacher education:

> To implement the TEAM Project new curriculum proposal . . . our first concerns are with instructional systems, materials to feed the system, and personnel to operate the system. We have defined an instructional system as the optimal blending of the demands of content, communication, and learning. While numerous models have been developed, our simplified model of an instructional system would look like Figure 2. . . . We look at the process of communication—communicating content to produce learning—as something involving the senses: . . . [aural, oral, tactile, visual]. And I think in teacher education we had better think of the communications aspect of the instructional system as a package that includes the teacher, textbook, new media, classroom, and environment. To integrate these elements to more effectively transmit content into permanent learning, new and better instructional materials are needed and a new focus on the teacher of teachers is required. The teacher of teachers must: (1) examine critically the content of traditional courses in relation to desired behavioral outcomes; (2) become more sophisticated in the techniques of communicating course content; and (3) learn to work in concert with media specialists to develop the materials and procedures requisite to the efficient instructional system. And if the media specialist were to be charged with the efficient operation of the system, his upgrading would demand a broad-based "media generalist" orientation.

I submit that the author of this passage was thinking of human beings as stimulus-response systems on the simplest possible model, and that he was thinking of the purpose of education as the transfer of information from one machine to another. Though he would certainly deny it if we asked him, he has come to think about the human mind so habitually in the mechanistic mode that he doesn't even know he's doing it.[5]

But it is time to move from the machine metaphor to animal metaphors. They are closely related, of course, because everybody who believes that man is a machine also believes that animals are machines, only simpler ones. But many people who would resist the word "machine" do tend to analogize man to one or another characteristic of animals. Since man is obviously an animal in one sense, he can be studied as an animal, and he can be taught as an animal is taught. Most of the fundamental research in learning theory underlying the use of teaching machines has been done, in fact, on animals like rats and pigeons. You can teach pigeons to play Ping-Pong rather quickly by rewarding every gesture they make that moves them toward success in the game and refusing to reward those gestures that you want to efface. Though everybody admits that human beings are more complicated than rats and pigeons, just as everyone admits that human beings are more complicated than computers, the basic picture of the animal as a collection of drives or instincts, "conditioned" to learn according to rewards or punishments, has underlain much modern educational theory.

15   The notion of the human being as a collection of drives different from animal drives only in being more complex carries with it implications for education planners. If you and I are motivated only by sex or hunger or more complex drives like desire for power or for ego-satisfaction, then of course all education depends on the provision of satisfactions along our route to knowledge. If our teachers can just program carrots along the path at the proper distance, we donkey-headed students will plod along the path from carrot to carrot and end up as educated men.

I cannot take time here to deal with this view adequately, but it seems to me that it is highly questionable even about animals themselves. What kind of thing, really, is a rat or a monkey? The question of whether animals have souls has been debated actively for at least nine centuries; now psychologists find themselves dealing with the same question under another guise: What *are* these little creatures that we kill so blithely for the sake of knowledge? What *are* these strangely resistant little bundles

5. I am not of course suggesting that *any* use of teaching machines implies a mechanistic reduction of persons to machines; programmers rightly point out that machines *can* free teachers from the mechanical and save time for the personal [Booth's note].

of energy that will prefer—as experiments with rats have shown—a complicated interesting maze without food to a dull one *with* food?

There are, in fact, many experiments by now showing that at the very least we must postulate, for animals, a strong independent drive for mastery of the environment or satisfaction of curiosity about it. All the more advanced animals will learn to push levers that produce interesting results—clicks or bells or flashing lights or sliding panels—when no other reward is offered. It seems clear that even to be a fulfilled animal, as it were, something more than "animal satisfaction" is needed!

I am reminded here of the experiments on mother-love in monkeys reported by Harry F. Harlow in the *Scientific American* some years ago. Harlow called his article "Love in Infant Monkeys," and the subtitle of his article read, "Affection in infants was long thought to be generated by the satisfactions of feeding. Studies of young rhesus monkeys now indicate that love derives mainly from close bodily contact." The experiment consisted of giving infant monkeys a choice between a plain wire figure that offered the infant milk and a terry-cloth covered figure without milk. There was a pathetic picture of an infant clinging to the terry-cloth figure, and a caption that read "The infants spent most of their time clinging to the soft cloth 'mother' even when nursing bottles were attached to the wire mother." The article concluded—rather prematurely, I thought—that "contact comfort" had been shown to be a "prime requisite in the formation of an infant's love for its mother," that the act of nursing had been shown to be unimportant if not totally irrelevant in forming such love (though it was evident to any reader, even at the time, that no genuine "*act* of nursing" had figured in the experiment at all), and that "our investigations have established a secure experimental approach to this realm of dramatic and subtle emotional relationships." The only real problem, Harlow said, was the availability of enough infant monkeys for experiment.

Now I would not want to underrate the importance of Harlow's demonstration to the scientific community that monkeys do not live by bread alone. But I think that most scientists and humanists reading the article would have been struck by two things. The first is the automatic assumption that the way to study a subject like love is to break it down into its component parts; nobody looking at that little monkey clinging to the terry-cloth could possibly have said, "This is love," unless he had been blinded by a hidden conviction that love in animals is—must be—a mere cumulative result of a collection of drive satisfactions. This assumption is given quite plainly in Harlow's concluding sentence: "Finally with such techniques established, there appears to be no reason why we cannot at some future time investigate the fundamental neurophysiological and biochemical variables underlying affection and love."

For Harlow monkeys (and people) seem to be mere collections of neuro-physiological and biochemical variables, and love will be best explained when we can explain the genesis of each of its parts. The second striking point is that for Harlow animals do not matter, except as they are useful for experiment. If he had felt that they mattered, he might have noticed the look on his infant's face—a look that predicted for me, and for other readers of the *Scientific American* I've talked with, that these monkeys were doomed.

20   And indeed they were. A year or so later another article appeared, reporting Harlow's astonished discovery that all of the little monkeys on which he had earlier experimented had turned out to be incurably psychotic. Not a single monkey could mate, not a single monkey could play, not a single monkey could in fact become anything more than the twisted half-creatures that Harlow's deprivations had made of them. Harlow's new discovery was that monkeys needed close association with their peers during infancy and that such association was even more important to their development than genuine mothering. There was no sign that Harlow had learned any fundamental lessons from his earlier gross mistakes; he had landed nicely on his feet, still convinced that the way to study love is to break it down into its component parts and that the way to study animals is to maim them or reduce them to something less than themselves. As Robert White says, summarizing his reasons for rejecting similar methods in studying human infancy, it is too often assumed that the scientific way is to analyze behavior until one can find a small enough unit to allow for detailed research, but in the process "very vital common properties" are lost from view.

I cite Harlow's two reports not, of course, to attack animal experimentation—though I must confess that I am horrified by much that goes on in its name—nor to claim that animals are more like human beings than they are. Rather, I want simply to suggest that the danger of thinking of men as animals is heightened if the animals we think of are reduced to machines on a simple model.

The effects of reducing education to conditioning can be seen throughout America today. Usually they appear in subtle forms, disguised with the language of personalism; you will look a long time before you find anyone (except a very few Skinnerians) saying that he thinks of education as exactly like conditioning pigeons. But there are plenty of honest, blunt folk around to let the cat out of the bag—like the author of an article this year in *College Composition and Communications:* "The Use of a Multiple Response Device in the Teaching of Remedial English." The author claimed to have evidence that if you give each student four buttons to be pushed on multiple-choice questions, with all the buttons wired into a lighted grid at the front of the room, the resulting "instantaneous feedback"—every child learning immediately whether he agrees with the rest of the class—speeds up the learning of grammatical rules considerably over the usual workbook procedures. I daresay it does—but meanwhile what has happened to education? Or take the author of an article on "Procedures and Techniques of Teaching," who wrote as follows: "If we expect students to learn skills, they have to practice, but practice doesn't make perfect. Practice works if the learner *learns the results* of his practice, i.e., if he receives feedback. Feedback is most effective when it is contiguous to the response being learned. One of the chief advantages of teaching machines is that the learner finds out quickly whether his response is right or wrong . . . [Pressey] has published the results of an extensive program of research with tests that students score for themselves by punching alternatives until they hit the correct one. . . . [Thus] teaching machines or workbooks have many theoretical advantages over lecturing or other conventional methods of instruction." But according to what theory, one must ask, *do* systematic feedback mechanisms, perfected to whatever degree, have "theoretical advantages" over human contact? Whatever else can be said for such a theory, it will be based on the simplest of comparisons with animal learning. Unfortunately, the author goes on, experimental evidence is on the whole rather discouraging: "Experiments at the Systems Development Corporation . . . suggest that teaching incorporating . . . human characteristics is more effective than the typical fixed-sequence machines. (In this experiment instead of using teaching machines to simulate human teachers, the experimenters used humans to simulate teaching machines.)"

So far I have dealt with analogies for man that apply only to individuals. My third analogy turns to the picture of men in groups, and it is given to me partly by discussions of education, like those of Admiral Rickover, that see it simply as filling society's needs. I know of only one prominent educator who has publicly praised the anthill as a model for the kind of society a university should serve—a society of specialists each trained to do his part. But the notion pervades many of the defenses of the emerging multiversities.[6]

If knowledge is needed to enable men to function as units in society, and if the health of society is taken as the purpose of their existence, then there is nothing wrong in training the ants to fill their niches; it would be wrong not to. "Education is our first line of defense—make it strong," so reads the title of the first chapter of Admiral Rickover's book, *Education and Freedom* (New York: Dutton, 1959). "We must upgrade our schools" in order to "guarantee the future prosperity and freedom of the Republic." You can tell whether the ant-analogy is

6. A 1960s term for the gargantuan universities which often set government and corporate research, and the training of graduate students to do that research, above undergraduate education.

dominating a man's thinking by a simple test of how he orders his ends and means. In Admiral Rickover's statement, the schools must be up-graded in order to guarantee future prosperity, that is, we improve education for the sake of some presumed social good.

25   I seldom find anyone putting it the other way round: we must guaran-tee prosperity so that we can improve the schools, and the reason we want to improve the schools is that we want to insure the development of certain kinds of persons, both as teachers and as students. You cannot even say what I just said so long as you are really thinking of ants and anthills. Ants are not ends in themselves, ultimately more valuable than the hills they live in (I *think* they are not; maybe to themselves, or in the eyes of God, even ants are ultimate, self-justifying ends). At least from our point of view, ants are expendable, or to put it another way, their society is more beautiful, more interesting, more admirable than they are. And I would want to argue that too many people think of human beings in the same way when they think of educating them. The Communists make this quite explicit: the ends of Communist society justify whatever distortion or destruction of individual purposes is neces-sary to achieve them; men are educated for the state, not for their own well-being. They are basically political animals, not in the Aristotelian sense that they require society if they are to achieve their full natures and thus their own special, human kind of happiness, but in the sense that they exist, like ants, for the sake of the body politic.

If the social order is the final justification of what we do in education, then a certain attitude toward teaching and research will result: all of us little workmen, down inside the anthill, will go on happily contribut-ing our tiny bit to the total scheme without worrying much about larger questions of the why and wherefore. I know a graduate student who says that she sometimes sees her graduate professors as an army of tiny industrious miners at the bottom of a vast mine, chipping away at the edges and shipping their bits of knowledge up to the surface, blindly hoping that someone up there will know what to do with it all. An order is received for such-and-such new organic compounds; society needs them. Another order is received for an atomic bomb; it is needed, and it is therefore produced. Often no orders come down, but the chipping goes on anyway, and the shipments are made, because everyone knows that the health of the mine depends on a certain tonnage of specialized knowledge each working day.

We have learned lately that "they" are going to establish a great new atom-smasher, perhaps near Chicago. The atom-smasher will employ two thousand scientists and technicians. I look out at you here, knowing that some of you are physics majors, and I wonder whether any of you will ultimately be employed in that new installation, and if you are, whether it will be as an ant or as a human being. Which it will be must depend not on your ultimate employers but on yourself and on what happens to your education between now and then: if you have been given nothing but training to be that ultimate unit in that ultimate system, only a miracle can save you from formic dissolution of your human lineaments.

But it is long past time for me to turn from these negative, truncated portraits of what man really is not and attempt to say what he is. And here we encounter a difficulty that I find very curious. You will note that each of these metaphors has reduced man to something less than man, or at least to a partial aspect of man. It is easy to say that man is not a machine, though he is in some limited respects organized like a machine and even to some degree "programmable." It is also easy to say that man is not simply a complicated rat or monkey, though he is in some ways like rats and monkeys. Nor is man an ant, though he lives and must function in a complicated social milieu. All these metaphors break down not because they are flatly false but because they *are* metaphors, and any metaphorical definition is inevitably misleading. The ones I have been dealing with are especially misleading, because in every case they have reduced something more complex to something much less complex. But even if we were to analogize man to something more complex, say, the universe, we would be dissatisfied. What we want is some notion of what man really *is,* so that we will know what or whom we are trying to educate.

And here it is that we discover something very important about man, something that even the least religious person must find himself mystified by: man is the one "thing" we know that is completely resistant to our efforts at metaphor or analogy or image-making. What seems to be the most important literal characteristic of man is his resistance to definitions in terms of anything else. If you call me a machine, even a very complicated machine, I know that you deny what I care most about, my selfhood, my sense of being a person, my consciousness, my conviction of freedom and dignity, my awareness of love, my laughter. Machines have none of these things, and even if we were generous to their prospects, and imagined machines immeasurably superior to the most complicated ones now in existence, we would still feel an infinite gap between them and what we know to be a basic truth about ourselves: machines are expendable, ultimately expendable, and men are mysteriously ends in themselves.

I hear people deny this, but when they do they always argue for their position by claiming marvelous feats of super-machine calculation that machines can now do or will someday be able to do. But that is not the point; of course machines can outcalculate us. The question to ask is entirely a different one: Will they ever outlove us, outlive us, outvalue

30

us? Do we build machines because machines are good things in them-selves? Do we nurture them for their own good, as we nurture our children? An obvious way to test our sense of worth in men and ma-chines is to ask ourselves whether we would ever campaign to liberate the poor downtrodden machines who have been enslaved. Shall we form a National Association for the Advancement of Machinery? Will anyone ever feel a smidgeon of moral indignation because this or that piece of machinery is not given equal rights before the law? Or put it another way: Does anyone value Gemini[7] more than the twins? There may be men now alive who would rather "destruct," as we say, the pilot than the experimental rocket, but most of us still believe that the human being in the space ship is more important than the space ship.

When college students protest the so-called depersonalization of edu-cation, what they mean, finally, is not simply that they want to meet their professors socially or that they want small classes or that they do not want to be dealt with by IBM machines. All these things are but symptoms of a deeper sense of a violation of their literal reality as persons, ends in themselves rather than mere expendable things. Simi-larly, the current deep-spirited revolt against racial and economic injus-tice seems to me best explained as a sudden assertion that people, of whatever color or class, are not reducible to social conveniences. When you organize your labor force or your educational system as if men were mere social conveniences, "human resources," as we say, contributors to the gross national product, you violate something that we all know, in a form of knowledge much deeper than our knowledge of the times tables or the second law of thermodynamics: those field hands, those children crowded into the deadening classroom, those men laboring without dignity in the city anthills are *men,* creatures whose worth is mysteriously more than any description of it we might make in justifying what we do to them.

Ants, rats, and machines can all learn a great deal. Taken together, they "know" a very great part of what our schools and colleges are now designed to teach. But is there any kind of knowledge that a creature must have to qualify as a man? Is there any part of the educational task that is demanded of us by virtue of our claim to educate this curious entity, this *person* that cannot be reduced to mechanism or animality alone?

You will not be surprised, by now, to have me sound, in my answer, terribly traditional, not to say square: the education that a *man* must have is what has traditionally been called liberal education. The knowl-edge it yields is the knowledge or capacity or power of how to act freely

7. Here referring not to the astrological sign but to the space rockets.

as a man. That's why we call liberal education liberal: it is intended to liberate from whatever it is that makes animals act like animals and machines act like machines.

I'll return in a moment to what it means to act freely as a man. But we are already in a position to say something about what knowledge a man must have—he must first of all be able to learn for himself. If he cannot learn for himself, he is enslaved by his teachers' ideas, or by the ideas of his more persuasive contemporaries, or by machines programmed by other men. He may have what we call a good formal education, yet still be totally bound by whatever opinions happen to have come his way in attractive garb. One wonders how many of our graduates have learned how to take hold of a subject and "work it up," so that they can make themselves experts on what other men have concluded. In some ways this is not a very demanding goal, and it is certainly not very exciting. It says nothing about that popular concept, creativity, or about imagination or originality. All it says is that anyone who is dependent on his teachers *is* dependent, not free, and that anyone who knows how to learn for himself is less like animals and machines than anyone who does not know how to learn for himself.

We see already that a college is not being merely capricious or arbitrary when it insists that some kinds of learning are more important than some others. The world is overflowing with interesting subjects and valuable skills, but surely any college worth the name will put first things first: it will try to insure, as one inescapable goal, that every graduate can dig out from the printed page what he needs to know. And it will not let the desire to tamp in additional tidbits of knowledge, however delicious, interfere with training minds for whom a formal teacher is no longer required.

To put our first goal in this way raises some real problems that we cannot solve. Obviously no college can produce self-learners in very many subjects. Are we not lucky if a graduate can learn for himself even in one field, now that knowledge in all areas has advanced as far as it has? Surely we cannot expect our graduates to reach a stage of independence in mathematics and physics, in political science and psychology, in philosophy and English, *and* in all the other nice subjects that one would like to master.

Rather than answer this objection right away, let me make things even more difficult by saying that it is not enough to learn how to learn. The man who cannot *think* for himself, going beyond what other men have learned or thought, is still enslaved to other men's ideas. Obviously the goal of learning to think is even more difficult than the goal of learning to learn. But difficult as it is we must add it to our list. It is simply not enough to be able to get up a subject on one's own, like a good encyclopedia employee, even though any college would take pride if all its

35

graduates could do so. To be fully human means in part to think one's own thoughts, to reach a point at which, whether one's ideas are different from or similar to other men's, they are truly one's own.

The art of asking oneself critical questions that lead either to new answers or to genuine revitalizing of old answers, the art of making thought live anew in each new generation, may not be entirely amenable to instruction. But it is a necessary art nonetheless, for any man who wants to be free. It is an art that all philosophers have tried to pursue, and many of them have given direct guidance in how to pursue it. Needless to say, it is an art the pursuit of which is never fully completed. No one thinks for himself very much of the time or in very many subjects. Yet the habitual effort to ask the right critical questions and to apply rigorous tests to our hunches is a clearer mark than any other of an educated man.

But again we stumble upon the question, "Learn to think about *what?*" The modern world presents us with innumerable subjects to think about. Does it matter whether anyone achieves this rare and difficult point in more than one subject? And if not, won't the best education simply be the one that brings a man into mastery of a narrow specialty as soon as possible, so that he can learn to think for himself as soon as possible? Even at best most of us are enslaved to opinions provided for us by experts in *most* fields. So far, it might be argued, I still have not shown that there is any kind of knowledge that a man must have, only that there are certain skills that he must be able to exercise in at least one field.

40   To provide a proper grounding for my answer to that objection would require far more time than I have left, and I'm not at all sure that I could do so even with all the time in the world. The question of whether it is possible to maintain a human stance toward any more than a tiny fraction of modern knowledge is not clearly answerable at this stage in our history. It will be answered, if at all, only when men have learned how to store and retrieve all "machinable" knowledge, freeing themselves for distinctively human tasks. But in the meantime, I find myself unable to surrender, as it were, three distinct kinds of knowledge that seem to me indispensable to being human.

To be a man, a man must first know something about his own nature and his place in Nature, with a capital N—something about the truth of things, as men used to say in the old-fashioned days before the word "truth" was banned from academia. Machines are not curious, so far as I can judge; animals are, but presumably they never go, in their philosophies, even at the furthest, beyond a kind of solipsistic existentialism. But in science, in philosophy (ancient and modern), in theology, in psychology and anthropology, and in literature (of some kinds), we are presented with accounts of our universe and of our place in it that as men we can respond to in only one manly way: by thinking about them, by speculating and testing our speculations.

We know before we start that our thought is doomed to incompleteness and error and downright chanciness. Even the most rigorously scientific view will be changed, we know, within a decade, or perhaps even by tomorrow. But to refuse the effort to understand is to resign from the human race; the unexamined life can no doubt be worth living in other respects—after all, it is no mean thing to be a vegetable, an oak tree, an elephant, or a lion.[8] But a man, a man will want to see, in this speculative domain, beyond his next dinner.

By putting it in this way, I think we can avoid the claim that to be a man I must have studied any one field—philosophy, science, theology. But to be a man, *I must speculate,* and I must learn how to test my speculations so that they are not simply capricious, unchecked by other men's speculations. A college education, surely, should throw every student into a regular torrent of speculation, and it should school him to recognize the different standards of validation proper to different kinds of claims to truth. You cannot distinguish a man who in this respect is educated from other men by whether or not he believes in God, or in UFO's. But you can tell an educated man by the way he takes hold of the question of whether God exists, or whether UFO's are from Mars. Do you know your own reasons for your beliefs, or do you absorb your beliefs from whatever happens to be in your environment, like plankton taking in nourishment?

Second, the man who has not learned how to make the great human achievements in the arts his own, who does not know what it means to *earn* a great novel or symphony or painting for himself, is enslaved either to caprice or to other men's testimony or to a life of ugliness. You will notice that as I turn thus to "beauty"—another old-fashioned term—I do not say that a man must know how to prove what is beautiful or how to discourse on aesthetics. Such speculative activities are pleasant and worthwhile in themselves, but they belong in my first domain. Here we are asking that a man be educated to the experience of beauty; speculation about it can then follow. My point is simply that a man is less than a man if he cannot respond to the art made by his fellow man.

Again I have tried to put the standard in a way that allows for the impossibility of any one man's achieving independent responses in very many arts. Some would argue that education should insure some minimal human competence in all of the arts, or at least in music, painting, and literature. I suppose I would be satisfied if all of our graduates had been "hooked" by at least one art, hooked so deeply that they could

45

8. Here Booth echoes the assertion of Socrates, defending his practice of probing students' conventional beliefs, that the unexamined life is not worth living.

never get free. As in the domain of speculation, we could say that the more types of distinctively human activity a man can master, the better, but we are today talking about floors, not ceilings, and I shall simply rest content with saying that to be a man, a man must know artistic beauty, in some form, and know it in the way that beauty can be known. (The distinction between natural and man-made beauty might give me trouble if you pushed me on it here, but let me just say, dogmatically, that I would not be satisfied simply to know natural beauty—women and sunsets, say—as a substitute for art.)

Finally, the man who has not learned anything about how to understand his own intentions and to make them effective in the world, who has not, through experience and books, learned something about what is possible and what impossible, what desirable and what undesirable, will be enslaved by the political and social intentions of other men, benign or malign. The domain of practical wisdom is at least as complex and troublesome as the other two, and at the same time it is even more self-evidently indispensable. How should a man live? How should a society be run? What direction should a university take in 1966? For that matter what should be the proportion, in a good university, of inquiry into truth, beauty, and "goodness"? What kind of knowledge of self or of society is pertinent to living the life proper to a man? In short, the very question of this conference falls within this final domain: What knowledge, if any, is most worthy of pursuit? You cannot distinguish the men from the boys according to any one set of conclusions, but you *can* recognize a man, in this domain, simply by discovering whether he can think for himself about practical questions, with some degree of freedom from blind psychological or political or economic compulsions. Ernest Hemingway tells somewhere of a man who had "moved one dollar's width to the [political] right for every dollar that he'd ever earned." Perhaps no man ever achieves the opposite extreme, complete freedom in his choices from irrelevant compulsions. But all of us who believe in education believe that it is possible for any man, through study and conscientious thought, to school his choices—that is, to free them through coming to understand the forces working on them.

Even from this brief discussion of the three domains, I think we are put in a position to see how it can be said that there is some knowledge that a man must have. The line I have been pursuing will not lead to a list of great books, or even to a list of indispensable departments in a university. Nor will it lead, in any clear-cut fashion, to a pattern of requirements in each of the divisions. Truth, beauty, and goodness (or "right choice") are relevant to study in every division within the university; the humanities, for example, have no corner on beauty or imagination or art, and the sciences have no corner on speculative truth. What is more, a man can be ignorant even of Shakespeare, Aristotle, Beethoven, and Einstein, and be a man for a' that—*if* he has learned how to think his own thoughts, experience beauty for himself, and choose his own actions.

It is not the business of a college to determine or limit what a man will know; if it tries to, he will properly resent its impositions, perhaps immediately, perhaps ten years later when the imposed information is outmoded. But I think that it *is* the business of a college to help teach a man how to use his mind for himself, in at least the three directions I have suggested. * * * To think for oneself is, as we all know, hard enough. To design a program and assemble faculty to assist rather than hinder students in their efforts to think for themselves is even harder. But in an age that is oppressed by huge accumulations of unassimilated knowledge, the task of discovering what it means to educate a man is perhaps more important than ever before.

William Bennett

ADDRESS

During the Roman Saturnalia [1] even slaves could speak freely. On the occasion of Harvard College's 350th anniversary, let me invoke ancient custom and ask that, I, a public servant, be permitted to speak freely. And so I shall speak about the condition, as I see it, of American higher education today. I am not confident that this condition is an entirely healthy one.

It gives me no pleasure to say this. I spent the majority of my adult years on college and university campuses, and my memories of those years are fine ones. Even now it is a special pleasure to get back onto college campuses, and talk to students and professors, and browse in the bookstores, and remind myself of all the reasons these institutions should be worthy of allegiance and esteem. And so I'm glad to be here, at Harvard, today, to help the College celebrate its 350th birthday.

I'm glad not simply because Harvard is a representative institution of American higher education. I'm personally glad to be back. I spent three very interesting years here, and it's good to return. I say this not out of excessive sentimentality about Harvard. In fact, I received some publicity for a comment I made soon after becoming Secretary of Education,

This address, delivered at Harvard University on the 350th anniversary of Harvard College, was reprinted in *The Chronicle of Higher Education* (Oct. 15, 1986).

1. The feast of the god Saturn, celebrated in ancient Rome with revelry and license.

that it is possible to live a fulfilled life without a Harvard degree. Well, it is. But it's also possible to live a fulfilled life with one. In any case, a fulfilled life depends on many things; an education is only one of them.

I want to discuss today the question of the extent to which our colleges and universities in general contribute seriously to the fulfillment, to the betterment, of the lives of their students, of the young men and women given over to their charge. I have been concerned with this question since I myself was an undergraduate and then a graduate student; but perhaps not so intensely until I arrived at Harvard in 1968. I came as a law student, and became also a proctor in Matthews, and a tutor in Social Studies.[2] I had a good time, and learned some things and treasure some memories.

5   Let me mention one set of memories in particular. My job as a freshman proctor was far and away the best part of my years here. I had a good time doing it, I made some fast friends, I learned a great deal, and I think I was able to be of some actual help to those whose well-being was my direct and ongoing responsibility. Every year, from the photographs and records that were available, I memorized my freshmen before they arrived, so that I could greet them by name, and be somewhat familiar with their interests and talents. I made it a point not to conform to the pretentious practice of keeping proctor's office hours— mere graduate or law students acting like full professors; my freshmen were always welcome in my room, and they made use of this welcome. We spent a lot of time together, at parties, at our own softball and football games, and in serious and considerably less-than-serious discussion. To some of them, I'm proud to say, I occasionally gave a hard time; I was tough on drugs, and I would not sign course-change cards if I thought a student was going after gut courses or otherwise undercutting his academic opportunities.

Proctoring was the highlight of my experience at Harvard, though I enjoyed the tutoring as well, and law school was at least interesting. But out of these various Harvard experiences, and especially from the intense experience and illuminating vantage point of a proctor, I formed some notions both about this university and about American higher education in general. My subsequent experiences at other colleges and universities have served to strengthen these notions into convictions.

One of my fundamental convictions is this: There is an extraordinary gap between the rhetoric and the reality of American higher education. The gap is so wide, in fact, that we face the real possibility—not today, perhaps not tomorrow, but someday—of an erosion of public support for the enterprise.

The rhetoric of contemporary American higher education, the terms

---

2. A resident adviser in Matthews Hall, a freshman dormitory, and a part-time instructor.

in which its practitioners and advocates speak of it, is often exceedingly pious, self-congratulatory, and suffused with the aura of moral superiority. The spokesmen for higher education tend to invoke the mission of the university as if they were reciting the Nicene Creed: one, holy, universal, and apostolic church.[3] To be sure, being modern and sophisticated, they also know the rhetorical uses of a little well-placed deprecation, and they can speak winningly of the need for constant self-inspection and self-improvement. But try, as I have tried, to criticize American higher education by the one yardstick that matters—namely, the relative success or failure of our colleges and universities at discharging the educational responsibilities that they bear. From the reaction, you would think I had hurled a rock through the stained-glass window of a cathedral. The response to my criticism was not "Prove it," or "You're wrong for the following reasons"; it was more like "How dare you"—"Who do you think you are?" Well, I know who I am, having been a student at three colleges and universities, and a teacher at six. I know who I am, but does the university know what it is? The university claims to educate, to improve the minds—even the hearts—of young men and women. Sometimes it does this, to be sure—but not as often, and not as wholeheartedly and as purposefully and as successfully as it should.

Let's take Harvard as an example. Considering the vast sums that parents pay for the privilege of sending their children to a college like Harvard, it may seem gauche and impertinent to ask whether the sacrifice is matched by the value of the education received in exchange. But the question is nevertheless worth asking, for the fact is that neither those fees themselves, nor a $3.1-billion endowment, nor a library system staggering in its holdings, nor research laboratories and scientific facilities that are the envy of the world, nor well-furnished centers for the study of domestic and international affairs, nor first-class museums and theaters, nor a faculty justly renowned for its scholarship and intellectual brilliance, nor even, for that matter, a brainy and resourceful student body—the fact is that none of these things is evidence that Harvard or any similarly situated university is really fulfilling its obligation *to its own students* of seeing to it that when they leave after four years, they leave as educated men and women.

That Harvard is a place where one *can* get a good education, no one   10
can doubt. The reason has largely to do with the presence here on one campus of all those resources I've just enumerated, and especially the final two items on the list: the bright young men and women whom the college attracts as students, and the gifted scholars with whom they are placed in proximity. From such a combination of active elements, exciting things will occur. It's a good bet. But it does not occur in other

3. The Apostles' Creed and the Nicene Creed set forth Christian doctrine; Bennett quotes the Roman Catholic translation of the Nicene Creed.

cases—and I would fault Harvard and other universities for this: there's not that much effort to see to it, systematically and devotedly, that real education occurs. Under the justification of deferring to individual decisions and choices, much is left to chance. Sometimes a proctor, a professor, a dean, steps in and takes a real interest in a student's education—but that's often the luck of the draw.

Our students deserve better. They deserve a university's real and sustained attention to their intellectual and their moral well-being. And they deserve a good general education—at a minimum, a systematic familiarization with our own, Western tradition of learning: with the classical and Jewish-Christian heritage, the facts of American and European history, the political organization of Western societies, the great works of Western art and literature, the major achievements of the scientific disciplines—in short, the basic body of knowledge which universities once took it upon themselves as their obligation to transmit, under the name of a liberal education, from ages past to ages present and future.

As the distinguished historian James H. Billington[4] has remarked, American universities have as a rule given up on this once-central task—with the result that not only do students now tend to lack a knowledge of their own tradition, they often have no tradition, they often have no standpoint from which to appreciate any other tradition, or even to *have* a sense of tradition. Billington characterizes the typical undergraduate curriculum of today as a "smorgasbord." If this Scandinavian metaphor betrays too Western a bias, I would propose instead the metaphor of an old-style Chinese menu, the kind that used to adorn the Hong Kong restaurant on Mass Ave, where a customer could pick at leisure from Column A and Column B. Whatever may be said of this as a meal, it is not a model for a college curriculum.

But one might respond, here at Harvard, we have the Core Curriculum. Well, I would respond in turn, do you? You have a symbolic nod, a head feint, in the direction of a core curriculum. I have studied the Harvard catalogue, and I agree that under the heading of the Core Curriculum we find an agglomeration of courses, many of them obviously meaty and important, taught by eminent scholars, on a wide variety of subjects. But it seems to me that many of them could more appropriately find their place among the individual offerings of the various departments of instruction, from where, indeed, they give every appearance of having been plucked, only to be regrouped in new combinations. In what sense, however, do these courses constitute a *core*—i.e., the central, foundational part of a liberal education? Some of the courses are real core courses—and my sense is that in fact students, to their credit, often flock to such classes. But they do not constitute a true

4. James Billington (1929–   ): historian of Russia, now Librarian of Congress; also taught at Harvard University.

curriculum. I think students would benefit from a real core curriculum—i.e., a *set* of fundamental courses, ordered, purposive, coherent. I cannot discern such a core curriculum here.

Now despite this, many Harvard students get an education—or at least they learn a lot. And of course there is a limit to what any curriculum can accomplish. But if Harvard were more intentional about it, more committed to ensuring that its undergraduates received an education commensurate with the promise held out by the Core Curriculum, it would be doing even better by its students, and it would set a clearer example for all the institutions that look to it. There are too many intellectual and educational casualties among the student body of Harvard. Of course there would be some under any plan; but there are more than there have to be, and that's because luck, serendipity, chance, peer pressure, and a kind of institutional negligence—often a very high-minded negligence—are not the best guarantors of a general education. Some people don't get educated here—too many for the greatest university in the country. If we say to parents and taxpayers and donors when we take their money—often large amounts of it—that we'll educate their sons and daughters—let's do so. Let's do what we promise.

After all, American colleges and universities are quick to proclaim their duty to address all sorts of things that are wrong in the world, to speak truth to power, to discourse on the most complex social and moral issues beyond their walls, and to instruct political and business and religious leaders on the proper path to follow. But they have a prior duty, which is to see to the education of the young people in their charge. They ought to be expected to take a proctor's interest in that education—this is, after all, what they are paid for. Some do—perhaps especially the smaller, less famous institutions. But too often our institutions—especially our most prestigious institutions—fail in the discharge of their educational responsibilities. And they ought to be held to account for this—not just by parents and trustees and donors and taxpayers, but above all by students.

I was interested to read in *The Chronicle of Higher Education* [5] of a recent, comprehensive survey of undergraduates that found the following: Two-fifths reported that *no* professor at their institution took a "special personal interest" in their academic progress; and fewer than one-fifth rated their institution's academic advisory programs "highly adequate," while nearly three of five rated them merely "adequate" or worse. Students should not accept this state of affairs as inevitable, or pre-ordained; I think that demanding greater guidance, a more serious assumption of responsibility by their institutions, is a worthy cause for student activism. Commencement exercises at Harvard College used to conclude—perhaps they still do—with the president's welcoming the

15

5. A weekly newspaper.

new graduates into the company of educated men and women. If students feel that their years at Harvard are failing to prepare them adequately for membership in that privileged company, they should let Harvard know.

Let me add that Harvard would, I think, be prepared to listen. One approach that may help foster quality and focus and purpose in undergraduate education goes by the name of assessment—that is, assessing what students actually learn. I suggested, near the beginning of my tenure as Secretary of Education, that more attention to this issue might be desirable. At the time many in higher education refused even to consider it. But I do want to pay tribute to your president, my former crackerjack labor-law teacher, Mr. Bok.[6] He thinks the question of quality and assessing quality is important, as he said in his last annual report, and he's beginning to do something about it, with a faculty seminar, among other things, here at Harvard. Good for him. That's leadership. I hope others will follow—and we in the Department of Education stand ready to help.

Students should make other demands of colleges and universities as well. William James[7] said the purpose of a college education is to help you to know a good man when you see him. (We can add "and a good woman.") He said a college education's best claim is that it helps you to value what deserves to be valued: "The only rational ground for preeminent admiration of any single college," James said, speaking of Harvard, "would be its preeminent spiritual tone." And James warned that all too often, "to be a college man, even a Harvard man, affords no sure guarantee for anything but a more educated cleverness in the service of popular idols and vulgar ends."

Notice that James is talking about both intellectual and moral discernment. What of moral discernment in particular? Most of our colleges would not dream of claiming to offer a moral education to their students, to their charges. Most do not seek to improve the individual moral sense of their students—much less their faculty. But there is no shortage of moralizing and moral posturing—especially the kind that does not cost anything of the individual, that does not take time or self-denial or effort. Chekhov[8] wrote, "You can't become a saint through other people's sins," but many seem to think that's just how you do it. I remember some teachers and tutors in the 70's who were at a fever pitch over international justice and the welfare of others in general, but in particular they did not want to give much time to those on their own campus whom they were charged to help. The advantage of a concern for justice in general, for justice somewhere else, is that it takes less time than

6. Derek Bok (1930–): also dean of Harvard Law School and president of Harvard University, 1971–91.
7. William James (1842–1910): psychologist and philosopher; also taught at Harvard University.
8. Anton Chekhov (1860–1904): Russian dramatist and short story writer.

pursuing justice in particular, and it has the added benefit of not interfering with meals, socializing, and other engagements.

Now where are many of our colleges and universities on the issues of their responsibility to protect their students and their obligation to foster moral discernment in their students? With the exception of relatively few places—mostly religious or military institutions, I gather—higher education is silent. Many colleges freely dispense guidance to those beyond their walls, and such guidance is to be welcomed in a free society; but colleges that aim, as they might put it, to "lead" society's conscience on various social problems should not, when faced by a real problem within their competence to deal with, duck or throw up their hands. When it comes to drugs on campus, too many college presidents say, well, that's a society-wide problem—there's little we can do about it. This unaccustomed modesty from higher education is puzzling. I think moral responsibility begins at home. To be interested—intensely interested—in broader issues is fine, but to neglect one's basic responsibilities is not. It is true that dealing with the drug problem requires a more sustained effort than signing a petition or mounting a demonstration; it requires individual and institutional time and long-term commitment. These have not been very forthcoming on very many of our college campuses.

Earlier on, I compared the modern university with the old church. Although I am known, generally and correctly, as a friend of religion, let me say this: the self-righteousness that has given so many religious institutions and spokesmen a bad name has found an even more secure and hospitable home in the modern university. Even more, because in the old churches most divines did not forget that the first injunction was, heal thyself; they knew they had to attend to their own souls, and then those of their parishioners, before preaching to the outside world. The residents of the modern university all too often take it upon themselves to preach, without even a cursory acknowledgment that they should first attend to healing themselves.

There is another analogy that can be drawn between the contemporary university and the old church. The old church fell into some disrepute because its exhortations to poverty and holiness were too often belied by the worldliness and sumptuousness of its clerics. Similarly, American higher education simply refuses to acknowledge the obvious fact that, in general, it is rich. Whether this refusal is due to calculation or self-deception, I do not know, but in all the debates over student aid and federal tax policy, somehow this basic fact has been neglected. Now reasonable people can differ over student aid or tax policies—but these differences should be based on facts. And the fact is that the American people have been very generous to higher education in this country. From higher education's publicity you would think that hosts of institutions are on the brink of collapse, others near the abyss; but this is not so. The number of institutions of higher education in the United States has increased from 1,852 in 1950 to 2,230 in 1965 to 3,231 in 1980 to 3,331 today. The number of public institutions continues to increase; the number of private institutions continues to increase. This is fine—but let's not pretend this is a shrinking enterprise, in a perilous state.

And let's not pretend the wealth of this increasing number of institutions is shrinking either. Gross national spending on higher education in this nation has gone, in constant 1985–1986 dollars, from $12 billion in 1950 to $53 billion in 1965 to over $100 billion today. The wealth—the endowments—of our institutions of higher education have also continued to increase—especially in the past few years. In fact, the Reagan-era stock market may be the best thing to have happened in a long while to American higher education.[9]

But to say this is to adopt a false criterion of well-being for our institutions of higher education, a criterion their spokesmen too often adopt. It is to mistake a means for an end. Now I work in Washington, and I see higher education much of the time through its representatives there. Of those representatives I would say this: I have never seen a greater interest in *money*—money, cash, bucks—among anybody. The higher education lobbyists put Harvard Square hawkers to shame. They are, admittedly, very good at getting their funds from a Congress seemingly enraptured by the pieties, pontifications, and poor-mouthings of American higher education. But very few words can be heard from any of these representatives about other aspects of higher education—issues like purpose, quality, curriculum, the moral authority and responsibilities of universities; most of the time, all we hear from them are pleas for money, for more money.

25   For example, just the other week, the American Council on Education appointed a 33-member national "Commission on National Challenges in Higher Education"; the purpose was to provide "a new and exciting agenda" for American higher education. But this agenda is limited in an interesting way: the commission will *not* deal with such issues as what should be taught or what students are learning. Rather, the president of the A.C.E. said, "We will be looking at such questions as 'What does higher education mean . . . to the people who fund us?' and 'What are their responsibilities?' Notice: their responsibilities. And the purpose of the exercise, it is reported, is that "it is hoped that, by highlighting the importance of education to the nation, the Commission can coax additional funds from Congress." Is it likely that this report will be an examination of the real national challenges in higher education?

Even supporters of increased government spending in higher educa-

9. The value of stocks—and consequently of college endowments—increased during Ronald Reagan's presidency.

tion are coming to find the spectacle in Washington a bit much. Thus the Washington *Post* recently took issue with colleges' objections to the new tax bill under the headline, "Crying Towel for Colleges." And there is some danger that higher education's tendency to cry "Wolf" so insistently and so tiresomely will lead even Congress, one of these days, to balk.

Money is a means. It can be used for good and ill. In some cases money has aided good things, but in others money has aided a kind of corruption. Money has meant growth and expansion, which in some places has meant a diffusion and loss of focus, a loss of central purpose. And more money has given many in our universities the opportunity to avoid doing one thing above all—actually teaching large numbers of students; or, in some cases, any students. Bennett's axiom: After a certain point, the more money you have, the fewer distinguished professors you will have in the classroom. This is an oddity of academic life. x dollars buys the students one professor, $2x$ dollars buys them two, but $3x$ and $4x$ and $5x$ dollars gradually remove the professor from the student, and $6x$ dollars may replace all the classroom professors with graduate students. So money is not an unambiguous good. In any case, it's often not that hard to get money—but to bring quality and focus and purpose to a place, now that's harder.

My final topic is tolerance: the university as home for the free exchange of ideas. We are all too familiar with the recent incidents of denial of free speech on college campuses. There was even an incident here at Harvard, last spring, though I was glad to see Harvard invited the victimized speakers back.[10] Still, as Wayne State University President David Adamany said earlier this year, "The whole nation knows that faculty members, students, academic administrators, and some governing boards have in recent years silenced unpopular speakers— especially speakers on the right. . . . The shame for those of us who are active liberals is that we do not join in a chorus of condemnation of our colleagues when right-leaning speakers are kept off our campuses by threat or are silenced by disorder." Perhaps such a chorus of condemnation may now—finally—begin to emerge, as in the recent speech by Yale President Benno Schmidt; such a chorus had better emerge, and triumph—or else the game really will be up.

And we should also be careful not to allow a more subtle and pervasive kind of conformism and intolerance to permeate our institutions of higher education. Let me put it simply. Prestigious, selective, leading universities—whatever modifier you wish—have a tendency in our time to show a liberal bias. This is partly because most of the people in the

10. Edwin Meese, attorney-general in Reagan's cabinet, was to receive an award from Harvard's Kennedy School of Government in the spring of 1986; his appearance was protested and then rescheduled for a later date.

humanities and social sciences departments in these universities stand to the left of center. A 1984 Carnegie Foundation survey of the professoriate found that, among philosophy faculty at four-year institutions, 21.7% designated themselves as "left," *none* as "strongly conservative;" for the sociologists, the percentages were 37% vs. .9%; for historians, 12.9% vs. 3.0%. As the values-forming teachers of the young, these professors may tend to tilt students in the direction of their own beliefs. (Also many students coming to such universities think that a general liberal bias is expected of them.) So certain views are in a minority, and indeed are unpopular.

30　　This need not be a great problem, as long as we are very careful that a generally shared political viewpoint does not lead to the explicit or implicit censorship of unpopular ideas. Unpopular views—views unpopular in the academy, that is—should not merely be grudgingly tolerated there; they should be respected, and fostered. Harvard professor James Q. Wilson [11] wrote over a decade ago that of the five institutions of which he had been a part—the Catholic Church, the University of Redlands, the U.S. Navy, the University of Chicago, and Harvard—it was Harvard that was perhaps the least open to free and uninhibited discussion. Combating this sort of intolerance, if it is present, requires more than allowing an occasional dissenting outside speaker to appear on campus. It requires self-criticism and self-examination; it requires a conscious striving by the academy against the tendency to become home to a "herd of independent minds." For if you cannot hold or express or argue for an unorthodox view at a university without risk of penalty, either explicit penalty or social disdain, the university will collapse like a deck of cards, falling of its own weight. If we cannot protect the basic principle of academic freedom, then we cannot even begin to hope that our colleges and universities will evolve into a recognizable imitation of what they claim to be.

Let me conclude: Universities deserve the kind of scrutiny they like to give to others. Universities cost a lot, and puff and boast a lot. From time to time, it's not a bad idea to look at what's really going on, and to ask some hard questions. I've tried to do a bit of that today, and I've tried to do it for the sake of our students. I hope that some in American higher education will take seriously the questions I've raised, and ask *themselves* how our colleges and universities today can do better by their students—who are after all the purpose of the enterprise. If we are not doing as well as we might by them, we should begin to see to it that we do better.

11. James Q. Wilson (1931–　): professor of government at UCLA; also taught at Harvard University.

Language and Communication

Casey Miller and Kate Swift

WHO'S IN CHARGE OF THE ENGLISH LANGUAGE?

In order to encourage the use of language that is free of gender bias, it's obviously necessary to get authors to *recognize* gender bias in their writing. The reason that's so difficult is that our culture is steeped in unconscious attitudes and beliefs about gender characteristics, a condition reflected in our use of words.

Every human society has recognized the relationship between power and naming: that the *act of naming* confers power over the thing named. In the Book of Genesis, Adam named all the animals and was given dominion over them, and then, later, the story says "Adam called his wife's name Eve." Those who have the power to name and define other things—animals, wives, whatever—inevitably take themselves as the norm or standard, the measure of all things.

English is androcentric because for centuries it has been evolving in a society where men have been dominant. They were the ones in charge of the major social institutions: government, law, commerce, education, religion. They shaped the course of history and were the subjects of history. It's natural that the languages of patriarchal societies should come to express a male-centered view. That's basic anthropology. Anthropologists know that the single best way to understand the culture of any society is to study the lexicon of its language: a people's words reflect their reality. But the question is: whose reality? The English language still reflects a world in which the power to define gender characteristics is a male prerogative.

From *The Exchange,* Association of American University Professors (No. 62, Fall 1990). Excerpted from a talk given at the AAUP annual meeting on June 26, 1990.

We all know that English contains a variety of words that identify and emphasize difference between the sexes. A number of English words actually express polarization of the sexes. Never mind that beyond having one or the other set of biological features necessary for reproduction, every individual is distinct in personality, combining in a unique way those polarized qualities called "masculine" and "feminine." Never mind that virtually no one fits the mold at either pole. It remains a cherished precept of our culture, semantically underlined in our lexicon and embraced by the purveyors of every commodity imaginable, that the sexes must be thought of as opposite.

Female-Negative-Trivial

5   This linguistic syndrome can be described as "female-negative-trivial" on the one hand, and "male-positive-important" on the other. If that strikes you as overly exaggerated, consider for a moment a group of people who are *not* in charge of the English language—that is, lexicographers—and the definitions they have come up with for a pair of words which relate to gender—the words *manly* and *womanly*. These definitions are from the most recently updated edition of *Webster's Third New International Dictionary* (copyright 1986).

> **Manly** 1. a: having qualities appropriate to a man: not effeminate or timorous: bold, resolute, and open in conduct or bearing . . . b. (1): belonging to or appropriate in character to man [*and they give as examples*] "manly sports," "beer is a manly drink," and "a big booming manly voice." (2): of undaunted courage: gallant, brave [*and among the quotations they give as examples*] "it seemed a big manly thing to say" and "a manly disregard of his enemies" . . .

Now compare the same dictionary's definition of *womanly*, remembering that lexicographers base their definitions on hundreds of examples of usage that have appeared in print.

> **Womanly** 1: marked by qualities characteristic of a woman, esp. marked by qualities becoming a well-balanced adult woman [*and their examples are*] "womanly manners" and "womanly advice." 2: possessed of the character or behavior befitting a grown woman: no longer childish or girlish: becoming to a grown woman [*and their example is from Charles Dickens*] "a little girl wearing a womanly sort of bonnet much too large for her" 3: characteristic of, belonging to, or suitable to women: conforming to or motivated by a woman's nature and attitudes rather than a man's. [*The first example here is*] "convinced that drawing was a waste of time, if not downright womanly, like painting on China." [*And another example*] "her usual womanly volubility."

What are these two supposedly parallel entries telling us? They're saying that in addition to defining characteristics appropriate to a man, like vocal pitch, *manly* is synonymous with admirable qualities that all of us might wish we had. "Bold, resolute, open in conduct or bearing; of undaunted courage, gallant, brave." And where is the list of comparable synonyms for *womanly?* There aren't any. Instead, *womanly* is defined only in a circular way—through characteristics seen to be appropriate or inappropriate to women, not to human beings in general. And the examples of usage cited give a pretty good picture of what is considered appropriate to, or characteristic of, a well-balanced adult woman: she's concerned with manners, advice, and hat styles (as distinguished from sports and beer, which are felt to be manly); she wastes time in trivial pursuits like painting on china; and she talks too much.

The Slippery Slope

Most writers and editors today recognize that the female-negative-trivial syndrome is clearly evident in the use of so-called feminine suffixes with nouns of common gender. In 1990 no publishable author would identify someone as "a poetess," except in ridicule. (Adrienne Rich says the word brings out the "terroristress" in her.) But respectable writers are still using *heroine, suffragette,* and *executrix* when referring to a hero, a suffragist, or an executor who is a woman.

These words illustrate what Douglas Hofstadter calls "the slippery slope" of meaning. In his book *Metamagical Themas,* Hofstadter shows diagramatically how the slippery slope works. A triangle represents the idea of, let's say, a heroic person. At one base angle of this triangle is the word *heroine,* representing the female heroic person. At the other base angle is the word *hero,* representing the male heroic person. And at the apex is the generic word, again *hero,* encompassing both. But because the *hero* at the apex and the *hero* at one base angle are identical in name, their separate meanings slip back and forth along one side of the triangle, the slippery slope. The meanings blend and absorb each other. They bond together on the slope. And *heroine,* at the other base angle, remains outside that bond.

Another word that comes to mind in this connection is *actress.* It's our impression that women performers in the theater and films today are tending more and more to refer to themselves and one another as "actors." It may be deliberate, conscious usage on the part of some. Considering that their union is called Actors Equity, and that they may have trained at Actors Studio, and performed at Actors Playhouse, they simply accept that the generic word for their profession is *actor.* But when this word appears in juxtaposition with *actress,* the generic meaning of *actor* is absorbed into the gender-specific meaning, and women are identified as nonactors, as being outside or marginal, in de Beauvoir's phrase, as "the other."

10   Many people will undoubtedly go on feeling that *actress* is a term without bias, but we would like to suggest that it is on its way to becoming archaic, or at least quaint, simply because people it has identified are abandoning it by a process that may be more visceral than cerebral. In a sense it's their word, it has defined them, and, whether intentionally or not, they are taking charge of it, perhaps dumping it. We'll see.

Because linguistic changes reflect changes in our ways of thinking, a living language is constantly being created and re-created by the people who speak it. Linguistic changes spring from nothing less than new perceptions of the world and of ourselves.

Obviously we all know that over time the "rules" of grammar have changed, and we know that words themselves change their meanings: they lose some and acquire others; new words come into existence and old ones disappear into that word heaven, the *Oxford English Dictionary*. Nevertheless, most people resist change, especially, it seems, changes in grammar and the meanings of words. What we tend to forget—or choose to forget—is that the only languages which don't change are the ones no one speaks any more, like classical Greek and Latin.

Take the narrowing process that turned the Old English word *man* into a synonym for "adult male human being." As long ago as 1752 the philosopher David Hume recognized how ambiguous that word had already become: "All men," he wrote, and then added, "both male and female." And you are probably familiar with the numerous experimental studies done in the last few years, primarily by psychologists and sociologists rather than linguists, which show that most native speakers of English simply do not conceptualize women and girls when they encounter *man* and *mankind* used generically. In fact the narrowing process is felt so strongly, at least at an existential level, that a growing number of women today strongly object to being subsumed under those male-gender terms. "We aren't men," they're saying; "we're women, and we're tired of being made invisible."

Yet despite women's objections, and despite the slippery, ambiguous nature of generic *man*, lots of people, especially formally educated people, have a hard time giving it up. They forget, it seems, that words have a power of their own—the power of taking over meaning. A writer starts out talking about the species as a whole and, more often than we'll ever know, ends up talking about males. Listen to this well-known author, for example, who was discussing aggressive behavior in human beings—all of us, *Homo sapiens*. "[M]an," he wrote, "can do several things which the animal cannot do. . . . Eventually, his vital interests are not only life, food, access to females, etc., but also values, symbols, institutions."

Resistance to Change and the Problem of Precision

It's probably helpful, once in a while, to look back at the way some   15
of the most familiar and accepted words in use today were greeted when they were newcomers.

Back in 1619, for example, the London schoolmaster Alexander Gil described what he called "the new mange in speaking and writing." What he was deploring was the introduction of newly coined, Latin-derived words to replace older English ones. According to him, the "new mange" included such terms as *virtue, justice, pity, compassion,* and *grace.* And he asked, "Whither have you banished those words our forefathers used for these new-fangled ones?" Alexander Gil was headmaster of St. Paul's school at the time, and it might be noted that one of his students was an eleven-year-old named John Milton who—fortunately—was not persuaded to reject Gil's "new-fangled" words.

And how about old terms that have lost favor, like the once-accepted use of the pronoun *they* with a singular referent, as in "If a person is born of a gloomy temper, they cannot help it." That was written in 1759 by none other than the very correct, well-educated British statesman, Lord Chesterfield. However, since most academics are not yet ready to revive that convenient usage—despite precedents ranging from Shakespeare to Shaw—it still isn't surprising to come across a recently published book about, let's say, the psychology of children, in which the distinguished author uses *he* and its inflected forms as all-purpose pronouns, leaving readers to guess whether a particular problem or development applies to boys only or to children of both sexes. We submit that such writing is not just unfortunate. It's inexcusable.

These days more and more writers acknowledge that *he* used generically is, like *man* used generically, both ambiguous and insidious, and they take the time and trouble to write more precisely. But sometimes, even after several polite but probably exhausting battles between author and editor, all the author will agree to do is add a disclaimer. Disclaimers can be helpful, of course (for example, those providing guidance as to what a writer of some previous century may have meant by a now-ambiguous term). More often, however, they are nothing but excuses for sloppiness.

There is also an element here which we don't think should be ignored: the deep if often unacknowledged *psychological* impact of the grammatical "rule" mandating masculine-gender pronouns for indefinite referents. As long ago as the 1950s, Lynn White, Jr., then the president of

Mills College, described with great perception the harm that rule can do to children when he wrote:

> The penetration of this habit of language into the minds of little girls as they grow up to be women is more profound than most people, including most women, have recognized; for it implies that personality is really a male attribute, and that women are a human subspecies. . . . It would be a miracle if a girl-baby, learning to use the symbols of our tongue, could escape some unverbalized wound to her self-respect; whereas a boy-baby's ego is bolstered by the pattern of our language.

20   Obviously many literate men (and some literate women) must find the truth of White's perception difficult to accept, or we wouldn't still be battling the generic use of masculine-gender pronouns. But since accuracy and precision are what we're talking about today, let us ask this question: what is one to make of a scholar—a professor of communications with a special interest in semantics, as a matter of fact—who dismissed the problem of sexist language as follows: "I tend to avoid 'gender-exclusive' words," he wrote, "except when in so doing, I would injure the rhythm of a sentence."

Has it never occurred to him that in writing a sentence, any sentence, he must choose both its words and the way those words, in their infinite variety, are put together? That the choice isn't between exclusionary language on the one hand and rhythm on the other? (Surely it's possible to write with style and still communicate accurately what it is you want to say.) The choice is between settling for an ambiguous or inaccurate term because it "sounds good"—and finding the exact combination of words to convey one's message with clarity and precision. It seems to us that editors have every right to expect nothing less than the latter.

English is a vigorously alive tongue, and it reflects a vigorously alive, dynamic society that is capable of identifying its ills and thereby trying to cope with them. Neither the term *sexism* nor the term *racism* existed fifty years ago—which, as you know, isn't the same as saying that the attitudes and practices they define didn't exist before; of course they did. But those attitudes and practices came to be widely examined and questioned, and finally to be widely acknowledged within the dominant culture, only after they were put into words.

Without precision, language can betray everything we stand for. As George Orwell put it in his essay "Politics and the English Language," we must "Let the meaning choose the word and not the other way about." And Orwell went on, "In prose the worst thing you can do with words is surrender to them."

With George Orwell giving us courage, may we be so bold, in closing, as to adapt his wisdom to the occasion by adding this final thought? In publishing, the worst thing you can do is surrender to some tyrannical author who lets the *word* choose the *meaning* rather than the other way about.

H. L. Mencken

GAMALIELESE[1]

On the question of the logical content of Dr. Harding's harangue of last Friday I do not presume to have views. The matter has been debated at great length by the editorial writers of the Republic, all of them experts in logic; moreover, I confess to being prejudiced. When a man arises publicly to argue that the United States entered the late war because of a "concern for preserved civilization," I can only snicker in a superior way and wonder why he isn't holding down the chair of history in some American university. When he says that the U.S. has "never sought territorial aggrandizement through force," the snicker rises to the virulence of a chuckle, and I turn to the first volume of General Grant's memoirs.[2] And when, gaining momentum, he gravely informs the boobery that "ours is a constitutional freedom where the popular will is supreme, and minorities are sacredly protected," then I abandon myself to a mirth that transcends, perhaps, the seemly, and send picture post-cards of A. Mitchell Palmer,[3] and the Atlanta Penitentiary to all of my enemies who happen to be Socialists.

But when it comes to the style of a great man's discourse, I can speak with a great deal less prejudice, and maybe with somewhat more competence, for I have earned most of my livelihood for twenty years past by translating the bad English of a multitude of authors into measurably better English. Thus qualified professionally, I rise to pay my small tribute to Dr. Harding. Setting aside a college professor or two and half a dozen dipsomaniacal newspaper reporters, he takes the first place in my Valhall of literati. That is to say, he writes the worst English that I have ever encountered. It reminds me of a string of wet sponges; it reminds me of tattered washing on the line; it reminds me of a stale bean-soup, of college yells, of dogs barking idiotically through endless

First printed in the *Baltimore Sun* (Mar. 7, 1921).

1. Gamaliel was President Warren Harding's middle name, here nominalized to identify his oratorical style.
2. Dealing with the Mexican-American War (1846–48), in some respects a land-grabbing venture.
3. Palmer, U.S. attorney general (1919–21), initiator of the "Palmer Raids" in which thousands of alleged subversives were arrested for deportation.

nights. It is so bad that a sort of grandeur creeps into it. It drags itself out of the dark abysm (I was about to write abscess!) of pish, and crawls insanely up the topmost pinnacle of posh. It is rumble and bumble. It is flap and doodle. It is balder and dash.

But I grow lyrical. More scientifically, what is the matter with it? Why does it seem so flabby, so banal, so confused and childish, so stupidly at war with sense? If you first read the inaugural address and then heard it intoned, as I did (at least in part), then you will perhaps arrive at an answer. That answer is very simple. When Dr. Harding prepares a speech he does not think it out in terms of an educated reader locked up in jail, but in terms of a great horde of stoneheads gathered around a stand. That is to say, the thing is always a stump speech; it is conceived as a stump speech and written as a stump speech. More, it is a stump speech addressed primarily to the sort of audience that the speaker has been used to all his life, to wit, an audience of small town yokels, of low political serfs, or morons scarcely able to understand a word of more than two syllables, and wholly unable to pursue a logical idea for more than two centimeters.

Such imbeciles do not want ideas—that is, new ideas, ideas that are unfamiliar, ideas that challenge their attention. What they want is simply a gaudy series of platitudes, of threadbare phrases terrifically repeated, of sonorous nonsense driven home with gestures. As I say, they can't understand many words of more than two syllables, but that is not saying that they do not esteem such words. On the contrary, they like them and demand them. The roll of incomprehensible polysyllables enchants them. They like phrases which thunder like salvos of artillery. Let that thunder sound, and they take all the rest on trust. If a sentence begins furiously and then peters out into fatuity, they are still satisfied. If a phrase has a punch in it, they do not ask that it also have a meaning. If a word slides off the tongue like a ship going down the ways, they are content and applaud it and wait for the next.

Brought up amid such hinds, trained by long practice to engage and delight them, Dr. Harding carries over his stump manner into everything he writes. He is, perhaps, too old to learn a better way. He is, more likely, too discreet to experiment. The stump speech, put into cold type, maketh the judicious to grieve. But roared from an actual stump, with arms flying and eyes flashing and the old flag overhead, it is certainly and brilliantly effective. Read the inaugural address, and it will gag you. But hear it recited through a sound-magnifier, with grand gestures to ram home its periods, and you will begin to understand it.

Let us turn to a specific example. I exhume a sentence from the latter half of the eminent orator's discourse:

"I would like government to do all it can to mitigate; then, in understanding, in mutuality of interest, in concern for the common good, our tasks will be solved."

I assume that you have read it. I also assume that you set it down as idiotic—a series of words without sense. You are quite right; it is. But now imagine it intoned as it was designed to be intoned. Imagine the slow tempo of a public speech. Imagine the stately unrolling of the first clause, the delicate pause upon the word "then"—and then the loud discharge of the phrases "in understanding," "in mutuality of interest," "in concern for the common good," each with its attendant glare and roll of the eyes, each with its sublime heave, each with its gesture of a blacksmith bringing down his sledge upon an egg—imagine all this, and then ask yourself where you have got. You have got, in brief, to a point where you don't know what it is all about. You hear and applaud the phrases, but their connection has already escaped you. And so, when in violation of all sequence and logic, the final phrase, "our tasks will be solved," assaults you, you do not notice its disharmony—all you notice is that, if this or that, already forgotten, is done, "our tasks will be solved." Whereupon, glad of the assurance and thrilled by the vast gestures that drive it home, you give a cheer.

That is, if you are the sort of man who goes to political meetings, which is to say, if you are the sort of man that Dr. Harding is used to talking to, which is to say, if you are a jackass.

The whole inaugural address reeked with just such nonsense. The thing started off with an error in English in its very first sentence—the confusion of pronouns in the *one-he* combination, so beloved of bad newspaper reporters. It bristled with words misused; *civic* for *civil*, *luring* for *alluring*, *womanhood* for *women*, *referendum* for *reference*, even *task* for *problem*. "The *task* is to be *solved* "—what could be worse? Yet I find it twice. "The expressed views of world opinion"— what irritating tautology! "The expressed conscience of progress"— what on earth does it mean? "This is not selfishness, it is sanctity"— what intelligible idea do you get out of that? "I know that Congress and the administration will favor every wise government policy to aid the resumption and encourage continued progress"—the resumption of what? "Service is the supreme *commitment* of life"—*ach, du heiliger!* [4]

But is such bosh out of place in a stump speech? Obviously not. It is precisely and thoroughly in place in a stump speech. A tight fabric of ideas would weary and exasperate the audience; what it wants is simply a loud burble of words, a procession of phrases that roar, a series of whoops. This is what it got in the inaugural address of the Hon. Warren Gamaliel Harding. And this is what it will get for four long years—unless God sends a miracle and the corruptible puts on incorruption . . . Almost I long for the sweeter song, the rubber-stamps of more familiar design, the gentler and more seemly bosh of the late Woodrow.

4. "Good Lord!"

THE READER

1. *What are the particular qualities of "Gamalielese," as Mencken uses the term? What are Mencken's specific objections to Gamalielese? Why, if it works so well as a political speech, should we care if the English isn't too good? Mencken says he is talking about the style rather than the content, but what does style matter except to people like Mencken and English teachers and language cops?*

2. *Mencken writes, "When a man arises publicly to argue that the United States entered the late war because of a 'concern for preserved civilization,' I can only snicker in a superior way and wonder why he isn't holding down the chair of history in some American university" (p. 369). In this sentence, Mencken is fighting on two fronts at once. What are the two objects of his attack? Why in his essay does he use "Dr. Harding" for "President Harding"?*

3. *Mencken characterizes President Harding's usual audience as "stone-heads," "yokels," "serfs," "morons," "imbeciles," and "hinds." Is this a fair characterization of the American public? Should Mencken have used euphemisms?*

THE WRITER

1. *What is the purpose of Mencken's essay? What is its tone? How would you describe its intended audience?*

2. *Write a brief essay explaining the following poem by e. e. cummings. Is the characterization of President Harding and his style similar to that in Mencken's characterization?*

XXVII

the first president to be loved by his
bitterest enemies" is dead

the only man woman or child who wrote
a simple declarative sentence with seven grammatical
errors "is dead"
beautiful Warren Gamaliel Harding
"is" dead
he's
"dead"
if he wouldn't have eaten them Yapanese Craps

somebody might hardly never have not been
                    unsorry,perhaps

—E. E. Cummings, from *ViVa*, 1931

Richard Mitchell

THE VOICE OF SISERA

The invention of discursive prose liberated the mind of man from the limitations of the individual's memory. We can now "know" not just what we can store in our heads, and, as often as not, misplace among the memorabilia and used slogans. Nevertheless, that invention made concrete and permanent one of the less attractive facts of language. It called forth a new "mode" of language and provided yet another way in which to distinguish social classes from one another.

Fleeing the lost battle on the plain of Megiddo, General Sisera is said to have stopped off at the tent of Heber the Kenite.[1] Heber himself was out, but his wife, Jael, was home and happy to offer the sweaty warrior a refreshing drink—"a bottle of milk" in fact, the Bible says. (That seems to find something in translation.) It was a kindly and generous gesture, especially since Sisera asked nothing more than a drink of water.

Having drunk his fill, the tired Sisera stretched out for a little nap and told Jael to keep careful watch, for he had good reason to expect that the Jews who had cut up his army that day were probably looking around for him. Jael said, Sure, sure, don't worry, and when Sisera fell asleep, that crafty lady took a hammer and a tent spike and nailed him through the temples fast to the earth.

I suppose that we are meant to conclude that the Kenites, not themselves Jews, were nevertheless right-thinking folk and that Jael's act had a meaning that was both political and religious. I'm not so sure. I'd like to know, before deciding, just what language it was that Sisera used when he asked for that drink of water.

Scholars think that Sisera was probably the leader of an invading Hittite army, but the details are not important. What is important is that he was obviously a would-be conqueror in a land not his own. He had, until quite recently, been successful; he had come a long way with his iron chariots, powerful weapons that the Jews lacked and that would have won yet another battle if it hadn't been for a spell of bad weather. He was a successful foreign invader from a technologically superior culture. Can you suppose that he felt any obligation or even curious desire to learn the language of the Jews? Wouldn't they have seemed to him just another bunch of local primitives, in no important way to be distinguished from other such bunches he had already overcome? As

5

Chapter 4 of *Less Than Words Can Say* (1979).

1. The story is told in Judges iv–v.

for the tent-dwelling Kenites, a meager clan of impoverished nomads, who would ever bother to learn their ignorant babble? I'm willing to bet a brand-new Fowler[2] against a D minus freshman theme that Sisera spoke to Jael in his language, not hers, and loudly. With gestures. What Jael did, a little later, was actually an early example of linguistic consciousness-raising. Hers, not his.

Now, your typical American tourist in Naples doesn't usually get a wooden spike through his head for shouting pidgin English at the natives—a little diarrhea, maybe, but that's about it. Roman legionnaires in Gaul, however, and British soldiers in India did get some of each, once in a while. Conquered peoples hate, along with everything else about them, the language of the conquerors, and with good reason, for the language is itself a weapon. It keeps the vanquished in the dark about meanings and intentions, and it makes it extremely difficult to obey commands that had damn well better be obeyed, and *schnell*, too. Whatever it was that Sisera said to Jael that afternoon, it must have had something like the emotional effect of *"Juden heraus!"*[3] shouted in the streets of a small village in eastern Poland.

History is rich in examples of Siseranism. The language of the Cro-Magnons must have had upon the Neanderthals the same effect as Norman French had upon the English after 1066. Furthermore, it isn't only the victors and the vanquished who dwell together speaking different tongues. The war doesn't really go on forever. When the fighting is over—for a while—the victors and the vanquished often settle down to become the rulers and the ruled. They continue to speak different languages. Their languages may in time merge and become one, but they will still find a way to speak different languages. That is the case with us.

The arrangement offers some advantages on both sides. The powerful can write the laws and the rules in their own language so that the weak come before the courts and the commissions at a double disadvantage. (You'll see what that means when they audit your tax return.) The ruling class also becomes the "better" class, and its language must be the language of literature and philosophy and science and all the gentle arts. The subjects, whose language is deemed insufficiently elegant or complex to express such matters, are thus excluded from the business of the intellect in all its forms and relegated to tradecraft and handiwork, for which their rudimentary babble is just about good enough. On the other hand, the rudimentary babble of the riffraff is, after all, a language that the rulers don't, and generally don't care to, understand. The language of the subjects serves them as a form of "secret" talking, so that servants

2. The influential *Dictionary of Modern English Usage* (1st ed., 1926) by Henry Watson Fowler (1858–1933), English lexicographer.

3. "Jews [come] out!" A Nazi command preceding and during World War II.

can mutter, not quite inaudibly, appropriate comments on the lord and his lady. It's the same kind of revenge that schoolboys used to take by learning fluent, rapid pig latin to use in the presence of pompous and pedantic masters.

The linguistic distinction between the rulers and the ruled seems so right, especially to the rulers, that where it doesn't occur naturally it gets invented. Thus the upper classes in Russia in the times of the czars were put to the trouble of learning French, a more "civilized" tongue, and reserved their Russian for speaking to servants, very small children, and domestic animals. Thus the French upper classes from time to time have gone through paroxysms of tortured elegance in language in order to distinguish themselves yet further from their inferiors. It would have seemed reasonable, and handsomely symmetrical, too, for the French aristocrats to have learned Russian, saving their French for servants, very small children, and domestic animals, but your standard everyday French aristocrat would rather drink out of his fingerbowl than learn a barbarous babble like Russian. It's interesting to notice that in both those cultures certain linguistic distinctions were ultimately obliterated, at least for a while, by bloody revolutions. True, there may have been some other causes as well, but these little lessons of history should cause at least an occasional sleepless night for those of our rulers who like to speak in a language not understood by the people.

We don't have two languages, of course, so those who rule us have the same problem that once troubled the French aristocracy. They have to devise an elaborate language-within-a-language that we can understand only sometimes and even then uncertainly. It is a mistake to think that the language of the bureaucrats is merely an ignorant, garbled jargon. They may not always know what they are doing, but what they are doing is not haphazard. It works, too.

We like to make jokes, for instance, about the language of the tax forms. Heh heh, we chuckle, ain't them bureaucrats a caution? Just listen to this here, Madge. Them bureaucrats, however, don't chuckle at all, and if you'd like to see just what the term "stony silence" really means, try chuckling at their jargon when they haul you down to the tax office to ask how you managed to afford that cabin cruiser. Even your own lawyer will start looking around for some lint to pick off his trousers.

And as long as we have a lawyer in view, ain't they something? We read with pitying shakes of the head the disclaimers and demurrers at the bottom of the contract. We like to imagine that we, just plain folks, are somehow, deep down where it really counts, superior to those pointy-headed word-mongers with all their hereinafters. Nevertheless, we do what they tell us to do. We always remember that if we can't figure out from their language what we're required to do, and if we therefore fail to do it, it isn't the writers of the jargon who will be called to account.

Our sense of superiority is an illusion, a convenient illusion from some-body's point of view; in fact, when we read the contract, we are afraid. It is the intent of that language to make us afraid. It works. Now *that* is effective writing.

Imagine that the postman brings you a letter from the Water and Sewer Department or the Bureau of Mines or some such place. Any right-thinking American will eye even the envelope in the same way he would eye some sticky substance dripping from the underparts of his automobile. Things get worse. You open the letter and see at once these words: "You are hereby notified . . ." How do you feel? Are you keen to read on? But you will, won't you? Oh, yes. You will.

Here comes another letter. This one doesn't even have a stamp. It carries instead the hint that something very bad will happen to any mere citizen caught using this envelope for his own subversive purposes. You open it and read: "It has been brought to the attention of this office . . ." Do you throw it out at that point because you find it too preposter-ous to think that an office can have an attention? Do you immediately write a reply: "Dear So-and-so, I am surprised and distressed by the rudeness of your first ten words, especially since they are addressed to one of those who pay your salary. Perhaps you're having a bad day. Why don't you write again and say something else?" You do not. In fact, you turn pale and wonder frantically which of your misdeeds has been revealed. Your anxiety is increased by that passive verb—that's what it's for—which suggests that this damaging exposure has been made not by an envious neighbor or a vengeful merchant or an ex-girlfriend or any other perfectly understandable, if detestable, human agent, but by the very nature of the universe. "It has been brought." This is serious.

15   Among the better class of Grammarians, that construction is known as the Divine Passive. It intends to suggest that neither the writer nor anyone else through whose head you might like to hammer a blunt wooden spike can be held accountable for anything in any way. Like an earthquake or a volcanic eruption, this latest calamity must be accepted as an act of God. God may well be keeping count of the appearances of the Divine Passive.

Another classic intimidation with which to begin a letter is: "Accord-ing to our records . . ." It reminds you at once, with that plural pronoun, that the enemy outnumbers you, and the reference to "records" makes it clear that they've got the goods. There is even a lofty pretense to fairness, as though you were being invited to bring forth *your* records to clear up this misunderstanding. You know, however, that they don't suspect for an instant that there's anything wrong in their records. Besides, you don't *have* any records, as they damn well know.

Such frightening phrases share an important attribute. They are not things that ordinary people are likely to say, or even write, to one another except, of course, in certain unpleasant circumstances. We can see their intentions when we put them into more human contexts: "My dear Belinda, You are hereby notified . . ." conveys a message that ought to infuriate even the dullest of Belindas. Why is it then that we are not infuriated when we hear or read such words addressed to us by bureaucrats? We don't even stop to think that those words make up a silly verbal paradox; the only context in which they can possibly appear is the one in which they are not needed at all. No meaning is added to "Your rent is overdue" when the landlord writes, "You are hereby notified that your rent is overdue." What *is* added is the tone of official legality, and the presumption that one of the rulers is addressing one of the ruled. The voice of Sisera puts you in your place, and, strangely enough, you go there.

We Americans make much of our egalitarian society, and we like to think we are not intimidated by wealth and power. Still, we are. There are surely many reasons for that, and about most of them we can do nothing, it seems. But one of the reasons is the very language in which the wealthy and powerful speak to us. When we hear it, something ancient stirs in us, and we take off our caps and hold them to our chests as we listen. About *that* we *could* do something—all it takes is some education. That must have been in Jefferson's mind when he thought about the importance of universal education in a society of free people. People who are automatically and unconsciously intimidated by the sound of a language that they cannot themselves use easily will never be free. Jefferson must have imagined an America in which all citizens would be able, when they felt like it, to address one another as members of the same class. That we cannot do so is a sore impediment to equality, but, of course, a great advantage to those who *can* use the English of power and wealth.

It would be easier to see bureaucratic language for what it is if only the governors and bureaucrats did in fact speak a foreign tongue. When the Normans ruled England anyone could tell the French was French and English, English. It was the government that might, rarely, pardon you for your crimes, but it needed a friend to forgive you for your sins. Words like "pardon" and "forgive" were clearly in different languages, and, while either might have been translated by the other, they still meant subtly different acts. They still do, even though they are both thought of as English words now. Modern English has swallowed up many such distinctions, but not all. We still know that hearts are broken, not fractured. This is the kind of distinction Winston Churchill had in mind when he advised writers to choose the native English word whenever possible rather than a foreign import. This is good advice, but few can heed it in these days. The standard American education does not provide the knowledge out of which to make such choices.

THE READER

1. Mitchell makes a rather unusual application of an Old Testament story to present-day affairs. What exactly does he mean by "the voice of Sisera"?
2. Occasionally Mitchell slips abruptly into a different level of usage, as in "Heh heh, we chuckle, ain't them bureaucrats a caution? Just listen to this here, Madge." Identify two or three other such instances and explain the effect Mitchell is trying for. Does he achieve it?
3. Mitchell gives us three examples of bureaucratic language: "You are hereby notified . . ." (p. 376), "It has been brought to the attention of this office . . ." (p. 376), and "According to our records . . ." (p. 376). What do these examples have in common? Can you recall (or perhaps invent) similar examples?

THE WRITER

1. Imagine a bureaucratic directive ordering you to do something and threatening you with unpleasant consequences if you are remiss. Then write a noncomplying reply that turns the language of the directive back on the sender.
2. Mitchell points out that "No meaning is added to 'Your rent is overdue' when the landlord writes, 'You are hereby notified that your rent is overdue.'" What is added, he says, is the presumption of a relationship: "one of the rulers is addressing one of the ruled." Think of other ways of using language primarily to establish a relationship rather than to convey meaning—to imply submissiveness, for example. Then write a paragraph illustrating such a use.
3. According to Mitchell, a letter beginning " 'My dear Belinda, You are hereby notified . . .' conveys a message that ought to infuriate even the dullest of Belindas." But one can imagine a letter in which such a beginning, along with what follows, might arouse Belinda's laughter rather than fury. Write that letter.

Gloria Naylor

"MOMMY, WHAT DOES 'NIGGER' MEAN?"

Language is the subject. It is the written form with which I've managed to keep the wolf away from the door and, in diaries, to keep my sanity. In spite of this, I consider the written word inferior to the

Originally appeared as a "Hers" column in the *New York Times* (Feb. 20, 1986).

spoken, and much of the frustration experienced by novelists is the awareness that whatever we manage to capture in even the most transcendent passages falls far short of the richness of life. Dialogue achieves its power in the dynamics of a fleeting moment of sight, sound, smell and touch.

I'm not going to enter the debate here about whether it is language that shapes reality or vice versa. That battle is doomed to be waged whenever we seek intermittent reprieve from the chicken and egg dispute. I will simply take the position that the spoken word, like the written word, amounts to a nonsensical arrangement of sounds or letters without a consensus that assigns "meaning." And building from the meanings of what we hear, we order reality. Words themselves are innocuous; it is the consensus that gives them true power.

I remember the first time I heard the word nigger. In my third-grade class, our math tests were being passed down the rows, and as I handed the papers to a little boy in back of me, I remarked that once again he had received a much lower mark than I did. He snatched his test from me and spit out that word. Had he called me a nymphomaniac or a necrophiliac, I couldn't have been more puzzled. I didn't know what a nigger was, but I knew that whatever it meant, it was something he shouldn't have called me. This was verified when I raised my hand, and in a loud voice repeated what he had said and watched the teacher scold him for using a "bad" word. I was later to go home and ask the inevitable question that every black parent must face—"Mommy, what does 'nigger' mean?"

And what exactly did it mean? Thinking back, I realize that this could not have been the first time the word was used in my presence. I was part of a large extended family that had migrated from the rural South after World War II and formed a close-knit network that gravitated around my maternal grandparents. Their ground-floor apartment in one of the buildings they owned in Harlem was a weekend mecca for my immediate family, along with countless aunts, uncles and cousins who brought along assorted friends. It was a bustling and open house with assorted neighbors and tenants popping in and out to exchange bits of gossip, pick up an old quarrel or referee the ongoing checkers game in which my grandmother cheated shamelessly. They were all there to let down their hair and put up their feet after a week of labor in the factories, laundries and shipyards of New York.

Amid the clamor, which could reach deafening proportions—two or three conversations going on simultaneously, punctuated by the sound of a baby's crying somewhere in the back rooms or out on the street— there was still a rigid set of rules about what was said and how. Older children were sent out of the living room when it was time to get into

5

the juicy details about "you-know-who" up on the third floor who had
gone and gotten herself "p-r-e-g-n-a-n-t!" But my parents, knowing that
I could spell well beyond my years, always demanded that I follow the
others out to play. Beyond sexual misconduct and death, everything else
was considered harmless for our young ears. And so among the anecdotes
of the triumphs and disappointments in the various workings of their
lives, the word nigger was used in my presence, but it was set within
contexts and inflections that caused it to register in my mind as something else.

In the singular, the word was always applied to a man who had
distinguished himself in some situation that brought their approval for
his strength, intelligence or drive:

"Did Johnny really do that?"

"I'm telling you, that nigger pulled in $6,000 of overtime last year.
Said he got enough for a down payment on a house."

When used with a possessive adjective by a woman—"my nigger"—it
became a term of endearment for husband or boyfriend. But it could
be more than just a term applied to a man. In their mouths it became
the pure essence of manhood—a disembodied force that channeled their
past history of struggle and present survival against the odds into a
victorious statement of being: "Yeah, that old foreman found out quick
enough—you don't mess with a nigger."

10   In the plural, it became a description of some group within the
community that had overstepped the bounds of decency as my family
defined it: Parents who neglected their children, a drunken couple who
fought in public, people who simply refused to look for work, those with
excessively dirty mouths or unkempt households were all "trifling niggers." This particular circle could forgive hard times, unemployment,
the occasional bout of depression—they had gone through all of that
themselves—but the unforgivable sin was lack of self-respect.

A woman could never be a "nigger" in the singular, with its connotation of confirming worth. The noun girl was its closest equivalent in that
sense, but only when used in direct address and regardless of the gender
doing the addressing. "Girl" was a token of respect for a woman. The
one-syllable word was drawn out to sound like three in recognition of
the extra ounce of wit, nerve or daring that the woman had shown in
the situation under discussion.

"G-i-r-l, stop. You mean you said that to his face?"

But if the word was used in a third-person reference or shortened so
that it almost snapped out of the mouth, it always involved some element of communal disapproval. And age became an important factor in
these exchanges. It was only between individuals of the same generation,
or from an older person to a younger (but never the other way around),
that "girl" would be considered a compliment.

I don't agree with the argument that use of the word nigger at this social stratum of the black community was an internalization of racism. The dynamics were the exact opposite: the people in my grandmother's living room took a word that whites used to signify worthlessness or degradation and rendered it impotent. Gathering there together, they transformed "nigger" to signify the varied and complex human beings they knew themselves to be. If the word was to disappear totally from the mouths of even the most liberal of white society, no one in that room was naïve enough to believe it would disappear from white minds. Meeting the word head-on, they proved it had absolutely nothing to do with the way they were determined to live their lives.

So there must have been dozens of times that the word "nigger" was spoken in front of me before I reached the third grade. But I didn't "hear" it until it was said by a small pair of lips that had already learned it could be a way to humiliate me. That was the word I went home and asked my mother about. And since she knew that I had to grow up in America, she took me in her lap and explained.

15

Maxine Hong Kingston

TONGUE-TIED

Long ago in China, knot-makers tied string into buttons and frogs, and rope into bell pulls. There was one knot so complicated that it blinded the knot-maker. Finally an emperor outlawed this cruel knot, and the nobles could not order it anymore. If I had lived in China, I would have been an outlaw knot-maker.

Maybe that's why my mother cut my tongue. She pushed my tongue up and sliced the frenum.[1] Or maybe she snipped it with a pair of nail scissors. I don't remember her doing it, only her telling me about it, but all during childhood I felt sorry for the baby whose mother waited with scissors or knife in hand for it to cry—and then, when its mouth was wide open like a baby bird's, cut. The Chinese say "a ready tongue is an evil."

I used to curl up my tongue in front of the mirror and tauten my frenum into a white line, itself as thin as a razor blade. I saw no scars in my mouth. I thought perhaps I had had two frena, and she had cut one. I made other children open their mouths so I could compare theirs

From *The Woman Warrior: Memoirs of a Girlhood among Ghosts* (1976)

1. The connecting fold of membrane on the underside of the tongue.

to mine. I saw perfect pink membranes stretching into precise edges that looked easy enough to cut. Sometimes I felt very proud that my mother committed such a powerful act upon me. At other times I was terrified—the first thing my mother did when she saw me was to cut my tongue.

"Why did you do that to me, Mother?"

"I told you."

"Tell me again."

"I cut it so that you would not be tongue-tied. Your tongue would be able to move in any language. You'll be able to speak languages that are completely different from one another. You'll be able to pronounce anything. Your frenum looked too tight to do those things, so I cut it."

"But isn't 'a ready tongue an evil'?"

"Things are different in this ghost country." [2]

"Did it hurt me? Did I cry and bleed?"

"I don't remember. Probably."

She didn't cut the other children's. When I asked cousins and other Chinese children whether their mothers had cut their tongues loose, they said, "What?"

"Why didn't you cut my brothers' and sisters' tongues?"

"They didn't need it."

"Why not? Were theirs longer than mine?"

"Why don't you quit blabbering and get to work?"

If my mother was not lying she should have cut more, scraped away the rest of the frenum skin, because I have a terrible time talking. Or she should not have cut at all, tampering with my speech. When I went to kindergarten and had to speak English for the first time, I became silent. A dumbness—a shame—still cracks my voice in two, even when I want to say "hello" casually, or ask an easy question in front of the check-out counter, or ask directions of a bus driver. I stand frozen, or I hold up the line with the complete, grammatical sentence that comes squeaking out at impossible length. "What did you say?" says the cab driver, or "Speak up," so I have to perform again, only weaker the second time. A telephone call makes my throat bleed and takes up that day's courage. It spoils my day with self-disgust when I hear my broken voice come skittering out into the open. It makes people wince to hear it. I'm getting better, though. Recently I asked the postman for special-issue stamps; I've waited since childhood for postmen to give me some of their own accord. I am making progress, a little every day.

My silence was thickest—total—during the three years that I covered my school paintings with black paint. I painted layers of black over

2. In Kingston's story, the Chinese immigrants see white Americans as "ghosts" whose language and values they must adopt in order to become American.

houses and flowers and suns, and when I drew on the blackboard, I put a layer of chalk on top. I was making a stage curtain, and it was the moment before the curtain parted or rose. The teachers called my parents to school, and I saw they had been saving my pictures, curling and cracking, all alike and black. The teachers pointed to the pictures and looked serious, talked seriously too, but my parents did not understand English. ("The parents and teachers of criminals were executed," said my father.) My parents took the pictures home. I spread them out (so black and full of possibilities) and pretended the curtains were swinging open, flying up, one after another, sunlight underneath, mighty operas.

During the first silent year I spoke to no one at school, did not ask before going to the lavatory, and flunked kindergarten. My sister also said nothing for three years, silent in the playground and silent at lunch. There were other quiet Chinese girls not of our family, but most of them got over it sooner than we did. I enjoyed the silence. At first it did not occur to me I was supposed to talk or to pass kindergarten. I talked at home and to one or two of the Chinese kids in class. I made motions and even made some jokes. I drank out of a toy saucer when the water spilled out of the cup, and everybody laughed, pointing at me, so I did it some more. I didn't know that Americans don't drink out of saucers.

I liked the Negro students (Black Ghosts) best because they laughed the loudest and talked to me as if I were a daring talker too. One of the Negro girls had her mother coil braids over her ears Shanghai-style like mine; we were Shanghai twins except that she was covered with black like my paintings. Two Negro kids enrolled in Chinese school, and the teachers gave them Chinese names. Some Negro kids walked me to school and home, protecting me from the Japanese kids, who hit me and chased me and stuck gum in my ears. The Japanese kids were noisy and tough. They appeared one day in kindergarten, released from concentration camp,[3] which was a tic-tac-toe mark, like barbed wire, on the map.

It was when I found out I had to talk that school became a misery, that the silence became a misery. I did not speak and felt bad each time that I did not speak. I read aloud in first grade, though, and heard the barest whisper with little squeaks come out of my throat. "Louder," said the teacher, who scared the voice away again. The other Chinese girls did not talk either, so I knew the silence had to do with being a Chinese girl.

Reading out loud was easier than speaking because we did not have to make up what to say, but I stopped often, and the teacher would think I'd gone quiet again. I could not understand "I." The Chinese "I" had

20

3. During World War II, more than 100,000 Japanese-Americans were imprisoned in "War Relocation Camps" in the United States.

seven strokes, intricacies. How could the American "I," assuredly wearing a hat like the Chinese, have only three strokes, the middle so straight? Was it out of politeness that this writer left off strokes the way a Chinese has to write her own name small and crooked? No, it was not politeness; "I" is a capital and "you" is a lower-case. I stared at that middle line and waited so long for its black center to resolve into tight strokes and dots that I forgot to pronounce it. The other troublesome word was "here," no strong consonant to hang on to, and so flat, when "here" is two mountainous ideographs. [4] The teacher, who had already told me every day how to read "I" and "here," put me in the low corner under the stairs again, where the noisy boys usually sat.

When my second grade class did a play, the whole class went to the auditorium except the Chinese girls. The teacher, lovely and Hawaiian, should have understood about us, but instead left us behind in the classroom. Our voices were too soft or nonexistent, and our parents never signed the permission slips anyway. They never signed anything unnecessary. We opened the door a crack and peeked out, but closed it again quickly. One of us (not me) won every spelling bee, though.

I remember telling the Hawaiian teacher, "We Chinese can't sing 'land where our fathers died.' " She argued with me about politics, while I meant because of curses. But how can I have that memory when I couldn't talk? My mother says that we, like the ghosts, have no memories.

After American school, we picked up our cigar boxes, in which we had arranged books, brushes, and an inkbox neatly, and went to Chinese school, from 5:00 to 7:30 P.M. There we chanted together, voices rising and falling, loud and soft, some boys shouting, everybody reading together, reciting together and not alone with one voice. When we had a memorization test, the teacher let each of us come to his desk and say the lesson to him privately, while the rest of the class practiced copying or tracing. Most of the teachers were men. The boys who were so well behaved in the American school played tricks on them and talked back to them. The girls were not mute. They screamed and yelled during recess, when there were no rules; they had fistfights. Nobody was afraid of children hurting themselves or of children hurting school property. The glass doors to the red and green balconies with the gold joy symbols were left wide open so that we could run out and climb the fire escapes. We played capture-the-flag in the auditorium, where Sun Yat-sen and Chiang Kai-shek's [5] pictures hung at the back of the stage, the Chinese flag on their left and the American flag on their right. We climbed the

4. Composite characters in Chinese writing made by combining two or more other characters for words of related meaning.
5. Sun Yat-sen (1866–1925) and his successor, Chiang Kai-shek (1888–1975), led the Guomindang (or Nationalist party) campaign to unify China in the 1920s and 1930s.

teak ceremonial chairs and made flying leaps off the stage. One flag headquarters was behind the glass door and the other on stage right. Our feet drummed on the hollow stage. During recess the teachers locked themselves up in their office with the shelves of books, copybooks, inks from China. They drank tea and warmed their hands at a stove. There was no play supervision. At recess we had the school to ourselves, and also we could roam as far as we could go—downtown, Chinatown stores, home—as long as we returned before the bell rang.

At exactly 7:30 the teacher again picked up the brass bell that sat on his desk and swung it over our heads, while we charged down the stairs, our cheering magnified in the stairwell. Nobody had to line up.

Not all of the children who were silent at American school found voice at Chinese school. One new teacher said each of us had to get up and recite in front of the class, who was to listen. My sister and I had memorized the lesson perfectly. We said it to each other at home, one chanting, one listening. The teacher called on my sister to recite first. It was the first time a teacher had called on the second-born to go first. My sister was scared. She glanced at me and looked away; I looked down at my desk. I hoped that she could do it because if she could, then I would have to. She opened her mouth and a voice came out that wasn't a whisper, but it wasn't a proper voice either. I hoped that she would not cry, fear breaking up her voice like twigs underfoot. She sounded as if she were trying to sing through weeping and strangling. She did not pause or stop to end the embarrassment. She kept going until she said the last word, and then she sat down. When it was my turn, the same voice came out, a crippled animal running on broken legs. You could hear splinters in my voice, bones rubbing jagged against one another. I was loud, though. I was glad I didn't whisper. There was one little girl who whispered.

Richard Rodriguez

ARIA

Supporters of bilingual education today imply that students like me miss a great deal by not being taught in their family's language. What they seem not to recognize is that, as a socially disadvantaged child, I considered Spanish to be a private language. What I needed to learn in school was that I had the right—and the obligation—to speak the public

From *Hunger of Memory: The Biography of Richard Rodriguez* (1982).

language of *los gringos*. [1] The odd truth is that my first-grade classmates could have become bilingual, in the conventional sense of that word, more easily than I. Had they been taught (as upper-middle-class children are often taught early) a second language like Spanish or French, they could have regarded it simply as that: another public language. In my case such bilingualism could not have been so quickly achieved. What I did not believe was that I could speak a single public language.

Without question, it would have pleased me to hear my teachers address me in Spanish when I entered the classroom. I would have felt much less afraid. I would have trusted them and responded with ease. But I would have delayed—for how long postponed?—having to learn the language of public society. I would have evaded—and for how long could I have afforded to delay?—learning the great lesson of school, that I had a public identity.

Fortunately, my teachers were unsentimental about their responsibility. What they understood was that I needed to speak a public language. So their voices would search me out, asking me questions. Each time I'd hear them, I'd look up in surprise to see a nun's face frowning at me. I'd mumble, not really meaning to answer. The nun would persist, "Richard, stand up. Don't look at the floor. Speak up. Speak to the entire class, not just to me!" But I couldn't believe that the English language was mine to use. (In part, I did not want to believe it.) I continued to mumble. I resisted the teacher's demands. (Did I somehow suspect that once I learned public language my pleasing family life would be changed?) Silent, waiting for the bell to sound, I remained dazed, diffident, afraid.

Because I wrongly imagined that English was intrinsically a public language and Spanish an intrinsically private one, I easily noted the difference between classroom language and the language of home. At school, words were directed to a general audience of listeners. ("Boys and girls.") Words were meaningfully ordered. And the point was not self-expression alone but to make oneself understood by many others. The teacher quizzed: "Boys and girls, why do we use that word in this sentence? Could we think of a better word to use there? Would the sentence change its meaning if the words were differently arranged? And wasn't there a better way of saying much the same thing?" (I couldn't say. I wouldn't try to say.)

Three months. Five. Half a year passed. Unsmiling, ever watchful, my teachers noted my silence. They began to connect my behavior with the difficult progress my older sister and brother were making. Until one Saturday morning three nuns arrived at the house to talk to our parents. Stiffly, they sat on the blue living room sofa. From the doorway of

5

1. Foreigners.

another room, spying the visitors, I noted the incongruity—the clash of two worlds, the faces and voices of school intruding upon the familiar setting of home. I overheard one voice gently wondering, "Do your children speak only Spanish at home, Mrs. Rodriguez?" While another voice added, "That Richard especially seems so timid and shy."

That Rich-heard!

With great tact the visitors continued, "Is it possible for you and your husband to encourage your children to practice their English when they are home?" Of course, my parents complied. What would they not do for their children's well-being? And how could they have questioned the Church's authority which those women represented? In an instant, they agreed to give up the language (the sounds) that had revealed and accentuated our family's closeness. The moment after the visitors left, the change was observed. "*Ahora*, speak to us *en inglés*,"[2] my father and mother united to tell us.

At first, it seemed a kind of game. After dinner each night, the family gathered to practice "our" English. (It was still then *inglés*, a language foreign to us, so we felt drawn as strangers to it.) Laughing, we would try to define words we could not pronounce. We played with strange English sounds, often overanglicizing our pronunciations. And we filled the smiling gaps of our sentences with familiar Spanish sounds. But that was cheating, somebody shouted. Everyone laughed. In school, meanwhile, like my brother and sister, I was required to attend a daily tutoring session. I needed a full year of special attention. I also needed my teachers to keep my attention from straying in class by calling out, *Rich-heard*—their English voices slowly prying loose my ties to my other name, its three notes, *Ri-car-do*. Most of all I needed to hear my mother and father speak to me in a moment of seriousness in broken—suddenly heartbreaking—English. The scene was inevitable: One Saturday morning I entered the kitchen where my parents were talking in Spanish. I did not realize that they were talking in Spanish however until, at the moment they saw me, I heard their voices change to speak English. Those *gringo* sounds they uttered startled me. Pushed me away. In that moment of trivial misunderstanding and profound insight, I felt my throat twisted by unsounded grief. I turned quickly and left the room. But I had no place to escape to with Spanish. (The spell was broken.) My brother and sisters were speaking English in another part of the house.

Again and again in the days following, increasingly angry, I was obliged to hear my mother and father: "Speak to us *en inglés*." (*Speak.*) Only then did I determine to learn classroom English. Weeks after, it happened: One day in school I raised my hand to volunteer an answer.

2. *"Now,* speak to us *in English."*

I spoke out in a loud voice. And I did not think it remarkable when the entire class understood. That day, I moved very far from the disadvantaged child I had been only days earlier. The belief, that calming assurance that I belonged in public, had at last taken hold.

10   Shortly after, I stopped hearing the high and loud sounds of *los gringos*. A more and more confident speaker of English, I didn't trouble to listen to *how* strangers sounded, speaking to me. And there simply were too many English-speaking people in my day for me to hear American accents anymore. Conversations quickened. Listening to persons who sounded eccentrically pitched voices, I usually noted their sounds for an initial few seconds before I concentrated on *what* they were saying. Conversations became content-full. Transparent. Hearing someone's *tone* of voice—angry or questioning or sarcastic or happy or sad—I didn't distinguish it from the words it expressed. Sound and word were thus tightly wedded. At the end of a day, I was often bemused, always relieved, to realize how "silent," though crowded with words, my day in public had been. (This public silence measured and quickened the change in my life.)

At last, seven years old, I came to believe what had been technically true since my birth: I was an American citizen.

But the special feeling of closeness at home was diminished by then. Gone was the desperate, urgent, intense feeling of being at home; rare was the experience of feeling myself individualized by family intimates. We remained a loving family, but one greatly changed. No longer so close; no longer bound tight by the pleasing and troubling knowledge of our public separateness. Neither my older brother nor sister rushed home after school anymore. Nor did I. When I arrived home there would often be neighborhood kids in the house. Or the house would be empty of sounds.

Following the dramatic Americanization of their children, even my parents grew more publicly confident. Especially my mother. She learned the names of all the people on our block. And she decided we needed to have a telephone installed in the house. My father continued to use the word *gringo*. But it was no longer charged with the old bitterness or distrust. (Stripped of any emotional content, the word simply became a name for those Americans not of Hispanic descent.) Hearing him, sometimes, I wasn't sure if he was pronouncing the Spanish word *gringo* or saying gringo in English.

Matching the silence I started hearing in public was a new quiet at home. The family's quiet was partly due to the fact that, as we children learned more and more English, we shared fewer and fewer words with our parents. Sentences needed to be spoken slowly when a child addressed his mother or father. (Often the parent wouldn't understand.) The child would need to repeat himself. (Still the parent misunderstood.) The young voice, frustrated, would end up saying, "Never mind"—the subject was closed. Dinners would be noisy with the clinking of knives and forks against dishes. My mother would smile softly between her remarks; my father at the other end of the table would chew and chew at his food, while he stared over the heads of his children.

My *mother!* My *father!* After English became my primary language, I no longer knew what words to use in addressing my parents. The old Spanish words (those tender accents of sound) I had used earlier—*mamá* and *papá*—I couldn't use anymore. They would have been too painful reminders of how much had changed in my life. On the other hand, the words I heard neighborhood kids call *their* parents seemed equally unsatisfactory. *Mother* and *Father; Ma, Papa, Pa, Dad, Pop* (how I hated the all American sound of that last word especially)—all these terms I felt were unsuitable, not really terms of address for *my* parents. As a result, I never used them at home. Whenever I'd speak to my parents, I would try to get their attention with eye contact alone, In public conversations, I'd refer to "my parents" or "my mother and father."

My mother and father, for their part, responded differently, as their children spoke to them less. She grew restless, seemed troubled and anxious at the scarcity of words exchanged in the house. It was she who would question me about my day when I came home from school. She smiled at small talk. She pried at the edges of my sentences to get me to say something more. (What?) She'd join conversations she overhead, but her intrusions often stopped her children's talking. By contrast, my father seemed reconciled to the new quiet. Though his English improved somewhat, he retired into silence. At dinner he spoke very little. One night his children and even his wife helplessly giggled at his garbled English pronunciation of the Catholic Grace before Meals. Thereafter he made his wife recite the prayer at the start of each meal, even on formal occasions, when there were guests in the house. Hers became the public voice of the family. On official business, it was she, not my father, one would usually hear on the phone or in stores, talking to strangers. His children grew so accustomed to his silence that, years later, they would speak routinely of his shyness. (My mother would often try to explain: Both his parents died when he was eight. He was raised by an uncle who treated him like little more than a menial servant. He was never encouraged to speak. He grew up alone. A man of few words.) But my father was not shy, I realized, when I'd watch him speaking Spanish with relatives. Using Spanish, he was quickly effusive. Especially when talking with other men, his voice would spark, flicker, flare alive with sounds. In Spanish, he expressed ideas and feelings he rarely revealed in English. With firm Spanish sounds, he conveyed confidence and authority English would never allow him.

The silence at home, however, was finally more than a literal silence.

15

Fewer words passed between parent and child, but more profound was the silence that resulted from my inattention to sounds. At about the time I no longer bothered to listen with care to the sounds of English in public, I grew careless about listening to the sounds family members made when they spoke. Most of the time I heard someone speaking at home and didn't distinguish his sounds from the words people uttered in public. I didn't even pay much attention to my parents' accented and ungrammatical speech. At least not at home. Only when I was with them in public would I grow alert to their accents. Though, even then, their sounds caused me less and less concern. For I was increasingly confident of my own public identity.

I would have been happier about my public success had I not sometimes recalled what it had been like earlier, when my family had conveyed its intimacy through a set of conveniently private sounds. Sometimes in public, hearing a stranger, I'd hark back to my past. A Mexican farmworker approached me downtown to ask directions to somewhere, *"¿Hijito . . . ?"*[3] he said. And his voice summoned deep longing. Another time, standing beside my mother in the visiting room of a Carmelite convent,[4] before the dense screen which rendered the nuns shadowy figures, I heard several Spanish-speaking nuns—their busy, singsong overlapping voices—assure us that yes, yes, we were remembered, all our family was remembered in their prayers. (Their voices echoed faraway family sounds.) Another day, a dark-faced old woman—her hand light on my shoulder—steadied herself against me as she boarded a bus. She murmured something I couldn't quite comprehend. Her Spanish voice came near, like the face of a never-before-seen relative in the instant before I was kissed. Her voice, like so many of the Spanish voices I'd hear in public, recalled the golden age of my youth. Hearing Spanish then, I continued to be a careful, if sad, listener to sounds. Hearing a Spanish-speaking family walking behind me, I turned to look. I smiled for an instant, before my glance found the Hispanic-looking faces of strangers in the crowd going by.

Today I hear bilingual educators say that children lose a degree of "individuality" by becoming assimilated into public society. (Bilingual schooling was popularized in the seventies, that decade when middle-class ethnics began to resist the process of assimilation—the American melting pot.) But the bilingualists simplistically scorn the value and necessity of assimilation. They do not seem to realize that there are *two* ways a person is individualized. So they do not realize that while one suffers a diminished sense of *private* individuality by becoming assimi-

3. "Little boy . . . ?"   Mount Carmel.
4. Of the Catholic Order of Our Lady of

lated into public society, such assimilation makes possible the achievement of *public* individuality.

The bilingualists insist that a student should be reminded of his   20
difference from others in mass society, his heritage. But they equate
mere separateness with individuality. The fact is that only in private—
with intimates—is separateness from the crowd a prerequisite for individuality. (An intimate draws me apart, tells me that I am unique,
unlike all others.) In public, by contrast, full individuality is achieved,
paradoxically, by those who are able to consider themselves members of
the crowd. Thus it happened for me: Only when I was able to think of
myself as an American, no longer an alien in *gringo* society, could I seek
the rights and opportunities necessary for full public individuality. The
social and political advantages I enjoy as a man result from the day that
I came to believe that my name, indeed, is *Rich-heard Road-ree-guess.*
It is true that my public society today is often impersonal. (My public
society is usually mass society). Yet despite the anonymity of the crowd
and despite the fact that the individuality I achieve in public is often
tenuous—because it depends on my being one in a crowd—I celebrate
the day I acquired my new name. Those middle-class ethnics who scorn
assimilation seem to me filled with decadent self-pity, obsessed by the
burden of public life. Dangerously, they romanticize public separateness
and they trivialize the dilemma of the socially disadvantaged.

My awkward childhood does not prove the necessity of bilingual
education. My story discloses instead an essential myth of childhood—
inevitable pain. If I rehearse here the changes in my private life after
my Americanization, it is finally to emphasize the public gain. The loss
implies the gain: The house I returned to each afternoon was quiet.
Intimate sounds no longer rushed to the door to greet me. There were
other noises inside. The telephone rang. Neighborhood kids ran past the
door of the bedroom where I was reading my schoolbooks—covered with
shopping-bag paper. Once I learned public language, it would never
again be easy for me to hear intimate family voices. More and more of
my day was spent hearing words. But that may only be a way of saying
that the day I raised my hand in class and spoke loudly to an entire
roomful of faces, my childhood started to end.

THE READER

1. *What did Rodriguez lose because his schooling was in English instead of in Spanish? What did he gain? Was there any pain connected
   with the loss and gain? Was it worth it?*
2. *Rodriguez writes of those "middle-class ethnics who scorn assimilation" that they seem to him "filled with decadent self-pity, obsessed
   by the burden of public life. Dangerously, they romanticize public*

separateness and they trivialize the dilemma of the socially disadvantaged." Explain what the terms and implications of this judgment are. Is it a fair judgment?

3. Could one argue from Rodriguez's view of the matter that encouragement or advocacy of bilingual education amounts to trying to ensure perpetual childhood for those schooled? If so, is Rodriguez's view a fair one? Is his position elitist? Is it bad to be elitist?

THE WRITER

1. What qualities does Rodriguez ascribe to private language? What is his tone in writing of these? What attitude has he toward them?
2. How does Rodriguez characterize the difference between private and public language? Does he show persuasively the need for public language? By what means does he seek to do this?
3. For Rodriguez, the private language is Spanish, the public English. Could similar considerations apply if both were different kinds of
⟨ English? Does the English you have learned at school differ from the English of your home and childhood? Do your parents, your friends, your teachers have different languages (all called "English")? Write an essay exploring your personal experience with private and public language.

Nancy Mairs

WHO ARE YOU?

In her stunning memoir of bicultural girlhood, *The Woman Warrior*, Maxine Hong Kingston writes, "There is a Chinese word for the female *I*—which is 'slave.' Break the women with their own tongues!" English contains no such dramatic instance of the ways in which language shapes women's reality. We can, after all, use the same "I" as men do. We can, but we're not supposed to, at least not often. In myriad ways the rules of polite discourse in this country serve, among other purposes, not to enslave but certainly to silence women and thus to prevent them from uttering the truth about their lives.

Seldom are such rules spoken out loud. Indeed, part of their force arises from their implicitness, which makes them seem natural and essential. They vary in detail, I think, from generation to generation,

Originally appeared in the *New York Times* (Aug. 13, 1987).

region to region, class to class, though they stifle communication in similiar ways.

Here, roughly put, are a few of the ones I've learned to obey in the company of men. (The issues of polite discourse among women deserve a study of their own.) If, in a fit of wishful thinking, you're inclined to dismiss them as passé, spend a few hours in the classrooms and corridors of a coeducational high school or college. We haven't actually come a long way, baby.

Rule 1: Keep quiet. If at all possible, a woman should remain perfectly mute. She should, however, communicate agreement with the men around her eloquently through gestures and demeanor. Think, for instance, of the Presidents' wives. The first First Lady I remember was Mamie Eisenhower, and from then on my head holds a gallery of film clips and still photos of women in the proper polite posture: Jackie and Lady Bird and Pat and Betty and Rosalynn and above all Nancy, eyes widened and glittering, polished lips slightly parted in breathless wonder, heads tilted to gaze upward at the sides of their husband's faces.

No one yawns or rolls her eyes (much less speaks unless spoken to). Now, if I were elected President, my husband (who dotes on me, by the way) would fall asleep during my inaugural address. There he'd be in the photos, eyes closed, mouth sagging, head rolled to one side, maybe a bit of spittle trickling into his beard. He wouldn't mean to be rude.

Even if you're tempted to break this rule of silence, some man will probably jump in and rescue you from yourself. As Carol Tavris and Carole Wade note in their text on sex differences, *The Longest War*, in mixed conversations men interrupt more freely, and speak at greater length, than women. So you won't get too much chance to be rude.

Rule 2: If you must talk at all, talk about something he's interested in. If your feelings are hurt by stifled yawns and retreating backs, dig out this old chestnut. It's still in force. Try not to think of all the women who have used up brain cells memorizing the batting averages of every outfielder in Red Sox history or the difference between the Apollonian and the Dionysian in Nietzsche,[1] depending on their intended target, instead of reflecting on the spiritual dilemma of women denied the priesthood by the Roman Catholic Church or the effect on human reproductive systems of even a "limited" nuclear war or the like.

Rule 3: If you must mention your own concerns, deprecate them prettily. The greatest rudeness in a woman is to appear to take herself seriously. My husband's indictment of feminism, for example—and he's not alone in it—is that feminists "lack a sense of humor." As members

5

1. Friedrich Nietzsche (1844–1900), German philosopher who (in *The Birth of Tragedy*) spoke of two strands in Greek art that he identified with the names of Apollo and Dionysius, the gods (respectively) of music and of wine.

of Catholics for Peace and Justice, we both support Sanctuary and Witness for Peace, two nonsectarian groups that work to promote international amity.

In our pained discussions of human-rights issues in Central America I have never heard him criticize Salvadoran and Guatemalan refugees or Sandinista peasants for lacking a sense of humor about their disappeared relatives, their burned infirmaries and bombed buses, their starvation and terror. Nor should he. And he shouldn't expect women to crack jokes when they are enraged by the malnutrition, rape and battering of their sisters and the system that makes such occurrences inevitable.

Actually, in the right places most of the women I know laugh heartily (even though a belly laugh isn't as polite as a giggle). But they weep in the right places, too.

"Lighten up," men tell women who grow passionate about the conditions of their lives. "What *is* all this whining?" one wrote to me. When we are the subjects of our speaking, our voices are too "shrill," "strident"; our tongues are too "sharp"; we are "shrews," "Xanthippes," [2] "termagants," "fishwives." All these words have in common the denigration of women's speech. By ridiculing or trivializing women's utterances, men seek to control what is and is not considered important, weighty, worthwhile in the world.

I, for one, was a well-bred girl who grew into a Yankee lady. From infancy, the language slipped into my mouth was scrubbed as clean as my rattles and teething rings. To this day, I wince at the possibility I might be thought rude. A man's sneer shrivels me. But I guess that's just what I'm going to have to be: rude. Because if women are ever going to be really heard, people (including women themselves) are going to have to get used to the sound of their voices and to the subjects they believe worth discussing.

So I, for one, intend to keep telling the truth about my life as a woman: what I see, whom I love, where I hurt, why I laugh.

And you? Tell me, out loud: who are you?

2. Wife of the Greek philosopher Socrates (470?–399 B.C.), her name has come to mean shrew.

Lewis Thomas

NOTES ON PUNCTUATION

There are no precise rules about punctuation (Fowler[1] lays out some general advice (as best he can under the complex circumstances of English prose (he points out, for example, that we possess only four stops (the comma, the semicolon, the colon and the period (the question mark and exclamation point are not, strictly speaking, stops; they are indicators of tone (oddly enough, the Greeks employed the semicolon for their question mark (it produces a strange sensation to read a Greek sentence which is a straightforward question: Why weepest thou; (instead of Why weepest thou? (and, of course, there are parentheses (which are surely a kind of punctuation making this whole much more complicated by having to count up the left-handed parentheses in order to be sure of closing with the right number (but if the parentheses were left out, with nothing to work with but the stops, we would have considerably more flexibility in the deploying of layers of meaning than if we tried to separate all the clauses by physical barriers (and in the latter case, while we might have more precision and exactitude for our meaning, we would lose the essential flavor of language, which is its wonderful ambiguity)))))))))))).

The commas are the most useful and usable of all the stops. It is highly important to put them in place as you go along. If you try to come back after doing a paragraph and stick them in the various spots that tempt you you will discover that they tend to swarm like minnows into all sorts of crevices whose existence you hadn't realized and before you know it the whole long sentence becomes immobilized and lashed up squirming in commas. Better to use them sparingly, and with affection, precisely when the need for each one arises, nicely, by itself.

I have grown fond of semicolons in recent years. The semicolon tells you that there is still some question about the preceding full sentence; something needs to be added; it reminds you sometimes of the Greek usage. It is almost always a greater pleasure to come across a semicolon than a period. The period tells you that that is that; if you didn't get all the meaning you wanted or expected, anyway you got all the writer intended to parcel out and now you have to move along. But with a

From *The Medusa and the Snail: More Notes of a Biology Watcher* (1979).

1. H. W. Fowler, author of *Modern English Usage* (1926, revised 1965 by Sir Ernest Gowers), a standard reference work.

semicolon there you get a pleasant little feeling of expectancy; there is more to come; read on; it will get clearer.

Colons are a lot less attractive, for several reasons: firstly, they give you the feeling of being rather ordered around, or at least having your nose pointed in a direction you might not be inclined to take if left to yourself, and, secondly, you suspect you're in for one of those sentences that will be labeling the points to be made: firstly, secondly and so forth, with the implication that you haven't sense enough to keep track of a sequence of notions without having them numbered. Also, many writers use this system loosely and incompletely, starting out with number one and number two as though counting off on their fingers but then going on and on without the succession of labels you've been led to expect, leaving you floundering about searching for the ninethly or seventeenthly that ought to be there but isn't.

Exclamation points are the most irritating of all. Look! they say, look at what I just said! How amazing is my thought! It is like being forced to watch someone else's small child jumping up and down crazily in the center of the living room shouting to attract attention. If a sentence really has something of importance to say, something quite remarkable, it doesn't need a mark to point it out. And if it is really, after all, a banal sentence needing more zing, the exclamation point simply emphasizes its banality!

Quotation marks should be used honestly and sparingly, when there is a genuine quotation at hand, and it is necessary to be very rigorous about the words enclosed by the marks. If something is to be quoted, the *exact* words must be used. If part of it must be left out because of space limitations, it is good manners to insert three dots to indicate the omission, but it is unethical to do this if it means connecting two thoughts which the original author did not intend to have tied together. Above all, quotation marks should not be used for ideas that you'd like to disown, things in the air so to speak. Nor should they be put in place around clichés; if you want to use a cliché you must take full responsibility for it yourself and not try to job it off on anon., or on society. The most objectionable misuse of quotation marks, but one which illustrates the dangers of misuse in ordinary prose, is seen in advertising, especially in advertisements for small restaurants, for example "just around the corner," or "a good place to eat." No single, identifiable, citable person ever really said, for the record, "just around the corner," much less "a good place to eat," least likely of all for restaurants of the type that use this type of prose.

The dash is a handy device, informal and essentially playful, telling you that you're about to take off on a different tack but still in some way connected with the present course—only you have to remember that the dash is there, and either put a second dash at the end of the notion to let the reader know that he's back on course, or else end the sentence, as here, with a period.

The greatest danger in punctuation is for poetry. Here it is necessary to be as economical and parsimonious with commas and periods as with the words themselves, and any marks that seem to carry their own subtle meanings, like dashes and little rows of periods, even semicolons and question marks, should be left out altogether rather than inserted to clog up the thing with ambiguity. A single exclamation point in a poem, no matter what else the poem has to say, is enough to destroy the whole work.

The things I like best in T. S. Eliot's poetry, especially in the *Four Quartets,* are the semicolons. You cannot hear them, but they are there, laying out the connections between the images and the ideas. Sometimes you get a glimpse of a semicolon coming, a few lines farther on, and it is like climbing a steep path through woods and seeing a wooden bench just at a bend in the road ahead, a place where you can expect to sit for a moment, catching your breath.

Commas can't do this sort of thing; they can only tell you how the different parts of a complicated thought are to be fitted together, but you can't sit, not even take a breath, just because of a comma,

10

THE READER

1. *Compare Thomas' statements about the various punctuation marks with a handbook's rules on the subject. How do they differ? Do they make any of the same points?*
2. *Compare the punctuation in two or more of the pieces in "An Album of Styles" (p. 429). You might look particularly at the selections by Bacon, Thurber, and White before making your choices.*
3. *Gertrude Stein once said: "There are two different ways of thinking about colons and semi-colons you can think of them as commas and as such they are purely servile or you can think of them as periods and then using them can make you feel adventurous." What might Thomas' comment on Stein's statement be?*

THE WRITER

1. *How soon in this essay do you realize that Thomas is playing a kind of game with the reader? Why doesn't he tell you at the beginning what he is going to do?*
2. *Here Thomas deals with a restricted, minor subject and, in "Humanities and Science" (p. 329), with one that is sweeping and important. Describe the personality he presents to you here and then the one he presents in "Humanities and Science." Are they similar? Different?*

Do they overlap? Is his analysis in "On Magic in Medicine" (p. 483) consistent with this personality or these personalities?

3. *The first paragraph in Thomas' essay is a single sentence. Rewrite the paragraph so that it is several sentences. What changes in punctuation did you make?*

4. *Write a short essay on "My Encounters with Punctuation" or "The Semicolon and I."*

Erich Fromm

THE NATURE OF SYMBOLIC LANGUAGE

Let us assume you want to tell someone the difference between the taste of white wine and red wine. This may seem quite simple to you. *You* know the difference very well; why should it not be easy to explain it to someone else? Yet you find the greatest difficulty putting this taste difference into words. And probably you will end up by saying, "Now look here, I can't explain it to you. Just drink red wine and then white wine, and you will know what the difference is." You have no difficulty in finding words to explain the most complicated machine, and yet words seem to be futile to describe a simple taste experience.

Are we not confronted with the same difficulty when we try to explain a feeling experience? Let us take a mood in which you feel lost, deserted, where the world looks gray, a little frightening though not really dangerous. You want to describe this mood to a friend, but again you find yourself groping for words and eventually feel that nothing you have said is an adequate explanation of the many nuances of the mood. The following night you have a dream. You see yourself in the outskirts of a city just before dawn, the streets are empty except for a milk wagon, the houses look poor, the surroundings are unfamiliar, you have no means of accustomed transportation to places familiar to you and where you feel you belong. When you wake up and remember the dream, it occurs to you that the feeling you had in that dream was exactly the feeling of lostness and grayness you tried to describe to your friend the day before. It is just one picture, whose visualization took less than a second. And yet this picture is a more vivid and precise description than you could have given by talking *about* it at length. The picture you see in the dream is a *symbol* of something you felt.

What is a symbol? A symbol is often defined as "something that stands for something else." This definition seems rather disappointing.

From *The Forgotten Language* (1951).

It becomes more interesting, however, if we concern ourselves with those symbols which are sensory expressions of seeing, hearing, smelling, touching, standing for a "something else" which is an inner experience, a feeling or thought. A symbol of this kind is something outside ourselves; that which it symbolizes is something inside ourselves. Symbolic language is language in which we express inner experience as if it were a sensory experience, as if it were something we were doing or something that was done to us in the world of things. Symbolic language is language in which the world outside is a symbol of the world inside, a symbol for our souls and our minds.

If we define a symbol as "something which stands for something else," the crucial question is: *What is the specific connection between the symbol and that which it symbolizes?*

In answer to this question we can differentiate between three kinds   5
of symbols: the *conventional,* the *accidental* and the *universal* symbol. As will become apparent presently, only the latter two kinds of symbols express inner experiences as if they were sensory experiences, and only they have the elements of symbolic language.

The *conventional* symbol is the best known of the three, since we employ it in everyday language. If we see the word "table" or hear the sound "table," the letters T-A-B-L-E stand for something else. They stand for the thing table that we see, touch and use. What is the connection between the *word* "table" and the *thing* "table"? Is there any inherent relationship between them? Obviously not. The thing table has nothing to do with the sound table, and the only reason the word symbolizes the thing is the convention of calling this particular thing by a particular name. We learn this connection as children by the repeated experience of hearing the word in reference to the thing until a lasting association is formed so that we don't have to think to find the right word.

There are some words, however, where the association is not only conventional. When we say "phooey," for instance, we make with our lips a movement of dispelling the air quickly. It is an expression of disgust in which our mouths participate. By this quick expulsion of air we imitate and thus express our intention to expel something, to get it out of our system. In this case, as in some others, the symbol has an inherent connection with the feeling it symbolizes. But even if we assume that originally many or even all words had their origins in some such inherent connection between symbol and the symbolized, most words no longer have this meaning for us when we learn a language.

Words are not the only illustration for conventional symbols, although they are the most frequent and best-known ones. Pictures also can be conventional symbols. A flag, for instance, may stand for a specific country, and yet there is no connection between the specific colors and the country for which they stand. They have been accepted as denoting that particular country, and we translate the visual impression of the flag into the concept of that country, again on conventional grounds. Some pictorial symbols are not entirely conventional; for example, the cross. The cross can be merely a conventional symbol of the Christian church and in that respect no different from a flag. But the specific content of the cross referring to Jesus' death or, beyond that, to the interpenetration of the material and spiritual planes, puts the connection between the symbol and what it symbolizes beyond the level of mere conventional symbols.

The very opposite to the conventional symbol is the *accidental* symbol, although they have one thing in common: there is no intrinsic relationship between the symbol and that which it symbolizes. Let us assume that someone has had a saddening experience in a certain city; when he hears the name of that city, he will easily connect the name with a mood of sadness, just as he would connect it with a mood of joy had his experience been a happy one. Quite obviously there is nothing in the nature of the city that is either sad or joyful. It is the individual experience connected with the city that makes it a symbol of a mood.

The same reaction could occur in connection with a house, a street, a certain dress, certain scenery, or anything once connected with a specific mood. We might find ourselves dreaming that we are in a certain city. In fact, there may be no particular mood connected with it in the dream; all we see is a street or even simply the name of the city. We ask ourselves why we happened to think of that city in our sleep and may discover that we had fallen asleep in a mood similar to the one symbolized by the city. The picture in the dream represents this mood, the city "stands for" the mood once experienced in it. Here the connection between the symbol and the experience symbolized is entirely accidental.

In contrast to the conventional symbol, the accidental symbol cannot be shared by anyone else except as we relate the events connected with the symbol. For this reason accidental symbols are rarely used in myths, fairy tales, or works of art written in symbolic language because they are not communicable unless the writer adds a lengthy comment to each symbol he uses. In dreams, however, accidental symbols are frequent. * * *

The *universal* symbol is one in which there is an intrinsic relationship between the symbol and that which it represents. We have already given one example, that of the outskirts of the city. The sensory experience of a deserted, strange, poor environment has indeed a significant relationship to a mood of lostness and anxiety. True enough, if we have never been in the outskirts of a city we could not use that symbol, just as the word "table" would be meaningless had we never seen a table.

This symbol is meaningful only to city dwellers and would be meaning-less to people living in cultures that have no big cities. Many other universal symbols, however, are rooted in the experience of every human being. Take, for instance, the symbol of fire. We are fascinated by certain qualities of fire in a fireplace. First of all, by its aliveness. It changes continuously, it moves all the time, and yet there is constancy in it. It remains the same without being the same. It gives the impression of power, of energy, of grace and lightness. It is as if it were dancing and had an inexhaustible source of energy. When we use fire as a symbol, we describe the inner experience characterized by the same elements which we notice in the sensory experience of fire; the mood of energy, lightness, movement, grace, gaiety—sometimes one, sometimes another of these elements being predominant in the feeling.

Similar in some ways and different in others is the symbol of water— of the ocean or of the stream. Here, too, we find the blending of change and permanence, of constant movement and yet of permanence. We also feel the quality of aliveness, continuity and energy. But there is a difference; where fire is adventurous, quick, exciting, water is quiet, slow and steady. Fire has an element of surprise; water an element of predict-ability. Water symbolizes the mood of aliveness, too, but one which is "heavier," "slower," and more comforting than exciting.

That a phenomenon of the physical world can be the adequate expres-sion of an inner experience, that the world of things can be a symbol of the world of the mind, is not surprising. We all know that our bodies express our minds. Blood rushes to our heads when we are furious, it rushes away from them when we are afraid; our hearts beat more quickly when we are angry, and the whole body has a different tonus if we are happy from the one it has when we are sad. We express our moods by our facial expressions and our attitudes and feelings by movements and gestures so precise that others recognize them more accurately from our gestures than from our words. Indeed, the body is a symbol—and not an allegory—of the mind. Deeply and genuinely felt emotion, and even any genuinely felt thought, is expressed in our whole organism. In the case of the universal symbol, we find the same connection between mental and physical experience. Certain physical phenomena suggest by their very nature certain emotional and mental experiences, and we express emotional experiences in the language of physical experiences, that is to say, symbolically.

The universal symbol is the only one in which the relationship be-tween the symbol and that which is symbolized is not coincidental but intrinsic. It is rooted in the experience of the affinity between an emo-tion or thought, on the one hand, and a sensory experience, on the other. It can be called universal because it is shared by all men, in contrast not only to the accidental symbol, which is by its very nature entirely

15

personal, but also to the conventional symbol, which is restricted to a group of people sharing the same convention. The universal symbol is rooted in the properties of our body, our senses, and our mind, which are common to all men and, therefore, not restricted to individuals or to specific groups. Indeed, the language of the universal symbol is the one common tongue developed by the human race, a language which it forgot before it succeeded in developing a universal conventional language.

There is no need to speak of a racial inheritance in order to explain the universal character of symbols. Every human being who shares the essential features of bodily and mental equipment with the rest of mankind is capable of speaking and understanding the symbolic language that is based upon these common properties. Just as we do not need to learn to cry when we are sad or to get red in the face when we are angry, and just as these reactions are not restricted to any particular race or group of people, symbolic language does not have to be learned and is not restricted to any segment of the human race. Evidence for this is to be found in the fact that symbolic language as it is employed in myths and dreams is found in all cultures—in so-called primitive as well as such highly developed cultures as Egypt and Greece. Furthermore, the symbols used in these various cultures are strikingly similar since they all go back to the basic sensory as well as emotional experiences shared by men of all cultures. Added evidence is to be found in recent experiments in which people who had no knowledge of the theory of dream interpretation were able, under hypnosis, to interpret the symbolism of their dreams without any difficulty. After emerging from the hypnotic state and being asked to interpret the same dreams, they were puzzled and said, "Well, there is no meaning to them—it is just nonsense."

The foregoing statement needs qualification, however. Some symbols differ in meaning according to the difference in their realistic significance in various cultures. For instance, the function and consequently the meaning of the sun is different in northern countries and in tropical countries. In northern countries, where water is plentiful, all growth depends on sufficient sunshine. The sun is the warm, life-giving, protecting, loving power. In the Near East, where the heat of the sun is much more powerful, the sun is a dangerous and even threatening power from which man must protect himself, while water is felt to be the source of all life and the main condition for growth. We may speak of dialects of universal symbolic language, which are determined by those differences in natural conditions which cause certain symbols to have a different meaning in different regions of the earth.

Quite different from these "symbolic dialects" is the fact that many symbols have more than one meaning in accordance with different kinds of experiences which can be connected with one and the same natural phenomenon. Let us take up the symbol of fire again. If we watch fire in the fireplace, which is a source of pleasure and comfort, it is expressive of a mood of aliveness, warmth, and pleasure. But if we see a building or forest on fire, it conveys to us an experience of threat or terror, of the powerlessness of man against the elements of nature. Fire, then, can be the symbolic representation of inner aliveness and happiness as well as of fear, powerlessness, or of one's own destructive tendencies. The same holds true of the symbol water. Water can be a most destructive force when it is whipped up by a storm or when a swollen river floods its banks. Therefore, it can be the symbolic expression of horror and chaos as well as of comfort and peace.

Another illustration of the same principle is a symbol of a valley. The valley enclosed between mountains can arouse in us the feeling of security and comfort, of protection against all dangers from the outside. But the protecting mountains can also mean isolating walls which do not permit us to get out of the valley and thus the valley can become a symbol of imprisonment. The particular meaning of the symbol in any given place can only be determined from the whole context in which the symbol appears, and in terms of the predominant experiences of the person using the symbol. * * *

A good illustration of the function of the universal symbol is a story, written in symbolic language, which is known to almost everyone in Western culture: the Book of Jonah. Jonah has heard God's voice telling him to go to Nineveh and preach to its inhabitants to give up their evil ways lest they be destroyed. Jonah cannot help hearing God's voice and that is why he is a prophet. But he is an unwilling prophet, who, though knowing what he should do, tries to run away from the command of God (or, as we may say, the voice of his conscience). He is a man who does not care for other human beings. He is a man with a strong sense of law and order, but without love.

How does the story express the inner processes in Jonah?

We are told that Jonah went down to Joppa and found a ship which should bring him to Tarshish. In mid-ocean a storm rises and, while everyone else is excited and afraid, Jonah goes into the ship's belly and falls into a deep sleep. The sailors, believing that God must have sent the storm because someone on the ship is to be punished, wake Jonah, who had told them he was trying to flee from God's command. He tells them to take him and cast him forth into the sea and that the sea would then become calm. The sailors (betraying a remarkable sense of humanity by first trying everything else before following his advice) eventually take Jonah and cast him into the sea, which immediately stops raging. Jonah is swallowed by a big fish and stays in the fish's belly three days and three nights. He prays to God to free him from this prison. God makes the fish vomit out Jonah unto the dry land and Jonah goes to Nineveh, fulfills God's command, and thus saves the inhabitants of the city.

The story is told as if these events had actually happened. However, it is written in symbolic language and all the realistic events described are symbols for the inner experiences of the hero. We find a sequence of symbols which follow one another: going into the ship, going into the ship's belly, falling asleep, being in the ocean, and being in the fish's belly. All these symbols stand for the same inner experience: for a condition of being protected and isolated, of safe withdrawal from communication with other human beings. They represent what could be represented in another symbol, the fetus in the mother's womb. Different as the ship's belly, deep sleep, the ocean, and a fish's belly are realistically, they are expressive of the same inner experience, of the blending between protection and isolation.

In the manifest story events happen in space and time: *first,* going into the ship's belly; *then,* falling asleep; *then,* being thrown into the ocean; *then,* being swallowed by the fish. One thing happens after the other and, although some events are obviously unrealistic, the story has its own logical consistency in terms of time and space. But if we understand that the writer did not intend to tell us the story of external events, but of the inner experience of a man torn between his conscience and his wish to escape from his inner voice, it becomes clear that his various actions following one after the other express the same mood in him; and that *sequence in time* is expressive of a *growing intensity* of the same feeling. In his attempt to escape from his obligation to his fellow men Jonah isolates himself more and more until, in the belly of the fish, the protective element has so given way to the imprisoning element that he can stand it no longer and is forced to pray to God to be released from where he had put himself. (This is a mechanism which we find so characteristic of neurosis. An attitude is assumed as a defense against a danger, but then it grows far beyond its original defense function and becomes a neurotic symptom from which the person tries to be relieved.) Thus Jonah's escape into protective isolation ends in the terror of being imprisoned, and he takes up his life at the point where he had tried to escape.

25   There is another difference between the logic of the manifest and of the latent story. In the manifest story the logical connection is one of causality of external events. Jonah wants to go overseas *because* he wants to flee from God, he falls asleep *because* he is tired, he is thrown overboard *because* he is supposed to be the reason for the storm, and he is swallowed by the fish *because* there are man-eating fish in the ocean. One event occurs because of a previous event. (The last part of the story is unrealistic but not illogical.) But in the latent story the logic

is different. The various events are related to each other by their association with the same inner experience. What appears to be a causal
sequence of external events stands for a connection of experiences linked
with each other by their association in terms of inner events. This is as
logical as the manifest story—but it is a logic of a different kind.

Wayne C. Booth

BORING FROM WITHIN: THE ART OF THE FRESHMAN ESSAY

Last week I had for about the hundredth time an experience that
always disturbs me. Riding on a train, I found myself talking with my
seat-mate, who asked me what I did for a living. "I teach English." Do
you have any trouble predicting his response? His face fell, and he
groaned, "Oh, dear, I'll have to watch my language." In my experience
there are only two other possible reactions. The first is even less inspirit-
ing: "I hated English in school; it was my worst subject." The second,
so rare as to make an honest English teacher almost burst into tears of
gratitude when it occurs, is an animated conversation about literature,
or ideas, or the American language—the kind of conversation that shows
a continuing respect for "English" as something more than being sure
about *who* and *whom, lie* and *lay.*

Unless the people you meet are a good deal more tactful or better liars
than the ones I meet, you've had the two less favorable experiences many
times. And it takes no master analyst to figure out why so many of our
fellow citizens think of us as unfriendly policemen: it is because too
many of us have seen ourselves as unfriendly policemen. I know of a high
school English class in Indiana in which the students are explicitly told
that their paper grades will not be affected by anything they say; required
to write a paper a week, they are graded simply on the number of spelling
and grammatical errors. What is more, they are given a standard form
for their papers: each paper is to have three paragraphs, a beginning, a
middle, and an end—or is it an introduction, a body, and a conclusion?
The theory seems to be that if the student is not troubled about having
to say anything, or about discovering a good way of saying it, he can then
concentrate on the truly important matter of avoiding mistakes.

What's wrong with such assignments? What's wrong with getting the

Adapted by Wayne C. Booth from a speech delivered in May 1963 to the Illinois Council
of College Teachers of English.

problem of correctness focused sharply enough so that we can really work on it? After all, we do have the job of teaching correct English, don't we? We can't possibly teach our hordes of students to be colorful writers, but by golly, we can beat the bad grammar out of them. Leaving aside the obvious fact that we *can't* beat the bad grammar out of them, not by direct assault, let's think a bit about what that kind of assignment does to the poor teacher who gives it. Those papers must be read, by someone, and unless the teacher has more trained assistance than you and I have, *she's* the victim. She can't help being bored silly by her own paper-reading, and we all know what an evening of being bored by a class's papers does to our attitude toward that class the next day. The old formula of John Dewey was that any teaching that bores the student is likely to fail. The formula was subject to abuse, quite obviously, since interest in itself is only one of many tests of adequate teaching. A safer formula, though perhaps also subject to abuse, might be: Any teaching that bores the teacher is sure to fail. And I am haunted by the picture of that poor woman in Indiana, week after week reading batches of papers written by students who have been told that nothing they say can possibly affect her opinion of those papers. Could any hell imagined by Dante or Jean-Paul Sartre[1] match this self-inflicted futility?

I call it self-inflicted, as if it were a simple matter to avoid receiving papers that bore us. But unfortunately it is not. It may be a simple matter to avoid the *total* meaninglessness that the students must give that Indiana teacher, but we all know that it is no easy matter to produce interesting papers; our pet cures for boredom never work as well as they ought to. Every beginning teacher learns quickly and painfully that nothing works with all students, and that on bad days even the most promising ideas work with nobody.

5   As I try to sort out the various possible cures for those batches of boredom—in ink, double-spaced, on one side of the sheet, only, please—I find them falling into three groups: efforts to give the students a sharper sense of writing to an audience, efforts to give them some substance to express, and efforts to improve their habits of observation and of approach to their task—what might be called improving their mental personalities.

This classification, both obvious and unoriginal, is a useful one not only because it covers—at least I hope it does—all of our efforts to improve what our students can do but also because it reminds us that no one of the three is likely to work unless it is related to each of the others. In fact each of the three types of cure—"develop an awareness of audience," "give them something to say," and "enliven their writing

1. Booth refers to the elaborately described hell of the *Inferno*, by the fourteenth-century Italian poet Dante Alighieri, and to the banal locked room in which the characters of Sartre's *No Exit* discover that hell is "other people."

personalities"—threatens us with characteristic dangers and distortions; all three together are indispensable to any lasting cure.

Perhaps the most obvious omission in that Indiana teacher's assignments is all sense of an audience to be persuaded, of a serious rhetorical purpose to be achieved. One tempting cure for this omission is to teach them to put a controversial edge on what they say. So we ask them to write a three-page paper arguing that China should be allowed into the UN or that women are superior to men or that American colleges are failing in their historic task. Then we are surprised when the papers turn out to be as boring as ever. The papers on Red China are full of abstract pomposities that the students themselves obviously do not understand or care about, since they have gleaned them in a desperate dash through the most readily available sources listed in the *Readers' Guide.* Except for the rare student who has some political background and awareness, and who thus might have written on the subject anyway, they manage to convey little more than their resentment at the assignment and their boredom in carrying it out. One of the worst batches of papers I ever read came out of a good idea we had at Earlham College for getting the whole student body involved in controversial discussion about world affairs. We required them to read Barbara Ward's *Five Ideas that Change the World;* we even had Lady Jackson [2] come to the campus and talk to everyone about her concern for the backward nations. The papers, to our surprise, were a discouraging business. We found ourselves in desperation collecting the boners that are always a sure sign, when present in great numbers, that students are thoroughly disengaged. "I think altruism is all right, so long as we practice it in our own interest." "I would be willing to die for anything fatal." "It sure is a doggie dog world."

It is obvious what had gone wrong: though we had ostensibly given the student a writing purpose, it had not become *his* purpose, and he was really no better off, perhaps worse, than if we had him writing about, say, piccolos or pizza. We might be tempted in revulsion from such overly ambitious failures to search for controversy in the students' own mundane lives. This may be a good move, but we should not be surprised when the papers on "Let's clean up the campus" or "Why must we have traffic fatalities?" turn out to be just as empty as the papers on the UN or the Congo. They may have more exclamation points and underlined adjectives, but they will not interest any teacher who would like to read papers for his own pleasure or edification. "People often fail to realize that nearly 40,000 people are killed on our highways each year. Must this carnage continue?" Well, I suppose it must, until people who write about it learn to see it with their own eyes, and hearts, instead of through

2. Barbara Ward.

a haze of cliché. The truth is that to make students assume a controversial pose before they have any genuine substance to be controversial about is to encourage dishonesty and slovenliness, and to ensure our own boredom. It may very well lead them into the kind of commercial concern for the audience which makes almost every *Reader's Digest* article intelligible to everyone over the chronological age of ten and boring to everyone over the mental age of fifteen. *Newsweek* magazine recently had a readability survey conducted on itself. It was found to be readable by the average twelfth grader, unlike *Time*, which is readable by the average eleventh grader. The editors were advised, and I understand are taking the advice, that by improving their "readability" by one year they could improve their circulation by several hundred thousand. Whether they will thereby lop off a few thousand adult readers in the process was not reported.

The only protection from this destructive type of concern for the audience is the control of substance, of having something solid to say. Our students bore us, even when they take a seemingly lively controversial tone, because they have nothing to say, to us or to anybody else. If and when they discover something to say, they will no longer bore us, and our comments will no longer bore them. Having something to say, they will be interested in learning how to say it better. Having something to say, they can be taught how to give a properly controversial edge to what will by its nature be controversial—nothing, after all, is worth saying that everybody agrees on already.

10   When we think of providing substance, we are perhaps tempted first to find some way of filling students' minds with a goodly store of general ideas, available on demand. This temptation is not necessarily a bad one. After all, if we think of the adult writers who interest us, most of them have such a store; they have read and thought about man's major problems, and they have opinions and arguments ready to hand about how men ought to live, how society ought to be run, how literature ought to be written. Edmund Wilson, for example, one of the most consistently interesting men alive, seems to have an inexhaustible flow of reasoned opinions on any subject that comes before him. Obviously our students are not going to interest us until they too have some ideas.

But it is not easy to impart ideas. It is not even easy to impart opinions, though a popular teacher can usually manage to get students to parrot his views. But ideas—that is, opinions backed with genuine reasoning—are extremely difficult to develop. If they were not, we wouldn't have a problem in the first place; we could simply send our students off with an assignment to prove their conviction that God does or does not exist or that the American high school system is the best on God's earth, and the interesting arguments would flow.

There is, in fact, no short cut to the development of reasoned ideas.

Years and years of daily contact with the world of ideas are required before the child can be expected to begin formulating his own ideas and his own reasons. And for the most part the capacity to handle abstract ideas comes fairly late. I recently saw a paper of a bright high school sophomore, from a good private school, relating the economic growth of China and India to their political development and relative supply of natural resources. It was a terrible paper; the student's hatred of the subject, his sense of frustration in trying to invent generalizations about processes that were still too big for him, showed in every line. The child's parent told me that when the paper was returned by the geography teacher, he had pencilled on the top of one page, "Why do you mix so many bad ideas with your good ones?" The son was almost in tears, his father told me, with anger and helplessness. "He talks as if I'd put bad ideas in on purpose. *I* don't know a bad idea from a good one on this subject."

Yet with all this said, I am still convinced that general ideas are not only a resource but also a duty that cannot be dodged just because it is a dangerous one. There is nothing we touch, as English teachers, that is immune to being tainted by our touch; all the difference lies in how we go about it.

Ideas are a resource because adolescents are surprisingly responsive to any real encouragement to think for themselves, *if* methods of forced feeding are avoided. The seventeen-year-old who has been given nothing but commonplaces and clichés all his life and who finally discovers a teacher with ideas of his own may have his life changed, and, as I shall say in my final point, when his life is changed his writing is changed. Perhaps some of you can remember, as I can, a first experience with a teacher who could think for himself. I can remember going home from a conversation with my high school chemistry teacher and audibly vowing to myself: "Someday I'm going to be able to think for myself like that." There was nothing especially unconventional about Luther Gidding's ideas—at least I can remember few of them now. But what I cannot forget is the way he had with an idea, the genuine curiosity with which he approached it, the pause while he gave his little thoughtful cough, and then the bulldog tenacity with which he would argue it through. And I am convinced that though he never required me to write a line, he did more to improve my writing during the high school years than all of my English teachers put together. The diary I kept to record my sessions with him, never read by anyone, was the best possible writing practice.

If ideas, in this sense of speculation backed up with an attempt to think about things rigorously and constructively, are a great and often neglected resource, they are also our civic responsibility—a far more serious responsibility than our duty to teach spelling and grammar. It is

15

a commonplace to say that democracy depends for its survival on an informed citizenry, but we all know that mere information is not what we are talking about when we say such things. What we mean is that democracy depends on a citizenry that can reason for themselves, on men who know whether a case has been proved, or at least made probable. Democracy depends, if you will forgive some truisms for a moment, on free choices, and choices cannot be in any sense free if they are made blind: free choice is, in fact, choice that is based on knowledge—not just opinions, but knowledge in the sense of reasoned opinion. And if that half of our population who do not go beyond high school do not learn from us how to put two and two together and how to test the efforts of others to do so, and if the colleges continue to fail with most of the other half, we are doomed to become even more sheeplike, as a nation, than we are already.

Papers about ideas written by sheep are boring; papers written by thinking boys and girls are interesting. The problem is always to find ideas at a level that will allow the student to *reason*, that is, to provide support for his ideas, rather than merely assert them in half-baked form. And this means something that is all too often forgotten by the most ambitious teachers—namely, that whatever ideas the student writes about must somehow be connected with his own experience. Teaching machines will never be able to teach the kind of writing we all want, precisely because no machine can ever know which general ideas relate, for a given student, to some meaningful experience. In the same class we'll have one student for whom philosophical and religious ideas are meaningful, another who can talk with confidence about entropy and the second law of thermodynamics, a third who can write about social justice, and a fourth who can discuss the phony world of Holden Caulfield.[3] Each of them can do a good job on his own subject, because he has as part of his equipment a growing awareness of how conclusions in that subject are related to the steps of argument that support conclusions. Ideally, each of these students ought to have the personal attention of a tutor for an hour or so each week, someone who can help him sharpen those connections, and not force him to write on topics not yet appropriate to his interests or experience. But when these four are in a class of thirty or forty others, taught by a teacher who has three or four other similar sections, we all know what happens: the teacher is forced by his circumstances to provide some sort of mold into which all of the students can be poured. Although he is still better able to adapt to individual differences than a machine, he is unfortunately subject to boredom and fatigue, as a machine would not be. Instead of being the philosopher, scientist, political analyst, and literary critic that these four

3. The hero of *The Catcher in the Rye*, by J. D. Salinger.

students require him to be, teaching them and learning from them at the same time, the teacher is almost inevitably tempted to force them all to write about the ideas he himself knows best. The result is that at least three of the four must write out of ignorance.

Now clearly the best way out of this impasse would be for legislatures and school boards and college presidents to recognize the teaching of English for what it is: the most demanding of all teaching jobs, justifying the smallest sections and the lightest course loads. No composition teacher can possibly concentrate on finding special interests, making imaginative assignments, and testing the effectiveness and cogency of papers if he has more than seventy-five students at a time; the really desirable limit would be about forty-five—three sections of fifteen students each. Nobody would ever expect a piano teacher, who has no themes to read, to handle the great masses of pupils that we handle. Everyone recognizes that for all other technical skills individual attention is required. Yet for this, the most delicate of all skills, the one requiring the most subtle interrelationships of training, character, and experience, we fling students and teachers into hopelessly impersonal patterns.

But if I'm not careful I'll find myself saying that our pupils bore us because the superintendents and college presidents hire us to be bored. Administrative neglect and misallocation of educational funds are basic to our problem, and we should let the citizenry know of the scandal on every occasion. But meanwhile, back at the ranch, we are faced with the situation as it now is: we must find some way to train a people to write responsibly even though the people, as represented, don't want this service sufficiently to pay for it.

The tone of political exhortation into which I have now fallen leads me to one natural large source of ideas as we try to encourage writing that is not just lively and controversial but informed and genuinely persuasive. For many students there is obviously more potential interest in social problems and forces, political controversy, and the processes of everyday living around them than in more general ideas. The four students I described a moment ago, students who can say something about philosophy, science, general political theory, or literary criticism, are rare. But most students, including these four, can in theory at least be interested in meaningful argument about social problems in which they are personally involved.

As a profession we have tried, over the past several decades, a variety of approaches attempting to capitalize on such interests. Papers on corruption in TV, arguments about race relations, analyses of distortions in advertising, descriptions of mass communication—these have been combined in various quantities with traditional subjects like grammar, rhetoric, and literature. The "communications" movement, which

20

looked so powerful only a few years ago and which now seems almost dead, had at its heart a perfectly respectable notion, a notion not much different from the one I'm working with today: get them to write about something they know about, and make sure that they see their writing as an act of communication, not as a meaningless exercise. And what better material than other acts of communication.

The dangers of such an approach are by now sufficiently understood. As subject matter for the English course, current "communications media" can at best provide only a supplement to literature and analysis of ideas. But they can be a valuable supplement. Analysis in class of the appeals buried in a *New Yorker* or *Life* advertisement followed by a writing assignment requiring similar analyses can be a far more interesting introduction to the intricacies of style than assignments out of a language text on levels of usage or emotion-charged adjectives. Analysis of a *Time* magazine account, purporting to be objective news but in actual fact a highly emotional editorial, can be not only a valuable experience in itself, but it can lead to papers in which the students do say something to us. Stylistic analysis of the treatment of the same news events by two newspapers or weeklies of different editorial policy can lead to an intellectual awakening of great importance, and thus to papers that will not, cannot, bore the teacher. But this will happen only if the students' critical powers are genuinely developed. It will not do simply to teach the instructor's own prejudices.

There was a time in decades not long past when many of the most lively English teachers thought of their job as primarily to serve as handmaids to liberalism. I had one teacher in college who confessed to me that his overriding purpose was to get students to read and believe *The Nation* rather than the editorials of their daily paper. I suppose that his approach was not entirely valueless. It seems preferable to the effort to be noncontroversial that marks too many English teachers in the '60's, and at least it stirred some of us out of our dogmatic slumbers. But unfortunately it did nothing whatever about teaching us to think critically. Though we graduated from his course at least aware—as many college graduates do not seem to be today—that you can't believe anything you read in the daily press until you have analyzed it and related it to your past experience and to other accounts, it failed to teach us that you can't believe what you read in *The Nation* either. It left the job undone of training our ability to think, because it concentrated too heavily on our opinions. The result was, as I remember, that my own papers in that course were generally regurgitated liberalism. I was excited by them, and that was something. But I can't believe that the instructor found reading them anything other than a chore. There was nothing in them that came from my own experience, my own notions of what would constitute evidence for my conclusions. There I was, in

Utah in the depths of the depression, writing about the Okies when I could have been writing about the impoverished farmers all around me. I wrote about race relations in the south without ever having talked with a Negro in my life and without recognizing that the bootblack I occasionally saw in Salt Lake City in the Hotel Utah was in any way related to the problem of race relations.

The third element that accounts for our boring papers is the lack of character and personality in the writer. My life, my observations, my insights were not included in those papers on the Okies and race relations and the New Deal. Every opinion was derivative, every observation second-hand. I had no real opinions of my own, and my eyes were not open wide enough for me to make first-hand observations on the world around me. What I wrote was therefore characterless, without true personality, though often full of personal pronouns. My opinions had been changed, my *self* had not. The style was the boy, the opinionated, immature, uninformed boy; whether my teacher knew it or not—and apparently he did not—his real job was to make a man of me if he wanted me to write like a man.

Putting the difficulty in this way naturally leads me to what perhaps many of you have been impatient about from the beginning. Are not the narrative arts, both as encountered in great literature and as practiced by the students themselves, the best road to the infusion of individuality that no good writing can lack? Would not a real look at the life of that bootblack, and an attempt to deal with him in narrative, have led to a more interesting paper than all of my generalized attacks on the prejudiced southerners?

I think it would, but once again I am almost more conscious of the dangers of the cure than of the advantages. As soon as we make our general rule something like, "Have the students write a personal narrative on what they know about, what they can see and feel at first hand," we have opened the floodgates for those dreadful assignments that we all find ourselves using, even though we know better: "My Summer Vacation," "Catching My First Fish," and "Our Trip to the Seattle World's Fair." Here are personal experiences that call for personal observation and narration. What's wrong with them?

Quite simply, they invite triviality, superficiality, puerility. Our students have been writing essays on such non-subjects all their lives, and until they have developed some sort of critical vision, some way of looking at the world they passed through on their vacations or fishing trips, they are going to feed us the same old bromides that have always won their passing grades. "My Summer Vacation" is an invitation to a grocery list of items, because it implies no audience, no point to be made, no point of view, no character in the speaker. A bright student will make something of such an invitation, by dramatizing the comic

25

family quarrel that developed two days out, or by comparing his view of the American motel system with Nabokov's in *Lolita*, or by remembering the types of people seen in the campgrounds. If he had his own eyes and ears open he might have seen, in a men's room in Grand Canyon last summer, a camper with a very thick French accent trying to convert a Brooklyn Jew into believing the story of the Mormon gold plates.[4] Or he could have heard, at Mesa Verde, a young park ranger, left behind toward the end of the season by all of the experienced rangers, struggling ungrammatically through a set speech on the geology of the area and finally breaking down in embarrassment over his lack of education. Such an episode, really *seen*, could be used narratively to say something to other high school students about what education really is.

But mere narration can be in itself just as dull as the most abstract theorizing about the nature of the universe or the most derivative opinion-mongering about politics. Even relatively skilful narration, used too obviously as a gimmick to catch interest, with no real relation to the subject, can be as dull as the most abstract pomposities. We all know the student papers that begin like *Reader's Digest* articles, with stereotyped narration that makes one doubt the event itself: "On a dark night last January, two teen agers were seen etc., etc." One can open any issue of *Time* and find this so-called narrative interest plastered throughout. From the March 29 issue I find, among many others, the following bits of fantasy: #1: "A Bolivian father sadly surveyed his nation's seven universities, then made up his mind. 'I don't want my son mixed up in politics.' . . . So saying, he sent his son off to West Germany to college." So writing, the author sends me into hysterical laughter: the quote is phony, made up for the occasion to disguise the generality of the news item. #2: "Around 12:30 P.M. every Monday and Friday, an aging Cubana Airlines turbo-prop Britannia whistles to a halt at Mexico City's International Airport. Squads of police stand by. All passengers . . . without diplomatic or Mexican passports are photographed and questioned. . . . They always dodge questions. 'Why are you here? Where are you going?' ask the Mexicans. 'None of your business,' answer the secretive travelers." "Why should I go on reading?" ask I. #3: "At 6:30 one morning early this month, a phone shrilled in the small office off the bedroom of Egypt's President. . . Nasser. [All early morning phones "shrill" for *Time*.] Already awake, he lifted the receiver to hear exciting news: a military coup had just been launched against the anti-Nasser government of Syria. The phone rang again. It was the Minister of Culture. . . . How should Radio Cairo handle the Syrian crisis? 'Support the rebels,' snapped Nasser." Oh lucky reporter, I sigh, to have such an

4. Bearing, according to Mormon tradition, the Book of Mormon, divinely revealed to the prophet Joseph Smith in Upstate New York in 1827.

efficient wiretapping service. #4: "In South Korea last week, a farmer named Song Kyu Il traveled all the way from the southern provinces to parade before Seoul's Duk Soo Palace with a placard scrawled in his own blood. . . . Farmer Song was thrown in jail, along with some 200 other demonstrators." That's the last we hear of Song, who is invented as an individual for this opening and then dropped. #5: "Defense Secretary Robert McNamara last spring stood beside President Kennedy on the tenth-deck bridge of the nuclear-powered carrier *Enterprise*. For as far as the eye could see, other U.S. ships deployed over the Atlantic seascape." Well, maybe. But for as far as the eye can see, the narrative clichés are piled, rank on rank. At 12:00 midnight last Thursday a gaunt, harried English professor could be seen hunched over his typewriter, a pile of *Time* magazines beside him on the floor. "What," he murmured to himself, sadly, "Whatever can we do about this trashy imitation of narration?"

Fortunately there is something we can do, and it is directly within our province. We can subject our students to models of genuine narration, with the sharp observation and penetrating critical judgment that underlies all good story telling, whether reportorial or fictional.

> It is a truth universally acknowledged, that a single man in possession of a good fortune must be in want of a wife.
> However little known the feelings or views of such a man may be on his first entering a neighborhood, this truth is so well fixed in the minds of the surrounding families, that he is considered as the rightful property of someone or other of their daughters.
> "My dear Mr. Bennet," said his lady to him one day, "have you heard that Netherfield Park is let at last?"

And already we have a strong personal tone established, a tone of mocking irony which leaves Jane Austen's Mrs. Bennet revealed before us as the grasping, silly gossip she is. Or try this one:

> I am an American, Chicago-born—Chicago, that somber city—and go at things as I have taught myself, free-style, and will make the record in my own way: first to knock, first admitted; sometimes an innocent knock, sometimes a not so innocent. But a man's character is his fate, says Heraclitus, and in the end there isn't any way to disguise the nature of the knocks by acoustical work on the door or gloving the knuckles.
> Everybody knows there is no fineness or accuracy of suppression; if you hold down one thing you hold down the adjoining.
> My own parents were not much to me, though I cared for my mother. She was simple-minded, and what I learned from her was not what she taught. . . .

Do you catch the accent of Saul Bellow here, beneath the accent of his Augie March? You do, of course, but the students, many of them, do not. How do you know, they will ask, that Jane Austen is being ironic? How do you know, they ask again, that Augie is being characterized by his author through what he says? In teaching them how we know, in exposing them to the great narrative voices, ancient and modern, and in teaching them to hear these voices accurately, we are, of course, trying to change their lives, to make them new, to raise their perceptions to a new level altogether. Nobody can really catch these accents who has not grown up sufficiently to see through cheap substitutes. Or, to put it another way, a steady exposure to such voices is the very thing that will produce the maturity that alone can make our students ashamed of beclouded, commercial, borrowed spectacles for viewing the world.

30   It is true that exposure to good fiction will not in itself transform our students into good writers. Even the best-read student still needs endless hours and years of practice, with rigorous criticism. Fiction will not do the job of discipline in reasoned argument and of practice in developing habits of addressing a living audience. But in the great fiction they will learn what it means to look at something with full attention, what it means to see beneath the surface of society's platitudes. If we then give them practice in writing about things close to the home base of their own honest observations, constantly stretching their powers of generalization and argument but never allowing them to drift into pompous inanities or empty controversiality, we may have that rare but wonderful pleasure of witnessing the miracle: a man and a style where before there was only a bag of wind or a bundle of received opinions. Even when, as with most of our students, no miracles occur, we can hope for papers that we can enjoy reading. And as a final bonus, we might hope that when our students encounter someone on a train who says that he teaches English, their automatic response may be something other than looks of pity or, cries of mock alarm.

THE READER

1. *What steps are necessary before an "opinion" can become a "reasoned opinion"? Select some subject on which you have a strong opinion, and decide whether it is a reasoned opinion.*
2. *Booth characterizes the writing in the* Reader's Digest *and* Time *(p. 414). What does he feel the two magazines have in common? Analyze an article from either one of these magazines to see how accurate Booth's characterization is.*

THE WRITER

1. *Booth is writing for an audience of English teachers. In what ways might the essay differ if he were writing for an audience of students?*
2. *On p. 411, Booth says he has "now fallen" into a "tone of political*

exhortation." (Tone *may be defined as the reflection in language of the attitude a writer takes toward his or her subject or audience or both.) What other "tones" are there in the essay? Why does Booth find it necessary to vary the tone?*

3. *Write an account of the process you went through in writing some paper recently or the process you typically go through in writing a paper. Then, in a paragraph or two, tell what you think Booth's comments on your process of writing might be.*

George Orwell

POLITICS AND THE ENGLISH LANGUAGE

Most people who bother with the matter at all would admit that the English language is in a bad way, but it is generally assumed that we cannot by conscious action do anything about it. Our civilization is decadent and our language—so the argument runs—must inevitably share in the general collapse. It follows that any struggle against the abuse of language is a sentimental archaism, like preferring candles to electric light or hansom cabs to aeroplanes. Underneath this lies the half-conscious belief that language is a natural growth and not an instrument which we shape for our own purposes.

Now, it is clear that the decline of a language must ultimately have political and economic causes: it is not due simply to the bad influence of this or that individual writer. But an effect can become a cause, reinforcing the original cause and producing the same effect in an intensified form, and so on indefinitely. A man may take to drink because he feels himself to be a failure, and then fail all the more completely because he drinks. It is rather the same thing that is happening to the English language. It becomes ugly and inaccurate because our thoughts are foolish, but the slovenliness of our language makes it easier for us to have foolish thoughts. The point is that the process is reversible. Modern English, especially written English, is full of bad habits which spread by imitation and which can be avoided if one is willing to take the necessary trouble. If one gets rid of these habits one can think more clearly, and to think clearly is a necessary first step towards political regeneration: so that the fight against bad English is not frivolous and is not the exclusive concern of professional writers. I will come back to this presently, and I hope that by that time the meaning of what I have

First published in *Horizon*, April 1946; reprinted in *Shooting an Elephant and Other Essays* (1950).

said here will have become clearer. Meanwhile, here are five specimens
of the English language as it is now habitually written.

These five passages have not been picked out because they are especially bad—I could have quoted far worse if I had chosen—but because
they illustrate various of the mental vices from which we now suffer.
They are a little below the average, but are fairly representative samples.
I number them so that I can refer back to them when necessary:

> "(1) I am not, indeed, sure whether it is not true to say that the
> Milton who once seemed not unlike a seventeenth-century Shelley had
> not become, out of an experience ever more bitter in each year, more
> alien [*sic*] to the founder of that Jesuit sect which nothing could induce
> him to tolerate."
>
> Professor Harold Laski (Essay in *Freedom of Expression*).

> "(2) Above all, we cannot play ducks and drakes with a native battery
> of idioms which prescribes such egregious collocations of vocables as the
> Basic *put up with* for *tolerate* or *put at a loss* for *bewilder.*"
>
> Professor Lancelot Hogben (*Interglossa*).

> "(3) On the one side we have the free personality: by definition it is not
> neurotic, for it has neither conflict nor dream. Its desires, such as they are,
> are transparent, for they are just what institutional approval keeps in the
> forefront of consciousness; another institutional pattern would alter their
> number and intensity; there is little in them that is natural, irreducible,
> or culturally dangerous. But *on the other side*, the social bond itself
> is nothing but the mutual reflection of these self-secure integrities. Recall
> the definition of love. Is not this the very picture of a small academic?
> Where is there a place in this hall of mirrors for either personality or fra-
> ternity?"
>
> Essay on psychology in *Politics* (New York).

> "(4) All the 'best people' from the gentlemen's clubs, and all the fran-
> tic fascist captains, united in common hatred of Socialism and bestial
> horror of the rising tide of the mass revolutionary movement, have
> turned to acts of provocation, to foul incendiarism, to medieval legends
> of poisoned wells, to legalize their own destruction of proletarian organi-
> zations, and rouse the agitated petty-bourgeoisie to chauvinistic fervour
> on behalf of the fight against the revolutionary way out of the crisis."
>
> Communist pamphlet.

> "(5) If a new spirit *is* to be infused into this old country, there is one
> thorny and contentious reform which must be tackled, and that is the
> humanization and galvanization of the B.B.C. Timidity here will bespeak
> cancer and atrophy of the soul. The heart of Britain may be sound and of
> strong beat, for instance, but the British lion's roar at present is like that
> of Bottom in Shakespeare's *Midsummer Night's Dream*—as gentle as any
> sucking dove. A virile new Britain cannot continue indefinitely to be

traduced in the eyes or rather ears, of the world by the effete languors of Langham Place, brazenly masquerading as 'standard English'. When the Voice of Britain is heard at nine o'clock, better far and infinitely less ludicrous to hear aitches honestly dropped than the present priggish, inflated, inhibited, school-ma'amish arch braying of blameless bashful mewing maidens!"

Letter in Tribune.

Each of these passages has faults of its own, but, quite apart from avoidable ugliness, two qualities are common to all of them. The first is staleness of imagery: the other is lack of precision. The writer either has a meaning and cannot express it, or he inadvertently says something else, or he is almost indifferent as to whether his words mean anything or not. This mixture of vagueness and sheer incompetence is the most marked characteristic of modern English prose, and especially of any kind of political writing. As soon as certain topics are raised, the concrete melts into the abstract and no one seems able to think of turns of speech that are not hackneyed: prose consists less and less of *words* chosen for the sake of their meaning, and more and more of *phrases* tacked together like the sections of a prefabricated hen-house. I list below, with notes and examples, various of the tricks by means of which the work of prose-construction is habitually dodged:

Dying Metaphors

A newly invented metaphor assists thought by evoking a visual image, while on the other hand a metaphor which is technically "dead" (e.g. *iron resolution*) has in effect reverted to being an ordinary word and can generally be used without loss of vividness. But in between these two classes there is a huge dump of worn-out metaphors which have lost all evocative power and are merely used because they save people the trouble of inventing phrases for themselves. Examples are: *Ring the changes on, take up the cudgels for, toe the line, ride roughshod over, stand shoulder to shoulder with, play into the hands of, no axe to grind, grist to the mill, fishing in troubled waters, on the order of the day, Achilles' heel, swan song, hotbed.* Many of these are used without knowledge of their meaning (what is a "rift," for instance?), and incompatible metaphors are frequently mixed, a sure sign that the writer is not interested in what he is saying. Some metaphors now current have been twisted out of their original meaning without those who use them even being aware of the fact. For example, *toe the line* is sometimes written *tow the line.* Another example is *the hammer and the anvil,* now always used with the implication that the anvil gets the worst of it. In real life it is always the anvil that breaks the hammer, never the other way about:

a writer who stopped to think what he was saying would be aware of this, and would avoid perverting the original phrase.

Operators or Verbal False Limbs

These save the trouble of picking out appropriate verbs and nouns, and at the same time pad each sentence with extra syllables which give it an appearance of symmetry. Characteristic phrases are: *render inoperative, militate against, make contact with, be subjected to, give rise to, give grounds for, have the effect of, play a leading part (role) in, make itself felt, take effect, exhibit a tendency to, serve the purpose of, etc., etc.* The keynote is the elimination of simple verbs. Instead of being a single word, such as *break, stop, spoil, mend, kill,* a verb becomes a *phrase,* made up of a noun or adjective tacked on to some general-purposes verb such as *prove, serve, form, play, render.* In addition, the passive voice is wherever possible used in preference to the active, and noun constructions are used instead of gerunds (*by examination of* instead of *by examining*). The range of verbs is further cut down by means of the *-ize* and *de-* formation, and the banal statements are given an appearance of profundity by means of the *not un-* formation. Simple conjunctions and prepositions are replaced by such phrases as *with respect to, having regard to, the fact that, by dint of, in view of, in the interests of, on the hypothesis that;* and the ends of sentences are saved from anticlimax by such resounding commonplaces as *greatly to be desired, cannot be left out of account, a development to be expected in the near future, deserving of serious consideration, brought to a satisfactory conclusion,* and so on and so forth.

Pretentious Diction

Words like *phenomenon, element, individual* (as noun), *objective, categorical, effective, virtual, basic, primary, promote, constitute, exhibit, exploit, utilize, eliminate, liquidate,* are used to dress up simple statements and give an air of scientific impartiality to biased judgments. Adjectives like *epoch-making, epic, historic, unforgettable, triumphant, age-old, inevitable, inexorable, veritable,* are used to dignify the sordid processes of international politics, while writing that aims at glorifying war usually takes on an archaic colour, its characteristic words being: *realm, throne, chariot, mailed fist, trident, sword, shield, buckler, banner, jackboot, clarion.* Foreign words and expressions such as *cul de sac, ancien régime, deus ex machina, mutatis mutandis, status quo, gleichschaltung, weltanschauung,* are used to give an air of culture and elegance. Except for the useful abbreviations *i.e., e.g.,* and *etc.,* there is no real need for any of the hundreds of foreign phrases now current in English. Bad writers, and especially scientific, political and sociological writers, are nearly always haunted by the notion that Latin or Greek words are grander than Saxon ones, and unnecessary words like *expedite, ameliorate, predict, extraneous, deracinated, clandestine, subaqueous* and hundreds of others constantly gain ground from their Anglo-Saxon opposite numbers.[1] The jargon peculiar to Marxist writing (*hyena, hangman, cannibal, petty bourgeois, these gentry, lacquey, flunkey, mad dog, White Guard,* etc.) consists largely of words and phrases translated from Russian, German or French; but the normal way of coining a new word is to use a Latin or Greek root with the appropriate affix and, where necessary, the *-ize* formation. It is often easier to make up words of this kind (*deregionalize, impermissible, extramarital, nonfragmentatory* and so forth) than to think up the English words that will cover one's meaning. The result, in general, is an increase in slovenliness and vagueness.

Meaningless Words

In certain kinds of writing, particularly in art criticism and literary criticism, it is normal to come across long passages which are almost completely lacking in meaning.[2] Words like *romantic, plastic, values, human, dead, sentimental, natural, vitality,* as used in art criticism, are strictly meaningless in the sense that they not only do not point to any discoverable object, but are hardly ever expected to do so by the reader. When one critic writes, "The outstanding feature of Mr. X's work is its living quality," while another writes, "The immediately striking thing about Mr. X's work is its peculiar deadness," the reader accepts this as a simple difference of opinion. If words like *black* and *white* were involved, instead of the jargon words *dead* and *living,* he would see at once that language was being used in an improper way. Many political words are similarly abused. The word *Fascism* has now no meaning except in so far as it signifies "something not desirable." The words *democracy, socialism, freedom, patriotic, realistic, justice,* have each of them several different meanings which cannot be reconciled with one another. In the case of a word like *democracy,* not only is there no agreed

1. An interesting illustration of this is the way in which the English flower names which were in use till very recently are being ousted by Greek ones, *snapdragon* becoming *antirrhinum, forget-me-not* becoming *myosotis,* etc. It is hard to see any practical reason for this change of fashion: it is probably due to an instinctive turning-away from the more homely word and a vague feeling that the Greek word is scientific [Orwell's note].

2. Example: "Comfort's catholicity of per-

ception and image, strangely Whitmanesque in range, almost the exact opposite in aesthetic compulsion, continues to evoke that trembling atmospheric accumulative hinting at a cruel, an inexorably serene timelessness. . . . Wrey Gardiner scores by aiming at simple bull's-eyes with precision. Only they are not so simple, and through this contented sadness- runs more than the surface bittersweet of resignation" (*Poetry Quarterly*) [Orwell's note].

definition, but the attempt to make one is resisted from all sides. It is
almost universally felt that when we call a country democratic we are
praising it: consequently the defenders of every kind of régime claim
that it is a democracy, and fear that they might have to stop using the
word if it were tied down to any one meaning. Words of this kind are
often used in a consciously dishonest way. That is, the person who uses
them has his own private definition, but allows his hearer to think he
means something quite different. Statements like *Marshal Pétain was a
true patriot, The Soviet Press is the freest in the world, The Catholic
Church is opposed to persecution,* are almost always made with intent
to deceive. Other words used in variable meanings, in most cases more
or less dishonestly, are: *class, totalitarian, science, progressive, reactionary, bourgeois, equality.*

Now that I have made this catalogue of swindles and perversions, let
me give another example of the kind of writing that they lead to. This
time it must of its nature be an imaginary one. I am going to translate
a passage of good English into modern English of the worst sort. Here
is a well-known verse from *Ecclesiastes:*

> "I returned and saw under the sun, that the race is not to the swift, nor
> the battle to the strong, neither yet bread to the wise, nor yet riches to
> men of understanding, nor yet favour to men of skill; but time and chance
> happeneth to them all."

10   Here it is in modern English:

> "Objective consideration of contemporary phenomena compels the con-
> clusion that success or failure in competitive activities exhibits no tendency
> to be commensurate with innate capacity, but that a considerable element
> of the unpredictable must invariably be taken into account."

This is a parody, but not a very gross one. Exhibit (3), above, for
instance, contains several patches of the same kind of English. It will
be seen that I have not made a full translation. The beginning and
ending of the sentence follow the original meaning fairly closely, but in
the middle the concrete illustrations—race, battle, bread—dissolve into
the vague phrase "success or failure in competitive activities." This had
to be so, because no modern writer of the kind I am discussing—no one
capable of using phrases like "objective consideration of contemporary
phenomena"—would ever tabulate his thoughts in that precise and
detailed way. The whole tendency of modern prose is away from con-
creteness. Now analyse these two sentences a little more closely. The
first contains forty-nine words but only sixty syllables, and all its words
are those of everyday life. The second contains thirty-eight words of
ninety syllables: eighteen of its words are from Latin roots, and one from
Greek. The first sentence contains six vivid images, and only one phrase

("time and chance") that could be called vague. The second contains not a single fresh, arresting phrase, and in spite of its ninety syllables it gives only a shortened version of the meaning contained in the first. Yet without a doubt it is the second kind of sentence that is gaining ground in modern English. I do not want to exaggerate. This kind of writing is not yet universal, and outcrops of simplicity will occur here and there in the worst-written page. Still, if you or I were told to write a few lines on the uncertainty of human fortunes, we should probably come much nearer to my imaginary sentence than to the one from *Ecclesiastes*.

As I have tried to show, modern writing at its worst does not consist in picking out words for the sake of their meaning and inventing images in order to make the meaning clearer. It consists in gumming together long strips of words which have already been set in order by someone else, and making the results presentable by sheer humbug. The attraction of this way of writing is that it is easy. It is easier—even quicker, once you have the habit—to say *In my opinion it is a not unjustifiable assumption that* than to say *I think*. If you use ready-made phrases, you not only don't have to hunt about for words; you also don't have to bother with the rhythms of your sentences, since these phrases are generally so arranged as to be more or less euphonious. When you are composing in a hurry—when you are dictating to a stenographer, for instance, or making a public speech—it is natural to fall into a pretentious, Latinized style. Tags like *a consideration which we should do well to bear in mind* or *a conclusion to which all of us would readily assent* will save many a sentence from coming down with a bump. By using stale metaphors, similes and idioms, you save much mental effort, at the cost of leaving your meaning vague, not only for your reader but for yourself. This is the significance of mixed metaphors. The sole aim of a metaphor is to call up a visual image. When these images clash—as in *The Fascist octopus has sung its swan song, the jackboot is thrown into the melting pot*—it can be taken as certain that the writer is not seeing a mental image of the objects he is naming; in other words he is not really thinking. Look again at the examples I gave at the beginning of this essay. Professor Laski (1) uses five negatives in fifty-three words. One of these is superfluous, making nonsense of the whole passage, and in addition there is the slip *alien* for akin, making further nonsense, and several avoidable pieces of clumsiness which increase the general vagueness. Professor Hogben (2) plays ducks and drakes with a battery which is able to write prescriptions, and, while disapproving of the everyday phrase *put up with*, is unwilling to look *egregious* up in the dictionary and see what it means. (3), if one takes an uncharitable attitude towards it, is simply meaningless: probably one could work out its intended meaning by reading the whole of the article in which it occurs. In (4), the writer knows more or less what he wants to say, but an accumulation of stale phrases chokes him like tea leaves blocking a sink. In (5), words and meaning have almost parted company. People who write in this manner usually have a general emotional meaning—they dislike one thing and want to express solidarity with another—but they are not interested in the detail of what they are saying. A scrupulous writer, in every sentence that he writes, will ask himself at least four questions, thus: What am I trying to say? What words will express it? What image or idiom will make it clearer? Is this image fresh enough to have an effect? And he will probably ask himself two more: Could I put it more shortly? Have I said anything that is avoidably ugly? But you are not obliged to go to all this trouble. You can shirk it by simply throwing your mind open and letting the ready-made phrases come crowding in. They will construct your sentences for you—even think your thoughts for you, to a certain extent—and at need they will perform the important service of partially concealing your meaning even from yourself. It is at this point that the special connection between politics and the debasement of language becomes clear.

In our time it is broadly true that political writing is bad writing. Where it is not true, it will generally be found that the writer is some kind of rebel, expressing his private opinions and not a "party line." Orthodoxy, of whatever colour, seems to demand a lifeless, imitative style. The political dialects to be found in pamphlets, leading articles, manifestos, White Papers and the speeches of under-secretaries do, of course, vary from party to party, but they are all alike in that one almost never finds in them a fresh, vivid, home-made turn of speech. When one watches some tired hack on the platform mechanically repeating the familiar phrases—*bestial atrocities, iron heel, bloodstained tyranny, free peoples of the world, stand shoulder to shoulder*—one often has a curious feeling that one is not watching a live human being but some kind of dummy: a feeling which suddenly becomes stronger at moments when the light catches the speaker's spectacles and turns them into blank discs which seem to have no eyes behind them. And this is not altogether fanciful. A speaker who uses that kind of phraseology has gone some distance towards turning himself into a machine. The appropriate noises are coming out of his larynx, but his brain is not involved as it would be if he were choosing his words for himself. If the speech he is making is one that he is accustomed to make over and over again, he may be almost unconscious of what he is saying, as one is when one utters the responses in church. And this reduced state of consciousness, if not indispensable, is at any rate favourable to political conformity.

In our time, political speech and writing are largely the defence of the indefensible. Things like the continuance of British rule in India, the Russian purges and deportations, the dropping of the atom bombs on Japan, can indeed be defended, but only by arguments which are too brutal for most people to face, and which do not square with the professed aims of political parties. Thus political language has to consist largely of euphemism, question-begging and sheer cloudy vagueness. Defenceless villages are bombarded from the air, the inhabitants driven out into the countryside, the cattle machine-gunned, the huts set on fire with incendiary bullets: this is called *pacification*. Millions of peasants are robbed of their farms and sent trudging along the roads with no more than they can carry: this is called *transfer of population* or *rectification of frontiers*. People are imprisoned for years without trial, or shot in the back of the neck or sent to die of scurvy in Arctic lumber camps: this is called *elimination of unreliable elements*. Such phraseology is needed if one wants to name things without calling up mental pictures of them. Consider for instance some comfortable English professor defending Russian totalitarianism. He cannot say outright, "I believe in killing off your opponents when you can get good results by doing so." Probably, therefore, he will say something like this:

"While freely conceding that the Soviet régime exhibits certain features which the humanitarian may be inclined to deplore, we must, I think, agree that a certain curtailment of the right to political opposition is an unavoidable concomitant of transitional periods, and that the rigors which the Russian people have been called upon to undergo have been amply justified in the sphere of concrete achievement."

The inflated style is itself a kind of euphemism. A mass of Latin words falls upon the facts like soft snow, blurring the outlines and covering up all the details. The great enemy of clear language is insincerity. When there is a gap between one's real and one's declared aims, one turns as it were instinctively to long words and exhausted idioms, like a cuttlefish squirting out ink. In our age there is no such thing as "keeping out of politics." All issues are political issues, and politics itself is a mass of lies, evasions, folly, hatred and schizophrenia. When the general atmosphere is bad, language must suffer. I should expect to find—this is a guess which I have not sufficient knowledge to verify—that the German, Russian and Italian languages have all deteriorated in the last ten or fifteen years, as a result of dictatorship.

But if thought corrupts language, language can also corrupt thought. A bad usage can spread by tradition and imitation, even among people who should and do know better. The debased language that I have been discussing is in some ways very convenient. Phrases like *a not unjustifiable assumption, leaves much to be desired, would serve no good purpose, a consideration which we should do well to bear in mind*, are a continuous temptation, a packet of aspirins always at one's elbow. Look back through this essay, and for certain you will find that I have again and again committed the very faults I am protesting against. By this morning's post I have received a pamphlet dealing with conditions in Germany. The author tells me that he "felt impelled" to write it. I open it at random, and here is almost the first sentence that I see: "(The Allies) have an opportunity not only of achieving a radical transformation of Germany's social and political structure in such a way as to avoid a nationalistic reaction in Germany itself, but at the same time of laying the foundations of a co-operative and unified Europe." You see, he "feels impelled" to write—feels, presumably, that he has something new to say—and yet his words, like cavalry horses answering the bugle, group themselves automatically into the familiar dreary pattern. This invasion of one's mind by ready-made phrases (*lay the foundations, achieve a radical transformation*) can only be prevented if one is constantly on guard against them, and every such phrase anaesthetizes a portion of one's brain.

I said earlier that the decadence of our language is probably curable. Those who deny this would argue, if they produced an argument at all, that language merely reflects existing social conditions, and that we cannot influence its development by any direct tinkering with words and constructions. So far as the general tone or spirit of a language goes, this may be true, but it is not true in detail. Silly words and expressions have often disappeared, not through any evolutionary process but owing to the conscious action of a minority. Two recent examples were *explore every avenue* and *leave no stone unturned,* which were killed by the jeers of a few journalists. There is a long list of flyblown metaphors which could similarly be got rid of if enough people would interest themselves in the job; and it should also be possible to laugh the *not un-* formation out of existence,[3] to reduce the amount of Latin and Greek in the average sentence, to drive out foreign phrases and strayed scientific words, and, in general, to make pretentiousness unfashionable. But all these are minor points. The defence of the English language implies more than this, and perhaps it is best to start by saying what it does *not* imply.

To begin with it has nothing to do with archaism, with the salvaging of obsolete words and turns of speech, or with the setting up of a "standard English" which must never be departed from. On the contrary, it is especially concerned with the scrapping of every word or idiom which has outworn its usefulness. It has nothing to do with correct grammar and syntax, which are of no importance so long as one makes one's meaning clear, or with the avoidance of Americanisms, or with having what is called a "good prose style." On the other hand it is not concerned with fake simplicity and the attempt to make written English colloquial. Nor does it even imply in every case preferring the Saxon

3. One can cure oneself of the *not un-* formation by memorizing this sentence: *A not unblack dog was chasing a not unsmall rabbit across a not ungreen field* [Orwell's note].

word to the Latin one, though it does imply using the fewest and shortest words that will cover one's meaning. What is above all needed is to let the meaning choose the word, and not the other way about. In prose, the worst thing one can do with words is to surrender to them. When you think of a concrete object, you think wordlessly, and then, if you want to describe the thing you have been visualizing you probably hunt about till you find the exact words that seem to fit. When you think of something abstract you are more inclined to use words from the start, and unless you make a conscious effort to prevent it, the existing dialect will come rushing in and do the job for you, at the expense of blurring or even changing your meaning. Probably it is better to put off using words as long as possible and get one's meaning as clear as one can through pictures or sensations. Afterwards one can choose—not simply *accept*—the phrases that will best cover the meaning, and then switch round and decide what impression one's words are likely to make on another person. This last effort of the mind cuts out all stale or mixed images, all prefabricated phrases, needless repetitions, and humbug and vagueness generally. But one can often be in doubt about the effect of a word or a phrase, and one needs rules that one can rely on when instinct fails. I think the following rules will cover most cases:

(i) Never use a metaphor, simile or other figure of speech which you are used to seeing in print.

(ii) Never use a long word where a short one will do.

(iii) If it is possible to cut a word out, always cut it out.

(iv) Never use the passive where you can use the active.

(v) Never use a foreign phrase, a scientific word or a jargon word if you can think of an everyday English equivalent.

(vi) Break any of these rules sooner than say anything outright barbarous.

These rules sound elementary, and so they are, but they demand a deep change of attitude in anyone who has grown used to writing in the style now fashionable. One could keep all of them and still write bad English, but one could not write the kind of stuff that I quoted in those five specimens at the beginning of this article.

I have not here been considering the literary use of language, but merely language as an instrument for expressing and not for concealing or preventing thought. Stuart Chase and others have come near to claiming that all abstract words are meaningless, and have used this as a pretext for advocating a kind of political quietism. Since you don't know what Fascism is, how can you struggle against Fascism? One need not swallow such absurdities as this, but one ought to recognize that the present political chaos is connected with the decay of language, and that one can probably bring about some improvement by starting at the

20

verbal end. If you simplify your English, you are freed from the worst follies of orthodoxy. You cannot speak any of the necessary dialects, and when you make a stupid remark its stupidity will be obvious, even to yourself. Political language—and with variations this is true of all political parties, from Conservatives to Anarchists—is designed to make lies sound truthful and murder respectable, and to give an appearance of solidity to pure wind. One cannot change this all in a moment, but one can at least change one's own habits, and from time to time one can even, if one jeers loudly enough, send some worn-out and useless phrase—some *jackboot, Achilles' heel, hotbed, melting pot, acid test, veritable inferno* or other lump of verbal refuse—into the dustbin where it belongs.

THE READER

1. *What is Orwell's pivotal point? Where is it best stated?*
2. *Discuss Orwell's assertion that "the decline of a language must ultimately have political and economic causes." Is this "clear," as he claims?*
3. *Orwell suggests that if you look back through his essay, you will find that he has "again and again committed the very faults" he is protesting against. Is this true? If it is, does it affect the validity of his major points?*

THE WRITER

1. *How can you be sure that a metaphor is dying, rather than alive or dead? Is Orwell's test of seeing it often in print a sufficient one? Can you defend any of his examples of dying metaphors as necessary or useful additions to our vocabularies?*
2. *Orwell gives a list of questions for the writer to ask himself (p. 424) and a list of rules for the writer to follow (p. 427). Why does he consider it necessary to give both kinds of advice? How much do the two overlap? Are both consistent with Orwell's major ideas expressed elsewhere in the essay? Does his injunction to "break any of these rules sooner than say anything outright barbarous" beg the question?*
3. *Words create a personality or confer a character. Write a brief essay describing the personality that would be created by following Orwell's six rules. Show that character in action.*

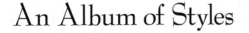

An Album of Styles

Francis Bacon: OF REVENGE

Revenge is a kind of wild justice; which the more man's nature runs to, the more ought law to weed it out. For as for the first wrong, it doth but offend the law; but the revenge of that wrong putteth the law out of office. Certainly, in taking revenge, a man is but even with his enemy; but in passing it over, he is superior; for it is a prince's part to pardon. And Salomon, I am sure, saith, *It is the glory of a man to pass by an offence.* That which is past is gone, and irrevocable; and wise men have enough to do with things present and to come: therefore they do but trifle with themselves, that labour in past matters. There is no man doth a wrong for the wrong's sake; but thereby to purchase himself profit, or pleasure, or honour, or the like. Therefore why should I be angry with a man for loving himself better than me? And if any man should do wrong merely out of ill nature, why, yet it is but like the thorn or briar, which prick and scratch, because they can do no other. The most tolerable sort of revenge is for those wrongs which there is no law to remedy; but then let a man take heed the revenge be such as there is no law to punish; else a man's enemy is still beforehand, and it is two for one. Some, when they take revenge, are desirous the party should know whence it cometh: this is the more generous. For the delight seemeth to be not so much in doing the hurt as in making the party repent: but base and crafty cowards are like the arrow that flieth in the dark. Cosmus, duke of Florence, had a desperate saying against perfidious or neglecting friends, as if those wrongs were unpardonable: *You shall read* (saith he) *that we are commanded to forgive our enemies; but you never read that we are commanded to forgive our friends.* But yet the spirit of Job was in a better tune: *Shall we* (saith he) *take good at God's hands, and not be content to take evil also?* And so of friends in a proportion. This is certain, that a man that studieth revenge keeps his own wounds green, which otherwise would heal and do well. Public

From *Essays* (various editions, 1597–1625).

revenges are for the most part fortunate; as that for the death of Caesar; for the death of Pertinax;[1] for the death of Henry the third of France;[2] and many more. But in private revenges it is not so. Nay rather, vindictive persons live the life of witches; who as they are mischievous, so end they infortunate.

1. Publius Helvius Pertinax became Emperor of Rome in 193 and was assassinated three months after his accession to the throne by a soldier in his praetorian Guard. 2. King of France 1574–89; assassinated during the Siege of Paris.

John Donne: NO MAN IS AN ISLAND

No man is an island, entire of itself; every man is a piece of the continent, a part of the main.[1] If a clod be washed away by the sea, Europe is the less, as well as if a promontory were, as well as if a manor of thy friend's or of thine own were. Any man's death diminishes me, because I am involved in mankind; and therefore never send to know for whom the bell tolls; it tolls for thee.

From *Meditation 17* of Donne's *Devotions upon Emergent Occasions* (1623).

1. Mainland.

Samuel Johnson: THE PYRAMIDS

Of the wall [of China] it is very easy to assign the motives. It secured a wealthy and timorous nation from the incursions of Barbarians, whose unskillfulness in arts made it easier for them to supply their wants by rapine than by industry, and who from time to time poured in upon the habitations of peaceful commerce, as vultures descend upon domestic fowl. Their celerity and fierceness made the wall necessary, and their ignorance made it efficacious.

But for the pyramids no reason has ever been given adequate to the cost and labor of the work. The narrowness of the chambers proves that it could afford no retreat from enemies, and treasures might have been reposited at far less expense with equal security. It seems to have been erected only in compliance with that hunger of imagination which preys

From *Rasselas* (1759).

incessantly upon life, and must be always appeased by some employment. Those who have already all that they can enjoy, must enlarge their desires. He that has built for use, till use is supplied must begin to build for vanity, and extend his plan to the utmost power of human performance, that he may not be soon reduced to form another wish.

I consider this mighty structure as a monument of the insufficiency of human enjoyments. A king, whose power is unlimited, and whose treasures surmount all real and imaginary wants, is compelled to solace, by the erection of a pyramid, the satiety of dominion and tastelessness of pleasures, and to amuse the tediousness of declining life, by seeing thousands laboring without end, and one stone, for no purpose, laid upon another. Whoever thou art, that, not content with a moderate condition, imaginest happiness in royal magnificence, and dreamest that command or riches can feed the appetite of novelty with perpetual gratifications, survey the pyramids, and confess thy folly!

Charles Lamb: THE TWO RACES OF MEN

The human species, according to the best theory I can form of it, is composed of two distinct races, *the men who borrow,* and *the men who lend.* To these two original diversities may be reduced all those impertinent classifications of Gothic and Celtic tribes, white men, black men, red men. All the dwellers upon earth, "Parthians, and Medes, and Elamites," flock hither, and do naturally fall in with one or other of these primary distinctions. The infinite superiority of the former, which I choose to designate as the *great race,* is discernible in their figure, port, and a certain instinctive sovereignty. The latter are born degraded. "He shall serve his brethren." There is something in the air of one of this cast, lean and suspicious; contrasting with the open, trusting, generous manners of the other.

Observe who have been the greatest borrowers of all ages—Alcibiades—Falstaff—Sir Richard Steele—our late incomparable Brinsley[1]—what a family likeness in all four!

One of Lamb's *Essays of Elia* published in the *London Magazine* (1820–23).

1. Alcibiades (c. 450–404 B.C.), brilliant but unscrupulous Athenian politician and military commander; John Falstaff, Shakespeare's most famous comic character, a monumentally self-indulgent braggart. Sir Richard Steele (1672–1729), Irish-born English essayist, dramatist, politician, and journalist; and Richard Brinsley Sheridan (1751–1816), Irish-born English dramatist (*The Rivals, The School for Scandal*), orator, and statesman, were both notoriously improvident men.

What a careless, even deportment hath your borrower! what rosy gills! what a beautiful reliance on Providence doth he manifest—taking no more thought than lilies![2] What contempt for money—accounting it (yours and mine especially) no better than dross. What a liberal confounding of those pedantic distinctions of *meum* and *tuum!* or rather, what a noble simplification of language (beyond Tooke), resolving these supposed opposites into one clear, intelligible pronoun adjective![3] What near approaches doth he make to the primitive *community*—to the extent of one half of the principle at least!

2. Matthew vi:28: "Consider the lilies of the field, how they grow; they toil not, neither do they spin."
3. "Mine and thine," the resolution "of these supposed opposites into one . . . pronoun adjective" would presumably be *meum* alone. John Horne Tooke (1736–1812), English philologist and politician.

John Henry Newman: KNOWLEDGE AND VIRTUE

Knowledge is one thing, virtue is another; good sense is not conscience, refinement is not humility, nor is largeness and justness of view faith. Philosophy, however enlightened, however profound, gives no command over the passions, no influential motives, no vivifying principles. Liberal Education makes not the Christian, not the Catholic, but the gentleman. It is well to be a gentleman, it is well to have a cultivated intellect, a delicate taste, a candid, equitable, dispassionate mind, a noble and courteous bearing in the conduct of life—these are the connatural qualities of a large knowledge; they are the objects of a University; I am advocating, I shall illustrate and insist upon them; but still, I repeat, they are no guarantee for sanctity or even for conscientiousness, they may attach to the man of the world, to the profligate, to the heartless, pleasant, alas, and attractive as he shows when decked out in them. Taken by themselves, they do but seem to be what they are not; they look like virtue at a distance, but they are detected by close observers, and on the long run; and hence it is that they are popularly accused of pretense and hypocrisy, not, I repeat, from their own fault, but because their professors and their admirers persist in taking them for what they are not, and are officious in arrogating for them a praise to which they have no claim. Quarry the granite rock with razors, or moor the vessel with a thread of silk; then may you hope with such keen and delicate instruments as human knowledge and human reason to contend against those giants, the passion and the pride of man.

From *The Idea of a University Defined and Illustrated* (1852).

Abraham Lincoln: THE GETTYSBURG ADDRESS

Four score and seven years ago our fathers brought forth on this continent, a new nation, conceived in Liberty, and dedicated to the proposition that all men are created equal.

Now we are engaged in a great civil war, testing whether that nation, or any nation so conceived and so dedicated, can long endure. We are met on a great battle-field of that war. We have come to dedicate a portion of that field, as a final resting place for those who here gave their lives that that nation might live. It is altogether fitting and proper that we should do this.

But, in a larger sense, we can not dedicate—we can not consecrate—we can not hallow—this ground. The brave men, living and dead, who struggled here, have consecrated it, far above our poor power to add or detract. The world will little note, nor long remember what we say here, but it can never forget what they did here. It is for us the living, rather, to be dedicated here to the unfinished work which they who fought here have thus far so nobly advanced. It is rather for us to be here dedicated to the great task remaining before us—that from these honored dead we take increased devotion to that cause for which they gave the last full measure of devotion—that we here highly resolve that these dead shall not have died in vain—that this nation, under God, shall have a new birth of freedom—and that government of the people, by the people, for the people, shall not perish from the earth.

Presidential address delivered in 1863 in Gettysburg, Pennsylvania.

Matthew Arnold: CULTURE

But there is of culture another view, in which not solely the scientific passion, the sheer desire to see things as they are, natural and proper in an intelligent being, appears as the ground of it. There is a view in which all the love of our neighbor, the impulses towards action, help, and beneficence, the desire for removing human error, clearing human confusion, and diminishing human misery, the noble aspiration to leave the world better and happier than we found it—motives eminently such as are called social—come in as part of the grounds of culture, and the main and pre-eminent part. Culture is then properly described not as having

From *Culture and Anarchy* (1869).

433

its origin in curiosity, but as having its origin in the love of perfection; it is *a study of perfection.* It moves by the force, not merely or primarily of the scientific passion for pure knowledge, but also of the moral and social passion for doing good. As, in the first view of it, we took for its worthy motto Montesquieu's words: "To render an intelligent being yet more intelligent!" so, in the second view of it, there is no better motto which it can have than these words of Bishop Wilson: "To make reason and the will of God prevail!"

Only, whereas the passion for doing good is apt to be overhasty in determining what reason and the will of God say, because its turn is for acting rather than thinking, and it wants to be beginning to act; and whereas it is apt to take its own conceptions, which proceed from its own state of development and share in all the imperfections and immaturities of this, for a basis of action; what distinguishes culture is, that it is possessed by the scientific passion as well as by the passion of doing good; that it demands worthy notions of reason and the will of God, and does not readily suffer its own crude conceptions to substitute themselves for them. And knowing that no action or institution can be salutary and stable which is not based on reason and the will of God, it is not so bent on acting and instituting, even with the great aim of diminishing human error and misery ever before its thoughts, but that it can remember that acting and instituting are of little use, unless we know how and what we ought to act and to institute.

Walter Pater: THE MONA LISA

The presence that rose thus so strangely beside the waters, is expressive of what in the ways of a thousand years men had come to desire. Hers is the head upon which all "the ends of the world are come," and the eyelids are a little weary. It is a beauty wrought out from within upon the flesh, the deposit, little cell by cell, of strange thoughts and fantastic reveries and exquisite passions. Set it for a moment beside one of those white Greek goddesses or beautiful women of antiquity, and how would they be troubled by this beauty, into which the soul with all its maladies has passed! All the thoughts and experience of the world have etched and molded there, in that which they have of power to refine and make expressive the outward form, the animalism of Greece, the lust of Rome, the mysticism of the middle ages with its spiritual ambition and imagina-

From Pater's essay on Leonardo da Vinci in his first book, *Studies in the History of the Renaissance* (1873).

tive loves, the return of the Pagan world, the sins of the Borgias. She is older than the rocks among which she sits; like the vampire, she has been dead many times, and learned the secrets of the grave; and has been a diver in deep seas, and keeps their fallen day about her; and trafficked for strange webs with Eastern merchants: and, as Leda, was the mother of Helen of Troy, and, as Saint Anne, the mother of Mary; and all this has been to her but as the sound of lyres and flutes, and lives only in the delicacy with which it has molded the changing lineaments, and tinged the eyelids and the hands. The fancy of a perpetual life, sweeping together ten-thousand experiences, is an old one; and modern philosophy has conceived the idea of humanity as wrought upon by, and summing up in itself, all modes of thought and life. Certainly Lady Lisa might stand as the embodiment of the old fancy, the symbol of the modern idea.

Ernest Hemingway: FROM A FAREWELL TO ARMS

* * * I was always embarrassed by the words sacred, glorious, and sacrifice and the expression in vain. We had heard them, sometimes standing in the rain almost out of earshot, so that only the shouted words came through, and had read them, on proclamations that were slapped up by billposters over other proclamations, now for a long time, and I had seen nothing sacred, and the things that were glorious had no glory and the sacrifices were like the stockyards at Chicago if nothing was done with the meat except to bury it. There were many words that you could not stand to hear and finally only the names of places had dignity. Certain numbers were the same way and certain dates and these with the names of places were all you could say and have them mean anything. Abstract words such as glory, honor, courage, or hallow were obscene beside the concrete names of villages, the numbers of roads, the names of rivers, the numbers of regiments and the dates.

From *A Farewell to Arms* (1929).

Virginia Woolf: What the Novelist Gives Us

It is simple enough to say that since books have classes—fiction, biography, poetry—we should separate them and take from each what it is right that each should give us. Yet few people ask from books what books can give us. Most commonly we come to books with blurred and divided minds, asking of fiction that it shall be true, of poetry that it shall be false, of biography that it shall be flattering, of history that it shall enforce our own prejudices. If we could banish all such preconceptions when we read, that would be an admirable beginning. Do not dictate to your author; try to become him. Be his fellow-worker and accomplice. If you hang back, and reserve and criticize at first, you are preventing yourself from getting the fullest possible value from what you read. But if you open your mind as widely as possible, then signs and hints of almost imperceptible fineness, from the twist and turn of the first sentences, will bring you into the presence of a human being unlike any other. Steep yourself in this, acquaint yourself with this, and soon you will find that your author is giving you, or attempting to give you, something far more definite. The thirty-two chapters of a novel—if we consider how to read a novel first—are an attempt to make something as formed and controlled as a building: but words are more impalpable than bricks; reading is a longer and more complicated process than seeing. Perhaps the quickest way to understand the elements of what a novelist is doing is not to read, but to write; to make your own experiment with the dangers and difficulties of words. Recall, then, some event that has left a distinct impression on you—how at the corner of the street, perhaps, you passed two people talking. A tree shook; an electric light danced; the tone of the talk was comic, but also tragic; a whole vision, an entire conception, seemed contained in that moment.

But when you attempt to reconstruct it in words, you will find that it breaks into a thousand conflicting impressions. Some must be subdued; others emphasized; in the process you will lose, probably, all grasp upon the emotion itself. Then turn from your blurred and littered pages to the opening pages of some great novelist—Defoe, Jane Austen, Hardy. Now you will be better able to appreciate their mastery. It is not merely that we are in the presence of a different person—Defoe, Jane Austen, or Thomas Hardy—but that we are living in a different world. Here, in *Robinson Crusoe*, we are trudging a plain high road; one thing happens after another; the fact and the order of the fact is enough. But if the open air and adventure mean everything to Defoe they mean nothing to Jane Austen. Hers is the drawing-room, and people talking,

From the essay "How Should One Read a Book?" in *The Second Common Reader* (1932).

and by the many mirrors of their talk revealing their characters. And if, when we have accustomed ourselves to the drawing-room and its reflections, we turn to Hardy, we are once more spun around. The moors are round us and the stars are above our heads. The other side of the mind is now exposed—the dark side that comes uppermost in solitude, not the light side that shows in company. Our relations are not towards people, but towards Nature and destiny. Yet different as these worlds are, each is consistent with itself. The maker of each is careful to observe the laws of his own perspective, and however great a strain they may put upon us they will never confuse us, as lesser writers so frequently do, by introducing two different kinds of reality into the same book. Thus to go from one great novelist to another—from Jane Austen to Hardy, from Peacock to Trollope, from Scott to Meredith—is to be wrenched and uprooted; to be thrown this way and then that. To read a novel is a difficult and complex art. You must be capable not only of great finesse of perception, but of great boldness of imagination if you are going to make use of all that the novelist—the great artist—gives you.

E. B. White: Progress and Change

In resenting progress and change, a man lays himself open to censure. I suppose the explanation of anyone's defending anything as rudimentary and cramped as a Pullman berth is that such things are associated with an earlier period in one's life and that this period in retrospect seems a happy one. People who favor progress and improvements are apt to be people who have had a tough enough time without any extra inconvenience. Reactionaries who pout at innovations are apt to be well-heeled sentimentalists who had the breaks. Yet for all that, there is always a subtle danger in life's refinements, a dim degeneracy in progress. I have just been refining the room in which I sit, yet I sometimes doubt that a writer should refine or improve his workroom by so much as a dictionary: one thing leads to another and the first thing you know he has a stuffed chair and is fast asleep in it. Half a man's life is devoted to what he calls improvements, yet the original had some quality which is lost in the process. There was a fine natural spring of water on this place when I bought it. Our drinking water had to be lugged in a pail, from a wet glade of alder and tamarack. I visited the spring often in those first years, and had friends there—a frog, a woodcock, and an

From "One Man's Meat," White's column for *Harper's Magazine* (Dec. 1938).

eel which had churned its way all the way up through the pasture creek to enjoy the luxury of pure water. In the normal course of development, the spring was rocked up, fitted with a concrete curb, a copper pipe, and an electric pump. I have visited it only once or twice since. This year my only gesture was the purely perfunctory one of sending a sample to the state bureau of health for analysis. I felt cheap, as though I were smelling an old friend's breath.

William Faulkner: NOBEL PRIZE AWARD SPEECH

I feel that this award was not made to me as a man but to my work—a life's work in the agony and sweat of the human spirit, not for glory and least of all for profit, but to create out of the materials of the human spirit something which did not exist before. So this award is only mine in trust. It will not be difficult to find a dedication for the money part of it commensurate with the purpose and significance of its origin. But I would like to do the same with the acclaim too, by using this moment as a pinnacle from which I might be listened to by the young men and women already dedicated to the same anguish and travail, among whom is already that one who will some day stand here where I am standing.

Our tragedy today is a general and universal physical fear so long sustained by now that we can even bear it. There are no longer problems of the spirit. There is only the question: When will I be blown up? Because of this, the young man or woman writing today has forgotten the problems of the human heart in conflict with itself which alone can make good writing because only that is worth writing about, worth the agony and the sweat.

He must learn them again. He must teach himself that the basest of all things is to be afraid; and, teaching himself that, forget it forever, leaving no room in his workshop for anything but the old verities and truths of the heart, the old universal truths lacking which any story is ephemeral and doomed—love and honor and pity and pride and compassion and sacrifice. Until he does so, he labors under a curse. He writes not of love but of lust, of defeats in which nobody loses anything of value, of victories without hope and, worst of all, without pity or compassion. His griefs grieve on no universal bones leaving no scars. He writes not of the heart but of the glands.

Until he relearns these things, he will write as though he stood alone

Given on acceptance of the Nobel Prize in 1949.

and watched the end of man. I decline to accept the end of man. It is easy enough to say that man is immortal simply because he will endure; that when the last ding-dong of doom has clanged and faded from the last worthless rock hanging tideless in the last red and dying evening, that even then there will still be one more sound: that of his puny inexhaustible voice, still talking. I refuse to accept this. I believe that man will not merely endure: he will prevail. He is immortal, not because he alone among creatures has an inexhaustible voice but because he has a soul, a spirit capable of compassion and sacrifice and endurance. The poet's, the writer's, duty is to write about these things. It is his privilege to help man endure by lifting his heart, by reminding him of the courage and honor and hope and pride and compassion and pity and sacrifice which have been the glory of his past. The poet's voice need not merely be the record of man, it can be one of the props, the pillars to help him endure and prevail.

James Thurber: A Dog's Eye View of Man

If Man has benefited immeasurably by his association with the dog, what, you may ask, has the dog got out of it? His scroll has, of course, been heavily charged with punishments: he has known the muzzle, the leash, and the tether; he has suffered the indignities of the show bench, the tin can on the tail, the ribbon in the hair; his love life with the other sex of his species has been regulated by the frigid hand of authority, his digestion ruined by the macaroons and marshmallows of doting women. The list of his woes could be continued indefinitely. But he has also had his fun, for he has been privileged to live with and study at close range the only creature with reason, the most unreasonable of creatures.

The dog has got more fun out of Man than Man has got out of the dog, for the clearly demonstrable reason that Man is the more laughable of the two animals. The dog has long been bemused by the singular activities and the curious practices of men, cocking his head inquiringly to one side, intently watching and listening to the strangest goings-on in the world. He has seen men sing together and fight one another in the same evening. He has watched them go to bed when it is time to get up, and get up when it is time to go to bed. He has observed them destroying the soil in vast areas, and nurturing it in small patches. He has stood by while men built strong and solid houses for rest and quiet,

From *Thurber's Dogs* (1955).

and then filled them with lights and bells and machinery. His sensitive nose, which can detect what's cooking in the next township, has caught at one and the same time the bewildering smells of the hospital and the munitions factory. He has seen men raise up great cities to heaven and then blow them to hell.

John Updike: Beer Can

This seems to be an era of gratuitous inventions and negative improvements. Consider the beer can. It was beautiful—as beautiful as the clothespin, as inevitable as the wine bottle, as dignified and reassuring as the fire hydrant. A tranquil cylinder of delightfully resonant metal, it could be opened in an instant, requiring only the application of a handy gadget freely dispensed by every grocer. Who can forget the small, symmetrical thrill of those two triangular punctures, the dainty *pfff*, the little crest of suds that foamed eagerly in the exultation of release? Now we are given, instead, a top beetling with an ugly, shmoo-shaped "tab," which, after fiercely resisting the tugging, bleeding fingers of the thirsty man, threatens his lips with a dangerous and hideous hole. However, we have discovered a way to thwart Progress, usually so unthwartable. *Turn the beer can upside down and open the bottom.* The bottom is still the way the top used to be. True, this operation gives the beer an unsettling jolt, and the sight of a consistently inverted beer can might make people edgy, not to say queasy. But the latter difficulty could be eliminated if manufacturers would design cans that looked the same whichever end was up, like playing cards. What we need is Progress with an escape hatch.

Originally appeared in *The New Yorker* (Jan. 18, 1964).

Robert Pirsig: Concrete, Brick, and Neon

The city closes in on him now, and in his strange perspective it becomes the antithesis of what he believes. The citadel not of Quality, the citadel of form and substance. Substance in the form of steel sheets

From *Zen and the Art of Motorcycle Maintenance* (1974).

and girders, substance in the form of concrete piers and roads, in the form of brick, of asphalt, of auto parts, old radios, and rails, dead carcasses of animals that once grazed the prairies. Form and substance without Quality. That is the soul of this place. Blind, huge, sinister and inhuman: seen by the light of fire flaring upward in the night from the blast furnaces in the south, through heavy coal smoke deeper and denser into the neon of BEER and PIZZA and LAUNDROMAT signs and unknown and meaningless signs along meaningless straight streets going off into other straight streets forever.

If it was all bricks and concrete, pure forms of substance, clearly and openly, he might survive. It is the little, pathetic attempts at Quality that kill. The plaster false fireplace in the apartment, shaped and waiting to contain a flame that can never exist. Or the hedge in front of the apartment building with a few square feet of grass behind it. A few square feet of grass, after Montana. If they just left out the hedge and grass it would be all right. Now it serves only to draw attention to what has been lost.

Along the streets that lead away from the apartment he can never see anything through the concrete and brick and neon but he knows that buried within it are grotesque, twisted souls forever trying the manners that will convince themselves they possess Quality, learning strange poses of style and glamour vended by dream magazines and other mass media, and paid for by the vendors of substance. He thinks of them at night alone with their advertised glamorous shoes and stockings and underclothes off, staring through the sooty windows at the grotesque shells revealed beyond them, when the poses weaken and the truth creeps in, the only truth that exists here, crying to heaven, God, there is nothing here but dead neon and cement and brick.

D. Keith Mano: How to Keep from Getting Mugged

Learn to walk gas-fast. Book it, baby: Lay a big batch behind. Not in panic, mind you: never run. A power-purposeful, elbow-out, crazy kind of stride. The way people moved in old silent films—you know, right before they fell into an open manhole. Wave one hand now and then, as if you'd just seen three armed friends and were about to hail a cab. Your attitude should be: "Busy signal, dit-dit-dit. Can't fit you in today,

Originally appeared in *Playboy* magazine (July 1982).

fellas. Catch me tomorrow." In a real halfway-house neighborhood, walk dead street center: follow that white line; avoid ambush cover. Who's gonna mug you when he might get hit by a truck while doing it? Oh, you should see me squeeze out sneaker juice: I am Rapid City: I have no staying power, g'bye. A thug will get depressed by energy. He'd rather come down on someone wearing orthopedic pants. Also, if you can manage it, be tall.

Sing aloud. Mutter a lot. Preach Jesus. Interrogate yourself. Say things like: "Oh, the onion bagel won't come off. Oh, it hurts. Mmmmmmm-huh. Mmmmm. Please, Ma, don't send me back to the nutria farm again. No. Oh, no. That three-foot roach is still swimming in my water bed. Ah. Oh. Ech." Muggers are superstitious. They don't like to attack loony people: Might be a cousin on the paternal side. Make sure your accent is very New York (or L. A. or Chicago or wherever). Tourists are considered table-grade meat: heck, who'd miss his super-saver flight to attend a three-month trial? Most of all, eschew eye contact. If your vision says, "Uh-oh, this creep is after my wallet," this creep may feel a *responsibility* to yank you off. Keep both pupils straight ahead, in close-order drill. Do not flash a bank-and-turn indicator. Sure, you may walk past the place you're headed for, but, *shees,* no system is perfect.

Dress way down. Mom-and-pop candy-store owners take their cash to deposit in an old brown Bohack[1] bag. Me, I *wear* the bag. I own two basic outfits: One has the *haute couture*[2] of some fourth-hand algebra-textbook cover; my second best was cut using three dish drainers as a pattern. If stagflation[3] were human, it'd look like me. No one messes with D.K.M.,[4] they figure I'm messed up enough now. But when you gotta go in finery, turn your tux jacket inside out and put a basketball kneepad around one trouser leg. Peg your collar. Stitch a white shoelace through your patent-leather pump. Recall what Jesus said about excessive glad-ragging (*Matthew,* chapter six): "Consider the lilies of the field . . . even Solomon in all his glory was not arrayed as one of these—so, *nu,*[5] what happens? They get picked, *Dummkopf.*"[6]

1. Supermarket chain in New York.
2. French, high fashion.
3. An economic condition combining relatively high unemployment with relatively high inflation.
4. The author's initials.
5. Yiddish, now.
6. German, stupid (literally, dumbhead).

Signs of the Times

Anthony Burgess

IS AMERICA FALLING APART?

I am back in Bracciano, a castellated town about 13 miles north of Rome, after a year in New Jersey. I find the Italian Government still unstable, gasoline more expensive than anywhere in the world, butchers and bank clerks and tobacconists (which also means saltsellers) ready to go on strike at the drop of a *cappello*, [1] neo-Fascists at their dirty work, the hammer and sickle painted on the rumps of public statues, a thousand-lire note (officially worth about $1.63) shrunk to the slightness of a dollar bill.

Nevertheless, it's delightful to be back. People are underpaid but they go through an act of liking their work, the open markets are luscious with esculent color, the community is more important than the state, the human condition is humorously accepted. The *tramontana* [2] blows viciously today, and there's no central heating to turn on, but it will be pleasant when the wind drops. The two television channels are inadequate, but next Wednesday's rerun of an old Western, with Gary Cooper coming into a saloon saying *"Ciao, ragazzi,"* [3] is something to look forward to. Manifold consumption isn't important here. The quality of life has nothing to do with the quantity of brand names. What matters is talk, family, cheap wine in the open air, the wresting of minimal sweetness out of the long-known bitterness of living. I was spoiled in New Jersey. The Italian for *spoiled* is *viziato*, cognate with *vitiated*, which has to do with vice.

Spoiled? Well, yes. I never had to shiver by a fire that wouldn't draw, or go without canned kraut juice or wild rice. America made me develop new appetites in order to make proper use of the supermarket. A charac-

From the *New York Times* (Nov. 7, 1971).

1. Hat.   3. "Howdy, boys," in Italian.
2. North wind.

443

ter in Evelyn Waugh's *Put Out More Flags* said that the difference between prewar and postwar life was that, prewar, if one thing went wrong the day was ruined; postwar, if one thing went right the day would be made. America is a prewar country, psychologically unprepared for one thing to go wrong. Now everything seems to be going wrong. Hence the neurosis, despair, the Kafka feeling that the whole marvelous fabric of American life is coming apart at the seams. Italy is used to everything going wrong. This is what the human condition is about.

Let me stay for a while on this subject of consumption. American individualism, on the face of it an admirable philosophy, wishes to manifest itself in independence of the community. You don't share things in common; you have your own things. A family's strength is signalized by its possessions. Herein lies a paradox. For the desire for possessions must eventually mean dependence on possessions. Freedom is slavery. Once let the acquisitive instinct burgeon (enough flour for the winter, not just for the week), and there are ruggedly individual forces only too ready to make it come to full and monstrous blossom. New appetites are invented; what to the European are bizarre luxuries become, to the American, plain necessities.

5   During my year's stay in New Jersey I let my appetites flower into full Americanism except for one thing. I did not possess an automobile. This self-elected deprivation was a way into the nastier side of the consumer society. Where private ownership prevails, public amenities decay or are prevented from coming into being. The wretched run-down rail services of America are something I try, vainly, to forget. The nightmare of filth, outside and in, that enfolds the trip from Springfield, Mass., to Grand Central Station would not be accepted in backward Europe. But far worse is the nightmare of travel in and around Los Angeles, where public transport does not exist and people are literally choking to death in their exhaust fumes. This is part of the price of the metaphysic of individual ownership.

But if the car owner can ignore the lack of public transport, he can hardly ignore the decay of services in general. His car needs mechanics, and mechanics grow more expensive and less efficient. The gadgets in the home are cheaper to replace than repair. The more efficiently self-contained the home, primary fortress of independence, seems to be, the more dependent it is on the great impersonal corporations, as well as a diminishing army of servitors. Skills at the lowest level have to be wooed slavishly and exorbitantly rewarded. Plumbers will not come. Nor, at the higher level, will doctors. And doctors and dentists, in a nation committed to maiming itself with sugar and cholesterol, know their scarcity value and behave accordingly.

Americans are at last realizing that the acquisition of goods is not the whole of life. Consumption, on one level, is turning insipid, especially as the quality of the artifacts themselves seems to be deteriorating. Planned obsolescence is not conducive to pride in workmanship. On another level, consumption is turning sour. There is a growing guilt about the masses of discarded junk—rusting automobiles and refrigerators and washing machines and dehumidifiers—that it is uneconomical to recycle. Indestructible plastic hasn't even the grace to undergo chemical change. America, the world's biggest consumer, is the world's biggest polluter. Awareness of this is a kind of redemptive grace, but it doesn't appreciably lead to repentance and a revolution in consumer habits. Citizens of Los Angeles are horrified by that daily pall of golden smog, but they don't noticeably clamor for a decrease in the number of owner-vehicles. There is no worse neurosis than that which derives from a consciousness of guilt and an inability to reform.

America is anachronistic in so many ways, and not least in its clinging to a belief—now known to be unviable—in the capacity of the individual citizen to do everything for himself. Americans are admirable in their distrust of the corporate state—they have fought both Fascism and Communism—but they forget that there is a use for everything, even the loathesome bureaucratic machine. America needs a measure of socialization, as Britain needed it. Things—especially those we need most—don't always pay their way, and it is here that the state must enter, dismissing the profit element. Part of the present American neurosis, again, springs from awareness of this but inability to do anything about practical implementation. Perhaps only a country full of bombed cities feels capable of this kind of social revolution.

It would be supererogatory for me to list those areas in which thoughtful Americans feel that collapse is coming. It is enough for me to concentrate on what, during my New Jersey stay, impinged on my own life. Education, for instance, since I have a 6-year-old son to be brought up. America has always despised its teachers and, as a consequence, it has been granted the teachers it deserves. The quality of first-grade education that my son received, in a New Jersey town noted for the excellence of its public schools, could not, I suppose, be faulted on the level of dogged conscientiousness. The principal had read all the right pedagogic books, and was ready to quote these in the footnotes to his circular exhortations to parents. The teachers worked rigidly from the approved rigidly programed primers, ensuring that school textbook publication remains the big business it is.

But there seemed to be no spark; no daring, no madness, no readiness to engage the individual child's mind as anything other than raw material for statistical reductions. The fear of being unorthodox is rooted in the American teacher's soul: you can be fired for treading the path of

10

experimental enterprise. In England, teachers cannot be fired, except for raping girl students and getting boy students drunk. In consequence, there is the kind of security that breeds eccentric genius, the capacity for firing mad enthusiasms.

I know that American technical genius, and most of all the moon landings, seems to give the lie to too summary a condemnation of the educational system, but there is more to education than the segmental equipping of the mind. There is that transmission of the value of the past as a force still miraculously fertile and moving—mostly absent from American education at all levels.

Of course, America was built on a rejection of the past. Even the basic Christianity which was brought to the continent in 1620 was of a novel and bizarre kind that would have nothing to do with the great rank river of belief that produced Dante and Michelangelo. America as a nation has never been able to settle to a common belief more sophisticated than the dangerous naiveté of the Declaration of Independence. "Life, liberty and the pursuit of happiness," indeed. And now America, filling in the vacuum left by the liquefied British Empire, has the task of telling the rest of the world that there's something better than Communism. The something better can only be money-making and consumption for its own sake. In the name of this ghastly creed the jungles must be defoliated.[4]

No wonder the guilt of the thoughtful Americans I met in Princeton and New York and, indeed, all over the Union tended to express itself as an extravagant masochism, a desire for flagellation. Americans want to take on all the blame they can find, gluttons for punishment. "What do Europeans really think of us?" is a common question at parties. The expected answer is: "They think you're a load of decadent, gross-lipped, potbellied, callous, overbearing neoimperialists." Then the head can be bowed and the chest smitten: "*Nostra culpa, nostra maxima culpa.* . . ."[5] But the fact is that such an answer, however much desired, would not be an honest one. Europeans think more highly of Americans now than they ever did. Let me try to explain why.

When Europe, after millennia of war, rapine, slavery, famine, intolerance, had sunk to the level of a sewer, America became the golden dream, the Eden where innocence could be recovered. Original sin was the monopoly of that dirty continent over there; in America man could glow in an aura of natural goodness, driven along his shining path by

4. That is, in order to deny the enemy protective cover—a part of American strategy during the Vietnam War.
5. "Through our fault, through our most grievous fault," a modification of *Mea culpa, mea maxima culpa* ("Through my fault . . ."), part of the act of confession in the Roman Catholic church.

divine reason. The Declaration of Independence itself is a monument
to reason. Progress was possible, and the wrongs committed against the
Indians, the wildlife, the land itself, could be explained away in terms
of the rational control of environment necessary for the building of a
New Jerusalem.[6] Right and wrong made up the moral dichotomy; evil—
that great eternal inextirpable entity—had no place in America.

At last, with the Vietnam war and especially the Mylai horror,[7]   15
Americans are beginning to realize that they are subject to original sin
as much as Europeans are. Some things—the massive crime figures, for
instance—can now be explained only in terms of absolute evil. Europe,
which has long known about evil and learned to live with it (*live* is *evil*
spelled backwards), is now grimly pleased to find that America is becoming like Europe. America is no longer Europe's daughter nor her rich
stepmother: she is Europe's sister. The agony that America is undergoing is not to be associated with breakdown so much as with the
parturition of self-knowledge.

It has been assumed by many that the youth of America has been in
the vanguard of the discovery of both the disease and the cure. The
various copping-out movements, however, from the Beats on, have committed the gross error of assuming that original sin rested with their
elders, their rulers, and that they themselves could manifest their essential innocence by building little neo-Edens. The drug culture could
confirm that the paradisal vision was available to all who sought it. But
instant ecstasy has to be purchased, like any other commodity, and, in
economic terms, that passive life of pure being involves parasitism.
Practically all of the crime I encountered in New York—directly or
through report—was a preying of the opium-eaters on the working
community. There has to be a snake in paradise. You can't escape the
heritage of human evil by building communes, usually on an agronomic
ignorance that, intended to be a rejection of inherited knowledge, that
suspect property of the elders, does violence to life. The American young
are well-meaning but misguided, and must not themselves be taken as
guides.

The guides, as always, lie among the writers and artists. And Americans ought to note that, however things may seem to be falling apart,
arts and the humane scholarship are flourishing here, as they are not, for
instance, in England. I'm not suggesting that Bellow, Mailer, Roth and
the rest have the task of finding a solution to the American mess, but
they can at least clarify its nature and show how it relates to the human
condition in general. Literature, that most directly human of the arts,

6. The holy city described by John in Revelation xxi, here a figurative expression for a
perfected society.

7. A massacre by American troops of over
a hundred Vietnamese civilians in the village of Mylai.

often reacts magnificently to an ambience of unease or apparent break-down. The Elizabethans, [8] to whose era we look back as to an irrecovera-ble Golden Age, were far more conscious than modern Americans of the chaos and corruption and incompetence of the state. Shakespeare's period was one of poverty, unemployment, ghastly inflation, violence in the streets. Twenty-six years after his death there was a bloody civil war, followed by a dictatorship of religious fanatics, followed by a calm respite in which the seeds of a revolution were sown. England survived. America will survive.

I'm not suggesting that Americans sit back and wait for a transient period of mistrust and despair to resolve itself, like a disease, through the unconscious healing forces which lie deep in organic nature. Man, as Thornton Wilder showed in *The Skin of Our Teeth*, [9] always comes through—though sometimes only just. Americans living here and now have a right to an improvement in the quality of their lives, and they themselves, not the remote governors, must do something about it. It is not right that men and women should fear to go on the streets at night, and that they should sometimes fear the police as much as the criminals, both of whom sometimes look like mirror images of each other. I have had too much evidence, in my year in New Jersey, of the police behaving like the "Fascist pigs" of the revolutionary press. There are too many guns about, and the disarming of the police should be a natural aspect of the disarming of the entire citizenry.

American politics, at both the state and the Federal levels, is too much concerned with the protection of large fortunes, America being the only example in history of a genuine timocracy. The wealth qualifi-cation for the aspiring politician is taken for granted; a governmental system dedicated to the promotion of personal wealth in a few selected areas will never act for the public good. The time has come, nevertheless, for citizens to demand, from their government, a measure of socializa-tion—the provision of amenities for the many, of which adequate state pensions and sickness benefits, as well as nationalized transport, should be priorities.

20   As for those remoter solutions to the American nightmare—only an aspect, after all, of the human nightmare—an Englishman must be diffident about suggesting that America made her biggest mistake in becoming America—meaning a revolutionary republic based on a ro-mantic view of human nature. To reject a limited monarchy in favor of an absolute one (which is, after all, what the American Presidency is) argues a trust in the disinterestedness of an elected ruler which is, of

8. The British during the reign of Elizabeth I, 1558–1603.
9. American play depicting man's tragi-comic struggle for survival from prehistoric times to the present.

course, no more than a reflection of belief in the innate goodness of man—so long as he happens to be American man. The American Constitution is out of date. Republics tend to corruption. Canada and Australia have their own problems, but they are happier countries than America.

This *Angst* [1] about America coming apart at the seams, which apparently is shared by nearly 50 per cent of the entire American population, is something to rejoice about. A sense of sin is always admirable, though it must not be allowed to become neurotic. If electric systems break down and gadgets disintegrate, it doesn't matter much. There is always wine to be drunk by candlelight, uniced. If America's position as a world power collapses, and the Union dissolves into independent states, there is still the life of the family or the individual to be lived. England has survived her own dissolution as an imperial power, and Englishmen seem to be happy enough. But I ask the reader to note that I, an Englishman, no longer live in England, and I can't spend more than six months at a stretch in Italy—or any other European country, for that matter. I come to America as to a country more stimulating than depressing. The future of mankind is being worked out there on a scale typically American—vast, dramatic, almost apocalyptical. I brave the brutality and the guilt in order to be in on the scene. I shall be back.

1. Anxiety.

THE READER

1. *Burgess wrote this piece in 1971. If he were writing it today, what might he want to leave out, add, or modify?*
2. *Burgess says that in the school his son attended, there was "no readiness to engage the individual child's mind as anything other than raw material for statistical reductions." Can you recall incidents from your early school days that would either support or counter Burgess' criticism of American education?*

THE WRITER

1. *Burgess writes as a visitor to America but a native of Great Britain. How might his account have differed if he had been an American?*
2. *Burgess' observation about the Italian word for* spoiled *implies a concern for etymology and precision of language. Is there evidence of that concern in his choice of English words?*
3. *Write your own brief characterization of one area of American life that Burgess talks about. How does your view differ from Burgess'?*
4. *Burgess refers to "the dangerous naiveté of the Declaration of Independence." Study the Declaration (p. 928), and write a brief argument either for considering it as a "naive" piece of writing or not.*

Ada Louise Huxtable

MODERN-LIFE BATTLE: CONQUERING CLUTTER

There are two kinds of people in the world—those who have a horror of a vacuum and those with a horror of the things that fill it. Translated into domestic interiors, this means people who live with, and without, clutter. (Dictionary definition: jumble, confusion, disorder.) The reasons for clutter, the need to be surrounded by things, goes deep, from security to status. The reasons for banning objects, or living in as selective and austere an environment as possible, range from the esthetic to the neurotic. This is a phenomenon of choice that relates as much to the psychiatrist as to the tastemaker.

Some people clutter compulsively, and others just as compulsively throw things away. Clutter in its highest and most organized form is called collecting. Collecting can be done as the Collyer brothers[1] did it, or it can be done with art and flair. The range is from old newspapers to Fabergé.[2]

This provides a third category, or what might be called calculated clutter, in which the objets d'art, the memorabilia that mark one's milestones and travels, the irresistible and ornamental things that speak to pride, pleasure and temptation, are constrained by decorating devices and hierarchal principles of value. This gives the illusion that one is in control.

Most of us are not in control. My own life is an unending battle against clutter. By that I do not mean to suggest that I am dedicated to any clean-sweep asceticism or arrangements of high art; I am only struggling to keep from drowning in the detritus of everyday existence, or at least to keep it separate from the possessions that are meant to be part of what I choose to believe is a functional-esthetic scheme.

5 Really living without clutter takes an iron will, plus a certain stoicism about the little comforts of life. I have neither. But my eye requires a modest amount of beauty and serenity that clutter destroys. This in-

Originally appeared in the "Design Notebook" column of the *New York Times* (Feb. 5, 1981).

1. In spring of 1947, the bodies of Langley and Homer Collyer, aged brothers living in a New York brownstone, were excavated by police along with 120 tons of newspapers and rubbish, hoarded over time, including fourteen grand pianos and the parts of a dismantled Model T Ford.

2. Peter Carl Fabergé (1846–1920), Russian court jeweler noted for delicate objects in gold and enamel.

volves eternal watchfulness and that oldest and most relentless of the housewife's occupations, picking up. I have a feeling that picking up will go on long after ways have been found to circumvent death and taxes.

I once saw a home in which nothing had ever been picked up. Daily vigilance had been abandoned a long time ago. Although disorder descends on the unwary with the speed of light, this chaos must have taken years to achieve; it was almost a new decorating art form.

The result was not, as one might suppose, the idiosyncratic disorder of a George Price[3] drawing, where things are hung from pipes and hooks in permanent arrangements of awesome convenience.

This was an expensive, thoughtful, architect-designed house where everything had simply been left where it landed. Pots and pans, linens and clothing, toys and utensils were tangled and piled everywhere, as well as all of those miscellaneous items that go in, and usually out, of most homes. No bare spot remained on furniture or floor. And no one who lived there found it at all strange, or seemed to require any other kind of domestic landscape. They had no hangups, in any sense of the word.

I know another house that is just as full of things, but the difference is instructive. This is a rambling old house lived in for many years by a distinguished scholar and his wife, whose love of the life of the mind and its better products has only been equaled by their love of life.

In this very personal and knowledgeable eclecticism, every shared intellectual and cultural experience led to the accumulation of discoveries, mementos and objets de vertu,[4] kept casually at hand or in unstudied places. Tabletops and floors are thickets of books and overflow treasures. There is enormous, overwhelming, profligate clutter. And everything has meaning, memory and style.

At the opposite extreme is the stripped, instant, homogeneous style, created whole and new. These houses and apartments, always well-published, either start with nothing, which is rare, or clear everything out that the owners have acquired, which must take courage, desperation, or both. This means jettisoning the personal baggage, and clutter, of a lifetime.

I confess to very mixed reactions when I see these sleek and shining couples in their sleek and shining rooms, with every perfect thing in its perfect place. Not the least of my feelings is envy. Do these fashionable people, elegantly garbed and posed in front of the lacquered built-ins with just the right primitive pot and piece of sculpture and the latest exotic tree, feel a tremendous sense of freedom and release? Have they been liberated by their seamless new look?

10

3. Price (1901–   ), cartoonist, whose jumbled interiors are typified in the rest of this sentence.

4. Art objects, especially if beautiful and rare.

More to the point, what have they done with their household lares and penates,[5] the sentimental possessions of their past? Did they give them away? Send them to auction galleries and thrift shops? Go on a trip while the decorator cleared them all out? Take a deduction for their memories? Were they tempted to keep nothing? Do they ever have any regrets?

This, of course, is radical surgery. The rest of us resort to more conventional forms of clutter combat. Houses have, or had, attics and cellars. Old apartments provide generous closets, which one fills with things that are permanently inaccessible and unneeded. In the city, there is stolen space, in elevator and service halls. And there is the ultimate catch-all—the house in the country.

Historically, clutter is a modern phenomenon, born of the industrial revolution. There was a time when goods were limited; and the rich and fashionable were few in number and objects were precious and hard to come by. Clutter is a 19th-century esthetic; it came with the abundance of products combined with the rise of purchasing power, and the shifts in society that required manifestations of status and style.

Victorian parlors were a jungle of elaborate furnishings and ornamental overkill. The reforms of the Arts and Crafts movement in the later 19th century only substituted a more "refined" kind of clutter—art pottery, embroidered mottos, handpainted tiles and porcelains, vases of bullrushes and peacock feathers. There were bewildering "artful" effects borrowed from the studio or atelier.

Clutter only became a bad word in the 20th century. The modern movement decreed a new simplicity—white walls, bare floors, and the most ascetic of furnishings in the most purified of settings. If ornament was crime, clutter was taboo.

Architects built houses and decorators filled them. Antiques were discovered and every kind of collecting boomed. There were even architects of impeccable modernist credentials—Charles Eames and Alexander Girard—who acquired and arranged vast numbers of toys and treasures. They did so with a discerning eye for the colorful and the primitive that added interest—and clutter—to modern rooms.

Today, clutter is oozing in at a record rate. Architect-collectors like Charles Moore are freewheeling and quixotic in their tastes; high seriousness has been replaced by eclectic whimsy. Nostalgia and fleamarkets coexist on a par with scholarship and accredited antiques. Turning the century on its head, the artifacts of early modernism are being collected by the post-modernist avant-garde. At the commercial level, sophisticated merchandising sells the endless new fashions and products em-

5. Valued household possessions; literally, household gods.

braced by an affluent consumer society. The vacuum must be filled. And the truth must be told. Our possessions possess us.

THE READER

1. What distinction does Huxtable make between clutter and collecting?
2. Why does Huxtable find it necessary to introduce the third category of "calculated clutter"?
3. Describe the most important differences between the house in the George Price cartoon and the house of the "distinguished scholar and his wife."
4. Look at the sentence in which Huxtable describes a home "in which nothing had ever been picked up": "Although disorder descends on the unwary with the speed of light, this chaos must have taken years to achieve; it was almost a new decorating art form." What is the tone or attitude in the sentence—straightforward? sarcastic? disapproving? amused? other?—and how has the tone been achieved?
5. Why does Huxtable have "mixed reactions" about the "sleek and shining couples in their sleek and shining rooms"? What are some of those reactions?
6. If what Huxtable says about the disadvantages of clutter is true, why does it take "an iron will" to live without clutter?
7. Taking the essay as a whole, how does Huxtable feel about clutter? How do you know?

THE WRITER

1. Why does Huxtable put the historical information contained in the last five paragraphs of her essay at the end rather than at the beginning? What effect would it have to put the history at the beginning and her personal experiences and feelings at the end?
2. Look closely at Huxtable's use of language in such phrases as "awesome convenience," "a jungle of elaborate furnishings, and ornamental overkill," and "clutter is oozing in at a record rate." What tone do these phrases help to establish? What other examples, similar to these, can you find in the essay? Try rewriting a short passage, using flatter, more matter-of-fact language. What is the difference in effect and effectiveness?
3. Huxtable refers to the Collyer brothers in her second paragraph. Author Malcolm Cowley describes their clutter in his essay, "The View from 80," After the brothers' deaths the police removed from their house "120 tons of rubbish, including . . . 14 grand pianos and the parts of a dismantled Model T Ford." Cowley speculates on why "so

many old people accumulate junk, not on the scale of Langley Collyer, but still in a dismaying fashion." He supposes that "*the piling up is partly from lethargy and partly from the feeling that everything once useful, including their own bodies, should be preserved.*" Compare this conclusion with Huxtable's conclusion that "*our possessions possess us.*"

4. *Charles Lamb begins one of his essays with this sentence:* "*The human species, according to the best theory I can form of it, is composed of two distinct races,* the men who borrow, *and* the men who lend." *Compare this with Huxtable's first sentence. What are the differences in tone and attitude between the two?*

5. *Write a short essay beginning with a sentence of the same pattern:* "*There are two kinds of people in the world—those who . . . and those who . . . ."*

John McMurtry

KILL 'EM! CRUSH 'EM! EAT 'EM RAW!

A few months ago my neck got a hard crick in it. I couldn't turn my head; to look left or right I'd have to turn my whole body. But I'd had cricks in my neck since I started playing grade-school football and hockey, so I just ignored it. Then I began to notice that when I reached for any sort of large book (which I do pretty often as a philosophy teacher at the University of Guelph) I had trouble lifting it with one hand. I was losing the strength in my left arm, and I had such a steady pain in my back I often had to stretch out on the floor of the room I was in to relieve the pressure.

A few weeks later I mentioned to my brother, an orthopedic surgeon, that I'd lost the power in my arm since my neck began to hurt. Twenty-four hours later I was in a Toronto hospital not sure whether I might end up with a wasted upper limb. Apparently the steady pounding I had received playing college and professional football in the late Fifties and early Sixties had driven my head into my backbone so that the discs had crumpled together at the neck—"acute herniation"—and had cut the nerves to my left arm like a pinched telephone wire (without nerve stimulation, of course, the muscles atrophy, leaving the arm crippled). So I spent my Christmas holidays in the hospital in heavy traction and much of the next three months with my neck in a brace. Today most of the pain has gone, and I've recovered most of the strength in my arm.

Originally appeared in *Macleans* (Oct. 1971).

But from time to time I still have to don the brace, and surgery remains a possibility.

Not much of this will surprise anyone who knows football. It is a sport in which body wreckage is one of the leading conventions. A few days after I went into hospital for that crick in my neck, another brother, an outstanding football player in college, was undergoing spinal surgery in the same hospital two floors above me. In his case it was a lower, more massive herniation, which every now and again buckled him so that he was unable to lift himself off his back for days at a time. By the time he entered the hospital for surgery he had already spent several months in bed. The operation was successful, but, as in all such cases, it will take him a year to recover fully.

These aren't isolated experiences. Just about anybody who has ever played football for any length of time, in high school, college or one of the professional leagues, has suffered for it later physically.

Indeed, it is arguable that body shattering is the very *point* of football, as killing and maiming are of war. (In the United States, for example, the game results in 15 to 20 deaths a year and about 50,000 major operations on knees alone.) To grasp some of the more conspicuous similarities between football and war, it is instructive to listen to the imperatives most frequently issued to the players by their coaches, team-mates and fans. "Hurt 'em!" "Level 'em!" "Kill 'em!" "Take 'em apart!" Or watch for the plays that are most enthusiastically applauded by the fans. Where someone is "smeared," "knocked silly," "creamed," "nailed," "broken in two," or even "crucified." (One of my coaches when I played corner linebacker with the Calgary Stampeders in 1961 elaborated, often very inventively, on this language of destruction: admonishing us to "unjoin" the opponent, "make 'im remember you" and "stomp 'im like a bug.") Just as in hockey, where a fight will bring fans to their feet more often than a skillful play, so in football the mouth waters most of all for the really crippling block or tackle. For the kill. Thus the good teams are "hungry," the best players are "mean," and "casualties" are as much a part of the game as they are of a war.

The family resemblance between football and war is, indeed, striking. Their languages are similar: "field general," "long bomb," "blitz," "take a shot," "front line," "pursuit," "good hit," "the draft" and so on. Their principles and practices are alike: mass hysteria, the art of intimidation, absolute command and total obedience, territorial aggression, censorship, inflated insignia and propaganda, blackboard maneuvers and strategies, drills, uniforms, formations, marching bands and training camps. And the virtues they celebrate are almost identical: hyper-aggressiveness, coolness under fire and suicidal bravery. All this has been implicitly recognized by such jock-loving Americans as media stars General Patton and President Nixon, who have talked about war as a football game.

5

Patton wanted to make his Second World War tank men look like football players. And Nixon, as we know, was fond of comparing attacks on Vietnam to football plays and drawing coachly diagrams on a blackboard for TV war fans.

One difference between war and football, though, is that there is little or no protest against football. Perhaps the most extraordinary thing about the game is that the systematic infliction of injuries excites in people not concern, as would be the case if they were sustained at, say, a rock festival, but a collective rejoicing and euphoria. Players and fans alike revel in the spectacle of a combatant felled into semiconsciousness, "blindsided," "clotheslined" or "decapitated." I can remember, in fact, being chided by a coach in pro ball for not "getting my hat" injuriously into a player who was already lying helpless on the ground. (On another occasion, after the Stampeders had traded the celebrated Joe Kapp to BC, we were playing the Lions in Vancouver and Kapp was forced on one play to run with the ball. He was coming "down the chute," his bad knee wobbling uncertainly, so I simply dropped on him like a blanket. After I returned to the bench I was reproved for not exploiting the opportunity to unhinge his bad knee.)

After every game, of course, the papers are full of reports on the day's injuries, a sort of post-battle "body count," and the respective teams go to work with doctors and trainers, tape, whirlpool baths, cortisone and morphine to patch and deaden the wounds before the next game. Then the whole drama is reenacted—injured athletes held together by adhesive, braces and drugs—and the days following it are filled with even more feverish activity to put on the show yet again at the end of the next week. (I remember being so taped up in college that I earned the nickname "mummy.") The team that survives this merry-go-round spectacle of skilled masochism with the fewest incapacitating injuries usually wins. It is a sort of victory by ordeal: "We hurt them more than they hurt us."

My own initiation into this brutal circus was typical. I loved the game from the moment I could run with a ball. Played shoeless on a green open field with no one keeping score and in a spirit of reckless abandon and laughter, it's a very different sport. Almost no one gets hurt and it's rugged, open and exciting (it still is for me). But then, like everything else, it starts to be regulated and institutionalized by adult authorities. And the fun is over.

So it was as I began the long march through organized football. Now there was a coach and elders to make it clear by their behavior that beating other people was the only thing to celebrate and that trying to shake someone up every play was the only thing to be really proud of. Now there were severe rule enforcers, audiences, formally recorded victors and losers, and heavy equipment to permit crippling bodily moves and collisions (according to one American survey, more than 80% of all football injuries occur to fully equipped players). And now there was the official "given" that the only way to keep playing was to wear suffocating armor, to play to defeat, to follow orders silently and to renounce spontaneity for joyless drill. The game had been, in short, ruined. But because I loved to play and play skillfully, I stayed. And progressively and inexorably, as I moved through high school, college and pro leagues, my body was dismantled. Piece by piece.

I started off with torn ligaments in my knee at 13. Then, as the organization and the competition increased, the injuries came faster and harder. Broken nose (three times), broken jaw (fractured in the first half and dismissed as a "bad wisdom tooth," so I played with it for the rest of the game), ripped knee ligaments again. Torn ligaments in one ankle and a fracture in the other (which I remember feeling relieved about because it meant I could honorably stop drill-blocking a 270-pound defensive end). Repeated rib fractures and cartilage tears (usually carried, again, through the remainder of the game). More dislocations of the left shoulder than I can remember (the last one I played with because, as the Calgary Stampeder doctor said, it "couldn't be damaged any more"). Occasional broken or dislocated fingers and toes. Chronically hurt lower back (I still can't lift with it or change a tire without worrying about folding). Separated right shoulder (as with many other injuries, like badly bruised hips and legs, needled with morphine for the games). And so on. The last pro grame I played—against Winnipeg Blue Bombers in the Western finals in 1961—I had a recently dislocated left shoulder, a more recently wrenched right shoulder and a chronic pain center in one leg. I was so tied up with soreness I couldn't drive my car to the airport. But it never occurred to me or anyone else that I miss a play as a corner linebacker.

By the end of my football career, I had learned that physical injury—giving it and taking it—is the real currency of the sport. And that in the final analysis the "winner" is the man who can hit to kill even if only half his limbs are working. In brief, a warrior game with a warrior ethos into which (like almost everyone else I played with) my original boyish enthusiasm had been relentlessly taunted and conditioned.

In thinking back on how all this happened, though, I can pick out no villains. As with the social system as a whole, the game has a life of its own. Everyone grows up inside it, accepts it and fulfills its dictates as obediently as helots. Far from ever questioning the principles of the activity, people simply concentrate on executing these principles more aggressively than anybody around them. The result is a group of people who, as the leagues become of a higher and higher class, are progressively insensitive to the possibility that things could be otherwise. Thus, in football, anyone who might question the wisdom or enjoyment of putting on heavy equipment on a hot day and running full speed at someone else with the intention of knocking him senseless would be regarded simply as not really a devoted athlete and probably "chicken." The choice is made straightforward. Either you, too, do your very utmost to efficiently smash and be smashed, or you admit incompetence or cowardice and quit. Since neither of these admissions is very pleasant, people generally keep any doubts they have to themselves and carry on.

Of course, it would be a mistake to suppose that there is more blind acceptance of brutal practices in organized football than elsewhere. On the contrary, a recent Harvard study has approvingly argued that football's characteristics of "impersonal acceptance of inflicted injury," an overriding "organization goal," the "ability to turn oneself on and off" and being, above all, "out to win" are of "inestimable value" to big corporations. Clearly, our sort of football is no sicker than the rest of our society. Even its organized destruction of physical well-being is not anomalous. A very large part of our wealth, work and time is, after all, spent in systematically destroying and harming human life. Manufacturing, selling and using weapons that tear opponents to pieces. Making ever bigger and faster predator-named cars with which to kill and injure one another by the million every year. And devoting our very lives to outgunning one another for power in an ever more destructive rat race. Yet all these practices are accepted without question by most people, even zealously defended and honored. Competitive, organized injuring is integral to our way of life, and football is simply one of the more intelligible mirrors of the whole process: a sort of colorful morality play showing us how exciting and rewarding it is to Smash Thy Neighbor.

15   Now it is fashionable to rationalize our collaboration in all this by arguing that, well, man *likes* to fight and injure his fellows and such games as football should be encouraged to discharge this original-sin urge into less harmful channels than, say, war. Public-show football, this line goes, plays the same sort of cathartic role as Aristotle said stage tragedy does: without real blood (or not much), it releases players and audience from unhealthy feelings stored up inside them.

As an ex-player in the seasonal coast-to-coast drama, I see little to recommend such a view. What organized football did to me was make me *suppress* my natural urges and re-express them in an alienating, vicious form. Spontaneous desires for free bodily exuberance and fraternization with competitors were shamed and forced under ("If it ain't hurtin' it ain't helpin' ") and in their place were demanded armored mechanical moves and cool hatred of all opposition. Endless authoritarian drill and dressing-room harangues (ever wonder why competing teams can't prepare for a game in the same dressing room?) were the kinds of mechanisms employed to reconstruct joyful energies into mean and alien shapes. I am quite certain that everyone else around me was being similarly forced into this heavily equipped military precision and angry antagonism, because there was always a mutinous attitude about full-dress practices, and everybody (the pros included) had to concentrate incredibly hard for days to whip themselves into just one hour's hostility a week against another club. The players never speak of these things, of course, because everyone is so anxious to appear tough.

The claim that men like seriously to battle one another to some sort of finish is a myth. It only endures because it wears one of the oldest and most propagandized of masks—the romantic combatant. I sometimes wonder whether the violence all around us doesn't depend for its survival on the existence and preservation of this tough-guy disguise.

As for the effect of organized football on the spectator, the fan is not released from supposed feelings of violent aggression by watching his athletic heroes perform it so much as encouraged in the view that people-smashing is an admirable mode of self-expression. The most savage attackers, after all, are, by general agreement, the most efficient and worthy players of all (the biggest applause I ever received as a football player occurred when I ran over people or slammed them so hard they couldn't get up). Such circumstances can hardly be said to lessen the spectators' martial tendencies. Indeed it seems likely that the whole show just further develops and titillates the North American addiction for violent self-assertion. . . . Perhaps, as well, it helps explain why the greater the zeal of U.S. political leaders as football fans (Johnson, Nixon, Agnew), the more enthusiastic the commitment to hard-line politics. At any rate there seems to be a strong correlation between people who relish tough football and people who relish intimidating and beating the hell out of commies, hippies, protest marchers and other opposition groups.

Watching well-advertised strong men knock other people round, make them hurt, is in the end like other tastes. It does not weaken with feeding and variation in form. It grows.

I got out of football in 1962. I had asked to be traded after Calgary had offered me a $25-a-week-plus-commissions off-season job as a clothing-store salesman. ("Dear Mr. Finks:" I wrote. [Jim Finks was then the Stampeders' general manager.] "Somehow I do not think the dialectical subtleties of Hegel, Marx and Plato would be suitably oriented amidst the environmental stimuli of jockey shorts and herringbone suits. I hope you make a profitable sale or trade of my contract to the East.") So the Stampeders traded me to Montreal. In a preseason intersquad game with the Alouettes I ripped the cartilages in my ribs on the hardest block I'd ever thrown. I had trouble breathing and I had to shuffle-walk with my torso on a tilt. The doctor in the local hospital said three weeks rest, the coach said scrimmage in two days. Three days later I was back home reading philosophy.

20

THE READER

1. What relationship does McMurtry see between football and war? Do you find his suggestion persuasive?
2. Does football, in McMurtry's view, provide for participants and spectators a harmless release of potentially harmful tensions and impulses, like "letting off steam"? Do you agree with McMurtry's view?
3. McMurtry says he can "pick out no villains" for the damage football does to its players. Do you agree? Explain.
4. To what extent is what McMurtry says of football true of any other sport?
5. What relationships does McMurtry see between football and society at large? Do his comparisons make sense to you?

THE WRITER

1. Is McMurtry's essay mainly about his personal experiences in football? What effect is produced by his recounting his experiences in detail?
2. What evidence in the essay, if any, do you find to show that McMurtry is not a "team player"? If he is not a "team player," would that account for the fact that he finds so much to criticize about football and about society?
3. McMurtry says that "our sort of football is no sicker than the rest of our society." Write a brief argument supporting or denying that view.
4. Write an essay drawing connections between "real life" and some kind of game or play familiar to you. Does this illuminate any social arrangements, help you to see them in a new light? How far can you truthfully generalize?

Russell Baker

SURELY NOT CIGAR-SHAPED!

They'll never get the world right. Take this summer's heat. The newspapers say it is hotter than most summers' heat, and the reason is a pool of hot air located at 20,000 feet over the middle of the United States.

That's right: "a pool of hot air" high in the sky. One report in a reputable paper said the pool was cigar-shaped and drifting around aimlessly, now moving up toward the Great Lakes, now sloshing back toward the Southwestern desert.

From the *New York Times* (Aug. 8, 1987).

Weather fans, I put it to you: Is this hot-air pool in the sky not a complete revision of everything we were taught at TV Weatherman College right after the Mickey Mouse Club went off and the news department clunks got through reading the daily A.P. leads about Communist nastiness?

What they told us was that summer's awful heat was caused by the notorious Bermuda high, right? Remember the maps with the gorgeous voluptuous curves and the big H for "high pressure" over Myrtle Beach, S.C.?

"We've got this big old Bermuda high," the weather professor always said. I can hear him now just as clear as Chet Huntley and Edward R. Murrow. "This big old Bermuda high," he always said, propagandizing us to think of it as an old friend, maybe a sort of meteorological sloppy, overweight uncle who came over on Saturday night and drank a lot of gin and sprawled all over the couch.

And what did we know about the air movement around a high? That the air moved clockwise!

"Right!" cried the weatherman. "With the air movement clockwise around the high, it'll keep pumping all this hot air up from the Southwest out of the Gulf of Mexico . . ."

Remember how you hated the Gulf of Mexico after two weeks of a big old Bermuda high pumping all that hot air up from the Southwest? After a week or so of hot air pumped up from the gulf, the smell of everything got close to intolerable. It gave you a terrible impression of the Gulf of Mexico.

You'd find yourself thinking, "If it smells this bad up here, the Gulf of Mexico must be a really stinking place."

Several years went by before they discovered the jet stream. That was a surprise. The old-time TV weather professor never told us about the jet stream. It was all fronts and pressure areas and wind blowing. Clockwise around a high, counterclockwise around a low.

Obviously, they hadn't even known the jet stream was up there. Probably they couldn't get up high enough to notice the jet stream until Chuck Yeager came along. After its discovery, the TV weather was not the same.

In the old days of the big sexy curves with the H's, the only drama came from vicious lines with cruel, pointed teeth coming out of Canada. No doubt what one of those was, eh, weather fans? It was the famous cold front, which just might, if we were lucky, blow that old Bermuda high out of here and give us a wind from the Northwest, which meant . . .

Relief! "Yes, there is a chance we're going to get a little relief," were the famous words that accompanied those cruel, pointed teeth.

Discovery of the jet stream created an entirely new view of the meteorological cataclysm. Now the map was dominated by a sinuously wriggling rope-like thing whose vermiform structure pulsated unpredictably north and south, south and north, sometimes buckling upward in a great loop toward Canada, others downward toward Mexico as though in a continent-wide state of peristalsis.

15   Pointing to this formidable display, the weatherman lectured on the quixotic nature of the jet stream. "Here's our jet stream staying well up over the northern tier, but there's a chance it could dip down here all the way to . . ."

We were now in weather graduate school. The difference between the old-time voluptuous curves and the jet stream was the difference between *The Cat in the Hat* and being at Yale with the theory of deconstruction.[1]

When children glistening with perspiration asked, "When's it going to be cool enough to breathe again?" you spoke with authority: "Not until the jet stream moves down off the Yukon and dips into Oklahoma so it can blow that old Bermuda high out of here."

You didn't know about that elevated pool of hot air, did you? Didn't know that regardless how the wind blows or where the jet stream lies, newly discovered hot-air pools could keep you roasting.

What's dispiriting about learning that nobody knew much when you were young is the logically ensuing conclusion that your grandchildren will someday learn that nobody knew much when you were old, either. It makes you realize there's no relief in sight.

1. A theory of literature and literary criticism, several of whose proponents were professors at Yale.

Jessica Mitford

BEHIND THE FORMALDEHYDE CURTAIN

The drama begins to unfold with the arrival of the corpse at the mortuary.

Alas, poor Yorick![1] How surprised he would be to see how his counterpart of today is whisked off to a funeral parlor and is in short order sprayed, sliced, pierced, pickled, trussed, trimmed, creamed, waxed, painted, rouged and neatly dressed—transformed from a common

From *The American Way of Death* (1963).

1. The phrase is Hamlet's (V.i.184) on the distinterment, identification, and perusal of the skull of the court clown he had known as a child.

corpse into a Beautiful Memory Picture. This process is known in the trade as embalming and restorative art, and is so universally employed in the United States and Canada that the funeral director does it routinely, without consulting corpse or kin. He regards as eccentric those few who are hardy enough to suggest that it might be dispensed with. Yet no law requires embalming, no religious doctrine commends it, nor is it dictated by considerations of health, sanitation, or even of personal daintiness. In no part of the world but in Northern America is it widely used. The purpose of embalming is to make the corpse presentable for viewing in a suitably costly container; and here too the funeral director routinely, without first consulting the family, prepares the body for public display.

Is all this legal? The processes to which a dead body may be subjected are after all to some extent circumscribed by law. In most states, for instance, the signature of next of kin must be obtained before an autopsy may be performed, before the deceased may be cremated, before the body may be turned over to a medical school for research purposes; or such provision must be made in the decedent's will. In the case of embalming, no such permission is required nor is it ever sought. A textbook, *The Principles and Practices of Embalming*, comments on this: "There is some question regarding the legality of much that is done within the preparation room." The author points out that it would be most unusual for a responsible member of a bereaved family to instruct the mortician, in so many words, to "embalm" the body of a deceased relative. The very term "embalming" is so seldom used that the mortician must rely upon custom in the matter. The author concludes that unless the family specifies otherwise, the act of entrusting the body to the care of a funeral establishment carries with it an implied permission to go ahead and embalm.

Embalming is indeed a most extraordinary procedure, and one must wonder at the docility of Americans who each year pay hundreds of millions of dollars for its perpetuation, blissfully ignorant of what it is all about, what is done, how it is done. Not one in ten thousand has any idea of what actually takes place. Books on the subject are extremely hard to come by. They are not to be found in most libraries or bookshops.

In an era when huge television audiences watch surgical operations in the comfort of their living rooms, when, thanks to the animated cartoon, the geography of the digestive system has become familiar territory even to the nursery school set, in a land where the satisfaction of curiosity about almost all matters is a national pastime, the secrecy surrounding embalming can, surely, hardly be attributed to the inherent gruesomeness of the subject. Custom in this regard has within this century suffered a complete reversal. In the early days of American

5

embalming, when it was performed in the home of the deceased, it was almost mandatory for some relative to stay by the embalmer's side and witness the procedure. Today, family members who might wish to be in attendance would certainly be dissuaded by the funeral director. All others, except apprentices, are excluded by law from the preparation room.

A close look at what does actually take place may explain in large measure the undertaker's intractable reticence concerning a procedure that has become his major *raison d'être*. [2] Is it possible he fears that public information about embalming might lead patrons to wonder if they really want this service? If the funeral men are loath to discuss the subject outside the trade, the reader may, understandably, be equally loath to go on reading at this point. For those who have the stomach for it, let us part the formaldehyde curtain. . . .

The body is first laid out in the undertaker's morgue—or rather, Mr. Jones is reposing in the preparation room—to be readied to bid the world farewell.

The preparation room in any of the better funeral establishments has the tiled and sterile look of a surgery, and indeed the embalmer-restorative artist who does his chores there is beginning to adopt the term "dermasurgeon" (appropriately corrupted by some mortician-writers as "demi-surgeon") to describe his calling. His equipment, consisting of scalpels, scissors, augers, forceps, clamps, needles, pumps, tubes, bowls and basins, is crudely imitative of the surgeon's, as is his technique, acquired in a nine- or twelve-month post-high-school course in an embalming school. He is supplied by an advanced chemical industry with a bewildering array of fluids, sprays, pastes, oils, powders, creams, to fix or soften tissue, shrink or distend it as needed, dry it here, restore the moisture there. There are cosmetics, waxes and paints to fill and cover features, even plaster of Paris to replace entire limbs. There are ingenious aids to prop and stabilize the cadaver: a Vari-Pose Head Rest, the Edwards Arm and Hand Positioner, the Repose Block (to support the shoulders during the embalming), and the Throop Foot Positioner, which resembles an old-fashioned stocks.

Mr. John H. Eckels, president of the Eckels College of Mortuary Science, thus describes the first part of the embalming procedure: "In the hands of a skilled practitioner, this work may be done in a comparatively short time and without mutilating the body other than by slight incision—so slight that it scarcely would cause serious inconvenience if made upon a living person. It is necessary to remove the blood, and doing this not only helps in the disinfecting, but removes the principal cause of disfigurements due to discoloration."

2. Reason for being.

Another textbook discusses the all-important time element: "The 10
earlier this is done, the better, for every hour that elapses between death
and embalming will add to the problems and complications encountered. . . ." Just how soon should one get going on the embalming? The
author tells us, "On the basis of such scanty information made available
to this profession through its rudimentary and haphazard system of
technical research, we must conclude that the best results are to be
obtained if the subject is embalmed before life is completely extinct—
that is, before cellular death has occurred. In the average case, this would
mean within an hour after somatic death." For those who feel that there
is something a little rudimentary, not to say haphazard, about this
advice, a comforting thought is offered by another writer. Speaking of
fears entertained in early days of premature burial, he points out, "One
of the effects of embalming by chemical injection, however, has been
to dispel fears of live burial." How true; once the blood is removed,
chances of live burial are indeed remote.

To return to Mr. Jones, the blood is drained out through the veins
and replaced by embalming fluid pumped in through the arteries. As
noted in *The Principles and Practices of Embalming*, "every operator
has a favorite injection and drainage point—a fact which becomes a
handicap only if he fails or refuses to forsake his favorites when conditions demand it." Typical favorites are the carotid artery, femoral artery,
jugular vein, subclavian vein. There are various choices of embalming
fluid. If Flextone is used, it will produce a "mild, flexible rigidity. The
skin retains a velvety softness, the tissues are rubbery and pliable. Ideal
for women and children." It may be blended with B. and G. Products
Company's Lyf-Lyk tint, which is guaranteed to reproduce "nature's
own skin texture . . . the velvety appearance of living tissue." Suntone
comes in three separate tints: Suntan; Special Cosmetic Tint, a pink
shade "especially indicated for young female subjects"; and Regular
Cosmetic Tint, moderately pink.

About three to six gallons of a dyed and perfumed solution of formaldehyde, glycerin, borax, phenol, alcohol and water is soon circulating
through Mr. Jones, whose mouth has been sewn together with a "needle
directed upward between the upper lip and gum and brought out
through the left nostril," with the corners raised slightly "for a more
pleasant expression." If he should be bucktoothed, his teeth are cleaned
with Bon Ami and coated with colorless nail polish. His eyes, meanwhile,
are closed with flesh-tinted eye caps and eye cement.

The next step is to have at Mr. Jones with a thing called a trocar. This
is a long, hollow needle attached to a tube. It is jabbed into the abdomen, poked around the entrails and chest cavity, the contents of which
are pumped out and replaced with "cavity fluid." This done, and the
hole in the abdomen sewn up, Mr. Jones's face is heavily creamed (to

protect the skin from burns which may be caused by leakage of the chemicals), and he is covered with a sheet and left unmolested for a while. But not for long—there is more, much more, in store for him. He has been embalmed, but not yet restored, and the best time to start the restorative work is eight to ten hours after embalming, when the tissues have become firm and dry.

The object of all this attention to the corpse, it must be remembered, is to make it presentable for viewing in an attitude of healthy repose. "Our customs require the presentation of our dead in the semblance of normality . . . unmarred by the ravages of illness, disease or mutilation," says Mr. J. Sheridan Mayer in his *Restorative Art.* This is rather a large order since few people die in the full bloom of health, unravaged by illness and unmarked by some disfigurement. The funeral industry is equal to the challenge: "In some cases the gruesome appearance of a mutilated or disease-ridden subject may be quite discouraging. The task of restoration may seem impossible and shake the confidence of the embalmer. This is the time for intestinal fortitude and determination. Once the formative work is begun and affected tissues are cleaned or removed, all doubts of success vanish. It is surprising and gratifying to discover the results which may be obtained."

15   The embalmer, having allowed an appropriate interval to elapse, returns to the attack, but now he brings into play the skill and equipment of sculptor and cosmetician. Is a hand missing? Casting one in plaster of Paris is a simple matter. "For replacement purposes, only a cast of the back of the hand is necessary; this is within the ability of the average operator and is quite adequate." If a lip or two, a nose or an ear should be missing, the embalmer has at hand a variety of restorative waxes with which to model replacements. Pores and skin texture are simulated by stippling with a little brush, and over this cosmetics are laid on. Head off? Decapitation cases are rather routinely handled. Ragged edges are trimmed, and head joined to torso with a series of splints, wires and sutures. It is a good idea to have a little something at the neck—a scarf or a high collar—when time for viewing comes. Swollen mouth? Cut out tissue as needed from inside the lips. If too much is removed, the surface contour can easily be restored by padding with cotton. Swollen necks and cheeks are reduced by removing tissue through vertical incisions made down each side of the neck. "When the deceased is casketed, the pillow will hide the suture incisions . . . as an extra precaution against leakage, the suture may be painted with liquid sealer."

The opposite condition is more likely to present itself—that of emaciation. His hypodermic syringe now loaded with massage cream, the embalmer seeks out and fills the hollowed and sunken areas by injection. In this procedure the backs of the hands and fingers and the under-chin area should not be neglected.

Positioning the lips is a problem that recurrently challenges the ingenuity of the embalmer. Closed too tightly, they tend to give a stern, even
disapproving expression. Ideally, embalmers feel, the lips should give the
impression of being ever so slightly parted, the upper lip protruding
slightly for a more youthful appearance. This takes some engineering,
however, as the lips tend to drift apart. Lip drift can sometimes be
remedied by pushing one or two straight pins through the inner margin
of the lower lip and then inserting them between the two front upper
teeth. If Mr. Jones happens to have no teeth, the pins can just as easily
be anchored in his Armstrong Face Former and Denture Replacer.
Another method to maintain lip closure is to dislocate the lower jaw,
which is then held in its new position by a wire run through holes which
have been drilled through the upper and lower jaws at the midline. As
the French are fond of saying, *il faut souffrir pour être belle.* [3]

If Mr. Jones has died of jaundice, the embalming fluid will very likely
turn him green. Does this deter the embalmer? Not if he has intestinal
fortitude. Masking pastes and cosmetics are heavily laid on, burial garments and casket interiors are color-correlated with particular care, and
Jones is displayed beneath rose-colored lights. Friends will say "How *well*
he looks." Death by carbon monoxide, on the other hand, can be rather
a good thing from the embalmer's viewpoint: "One advantage is the fact
that this type of discoloration is an exaggerated form of a natural pink
coloration." This is nice because the healthy glow is already present and
needs but little attention.

The patching and filling completed, Mr. Jones is now shaved, washed
and dressed. Cream-based cosmetic, available in pink, flesh, suntan,
brunette and blond, is applied to his hands and face, his hair is sham-
pooed and combed (and, in the case of Mrs. Jones, set), his hands
manicured. For the horny-handed son of toil special care must be taken;
cream should be applied to remove ingrained grime, and the nails
cleaned. "If he were not in the habit of having them manicured in life,
trimming and shaping is advised for better appearance—never questioned by kin."

Jones is now ready for casketing (this is the present participle of the
verb "to casket"). In this operation his right shoulder should be depressed slightly "to turn the body a bit to the right and soften the
appearance of lying flat on the back." Positioning the hands is a matter
of importance, and special rubber positioning blocks may be used. The
hands should be cupped slightly for a more lifelike, relaxed apearance.
Proper placement of the body requires a delicate sense of balance. It
should lie as high as possible in the casket, yet not so high that the lid,
when lowered, will hit the nose. On the other hand, we are cautioned,

20

3. It's necessary to suffer to be beautiful.

placing the body too low "creates the impression that the body is in a box."

Jones is next wheeled into the appointed slumber room where a few last touches may be added—his favorite pipe placed in his hand or, if he was a great reader, a book propped into position. (In the case of little Master Jones a Teddy bear may be clutched.) Here he will hold open house for a few days, visiting hours 10 A.M. to 9 P.M.

All now being in readiness, the funeral director calls a staff conference to make sure that each assistant knows his precise duties. Mr. Wilber Kriege writes: "This makes your staff feel that they are a part of the team, with a definite assignment that must be properly carried out if the whole plan is to succeed. You never heard of a football coach who failed to talk to his entire team before they go on the field. They have drilled on the plays they are to execute for hours and days, and yet the successful coach knows the importance of making even the bench-warming third-string substitute feel that he is important if the game is to be won." The winning of *this* game is predicated upon glass-smooth handling of the logistics. The funeral director has notified the pallbearers whose names were furnished by the family, has arranged for the presence of clergy-man, organist, and soloist, has provided transportation for everybody, has organized and listed the flowers sent by friends. In *Psychology of Funeral Service* Mr. Edward A. Martin points out: "He may not always do as much as the family thinks he is doing, but it is his helpful guidance that they appreciate in knowing they are proceeding as they should. . . . The important thing is how well his services can be used to make the family believe they are giving unlimited expression to their own sentiment."

The religious service may be held in a church or in the chapel of the funeral home; the funeral director vastly prefers the latter arrangement, for not only is it more convenient for him but it affords him the opportunity to show off his beautiful facilities to the gathered mourners. After the clergyman has had his say, the mourners queue up to file past the casket for a last look at the deceased. The family is *never* asked whether they want an open-casket ceremony; in the absence of their instruction to the contrary, this is taken for granted. Consequently well over 90 per cent of all American funerals feature the open casket—a custom unknown in other parts of the world. Foreigners are astonished by it. An English woman living in San Francisco described her reaction in a letter to the writer:

> I myself have attended only one funeral here—that of an elderly fellow worker of mine. After the service I could not understand why everyone was walking towards the coffin (sorry, I mean casket), but thought I had better follow the crowd. It shook me rigid to get there and find the casket open

and poor old Oscar lying there in his brown tweed suit, wearing a suntan makeup and just the wrong shade of lipstick. If I had not been extremely fond of the old boy, I have a horrible feeling that I might have giggled. Then and there I decided that I could never face another American funeral—even dead.

The casket (which has been resting throughout the service on a Classic Beauty Ultra Metal Casket Bier) is now transferred by a hydraulically operated device called Porto-Lift to a balloon-tired, Glide Easy casket carriage which will wheel it to yet another conveyance, the Cadillac Funeral Coach. This may be lavender, cream, light green—anything but black. Interiors, of course, are color-correlated, "for the man who cannot stop short of perfection."

At graveside, the casket is lowered into the earth. This office, once the prerogative of friends of the deceased, is now performed by a patented mechanical lowering device. A "Lifetime Green" artificial grass mat is at the ready to conceal the sere earth, and overhead, to conceal the sky, is a portable Steril Chapel Tent ("resists the intense heat and humidity of summer and the terrific storms of winter . . . available in Silver Grey, Rose or Evergreen"). Now is the time for the ritual scattering of earth over the coffin, as the solemn words "earth to earth, ashes to ashes, dust to dust" are pronounced by the officiating cleric. This can today be accomplished "with a mere flick of the wrist with the Gordon Leak-Proof Earth Dispenser. No grasping of a handful of dirt, no soiled fingers. Simple, dignified, beautiful, reverent! The modern way!" The Gordon Earth Dispenser (at $5) is of nickel-plated brass construction. It is not only "attractive to the eye and long wearing"; it is also "one of the 'tools' for building better public relations" if presented as "an appropriate non-commercial gift" to the clergyman. It is shaped something like a saltshaker.

Untouched by human hand, the coffin and the earth are now united.

It is in the function of directing the participants through this maze of gadgetry that the funeral director has assigned to himself his relatively new role of "grief therapist." He has relieved the family of every detail, he has revamped the corpse to look like a living doll, he has arranged for it to nap for a few days in a slumber room, he has put on a well-oiled performance in which the concept of *death* has played no part whatsoever—unless it was inconsiderately mentioned by the clergyman who conducted the religious service. He has done everything in his power to make the funeral a real pleasure for everybody concerned. He and his team have given their all to score an upset victory over death.

25

Tom Wolfe

LAND OF WIZARDS

The threat was delivered to Lemelson's lawyer. "Tell your client we're gonna bury him under a ton of paper." Lemelson wasn't too worried. He thought it was a figure of speech.

So the next day, Lemelson is in the courtroom, sitting at the plaintiff's table with his lawyer, waiting for the proceedings to begin. Lemelson is an inventor. He invented the automated warehouse, the automated machine shop, one of the first two industrial robots, several robot-vision machines, the drive mechanism of the audio cassette player, and 380 other things. He holds more patents than anybody except the great Edison himself and Edwin Land, inventor of the Polaroid camera. This causes him to be in courtrooms a great deal.

Many corporations manufacture his inventions, but not many mention it to him beforehand.

So it is on this particular day Jerome H. Lemelson is in a court of law under the usual circumstances, charging a manufacturer with patent infringement. The lawyers for the manufacturer are right across from him at the defendant's table. Between the two tables and the judge's bench is a fifteen-foot stretch of floor.

5   The next thing Lemelson knows, the door to the courtroom opens, and here comes a trucker's helper pushing a hand truck with archive boxes piled from the fender on the bottom to the curve of the handles at the top.

An archive box is a box made of heavy cardboard with oak-grain patterns printed on it to make it look like wood. On one end of the box is a little metal frame that holds a card describing the contents. The box has a lid, like a shoe box. Inside, there is room for a dozen reams of documents, usually arranged in file folders with little tabs sticking up. However you want to arrange it, you can get about forty pounds of paper into each box.

Fascinated, the way the chickadee is fascinated by the snake, Lemelson watches as the trucker's helper begins unloading the boxes. He puts them right on the floor between the tables and the judge's bench. One of the lawyers is out there like a field commander, pointing to spots on the floor. This one goes here. That one goes there. No sooner is that load arranged than the courtroom door opens again, and here comes another teamster, puffing and pushing a fresh load of archive boxes on a hand

Originally appeared in *Popular Mechanics* (July 1986).

truck. Now he's lugging his stack off the hand truck and putting it on the floor. The door opens again. Here comes another yobbo[1] pushing a hand truck with archive boxes piled as tall as he is. You can hear the floor groaning from the weight of the load as the wheels roll over the hardwood.

The field commander is out there, and the archive boxes are lining up in rows like a tank formation. Lemelson's pale gray-blue eyes are the size of radar dishes. He's speechless. The cargo humpers keep coming. Pretty soon seventy or eighty square feet of floor is occupied by this squat battalion of archive boxes. You don't have to be an engineering genius like Lemelson to figure out that there is now a ton of paper sitting there. More than a ton, perhaps a ton and a half.

"Well," Lemelson says to his lawyer, "at least it's not on top of me."

Neither of them laughed. They both had the feeling it was only a matter of time. There was a judge but no jury. Apparently the ton of paper was supposed to impress the judge and intimidate Lemelson.

Something impressed the judge; no question about that. Lemelson lost. It wasn't even close.

He gritted his teeth and announced he was going to appeal. The next message said: "O.K., go ahead. We'll search for evidence in Europe."

That meant they would send a lawyer to Europe to take depositions from anybody they could find who had dealings with Jerome H. Lemelson or his invention. Here you have the greatest device for generating paper ever thought up by the legal profession: the deposition. All successful inventors know about depositions. They learn to live with them the way one learns to live with arthritis.

A deposition is a pretrial maneuver in which lawyers take sworn testimony from people out of court, usually in somebody's office. A court reporter records the testimony on a stenotype machine and then types up a transcript. The number of pages of testimony that can come out of an hour of this is fabulous, and some depositions go on for a week. What might actually be divulged about Jerome H. Lemelson or his works on any of these thousands of pieces of paper was beside the point. The point was that Lemelson would have to hire a lawyer to represent his interests during each deposition, day after day, city after city, across the map of Europe. The sheets of paper would go into archive boxes, and every sheet meant another little hemorrhage in Lemelson's net worth.

This case began in the 1970s. It grinds on still. So far it has cost Lemelson $250,000 in lawyers' fees, and the meter is still ticking. It sounds like something from out of *Bleak House,* which Charles Dickens wrote in 1852 and 1853, but it is merely a typical episode in the life of

1. British slang for a teenage lout or hooligan.

an American inventor in the 1980s. Which is to say, it is the story of a man trying to dig his way out from under a ton of paper.

Is there any more feverish dream of glory in the world, outside of Islam,[2] than the dream of being an inventor? Certainly not in the United States, and probably not in Japan or in any other industrial country. An invention is one of those superstrokes, like discovering a platinum deposit or a gas field or writing a novel, through which an individual, the hungriest loner, can transform his life, overnight, and light up the sky. The inventor needs only one thing, which is as free as the air: a terrific idea.

He doesn't need connections. The great American inventors of the past hundred years, the so-called age of technology, have not come from prominent families. They have not had money. They have not been part of the highly touted, highly financed research teams of industry and the universities. They have not been adept politically or socially. Many have been breathtakingly deficient in charm.

Thomas Edison was scarcely educated at all; three years in public school, and that was it. Alexander Graham Bell was a teacher who began his experiments, leading to the telephone, in the cellar of a house in Boston, where he rented a room. Steven Jobs and Steven Wozniak, of Apple Computer fame, were a pair of public high school A-V types. A-V types are audio-visual nerds who wear windbreakers, carry a lot of keys, and wire up directional mikes for the drama club. The Silicon Valley of California, center of the most spectacular new industry of the second half of the twentieth century, computers and semiconductors, is known as the Land of Nerd, the Planet of the Nerds, and the Emerald City of Nerdz. The centimillionaires of the Silicon Valley want nothing to do with the traditional Society of nearby San Francisco. They can't get into Trader Vic's wearing their nerd shirts, which are short-sleeved white sport shirts with pencil guards on the pockets.

Wilbur and Orville Wright were regarded as two wet smacks who ran a bicycle repair shop in Dayton, Ohio, when they arrived at Kitty Hawk for their airplane experiment in 1903. Neither had graduated from high school. But theirs was the invention that dazzled Jerome H. Lemelson and thousands of other boys who were born in the early 1920s.

20   As a teenager, Lemelson was typical of the airplane "hobbyists," as they were known, quiet boys who built gasoline-powered model airplanes, took them out in the fields, and flew them by wire or remote control. There were still a lot of open fields on Staten Island, where he grew up. His father was a doctor, a general practitioner, but Lemelson's passion was airplanes. During the Second World War he found his way

2. A reference to the Islamic concept of the joys of Paradise or Heaven.

into the engineering department of the Army Air Corps. After the war he earned a bachelor's degree in aeronautical engineering at New York University, then went to work at NYU for the Office of Naval Research's Project Squid. Project Squid was supposed to develop rocket and pulse jet engines.

One day in 1951, Lemelson took the subway over to the Arma factory in Brooklyn, which made control mechanisms for aircraft, to see a demonstration of a fully automatic, feedback-controlled metal lathe. "Feedback" was a hot new word in engineering circles. Nobody there on the work way at Arma took a second look at Jerome H. Lemelson. He was twenty-eight years old, neither far nor thin, neither very tall nor very short, not bad looking and not Tyrone Power, either. He had a broad forehead, light brown curly hair, large eyes, and a long, straight nose. He was quiet, polite, reserved, and a typical hard-working young engineer, by the looks of him, if you looked at all.

Lemelson took more than a second look at the metal lathe, however. An ordinary metal lathe turned a metal rod while an operator shaved it down to whatever diameter or shape he wanted by adjusting a tool bit. In the case of the feedback-controlled lathe, the bit was controlled automatically by punch cards. The crowd murmured a lot as the bit rose and fell to unseen commands.

Lemelson began wondering how far you could take this idea of a programmed factory machine. Over the next three years he developed the designs for a "universal robot." The robot would have an arm with joints. It would rivet, weld, drill, measure, pick things up and move them. He drew up a 150-page patent application and submitted it to the U.S. Patent Office in Washington, D.C., on Christmas Eve, 1954. Unbeknownst to Lemelson, an inventor named George Devol had filed an application for a robot two weeks earlier. Theirs were the first industrial robots. As it turned out, both men had a long wait ahead of them.

In the meantime, Lemelson was already working on a second application for an offshoot of the universal robot, a "flexible manufacturing system," which was the automated machine shop.

That same year, 1954, Lemelson married an interior decorator named Dolly Ginsberg. The first stop on their honeymoon was Bermuda. The second stop was the Willard Hotel in Washington because it happened to be across the street from the Search Room of the Patent Office. Lemelson was already deep in the grip of The Dream.

The Search Room was an enormous archive the size of Uline Arena, where the Washington Capitols, the professional basketball team, played their games. It was full of ancient wooden shelves and boxes, known as shoes, containing nearly 150 years' worth of patent documents. The spaces between the stacks of shelves were so narrow that the clerks had to shimmy past each other to fetch the shoes for people doing patent searches. This led to a lot of waiting and sighing. Dolly heard one patent lawyer complaining to another: "There ought to be some way to mechanize this place."

She happened to mention this to Lemelson. That started him off on another track, resulting in his "video filing system." The documents would be recorded on reels of videotape or magnetic tape. The average patent application was ten pages long. You could store 100,000 applications on just four reels of tape. You would look at them on a television screen in stop-frame pictures. (His conception of the stop-frame picture would lead, during the 1960s, to filmless photography, still pictures created from video images.)

Instead of having GS-8 civil servants shimmying between stacks of shelves, you would press a few buttons and send a playback device along a track to a slot where the tape was. But how could the device connect with the tape and enable you to play it and wind it back and forth? Lemelson thought about that awhile and conceived of the mechanism that eventually became the core of the audio cassette player. He presented video filing and its components in a sixty-page patent application in 1955.

And he waited some more. Several years went by, and the Patent Office still had not issued any patents for all these brilliant ideas. Lemelson was now learning one of the facts of life about being an inventor in America. The first flash of genius lights up only a few yards of the road. The road is long and uphill.

More than once, he and Dolly had to fall back on her earnings as an interior decorator. There was only one way an inventor could make money rapidly without waiting for the patent process to go its course, and that was to design toys. In the case of a toy, you prudently filed for a patent but went ahead and sold the design immediately, if you could. Lemelson had an idea for a face-mask kit for children that would be printed on a cereal box. A child could cut out the pieces, assemble them in different combinations and put on the mask. He filed for a patent and took his drawings to one of the cereal manufacturers. The company said it wasn't interested, and so he put the drawings away and forgot about them.

One day, three years later, he is in the grocery store, and there on the shelf is a cereal box with a face-mask kit on it. It's put out by the very people he showed his drawings to. He can't believe it. The way he sees it, he's staring at as blatant a case of patent infringement as you could imagine. He files suit. So now he's in court. It's a jury trial. The judge comes in, and he gives Lemelson and the lawyers a long look down his nose.

"This is a patent case," he says. He lets the term "patent case" hang in the air for a moment, like a bad smell. "I have better things to do with my time than listen to patent cases. It is now ten-fifteen. You have until three o'clock this afternoon to complete your arguments."

Sure enough, at three o'clock on the dot he looks at his watch, stands up, and, without saying a word, walks out. Lemelson has an expert witness testifying for him at the time, and the fellow is sitting there on the stand with his mouth hanging open.

Then the judge pops back in. "Ladies and gentlemen of the jury, my apologies. I neglected to dismiss you. You are dismissed."

It turns out the case has been dismissed, too. Lemelson appeals, and a new trial is called—before the same judge, who summarily dismisses the suit, this time for good.

When Lemelson spoke of these things to other inventors, they smiled without joy. He was just getting the picture. First, many American corporations, including many of the most respected, ignored patent rights without batting an eye. They didn't give you so much as a sporting wink. Second, the courts couldn't be bothered. Practically none of the judges who heard patent cases had any background in patent law, much less engineering. It was unfamiliar terrain, which seemed to make them irritable. On the one hand, they couldn't stand all these obsessive small-fry inventors, these parasites on the hide of Science, with their endless theories and their transducers and capacitive-sensitive relays and the rest of that paralyzing jargon. But on the other hand, if they, the judges, could understand an invention, then it must not be much of an invention. They had developed "the doctrine of obviousness." If an invention looked obvious, they declared the patent invalid.

The inventors kept ratings of the chances of having their patent rights upheld in the various federal jurisdictions. Back when Lemelson was starting out, your chances ran from zero in the Eighth Circuit, which covered most of the Midwest, to 45 percent in the South. The Second Circuit, covering New York, was rated about average, one chance in four.

But what about the corporations? How could they get away with flouting the patent system and patent law? It was simple, the inventors told Lemelson. All that the corporations needed to overcome was their scruples, if any. In the United States, unlike Japan and parts of Europe, patent infringement was not considered a form of theft, so there were no criminal penalties. There were not even punitive damages in patent cases unless the inventor could prove "willful infringement." To avoid that, a manufacturer merely had to take the precaution of going to its own lawyer and having him write an opinion saying that such and such a product did not infringe upon any existing patents for such and such reasons. It didn't matter how cockeyed the reasons were. That was what lawyers were for.

Once the manufacturer had that document in hand, the worst that could have happened, even if the firm had been found guilty in court, was that the manufacturer would have had to pay the inventor the royalties he would have received if a license had been obtained. There were lawyers who would actually advise their corporate clients to ignore patents, calling it a no-risk strategy.

40   Just in case the inventor was new at this game, the manufacturer would let him know the odds, discreetly, or, if he looked a little thick, bluntly. To get a case as far as the trial stage was going to cost $40,000. Was he ready for that? To get a case through the trial and all the appeal stages—was he ready for $250,000? For good measure, the manufacturer usually added some variation of the theme, "We're gonna bury you under a ton of paper." If a corporation was big enough, it would threaten anybody, not merely little lone-wolf inventors but even another, smaller corporation. When J. Reid Anderson, the chief executive officer of Verbatim, a company specializing in computer storage devices, went to a big manufacturer complaining of patent infringement, he was told: "We have more patent attorneys than you have people in your company, and they are just sitting back waiting for someone to start a patent fight like this."

Lemelson's saving grace was that he was not a cynic. He didn't have a cynical or even a morbidly pessimistic bone in his body. Despite everything, he believed that it wasn't a bad world. His most important inventions had disappeared somewhere in the papyraphagous mew[3] of the Patent Office. A manufacturer had just walked right over him, without stopping, and the court he had gone to for help hadn't even been able to hide its contempt for Jerome H. Lemelson. Moreover, he had just learned that this was the customary state of affairs for small-fries of his vocation.

But that was just what it was—a vocation, a calling. By now, Lemelson derived an aesthetic or spiritual—or some kind of—satisfaction that went beyond the money he wasn't making from inventing. He was irrepressible. He was thinking up new inventions at the rate of one a month, a pace that he managed to keep up for the next thirty years.

Once Lemelson had designed robots that did every imaginable industrial chore, he designed a robot that inspected what the other robots had done. He invented robot-vision or "image analysis" machines that could, among other things, detect diseased blood or tissue cells, such as cancer cells. He invented the "computer-controlled coordinate measuring machine," which would later be used to measure and align the tiles on the exterior of the space shuttles. He invented a computerized tourniquet

3. "Paper-eating hiding place"—from *papyrus*, the source of paper in ancient Egypt, and *-phagous*, a combining form meaning "eating."

that would allow a surgeon to perform an operation without stopping to turn valves to alter the flow of a patient's blood. He designed several systems for transfer of information between computers. He designed two laser-powered recording and reproduction systems, Lasercard and Videocard, to perform the computer functions now performed by floppy disks. He invented a widely used "automated teller machine" that scans credit cards and checks out their credit status. He invented both a cordless telephone and a cordless videophone.

At the same time, he was turning out toy and novelty designs. He designed the "watchpen," a ballpoint pen with a watch built into it. He invented the flexible-track car toy—one of the biggest-selling toys of all time—manufactured by at least five companies under different names, Hot Wheels being the best known. He invented the Velcro dart game, in which you throw a Velcro-covered ball, instead of a steel-tipped dart, at a Velcro-covered dart board. He invented the "printing putty toy," best known under the brand name Monster Print Putty, with which you can remove words and pictures from a newspaper and reprint them on another piece of paper. Lemelson was thinking up these things, doing the drawings, writing the descriptions, and dispatching them to the Patent Office so fast, his two sons called him The Blur.

During the early 1960s, when Lemelson was pushing forty, the patents finally started rolling in. First was his video filing system in 1961. Then the automated warehouse in 1962. In 1966, almost twelve years after he had submitted the application, his universal robot patent was issued. Devol's had come through five years earlier. ⁴⁵

Lemelson closed his first major deal in 1964, selling an exclusive license for his automated warehouse system to a firm called Triax, but almost immediately he was up to his neck in lawsuits. Other firms, he and Triax charged, had already begun pirating the invention in violation of Triax's license. That litigation continues today, twenty-two years later.

In 1967, he sold an exclusive license to an English company, Molins, for the automated machine shop. In 1973, he made the best deal of his career, selling an exclusive license for his cassette drive mechanism to Sony. Sony sublicensed it to more than a hundred Japanese firms. Today, practically every audio cassette player on the market operates with the Lemelson drive.

None of this brought any dramatic improvement in Lemelson's style of living. In 1959, after the birth of their second son, he and Dolly moved from a garden apartment in Metuchen, New Jersey, looking out not onto a garden but U.S. Route 1, to an eight-room house in Metuchen on a quarter of an acre. It wasn't until 1985 that they moved to greener, grander scenery in Princeton. No small part of the picture was the hundreds of thousands of dollars that Lemelson was spending on legal fees, trying to deal with American firms.

From the first, there were cases of what he regarded as the most arrant infringement. It absolutely stupefied him. The retort of "go ahead and sue" (. . . "and we'll bury you under a ton of paper") was standard practice. Some firms were bluffing. If you brought suit, they would settle. But there was only one way to find out, which was to sue. Other firms were not bluffing. They would spend half a million dollars in legal fees to keep from taking a license and paying royalties they knew wouldn't run over $150,000. Lemelson couldn't figure these people out. He didn't know whether they were trying to teach a lesson to other small-fry inventors—the lesson being that Lemelson's legal bills were running well over $150,000—or whether these were displays of sheer competitive ego.

50   Sometimes the lawsuits sprang up on so many fronts, it was hard to keep track of them. Lemelson found himself suing all the major manufacturers of the flexible-track car toy. These cases live on today. Some of the suits turned ludicrous, but the laughs never came cheaply.

In one case, Lemelson was suing the U.S. government and two private manufacturers over the same invention. He decided to abandon the case against the government and grant it a license free of charge. The private firms sought to block this move, apparently on the grounds that the government's acceptance of the license implied recognition of Lemelson's patent rights.

He ended up spending $18,000 in lawyers' fees to give the license away.

Lemelson was in noble, but expensive, company. Robert Goddard, now called—officially, by the U.S. government—the father of American rocketry, ran a lone-wolf rocket program west of nowhere in the New Mexico desert in no small part to try to put an end to the pirating of his patented inventions—chiefly by the U.S. government.

Fifteen years after his death, the government gave his wife $1 million to settle his many claims of infringement. There was something melancholy about this refrain of the widow and the million dollars.

55   One day Lemelson met a lawyer who had been in on the Armstrong case. Edwin Armstrong was the inventor of FM, frequency modulation, the greatest advance in broadcasting since the invention of the radio itself. In 1940, the Radio Corporation of America offered Armstrong a flat fee of $1 million for his FM patents. The lawyer had been in the room when Armstrong was handed the check. Armstrong looked at it and then, with great deliberation, tore it up and dropped the pieces on the floor.

In 1948, Armstrong sued RCA, Motorola, and several other corporations for patent infringement. The lawyers rubbed their hands and licked their chops and started manufacturing a ton of paper. By the early

1950s, Armstrong was lamenting, "They will stall this along until I am dead or broke." It was the former. On the night of January 31, 1954, he jumped out the window of his Manhattan apartment ten stories above the East River. For some reason, he put on his overcoat, scarf, hat, and gloves before he jumped. Late that year, his widow accepted a million-dollar settlement. It was the merest fraction of what his invention had come to be worth.

Then there was the case of another loner, Gordon Gould, one of the three main holders of patents on the laser. Gould and Lemelson were about the same age. They had hit upon their major concepts at about the same time, the mid-1950s. Gould had been a thirty-six-year-old graduate student at Columbia University when what he called "the fire" first possessed him. He was the one who thought up the acronym LASER (for Light Amplification by Stimulated Emission of Radiation). For twenty-seven years he was embroiled in legal battles on two fronts, with the Patent Office and with laser manufacturers.

By the time a court ordered the Patent Office to grant him his key patents, Gould had retired. He was spending his golden years with his lawyers. He had twelve lawsuits going in the United States and Canada. His legal bills had come to $2.5 million, much of it paid for by a firm that would get 64 percent of his income—down the road—if he won the suits.

As for himself, Gould indicated in an interview, he was long past the stage of life in which the big money would interest him, even if it ever came.

Lemelson's problems were still more complicated, because he had so many patents. He lived like a chess player who takes on forty opponents at once, walking from board to board, trying to keep straight in his mind what threats are coming up where.

Well, at least Lemelson had had enough victories to be able to keep breathing in the avalanche of paper and lawyers' bills. Very few independent inventors had the money even to get in the game.

In the late 1970s, it began to dawn on government statisticians that the United States was no longer the great world center of technological innovation. Over a single five-year stretch, 1971 to 1976, the number of American citizens receiving U.S. patents declined by 21 percent. The number of foreign citizens receiving U.S. patents increased by 16 percent. By 1979, about four of every ten new U.S. patents were going to foreigners. That year, the subject began to break out in the press. *Newsweek* ran a cover story titled "Innovation: Has America Lost Its Edge?" The conclusion was that it had lost it, or was losing it, to the Japanese. That was not news to Lemelson. The underlying problem, as he saw it, was the sad fate of the independent inventor.

By the late 1970s, the corporations had managed to create the impres-

sion that in the twentieth century the greatest technological innovations
were no longer coming from the loners but from the corporate and
university research teams. But this had never been true. Innovation and
corporate research were very nearly a contradiction in terms; at bottom,
the corporations were interested only in improvements in existing product lines. As for the universities, they actually looked down upon invention as an amateur pastime, despite the fact that much scientific study,
especially in the area of electronics, was nothing more than the analysis
of discoveries made by inventors.

In 1975, Lemelson was appointed to the Patent and Trademark
Office Advisory Committee. In July 1979, he testified at Senate hearings
investigating what was beginning to be called "the innovation crisis."
In a prepared statement, he said that corporations and the courts had
combined to create an "antipatent philosophy" in the United States.
"Company managers know that the odds of an inventor being able to
afford the costly litigation are less than one in ten; and even if the suit
is brought, four times out of five the courts will hold the patent invalid.
When the royalties are expected to exceed the legal expense, it makes
good business sense to attack the patent."

65   He contrasted this with the situation in Japan, where patent law was
taken seriously, both morally and legally. "Although the majority of my
income is derived from foreign licenses, I have *never* had to enforce a
patent against a foreign infringer. I leave it to you to conclude the reason
as to why the attitude is so different. My licensees have told me that
they recognize the clear value of invention from an economic point of
view. They feel that the United States has lived off the fat of its own
technology for so long that we don't recognize that the consequence of
the legal destruction of patents is a decline in innovation, a situation that
is not within anyone's economic interest.

"What all this means to the inventor is that he either quits inventing
or he licenses foreign."

One fine day a few months ago, Lemelson was in his New York office
on Park Avenue, near Grand Central Terminal, talking to a reporter
from a magazine. The two of them were sitting on a couch across from
Lemelson's desk. The reporter had on a checked suit and a shirt collar
like Herbert Hoover's. It looked about four inches high. Underneath his
necktie you could see a brass-plated collar button of the sort that went
out forty-six years ago. Lemelson's office, on the other hand, had a cool,
immaculate, low-slung, modern look in tones of beige, gray, taupe, and
teak. Lemelson himself was just as neatly composed. He was wearing a
navy blazer, dark gray pants, a blue shirt, and a sincere necktie. He was
now sixty-two years old and what remained of his curly hair was turning

gray. But he was as trim as a digital watch. That morning, as usual, he
had run a mile and a half and done forty push-ups, fifty sit-ups, and a
hundred sidesaddle hops. His face had the gaunt athletic look of those
who stare daily down the bony gullet of the great god Aerobics.

The reporter with the collar was wrapping his eyebrows around his
nose as he tried to think of the technical terms concerning Lemelson's
inventions. Lemelson listened patiently and sipped a glass of orange
juice. Every now and then, one of the two telephones on the desk would
ring. Lemelson would excuse himself and walk to the desk. One telephone had an ordinary ring, and he would answer that one by saying
hello. The other one rang with an electronic burble. That one he would
answer by saying, "Licensing Management." Licensing Management
Corp. was a firm he had created chiefly to sell licenses for his own
inventions to manufacturers.

"Licensing Management . . . Yes . . . This is Jerry Lemelson . . . Oh,
hi . . . No, I can't do it this week. I have three days of depositions coming up."

The other telephone rings.   70

"Hello? . . . Oh, hi . . . Thursday of next week? I can't make it. I have
to be in Cleveland . . . What for? For a deposition."

It goes on like that.

"Hello? . . . Yes . . . Oh, hi . . . This afternoon? . . . . I won't be here
that late. I have an appointment with my lawyer in half an hour."

Lemelson walks back to the couch. The reporter with the trick collar
says, "If you don't mind my asking, when do you . . . *invent?*"

"On the train."   75

"On the train?"

"On the train out to Princeton, where I live."

"On the train," the fellow with the collar repeats it, all the while
staring at him, apparently wondering if Lemelson is putting him on. But
Lemelson isn't the type.

Then the fellow says, "Your opponents say, or they imply, that you
make your money by filing lawsuits."

Not much ruffles Jerome H. Lemelson, but this gets under his skin.   80
"Who said that?"

"One of the lawyers."

Lemelson shakes his head. "Oh, sure. They accuse me of being liti-
gious. But I've *lost* money on litigation. I've spent more than a million
dollars on it, and I don't even like to think about the time."

"Then why get involved in it?"

"*Why?* To protect my rights. What do you do when your rights are   85
being violated? Lie down? Walk away? You show me a successful inventor who hasn't been a scrapper."

Then his expression changes. "I don't know if I should even stress this side of it. It all sounds so negative. I don't want to discourage inventors. I want to encourage them. I think we ought to have something like the National Inventors Council that we had during World War II. The government called upon our people for inventions to help win the war. They received four hundred thousand ideas during World War II alone, and over four thousand of them actually went into production, and they helped win the war. I'd like to see this type of thing revived to see if we can win the technological battle with the rest of the world."

He thinks a moment. "There's nothing wrong with our patent system itself. We just need to protect patents. And actually things are getting a little better. There's a new federal court for handling patent cases now, the court of appeals for the federal circuit, and the judges know patent law. Your chances are much better now. They're about fifty-fifty."

"If every opponent in every piece of litigation you have going right now decided to settle in your favor, how much money would you receive?"

The thought of the corporations suffering this sudden mass attack of equity makes Lemelson laugh. "Millions. It won't turn out that way, of course.

"But I don't have any regrets. This has been a good life. I've been independent, and I've done exactly what I wanted to do."

The train to Princeton was fifteen or twenty minutes out of Penn Station, and everybody was settling into the dim blue haze of the car and the jouncing and bouncing. The roadbed was in a little better shape than it used to be. They were starting to replace the old wooden ties with concrete. It would be easy enough to invent better rail systems, and no doubt plenty of people had, but they would never be built, and so it wasn't worth thinking about.

A little more of the lurching there in the haze, a few more metal shrieks from between the cars, and—bango!—it came to Lemelson, just like that. The drug delivery system, the whole thing—it all came to him while he was sitting there. For a long time he had been trying to think of a way to use drugs to treat a diseased area of the body without having to diffuse the chemicals and subject the entire body to their effects, as happens in chemotherapy. For people with certain forms of cancer, it would be a godsend. And now he had it! The time-release thing! The insertion system! All the parts were in place!

Lemelson reached into his briefcase and pulled out the pad he always kept on hand for such moments as these. He was aware for the first time of the man sitting next to him. The man looked like nothing more than a dead-average New Jersey commuter, but you never knew. You just never knew. Lemelson began writing it all down in a shorthand he had created for himself. The drug delivery. The time release. He was no longer aware of the haze and the motion of the car. He was soaring. It was like the beginning, once more, of a dream come true.

Lewis Thomas

ON MAGIC IN MEDICINE

Medicine has always been under pressure to provide public explanations for the diseases with which it deals, and the formulation of comprehensive, unifying theories has been the most ancient and willing preoccupation of the profession. In the earliest days, hostile spirits needing exorcism were the principal pathogens, and the shaman's duty was simply the development of improved techniques for incantation. Later on, especially in the Western world, the idea that the distribution of body fluids among various organs determined the course of all illnesses took hold, and we were in for centuries of bleeding, cupping, sweating, and purging in efforts to intervene. Early in this century the theory of autointoxication evolved, and a large part of therapy was directed at emptying the large intestine and keeping it empty. Then the global concept of focal infection became popular, accompanied by the linked notion of allergy to the presumed microbial pathogens, and no one knows the resulting toll of extracted teeth, tonsils, gallbladders, and appendixes: the idea of psychosomatic influences on disease emerged in the 1930s and, for a while, seemed to sweep the field.

Gradually, one by one, some of our worst diseases have been edited out of such systems by having their causes indisputably identified and dealt with. Tuberculosis was the paradigm. This was the most chronic and inexorably progressive of common human maladies, capable of affecting virtually every organ in the body and obviously influenced by crowding, nutrition, housing, and poverty; theories involving the climate in general, and night air and insufficient sunlight in particular, gave rise to the spa as a therapeutic institution. It was not until the development of today's effective chemotherapy that it became clear to everyone that the disease had a single, dominant, central cause. If you got rid of the tubercle bacillus you were rid of the disease.

But that was some time ago, and today the idea that complicated diseases can have single causes is again out of fashion. The microbial infections that can be neatly coped with by antibiotics are regarded as lucky anomalies. The new theory is that most of today's human illnesses, the infections aside, are multifactorial in nature, caused by two great

From *The Medusa and the Snail* (1979).

arrays of causative mechanisms: 1) the influence of things in the environment and 2) one's personal life-style. For medicine to become effective in dealing with such diseases, it has become common belief that the environment will have to be changed, and personal ways of living will also have to be transformed, and radically.

These things may turn out to be true, for all I know, but it will take a long time to get the necessary proofs. Meanwhile, the field is wide open for magic.

One great difficulty in getting straightforward answers is that so many of the diseases in question have unpredictable courses, and some of them have a substantial tendency toward spontaneous remission. In rheumatoid arthritis, for instance, when such widely disparate therapeutic measures as copper bracelets, a move to Arizona, diets low in sugar or salt or meat or whatever, and even an inspirational book have been accepted by patients as useful, the trouble in evaluation is that approximately 35 percent of patients with this diagnosis are bound to recover no matter what they do. But if you actually have rheumatoid arthritis or, for that matter, schizophrenia, and then get over it, or if you are a doctor and observe this to happen, it is hard to be persuaded that it wasn't *something* you did that was responsible. Hence you need very large numbers of patients and lots of time, and a cool head.

Magic is back again, and in full force. Laetrile cures cancer, acupuncture is useful for deafness and low-back pain, vitamins are good for anything, and meditation, yoga, dancing, biofeedback, and shouting one another down in crowded rooms over weekends are specifics for the human condition. Running, a good thing to be doing for its own sake, has acquired the medicinal value formerly attributed to rare herbs from Indonesia.

There is a recurring advertisement, placed by Blue Cross on the op-ed page of *The New York Times,* which urges you to take advantage of science by changing your life habits, with the suggestion that if you do so, by adopting seven easy-to-follow items of life-style, you can achieve eleven added years beyond what you'll get if you don't. Since today's average figure is around seventy-two for all parties in both sexes, this might mean going on until at least the age of eighty-three. You can do this formidable thing, it is claimed, by simply eating breakfast, exercising regularly, maintaining normal weight, not smoking cigarettes, not drinking excessively, sleeping eight hours each night, and not eating between meals.

The science which produced this illumination was a careful study by California epidemiologists, based on a questionnaire given to about seven thousand people. Five years after the questionnaire, a body count was made by sorting through the county death certificates, and the 371 people who had died were matched up with their answers to the questions. To be sure, there were more deaths among the heavy smokers and drinkers, as you might expect from the known incidence of lung cancer in smokers and cirrhosis and auto accidents among drinkers. But there was also a higher mortality among those who said they didn't eat breakfast, and even higher in those who took no exercise, no exercise at all, not even going off in the family car for weekend picnics. Being up to 20 percent overweight was not so bad, surprisingly, but being *underweight* was clearly associated with a higher death rate.

The paper describing these observations has been widely quoted, and not just by Blue Cross. References to the Seven Healthy Life Habits keep turning up in popular magazines and in the health columns of newspapers, always with that promise of eleven more years.

The findings fit nicely with what is becoming folk doctrine about   10
disease. You become ill because of not living right. If you get cancer it is, somehow or other, your own fault. If you didn't cause it by smoking or drinking or eating the wrong things, it came from allowing yourself to persist with the wrong kind of personality, in the wrong environment. If you have a coronary occlusion, you didn't run enough. Or you were too tense, or you *wished* too much, and didn't get a good enough sleep. Or you got fat. Your fault.

But eating breakfast? It is a kind of enchantment, pure magic.

You have to read the report carefully to discover that there is another, more banal way of explaining the findings. Leave aside the higher deaths in heavy smokers and drinkers, for there is no puzzle in either case; these are dangerous things to do. But it is hard to imagine any good reason for dying within five years from not eating a good breakfast, or any sort of breakfast.

The other explanation turns cause and effect around. Among the people in that group of seven thousand who answered that they don't eat breakfast, don't go off on picnics, are underweight, and can't sleep properly, there were surely some who were already ill when the questionnaire arrived. They didn't eat breakfast because they couldn't stand the sight of food. They had lost their appetites, were losing weight, didn't feel up to moving around much, and had trouble sleeping. They didn't play tennis or go off on family picnics because they didn't *feel* good. Some of these people probably had an undetected cancer, perhaps of the pancreas; others may have had hypertension or early kidney failure or some other organic disease which the questionnaire had no way of picking up. The study did not ascertain the causes of death in the 371, but just a few deaths from such undiscerned disorders would have made a significant statistical impact. The author of the paper was careful to note these possible interpretations, although the point was not made strongly, and the general sense you have in reading it is that you can live on and on if only you will eat breakfast and play tennis.

The popular acceptance of the notion of Seven Healthy Life Habits, as a way of staying alive, says something important about today's public attitudes, or at least the attitudes in the public mind, about disease and dying. People have always wanted causes that are simple and easy to comprehend, and about which the individual can *do* something. If you believe that you can ward off the common causes of premature death— cancer, heart disease, and stroke, diseases whose pathogenesis we really do not understand—by jogging, hoping, and eating and sleeping regularly, these are good things to believe even if not necessarily true. Medicine has survived other periods of unifying theory, constructed to explain all of human disease, not always as benign in their effects as this one is likely to be. After all, if people can be induced to give up smoking, stop overdrinking and overeating, and take some sort of regular exercise, most of them are bound to feel the better for leading more orderly, regular lives, and many of them are surely going to look better.

15   Nobody can say an unfriendly word against the sheer goodness of keeping fit, but we should go carefully with the promises.

There is also a bifurcated ideological appeal contained in the seven-life-habits doctrine, quite apart from the subliminal notion of good luck in the numbers involved (7 come 11). Both ends of the political spectrum can find congenial items. At the further right, it is attractive to hear that the individual, the good old freestanding, free-enterprising American citizen, is responsible for his own health and when things go wrong it is his own damn fault for smoking and drinking and living wrong (and he can jolly well pay for it). On the other hand, at the left, it is nice to be told that all our health problems, including dying, are caused by failure of the community to bring up its members to live properly, and if you really want to improve the health of the people, research is not the answer; you should upheave the present society and invent a better one. At either end, you can't lose.

In between, the skeptics in medicine have a hard time of it. It is much more difficult to be convincing about ignorance concerning disease mechanisms than it is to make claims for full comprehension, especially when the comprehension leads, logically or not, to some sort of action. When it comes to serious illness, the public tends, understandably, to be more skeptical about the skeptics, more willing to believe the true believers. It is medicine's oldest dilemma, not to be settled by candor or by any kind of rhetoric; what it needs is a lot of time and patience, waiting for science to come in, as it has in the past, with the solid facts.

THE READER

1. *What would be a sensible response to a recommendation of the Seven Healthy Life Habits?*
2. *Thomas speaks of "folk doctrine about disease" (p. 485). Are there folk doctrines about other things? How are they similar or different?*
3. *In this essay, Thomas calls himself a skeptic. What evidence does he*

give of a similar skepticism in "The Long Habit" (p. 247)? What other features of his presumed personality are common to both essays?

THE WRITER

1. *In the second paragraph, Thomas uses the word* paradigm. *First define the term from the way Thomas uses it in that paragraph, and then compare that definition with what you find in the dictionary. Explain how Thomas might say that the study by the California epidemiologists that defined the Seven Healthy Life Habits (p. 484) was also a paradigm—for successful research, in their case. Does such an explanation require that you define a place for magic in the paradigm for successful research? Consult Kuhn's "The Route to Normal Science" (p. 1033) for help.*
2. *On p. 485, Thomas argues for turning cause and effect (in the California study) around so that, for example, what was the effect (sickness) becomes a cause and what was a cause (failure to exercise) becomes an effect. This is obviously a potent argumentative tactic. Suggest some other applications in politics or international affairs. Explain one of your examples in a paragraph or two.*

Alistair Cooke

DOCTOR AND PATIENT: FACE TO FACE

What I have in mind is the daily relation of the doctor (most especially the internist or general practitioner) to the patients he sees, and the cures or placebos he offers them. Most of all I want to address myself to the psychological assumptions on which both doctor and patient gauge each other's character and temperament and adjust their attitudes accordingly. If I have anything to offer to doctors, who have spent their lifetimes with this problem, it may be to sharpen some of the differences that I have noticed, in Britain and America, between what the doctor expects of the patient and what the patient expects of the doctor.

Some of you may be disappointed to infer—correctly—that I am not going to discuss the big social themes that have been well aired by people far more knowledgeable than I: such things as the proper distribution of rural and city doctors, and profit-making private clinics; let alone the large and universal problems of socialized medicine versus private practice, and the never-ending arguments that flow from a national health insurance system about how thorough a clinical routine can be applied

From *The Patient Has the Floor* (1986), originally published in the *Mayo Clinic Proceedings* (Vol. 41, No. 2, 1966).

to a horde of people in the waiting room who are there because the service is free. I will only say in passing that very few people I have ever heard of are willing to put money aside for health insurance. All systems so-called would be better labeled sickness-insurance programs.

One of the sharpest differences between Britain and America is how much the doctor expects the patient to know about the working of his body in general and the particular troubles he is susceptible to. Nobody has written more aptly about this—as about many other relations between doctors and patients—than the late Richard Asher. At your annual meeting twenty-two years ago, he said: "Indirectly, a little knowledge of medicine in the hands of our patients may benefit doctors. It is hard for a salesman to remain honest if his customers have no idea whether his goods are satisfactory or not. Blind, ignorant faith in doctors is not always to their benefit, although we appreciate it highly on the rare occasions we obtain it. Heaven defend us from the kind of patient who comes to us and says: 'I want you to have my 17-keto-steroids estimated.' How much we prefer the patient who says: 'I leave it to you, doctor.'"

I am sure that while these two types stake out the extremes of the general practitioner's experience, there are many more varied types in between—suppliants, admirers, doubting Thomases, paranoiacs, pests. The technically inquisitive patient is, I suspect, far more common in the United States. In my frequent shuttling between the two countries, I have often thought that British doctors are lucky in having, in their educated patients especially, an ignorant laity that would rather remain so. This must have something to do with the persistence in Britain of C. P. Snow's[1] two cultures, which encourage the automatic decision among university students to go into the arts or sciences on the presumption that the twain are never meant to meet, and with the general presumption of writers, lawyers, musicians, artists that no intellectual or social prestige is lost by regarding the sciences as beneath their notice. In glaring contrast to this national prejudice, I think of the not unusual American career of the late Robert Tyre Jones, Jr., of Atlanta, Georgia. If he had been an Englishman, I doubt whether before he became the greatest golfer in the world he would have acquired an honors degree in English literature from Oxford, a law degree from the Middle Temple, and an engineering degree from Manchester.

5   I find that in even the most distinguished British biographies of literary figures, musicians, and artists, five hundred pages of the most scrupulous scholarship will end with the note that the great man or

1. C. P. Snow (Charles Percy, 1905–80), British novelist, scientist, and government administrator. His books *The Two Cultures and the Scientific Revolution* (1959) and *Second Look* (1964) argue that humanists and scientists know little about each other's disciplines and that communication between them is difficult, if not impossible.

woman tired easily, was in increasing pain, and friends knew that "the end was near." Nearly fifty years ago my first American friend, who was then a premedical student at Yale, on coming to the end of a biography of some eighteenth-century writer (it could just as well have been a twentieth-century figure) said: "What *is* this listlessness that killed him? Was it an anemia, diabetes, encephalitis, or what?" An annoyingly large number of Americans, from all sorts of backgrounds, tend to want to know. And so the American internist expects to be burdened by this nagging demand—from a lawyer, a housewife, an actor, or a real estate broker—for a technical explanation that would bore or bewilder the more stoical Briton.

American curiosity is fed daily at high and low levels. At the lowest it is fed by the preposterous magical cures propounded by weekly junk magazines that litter the display shelves of supermarkets. At the highest level it is fed by television documentaries and by the excellent and wide-ranging articles on health and disease that appear in the best of the American press. In how many other countries, I wonder, is a weekly scientific supplement enclosed in the daily newspaper, as it is every Tuesday in *The New York Times?*

As for television, it is at once a curse and a blessing. The curse is television commercials, from which viewers pick up, subliminally, in the moment of ridicule, quick fixes for indigestion, headaches, hemorrhoids, lower backache, insomnia, and what is guardedly called "minor arthritis pain." The blessing, not unmixed, lies in the frequent television documentaries on how the body works and how it doesn't. Here again, it is the nature of the medium to be most engrossing when it is most visually dramatic. Few inquisitive people can resist the marvelous world revealed to us by microphotography, and the most memorable medical documentaries I have seen have been of performances of microsurgery. Inevitably, these deal with impaired function which, without the intervention of the skilled surgeon, would kill the patient. Before television, something of the sort was done by documentary-film makers. I remember how enthusiastically, before the last war, the Roosevelt administration discovered the virtues, or rather the propaganda uses, of documentary film. One of the ablest of the directors hired by the government did a film called *The Birth of a Baby*. It was quite brilliant and received ecstatic reviews from everybody but—I should guess—expectant mothers. Throughout the film the heartbeat was amplified on the sound track and provided a relentless bass rhythm. The effect of it—as it pounded at a gallop and then perilously slowed—was ominous. For what the director was filming was not the normal birth of a baby but a terrifying case of eclampsia.[2] It was, in other words, a film about disease. I should think

2. Rare disorder affecting women in the last ten weeks of pregnancy.

it contributed powerfully to the abortion rate of the time—which was not its original purpose.

But the effects of television in general—its dramas, soap operas, its fictional life—go much further than most of us had guessed in implanting in the general public new attitudes toward the doctor. We have just learned this from a study conducted over the past ten years by the University of Pennsylvania. It is serious enough to merit its being published in full, later this year, by the United States Public Health Service. Its conclusions are at once flattering to the doctor and a threat to his honesty and patience. Here are the main ones:

Characters on evening prime-time serials are shown as healthy "despite all the mayhem, eating, and drinking" and are relatively sober, safe from accidents, and slim at all ages.

10   The image of mentally ill people presented by television fits erroneously into stereotypes and popular prejudice.

There are five times as many doctors, nurses, and other health professionals on television as there are in real life.

Daytime soap operas rely for their cliff-hanging tension on so much illness, major and minor, that "they could well be the largest source of medical advice in the United States."

These characteristics alone, by reinforcing the preconception that doctors are available in all places at all hours, could well make the patient who suddenly falls ill all the more outraged by the reality of the unreachable doctor and the tedium and trauma of the emergency clinic; they may have done much to stimulate what is called "roadside medicine" and the mushrooming growth of freestanding emergency centers, or walk-in clinics, with a promised limit of fifteen minutes' waiting time.

The most somber and threatening—threatening to you—sentence in the report is this one, which starts out as a seeming compliment: "Television contributes to a syndrome in which high levels of confidence in the medical profession seem to justify live-for-today attitudes. . . . This cultivation of complacency, coupled with an unrealistic belief in the 'magic of medicine,' is likely to perpetuate unhealthy life-styles and to leave both patients and doctors vulnerable to disappointment, frustration—and litigation."

15   Litigation! The dread word reminds us of the enormous increase in this country, in the past twenty years or so, of suits for malpractice, and a corresponding increase in protective premiums, so stiff in some states that there are skillful surgeons who have quit their practices and turned to more dependable ways of providing for their families.[3] It is taken, by

3. By 1985, of all medical specialists, obstetricians had become the most vulnerable to legal action. In some states, their annual malpractice insurance premiums were as high as $70,000, and as many as one in four were quitting their practices [Cooke's note].

many newspapers and other media, as a grisly reflection of rampant malpractice. And it may be that as people come to expect more from doctors, more doctors take bigger risks to accommodate them. But many of these suits reflect rather the bitter disillusion of a generation lulled by the popular education we have been talking about into believing that doctors can cure any disease, and that almost any organ of the body can be replaced as readily as a punctured tire or a shock absorber.

So one big social question that the modern doctor has to face is: who will help him adjust to these rosy expectations and regain the realistic confidence of his patients? Well, there is good news. The answer is—the sociologists, whose main job, after all, is to tell us how society works and, by the disinterestedness of their findings, point the way to its behaving better. In the past ten years the sociologists have turned their expertise to the doctor-patient relationship. The studies I have seen are based on the premise, which seems to me a sensible one, that the root of a trusting relationship or a suspicious one lies in the first interview. Consequently, they went out with microphones and tape recorders, in Southern and Northern California, in Washington, D.C., in Massachusetts, and in West Germany, to tape the dialogues between doctors and their new patients.

The reports I have looked over should not raise your hopes for enlightenment too high. They appear to me to share two initial flaws. The first is almost inevitable in a procedure that requires both the doctor and the patient to be told that they are going to be recorded. The happy injunction to "just be yourself" is one with which naive radio and television producers hope to comfort beginning broadcasters. The truth is that to ninety-nine human beings in a hundred, however emotionally secure or blithe they may be in life, a microphone is a sword of Damocles that instantly heightens self-consciousness and produces a tune (what the phoneticians call an "intonation pattern") which is not the natural tune of a person talking to one or two friends in a room—and that, to me, is the ideal condition for all successful broadcasting. It takes years to forget the microphone and any awareness of an outside audience.

So, in the transcripts of the interviews I have read there is an unnatural strain on both sides, which is in itself a source of suspicion. Many doctors seem to overcome this better than their patients, however, and this leads the recording angels—the sociologists—into their second flaw: the presumption, reported as an observation, that doctors tend, especially with less-educated patients, to be intimidating, to be exercising power. But surely the first meeting between a patient and a doctor, between the learner and the teacher, between the anxious ignoramus and the one who knows, cannot possibly be an equal emotional and psychological exchange.

Whatever else the sociologists can usefully tell us is befogged by their own appalling jargon. Let me recite—not for long—some of the discoveries which they seem to offer as being most relevant, if not profound.

20   They notice that patients develop an "attitude" to the doctor: "Specific aspects of the doctor's talk obviously contribute to this notion of attitude." The only comment I can make on that is: obviously. Some investigators, we are told, "use a scale of 1 to 6 to score . . . the least to the most technical remarks . . . [and] the same scale is used to decide the globality or specificity of the patient's questions and the doctor's responses. . . . Additional scoring is used about the causal or noncausal nature of the explanation and its probabilistic or nonprobabilistic nature." Well, fancy that!

One original study "involved longitudinal observations of doctor-patient interaction between six internists and thirty-six patients over a nine-month period." What they were doing discussing longitude I have no idea, unless—as I can well imagine—the patients were so disoriented after nine months that they had to be told where they were at.

I am afraid there is no succor for us from the sociologists. I should like some doctors—neuropsychiatrists preferably—to do a study on the problems of communication that are peculiar to sociologists: why they fail to get anything at all across to poor us, their abject subjects.

Any of you frightened by these strictures may take decent consolation from the wiser words of Franz Ingelfinger, who four years ago, meeting the charge that doctors are more arrogant than most professionals, had this to say: "Physicians as a class are, I suspect, no more vain or insolent than any other people. Some are presumptuous and condescending, others self-effacing and sympathetic . . . [but] if the physician is to be effective in alleviating the patient's complaints, it follows that the patient has to believe . . . that his physician not only can be trusted but has also some special knowledge that the patient does not possess. He needs, if the treatment is to succeed, a physician whom he invests with authoritative experience and competence. He needs a physician from whom he will accept some domination. If I am going to give up eating eggs for the rest of my life, I must be convinced, as an ovophile, that a higher authority than I will influence my eating habits. I do not want to be in the position of the shopper at the casbah[4] who negotiates and haggles with the physician about what is best. . . . In fact, if you agree that the physician's primary function is to make the patient feel better, a certain amount of authoritarianism, paternalism, and domination are the essence of the physician's effectiveness."

This must be so, though we have only to look around at any dozen, and apparently happy, marriages we know to see that for some people authority does not reside in domination but rather in the partner's

4. Arabic, meaning "metropolis," "capital," or "citadel."

serene temperament, or in humor, or in simply a pair of beautiful brown eyes. For me, medical authority is most acceptable in a doctor who is a skeptic.

I should like to end by considering briefly the special temptation that   25
is offered by the present great age of biochemical medicine—the temptation to become what the late Dr. Haven Emerson called "the Ph.D.": the pharmacopoeia doctor, who listens to a recital of the symptoms, retires to the back room, matches the most distressing symptom with the latest drug, and prescribes it. The layman does not know that about a half of today's prescriptions are for drugs that did not exist ten years ago. With his preconceived trust in the doctor as a sainted healer, he is not disposed to discover that, according to a survey done as long ago as 1964, one in three prescriptions handed out by general practitioners is based on the information folders that come with the drug company's sample. Luckily for doctors, the time it takes for each succeeding wonder drug to be discredited, or restricted to its rare and proper use, is so long or so masked by gradual disease that the disappointment or damage in the old drug is forgotten in the glowing promise of the new. I am thinking of those drugs which are seized on as God-sent solutions to ancient or particular problems and which, in time, reveal not so much that they have bad side effects but that the *effect on the ailments they are prescribed for may be the side effect*, the main effect being the damage done to some organ that was not considered in the original research or manufacture.

The example of thalidomide[5] is too gross to enlarge on, although for a year or two its potential merit was seriously weighed and attested by some very competent physicians in the Western world. Those in active practice in the 1950s will recall chloramphenicol, a wonder drug indeed until it was seen to shut down the bone marrow. Those of us with any interest in athletics vividly recall the miracle we saw with our very eyes, when some football player received a brutal injury, limped or was carried off the field, and within ten minutes or so was trotting happily back into combat after a massive shot of hydrocortisone. We never noticed how many of these heroes went off into early retirement. More recently, phenylbutazone (Butazolidin) has been joyfully prescribed as the most magical of the anti-inflammatory drugs. Crippling muscle spasms vanish overnight! No wonder: as one orthopedic surgeon put it: "It's like killing a gnat with an atom bomb." And to this day, it takes courage for the good doctor to refuse to pump penicillin into patients with self-limiting ailments such as the common cold. The belief in fashionable magic has come so far in the United States that there are rich people, from Palm

5. Sleep-producing drug used widely from 1958 on, until it was discovered to cause severe fetal malformations.

Beach to Beverly Hills, who at the onset of a headache demand a computed axial tomography (CAT) scan.[6]

As for the vitamins—apart from the weekly shots of vitamin B_{12} given patients who feel out of sorts but could not possibly have pernicious anemia—all but the most cynical doctors can be excused from blame, since vitamins constitute the most flourishing branch of the self-medication industry. First it was C, then the B complex, and now—in the United States—the magical E. I once tried to tell a devoted addict of vitamin E how Evans and Emerson,[7] so long ago as 1936, labored to find for rats a diet deficient in vitamin E; how difficult this effort was; how the thing seemed to exist in cardboard, ground glass, and dust; how in the end those two pioneers isolated such a diet, so deficient in everything that the rats grew lackadaisical and some developed muscular dystrophy. Moreover, Mr. Rat was no longer interested in Mrs. Rat. *That* was the detail that excited the industry and the laggard lover. If you took lots of vitamin E surely your potency would be enhanced. It followed, did it not? It did not. But it was useless to suggest to my addict that the logic in this inference was about as sensible as deducing that if Neville Chamberlain had gone to Munich *without his umbrella* he would not have appeased Hitler. In fact, I believe that nothing at all can be done for patients, or nonpatients, who believe that with vitamins, more is better.

But as I travel from place to place and country to country, I am constantly struck by finding that this friend in London, and that one in Dallas, another in Paris, and yet another in Glasgow are all getting the same, the latest, antibiotic though their ailments seem to be different. My conclusion is that, because this is an era of intensifying specialization and widespread biochemical experiment, there never was a time when the ordinary doctor, the general practitioner, needed to do more homework, to exercise more patience, and to direct his own and his patients' attention to the human body's subtle, and, indeed, preponderant capacity for *health*. Lewis Thomas has said it as well as anyone:

> It is a distortion . . . to picture the human being as a teetering, fallible contraption, always needing watching and patching, always on the verge of flapping to pieces; this is the doctrine that people hear most often, and most eloquently, on all our information media. We ought to be developing a much better system of general education about human health, with more

6. Once the word gets around such chic environs that magnetic resonance imaging (MRI) could eventually replace both CAT scans and X rays, the MRI procedure may become as obligatory as access to a sauna [Cooke's note].

7. Herbert Mclean Evans (1882–1971), American anatomist and embryologist, and Gladys Anderson Emerson (1903–84), American biochemist and nutritionist.

curricular time for acknowledgment, and even some celebration, of the absolute marvel of good health that is the real lot of most of us, most of the time.

Well, I seem to be asking of doctors inhumanly high standards of skill, intelligence, imagination, patience, and honor. This is unfair, but it is only because of an illusion that doctors themselves have fostered as much as anybody: the illusion of modest infallibility. I noticed as a student, first at my own English university and then at two others in the United States, that medical students were notable for high spirits, coarse humor, and general affability, but not particularly for intellectual brilliance. This cruel reputation must have been planted long ago because practitioners of medicine were regarded for hundreds of years as journeymen, on a level with butchers, carpenters, and barbers, and were denied the term "doctor" for two centuries after it had been bestowed on theologians and lawyers.

But sometime during the nineteenth century—perhaps after surgery turned from amputation to repair—a medical degree descended like a small halo; and ever since, the ordinary citizen has secretly resented it or been dazzled by it. The retention of the serpent as a logo has certainly helped to keep alive the notion of the doctor as the possessor of a strange and subtle wisdom. Cherish and protect this illusion. It has not yet occurred to the layman that doctors—like cab drivers, schoolmasters, politicians, and television repairmen—can be very good, good, indifferent, bad, or downright stupid. Do not let the word get out!

In the meantime, let the conscientious doctor, harried by an excess of sick patients and by his usual large allotment of hypochondriacs, make the most of the peculiar boon offered today by the increasingly numerous varieties of antibiotics and steroids: when you are baffled by the patient's primary affliction, give him another disease and cure that.

Adrienne Rich

WHEN WE DEAD AWAKEN: WRITING AS RE-VISION

Ibsen's *When We Dead Awaken* is a play about the use that the male artist and thinker—in the process of creating culture as we know it—has

Written for a forum on "The Woman Writer in the Twentieth Century" in 1971, and later published in *College English* (Vol. 34, No. 1, Oct. 1972); this revision, slightly revised, is included in *On Lies, Secrets, and Silence: Selected Prose: 1966–1978* (1979).

made of women, in his life and in his work; and about a woman's slow struggling awakening to the use to which her life has been put. Bernard Shaw wrote in 1900 of this play: "[Ibsen] shows us that no degradation ever devized or permitted is as disastrous as this degradation; that through it women can die into luxuries for men and yet can kill them; that men and women are becoming conscious of this: and that what remains to be seen as perhaps the most interesting of all imminent social developments is what will happen 'when we dead awaken.'"

It's exhilarating to be alive in a time of awakening consciousness; it can also be confusing, disorienting, and painful. This awakening of dead or sleeping consciousness has already affected the lives of millions of women, even those who don't know it yet. It is also affecting the lives of men, even those who deny its claims upon them. The argument will go on whether an oppressive economic class system is responsible for the oppressive nature of male/female relations, or whether, in fact, the sexual class system is the original model on which all the others are based. But in the last few years connections have been drawn between our sexual lives and our political institutions which are inescapable and illuminating. The sleepwalkers are coming awake, and for the first time this awakening has a collective reality; it is no longer such a lonely thing to open one's eyes.

Re-vision—the act of looking back, of seeing with fresh eyes, of entering an old text from a new critical direction—is for us more than a chapter in cultural history: it is an act of survival. Until we can understand the assumptions in which we are drenched we cannot know ourselves. And this drive to self-knowledge, for woman, is more than a search for identity: it is part of her refusal of the destructiveness of male-dominated society. A radical critique of literature, feminist in its impulse, would take the work first of all as a clue to how we live, how we have been living, how we have been led to imagine ourselves, how our language has trapped as well as liberated us; and how we can begin to see—and therefore live—afresh. A change in the concept of sexual identity is essential if we are not going to see the old political order reassert itself in every new revolution. We need to know the writing of the past, and know it differently than we have ever known it; not to pass on a tradition but to break its hold over us.

For writers, and at this moment for women writers in particular, there is the challenge and promise of a whole new psychic geography to be explored. But there is also a difficult and dangerous walking on the ice, as we try to find language and images for a consciousness we are just coming into, and with little in the past to support us. I want to talk about some aspects of this difficulty and this danger.

Jane Harrison, the great classical anthropologist, wrote in 1914 in a letter to her friend Gilbert Murray: "By the by, about 'Women,' it has bothered me often—why do women never want to write poetry about Man as a sex—why is Woman a dream and a terror to man and not the other way around? . . . Is it mere convention and propriety, or something deeper?" I think Jane's question cuts deep into the myth-making tradition, the romantic tradition; deep into what women and men have been to each other; and deep into the psyche of the woman writer. Thinking about that question, I began thinking of the work of two twentieth-century women poets, Sylvia Plath and Diane Wakoski. It strikes me that in the work of both Man appears as, if not a dream, a fascination, and a terror; and that the source of the fascination and the terror is, simply, Man's power—to dominate, tyrannize, choose or reject the woman. The charisma of Man seems to come purely from his power over her, and his control of the world by force; not from anything fertile or life-giving in him. And, in the work of both these poets, it is finally the woman's sense of *herself*—embattled, possessed—that gives the poetry its dynamic charge, its rhythms of struggle, need, will and female energy. Convention and propriety are perhaps not the right words, but until recently this female anger, this furious awareness of the Man's power over her, were not available materials to the female poet, who tended to write of Love as the source of her suffering, and to view that victimization by Love as an almost inevitable fate. Or, like Marianne Moore and Elizabeth Bishop, she kept human sexual relationships at a measured and chiselled distance in her poems.

One answer to Jane Harrison's question has to be that historically men and women have played very different parts in each others' lives. Where woman has been a luxury for man, and has served as the painter's model and the poet's muse, but also as comforter, nurse, cook, bearer of his seed, secretarial assistant, and copyist of manuscripts, man has played a quite different role for the female artist. Henry James repeats an incident which the writer Prosper Mérimée described, of how, while he was living with George Sand,

> he once opened his eyes, in the raw winter dawn, to see his companion, in a dressing-gown, on her knees before the domestic hearth, a candle-stick beside her and a red *madras* round her head, making bravely, with her own hands, the fire that was to enable her to sit down betimes to urgent pen and paper. The story represents him as having felt that the spectacle chilled his ardor and tried his taste; her appearance was unfortunate, her occupation an inconsequence, and her industry a reproof—the result of all of which was a lively irritation and an early rupture.

I am suggesting that the specter of this kind of male judgment, along with the active discouragement and thwarting of her needs by a culture controlled by males, has created problems for the woman writer: problems of contact with herself, problems of language and style, problems of energy and survival.

In rereading Virginia Woolf's *A Room of One's Own* for the first time in some years, I was astonished at the sense of effort, of pains taken, of dogged tentativeness, in the tone of that essay. And I recognized that tone. I had heard it often enough, in myself and in other women. It is the tone of a woman almost in touch with her anger, who is determined not to appear angry, who is *willing* herself to be calm, detached, and even charming in a roomful of men where things have been said which are attacks on her very integrity. Virginia Woolf is addressing an audience of women, but she is acutely conscious—as she always was—of being overheard by men: by Morgan and Lytton and Maynard Keynes[1] and for that matter by her father, Leslie Stephen. She drew the language out into an exacerbated thread in her determination to have her own sensibility yet protect it from those masculine presences. Only at rare moments in that essay do you hear the passion in her voice; she was trying to sound as cool as Jane Austen, as Olympian as Shakespeare, because that is the way the men of the culture thought a writer should sound.

No male writer has written primarily or even largely for women, or with the sense of women's criticism as a consideration when he chooses his materials, his theme, his language. But to a lesser or greater extent, every woman writer has written for men even when, like Virginia Woolf, she was supposed to be addressing women. If we have come to the point when this balance might begin to change, when women can stop being haunted, not only by "convention and propriety" but by internalized fears of being and saying themselves, then it is an extraordinary moment for the woman writer—and reader.

I have hesitated to do what I am going to do now, which is to use myself as an illustration. For one thing, it's a lot easier and less dangerous to talk about other women writers. But there is something else. Like Virginia Woolf, I am aware of the women who are not with us here because they are washing the dishes and looking after the children. Nearly fifty years after she spoke, that fact remains largely unchanged. And I am thinking also of women whom she left out of the picture altogether—women who are washing other people's dishes and caring for other people's children, not to mention women who went on the streets last night in order to feed their children. We seem to be special women here, we have liked to think of ourselves as special, and we have

---

1. E. M. Forster, novelist, and Lytton Strachey, biographer, and John Maynard Keynes, economist—all members of the Bloomsbury group in London during the 1920s and 1930s.

known that men would tolerate, even romanticize us as special, as long as our words and actions didn't threaten their privilege of tolerating or rejecting us according to *their* ideas of what a special woman ought to be. An important insight of the radical women's movement, for me, has been how divisive and how ultimately destructive is this myth of the special woman, who is also the token woman. Every one of us here in this room has had great luck; our own gifts could not have been enough, for we all know women whose gifts are buried or aborted. Our struggles can have meaning only if they can help to change the lives of women whose gifts—and whose very being—continues to be thwarted.

My own luck was being born white and middle-class into a house full   10
of books, with a father who encouraged me to read and write. So for about twenty years I wrote for a particular man, who criticized and praised me and made me feel I was indeed "special." The obverse side of this, of course, was that I tried for a long time to please him, or rather, not to displease him. And then of course there were other men—writers, teachers—the Man, who was not a terror or a dream but a literary master and a master in other ways less easy to acknowledge. And there were all those poems about women, written by men: it seemed to be a given that men wrote poems and women frequently inhabited them. These women were almost always beautiful, but threatened with the loss of beauty, the loss of youth—the fate worse than death. Or, they were beautiful and died young, like Lucy and Lenore.[2] Or, the woman was like Maud Gonne,[3] cruel and disastrously mistaken, and the poem reproached her because she had refused to become a luxury for the poet.

A lot is being said today about the influence that the myths and images of women have on all of us who are products of culture. I think it has been a peculiar confusion to the girl or woman who tries to write, because she is peculiarly susceptible to language. She goes to poetry or fiction looking for *her* way of being in the world, since she too has been putting words and images together; she is looking eagerly for guides, maps, possibilities; and over and over in the "words' masculine persuasive force" of literature she comes up against something that negates everthing she is about: she meets the image of Woman in books written by men. She finds a terror and a dream, she finds a beautiful pale face, she finds La Belle Dame Sans Merci, she finds Juliet or Tess or Salomé,[4] but precisely what she does not find is that absorbed, drudging, puzzled,

2. In poems by William Wordsworth and Edgar Allan Poe.
3. Irish revolutionary activist, subject of many love poems by William Butler Yeats.
4. These female figures appear respectively in the poem "La Belle Dame sans Merci"

by John Keats, Shakespeare's play *Romeo and Juliet*, Thomas Hardy's novel *Tess of the D'Urbervilles*, and Oscar Wilde's play *Salomé*. The men whom they love, or who love them, all sicken or die.

sometimes inspired creature, herself, who sits at a desk trying to put words together.

So what does she do? What did I do? I read the older women poets with their peculiar keenness and ambivalence: Sappho, Christina Rossetti, Emily Dickinson, Elinor Wylie, Edna Millay, H.D. I discovered that the woman poet most admired at the time (by men) was Marianne Moore, who was maidenly, elegant, intellectual, discreet. But even in reading these women I was looking in them for the same things I had found in the poetry of men, because I wanted women poets to be the equals of men, and to be equal was still confused with sounding the same.

I know that my style was formed first by male poets: by the men I was reading as an undergraduate—Frost, Dylan Thomas, Donne, Auden, MacNiece, Stevens, Yeats. What I chiefly learned from them was craft. But poems are like dreams: in them you put what you don't know you know. Looking back at poems I wrote before I was twenty-one, I'm startled because beneath the conscious craft are glimpses of the split I even then experienced between the girl who wrote poems, who defined herself in writing poems, and the girl who was to define herself by her relationships with men. "Aunt Jennifer's Tigers," written while I was a student, looks with deliberate detachment at this split.

> Aunt Jennifer's tigers stride across ascreen,
> Bright topaz denizens of a world of green.
> They do not fear the men beneath the tree,
> They pace in sleek chivalric certainty.
>
> Aunt Jennifer's fingers, fluttering through her wool,
> Find even the ivory needle hard to pull.
> The massive weight of Uncle's wedding-band
> Sits heavily upon Aunt Jennifer's hand.
>
> When Aunt is dead, her terrified hands will lie
> Still ringed with ordeals she was mastered by.
> The tigers in the panel that she made
> Will go on striding, proud and unafraid.

In writing this poem, composed and apparently cool as it is, I thought I was creating a portrait of an imaginary woman. But this woman suffers from the opposition of her imagination, worked out in tapestry, and her life-style, "ringed with ordeals she was mastered by." It was important to me that Aunt Jennifer was a person as distinct from myself as possible—distanced by the formalism of the poem; by its objective, observant tone; even by putting the woman in a different generation.

In those years formalism was part of the strategy—like asbestos gloves, it allowed me to handle materials I couldn't pick up barehanded. (A later strategy was to use the persona of a man, as I did in "The Loser.")

A man thinks of the woman he once loved: first, after her wedding, and then nearly a decade later.

I

I kissed you, bride and lost, and went
home from that bourgeois sacrament,
your cheek still tasting cold upon
my lips that gave you benison
with all the swagger that they knew—
as losers somehow learn to do.

Your wedding made my eyes ache; soon
the world would be worse off for one
more golden apple dropped to ground
without the least protesting sound,
and you would windfall lie, and we
forget your shimmer on the tree.

Beauty is always wasted: if
not Mignon's song sung to the deaf,
at all events to the unmoved.
A face like yours cannot be loved
long or seriously enough.
Almost, we seem to hold it off.

II

Well, you are tougher than I thought.
Now when the wash with ice hangs taut
this morning of St. Valentine,
I see you strip the squeaking line,
your body weighed against the load,
and all my groans can do no good.

Because you still are beautiful,
though squared and stiffened by the pull
of what nine windy years have done.
You have three daughters, lost a son.
I see all your intelligence
flung into that unwearied stance.

My envy is of no avail.
I turn my head and wish him well
who chafed your beauty into use
and lives forever in a house
lit by the friction of your mind.
You stagger in against the wind.

1958

15   I finished college, published my first book by a fluke, as it seemed to me, and broke off a love-affair. I took a job, lived alone, went on writing, fell in love. I was young, full of energy, and the book seemed to mean that others agreed I was a poet. Because I was also determined to have a "full" woman's life, I plunged in my early twenties into marriage and had three children before I was thirty. There was nothing overt in the environment to warn me: these were the fifties, and in reaction to the earlier wave of feminism, middle-class women were making careers of domestic perfection, working to send their husbands through professional schools, then retiring to raise large families. People were moving out to the suburbs, technology was going to be the answer to everything, even sex; the family was in its glory. Life was extremely private; women were isolated from each other by the loyalties of marriage. I have a sense that women didn't talk to each other much in the fifties—not about their secret emptinesses, their frustrations. I went on trying to write, my second book and first child appeared in the same month. But by the time that book came out I was already dissatisfied with those poems, which seemed to me mere exercises for poems I hadn't written. The book was praised, however, for its "gracefulness"; I had a marriage and a child. If there were doubts, if there were periods of null depression or active despairing, these could only mean that I was ungrateful, insatiable, perhaps a monster.

About the time my third child was born, I felt that I had either to consider myself a failed woman and a failed poet, or try to find some synthesis by which to understand what was happening to me. What frightened me most was the sense of drift, of being pulled along on a current which called itself my destiny, but in which I seemed to be losing touch with whoever I had been, with the girl who had experienced her own will and energy almost ecstatically at times, walking around a city or riding a train at night or typing in a student room. In a poem about my grandmother, I wrote (of myself): "A young girl, thought sleeping, is certified dead." I was writing very little, partly from fatigue, that female fatigue of suppressed anger and the loss of contact with her own being; partly from the discontinuity of female life with its attention to small chores, errands, work that others constantly undo, small children's constant needs. What I did write was unconvincing to me; my anger and frustration were hard to acknowledge in or out of poem, because in fact I cared a great deal about my husband and my children. Trying to look back and understand that time I have tried to analyze the real nature of the conflict. Most, if not all, human lives are full of fantasy—passive daydreaming which need not be acted on. But to write poetry or fiction, or even to think well, is not to fantasize, or to put fantasies on paper. For a poem to coalesce, for a character or an action to take shape, there has to be an imaginative transformation of reality which is in no way passive. And a certain freedom of the mind is needed—freedom to press on, to enter the currents of your thought like a glider pilot, knowing that your motion can be sustained, that the buoyancy of your attention will not be suddenly snatched away. Moreover, if the imagination is to transcend and transform experience it has to question, to challenge, to conceive of alternatives, perhaps to the very life you are living at that moment. You have to be free to play around with the notion that day might be night, love might be hate; nothing can be too sacred for the imagination to turn into its opposite or to call experimentally by another name. For writing is re-naming. Now, to be maternally with small children all day in the old way, to be with a man in the old way of marriage, requires a holding-back, a putting-aside of that imaginative activity, and seems to demand instead a kind of conservatism. I want to make it clear that I am *not* saying that in order to write well, or think well, it is necessary to become unavailable to others, or to become a devouring ego. This has been the myth of the masculine artist and thinker; and I repeat, I do not accept it. But to be a female human being trying to fulfill traditional female functions in a traditional way *is* in direct conflict with the subversive function of the imagination. The word *traditional* is important here. There must be ways, and we will be finding out more and more about them, in which the energy of creation and the energy of relation can be united. But in those earlier years I always felt the conflict as a failure of love in myself. I had thought I was choosing a full life: the life available to most men, in which sexuality, work and parenthood could coexist. But I felt, at twenty-nine, guilt toward the people closest to me, and guilty toward my own being.

I wanted, then, more than anything, the one thing of which there was never enough: time to think, time to write. The fifties and early sixties were years of rapid revelations: the sit-ins and marches in the South, the Bay of Pigs,[5] the early anti-war movement raised large questions— questions for which the masculine world of the academy around me seemed to have expert and fluent answers. But I needed desperately to think for myself—about pacifism and dissent and violence, about poetry and society and about my own relationship to all these things. For about ten years I was reading in fierce snatches, scribbling in notebooks, writing poetry in fragments; I was looking desperately for clues, because if there were no clues then I thought I might be insane. I wrote in a notebook about this time: "Paralyzed by the sense that there exists a mesh of relationships—e.g. between my anger at the children, my sensual life, pacifism, sex, (I mean sex in its broadest significance, not merely sexual desire)—an interconnectedness which, if I could see it, make it valid, would give me back myself, make it possible to function lucidly

---

5. Site of a failed American invasion of Cuba, intended to overthrow the Castro regime.

and passionately. Yet I grope in and out among these dark webs." I think I began at this point to feel that politics was not something "out there" but something "in here" and of the essence of my condition.

In the late fifties I was able to write, for the first time, directly about experiencing myself as a woman. The poem was jotted in fragments during children's naps, brief hours in a library, or at 3 A.M. after rising with a wakeful child. I despaired of doing any continuous work at this time. Yet I began to feel that my fragments and scraps had a common consciousness and a common theme, one which I would have been very unwilling to put on paper at an earlier time because I had been taught that poetry should be "universal," which meant, of course, non-female. Until then I had tried very much *not* to identify myself as a female poet. Over two years I wrote a ten-part poem called "Snapshots of A Daughter-in-Law," in a longer, looser mode than I've ever trusted myself with before. It was an extraordinary relief to write that poem. It strikes me now as too literary, too dependent on allusion; I hadn't found the courage yet to do without authorities, or even to use the pronoun *I*—the woman in the poem is *always she*. One section of it, 2, concerns a woman who thinks she is going mad; she is haunted by voices telling her to resist and rebel, voices which she can hear but not obey.

> 2.
>
> Banging the coffee-pot into the sink
> she hears the angels chiding, and looks out
> past the raked gardens to the sloppy sky.
> Only a week since They said: *Have no patience.*
>
> The next time it was: *Be insatiable.*
> Then: *Save yourself; others you cannot save.*
> Sometimes she's let the tapstream scald her arm,
> a match burn to her thumbnail,
>
> or held her hand above the kettle's spout
> right in the woolly steam. They are probably angels,
> since nothing hurts her any more, except
> each morning's grit blowing into her eyes.

The poem "Orion," written five years later, is a poem of reconnection with a part of myself I had felt I was losing—the active principle, the energetic imagination, the "half-brother" whom I projected, as I had for many years, into the constellation Orion.

> Far back when I went zig-zagging
> through tamarack pastures
> you were my genius, you
> my cast-iron Viking, my helmed
> lion-heart king in prison.
> Years later now you're young

my fierce half-brother, staring
down from that simplified west
your breast open, your belt dragged down
by an oldfashioned thing, a sword
the last bravado you won't give over
though it weighs you down as you stride

and the stars in it are dim
and maybe have stopped burning.
But you burn, and I know it;
as I throw back my head to take you in
an old transfusion happens again:
divine astronomy is nothing to it.

Indoors I bruise and blunder,
break faith, leave ill enough
alone, a dead child born in the dark.
Night cracks up over the chimney,
pieces of time, frozen geodes
come showering down in the grate.

A man reaches behind my eyes
and finds them empty
a woman's head turns away
from my head in the mirror
children are dying my death
and eating crumbs of my life.

Pity is not your forte.
Calmly you ache up there
pinned aloft in your crow's nest,
my speechless pirate!
You take it all for granted
and when I look you back

it's with a starlike eye
shooting its cold and egotistical spear
where it can do least damage.
Breathe deep! No hurt, no pardon
out here in the cold with you
you with your back to the wall.

It's no accident that the words *cold and egotistical* appear in this   20
poem, and are applied to myself. The choice still seemed to be between
"love"—womanly, maternal love, altruistic love—a love defined and
ruled by the weight of an entire culture—and egotism—a force directed
by men into creation, achievement, ambition, often at the expense of
others, but justifiably so. For weren't they men, and wasn't that their
destiny as womanly love was ours? I know now that the alternatives are
false ones—that the word *love* is itself in need of re-vision.

There is a companion poem to "Orion," written three years later, in which at last the woman in the poem and the woman writing the poem become the same person. It is called "Planetarium," and it was written after a visit to a real planetarium, where I read an account of the work of Caroline Herschel, the astronomer, who worked with her brother William, but whose name remained obscure, as his did not.

(Thinking of Caroline
Herschel, 1750–1848,
astronomer, sister of
William; and others)

A woman in the shape of a monster
a monster in the shape of a woman
the skies are full of them

a woman   'in the snow
among the Clocks and instruments
or measuring the ground with poles'

in her 98 years to discover
8 comets

she whom the moon ruled
like us
levitating into the night sky
riding the polished lenses

Galaxies of women, there
doing penance for impetuousness
ribs chilled
in those spaces   of the mind

An eye,
          'virile, precise and absolutely certain'
          from the mad webs of Uranisborg
                    encountering the NOVA

every impulse of light exploding
from the core
as life flies out of us

          Tycho whispering at last
          'Let me not seem to have lived in vain'

What we see, we see
and seeing is changing

the light that shrivels a mountain
and leaves a man alive

Heartbeat of the pulsar
heart sweating through my body

The radio impulse
pouring in from Taurus

      I am bombarded yet   I stand

I have been standing all my life in the
direct path of a battery of signals
the most accurately transmitted most
untranslatable language in the universe
I am a galactic cloud so deep   so invo-
luted that a light wave could take 15
years to travel through me   And has
taken   I am an instrument in the shape
of a woman trying to translate pulsations
into images   for the relief of the body
and the reconstruction of the mind.

In closing I want to tell you about a dream I had last summer. I dreamed I was asked to read my poetry at a mass women's meeting; but when I began to read, what came out were the lyrics of a blues song. I share this dream with you because it seemed to me to say a lot about the problems and the future of the woman writer, and probably of women in general. The awakening of consciousness is not like the crossing of a frontier—one step, and you are in another country. Much of women's poetry has been of the nature of the blues song: a cry of pain, of victimization, or a lyric of seduction. And today, much poetry by women—and prose for that matter—is charged with anger. I think we need to go through that anger, and we will betray our own reality if we try, as Virginia Woolf was trying, for an objectivity, a detachment; that would make us sound more like Jane Austen or Shakespeare. We know more than Jane Austen or Shakespeare knew: more than Jane Austen because our lives are more complex, more than Shakespeare because we know more about the lives of women, Jane Austen and Virginia Woolf included.

Both the victimization and the anger experienced by women are real, and have real sources, everywhere in the environment, built into society. They must go on being tapped and explored by poets, among others. We can neither deny them, nor can we rest there. They are our birth-pains, and we are bearing ourselves. We would be failing each other as writers and as women, if we neglected or denied what is negative, regressive or Sisyphean [5] in our inwardness.

We all know that there is another story to be told. I am curious and expectant about the future of the masculine consciousness. I feel in the

5. The reference is to the Greek myth of Sisyphus. He was condemned to roll a huge rock to the top of a hill, but the rock always rolled back down before the top was reached.

work of the men whose poetry I read today a deep pessimism and fatalistic grief; and I wonder if it isn't the masculine side of what women have experienced, the price of masculine dominance. One thing I am sure of: just as woman is becoming her own midwife, creating herself anew, so man will have to learn to gestate and give birth to his own subjectivity—something he has frequently wanted woman to do for him. We can go on trying to talk to each other, we can sometimes help each other, poetry and fiction can show us what the other is going through; but women can no longer be primarily mothers and muses for men: we have our own work cut out for us.

THE READER

1. A typical male-chauvinist cliché is that women take everything too personally, that they lack the larger (i.e., male) perspective. Does this essay tend to confirm or deny that belief?
2. In the eighth paragraph, Rich asserts that "no male writer has written primarily or even largely for women, or with the sense of women's criticism as a consideration when he chooses his materials, his theme, his langue." How can she know this? Do you think she is right? How do you know?
3. In saying that the need is to break tradition's hold over us (p. 496), Rich clearly implies her assessment of tradition. Looking to the future she says, "Woman is becoming her own midwife, creating herself anew." What view of history is implicit here? What role does the speaker create for herself?

THE WRITER

1. Why does Rich include some of her own poetry? Explain whether you think she is able to make points through it that she couldn't make otherwise.
2. On p. 498, Rich describes Virginia Woolf as being conscious of male listeners even as she addressed women. Can you detect signs of this in Woolf's "In Search of a Room of One's Own" (p. 1111)? Rich will try to avoid this way of speaking and writing. Does she succeed? Find passages to support your answer.
3. Why does Rich use the hyphen in re-vision? What does she wish to imply about writing?
4. On p. 499, Rich refers to "the influence that the myths and images of women have on all of us." Presumably there are also myths and images of men. Write a brief account of either a male or a female myth and its influence upon attitudes and actions of the other sex.

Herb Goldberg

IN HARNESS: THE MALE CONDITION

Most men live in harness. Richard was one of them. Typically he had no awareness of how his male harness was choking him until his personal and professional life and his body had nearly fallen apart.

Up to that time he had experienced only occasional short bouts of depression that a drink would bring him out of. For Richard it all crashed at an early age, when he was thirty-three. He came for psychotherapy with resistance, but at the instruction of his physician. He had a bad ulcer, was losing weight, and, in spite of repeated warnings that it could kill him, he was drinking heavily.

His personal life was also in serious trouble. He had recently lost his job as a disc jockey on a major radio station because he'd been arrested for drunk driving. He had totaled his car against a tree and the newspapers had a picture of it on the front page. Shortly thereafter his wife moved out, taking with her their eight-year-old daughter. She left at the advice of friends who knew that he had become violent twice that year while drunk.

As he began to talk about himself it became clear that he had been securely fitted into his male harness early in his teens. In high school he was already quite tall and stronger than most. He was therefore urged to go out for basketball, which he did, and he got lots of attention for it.

He had a deep, resonant voice that he had carefully cultivated. He was told that he should go into radio announcing and dramatics, so he got into all the high school plays. In college he majored in theater arts.

In his senior year in college he dated one of the most beautiful and sought-after girls in the junior class. His peer group envied him, which reassured Richard that he had a good thing going. So he married Joanna a year after graduating and took a job with a small radio station in Fresno, California. During the next ten years he played out the male role; he fathered a child and fought his way up in a very competitive profession.

It wasn't until things had fallen apart that he even let himself know that he had any feelings of his own, and in therapy he began to see why it had been so necessary to keep his feelings buried. They were confusing and frightening.

More than anything else, there was a hypersensitive concern over

5

From *The Hazards of Being Male* (1976).

what others thought about him as a "man." As other suppressed feelings began to surface they surprised him. He realized how he had hated the pressures of being a college basketball player. The preoccupation with being good and winning had distorted his life in college.

Though he had been to bed with many girls before marriage and even a few afterward, he acknowledged that rarely was it a genuine turn-on for him. He liked the feeling of being able to seduce a girl but the experience itself was rarely satisfying, so he would begin the hunt for another as soon as he succeeded with one. "Some of those girls were a nightmare," he said, "I would have been much happier without them. But I was caught in the bag of proving myself and I couldn't seem to control it."

10   The obsessive preoccupation in high school and college with cultivating a deep, resonant "masculine" voice he realized was similar to the obsession some women have with their figures. Though he thought he had enjoyed the attention he got being on stage, he acknowledged that he had really disliked being an entertainer, or "court jester," as he put it.

When he thought about how he had gotten married he became particularly uncomfortable. "I was really bored with Joanna after the first month of dating but I couldn't admit it to myself because I thought I had a great thing going. I married her because I figured if I didn't one of the other guys would. I couldn't let that happen."

Richard had to get sick in his harness and nearly be destroyed by role-playing masculinity before he could allow himself to be a person with his own feelings, rather than just a hollow male image. Had it not been for a bleeding ulcer he might have postponed looking at himself for many years more.

Like many men, Richard had been a zombie, a daytime sleepwalker. Worse still, he had been a highly "successful" zombie, which made it so difficult for him to risk change. Our culture is saturated with successful male zombies, businessmen zombies, golf zombies, sports car zombies, playboy zombies, etc. They are playing by the rules of the male game plan. They have lost touch with, or are running away from, their feelings and awareness of themselves as people. They have confused their social masks for their essence and they are destroying themselves while fulfilling the traditional definitions of masculine-appropriate behavior. They set their life sails by these role definitions. They are the heroes, the studs, the providers, the warriors, the empire builders, the fearless ones. Their reality is always approached through these veils of gender expectations.

When something goes seriously wrong, they discover that they are shadows to themselves as well as to others. They are unknown because they have been so busy manipulating and masking themselves in order to maintain and garner more status that a genuine encounter with another person would threaten them, causing them to flee or to react with extreme defensiveness.

Men evaluate each other and are evaluated by many women largely by the degree to which they approximate the ideal masculine model. Women have rightfully lashed out against being placed into a mold and being related to as a sex object. Many women have described their roles in marriage as a form of socially approved prostitution. They assert that they are selling themselves out for an unfulfilling portion of supposed security. For psychologically defensive reasons the male has not yet come to see himself as a prostitute, day in and day out, both in and out of the marriage relationship.

The male's inherent survival instincts have been stunted by the seemingly more powerful drive to maintain his masculine image. He would, for example, rather die in the battle than risk living in a different way and being called a "coward" or "not a man." He would rather die at his desk prematurely than free himself from his compulsive patterns and pursuits. As a recently published study concluded, "A surprising number of men approaching senior citizenship say they would rather die than be buried in retirement."

The male in our culture is at a growth impasse. He won't move—not because he is protecting his cherished central place in the sun, but because he *can't* move. He is a cardboard Goliath precariously balanced and on the verge of toppling over if he is pushed even ever so slightly out of his well-worn path. He lacks the fluidity of the female who can readily move between the traditional definitions of male or female behavior and roles. She can be wife and mother or a business executive. She can dress in typically feminine fashion or adopt the male styles. She will be loved for having "feminine" interests such as needlework or cooking, or she will be admired for sharing with the male in his "masculine" interests. That will make her a "man's woman." She can be sexually assertive or sexually passive. Meanwhile, the male is rigidly caught in his masculine pose and, in many subtle and direct ways, he is severely punished when he steps out of it.

Unlike some of the problems of women, the problems of men are not readily changed through legislation. The male has no apparent and clearly defined targets against which he can vent his rage. Yet he is oppressed by the cultural pressures that have denied him his feelings, by the mythology of the woman and the distorted and self-destructive way he sees and relates to her, by the urgency for him to "act like a man" which blocks his ability to respond to his inner promptings both emo-

15

tionally and physiologically, and by a generalized self-hate that causes him to feel comfortable only when he is functioning well in harness, or when he lives for joy and for personal growth.

The prevalent "enlightened" male's reaction to the women's liberation movement bears testimony to his inability to mobilize himself on his own behalf. He has responded to feminist assertions by donning sack cloth, sprinkling himself with ashes, and flagellating himself—accusing himself of the very things she is accusing him of. An article entitled, "You've Come a Long Way, Buddy," perhaps best illustrates the male self-hating attitude. In it, the writer said,

> The members of the men's liberation movement are . . . a kind of embarrassing vanguard, the first men anywhere on record to take a political stand based on the idea that what the women are saying is right—men are a bunch of lazy, selfish, horny, unhappy oppressors.

20   Many other undoubtedly well-intentioned writers on the male condition have also taken a basically guilt- and shame-oriented approach to the male, alternately scolding him, warning him, and preaching to him that he better change and not be a male chauvinist pig anymore. During many years of practice as a psychotherapist, I have never seen a person grow or change in a self-constructive, meaningful way when he was motivated by guilt, shame, or self-hate. That manner of approach smacks of old-time religion and degrades the male by ignoring the complexity of the binds and repressions that are his emotional heritage.

Precisely because the tenor and mood of the male liberation efforts so far have been one of self-accusation, self-hate, and a repetition of feminist assertions, I believe it is doomed to failure in its present form. It is buying the myth that the male is culturally favored—a notion that is clung to despite the fact that every critical statistic in the area of longevity, disease, suicide, crime, accidents, childhood emotional disorders, alcoholism, and drug addiction shows a disproportionately higher male rate.

Many men who join male liberation groups do so to please or impress their women or to learn how to deal with and hold onto their recently liberated wives or girlfriends. Once in a male liberation group they intellectualize their feelings and reactions into lifelessness. In addition, the men tend to put each other down for thinking like "typical male chauvinists" or using words like "broad," "chick," "dike," etc. They have introjected the voices of their feminist accusers and the result is an atmosphere that is joyless, self-righteous, cautious, and lacking in a vitalizing energy. A new, more subtle kind of competitiveness pervades the atmosphere: the competition to be the least competitive and most free of the stereotyped version of male chauvinism.

The women's liberation movement did not effect its astounding impact via self-hate, guilt, or the desire to placate the male. Instead it has been energized by anger and outrage. Neither will the male change in any meaningful way until he experiences his underlying rage toward the endless, impossible binds under which he lives, the rigid definitions of his role, the endless pressure to be all things to all people, and the guilt-oriented, self-denying way he has traditionally related to women, to his feelings, and to his needs.

Because it is so heavily repressed, male rage only manifests itself indirectly and in hidden ways. Presently it is taking the form of emotional detachment, interpersonal withdrawal, and passivity in relationship to women. The male has pulled himself inward in order to deny his anger and to protect himself and others from his buried cascade of resentment and fury. Pathetic, intellectualized attempts not to be a male chauvinist pig will *never* do the job.

There is also a commonly expressed notion that men will somehow be freed as a by-product of the feminist movement. This is a comforting fantasy for the male but I see no basis for it becoming a reality. It simply disguises the fear of actively determining his own change. Indeed, by responding inertly and passively, the male will be moved, but not in a meaningful and productive direction. If there is to be a constructive change for the male he will have to chart his own way, develop his own style and experience his own anxieties, fear, and rage because *this time mommy won't do it!*

Recently, I asked a number of men to write to me about how they see their condition and what liberation would mean to them. A sense of suffocation and confusion was almost always present.

A forty-six-year-old businessman wrote: "From what do I need to be liberated? I'm too old and tired to worry about myself. I know that I'm only a high-grade mediocrity. I've come to accept a life where the dreams are now all revealed as unreality. I don't know how my role or my son's role should change. If I knew I suppose it would be in any way that would make my wife happier and less of a shrew."

A thirty-nine-year-old carpenter discussing the "joys" of working responded: "I contend that the times in which it is fun and rewarding in a healthy way have been fairly limited. Most of the time it has been a question of running in fear of failure." Referring to his relationships, he continued. "There is another aspect of women's and men's lib that I haven't experienced extensively. This is the creation of close friendships outside of the marriage. My past experiences have been stressful to the point where I am very careful to limit any such contact. What's the fear? I didn't like the sense of insecurity developed by my wife and the internal stresses that I felt. It created guilt feelings."

A fifty-seven-year-old college professor expressed it this way: "Yes, there's a need for male lib and hardly anyone writes about it the way it really is, though a few make jokes. My gut reaction, which is what you asked for, is that men—the famous male chauvinist pigs who neglect their wives, underpay their women employees, and rule the world—are literally slaves. They're out there picking that cotton, sweating, swearing, taking lashes from the boss, working fifty hours a week to support themselves and the plantation, only then to come back to the house to do another twenty hours a week rinsing dishes, toting trash bags, writing checks, and acting as butlers at the parties. It's true of young husbands and middle-aged husbands. Young bachelors may have a nice deal for a couple of years after graduating, but I've forgotten, and I'll never again be young! Old men. Some have it sweet, some have it sour.

30   "Man's role—how has it affected my life? At thirty-five, I chose to emphasize family togetherness and income and neglect my profession if necessary. At fifty-seven, I see no reward for time spent with and for the family, in terms of love or appreciation. I see a thousand punishments for neglecting my profession. I'm just tired and have come close to just walking away from it and starting over; just research, publish, teach, administer, play tennis, and travel. Why haven't I? Guilt. And love. And fear of loneliness. How should the man's role in my family change? I really don't know how it can, but I'd like a lot more time to do my thing."

The most remarkable and significant aspect of the feminist movement to date has been woman's daring willingness to own up to her resistances and resentment toward her time-honored, sanctified roles of wife and even mother. The male, however, has yet to fully realize, acknowledge, and rebel against the distress and stifling aspects of many of the roles he plays—from good husband, to good daddy, to good provider, to good lover, etc. Because of the inner pressure to constantly affirm his dominance and masculinity, he continues to act as if he can stand up under, fulfill, and even enjoy all the expectations placed on him no matter how contradictory and devitalizing they are.

It's time to remove the disguises of privilege and reveal the male condition for what it really is.

THE READER

1. Betty Rollin, in "Motherhood: Who Needs It?" (p. 521), talks about extinguishing the "Motherhood Myth" to encourage women to discover and be themselves. What does Goldberg imply about extinguishing fatherhood? How do these two ideas differ? Which would have a greater impact on society?

2. Compare the approach to human personality taken by Goldberg with

that of Willard Gaylin, also a psychotherapist, in "What You See Is the Real You" (p. 675). Do they seem to agree on the nature of human personality? Explain.

THE WRITER

1. *From what sort of evidence or experience does Goldberg draw his conclusions? Do the men who seek help from a psychotherapist represent a good cross section of all males? What biases might be encountered in such a group of subjects?*
2. *Construct a dialogue in which Goldberg's "harnessed" man and a "liberated" woman discuss birth control, the proper role of parents, platonic relationships between men and women, or some similar topic.*

Gloria Steinem

THE GOOD NEWS IS: THESE ARE NOT THE BEST YEARS OF YOUR LIFE

If you had asked me a decade or more ago, I certainly would have said the campus was the first place to look for the feminist or any other revolution. I also would have assumed that student-age women, like student-age men, were much more likely to be activist and open to change than their parents. After all, campus revolts have a long and well-publicized tradition, from the students of medieval France, whose "heresy" was suggesting that the university be separate from the church, through the anticolonial student riots of British India; from students who led the cultural revolution of the People's Republic of China, to campus demonstrations against the Shah of Iran. Even in this country, with far less tradition of student activism, the populist movement to end the war in Vietnam was symbolized by campus protests and mistrust of anyone over thirty.

It has taken me many years of traveling as a feminist speaker and organizer to understand that I was wrong about women; at least, about women acting on their own behalf. In activism, as in so many other things, I had been educated to assume that men's cultural pattern was the natural or the only one. If student years were the peak time of rebellion and openness to change for men, then the same must be true for women. In fact, a decade of listening to every kind of women's group—from brown-bag lunchtime lectures organized by office workers

First appeared in *Ms.* magazine (Sept. 1979).

to all-night rap sessions at campus women's centers; from housewives' self-help groups to campus rallies—has convinced me that the reverse is more often true. Women may be the one group that grows more radical with age. Though some students are big exceptions to this rule, women in general don't begin to challenge the politics of our own lives until later.

Looking back, I realize that this pattern has been true for my life, too. My college years were full of uncertainties and the personal conservatism that comes from trying to win approval and fit into the proper grown-up and womanly role whether that means finding a well-to-do man to be supported by or a male radical to support. Nonetheless, I went right on assuming that brave exploring youth and cowardly conservative old age were the norms for everybody, and that I must be just an isolated and guilty accident. Though every generalization based on female culture has many exceptions, and should never be used as a crutch or excuse, I think we might be less hard on ourselves and each other as students, feel better about our potential for change as we grow older—and educate reporters who announce feminism's demise because its red-hot center is not on campus—if we figured out that for most of us as women, the traditional college period is an unrealistic and cautious time. Consider a few of the reasons.

As students, women are probably treated with more equality than we ever will be again. For one thing, we're consumers. The school is only too glad to get the tuitions we pay, or that our families or government grants pay on our behalf. With population rates declining because of women's increased power over childbearing, that money is even more vital to a school's existence. Yet more than most consumers, we're too transient to have much power as a group. If our families are paying our tuition, we may have even less power.

5   As young women, whether students or not, we're still in the stage most valued by male-dominant cultures: We have our full potential as workers, wives, sex partners, and childbearers.

That means we haven't yet experienced the life events that are most radicalizing for women: entering the paid-labor force and discovering how women are treated there; marrying and finding out that it is not yet an equal partnership; having children and discovering who is responsible for them and who is not; and aging, still a greater penalty for women than for men.

Furthermore, new ambitions nourished by the rebirth of feminism may make young women feel and behave a little like a classical immigrant group. We are determined to prove ourselves, to achieve academic excellence, and to prepare for interesting and successful careers. More noses are kept to more grindstones in an effort to demonstrate newfound abilities, and perhaps to allay suspicions that women still have to have more and better credentials than men. This doesn't leave much time for activism. Indeed, we may not yet know that it is necessary.

In addition, the very progress into previously all-male careers that may be revolutionary for women is seen as conservative and conformist by outside critics. Assuming male radicalism to be the measure of change, they interpret any concern with careers as evidence of "campus conservatism." In fact, "dropping out" may be a departure for men, but "dropping in" is a new thing for women. Progress lies in the direction we have not been.

Like most groups of the newly arrived or awakened, our faith in education and paper degrees also has yet to be shaken. For instance, the percentage of women enrolled in colleges and universities has been increasing at the same time that the percentage of men has been decreasing. Among students entering college in 1978, women *outnumbered* men for the first time. This hope of excelling at the existing game is probably reinforced by the greater cultural pressure on females to be "good girls" and observe somebody else's rules.

Though we may know intellectually that we need to have new games with new rules, we probably haven't quite absorbed such facts as the high unemployment rate among female Ph.D.s; the lower average salary among women college graduates of all races than among counterpart males who graduated from high school or less; the middle-management ceiling against which even those eagerly hired new business-school graduates seem to bump their heads after five or ten years; and the barrier-breaking women in nontraditional fields who become the first fired when recession hits. Sadly enough, we may have to personally experience some of these reality checks before we accept the idea that lawsuits, activism, and group pressure will have to accompany our individual excellence and crisp new degrees.

Then there is the female guilt trip, student edition. If we're not sailing along as planned, it must be *our* fault. If our mothers didn't "do anything" with their educations, it must have been *their* fault. If we can't study as hard as we think we must (because women still have to be better prepared than men), and have a substantial personal and sexual life at the same time (because women are supposed to care more about relationships than men do), then we feel inadequate, as if each of us were individually at fault for a problem that is actually culture-wide.

I've yet to be on a campus where most women weren't worrying about some aspect of combining marriage, children, and a career. I've yet to find one where many men were worrying about the same thing. Yet women will go right on suffering from the double-role problem and terminal guilt until men are encouraged, pressured, or otherwise forced,

10

individually and collectively, to integrate themselves into the "women's work" of raising children and homemaking. Until then, and until there are changed job patterns to allow equal parenthood, children will go right on growing up with the belief that only women can be loving and nurturing, and only men can be intellectual or active outside the home. Each half of the world will go on limiting the full range of its human talent.

Finally, there is the intimate political training that hits women in the teens and early twenties: the countless ways we are still brainwashed into assuming that women are dependent on men for our basic identities, both in our work and our personal lives, much more than vice versa. After all, if we're going to enter a marriage system that's still legally designed for a person and a half, submit to an economy in which women still average about fifty-nine cents on the dollar earned by men, and work mainly as support staff and assistants, or *co*-directors and *vice*-presidents at best, then we have to be convinced that we are not whole people on our own.

In order to make sure that we will see ourselves as half-people, and thus be addicted to getting our identity from serving others, society tries hard to convert us as young women into "man junkies"; that is, into people who are addicted to regular shots of male-approval and presence, both professionally and personally. We need a man standing next to us, actually and figuratively, whether it's at work, on Saturday night, or throughout life. (If only men realized how little it matters *which* man is standing there, they would understand that this addiction depersonalizes them, too.) Given the danger to a male-dominant system if young women stop internalizing this political message of derived identity, it's no wonder that those who try to kick the addiction—and, worse yet, to help other women do the same—are likely to be regarded as odd or dangerous by everyone from parents to peers.

15   With all that pressure combined with little experience, it's no wonder that younger women are often less able to support each other. Even young women who espouse feminist goals as individuals may refrain from identifying themselves as "feminist": it's okay to want equal pay for yourself (just one small reform) but it's not okay to want equal pay for women as a group (an economic revolution). Some retreat into individualized career obsessions as a way of avoiding this dangerous discovery of shared experience with women as a group. Others retreat into the safe middle ground of "I'm not a feminist but. . . ." Still others become politically active, but only on issues that are taken seriously by their male counterparts.

The same lesson about the personal conservatism of younger women is taught by the history of feminism. If I hadn't been conned into believing the masculine stereotype of youth as the "natural" time for freedom and rebellion, a time of "sowing wild oats" that actually is made possible by the assurance of power and security later on, I could have figured out the female pattern of activism by looking at women's movements of the past.

In this country, for instance, the nineteenth-century wave of feminism was started by older women who had been through the radicalizing experience of getting married and becoming the legal chattel of their husbands (or the equally radicalizing experience of *not* getting married and being treated as spinsters). Most of them had also worked in the antislavery movement and learned from the political parallels between race and sex. In other countries, that wave was also led by women who were past the point of maximum pressure toward marriageability and conservatism.

Looking at the first decade of this second wave, it's clear that the early feminist activist and consciousness-raising groups of the 1960s were organized by women who had experienced the civil rights movement, or homemakers who had discovered that raising kids and cooking didn't occupy all their talents. While most campuses of the late sixties were still circulating the names of illegal abortionists privately (after all, abortion could damage our marriage value), slightly older women were holding press conferences and speak-outs about the reality of abortions (including their own, even though that often meant confessing to an illegal act) and demanding reform or repeal of antichoice laws. Though rape had been a quiet epidemic on campus for generations, younger women victims were still understandably fearful of speaking up, and campuses encouraged silence in order to retain their reputation for safety with tuition-paying parents. It took many off-campus speak-outs, demonstrations against laws of evidence and police procedures, and testimonies in state legislatures before most student groups began to make demands on campus and local cops for greater rape protection. In fact, "date rape"— the common campus phenomenon of a young woman being raped by someone she knows, perhaps even by several students in a fraternity house—is just now being exposed. Marital rape, a more difficult legal issue, was taken up several years ago. As for battered women and the attendant exposé of husbands and lovers as more statistically dangerous than unknown muggers in the street, that issue still seems to be thought of as a largely noncampus concern, yet at many of the colleges and universities where I've spoken, there has been at least one case within current student memory of a young woman beaten or murdered by a jealous lover.

This cultural pattern of youthful conservatism makes the growing number of older women going back to school very important. They are life examples and pragmatic activists who radicalize women young enough to be their daughters. Now that the median female undergraduate age in this country is twenty-seven because so many older women have returned, the campus is becoming a major place for cross-generational connections.

20   None of this should denigrate the courageous efforts of young women, especially women on campus, and the many changes they've pioneered. On the contrary, they should be seen as even more remarkable for surviving the conservative pressures, recognizing societal problems they haven't yet fully experienced, and organizing successfully in the midst of a transient student population. Every women's history course, rape hot line, or campus newspaper that is finally covering *all* the news; every feminist professor whose job has been created or tenure saved by student pressure, or male administrator whose consciousness has been permanently changed; every counselor who's stopped guiding women one way and men another; every lawsuit that's been fueled by student energies against unequal athletic funds or graduate school requirements: all those accomplishments are even more impressive when seen against the backdrop of the female pattern of activism.

Finally, it would help to remember that a feminist revolution rarely resembles a masculine-style one—just as a young woman's most radical act toward her mother (that is, connecting as women in order to help each other get some power) doesn't look much like a young man's most radical act toward his father (that is, breaking the father-son connection in order to separate identities or take over existing power).

It's those father-son conflicts at a generational, national level that have often provided the conventional definition of revolution; yet they've gone on for centuries without basically changing the role of the female half of the world. They have also failed to reduce the level of violence in society, since both fathers and sons have included some degree of aggressiveness and superiority to women in their definition of masculinity, thus preserving the anthropological model of dominance.

Furthermore, what current leaders and theoreticians define as revolution is usually little more than taking over the army and the radio stations. Women have much more in mind than that. We have to uproot the sexual caste system that is the most pervasive power structure in society, and that means transforming the patriarchal values of those who run the institutions, whether they are politically the "right" or the "left," the fathers or the sons. This cultural part of the change goes very deep, and is often seen as too intimate, and perhaps too threatening, to be considered as either serious or possible. Only conflicts among men are "serious." Only a takeover of existing institutions is "possible."

That's why the definition of "political," on campus as elsewhere, tends to be limited to who's running for president, who's demonstrating against corporate investments in South Africa, or which is the "moral"

side of some conventional revolution, preferably one that is thousands
of miles away.

As important as such activities are, they are also the most comfortable   25
ones when we're young. They provide a sense of virtue without much
disruption in the power structure of our daily lives. Even when the most
consistent energies on campus are actually concentrated around feminist
issues, they may be treated as apolitical and invisible. Asked "What's
happening on campus?" a student may reply, "The antinuke movement," even though that resulted in one demonstration of two hours,
while student antirape squads have been patrolling the campus every
night for two years and women's studies have begun to transform the
very textbooks we read.

No wonder reporters and sociologists looking for revolution on campus often miss the depth of feminist change and activity that is really
there. Women students themselves may dismiss it as not political and
not serious. Certainly, it rarely comes in the masculine sixties style of
bombing buildings or burning draft cards. In fact, it goes much deeper
than protesting a temporary sympton—say, the draft—and challenges
the right of one group to dominate another, which is the disease itself.

Young women have a big task of resisting pressures and challenging
definitions. Their increasing success is a miracle of foresight and courage
that should make us all proud. But they should know that they, too, may
grow more radical with age.

One day, an army of gray-haired women may quietly take over the
earth.

Betty Rollin

MOTHERHOOD: WHO NEEDS IT?

Motherhood is in trouble, and it ought to be. A rude question is long
overdue: Who needs it? The answer used to be (1) society and (2)
women. But now, with the impending horrors of overpopulation, society
desperately *doesn't* need it. And women don't need it either. Thanks
to the Motherhood Myth—the idea that having babies is something
that all normal women instinctively want and need and will enjoy
doing—they just *think* they do.

The notion that the maternal wish and the activity of mothering are
instinctive or biologically predestined is baloney. Try asking most sociologists, psychologists, psychoanalysts, biologists—many of whom are

First appeared in *Look* (Sept. 22, 1970).

mothers—about motherhood being instinctive: it's like asking department store presidents if their Santa Clauses are real. "Motherhood—
instinctive?" shouts distinguished sociologist/author Dr. Jessie Bernard.
"Biological destiny? Forget biology! If it were biology, people would die
from not doing it."

"Women don't need to be mothers any more than they need spaghetti," says Dr. Richard Rabkin, a New York psychiatrist. "But if
you're in a world where everyone is eating spaghetti, thinking they need
it and want it, you will think so too. Romance has really contaminated
science. So-called instincts have to do with stimulation. They are not
things that well up inside of you."

"When a woman says with feeling that she craved her baby from
within, she is putting into biological language what is psychological,"
says University of Michigan psychoanalyst and motherhood-researcher
Dr. Frederick Wyatt. "There are no instincts," says Dr. William Goode,
president-elect of the American Sociological Association. "There are
reflexes, like eye-blinking, and drives, like sex. There is no innate drive
for children. Otherwise, the enormous cultural pressures that there are
to reproduce wouldn't exist. There are no cultural pressures to sell you
on getting your hand out of the fire."

5   There are, to be sure, biologists and others who go on about biological
destiny, that is, the innate or instinctive goal of motherhood. (At the
turn of the century, even good old capitalism was explained by a theorist
as "the *instinct* of acquisitiveness.") And many psychoanalysts will hold
the Freudian view that women feel so rotten about not having a penis
that they are necessarily propelled into the child-wish to replace the
missing organ. Psychoanalysts also make much of the psychological need
to repeat what one's parent of the same sex has done. Since every woman
has a mother, it is considered normal to wish to imitate one's mother
by being a mother.

There is, surely, a wish to pass on love if one has received it, but to
insist women must pass it on in the same way is like insisting that every
man whose father is a gardener has to be a gardener. One dissenting
psychoanalyst says, simply, "There is a wish to comply with one's biology, yes, but we needn't and sometimes we shouldn't." (Interestingly,
the woman who has been the greatest contributor to child therapy and
who has probably given more to children than anyone alive is Dr. Anna
Freud, Freud's magnificent daughter, who is not a mother.)

Anyway, what an expert cast of hundreds is telling us is, simply, that
biological *possibility* and desire are not the same as biological *need*.
Women have childbearing equipment. To choose not to use the equipment is no more blocking what is instinctive than it is for a man who,
muscles or no, chooses not to be a weight lifter.

So much for the wish. What about the "instinctive" *activity* of mothering? One animal study shows that when a young member of a species is put in a cage, say, with an older member of the same species, the latter will act in a protective, "maternal" way. But that goes for both males and females who have been "mothered" themselves. And studies indicate that a human baby will also respond to whoever is around playing mother—even if it's father. Margaret Mead and many others frequently point out that mothering can be a fine occupation, if you want it, for either sex. Another experiment with monkeys who were brought up without mothers found them lacking in maternal behavior toward their own offspring. A similar study showed that monkeys brought up without other monkeys of the opposite sex had no interest in mating—all of which suggests that both mothering and mating behavior are learned, not instinctual. And, to turn the cart (or the baby carriage) around, baby ducks who lovingly follow their mothers seemed, in the mother's absence, to just as lovingly follow wooden ducks or even vacuum cleaners.

If motherhood isn't instinctive, when and why, then, was the Motherhood Myth born? Until recently, the entire question of maternal motivation was academic. Sex, like it or not, meant babies. Not that there haven't always been a lot of interesting contraceptive tries. But until the creation of the diaphragm in the 1880's, the birth of babies was largely unavoidable. And, generally speaking, nobody really seemed to mind. For one thing, people tend to be sort of good sports about what seems to be inevitable. For another, in the past, the population needed beefing up. Mortality rates were high, and agricultural cultures, particularly, have always needed children to help out. So because it "just happened" and because it was needed, motherhood was assumed to be innate.

Originally, it was the word of God that got the ball rolling with "Be fruitful and multiply," a practical suggestion, since the only people around then were Adam and Eve. But in no time, supermoralists like St. Augustine changed the tone of the message: "Intercourse, even with one's legitimate wife, is unlawful and wicked where the conception of the offspring is prevented," he, we assume, thundered. And the Roman Catholic position was thus cemented. So then and now, procreation took on a curious value among people who viewed (and view) the pleasures of sex as sinful. One could partake in the sinful pleasure, but feel vindicated by the ensuing birth. Motherhood cleaned up sex. Also, it cleaned up women, who have always been considered somewhat evil, because of Eve's transgression (". . . but the woman was deceived and became a transgressor. Yet woman will be saved through bearing children . . . ," I Timothy, 2:14–15), and somewhat dirty because of menstruation.

And so, based on need, inevitability, and pragmatic fantasy—the Myth *worked,* from society's point of view—the Myth grew like corn in Kansas. And society reinforced it with both laws and propaganda—

10

laws that made woman a chattel, denied her education and personal mobility, and madonna propaganda that she was beautiful and wonderful doing it and it was all beautiful and wonderful to do. (One rarely sees a madonna washing dishes.)

In fact, the Myth persisted—breaking some kind of record for long-lasting fallacies—until something like yesterday. For as the truth about the Myth trickled in—as women's rights increased, as women gradually got the message that it was certainly possible for them to do most things that men did, that they live longer, that their brains were not tinier—then, finally, when the really big news rolled in, that they could *choose* whether or not to be mothers—what happened? The Motherhood Myth soared higher than ever. As Betty Friedan made oh-so-clear in *The Feminine Mystique,* the '40's and '50's produced a group of ladies who not only had babies as if they were going out of style (maybe they were) but, as never before, they turned motherhood into a cult. First, they wallowed in the aesthetics of it all—natural childbirth and nursing became maternal musts. Like heavy-bellied ostriches, they grounded their heads in the sands of motherhood, only coming up for air to say how utterly happy and fulfilled they were. But, as Mrs. Friedan says only too plainly, they weren't. The Myth galloped on, moreover, long after making babies had turned from practical asset to liability for both individual parents *and* society. With the average cost of a middle-class child figured conservatively at $30,000 (not including college), any parent knows that the only people who benefit economically from children are manufacturers of consumer goods. Hence all those gooey motherhood commercials. And the Myth gathered momentum long after sheer numbers, while not yet extinguishing us, have made us intensely uncomfortable. Almost all of our societal problems, from minor discomforts like traffic to major ones like hunger, the population people keep reminding us, have to do with there being too many people. And who suffers most? The kids who have been so mindlessly brought into the world, that's who. They are the ones who have to cope with all of the difficult and dehumanizing conditions brought on by overpopulation. They are the ones who have to cope with the psychological nausea of feeling unneeded by society. That's not the only reason for drugs, but, surely, it's a leading contender.

Unfortunately, the population curbers are tripped up by a romantic, stubborn, ideological hurdle. How can birth-control programs really be effective as long as the concept of glorious motherhood remains unchanged? (Even poor old Planned Parenthood has to euphemize—why not Planned Unparenthood?) Particularly among the poor, motherhood is one of the few inherently positive institutions that are accessible. As Berkeley demographer Judith Blake points out, "Poverty-oriented birth control programs do not make sense as a welfare measure . . . as long as existing pronatalist policies . . . encourage mating, pregnancy, and the care, support, and rearing of children." Or, she might have added, as long as the less-than-idyllic child-rearing part of motherhood remains "in small print."

Sure, motherhood gets dumped on sometimes: Philip Wylie's Momism[1] got going in the '40's and Philip Roth's *Portnoy's Complaint* did its best to turn rancid the chicken-soup concept of Jewish motherhood. But these are viewed as the sour cries of a black humorist here, a malcontent there. Everyone shudders, laughs, but it's like the mouse and the elephant joke. Still, the Myth persists. Last April, a Brooklyn woman was indicted on charges of manslaughter and negligent homicide— eleven children died in a fire in a building she owned and criminally neglected—"But," sputtered her lawyer, "my client, Mrs. Breslow, is a mother, a grandmother, and a great-grandmother!"

Most remarkably, the Motherhood Myth persists in the face of the most overwhelming maternal unhappiness and incompetence. If reproduction were merely superfluous and expensive, if the experience were as rich and rewarding as the cliché would have us believe, if it were a predominantly joyous trip for everyone riding—mother, father, child— then the going everybody-should-have-two-children plan would suffice. Certainly, there are a lot of joyous mothers, and their children and (sometimes, not necessarily) their husbands reflect their joy. But a lot of evidence suggests that for more women than anyone wants to admit, motherhood can be miserable. ("If it weren't," says one psychiatrist wryly, "the world wouldn't be in the mess it's in.")

There is a remarkable statistical finding from a recent study of Dr. Bernard's, comparing the mental illness and unhappiness of married mothers and single women. The latter group, it turned out, was both markedly less sick and overtly more happy. Of course, it's not easy to measure slippery attitudes like happiness. "Many women have achieved a kind of reconciliation—a conformity," says Dr. Bernard,

> that they interpret as happiness. Since feminine happiness is supposed to lie in devoting one's life to one's husband and children, they do that; so *ipso facto*, they assume they are happy. And for many women, untrained for independence and "processed" for motherhood, they find their state far preferable to the alternatives, which don't really exist.

Also, unhappy mothers are often loath to admit it. For one thing, if in society's view not to be a mother is to be a freak, not to be a *blissful* mother is to be a witch. Besides, unlike a disappointing marriage, disappointing motherhood cannot be terminated by divorce. Of course, none of that stops such a woman from expressing her dissatisfaction in a

15

1. Philip Wylie's *A Generation of Vipers* (1942) blamed many of the ills of American society on dominating mothers.

variety of ways. Again, it is not only she who suffers but her husband and children as well. Enter the harridan housewife, the carping shrew. The realities of motherhood can turn women into terrible people. And, judging from the 50,000 cases of child abuse in the U.S. each year, some are worse than terrible.

In some cases, the unpleasing realities of motherhood begin even before the beginning. In *Her Infinite Variety*, Morton Hunt describes young married women pregnant for the first time as "very likely to be frightened and depressed, masking these feelings in order not to be considered contemptible. The arrival of pregnancy interrupts a pleasant dream of motherhood and awakens them to the realization that they have too little money, or not enough space, or unresolved marital problems. . . ."

The following are random quotes from interviews with some mothers in Ann Arbor, Mich., who described themselves as reasonably happy. They all had positive things to say about their children, although when asked about the best moment of their day, they *all* confessed it was when the children were in bed. Here is the rest:

> Suddenly I had to devote myself to the child totally. I was under the illusion that the baby was going to fit into my life, and I found that I had to switch my life and my schedule to fit *him*. You think, "I'm in love, I'll get married, and we'll have a baby." First there's two, then three, it's simple and romantic. You don't even think about the work. . . .

> You never get away from the responsibility. Even when you leave the children with a sitter, you are not out from under the pressure of the responsibility. . . .

> I hate ironing their pants and doing their underwear, and they never put their clothes in the laundry basket. . . . As they get older, they make less demands on our time because they're in school, but the demands are greater in forming their values. . . . Best moment of the day is when all the children are in bed. . . . The worst time of the day is 4 P.M., when you have to get dinner started, the kids are tired, hungry and crabby—everybody wants to talk to you about *their* day . . . your day is only half over.

> Once a mother, the responsibility and concern for my children became so encompassing. . . . It took a great deal of will to keep up other parts of my personality. . . . To me, motherhood gets harder as they get older because you have less control. . . . In an abstract sense, I'd have several. . . . In the non-abstract, I would not have any . . . .

> I had anticipated that the baby would sleep and eat, sleep and eat. Instead, the experience was overwhelming. I really had not thought particularly about what motherhood would mean in a realistic sense. I want to do *other* things, like to become involved in things that are worthwhile—I don't mean women's clubs—but I don't have the physical energy to go out

in the evenings. I feel like I'm missing something . . . the experience of being somewhere with people and having them talking about something—something that's going on in the world.

Every grownup person expects to pay a price for his pleasures, but seldom is the price as vast as the one endured "however happily" by most mothers. We have mentioned the literal cost factor. But what does that mean? For middle-class American women, it means a life style with severe and usually unimagined limitations; i.e., life in the suburbs, because who can afford three bedrooms in the city? And what do suburbs mean? For women, suburbs mean other women and children and left-over peanut-butter sandwiches and car pools and seldom-seen husbands. Even the Feminine Mystiqueniks—the housewives who finally admitted that their lives behind brooms (OK, electric brooms) were driving them crazy—were loath to trace their predicament to their children. But it is simply a fact that a childless married woman has no child-work and little housework. She can live in a city, or, if she still chooses the suburbs or the country, she can leave on the commuter train with her husband if she wants to. Even the most ardent job-seeking mother will find little in the way of great opportunities in Scarsdale.[2] Besides, by the time she wakes up, she usually lacks both the preparation for the outside world and the self-confidence to get it. You will say there are plenty of city-dwelling working mothers. But most of those women do additional-funds-for-the-family kind of work, not the interesting career kind that takes plugging during childbearing years.

Nor is it a bed of petunias for the mother who does make it professionally. Says writer critic Marya Mannes:

20

> If the creative woman has children, she must pay for this indulgence with a long burden of guilt, for her life will be split three ways between them and her husband and her work. . . . No woman with any heart can compose a paragraph when her child is in trouble. . . . The creative woman has no wife to protect her from intrusion. A man at his desk in a room with closed door is a man at work. A woman at a desk in any room is available.

Speaking of jobs, do remember that mothering, salary or not, is a job. Even those who can afford nurses to handle the nitty-gritty still need to put out emotionally. "Well-cared-for" neurotic rich kids are not exactly unknown in our society. One of the more absurd aspects of the Myth is the underlying assumption that, since most women are biologically equipped to bear children, they are psychologically, mentally, emotionally, and technically equipped (or interested) to rear them. Never mind happiness. To assume that such an exacting, consuming, and important task is something almost all women are equipped to do is far more

2. A wealthy suburb of New York City.

dangerous and ridiculous than assuming that everyone with vocal chords should seek a career in the opera.

A major expectation of the Myth is that children make a not-so-hot marriage hotter, or a hot marriage, hotter still. Yet almost every available study indicates that childless marriages are far happier. One of the biggest, of 850 couples, was conducted by Dr. Harold Feldman of Cornell University, who states his finding in no uncertain terms: "Those couples with children had a significantly lower level of marital satisfaction than did those without children." Some of the reasons are obvious. Even the most adorable children make for additional demands, complications, and hardships in the lives of even the most loving parents. If a woman feels disappointed and trapped in her mother role, it is bound to affect her marriage in any number of ways: she may take out her frustrations directly on her husband, or she may count on him too heavily for what she feels she is missing in her daily life.

". . . You begin to grow away from your husband," says one of the Michigan ladies. "He's working on his career and you're working on your family. But you both must gear your lives to the children. You do things the children enjoy, more than things you might enjoy." More subtle and possibly more serious is what motherhood may do to a woman's sexuality. Often when the stork flies in, sexuality flies out. Both in the emotional minds of some women *and* in the minds of their husbands, when a woman becomes a mother, she stops being a woman. It's not only that motherhood may destroy her physical attractiveness, but its madonna concept may destroy her *feelings* of sexuality.

And what of the payoff? Usually, even the most self-sacrificing of maternal self-sacrificers expects a little something back. Gratified parents are not unknown to the Western world, but there are probably at least just as many who feel, to put it crudely, shortchanged. The experiment mentioned earlier—where the baby ducks followed vacuum cleaners instead of their mothers—indicates that what passes for love from baby to mother is merely a rudimentary kind of object attachment. Without necessarily feeling like a Hoover, a lot of women become disheartened because babies and children are not only not interesting to talk to (not everyone thrills at the wonders of da-da-ma-ma talk) but they are generally not empathetic, considerate people. Even the nicest children are not capable of empathy, surely a major ingredient of love, until they are much older. Sometimes they're never capable of it. Dr. Wyatt says that often, in later years particularly, when most of the "returns" are in, it is the "good mother" who suffers most of all. It is then she must face a reality: The child—the appendage with her genes—is not an appendage, but a separate person. What's more, he or she may be a separate person who doesn't even like her—or whom she doesn't really like.

So if the music is lousy, how come everyone's dancing? Because the   25
motherhood minuet is taught freely from birth, and whether or not she
has rhythm or likes the music, every woman is expected to do it. Indeed,
she *wants* to do it. Little girls start learning what to want—and what
to be—when they are still in their cribs. Dr. Miriam Keiffer, a young
social psychologist at Bensalem, the Experimental College of Fordham
University, points to studies showing that

> at six months of age, mothers are already treating their baby girls and boys
> quite differently. For instance, mothers have been found to touch, com-
> fort, and talk to their females more. If these differences can be found at
> such an early stage, it's not surprising that the end product is as different
> as it is. What is surprising is that men and women are, in so many ways,
> similar.

Some people point to the way little girls play with dolls as proof of their
innate motherliness. But remember, little girls are *given* dolls. When
Margaret Mead presented some dolls to New Guinea children, it was
the boys, not the girls, who wanted to play with them, which they did
by crooning lullabies and rocking them in the most maternal fashion.

By the time they reach adolescence, most girls, unconsciously or not,
have learned enough about role definition to qualify for a master's
degree. In general, the lesson has been that no matter what kind of
career thoughts one may entertain, one must, first and foremost, be a
wife and mother. A girl's mother is usually her first teacher. As Dr.
Goode says, "A woman is not only taught by society to have a child; she
is taught to have a child who will have a child." A woman who has hung
her life on the Motherhood Myth will almost always reinforce her young
married daughter's early training by pushing for grandchildren. Prospec-
tive grandmothers are not the only ones. Husbands, too, can be effective
sellers. After all, they have the Fatherhood Myth to cope with. A
married man is *supposed* to have children. Often, particularly among
Latins, children are a sign of potency. They help him assure the world—
and himself—that he is the big man he is supposed to be. Plus, children
give him both immortality (whatever that means) and possibly the
chance to become more in his lifetime through the accomplishments of
his children, particularly his son. (Sometimes it's important, however,
for the son to do better, but not *too* much better.)

Friends, too, can be counted on as myth-pushers. Naturally one wants
to do what one's friends do. One study, by the way, found a correlation
between a woman's fertility and that of her three closest friends. The
negative sell comes into play here, too. We have seen what the concept
of non-mother means (cold, selfish, unwomanly, abnormal). In practice,
particulary in the suburbs, it can mean, simply, exclusion—both from
child-centered activities (that is, most activities) and child-centered

conversations (that is, most conversations). It can also mean being the butt of a lot of unfunny jokes. ("Whaddya waiting for? An immaculate conception? Ha ha.") Worst of all, it can mean being an object of pity.

In case she's escaped all those pressures (that is, if she was brought up in a cave), a young married woman often wants a baby just so that she'll (1) have something to do (motherhood is better than clerk/typist, which is often the only kind of job she can get, since little more has been expected of her and, besides, her boss also expects her to leave and be a mother); (2) have something to hug and possess, to be needed by and have power over; and (3) have something to *be*—e.g., a baby's mother. Motherhood affords an instant identity. First, through wifehood, you are somebody's wife; then you are somebody's mother. Both give not only identity and activity, but status and stardom of a kind. During pregnancy, a woman can look forward to the kind of attention and pampering she may not ever have gotten or may never otherwise get. Some women consider birth the biggest accomplishment of their lives, which may be interpreted as saying not much for the rest of their lives. As Dr. Goode says, "It's like the gambler who may know the roulette wheel is crooked, but it's the only game in town." Also, with motherhood, the feeling of accomplishment is immediate. It is really much faster and easier to make a baby than paint a painting, or write a book, or get to the point of accomplishment in a job. It is also easier in a way to shift focus from self-development to child development—particularly since, for women, self-development is considered selfish. Even unwed mothers may achieve a feeling of this kind. (As we have seen, little thought is given to the aftermath.) And, again, since so many women are underdeveloped as people, they feel that, besides children, they have little else to give—to themselves, their husbands, to their world.

You may ask why then, when the realities do start pouring in, does a woman want to have a second, third, even fourth child? OK, (1) just because reality is pouring in doesn't mean she wants to *face* it. A new baby can help bring back some of the old illusions. Says psychoanalyst Dr. Natalie Shainess, "She may view each successive child as a knight in armor that will rescue her from being a 'bad unhappy mother.'" (2) Next on the horror list of having no children, is having one. It suffices to say that only children are not only OK, they even have a high rate of exceptionality. (3) Both parents usually want at least one child of each sex. The husband, for reasons discussed earlier, probably wants a son. (4) The more children one has, the more of an excuse one has not to develop in any other way.

30   What's the point? A world without children? Of course not. Nothing could be worse or more unlikely. No matter what anyone says in *Look* or anywhere else, motherhood isn't about to go out like a blown bulb, and who says it should? Only the Myth must go out, and now it seems to be dimming.

The younger-generation females who have been reared on the Myth have not rejected it totally, but at least they recognize it can be more loving to children not to have them. And at least they speak of adopting children instead of bearing them. Moreover, since the new nonbreeders are "less hung-up" on ownership, they seem to recognize that if you dig loving children, you don't necessarily have to own one. The end of the Motherhood Myth might make available more loving women (and men!) for those children who already exist.

When motherhood is no longer culturally compulsory, there will, certainly, be less of it. Women are now beginning to think and do more about development of self, of their individual resources. Far from being selfish, such development is probably our only hope. That means more alternatives for women. And more alternatives mean more selective, better, happier, motherhood—and childhood and husbandhood (or manhood) and peoplehood. It is not a question of whether or not children are sweet and marvelous to have and rear; the question is, even if that's so, whether or not one wants to pay the price for it. It doesn't make sense any more to pretend that women need babies, when what they really need is themselves. If God were still speaking to us in a voice we could hear, even He would probably say, "Be fruitful. Don't multiply."

THE READER

1. *Why does Rollin use the term "myth" to describe what she believes is the common attitude toward motherhood?*
2. *What kinds of evidence does Rollin use? Are some kinds more persuasive than others?*
3. *How would you characterize Rollin's tone? What effect does that tone have on the persuasiveness of her argument?*
4. *Herb Goldberg (see "In Harness: the Male Condition," p. 509) suggests that men are trapped in stereotyped roles in much the same way that Rollin believes women are. What differences and similarities do you see between the two writers in their analyses, their use of evidence, and their persuasiveness in their final conclusions?*
5. *Toward the end of her essay Rollin asserts that "nothing could be worse or more unlikely" than "a world without children." Does this contradict her previous argument? Explain.*

THE WRITER

1. *What special problems does Rollin face in persuading her audience? How does she try to meet these?*
2. *What possible counterarguments to her position does Rollin take account of and try to meet? Does she ignore any possible counterarguments?*
3. *In an interview a few years ago Rollin said, "Nothing comes easily in*

writing, nothing. . . . What looks natural and easy is not. But I do write
somewhat the way I talk; I try to just 'talk' on paper, to let it come
out and not be intellectual about it. . . . I feel pretty uninhibited about
it all." (Telephone interview by Jean W. Ross, Contemporary Authors, New Revision Series, Vol. 22, Gale Research Co., Detroit,
1988). Does this description of her writing correspond with her essay
"Motherhood"? What are the possible advantages and disadvantages
of writing this way?

4. *Write a dialogue between Rollin and Goldberg in which they discuss*
   male and female stereotyped roles.

5. *Read this passage from author Philip Wylie, who attacked "Momism"*
   in 1942:

   > Megaloid momworship has got completely out of hand. Our land, subjec-
   > tively mapped, would have more silver cords and apron strings crisscrossing
   > it than railroads and telephone wires. Mom is everywhere and everything
   > and damned near everybody, and from her depends all the rest of the U.S.
   > Disguised as good old mom, sweet old mom, your loving mom, and so on,
   > she is the bride at every funeral and the corpse at every wedding. Men live
   > for her and die for her, dote upon her and whisper her name as they pass
   > away, and I believe she has now achieved, in the hierarchy of miscellaneous
   > articles, a spot next to the Bible and the Flag, being reckoned part of both
   > in a way. (*Generation of Vipers,* New York: Rinehart & Co., Inc., 1942).

   How are Wylie's criticisms of "Mom" different from Rollin's attack
   on the myth of motherhood? How are they similar? Could you tell that
   one piece is written by a woman, the other by a man? Explore one or
   more of these questions in a brief essay.

6. *Write an essay in which you discuss another "myth" in our society.*

Letty Cottin Pogrebin

IT STILL TAKES A BRIDE AND GROOM

Now that June is over, I may as well confess my secret vice: reading
newspaper accounts of weddings and engagements.

During the counterculture years of the 60's and 70's—when radical
feminists were deconstructing the institution of marriage and demonstrating against bridal shows—to admit a fondness for wedding announcements was tantamount to being caught reading *Playboy.*

Weddings were politically incorrect. Weddings were rites of passage
codifying patriarchal authoritarianism. Weddings were prettied-up rituals built upon the symbols of the dowry, the virgin bride, and vows of

First appeared in the *New York Times Magazine* (July 12, 1989).

wifely obedience. As much as I might agree with this analysis and favor nonsexist ceremonial reforms, I also found weddings to be among life's most uplifting experiences. Mine felt like a coronation.

Thus burdened by romanticism and a fondness for new beginnings, I never gave up my secret addiction. Ironically, in this age of "post-feminism," [1] I now read wedding announcements not just for pleasure but as documents of social history and feminist archeology.

Don't be deceived by the fact that they still show brides wearing pearls and lace. Cumulatively, these brief news items delineate the progress of women with more clarity than mountains of polls or statistics. Each minibiography of a particular couple may be read as a microsummary of social change—at least among the white, educated people who tend to report their matrimonial activities to the local press.

Some developments are easy to notice: the growing number of bridal couples who were "previously married and divorced"; the proliferation of step-parents; the increased use of the honorific Ms., which masks a woman's marital history; photographs of the couple rather than just the bride; racial, ethnic and religious intermarriage cued by the couple's picture, disparate ethnic names, or the mention of two officiating clergy, one from each partner's faith; an occasional cross-class marriage where the daughter of a physician marries the son of an electrician, or a California schoolteacher marries an Italian count.

Most striking to me is the evidence of women's professional progress and growing autonomy. When I graduated from college in 1959, men listed their diplomas and job titles, brides listed their diplomas and dress designs. Most women had no jobs, other than planning the wedding. Those who did considered their work too menial to mention, or potentially threatening to the egos of their husbands who thought an employed wife reflected badly on a man's breadwinning powers.

In contrast, today's announcements present brides who are lawyers, doctors, corporate vice presidents, financial analysts, marketing managers, bankers, management consultants, architects, business owners, computer specialists, editors, psychologists, curators, athletic coaches, veterinarians and chefs. (Nurses, secretaries and teachers are few and far between—mirroring the shortage of nurses, secretaries and teachers in the labor force.)

Wedding announcements also proclaim the new reality of male-female equality. He's a radiologist, she a cardiologist. (In my day, that would be a misprint, not a marriage.) Both graduated from Harvard and got their M.B.A.'s from Wharton. She's an airline pilot and he's a meteorologist. She's a Eurodollar broker and he's an international trade analyst. Often, bride and groom both are law associates. Or it's a bank merger: he's at Citicorp and she's at Bankers Trust. In other words, they

1. Some commentators argue that the feminist revolution has been won; hence "post-feminism."

are peers. They share common interests or workloads, understand each other's tensions and dreams.

10　　This seems true whether the couple come across as yuppies or public-service types. In one recent announcement, both served in the Peace Corps in Senegal; in another it was Honduras. He's a drug counselor for adolescents and she works at a women's health clinic. They run a retail store together. Besides documenting this generation's occupational propensities, the text tells us that men and women are coming together as equal human beings, not sex-role stereotypes—and that equality breeds love as readily as did the old ethic of the woman marrying up and the man marrying down. Maybe better.

More and more often, the bride "will retain her name"—or retain it "professionally." Some women choose to hyphenate: for example, "Mrs. Smith-Jones, as the bride will be known, is a graphics designer." Others say, "Ms. Smith-Jones."

If one thing can sweeten an already inspiring wedding announcement, it's the appearance of a Reverend Janet or a Rabbi Emily or a Judge Ruth to perform the ceremony. Indeed, newspapers in a half-dozen cities report that women are officiating at Lutheran, Presbyterian, Episcopalian, Jewish, Unitarian, Ethical Humanist, nondenominational and civil weddings. For one who remembers the bitter ordination battles of not long ago, and the resistance to women on the bench, such reading compounds the gender pride.

Another feminist bellwether is the fate of the mothers. Traditionally, wedding announcements described the occupations of the fathers of the bride and groom, but never mentioned the women who bore and reared them. Mothers were invisible because they were wives, their identities subsumed in their husband's ("Mrs. John Smith"), their work at home unacknowledged.

Lately, however, the mothers of my generation have come forward with a vengeance. Those who do not list a profession cite volunteer activities that range from the opera and library to projects for battered women and the homeless. While some mothers are nurses, secretaries and teachers, many more seem to be C.P.A.'s, art historians, insurance executives, real-estate agents, and, yes, lawyers and bankers, too. In *The Times* recently, one mother of a bride had been the Democratic candidate for Vice President.[2]

15　　When it comes to divulging personal information, some newspapers provide minimal descriptions of the couple's educational and professional life but don't hesitate to reveal that the reception was held at the firehouse, or what the bride wore and carried down to the last baby's breath, where the couple went on their honeymoon and where they will "be at home."

When I'm out of town, I enjoy reading these old-style announce-

2. Geraldine Ferraro ran on a ticket with Walter Mondale in 1984.

ments almost as much as the curriculum vitae[3] listings in big-city papers. How else would I know that "in her shoe was a sixpence her mother brought from England?" Or that "the bride is an executive secretary and gospel contralto"?

Where attendants are concerned, custom still decrees women friends for the bride and men friends for the groom. Every now and then parents are attended by their children, brides by their mothers, and grooms by their fathers. I once heard of a bridegroom whose best man was a woman—eminently sensible if the woman was his best friend. But judging by the announcement texts, such gender crossing remains an uncrossed frontier.

When it happens, I'll know about it. Wedding announcements may appear stylized and perfunctory but if you read between the lines, they tell quite a story.

3. Or c.v.; literally, course of life; a résumé.

Andrew Holleran

THE NAMES OF FLOWERS

It's the sort of party I worked as a bartender my first few years in the city, and which I attend as a guest only a decade later. There's someone by the elevator with a list, checking names when I enter the building. There's a handsome young man in black tie running the elevator. There's a woman in a bathrobe who says she got stuck in the elevator between the basement and the first floor—a neighbor of my host, who goes up with me to the party in her bathrobe, smelling of Pepsodent. I never see her again, but the fragrance of toothpaste softens the formality of the loft filled with guests, the waiters in black tie, when the elevator operator pulls back the metal grille and I step forward. The invitation said Food and Music. Hurrying downtown through deserted streets, later than I wished to be, I had visions of a concert one could not enter till the first movement was finished. It is much more chaotic than that. The thirty-five guests I imagined are one hundred thirty-five; the music can barely be heard; the room is roaring. It is a cold April night. There are sprays of spring flowers throughout the room—more irises than I have ever seen at one time in a cylindrical glass vase; strange lilies in a spotlight; flowers whose names I do not know, which remind me of the Age of Parties—there were always flowers whose names I didn't know.

Of people I know the names of ten. They are clustered together in

From *Ground Zero* (1988).

a corner beyond the table on which the glasses are lined up in neat rows beside the bottles and the waiters. I stand there on the edge of the party looking at it like a man selecting a spot on a crowded beach before he puts his blanket and books down, and then I ask one of the two waiters at the long table for a drink. For a long time parties were more enjoyable to me when I worked them than when I came as a guest, but I've not been to a party of this sort in so long, or seen certain friends, that this evening is welcome. "No one has given a party like this in five years!" a friend said on the phone earlier that day. (Parties are like books, like plays: Occasionally the right one comes along at the right time.) This one's got everything: flowers whose names I have to ask, in thin spotlights; a quartet playing chamber music; waiters. It's as if the Age of Parties had been re-created—with one pleasant change: This one doesn't terrify. They used to. I used to attach myself like a leech to the only person I knew in the room—in the Age of Parties I only knew one—till he pried me loose with a lighted match and went off to talk, quite sensibly, to someone else, at which I felt he had left me alone on a small ice floe, like Little Eva,[1] in full view of the plantation owner's dogs. Now I can stand alone and survey the room before going over to join the group I know—mainly because there is a group I know. No need to panic (though some never did; were poised from the start). It strikes me as I pause there looking at the room, moreover, that this is something to look at a while longer; that what we once took for granted now seems extraordinary.

Even the friends who ten years ago did not know each other now do, and I tell myself to speak with the ones I see once a year, rather than those I saw the previous evening—and this practical thought as I walk over to join them makes me aware, too, of how time has passed. Working a room is not nice. But after many parties one learns there is nothing sillier than the reprimand, once the door has shut behind you, that your life might have been different had you only had the nerve to introduce yourself to Him. Perhaps this time I can introduce myself to the one in the red bow tie: one of several faces I have seen for years but never spoken to, and which now surprise, reassure, and comfort because they are still alive. This is no small achievement in New York in 1985. Life here has assumed the suspense of a summer Sunday's tea dance—you're not sure who is going to disappear on the next boat. In this loft once lived a man who died bravely at home, in complete secrecy, where now more than a hundred people go on with the next installment of the soap opera. He is in some sense still here. He was a handsome, kind, witty man who came to New York from Boston, a famous university, a close-knit family, to write about and live a homosexual life—and he collided

1. A character in Harriet Beecher Stowe's novel *Uncle Tom's Cabin* (1852).

with the thing that no artist's dream ever included. It was thought this might be a memorial service, but I learn instead it is a birthday, and the message of the party seems to be: Life goes on, with lots of irises. This seems obvious but is not. I spot an old friend across the room and wonder if I should say hello—because I've not seen him since the mutual friend died. I do and we don't dwell long on the fact. The people who have introduced new mourning customs—replaced wakes with dinner parties at which slides of Fire Island are shown—refuse to give death more than its due. They refuse to be lugubrious. They refuse to be stupid, too, for the most part—and, if before the hidden agenda of these gatherings was the pursuit of sex, now it is the avoidance of it. As a friend said, "No one in New York is having much sex anymore." This makes the party even more curious: An odd reticence pervades the room. What we are not speaking of we are not speaking of by mutual agreement. The collective ego has been dampened. We're all afraid and grateful to be mobile and nervous because we can't say what the future holds. The curious thing is that, though one would think the decision that we are all so vulnerable would make us stay home and give up each other's company—the opposite is true: I enjoy more than ever the sight of homosexuals together. And if a way of life that was once high-spirited, hilarious, is now restrained, solicitous (as if someone went from adolescence to late middle age without the intervening gradations)—we are therefore more grateful for the party. Its taste and generosity and style remind us: Life was once like this. We talk about everything but It. And instead of asking what someone does in bed, we inquire, "Will there be chocolate for dessert?"

For there is more than the names of flowers I do not know as I look out over this noisy, happy crowd. The old assumptions that bound this group together are changed. Our community has been broken up—like the phone company—into different systems of communications. Looking at some of the guests I can tell which ones are celibate; which ones are having little, more cautious sex; and which ones are going right on with the old ways. It has nothing to do with one's degree of personal exposure to the dying; it has to do with temperament, with the way different minds respond to the same facts. We face each other, after all, over freshly dug graves. There are ghosts among us. We're the actresses who meet in the ruined theater in *Follies*.[2] We're tourists who have been admitted to an exhibit of our own former lives. Here are the flowers, the lights, the faces—just as they used to be, when everyone was sleeping with one another. (Gay life without sex is a theme park.) Watching *The Normal Heart* the previous evening, I stared—across the

2. A Stephen Sondheim musical of 1971 in which an old theater about to be demolished is visited by some performers who had played there in the past.

stage between my seat and those opposite—at a handsome man in a long-sleeved, button-down, neatly pressed shirt. He had thick, dark hair; a mustache; watchful, dark eyes; and—beneath his clean clothes—one of those substantial bodies whose broad shoulders, swelling thighs, represent meat, flesh, life. *"Stop screwing!"* the doctor on stage was telling the hero. *"Until this is over!"* And I looked at the man in the first row in the button-down shirt, as if at an éclair on the bakery shelf, and thought, *"Someday, when this is over, perhaps I can have just . . . one . . . more . . . of those."*

5   That's because there seems to be a lull on this spring evening—which, in this room full of flowers and handsome men, encourages fantasy. Someday life will be as it was again. In fact, on the surface of this city it seems exactly the same. In the past few days I have spent an afternoon in Central Park; seen the Caravaggios[3] at the Metropolitan, the Mayan artifacts at the Museum of Natural History, *The Normal Heart* and *Parsifal* (two works with, strangely, a common theme); had lunch with friends on Second Avenue; watched men meet in my local park at night and leave together; even visited the baths and seen men too numerous to count. Anyone would say nothing has changed. The city goes on: The baths and bars and parks are busy. But there is another city. The doppelgänger[4] that coexists with us: invisible, mental, it draws attention to itself when I pass certain apartment buildings, a baths that has closed, or enter a room in which someone used to live. So if this party seems to re-create a former life—whose felicities we took for granted—there is a mood in the room: the same sentimental delicacy two lovers feel who haven't seen each other in five years but meet in a restaurant they first went to every night the first month of their affair. It's not just that, as another friend said, "New Yorkers have a solution for every dilemma. But not this one." It's that what has happened has left its mark. What has happened to us in New York the past five years has made those who still remain *careful* with each other in a way they weren't before—almost tender. Gone is the old, caustic gossip, the sexual current that lay beneath a party like this to such a degree that reaching for an hors d'oeuvre, you were always wondering, *Who's in the bathroom now, and how long have they been in there?*

That's all passé—and in its place a new reserve based on the simple truth that everyone has adjusted to new facts. Each one of us is Diseased Meat. Diseased Meat is blue-green; it stinks. It makes us think we shouldn't sleep with the man in the red bow tie even if we meet him. Now, there's Clorox and Oxynol-9 and hydrogen peroxide and condoms, and mutual masturbation at ten paces, but that's not what meeting

3. Michelangelo Merisi da Caravaggio (also Amerigi, 1573–1610), Italian painter.
4. In German folklore, a character's appari-tion or "twin" character that generally represents another side of his or her person-ality.

someone in the Age of Parties led to. That's why the Age of Parties ended. That's why it took at least five years for the enormous impetus—the assumptions, standards, freedom, egotism—of Promiscuity, Inc., to slow. The men—who used to be hors d'oeuvres—are no longer edible. So the real hors d'oeuvres become the focus of our mouths. We praise the food, we talk about someone's student days in Paris in the pissoirs that are no longer there, and finally, the cakes on the table lined with bowls of strawberries.

Later someone I've just met remarks he recently began reading a novel by Henry James[5]—a novel in which the heroine dies of an unnamed illness when she is still young, and her life is all before her. The model for this character, it's said, was James's cousin, who died of the disease that in the previous century eclipsed lives before they had run their course or achieved their purpose: tuberculosis. Her death haunted James all his life. The death of people before their time often does. The young writer who lived here had his career still before him; we will never know what he might have written. But it seems to me he was following the advice the doctor gives the heroine of *The Wings of the Dove:* "You must be happy. Any way you can!" How ironic! As I look out over the room at the guests, the flowers, the food assembled by a host who brought to his dead lover's illness the same tact and imagination he has shown in re-creating the Age of Parties, I remember something else from *The Wings of the Dove*—the very last lines. As the quartet saws away at its instruments in the flower-banked corner, I think of the two lovers who meet each other in the final scene of the book and realize their plan to defraud the heroine of her millions has failed in a way that not only turns their world upside down but introduces a certain estrangement between them. "I'll marry you, mind you," says the man in an attempt to reassure the woman, "in an hour."

"As we were?" she says.

"As we were," he says.

And then, with the finality the plague has introduced to life: "We shall never," she says, "be again as we were!"

That's kind of it. And with this I walk across the room to find my host, whom I half hope not to find, since the right mixture of condolences and gratitude—the referring, or not referring, to the person he's lost; the thank-you for his party—is still not one I've grasped. The room is so crowded I give up with a good conscience. The man in the red bow tie gives me that blank look that seems to convey the sense that men are as nameless and perishable as the flowers I will not learn the names of tonight, either. The tall windows of the loft gaze down on the cold,

10

---

5. James (1843–1916), American novelist, short-story writer, and critic whose novel *The Wings of the Dove* appeared in 1902.

empty street outside: the street that can no longer promise, when you leave the party, a man to sleep with, in place of the one you did not have the nerve to introduce yourself to here. In the Age of Parties there were lots of substitutes. As I go to the coatroom the refrain of a song that's been going through my mind since this began repeats itself: *The Party's Over.* But is that right? It goes on behind me with laughter and talk and introductions, louder than ever. Perhaps everything *but* the party's over.

James Baldwin

STRANGER IN THE VILLAGE

From all available evidence no black man had ever set foot in this tiny Swiss village before I came. I was told before arriving that I would probably be a "sight" for the village; I took this to mean that people of my complexion were rarely seen in Switzerland, and also that city people are always something of a "sight" outside of the city. It did not occur to me—possibly because I am an American—that there could be people anywhere who had never seen a Negro.

It is a fact that cannot be explained on the basis of the inaccessibility of the village. The village is very high, but it is only four hours from Milan and three hours from Lausanne. It is true that it is virtually unknown. Few people making plans for a holiday would elect to come here. On the other hand, the villagers are able, presumably, to come and go as they please—which they do: to another town at the foot of the mountain, with a population of approximately five thousand, the nearest place to see a movie or go to the bank. In the village there is no movie house, no bank, no library, no theater; very few radios, one jeep, one station wagon; and at the moment, one typewriter, mine, an invention which the woman next door to me here had never seen. There are about six hundred people living here, all Catholic—I conclude this from the fact that the Catholic church is open all year round, whereas the Protestant chapel, set off on a hill a little removed from the village, is open only in the summertime when the tourists arrive. There are four or five hotels, all closed now, and four or five *bistros,* of which, however, only two do any business during the winter. These two do not do a great deal, for life in the village seems to end around nine or ten o'clock. There are a few stores, butcher, baker, *épicerie,* a hardware store, and a money-changer—who cannot change travelers' checks, but must send them down to the bank, an operation which takes two or three days. There

From *Notes of a Native Son* (1955).

is something called the *Ballet Haus*, closed in the winter and used for God knows what, certainly not ballet, during the summer. There seems to be only one schoolhouse in the village, and this for the quite young children; I suppose this to mean that their older brothers and sisters at some point descend from these mountains in order to complete their education—possibly, again, to the town just below. The landscape is absolutely forbidding, mountains towering on all four sides, ice and snow as far as the eye can reach. In this white wilderness, men and women and children move all day, carrying washing, wood, buckets of milk or water, sometimes skiing on Sunday afternoons. All week long boys and young men are to be seen shoveling snow off the rooftops, or dragging wood down from the forest in sleds.

The village's only real attraction, which explains the tourist season, is the hot spring water. A disquietingly high proportion of these tourists are cripples, or semi-cripples, who come year after year—from other parts of Switzerland, usually—to take the waters. This lends the village, at the height of the season, a rather terrifying air of sanctity, as though it were a lesser Lourdes. There is often something beautiful, there is always something awful, in the spectacle of a person who has lost one of his faculties, a faculty he never questioned until it was gone, and who struggles to recover it. Yet people remain people, on crutches or indeed on deathbeds; and wherever I passed, the first summer I was here, among the native villagers or among the lame, a wind passed with me—of astonishment, curiosity, amusement, and outrage. That first summer I stayed two weeks and never intended to return. But I did return in the winter, to work; the village offers, obviously, no distractions whatever and has the further advantage of being extremely cheap. Now it is winter again, a year later, and I am here again. Everyone in the village knows my name, though they scarcely ever use it, knows that I come from America—though, this, apparently, they will never really believe: black men come from Africa—and everyone knows that I am the friend of the son of a woman who was born here, and that I am staying in their chalet. But I remain as much a stranger today as I was the first day I arrived, and the children shout *Neger! Neger!* as I walk along the streets.

It must be admitted that in the beginning I was far too shocked to have any real reaction. In so far as I reacted at all, I reacted by trying to be pleasant—it being a great part of the American Negro's education (long before he goes to school) that he must make people "like" him. This smile-and-the-world-smiles-with-you routine worked about as well in this situation as it had in the situation for which it was designed, which is to say that it did not work at all. No one, after all, can be liked whose human weight and complexity cannot be, or has not been, admitted. My smile was simply another unheard-of phenomenon which allowed them to see my teeth—they did not, really, see my smile and I began to think that, should I take to snarling, no one would notice any difference. All of the physical characteristics of the Negro which had caused me, in America, a very different and almost forgotten pain were nothing less than miraculous—or infernal—in the eyes of the village people. Some thought my hair was the color of tar, that it had the texture of wire, or the texture of cotton. It was jocularly suggested that I might let it all grow long and make myself a winter coat. If I sat in the sun for more than five minutes some daring creature was certain to come along and gingerly put his fingers on my hair, as though he were afraid of an electric shock, or put his hand on my hand, astonished that the color did not rub off. In all of this, in which it must be conceded there was the charm of genuine wonder and in which there were certainly no element of intentional unkindness, there was yet no suggestion that I was human: I was simply a living wonder.

5   I knew that they did not mean to be unkind, and I know it now; it is necessary, nevertheless, for me to repeat this to myself each time that I walk out of the chalet. The children who shout *Neger!* have no way of knowing the echoes this sound raises in me. They are brimming with good humor and the more daring swell with pride when I stop to speak with them. Just the same, there are days when I cannot pause and smile, when I have no heart to play with them; when, indeed, I mutter sourly to myself, exactly as I muttered on the streets of a city these children have never seen, when I was no bigger than these children are now: *Your mother was a nigger.* Joyce is right about history being a nightmare—but it may be the nightmare from which no one *can* awaken. People are trapped in history and history is trapped in them.

There is a custom in the village—I am told it is repeated in many villages—of "buying" African natives for the purpose of converting them to Christianity. There stands in the church all year round a small box with a slot for money, decorated with a black figurine, and into this box the villagers drop their francs. During the *carnaval* which precedes Lent, two village children have their faces blackened—out of which bloodless darkness their blue eyes shine like ice—and fantastic horsehair wigs are placed on their blond heads; thus disguised, they solicit among the villagers for money for the missionaries in Africa. Between the box in the church and the blackened children, the village "bought" last year six or eight African natives. This was reported to me with pride by the wife of one of the *bistro* owners and I was careful to express astonishment and pleasure at the solicitude shown by the village for the souls of black folks. The *bistro* owner's wife beamed with a pleasure far more genuine than my own and seemed to feel that I might now breathe more easily concerning the souls of at least six of my kinsmen.

I tried not to think of these so lately baptized kinsmen, of the price paid for them, or the peculiar price they themselves would pay, and said nothing about my father, who having taken his own conversion too literally never, at bottom, forgave the white world (which he described as heathen) for having saddled him with a Christ in whom, to judge at least from their treatment of him, they themselves no longer believed. I thought of white men arriving for the first time in an African village, strangers there, as I am a stranger here, and tried to imagine the astounded populace touching their hair and marveling at the color of their skin. But there is a great difference between being the first white man to be seen by Africans and being the first black man to be seen by whites. The white man takes the astonishment as tribute, for he arrives to conquer and to convert the natives, whose inferiority in relation to himself is not even to be questioned; whereas I, without a thought of conquest, find myself among a people whose culture controls me, has even, in a sense, created me, people who have cost me more in anguish and rage than they will ever know, who yet do not even know of my existence. The astonishment with which I might have greeted them, should they have stumbled into my African village a few hundred years ago, might have rejoiced their hearts. But the astonishment with which they greet me today can only poison mine.

And this is so despite everything I may do to feel differently, despite my friendly conversations with the *bistro* owner's wife, despite their three-year-old son who has at last become my friend, despite the *saluts* and *bonsoirs* [1] which I exchange with people as I walk, despite the fact that I know that no individual can be taken to task for what history is doing, or has done. I say that the culture of these people controls me—but they can scarcely be held responsible for European culture. America comes out of Europe, but these people have never seen America, nor have most of them seen more of Europe than the hamlet at the foot of their mountain. Yet they move with an authority which I shall never have; and they regard me, quite rightly, not only as a stranger in their village but as a suspect latecomer, bearing no credentials, to everything they have—however unconsciously—inherited.

For this village, even were it incomparably more remote and incredibly more primitive, is the West, the West onto which I have been so strangely grafted. These people cannot be, from the point of view of power, strangers anywhere in the world; they have made the modern world, in effect, even if they do not know it. The most illiterate among them is related, in a way that I am not, to Dante, Shakespeare, Michelangelo, Aeschylus, Da Vinci, Rembrandt, and Racine; the cathedral at Chartres says something to them which it cannot say to me, as indeed would New York's Empire State Building, should anyone here ever see it. Out of their hymns and dances come Beethoven and Bach. Go back

---

1. "Hellos" and "good evenings."

a few centuries and they are in their full glory—but I am in Africa, watching the conquerors arrive.

10   The rage of the disesteemed is personally fruitless, but it is also absolutely inevitable; this rage, so generally discounted, so little understood even among the people whose daily bread it is, is one of the things that makes history. Rage can only with difficulty, and never entirely, be brought under the domination of the intelligence and is therefore not susceptible to any arguments whatever. This is a fact which ordinary representatives of the *Herrenvolk*, [2] having never felt this rage and being unable to imagine, quite fail to understand. Also, rage cannot be hidden, it can only be dissembled. This dissembling deludes the thoughtless, and strengthens rage and adds, to rage, contempt. There are, no doubt, as many ways of coping with the resulting complex of tensions as there are black men in the world, but no black man can hope ever to be entirely liberated from this internal warfare—rage, dissembling, and contempt having inevitably accompanied his first realization of the power of white men. What is crucial here is that, since white men represent in the black man's world so heavy a weight, white men have for black men a reality which is far from being reciprocal; and hence all black men have toward all white men an attitude which is designed, really, either to rob the white man of the jewel of his naïveté, or else to make it cost him dear.

The black man insists, by whatever means he finds at his disposal, that the white man cease to regard him as an exotic rarity and recognize him as a human being. This is a very charged and difficult moment, for there is a great deal of will power involved in the white man's naïveté. Most people are not naturally reflective any more than they are naturally malicious, and the white man prefers to keep the black man at a certain human remove because it is easier for him thus to preserve his simplicity and avoid being called to account for crimes committed by his forefathers, or his neighbors. He is inescapably aware, nevertheless, that he is in a better position in the world than black men are, nor can he quite put to death the suspicion that he is hated by black men therefore. He does not wish to be hated, neither does he wish to change places, and at this point in his uneasiness he can scarcely avoid having recourse to those legends which white men have created about black men, the most usual effect of which is that the white man finds himself enmeshed, so to speak, in his own language which describes hell, as well as the attributes which lead one to hell, as being as black as night.

Every legend, moreover, contains its residuum of truth, and the root function of language is to control the universe by describing it. It is of quite considerable significance that black men remain, in the imagination, and in overwhelming numbers in fact, beyond the disciplines of

2. Master race.

salvation; and this despite the fact that the West has been "buying" African natives for centuries. There is, I should hazard, an instantaneous necessity to be divorced from this so visibly unsaved stranger, in whose heart, moreover, one cannot guess what dreams of vengeance are being nourished; and, at the same time, there are few things on earth more attractive than the idea of the unspeakable liberty which is allowed the unredeemed. When, beneath the black mask, a human being begins to make himself felt one cannot escape a certain awful wonder as to what kind of human being it is. What one's imagination makes of other people is dictated, of course, by the laws of one's own personality and it is one of the ironies of black-white relations that, by means of what the white man imagines the black man to be, the black man is enabled to know who the white man is.

I have said, for example, that I am as much a stranger in this village today as I was the first summer I arrived, but this is not quite true. The villagers wonder less about the texture of my hair than they did then, and wonder rather more about me. And the fact that their wonder now exists on another level is reflected in their attitudes and in their eyes. There are the children who make those delightful, hilarious, sometimes astonishingly grave overtures of friendship in the unpredictable fashion of children; other children, having been taught that the devil is a black man, scream in genuine anguish as I approach. Some of the older women never pass without a friendly greeting, never pass, indeed, if it seems that they will be able to engage me in conversation; other women look down or look away or rather contemptuously smirk. Some of the men drink with me and suggest that I learn how to ski—partly, I gather, because they cannot imagine what I would look like on skis—and want to know if I am married, and ask questions about my *métier*. But some of the men have accused *le sale nègre* [3]—behind my back—of stealing wood and there is already in the eyes of some of them that peculiar, intent, paranoiac malevolence which one sometimes surprises in the eyes of American white men when, out walking with their Sunday girl, they see a Negro male approach.

There is a dreadful abyss between the streets of this village and the streets of the city in which I was born, between the children who shout *Neger!* today and those who shouted *Nigger!* yesterday—the abyss is experience, the American experience. The syllable hurled behind me today expresses, above all, wonder: I am a stranger here. But I am not a stranger in America and the same syllable riding on the American air expresses the war my presence has occasioned in the American soul.

For this village brings home to me this fact: that there was a day, and not really a very distant day, when Americans were scarcely Americans

15

---

3. The dirty Negro.

at all but discontented Europeans, facing a great unconquered continent and strolling, say, into a marketplace and seeing black men for the first time. The shock this spectacle afforded is suggested, surely, by the promptness with which they decided that these black men were not really men but cattle. It is true that the necessity on the part of the settlers of the New World of reconciling their moral assumptions with the fact—and the necessity—of slavery enhanced immensely the charm of this idea, and it is also true that this idea expresses, with a truly American bluntness, the attitude which to varying extents all masters have had toward all slaves.

But between all former slaves and slave-owners and the drama which begins for Americans over three hundred years ago at Jamestown, there are at least two differences to be observed. The American Negro slave could not suppose, for one thing, as slaves in past epochs had supposed and often done, that he would ever be able to wrest the power from his master's hands. This was a supposition which the modern era, which was to bring about such vast changes in the aims and dimensions of power, put to death; it only begins, in unprecedented fashion, and with dreadful implications, to be resurrected today. But even had this supposition persisted with undiminished force, the American Negro slave could not have used it to lend his condition dignity, for the reason that this supposition rests on another: that the slave in exile yet remains related to his past, has some means—if only in memory—of revering and sustaining the forms of his former life, is able, in short, to maintain his identity.

This was not the case with the American Negro slave. He is unique among the black men of the world in that his past was taken from him, almost literally, at one blow. One wonders what on earth the first slave found to say to the first dark child he bore. I am told that there are Haitians able to trace their ancestry back to African kings, but any American Negro wishing to go back so far will find his journey through time abruptly arrested by the signature on the bill of sale which served as the entrance paper for his ancestor. At the time—to say nothing of the circumstances—of the enslavement of the captive black man who was to become the American Negro, there was not the remotest possibility that he would ever take power from his master's hands. There was no reason to suppose that his situation would ever change, nor was there, shortly, anything to indicate that his situation had ever been different. It was his necessity, in the words of E. Franklin Frazier, to find a "motive for living under American culture or die." The identity of the American Negro comes out of this extreme situation, and the evolution of this identity was a source of the most intolerable anxiety in the minds and the lives of his masters.

For the history of the American Negro is unique also in this: that the question of his humanity, and of his rights therefore as a human being, became a burning one for several generations of Americans, so burning a question that it ultimately became one of those used to divide the nation. It is out of this argument that the venom of the epithet *Nigger!* is derived. It is an argument which Europe has never had, and hence Europe quite sincerely fails to understand how or why the argument arose in the first place, why its effects are frequently disastrous and always so unpredictable, why it refuses until today to be entirely settled. Europe's black possessions remained—and do remain—in Europe's colonies, at which remove they represented no threat whatever to European identity. If they posed any problem at all for the European conscience it was a problem which remained comfortingly abstract: in effect, the black man, as a *man* did not exist for Europe. But in America, even as a slave, he was an inescapable part of the general social fabric and no American could escape having an attitude toward him. Americans attempt until today to make an abstraction of the Negro, but the very nature of these abstractions reveals the tremendous effects the presence of the Negro has had on the American character.

When one considers the history of the Negro in America it is of the greatest importance to recognize that the moral beliefs of a person, or a people, are never really as tenuous as life—which is not moral—very often causes them to appear; these create for them a frame of reference and a necessary hope, the hope being that when life has done its worst they will be enabled to rise above themselves and to triumph over life. Life would scarcely be bearable if this hope did not exist. Again, even when the worst has been said, to betray a belief is not by any means to have put oneself beyond its power; the betrayal of a belief is not the same thing as ceasing to believe. If this were not so there would be no moral standards in the world at all. Yet one must also recognize that morality is based on ideas and that all ideas are dangerous—dangerous because ideas can only lead to action and where the action leads no man can say. And dangerous in this respect: that confronted with the impossibility of remaining faithful to one's beliefs, and the equal impossibility of becoming free of them, one can be driven to the most inhuman excesses. The ideas on which American beliefs are based are not, though Americans often seem to think so, ideas which originated in America. They came out of Europe. And the establishment of democracy on the American continent was scarcely as radical a break with the past as was the necessity, which Americans faced, of broadening this concept to include black men.

This was, literally, a hard necessity. It was impossible, for one thing, for Americans to abandon their beliefs, not only because these beliefs alone seemed able to justify the sacrifices they had endured and the blood that they had spilled, but also because these beliefs afforded them

20

their only bulwark against a moral chaos as absolute as the physical chaos of the continent it was their destiny to conquer. But in the situation in which Americans found themselves, these beliefs threatened an idea which, whether or not one likes to think so, is the very warp and woof of the heritage of the West, the idea of white supremacy.

Americans have made themselves notorious by the shrillness and the brutality with which they have insisted on this idea, but they did not invent it; and it has escaped the world's notice that those very excesses of which Americans have been guilty imply a certain, unprecedented uneasiness over the idea's life and power, if not, indeed, the idea's validity. The idea of white supremacy rests simply on the fact that white men are the creators of civilization (the present civilization, which is the only one that matters; all previous civilizations are simply "contributions" to our own) and are therefore civilization's guardians and defenders. Thus it was impossible for Americans to accept the black man as one of themselves, for to do so was to jeopardize their status as white men. But not so to accept him was to deny his human reality, his human weight and complexity, and the strain of denying the overwhelmingly undeniable forced Americans into rationalizations so fantastic that they approached the pathological.

At the root of the American Negro problem is the necessity of the American white man to find a way of living with the Negro in order to be able to live with himself. And the history of this problem can be reduced to the means used by Americans—lynch law and law, segregation and legal acceptance, terrorization and concession—either to come to terms with this necessity, or to find a way around it, or (most usually) to find a way of doing both these things at once. The resulting spectacle, at once foolish and dreadful, led someone to make the quite accurate observation that "the Negro-in-America is a form of insanity which overtakes white men."

In this long battle, a battle by no means finished, the unforeseeable effects of which will be felt by many future generations, the white man's motive was the protection of his identity; the black man was motivated by the need to establish an identity. And despite the terrorization which the Negro in America endured and endures sporadically until today, despite the cruel and totally inescapable ambivalence of his status in his country, the battle for his identity has long ago been won. He is not a visitor to the West, but a citizen there, an American; as American as the Americans who despise him, the Americans who fear him, the Americans who love him—the Americans who became less than themselves, or rose to be greater than themselves by virtue of the fact that the challenge he represented was inescapable. He is perhaps the only black man in the world whose relationship to white men is more terrible, more subtle, and more meaningful than the relationship of bitter possessed to uncertain possessors. His survival depended, and his development depends, on his ability to turn his peculiar status in the Western world to his own advantage and, it may be, to the very great advantage of that world. It remains for him to fashion out of his experience that which will give him sustenance, and a voice.

The cathedral at Chartres, I have said, says something to the people of this village which it cannot say to me; but it is important to understand that this cathedral says something to me which it cannot say to them. Perhaps they are struck by the power of the spires, the glory of the windows; but they have known God, after all, longer than I have known him, and in a different way, and I am terrified by the slippery bottomless well to be found in the crypt, down which heretics were hurled to death, and by the obscene, inescapable gargoyles jutting out of the stone and seeming to say that God and the devil can never be divorced. I doubt that the villagers think of the devil when they face a cathedral because they have never been identified with the devil. But I must accept the status which myth, if nothing else, gives me in the West before I can hope to change the myth.

Yet, if the American Negro has arrived at his identity by virtue of the   25 absoluteness of his estrangement from his past, American white men still nourish the illusion that there is some means of recovering the European innocence, of returning to a state in which black men do not exist. This is one of the greatest errors Americans can make. The identity they fought so hard to protect has, by virtue of that battle, undergone a change: Americans are as unlike any other white people in the world as it is possible to be. I do not think, for example, that it is too much to suggest that the American vision of the world—which allows so little reality, generally speaking, for any of the darker forces in human life, which tends until today to paint moral issues in glaring black and white—owes a great deal to the battle waged by Americans to maintain between themselves and black men a human separation which could not be bridged. It is only now beginning to be borne in on us—very faintly, it must be admitted, very slowly, and very much against our will—that this vision of the world is dangerously inaccurate, and perfectly useless. For it protects our moral high-mindedness at the terrible expense of weakening our grasp of reality. People who shut their eyes to reality simply invite their own destruction, and anyone who insists on remaining in a state of innocence long after that innocence is dead turns himself into a monster.

The time has come to realize that the interracial drama acted out on the American continent has not only created a new black man, it has created a new white man, too. No road whatever will lead Americans back to the simplicity of this European village where white men still have the luxury of looking on me as a stranger. I am not, really, a stranger any longer for any American alive. One of the things that distinguishes Americans from other people is that no other people has ever been so deeply involved in the lives of black men, and vice versa. This fact faced, with all its implications, it can be seen that the history of the American Negro problem is not merely shameful, it is also something of an achievement. For even when the worst has been said, it must also be added that the perpetual challenge posed by this problem was always, somehow, perpetually met. It is precisely this black-white experience which may prove of indispensable value to us in the world we face today. This world is white no longer, and it will never be white again.

THE READER

1. *Baldwin begins with the narration of his experience in a Swiss village. At what point do you become aware that he is going to do more than tell the story of his stay in the village? What purpose does he make his experience serve?*
2. *On p. 547, Baldwin says that Americans have attempted to make an abstraction of the Negro. To what degree has his purpose forced Baldwin to make an abstraction of the white man? What are the components of that abstraction?*

THE WRITER

1. *Baldwin intimately relates the white man's language and legends about black men to the "laws" of the white man's personality. What conviction about the nature of language does this reveal?*
2. *Define* alienation *in a paragraph or two.*
3. *Describe some particular experience that raises a large social question or shows the working of large social forces. Does Baldwin offer any help in the problem of connecting the particular and the general?*

Brent Staples

BLACK MEN AND PUBLIC SPACE

My first victim was a woman—white, well dressed, probably in her early twenties. I came upon her late one evening on a deserted street in Hyde Park, a relatively affluent neighborhood in an otherwise mean, impoverished section of Chicago. As I swung onto the avenue behind

Staples' essay "Just Walk on By" appeared in *Ms.* magazine (Sept. 1986); an excerpt, titled "Black Men and Public Space," was published in *Harper's* (Dec. 1986).

her, there seemed to be a discreet, uninflammatory distance between us. Not so. She cast back a worried glance. To her, the youngish black man—a broad six feet two inches with a beard and billowing hair, both hands shoved into the pockets of a bulky military jacket—seemed menacingly close. After a few more quick glimpses, she picked up her pace and was soon running in earnest. Within seconds she disappeared into a cross street.

That was more than a decade ago, I was twenty-two years old, a graduate student newly arrived at the University of Chicago. It was in the echo of that terrified woman's footfalls that I first began to know the unwieldy inheritance I'd come into—the ability to alter public space in ugly ways. It was clear that she thought herself the quarry of a mugger, a rapist, or worse. Suffering a bout of insomnia, however, I was stalking sleep, not defenseless wayfarers. As a softy who is scarcely able to take a knife to a raw chicken—let alone hold one to a person's throat—I was surprised, embarrassed, and dismayed all at once. Her flight made me feel like an accomplice in tyranny. It also made it clear that I was indistinguishable from the muggers who occasionally seeped into the area from the surrounding ghetto. That first encounter, and those that followed, signified that a vast, unnerving gulf lay between nighttime pedestrians—particularly women—and me. And I soon gathered that being perceived as dangerous is a hazard in itself. I only needed to turn a corner into a dicey situation, or crowd some frightened, armed person in a foyer somewhere, or make an errant move after being pulled over by a policeman. Where fear and weapons meet—and they often do in urban America—there is always the possibility of death.

In that first year, my first away from my hometown, I was to become thoroughly familiar with the language of fear. At dark, shadowy intersections, I could cross in front of a car stopped at a traffic light and elicit the *thunk, thunk, thunk, thunk* of the driver—black, white, male, or female—hammering down the door locks. On less traveled streets after dark, I grew accustomed to but never comfortable with people crossing to the other side of the street rather than pass me. Then there were the standard unpleasantries with policemen, doormen, bouncers, cabdrivers, and others whose business it is to screen out troublesome individuals *before* there is any nastiness.

I moved to New York nearly two years ago and I have remained an avid night walker. In central Manhattan, the near-constant crowd cover minimizes tense one-on-one street encounters. Elsewhere—in SoHo, for example, where sidewalks are narrow and tightly spaced buildings shut out the sky—things can get very taut indeed.

After dark, on the warrenlike streets of Brooklyn where I live, I often see women who fear the worst from me. They seem to have set their faces on neutral, and with their purse straps strung across their chests

5

bandolier-style, they forge ahead as though bracing themselves against being tackled. I understand, of course, that the danger they perceive is not a hallucination. Women are particularly vulnerable to street violence, and young black males are drastically overrepresented among the perpetrators of that violence. Yet these truths are no solace against the kind of alienation that comes of being ever the suspect, a fearsome entity with whom pedestrians avoid making eye contact.

It is not altogether clear to me how I reached the ripe old age of twenty-two without being conscious of the lethality nighttime pedestrians attributed to me. Perhaps it was because in Chester, Pennsylvania, the small, angry industrial town where I came of age in the 1960s, I was scarcely noticeable against a backdrop of gang warfare, street knifings, and murders. I grew up one of the good boys, had perhaps a half-dozen fistfights. In retrospect, my shyness of combat has clear sources.

As a boy, I saw countless tough guys locked away; I have since buried several, too. They were babies, really—a teenage cousin, a brother of twenty-two, a childhood friend in his mid-twenties—all gone down in episodes of bravado played out in the streets. I came to doubt the virtues of intimidation early on. I chose, perhaps unconsciously, to remain a shadow—timid, but a survivor.

The fearsomeness mistakenly attributed to me in public places often has a perilous flavor. The most frightening of these confusions occurred in the late 1970s and early 1980s, when I worked as a journalist in Chicago. One day, rushing into the office of a magazine I was writing for with a deadline story in hand, I was mistaken for a burglar. The office manager called security and, with an ad hoc [1] posse, pursued me through the labyrinthine halls, nearly to my editor's door. I had no way of proving who I was. I could only move briskly toward the company of someone who knew me.

Another time I was on assignment for a local paper and killing time before an interview. I entered a jewelry store on the city's affluent Near North Side. The proprietor excused herself and returned with an enormous red Doberman pinscher straining at the end of a leash. She stood, the dog extended toward me, silent to my questions, her eyes bulging nearly out of her head. I took a cursory look around, nodded, and bade her good night.

10   Relatively speaking, however, I never fared as badly as another black male journalist. He went to nearby Waukegan, Illinois, a couple of summers ago to work on a story about a murderer who was born there. Mistaking the reporter for the killer, police officers hauled him from his car at gunpoint and but for his press credentials would probably have tried to book him. Such episodes are not uncommon. Black men trade tales like this all the time.

1. For a particular purpose.

Over the years, I learned to smother the rage I felt at so often being taken for a criminal. Not to do so would surely have led to madness. I now take precautions to make myself less threatening. I move about with care, particularly late in the evening. I give a wide berth to nervous people on subway platforms during the wee hours, particularly when I have exchanged business clothes for jeans. If I happen to be entering a building behind some people who appear skittish, I may walk by, letting them clear the lobby before I return, so as not to seem to be following them. I have been calm and extremely congenial on those rare occasions when I've been pulled over by the police.

And on late-evening constitutionals I employ what has proved to be an excellent tension-reducing measure: I whistle melodies from Beethoven and Vivaldi and the more popular classical composers. Even steely New Yorkers hunching toward nighttime destinations seem to relax, and occasionally they even join in the tune. Virtually everybody seems to sense that a mugger wouldn't be warbling bright, sunny selections from Vivaldi's *Four Seasons.* [2] It is my equivalent of the cowbell that hikers wear when they know they are in bear country.

2. Work by eighteenth-century composer Antonio Vivaldi celebrating the seasons.

THE READER

1. *In his essay, Staples writes of situations correctly perceived as dangerous and situations misperceived as dangerous. Give specific instances of each. How are they related?*

2. *Staples shows that his personal background and experiences led him to see things in a particular way. To what degree is that particular way idiosyncratic—specific to him? To what degree is that particular way expressive of general truth—experience common to all or most persons?*

THE WRITER

1. *Does Staples take a humorous approach to his subject at certain points in the essay? If so, does this distract from or contribute to the seriousness of the matter? Explain.*

2. *Is the concluding sentence an effective close? Draw out its implications, showing how these relate to the details of his discussion.*

3. *Do you have perceptions and apprehensions similar to or largely different from those described by Staples? Write an essay on this topic, placing yourself in familiar or in unusual surroundings.*

Shelby Steele

THE RECOLORING OF CAMPUS LIFE

In the past few years, we have witnessed what the National Institute Against Prejudice and Violence calls a "proliferation" of racial incidents on college campuses around the country. Incidents of on-campus "intergroup conflict" have occurred at more than 160 colleges in the last three years, according to the institute. The nature of these incidents has ranged from open racial violence—most notoriously, the October 1986 beating of a black student at the University of Massachusetts at Amherst after an argument about the World Series turned into a racial bashing, with a crowd of up to 3,000 whites chasing twenty blacks—to the harassment of minority students, to acts of racial or ethnic insensitivity, with by far the greatest number falling in the last two categories. At Dartmouth College, three editors of the *Dartmouth Review*, the off-campus right-wing student weekly, were suspended last winter for harassing a black professor in his lecture hall. At Yale University last year a swastika and the words "white power" were painted on the school's Afro-American cultural center. Racist jokes were aired not long ago on a campus radio station at the University of Michigan. And at the University of Wisconsin at Madison, members of the Zeta Beta Tau fraternity held a mock slave auction in which pledges painted their faces black and wore Afro wigs. Two weeks after the president of Stanford University informed the incoming freshmen class last fall that "bigotry is out, and I mean it," two freshmen defaced a poster of Beethoven— gave the image thick lips—and hung it on a black student's door.

In response, black students around the country have rediscovered the militant protest strategies of the Sixties. At the University of Massachusetts at Amherst, Williams College, Penn State University, UC Berkeley, UCLA, Stanford, and countless other campuses, black students have sat in, marched, and rallied. But much of what they were marching and rallying about seemed less a response to specific racial incidents than a call for broader action on the part of the colleges and universities they were attending. Black students have demanded everything from more black faculty members and new courses on racism to the addition of "ethnic" foods in the cafeteria. There is the sense in these demands that racism runs deep.

Of course, universities are not where racial problems tend to arise. When I went to college in the mid-Sixties, colleges were oases of calm

First published in *Harper's* (Feb. 1989).

and understanding in a racially tense society; campus life—with its traditions of tolerance and fairness, its very distance from the "real" world—imposed a degree of broad-mindedness on even the most provincial students. If I met whites who were not anxious to be friends with blacks, most were at least vaguely friendly to the cause of our freedom. In any case, there was no guerrilla activity against our presence, no "mine field of racism" (as one black student at Berkeley recently put it) to negotiate. I wouldn't say that the phrase "campus racism" is a contradiction in terms, but until recently it certainly seemed an incongruence.

But a greater incongruence is the generational timing of this new problem on the campuses. Today's undergraduates were born after the passage of the 1964 Civil Rights Act. They grew up in an age when racial equality was for the first time enforceable by law. This too was a time when blacks suddenly appeared on television, as mayors of big cities, as icons of popular culture, as teachers, and in some cases even as neighbors. Today's black and white college students, veterans of *Sesame Street* and often of integrated grammar and high schools, have had more opportunities to know each other—whites and blacks—than any previous generation in American history. Not enough opportunities, perhaps, but enough to make the notion of racial tension on campus something of a mystery, at least to me.

To try to unravel this mystery I left my own campus, where there have been few signs of racial tension, and talked with black and white students at California schools where racial incidents had occurred: Stanford, UCLA, Berkeley. I spoke with black and white students—and not with Asians and Hispanics—because, as always, blacks and whites represent the deepest lines of division, and because I hesitate to wander onto the complex territory of other minority groups. A phrase by William H. Gass[1]—"the hidden internality of things"—describes with maybe a little too much grandeur what I hoped to find. But it *is* what I wanted to find, for this is the kind of problem that makes a black person nervous, which is not to say that it doesn't unnerve whites as well. Once every six months or so someone yells "nigger" at me from a passing car. I don't like to think that these solo artists might soon make up a chorus or, worse, that this chorus might one day soon sing to me from the paths of my own campus.

5

I have long believed that trouble between the races is seldom what it appears to be.[2] It was not hard to see after my first talks with students that racial tension on campus is a problem that misrepresents itself. It has the same look, the archetypal pattern, of America's timeless racial

1. A contemporary American novelist.
2. See my essay, "I'm Black, You're White, Who's Innocent? Race and Power in an Era of Blame," *Harper's Magazine,* June 1988 [Steele's note].

conflict—white racism and black protest. And I think part of our concern over it comes from the fact that it has the feel of a relapse, illness gone and come again. But if we are seeing the same symptoms, I don't believe we are dealing with the same illness. For one thing, I think racial tension on campus is the result more of racial equality than inequality.

How to live with racial difference has been America's profound social problem. For the first 100 years or so following emancipation it was controlled by a legally sanctioned inequality that acted as a buffer between the races. No longer is this the case. On campuses today, as throughout society, blacks enjoy equality under the law—a profound social advancement. No student may be kept out of a class or a dormitory or an extracurricular activity because of his or her race. But there is a paradox here: On a campus where members of all races are gathered, mixed together in the classroom as well as socially, differences are more exposed than ever. And this is where the trouble starts. For members of each race—young adults coming into their own, often away from home for the first time—bring to this site of freedom, exploration, and now, today, equality very deep fears and anxieties, inchoate feelings of racial shame, anger, and guilt. These feelings could lie dormant in the home, in familiar neighborhoods, in simpler days of childhood. But the college campus, with its structures of interaction and adult-level competition—the big exam, the dorm, the "mixer"—is another matter. I think campus racism is born of the rub between racial difference and a setting, the campus itself, devoted to interaction and equality. On our campuses, such concentrated micro-societies, all that remains unresolved between blacks and whites, all the old wounds and shames that have never been addressed, present themselves for attention—and present our youth with pressures they cannot always handle.

I have mentioned one paradox: racial fears and anxieties among blacks and whites bubbling up in an era of racial equality under the law, in settings that are among the freest and fairest in society. And there is another, related paradox, stemming from the notion of—and practice of—affirmative action. Under the provisions of the Equal Employment Opportunity Act of 1972, all state governments and institutions (including universities) were forced to initiate plans to increase the proportion of minority and women employees—in the case of universities, of students too. Affirmative action plans that establish racial quotas were ruled unconstitutional more than ten years ago in *University of California Regents v. Bakke*. But quotas are only the most controversial aspect of affirmative action; the principle of affirmative action is reflected in various university programs aimed at redressing and overcoming past patterns of discrimination. Of course, to be conscious of patterns of discrimination—the fact, say, that public schools in the black inner cities are more crowded and employ fewer top-notch teachers than white

suburban public schools, and that this is a factor in student performance—is only reasonable. However, in doing this we also call attention
quite obviously to difference: in the case of blacks and whites, racial
difference. What has emerged on campus in recent years—as a result
of the new equality and affirmative action, in a sense, as a result of
progress—is a *politics of difference,* a troubling, volatile politics in which
each group justifies itself, its sense of worth and its pursuit of power,
through difference alone.

In this context, racial, ethnic, and gender differences become forms
of sovereignty, campuses become balkanized, and each group fights with
whatever means are available. No doubt there are many factors that have
contributed to the rise of racial tension on campus: What has been the
role of fraternities, which have returned to campus with their inclusions
and exclusions? What role has the heightened notion of college as some
first step to personal, financial success played in increasing competition,
and thus tension? Mostly what I sense, though, is that in interactive
settings, while fighting the fights of "difference," old ghosts are stirred,
and haunt again. Black and white Americans simply have the power to
make each other feel shame and guilt. In the "real" world, we may be
able to deny these feelings, keep them at bay. But these feelings are
likely to surface on college campuses, where young people are groping
for identity and power, and where difference is made to matter so
greatly. In a way, racial tension on campus in the Eighties might have
been inevitable.

I would like, first, to discuss black students, their anxieties and vul-   10
nerabilities. The accusation that black Americans have always lived with
is that they are inferior—inferior simply because they are black. And this
accusation has been too uniform, too ingrained in cultural imagery, too
enforced by law, custom, and every form of power not to have left a
mark. Black inferiority was a precept accepted by the founders of this
nation; it was a principle of social organization that relegated blacks to
the sidelines of American life. So when today's young black students find
themselves on white campuses, surrounded by those who historically
have claimed superiority, they are also surrounded by the myth of their
inferiority.

Of course it is true that many young people come to college with some
anxiety about not being good enough. But only blacks come wearing a
color that is still, in the minds of some, a sign of inferiority. Poles, Jews,
Hispanics, and other groups also endure degrading stereotypes. But two
things make the myth of black inferiority a far heavier burden—the
broadness of its scope and its incarnation in color. There are not only
more stereotypes of blacks than of other groups, but these stereotypes
are also more dehumanizing, more focused on the most despised of

human traits—stupidity, laziness, sexual immorality, dirtiness, and so on. In America's racial and ethnic hierarchy, blacks have clearly been relegated to the lowest level—have been burdened with an ambiguous, animalistic humanity. Moreover, this is made unavoidable for blacks by the sheer visibility of black skin, a skin that evokes the myth of inferiority on sight. And today this myth is sadly reinforced for many black students by affirmative action programs, under which blacks may often enter college with lower test scores and high-school grade point averages than whites. "They see me as an affirmative action case," one black student told me at UCLA.

So when a black student enters college, the myth of inferiority compounds the normal anxiousness over whether he or she will be good enough. This anxiety is not only personal but also racial. The families of these students will have pounded into them the fact that blacks are not inferior. And probably more than anything, it is this pounding that finally leaves a mark. If I am not inferior, why the need to say so?

This myth of inferiority constitutes a very sharp and ongoing anxiety for young blacks, the nature of which is very precise: It is the terror that somehow, through one's actions or by virtue of some "proof" (a poor grade, a flubbed response in class), one's fear of inferiority—inculcated in ways large and small by society—will be confirmed as real. On a university campus, where intelligence itself is the ultimate measure, this anxiety is bound to be triggered.

A black student I met at UCLA was disturbed a little when I asked him if he ever felt vulnerable—anxious about "black inferiority"—as a black student. But after a long pause, he finally said, "I think I do." The example he gave was of a large lecture class he'd taken with more than 300 students. Fifty or so black students sat in the back of the lecture hall and "acted out every stereotype in the book." They were loud, ate food, came in late—and generally got lower grades than the whites in the class. "I knew I would be seen like them, and I didn't like it. I never sat by them." Seen like what? I asked, though we both knew the answer. "As lazy, ignorant, and stupid," he said sadly.

15   Had the group at the back been white fraternity brothers, they would not have been seen as dumb *whites,* of course. And a frat brother who worried about his grades would not worry that he would be seen "like them." The terror in this situation for the student I spoke with was that his own deeply buried anxiety would be given credence, that the myth would be verified, and that he would feel shame and humiliation not because of who he was but simply because he was black. In this lecture hall his race, quite apart from his performance, might subject him to four unendurable feelings—diminishment, accountability to the preconceptions of whites, a powerlessness to change those preconceptions, and, finally, shame. These are the feelings that make up his racial anxiety, and

that of all blacks on any campus. On a white campus a black is never far from these feelings, and even his unconscious knowledge that he is subject to them can undermine his self-esteem. There are blacks on every campus who are not up to doing good college-level work. Certain black students may not be happy or motivated or in the appropriate field of study—*just like whites*. (Let us not forget that many white students get poor grades, fail, drop out.) Moreover, many more blacks than whites are not quite prepared for college, may have to catch up, owing to factors beyond their control: poor previous schooling, for example. But the white who has to catch up will not be anxious that his being behind is a matter of his whiteness, of his being *racially* inferior. The black student may well have such a fear.

This, I believe, is one reason why black colleges in America turn out 34 percent of all black college graduates, though they enroll only 17 percent of black college students. Without whites around on campus the myth of inferiority is in abeyance and, along with it, a great reservoir of culturally imposed self-doubt. On black campuses feelings of inferiority are personal; on campuses with a white majority, a black's problems have a way of becoming a "black" problem.

But this feeling of vulnerability a black may feel in itself is not as serious a problem as what he or she does with it. To admit that one is made anxious in integrated situations about the myth of racial inferiority is difficult for young blacks. It seems like admitting that one *is* racially inferior. And so, most often, the student will deny harboring these feelings. This is where some of the pangs of racial tension begin, because denial always involves distortion.

In order to deny a problem we must tell ourselves that the problem is something different than what it really is. A black student at Berkeley told me that he felt defensive every time he walked into a class and saw mostly white faces. When I asked why, he said, "Because I know they're all racists. They think blacks are stupid." Of course it may be true that some whites feel this way, but the singular focus on white racism allows this student to obscure his own underlying racial anxiety. He can now say that his problem—facing a class full of white faces, *fearing* that they think he is dumb—is entirely the result of certifiable white racism and has nothing to do with his own anxieties, or even that this particular academic subject may not be his best. Now all the terror of his anxiety, its powerful energy, is devoted to simply *seeing* racism. Whatever evidence of racism he finds—and looking this hard, he will no doubt find some—can be brought in to buttress his distorted view of the problem, while his actual deep-seated anxiety goes unseen.

Denial, and the distortion that results, places the problem *outside* the self and in the world. It is not that I have any inferiority anxiety because of my race; it is that I am going to school with people who don't like blacks. This is the shift in thinking that allows black students to reenact the protest pattern of the Sixties. Denied racial anxiety-distortion-reenactment is the process by which feelings of inferiority are transformed into an exaggerated white menace—which is then protested against with the techniques of the past. Under the sway of this process, black students believe that history is repeating itself, that it's just like the Sixties, or Fifties. In fact, it is the not yet healed wounds from the past, rather than the inequality that created the wounds, that is the real problem.

This process generates an unconscious need to exaggerate the level of racism on campus—to make it a matter of the system, not just a handful of students. Racism is the avenue away from the true inner anxiety. How many students demonstrating for a black "theme house"—demonstrating in the style of the Sixties, when the battle was to win for blacks a place on campus—might be better off spending their time reading and studying? Black students have the highest dropout rate and lowest grade point average of any group in American universities. This need not be so. And it is not the result of not having black theme houses.

It was my very good fortune to go to college in 1964, when the question of black "inferiority" was openly talked about among blacks. The summer before I left for college I heard Martin Luther King Jr. speak in Chicago, and he laid it on the line for black students everywhere. "When you are behind in a footrace, the only way to get ahead is to run faster than the man in front of you. So when your white roommate says he's tired and goes to sleep, you stay up and burn the midnight oil." His statement that we were "behind in a footrace" acknowledged that because of history, of few opportunities, of racism, we were, in a sense, "inferior." But this had to do with what had been done to our parents and their parents, not with inherent inferiority. And because it was acknowledged, it was presented to us as a challenge rather than a mark of shame.

Of the eighteen black students (in a student body of 1,000) who were on campus in my freshman year, all graduated, though a number of us were not from the middle class. At the university where I currently teach, the dropout rate for black students is 72 percent, despite the presence of several academic-support programs; a counseling center with black counselors; an Afro-American studies department; black faculty, administrators, and staff; a general education curriculum that emphasizes "cultural pluralism"; an Educational Opportunities Program; a mentor program; a black faculty and staff association; and an administration and faculty that often announce the need to do more for black students.

It may be unfair to compare my generation with the current one. Parents do this compulsively and to little end but self-congratulation.

But I don't congratulate my generation. I think we were advantaged. We came along at a time when racial integration was held in high esteem. And integration was a very challenging social concept for both blacks and whites. We were remaking ourselves—that's what one did at college—and making history. We had something to prove. This was a profound advantage; it gave us clarity and a challenge. Achievement in the American mainstream was the goal of integration, and the best thing about this challenge was its secondary message—that we *could* achieve.

There is much irony in the fact that black power would come along in the late Sixties and change all this. Black power was a movement of uplift and pride, and yet it also delivered the weight of pride—a weight that would burden black students from then on. Black power "nationalized" the black identity, made blackness itself an object of celebration and allegiance. But if it transformed a mark of shame into a mark of pride, it also, in the name of pride, required the denial of racial anxiety. Without a frank account of one's anxieties, there is no clear direction, no concrete challenge. Black students today do not get as clear a message from their racial identity as my generation got. They are not filled with the same urgency to prove themselves, because black pride has said, You're already proven, already equal, as good as anybody.

The "black identity" shaped by black power most powerfully contributes to racial tensions on campuses by basing entitlement more on race than on constitutional rights and standards of merit. With integration, black entitlement was derived from constitutional principles of fairness. Black power changed this by skewing the formula from rights to color— if you were black, you were entitled. Thus, the United Coalition Against Racism (UCAR) at the University of Michigan could "demand" two years ago that all black professors be given immediate tenure, that there be special pay incentives for black professors, and that money be provided for an all-black student union. In this formula, black becomes the very color of entitlement, an extra right in itself, and a very dangerous grandiosity is promoted in which blackness amounts to specialness.

Race is, by any standard, an unprincipled source of power. And on campuses the use of racial power by one group makes racial or ethnic or gender *difference* a currency of power for all groups. When I make my difference into power, other groups must seize upon their difference to contain my power and maintain their position relative to me. Very quickly a kind of politics of difference emerges in which racial, ethnic, and gender groups are forced to assert their entitlement and vie for power based on the single quality that makes them different from one another.

On many campuses today academic departments and programs are established on the basis of difference—black studies, women's studies, Asian studies, and so on—despite the fact that there is nothing in these

25

"difference" departments that cannot be studied within traditional academic disciplines. If their rationale truly is past exclusion from the mainstream curriculum, shouldn't the goal now be complete inclusion rather than separateness? I think this logic is overlooked because these groups are too interested in the power their difference can bring, and they insist on separate departments and programs as a tribute to that power.

This politics of difference makes everyone on campus a member of a minority group. It also makes racial tensions inevitable. To highlight one's difference as a source of advantage is also, indirectly, to inspire the enemies of that difference. When blackness (and femaleness) becomes power, then white maleness is also sanctioned as power. A white male student at Stanford told me, "One of my friends said the other day that we should get together and start up a white student union and come up with a list of demands."

It is certainly true that white maleness has long been an unfair source of power. But the sin of white male power is precisely its use of race and gender as a source of entitlement. When minorities and women use their race, ethnicity, and gender in the same way, they not only commit the same sin but also, indirectly, sanction the very form of power that oppressed them in the first place. The politics of difference is based on a tit-for-tat sort of logic in which every victory only calls one's enemies to arms.

This elevation of difference undermines the communal impulse by making each group foreign and inaccessible to others. When difference is celebrated rather than remarked, people must think in terms of difference, they must find meaning in difference, and this meaning comes from an endless process of contrasting one's group with other groups. Blacks use whites to define themselves as different, women use men. Hispanics use whites and blacks, and on it goes. And in the process each group mythologizes and mystifies its difference, puts it beyond the full comprehension of outsiders. Difference becomes an inaccessible preciousness toward which outsiders are expected to be simply and uncomprehendingly reverential. But beware: In this world, even the insulated world of the college campus, preciousness is a balloon asking for a needle. At Smith College, graffiti appears: "Niggers, Spics, and Chinks quit complaining or get out."

30   Most of the white students I talked with spoke as if from under a faint cloud of accusation. There was always a ring of defensiveness in their complaints about blacks. A white student I spoke with at UCLA told me: "Most white students on this campus think the black student leadership here is made up of oversensitive crybabies who spend all their time looking for things to kick up a ruckus about." A white student at

Stanford said: "Blacks do nothing but complain and ask for sympathy when everyone really knows they don't do well because they don't try. If they worked harder, they could do as well as everyone else."

That these students felt accused was most obvious in their compulsion to assure me that they were not racists. Oblique versions of some-of-my-best-friends-are stories came ritualistically before or after critiques of black students. Some said flatly, "I am not a racist, but . . ." Of course, we all deny being racists, but we only do this compulsively, I think, when we are working against an accusation of bias. I think it was the color of my skin, itself, that accused them.

This was the meta-message that surrounded these conversations like an aura, and in it, I believe, is the core of white American racial anxiety. My skin not only accused them, it judged them. And this judgment was a sad gift of history that brought them to account whether they deserved such an accounting or not. It said that wherever and whenever blacks were concerned, they had reason to feel guilt. And whether it was earned or unearned, I think it was guilt that set off the compulsion in these students to disclaim. I believe it is true that in America black people make white people feel guilty.

Guilt is the essence of white anxiety, just as inferiority is the essence of black anxiety. And the terror that it carries for whites is the terror of discovering that one has reason to feel guilt where blacks are concerned—not so much because of what blacks might think but because of what guilt can say about oneself. If the darkest fear of blacks is inferiority, the darkest fear of whites is that their better lot in life is at least partially the result of their capacity for evil—their capacity to dehumanize an entire people for their own benefit, and then to be indifferent to the devastation their dehumanization has wrought on successive generations of their victims. This is the terror that whites are vulnerable to regarding blacks. And the mere fact of being white is sufficient to feel it, since even whites with hearts clean of racism benefit from being white—benefit at the expense of blacks. This is a conditional guilt having nothing to do with individual intentions or actions. And it makes for a very powerful anxiety because it threatens whites with a view of themselves as inhuman, just as inferiority threatens blacks with a similar view of themselves. At the dark core of both anxieties is a suspicion of incomplete humanity.

So the white students I met were not just meeting me; they were also meeting the possibility of their own inhumanity. And this, I think, is what explains how some young white college students in the late Eighties can so frankly take part in racially insensitive and outright racist acts. They were expected to be cleaner of racism than any previous generation—they were born into the Great Society. But this expectation overlooks the fact that, for them, color is still an accusation and judgment.

In black faces there is a discomforting reflection of white collective shame. Blacks remind them that their racial innocence is questionable, that they are the beneficiaries of past and present racism, and that the sins of the father may well have been visited on the children.

35   And yet young whites tell themselves that they had nothing to do with the oppression of black people. They have a stronger belief in their racial innocence than any previous generation of whites, and a natural hostility toward anyone who would challenge that innocence. So (with a great deal of individual variation) they can end up in the paradoxical position of being hostile to blacks as a way of defending their own racial innocence.

I think this is what the young white editors of the *Dartmouth Review* were doing when they shamelessly harassed William Cole, a black music professor. Weren't they saying, in effect, I am so free of racial guilt that I can afford to ruthlessly attack blacks and still be racially innocent? The ruthlessness of that attack was a form of denial, a badge of innocence. The more they were charged with racism, the more ugly and confrontational their harassment became. Racism became a means of rejecting racial guilt, a way of showing that they were not ultimately racists.

The politics of difference sets up a struggle for innocence among all groups. When difference is the currency of power, each group must fight for the innocence that entitles it to power. Blacks sting whites with guilt, remind them of their racist past, accuse them of new and more subtle forms of racism. One way whites retrieve their innocence is to discredit blacks and deny their difficulties, for in this denial is the denial of their own guilt. To blacks this denial looks like racism, a racism that feeds black innocence and encourages them to throw more guilt at whites. And so the cycle continues. The politics of difference leads each group to pick at the sore spots of the other.

Men and women who run universities—whites, mostly—also participate in the politics of difference, although they handle their guilt differently than many of their students. They don't deny it, but still they don't want to *feel* it. And to avoid this *feeling* of guilt they have tended to go along with whatever blacks put on the table rather than work with them to assess their real needs. University administrators have too often been afraid of their own guilt and have relied on negotiation and capitulation more to appease that guilt than to help blacks and other minorities. Administrators would never give white students a racial theme house where they could be "more comfortable with people of their own kind," yet more and more universities are doing this for black students, thus fostering a kind of voluntary segregation. To avoid the anxieties of integrated situations, blacks ask for theme houses; to avoid guilt, white administrators give them theme houses.

When everyone is on the run from his anxieties about race, race relations on campus can be reduced to the negotiation of avoidances. A pattern of demand and concession develops in which each side uses the other to escape itself. Black studies departments, black deans of student affairs, black counseling programs, Afro houses, black theme houses, black homecoming dances and graduation ceremonies—black students and white administrators have slowly engineered a machinery of separatism that, in the name of sacred difference, redraws the ugly lines of segregation.

Black students have not sufficiently helped themselves, and universities, despite all their concessions, have not really done much for blacks. If both faced their anxieties, I think they would see the same thing: Academic parity with all other groups should be the overriding mission of black students, and it should also be the first goal that universities have for their black students. Blacks can only *know* they are as good as others when they are, in fact, as good—when their grades are higher and their dropout rate lower. Nothing under the sun will substitute for this, and no amount of concessions will bring it about.

Universities and colleges can never be free of guilt until they truly help black students, which means leading and challenging them rather than negotiating and capitulating. It means inspiring them to achieve academic parity, nothing less, and helping them see their own weaknesses as their greatest challenge. It also means dismantling the machinery of separatism, breaking the link between difference and power, and skewing the formula for entitlement away from race and gender and back to constitutional rights.

As for the young white students who have rediscovered swastikas and the word "nigger," I think they suffer from an exaggerated sense of their own innocence, as if they were incapable of evil and beyond the reach of guilt. But it is also true that the politics of difference creates an environment which threatens their innocence and makes them defensive. White students are not invited to the negotiating table from which they see blacks and others walk away with concessions. The presumption is that they do not deserve to be there because they are white. So they can only be defensive, and the less mature among them will be aggressive. Guerrilla activity will ensue. Of course this is wrong, but it is also a reflection of an environment where difference carries power and where whites have the wrong "difference."

I think universities should emphasize commonality as a higher value than "diversity" and "pluralism"—buzzwords for the politics of difference. Difference that does not rest on a clearly delineated foundation of commonality not only is inaccessible to those who are not part of the ethnic or racial group but is antagonistic to them. Difference can enrich only the common ground.

Integration has become an abstract term today, having to do with little more than numbers and racial balances. But it once stood for a high and admirable set of values. It made difference second to commonality, and it asked members of all races to face whatever fears they inspired in each other. I doubt the word will have a new vogue, but the values, under whatever name, are worth working for.

THE READER

1. After reviewing racial incidents on American campuses in the late 1980s, Steele makes two important assertions: one about racial tension and one about the campus. What are they? What is their function in his argument?
2. Restate Steele's conclusion in your own words.
3. What did Steele do to learn about racial tension on campus? What are the advantages and disadvantages of this approach, as opposed, say, to a carefully designed social survey?
4. What leads Steele to his observation that the campus is given over to "politics of difference"? What are "the politics of difference"?
5. James Baldwin's "Stranger in the Village" (p. 540), written before the 1960s and about a place very unlike a contemporary campus, is a meditation on racial tension. Does Steele share any of Baldwin's perceptions?

THE WRITER

1. How does Steele organize this essay? What are the main points he makes and in what order?
2. Write a brief essay setting out what you think, on the basis of "Stranger in the Village" (p. 540), Baldwin's assessment of the politics of difference would have been.
3. Write a paragraph defending the politics of difference. You don't have to rebut Steele, but you do need to be aware of his argument.

Nature and the Environment

Robert Finch

BEING AT TWO WITH NATURE

On Cape Cod, where I live, most people still enter their houses through the back door. This is a holdover from the old days when the front door, the formal entrance, was used only rarely—usually by the minister, the sheriff, or the undertaker. These figures were greeted with ceremony and good china, but they were kept in the front parlor and were not expected to stay long. The inhabitants, on the other hand, tended naturally to use the rear entrance, up a dirt path lined with dogs and chickens and the day's wash.

In this respect, at least, the field of nature writing is something like the traditional Cape Cod house. Most of what I would call nature writing is done not by scientists or formally trained naturalists, or even by writers with substantial scientific backgrounds, but by writers who slip in through the back door of the humanities. There have been notable exceptions, of course—Aldo Leopold, Rachel Carson, Loren Eiseley, Rene Dubos, E. O. Wilson, for example—who had established credentials in the natural sciences before being recognized as literary figures. But most of us are novelists, poets, artists, journalists, actors, philosophers, theologians. We tend to get our grounding in natural history on our own or secondhand, leading somewhat parasitical lives by associating with, and appropriating material and ideas from professional scientists and naturalists.

My own case is fairly typical. I grew up along the glass-littered, oil-sheened banks of the Passaic River in industrial New Jersey. Until I was twenty-five years old I could not tell a maple from an oak (or imagine why anyone would care to know). I did read *Walden* in high

First published in *The Georgia Review* (Mar. 1991).

school, not as a "nature book" but, like most adolescents, as a blueprint for making my own life memorable and extraordinary.

In college I took only one elective science course: an introductory class in ecology (this in the days when only scientists used the word *ecology*) taught by the late George C. Clarke, a wonderful old-school marine biologist long associated with the Woods Hole Oceanographic Institute. From that course I remember only two facts, both about wind: that in parts of Texas on a windy day it is possible for a man to expectorate for half a mile; and that the highest wind velocity ever recorded was on Mt. Washington in New Hampshire during the hurricane of 1938, when the anemometer reached a wind velocity of 213 mph—and then was blown off the mountain.

5   In graduate school I took one other natural-history course, this time in ornithology. I had an instructor who was doing his doctoral dissertation on the feeding habits of vultures in the Caribbean. One day he passed out a reprint of an article he had written on his research methods. It described how he had trapped the birds, massaged their crops to force them to throw up, and then carefully analyzed the vomit—which showed a predominance of coconut, followed by the remains of rodents, insects, and some other vegetable matter. I remember thinking, as an English graduate student, that his methods and results were not all that different from those we were being taught to employ in our own discipline.

These minimal formal experiences with the biological sciences may have had something to do with my eventual gravitation into nature writing, but I doubt it. Instead I seem to have backed into the field through a general love of literature, a desire to be a writer, an early habit of keeping journals, and the gradual discovery that I possessed a strong feeling for place. Only several years after leaving the academic arena did I begin shaping my accumulated bulk of notes and sketches into a form that is generally known as "the nature essay."

Such a hybridized history, like that of so many nature writers, is reflected in the awkward and unhelpful array of binomial name-tags that have been pinned on us. Nature writers are labeled variously as poet-naturalists, natural-history writers, literary naturalists, nature essayists, creative naturalists, and so on. The preponderance of double terms used to describe the genre's practitioners suggests, I believe, some inner dichotomy in the minds of those who use them, some not-quite-comfortable amalgam of the humanities and science. This confusion reaches even to *Walden,* that supreme icon of American nature writing, which has remained something of a wandering orphan on the shelves of most libraries. One might think it could always be found under American Letters, but over the years I have found it shelved with general nature writing, New England regional literature, personal essays, travel, philosophy, economics, science and technology, limnology, even pets (well, Thoreau *did* keep some ants inside for a while . . .).

What is nature writing anyway? Like fall warblers, works of nature writing are not always easy to recognize. From a distance their characteristic outlines may seem distinct, but individual birds tend to be difficult to identify. I suspect that, in addition to *Walden*, most readers would agree to include under the general rubric of nature writing such works as Gilbert White's *The Natural History of Selborne*, Charles Darwin's *Voyage of the Beagle*, John Muir's *My First Summer in the Sierra*, Mary Austin's *The Land of Little Rain*, Aldo Leopold's *Sand County Almanac*, Loren Eiseley's *The Immense Journey*, Edward Abbey's *Desert Solitaire*, and Barry Lopez' *Arctic Dreams*. But what about Coleridge's *Anima Poetae*, or Mark Twain's *Life on the Mississippi*, or Gerard Manley Hopkins' journals and diaries, or Isak Dinesen's *Out of Africa*, or D. H. Lawrence's *Etruscan Places*, or Norman Maclean's *A River Runs Through It*? And should we mention *Moby-Dick*, *Leaves of Grass*, or the novels of Willa Cather and William Faulkner? Clearly nature writing is not simply a question of subject matter, but of the writer's intent and treatment of that matter.

Consider for a moment those two "facts" about wind I cited at the start of this essay. What they have in common is not just the same environmental vector but a more significant characteristic. In each case scientific information is coupled with a peculiarly human element: wind force defined on one hand by human spit and on the other by man-made machines that are themselves overwhelmed by the very power they are designed to measure. These, I would suggest, are the kinds of "natural facts" that attract nature writers—data or experiences with human meaning attached to them, or on which they can bring some human meaning to bear.

John Steinbeck illustrates this idea in his introduction to *The Log from the Sea of Cortez* (1951), an account of an expedition with his friend, the biologist Ed Ricketts, to study the marine life of the Gulf of California. He also points toward a definition of nature writing by focusing on the crucial distinction between scientific and literary natural history: 10

> We wanted to see everything our eyes would accommodate, to think what we could, and, out of our seeing and thinking, to build some kind of structure in modeled imitation of the observed reality. We knew that what we would see and record and construct would be warped, as all knowledge patterns are warped, first, by the collective pressure and stream of our time and race, second, by the thrust of our individual personalities. But knowing this, we might not fall into too many holes—we might maintain some balance between our warp and the separate thing, the external reality. The

oneness of these two might take its contribution from both. For example: the Mexican Sierra has "XVII-15-IX" spines in the dorsal fin. These can easily be counted. But if the sierra strikes hard on the line so that our hands are burned, if the fish sounds and nearly escapes and finally comes in over the rail, his colors pulsing and his tail beating the air, a whole new relational externality has come into being—an entity which is more than the sum of the fish plus the fisherman.

In other words, both scientists and nature writers impose patterns upon their subjects. But it is the nature writer's deliberate intent to include that "relational externality" between self and nature, to filter natural experience through an individual sensibility, that makes the undertaking a literary one.

Yet despite the high literary caliber of such contemporary practitioners as Wallace Stegner, Annie Dillard, Barry Lopez, Peter Matthiessen, John Hay, John Fowles, Edward Hoagland, and John McPhee, many critics still seem uneasy evaluating nature writing as literature. Rather, its authors tend to be judged on such things as their perception and sensitive recording of natural fact ("Her book contains a wealth of observation on the little-understood ecosystems of southern Minnesota"), their defense of endangered species ("An eloquent effort to understand a despised, feared and heavily mythologized beast"), their philosophical and moral stands on current environmental crises ("An important warning towards an uncertain future")—even for their ability to chop wood or survive alone in the desert or build a birch-bark canoe, things most of them are not especially good at. Though token acknowledgement is frequently given to an author's style ("Fleshy, quite often rapt"), nature writers are too seldom recognized for being—as much as any lyric poet or short-story writer—conscious literary craftsmen, shapers of experience.

What sets off nature writing from all other kinds of writing about nature, I think, is that it tries to suggest a relationship with the natural environment that is more than strictly intellectual, biological, cultural, or even ethical—though it pays due attention to these aspects. This is not to denigrate other forms of natural history, especially the basic field research that provides much of the grist for the contemporary nature writers' mills. But nature writers tend to see nature as more then a subject for scientific research or a life-support system for human society which must be managed wisely, more than a source of aesthetic and recreational pleasure or a topic for philosophical speculation, more even than something which has basic "rights" and "values" and which we have a moral obligation to protect and pass on to posterity. Rather, they sense that nature is, at its very heart, an enduring mystery—a mystery, as Henry Beston put it, for which "poetry is as necessary to comprehension as science." They sense a fundamental connection in the physical and biological world not just with human existence but with human identity. They suspect that, despite the urban lives most of us live today, we must look to the sounds and images of unedited natural experience for the true sources of our emotions, our impulses, our longings—even for the very language of imagination itself. In other words, what the nature writer seeks is as whole and immediate and integrated a response to nature as most other writers seek with other human beings, real or fictional.

This is why nature writers, as opposed to environmental writers, tend to have no agenda—no theory to test, no point to prove, no program or plan for salvation to push. Or if they do, as in a book like Farley Mowat's *Never Cry Wolf*, the agenda tends to be subordinated to or eventually overwhelmed by the larger human experience related. This is why, in my mind at least, Rachel Carson's *Silent Spring* is important as a work of environmental writing, but *The Edge of the Sea* stands as one of the finest books of twentieth-century nature writing.

This is not to say that the propagandist or the moralist does not often exist within the same set of covers with the nature writer. Thoreau himself was no slouch at lecturing the reader, and part of the pleasure of reading a writer like Edward Abbey is being hit full in the face with his unbridled and outrageous Old Testament fury. But at its core, nature writing does not so much seek to express didactic certainty, or even unambiguous meaning, as to find imaginative connection with what D. H. Lawrence called the "circumambient universe"—the plants, animals, and natural forces with which we share existence. 15

This desire to restore nature to its central place in individual, personal experience can be seen as part of a broader attempt, by writers from many fields, to bridge the notorious "science/humanities gap" first popularized three decades ago in C. P. Snow's *The Two Cultures* (although the discussion actually goes back at least to the lectures of Thomas Huxley and Matthew Arnold over a century ago). Nature writing in a sense serves as a melting-pot genre, where scientists and humanists can meet on congenial ground.

Of course during the golden age of natural-history writing—the latter eighteenth and early nineteenth centuries—there was no such gap to be bridged. Pick up a volume from any of the leading naturalists of that era—John or William Bartram, Mark Catesby, Alexander Wilson, John James Audubon, Philip Gosse, Louis Agassiz, Charles Darwin, Thomas Nuttall—and you will find a human sensibility, a full and engaging personality, behind it. Here, for example, is the final paragraph from Darwin's *The Descent of Man* (1871):

> Man may be excused from feeling some pride at having risen, though not through his own exertions, to the very summit of the organic scale; and

the fact of his having thus risen, instead of having been aboriginally placed there, may give him hopes for a still higher destiny in the distant future. But we are not here concerned with hopes or fears, only with the truth as far as our reason allows us to discover it. I have given the evidence to the best of my ability; and we must acknowledge, as it seems to me, that man with all his noble qualities, with sympathy which feels for the most debased, with benevolence which extends not only to other men but to the humblest living creatures, with his godlike intellect which has penetrated into the movements and constitution of the solar system—with all these exalted powers—Man still bears in his bodily frame the indelible stamp of his lowly origin.

What unabashed humanity there is in a passage like this!—so full of personal humility, racial hubris, deliberate rhetorical heuristics, compassion, and a sense of the enormity of his subject. One can easily forgive what now seem its faults—such as its ingrained Victorian sense of progress—because of Darwin's fullness of response to the philosophical as well as the scientific implications of man's evolutionary nature. It is ironic that the man who was responsible for the transformation of the study of modern biological science employed language in his landmark works that today would be "unacceptable" in most scientific papers.

Earlier I suggested that the awkward hybrid terminology that has evolved to describe nature writing implied a more profound and disturbing dichotomy in our contemporary concept of nature. If the underlying intent of the genre is, as I have said, to reintegrate the human personality in its response to nature, then one reason why nature writing has been so difficult to categorize (and why there has been such resistance to its acceptance as genuine literature) may be precisely because it threatens to break down traditional Western categories that we have come to hold dear: the divisions between literature and science, between fiction and nonfiction, and above all, between human culture and nature.

20   There is now almost universal intellectual acceptance of the premise that humanity is a part of nature. Yet every day, as global ecological crises worsen, we wonder why we have paid little more than lip service to that idea in our individual and communal actions. It is easy enough to point the finger at the vast structure of vested economic and political interests, or at the apathy and sense of helplessness of the individual in the face of overwhelming environmental problems. But I think there is a more fundamental problem in our refusal to internalize what we know to be true. There seems to remain, on a deep emotional level, something in us that does not want the barriers broken down, that resists the notion that we are, in the most literal sense, not only a part but a *product* of physical creation. Nature writing poses problems beyond those of classification or evaluation by touching something extremely basic in the

human psyche. The nature writer is not merely exploring the natural world and offering an individual response; he is asserting his, and our, undeniable connection to that world—which is nonhuman, which is otherness, which is *not us.*

We resist this connection in large part because we recognize in the natural a world where human moral structures and value systems do not apply, at least as we usually apply them. It is this sense of an unbridgeable gap—between ourselves and a natural order which seems to fly in the face of human sensibilities—that leads most of us to attempt to view nature with scientific detachment, to imbue it with human values, or simply to avoid it. Yet it is this same simultaneous gap/connection between the human and natural world that nature writers both delight in and recoil from. The best are honest enough to record and explore both responses. At one place in *Pilgrim at Tinker Creek* Annie Dillard can say, "The great hurrah about wild animals is that they exist at all." In another, after watching a praying mantis devour its mate during the act of copulation, she can protest that "The universe that suckled us is a monster that does not care if we live or die . . . we can only try to outwit it at every turn to save our skins."

The naturalist imagination always makes the basic assumption, first deliberately tested by Thoreau, that nature (or the nonhuman environment) has something fundamentally important to teach us about ourselves as human beings—not because of its scientific or poetic potential, not as anything that we can directly use, but precisely because we have fundamental connections to it. Nature is the source from which our consciousness and identity have sprung—and which still informs them, whether we recognize it or not.

John Hay, one of our finest contemporary nature writers, put the intent of much nature writing in a nutshell when he wrote, "One ought to be able to say, Here is a life not mine, I am enriched." This, I think, expresses the essential task of nature writers. Nature is a continual challenge to our very image of ourselves, to all we have created and set apart from it. Our instinct is to hide from nature by covering it up with our works or our words, to control it with our simplistic technology or our narrow ideas, to cut it down to our size—which, as Hay says elsewhere, may be making too little of too much. The nature writer's job is not to limit or encompass nature, not even necessarily to explain or interpret it, but to show it to us in all its scope: its beauty and repulsiveness, its sociability and its utter alienness, its nurturing and its destructive elements, its immeasurable providence and (more terrifying than any malice) its indifference to human aspirations—and in so doing to extend our own humanity.

But this, after all, has always been the job of artists everywhere: to make us see in new ways, to make us comfortable with the uncomfortable and uncomfortable with the comfortable, familiar with the unfamiliar and unfamiliar with the familiar, responsive to what we have ignored and skeptical—or at least questioning—of what we have loved without examination. This is at once the challenge, the risk, and at times the great reward of the nature writer. For he is always putting his human values on the line, always placing himself and his viewpoint at the center of the universe (though fully aware of the immense folly of doing so), and then waiting with glad suspense, open-eyed, with pencil or word processor in hand, to see which universal force—an earthquake or an ant—will be the next one to knock him right back on his assumptions.

Gretel Ehrlich

SPRING

We have a nine-acre lake on our ranch and a warm spring that feeds it all winter. By mid-March the lake ice begins to melt where the spring feeds in, and every year the same pair of mallards come ahead of the others and wait. Though there is very little open water they seem content. They glide back and forth through a thin estuary, brushing watercress with their elegant folded wings, then tip end-up to eat and, after, clamber onto the lip of ice that retreats, hardens forward, and retreats again.

Mornings, a transparent pane of ice lies over the meltwater. I peer through and see some kind of waterbug—perhaps a leech—paddling like a sea turtle between green ladders of lakeweed. Cattails and sweetgrass from the previous summer are bone dry, marked with black mold spots, and bend like elbows into the ice. They are swords that cut away the hard tenancy of winter. At the wide end a mat of dead waterplants has rolled back into a thick, impregnable breakwater. Near it, bubbles trapped under the ice are lenses focused straight up to catch the coming season.

It's spring again and I wasn't finished with winter. That's what I said at the end of summer too. I stood on the twenty-foot-high haystack and yelled "No!" as the first snow fell. We had been up since four in the morning picking the last bales of hay from the oatfield by hand, slipping under the weight of them in the mud, and by the time we finished the stack, six inches of snow had fallen.

It's spring but I was still cataloguing the different kinds of snow: snow that falls dry but is rained on; snow that melts down into hard crusts;

First published in *Antaeus* (1986), "On Nature" issue.

wind-driven snow that looks blue; powder snow on hardpack on powder—a Linzertorte[1] of snow. I look up. The troposphere is the seven-to-
ten-mile-wide sleeve of air out of which all our weather shakes. A bank
of clouds drives in from the south. Where in it, I wonder, does a
snowflake take on its thumbprint uniqueness? Inside the cloud where
schools of flakes are flung this way and that like schools of fish? What
gives the snowflake its needle, plate, column, branching shapes—the
battering wind or the dust particles around which water vapor clings?

Near town the river ice breaks up and lies stacked in industrial-sized   5
hunks—big as railway cars—on the banks, and is flecked black by wheeling hurricanes of newly plowed topsoil. That's how I feel when winter
breaks up inside me: heavy, onerous, upended, inert against the flow of
water. I had thought about ice during the cold months too. How it is
movement betrayed, water seized in the moment of falling. In November, ice thickened over the lake like a cataract, and from the air looked
like a Cyclops,[2] one bad eye. Under its milky spans over irrigation
ditches, the sound of water running south was muffled. One solitary spire
of ice hung noiselessly against dark rock at the Falls as if mocking or
mirroring the broom-tail comet on the horizon. Then, in February, I
tried for words not about ice, but words hacked from it—the ice at the
end of the mind, so to speak—and failed.

Those were winter things and now it is spring, though one name can't
describe what, in Wyoming, is a three-part affair: false spring, the vernal
equinox, and the spring when flowers come and the grass grows.

Spring means restlessness. The physicist I've been talking to all winter
says if I look more widely, deeply, and microscopically all at once I might
see how springlike the whole cosmos is. What I see as order and stillness—the robust, time-bound determinacy of my life—is really a mirage
suspended above chaos. "There's a lot of random jiggling going on all
the time, everywhere," he tells me. Winter's tight sky hovers. Under it,
the hayfields are green, then white, then green growing under white.
The confinement I've felt since November resembles the confinement
of subatomic particles, I'm told. A natural velocity finally shows itself.
The particle moves; it becomes a wave.

The sap rises in trees and in me and the hard knot of perseverance
I cultivated to meet winter dissipates; I walk away from the obsidian of
bitter nights. Now, when snow comes, it is wet and heavy, but the air
it traverses feels light. I sleep less and dream not of human entangle-
ments, but of animals I've never seen: a caterpillar fat as a man's thumb,
made of linked silver tubes, has two heads—one human, one a butterfly's.

---

1. An Austrian cake made with multiple   2. A mythical giant with a single eye set in
layers.   the middle of its forehead.

Last spring at this time I was coming out of a bout with pneumonia. I went to bed on January first and didn't get up until the end of February. Winter was a cocoon in which my gagging, basso cough shook the dark figures at the end of my bed. Had I read too much Hemingway? Or was I dying? I'd lie on my stomach and look out. Nothing close up interested me. All engagements of mind—the circumlocutions of love interests and internal gossip—appeared false. Only my body was true. And my body was trying to close down, go out the window without me.

10   I saw things out there. Our ranch faces south down a long treeless valley whose vanishing point is two gray hills, folded one in front of the other like two hands, and after that—space, cerulean air, clouds like pleated skirts, and red mesas standing up like breaching whales in a valley three thousand feet below. Afternoons, our young horses played, rearing up on back legs and pawing oh so carefully at each other, reaching around, ears flat back, nipping manes and withers. One of those times their falsetto squeals looped across the pasture and hung on frozen currents of air. But when I tried to ingest their sounds of delight, I found my lungs had no air.

It was thirty-five below zero that night. Our plumbing froze, and because I was very weak my husband had to bundle me up and help me to the outhouse. Nothing close at hand seemed to register with me: neither the cold nor the semicoziness of an uninsulated house. But the stars were lurid. For a while I thought I saw the horses, dead now, and eating each other, and spinning round and round in the ice of the air.

My scientists friends talk with relish about how insignificant we humans are when placed against the time-scale of geology and the cosmos. I had heard it a hundred times, but never felt it truly. As I lay in bed, the black room was a screen through which some part of my body traveled, leaving the rest behind. I thought I was a sun flying over a barge whose iron holds soaked me up until I became rust floating on a bright river.

A ferocious loneliness took hold of me. I felt spring-inspired desire, a sense of trajectory, but no interception was in sight. In fact, I wanted none. My body was a parenthetical dash laid against a landscape so spacious it defied space as we know it—space as a membrane—and curved out of time. That night a luscious, creamy fog rolled in, like a roll of fat, hugging me, but it was snow.

Recuperation is like spring: dormancy and vitality collide. In any year I'm like a bear, a partial hibernator. During January thaws I stick my nose out and peruse the frozen desolation as if reading a book whose language I don't know. In March I'm ramshackle, weak in the knees, giddy, dazzled by broken-backed clouds, the passing of Halley's comet, the on-and-off strobe of sun. Like a sheepherder I X out each calendar day as if time were a forest through which I could clear-cut a way to the future. My physicist friend straightens me out on this point too. The notion of "time passing," like a train through a landscape, is an illusion, he says. I hold the Big Ben clock taken from a dead sheepherder's wagon and look at it. The clock measures intervals of time, not the speed of time, and the calendar is a scaffolding we hang as if time were rushing water we could harness. Time-bound, I hinge myself to a linear bias— cause and effect all laid out in a neat row—and in this we learn two things: blame and shame.

Julius Caesar had a sense of humor about time. The Roman calendar with its calends, nones, and ides—counting days—changed according to who was in power. Caesar serendipitously added days, changed the names of certain months, and when he was through, the calendar was so skewed that January fell in autumn.

Einsteinian time is too big for even Julius Caesar to touch. It stretches and shrinks and dilates. In fact, it is the antithesis of the mechanistic concept we've imposed on it. Time, indecipherable from space, is not one thing but an infinity of spacetimes, overlapping, interfering, wave-like. There is no future that is not now, no past that is not now. Time includes every moment.

It's the ides of March today.

I've walked to a hill a mile from the house. It's not really a hill but a mountain slope that heaves up, turns sideways, and comes down again, straight down to a foot-wide creek. Everything I can see from here used to be a flatland covered with shallow water. "Used to be" means several hundred million years ago, and the land itself was not really "here" at all, but part of a continent floating near Bermuda. On top is a fin of rock, a marine deposition created during Jurassic[3] times by small waves moving in and out slapping the shore.

I've come here for peace and quiet and to see what's going on in this secluded valley, away from ranch work and sorting corrals, but what I get is a slap on the ass by a prehistoric wave, gains and losses in altitude and aridity, outcrops of mud composed of rotting volcanic ash that fell continuously for ten thousand years a hundred million years ago. The soils are a geologic flag—red, white, green, and gray. On one side of the hill, mountain mahogany gives off a scent like orange blossoms; on the other, colonies of sagebrush root wide in ground the color of Spanish roof tiles. And it still looks like the ocean to me. "How much truth can a man stand, sitting by the ocean, all that perpetual motion," Mose Allison, the jazz singer, sings.

The wind picks up and blusters. Its fat underbelly scrapes the uneven ground, twisting like taffy toward me, slips up over the mountain, and

3. The second period of the Mesozoic era, characterized by the dominance of the dinosaur.

showers out across the Great Plains. The sea smell it carried all the way from Seattle has long since been absorbed by pink gruss—the rotting granite that spills down the slopes of the Rockies. Somewhere over the Midwest the wind slows, tangling in the hair of hardwood forests, and finally drops into the corridors of the cities, past Manhattan's World Trade Center, ripping free again as it crosses the Atlantic's green swell.

Spring jitterbugs inside me. Spring *is* wind, symphonic and billowing. A dark cloud pops like a blood blister over me, letting hail down. It comes on a piece of wind that seems to have widened the sky, comes so the birds have something to fly on.

A message reports to my brain but I can't believe my eyes. The sheet of wind had a hole in it: an eagle just fell out of the sky. It fell as if down the chute of a troubled airplane. Landed, falling to one side as if a leg were broken. I was standing on the hill overlooking the narrow valley that had been a seashore 170 million years ago, whose sides had lifted like a medic's litter to catch up this eagle now.

She hops and flaps seven feet of wing and closes them down and sways. She had come down (on purpose?) near a dead fawn whose carcass had recently been feasted upon. When I walked closer, all I could see of the animal was a ribcage rubbed red with fine tissue and the decapitated head lying peacefully against sagebrush, eyes closed.

At twenty yards the eagle opened her wings halfway and rose up, her whole back lengthening and growing stiff. At forty feet she looked as big as a small person. She craned her neck, first to one side, then the other, and stared hard. She's giving me the eagle eye, I thought.

Friends who have investigated eagles' nests have literally feared for their lives. It's not that they were in danger of being pecked to death but, rather, grabbed. An eagle's talons are a powerful jaw. Their grip is so strong the talons can slice down through flesh to bone in one motion.

25   But I had come close only to see what was wrong, to see what I could do. An eagle with a bum leg will starve to death. Was it broken, bruised, or sprained? How could I get close enough to know? I approached again. She hopped up in the air, dashing the critical distance between us with her great wings. Best to leave her alone, I decided. My husband dragged a road-killed deer up the mountain slope so she could eat, and I brought a bucket of water. Then we turned toward home.

A golden eagle is not golden but black with yellow spots on the neck and wings. Looking at her, I had wondered how feathers came to be, how their construction—the rachis, vane, and quill—is unlike anything else in nature.

Birds are glorified flying lizards. The remarkable feathers that, positioned together, are like hundreds of smaller wings, evolved from reptilian scales. Ancestral birds had thirteen pairs of cone-shaped teeth that grew in separate sockets like a snake's, rounded ribs, and bony tails.

Archaeopteryx was half bird, half dinosaur who glided instead of flying; ichthyornis was a fish-bird, a relative of the pelican; diatryma was a giant, seven feet tall with a huge beak and wings so absurdly small they must have been useless, though later the wingbone sprouted from them. *Aquila chrysaëtos*, the modern golden eagle, has seven thousand contour feathers, no teeth, and weighs about eight pounds.

I think about the eagle. How big she was, how each time she spread her wings it was like a thought stretching between two seasons.

Back at the house I relax with a beer. At 5:03 the vernal equinox occurs. I go outside and stand in the middle of a hayfield with my eyes closed. The universe is restless but I want to feel celestial equipoise: twelve hours of daylight, twelve of dark, and the earth ramrod straight on its axis. In celebration I straighten my posture in an effort to resist the magnetic tilt back into dormancy, spiritual and emotional reticence. Far to the south I imagine the equatorial sash, now nose to nose with the sun, sizzling like a piece of bacon, then the earth slowly tilting again.

In the morning I walk up to the valley again. I glass both hillsides, back and forth through the sagebrush, but the eagle isn't there. The hindquarters of the road-killed deer have been eaten. Coyote tracks circle the carcass. Did they have eagle for dinner too?

Afternoon. I return. Far up on the opposite hill I see her, flapping and hopping to the top. When I stop, she stops and turns her head. Her neck is the plumbline on which earth revolves. Even at two hundred yards, I can feel her binocular vision zeroing in; I can feel the heat of her stare.

Later, I look through my binoculars at all sorts of things. I'm seeing the world with an eagle eye. I glass the crescent moon. How jaded I've become, taking the moon at face value only, forgetting the charcoal, shaded backside, as if it weren't there at all.

That night I dream about two moons. One is pink and spins fast; the other is an eagle's head, farther away and spinning in the opposite direction. Slowly, both moons descend and then it is day.

At first light I clamber up the hill. Now the dead deer my husband brought is only a hoop of ribs, two forelegs, and hair. The eagle is not here or along the creek or on either hill. I go to the hill and sit. After a long time an eagle careens out from the narrow slit of the red-walled canyon whose creek drains into this valley. Surely it's the same bird. She flies by. I can hear the bone-creak and whoosh of air under her wings. She cocks her head and looks at me. I smile. What is a smile to her? Now she is not so much flying as lifting above the planet, far from me.

Late March. The emerald of the hayfields brightens. A flock of gray-capped rosy finches who overwintered here swarms a leafless apple tree, then falls from the smooth boughs like cut grass. the tree was planted by the Texan who homesteaded this ranch. As I walk past, one of the boughs, shaped like an undulating dragon, splits off from the trunk and falls.

Space is an arena in which the rowdy particles that are the building blocks of life perform their antics. All spring, things fall; the general law of increasing disorder is on the take. I try to think of what it is to be a cause without an effect, an effect without a cause. To abandon time-bound thinking, the use of tenses, the temporally related emotions of impatience, expectation, hope, and fear. But I can't. I go to the edge of the lake and watch the ducks. Like them, my thinking rises and falls on the same water.

Another day. Sometimes when I'm feeling small-minded I take a plane ride over Wyoming. As we take off I feel the plane's resistance to accepting air under its wings. Is this how an eagle feels? Ernst Mach's[4] principle tells me that an object's resistance against being accelerated is not the intrinsic property of matter, but a measure of its interaction with the universe; that matter has inertia only because it exists in relation to other matter.

Airborne, then, I'm not aloof but in relation to everything—like Wallace Steven's floating eagle for whom the whole, intricate Alps is a nest. We fly southeast from Heart Mountain across the Big Horn River, over the long red wall where Butch Cassidy trailed stolen horses, across the high plains to Laramie. Coming home the next day, we hit clouds. Turbulence, like many forms of trouble, cannot always be seen. We bounce so hard my arms sail helplessly above my head. In evolution, wingbones became arms and hands; perhaps I'm de-evolving.

From ten thousand feet I can see that spring is only half here: the southern part of the state is white, the northern half is green. Land is also time. The greening of time is a clock whose hands are blades of grass moving vertically, up through the fringe of numbers, spreading across the middle of the face, sinking again as the sun moves from one horizon to the other. Time doesn't go anywhere; the shadow of the plane, my shadow, moves across it.

40

To sit on a plane is to sit on the edge of sleep where the mind's forge brightens into incongruities. Down there I see disparate wholenesses strung together and the string dissolving. Mountains run like rivers; I fly through waves and waves of chiaroscuro light. The land looks bare but is articulate. The body of the plane is my body, pressing into spring, pressing matter into relation with matter. Is it even necessary to say the obvious? That spring brings on surges of desire? From this disinterested height I say out loud what Saint Augustine wrote: "My love is my weight. Because of it I move."

4. Mach (1836–1916), Austrian physicist who formulated the principle that the inertial and other properties of a system any-where in the universe are determined by the interaction of that system with the rest of the universe.

Directly below us now is the fine old Wyoming ranch where Joel, Mart, Dave, Hughy, and I have moved thousands of head of cattle. Joel's father, Smokey, was one of two brothers who put the outfit together. They worked hard, lived frugally, and even after Fred died, Smokey did not marry until his late fifties. As testimony to a long bachelorhood, there is no kitchen in the main house. The cookhouse stands separate from all the other buildings. In back is a bedroom and bath, which have housed a list of itinerant cooks ten pages long.

Over the years I've helped during roundup and branding. We'd rise at four. Smokey, now in his eighties, cooked flapjacks and boiled coffee on the wood cookstove. There was a long table. Joel and Smokey always sat at one end. They were lookalikes, both skin-and-bones tall with tipped-up dark eyes set in narrow faces. Stern and vigilant, Smokey once threw a young hired hand out of the cookhouse because he hadn't grained his saddle horse after a long day's ride. "On this outfit we take care of our animals first," he said. "Then if there's time, we eat."

Even in his early twenties, Joel had his father's dignity and razor-sharp wit. They both wore white Stetsons identically shaped. Only their hands were different: Joel had eight fingers and one thumb—the other he lost while roping.

Eight summers ago my parents visited their ranch. We ate a hearty meal of homemade whiskey left over from Prohibition days, steaks cut from an Angus bull, four kinds of vegetables, watermelon, ice cream, and pie. Despite a thirteen-year difference in our ages, Smokey wanted Joel and me to marry. As we rose from the meal, he shook my father's hand. "I guess you'll be my son's father-in-law," he said. That was news to all of us. Joel's face turned crimson. My father threw me an astonished look, cleared his throat, and thanked his host for the fine meal.

One night Joel did come to my house and asked me if I would take him into my bed. It was a gentlemanly proposition—doffed hat, moist eyes, a smile almost grimacing with loneliness. "You're an older woman. Think of all you could teach me," he said jauntily, but with a blush. He stood ramrod straight waiting for an answer. My silence turned him away like a rolling wave and he drove to the home ranch, spread out across the Emblem Bench thirty-five miles away.

The night Joel died I was staying at a writer's farm in Missouri. I had fallen asleep early, then awakened suddenly, feeling claustrophobic. I jumped out of bed and stood in the dark. I wanted to get out of there, drive home to Wyoming, and I didn't know why. Finally, at seven in the morning, I was able to sleep. I dreamed about a bird landing, then lifting out of a tree along a river bank. That was the night Joel's pickup rolled. He was found five hours after the accident occurred—just about daylight—and died on the way to the hospital.

45

Now I'm sitting on a fin of Gypsum Springs rock looking west. The sun is setting. What I see are three gray cloud towers letting rain down at the horizon. The sky behind these massifs is gilded gold, and long fingers of land—benches where the Hunt Oil Company's Charolais cattle graze—are pink. Somewhere over Joel's grave the sky is bright. The road where he died shines like a dash in a Paul Klee painting. Over my head, it is still winter: snow so dry it feels like Styrofoam when squeezed together, tumbles into my lap. I think about flying and falling. The place in the sky where the eagle fell is dark, as if its shadow had burned into the backdrop of rock—Hiroshima style. Why does a wounded eagle get well and fly away; why do the head wounds of a young man cut him down? Useless questions.

Sex and death are the riddles thrown into the hopper, thrown down on the planet like hailstones. Where one hits the earth, it makes a crater and melts, perhaps a seed germinates, perhaps not. If I dice life down into atoms, the trajectories I find are so wild, so random, anything could happen: life or nonlife. But once we have a body, who can give it up easily? Our own or others? We check our clocks and build our beautiful narratives, under which indeterminacy seethes.

Sometimes, lying in bed, I feel like a flounder with its two eyes on one side pointing upward into nothingness. The casings of thought rattle. Then I realize there are no casings at all. Is it possible that the mind, like space, is finite, but has no boundaries, no center or edge? I sit cross-legged on old blankets. My bare feet strain against the crotch of my knees. Time is between my toes, it seems. Just as morning comes and the indigo lifts, the leaflessness of the old apple tree looks ornate. Nothing in this world is plain.

"Every atom in your body was once inside a star," another physicist says, but he's only trying to humor me. Not all atoms in all kinds of matter are shared. But who wouldn't find that idea appealing? Outside, shadows trade places with a sliver of sun that trades places with shadow. Finally the lake ice goes and the water—pale and slate blue—wears its coat of diamonds all day. The mallards number twenty-six pairs now. They nest on two tiny islands and squabble amicably among themselves. A Pacific storm blows in from the south like a jibsail reaching far out, backhanding me with a gust of something tropical. It snows into my mouth, between my breasts, against my shins. Spring teaches me what space and time teach me: that I am a random multiple; that the many fit together like waves; that my swell is a collision of particles. Spring is a kind of music, a seething minor, a twelve-tone scale. Even the odd harmonies amassed only lift up to dissolve.

Spring passes harder and harder and is feral. The first thunder cracks the sky into a larger domain. Sap rises in obdurateness. For the first time in seven months, rain slants down in a slow pavane—sharp but soft—like

desire, like the laying on of hands. I drive the highway that crosses the
wild-horse range. Near Emblem I watch a black studhorse trot across the
range all alone. He travels north, then turns in my direction as if trotting
to me. Now, when I dream of Joel, he is riding that horse and he knows
he is dead. One night he rides to my house, all smiles and shyness. I let
him in.

Diane Ackerman

MASS MEETING ON THE COAST

In a eucalyptus grove near Santa Barbara, the towering trees are
strung with gaudy lights. Long, thick garlands of orange and yellow sway
among the bluish leaves. A warm coastal breeze puffs hard, and all at
once the lights scatter, exploding in the sky and then falling like embers.
Fire from the trees? When they rise again, your mouth opens in silent
surprise. Butterflies! Thousands and thousands of butterflies.

Some of the monarchs recluster in the scimitar leaves. Others flutter
to the open field beside the ocean, sip dew from the grass with hollow
proboscises, which unfurl from their mouths like party favors, or drink
nectar from the frilly yellow eucalyptus flowers. They smear the field
with orange and fly up like a cloud of bright coins. Only Bambi is missing
from this fantasia of murmuring wings and unearthly calm. Trees, field
and sky are all drenched with butterflies. How did they get here?

A hundred million monarchs migrate each year. Gliding, flapping,
hitching rides on thermals like any hawk or eagle, they fly as far as 4,000
miles, as high as 2,000 feet. They rival the great animal migrations of
Africa, the great flocking of birds across North America. Occasionally
one will be bamboozled by high winds and end up in Mauritius or
England. Monarchs need only water and nectar to thrive but are sensitive to cold and must spend the winter somewhere warm or die. So in
the fall those west of the Rocky Mountains fly to the coast of California,
to cluster in select stands of eucalyptus and pine, while Eastern monarchs migrate to Mexico. The routes are not learned—it's straight genetics. The butterflies that leave the grove this spring are four or five
generations removed from the ones that were here last year.

Each monarch site in California is different, but together they make
an archipelago of roosts, a single winter address. One is the elaborately
landscaped front yard of an abandoned $3.5 million Santa Barbara beach
house, rumbled past by trains. One is a campground in Big Sur, under

From *Life* magazine (May 1987).

the gaze of wild boars, coyotes, red-tailed hawks, whales and wide-eyed schoolchildren. One is in back of a Pacific Grove motel, where every door is decorated with a large wooden butterfly. One is a park right on the highway in Pismo Beach, complete with a kiosk with butterfly brochures and a ranger who gives butterfly talks. One is the yard of a white hacienda in Hope Ranch, where the monarch-appreciating owner beams as if from a visitation of orange angels. One is a wild, windswept outcropping at Morro Bay, where no butterfly ought to be able to survive. One is tucked behind a Zen-inspired bridge near a small waterfall on the manicured estate of the Esalen Institute, where people go to find self-awareness, and though the catalog promises such activities as the gestalt of singing, there is apparently no butterfly communing, no mapping of the monarchs' auras.

5   One site is in the Natural Bridges park at Santa Cruz, where butterfly rangers man a redwood viewing platform. Each October there is a festival in town, featuring a balloon-and-cake party and a concert from the 5 M Band (Mostly Mediocre Musical Monarch Mariposas). The mayor gives a speech, local poets read, and a person dubbed Monarch Man, dressed in orange and black with dangling antennae, flies down a wire from a tree into the waiting crowd. He bursts through a paper banner and hands out black and orange taffy. On the day the monarchs arrive, the rangers hoist a monarch flag on their monarch pole and fly it for six months until the last monarch leaves. In a typical season 60,000 visitors come to the Natural Bridges site. One day last December, though it was raining heavily, about 40,000 butterflies hung in clusters from the trees and visitors kept arriving, their eyes full of amazement.

Pacific Grove, with two roosts, challenges Santa Cruz up the coast by billing itself Butterfly Town, U.S.A. Many of its businesses are named monarch this and that, and there is a parade each year with schoolchildren dressed in butterfly costumes. The town is serious about its winged visitors, which have brought in many binocular-slung tourists. There is a $500 fine for "molesting a butterfly in any way," and there are signs cautioning people to whisper around the butterflies, not to spook or yell at them. This even though butterflies don't hear sound the way vertebrates do. There are healthy roosts under the final approach path to Santa Barbara Airport, beside a clanking highway and in the concussive racket of Big Sur's waves.

Many other coastal sites have vanished under condominiums, business parks, avocado ranches, horse farms, golf courses, trailer parks. Unlike Mexico, the United States has no laws yet to protect its migrating insects. In the last three years, seven butterfly groves have been cut down, four around Santa Barbara. Butterfly Lane in town, next to Butterfly Beach, once boasted the most famous site in America, but now there are beautiful homes instead, with small lawns, and *"wing"* means only an additional set of rooms.

To the butterflies' defense comes the privately funded Monarch Project. Its several scores of volunteers spend the winter visiting the roosts. They tag thousands of butterflies to track how fast and how far they fly (some travel up to 80 miles a day), where they gather to roost, how their populations may be changing. Last November the project held a tag-off and set a world record, marking 5,874 butterflies in one day. (That is, they claimed it as a record—the people at the *Guinness Book* haven't decided whether it's worthy of listing.) A 10 percent return on the tagged insects is good; people find them in their backyards and fields. The tiny white message on the butterflies' wings gives the address of the Natural History Museum in Los Angeles, which is the roost of Chris Nagano, the project's chief entomologist.

Chris is a slender, mustachioed young scientist with a lively sense of wonder. He takes me to the Ellwood site in Santa Barbara, where monarchs have been monitored for the past 30 years. A cloud of butterflies drifts low through a wash and up a bank, which is littered with eucalyptus bark like rolls of papyrus. There are few crawling insects; the eucalyptus oil keeps them away. The pungent smell fills me with memories of mentholated rub and childhood colds. A Pacific tree frog begins a long croak that sounds like someone working the tumblers of a safe. There is an artillery of falling eucalyptus seeds; the hard, sharp nose cones hit the soft dirt with a relentless plopping. Timbers are creaking constantly, like the opening and shutting of a door.

We must tag at least 200 butterflies at each site for it to be statistically useful. Chris takes a pole that extends like a telescope, with a long net at one end, and pushes it high into one of the trees. He scoops up about 75 butterflies. Fluttering madly in the mesh, their wings sound like drizzle falling on dry leaves. Chris lays his green army jacket gently over them, "so they don't get agitated," he says. We sit down in the sunlight, in what might be an Indonesian forest, and begin lifting the butterflies out of the net one by squirming one.

There is an art to tagging a butterfly. First you hold its soft, slender body in your left hand, securely, although you can feel it gently quivering. With your right hand, you separate the front and back wings as if you were sliding one playing card behind the other. Then you rub off a small oval of colored scales with your thumb and forefinger, until the clear cellophane of the wing appears. Children often are taught the old wives' tale that if you touch a butterfly's wing, you'll wipe off its "flying dust" and ground it permanently. But the microscopic scales are dead, like fingernails or hair. Tagging doesn't hurt the monarchs, nor does

10

handling. Onto the clear window in the wing you press one half of the sticky stamplike tag, then fold the other half over the top of the wing and press it firmly. Next, with both hands, open the wings of the butterfly to see if it's a male or female. Males have two black dots low on their wings and black scent pouches (the scent is probably to alert other males rather than to attract females). The females have no pouches but thicker black veins for conducting heat to the body. On a prenumbered sheet record whether you have a male or female and its condition. A one is perfect, a three is battered and worn. The flawless specimen will have a radiant blue sheen, heart-stoppingly vibrant; the velvety wings will be of deep orange and buff on which loud islands of color float, some blurred, some clear-edged; a white-spotted frill will hem the bottom of each wing; and the body will be covered in a thick, minky brown fur.

If it's a female monarch, check to see if it's pregnant by lifting up its soft abdomen and feeling it between thumb and forefinger. The deposit of sperm a male leaves inside a female is thick with protein and vitamins, and it feels like a ball bearing. I jot down "F2V," which means I've just tagged a female virgin in average condition; other numbers indicate the capture site.

It can get chilly in southern California in the winter, and monarchs can't fly much if it's below 55°F. They would rather cluster to stay warm than shiver the way animals do, but they will shiver if they have to. One stands quaking on a log. Chris lifts it up, places it like a fluttering gold cookie in his open mouth and breathes warm air over its muscles. Its four tiny black feet flex, and when he tosses it into the air it flies at once back to its cluster high in the tree. As it approaches, all the other butterflies flap their wings to warn it not to land on them. It hovers, finds a free spot lower down and clings with its sticky feet. The feet are double-pronged like a longshoreman's grapple. Lift one foot free and the other three will snag tight.

Over the hill appears a class of teenagers from Bishop, about six hours' drive inland. They are on a biology field trip to see the creatures of tide pools and the monarch butterflies. Chris adlibs a lecture on the insects' life cycle, noting that the black-and-white-striped caterpillars feed only on milkweed, which contains a digitalislike poison that was favored by assassins in ancient Rome. In turn the butterflies' bodies will contain enough poison to sicken a hungry bird. He shows them a monarch with a beak-shaped bit of wing missing; the butterfly could still fly, and the bird would have learned not to attack others of that color and pattern. Indeed, viceroys are mock-monarch butterflies that are not poisonous to birds at all, though they mimic the others' color as a defensive sleight of hand. It is opportunistic chemistry on the butterfly's part to use the poison of the milkweed to defend itself. A couple of the boys pass a football back and forth, but most of the students are rapt. Chris urges them to try their hands at tagging.

"Sometimes it takes a long time to go through a whole class and give everyone a turn," he explains after the students have left for the beach, "but one day when an environmental issue comes up, they'll remember. It's hard to learn about animals if you only see them dead on dissecting trays."

Classes seem to be attracted to Chris when he is tagging. When we get to Pismo Beach, just up the coast, a park ranger comes by with preschoolers on a butterfly tour. It is a brilliantly sunny day, and the butterflies are busy running all of their errands. Some arch their wings wide, like solar collectors, and sit directly in the sun. Some cluster upside down high in the trees. Some sip dew from the grass. (They must be alert to the yellow jackets patrolling under the trees for injured monarchs to kill and eat.) Some feed on nectar among the wildflowers. Some mate. Monarchs don't go in much for courtship. The male yanks the female right out of the air, hurls her to the ground and attaches himself. Then he flies off with her still hooked and dangling below, her wings folded closed, as if she were a tan purse he was carrying or a dropped hankie that must be returned.

Seated on the fragrant floor of the eucalyptus grove, where the ground is covered with the South African ice plant (one of the few that can tolerate the drops of heavy oils), we settle down to serious tagging. I deliver the kiss of life to each butterfly to warm its muscles before flinging it back up at the sky like a piece of confetti. Some insects have faces smeared with white or yellow grains of pollen—they all differ slightly in shape, coloring and (to me) personality. These overwhelming monarchs live six to nine months, considerably longer than the hasty generations they will beget throughout the West this summer. After tagging the first hundred, my fingertips are coated yellow from the scales.

It's easy to be mesmerized watching them glide overhead, with the sun shining through their wings, as if they were small rooms in which a light had been turned on. A cluster trembles on a branch, then in a silent explosion they burst into the air and fly down to a Christmas pine in the full sun near the road. They sit on the very tips of the branches like orange and gold ornaments and spread their wings wide. They are silent, they are beautiful, they are fragile, they are harmless, they are clean, they are determined, they are graceful, they stalk nothing, they are ingenious chemists, they are the symbols of innocence in the world of cartoons, they are the first butterfly we learn to call by name. Like the imagination, they dart from one brightly lit spot to another. To the Mexicans, who call them *Las Palomas,* they are the souls of children who died during the past year, fluttering on their way to heaven.

Konrad Z. Lorenz

THE TAMING OF THE SHREW

Though Nature, red in tooth and claw,
With ravine, shrieked against his creed.

TENNYSON, *In Memoriam*

All shrews are particularly difficult to keep; this is not because, as we are led proverbially to believe, they are hard to tame, but because the metabolism of these smallest of mammals is so very fast that they will die of hunger within two or three hours if the food supply fails. Since they feed exclusively on small, living animals, mostly insects, and demand, of these, considerably more than their own weight every day, they are most exacting charges. At the time of which I am writing, I had never succeeded in keeping any of the terrestrial shrews alive for any length of time; most of those that I happened to obtain had probably only been caught because they were already ill and they died almost at once. I had never succeeded in procuring a healthy specimen. Now the order Insectivora is very low in the genealogical hierarchy of mammals and is, therefore, of particular interest to the comparative ethologist. Of the whole group, there was only one representative with whose behavior I was tolerably familiar, namely the hedgehog, an extremely interesting animal of whose ethology Professor Herter of Berlin has made a very thorough study. Of the behavior of all other members of the family practically nothing is known. Since they are nocturnal and partly subterranean animals, it is nearly impossible to approach them in field observation, and the difficulty of keeping them in captivity had hitherto precluded their study in the laboratory. So the Insectivores were officially placed on my program.

First I tried to keep the common mole. It was easy to procure a healthy specimen, caught to order in the nursery gardens of my father-in-law, and I found no difficulty in keeping it alive. Immediately on its arrival, it devoured an almost incredible quantity of earthworms which, from the very first moment, it took from my hand. But, as an object of behavior study, it proved most disappointing. Certainly, it was interesting to watch its method of disappearing in the space of a few seconds under the surface of the ground, to study its astoundingly efficient use of its strong, spadeshaped fore-paws, and to feel their amazing strength when one held the little beast in one's hand. And again, it was remarkable with what surprising exactitude it located, by smell, from under-

From *King Solomon's Ring* (1952), translated by Marjorie Kerr Wilson.

ground, the earthworms which I put on the surface of the soil in its terrarium. But these observations were the only benefits I derived from it. It never became any tamer and it never remained above ground any longer than it took to devour its prey; after this, it sank into the earth as a submarine sinks into the water. I soon grew tired of procuring the immense quantities of living food it required and, after a few weeks, I set it free in the garden.

It was years afterwards, on an excursion to that extraordinary lake, the Neusiedlersee, which lies on the Hungarian border of Austria, that I again thought of keeping an insectivore. This large stretch of water, though not thirty miles from Vienna, is an example of the peculiar type of lake found in the open steppes of Eastern Europe and Asia. More than thirty miles long and half as broad, its deepest parts are only about five feet deep and it is much shallower on the average. Nearly half its surface is overgrown with reeds which form an ideal habitat for all kinds of water birds. Great colonies of white, purple, and grey heron and spoonbills live among the reeds and, until a short while ago, glossy ibis were still to be found here. Greylag geese breed here in great numbers and, on the eastern, reedless shore, avocets and many other rare waders can regularly be found. On the occasion of which I am speaking, we, a dozen tired zoologists, under the experienced guidance of my friend Otto Koenig, were wending our way, slowly and painfully, through the forest of reeds. We were walking in single file, Koenig first, I second, with a few students in our wake. We literally left a wake, an inky-black one in pale grey water. In the reed forests of Lake Neusiedel, you walk knee deep in slimy, black ooze, wonderfully perfumed by sulphureted-hydrogen-producing bacteria. This mud clings tenaciously and only releases its hold on your foot with a loud, protesting plop at every step.

After a few hours of this kind of wading you discover aching muscles whose very existence you had never suspected. From the knees to the hips you are immersed in the milky, clay-colored water characteristic of the lake, which, among the reeds, is populated by myriads of extremely hungry leeches conforming to the old pharmaceutical recipe, *"Hirudines medicinales maxime affamati."* [1] The rest of your person inhabits the upper air, which here consists of clouds of tiny mosquitoes whose blood-thirsty attacks are all the more exasperating because you require both your hands to part the dense reeds in front of you and can only slap your face at intervals. The British ornithologist who may perhaps have envied us some of our rare specimens will perceive that bird watching on Lake Neusiedel is not, after all, an entirely enviable occupation.

We were thus wending our painful way through the rushes when

5

---

1. "In medicine, the hungriest leech is best." Until modern times, patients were bled as a remedy for various ills, and doctors kept live leeches for the purpose.

suddenly Koenig stopped and pointed mutely towards a pond, free from reeds, that stretched in front of us. At first, I could only see whitish water, dark blue sky and green reeds, the standard colors of Lake Neusiedel. Then, suddenly, like a cork popping up on to the surface, there appeared, in the middle of the pool, a tiny black animal, hardly bigger than a man's thumb. And for a moment I was in the rare position of a zoologist who sees a specimen and is not able to classify it, in the literal sense of the word: I did not know to which class of vertebrates the object of my gaze belonged. For the first fraction of a second I took it for the young of some diving bird of a species unknown to me. It appeared to have a beak and it swam on the water like a bird, not in it as a mammal. It swam about in narrow curves and circles, very much like a whirligig beetle, creating an extensive wedge-shaped wake, quite out of proportion to the tiny animal's size. Then a second little beast popped up from below, chased the first one with a shrill, bat-like twitter, then both dived and were gone. The whole episode had not lasted five seconds.

I stood open-mouthed, my mind racing. Koenig turned round with a broad grin, calmly detached a leech that was sticking like a leech to his wrist, wiped away the trickle of blood from the wound, slapped his cheek, thereby killing thirty-five mosquitoes, and asked, in the tone of an examiner, "What was that?" I answered as calmly as I could, "water shrews," thanking, in my heart, the leech and the mosquitoes for the respite they had given me to collect my thoughts. But my mind was racing on: water shrews ate fishes and frogs which were easy to procure in any quantity; water shrews were less subterranean than most other insectivores; they were the very insectivore to keep in captivity. "That's an animal I must catch and keep," I said to my friend. "That is easy," he responded. "There is a nest with young under the floor mat of my tent." I had slept that night in his tent and Koenig had not thought it worth-while to tell me of the shrews; such things are, to him, as much a matter of course as wild little spotted crakes feeding out of his hand, or as any other wonders of his queer kingdom in the reeds.

On our return to the tent that evening, he showed me the nest. It contained eight young which, compared with their mother, who rushed away as we lifted the mat, were of enormous size. They were considerably more than half her length and must each have weighed well between a fourth and a third of their dam: that is to say, the whole litter weighed, at a very modest estimate, twice as much as the old shrew. Yet they were still quite blind and the tips of their teeth were only just visible in their rosy mouths. And two days later when I took them under my care, they were still quite unable to eat even the soft abdomens of grasshoppers, and in spite of evident greed, they chewed interminably on a soft piece of frog's meat without succeeding in detaching a morsel from it. On our journey home, I fed them on the squeezed-out insides of grasshoppers and finely minced frog's meat, a diet on which they obviously throve. Arrived home in Altenberg, I improved on this diet by preparing a food from the squeezed-out insides of mealworm larvae, with some finely chopped small, fresh fishes, worked into a sort of gravy with a little milk. They consumed large quantities of this food, and their little nest-box looked quite small in comparison with the big china bowl whose contents they emptied three times a day. All these observations raise the problem of how the female water shrew succeeds in feeding her gigantic litter. It is absolutely impossible that she should do so on milk alone. Even on a more concentrated diet my young shrews devoured the equivalent of their own weight daily and this meant nearly twice the weight of a grown shrew. Yet, at that time of their lives, young shrews could not possibly engulf a frog or a fish brought whole to them by their mother, as my charges indisputably proved. I can only think that the mother feeds her young by regurgitation of chewed food. Even thus, it is little short of miraculous that the adult female should be able to obtain enough meat to sustain herself and her voracious progeny.

When I brought them home, my young watershrews were still blind. They had not suffered from the journey and were as sleek and fat as one could wish. Their black, glossy coats were reminiscent of moles, but the white color of their underside, as well as the round, streamlined contours of their bodies, reminded me distinctly of penguins, and not, indeed, without justification: both the streamlined form and the light underside are adaptations to a life in the water. Many free-swimming animals, mammals, birds, amphibians and fishes, are silvery-white below in order to be invisible to enemies swimming in the depths. Seen from below, the shining white belly blends perfectly with the reflecting surface film of the water. It is very characteristic of these water animals that the dark dorsal and the white ventral colors do not merge gradually into each other as is the case in "counter-shaded" land animals whose coloring is calculated to make them invisible by eliminating the contrasting shade on their undersides. As in the killer whale, in dolphins, and in penguins, the white underside of the watershrew is divided from the dark upper side by a sharp line which runs, often in very decorative curves, along the animal's flank. Curiously enough, this borderline between black and white showed considerable variations in individuals and even on both sides of one animal's body. I welcomed this, since it enabled me to recognize my shrews personally.

Three days after their arrival in Altenberg my eight shrew babies opened their eyes and began, very cautiously, to explore the precincts of their nest-box. It was now time to remove them to an appropriate container, and on this question I expended much hard thinking. The enormous quantity of food they consumed and, consequently, of excrement they produced, made it impossible to keep them in an ordinary aquarium whose water, within a day, would have become a stinking brew. Adequate sanitation was imperative for particular reasons; in ducks, grebes, and all waterfowl, the plumage must be kept perfectly dry if the animal is to remain in a state of health, and the same premise may reasonably be expected to hold good of the shrew's fur. Now water which has been polluted soon turns strongly alkaline and this I knew to be very bad for the plumage of waterbirds. It causes saponification of the fat to which the feathers owe their waterproof quality, and the bird becomes thoroughly wet and is unable to stay on the water. I hold the record, as far as I know hitherto unbroken by any other birdlover, for having kept dabchicks alive and healthy in captivity for nearly two years, and even then they did not die but escaped, and may still be living. My experience with these birds proved the absolute necessity of keeping the water perfectly clean: whenever it became a little dirty I noticed their feathers beginning to get wet, a danger which they anxiously tried to counteract by constantly preening themselves. I had, therefore, to keep these little grebes in crystal clear water which was changed every day, and I rightly assumed that the same would be necessary for my water shrews.

10   I took a large aquarium tank, rather over a yard in length and about two feet wide. At each end of this, I placed two little tables, and weighed them down with heavy stones so that they would not float. Then I filled up the tank until the water was level with the tops of the tables. I did not at first push the tables close against the panes of the tank, which was rather narrow, for fear that the shrews might become trapped underwater in the blind alley beneath a table and drown there; this precaution, however, subsequently proved unnecessary. The water shrew which, in its natural state, swims great distances under the ice, is quite able to find its way to the open surface in much more difficult situations. The nest-box, which was placed on one of the tables, was equipped with a sliding shutter, so that I could imprison the shrews whenever the container had to be cleaned. In the morning, at the hour of general cage-cleaning, the shrews were usually at home and asleep, so that the procedure caused them no appreciable disturbance. I will admit that I take great pride in devising, by creative imagination, suitable containers for animals of which nobody, myself included, has had any previous experience, and it was particularly gratifying that the contraption described above proved so satisfactory that I never had to alter even the minutest detail.

When first my baby shrews were liberated in this container they took a very long time to explore the top of the table on which their nest-box was standing. The water's edge seemed to exert a strong attraction; they approached it ever and again, smelled the surface and seemed to feel along it with the long, fine whiskers which surround their pointed snouts like a halo and represent not only their most important organ of touch but the most important of all their sensory organs. Like other aquatic mammals, the water shrew differs from the terrestrial members of its class in that its nose, the guiding organ of the average mammal, is of no use whatsoever in its underwater hunting. The water shrew's whiskers are actively mobile like the antennae of an insect or the fingers of a blind man.

Exactly as mice and many other small rodents would do under similar conditions, the shrews interrupted their careful exploration of their new surroundings every few minutes to dash wildly back into the safe cover of their nest-box. The survival value of this peculiar behavior is evident: the animal makes sure, from time to time that it has not lost its way and that it can, at a moment's notice, retreat to the one place it knows to be safe. It was a queer spectacle to see those podgy black figures slowly and carefully whiskering their way forward and, in the next second, with lightning speed, dash back to the nest-box. Queerly enough, they did not run straight through the little door, as one would have expected, but in their wild dash for safety they jumped, one and all, first onto the roof of the box and only then, whiskering along its edge, found the opening and slipped in with a half somersault, their back turned nearly vertically downward. After many repetitions of this maneuver, they were able to find the opening without feeling for it; they "knew" perfectly its where-abouts yet still persisted in the leap onto the roof. They jumped onto it and immediately vaulted in through the door, but they never, as long as they lived, found out that the leap and vault which had become their habit was really quite unnecessary and that they could have run in directly without this extraordinary detour. We shall hear more about this dominance of path habits in the water shrew presently.

It was only on the third day, when the shrews had become thoroughly acquainted with the geography of their little rectangular island, that the largest and most enterprising of them ventured into the water. As is so often the case with mammals, birds, reptiles, and fishes, it was the largest and most handsomely colored male which played the role of leader. First he sat on the edge of the water and thrust in the fore part of his body, at the same time frantically paddling with his forelegs but still clinging with his hind ones to the board. Then he slid in, but in the next moment took fright, scampered madly across the surface very much after the manner of a frightened duckling, and jumped out onto the board at the opposite end of the tank. There he sat, excitedly grooming his belly with one hind paw, exactly as coypus and beavers do. Soon he quieted down and sat still for a moment. Then he went to the water's edge a second time, hesitated for a moment, and plunged in; diving immediately, he swam ecstatically about underwater, swerving upward and downward again, running quickly along the bottom, and finally jumping out of the water at the same place as he had first entered it.

When I first saw a water shrew swimming I was most struck by a thing which I ought to have expected but did not: at the moment of diving, the little black and white beast appears to be made of silver. Like the plumage of ducks and grebes, but quite unlike the fur of most water mammals, such as seals, otters, beavers or coypus, the fur of the water shrew remains absolutely dry under water, that is to say, it retains a thick layer of air while the animal is below the surface. In the other mammals mentioned above, it is only the short, woolly undercoat that remains dry, the superficial hair tips becoming wet, wherefore the animal looks its natural color when underwater and is superficially wet when it emerges. I was already aware of the peculiar qualities of the waterpfoof fur of the shrew, and, had I given it a thought, I should have known that it would look, under water, exactly like the air-retaining fur on the underside of a water beetle or on the abdomen of a water spider. Nevertheless the wonderful, transparent silver coat of the shrew was, to me, one of those delicious surprises that nature has in store for her admirers.

15   Another surprising detail which I only noticed when I saw my shrews in the water was that they have a fringe of stiff, erectile hairs on the outer side of their fifth toes and on the underside of their tails. These form collapsible oars and a collapsible rudder. Folded and inconspicuous as long as the animal is on dry land, they unfold the moment it enters the water and broaden the effective surface of the propelling feet and of the steering tail by a considerable area.

Like penguins, the water shrews looked rather awkward and ungainly on dry land but were transformed into objects of elegance and grace on entering the water. As long as they walked, their strongly convex underside made them look pot-bellied and reminiscent of an old, overfed dachshund. But under water, the very same protruding belly balanced harmoniously the curve of their back and gave a beautifully symmetrical streamline which, together with their silver coating and the elegance of their movements, made them a sight of entrancing beauty.

When they had all become familiar with the water, their container was one of the chief attractions that our research station had to offer to any visiting naturalists or animal lovers. Unlike all other mammals of their size, the water shrews were largely diurnal and, except in the early hours of the morning, three or four of them were constantly on the scene. It was exceedingly interesting to watch their movements upon and under the water. Like the whirligig beetle, Gyrinus, they could turn in an extremely small radius without diminishing their speed, a faculty for which the large rudder surface of the tail with its fringe of erectile hairs is evidently essential. They had two different ways of diving, either by taking a little jump as grebes or coots do and working their way down at a steep angle, or by simply lowering their snout under the surface and paddling very fast till they reached "planing speed," thus working their way downward on the principle of the inclined plane—in other words, performing the converse movement of an ascending airplane. The water shrew must expend a large amount of energy in staying down since the air contained in its fur exerts a strong pull upwards. Unless it is paddling straight downwards, a thing it rarely does, it is forced to maintain a constant minimum speed, keeping its body at a slightly downward angle in order not to float to the surface. While swimming under water the shrew seems to flatten, broadening its body in a peculiar fashion, in order to present a better planing surface to the water. I never saw my shrews try to cling by their claws to any underwater objects, as the dipper is alleged to do. When they seemed to be running along the bottom, they were really swimming close above it, but perhaps the smooth gravel on the bottom of the tank was unsuitable for holding on to and it did not occur to me then to offer them a rougher surface. They were very playful when in the water and chased one another loudly twittering on the surface, or silently in the depths. Unlike any other mammal, but just like water birds, they could rest on the surface; this they used to do, rolling partly over and grooming themselves. Once out again, they instantly proceeded to clean their fur—one is almost tempted to say "preen" it, so similar was their behavior to that of ducks which have just left the water after a long swim.

Most interesting of all was their method of hunting under water. They came swimming along with an erratic course, darting a foot or so forward very swiftly in a straight line, then starting to gyrate in looped turns at reduced speed. While swimming straight and swiftly their whiskers were, as far as I could see, laid flat against their head, but while circling they were erect and bristled out in all directions, as they sought contact with some prey. I have no reason to believe that vision plays any part in the water shrew's hunting, except perhaps in the activation of its tactile search. My shrews may have noticed visually the presence of the live tadpoles or little fishes which I put in the tank, but in the actual hunting of its prey the animal is exclusively guided by its sense of touch, located in the wide-spreading whiskers on its snout. Certain small free-swimming species of catfish find their prey by exactly the same method. When these fishes swim fast and straight, the long feelers on their snout are depressed but, like the shrew's whiskers, are stiffly spread out when the fish becomes conscious of the proximity of potential prey; like the shrew, the fish then begins to gyrate blindly in order to establish contact with its prey. It may not even be necessary for the water shrew actually to touch its prey with one of its whiskers. Perhaps, at very close range, the water vibration caused by the movements of a small fish, a tadpole or a water insect is perceptible by those sensitive tactile organs. It is quite impossible to determine this question by mere observation, for the action is much too quick for the human eye. There is a quick turn and a snap and the shrew is already paddling shorewards with a wriggling creature in its maw.

In relation to its size, the water shrew is perhaps the most terrible predator of all vertebrate animals, and it can even vie with the invertebrates, including the murderous Dytiscus larva. It has been reported by A. E. Brehm that water shrews have killed fish more than sixty times heavier than themselves by biting out their eyes and brain. This happened only when the fish were confined in containers with no room for escape. The same story has been told to me by fishermen on Lake Neusiedel, who could not possibly have heard Brehm's report. I once offered to my shrews a large edible frog. I never did it again, nor could I bear to see out to its end the cruel scene that ensued. One of the shrews encountered the frog in the basin and instantly gave chase, repeatedly seizing hold of the creature's legs; although it was kicked off again it did not cease in its attack and finally, the frog, in desperation, jumped out of the water and onto one of the tables, where several shrews raced to the pursuer's assistance and buried their teeth in the legs and hindquarters of the wretched frog. And now, horribly, they began to eat the frog alive, beginning just where each one of them happened to have hold of it; the poor frog croaked heartrendingly, as the jaws of the shrews munched audibly in chorus. I need hardly be blamed for bringing this experiment to an abrupt and agitated end and putting the lacerated frog out of its misery. I never offered the shrews large prey again but only such as would be killed at the first bite or two. Nature can be very cruel indeed; it is not out of pity that most of the larger predatory animals kill their prey quickly. The lion has to finish off a big antelope or a buffalo very quickly indeed in order not to get hurt itself, for a beast of prey which has to hunt daily cannot afford to receive even a harmless scratch in effecting a kill; such scratches would soon add up to such an extent as to put the killer out of action. The same reason has forced the python and other large snakes to evolve a quick and really humane method of killing the well-armed mammals that are their natural prey. But where there is no danger of the victim doing damage to the killer, the latter shows no pity whatsoever. The hedgehog which, by virtue of its armor, is quite immune to the bite of a snake, regularly proceeds to eat it, beginning at the tail or in the middle of its body, and in the same way the water shrew treats its innocuous prey. But man should abstain from judging his innocently-cruel fellow creatures, for even if nature sometimes "shrieks against his creed," what pain does he himself not inflict upon the living creatures that he hunts for pleasure and not for food?

20   The mental qualities of the water shrew cannot be rated very high. They were quite tame and fearless of me and never tried to bite when I took them in my hand, nor did they ever try to evade it, but, like little

tame rodents, they tried to dig their way out if I held them for too long in the hollow of my closed fist. Even when I took them out of their container and put them on a table or on the floor, they were by no means thrown into a panic but were quite ready to take food out of my hand and even tried actively to creep into it if they felt a longing for cover. When, in such an unwonted environment, they were shown their nest-box, they plainly showed that they knew it by sight and instantly made for it, and even pursued it with upraised heads if I moved the box along above them, just out of their reach. All in all, I really may pride myself that I have tamed the shrew, or at least one member of that family.

In their accustomed surroundings, my shrews proved to be very strict creatures of habit. I have already mentioned the remarkable conservatism with which they persevered in their unpractical way of entering their nest-box by climbing onto its roof and then vaulting, with a half turn, in through the door. Something more must be said about the unchanging tenacity with which these animals cling to their habits once they have formed them. In the water shrew, the path habits, in particular, are of a really amazing immutability; I hardly know another instance to which the saying, "As the twig is bent, so the tree is inclined," applies so literally.

In a territory unknown to it, the water shrew will never run fast except under pressure of extreme fear, and than it will run blindly along, bumping into objects and usually getting caught in a blind alley. But, unless the little animal is severely frightened, it moves in strange surroundings, only step by step, whiskering right and left all the time and following a path that is anything but straight. Its course is determined by a hundred fortuitous factors when it walks that way for the first time. But, after a few repetitions, it is evident that the shrew recognizes the locality in which it finds itself and that it repeats, with the utmost exactitude, the movements which it performed the previous time. At the same time, it is noticeable that the animal moves along much faster whenever it is repeating what it has already learned. When placed on a path which it has already traversed a few times, the shrew starts on its way slowly, carefully whiskering. Suddenly it finds known bearings, and now rushes forward a short distance, repeating exactly every step and turn which it executed on the last occasion. Then, when it comes to a spot where it ceases to know the way by heart, it is reduced to whiskering again and to feeling its way step by step. Soon, another burst of speed follows and the same thing is repeated, bursts of speed alternating with very show progress. In the beginning of this process of learning their way, the shrews move along at an extremely slow average rate and the little bursts of speed are few and far between. But gradually the little laps of the course which have been "learned by heart" and which can be covered quickly begin to increase in length as well as in number until they fuse and the whole course can be completed in a fast, unbroken rush.

Often, when such a path habit is almost completely formed, there still remains one particularly difficult place where the shrew always loses its bearings and has to resort to its senses of smell and touch, sniffing and whiskering vigorously to find out where the next reach of its path "joins on." Once the shrew is well settled in its path habits it is as strictly bound to them as a railway engine to its tracks and as unable to deviate from them by even a few centimeters. If it diverges from its path by so much as an inch, it is forced to stop abruptly, and laboriously regain its bearings. The same behavior can be caused experimentally by changing some small detail in the customary path of the animal. Any major alteration in the habitual path threw the shrews into complete confusion. One of their paths ran along the wall adjoining the wooden table opposite to that on which the nest box was situated. This table was weighted with two stones lying close to the panes of the tank, and the shrews, running along the wall, were accustomed to jump on and off the stones which lay right in their path. If I moved the stones out of the runway, placing both together in the middle of the table, the shrews would jump right up into the air in the place where the stone should have been; they came down with a jarring bump, were obviously disconcerted and started whiskering cautiously right and left, just as they behaved in an unknown environment. And then they did a most interesting thing: they went back the way they had come, carefully feeling their way until they had again got their bearings. Then, facing round again, they tried a second time with a rush and jumped and crashed down exactly as they had done a few seconds before. Only then did they seem to realize that the first fall had not been their own fault but was due to a change in the wonted pathway, and now they proceeded to explore the alteration, cautiously sniffing and bewhiskering the place where the stone ought to have been. This method of going back to the start, and trying again always reminded me of a small boy who, in reciting a poem, gets stuck and begins again at an earlier verse.

In rats, as in many small mammals, the process of forming a path habit, for instance in learning a maze, is very similar to that just described; but a rat is far more adaptable in its behavior and would not dream of trying to jump over a stone which was not there. The preponderance of motor habit over present perception is a most remarkable peculiarity of the water shrew. One might say that the animal actually disbelieves its senses if they report a change of environment which necessitates a sudden alteration in its motor habits. In a new environment a water shrew would be perfectly able to see a stone of that size and consequently to avoid it or to run over it in a manner well adapted to the spatial conditions; but once a habit is formed and has become ingrained, it supersedes all better knowledge. I know of no animal that is a slave to its habits in so literal a sense as the water shrew. For this animal the geometric axiom that a straight line is the shortest distance between two points simply does not hold good. To them, the shortest line is always the accustomed path and, to a certain extent, they are justified in adhering to this principle: they run with amazing speed along their pathways and arrive at their destination much sooner than they would if, by whiskering and nosing, they tried to go straight. They will keep to the wonted path, even though it winds in such a way that it crosses and recrosses itself. A rat or mouse would be quick to discover that it was making an unnecessary detour, but the water shrew is no more able to do so than is a toy train to turn off at right angles at a level crossing. In order to change its route, the water shrew must change its whole path habit, and this cannot be done at a moment's notice but gradually, over a long period of time. An unnecessary, loop-shaped detour takes weeks and weeks to become a little shorter, and after months it is not even approximately straight. The biological advantage of such a path habit is obvious: it compensates the shrew for being nearly blind and enables it to run exceedingly fast without wasting a minute on orientation. On the other hand it may, under unusual circumstances, lead the shrew to destruction. It has been reported, quite plausibly, that water shrews have broken their necks by jumping into a pond which had been recently drained. In spite of the possibility of such mishaps, it would be shortsighted if one were simply to stigmatize the water shrew as stupid because it solves the spatial problems of its daily life in quite a different way from man. On the contrary, if one thinks a little more deeply, it is very wonderful that the same result, namely a perfect orientation in space, can be brought about in two so widely divergent ways: by true observation, as we achieve it, or, as the water shrew does, by learning by heart every possible spatial contingency that may arise in a given territory.

Among themselves, my water shrews were surprisingly good-natured. Although, in their play, they would often chase each other, twittering with a great show of excitement, I never saw a serious fight between them until an unfortunate accident occurred: one morning, I forgot to reopen the little door of the nest-box after cleaning out their tank. When at last I remembered, three hours had elapsed—a very long time for the swift metabolism of such small insectivores. Upon the opening of the door, all the shrews rushed out and made a dash for the food tray. In their haste to get out, not only did they soil themselves all over but they apparently discharged, in their excitement, some sort of glandular secretion, for a strong, musk-like odor accompanied their exit from the box. Since they appeared to have incurred no damage by their three hours' fasting, I turned away from the box to occupy myself with other things. However, on nearing the container soon afterwards, I heard an unusually loud, sharp twittering and, on my hurried approach, found my eight shrews locked in deadly battle. Two were even then dying and, though I consigned them at once to separate cages, two more died in the course of the day. The real cause of this sudden and terrible battle is hard to ascertain but I cannot help suspecting that the shrews, owing to the sudden change in the usual odor, had failed to recognize each other and had fallen upon each other as they would have done upon strangers. The four survivors quieted down after a certain time and I was able to reunite them in the original container without fear of further mishap.

I kept those four remaining shrews in good health for nearly seven months and would probably have had them much longer if the assistant whom I had engaged to feed them had not forgotten to do so. I had been obliged to go to Vienna and, on my return in the late afternoon, was met by that usually reliable fellow who turned pale when he saw me, thereupon remembering that he had forgotten to feed the shrews. All four of them were alive but very weak; they ate greedily when we fed them but died nonetheless within a few hours. In other words, they showed exactly the same symptoms as the shrews which I had formerly tried to keep; this confirmed my opinion that the latter were already dying of hunger when they came into my possession.

To any advanced animal keeper who is able to set up a large tank, preferably with running water, and who can obtain a sufficient supply of small fish, tadpoles, and the like, I can recommend the water shrew as one of the most gratifying, charming, and interesting objects of care. Of course it is a somewhat exacting charge. It will eat raw chopped heart (the customary substitute for small live prey) only in the absence of something better and it cannot be fed exclusively on this diet for long periods. Moreover, really clean water is indispensable. But if these clear-cut requirements be fulfilled, the water shrew will not merely remain alive but will really thrive, nor do I exclude the possibility that it might even breed in captivity.

THE READER

1. *What features of the shrew's behavior does Lorenz select for special emphasis? What conclusions does he draw about these features?*
2. *Lorenz employs a narrative framework in which to describe the shrews. Make a list of narrative events and a list of major characteristics of the shrew. Do you as a reader react differently to the facts about shrew behavior because they are embedded in narrative?*

THE WRITER

1. *Lorenz discusses a field trip and some other matters before he reports his laboratory observations. What is the effect of this organization?*
2. *Though this is mainly a report of his observations, Lorenz includes matters that are not necessary to the report of strictly controlled observation of the shrew's habits. Indicate some of the places where his discussion moves beyond strict reporting. Characterize the roles he assumes in these passages. Do these other roles or revelations of personality compromise or support his claim to being a scientist?*
3. *Write an account of the characteristics of some animal, either domesticated or wild, embedding them in a brief narrative.*

Alexander Petrunkevitch

THE SPIDER AND THE WASP

In the feeding and safeguarding of their progeny insects and spiders exhibit some interesting analogies to reasoning and some crass examples of blind instinct. The case I propose to describe here is that of the tarantula spiders and their archenemy, the digger wasps of the genus Pepsis. It is a classic example of what looks like intelligence pitted against instinct—a strange situation in which the victim, though fully able to defend itself, submits unwittingly to its destruction.

Most tarantulas live in the tropics, but several species occur in the temperate zone and a few are common in the southern U.S. Some varieties are large and have powerful fangs with which they can inflict a deep wound. These formidable looking spiders do not, however, attack man; you can hold one in your hand, if you are gentle, without being bitten. Their bite is dangerous only to insects and small mammals such as mice; for man it is no worse than a hornet's sting.

Tarantulas customarily live in deep cylindrical burrows, from which they emerge at dusk and into which they retire at dawn. Mature males wander about after dark in search of females and occasionally stray into houses. After mating, the male dies in a few weeks, but a female lives much longer and can mate several years in succession. In a Paris museum is a tropical specimen which is said to have been living in captivity for 25 years.

A fertilized female tarantula lays from 200 to 400 eggs at a time; thus it is possible for a single tarantula to produce several thousand young.

From *Scientific American* (Aug. 1952).

She takes no care of them beyond weaving a cocoon of silk to enclose the eggs. After they hatch, the young walk away, find convenient places in which to dig their burrows and spend the rest of their lives in solitude. The eyesight of tarantulas is poor, being limited to a sensing of change in the intensity of light and to the perception of moving objects. They apparently have little or no sense of hearing, for a hungry tarantula will pay no attention to a loudly chirping cricket placed in its cage unless the insect happens to touch one of its legs.

But all spiders, and especially hairy ones, have an extremely delicate sense of touch. Laboratory experiments prove that tarantulas can distinguish three types of touch: pressure against the body wall, stroking of the body hair, and riffling of certain very fine hairs on the legs called trichobothria. Pressure against the body, by the finger or the end of a pencil, causes the tarantula to move off slowly for a short distance. The touch excites no defensive response unless the approach is from above where the spider can see the motion, in which case it rises on its hind legs, lifts its front legs, opens its fangs and holds this threatening posture as long as the object continues to move.

The entire body of a tarantula, especially its legs, is thickly clothed with hair. Some of it is short and wooly, some long and stiff. Touching this body hair produces one of two distinct reactions. When the spider is hungry, it responds with an immediate and swift attack. At the touch of a cricket's antennae the tarantula seizes the insect so swiftly that a motion picture taken at the rate of 64 frames per second shows only the result and not the process of capture. But when the spider is not hungry, the stimulation of its hairs merely causes it to shake the touched limb. An insect can walk under its hairy belly unharmed.

The trichobothria, very fine hairs growing from dislike[1] membranes on the legs, are sensitive only to air movement. A light breeze makes them vibrate slowly, without disturbing the common hair. When one blows gently on the trichobothria, the tarantula reacts with a quick jerk of its four front legs. If the front and hind legs are stimulated at the same time, the spider makes a sudden jump. This reaction is quite independent of the state of its appetite.

These three tactile responses—to pressure on the body wall, to moving of the common hair, and to flexing of the trichobothria—are so different from one another that there is no possibility of confusing them. They serve the tarantula adequately for most of its needs and enable it to avoid most annoyances and dangers. But they fail the spider completely when it meets its deadly enemy, the digger wasp Pepsis.

These solitary wasps are beautiful and formidable creatures. Most species are either a deep shiny blue all over, or deep blue with rusty

---

1. Unlike or dissimilar.

wings. The largest have a wing span of about four inches. They live on nectar. When excited, they give off a pungent odor—a warning that they are ready to attack. The sting is much worse than that of a bee or common wasp, and the pain and swelling last longer. In the adult stage the wasp lives only a few months. The female produces but a few eggs, one at a time at intervals of two or three days. For each egg the mother must provide one adult tarantula, alive but paralyzed. The mother wasp attaches the egg to the paralyzed spider's abdomen. Upon hatching from the egg, the larva is many hundreds of times smaller than its living but helpless victim. It eats no other food and drinks no water. By the time it has finished its single Gargantuan meal and become ready for wasp-hood, nothing remains of the tarantula but its indigestible chitinous skeleton.

The mother wasp goes tarantula-hunting when the egg in her ovary is almost ready to be laid. Flying low over the ground late on a sunny afternoon, the wasp looks for its victim or for the mouth of a tarantula burrow, a round hole edged by a bit of silk. The sex of the spider makes no difference, but the mother is highly discriminating as to species. Each species of Pepsis requires a certain species of tarantula, and the wasp will not attack the wrong species. In a cage with a tarantula which is not its normal prey, the wasp avoids the spider and is usually killed by it in the night.

Yet when a wasp finds the correct species, it is the other way about. To identify the species the wasp apparently must explore the spider with her antennae. The tarantula shows an amazing tolerance to this exploration. The wasp crawls under it and walks over it without evoking any hostile response. The molestation is so great and so persistent that the tarantula often rises on all eight legs, as if it were on stilts. It may stand this way for several minutes. Meanwhile the wasp, having satisfied itself that the victim is of the right species, moves off a few inches to dig the spider's grave. Working vigorously with legs and jaws, it excavates a hole 8 to 10 inches deep with a diameter slightly larger than the spider's girth. Now and again the wasp pops out of the hole to make sure that the spider is still there.

When the grave is finished, the wasp returns to the tarantula to complete her ghastly enterprise. First she feels it all over once more with her antennae. Then her behavior becomes more aggressive. She bends her abdomen, protruding her sting, and searches for the soft membrane at the point where the spider's legs join its body—the only spot where she can penetrate the horny skeleton. From time to time, as the exasperated spider slowly shifts ground, the wasp turns on her back and slides along with the aid of her wings, trying to get under the tarantula for a shot at the vital spot. During all this maneuvering, which can last for several minutes, the tarantula makes no move to save itself. Finally the wasp corners it against some obstruction and grasps one of its legs in her powerful jaws. Now at last the harassed spider tries a desperate but vain defense. The two contestants roll over and over on the ground. It is a terrifying sight and the outcome is always the same. The wasp finally manages to thrust her sting into the soft spot and holds it there for a few seconds while she pumps in the poison. Almost immediately the tarantula falls paralyzed on its back. Its legs stop twitching; its heart stops beating. Yet it is not dead, as is shown by the fact that if taken from the wasp it can be restored to some sensitivity by being kept in a moist chamber for several months.

After paralyzing the tarantula, the wasp cleans herself by dragging her body along the ground and rubbing her feet, sucks the drop of blood oozing from the wound in the spider's abdomen, then grabs a leg of the flabby, helpless animal in her jaws and drags it down to the bottom of the grave. She stays there for many minutes, sometimes for several hours, and what she does all that time in the dark we do not know. Eventually she lays her egg and attaches it to the side of the spider's abdomen with a sticky secretion. Then she emerges, fills the grave with soil carried bit by bit in her jaws, and finally tramples the ground all around to hide any trace of the grave from prowlers. Then she flies away, leaving her descendant safely started in life.

In all this the behavior of the wasp evidently is qualitatively different from that of the spider. The wasp acts like an intelligent animal. This is not to say that instinct plays no part or that she reasons as man does. But her actions are to the point; they are not automatic and can be modified to fit the situation. We do not know for certain how she identifies the tarantula—probably it is by some olfactory or chemo-tactile sense—but she does it purposefully and does not blindly tackle a wrong species.

15   On the other hand, the tarantula's behavior shows only confusion. Evidently the wasp's pawing gives it no pleasure, for it tries to move away. That the wasp is not simulating sexual stimulation is certain because male and female tarantulas react in the same way to its advances. That the spider is not anesthetized by some odorless secretion is easily shown by blowing lightly at the tarantula and making it jump suddenly. What, then, makes the tarantula behave as stupidly as it does?

No clear, simple answer is available. Possibly the stimulation by the wasp's antennae is masked by a heavier pressure on the spider's body, so that it reacts as when prodded by a pencil. But the explanation may be much more complex. Initiative in attack is not in the nature of tarantulas; most species fight only when cornered so that escape is impossible. Their inherited patterns of behavior apparently prompt them to avoid problems rather than attack them. For example, spiders always weave their webs in three dimensions, and when a spider finds that there is insufficient space to attach certain threads in the third dimension, it leaves the place and seeks another, instead of finishing the web in a single plane. This urge to escape seems to arise under all circumstances, in all phases of life, and to take the place of reasoning. For a spider to change the pattern of its web is as impossible as for an inexperienced man to build a bridge across a chasm obstructing his way.

In a way the instinctive urge to escape is not only easier but often more efficient than reasoning. The tarantula does exactly what is most efficient in all cases except in an encounter with a ruthless and determined attacker dependent for the existence of her own species on killing as many tarantulas as she can lay eggs. Perhaps in this case the spider follows its usual pattern of trying to escape, instead of seizing and killing the wasp, because it is not aware of its danger. In any case, the survival of the tarantula species as a whole is protected by the fact that the spider is much more fertile than the wasp.

THE READER

1. *What are the major points of contrast between the spider and the wasp? Why does Petrunkevitch emphasize these particular points and neglect other possible differences?*
2. *Petrunkevitch suggests more than one hypothesis or possible explanation for the behavior of the tarantula, and he says that "no clear, simple answer is available." How does he test the possible explanations? Explain which one you think he prefers.*
3. *What evidence do you have that Petrunkevitch sees the tarantula and the wasp at least partly in human terms? Explain why you think this is or is not legitimate for a scientist.*

THE WRITER

1. *Petrunkevitch says that "insects and spiders exhibit some interesting analogies to reasoning and some crass examples of blind instinct." Why does he use the words* analogies *and* crass?
2. *Why is Petrunkevitch's initial description of the tarantula longer than his initial description of the wasp?*
3. *Petrunkevitch says that the wasp behaves "like an intelligent animal," while the spider behaves "stupidly" and "shows only confusion." Rewrite the tenth, eleventh, twelfth, and thirteenth paragraphs, reversing the characteristics of the two so that the spider acts intelligently and the wasp behaves stupidly. What other changes are necessary?*

David Rains Wallace

THE MIND OF THE BEAVER

One of my early memories is of walking across a frozen Connecticut pond with a friend and his father and coming upon a conical mound of sticks. When my friend's father told us it was a beaver lodge, I was fascinated. The snow-covered pond and bare woods seemed more alive because of this evidence of hidden, furry swimmers beneath the ice. I took a stick from the lodge home and kept it in my closet for years, occasionally taking it out to look at the tooth marks on the dry, gray wood. They seemed to promise new worlds to discover beyond the routines of schoolwork and suburban chores.

No wild animal has been a greater incitement to the discovery of new worlds than the beaver. North America was largely explored by men seeking to profit from an insatiable European market for felt hats made from shorn and pressed beaver fur. The Hudson's Bay Company, established in 1669 to trade with the Indians for beaver pelts, was the effective government of most of Canada from the French and Indian War until the mid-nineteenth century. American beaver traders such as Jedediah Smith preceded gold miners and settlers to the West Coast by several decades. During the height of the beaver trade, after the steel trap began to be produced industrially and before new felt-making processes depressed the price of a beaver pelt by some 80 percent, a beaver trapper could average a daily income estimated at thirty-two times that of a farm laborer. It's no wonder that mountain men explored every watershed from Santa Fe to Vancouver in the 1820s. Even after beaver prices fell in the 1840s, an estimated 500,000 beavers were being killed every year, primarily for their fur, which was (and is) used to make coats and collars.

Beaver trappers generally discovered more about geography than they did about beavers. It is one thing to catch a beaver in a trap or deadfall, another to discern its way of life. Beavers were a subject of lively scientific and popular interest in Colonial days, but early beaver lore was based as much on hearsay and imagination as on observation. Writing on the eve of the American Revolution, Captain Jonathan Carver described how, "after mature deliberation," troops of two or three hundred beavers assembled to build dams; how they plastered their dams with "a kind of mortar . . . laid on with their tails;" and how they built their "cabins . . . on poles." This anthropomorphized picture, in which bea-

From *The Untamed Garden and Other Personal Essays* (1986).

vers seemed more like a pond-dwelling tribe of people than wild animals, was repeated in dozens of accounts and illustrations, some of which showed beaver lodges with square-frame windows and second stories. The American historian George Bancroft considered beavers superior to Indians in cleanliness, thrift, industry, and architectural skill.

Beavers do have many traits that, viewed from a human standpoint, seem admirable. They spend a lot of time grooming, although their purpose is as much to waterproof their fur with oil as it is to keep clean. They are family animals, generally mating for life; and they are protective of their young, which remain with the parents until two years old. Where food is abundant, large beaver colonies grow up, consisting of many families that coexist peacefully in separate but neighboring quarters. These beaver towns may have evolved as a way of guarding against wolves, otters, bobcats, and other natural predators, although they proved a liability when trappers became the beavers' most deadly predator.

The high regard in which beavers came to be held collided with the fur trade in the late nineteenth century. Beavers were rapidly disappearing from the United States as trappers competed for the last scattered populations. Complete extinction was predicted, and a beaver preservation movement, comparable to the present campaign to save the whales, grew up. The beaver was seen as a paragon of wilderness virtue. Former trappers such as Joseph Henry Taylor and Gray Owl wrote books deploring the beaver trade and romanticizing their own exploits in it. Naturalists, particularly Arthur Dugmore (*The Romance of the Beaver*, 1914) and Enos Mills (*The Beaver World*, 1913), made the first detailed studies of beaver life.

What the naturalists discovered did not have the science-fiction glamour of Colonial accounts, but in a way it was equally extraordinary. Beavers are rodents, the largest in North America, reaching a length of more than four feet, including the tail, and a weight of more than eighty pounds. But they still have rodent brains, which are not particularly large and which lack the abundant convolutions that characterize human (and dolphin) brains. (Brain convolutions are believed to be a sign of intelligence because they increase the surface area of the cerebrum, where thinking is supposed to occur.) Yet Dugmore and Mills watched beavers do things that seemed to require considerable foresight. When their dams were threatened by high water, beavers promptly opened spillways or built smaller dams downstream to relieve the pressure of the fast current. Beavers dug canals as much as 1,000 feet long to divert an extra stream into their pond or to reach a source of food (beavers eat the inner bark of aspens, maples, willows, and other trees). If the canals were dug on sloping terrain, the beavers built small check dams at intervals along them so the water wouldn't flow too fast. Mills quoted Alexander Ma-

5

jors, the originator of the Pony Express, as saying often that beavers "had more engineering skill than the entire Corps of Engineers who were connected with General Grant's army when he besieged Vicksburg."

Before I read Mills and Dugmore, I saw a beaver canal in a marsh along the Stillwater River in Montana's Beartooth–Absaroka Wilderness. It was so straight and tidy, the spoil piled along its bank as if by a dredge, that I didn't think beavers could have made it, although the river was full of beavers. I thought the Forest Service had sent a crew to dig a canal through the marsh, although I couldn't imagine why, since it was a day's walk from a road. Beavers kept puzzling me on that trip. I had conventional notions of low beaver dams across gentle New England streams, with lodges in the centers of ponds. But the Montana beavers had adapted their engineering works to the steep ruggedness of the Beartooth Mountains. I found a large beaver lodge in a dry gully right beside the trail. The only explanation for this I could think of was that the gully might be flooded in winter, which is when beavers live in lodges. (They spend warm weather "on vacation," wandering about and eating water plants.) I passed another gully that looked as though it had been terraced by Asian rice farmers. A series of beaver dams ran as far as I could see up the gully, so that it contained no longer a stream but a string of quiet ponds. Some of the dams were considerably taller than I am, reminding me of miniature Grand Coulees. This terracing presumably made it easier for beavers to ascend the gully and bring back aspens from farther up the mountainside.

Canals are considered the most striking examples of beaver ingenuity because they seem to require more planning than anything else beavers do. They usually appear to have some definite objective, making it unlikely that the beavers could simply be carrying on instinctive, unplanned activity in building them. Dugmore noted that, when they dig a canal to a grove of food trees, beavers build the canal *before* they cut the trees. The canal is thus not dug inadvertently while the beavers are going back and forth to cut and haul trees. It is built with an apparently conscious intention of providing access to a planned "timber sale." That is not to say that there isn't an instinctive element in beaver canal-building. Most aquatic rodents make canallike paths as they move about their territories; but other rodents don't deliberately divert streams with their canals, and they don't build locks in their canals if they happen to be on sloping ground.

There are other examples of beaver "thinking." Enos Mills, who spent twenty-seven years watching beavers, described several ways that a beaver's tree-cutting can show foresight: "He occasionally endeavors to fell trees in a given direction. . . . He avoids cutting those entangled at the top. . . . Sometimes he will, on a windy day, fell trees on the leeward side of the grove. . . . He commonly avoids felling trees in the heart of the grove, but cuts on the outskirts of it." Mills also saw beavers display just the opposite of this sagacity, cutting trees that were entangled at the top, or in the heart of a grove, so the trees were impossible to move. He found dead beavers that had felled trees on top of themselves. Individually stupid behavior doesn't prove lack of intelligence in a species, though; otherwise, *Homo sapiens* would have to change its scientific name. Indeed, the fact that some beavers are incompetent tree-fellers suggests that tree felling involves thoughtful as well as instinctive behavior. If it were a purely instinctive activity, then all beavers should do it equally well. Wide variation in complex behavior implies a capacity for learning and innovating.

The dam and lodge building that so impressed Colonial writers requires less foresight than canal-building and tree-felling. Like many rodents, beavers are compulsive pilers of sticks during nesting and food-storing. Lodges may have evolved from piles of sticks raised for protection over the stream bank holes that ancestral beavers lived in (and that modern beavers revert to if heavily persecuted or if living along rivers too big to dam). Such primitive dens probably evolved gradually into full-fledged lodges as beavers dug their burrows on small islands or on banks that were seasonally flooded. A beaver lodge is essentially an artificial island with a burrow in it (or several burrows: early explorers found beaver apartment houses—giant lodges with dozens of burrows, accommodating several families).

Dams may have evolved from the beaver's habit of storing cut branches underwater for a winter food supply. (Such storage assures that the bark will not decay, but will remain nutritious throughout the winter.) Dams are not built of whole trees felled across a stream, as some Colonial writers thought, but of many limbs set parallel to the current with their butt ends facing upstream, so their branches interlace and hold the limbs firmly to the stream bottom. That method of anchoring the dam may have begun as a way of assuring that the winter's food supply wouldn't be swept away. Beavers that made food piles big enough to slow or dam their stream might have had better survival rates in the artifical ponds they thus created, and might then have passed on a predilection for such piles to their young. That is all conjecture, of course. We have no way of knowing how beaver dams evolved. Dams and lodges are more a part of the beaver's normal biological activities than canals, though, so they seem less planned and rational.

Even if dam and lodge building are largely instinctive activities, however, they show a great deal of individual variation. Some beavers, especially young or solitary old ones, are sloppy and perfunctory builders. Beavers don't always choose the best possible sites for dams. They'll even build dams where it's obvious that none is required—for example, when they are transplanted to already-existing ponds. On the other hand, dams often are sited as though the best engineering techniques had been used. Beavers have also been known to build lodges over springs, a sagacious way of eliminating the danger that the water at the lodge's entrance might freeze, shutting the resident beavers inside to die of slow starvation. And beavers generally take excellent care of their dams and lodges, plastering them with mud (although not by using their tails as trowels, as Captain Carver thought) and promptly repairing damage, as though mindful that the continued value of property depends on good maintenance.

The likeliest conclusion that I can draw from all this evidence is that beavers are animals with minds, animals that think. They seem to confront their environment in a conscious, deliberate way: they plan, they choose, they solve problems.

An experimental scientist might spend an entire career, or more, on the mysteries of beaver psychology. If the beaver thinks, then *how* does it think? We humans think with language. We can't build dams or canals without it. There's no evidence that beavers have language, though; they're quiet creatures, even for wild animals. They do make various communicative noises, including the well-known tail slap on the water, but such noises don't seem complex enough to communicate canal-building techniques. The sloppy dam-building of young beavers suggests that engineering techniques may be passed down somehow from parents to young, perhaps simply by the young beavers' watching their parents. We don't know enough about beavers to be sure about that, though. Mills saw little evidence of leadership when he watched groups of beavers at work, although he noted one instance in which parents accompanied their maturing offspring to a new location, helped them build a dam and lodge, and then returned to their old pond, leaving the youngsters in the new one.

15   Whether beaver "thinking" is handed down from generation to generation or simply occurs in individuals as an adjunct to instinctive behavior, it has had a long time to evolve, much longer than human intelligence. The beaver's first ancestors appeared in the Oligocene Epoch, some 35 million years ago, and the genus *Castor,* to which the modern beaver belongs, was fully developed by the Pliocene Epoch, which began 13 million years ago. During the Ice Age, giant beavers up to nine feet long lived in North American rivers. Assuming (as is not necessarily the case) that these giant beavers had giant beaver brains, I wonder what kind of engineering feats they may have accomplished? They evidently built lodges, since fossil mounds of willow poles capable of housing giant beavers have been unearthed.

Of course, my conclusion that the beaver has a mind isn't the only possible one. An instinct-versus-intelligence controversy has raged around the beaver since modern science discovered it. Baron Cuvier, the early-nineteenth-century French anatomist, "proved" that beavers are purely instinctive creatures by raising baby beavers in isolation. Cuvier claimed that the isolated beavers demonstrated all the talents and abilities of wild beavers. I don't know if Cuvier's beavers built 1,000-foot-long canals complete with check dams to divert entire streams. It seems unlikely they'd have had much scope to do so in captivity. Even if they did, though, that wouldn't necessarily prove that they weren't thinking as they built their canals. It would prove only that they built them without having learned how from other beavers. Cuvier was judging his beavers in anthropomorphic terms. Human intelligence depends heavily on cultural conditioning for its development; people who are raised in isolation, such as the so-called wolf children of India, remain subhuman in behavior, unable to use language or other tools. But that doesn't prove that there couldn't be another kind of intelligence, less dependent on cultural conditioning. After all, no amount of education can turn a truly stupid human into a good engineer. Intelligence requires innate capacity as well as learning.

One has only to spend a little time watching beavers to sense that, rational or not, these are sharp animals. I've never been able to catch beavers off guard, as I've sometimes caught muskrats. Beavers go about their business as I watch, seemingly oblivious of me; but if I begin to edge into a position that might give me an advantage over them, the beavers are gone. Muskrats, on the other hand, bumble right up to my feet as I stand beside their den holes, then panic when they realize they're not alone, tumbling comically into the water.

Beavers seem able to adapt to the worst that humans can do to land. Once while hiking the lunar landscape of an Ohio strip mine, I came upon an eroded, muddy gully that beavers had improved in much the same way that they'd treated the rocky gully in the Beartooth Mountains. They had built a series of check dams across the gully, turning it into a string of pools instead of an eroded watercourse. The fact that the water was opaque with mud and yellowboy (residual sulfur from the coal seam) hadn't stopped them. It was confusing to come upon something as "natural" as beaver dams in such a ravaged landscape.

The beaver's activity on strip-mined land is valued because it reduces erosion and water pollution. Sediment settles behind beaver dams instead of choking rivers. Strip-mining companies prohibit beaver trapping on their land. Of course, the beavers aren't working to conserve soil; they're simply trying to survive in what must be a challenging, if not harsh, environment for them. But that they are surviving, as they've survived the 300-year war that civilization has waged on them, is at least partly a measure of their ingenuity. It might not be so easy to exterminate beavers. While visiting France, after having been told by his hosts that beavers had been extinct in their region for many years, Enos Mills found a piece of beaver-chewed wood in the River Seine.

Accounts of beaver wisdom sometimes challenge belief. There are [20] reports that beavers may learn to spring traps with sticks, and in fact there have been beaver populations that proved virtually untrappable. Trappers believed that beavers could forecast the weather, could predict whether winters would be mild or severe. Mills and Dugmore both failed to see evidence of that, and I'm more inclined to believe them than the trappers. Still, who can say what a mode of thought so different from our own might perceive?

I certainly don't pretend to know how beavers think. We understand little enough about how our own gray matter produces canals and dams. Scientific attention has shifted from the question of beaver intelligence to that of whale and dolphin intelligence, partly because whales have big, convoluted brains like ours, partly because we are in danger of exterminating them, as we were in danger of exterminating the beaver 100 years ago. Whales certainly deserve our attention. I sometimes think, though, that our shifting interest in various animals reflects our vanity as well as our concern. We wanted to save the beaver because it builds dams, lodges, and canals—as we do. Now we want to save the whales because they have big brains and (possibly) language—as we do. But there are many things deserving our attention that are quite unlike us. The beaver's solitary, silent way of thinking may be one of them.

THE READER

1. On pp. 608–609 Wallace cites examples of both "thinking" and "stupid behavior" on the part of beavers. Explain how both kinds of examples can be taken as evidence of beaver intelligence.
2. Explain how an anthropomorphizing tendency on the part of a human observer can produce opposite results, as in the cases of Captain Jonathan Carver (p. 606) and Baron Cuvier (p. 610).

THE WRITER

1. Why does Wallace begin by telling of the boyish wonder he experienced at his first encounter with evidence of beavers?
2. Write an essay on anthropomorphism. (For further examples see Lorenz, "The Taming of the Shrew," p. 588.) If your experience with wild nature is limited, you might want to consider how the concept applies to things both "below" and "above": to pets, or flowers, or inanimate things, for example, or to ideas of God.

Carl Sagan

THE ABSTRACTIONS OF BEASTS

"Beasts abstract not," announced John Locke, expressing mankind's prevailing opinion throughout recorded history: Bishop Berkeley[1] had, however, a sardonic rejoinder: "If the fact that brutes abstract not be made the distinguishing property of that sort of animal, I fear a great many of those that pass for men must be reckoned into their numbers." Abstract thought, at least in its more subtle varieties, is not an invariable accompaniment of everyday life for the average man. Could abstract thought be a matter not of kind but of degree? Could other animals be capable of abstract thought but more rarely or less deeply than humans?

We have the impression that other animals are not very intelligent. But have we examined the possibility of animal intelligence carefully enough, or, as in François Truffaut's poignant film *The Wild Child*, do we simply equate the absence of our style of expression of intelligence with the absence of intelligence? In discussing communication with the animals, the French philosopher Montaigne remarked, "The defect that hinders communication betwixt them and us, why may it not be on our part as well as theirs?"

There is, of course, a considerable body of anecdotal information suggesting chimpanzee intelligence. The first serious study of the behavior of simians—including their behavior in the wild—was made in Indonesia by Alfred Russel Wallace, the co-discoverer of evolution by natural selection. Wallace concluded that a baby orangutan he studied behaved "exactly like a human child in similar circumstances." In fact, "orangutan" is a Malay phrase meaning not ape but "man of the woods." Teuber recounted many stories told by his parents, pioneer German ethologists who founded and operated the first research station devoted to chimpanzee behavior on Tenerife in the Canary Islands early in the second decade of this century. It was here that Wolfgang Kohler performed his famous studies of Sultan, a chimpanzee "genius" who was able to connect two rods in order to reach an otherwise inaccessible banana. On Tenerife, also, two chimpanzees were observed maltreating a chicken: One would extend some food to the fowl, encouraging it to approach; whereupon the other would thrust at it with a piece of wire

From *The Dragons of Eden* (1977).

1. John Locke, English philosopher, author of *An Essay Concerning Human Understanding* (1690); Bishop George Berkeley, Irish philosopher, author of *A Treatise Concerning the Principles of Human Knowledge* (1710).

it had concealed behind its back. The chicken would retreat but soon allow itself to approach once again—and be beaten once again. Here is a fine combination of behavior sometimes thought to be uniquely human: cooperation, planning a future course of action, deception and cruelty. It also reveals that chickens have a very low capacity for avoidance learning.

Until a few years ago, the most extensive attempt to communicate with chimpanzees went something like this: A newborn chimp was taken into a household with a newborn baby, and both would be raised together—twin cribs, twin bassinets, twin high chairs, twin potties, twin diaper pails, twin babypowder cans. At the end of three years, the young chimp had, of course, far outstripped the young human in manual dexterity, running, leaping, climbing and other motor skills. But while the child was happily babbling away, the chimp could say only, and with enormous difficulty, "Mama," "Papa," and "cup." From this it was widely concluded that in language, reasoning and other higher mental functions, chimpanzees were only minimally competent: "Beasts abstract not."

5   But in thinking over these experiments, two psychologists, Beatrice and Robert Gardner, at the University of Nevada, realized that the pharynx and larynx of the chimp are not suited for human speech. Human beings exhibit a curious multiple use of the mouth for eating, breathing and communicating. In insects such as crickets, which call to one another by rubbing their legs, these three functions are performed by completely separate organ systems. Human spoken language seems to be adventitious. The exploitation of organ systems with other functions for communication in humans is also indicative of the comparatively recent evolution of our linguistic abilities. It might be, the Gardners reasoned, that chimpanzees have substantial language abilities which could not be expressed because of the limitations of their anatomy. Was there any symbolic language, they asked, that could employ the strengths rather than the weaknesses of chimpanzee anatomy?

The Gardners hit upon a brilliant idea: Teach a chimpanzee American sign language, known by its acronym Ameslan, and sometimes as "American deaf and dumb language" (the "dumb" refers, of course, to the inability to speak and not to any failure of intelligence). It is ideally suited to the immense manual dexterity of the chimpanzee. It also may have all the crucial design features of verbal languages.

There is by now a vast library of described and filmed conversations, employing Ameslan and other gestural languages, with Washoe, Lucy, Lana and other chimpanzees studied by the Gardners and others. Not only are there chimpanzees with working vocabularies of 100 to 200 words; they are also able to distinguish among nontrivially different grammatical patterns and syntaxes. What is more, they have been remarkably inventive in the construction of new words and phrases.

On seeing for the first time a duck land quacking in a pond, Washoe gestured "waterbird," which is the same phrase used in English and other languages, but which Washoe invented for the occasion. Having never seen a spherical fruit other than an apple, but knowing the signs for the principal colors, Lana, upon spying a technician eating an orange, signed "orange apple." After tasting a watermelon, Lucy described it as "candy drink" or "drink fruit," which is essentially the same word form as the English "water melon." But after she had burned her mouth on her first radish, Lucy forever after described them as "cry hurt food." A small doll placed unexpectedly in Washoe's cup elicited the response "Baby in my drink." When Washoe soiled, particularly clothing or furniture, she was taught the sign "dirty," which she then extrapolated as a general term of abuse. A rhesus monkey that evoked her displeasure was repeatedly signed at: "Dirty monkey, dirty monkey, dirty monkey." Occasionally Washoe would say things like "Dirty Jack, gimme drink." Lana, in a moment of creative annoyance, called her trainer "You green shit." Chimpanzees have invented swear words. Washoe also seems to have a sort of sense of humor; once, when riding on her trainer's shoulders and, perhaps inadvertently, wetting him, she signed: "Funny, funny."

Lucy was eventually able to distinguish clearly the meanings of the phrases "Roger tickle Lucy" and "Lucy tickle Roger," both of which activities she enjoyed with gusto. Likewise, Lana extrapolated from "Tim groom Lana" to "Lana groom Tim." Washoe was observed "reading" a magazine—i.e., slowly turning the pages, peering intently at the pictures and making, to no one in particular, an appropriate sign, such as "cat" when viewing a photograph of a tiger, and "drink" when examining a Vermouth advertisement. Having learned the sign "open" with a door, Washoe extended the concept to a briefcase. She also attempted to converse in Ameslan with the laboratory cat, who turned out to be the only illiterate in the facility. Having acquired this marvelous method of communication, Washoe may have been surprised that the cat was not also competent in Ameslan. And when one day Jane, Lucy's foster mother, left the laboratory, Lucy gazed after her and signed: "Cry me. Me cry."

Boyce Rensberger is a sensitive and gifted reporter for the *New York Times* whose parents could neither speak nor hear, although he is in both respects normal. His first language, however, was Ameslan. He had been abroad on a European assignment for the *Times* for some years. On his return to the United States, one of his first domestic duties was to look into the Gardners' experiments with Washoe. After some little

10

time with the chimpanzee, Rensberger reported, "Suddenly I realized I was conversing with a member of another species in my native tongue." The use of the word tongue is, of course, figurative: it is built deeply into the structure of the language (a word that also means "tongue"). In fact, Rensberger was conversing with a member of another species in his native "hand." And it is just this transition from tongue to hand that has permitted humans to regain the ability—lost, according to Josephus,[2] since Eden—to communicate with the animals.

In addition to Ameslan, chimpanzees and other nonhuman primates are being taught a variety of other gestural languages. At the Yerkes Regional Primate Research Center in Atlanta, Georgia, they are learning a specific computer language called (by the humans, not the chimps) "Yerkish." The computer records all of its subjects' conversations, even during the night when no humans are in attendance; and from its ministrations we have learned that chimpanzees prefer jazz to rock and movies about chimpanzees to movies about human beings. Lana had, by January 1976, viewed *The Developmental Anatomy of the Chimpanzee* 245 times. She would undoubtedly appreciate a larger film library.

* * * The machine provides for many of Lana's needs, but not all. Sometimes, in the middle of the night, she forlornly types out: "Please, machine, tickle Lana." More elaborate requests and commentaries, each requiring a creative use of a set grammatical form, have been developed subsequently.

Lana monitors her sentences on a computer display, and erases those with grammatical errors. Once, in the midst of Lana's construction of an elaborate sentence, her trainer mischievously and repeatedly interposed, from his separate computer console, a word that made nonsense of Lana's sentence. She gazed at her computer display, spied her trainer at his console, and composed a new sentence: "Please, Tim, leave room." Just as Washoe and Lucy can be said to speak, Lana can be said to write.

At an early stage in the development of Washoe's verbal abilities, Jacob Bronowski and a colleague wrote a scientific paper denying the significance of Washoe's use of gestural language because, in the limited data available to Bronowski, Washoe neither inquired nor negated. But later observations showed that Washoe and other chimpanzees were perfectly able both to ask questions and to deny assertions put to them. And it is difficult to see any significant difference in quality between chimpanzee use of gestural language and the use of ordinary speech by children in a manner that we unhesitatingly attribute to intelligence. In reading Bronowski's paper I cannot help but feel that a little pinch of human chauvinsim has crept in, an echo of Locke's "Beasts abstract

---

2. First-century Jewish general and historian.

not." In 1949, the American anthropologist Leslie White stated unequivocally: "Human behavior is symbolic behavior; symbolic behavior is human behavior." What would White have made of Washoe, Lucy and Lana?

These findings on chimpanzee language and intelligence have an intriguing bearing on "Rubicon" arguments[3]—the contention that the total brain mass, or at least the ratio of brain to body mass, is a useful index of intelligence. Against this point of view it was once argued that the lower range of the brain masses of microcephalic humans overlaps the upper range of brain masses of adult chimpanzees and gorillas; and yet, it was said, microcephalics have some, although severely impaired, use of language—while the apes have none. But in only relatively few cases are microcephalics capable of human speech. One of the best behavioral descriptions of microcephalics was written by a Russian physician, S. Korsakov, who in 1893 observed a female microcephalic named "Masha." She could understand a very few questions and commands and could occasionally reminisce on her childhood. She sometimes chattered away, but there was little coherence to what she uttered. Korsakov characterized her speech as having "an extreme poverty of logical associations." As an example of her poorly adapted and automaton-like intelligence, Korsakov described her eating habits. When food was present on the table, Masha would eat. But if the food was abruptly removed in the midst of a meal, she would behave as if the meal had ended, thanking those in charge and piously blessing herself. If the food were returned, she would eat again. The pattern apparently was subject to indefinite repetition. My own impression is that Lucy or Washoe would be a far more interesting dinner companion than Masha, and that the comparison of microcephalic humans with normal apes is not inconsistent with some sort of "Rubicon" of intelligence. Of course, both the quality and the quantity of neural connections are probably vital for the sorts of intelligence that we can easily recognize.

Recent experiments performed by James Dewson of the Stanford University School of Medicine and his colleagues give some physiological support to the idea of language centers in the simian neocortex—in particular, like humans, in the left hemisphere. Monkeys were trained to press a green light when they heard a hiss and a red light when they heard a tone. Some seconds after a sound was heard, the red or the green light would appear at some unpredictable position—different each time—on the control panel. The monkey pressed the appropriate light and, in the case of a correct guess, was rewarded with a pellet of food.

15

3. Those assuming a definitive boundary between different kinds of intelligence. The allusion is to the river Rubicon, in ancient times the boundary between Rome and its "barbaric" Germanic provinces.

Then the time interval between hearing the sound and seeing the light was increased up to twenty seconds. In order to be rewarded, the monkeys now had to remember for twenty seconds which noise they had heard. Dewson's team then surgically excised part of the so-called auditory association cortex from the left hemisphere of the neocortex in the temporal lobe. When retested, the monkeys had very poor recall of which sound they were then hearing. After less than a second they could not recall whether it was a hiss or a tone. The removal of a comparable part of the temporal lobe from the right hemisphere produced no effect whatever on this task. "It looks," Dewson was reported to say, "as if we removed the structure in the monkeys' brains that may be analogous to human language centers." Similar studies on rhesus monkeys, but using visual rather than auditory stimuli, seem to show no evidence of a difference between the hemispheres of the neocortex.

Because adult chimpanzees are generally thought (at least by zoo-keepers) to be too dangerous to retain in a home or home environment, Washoe and other verbally accomplished chimpanzees have been involuntarily "retired" soon after reaching puberty. Thus we do not yet have experience with the adult language abilities of monkeys and apes. One of the most intriguing questions is whether a verbally accomplished chimpanzee mother will be able to communicate language to her off-spring. It seems very likely that this should be possible and that a community of chimps initially competent in gestural language could pass down the language to subsequent generations.

Where such communication is essential for survival, there is already some evidence that apes transmit extragenetic or cultural information. Jane Goodall observed baby chimps in the wild emulating the behavior of their mothers and learning the reasonably complex task of finding an appropriate twig and using it to prod into a termite's nest so as to acquire some of these tasty delicacies.

Differences in group behavior—something that it is very tempting to call cultural differences—have been reported among chimpanzees, ba-boons, macaques and many other primates. For example, one group of monkeys may know how to eat bird's eggs, while an adjacent band of precisely the same species may not. Such primates have a few dozen sounds or cries, which are used for intra-group communication, with such meanings as "Flee; here is a predator." But the sound of the cries differs somewhat from group to group: there are regional accents.

20   An even more striking experiment was performed accidentally by Japanese primatologists attempting to relieve an overpopulation and hunger problem in a community of macaques on an island in south Japan. The anthropologists threw grains of wheat on a sandy beach. Now it is very difficult to separate wheat grains one by one from sand grains; such an effort might even expend more energy than eating the collected

wheat would provide. But one brilliant macaque, Imo, perhaps by accident or out of pique, threw handfuls of the mixture into the water. Wheat floats; sand sinks, a fact that Imo clearly noted. Through the sifting process she was able to eat well (on a diet of soggy wheat, to be sure). While older macaques, set in their ways, ignored her, the younger monkeys appeared to grasp the importance of her discovery, and imitate it. In the next generation, the practice was more widespread; today all macaques on the island are competent at water sifting, an example of a cultural tradition among the monkeys.

Earlier studies on Takasakiyama, a mountain in northeast Kyushu inhabited by macaques, show a similar pattern in cultural evolution. Visitors to Takasakiyama threw caramels wrapped in paper to the monkeys—a common practice in Japanese zoos, but one the Takasakiyama macaques had never before encountered. In the course of play, some young monkeys discovered how to unwrap the caramels and eat them. The habit was passed on successively to their playmates, their mothers, the dominant males (who among the macaques act as babysitters for the very young) and finally to the subadult males, who were at the furthest social remove from the monkey children. The process of acculturation took more than three years. In natural primate communities, the existing nonverbal communications are so rich that there is little pressure for the development of a more elaborate gestural language. But if gestural language were necessary for chimpanzee survival, there can be little doubt that it would be transmitted culturally down through the generations.

I would expect a significant development and elaboration of language in only a few generations if all the chimps unable to communicate were to die or fail to reproduce. Basic English corresponds to about 1,000 words. Chimpanzees are already accomplished in vocabularies exceeding 10 percent of that number. Although a few years ago it would have seemed the most implausible science fiction, it does not appear to me out of the question that, after a few generations in such a verbal chimpanzee community, there might emerge the memoirs of the natural history and mental life of a chimpanzee, published in English or Japanese (with perhaps an "as told to" after the by-line).

If chimpanzees have consciousness, if they are capable of abstractions, do they not have what until now has been described as "human rights"? How smart does a chimpanzee have to be before killing him constitutes murder? What further properties must he show before religious missionaries must consider him worthy of attempts at conversion?

I recently was escorted through a large primate research laboratory by its director. We approached a long corridor lined, to the vanishing point as in a perspective drawing, with caged chimpanzees. They were one, two or three to a cage, and I am sure the accommodations were exemplary as far as such institutions (or for that matter traditional zoos) go. As we approached the nearest cage, its two inmates bared their teeth and with incredible accuracy let fly great sweeping arcs of spittle, fairly drenching the lightweight suit of the facility's director. They then uttered a staccato of short shrieks, which echoed down the corridor to be repeated and amplified by other caged chimps, who had certainly not seen us, until the corridor fairly shook with the screeching and banging and rattling of bars. The director informed me that not only spit is apt to fly in such a situation; and at his urging we retreated.

25   I was powerfully reminded of those American motion pictures of the 1930s and '40s, set in some vast and dehumanized state or federal penitentiary, in which the prisoners banged their eating utensils against the bars at the appearance of the tyrannical warden. These chimps are healthy and well-fed. If they are "only" animals, if they are beasts which abstract not, then my comparison is a piece of sentimental foolishness. But chimpanzees *can* abstract. Like other mammals, they are capable of strong emotions. They have certainly committed no crimes. I do not claim to have the answer, but I think it is certainly worthwhile to raise the question: Why, exactly, all over the civilized world, in virtually every major city, are apes in prison?

For all we know, occasional viable crosses between humans and chimpanzees are possible. The natural experiment must have been tried very infrequently, at least recently. If such off-spring are ever produced, what will their legal status be? The cognitive abilities of chimpanzees force us, I think, to raise searching questions about the boundaries of the community of beings to which special ethical considerations are due, and can, I hope, help to extend our ethical perspectives downward through the taxa on Earth and upwards to extraterrestial organisms, if they exist.

Edward Abbey

THE SERPENTS OF PARADISE

The April mornings are bright, clear and calm. Not until the afternoon does the wind begin to blow, raising dust and sand in funnel-shaped twisters that spin across the desert briefly, like dancers, and then collapse—whirlwinds from which issue no voice or word except the forlorn moan of the elements under stress. After the reconnoitering dust devils comes the real the serious wind, the voice of the desert rising to a demented howl and blotting out sky and sun behind yellow clouds of

From *Desert Solitaire: A Season in the Wilderness* (1968).

dust, sand, confusion, embattled birds, last year's scrub-oak leaves, pollen, the husks of locusts, bark of juniper. . . .

Time of the red eye, the sore and bloody nostril, the sand-pitted windshield, if one is foolish enough to drive his car into such a storm. Time to sit indoors and continue that letter which is never finished—while the fine dust forms neat little windrows under the edge of the door and on the windowsills. Yet the springtime winds are as much a part of the canyon country as the silence and the glamorous distances, you learn, after a number of years, to love them also.

The mornings therefore, as I started to say and meant to say, are all the sweeter in the knowledge of what the afternoon is likely to bring. Before beginning the morning chores I like to sit on the sill of my doorway, bare feet planted on the bare ground and a mug of hot coffee in hand, facing the sunrise. The air is gelid, not far above freezing, but the butane heater inside the trailer keeps my back warm, the rising sun warms the front, and the coffee warms the interior.

Perhaps this is the loveliest hour of the day, though it's hard to choose. Much depends on the season. In midsummer the sweetest hour begins at sundown, after the awful heat of the afternoon. But now, in April, we'll take the opposite, that hour beginning with the sunrise. The birds, returning from wherever they go in winter, seem inclined to agree. The pinyon jays are whirling in garrulous, gregarious flocks from one stunted tree to the next and back again, erratic exuberant games without any apparent practical function. A few big ravens hang around and croak harsh clanking statements of smug satisfaction from the rimrock, lifting their greasy wings now and then to probe for lice. I can hear but seldom see the canyon wrens singing their distinctive song from somewhere up on the cliffs: a flutelike descent—never ascent—of the whole tone scale. Staking out new nesting claims, I understand. Also invisible but invariably present at some indefinable distance are the mourning doves whose plaintive call suggests irresistibly a kind of seeking out, the attempt by separated souls to restore a lost communion:

Hello . . . they seem to cry, *who . . . are . . . you?*   5

And the reply from a different quarter. *Hello . . .* (pause) *where . . . are . . . you?*

No doubt this line of analogy must be rejected. It's foolish and unfair to impute to the doves, with serious concerns of their own, an interest in questions more appropriate to their human kin. Yet their song, if not a mating call or a warning, must be what it sounds like, a brooding meditation on space, on solitude. The game.

Other birds, silent, which I have not yet learned to identify, are also lurking in the vicinity, watching me. What the ornithologist terms l.g.b.'s—little gray birds—they flit about from point to point on noiseless wings, their origins obscure.

* * * I share the housetrailer with a number of mice. I don't know how many but apparently only a few, perhaps a single family. They don't disturb me and are welcome to my crumbs and leavings. Where they came from, how they got into the trailer, how they survived before my arrival (for the trailer had been locked up for six months), these are puzzling matters I am not prepared to resolve. My only reservation concerning the mice is that they do attract rattlesnakes.

10   I'm sitting on my doorstep early one morning, facing the sun as usual, drinking coffee, when I happen to look down and see almost between my bare feet, only a couple of inches to the rear of my heels, the very thing I had in mind. No mistaking that wedgelike head, that tip of horny segmented tail peeping out of the coils. He's under the doorstep and in the shade where the ground and air remain very cold. In his sluggish condition he's not likely to strike unless I rouse him by some careless move of my own.

There's a revolver inside the trailer, a huge British Webley .45, loaded, but it's out of reach. Even if I had it in my hands I'd hesitate to blast a fellow creature at such close range, shooting between my own legs at a living target flat on solid rock thirty inches away. It would be like murder; and where would I set my coffee? My cherrywood walking stick leans against the trailerhouse wall only a few feet away, but I'm afraid that in leaning over for it I might stir up the rattler or spill some hot coffee on his scales.

Other considerations come to mind. Arches National Monument[1] is meant to be among other things a sanctuary for wildlife—for all forms of wildlife. It is my duty as a park ranger to protect, preserve and defend all living things within the park boundaries, making no exceptions. Even if this were not the case I have personal convictions to uphold. Ideals, you might say. I prefer not to kill animals. I'm a humanist; I'd rather kill a *man* than a snake.

What to do. I drink some more coffee and study the dormant reptile at my heels. It is not after all the mighty diamondback, *Crotalus atrox,* I'm confronted with but a smaller species known locally as the horny rattler or more precisely as the Faded Midget. An insulting name for a rattlesnake, which may explain the Faded Midget's alleged bad temper. But the name is apt: he is small and dusty-looking, with a little knob above each eye—the horns. His bite though temporarily disabling would not likely kill a full-grown man in normal health. Even so I don't really want him around. Am I to be compelled to put on boots or shoes every time I wish to step outside? The scorpions, tarantulas, centipedes, and black widows are nuisance enough.

I finish my coffee, lean back and swing my feet up and inside the doorway of the trailer. At once there is a buzzing sound from below and

1. Near Moab, Utah, in the spectacular Canyonlands region.

the rattler lifts his head from his coils, eyes brightening, and extends his narrow black tongue to test the air.

After thawing out my boots over the gas flame I pull them on and come back to the doorway. My visitor is still waiting beneath the doorstep, basking in the sun, fully alert. The trailerhouse has two doors. I leave by the other and get a long-handled spade out of the bed of the government pickup. With this tool I scoop the snake into the open. He strikes, I can hear the click of the fangs against steel, see the stain of venom. He wants to stand and fight, but I am patient; I insist on herding him well away from the trailer. On guard, head aloft—that evil slit-eyed weaving head shaped like the ace of spades—tail whirring, the rattler slithers sideways, retreating slowly before me until he reaches the shelter of a sandstone slab. He backs under it.

You better stay there, cousin, I warn him; if I catch you around the trailer again I'll chop your head off.

A week later he comes back. If not him his twin brother. I spot him one morning under the trailer near the kitchen drain, waiting for a mouse. I have to keep my promise.

This won't do. If there are midget rattlers in the area there may be diamondbacks too—five, six or seven feet long, thick as a man's wrist, dangerous. I don't want them camping under my home. It looks as though I'll have to trap the mice.

However, before being forced to take that step I am lucky enough to capture a gopher snake. Burning garbage one morning at the park dump, I see a long slender yellow-brown snake emerge from a mound of old tin cans and plastic picnic plates and take off down the sandy bed of a gulch. There is a burlap sack in the cab of the truck which I carry when plucking Kleenex flowers from the brush and cactus along the road; I grab that and my stick, run after the snake and corner it beneath the exposed roots of a bush. Making sure it's a gopher snake and not somethng less useful, I open the neck of the sack and with a great deal of coaxing and prodding get the snake into it. The gopher snake, *Drymarchon corais couperi*, or bull snake, has a reputation as the enemy of rattlesnakes, destroying or driving them away whenever encountered.

Hoping to domesticate this sleek, handsome and docile reptile, I release him inside the trailerhouse and keep him there for several days. Should I attempt to feed him? I decide against it—let him eat mice. What little water he may need can also be extracted from the flesh of his prey.

The gopher snake and I get along nicely. During the day he curls up like a cat in the warm corner behind the heater and at night he goes about his business. The mice, singularly quiet for a change, make themselves scarce. The snake is passive, apparently contented, and makes no resistance when I pick him up with my hands and drape him over an

15

20

arm or around my neck. When I take him outside into the wind and sunshine his favorite place seems to be inside my shirt, where he wraps himself around my waist and rests on my belt. In this position he sometimes sticks his head out between shirt buttons for a survey of the weather, astonishing and delighting any tourists who may happen to be with me at the time. The scales of a snake are dry and smooth, quite pleasant to the touch. Being a cold blooded creature, of course, he takes his temperature from that of the immediate environment—in this case my body.

We are compatible. From my point of view, friends. After a week of close association I turn him loose on the warm sandstone at my doorstep and leave for a patrol of the park. At noon when I return he is gone. I search everywhere beneath, nearby and inside the trailerhouse, but my companion has disappeared. Has he left the area entirely or is he hiding somewhere close by? At any rate I am troubled no more by rattlesnakes under the door.

The snake story is not yet ended.

In the middle of May, about a month after the gopher snake's disappearance, in the evening of a very hot day, with all the rosy desert cooling like a griddle with the fire turned off, he reappears. This time with a mate.

I'm in the stifling heat of the trailer opening a can of beer, barefooted, about to go outside and relax after a hard day watching cloud formations. I happen to glance out the little window near the refrigerator and see two gopher snakes on my verandah engaged in what seems to be a kind of ritual dance. Like a living caduceus they wind and unwind about each other in undulant, graceful, perpetual motion, moving slowly across a dome of sandstone. Invisible but tangible as music is the passion which joins them—sexual? combative? both? A shameless *voyeur,* I stare at the lovers, and then to get a closer view run outside and around the trailer to the back. There I get down on hands and knees and creep toward the dancing snakes, not wanting to frighten or disturb them. I crawl to within six feet of them and stop, flat on my belly, watching from the snake's eye level. Obsessed with their ballet, the serpents seem unaware of my presence.

The two gopher snakes are nearly identical in length and coloring; I cannot be certain that either is actually my former household pet. I cannot even be sure that they are male and female, though their performance resembles so strongly a *pas de deux* by formal lovers. They intertwine and separate, glide side by side in perfect congruence, turn like mirror images of each other and glide back again, wind and unwind again. This is the basic pattern but there is a variation: at regular intervals the snakes elevate their heads, facing one another, as high as they can go, as if each is trying to outreach or overawe the other. Their heads and bodies rise, higher and higher, then topple together and the rite goes on.

I crawl after them, determined to see the whole thing. Suddenly and simultaneously they discover me, prone on my belly a few feet away. The dance stops. After a moment's pause the two snakes come straight toward me, still in flawless unison, straight toward my face, the forked tongues flickering, their intense wild yellow eyes staring directly into my eyes. For an instant I am paralyzed by wonder; then, stung by a fear too ancient and powerful to overcome I scramble back, rising, to my knees. The snakes veer and turn and race away from me in parallel motion, their lean elegant bodies making a soft hissing noise as they slide over the sand and stone. I follow them for a short distance, still plagued by curiosity, before remembering my place and the requirements of common courtesy. For godsake let them go in peace, I tell myself. Wish them luck and (if lovers) innumerable offspring, a life of happily ever after. Not for their sake alone but for your own.

In the long hot day and cool evenings to come I will not see the gopher snakes again. Nevertheless I will feel their presence watching over me like totemic deities, keeping the rattlesnakes far back in the brush where I like them best, cropping off the surplus mouse population, maintaining useful connections with the primeval. Sympathy, mutual aid, symbiosis, continuity.

How can I descend to such anthropomorphism? Easily—but is it, in this case, entirely false? Perhaps not. I am not attributing human motives to my snake and bird acquaintances. I recognize that when and where they serve purposes of mine they do so for beautifully selfish reasons of their own. Which is exactly the way it should be. I suggest, however, that it's a foolish, simple-minded rationalism which denies any form of emotion to all animals but man and his dog. This is no more justified than the Moslems are in denying souls to women. It seems to me possible, even probable, that many of the nonhuman undomesticated animals experience emotions unknown to us. What do the coyotes mean when they yodel at the moon? What are the dolphins trying so patiently to tell us? Precisely what did those two enraptured gopher snakes have in mind when they came gliding toward my eyes over the naked sandstone? If I had been as capable of trust as I am susceptible to fear I might have learned something new or some truth so very old we have all forgotten it.

> They do not sweat and whine about their condition.
> They do not lie awake in the dark and weep for their sins. . . .

All men are brothers, we like to say, half-wishing sometimes in secret it were not true. But perhaps it is true. And is the evolutionary hue from

30

protozoan to Spinoza[2] any less certain? That also may be true. We are obliged, therefore, to spread the news, painful and bitter though it may be for some to hear, that all living things on hand are kindred. . . .

2. Baruch Spinoza (1632–77), Dutch philosopher known today for his writings on the doctrine of pantheism.

THE READER

1. "I'd rather kill a man than a snake," writes Abbey (p. 622). Can he be serious? What rhetorical purpose might such a statement serve?
2. Three paragraphs later Abbey threatens a rattlesnake: "If I catch you around the trailer again I'll chop your head off." (p. 623). How does he attempt to justify this apparent inconsistency in his attitude?
3. What exactly is Abbey referring to in his own text when he says "How can I descend to such anthropomorphism?"
4. Check the various senses of sentimental in a good dictionary. Can any of these be fairly applied to this essay?

THE WRITER

1. Why does Abbey begin with a description of desert windstorms and their unpleasant effects?
2. Abbey has called himself an "ecological terrorist" and has taken an aggressive stance against forces that would "develop" wild areas. Can this essay be viewed as propaganda for such a cause?
3. Write an essay in which you use your own experience in nature to defend an ecological or environmental cause.

Chief Seattle

LETTER TO PRESIDENT PIERCE, 1855

We know that the white man does not understand our ways. One portion of the land is the same to him as the next, for he is a stranger who comes in the night and takes from the land whatever he needs. The earth is not his brother, but his enemy, and when he has conquered it, he moves on. He leaves his fathers' graves, and his children's birthright is forgotten. The sight of your cities pains the eyes of the red man. But perhaps it is because the red man is a savage and does not understand.

From *Native American Testimony: An Anthology of Indian and White Relations*, edited by Peter Nabokov (1977).

There is no quiet place in the white man's cities. No place to hear the leaves of spring or the rustle of insect's wings. But perhaps because I am a savage and do not understand, the clatter only seems to insult the ears. The Indian prefers the soft sound of the wind darting over the face of the pond, the smell of the wind itself cleansed by a mid-day rain, or scented with the piñon pine. The air is precious to the red man. For all things share the same breath—the beasts, the trees, the man. Like a man dying for many days, he is numb to the stench.

What is man without the beasts? If all the beasts were gone, men would die from great loneliness of spirit, for whatever happens to the beasts also happens to man. All things are connected. Whatever befalls the earth befalls the sons of the earth.

It matters little where we pass the rest of our days; they are not many. A few more hours, a few more winters, and none of the children of the great tribes that once lived on this earth, or that roamed in small bands in the woods, will be left to mourn the graves of a people once as powerful and hopeful as yours.

The whites, too, shall pass—perhaps sooner than other tribes. Continue to contaminate your bed, and you will one night suffocate in your own waste. When the buffalo are all slaughtered, the wild horses all tamed, the secret corners of the forest heavy with the scent of many men, and the view of the ripe hills blotted by talking wires,[1] where is the thicket? Gone. Where is the eagle? Gone. And what is it to say goodby to the swift and the hunt, the end of living and the beginning of survival? We might understand if we knew what it was that the white man dreams, what he describes to his children on the long winter nights, what visions he burns into their minds, so they will wish for tomorrow. But we are savages. The white man's dreams are hidden from us.

5

1. I.e., the telegraph.

THE READER

1. *In his second sentence Chief Seattle says of the white man, "One portion of the land is the same to him as the next." The red man's attitude, presumably, is that each portion is different. Explain more fully just what the contrasting attitudes are.*
2. *Chief Seattle repeatedly refers to the red man as "a savage" who "does not understand," yet in the course of this letter he gives evidence of a great deal of understanding. What is his purpose in such self-disparaging and apparently inaccurate references?*
3. *A surprisingly modern note of ecological awareness resounds in "whatever happens to the beasts also happens to man. All things are connected." Locate two or three similar observations.*

THE WRITER

1. Study Chief Seattle's use of rhetorical questions ("What is man without the beasts?"). Then write a brief appeal of your own about some other subject, making similar use of rhetorical questions.
2. Chief Seattle says that the red man might understand the white man better "if we knew what it was that the white man dreams, what he describes to his children on the long winter nights, what visions he burns into their minds, so they will wish for tomorrow." Write a short essay explaining, either straightforwardly or ironically, how "the white man" might reply. If you prefer, write the reply itself.

Aldo Leopold

THINKING LIKE A MOUNTAIN

A deep chesty bawl echoes from rimrock to rimrock, rolls down the mountain, and fades into the far blackness of the night. It is an outburst of wild defiant sorrow, and of contempt for all the adversities of the world.

Every living thing (and perhaps many a dead one as well) pays heed to that call. To the deer it is a reminder of the way of all flesh, to the pine a forecast of midnight scuffles and of blood upon the snow, to the coyote a promise of gleanings to come, to the cowman a threat of red ink at the bank, to the hunter a challenge of fang against bullet. Yet behind these obvious and immediate hopes and fears there lies a deeper meaning, known only to the mountain itself. Only the mountain has lived long enough to listen objectively to the howl of a wolf.

Those unable to decipher the hidden meaning know nevertheless that it is there, for it is felt in all wolf country, and distinguishes that country from all other land. It tingles in the spine of all who hear wolves by night, or who scan their tracks by day. Even without sight or sound of wolf, it is implicit in a hundred small events: the midnight whinny of a pack horse, the rattle of rolling rocks, the bound of a fleeing deer, the way shadows lie under the spruces. Only the ineducable tyro can fail to sense the presence or absence of wolves, or the fact that mountains have a secret opinion about them.

My own conviction on this score dates from the day I saw a wolf die. We were eating lunch on a high rimrock, at the foot of which a turbu-

From Leopold's journals, published posthumously as *A Sand County Almanac* (1949). Sand County was Leopold's fictional name for family property outside of Madison, Wisconsin.

lent river elbowed its way. We saw what we thought was a doe fording the torrent, her breast awash in white water. When she climbed the bank toward us and shook out her tail, we realized our error: it was a wolf. A half-dozen others, evidently grown pups sprang from the willows and all joined in a welcoming mêlée of wagging tails and playful maulings. What was literally a pile of wolves writhed and tumbled in the center of an open flat at the foot of our rimrock.

In those days we had never heard of passing up a chance to kill a wolf. In a second we were pumping lead into the pack, but with more excitement than accuracy: how to aim a steep downhill shot is always confusing. When our rifles were empty, the old wolf was down, and a pup was dragging a leg into impassable slide-rocks.

We reached the old wolf in time to watch a fierce green fire dying in her eyes. I realized then, and have known ever since, that there was something new to me in those eyes—something known only to her and to the mountain. I was young then, and full of trigger-itch; I thought that because fewer wolves meant more deer, that no wolves would mean hunters' paradise. But after seeing the green fire die, I sensed that neither the wolf nor the mountain agreed with such a view.

Since then I have lived to see state after state extirpate its wolves. I have watched the face of many a newly wolfless mountain, and seen the south-facing slopes wrinkle with a maze of new deer trails. I have seen every edible bush and seedling browsed, first to anemic desuetude, and then to death. I have seen every edible tree defoliated to the height of a saddle-horn. Such a mountain looks as if someone had given God a new pruning shears, and forbidden Him all other exercise. In the end the starved bones of the hoped for deer herd, dead of its own too much, bleach with the bones of the dead sage, or molder under the high-lined junipers.

I now suspect that just as a deer herd lives in mortal fear of its wolves, so does a mountain live in mortal fear of its deer. And perhaps with better cause, for while a buck pulled down by wolves can be replaced in two or three years, a range pulled down by too many deer may fail of replacement in as many decades.

So also with cows. The cowman who cleans his range of wolves does not realize that he is taking over the wolf's job of trimming the herd to fit the range. He has not learned to think like a mountain. Hence we have dustbowls, and rivers washing the future into the sea.

We all strive for safety, prosperity, comfort, long life, and dullness. The deer strives with his supple legs, the cowman with trap and poison, the statesman with pen, the most of us with machines, votes, and dollars, but it all comes to the same thing: peace in our time. A measure of success in this is all well enough, and perhaps is a requisite to objective thinking, but too much safety seems to yield only danger in the long run. Perhaps this is behind Thoreau's dictum: In wildness is the salvation of the world. Perhaps this is the hidden meaning in the howl of the wolf, long known among mountains, but seldom perceived among men.

Joseph Wood Krutch

THE MOST DANGEROUS PREDATOR

In the United States the slaughter of wild animals for fun is subject to certain restrictions fairly well enforced. In Mexico the laws are less strict and in many regions there is little or no machinery for enforcement. Hence an automobile club in southern California distributes to its members an outline map of Baja [1] purporting to indicate in detail just where various large animals not yet quite extinct may be found by those eager to do their bit toward eliminating them completely. This map gives the impression that pronghorn antelopes, mountain sheep, and various other "game animals" abound.

In actual fact, the country can never have supported very many such and today the traveler accustomed to the open country of our own Southwest would be struck by the fact that, except for sea birds, sea mammals and fish, wildlife of any kind is far scarcer than at home. This is no doubt due in part to American hunters but also in part to the fact that native inhabitants who once could not afford the cartridges to shoot anything they did not intend to eat now get relatively cheap ammunition from the United States and can indulge in what seems to be the almost universal human tendency to kill anything that moves.

Someday—probably a little too late—the promoters of Baja as a resort area will wake up to the fact that wildlife is a tourist attraction and that though any bird or beast can be observed or photographed an unlimited number of times it can be shot only once. The Mexican government is cooperating with the government of the United States in a successful effort to save the gray whale and the sea elephant but to date does not seem much interested in initiating its own measures of protection. As long ago as 1947, Lewis Wayne Walker (who guided me on our innocent hunt for the boojum trees he had previously photographed) wrote for

Written in 1961; reprinted in *The Best Nature Writing of Joseph Wood Krutch* (1969).

1. A Mexican peninsula extending some 760 miles south from the U.S. border and separating the Gulf of California from the Pacific Ocean.

Natural History Magazine a survey of the situation, particularly as it concerns the pronghorn and the mountain sheep. A quarter of a century before, herds of antelope were to be found within thirty or forty miles of the United States border. But by 1933 they had all, so a rancher told him, been killed after a party of quail hunters had discovered them. In the roadless areas some bands of mountain sheep still existed (and doubtless do even today) but the water holes near traversable areas were already deserted by the mid forties. All the large animals of a given region must come to drink at the only pool or spring for many miles around, hence a single party need only wait beside it to exterminate the entire population inhabiting that area. Though Walker had driven more than ten thousand miles on the Baja trails during the two years preceding the writing of his letter, he saw only one deer, no sheep, and no antelope. Despite the publicity given it, "Baja is," he wrote, "the poorest game area I have ever visited."

The depredations of the hunter are not always the result of any fundamental blood lust. Perhaps he is only, more often than not, merely lacking in imagination. The exterminator of the noble animals likes the out-of-doors and thrills at the sight of something which suggests the world as it once was. But contemplation is not widely recognized as an end in itself. Having seen the antelope or the sheep, he must "do something about it." And the obvious thing to do is to shoot.

In the *Sea of Cortez* John Steinbeck[2] describes how a Mexican rancher invited his party to a sheep hunt. They were reluctant to accept until they realized that the rancher himself didn't really want to kill the animals—he merely didn't know what other excuse to give for seeking them out. When his Indians returned empty-handed he said with only mild regret: "If they had killed one we could have had our pictures taken with it." Then Steinbeck adds: "They had taught us the best of all ways to go hunting and we shall never use any other. We have, however, made one slight improvement on their method; we shall not take a gun, thereby obviating the last remote possibility of having the hunt cluttered up with game. We have never understood why men mount the heads of animals and hang them up to look down on their conquerors. Possibly it feels good to these men to be superior to animals but it does seem that if they were sure of it they would not have to prove it." Later, when one of the Indians brought back some droppings which he seemed to treasure and presented a portion of them to the white men, Steinbeck adds: "Where another man can say, 'there was an animal but because I am greater than he, he is dead and I am alive and there is his head to prove it' we can say, 'there was an

5

---

2. Steinbeck (1902–68), American author. California, his birthplace, was the setting of many of his books.

animal, and for all we know there still is and here is proof of it. He was very healthy when we last heard of him.' "

"Very pretty," so the tough-minded will say, "but hardly realistic. Man is a predator, to be sure, but he isn't the only one. The mountain lion killed sheep long before even the Indian came to Baja. The law of life is also a law of death. Nature is red in tooth and claw. You can't get away from that simple fact and there is no use in trying. Whatever else he may be, man is an animal; and like the other animals he is the enemy of all other living things. You talk of 'the balance of nature' but we are an element in it. As we increase, the mountain sheep disappear. The fittest, you know, survive."

Until quite recent times this reply would have been at least a tenable one. Primitive man seems to have been a rather unsuccessful animal, few in numbers and near the ragged edge of extinction. But gradually the balance shifted. He held his own; then he increased in numbers; then he developed techniques of aggression as well as of protection incomparably more effective than any which nature herself had ever been able to devise before the human mind intervened. Up until then, animals had always been a match, one for another. But they were no match for him. The balance no longer worked. Though for another 500,000 years "coexistence" still seemed to be a *modus vivendi* [3] the time came, only a short while ago, when man's strength, his numbers, and his skill made him master and tyrant. He now dominated the natural world of which he had once been only a part. Now for the first time he could exterminate, if he wished to do so, any other living creature—perhaps even (as we learned just yesterday) his fellow man. What this means in a specific case; what the difference is between nature, however red she may be in tooth and claw, and the terrifying predator who is no longer subject to the limitations she once imposed, can readily be illustrated on the Baja peninsula. In neither case is the story a pretty one. Both involve a ruthless predator and the slaughter of innocents. But nature's far from simple plan does depend upon a coexistence. Man is, on the other hand, the only animal who habitually exhausts or exterminates what he has learned to exploit.

Let us, then, take first a typical dog-eat-story as nature tells it, year after year, on Rasa Island, where confinement to a small area keeps it startlingly simple, without any of these sub-plots which make nature's usual stories so endlessly complicated.

This tiny island—less than a mile square in area and barely one hundred feet above sea level at its highest point—lies in the Gulf fifteen

3. Latin, "way of getting along."

or twenty miles away from the settlement at Los Angeles Bay. It is rarely visited because even in fair weather the waters round about it are treacherous. Currents up to eight knots create whirlpools between it and other small islands and there is a tide drop of twelve to thirty feet, depending upon the season. It is almost bare of vegetation except for a little of the salt weed or Salicornia which is found in so many of the saline sands in almost every climate. But it is the nesting place of thousands of Heermann gulls who, after the young are able to fend for themselves, migrate elswhere—a few southward as far as Central America but most of them north to various points on the Pacific coast. A few of the latter take the shortest route across the Baja peninsula but most take what seems an absurd detour by going first some 450 miles south to the tip of Baja and then the eight hundred or a thousand miles up its west coast to the United States—perhaps, as seems to be the case in various other paradoxes of migration—because they are following some ancestral habit acquired when the climate or the lay of the land was quite different.

My travels in Baja are, I hope, not finished, and I intend someday to set foot on Rasa to see what goes on there for myself. So far, however, I have observed the huge concentration of birds only from a low-flying plane and what I have to describe is what Walker has told me and what he wrote some ten years ago in an illustrated account for the *National Geographic Magazine.*

In late April, when the breeding season is at its height, the ground is crowded with innumerable nests—in some places no more than a yard apart, nowhere with more than twenty feet between them. Because man has so seldom disturbed the gulls here they show little fear of him though once they have reached the northern shore they rise and fly out to sea at the first sight of a human being.

If this were all there was to tell, Rasa might seem to realize that idyllic state of nature of which man, far from idyllic though he has made his own society, often loves to dream. Though on occasion gulls are predators as well as scavengers they respect one another's eggs and offspring on Rasa and live together in peace. But like most animals (and like most men) they are ruthless in their attitude toward other species though too utterly nature's children to rationalize as man does that ruthlessness. They know in their nerves and muscles without even thinking about it that the world was made for the exclusive use and convenience of gulls.

In the present case the victims of that egomania of the species are the two kinds of tern which share the island with them and have chosen to lay their eggs in a depression surrounded by gulls.

Here Walker had best tell his own story: "In the early morning of the second day a few eggs were seen under the terns but even as we watched, several were stolen by gulls. By late afternoon not an egg remained.

Nightfall brought on an influx of layers, and morning found twice as many eggs dotting the ground. By dusk only a fraction of the number in the exact center of the plot had escaped the inroads of the egg-eating enemy.

15   "The new colony had now gained a permanent foothold. Accordion-like it expanded during the night, contracted by evening. Each twenty-four hour period showed a gain for the terns and a corresponding retreat in the waiting ranks of the killing gulls.

"By the end of a week the colony had expanded from nothing to approximately four hundred square feet of egg-spotted ground and it continued to spread. The gulls seemed to be losing their appetites. Like children sated with ice cream, they had found that a single diet can be over-done."

What an absurd—some would say what a horrid—story that is. How decisively it gives the lie to what the earliest idealizers of nature called her "social union." How difficult it makes it to believe that some all-good, omnipotent, conscious, and transcendental power consciously chose to set up a general plan of which this is a typical detail. How much more probable it makes it seem that any purpose that may exist in the universe is one emerging from a chaos rather than one which had deliberately created that chaos.

But a fact remains: one must recognize that the scheme works—for the terns as well as for the gulls. If it is no more than the mechanism which so many call it, then it is at least (to use the newly current terminology) a cybernetic or self–regulating mechanism. If the gulls destroyed so many eggs that the tern population began to decline, then the gulls, deprived of their usual food supply, would also decline in numbers and the terns would again increase until the balance had been reached. "How careful of the type she seems; how careless of the single life"—as Tennyson observed some years before Darwin[4] made the same humanly disturbing fact a cornerstone of his theories.

Absurd as the situation on Rasa may seem, it has probably existed for thousands of years and may well continue for thousands more—if left to itself, undisturbed by the only predator who almost invariably renders the "cybernetic" system inoperable.

20   Consider now the case of the elephant seal, a great sea beast fourteen to sixteen feet long and nearly three tons in weight. Hardly more than a century ago it bred in enormous numbers on the rocky coast and on the islands from Point Reyes, just north of San Francisco, almost to the Magdalena Bay on the Pacific coast of Baja. Like the gray whale it was

4. Alfred, Lord Tennyson (1809–92), English poet. Charles Darwin (1809–82), English naturalist whose *Origin of Species* (1859) and *The Descent of Man* (1871) set forth his theory of evolution.

preyed upon by the ferocious killer whale which is, perhaps, the most formidable of all the predators of the sea. But a balance had been reached and the two coexisted in much the same fashion as the gulls and the terns of Rasa.

Unfortunately (at least for them) human enterprise presently discovered that sea elephants could become a source of oil second in importance to the whale alone. And against this new predator nature afforded no protection. The elephant seals had learned to be wary of the killer whale but they had known no enemy on land and they feared none. Because instinct is slow while the scheming human brain works fast, those who must depend upon instinct are lost before it can protect them against any new threat. Captain Scammon, always clear, vivid, and businesslike, describes how easy and how profitable it was to bring the seals as near to extinction as the gray whales were brought at approximately the same time:

"The mode of capturing them is thus; the sailors get between the herd and the water; then raising all possible noise by shouting, and at the same time flourishing clubs, guns, and lances, the party advances slowly towards the rookery, when the animals will retreat, appearing in a state of great alarm. Occasionally, an overgrown male will give battle, or attempt to escape; but a musket ball through the brain dispatches it; or someone checks its progress by thrusting a lance into the roof of its mouth, which causes it to settle on its haunches, when two men with heavy oaken clubs give the creature repeated blows about the head, until it is stunned or killed. After securing those that are disposed to showing resistance, the party rush on the main body. The onslaught creates such a panic among these peculiar creatures, that, losing all control of their actions, they climb, roll, and tumble over each other, when prevented from further retreat by the projecting cliffs. We recollect in one instance, where sixty-five were captured, that several were found showing no signs of having been either clubbed or lanced but were smothered by numbers of their kind heaped upon them. The whole flock, when attacked, manifested alarm by their peculiar roar, the sound of which, among the largest males, is nearly as loud as the lowing of an ox, but more prolonged in one strain, accompanied by a rattling noise in the throat. The quantity of blood in this species of the seal tribe is supposed to be double that contained in an ox, in proportion to its size.

"After the capture, the flay begins. First, with a large knife, the skin is ripped along the upper side of the body its whole length, and then cut down as far as practicable, without rolling it over; then the coating of fat that lies between the skin and flesh—which may be from one to seven inches in thickness, according to the size and condition of the animal—is cut into 'horse pieces,' about eight inches wide and twelve to fifteen long, and a puncture is made in each piece sufficiently large to pass a rope through. After flensing the upper portion of the body, it is rolled over, and cut all around as above described. Then the 'horse pieces' are strung on a raft rope (a rope three fathoms long, with an eye splice in one end) and taken to the edge of the surf; a long line is made fast to it, the end of which is thrown to a boat lying just outside of the breakers; they are then hauled through the rollers and towed to the vessel, where the oil is tried out by boiling the blubber, or fat, in large pots set in a brick furnace. . . . The oil produced is superior to whale oil for lubricating purposes. Owing to the continual pursuit of the animals, they have become nearly if not quite extinct on the California coast, or the few remaining have fled to some unknown point for security."

Captain Scammon's account was first published in the *Overland Monthly* in 1870. A few members of the herds he had helped to slaughter must have survived because in 1884 the zoologist Charles Haskins Townsend accompanied a party of sealers who hunted for two months and succeeded in killing sixty. Then, eight years later, he found eight elephant seals on Guadalupe, the lonely lava-capped island twenty-two by seven miles in extent which lies 230 miles southwest of Ensenada in Baja and is the most westerly of Mexican possessions.

25   It seems to be a biological law that if a given species diminishes in numbers, no matter how slowly, it presently reaches a point of no return from which even the most careful fostering cannot bring it back. Eight elephant seals would probably have been far too few to preserve the species; but there must have been others somewhere because when Townsend visited the islands again in 1911 he found 125, and in 1922 scientists from the Scripps Institution and the California Academy of Sciences counted 264 males at a time of year when the females had already left the breeding grounds.

Had Guadalupe not happened to be one of the most remote and inaccessible islands in our part of the world, the few refugees could hardly have survived. By the time it became known that on Guadalupe they had not only survived but multiplied into the hundreds, sealers would almost certainly have sought them out again to finish the job of extermination had not the Mexican government agreed to make Guadalupe a closed area. Because the elephant seal has again no enemy except the killer whale it now occupies all the beaches of the island to which it fled and has established new colonies on various other small islands in the same Pacific area, especially on the San Benitos group nearly two hundred miles to the east. By 1950 the total population was estimated at one thousand.

The earliest voyagers described Guadalupe, rising majestically from the sea to its four-thousand-foot summit, as a true island paradise and also, like other isolated islands, so rich in the unique forms of life which had been slowly evolved in isolation that half the birds and half the plants were unknown anywhere else. So far, I know it only by reputation and have not even seen it, as I have seen Rasa, from the air; but it is said to be very far from a paradise today. Though inhabited only by a few officers of the Mexican Navy who operate a meteorological station, whalers had begun to visit it as early as 1700 and disastrously upset the balance of nature by intentionally introducing goats to provide food for subsequent visits and unintentionally allowing cats and rats to escape from their ships. Several thousand wild goats as well as innumerable cats and rats now manage to exist there, but it is said that almost nothing of the original flora and fauna remains. Most of the unique birds are extinct; the goats have nibbled the trees as high as they are able to reach, and have almost completely destroyed all other plant life. In the absence of the natural predators necessary to establish a tolerable balance, many of the goats are said to die of starvation every year for the simple reason that any animal population will ultimately destroy its own food supply unless multiplication is regulated by either natural or artificial means. Guadalupe is, in short, a perfect demonstration of three truths: (1) That nature left to herself establishes a *modus vivendi* which may be based upon tooth and claw but which nevertheless does permit a varied flora and fauna to live and flourish; (2) that man easily upsets the natural balance so quickly and drastically that nature herself cannot reestablish it in any fashion so generally satisfactory as that which prevailed before the balance was destroyed; (3) that man, if he wishes, can mitigate to some extent the destructive effects of his intervention by intervening again to save some individual species as he seems now to have saved the gray whale and the elephant seal.

How important is it that he should come to an adequate realization of these three truths? Of the second he must take some account if he is not, like the goats of Guadalupe, to come up against the fact that any species may become so "successful" that starvation is inevitable as the ultimate check upon its proliferation and that from this fate not even his technology can save him ultimately, because even those cakes of sewage-grown algae with which he is already experimenting could do no more than postpone a little longer the final day of reckoning. He has proved himself so much cleverer than nature that, once he has intervened, she can no longer protect him just as she could not protect either the life indigenous to Guadalupe or the goats man had introduced there. Having decided to go it alone, he needs for his survival to become more clever still and, especially, more farseeing.

On the other hand, and if he so wishes, he can, perhaps, disregard the other two laws that prevent the gradual disappearance of every area which illustrates the profusion and variety which nature achieves by her own methods and he may see no reason why he should preserve from extinction the elephant seal, which will probably never again be commercially valuable, or for that matter any other of the plants and animals which supply none of his physical needs. None of them may be necessary to his survival, all of them merely "beautiful" or "curious," rather than "useful."

30   Many arguments have been advanced by those who would persuade him to take some thought before it is too late. But the result may depend less upon arguments than upon the attitudes which are essentially emotional and aesthetic.

Thoreau[5]—perhaps the most eloquent exponent we have ever had of the practical, the aesthetic, and the mystical goods which man can receive from the contemplation of the natural as opposed to the man-made or man-managed—once wrote as follows:

"When I consider that the nobler animals have been exterminated here—the cougar, the panther, lynx, wolverine, wolf, bear, moose, deer, the beaver, the turkey and so forth and so forth, I cannot but feel as if I lived in a tamed and, as it were, emasculated country. . . . Is it not a maimed and imperfect nature that I am conversing with? As if I were to study a tribe of Indians that had lost all its warriors. . . . I take infinite pains to know all the phenomena of the spring, for instance, thinking that I have here the entire poem, and then, to my chagrin, I hear that it is but an imperfect copy that I possess and have read, that my ancestors had torn out many of the first leaves and grandest passages, and mutilated it in many places. I should not like to think that some demigod had come before me and picked out some of the best of the stars. I wish to know an entire heaven and an entire earth."

To what proportion of the human race such a statement is, or could be made, meaningful I do not know. But upon the answer that time is already beginning to give will depend how much, if any, of the "poem" will be legible even a few generations hence.

Many of us now talk as if, until recently, there was no need to talk about "conservation." Probably there are today more men than ever before who could answer in the affirmative Emerson's[6] question:

35   "Hast thou named all the birds without a gun?
Loved the wild rose, and left it on its stalk?"
But in absolute rather than relative numbers there are vastly more men today equipped with vastly more efficient instruments of destruction than there ever were before and many of them respect neither the bird nor the wild rose. As of this moment it is they who are winning

5. Henry David Thoreau (1817–62), American author and naturalist.

6. Ralph Waldo Emerson (1803–82), American poet and essayist, friend of Thoreau.

against everything those of us who would like to preserve the poem are able to say or do.

THE READER

1. What is the essential distinction Krutch makes between predation within the nonhuman world of nature and predation on the creatures of that world by man?
2. Krutch calls the story of the gulls and terns on Rasa Island "absurd" and adds, "How decisively it gives the lie to what the earliest idealizers of nature called her 'social union.'" Explain the concept of "nature's social union" and the point Krutch makes about it here.
3. Taking the gulls and terns as a kind of model, explore the similarities and differences in these other examples of predation: birds and mosquitoes, mosquitoes and people, hunters and deer.

THE WRITER

1. Analyze the rhetorical effectiveness of this sentence: "Someday— probably a little too late—the promoters of Baja as a resort area will wake up to the fact that wildlife is a tourist attraction and that though any bird or beast can be observed or photographed an unlimited number of times it can be shot only once" (p. 630). Try to locate and analyze two or three similar examples of Krutch's style.
2. On p. 632 Krutch makes use of a familiar and often effective argumentative technique: he states the case that a "tough-minded" opponent might make and then goes on to show why that case is not convincing. Write a short argumentative essay of your own by starting with an imagined opposing argument and then rebutting it. Take care not to set up a straw man; that is, don't make the opposing argument too easy to knock down.

Terry Tempest Williams

THE CLAN OF ONE-BREASTED WOMEN

I belong to a Clan of One-breasted Women. My mother, my grandmothers, and six aunts have all had mastectomies. Seven are dead. The two who survive have just completed rounds of chemotherapy and radiation.

First published in *Witness* (Vol. 3, No. 4, Winter 1989).

I've had my own problems: two biopsies for breast cancer and a small tumor between my ribs diagnosed as "a border-line malignancy."

This is my family history.

Most statistics tell us breast cancer is genetic, hereditary, with rising percentages attached to fatty diets, childlessness, or becoming pregnant after thirty. What they don't say is living in Utah may be the greatest hazard of all.

We are a Mormon family with roots in Utah since 1847. The word-of-wisdom, a religious doctrine of health, kept the women in my family aligned with good foods: no coffee, no tea, tobacco, or alcohol. For the most part, these women were finished having their babies by the time they were thirty. And only one faced breast cancer prior to 1960. Traditionally, as a group of people, Mormons have a low rate of cancer.

Is our family a cultural anomaly? The truth is we didn't think about it. Those who did, usually the men, simply said, "bad genes." The women's attitude was stoic. Cancer was part of life. On February 16, 1971, the eve before my mother's surgery, I accidently picked up the telephone and overheard her ask my grandmother what she could expect.

"Diane, it is one of the most spiritual experiences you will ever encounter."

I quietly put down the receiver.

Two days later, my father took my three brothers and me to the hospital to visit her. She met us in the lobby in a wheelchair. No bandages were visible. I'll never forget her radiance, the way she held herself in a purple velour robe and how she gathered us around her.

"Children, I am fine. I want you to know I felt the arms of God around me."

We believed her. My father cried. Our mother, his wife, was thirty-eight years old.

Two years ago, after my mother's death from cancer, my father and I were having dinner together. He had just returned from St. George where his construction company was putting in natural gas lines for towns in southern Utah. He spoke of his love for the country: the sandstoned landscape, bare-boned and beautiful. He had just finished hiking the Kolob trail in Zion National Park. We got caught up in reminiscing, recalling with fondness our walk up Angel's Landing on his fiftieth birthday and the years our family had vacationed there. This was a remembered landscape where we had been raised.

Over dessert, I shared a recurring dream of mine. I told my father that for years, as long as I could remember, I saw this flash of light in the night in the desert. That this image had so permeated my being, I could not venture south without seeing it again, on the horizon, illuminating buttes and mesas.

"You did see it," he said.

"Saw what?" I asked, a bit tentative.

"The bomb. The cloud. We were driving home from Riverside, California. You were sitting on your mother's lap. She was pregnant. In fact, I remember the date, September 7, 1957. We had just gotten out of the Service. We were driving north, past Las Vegas. It was an hour or so before dawn, when this explosion went off. We not only heard it, but felt it. I thought the oil tanker in front of us had blown up. We pulled over and suddenly, rising from the desert floor, we saw it, clearly, this golden-stemmed cloud, the mushroom. The sky seemed to vibrate with an eerie pink glow. Within a few minutes, a light ash was raining on the car."

I stared at my father. This was new information to me.

"I thought you knew that," my father said. "It was a common occurrence in the fifties."

It was at this moment I realized the deceit I had been living under. Children growing up in the American Southwest, drinking contaminated milk from contaminated cows, even from the contaminated breasts of their mother, my mother—members, years later, of the Clan of One-breasted Women.

It is a well-known story in the Desert West, "The Day We Bombed Utah," or perhaps, "The Years We Bombed Utah."[1] Above ground atomic testing in Nevada took place from January 27, 1951, through July 11, 1962. Not only were the winds blowing north, covering "low use segments of the population" with fallout and leaving sheep dead in their tracks, but the climate was right.[2] The United States of the 1950s was red, white, and blue. The Korean War was raging. McCarthyism was rampant. Ike was it and the Cold War was hot.[3] If you were against nuclear testing, you were for a Communist regime.

---

1. Fuller, John G., *The Day We Bombed Utah* (New York: New American Library, 1984) [Williams' note].

2. Discussion on March 14, 1988, with Carole Gallagher, photographer and author, *Nuclear Towns: The Secret War in the American Southwest*, to be published by Doubleday, Spring, 1990 [Williams' note].

3. Events and figures of the 1950s: the Korean War (1950–53) pitted the combined forces of the Republic of Korea and the United Nations (primarily the United States) against the invading armies of communist North Korea; McCarthyism, after Republican senator Joseph S. McCarthy, refers to the Communist "witch-hunt" led by the senator; Ike is the nickname of Dwight D. Eisenhower, president from 1953 to 1961; the Cold War refers to the power struggle between the Western powers and the Communist bloc that began at the end of World War II.

Much has been written about this "American nuclear tragedy." Public health was secondary to national security. The Atomic Energy Commissioner, Thomas Murray said, "Gentlemen, we must not let anything interfere with this series of tests, nothing."[4]

Again and again, the American public was told by its government, in spite of burns, blisters, and nausea, "It has been found that the tests may be conducted with adequate assurance of safety under conditions prevailing at the bombing reservations."[5] Assuaging public fears was simply a matter of public relations. "Your best action," an Atomic Energy Commission booklet read, "is not to be worried about fallout." A news release typical of the times stated, "We find no basis for concluding that harm to any individual has resulted from radioactive fallout."[6]

On August 30, 1979, during Jimmy Carter's presidency, a suit was filed entitled "Irene Allen vs. the United States of America." Mrs. Allen was the first to be alphabetically listed with twenty-four test cases, representative of nearly 1200 plaintiffs seeking compensation from the United States government for cancers caused from nuclear testing in Nevada.

Irene Allen lived in Hurricane, Utah. She was the mother of five children and had been widowed twice. Her first husband with their two oldest boys had watched the tests from the roof of the local high school. He died of leukemia in 1956. Her second husband died of pancreatic cancer in 1978.

In a town meeting conducted by Utah Senator Orrin Hatch, shortly before the suit was filed, Mrs. Allen said, "I am not blaming the government, I want you to know that, Senator Hatch. But I thought if my testimony could help in any way so this wouldn't happen again to any of the generations coming up after us . . . I am really happy to be here this day to bear testimony of this."[7]

God-fearing people. This is just one story in an anthology of thousands.

On May 10, 1984, Judge Bruce S. Jenkins handed down his opinion. Ten of the plaintiffs were awarded damages. It was the first time a federal court had determined that nuclear tests had been the cause of cancers. For the remaining fourteen test cases, the proof of causation was not sufficient. In spite of the split decision, it was considered a landmark ruling.[8] It was not to remain so for long.

4. Szasz, Ferenc M., "Downwind From the Bomb," *Nevada Historical Society Quarterly*, Fall, 1987 Vol. XXX, No. 3, p. 185 [Williams' note].
5. Fradkin, Philip L., *Fallout* (Tucson: University of Arizona Press, 1989), 98 [Williams' note].
6. Ibid., 109 [Williams' note].
7. Town meeting held by Senator Orrin Hatch in St. George, Utah, April 17, 1979, transcript, 26–28 [Williams' note].
8. Fradkin, Op. cit., 228 [Williams' note].

In April, 1987, the 10th Circuit Court of Appeals overturned Judge Jenkins' ruling on the basis that the United States was protected from suit by the legal doctrine of sovereign immunity, the centuries-old idea from England in the days of absolute monarchs.[9]

In January, 1988, the Supreme Court refused to review the Appeals Court decision. To our court system, it does not matter whether the United States Government was irresponsible, whether it lied to its citizens or even that citizens died from the fallout of nuclear testing. What matters is that our government is immune. "The King can do no wrong."

In Mormon culture, authority is respected, obedience is revered, and   30
independent thinking is not. I was taught as a young girl not to "make waves" or "rock the boat."

"Just let it go—" my mother would say. "You know how you feel, that's what counts."

For many years, I did just that—listened, observed, and quietly formed my own opinions within a culture that rarely asked questions because they had all the answers. But one by one, I watched the women in my family die common, heroic deaths. We sat in waiting rooms hoping for good news, always receiving the bad. I cared for them, bathed their scarred bodies and kept their secrets. I watched beautiful women become bald as cytoxan, cisplatin and adriamycin were injected into their veins. I held their foreheads as they vomited green-black bile and I shot them with morphine when the pain became inhuman. In the end, I witnessed their last peaceful breaths, becoming a midwife to the rebirth of their souls. But the price of obedience became too high.

The fear and inability to question authority that ultimately killed rural communities in Utah during atmospheric testing of atomic weapons was the same fear I saw being held in my mother's body. Sheep. Dead sheep. The evidence is buried.

I cannot prove that my mother, Diane Dixon Tempest, or my grandmothers, Lettie Romney Dixon and Kathryn Blackett Tempest, along with my aunts contracted cancer from nuclear fallout in Utah. But I can't prove they didn't.

My father's memory was correct, the September blast we drove   35
through in 1957 was part of Operation Plumbbob, one of the most intensive series of bomb tests to be initiated. The flash of light in the night in the desert I had always thought was a dream developed into a family nightmare. It took fourteen years, from 1957 to 1971, for cancer

9. U.S. vs. Allen, 816 Federal Reporter, 2d/1417 (10th Circuit Court 1987), cert. denied, 108 S. CT. 694 (1988) [Williams' note].

to show up in my mother—the same time, Howard L. Andrews, an authority on radioactive fallout at the National Institutes of Health, says radiation cancer requires to become evident.[1] The more I learn about what it means to be a "downwinder," the more questions I drown in.

What I do know, however, is that as a Mormon woman of the fifth generation of "Latter-Day-Saints," I must question everything, even if it means losing my faith, even if it means becoming a member of a border tribe among my own people. Tolerating blind obedience in the name of patriotism or religion ultimately takes our lives.

When the Atomic Energy Commission described the country north of the Nevada Test Site as "virtually uninhabited desert terrain," my family members were some of the "virtual uninhabitants."

One night, I dreamed women from all over the world circling a blazing fire in the desert. They spoke of change, of how they hold the moon in their bellies and wax and wane with its phases. They mocked at the presumption of even-tempered beings and made promises that they would never fear the witch inside themselves. The women danced wildly as sparks broke away from the flames and entered the night sky as stars.

And they sang a song given to them by Shoshoni grandmothers:

> *Ah ne nah, nah*
> *nin nah nah—*
> *Ah ne nah, nah*
> *nin nah nah—*
> *Nyaga mutzi*
> *oh ne nay—*
> *Nyaga mutzi*
> *oh ne nay—* [2]

40   The women danced and drummed and sang for weeks, preparing themselves for what was to come. They would reclaim the desert for the sake of their children, for the sake of the land.

A few miles downwind from the fire circle, bombs were being tested. Rabbits felt the tremors. Their soft leather pads on paws and feet recognized the shaking sands while the roots of mesquite and sage were smoldering. Rocks were hot from the inside out and dust devils hummed unnaturally. And each time there was another nuclear test, ravens

1. Fradkin, Op. cit., 116 [Williams' note].

2. This song was sung by the Western Shoshone women as they crossed the line at the Nevada Test Site on March 18, 1988, as part of their "Reclaim the Land" action. The translation they gave was: "Consider the rabbits how gently they walk on the earth. Consider the rabbits how gently they walk on the earth. We remember them. We can walk gently also. We remember them. We can walk gently also." [Williams' note].

watched the desert heave. Stretch marks appeared. The land was losing its muscle.

The women couldn't bear it any longer. They were mothers. They had suffered labor pains but always under the promise of birth. The red hot pains beneath the desert promised death only as each bomb became a stillborn. A contract had been broken between human beings and the land. A new contract was being drawn by the women who understood the fate of the earth as their own.

Under the cover of darkness, ten women slipped under the barbed wire fence and entered the contaminated country. They were trespassing. They walked toward the town of Mercury in moonlight, taking their cues from coyote, kit fox, antelope squirrel, and quail. They moved quietly and deliberately through the maze of Joshua trees. When a hint of daylight appeared they rested, drinking tea and sharing their rations of food. The women closed their eyes. The time had come to protest with the heart, that to deny one's genealogy with the earth was to commit treason against one's soul.

At dawn, the women draped themselves in mylar, wrapping long streamers of silver plastic around their arms to blow in the breeze. They wore clear masks that became the faces of humanity. And when they arrived on the edge of Mercury, they carried all the butterflies of a summer day in their wombs. They paused to allow their courage to settle.

The town which forbids pregnant women and children to enter because of radiation risks to their health was asleep. The women moved through the streets as winged messengers, twirling around each other in slow motion, peeking inside homes and watching the easy sleep of men and women. They were astonished by such stillness and periodically would utter a shrill note or low cry just to verify life.

The residents finally awoke to what appeared as strange apparitions. Some simply stared. Others called authorities, and in time, the women were apprehended by wary soldiers dressed in desert fatigues. They were taken to a white, square building on the other edge of Mercury. When asked who they were and why they were there, the women replied, "We are mothers and we have come to reclaim the desert for our children."

The soldiers arrested them. As the ten women were blindfolded and handcuffed, they began singing:

> *You can't forbid us everything*
> *You can't forbid us to think—*
> *You can't forbid our tears to flow*
> *And you can't stop the songs that we sing.*

The women continued to sing louder and louder, until they heard the voices of their sisters moving across the mesa.

Ah ne nah, nah
nin nah nah—
Ah ne nah, nah
nin nah nah—
Nyaga mutzi
oh ne nay—
Nyaga mutzi
oh ne nay—

"Call for re-enforcement," one soldier said.

50 "We have," interrupted one woman. "We have—and you have no idea of our numbers."

On March 18, 1988, I crossed the line at the Nevada Test Site and was arrested with nine other Utahns for trespassing on military lands. They are still conducting nuclear tests in the desert. Ours was an act of civil disobedience. But as I walked toward the town of Mercury, it was more than a gesture of peace. It was a gesture on behalf of the Clan of One-breasted Women.

As one officer cinched the handcuffs around my wrists, another frisked my body. She found a pen and a pad of paper tucked inside my left boot.

"And these?" she asked sternly.

"Weapons," I replied.

55 Our eyes met. I smiled. She pulled the leg of my trousers back over my boot.

"Step forward, please," she said as she took my arm.

We were booked under an afternoon sun and bussed to Tonapah, Nevada. It was a two-hour ride. This was familiar country to me. The Joshua trees standing their ground had been named by my ancestors who believed they looked like prophets pointing west to the promised land. These were the same trees that bloomed each spring, flowers appearing like white flames in the Mojave. And I recalled a full moon in May when my mother and I had walked among them, flushing out mourning doves and owls.

The bus stopped short of town. We were released. The officials thought it was a cruel joke to leave us stranded in the desert with no way to get home. What they didn't realize is that we were home, soul-centered and strong, women who recognized the sweet smell of sage as fuel for our spirits.

Ethics

Gary Soto

THE PIE

I knew enough about hell to stop me from stealing. I was holy in almost every bone. Some days I recognized the shadows of angels flopping on the backyard grass, and other days I heard faraway messages in the plumbing that howled underneath the house when I crawled there looking for something to do.

But boredom made me sin. Once, at the German Market, I stood before a rack of pies, my sweet tooth gleaming and the juice of guilt wetting my underarms. I gazed at the nine kinds of pie, pecan and apple being my favorites, although cherry looked good, and my dear, fat-faced chocolate was always a good bet. I nearly wept trying to decide which to steal and, forgetting the flowery dust priests give off, the shadow of angels and the proximity of God howling in the plumbing underneath the house, sneaked a pie behind my coffee-lid frisbee and walked to the door, grinning to the bald grocer whose forehead shone with a window of light.

"No one saw," I muttered to myself, the pie like a discus in my hand, and hurried across the street, where I sat on someone's lawn. The sun wavered between the branches of a yellowish sycamore. A squirrel nailed itself high on the trunk, where it forked into two large bark-scabbed limbs. Just as I was going to work my cleanest finger into the pie, a neighbor came out to the porch for his mail. He looked at me, and I got up and headed for home. I raced on skinny legs to my block, but slowed to a quick walk when I couldn't wait any longer. I held the pie to my nose and breathed in its sweetness. I licked some of the crust and closed my eyes as I took a small bite.

In my front yard, I leaned against a car fender and panicked about stealing the apple pie. I knew an apple got Eve in deep trouble with snakes because Sister Marie had shown us a film about Adam and Eve

From *A Summer Life* (1990).

being cast into the desert, and what scared me more than falling from grace was being thirsty for the rest of my life. But even that didn't stop me from clawing a chunk from the pie tin and pushing it into the cavern of my mouth. The slop was sweet and gold-colored in the afternoon sun. I laid more pieces on my tongue, wet finger-dripping pieces, until I was finished and felt like crying because it was about the best thing I had ever tasted. I realized right there and then, in my sixth year, in my tiny body of two hundred bones and three or four sins, that the best things in life came stolen. I wiped my sticky fingers on the grass and rolled my tongue over the corners of my mouth. A burp perfumed the air.

5   I felt bad not sharing with Cross-Eyed Johnny, a neighbor kid. He stood over my shoulder and asked, "Can I have some?" Crust fell from my mouth, and my teeth were bathed with the jam-like filling. Tears blurred my eyes as I remembered the grocer's forehead. I remembered the other pies on the rack, the warm air of the fan above the door and the car that honked as I crossed the street without looking.

"Get away," I had answered Cross-Eyed Johnny. He watched my fingers greedily push big chunks of pie down my throat. He swallowed and said in a whisper, "Your hands are dirty," then returned home to climb his roof and sit watching me eat the pie by myself. After a while, he jumped off and hobbled away because the fall had hurt him.

I sat on the curb. The pie tin glared at me and rolled away when the wind picked up. My face was sticky with guilt. A car honked, and the driver knew. Mrs. Hancock stood on her lawn, hands on hip, and she knew. My mom, peeling a mountain of potatoes at the Redi-Spud factory, knew. I got to my feet, stomach taut, mouth tired of chewing, and flung my frisbee across the street, its shadow like the shadow of an angel fleeing bad deeds. I retrieved it, jogging slowly. I flung it again until I was bored and thirsty.

I returned home to drink water and help my sister glue bottle caps onto cardboard, a project for summer school. But the bottle caps bored me, and the water soon filled me up more than the pie. With the kitchen stifling with heat and lunatic flies, I decided to crawl underneath our house and lie in the cool shadows listening to the howling sound of plumbing. Was it God? Was it Father, speaking from death, or Uncle with his last shiny dime? I listened, ear pressed to a cold pipe, and heard a howl like the sea. I lay until I was cold and then crawled back to the light, rising from one knee, then another, to dust off my pants and squint in the harsh light. I looked and saw the glare of a pie tin on a hot day. I knew sin was what you take and didn't give back.

James Thurber

THE BEAR WHO LET IT ALONE

In the woods of the Far West there once lived a brown bear who could take it or let it lone. He would go into a bar where they sold mead, a fermented drink made of honey, and he would have just two drinks. Then he would put some money on the bar and say, "See what the bears in the back room will have," and he would go home. But finally he took to drinking by himself most of the day. He would reel home at night, kick over the umbrella stand, knock down the bridge lamps, and ram his elbows through the windows. Then he would collapse on the floor and lie there until he went to sleep. His wife was greatly distressed and his children were very frightened.

At length the bear saw the error of his ways and began to reform. In the end he became a famous teetotaller and a persistent temperance lecturer. He would tell everybody that came to his house about the awful effects of drink, and he would boast about how strong and well he had become since he gave up touching the stuff. To demonstrate this, he would stand on his head and on his hands and he would turn cartwheels in the house, kicking over the umbrella stand, knocking down the bridge lamps, and ramming his elbows through the windows. Then he would lie down on the floor, tired by his healthful exercise, and go to sleep. His wife was greatly distressed and his children were very frightened.

Moral: You might as well fall flat on your face as lean over too far backward.

From *Fables of Our Time* (1940).

Samuel Johnson

ON SELF-LOVE AND INDOLENCE

—Steriles transmisimus annos,
Haec aevi mihi prima dies, haec limina vitae.

STAT. [1.362]

—Our barren years are past;
Be this of life the first, of sloth the last.

ELPHINSTON [1]

No weakness of the human mind has more frequently incurred animadversion, than the negligence with which men overlook their own faults, however flagrant, and the easiness with which they pardon them, however frequently repeated.

It seems generally believed, that, as the eye cannot see itself, the mind has no faculties by which it can contemplate its own state, and that therefore we have not means of becoming acquainted with our real characters; an opinion which, like innumerable other postulates, an inquirer finds himself inclined to admit upon very little evidence, because it affords a ready solution of many difficulties. It will explain why the greatest abilities frequently fail to promote the happiness of those who possess them; why those who can distinguish with the utmost nicety the boundaries of vice and virtue, suffer them to be confounded in their own conduct; why the active and vigilant resign their affairs implicitly to the management of others; and why the cautious and fearful make hourly approaches toward ruin, without one sigh of solicitude or struggle for escape.

When a position teems thus with commodious consequences, who can without regret confess it to be false? Yet it is certain that declaimers have indulged a disposition to describe the dominion of the passions as extended beyond the limits that nature assigned. Self-love is often rather arrogant than blind; it does not hide our faults from ourselves, but persuades us that they escape the notice of others, and disposes us to resent censures lest we would confess them to be just. We are secretly conscious of defects and vices which we hope to conceal from the public

From *The Rambler* (1751).

1. The author of these lines is Publius Papinius Statius, a first-century Latin poet. They are given first in the original and then in William Elphinstone's sixteenth-century translation.

eye, and please ourselves with innumerable impostures, by which, in reality, no body is deceived.

In proof of the dimness of our internal sight, or the general inability of man to determine rightly concerning his own character, it is common to urge the success of the most absurd and incredible flattery, and the resentment always raised by advice, however soft, benevolent, and reasonable. But flattery, if its operation be nearly examined, will be found to owe its acceptance not to our ignorance but knowledge of our failures, and to delight us rather as it consoles our wants than displays our possessions. He that shall solicit the favor of his patron by praising him for qualities which he can find in himself, will be defeated by the more daring panegyrist who enriches him with adscititious excellence. Just praise is only a debt, but flattery is a present. The acknowledgment of those virtues on which conscience congratulates us, is a tribute that we can at any time exact with confidence, but the celebration of those which we only feign, or desire without any vigorous endeavors to attain them, is received as a confession of sovereignty over regions never conquered, as a favorable decision of disputable claims, and is more welcome as it is more gratuitous.

Advice is offensive, not because it lays us open to unexpected regret, or convicts us of any fault which had escaped our notice, but because it shows us that we are known to others as well as to ourselves; and the officious monitor is persecuted with hatred, not because his accusation is false, but because he assumes that superiority which we are not willing to grant him, and has dared to detect what we desired to conceal.

For this reason advice is commonly ineffectual. If those who follow the call of their desires, without inquiry whither they are going, had deviated ignorantly from the paths of wisdom, and were rushing upon dangers unforeseen, they would readily listen to information that recalls them from their errors, and catch the first alarm by which destruction or infamy is denounced. Few that wander in the wrong way mistake it for the right; they only find it more smooth and flowery, and indulge their own choice rather than approve it: therefore few are persuaded to quit it by admonition or reproof, since it impresses no new conviction, nor confers any powers of action or resistance. He that is gravely informed how soon profusion will annihilate his fortune, hears with little advantage what he knew before, and catches at the next occasion of expense, because advice has no force to suppress his vanity. He that is told how certainly intemperance will hurry him to the grave, runs with his usual speed to a new course of luxury, because his reason is not invigorated, nor his appetite weakened.

The mischief of Flattery is, not that it persuades any man that he is what he is not, but that it suppresses the influence of honest ambition,

5

by raising an opinion that honor may be gained without the toil of merit; and the benefit of advice arises commonly, not from any new light imparted to the mind, but from the discovery which it affords, of the publick suffrages. He that could withstand conscience, is frighted at infamy, and shame prevails where reason was defeated.

As we all know our own faults, and know them commonly with many aggravations which human perspicacity cannot discover, there is, perhaps, no man, however hardened by impudence or dissipated by levity, sheltered by hypocrisy, or blasted by disgrace, who does not intend some time to review his conduct, and to regulate the remainder of his life by the laws of virtue. New temptations indeed attack him, new invitations are offered by pleasure and interest, and the hour of reformation is always delayed; every delay gives vice another opportunity of fortifying itself by habit; and the change of manners, though sincerely intended and rationally planned, is referred to the time when some craving passion shall be fully gratified, or some powerful allurement cease its importunity.

Thus procrastination is accumulated on procrastination, and one impediment succeeds another, till age shatters our resolution, or death intercepts the project of amendment. Such is often the end of salutary purposes, after they have long delighted the imagination, and appeased that disquiet which every mind feels from known misconduct, when the attention is not diverted by business or by pleasure.

10 Nothing surely can be more unworthy of a reasonable nature, than to continue in a state so opposite to real happiness, as that all the peace of solitude and felicity of meditation, must arise from resolutions of forsaking it. Yet the world will often afford examples of men, who pass months and years in a continual war with their own convictions, and are daily dragged by habit or betrayed by passion into practices, which they closed and opened their eyes with purposes to avoid; purposes which, though settled on conviction, the first impulse of momentary desire totally overthrows.

The influence of custom is indeed such that to conquer it will require the utmost efforts of fortitude and virtue, nor can I think any man more worthy of veneration and renown, than those who have burst the shackles of habitual vice. This victory however has different degrees of glory as of difficulty; it is more heroic as the objects of guilty gratification are more familiar, and the recurrence of solicitation more frequent. He that from experience of the folly of ambition resigns his offices, may set himself free at once from temptation to squander his life in courts, because he cannot regain his former station. He who is enslaved by an amorous passion, may quit his tyrant in disgust, and absence will without the help of reason overcome by degrees the desire of returning. But those appetites to which every place affords their proper object, and which require no preparatory measures or gradual advances, are more tenaciously adhesive; the wish is so near the enjoyment, that compliance often precedes consideration, and before the powers of reason can be summoned, the time for employing them is past.

Indolence is therefore one of the vices from which those whom it once infects are seldom reformed. Every other species of luxury operates upon some appetite that is quickly satiated, and requires some concurrence of art or accident which every place will not supply; but the desire of ease acts equally at all hours, and the longer it is indulged in the more increased. To do nothing is in every man's power; we can never want an opportunity of omitting duties. The lapse to indolence is soft and imperceptible, because it is only a mere cessation of activity; but the return to diligence is difficult, because it implies a change from rest to motion, from privation to reality.

> —*Facilis descensus Averni:*
> *Noctes atque dies patet atri janua Ditis:*
> *Sed revocare gradum, superasque evadere ad auras,*
> *Hoc opus, hic labor est.—*
>
> [vir. *Aeneid VI. 126*]

> The gates of *Hell* are open night and day;
> Smooth the descent, and easy is the way:
> But, to return, and view the chearful skies;
> In this, the task and mighty labour lies.
>
> DRYDEN

Of this vice, as of all others, every man who indulges it is conscious; we all know our own state, if we could be induced to consider it; and it might perhaps be useful to the conquest of all these ensnarers of the mind, if at certain stated days life was reviewed. Many things necessary are omitted, because we vainly imagine that they may be always performed, and what cannot be done without pain will for ever be delayed if the time of doing it be left unsettled. No corruption is great but by long negligence, which can scarcely prevail in a mind regularly and frequently awakened by periodical remorse. He that thus breaks his life into parts, will find in himself a desire to distinguish every stage of his existence by some improvement, and delight himself with the approach of the day of recollection, as of the time which is to begin a new series of virtue and felicity.

Francis Bacon

OF SIMULATION AND DISSIMULATION

Dissimulation is but a faint kind of policy or wisdom; for it asketh a strong wit and a strong heart to know when to tell truth, and to do it. Therefore it is the weaker sort of politics[1] that are the great dissemblers.

Tacitus saith, *Livia sorted well with the arts of her husband and dissimulation of her son;* attributing arts or policy to Augustus, and dissimulation to Tiberius. And again, when Mucianus encourageth Vespasian to take arms against Vitellius, he saith, *We rise not against the piercing judgment of Augustus, nor the extreme caution or closeness of Tiberius.*[2] These properties, of arts or policy and dissimulation or closeness, are indeed habits and faculties several, and to be distinguished. For if a man have that penetration of judgment as he can discern what things are to be laid open, and what to be secreted, and what to be shewed at half lights, and to whom and when (which indeed are arts of state and arts of life, as Tacitus well calleth them), to him a habit of dissimulation is a hinderance and a poorness. But if a man cannot obtain to that judgment, then it is left to him generally to be close, and a dissembler. For where a man cannot choose or vary in particulars, there it is good to take the safest and wariest way in general; like the going softly, by one that cannot well see. Certainly the ablest men that ever were have had all an openness and frankness of dealing; and a name of certainty and veracity; but then they were like horses well managed; for they could tell passing well when to stop or turn; and at such times when they thought the case indeed required dissimulation, if then they used it, it came to pass that the former opinion spread abroad of their good faith and clearness of dealing made them almost invisible.

There be three degrees of this hiding and veiling of a man's self. The first, Closeness, Reservation, and Secrecy; when a man leaveth himself without observation, or without hold to be taken, what he is. The second, Dissimulation, in the negative; when a man lets fall signs and arguments, that he is not that he is. And the third, Simulation, in the affirmative; when a man industriously and expressly feigns and pretends to be that he is not.

From *Novum Organum* (1620).

1. Politicians.
2. The Roman historian Tacitus here speaks of the plottings of Livia, wife of the emperor Augustus Caesar and mother of his successor Tiberius; and of the Roman official Mucianus, who in A.D. 69 supported Vespasian in his successful struggle against Vitellius to gain the imperial throne.

For the first of these, Secrecy; it is indeed the virtue of a confessor.[3] And assuredly the secret man heareth many confessions. For who will open himself to a blab or babbler? But if a man be thought secret, it inviteth discovery; as the more close air sucketh in the more open; and as in confession the revealing is not for worldly use, but for the ease of a man's heart, so secret men come to the knowledge of many things in that kind; while men rather discharge their minds than impart their minds. In few words, mysteries are due to secrecy. Besides (to say truth) nakedness is uncomely, as well in mind as body; and it addeth no small reverence to men's manners and actions, if they be not altogether open. As for talkers and futile persons, they are commonly vain and credulous withal. For he that talketh what he knoweth, will also talk what he knoweth not. Therefore set it down, *that an habit of secrecy is both politic and moral.* And in this part, it is good that a man's face give his tongue leave to speak. For the discovery of a man's self by the tracts of his countenance is a great weakness and betraying; by how much it is many times more marked and believed than a man's words.

For the second, which is Dissimulation; it followeth many times upon secrecy by a necessity; so that he that will be secret must be a dissembler in some degree. For men are too cunning to suffer a man to keep an indifferent carriage between both, and to be secret, without swaying the balance on either side. They will so beset a man with questions, and draw him on, and pick it out of him, that, without an absurd silence, he must shew an inclination one way; or if he do not, they will gather as much by his silence as by his speech. As for equivocations, or oraculous speeches, they cannot hold out for long. So that no man can be secret, except he give himself a little scope of dissimulation; which is, as it were, but the skirts or train of secrecy. 5

But for the third degree, which is Simulation and false profession; that I hold more culpable, and less politic; except it be in great and rare matters. And therefore a general custom of simulation (which is this last degree) is a vice, rising either of a natural falseness or fearfulness, or of a mind that hath some main faults, which because a man must needs disguise, it maketh him practice simulation in other things, lest his hand should be out of ure.[4]

The great advantages of simulation and dissimulation are three. First, to lay asleep opposition, and to surprise. For where a man's intentions are published, it is an alarum to call up all that are against them. The second is, to reserve to a man's self a fair retreat. For if a man engage himself by a manifest declaration, he must go through or take a fall. The third is, the better to discover the mind of another. For to him that opens himself men will hardly shew themselves adverse; but will (fair)

3. One to whom confession is made.   4. Practice.

let him go on, and turn their freedom of speech to freedom of thought. And therefore it is a good shrewd proverb of the Spaniard, *Tell a lie and find a troth.* As if there were no way of discovery but by simulation. There be also three disadvantages, to set it even. The first, that simulation and dissimulation commonly carry with them a shew of fearfulness, which in any business doth spoil the feathers of round flying up to the mark. The second, that it puzzleth and perplexeth the conceits[5] of many, that perhaps would otherwise co-operate with him; and makes a man walk almost alone to his own ends. The third and greatest is, that it depriveth a man of one of the most principal instruments for action; which is trust and belief. The best composition and temperature is to have openness in fame and opinion; secrecy in habit; dissimulation in seasonable use; and a power to feign, if there be no remedy.

5. Conceptions, thoughts.

THE READER

1. Explain Bacon's distinction, drawn in the first two paragraphs, between dissembling, on the one hand, and, on the other, arts and policy. How does this opening prepare the way for the remainder of the essay?
2. How is the word dissimulation as used in the third paragraph and thereafter to be distinguished from its use in the first two paragraphs?
3. In what connection and to what purpose does Bacon use the following expressions? Explain the image or allusion in each:
   a) "like the going softly, by one that cannot well see" (p. 654)
   b) "like horses well managed; for they could tell passing well when to stop or turn" (p. 654)
   c) "as the more close air sucketh in the more open" (p. 655)
   d) "it is good that a man's face give his tongue leave to speak" (p. 655)
   e) "he must go through or take a fall" (p. 655)
   f) "fearfulness, which in any business doth spoil the feathers of round flying up to the mark" (p. 656)

THE WRITER

1. What are the three degrees of hiding of a man's self? According to what principles does Bacon arrange these degrees? What accounts for his according unequal amounts of space to the exposition of them?
2. Make a close analysis of Bacon's closing paragraph, indicating the ways Bacon achieves symmetry, balance. How does that effect contribute to his tone and purpose? What elements in the paragraph offset a mere symmetry?
3. Bacon would allow "Simulation and false profession" in "great and rare matters." Would you? Give an example of such matters. Write a brief essay explaining your position.

4. What view of the world underlies Bacon's essay? Write an essay showing what Bacon's assumptions about the world seem to be. Be careful to show how you draw on the essay to find out Bacon's assumptions.

Samuel Johnson

LETTER TO LORD CHESTERFIELD

February 1755

MY LORD

I have been lately informed by the proprietor of *The World* [1] that two papers in which my *Dictionary* is recommended to the public were written by your Lordship. To be so distinguished is an honor which, being very little accustomed to favors from the great, I know not well how to receive, or in what terms to acknowledge.

When upon some slight encouragement I first visited your Lordship I was overpowered like the rest of mankind by the enchantment of your address, [2] and could not forbear to wish that I might boast myself *le vainqueur du vainqueur de la terre*, [3] that I might obtain that regard for which I saw the world contending, but found my attendance so little encouraged that neither pride nor modesty would suffer me to continue it. When I had once addressed your Lordship in public, I had exhausted all the art of pleasing which a retired and uncourtly scholar can possess. I had done all that I could, and no man is well pleased to have his all neglected, be it ever so little.

Seven years, my lord, have now past since I waited in your outward rooms or was repulsed from your door, during which time I have been pushing on my work through difficulties of which it is useless to complain, and have brought it at last to the verge of publication without one act of assistance, one word of encouragement, or one smile of favor. Such treatment I did not expect, for I never had a patron before.

The shepherd in Virgil grew at last acquainted with Love, and found him a native of the rocks. [4] Is not a patron, my lord, one who looks with unconcern on a man struggling for life in the water and when he has

1. A journal in which Lord Chesterfield had recently praised Johnson's *Dictionary of the English Language.* Johnson had been at work on the dictionary for nine years.
2. Here in the old sense of "courtesy."
3. The conqueror of the conqueror of the world.
4. Or deserts; an allusion to Virgil's eighth eclogue, line 43.

reached ground encumbers him with help. The notice which you have been pleased to take of my labors, had it been early, had been kind; but it has been delayed till I am indifferent and cannot enjoy it, till I am solitary and cannot impart it, till I am known and do not want[5] it.

I hope it is no very cynical asperity not to confess obligation where no benefit has been received, or to be unwilling that the public should consider me as owing that to a patron, which Providence has enabled me to do for myself.

Having carried on my work thus far with so little obligation to any favorer of learning I shall not be disappointed though I should conclude it, if less be possible, with less, for I have been long wakened from that dream of hope, in which I once boasted myself with so much exultation, my lord your Lordship's most humble most obedient servant,

SAM:JOHNSON

5. Need.

Lord Chesterfield

LETTER TO HIS SON

London, October 16, O.S. 1747

DEAR BOY

The art of pleasing is a very necessary one to possess, but a very difficult one to acquire. It can hardly be reduced to rules; and your own good sense and observation will teach you more of it than I can. "Do as you would be done by," is the surest method that I know of pleasing. Observe carefully what pleases you in others, and probably the same things in you will please others. If you are pleased with the complaisance and attention of others to your humors, your tastes, or your weaknesses, depend upon it, the same complaisance and attention on your part to theirs will equally please them. Take the tone of the company that you are in, and do not pretend to give it; be serious, gay, or even trifling, as you find the present humor of the company; this is an attention due from every individual to the majority. Do not tell stories in company; there is nothing more tedious and disagreeable; if by chance you know a very short story, and exceedingly applicable to the present subject of conversation, tell it in as few words as possible; and even then, throw out that you do not love to tell stories, but that the shortness of it tempted you.

Of all things banish the egotism out of your conversation, and never think of entertaining people with your own personal concerns or private affairs; though they are interesting to you, they are tedious and imperti-

From Chesterfield's *Letters* (published in 1774).

nent to everybody else; besides that, one cannot keep one's own private affairs too secret. Whatever you think your own excellencies may be, do not affectedly display them in company; nor labor, as many people do, to give that turn to the conversation, which may supply you with an opportunity of exhibiting them. If they are real, they will infallibly be discovered, without your pointing them out yourself, and with much more advantage. Never maintain an argument with heat and clamor, though you think or know yourself to be in the right; but give your opinion modestly and coolly, which is the only way to convince; and, if that does not do, try to change the conversation, by saying, with good-humor, "We shall hardly convince one another; nor is it necessary that we should, so let us talk of something else."

Remember that there is a local propriety to be observed in all companies; and that what is extremely proper in one company may be, and often is, highly improper in another.

The jokes, the *bon-mots*, the little adventures, which may do very well in one company, will seem flat and tedious, when related in another. The particular characters, the habits, the cant of one company may give merit to a word, or a gesture, which would have none at all if divested of those accidental circumstances. Here people very commonly err; and fond of something that has entertained them in one company, and in certain circumstances, repeat it with emphasis in another, where it is either insipid, or, it may be, offensive, by being ill-timed or misplaced. Nay, they often do it with this silly preamble: "I will tell you an excellent thing," or, "I will tell you the best thing in the world." This raises expectations, which, when absolutely disappointed, make the relator of this excellent thing look, very deservedly, like a fool.

If you would particularly gain the affection and friendship of particular people, whether men or women, endeavor to find out their predominant excellency, if they have one, and their prevailing weakness, which everybody has; and do justice to the one, and something more than justice to the other. Men have various objects in which they may excel, or at least would be thought to excel; and, though they love to hear justice done to them, where they know that they excel, yet they are most and best flattered upon those points where they wish to excel, and yet are doubtful whether they do or not. As for example: Cardinal Richelieu, who was undoubtedly the ablest statesman of his time, or perhaps of any other, had the idle vanity of being thought the best poet too; he envied the great Corneille his reputation, and ordered a criticism to be written upon the *Cid.* [1] Those, therefore, who flattered skillfully, said little to him of his abilities in state affairs, or at least but *en passant,* and as it

5

---

1. When the French classic tragedy *The Cid,* founded upon the legendary exploits of the medieval Castilian warrior-hero, was published in 1636 by its author Pierre Cor-   neille (1606–84), it was the subject of violent criticism, led by the French minister of state Richelieu (1585–1642).

might naturally occur. But the incense which they gave him, the smoke of which they knew would turn his head in their favor, was as a *bel esprit* and a poet. Why? Because he was sure of one excellency, and distrustful as to the other.

You will easily discover every man's prevailing vanity by observing his favorite topic of conversation; for every man talks most of what he has most a mind to be thought to excel in. Touch him but there, and you touch him to the quick. The late Sir Robert Walpole[2] (who was certainly an able man) was little open to flattery upon that head, for he was in no doubt himself about it; but his prevailing weakness was, to be thought to have a polite and happy turn to gallantry—of which he had undoubtedly less than any man living. It was his favorite and frequent subject of conversation, which proved to those who had any penetration that it was his prevailing weakness, and they applied to it with success.

Women have, in general, but one object, which is their beauty; upon which scarce any flattery is too gross for them to follow. Nature has hardly formed a woman ugly enough to be insensible to flattery upon her person; if her face is so shocking that she must, in some degree, be conscious of it, her figure and air, she trusts, make ample amends for it. If her figure is deformed, her face, she thinks, counterbalances it. If they are both bad, she comforts herself that she has graces, a certain manner, a *je ne sais quoi*[3] still more engaging than beauty. This truth is evident from the studied and elaborate dress of the ugliest woman in the world. An undoubted, uncontested, conscious beauty is, of all women, the least sensible of flattery upon that head; she knows it is her due, and is therefore obliged to nobody for giving it her. She must be flattered upon her understanding; which, though she may possibly not doubt of herself, yet she suspects that men may distrust.

Do not mistake me, and think that I mean to recommend to you abject and criminal flattery: no; flatter nobody's vices or crimes: on the contrary, abhor and discourage them. But there is no living in the world without a complaisant indulgence for people's weaknesses, and innocent, though ridiculous vanities. If a man has a mind to be thought wiser, and a woman handsomer, than they really are, their error is a comfortable one to themselves, and an innocent one with regard to other people; and I would rather make them my friends by indulging them in it, than my enemies by endeavoring (and that to no purpose) to undeceive them.

There are little attentions, likewise, which are infinitely engaging, and which sensibly affect that degree of pride and self-love, which is inseparable from human nature, as they are unquestionable proofs of the regard and consideration which we have for the persons to whom we pay

2. For two decades a powerful prime minister, Walpole (1676–1745) was also a patron of the arts and prided himself on his taste.
3. A certain inexpressible quality.

them. As, for example, to observe the little habits, the likings, the antipathies, and the tastes of those whom we would gain; and then take care to provide them with the one, and to secure them from the other; giving them, genteelly, to understand, that you had observed they liked such a dish, or such a room, for which reason you had prepared it: or, on the contrary, that having observed they had an aversion to such a dish, a dislike to such a person, etc., you had taken care to avoid presenting them. Such attention to such trifles flatters self-love much more than greater things, as it makes people think themselves almost the only objects of your thoughts and care.

These are some of the arcana[4] necessary for your initiation in the great society of the world. I wish I had known them better at your age; I have paid the price of three and fifty years for them, and shall not grudge it if you reap the advantage. Adieu.

4. Secret things.

THE READER

1. *Chesterfield's letter is negatively phrased. What is the underlying evil he is advising his son to avoid?*
2. *Gaylin (p. 675) maintains that our behavior defines our identity. Would Chesterfield agree?*
3. *In question 2, "The Writer" (below), you are asked to rewrite a paragraph both positively and negatively. What ethical principle would you appeal to in each case?*

THE WRITER

1. *Is this letter unified around a central concern, or is it a series of separate observations?*
2. *An eighteenth-century aristocrat probably needs translation into modern terms. Rewrite a paragraph from Lord Chesterfield's letter so as to make it as appealing and persuasive as possible. Then do the opposite—make it as offensive as possible.*

Samuel L. Clemens

ADVICE TO YOUTH

Being told I would be expected to talk here, I inquired what sort of a talk I ought to make. They said it should be something suitable to youth—something didactic, instructive, or something in the nature of good advice. Very well. I have a few things in my mind which I have often longed to say for the instruction of the young; for it is in one's tender early years that such things will best take root and be most enduring and most valuable. First, then, I will say to you, my young friends—and I say it beseechingly, urgingly—

Always obey your parents, when they are present. This is the best policy in the long run, because if you don't they will make you. Most parents think they know better than you do, and you can generally make more by humoring that superstition than you can by acting on your own better judgment.

Be respectful to your superiors, if you have any, also to strangers, and sometimes to others. If a person offend you, and you are in doubt as to whether it was intentional or not, do not resort to extreme measures; simply watch your chance and hit him with a brick. That will be sufficient. If you shall find that he had not intended any offense, come out frankly and confess yourself in the wrong when you struck him; acknowledge it like a man and say you didn't mean to. Yes, always avoid violence; in this age of charity and kindliness, the time has gone by for such things. Leave dynamite to the low and unrefined.

Go to bed early, get up early—this is wise. Some authorities say get up with the sun; some others say get up with one thing, some with another. But a lark is really the best thing to get up with. It gives you a splendid reputation with everybody to know that you get up with the lark; and if you get the right kind of a lark, and work at him right, you can easily train him to get up at half past nine, every time—it is no trick at all.

5   Now as to the matter of lying. You want to be very careful about lying; otherwise you are nearly sure to get caught. Once caught, you can never again be, in the eyes of the good and the pure, what you were before. Many a young person has injured himself permanently through a single clumsy and illfinished lie, the result of carelessness born of incomplete training. Some authorities hold that the young ought not to lie at all. That, of course, is putting it rather stronger than necessary; still, while

Text of a lecture given by Clemens in 1882.

I cannot go quite so far as that, I do maintain, and I believe I am right, that the young ought to be temperate in the use of this great art until practice and experience shall give them that confidence, elegance, and precision which alone can make the accomplishment graceful and profitable. Patience, diligence, painstaking attention to detail—these are the requirements; these, in time, will make the student perfect; upon these, and upon these only, may he rely as the sure foundation for future eminence. Think what tedious years of study, thought, practice, experience, went to the equipment of that peerless old master who was able to impose upon the whole world the lofty and sounding maxim that "truth is mighty and will prevail"—the most majestic compound fracture of fact which any of woman born has yet achieved. For the history of our race, and each individual's experience, are sown thick with evidence that a truth is not hard to kill and that a lie told well is immortal. There is in Boston a monument of the man who discovered anaesthesia; many people are aware, in these latter days, that that man didn't discover it at all, but stole the discovery from another man. Is this truth mighty, and will it prevail? Ah no, my hearers, the monument is made of hardy material, but the lie it tells will outlast it a million years. An awkward, feeble, leaky lie is a thing which you ought to make it your unceasing study to avoid; such a lie as that has no more real permanence than an average truth. Why, you might as well tell the truth at once and be done with it. A feeble, stupid, preposterous lie will not live two years—except it be a slander upon somebody. It is indestructible, then, of course, but that is no merit of yours. A final word: begin your practice of this gracious and beautiful art early—begin now. If I had begun earlier, I could have learned how.

Never handle firearms carelessly. The sorrow and suffering that have been caused through the innocent but heedless handling of firearms by the young! Only four days ago, right in the next farmhouse to the one where I am spending the summer, a grandmother, old and gray and sweet, one of the loveliest spirits in the land, was sitting at her work, when her young grandson crept in and got down an old, battered, rusty gun which had not been touched for many years and was supposed not to be loaded, and pointed it at her, laughing and threatening to shoot. In her fright she ran screaming and pleading toward the door on the other side of the room; but as she passed him he placed the gun almost against her very breast and pulled the trigger! He had supposed it was not loaded. And he was right—it wasn't. So there wasn't any harm done. It is the only case of that kind I ever heard of. Therefore, just the same, don't you meddle with old unloaded firearms; they are the most deadly and unerring things that have ever been created by man. You don't have to take any pains at all with them; you don't have to have a rest, you don't have to have any sights on the gun, you don't have to take aim, even. No, you just pick out a relative and bang away, and you are sure to get him. A youth who can't hit a cathedral at thirty yards with a Gatling gun in three-quarters of an hour, can take up an old empty musket and bag his grandmother every time, at a hundred. Think what Waterloo[1] would have been if one of the armies had been boys armed with old muskets supposed not to be loaded, and the other army had been composed of their female relations. The very thought of it makes one shudder.

There are many sorts of books; but good ones are the sort for the young to read. Remember that. They are a great, an inestimable, an unspeakable means of improvement. Therefore be careful in your selection, my young friends; be very careful; confine yourselves exclusively to Robertson's Sermons, Baxter's *Saint's Rest*, *The Innocents Abroad*, and works of that kind.[2]

But I have said enough. I hope you will treasure up the instructions which I have given you, and make them a guide to your feet and a light to your understanding. Build your character thoughtfully and painstakingly upon these precepts, and by and by, when you have got it built, you will be surprised and gratified to see how nicely and sharply it resembles everybody else's.

1. The bloody battle (1815) in which Napoleon suffered his final defeat at the hands of English and German troops under the Duke of Wellington.
2. The five volumes of sermons by Frederick William Robertson (1816–53), an English clergyman, and Richard Baxter's *Saints' Everlasting Rest* (1650) were once well-known religious works. *The Innocents Abroad* is Clemens's own collection of humorous travel sketches.

THE READER

1. *How much of Clemens' advice applies only to the young? How much of it is to be taken seriously?*
2. *What does Clemens assume about his audience? How many of these assumptions would hold true today?*

THE WRITER

1. *Is this piece unified? Does it have a thesis sentence? If you think it is unified, in what does the unity consist? If you think it is not unified, where are the breaks? Would it have seemed more unified when it was given as a speech?*
2. *What "image" or "personality" does Clemens project or assume? What does he do that creates his image or personality?*
3. *Write a brief essay comparing what Clemens says about lying with what Didion says about it in "On Keeping a Notebook" (p. 68).*

Mary Midgley

TRYING OUT ONE'S NEW SWORD

All of us are, more or less, in trouble today about trying to understand cultures strange to us. We hear constantly of alien customs. We see changes in our lifetime which would have astonished our parents. I want to discuss here one very short way of dealing with this difficulty, a drastic way which many people now theoretically favor. It consists in simply denying that we can ever understand any culture except our own well enough to make judgments about it. Those who recommend this hold that the world is sharply divided into separate societies, sealed units, each with its own system of thought. They feel that the respect and tolerance due from one system to another forbids us ever to take up a critical position to any other culture. Moral judgment, they suggest, is a kind of coinage valid only in its country of origin.

I shall call this position "moral isolationism." I shall suggest that it is certainly not forced upon us, and indeed that it makes no sense at all. People usually take it up because they think it is a respectful attitude to other cultures. In fact, however, it is not respectful. Nobody can respect what is entirely unintelligible to them. To respect someone, we have to know enough about him to make a *favorable* judgment, however general and tentative. And we do understand people in other cultures to this extent. Otherwise a great mass of our most valuable thinking would be paralyzed.

To show this, I shall take a remote example, because we shall probably find it easier to think calmly about it than we should with a contemporary one, such as female circumcision in Africa or the Chinese Cultural Revolution. The principles involved will still be the same. My example is this. There is, it seems, a verb in classical Japanese which means "to try out one's new sword on a chance wayfarer." (The word is *tsujigiri*, literally "crossroads-cut.") A samurai sword had to be tried out because, if it was to work properly, it had to slice through someone at a single blow, from the shoulder to the opposite flank. Otherwise, the warrior bungled his stroke. This could injure his honor, offend his ancestors, and even let down his emperor. So tests were needed, and wayfarers had to be expended. Any wayfarer would do—provided, of course, that he was not another Samurai. Scientists will recognize a familiar problem about the rights of experimental subjects.

Now when we hear of a custom like this, we may well reflect that we

From *Heart and Mind: The Varieties of Moral Experience* (1981).

simply do not understand it; and therefore are not qualified to criticize it at all, because we are not members of that culture. But we are not members of any other culture either, except our own. So we extend the principle to cover all extraneous cultures, and we seem therefore to be moral isolationists. But this is, as we shall see, an impossible position. Let us ask what it would involve.

5   We must ask first: Does the isolating barrier work both ways? Are people in other cultures equally unable to criticize *us*? This question struck me sharply when I read a remark in *The Guardian* [1] by an anthropologist about a South American Indian who had been taken into a Brazilian town for an operation, which saved his life. When he came back to his village, he made several highly critical remarks about the white Brazilians' way of life. They may very well have been justified. But the interesting point was that the anthropologist called these remarks "a damning indictment of Western civilization." Now the Indian had been in that town about two weeks. Was he in a position to deliver a damning indictment? Would we ourselves be qualified to deliver such an indictment on the Samurai, provided we could spend two weeks in ancient Japan? What do we really think about this?

My own impression is that we believe that outsiders can, in principle, deliver perfectly good indictments—only, it usually takes more than two weeks to make them damning. Understanding has degrees. It is not a slapdash yes-or-no matter. Intelligent outsiders can progress in it, and in some ways will be at an advantage over the locals. But if this is so, it must clearly apply to ourselves as much as anybody else.

Our next question is this: Does the isolating barrier between cultures block praise as well as blame? If I want to say that the Samurai culture has many virtues, or to praise the South American Indians, am I prevented from doing *that* by my outside status? Now, we certainly do need to praise other societies in this way. But it is hardly possible that we could praise them effectively if we could not, in principle, criticize them. Our praise would be worthless if it rested on no definite grounds, if it did not flow from some understanding. Certainly we may need to praise things which we do not *fully* understand. We say "there's something very good here, but I can't quite make out what it is yet." This happens when we want to learn from strangers. And we can learn from strangers. But to do this we have to distinguish between those strangers who are worth learning from and those who are not. Can we then judge which is which?

This brings us to our third question: What is involved in judging? Now plainly there is no question here of sitting on a bench in a red robe and sentencing people. Judging simply means forming an opinion, and

1. A British daily newspaper published in Manchester.

expressing it if it is called for. Is there anything wrong about this? Naturally, we ought to avoid forming—and expressing—*crude* opinions, like that of a simple-minded missionary, who might dismiss the whole Samurai culture as entirely bad, because non-Christian. But this is a different objection. The trouble with crude opinions is that they are crude, whoever forms them, not that they are formed by the wrong people. Anthropologists, after all, are outsiders quite as much as missionaries. Moral isolationism forbids us to form *any* opinions on these matters. Its ground for doing so is that we don't understand them. But there is much that we don't understand in our own culture too. This brings us to our last question: If we can't judge other cultures, can we really judge our own? Our efforts to do so will be much damaged if we are really deprived of our opinions about other societies, because these provide the range of comparison, the spectrum of alternatives against which we set what we want to understand. We would have to stop using the mirror which anthropology so helpfully holds up to us.

In short, moral isolationism would lay down a general ban on moral reasoning. Essentially, this is the program of immoralism, and it carries a distressing logical difficulty. Immoralists like Nietzsche are actually just a rather specialized sect of moralists. [2] They can no more afford to put moralizing out of business than smugglers can afford to abolish customs regulations. The power of moral judgment is, in fact, not a luxury, not a perverse indulgence of the self-righteous. It is a necessity. When we judge something to be bad or good, better or worse than something else, we are taking it as an example to aim at or avoid. Without opinions of this sort, we would have no framework of comparison for our own policy, no chance of profiting by other people's insights or mistakes. In this vacuum, we could form no judgments on our own actions.

Now it would be odd if *Homo sapiens* [3] had really got himself into a position as bad as this—a position where his main evolutionary asset, his brain, was so little use to him. None of us is going to accept this sceptical diagnosis. We cannot do so, because our involvement in moral isolationism does not flow from apathy, but from a rather acute concern about human hypocrisy and other forms of wickedness. But we polarize that concern around a few selected moral truths. We are rightly angry with those who despise, oppress or steamroll other cultures. We think that doing these things is actually *wrong*. But this is itself a moral judgment. We could not condemn oppression and insolence if we thought that all our condemnations were just a trivial local quirk of our own culture. We could still less do it if we tried to stop judging altogether.

10

2. Friedrich Nietzsche (1844–1900), German philosopher who challenged Christian ethics.

3. Latin taxonomic designation; genus *homo* (man), species *sapiens* (thinking).

Real moral scepticism, in fact, could lead only to inaction, to our losing all interest in moral questions, most of all in those which concern other societies. When we discuss these things, it becomes instantly clear how far we are from doing this. Suppose, for instance, that I criticize the bisecting Samurai, that I say his behavior is brutal. What will usually happen next is that someone will protest, will say that I have no right to make criticisms like that of another culture. But it is most unlikely that he will use this move to end the discussion of the subject. Instead, he will justify the Samurai. He will try to fill in the background, to make me understand the custom, by explaining the exalted ideals of discipline and devotion which produced it. He will probably talk of the lower value which the ancient Japanese placed on individual life generally. He may well suggest that this is a healthier attitude than our own obsession with security. He may add, too, that the wayfarers did not seriously mind being bisected, that in principle they accepted the whole arrangement.

Now an objector who talks like this is implying that it *is* possible to understand alien customs. That is just what he is trying to make me do. And he implies, too, that if I do succeed in understanding them, I shall do something better than giving up judging them. He expects me to change my present judgment to a truer one—namely, one that is favorable. And the standards I must use to do this cannot just be Samurai standards. They have to be ones current in my own culture. Ideals like discipline and devotion will not move anybody unless he himself accepts them. As it happens, neither discipline nor devotion is very popular in the West at present. Anyone who appeals to them may well have to do some more arguing to make *them* acceptable, before he can use them to explain the Samurai. But if he does succeed here, he will have persuaded us, not just that there was something to be said for them in ancient Japan, but that there would be here as well.

Isolating barriers simply cannot arise here. If we accept something as a serious moral truth about one culture, we can't refuse to apply it—in however different an outward form—to other cultures as well, wherever circumstances admit it. If we refuse to do this, we just are not taking the other culture seriously. This becomes clear if we look at the last argument used by my objector—that of justification by consent of the victim. It is suggested that sudden bisection is quite in order, *provided* that it takes place between consenting adults. I cannot now discuss how conclusive this justification is. What I am pointing out is simply that it can only work if we believe that *consent* can make such a transaction respectable—and this is a thoroughly modern and Western idea. It would probably never occur to a Samurai; if it did, it would surprise him very much. It is *our* standard. In applying it, too, we are likely to make another typically Western demand. We shall ask for good factual evidence that the wayfarers actually do have this rather surprising taste—

that they are really willing to be bisected. In applying Western standards in this way, we are not being confused or irrelevant. We are asking the questions which arise *from where we stand*, questions which we can see the sense of. We do this because asking questions which you can't see the sense of is humbug. Certainly we can extend our questioning by imaginative effort. We can come to understand other societies better. By doing so, we may make their questions our own, or we may see that they are really forms of the questions which we are asking already. This is not impossible. It is just very hard work. The obstacles which often prevent it are simply those of ordinary ignorance, laziness and prejudice.

If there were really an isolating barrier, of course, our own culture could never have been formed. It is no sealed box, but a fertile jungle of different influences—Greek, Jewish, Roman, Norse, Celtic and so forth, into which further influences are still pouring—American, Indian, Japanese, Jamaican, you name it. The moral isolationist's picture of separate, unmixable cultures is quite unreal. People who talk about British history usually stress the value of this fertilizing mix, no doubt rightly. But this is not just an odd fact about Britain. Except for the very smallest and most remote, all cultures are formed out of many streams. All have the problem of digesting and assimilating things which, at the start, they do not understand. All have the choice of learning something from this challenge, or, alternatively, of refusing to learn, and fighting it mindlessly instead.

This universal predicament has been obscured by the fact that an- 15 thropologists used to concentrate largely on very small and remote cultures, which did not seem to have this problem. These tiny societies, which had often forgotten their own history, made neat, self-contained subjects for study. No doubt it was valuable to emphasize their remoteness, their extreme strangeness, their independence of our cultural tradition. This emphasis was, I think, the root of moral isolationism. But, as the tribal studies themselves showed, even there the anthropologists were able to interpret what they saw and make judgments—often favorable—about the tribesmen. And the tribesmen, too, were quite equal to making judgments about the anthropologists—and about the tourists and Coca-Cola salesmen who followed them. Both sets of judgments, no doubt, were somewhat hasty, both have been refined in the light of further experience. A similar transaction between us and the Samurai might take even longer. But that is no reason at all for deeming it impossible. Morally as well as physically, there is only one world, and we all have to live in it.

Carol Bly

BRUNO BETTELHEIM: THREE IDEAS TO TRY IN MADISON, MINNESOTA

It is exhilarating to spend a few days thinking about the ideas of Bruno Bettleheim,[1] not just because he has such energy and moral genius, but because he is so out of style at the moment. The attention, and certainly the affections, of the liberal intelligentsia are somewhere else, and I feel private and quiet among Bettelheim's findings, instead of feeling like one of a cheering crowd at the arena. There is no distraction.

I expect Bettelheim owes his unpopularity to the fact that he is such a mixed bag: he gets off some of the coarsest censures of young people, leftists, and women that you can come across. He is good and out of fashion. What I like and honor in him is his constant work on *decency.* In a decade given to opening up the unconscious almost as an end in itself, Bettelheim still goes on working on decency between people, decency based squarely on the moral well-being within each person. He calls this moral well-being "individual autonomy." Roughly, it means that no matter how sensibly some insane or cruel proposition is presented to you, you make up your own mind that it is not acceptable, and you do not do the insane or cruel thing.

Applying Bruno Bettelheim's perspective to life in rural Minnesota means taking ideas learned *in great straits* (in the concentration camp at Dachau and later, in the Orthogenic School of the University of Chicago, where he treated autistic children) and deliberately using them *in little straits.* I commend this idea because the countryside, despite its apparent culture lag, is doomed to be wrecked in the mass culture just as surely as the cities are being wrecked. We need major thinking, but our habit is to listen only to the local prophets—mild-mannered provincial professionals living among us, regional poets with their evident faith in nature, local administrators of community education projects. Our habit is to listen to those nearby who are affable and low-key. They can't save our personalities, though, any better than fervent quilt making can save our artistic nature or Solarcaine can set a broken leg.

Certainly life in western Minnesota must be about as untroublesome

First published in *Minnesota Monthly* (Jan. 1974); reprinted in *Letters from the Country* (1981).

1. Dr. Bettelheim has written many books. I've taken some of his ideas here from *The Informed Heart, The Empty Fortress,* and some recent newspaper interviews [Bly's note].

as life anywhere in the twentieth century. It is only luck; we haven't ourselves done anything, psychically or morally, to protect us from the coarsening of life that comes with more population. We are all set to become "mass men"—or at least we have no proofs that we won't give way to impersonal relations, increasing rudeness, increasing distrust, ill-temper while queuing up for everything from tennis courts to funeral reservations. Bettelheim's ideas—and I've chosen three of them to think about—have to do with how to keep the self from succumbing to the mass state. The three ideas are (1) replacing the feeling of "business as usual" with crisis thinking, (2) forcing ourselves to have a sense of time in our lives, and (3) understanding the power of negative thinking.

Even when the Germans began arresting Jews in the 1930s, many of the Jews refused to leave Germany because the aura of their posses- sions—the rooms, the rugs, the paintings—gave them a sense of nor- malcy in things: they'd projected some of themselves into these objects around them, so if the objects were still there, surely everything was usual? What they needed to do was to switch to *crisis thinking:* they needed to say to themselves, "This is *not* business as usual. We must run away at night, or join the Underground, or separate and plan to meet in Switzerland."

Bettelheim says we must speak or fight, whichever is called for, at the *first moment of our anxiety.* National Socialism looked like "business as usual" in 1932 and 1933; by 1934 it was too late. The Gestapo's inten- tion to terrify eighty million Germans through the constant threat of the camps was published long before they actually did it, but few paid attention. *Mein Kampf*[2] should have been lots of warning: very few people took it seriously. So Bettelheim suggests we must ask ourselves at every other moment, Is this business as usual? Is this a crisis? Is it O.K. to go on just maintaining my life today, or must I act in a political way? So here are some questions we can ask in rural Minnesota:

1. Should the President[3] be impeached? Now in the moment of our anxiety over his crookedness: should we impeach? If not, is there something else we should be doing? Is it really O.K. just to be sitting here?

2. Is TV watching turning our children into mass men or is it not? Many parents in Madison have said explicitly they think TV watching is bad for their children, but only two families I know of have got rid of the set. Somehow, the course of each day's activity disperses the parents' anxiety. Since they do not act in the moment of anxiety, then the children go on dully taking in the commercials and the vulgarity of

2. Adolf Hitler's statement of his theories and program, published 1925–27.   3. Richard M. Nixon, who resigned the presidency in 1974.

feeling and another week goes by, a year goes by, and the day after tomorrow, or perhaps it was yesterday, the children are eighteen and they have been watching television for seventeen years. They saw eighteen thousand murders by the time they were fourteen (according to *TV Generation,* by Gerald Loomey), and all the while the parents sincerely felt that TV watching was bad for them.

3. Is the American diet really "well balanced" as the Department of Agriculture would have us believe, or have the grain-milling companies (who systematically began degerminating all wheat flour on the market in the second decade of the century) caused a deficiency of Vitamin E (and other vitamins as well) which is responsible for the multiplying incidence of certain diseases and a sharp rise in fatalities from them? Does it mean anything that in the pamphlets given 4-H children, telling them how to make bread, the picture credits are nearly all to those very grain-milling companies?

A sense of time warns that now is the time; it is not business as usual. Thinking of time leads to the second idea of Bettelheim's I'd like to bring in: a sense of *time left.* The Gestapo cleverly realized that if you never know *when* something will happen, such as the release of a prisoner from camp or the end of a slave-work detail, you can't organize your own thoughts. A crude example that comes to my mind is the dilemma of a runner; if he doesn't know how many laps remain, how shall he husband his diminishing strength? When shall he make his final spurt? Christianity feels the sense of *time left* so strongly that the Church teaches that you must regard every moment as your last, so that you will make the final, mortal spurt always. But mass society, which tends to make people relaxed and low-key and unambitious, encourages a slack time sense. Here's an example from my town.

As soon as a Madison girl marries she will be asked to join most if not all of the following groups:

1. A circle of church women
2. The large Ladies' Aid, which meets monthly.
3. A homemakers' group
4. An auxiliary of the American Legion or the VFW
5. Mrs. Jaycees
6. A study club (Federated Women's Clubs of America)
7. Women's—or couples'—bridge club

I have omitted community groups that do useful work, such as teaching released-time school, or shampooing at the Home, filling hospital bird-feeding stations, or working in the hospital auxiliary. These projects are self-justifying.

If the young woman doesn't say to herself: I am twenty-five and in seventy years I will probably be dead, she is likely to join the organizations listed. If she has a sense of *time left,* however, she may ask the right questions: How much of my life do I want to spend in solitude? Most women in town also drink coffee with two or more other women at 10 A.M. and at 3 P.M. every day. This means another three hours a day of time spent in idle social intercourse. Yet, whenever we ask these young women if they think they might on their deathbeds regret this casual frittering away of time, they grin and say, "Oh, let's not be morbid now!"

Still, forty-five-year-old women do start dropping out of the artificially structured social life in Madison: people who have dazedly accepted belonging to clubs for twenty years now choose to topple into their own inner lives instead. They simply have finally learned a sense of *time left*—and the tragedy of it is that a spiritually dormant society ever allowed them to waste twenty years.

A few years ago we had a constantly cheerful minister in town; no one was less apprehensive than he. He wasn't nervous about the hydrogen bomb and he wasn't nervous about our participation in the Vietnam War. Then he became critically ill, and upon recovery he preached for an entire winter the first serious, thoughtful sermons of his life, or at least of his life here. Any number of people complained that the sermons had gone morbid and "negative." They hadn't. He simply had learned a sense of *time left.*

Complaints about "negative" sermons bring me to the third of Bettelheim's ideas: the usefulness of negative or critical thinking. Bettelheim objects to everyone's seizing on Anne Frank's "All men are basically good." He argues that they wish to derive comfort from their admiration of her positive attitude under such awful circumstances, instead of feeling uncomfortable with the truth—which is that men are basically good and they are basically bad. They can be ghastly. Stanley Milgram's *Obedience to Authority* describes an experiment in which subjects were directed to "administer pain" to people strapped in chairs in the next room who were visible through the window. The subjects believed that the dials they operated gave pain whenever the people strapped to the chair failed to learn a given piece of information. Some of the subjects repeatedly turned the dial to the "danger" markings on the machine. They were sadistic without even noticing. If we keep in mind such left-handed inhumanity—Americans just obeying orders—and then repeat to ourselves Anne Frank's remark about men being basically good, we are irritated: naïveté, which ever wants to preserve its artless high, is ignoring rank cruelty. Positive thinking is that kind of naïveté. People who practice or commend it are interested in feeling no pain and in preserving a high. Sometimes a whole culture wishes to preserve this high: then its art and doctrines turn not into positive thinking but into positive pretending.

We haven't got a Germany here, but we do have a TV space-selling society. Hence a generation has grown up on mostly happy, bland, evasive propaganda. No wonder this beastly positive thinking, which means positive *pretending,* has become the crutch of church and club. The other day a clergyman told me he "preferred to think of the Ten Commandments as positive, not negative." Marvelous! What is the *positive* way not to commit adultery? How do you *positively* not covet your neighbor's husband? How do you *positively* not steal from the Klein National Bank?

Bettelheim noted that, when he first wrote his interpretations of the concentration camps, his readers told him they felt "a strange relief," gruesome as the subject was. No matter how oppressive the facts, facing them, calling evil evil, safeguards our personalities.

15   Why read a set of ideas based on imprisonment in Dachau in 1938? When I first began reading Bettelheim years ago I had the uncanny sensation he was handing me a beautifully thought-out set of bright tools, to keep me (or anyone) in one piece. He showed a way not to sit around absent-mindedly while a gross society raveled away decency like a yarn ball. As much as anyone I've read, Bettelheim helps us not to be wrecked. It takes affection to keep preventing wrecks, and saving people already wrecked. You feel this tough affection in his ideas.

THE READER

1. *Although Bly recognizes that what Bettelheim saw in Hitler's Germany was far worse than what she sees in Minnesota, she is still upset by what she sees. Yet her tone is not angry. How do you account for that? Would the essay be more effective if she were angry?*
2. *Bly raises three questions (pp. 671–672). Do they seem to require crisis thinking? If you think not, how can you be sure that your rejection of the idea is not what she calls "business as usual?"*
3. *Bly's question about how ideas based on experience at Dachau in 1938 apply to life in Minnesota in the 1970s is a good one. What answers are suggested by Bettelheim's description of his concentration camp experience in "A Victim" (p. 29)? Bettelheim himself has been accused of behaving like a brutal tyrant at his school; what, if any, effect does this fact have on your reading of Bly's essay?*

THE WRITER

1. *Do the three ideas Bly discusses unite? How does Bly supply transitions: Are they logical, or are they merely verbal echoes?*
2. *Write an analysis of a question that you believe requires crisis thinking or "an understanding of the power of negative thinking."*

Willard Gaylin

WHAT YOU SEE IS THE REAL YOU

It was, I believe, the distinguished Nebraska financier Father Edward J. Flanagan[1] who professed to having "never met a bad boy." Having, myself, met a remarkable number of bad boys, it might seem that either our experiences were drastically different or we were using the word "bad" differently. I suspect neither is true, but rather that the Father was appraising the "inner man," while I, in fact, do not acknowledge the existence of inner people.

Since we psychoanalysts have unwittingly contributed to this confusion, let one, at least, attempt a small rectifying effort. Psychoanalytic data—which should be viewed as supplementary information—is, unfortunately, often viewed as alternative (and superior) explanation. This has led to the prevalent tendency to think of the "inner" man as the real man and the outer man as an illusion or pretender.

While psychoanalysis supplies us with an incredibly useful tool for explaining the motives and purposes underlying human behavior, most of this has little bearing on the moral nature of that behavior.

Like roentgenology, psychoanalysis is a fascinating, but relatively new, means of illuminating the person. But few of us are prepared to substitute an X-ray of Grandfather's head for the portrait that hangs in the parlor. The inside of the man represents another view, not a truer one. A man may not always be what he appears to be, but what he appears to be is always a significant part of what he is. A man is the sum total of *all* his behavior. To probe for unconscious determinants of behavior and then define *him* in their terms exclusively, ignoring his overt behavior altogether, is a greater distortion than ignoring the unconscious completely.

Kurt Vonnegut has said, "You are what you pretend to be," which is simply another way of saying, you are what we (all of us) perceive you to be, not what you think you are.

Consider for a moment the case of the ninety-year-old man on his deathbed (surely the Talmud must deal with this?) joyous and relieved over the success of his deception. For ninety years he has shielded his evil nature from public observation. For ninety years he has affected courtesy, kindness, and generosity—suppressing all the malice he knew

5

From the *New York Times* (Oct. 7, 1977).

1. Founder (1917) of Boys Town, a self-governing community for homeless and abandoned boys, for which he was also an energetic fund raiser.

was within him while he calculatedly and artificially substituted grace and charity. All his life he had been fooling the world into believing he was a good man. This "evil" man will, I predict, be welcomed into the Kingdom of Heaven.

Similarly, I will not be told that the young man who earns his pocket money by mugging old ladies is "really" a good boy. Even my generous and expansive definition of goodness will not accommodate that particular form of self-advancement.

It does not count that beneath the rough exterior he has a heart—or, for that matter, an entire innards—of purest gold, locked away from human perception. You are for the most part what you seem to be, not what you would wish to be, nor, indeed, what you believe yourself to be.

Spare me, therefore, your good intentions, your inner sensitivities, your unarticulated and unexpressed love. And spare me also those tedious psychohistories which—by exposing the goodness inside the bad man, and the evil in the good—invariably establish a vulgar and perverse egalitarianism, as if the arrangement of what is outside and what inside makes no moral difference.

Saint Francis[2] may, in his unconscious, indeed have been compensating for, and denying, destructive, unconscious Oedipal impulses identical to those which Atilla projected and acted on. But the similarity of the unconscious constellations in the two men matters precious little, if it does not distinguish between them.

I do not care to learn that Hitler's heart was in the right place. A knowledge of the unconscious life of the man may be an adjunct to understanding his behavior. It is *not* a substitute for his behavior in describing him.

The inner man is a fantasy. If it helps you to identify with one, by all means, do so; preserve it, cherish it, embrace it, but do not present it to others for evaluation or consideration, for excuse or exculpation, or, for that matter, for punishment or disapproval.

Like any fantasy, it serves your purposes alone. It has no standing in the real world which we share with each other. Those character traits, those attitudes, that behavior—that strange and alien stuff sticking out all over you—*that's the real you!*

2. Saint Francis of Assisi, who early in the thirteenth century renounced parental wealth, entered on a life of poverty, and founded the Franciscan order of begging friars.

THE READER

1. *Gaylin makes a key distinction between the inner and the outer man. Why is it necessary for him to start with this distinction?*

2. *Gaylin says in his first paragraph that he does "not acknowledge the existence of inner people," while in his fourth paragraph he says that*

"the inside of the man represents another view, not a truer one." How can you account for this seeming contradiction?

3. *Compare the approach to human personality taken by Gaylin with that of Goldberg, also a psychotherapist, in "In Harness: The Male Condition" (p. 509). Do they seem to agree on the nature of human personality? Explain.*

THE WRITER

1. *Gaylin finds in the relation between an X ray and a portrait an analogy for the relation between the inner man and the outer man. How accurate is this analogy?*
2. *Discuss the effectiveness of the examples in the essay, and suggest others that Gaylin might have used.*
3. *Write a paragraph commenting on the appropriateness of Gaylin's title.*

Michael Levin

THE CASE FOR TORTURE

It is generally assumed that torture is impermissible, a throwback to a more brutal age. Enlightened societies reject it outright, and regimes suspected of using it risk the wrath of the United States.

I believe this attitude is unwise. There are situations in which torture is not merely permissible but morally mandatory. Moreover, these situations are moving from the realm of imagination to fact.

Death: Suppose a terrorist has hidden an atomic bomb on Manhattan Island which will detonate at noon on July 4 unless . . . (here follow the usual demands for money and release of his friends from jail). Suppose, further, that he is caught at 10 a.m. of the fateful day, but—preferring death to failure—won't disclose where the bomb is. What do we do? If we follow due process—wait for his lawyer, arraign him—millions of people will die. If the only way to save those lives is to subject the terrorist to the most excruciating possible pain, what grounds can there be for not doing so? I suggest there are none. In any case, I ask you to face the question with an open mind.

Torturing the terrorist is unconstitutional? Probably. But millions of lives surely outweigh constitutionality. Torture is barbaric? Mass murder is far more barbaric. Indeed, letting millions of innocents die in deference to one who flaunts his guilt is moral cowardice, an unwillingness

Originally appeared in *Newsweek* (June 7, 1982).

to dirty one's hands. If *you* caught the terrorist, could you sleep nights knowing that millions died because you couldn't bring yourself to apply the electrodes?

Once you concede that torture is justified in extreme cases, you have admitted that the decision to use torture is a matter of balancing innocent lives against the means needed to save them. You must now face more realistic cases involving more modest numbers. Someone plants a bomb on a jumbo jet. He alone can disarm it, and his demands cannot be met (or if they can, we refuse to set a precedent by yielding to his threats). Surely we can, we must, do anything to the extortionist to save the passengers. How can we tell 300, or 100, or 10 people who never asked to be put in danger, "I'm sorry, you'll have to die in agony, we just couldn't bring ourselves to . . ."

Here are the results of an informal poll about a third, hypothetical, case. Suppose a terrorist group kidnapped a newborn baby from a hospital. I asked four mothers if they would approve of torturing kidnappers if that were necessary to get their own newborns back. All said yes, the most "liberal" adding that she would like to administer it herself.

I am not advocating torture as punishment. Punishment is addressed to deeds irrevocably past. Rather, I am advocating torture as an acceptable measure for preventing future evils. So understood, it is far less objectionable than many extant punishments. Opponents of the death penalty, for example, are forever insisting that executing a murderer will not bring back his victim (as if the purpose of capital punishment were supposed to be resurrection, not deterrence or retribution). But torture, in the cases described, is intended not to bring anyone back but to keep innocents from being dispatched. The most powerful argument against using torture as a punishment or to secure confessions is that such practices disregard the rights of the individual. Well, if the individual is all that important—and he is—it is correspondingly important to protect the rights of individuals threatened by terrorists. If life is so valuable that it must never be taken, the lives of the innocents must be saved even at the price of hurting the one who endangers them.

Better precedents for torture are assassination and pre-emptive attack. No Allied leader would have flinched at assassinating Hitler, had that been possible. (The Allies did assassinate Heydrich.) Americans would be angered to learn that Roosevelt could have had Hitler killed in 1943—thereby shortening the war and saving millions of lives—but refused on moral grounds. Similarly, if nation A learns that nation B is about to launch an unprovoked attack, A has a right to save itself by destroying B's military capability first. In the same way, if the police can by torture save those who would otherwise die at the hands of kidnappers or terrorists, they must.

Idealism: There is an important difference between terrorists and their victims that should mute talk of the terrorists' "rights." The terrorist's victims are at risk unintentionally, not having asked to be endangered. But the terrorist knowingly initiated his actions. Unlike his victims, he volunteered for the risks of his deed. By threatening to kill for profit or idealism, he renounces civilized standards, and he can have no complaint if civilization tries to thwart him by whatever means necessary.

Just as torture is justified only to save lives (not extort confessions or   10
recantations), it is justifiably administered only to those *known* to hold innocent lives in their hands. Ah, but how can the authorities ever be sure they have the right malefactor? Isn't there a danger of error and abuse? Won't We turn into Them?

Questions like these are disingenuous in a world in which terrorists proclaim themselves and perform for television. The name of their game is public recognition. After all, you can't very well intimidate a government into releasing your freedom fighters unless you announce that it is your group that has seized its embassy. "Clear guilt" is difficult to define, but when 40 million people see a group of masked gunmen seize an airplane on the evening news, there is not much question about who the perpetrators are. There will be hard cases where the situation is murkier. Nonetheless, a line demarcating the legitimate use of torture can be drawn. Torture only the obviously guilty, and only for the sake of saving innocents, and the line between Us and Them will remain clear.

There is little danger that the Western democracies will lose their way if they choose to inflict pain as one way of preserving order. Paralysis in the face of evil is the greater danger. Some day soon a terrorist will threaten tens of thousands of lives, and torture will be the only way to save them. We had better start thinking about this.

THE READER

1. *When, in the author's view, is torture permissible? When is it not permissible? What distinguishes the two situations?*
2. *Why is torture justified to save lives? That is, what assumption is made in this case?*
3. *Why is torture not justified as punishment or to extort confessions? That is, what assumption is being made in these cases?*
4. *Who will judge as to when torture is permissible and, indeed, "morally mandatory"? What ensures that that judgment will be correct?*

THE WRITER

1. *Why does Levin need to ask the reader to face the question posed in his third paragraph "with an open mind"?*
2. *In the first part of his essay, Levin gives three hypothetical examples. Why does he arrange them in the order he does?*

3. *Write a brief essay in which you discuss what effect the use of torture has upon the persons applying torture.*

Tom Regan

THE CASE FOR ANIMAL RIGHTS

I regard myself as an advocate of animal rights—as a part of the animal rights movement. That movement, as I conceive it, is committed to a number of goals, including:

- the total abolition of the use of animals in science;
- the total dissolution of commercial animal agriculture;
- the total elimination of commercial and sport hunting and trapping.

There are, I know, people who profess to believe in animal rights but do not avow these goals. Factory farming, they say, is wrong—it violates animals' rights—but traditional animal agriculture is all right. Toxicity tests of cosmetics on animals violates their rights, but important medical research—cancer research, for example—does not. The clubbing of baby seals is abhorrent, but not the harvesting of adult seals. I used to think I understood this reasoning. Not any more. You don't change unjust institutions by tidying them up.

What's wrong—fundamentally wrong—with the way animals are treated isn't the details that vary from case to case. It's the whole system. The forlornness of the veal calf is pathetic, heart-wrenching; the pulsing pain of the chimp with electrodes planted deep in her brain is repulsive; the slow, tortuous death of the racoon caught in the leg-hold trap is agonizing. But what is wrong isn't the pain, isn't the suffering, isn't the deprivation. These compound what's wrong. Sometimes—often—they make it much, much worse. But they are not the fundamental wrong.

The fundamental wrong is the system that allows us to view animals as *our resources,* here for *us*—to be eaten, or surgically manipulated, or exploited for sport or money. Once we accept this view of animals—as our resources—the rest is as predictable as it is regrettable. Why worry about their loneliness, their pain, their death? Since animals exist for us, to benefit us in one way or another, what harms them really doesn't matter—or matters only if it starts to bother us, makes us feel a trifle uneasy when we eat our veal escalope, for example. So, yes, let us get veal calves out of solitary confinement, give them more space, a little straw, a few companions. But let us keep our veal escalope.

From *In Defense of Animals* (1985).

But a little straw, more space and a few companions won't eliminate—won't even touch—the basic wrong that attaches to our viewing
and treating these animals as our resources. A veal calf killed to be eaten
after living in close confinement is viewed and treated in this way: but
so, too, is another who is raised (as they say) "more humanely." To right
the wrong of our treatment of farm animals requires more than making
rearing methods "more humane"; it requires the total dissolution of
commercial animal agriculture.

How we do this, whether we do it or, as in the case of animals in
science, whether and how we abolish their use—these are to a large
extent political questions. People must change their beliefs before they
change their habits. Enough people, especially those elected to public
office, must believe in change—must want it—before we will have laws
that protect the rights of animals. This process of change is very complicated, very demanding, very exhausting, calling for the efforts of many
hands in education, publicity, political organization and activity, down
to the licking of envelopes and stamps. As a trained and practicing
philosopher, the sort of contribution I can make is limited but, I like to
think, important. The currency of philosophy is ideas—their meaning
and rational foundation—not the nuts and bolts of the legislative process, say, or the mechanics of community organization. That's what I
have been exploring over the past ten years or so in my essays and talks
and, most recently, in my book, *The Case for Animal Rights*. I believe
the major conclusions I reach in the book are true because they are
supported by the weight of the best arguments. I believe the idea of
animal rights has reason, not just emotion, on its side.

In the space I have at my disposal here I can only sketch, in the barest
outline, some of the main features of the book. Its main themes—and
we should not be surprised by this—involve asking and answering deep,
foundational moral questions about what morality is, how it should be
understood and what is the best moral theory, all considered. I hope I
can convey something of the shape I think this theory takes. The
attempt to do this will be (to use a word a friendly critic once used to
describe my work) cerebral, perhaps too cerebral. But this is misleading.
My feelings about how animals are sometimes treated run just as deep
and just as strong as those of my more volatile compatriots. Philosophers
do—to use the jargon of the day—have a right side to their brains. If
it's the left side we contribute (or mainly should), that's because what
talents we have reside there.

How to proceed? We begin by asking how the moral status of animals
has been understood by thinkers who deny that animals have rights.
Then we test the mettle of their ideas by seeing how well they stand up
under the heat of fair criticism. If we start our thinking in this way, we
soon find that some people believe that we have no duties directly to

animals, that we owe nothing to them, that we can do nothing that wrongs them. Rather, we can do wrong acts that involve animals, and so we have duties regarding them, though none to them. Such views may be called indirect duty views. By way of illustration: suppose your neighbor kicks your dog. Then your neighbor has done something wrong. But not to your dog. The wrong that has been done is a wrong to you. After all, it is wrong to upset people, and your neighbor's kicking your dog upsets you. So you are the one who is wronged, not your dog. Or again: by kicking your dog your neighbor damages your property. And since it is wrong to damage another person's property, your neighbor has done something wrong—to you, of course, not to your dog. Your neighbor no more wrongs your dog than your car would be wronged if the windshield were smashed. Your neighbor's duties involving your dog are indirect duties to you. More generally, all of our duties regarding animals are indirect duties to one another—to humanity.

How could someone try to justify such a view? Someone might say that your dog doesn't feel anything and so isn't hurt by your neighbor's kick, doesn't care about the pain since none is felt, is as unaware of anything as is your windshield. Someone might say this, but no rational person will, since, among other considerations, such a view will commit anyone who holds it to the position that no human being feels pain either—that human beings also don't care about what happens to them. A second possibility is that though both humans and your dog are hurt when kicked, it is only human pain that matters. But, again, no rational person can believe this. Pain is pain wherever it occurs. If your neighbor's causing you pain is wrong because of the pain that is caused, we cannot rationally ignore or dismiss the moral relevance of the pain that your dog feels.

Philosophers who hold indirect duty views—and many still do—have come to understand that they must avoid the two defects just noted: that is, both the view that animals don't feel anything as well as the idea that only human pain can be morally relevant. Among such thinkers the sort of view now favored is one or other form of what is called *contractarianism*.

10   Here, very crudely, is the root idea: morality consists of a set of rules that individuals voluntarily agree to abide by, as we do when we sign a contract (hence the name contractarianism). Those who understand and accept the terms of the contract are covered directly; they have rights created and recognized by, and protected in, the contract. and these contractors can also have protection spelled out for others who, though they lack the ablity to understand morality and so cannot sign the contract themselves, are loved or cherished by those who can. Thus young children, for example, are unable to sign contracts and lack rights. But they are protected by the contract none the less because of the

sentimental interests of others, most notably their parents. So we have, then, duties involving these children, duties regarding them, but no duties to them. Our duties in their case are indirect duties to other human beings, usually their parents.

As for animals, since they cannot understand contracts, they obviously cannot sign; and since they cannot sign, they have no rights. Like children, however, some animals are the objects of the sentimental interest of others. You, for example, love your dog or cat. So those animals that enough people care about (companion animals, whales, baby seals, the American bald eagle), though they lack rights themselves, will be protected because of the sentimental interests of people. I have, then, according to contractarianism, no duty directly to your dog or any other animal, not even the duty not to cause them pain or suffering; my duty not to hurt them is a duty I have to those people who care about what happens to them. As for other animals, where no or little sentimental interest is present—in the case of farm animals, for example, or laboratory rats—what duties we have grow weaker and weaker, perhaps to vanishing point. The pain and death they endure, though real, are not wrong if no one cares about them.

When it comes to the moral status of animals, contractarianism could be a hard view to refute if it were an adequate theoretical approach to the moral status of human beings. It is not adequate in this latter respect, however, which makes the question of its adequacy in the former case, regarding animals, utterly moot. For consider: morality, according to the (crude) contractarian position before us, consists of rules that people agree to abide by. What people? Well, enough to make a difference—enough, that is, *collectively* to have the power to enforce the rules that are drawn up in the contract. This is very well and good for the signatories but not so good for anyone who is not asked to sign. And there is nothing in contractarianism of the sort we are discussing that guarantees or requires that everyone will have a chance to participate equally in framing the rules of morality. The result is that this approach to ethics could sanction the most blatant forms of social, economic, moral and political injustice, ranging from a repressive caste system to systematic racial or sexual discrimination. Might, according to this theory, does make right. Let those who are the victims of injustice suffer as they will. It matters not so long as no one else—no contractor, or too few of them—cares about it. Such a theory takes one's moral breath away . . . as if, for example, there would be nothing wrong with apartheid in South Africa if few white South Africans were upset by it. A theory with so little to recommend it at the level of the ethics of our treatment of our fellow humans cannot have anything more to recommend it when it comes to the ethics of how we treat our fellow animals.

The version of contractarianism just examined is, as I have noted, a crude variety, and in fairness to those of a contractarian persuasion it must be noted that much more refined, subtle and ingenious varieties are possible. For example, John Rawls, in his *A Theory of Justice*, sets forth a version of contractarianism that forces contractors to ignore the accidental features of being a human being—for example, whether one is white or black, male or female, a genius or of modest intellect. Only by ignoring such features, Rawls believes, can we ensure that the principles of justice that contractors would agree upon are not based on bias or prejudice. Despite the improvement a view such as Rawls's represents over the cruder forms of contractarianism, it remains deficient: it systematically denies that we have direct duties to those human beings who do not have a sense of justice—young children, for instance, and many mentally retarded humans. And yet it seems reasonably certain that, were we to torture a young child or a retarded elder, we would be doing something that wronged him or her, not something that would be wrong if (and only if) other humans with a sense of justice were upset. And since this is true in the case of these humans, we cannot rationally deny the same in the case of animals.

Indirect duty views, then, including the best among them, fail to command our rational assent. Whatever ethical theory we should accept rationally, therefore, it must at least recognize that we have some duties directly to animals, just as we have some duties directly to each other. The next two theories I'll sketch attempt to meet this requirement.

15   The first I call the cruelty-kindness view. Simply stated, this says that we have a direct duty to be kind to animals and a direct duty not to be cruel to them. Despite the familiar, reassuring ring of these ideas, I do not believe that this view offers an adequate theory. To make this clearer, consider kindness. A kind person acts from a certain kind of motive—compassion or concern, for example. And that is a virtue. But there is no guarantee that a kind act is a right act. If I am a generous racist, for example, I will be inclined to act kindly towards members of my own race, favoring their interests above those of others. My kindness would be real and, so far as it goes, good. But I trust it is too obvious to require argument that my kind acts may not be above moral reproach—may, in fact, be positively wrong because rooted in injustice. So kindness, notwithstanding its status as a virtue to be encouraged, simply will not carry the weight of a theory of right action.

Cruelty fares no better. People or their acts are cruel if they display either a lack of sympathy for or, worse, the presence of enjoyment in another's suffering. Cruelty in all its guises is a bad thing, a tragic human failing. But just as a person's being motivated by kindness does not guarantee that he or she does what is right, so the absence of cruelty does not ensure that he or she avoids doing what is wrong. Many people who perform abortions, for example, are not cruel, sadistic people. But that fact alone does not settle the terribly difficult question of the morality of abortion. The case is no different when we examine the ethics of our treatment of animals. So, yes, let us be for kindness and against cruelty. But let us not suppose that being for the one and against the other answers questions about moral right and wrong.

Some people think that the theory we are looking for is utilitarianism. A utilitarian accepts two moral principles. The first is that of equality: everyone's interests count, and similar interests must be counted as having similar weight or importance. White or black, American or Iranian, human or animal—everyone's pain or frustration matter, and matter just as much as the equivalent pain or frustration of anyone else. The second principle a utilitarian accepts is that of utility: do the act that will bring about the best balance between satisfaction and frustration for everyone affected by the outcome.

As a utilitarian, then, here is how I am to approach the task of deciding what I morally ought to do: I must ask who will be affected if I choose to do one thing rather than another, how much each individual will be affected, and where the best results are most likely to lie—which option, in other words, is most likely to bring about the best results, the best balance between satisfaction and frustration. That option, whatever it may be, is the one I ought to choose. That is where my moral duty lies.

The great appeal of utilitarianism rests with its uncompromising *egalitarianism:* everyone's interests count and count as much as the like interests of everyone else. The kind of odious discrimination that some forms of contractarianism can justify—discrimination based on race or sex, for example—seems disallowed in principle by utilitarianism, as is speciesism, systematic discrimination based on species membership.

The equality we find in utilitarianism, however, is not the sort an advocate of animal or human rights should have in mind. Utilitarianism has no room for the equal moral rights of different individuals because it has no room for their equal inherent value or worth. What has value for the utilitarian is the satisfaction of an individual's interests, not the individual whose interests they are. A universe in which you satisfy your desire for water, food and warmth is, other things being equal, better than a universe in which these desires are frustrated. And the same is true in the case of an animal with similar desires. But neither you nor the animal have any value in your own right. Only your feelings do.

Here is an analogy to help make the philosophical point clearer: a cup contains different liquids, sometimes sweet, sometimes bitter, sometimes a mix of the two. What has value are the liquids: the sweeter the better, the bitterer the worse. The cup, the container, has no value. It is what goes into it, not what they go into, that has value. For the utilitarian you and I are like the cup; we have no value as individuals and

20

thus no equal value. What has value is what goes into us, what we serve as receptacles for; our feelings of satisfaction have positive value, our feelings of frustration negative value.

Serious problems arise for utilitarianism when we remind ourselves that it enjoins us to bring about the best consequences. What does this mean? It doesn't mean the best consequences for me alone, or for my family or friends, or any other person taken individually. No, what we must do is, roughly, as follows: we must add up (somehow!) the separate satisfactions and frustrations of everyone likely to be affected by our choice, the satisfactions in one column, the frustrations in the other. We must total each column for each of the options before us. That is what it means to say the theory is aggregative. And then we must choose that option which is most likely to bring about the best balance of totaled satisfactions over totaled frustrations. Whatever act would lead to this outcome is the one we ought morally to perform—it is where our moral duty lies. And that act quite clearly might not be the same one that would bring about the best results for me personally, or for my family or friends, or for a lab animal. The best aggregated consequences for everyone concerned are not necessarily the best for each individual.

That utilitarianism is an aggregative theory—different individuals' satisfactions or frustrations are added, or summed, or totaled—is the key objection to this theory. My Aunt Bea is old, inactive, a cranky, sour person, though not physically ill. She prefers to go on living. She is also rather rich. I could make a fortune if I could get my hands on her money, money she intends to give me in any event, after she dies, but which she refuses to give me now. In order to avoid a huge tax bite, I plan to donate a handsome sum of my profits to a local children's hospital. Many, many children will benefit from my generosity, and much joy will be brought to their parents, relatives and friends. If I don't get the money rather soon, all these ambitions will come to naught. The once-in-a-lifetime opportunity to make a real killing will be gone. Why, then, not kill my Aunt Bea? Oh, of course I *might* get caught. But I'm no fool and, besides, her doctor can be counted on to co-operate (he has an eye for the same investment and I happen to know a good deal about his shady past). The deed can be done . . . professionally, shall we say. There is *very* little chance of getting caught. And as for my conscience being guilt-ridden, I am a resourceful sort of fellow and will take more than sufficient comfort—as I lie on the beach at Acapulco—in contemplating the joy and health I have brought to so many others.

Suppose Aunt Bea is killed and the rest of the story comes out as told. Would I have done anything wrong? Anything immoral? One would have thought that I had. Not according to utilitarianism. Since what I have done has brought about the best balance between totaled satisfaction and frustration for all those affected by the outcome, my action is not wrong. Indeed, in killing Aunt Bea the physician and I did what duty required.

This same kind of argument can be repeated in all sorts of cases, illustrating, time after time, how the utilitarian's position leads to results that impartial people find morally callous. It *is* wrong to kill my Aunt Bea in the name of bringing about the best results for others. A good end does not justify an evil means. Any adequate moral theory will have to explain why this is so. Utilitarianism fails in this respect and so cannot be the theory we seek.

What do do? Where to begin anew? The place to begin, I think, is with the utilitarian's view of the value of the individual—or, rather, lack of value. In its place, suppose we consider that you and I, for example, do have value as individuals—what we'll call *inherent value*. To say we have such value is to say that we are something more than, something different from, mere receptacles. Moreover, to ensure that we do not pave the way for such injustices as slavery or sexual discrimination, we must believe that all who have inherent value have it equally, regardless of their sex, race, religion, birthplace and so on. Similarly to be discarded as irrelevant are one's talents or skills, intelligence and wealth, personality or pathology, whether one is loved and admired or despised and loathed. The genius and the retarded child, the prince and the pauper, the brain surgeon and the fruit vendor, Mother Teresa and the most unscrupulous used-car salesman—all have inherent value, all possess it equally, and all have an equal right to be treated with respect, to be treated in ways that do not reduce them to the status of things, as if they existed as resources for others. My value as an individual is independent of my usefulness to you. Yours is not dependent on your usefulness to me. For either of us to treat the other in ways that fail to show respect for the other's independent value is to act immorally, to violate the individual's rights.

Some of the rational virtues of this view—what I call the rights view—should be evident. Unlike (crude) contractarianism, for example, the rights view *in principle* denies the moral tolerability of any and all forms of racial, sexual or social discrimination; and unlike utilitarianism, this view *in principle* denies that we can justify good results by using evil means that violate an individual's rights—denies, for example, that it could be moral to kill my Aunt Bea to harvest beneficial consequences for others. That would be to sanction the disrespectful treatment of the individual in the name of the social good, something the rights view will not—categorically will not—ever allow.

The rights view, I believe, is rationally the most satisfactory moral theory. It surpasses all other theories in the degree to which it illuminates and explains the foundation of our duties to one another—the domain of human morality. On this score it has the best reasons, the best arguments, on its side. Of course, if it were possible to show that only human beings are included within its scope, then a person like myself, who believes in animal rights, would be obliged to look elsewhere.

But attempts to limit its scope to humans only can be shown to be rationally defective. Animals, it is true, lack many of the abilities humans possess. They can't read, do higher mathematics, build a bookcase or make *baba ghanoush*. [1] Neither can many human beings, however, and yet we don't (and shouldn't) say that they (these humans) therefore have less inherent value, less of a right to be treated with respect, than do others. It is the *similarities* between those human beings who most clearly, most non-controversially have such value (the people reading this, for example), not our differences, that matter most. And the really crucial, the basic similarity is simply this: we are each of us the experiencing subject of a life, a conscious creature having an individual welfare that has importance to us whatever our usefulness to others. We want and prefer things, believe and feel things, recall and expect things. And all these dimensions of our life, including our pleasure and pain, our enjoyment and suffering, our satisfaction and frustration, our continued existence or our untimely death—all make a difference to the quality of our life as lived, as experienced, by us as individuals. As the same is true of those animals that concern us (the ones that are eaten and trapped, for example), they too must be viewed as the experiencing subjects of a life, with inherent value of their own.

30   Some there are who resist the idea that animals have inherent value. "Only humans have such value," they profess. How might this narrow view be defended? Shall we say that only humans have the requisite intelligence, or autonomy, or reason? But there are many, many humans who fail to meet these standards and yet are reasonably viewed as having value above and beyond their usefulness to others. Shall we claim that only humans belong to the right species, the species *Homo sapiens*? [2] But this is blatant speciesism. Will it be said, then, that all—and only—humans have immortal souls? Then our opponents have their work cut out for them. I am myself not ill-disposed to the proposition that there are immortal souls. Personally, I profoundly hope I have one. But I would not want to rest my position on a controversial ethical issue on the even more controversial question about who or what has an immortal soul. That is to dig one's hole deeper, not to climb out. Rationally, it is better to resolve moral issues without making more controversial assumptions than are needed. The question of who has inherent value

1. An eggplant-sesame oil spread or dip popular in the Middle East.
2. Latin for man with intellect, the taxo-
nomic designation for the modern human species.

is such a question, one that is resolved more rationally without the introduction of the idea of immortal souls than by its use.

Well, perhaps some will say that animals have some inherent value, only less than we have. Once again, however, attempts to defend this view can be shown to lack rational justification. What could be the basis of our having more inherent value than animals? Their lack of reason, or autonomy, or intellect? Only if we are willing to make the same judgment in the case of humans who are similarly deficient. But it is not true that such humans—the retarded child, for example, or the mentally deranged—have less inherent value than you or I. Neither, then, can we rationally sustain the view that animals like them in being the experiencing subjects of a life have less inherent value. *All* who have inherent value have it *equally*, whether they be human animals or not.

Inherent value, then, belongs equally to those who are the experiencing subjects of a life. Whether it belongs to others—to rocks and rivers, trees and glaciers, for example—we do not know and may never know. But neither do we need to know, if we are to make the case for animal rights. We do not need to know, for example, how many people are eligible to vote in the next presidential election before we can know whether I am. Similarly, we do not need to know how many individuals have inherent value before we can know that some do. When it comes to the case for animal rights, then, what we need to know is whether the animals that, in our culture, are routinely eaten, hunted and used in our laboratories, for example, are like us in being subjects of a life. And we do know this. We do know that many—literally, billions and billions—of these animals are the subjects of a life in the sense explained and so have inherent value if we do. And since, in order to arrive at the best theory of our duties to one another, we must recognize our equal inherent value as individuals, reason—not sentiment, not emotion— reason compels us to recognize the equal inherent value of these animals and, with this, their equal right to be treated with respect.

That, *very* roughly, is the shape and feel of the case for animal rights. Most of the details of the supporting argument are missing. They are to be found in the book to which I alluded earlier. Here, the details go begging, and I must, in closing, limit myself to four final points.

The first is how the theory that underlies the case for animal rights shows that the animal rights movement is a part of, not antagonistic to, the human rights movement. The theory that rationally grounds the rights of animals also grounds the rights of humans. Thus those involved in the animal rights movement are partners in the struggle to secure respect for human rights—the rights of women, for example, or minorities, or workers. The animal rights movement is cut from the same moral cloth as these.

35 Second, having set out the broad outlines of the rights view, I can now say why its implications for farming and science, among other fields, are both clear and uncompromising. In the case of the use of animals in science, the rights view is categorically abolitionist. Lab animals are not our tasters; we are not their kings. Because these animals are treated routinely, systematically as if their value were reducible to their usefulness to others, they are routinely, systematically treated with a lack of respect, and thus are their rights routinely, systematically violated. This is just as true when they are used in trivial, duplicative, unnecessary or unwise research as it is when they are used in studies that hold out real promise of human benefits. We can't justify harming or killing a human being (my Aunt Bea, for example) just for these sorts of reason. Neither can we do so even in the case of so lowly a creature as a laboratory rat. It is not just refinement or reduction that is called for, not just larger, cleaner cages, not just more generous use of anaesthetic or the elimination of multiple surgery, not just tidying up the system. It is complete replacement. The best we can do when it comes to using animals in science is—not to use them. That is where our duty lies, according to the rights view.

As for commercial animal agriculture, the rights view takes a similar abolitionist position. The fundamental moral wrong here is not that animals are kept in stressful close confinement or in isolation, or that their pain and suffering, their needs and preferences are ignored or discounted. All these *are* wrong, of course, but they are not the fundamental wrong. They are symptoms and effects of the deeper, systematic wrong that allows these animals to be viewed and treated as lacking independent value, as resources for us—as, indeed, a renewable resource. Giving farm animals more space, more natural environments, more companions does not right the fundamental wrong, any more than giving lab animals more anaesthesia or bigger, cleaner cages would right the fundamental wrong in their case. Nothing less than the total dissolution of commercial animal agriculture will do this, just as, for similar reasons I won't develop at length here, morality requires nothing less than the total elimination of hunting and trapping for commercial and sporting ends. The rights view's implications, then, as I have said, are clear and uncompromising.

My last two points are about philosophy, my profession. It is, most obviously, no substitute for political action. The words I have written here and in other places by themselves don't change a thing. It is what we do with the thoughts that the words express—our acts, our deeds— that changes things. All that philosophy can do, and all I have attempted, is to offer a vision of what our deeds should aim at. And the why. But not the how.

Finally, I am reminded of my thoughtful critic, the one I mentioned earlier, who chastised me for being too cerebral. Well, cerebral I have been: indirect duty views, utilitarianism, contractarianism—hardly the stuff deep passions are made of. I am also reminded, however, of the image another friend once set before me—the image of the ballerina as expressive of disciplined passion. Long hours of sweat and toil, of loneliness and practice, of doubt and fatigue: those are the discipline of her craft. But the passion is there too, the fierce drive to excel, to speak through her body, to do it right, to pierce our minds. That is the image of philosophy I would leave with you, not "too cerebral" but *disciplined passion.* Of the discipline enough has been seen. As for the passion: there are times, and these not infrequent, when tears come to my eyes when I see, or read, or hear of the wretched plight of animals in the hands of humans. Their pain, their suffering, their loneliness, their innocence, their death. Anger. Rage. Pity. Sorrow. Disgust. The whole creation groans under the weight of the evil we humans visit upon these mute, powerless creatures. It *is* our hearts, not just our heads, that call for an end to it all, that demand of us that we overcome, for them, the habits and forces behind their systematic oppression. All great movements, it is written, go through three stages: ridicule, discussion, adoption. It is the realization of this third stage, adoption, that requires both our passion and our discipline, our hearts and our heads. The fate of animals is in our hands. God grant we are equal to the task.

Carl Cohen

THE CASE FOR THE USE OF ANIMALS IN BIOMEDICAL RESEARCH*

Using animals as research subjects in medical investigations is widely condemned on two grounds: first, because it wrongly violates the *rights* of animals,[1] and second, becuse it wrongly imposes on sentient creatures much avoidable *suffering.*[2] Neither of these arguments is sound. The first relies on a mistaken understanding of rights; the second relies on a mistaken calculation of consequences. Both deserve definitive dismissal.

From the *New England Journal of Medicine* (Vol. 315, Oct. 1986).

*The notes to this essay are all Cohen's and are collected at the end as "References," as is the style of the *New England Journal of Medicine,* in which this essay appeared.

Why Animals Have No Rights

A right, properly understood, is a claim, or potential claim, that one party may exercise against another. The target against whom such a claim may be registered can be a single person, a group, a community, or (perhaps) all humankind. The content of rights claims also varies greatly: repayment of loans, nondiscrimination by employers, noninterference by the state, and so on. To comprehend any genuine right fully, therefore, we must know *who* holds the right, *against whom* it is held, and *to what* it is a right.

Alternative sources of rights add complexity. Some rights are grounded in constitution and law (e.g., the right of an accused to trial by jury); some rights are moral but give no legal claims (e.g., my right to your keeping the promise you gave me); and some rights (e.g., against theft or assault) are rooted both in morals and in law.

The different targets, contents, and sources of rights, and their inevitable conflict, together weave a tangled web. Notwithstanding all such complications, this much is clear about rights in general: they are in every case claims, or potential claims, within a community of moral agents. Rights arise, and can be intelligibly defended, only among beings who actually do, or can, make moral claims against one another. Whatever else rights may be, therefore, they are necessarily human; their possessors are persons, human beings.

The attributes of human beings from which this moral capability arises have been described variously by philosophers, both ancient and modern: the inner consciousness of a free will (Saint Augustine[3]); the grasp, by human reason, of the binding character of moral law (Saint Thomas[4]); the self-conscious participation of human beings in an objective ethical order (Hegel[5]); human membership in an organic moral community (Bradley[6]); the development of the human self through the consciousness of other moral selves (Mead[7]); and the underivative, intuitive cognition of the rightness of an action (Prichard[8]). Most influential has been Immanuel Kant's emphasis on the universal human possession of a uniquely moral will and the autonomy its use entails.[9] Humans confront choices that are purely moral; humans—but certainly not dogs or mice—lay down moral laws, for others and for themselves. Human beings are self-legislative, morally *auto-nomous.*

Animals (that is, nonhuman animals, the ordinary sense of that word) lack this capacity for free moral judgment. They are not beings of a kind capable of exercising or responding to moral claims. Animals therefore have no rights, and they can have none. This is the core of the argument about the alleged rights of animals. The holders of rights must have the capacity to comprehend rules of duty, governing all including themselves. In applying such rules, the holders of rights must recognize possible conflicts between what is in their own interest and what is just. Only in a community of beings capable of self-restricting moral judgments can the concept of a right be correctly invoked.

Humans have such moral capacities. They are in this sense self-legislative, are members of communities governed by moral rules, and do possess rights. Animals do not have such moral capacities. They are not morally self-legislative, cannot possibly be members of a truly moral community, and therefore cannot possess rights. In conducting research on animal subjects, therefore, we do not violate their rights, because they have none to violate.

To animate life, even in its simplest forms, we give a certain natural reverence. But the possession of rights presupposes a moral status not attained by the vast majority of living things. We must not infer, therefore, that a live being has, simply in being alive, a "right" to its life. The assertion that all animals, only because they are alive and have interests, also possess the "right to life" [10] is an abuse of that phrase, and wholly without warrant.

It does not follow from this, however, that we are morally free to do anything we please to animals. Certainly not. In our dealings with animals, as in our dealings with other human beings, we have obligations that do not arise from claims against us based on rights. Rights entail obligations, but many of the things one ought to do are in no way tied to another's entitlement. Rights and obligations are not reciprocals of one another, and it is a serious mistake to suppose that they are.

Illustrations are helpful. Obligations may arise from internal commitments made: physicians have obligations to their patients not grounded merely in their patients' rights. Teachers have such obligations to their students, shepherds to their dogs, and cowboys to their horses. Obligations may arise from differences of status: adults owe special care when playing with young children, and children owe special care when playing with young pets. Obligations may arise from special relationships: the payment of my son's college tuition is something to which he may have no right, although it may be my obligation to bear the burden if I reasonably can; my dog has no right to daily exercise and veterinary care, but I do have the obligation to provide these things for her. Obligations may arise from particular acts or circumstances: one may be obliged to another for a special kindness done, or obliged to put an animal out of its misery in view of its condition—although neither the human benefactor nor the dying animal may have had a claim of right.

Plainly, the grounds of our obligations to humans and to animals are manifold and cannot be formulated simply. Some hold that there is a general obligation to do no gratuitous harm to sentient creatures (the principle of nonmaleficence); some hold that there is a general obligation to do good to sentient creatures when that is reasonably within one's

10

power (the pinciple of beneficence). In our dealings with animals, few will deny that we are at least obliged to act humanely—that is, to treat them with the decency and concern that we owe, as sensitive human beings, to other sentient creatures. To treat animals humanely, however, is not to treat them as humans or as the holders of rights.

A common objection, which deserves a response, may be paraphrased as follows:

> If having rights requires being able to make moral claims, to grasp and apply moral laws, then many humans—the brain-damaged, the comatose, the senile—who plainly lack those capacities must be without rights. But that is absurd. This proves [the critic concludes] that rights do not depend on the presence of moral capacities. [1,10]

This objection fails; it mistakenly treats an essential feature of humanity as though it were a screen for sorting humans. The capacity for moral judgment that distinguishes humans from animals is not a test to be administered to human beings one by one. Persons who are unable, because of some disability, to perform the full moral functions natural to human beings are certainly not for that reason ejected from the moral community. The issue is one of kind. Humans are of such a kind that they may be the subject of experiments only with their voluntary consent. The choices they make freely must be respected. Animals are of such a kind that it is impossible for them, in principle, to give or withhold voluntary consent or to make a moral choice. What humans retain when disabled, animals have never had.

A second objection, also often made, may be paraphrased as follows:

> Capacities will not succeed in distinguishing humans from the other animals. Animals also reason; animals also communicate with one another; animals also care passionately for their young; animals also exhibit desires and preferences, [11,12] Features of moral relevance—rationality, interdependence, and love—are not exhibited uniquely by human beings. Therefore [this critic concludes], there can be no solid moral distinction between humans and other animals. [10]

15   This criticism misses the central point. It is not the ability to communicate or to reason, or dependence on one another, or care for the young, or the exhibition of preference, or any such behavior that marks the critical divide. Analogies between human families and those of monkeys, or between human communities and those of wolves, and the like, are entirely beside the point. Patterns of conduct are not at issue. Animals do indeed exhibit remakable behavior at times. Conditioning, fear, instinct, and intelligence all contribute to species survival. Membership in a community of moral agents nevertheless remains impossible for them. Actors subject to moral judgment must be capable of grasping the

generality of an ethical premise in a practical syllogism. Humans act immorally often enough, but only they—never wolves or monkeys—can discern, by applying some moral rule to the facts of a case, that a given act ought or ought not to be performed. The moral restraints imposed by humans on themselves are thus highly abstract and are often in conflict with the self-interest of the agent. Communal behavior among animals, even when most intelligent and most endearing, does not approach autonomous morality in this fundamental sense.

Genuinely moral acts have an internal as well as an external dimension. Thus, in law, an act can be criminal only when the guilty deed, the actus reus, is done with a guilty mind, mens rea. No animal can ever commit a crime; bringing animals to criminal trial is the mark of primitive ignorance. The claims of moral right are similarly inapplicable to them. Does a lion have a right to eat a baby zebra? Does a baby zebra have a right not to be eaten? Such questions, mistakenly invoking the concept of right where it does not belong, do not make good sense. Those who condemn biomedical research because it violates "animal rights" commit the same blunder.

In Defense of "Speciesism"

Abandoning reliance on animal rights, some critics resort instead to animal sentience—their feelings of pain and distress. We ought to desist from imposition of pain insofar as we can. Since all or nearly all experimentation on animals does impose pain and could be readily forgone, say these critics, it should be stopped. The ends sought may be worthy, but those ends do not justify imposing agonies on humans, and by animals the agonies are felt no less. The laboratory use of animals (these critics conclude) must therefore be ended—or at least very sharply curtailed.

Argument of this variety is essentially utilitarian, often expressly so;[13] it is based on the calculation of the net product, in pains and pleasures, resulting from experiments on animals. Jeremy Bentham, comparing horses and dogs with other sentient creatures, is thus commonly quoted: "The question is not, Can they reason? nor Can they talk? but, Can they suffer?"[14]

Animals certainly can suffer and surely ought not to be made to suffer needlessly. But in inferring, from these uncontroversial premises, that biomedical research causing animal distress is largely (or wholly) wrong, the critic commits two serious errors.

The first error is the assumption, often explicitly defended, that all sentient animals have equal moral standing. Between a dog and a human being, according to this view, there is no moral difference; hence the pains suffered by dogs must be weighed no differently from the pains

20

suffered by humans. To deny such equality, according to this critic, is to give unjust preference to one species over another; it is "speciesism." The most influential statement of this moral equality of species was made by Peter Singer:

> The racist violates the principle of equality by giving greater weight to the interests of members of his own race when there is a clash between their interests and the interests of those of another race. The sexist violates the principle of equality by favoring the interests of his own sex. Similarly the speciesist allows the interests of his own species to override the greater interests of members of other species. The pattern is identical in each case. [2]

This argument is worse than unsound; it is atrocious. It draws an offensive moral conclusion from a deliberately devised verbal parallelism that is utterly specious. Racism has no rational ground whatever. Differing degrees of respect or concern for humans for no other reason than that they are members of different races is an injustice totally without foundation in the nature of the races themselves. Racists, even if acting on the basis of mistaken factual beliefs, do grave moral wrong precisely because there is no morally relevant distinction among the races. The supposition of such differences has led to outright horror. The same is true of the sexes, neither sex being entitled by right to greater respect or concern than the other. No dispute here.

Between species of animate life, however—between (for example) humans on the one hand and cats or rats on the other—the morally relevant differences are enormous, and almost universally appreciated. Humans engage in moral reflection; humans are morally autonomous; humans are members of moral communities, recognizing just claims against their own interest. Human beings do have rights, theirs is a moral status very different from that of cats or rats.

I am a speciesist. Speciesism is not merely plausible; it is essential for right conduct, because those who will not make the morally relevant distinctions among species are almost certain, in consequence, to misapprehend their true obligations. The analogy between speciesism and racism is insidious. Every sensitive moral judgment requires that the differing natures of the beings to whom obligations are owed be considered. If all forms of animate life—or vertebrate animal life?—must be treated equally, and if therefore in evaluating a research program the pains of a rodent count equally with the pains of a human, we are forced to conclude (1) that neither humans nor rodents possess rights, or (2) that rodents possess all the rights that humans possess. Both alternatives are absurd. Yet one or the other must be swallowed if the moral equality of all species is to be defended.

Humans owe to other humans a degree of moral regard that cannot be owed to animals. Some humans take on the obligation to support and heal others, both humans and animals, as a principal duty in their lives; the fulfillment of that duty may require the sacrifice of many animals. If biomedical investigators abandon the effective pursuit of their professional objectives because they are convinced that they may not do to animals what the service of humans requires, they will fail, objectively, to do their duty. Refusing to recognize the moral differences among species is a sure path to calamity. (The largest animal rights group in the country is People for the Ethical Treatment of Animals; its codirector, Ingrid Newkirk, calls research using animal subjects "fascism" and "supremacism." "Animal liberationists do not separate out the *human* animal," she says, "so there is no rational basis for saying that a human being has special rights. A rat is a pig is a dog is a boy. They're all mammals." [15])

Those who claim to base their objection to the use of animals in biomedical research on their reckoning of the net pleasures and pains produced make a second error, equally grave. Even if it were true—as it is surely not—that the pains of all animal beings must be counted equally, a cogent utilitarian calculation requires that we weigh all the consequences of the use, and of the nonuse, of animals in laboratory research. Critics relying (however mistakenly) on animal rights may claim to ignore the beneficial results of such research, rights being trump cards to which interest and advantage must give way. But an argument that is explicitly framed in terms of interest and benefit for all over the long run must attend also to the disadvantageous consequences of not using animals in research, and to all the achievements attained and attainable only through their use. The sum of the benefits of their use is utterly beyond quantification. The elimination of horrible disease, the increase of longevity, the avoidance of great pain, the saving of lives, and the improvement of the quality of lives (for humans and for animals) achieved through research using animals is so incalculably great that the argument of these critics, systematically pursued, establishes not their conclusion but its reverse: to refrain from using animals in biomedical research is, on utilitarian grounds, morally wrong.

When balancing the pleasures and pains resulting from the use of animals in research, we must not fail to place on the scales the terrible pains that would have resulted, would be suffered now, and would long continue had animals not been used. Every disease eliminated, every vaccine developed, every method of pain relief devised, every surgical procedure invented, every prosthetic device implanted—indeed, virtually every modern medical therapy is due, in part or in whole, to experimentation using animals. Nor may we ignore, in the balancing process,

25

the predictable gains in human (and animal) well-being that are probably achievable in the future but that will not be achieved if the decision is made now to desist from such research or to curtail it.

Medical investigators are seldom insensitive to the distress their work may cause animal subjects. Opponents of research using animals are frequently insensitive to the cruelty of the results of the restrictions they would impose.[2] Untold numbers of human beings—real persons, although not now identifiable—would suffer grievously as the consequence of this well-meaning but shortsighted tenderness. If the morally relevant differences between humans and animals are borne in mind, and if all relevant considerations are weighed, the calculation of long-term consequences must give overwhelming support for biomedical research using animals.

Concluding Remarks

Substitution. The humane treatment of animals requires that we desist from experimenting on them if we can accomplish the same result using alternative methods—in vitro experimentation, computer simulation, or others. Critics of some experiments using animals rightly make this point.

It would be a serious error to suppose, however, that alternative techniques could soon be used in most research now using live animal subjects. No other methods now on the horizon—or perhaps ever to be available—can fully replace the testing of a drug, a procedure, or a vaccine, in live organisms. The flood of new medical possibilities being opened by the successes of recombinant DNA technology will turn to a trickle if testing on live animals is forbidden. When initial trials entail great risks, there may be no forward movement whatever without the use of live animal subjects. In seeking knowledge that may prove critical in later clinical applications, the unavailability of animals for inquiry may spell complete stymie. In the United States, federal regulations require the testing of new drugs and other products on animals, for efficacy and safety, before human beings are exposed to them.[16,17] We would not want it otherwise.

Every new advance in medicine—every new drug, new operation, new therapy of any kind—must sooner or later be tried on a living being for the first time. That trial, controlled or uncontrolled, will be an experiment. The subject of that experiment, if it is not an animal, will be a human being. Prohibiting the use of live animals in biomedical research, therefore, or sharply restricting it, must result either in the blockage of much valuable research or in the replacement of animal subjects with human subjects. These are the consequences—unacceptable to most reasonable persons—of not using animals in research.

Reduction. Should we not at least reduce the use of animals in biomedical research? No, we should increase it, to avoid when feasible the use of humans as experimental subjects. Medical investigations putting human subjects at some risk are numerous and greatly varied. The risks run in such experiments are usually unavoidable, and (thanks to earlier experiments on animals) most such risks are minimal or moderate. But some experimental risks are substantial.

When an experimental protocol that entails substantial risk to humans comes before an institutional review board, what response is appropriate? The investigation, we may suppose, is promising and deserves support, so long as its human subjects are protected against unnecessary dangers. May not the investigators be fairly asked, Have you done all that you can do to eliminate risk to humans by the extensive testing of that drug, that procedure, or that device on animals? To achieve maximal safety for humans we are right to require thorough experimentation on animal subjects before humans are involved.

Opportunities to increase human safety in this way are commonly missed; trials in which risks may be shifted from humans to animals are often not devised, sometimes not even considered. Why? For the investigator, the use of animals as subjects is often more expensive, in money and time, than the use of human subjects. Access to suitable human subjects is often quick and convenient, whereas access to appropriate animal subjects may be awkward, costly, and burdened with red tape. Physician-investigators have often had more experience working with human beings and know precisely where the needed pool of subjects is to be found and how they may be enlisted. Animals, and the procedures for their use, are often less familiar to these investigators. Moreover, the use of animals in place of humans is now more likely to be the target of zealous protests from without. The upshot is that humans are sometimes subjected to risks that animals could have borne, and should have borne, in their place. To maximize the protection of human subjects, I conclude, the wide and imaginative use of live animal subjects should be encouraged rather than discouraged. This enlargement in the use of animals is our obligation.

Consistency. Finally, inconsistency between the profession and the practice of many who oppose research using animals deserves comment. This frankly ad hominem observation aims chiefly to show that a coherent position rejecting the use of animals in medical research imposes costs so high as to be intolerable even to the critics themselves.

One cannot coherently object to the killing of animals in biomedical investigations while continuing to eat them. Anesthetics and thoughtful animal husbandry render the level of actual animal distress in the laboratory generally lower than that in the abattoir. So long as death and discomfort do not substantially differ in the two contexts, the consistent objector must not only refrain from all eating of animals but also protest as vehemently against others eating them as against others experimenting on them. No less vigorously must the critic object to the wearing of animal hides in coats and shoes, to employment in any industrial enterprise that uses animal parts, and to any commercial development that will cause death or distress to animals.

Killing animals to meet human needs for food, clothing, and shelter is judged entirely reasonable by most persons. The ubiquity of these uses and the virtual universality of moral support for them confront the opponent of research using animals with an inescapable difficulty. How can the many common uses of animals be judged morally worthy, while their use in scientific investigation is judged unworthy?

The number of animals used in research is but the tiniest fraction of the total used to satisfy assorted human appetites. That these appetites, often base and satisfiable in other ways, morally justify the far larger consumption of animals, whereas the quest for improved human health and understanding cannot justify the far smaller, is wholly implausible. Aside from the numbers of animals involved, the distinction in terms of worthiness of use, drawn with regard to any single animal, is not defensible. A given sheep is surely not more justifiably used to put lamb chops on the supermarket counter than to serve in testing a new contraceptive or a new prosthetic device. The needless killing of animals is wrong; if the common killing of them for our food or convenience is right, the less common but more humane uses of animals in the service of medical science are certainly not less right.

Scrupulous vegetarianism, in matters of food, clothing, shelter, commerce, and recreation, and in all other spheres, is the only fully coherent position the critic may adopt. At great human cost, the lives of fish and crustaceans must also be protected, with equal vigor, if speciesism has been forsworn. A very few consistent critics adopt this position. It is the reductio ad absurdum of the rejection of moral distinctions between animals and human beings.

Opposition to the use of animals in research is based on arguments of two different kinds—those relying on the alleged rights of animals and those relying on the consequences for animals. I have argued that arguments of both kinds must fail. We surely do have obligations to animals, but they have, and can have, no rights against us on which research can infringe. In calculating the consequences of animal research, we must weigh all the long-term benefits of the results achieved—to animals and to humans—and in that calculation we must not assume the moral equality of all animate species.

References

1. Regan T. The case for animal rights. Berkeley, Calif.: University of California Press, 1983.
2. Singer P. Animal liberation. New York: Avon Books, 1977.
3. St. Augustine. Confessions. Book Seven. 397 A.D. New York: Pocket books, 1957: 104–26.
4. St. Thomas Aquinas. Summa theologica. 1273 A.D. Philosophic texts. New York. Oxford University Press, 1960:353–66.
5. Hegel GWF. Philosophy of right. 1821. London: Oxford University Press, 1952: 105–10.
6. Bradley FH. Why should I be moral? 1876. In: Melden AI, ed. Ethical theories. New York: Prentice Hall, 1950:345–59.
7. Mead GH. The genesis of the self and social control. 1925. In: Reck AJ, ed. Selected writings. Indianapolis: Bobbs-Merrill, 1964:264–93.
8. Prichard HA. Does moral philosophy rest on a mistake? 1912. In: Cellars W, Hospers J, eds. Readings in ethical theory. New York: Appleton-Century-Crofts, 1952:149–63.
9. Kant I. Fundamental principles of the metaphysic of morals. 1785. New York: Liberal Arts Press, 1949.
10. Rollin BE. Animal rights and human morality. New York: Prometheus Books, 1981.
11. Hoff C. Immoral and moral uses of animals. N Engl J Med 1980; 302:115–8.
12. Jamieson D. Killing persons and other beings. In: Miller HB, Williams WH, eds. Ethics and animals. Clifton, N.J.: Humana Press, 1983:135–46.
13. Singer P. Ten years of animal liberation. New York Review of Books. 1985; 31:46–52.
14. Bentham J. Introduction to the principles of morals and legislation. London: Athlone Press, 1970.
15. McCabe K. Who will live, who will die? Washingtonian Magazine. August 1986:115.
16. U.S. Code of Federal Regulations, Title 21, Sect. 505(i). Food, drug and cosmetic regulations.
17. U.S. Code of Federal Regulations, Title 16, Sect. 1500.40–2. Consumer product regulations.

THE READER

1. *According to Cohen, what two grounds are widely used for arguing against the use of animals in medical research? What arguments on these grounds are put forth by opponents of animal research? Are there grounds other than these two on which such argument might be based?*

2. *How does Cohen distinguish between racism and sexism on the one hand and speciesism on the other? How does he defend this distinction?*

3. *Look at Cohen's concluding remarks (p. 698). How are they related to the argument that precedes them?*

THE WRITER

1. *What are the advantages of Cohen's concentration on only two grounds for argument against the use of animals in medical research? Are there disadvantages to this strategy?*

2. *Compare Cohen's defense of speciesism (p. 695) with Levin's "The*

Case for Torture" (p. 677) or Fussell's "Thank God for the Atom Bomb" (p. 711).
3. Write either a rebuttal of Cohen's defense of speciesism or an argument against speciesism without reference to Cohen's defense.

Stephen Jay Gould

THE TERRIFYING NORMALCY OF AIDS

Disney's Epcot Center in Orlando, Fla., is a technological tour de force and a conceptual desert. In this permanent World's Fair, American industrial giants have built their versions of an unblemished future. These masterful entertainments convey but one message, brilliantly packaged and relentlessly expressed: progress through technology is the solution to all human problems. G.E. proclaims from Horizons: "If we can dream it, we can do it." A.T.&T. speaks from on high within its giant golf ball: We are now "unbounded by space and time." United Technologies bubbles from the depths of Living Seas: "With the help of modern technology, we feel there's really no limit to what can be accomplished."

Yet several of these exhibits at the Experimental Prototype Community of Tomorrow, all predating last year's space disaster, belie their stated message from within by using the launch of the shuttle as a visual metaphor for technological triumph. The Challenger disaster may represent a general malaise, but it remains an incident. The AIDS pandemic, an issue that may rank with nuclear weaponry as the greatest danger of our era, provides a more striking proof that mind and technology are not omnipotent and that we have not canceled our bond to nature.

In 1984, John Platt, a biophysicist who taught at the University of Chicago for many years, wrote a short paper for private circulation. At a time when most of us were either ignoring AIDS, or viewing it as a contained and peculiar affliction of homosexual men, Platt recognized that the limited data on the origin of AIDS and its spread in America suggested a more frightening prospect: we are all susceptible to AIDS, and the disease has been spreading in a simple exponential manner.

Exponential growth is a geometric increase. Remember the old kiddy problem: if you place a penny on square one of a checkerboard and double the number of coins on each subsequent square—2, 4, 8, 16, 32 . . . —how big is the stack by the 64th square? The answer: about as

From the *New York Times Magazine* (Apr. 19, 1987).

high as the universe is wide. Nothing in the external environment inhibits this increase, thus giving to exponential processes their relentless character. In the real, noninfinite world, of course, some limit will eventually arise, and the process slows down, reaches a steady state, or destroys the entire system: the stack of pennies falls over, the bacterial cells exhaust their supply of nutrients.

Platt noticed that data for the initial spread of AIDS fell right on an exponential curve. He then followed the simplest possible procedure of extrapolating the curve unabated into the 1990's. Most of us were incredulous, accusing Platt of the mathematical gamesmanship that scientists call "curve fitting." After all, aren't exponential models unrealistic? Surely we are not all susceptible to AIDS. Is it not spread only by odd practices to odd people? Will it not, therefore, quickly run its short course within a confined group?

Well, hello 1987—worldwide data still match Platt's extrapolated curve. This will not, of course, go on forever. AIDS has probably already saturated the African areas where it probably originated, and where the sex ratio of afflicted people is 1-to-1, male-female. But AIDS still has far to spread, and may be moving exponentially, through the rest of the world. We have learned enough about the cause of AIDS to slow its spread, if we can make rapid and fundamental changes in our handling of that most powerful part of human biology—our own sexuality. But medicine, as yet, has nothing to offer as a cure and precious little even for palliation.

This exponential spread of AIDS not only illuminates its, and our, biology, but also underscores the tragedy of our moralistic misperception. Exponential processes have a definite time and place of origin, an initial point of "inoculation"—in this case, Africa. We didn't notice the spread at first. In a population of billions, we pay little attention when 1 increases to 2, or 8 to 16, but when 1 million becomes 2 million, we panic, even though the *rate* of doubling has not increased.

The infection has to start somewhere, and its initial locus may be little more than an accident of circumstance. For a while, it remains confined to those in close contact with the primary source, but only by accident of proximity, not by intrinsic susceptibility. Eventually, given the power and lability of human sexuality, it spreads outside the initial group and into the general population. And now AIDS has begun its march through our own heterosexual community.

What a tragedy that our moral stupidity caused us to lose precious time, the greatest enemy in fighting an exponential spread, by downplaying the danger because we thought that AIDS was a disease of three irregular groups of minorities: minorities of life style (needle users), of sexual preference (homosexuals) and of color (Haitians). If AIDS had first been imported from Africa into a Park Avenue apartment, we would not have dithered as the exponential march began.

10   The message of Orlando—the inevitability of technological solutions—is wrong, and we need to understand why.

Our species has not won its independence from nature, and we cannot do all that we can dream. Or at least we cannot do it at the rate required to avoid tragedy, for we are not unbounded from time. Viral diseases are preventable in principle, and I suspect that an AIDS vaccine will one day be produced. But how will this discovery avail us if it takes until the millenium, and by then AIDS has fully run its exponential course and saturated our population, killing a substantial percentage of the human race? A fight against an exponential enemy is primarily a race against time.

We must also grasp the perspective of ecology and evolutionary biology and recognize, once we reinsert ourselves properly into nature, that AIDS represents the ordinary workings of biology, not an irrational or diabolical plague with a moral meaning. Disease, including epidemic spread, is a natural phenomenon, part of human history from the beginning. An entire subdiscipline of my profession, paleopathology, studies the evidence of ancient diseases preserved in the fossil remains of organisms. Human history has been marked by episodic plagues. More native peoples died of imported disease than ever fell before the gun during the era of colonial expansion. Our memories are short, and we have had a respite, really, only since the influenza pandemic at the end of World War I, but AIDS must be viewed as a virulent expression of an ordinary natural phenomenon.

I do not say this to foster either comfort or complacency. The evolutionary perspective is correct, but utterly inappropriate for our human scale. Yes, AIDS is a natural phenomenon, one of a recurring class of pandemic diseases. Yes, AIDS may run through the entire population, and may carry off a quarter or more of us. Yes, it may make no *biological* difference to Homo sapiens in the long run: there will still be plenty of us left and we can start again. Evolution cares as little for its agents—organisms struggling for reproductive success—as physics cares for individual atoms of hydrogen in the sun. But *we* care. These atoms are our neighbors, our lovers, our children and ourselves. AIDS is both a natural phenomenon and, potentially, the greatest natural tragedy in human history.

The cardboard message of Epcot fosters the wrong attitudes; we must both reinsert ourselves into nature and view AIDS as a natural phenomenon in order to fight properly. If we stand above nature and if technology is all-powerful, then AIDS is a horrifying anomaly that must be trying to tell us something. If so, we can adopt one of two attitudes, each potentially fatal. We can either become complacent, because we believe the message of Epcot and assume that medicine will soon generate a cure, or we can panic in confusion and seek a scapegoat for something so irregular that it must have been visited upon us to teach us a moral lesson.

But AIDS is not irregular. It is part of nature. So are we. This should   15 galvanize us and give us hope, not prompt the worst of all responses: a kind of "new-age" negativism that equates natural with what we must accept and cannot, or even should not, change. When we view AIDS as natural, and when we recognize both the exponential property of its spread and the accidental character of its point of entry into America, we can break through our destructive tendencies to blame others and to free ourselves of concern.

If AIDS is natural, then there is no *message* in its spread. But by all that science has learned and all that rationality proclaims, AIDS works by a *mechanism*—and we can discover it. Victory is not ordained by any principle of progress, or any slogan of technology, so we shall have to fight like hell, and be watchful. There is no message, but there is a mechanism.

Kildare Dobbs

THE SHATTERER OF WORLDS

Before that morning in 1945 only a few conventional bombs, none of which did any great damage, had fallen on the city. Fleets of U.S. bombers had, however, devastated many cities round about, and Hiroshima had begun a program of evacuation which had reduced its population from 380,000 to some 245,000. Among the evacuees were Emiko and her family.

"We were moved out to Otake, a town about an hour's train-ride out of the city," Emiko told me. She had been a fifteen-year-old student in 1945. Fragile and vivacious, versed in the gentle traditions of the tea ceremony and flower arrangement, Emiko still had an air of the frail school-child when I talked with her. Every day, she and her sister Hideko used to commute into Hiroshima to school. Hideko was thirteen. Their father was an antique-dealer and he owned a house in the city, although it was empty now. Tetsuro, Emiko's thirteen-year-old brother, was at the Manchurian front with the Imperial Army. Her mother was kept busy

From *Reading the Time* (1968).

looking after the children, for her youngest daughter Eiko was sick with heart trouble, and rations were scarce. All of them were undernourished.

The night of August 5, 1945, little Eiko was dangerously ill. She was not expected to live. Everybody took turns watching by her bed, soothing her by massaging her arms and legs. Emiko retired at 8:30 (most Japanese people go to bed early) and at midnight was roused to take her turn with the sick girl. At 2 A.M. she went back to sleep.

While Emiko slept, the *Enola Gay,* a U.S. B-29 carrying the world's first operational atom bomb, was already in the air. She had taken off from the Pacific island of Iwo Jima at 1:45 A.M., and now Captain William Parsons, U.S.N. ordnance expert, was busy in her bomb-hold with the final assembly of Little Boy. Little Boy looked much like an outsize T.N.T. block-buster but the crew knew there was something different about him. Only Parsons and the pilot, Colonel Paul Tibbets, knew exactly in what manner Little Boy was different. Course was set for Hiroshima.

5   Emiko slept.

On board the *Enola Gay* co-pilot Captain Robert Lewis was writing up his personal log. "After leaving Iwo," he recorded, "we began to pick up some low stratus and before very long we were flying on top of an under-cast. Outside of a thin, high cirrus and the low stuff, it's a very beautiful day."

Emiko and Hideko were up at six in the morning. They dressed in the uniform of their women's college—white blouse, quilted hat, and black skirt—breakfasted and packed their aluminum lunch-boxes with white rice and eggs. These they stuffed into their shoulder bags as they hurried for the seven-o'clock train to Hiroshima. Today there would be no classes. Along with many women's groups, high school students, and others, the sisters were going to work on demolition. The city had begun a project of clearance to make fire-breaks in its downtown huddle of wood and paper buildings.

It was a lovely morning.

While the two young girls were at breakfast, Captain Lewis, over the Pacific, had made an entry in his log. "We are loaded. The bomb is now alive, and it's a funny feeling knowing it's right in back of you. Knock wood!"

10   In the train Hideko suddenly said she was hungry. She wanted to eat her lunch. Emiko dissuaded her: she'd be much hungrier later on. The two sisters argued, but Hideko at last agreed to keep her lunch till later. They decided to meet at the main station that afternoon and catch the five-o'clock train home. By now they had arrived at the first of Hiroshima's three stations. This was where Hideko got off, for she was to work in a different area from her sister. "Sayonara!" she called. "Goodbye." Emiko never saw her again.

There had been an air-raid at 7 A.M., but before Emiko arrived at Hiroshima's main station, two stops farther on, the sirens had sounded the all-clear. Just after eight, Emiko stepped off the train, walked through the station, and waited in the morning sunshine for her streetcar.

At about the same moment Lewis was writing in his log. "There'll be a short intermission while we bomb our target."

It was hot in the sun, Emiko saw a class-mate and greeted her. Together they moved back into the shade of a high concrete wall to chat. Emiko looked up at the sky and saw, far up in the cloudless blue, a single B-29.

It was exactly 8:10 A.M. The other people waiting for the streetcar saw it too and began to discuss it anxiously. Emiko felt scared. She felt that at all costs she must go on talking to her friend. Just as she was thinking this, there was a tremendous greenish-white flash in the sky. It was far brighter than the sun. Emiko afterwards remembered vaguely that there was a roaring or a rushing sound as well, but she was not sure, for just at that moment she lost consciousness.

"About 15 seconds after the flash," noted Lewis, 30,000 feet high and several miles away, "there were two very distinct slaps on the ship from the blast and the shock wave. That was all the physical effect we felt. We turned the ship so that we could observe the results." 15

When Emiko came to, she was lying on her face about forty feet away from where she had been standing. She was not aware of any pain. Her first thought was: "I'm alive!" She lifted her head slowly and looked about her. It was growing dark. The air was seething with dust and black smoke. There was a smell of burning. Emiko felt something trickle into her eyes, tested it in her mouth. Gingerly she put a hand to her head, then looked at it. She saw with a shock that it was covered with blood.

She did not give a thought to Hideko. It did not occur to her that her sister who was in another part of the city could possibly have been in danger. Like most of the survivors, Emiko assumed she had been close to a direct hit by a conventional bomb. She thought it had fallen on the post-office next to the station. With a hurt child's panic, Emiko, streaming with blood from gashes in her scalp, ran blindly in search of her mother and father.

The people standing in front of the station had been burned to death instantly (a shadow had saved Emiko from the flash). The people inside the station had been crushed by falling masonry. Emiko heard their faint cries, saw hands scrabbling weakly from under the collapsed platform. All around her the maimed survivors were running and stumbling away from the roaring furnace that had been a city. She ran with them toward the mountains that ring the landward side of Hiroshima.

From the *Enola Gay*, the strangers from North America looked down at their handiwork. "There, in front of our eyes," wrote Lewis, "was without a doubt the greatest explosion man had ever witnessed. The city was nine-tenths covered with smoke of a boiling nature, which seemed to indicate buildings blowing up, and a large white cloud which in less than three minutes reached 30,000 feet, then went to at least 50,000 feet."

20   Far below, on the edge of this cauldron of smoke, at a distance of some 2,500 yards from the blast's epicenter, Emiko ran with the rest of the living. Some who could not run limped or dragged themselves along. Others were carried. Many, hideously burned, were screaming with pain; when they tripped they lay where they had fallen. There was a man whose face had been ripped open from mouth to ear, another whose forehead was a gaping wound. A young soldier was running with a foot-long splinter of bamboo protruding from one eye. But these, like Emiko, were the lightly wounded.

Some of the burned people had been literally roasted. Skin hung from their flesh like sodden tissue paper. They did not bleed but plasma dripped from their seared limbs.

The *Enola Gay,* mission completed, was returning to base. Lewis sought words to express his feelings, the feelings of all the crew. "I might say," he wrote, "I might say 'My God! What have we done?' "

Emiko ran. When she had reached the safety of the mountain she remembered that she still had her shoulder bag. There was a small first-aid kit in it and she applied ointment to her wounds and to a small cut in her left hand. She bandaged her head.

Emiko looked back at the city. It was a lake of fire. All around her the burned fugitives cried out in pain. Some were scorched on one side only. Others, naked and flayed, were burned all over. They were too many to help and most of them were dying. Emiko followed the walking wounded along a back road, still delirious, expecting suddenly to meet her father and mother.

25   The thousands dying by the roadside called feebly for help or water. Some of the more lightly injured were already walking in the other direction, back towards the flames. Others, with hardly any visible wounds, stopped, turned ashy pale, and died within minutes. No one knew then that they were victims of radiation.

Emiko reached the suburb of Nakayama.

Far off in the *Enola Gay,* Lewis, who had seen none of this, had been writing, "If I live a hundred years, I'll never get those few minutes out of my mind. Looking at Captain Parsons, why he is as confounded as the rest, and he is supposed to have known everything and expected this to happen. . . ."

At Nakayama, Emiko stood in line at a depot where rice-balls were being distributed. Though it distressed her that the badly maimed could hardly feed themselves, the child found she was hungry. It was about 6 P.M. now. A little farther on, at Gion, a farmer called her by name. She did not recognize him, but it seemed he came monthly to her home to collect manure. The farmer took Emiko by the hand, led her to his own house, where his wife bathed her and fed her a meal of white rice. Then the child continued on her way. She passed another town where there were hundreds of injured. The dead were being hauled away in trucks. Among the injured a woman of about forty-five was waving frantically and muttering to herself. Emiko brought this woman a little water in a pumpkin leaf. She felt guilty about it; the schoolgirls had been warned not to give water to the seriously wounded. Emiko comforted herself with the thought that the woman would die soon anyway.

At Koi, she found standing-room in a train. It was heading for Otake with a full load of wounded. Many were put off at Ono, where there was a hospital; and two hours later the train rolled into Otake station. It was around 10 P.M.

A great crowd had gathered to look for their relations. It was a nightmare, Emiko remembered years afterwards; people were calling their dear kinfolk by name, searching frantically. It was necessary to call them by name, since most were so disfigured as to be unrecognizable. Doctors in the town council offices stitched Emiko's head-wounds. The place was crowded with casualties lying on the floor. Many died as Emiko watched.

The town council authorities made a strange announcement. They said a new and mysterious kind of bomb had fallen in Hiroshima. People were advised to stay away from the ruins.

Home at midnight, Emiko found her parents so happy to see her that they could not even cry. They could only give thanks that she was safe. Then they asked, "Where is your sister?"

For ten long days, while Emiko walked daily one and a half miles to have her wounds dressed with fresh gauze, her father searched the rubble of Hiroshima for his lost child. He could not have hoped to find her alive. All, as far as the eye could see, was a desolation of charred ashes and wreckage, relieved only by a few jagged ruins and by the seven estuarial rivers that flowed through the waste delta. The banks of these rivers were covered with the dead and in the rising tidal waters floated thousands of corpses. On one broad street in the Hakushima district the crowds who had been thronging there were all naked and scorched cadavers. Of thousands of others there was no trace at all. A fire several times hotter than the surface of the sun had turned them instantly to vapor.

On August 11 came the news that Nagasaki had suffered the same fate as Hiroshima; it was whispered that Japan had attacked the United States mainland with similar mysterious weapons. With the lavish circumstantiality of rumor, it was said that two out of a fleet of six-engined trans-Pacific bombers had failed to return. But on August 15, speaking for the first time over the radio to his people, the Emperor Hirohito announced his country's surrender. Emiko heard him. No more bombs! she thought. No more fear! The family did not learn till June the following year that this very day young Tetsuro had been killed in action in Manchuria.

Emiko's wounds healed slowly. In mid-September they had closed with a thin layer of pinkish skin. There had been a shortage of antiseptics and Emiko was happy to be getting well. Her satisfaction was short-lived. Mysteriously she came down with diarrhea and high fever. The fever continued for a month. Then one day she started to bleed from the gums, her mouth and throat became acutely inflamed, and her hair started to fall out. Through her delirium the child heard the doctors whisper by her pillow that she could not live. By now the doctors must have known that ionizing radiation caused such destruction of the blood's white cells that victims were left with little or no resistance against infection.

Yet Emiko recovered.

The wound on her hand, however, was particularly troublesome and did not heal for a long time.

As she got better, Emiko began to acquire some notion of the fearful scale of the disaster. Few of her friends and acquaintances were still alive. But no one knew precisely how many had died in Hiroshima. To this day the claims of various agencies conflict.

According to General Douglas MacArthur's headquarters, there were 78,150 dead and 13,083 missing.[1] The United States Atomic Bomb Casualty Commission claims there were 79,000 dead. Both sets of figures are probably far too low. There's reason to believe that at the time of the surrender Japanese authorities lied about the number of survivors, exaggerating it to get extra medical supplies. The Japanese welfare ministry's figures of 260,000 dead and 163,263 missing may well be too high. But the very order of such discrepancies speaks volumes about the scale of the catastrophe. The dead were literally uncountable.

This appalling toll of human life had been exacted from a city that had been prepared for air attack in a state of full wartime readiness. All civil-defense services had been overwhelmed from the first moment and it was many hours before any sort of organized rescue and relief could be put into effect.

It's true that single raids using so-called conventional weapons on other cities such as Tokyo and Dresden inflicted far greater casualties.

1. MacArthur (1880–1964), American army officer, Allied Supreme Commander in the Southwest Pacific (1942) and of oc- cupied Japan following World War II (1945–51).

And that it could not matter much to a victim whether he was burnt alive by a fire-storm caused by phosphorus, or by napalm or by nuclear fission. Yet in the whole of human history so savage a massacre had never before been inflicted with a single blow. And modern thermonuclear weapons are upwards of 1,000 times more powerful and deadly than the Hiroshima bomb.

The white scar I saw on Emiko's small, fine-boned hand was a tiny metaphor, a faint but eloquent reminder of the scar on humanity's conscience.

Paul Fussell

THANK GOD FOR THE ATOM BOMB

Many years ago in New York I saw on the side of a bus a whiskey ad I've remembered all this time. It's been for me a model of the short poem, and indeed I've come upon few short poems subsequently that exhibited more poetic talent. The ad consisted of two eleven-syllable lines of "verse," thus:

> In life, experience is the great teacher.
> In Scotch, Teacher's is the great experience.

For present purposes we must jettison the second line (licking our lips, to be sure, as it disappears), leaving the first to register a principle whose banality suggests that it enshrines a most useful truth. I bring up the matter because, writing on the forty-second anniversary of the atom-bombing of Hiroshima and Nagasaki, I want to consider something suggested by the long debate about the ethics, if any, of that ghastly affair. Namely, the importance of experience, sheer, vulgar experience, in influencing, if not determining, one's views about that use of the atom bomb.

The experience I'm talking about is having to come to grips, face to face, with an enemy who designs your death. The experience is common to those in the marines and the infantry and even the line navy, to those, in short, who fought the Second World War mindful always that their mission was, as they were repeatedly assured, "to close with the enemy and destroy him." *Destroy*, notice: not hurt, frighten, drive away, or capture. I think there's something to be learned about that war, as well as about the tendency of historical memory unwittingly to resolve ambiguity and generally clean up the premises, by considering the way tes-

Originally published in *The New Republic* (Aug. 22, 1981).

timonies emanating from real war experience tend to complicate attitudes about the most cruel ending of that most cruel war.

"What did you do in the Great War, Daddy?" The recruiting poster deserves ridicule and contempt, of course, but here its question is embarrassingly relevant, and the problem is one that touches on the dirty little secret of social class in America. Arthur T. Hadley said recently that those for whom the use of the A-bomb was "wrong" seem to be implying "that it would have been better to allow thousands on thousands of American and Japanese infantrymen to die in honest hand-to-hand combat on the beaches than to drop those two bombs." People holding such views, he notes, "do not come from the ranks of society that produce infantrymen or pilots." And there's an eloquence problem: most of those with firsthand experience of the war at its worst were not elaborately educated people. Relatively inarticulate, most have remained silent about what they know. That is, few of those destined to be blown to pieces if the main Japanese islands had been invaded went on to become our most effective men of letters or impressive ethical theorists or professors of contemporary history or of international law. The testimony of experience has tended to come from rough diamonds—James Jones[1] is an example—who went through the war as enlisted men in the infantry or the Marine Corps.

Anticipating objections from those without such experience, in his book *WWII* Jones carefully prepares for his chapter on the A-bombs by detailing the plans already in motion for the infantry assaults on the home islands of Kyushu (thirteen divisions scheduled to land in November 1945) and ultimately Honshu (sixteen divisions scheduled for March 1946). Planners of the invasion assumed that it would require a full year, to November 1946, for the Japanese to be sufficiently worn down by land-combat attrition to surrender. By that time, one million American casualties was the expected price. Jones observes that the forthcoming invasion of Kyushu "was well into its collecting and stockpiling stages before the war ended." (The island of Saipan was designated a main ammunition and supply base for the invasion, and if you go there today you can see some of the assembled stuff still sitting there.) "The assault troops were chosen and already in training," Jones reminds his readers, and he illuminates by the light of experience what this meant:

> What it must have been like to some old-timer buck sergeant or staff sergeant who had been through Guadalcanal or Bougainville or the Philippines, to stand on some beach and watch this huge war machine beginning to stir and move all around him and know that he very likely had survived this far only to fall dead on the dirt of Japan's home islands, hardly bears thinking about.

1. Jones (1921–77), American novelist, author of *From Here to Eternity* (1951), the first volume in a trilogy about World War II.

Another bright enlisted man, this one an experienced marine destined for the assault on Honshu, adds his testimony. Former Pfc. E. B. Sledge, author of the splendid memoir *With the Old Breed at Peleliu and Okinawa*, noticed at the time that the fighting grew "more vicious the closer we got to Japan," with the carnage of Iwo Jima and Okinawa worse than what had gone before. He points out that

> what we had *experienced* [my emphasis] in fighting the Japs (pardon the expression) on Peleliu and Okinawa caused us to formulate some very definite opinions that the invasion . . . would be a ghastly bloodletting. . . . It would shock the American public and the world. [Every Japanese] soldier, civilian, woman, and child would fight to the death with whatever weapons they had, rifle, grenade, or bamboo spear.

The Japanese pre-invasion patriotic song, "One Hundred Million Souls for the Emperor," says Sledge, "meant just that." Universal national kamikaze was the point. One kamikaze pilot, discouraged by his unit's failure to impede the Americans very much despite the bizarre casualties it caused, wrote before diving his plane onto an American ship, "I see the war situation becoming more desperate. All Japanese must become soldiers and die for the Emperor." Sledge's First Marine Division was to land close to the Yokosuka Naval Base, "one of the most heavily defended sectors of the island." The marines were told, he recalls, that

> due to the strong beach defenses, caves, tunnels, and numerous Jap suicide torpedo boats and manned mines, few Marines in the first five assault waves would get ashore alive—my company was scheduled to be in the first and second waves. The veterans in the outfit felt we had already run out of luck anyway. . . . We viewed the invasion with complete resignation that we would be killed—either on the beach or inland.

And the invasion was going to take place: there's no question about that. It was not theoretical or merely rumored in order to scare the Japanese. By July 10, 1945, the prelanding naval and aerial bombardment of the coast had begun, and the battleships *Iowa*, *Missouri*, *Wisconsin*, and *King George V* were steaming up and down the coast, softening it up with their sixteen-inch shells.

On the other hand, John Kenneth Galbraith is persuaded that the Japanese would have surrendered surely by November without an invasion. He thinks the A-bombs were unnecessary and unjustified because the war was ending anyway. The A-bombs meant, he says, "a difference, at most, of two or three weeks." But at the time, with no indication that surrender was on the way, the kamikazes were sinking American vessels, the *Indianapolis* was sunk (880 men killed), and Allied casualties were running to over 7,000 per week. "Two or three weeks," says Galbraith.

Two weeks more means 14,000 more killed and wounded, three weeks more, 21,000. Those weeks mean the world if you're one of those thousands or related to one of them. During the time between the dropping of the Nagasaki bomb on August 9 and the actual surrender on the fifteenth, the war pursued its accustomed course: on the twelfth of August eight captured American fliers were executed (heads chopped off); the fifty-first United States submarine, *Bonefish*, was sunk (all aboard drowned); the destroyer *Callaghan* went down, the seventieth to be sunk, and the Destroyer Escort *Underhill* was lost. That's a bit of what happened in six days of the two or three weeks posited by Galbraith. What did he do in the war? He worked in the Office of Price Administration in Washington. I don't demand that he experience having his ass shot off. I merely note that he didn't.

Likewise, the historian Michael Sherry, author of a recent book on the rise of the American bombing mystique, *The Creation of Armageddon*, argues that we didn't delay long enough between the test explosion in New Mexico and the mortal explosions in Japan. More delay would have made possible deeper moral considerations and perhaps laudable second thoughts and restraint. "The risks of delaying the bomb's use," he says, "would have been small—not the thousands of casualties expected of invasion but only a few days or weeks of relatively routine operations." While the mass murders represented by these "relatively routine operations" were enacting, Michael Sherry was safe at home. Indeed, when the bombs were dropped he was going on eight months old, in danger only of falling out of his pram. In speaking thus of Galbraith and Sherry, I'm aware of the offensive implications *ad hominem*. But what's at stake in an infantry assault is so entirely unthinkable to those without the experience of one, or several, or many, even if they possess very wide-ranging imaginations and warm sympathies, that experience is crucial in this case.

10   In general, the principle is, the farther from the scene of horror, the easier the talk. One young combat naval officer close to the action wrote home in the fall of 1943, just before the marines underwent the agony of Tarawa: "When I read that we will fight the Japs for years if necessary and will sacrifice hundreds of thousands if we must, I always like to check from where he's talking: it's seldom out here." That was Lieutenant (j.g.) John F. Kennedy. And Winston Churchill, with an irony perhaps too broad and easy, noted in Parliament that the people who preferred invasion to A-bombing seemed to have "no intention of proceeding to the Japanese front themselves."

A remoteness from experience like Galbraith's and Sherry's, and a similar rationalistic abstraction from actuality, seem to motivate the reaction of an anonymous reviewer of William Manchester's *Goodbye Darkness: A Memoir of the Pacific War* for *The New York Review of*

Books. The reviewer naturally dislikes Manchester's still terming the enemy Nips or Japs, but what really shakes him (her?) is this passage of Manchester's:

> After Biak the enemy withdrew to deep caverns. Rooting them out became a bloody business which reached its ultimate horrors in the last months of the war. You think of the lives which would have been lost in an invasion of Japan's home islands—a staggering number of Americans but millions more of Japanese—and you thank God for the atomic bomb.

Thank God for the atom bomb. From this, "one recoils," says the reviewer. One does, doesn't one?

And not just a staggering number of Americans would have been killed in the invasion. Thousands of British assault troops would have been destroyed too, the anticipated casualties from the almost 200,000 men in the six divisions (the same number used to invade Normandy) assigned to invade the Malay Peninsula on September 9. Aimed at the reconquest of Singapore, this operation was expected to last until about March 1946—that is, seven more months of infantry fighting. "But for the atomic bombs," a British observer intimate with the Japanese defenses notes, "I don't think we would have stood a cat in hell's chance. We would have been murdered in the biggest massacre of the war. They would have annihilated the lot of us."

The Dutchman Laurens van der Post had been a prisoner of the Japanese for three and a half years. He and thousands of his fellows, enfeebled by beriberi and pellagra, were being systematically starved to death, the Japanese rationalizing this treatment not just because the prisoners were white men but because they had allowed themselves to be captured at all and were therefore moral garbage. In the summer of 1945 Field Marshal Terauchi issued a significant order: at the moment the Allies invaded the main islands, all prisoners were to be killed by the prison-camp commanders. But thank God that did not happen. When the A-bombs were dropped, van der Post recalls, "This cataclysm I was certain would make the Japanese feel that they could withdraw from the war without dishonor, because it would strike them, as it had us in the silence of our prison night, as something supernatural."

In an exchange of views not long ago in *The New York Review of Books*, Joseph Alsop and David Joravsky set forth the by now familiar argument on both sides of the debate about the "ethics" of the bomb. It's not hard to guess which side each chose once you know that Alsop experienced capture by the Japanese at Hong Kong early in 1942, while Joravsky came into no deadly contact with the Japanese: a young, combat-innocent soldier, he was on his way to the Pacific when the war ended. The editors of *The New York Review* gave the debate the

tendentious title "Was the Hiroshima Bomb Necessary?" surely an
unanswerable question (unlike "Was It Effective?") and one precisely
indicating the intellectual difficulties involved in imposing *ex post facto*
a rational and even a genteel ethics on this event. In arguing the acceptability of the bomb, Alsop focuses on the power and fanaticism of War
Minister Anami, who insisted that Japan fight to the bitter end, defending the main islands with the same techniques and tenacity employed
at Iwo and Okinawa. Alsop concludes: "Japanese surrender could never
have been obtained, at any rate without the honor-satisfying bloodbath
envisioned by . . . Anami, if the hideous destruction of Hiroshima and
Nagasaki had not finally galvanized the peace advocates into tearing up
the entire Japanese book of rules." The Japanese plan to deploy the
undefeated bulk of their ground forces, over two million men, plus
10,000 kamikaze planes, plus the elderly and all the women and children
with sharpened spears they could muster in a suicidal defense makes it
absurd, says Alsop, to "hold the common view, by now hardly challenged
by anyone, that the decision to drop the two bombs on Japan was wicked
in itself, and that President Truman and all others who joined in making
or who [like Robert Oppenheimer] assented to this decision shared in
the wickedness." And in explanation of "the two bombs," Alsop adds:
"The true, climactic, and successful effort of the Japanese peace advocates . . . did not begin in deadly earnest until *after* the second bomb
had destroyed Nagasaki. The Nagasaki bomb was thus the trigger to all
the developments that led to peace." At this time the army was so
unready for surrender that most looked forward to the forthcoming
invasion as an indispensable opportunity to show their mettle, enthusiastically agreeing with the army spokesman who reasoned early in 1945,
"Since the retreat from Guadalcanal, the Army has had little opportunity to engage the enemy in land battles. But when we meet in Japan
proper, our Army will demonstrate its invincible superiority." This possibility foreclosed by the Emperor's post-A-bomb surrender broadcast, the
shocked, disappointed officers of one infantry battalion, anticipating a
professionally impressive defense of the beaches, killed themselves in the
following numbers: one major, three captains, ten first lieutenants, and
twelve second lieutenants.

15   David Joravsky, now a professor of history at Northwestern, argued
on the other hand that those who decided to use the A-bombs on cities
betray defects of "reason and self-restraint." It all needn't have happened, he says, "if the U.S. government had been willing to take a few
more days and to be a bit more thoughtful in opening up the age of
nuclear warfare." I've already noted what "a few more days" would
mean to the luckless troops and sailors on the spot, and as to being
thoughtful when "opening up the age of nuclear warfare," of course no
one was focusing on anything as portentous as that, which reflects a

historian's tidy hind-sight. The U.S. government was engaged not in that sort of momentous thing but in ending the war conclusively, as well as irrationally Remembering Pearl Harbor with a vengeance. It didn't know then what everyone knows now about leukemia and various kinds of carcinoma and birth defects. Truman was not being sly or coy when he insisted that the bomb was "only another weapon." History, as Eliot's "Gerontion" notes,

> . . . has many cunning passages, contrived corridors
> And issues, deceives with whispering ambitions,
> Guides us by vanities. . . .
> > > > Think
> Neither fear nor courage saves us.
> > Unnatural vices
> Are fathered by our heroism. Virtues
> Are forced upon us by our impudent crimes.

Understanding the past requires pretending that you don't know the present. It requires feeling its own pressure on your pulses without any *ex post facto* illumination. That's a harder thing to do than Joravsky seems to think.

The Alsop-Joravsky debate, reduced to a collision between experience and theory, was conducted with a certain civilized respect for evidence. Not so the way the scurrilous, agitprop *New Statesman* conceives those justifying the dropping of the bomb and those opposing. They are, on the one hand, says Bruce Page, "the imperialist class-forces acting through Harry Truman" and, on the other, those representing "the humane, democratic virtues"—in short, "fascists" as opposed to "populists." But ironically the bomb saved the lives not of any imperialists but only of the low and humble, the quintessentially democratic huddled masses—the conscripted enlisted men manning the fated invasion divisions and the sailors crouching at their gun-mounts in terror of the Kamikazes. When the war ended, Bruce Page was nine years old. For someone of his experience, phrases like "imperialist class forces" come easily, and the issues look perfectly clear.

He's not the only one to have forgotten, if he ever knew, the unspeakable savagery of the Pacific war. The dramatic postwar Japanese success at hustling and merchandising and tourism has (happily, in many ways) effaced for most people the vicious assault context in which the Hiroshima horror should be viewed. It is easy to forget, or not to know, what Japan was like before it was first destroyed, and then humiliated, tamed, and constitutionalized by the West. "Implacable, treacherous, barbaric"—those were Admiral Halsey's characterizations of the enemy, and at the time few facing the Japanese would deny that they fit to a T. One remembers the captured American airmen—the lucky ones who escaped decapitation—locked for years in packing crates. One remembers the gleeful use of bayonets on civilians, on nurses and the wounded, in Hong Kong and Singapore. Anyone who actually fought in the Pacific recalls the Japanese routinely firing on medics, killing the wounded (torturing them first, if possible), and cutting off the penises of the dead to stick in the corpses' mouths. The degree to which Americans register shock and extraordinary shame about the Hiroshima bomb correlates closely with lack of information about the Pacific war.

And of course the brutality was not just on one side. There was much sadism and cruelty, undeniably racist, on ours. (It's worth noting in passing how few hopes blacks could entertain of desegregation and decent treatment when the U.S. Army itself slandered the enemy as "the little brown Jap.") Marines and soldiers could augment their view of their own invincibility by possessing a well-washed Japanese skull, and very soon after Guadalcanal it was common to treat surrendering Japanese as handy rifle targets. Plenty of Japanese gold teeth were extracted—some from still living mouths—with Marine Corps Ka-Bar Knives,[2] and one of E. B. Sledge's fellow marines went around with a cut-off Japanese hand. When its smell grew too offensive and Sledge urged him to get rid of it, he defended his possession of this trophy thus: "How many Marines you reckon that hand pulled the trigger on?" (It's hardly necessary to observe that a soldier in the ETO would probably not have dealt that way with a German or Italian—that is, a "white person's"—hand.) In the Pacific the situation grew so public and scandalous that in September 1942, the Commander in Chief of the Pacific Fleet issued this order: "No part of the enemy's body may be used as a souvenir. Unit Commanders will take stern disciplinary action. . . ."

Among Americans it was widely held that the Japanese were really subhuman, little yellow beasts, and popular imagery depicted them as lice, rats, bats, vipers, dogs, and monkeys. What was required, said the Marine Corps journal *The Leatherneck* in May 1945, was "a gigantic task of extermination." The Japanese constituted a "pestilence," and the only appropriate treatment was "annihilation." Some of the marines landing on Iwo Jima had "Rodent Exterminator" written on their helmet covers, and on one American flagship the naval commander had erected a large sign enjoining all to "KILL JAPS! KILL JAPS! KILL MORE JAPS!" Herman Wouk remembers the Pacific war scene correctly while analyzing ensign Keith in *The Caine Mutiny:* "Like most of the naval executioners of Kwajalein, he seemed to regard the enemy as a species of animal pest." And the feeling was entirely reciprocal: "From the grim and desperate taciturnity with which the Japanese died,

---

2. High-carbon steel knives carried by Marines (officers and gunners) who did not carry bayonet-bearing rifles.

they seemed on their side to believe that they were contending with an invasion of large armed ants." Hiroshima seems to follow in natural sequence: "This obliviousness of both sides to the fact that the opponents were human beings may perhaps be cited as the key to the many massacres of the Pacific war." Since the Jap vermin resist so madly and have killed so many of us, let's pour gasoline into their bunkers and light it and then shoot those afire who try to get out. Why not? Why not blow them all up, with satchel charges or with something stronger? Why not, indeed, drop a new kind of bomb on them, and on the un-uniformed ones too, since the Japanese government has announced that women from ages of seventeen to forty are being called up to repel the invasion? The intelligence officer of the U.S. Fifth Air Force declared on July 21, 1945, that "the entire population of Japan is a proper military target," and he added emphatically, *"There are no civilians in Japan."* Why delay and allow one more American high school kid to see his own intestines blown out of his body and spread before him in the dirt while he screams and screams when with the new bomb we can end the whole thing just like that?

On Okinawa, only weeks before Hiroshima, 123,000 Japanese and Americans *killed* each other. (About 140,000 Japanese died at Hiroshima.) "Just awful" was the comment on the Okinawa slaughter not of some pacifist but of General MacArthur. On July 14, 1945, General Marshall sadly informed the Combined Chiefs of Staff—he was not trying to scare the Japanese—that it's "now clear . . . that in order to finish with the Japanese quickly, it will be necessary to invade the industrial heart of Japan." The invasion was definitely on, as I know because I was to be in it.

When the atom bomb ended the war, I was in the Forty-fifth Infantry Division, which had been through the European war so thoroughly that it had needed to be reconstituted two or three times. We were in a staging area near Rheims, ready to be shipped back across the United States for refresher training at Fort Lewis, Washington, and then sent on for final preparation in the Philippines. My division, like most of the ones transferred from Europe, was to take part in the invasion of Honshu. (The earlier landing on Kyushu was to be carried out by the 700,000 infantry already in the Pacific, those with whom James Jones has sympathized.) I was a twenty-one-year-old second lieutenant of infantry leading a rifle platoon. Although still officially fit for combat, in the German war I had already been wounded in the back and the leg badly enough to be adjudged, after the war, 40 percent disabled. But even if my leg buckled and I fell to the ground whenever I jumped out of the back of a truck, and even if the very idea of more combat made me breathe in gasps and shake all over, my condition was held to be adequate for the next act. When the atom bombs were dropped and news began to

20

circulate that "Operation Olympic" would not, after all, be necessary, when we learned to our astonishment that we would not be obliged in a few months to rush up the beaches near Tokyo assault-firing while being machine-gunned, mortared, and shelled, for all the practiced phlegm of our tough façades we broke down and cried with relief and joy. We were going to live. We were going to grow to adulthood after all. The killing was all going to be over, and peace was actually going to be the state of things. When the *Enola Gay* dropped its package, "There were cheers," says John Toland, "over the intercom; it meant the end of the war." Down on the ground the reaction of Sledge's marine buddies when they heard the news was more solemn and complicated. They heard about the end of the war

> with quiet disbelief coupled with an indescribable sense of relief. We thought the Japanese would never surrender. Many refused to believe it. . . . Sitting in stunned silence, we remembered our dead. So many dead. So many maimed. So many bright futures consigned to the ashes of the past. So many dreams lost in the madness that had engulfed us. Except for a few widely scattered shouts of joy, the survivors of the abyss sat hollow-eyed and silent, trying to comprehend a world without war.

These troops who cried and cheered with relief or who sat stunned by the weight of their experience are very different from the high-minded, guilt-ridden GIs we're told about by J. Glenn Gray in his sensitive book *The Warriors.* During the war in Europe Gray was an interrogator in the Army Counterintelligence Corps, and in that capacity he experienced the war at Division level. There's no denying that Gray's outlook on everything was admirably noble, elevated, and responsible. After the war he became a much-admired professor of philosophy at Colorado College and an esteemed editor of Heidegger. But *The Warriors,* his meditation on the moral and psychological dimensions of modern soldiering, gives every sign of error occasioned by remoteness from experience. Division headquarters is miles—*miles*—behind the line where soldiers experience terror and madness and relieve those pressures by crazy brutality and sadism. Indeed, unless they actually encountered the enemy during the war, most "soldiers" have very little idea what "combat" was like. As William Manchester says, "All who wore uniforms are called veterans, but more than 90 percent of them are as uninformed about the killing zones as those on the home front." Manchester's fellow marine E. B. Sledge thoughtfully and responsibly invokes the terms *drastically* and *totally* to underline the differences in experience between front and rear, and not even the far rear, but the close rear. "Our code of conduct toward the enemy," he notes, "differed drastically from that prevailing back at the division CP." (He's describing gold-tooth extraction from still-living Japanese.) Again he writes: "We existed in an environment totally incomprehensible to men behind the lines . . . ," even, he would insist, to men as intelligent and sensitive as Glenn Gray, who missed seeing with his own eyes Sledge's marine friends sliding under fire down a shell-pocked ridge slimy with mud and liquid dysentery shit into the maggoty Japanese and USMC corpses at the bottom, vomiting as the maggots burrowed into their own foul clothing. "We didn't talk about such things," says Sledge. "They were too horrible and obscene even for hardened veterans. . . . Nor do authors normally write about such vileness; unless they have seen it with their own eyes, it is too preposterous to think that men could actually live and fight for days and nights on end under such terrible conditions and not be driven insane." And Sledge has added a comment on such experience and the insulation provided by even a short distance: "Often people just behind our rifle companies couldn't understand what we knew." Glenn Gray was not in a rifle company, or even just behind one. "When the news of the atomic bombing of Hiroshima and Nagasaki came," he asks us to believe, "many an American soldier felt shocked and ashamed." Shocked, OK, but why ashamed? Because we'd destroyed civilians? We'd been doing that for years, in raids on Hamburg and Berlin and Cologne and Frankfurt and Mannheim and Dresden, and Tokyo, and besides, the two A-bombs wiped out 10,000 Japanese troops, not often thought of now, John Hersey's kindly physicians and Jesuit priests being more touching. If around division headquarters some of the people Gray talked to felt ashamed, down in the rifle companies no one did, despite Gray's assertions. "The combat soldier," he says,

> knew better than did Americans at home what those bombs meant in suffering and injustice. The man of conscience realized intuitively that the vast majority of Japanese in both cities were no more, if no less, guilty of the war than were his own parents, sisters, or brothers.

I find this canting nonsense. The purpose of the bombs was not to "punish" people but to stop the war. To intensify the shame Gray insists we feel, he seems willing to fiddle the facts. The Hiroshima bomb, he says, was dropped "without any warning." But actually, two days before, 720,000 leaflets were dropped on the city urging everyone to get out and indicating that the place was going to be (as the Potsdam Declaration had promised) obliterated. Of course few left.

Experience whispers that the pity is not that we used the bomb to end the Japanese war but that it wasn't ready in time to end the German one. If only it could have been rushed into production faster and dropped at the right moment on the Reich Chancellery or Berchtesgaden or Hitler's military headquarters in East Prussia (where Colonel Stauffenberg's July 20 bomb didn't do the job because it wasn't big enough), much of the Nazi hierarchy could have been pulverized immediately, saving not just the embarrassment of the Nuremberg trials but the lives of around four million Jews, Poles, Slavs, and gypsies, not to mention the lives and limbs of millions of Allied and German soldiers. If the bomb had only been ready in time, the young men of my infantry platoon would not have been so cruelly killed and wounded.

25   All this is not to deny that like the Russian Revolution, the atom-bombing of Japan was a vast historical tragedy, and every passing year magnifies the dilemma into which it has lodged the contemporary world. As with the Russian Revolution, there are two sides—that's why it's a tragedy instead of a disaster—and unless we are, like Bruce Page, simple-mindedly unimaginative and cruel, we will be painfully aware of both sides at once. To observe that from the viewpoint of the war's victims-to-be the bomb seemed precisely the right thing to drop is to purchase no immunity from horror. To experience both sides, one might study the book *Unforgettable Fire: Pictures Drawn by Atomic Bomb Survivors,* which presents a number of amateur drawings and watercolors of the Hiroshima scene made by middle-aged and elderly survivors for a peace exhibition in 1975. In addition to the almost unbearable pictures, the book offers brief moments of memoir not for the weak-stomached:

> While taking my severely wounded wife out to the river bank . . ., I was horrified indeed at the sight of a stark naked man standing in the rain with his eyeball in his palm. He looked to be in great pain but there was nothing that I could do for him. I wonder what became of him. Even today, I vividly remember the sight. I was simply miserable.

These childlike drawings and paintings are of skin hanging down, breasts torn off, people bleeding and burning, dying mothers nursing dead babies. A bloody woman holds a bloody child in the ruins of a house, and the artist remembers her calling, "Please help this child! Someone, please help this child. Please help! Someone, please." As Samuel Johnson said of the smothering of Desdemona, the innocent in another tragedy, "It is not to be endured." Nor, it should be noticed, is an infantryman's account of having his arm blown off in the Arno Valley in Italy in 1944:

> I wanted to die and die fast. I wanted to forget this miserable world. I cursed the war, I cursed the people who were responsible for it, I cursed God for putting me here . . . to suffer for something I never did or knew anything about.

(A good place to interrupt and remember Glenn Gray's noble but hopelessly one-sided remarks about "injustice," as well as "suffering.") "For this was hell," the soldier goes on,

> and I never imagined anything or anyone could suffer so bitterly. I screamed and cursed. Why? What had I done to deserve this? But no answer came. I yelled for medics, because subconsciously I wanted to live. I tried to apply my right hand over my bleeding stump, but I didn't have

the strength to hold it. I looked to the left of me and saw the bloody mess that was once my left arm; its fingers and palm were turned upward, like a flower looking to the sun for its strength.

The future scholar-critic who writes *The History of Canting in the Twentieth Century* will find much to study and interpret in the utterances of those who dilate on the special wickedness of the A-bomb-droppers. He will realize that such utterance can perform for the speaker a valuable double function. First, it can display the fineness of his moral weave. And second, by implication it can also inform the audience that during the war he was not socially so unfortunate as to find himself down there with the ground forces, where he might have had to compromise the purity and clarity of his moral system by the experience of weighing his own life against someone else's. Down there, which is where the other people were, is the place where coarse self-interest is the rule. When the young soldier with the wild eyes comes at you, firing, do you shoot him in the foot, hoping he'll be hurt badly enough to drop or mis-aim the gun with which he's going to kill you, or do you shoot him in the chest (or, if you're a prime shot, in the head) and make certain that you and not he will be the survivor of that mortal moment?

It would be not just stupid but would betray a lamentable want of human experience to expect soldiers to be very sensitive humanitarians. The Glenn Grays of this world need to have their attention directed to the testimony of those who know, like, say, Admiral of the Fleet Lord Fisher, who said, "Moderation in war is imbecility," or Sir Arthur Harris, director of the admittedly wicked aerial-bombing campaign designed, as Churchill put it, to "de-house" the German civilian population, who observed that "War is immoral," or our own General W. T. Sherman: "War is cruelty, and you cannot refine it." Lord Louis Mountbatten, trying to say something sensible about the dropping of the A-bomb, came up only with "War is crazy." Or rather, it requires choices among crazinesses. "It would seem even more crazy," he went on, "if we were to have more casualties on our side to save the Japanese." One of the unpleasant facts for anyone in the ground armies during the war was that you had to become pro tem a subordinate of the very uncivilian George S. Patton and respond somehow to his unremitting insistence that you embrace his view of things. But in one of his effusions he was right, and his observation tends to suggest the experimental dubiousness of the concept of "just wars." "War is not a contest with gloves," he perceived. "It is resorted to only when laws, which are rules, have failed." Soldiers being like that, only the barest decencies should be expected of them. They did not start the war, except in the terrible sense hinted at in Frederic Manning's observation based on his front-line experience in the Great War: "War is waged by men; not by beasts, or by gods. It is a peculiarly human activity. To call it a crime against

30

mankind is to miss at least half its significance; it is also the punishment of a crime." Knowing that unflattering truth by experience, soldiers have every motive for wanting a war stopped, by any means.

The stupidity, parochialism, and greed in the international mismanagement of the whole nuclear challenge should not tempt us to misimagine the circumstances of the bomb's first "use." Nor should our well-justified fears and suspicions occasioned by the capture of the nuclear-power trade by the inept and the mendacious (who have fucked up the works at Three Mile Island, Chernobyl, etc.) tempt us to infer retrospectively extraordinary corruption, imbecility, or motiveless malignity in those who decided, all things considered, to drop the bomb. Times change. Harry Truman . . . knew war, and he knew better than some of his critics then and now what he was doing and why he was doing it. "Having found the bomb," he said, "we have used it. . . . We have used it to shorten the agony of young Americans."

The past, which as always did not know the future, acted in ways that ask to be imagined before they are condemned. Or even simplified.

THE READER

1. Why does Fussell thank God for the atom bomb?
2. Fussell speaks as a former combat soldier. His experience leads him to an argument from numbers: he weighs the cost in lives and destruction from having dropped the two bombs on Japan against the cost of having continued the war with an invasion of Japan. The one cost we know from history; the other is a matter of hypothesis and projection. What are the strengths and weaknesses of the argument from numbers? Are there other arguments for or against dropping the atom bomb?
3. Fussell is hard on those who oppose his viewpoint; cite some examples. Is this simply aggressive debating, or is there something more basic at issue? Consider the definition of canting (p. 721), either as a noun or a verb. What does Fussell regard as cant?

THE WRITER

1. Fussell argues vehemently and projects a definite personality in doing so; describe that personality by reference to the essay. Would his argument be more effective if he modified that personality?
2. Is the last paragraph consistent with the title?
3. Fussell devotes a good deal of his essay to detailed description. How does it affect his argument? Choose a descriptive passage and rewrite it without the detail. What difference do your changes make?

Prose Forms: Apothegms

At the beginning of Bacon's essay "Of Truth," jesting Pilate asks, "What is truth?" and does not stay for an answer. Perhaps Pilate asked in jest because he thought the question foolish; perhaps because he thought an answer impossible. Something of Pilate's skepticism is in most of us, but something too of a belief that there is truth, even if—as the history of philosophy teaches us—determining its nature may be enormously difficult. We readily assume some things to be true even if we hesitate to say what ultimately is Truth.

The test of truth most often is an appeal to the observed facts of experience. The observation of experience yields knowledge; the generalized statement of that knowledge yields a concept of the experience; the concise, descriptive form in which that concept is expressed we call variously, apothegm, proverb, maxim, or aphorism. Thus Sir James Mackintosh can speak of apothegms as "the condensed good sense of nations," because the apothegm conveys the distilled observations of people about their own persistent conduct. To hear the familiar "Absence makes the heart grow fonder" is to be reminded of a general truth which you and the world acknowledge. It does not matter that the equally familiar "Out of sight, out of mind" seems to contradict the other saying; both are true but applicable to different situations. Both statements are immediately recognizable as true and neither requires to be argued for, representing as they do the collective experience of humankind intelligently observed.

Aphoristic statements often occur within the context of more extended pieces of writing, and while not apothegms in the strictest sense, but rather propositions, they have the force of apothegms. For example, Percy Shelley's "Defence of Poetry" (1821) concludes that "Poets are the unacknowledged legislators of the world." Seventy years later in his Preface to The Picture of Dorian Gray Oscar Wilde asserts that "All art is quite useless." Although these statements seem contradictory, each is unarguable within its own context.

Not everyone is as astute an observer as the writer of apothegms and maxims, of course, but everyone is presumably capable of perceiving

725

their rightness. What we perceive first is the facts to which the saying applies. When Franklin says "An empty bag cannot stand upright" (in 1740 he obviously had in mind a cloth bag), we acknowledge that this is the condition of the empty bag—and of ourselves when we are empty. Or when La Rochefoucauld says "We are all strong enough to endure the misfortunes of others," he too observes a condition that exists among people.

Many aphoristic assertions claim their validity primarily in descriptive terms. But the descriptive "is" in most apothegms and maxims is joined to a normative "ought" and the sayings therefore convey admonitions about and judgments of the conditions they describe. "Waste not, want not" is a simple illustration of this use of fact to admonish. Samuel Butler briefly gives us the presumed fact that "the world will always be governed by self-interest." Then he quickly advises: "We should not try to stop this, we should try to make the self-interest of cads a little more consistent with that of decent people." The condition of "ought" need not always be admonitory; it may be the implied judgment in La Rochefoucauld's assertion that "It is the habit of mediocre minds to condemn all that is beyond their grasp." The judgment is explicit in Franklin's "Fish and visitors stink in three days." And Bierce's definitions of ordinary words are not specifications of meanings in the way of ordinary dictionaries, but critical concepts of the experiences to which the words point.

"Wisdom" or "good sense," then, is the heart of the apothegm or maxim, the conjunction of "is" and "ought" in an assertion of universal truth. Unlike ordinary assertions of fact or opinion usually concerned with particular rather than universal experience, the wise saying is complete in its brevity. Before the ordinary assertion is allowed to hold, we require that the assumptions on which it rests, the implications it carries, the critical concepts and terms it contains, be examined closely and explored or justified. If someone says that the modern college student wants most to succeed materially in life, we want to be satisfied about what constitutes "modern," which college students (and where) are referred to, what else is involved in the comparative "most," what specifically is meant by "materially." But the apothegm assumes facts widely known and accepted, and in its judgments invokes values or attitudes readily intelligible to the great majority. It is the truth as most people experience it.

In a sense, every writer's concern is ultimately with truth. Certainly the essayist is directly concerned, in defining and ordering ideas, to say what is true and, somehow, to say it "new." Much of what he or she says is of the nature of assertion about particular experience; he or she must therefore be at pains to handle such matters as assump-

tions and logical proofs carefully and deliberately. But one cannot always be starting from scratch, not daring to assume anything, trusting no certain knowledge or experience or beliefs held in common with other people. Careful one must be, but also aware that there is available, in addition to methods of logical analysis and proof, rules of evidence, and the other means to effective exposition, the whole memory and record of the vast experience of the race contained in a people's apothegms and aphorisms. In them is a treasury of truths useful to many demands of clarity and precision. And in them, too, is a valuable lesson in the way a significantly large body of experience—direct, in a person's day-to-day encounters; indirect, in the study of all forms of history—can be observed, conceptualized, and then expressed in an economy of language brief in form, comprehensive in meaning, and satisfyingly true.

W. H. Auden: APOTHEGMS

Some books are undeservedly forgotten; none are undeservedly re-membered.

You do not educate a person's palate by telling him that what he has been in the habit of eating—watery, overboiled cabbage, let us say—is disgusting, but by persuading him to try a dish of vegetables which have been properly cooked. With some people, it is true, you seem to get quicker results by telling them—"Only vulgar people like overcooked cabbage; the best people like cabbage as the Chinese cook it"—but the results are less likely to be lasting.

No poet or novelist wishes he were the only one who ever lived, but most of them wish they were the only one alive, and quite a number fondly believe their wish has been granted.

The integrity of a writer is more threatened by appeals to his social conscience, his political or religious convictions, than by appeals to his cupidity. It is morally less confusing to be goosed by a traveling salesman than by a bishop.

Only a minor talent can be a perfect gentleman; a major talent is always more than a bit of a cad. Hence the importance of minor writers—as teachers of good manners. Now and again, an exquisite minor work can make a master feel thoroughly ashamed of himself.

Narcissus does not fall in love with his reflection because it is beautiful, but because it is *his.* If it were his beauty that enthralled him he would be set free in a few years by its fading.

"After all," sighed Narcissus the hunchback, "on *me* it looks good."

Our sufferings and weaknesses, in so far as they are personal, *our* sufferings, *our* weaknesses, are of no literary interest whatsoever. They are only interesting in so far as we can see them as typical of the human condition. A suffering, a weakness, which cannot be expressed as an aphorism should not be mentioned.

The same rules apply to self-examination as apply to confession to a

From *The Dyer's Hand* (1962).

728

priest: *be brief, be blunt, be gone.* Be brief, be blunt, forget. The scrupuland is a nasty specimen.

In a state of panic, a man runs round in circles by himself. In a state of joy, he links hands with others and they dance round in a circle together.

A sense of humor develops in a society to the degree that its members are simultaneously conscious of being each a unique person and of being all in common subjection to unalterable laws.

Among those whom I like or admire, I can find no common denominator, but among those whom I love, I can: all of them make me laugh.

If Homer had tried reading the *Iliad* to the gods on Olympus, they would either have started to fidget and presently asked if he hadn't got something a little lighter, or, taking it as a comic poem, would have roared with laughter or possibly, even, reacting like ourselves to a tear-jerking movie, have poured pleasing tears.

Ambrose Bierce: FROM THE DEVIL'S DICTIONARY

abdication, *n.* An act whereby a sovereign attests his sense of the high temperature of the throne.

abscond, *v.i.* To "move in a mysterious way," commonly with the property of another.

absent, *adj.* Peculiarly exposed to the tooth of detraction; vilified; hopelessly in the wrong; superseded in the consideration and affection of another.

accident, *n.* An inevitable occurrence due to the action of immutable natural laws.

accordion, *n.* An instrument in harmony with the sentiments of an assassin.

achievement, *n.* The death of endeavor and the birth of disgust.

admiration, *n.* Our polite recognition of another's resemblance to ourselves.

alone, *adj.* In bad company.

From *The Devil's Dictionary* (1906).

applause, *n.* The echo of a platitude.

ardor, *n.* The quality that distinguishes love without knowledge.

bore, *n.* A person who talks when you wish him to listen.

cemetery, *n.* An isolated suburban spot where mourners match lies, poets write at a target and stone-cutters spell for a wager. The inscription following will serve to illustrate the success attained in these Olympian games:

> His virtues were so conspicuous that his enemies, unable to overlook them, denied them, and his friends, to whose loose lives they were a rebuke, represented them as vices. They are here commemorated by his family, who shared them.

childhood, *n.* The period of human life intermediate between the idiocy of infancy and the folly of youth—two removes from the sin of manhood and three from the remorse of age.

Christian, *n.* One who believes that the New Testament is a divinely inspired book admirably suited to the spiritual needs of his neighbor. One who follows the teachings of Christ in so far as they are not inconsistent with a life of sin.

compulsion, *n.* The eloquence of power.

congratulation, *n.* The civility of envy.

conservative, *n.* A statesman who is enamored of existing evils, as distinguished from the Liberal, who wishes to replace them with others.

consult, *v.t.* To seek another's approval of a course already decided on.

contempt, *n.* The feeling of a prudent man for an enemy who is too formidable safely to be opposed.

coward, *n.* One who in a perilous emergency thinks with his legs.

debauchee, *n.* One who has so earnestly pursued pleasure that he has had the misfortune to overtake it.

destiny, *n.* A tyrant's authority for crime and a fool's excuse for failure.

diplomacy, *n.* The patriotic art of lying for one's country.

distance, *n.* The only thing that the rich are willing for the poor to call theirs and keep.

duty, *n.* That which sternly impels us in the direction of profit, along the line of desire.

education, *n.* That which discloses to the wise and disguises from the foolish their lack of understanding.

erudition, *n.* Dust shaken out of a book into an empty skull.

extinction, *n.* The raw material out of which theology created the future state.

faith, *n.* Belief without evidence in what is told by one who speaks without knowledge, of things without parallel.

genealogy, *n.* An account of one's descent from an ancestor who did not particularly care to trace his own.

ghost, *n.* The outward and visible sign of an inward fear.

habit, *n.* A shackle for the free.

heaven, *n.* A place where the wicked cease from troubling you with talk of their personal affairs, and the good listen with attention while you expound your own.

historian, *n.* A broad-gauge gossip.

hope, *n.* Desire and expectation rolled into one.

hypocrite, *n.* One who, professing virtues that he does not respect, secures the advantage of seeming to be what he despises.

impiety, *n.* Your irreverence toward my deity.

impunity, *n.* Wealth.

language, *n.* The music with which we charm the serpents guarding another's treasure.

logic, *n.* The art of thinking and reasoning in strict accordance with the limitations and incapacities of the human misunderstanding.

The basis of logic is the syllogism, consisting of a major and a minor premise and a conclusion—thus:

Major Premise: Sixty men can do a piece of work sixty times as quickly as one man.

Minor Premise: One man can dig a post-hole in sixty seconds; therefore—

Conclusion: Sixty men can dig a post-hole in one second.

This may be called the syllogism arithmetical, in which, by combining logic and mathematics, we obtain a double certainty and are twice blessed.

love, *n.* A temporary insanity curable by marriage or by removal of the patient from the influences under which he incurred the disorder. This disease, like *caries* and many other ailments, is prevalent only among civilized races living under artificial conditions; barbarous nations breathing pure air and eating simple food enjoy immunity from its ravages. It is sometimes fatal, but more frequently to the physician than to the patient.

miracle, *n.* An act or event out of the order of nature and unaccountable, as beating a normal hand of four kings and an ace with four aces and a king.

monkey, *n.* An arboreal animal which makes itself at home in genealogical trees.

mouth, *n.* In man, the gateway to the soul; in woman, the outlet of the heart.

non-combatant, *n.* A dead Quaker.

platitude, *n.* The fundamental element and special glory of popular literature. A thought that snores in words that smoke. The wisdom of a million fools in the diction of a dullard. A fossil sentiment in artificial rock. A moral without the fable. All that is mortal of a departed truth. A demi-tasse of milk-and-morality. The Pope's-nose of a featherless peacock. A jelly-fish withering on the shore of the sea of thought. The cackle surviving the egg. A dessicated epigram.

pray, *v.* To ask that the laws of the universe be annulled in behalf of a single petitioner confessedly unworthy.

presidency, *n.* The greased pig in the field game of American politics.

prude, *n.* A bawd hiding behind the back of her demeanor.

rapacity, *n.* Providence without industry. The thrift of power.

reason, *v.i.* To weigh probabilities in the scales of desire.

religion, *n.* A daughter of Hope and Fear, explaining to Ignorance the nature of the Unknowable.

resolute, *adj.* Obstinate in a course that we approve.

retaliation, *n.* The natural rock upon which is reared the Temple of Law.

saint, *n.* A dead sinner revised and edited.

> The Duchess of Orleans relates that the irreverent old calumniator, Marshal Villeroi, who in his youth had known St. Francis de Sales, said, on hearing him called saint: "I am delighted to hear that Monsieur de Sales is a saint. He was fond of saying indelicate things, and used to cheat at cards. In other respects he was a perfect gentleman, though a fool."

valor, *n.* A soldierly compound of vanity, duty and the gambler's hope:

> "Why have you halted?" roared the commander of a division at Chickamauga, who had ordered a charge; "move forward, sir, at once."
>
> "General," said the commander of the delinquent brigade, "I am persuaded that any further display of valor by my troops will bring them into collision with the enemy."

William Blake: PROVERBS OF HELL

In seed time learn, in harvest teach, in winter enjoy.
Drive your cart and your plough over the bones of the dead.
The road of excess leads to the palace of wisdom.
Prudence is a rich, ugly old maid courted by Incapacity.
He who desires but acts not, breeds pestilence.

From *The Marriage of Heaven and Hell* (1790–93).

The cut worm forgives the plough.

Dip him in the river who loves water.

A fool sees not the same tree that a wise man sees.

He whose face gives no light, shall never become a star.

Eternity is in love with the productions of time.

The busy bee has no time for sorrow.

The hours of folly are measur'd by the clock; but of wisdom, no clock can measure.

All wholesome food is caught without a net or a trap.

Bring out number, weight, and measure in a year of dearth.

No bird soars too high, if he soars with his own wings.

A dead body revenges not injuries.

The most sublime act is to set another before you.

If the fool would persist in his folly he would become wise.

Folly is the cloak of knavery.

Shame is Pride's cloak.

Prisons are built with stones of Law, brothels with bricks of Religion.

The pride of the peacock is the glory of God.

The lust of the goat is the bounty of God.

The wrath of the lion is the wisdom of God.

The nakedness of woman is the work of God.

Excess of sorrow laughs. Excess of joy weeps.

The roaring of lions, the howling of wolves, the raging of the stormy sea, and the destructive sword are portions of eternity too great for the eye of man.

The fox condemns the trap, not himself.

Joys impregnate. Sorrows bring forth.

Let man wear the fell of the lion, woman the fleece of the sheep.

The bird a nest, the spider a web, man friendship.

The selfish, smiling fool, and the sullen, frowning fool shall be both thought wise, that they may be a rod.

What is now proved was once only imagin'd.

The rat, the mouse, the fox, the rabbit watch the roots; the lion, the tiger, the horse, the elephant watch the fruits.

The cistern contains: the fountain overflows.

One thought fills immensity.

Always be ready to speak your mind, and a base man will avoid you.

Everything possible to be believ'd is an image of truth.

The eagle never lost so much time as when he submitted to learn of the crow.

The fox provides for himself; but God provides for the lion.

Think in the morning. Act in the noon. Eat in the evening. Sleep in the night.

He who has suffer'd you to impose on him, knows you.

As the plough follows words, so God rewards prayers.

The tigers of wrath are wiser than the horses of instruction.

Expect poison from the standing water.

You never know what is enough unless you know what is more than enough.

Listen to the fool's reproach! it is a kingly title!

The eyes of fire, the nostrils of air, the mouth of water, the beard of earth.

The weak in courage is strong in cunning.

The apple tree never asks the beech how he shall grow; nor the lion, the horse, how he shall take his prey.

The thankful receiver bears a plentiful harvest.

If others had not been foolish, we should be so.

The soul of sweet delight can never be defil'd.

When thou seest an eagle, thou seest a portion of Genius; lift up thy head!

As the caterpillar chooses the fairest leaves to lay her eggs on, so the priest lays his curse on the fairest joys.

To create a little flower is the labor of ages.

Damn braces. Bless relaxes.

The best wine is the oldest, the best water the newest.

Prayers plough not! Praises reap not!

Joys laugh not! Sorrows weep not!

The head Sublime, the heart Pathos, the genitals Beauty, the hands and feet Proportion.

As the air to a bird or the sea to a fish, so is contempt to the contemptible.

The crow wish'd everything was black, the owl that everything was white.

Exuberance is Beauty.

If the lion was advised by the fox, he would be cunning.

Improvement makes straight roads; but the crooked roads without improvement are roads of Genius.

Sooner murder an infant in its cradle than nurse unacted desires.

Where man is not, nature is barren.

Truth can never be told so as to be understood, and not be believ'd.

Enough! or Too much.

Benjamin Franklin: FROM POOR RICHARD'S ALMANACK

Light purse, heavy heart.   1733
He's a fool that makes his doctor his heir.
Love well, whip well.
Hunger never saw bad bread.
Fools make feasts, and wise men eat 'em.
He that lies down with dogs, shall rise up with fleas.
He is ill clothed, who is bare of virtue.
There is no little enemy.

Without justice courage is weak.   1734
Where there's marriage without love, there will be love without
marriage.
Do good to thy friend to keep him, to thy enemy to gain him.
He that cannot obey, cannot command.
Marry your son when you will, but your daughter when you can.

Approve not of him who commends all you say.   1735
Necessity never made a good bargain.
Be slow in choosing a friend, slower in changing.
Three may keep a secret, if two of them are dead.
Deny self for self's sake.
To be humble to superiors is duty, to equals courtesy, to inferiors
nobleness.

Fish and visitors stink in three days.   1736
Do not do that which you would not have known.
Bargaining has neither friends nor relations.
Now I've a sheep and a cow, every body bids me good morrow.
God helps them that help themselves.
He that speaks much, is much mistaken.
God heals, and the doctor takes the fees.

There are no ugly loves, nor handsome prisons.   1737
Three good meals a day is bad living.

Who has deceiv'd thee so oft as thyself?   1738
Read much, but not many books.

From *Poor Richard's Almanack* (1733–57).

Let thy vices die before thee.

He that falls in love with himself, will have no rivals.   1739
Sin is not hurtful because it is forbidden, but it is forbidden because it's hurtful.

An empty bag cannot stand upright.   1740

Learn of the skilful: he that teaches himself, hath a fool for his master.
     1741

Death takes no bribes.   1742

An old man in a house is a good sign.   1744
Fear God, and your enemies will fear you.

He's a fool that cannot conceal his wisdom.   1745
Many complain of their memory, few of their judgment.

When the well's dry, we know the worth of water.   1746
The sting of a reproach is the truth of it.

Write injuries in dust, benefits in marble.   1747

Nine men in *ten* are suicides.   1749
A man in a passion rides a mad horse.

He is a governor that governs his passions, and he is a servant that serves them.   1750
Sorrow is good for nothing but sin.

Calamity and prosperity are the touchstones of integrity.   1752
Generous minds are all of kin.

Haste makes waste.   1753

The doors of wisdom are never shut.   1755

The way to be safe, is never to be secure.   1757

La Rochefoucauld: FROM MAXIMS

Our virtues are mostly but vices in disguise.

14. Men not only forget benefits received and injuries endured; they even come to dislike those to whom they are indebted, while ceasing to hate those others who have done them harm. Diligence in returning good for good, and in exacting vengeance for evil, comes to be a sort of servitude which we do not readily accept.

19. We are all strong enough to endure the misfortunes of others.

20. The steadiness of the wise man is only the art of keeping his agitations locked within his breast.

25. Firmer virtues are required to support good fortune than bad.

28. Jealousy is, in its way, both fair and reasonable, since its intention is to preserve for ourselves something which is ours, or which we believe to be ours; envy, on the other hand, is a frenzy which cannot endure contemplating the possessions of others.

31. Were we faultless, we would not derive such satisfaction from remarking the faults of others.

38. Our promises are made in hope, and kept in fear.

50. A man convinced of his own merit will accept misfortune as an honor, for thus can he persuade others, as well as himself, that he is a worthy target for the arrows of fate.

56. To achieve a position in the world a man will do his utmost to appear already arrived.

59. There is no accident so disastrous that a clever man cannot derive some profit from it: nor any so fortunate that a fool cannot turn it to his disadvantage.

62. Sincerity comes from an open heart. It is exceedingly rare; what usually passes for sincerity is only an artful pretense designed to win the confidence of others.

67. Grace is to the body what sense is to the mind.

71. When two people have ceased to love, the memory that remains is almost always one of shame.

72. Love, to judge by most of its effects, is closer to hatred than to friendship.

75. Love, like fire, needs constant motion; when it ceases to hope, or to fear, love dies.

78. For most men the love of justice is only the fear of suffering injustice.

79. For a man who lacks self-confidence, silence is the wisest course.

From *Reflexions ou sentences et maximes morales,* or *Maxims,* (1655–78).

83. What men have called friendship is only a social arrangement, a mutual adjustment of interests, an interchange of services given and received; it is, in sum, simply a business from which those involved purpose to derive a steady profit for their own self-love.

89. Everyone complains of his memory, none of his judgment.

90. In daily life our faults are frequently more pleasant than our good qualities.

93. Old people love to give good advice: it compensates them for their inability nowadays to set a bad example.

119. We are so accustomed to adopting a mask before others that we end by being unable to recognize ourselves.

122. If we master our passions it is due to their weakness, not our strength.

134. We are never so ridiculous through what we are as through what we pretend to be.

138. We would rather speak ill of ourselves than not at all.

144. We do not like to give praise, and we never do so without reasons of self-interest. Praise is a cunning, concealed and delicate form of flattery which, in different ways, gratifies both the giver and the receiver; the one accepts it as the reward for merit; the other bestows it to display his sense of justice and his powers of discernment.

146. We usually only praise that we may be praised.

149. The refusal to accept praise is the desire to be praised twice over.

150. The wish to deserve the praise we receive strengthens our virtues; and praise bestowed upon wit, courage and beauty contributes to their increase.

167. Avarice, more than open-handedness, is the opposite of economy.

170. When a man's behavior is straightforward, sincere and honest it is hard to be sure whether this is due to rectitude or cleverness.

176. In love there are two sorts of constancy: the one comes from the perpetual discovery of new delights in the beloved: the other, from the self-esteem which we derive from our own fidelity.

180. Our repentance is less a regret for the evil we have done than a precaution against the evil that may be done to us.

185. Evil, like good, has its heroes.

186. Not all who have vices are contemptible: all without a trace of virtue are.

190. Only great men are marked with great faults.

192. When our vices depart from us, we flatter ourselves that it is we who have rid ourselves of them.

200. Virtue would not go so far did vanity not keep her company.

205. Virtue, in women, is often love of reputation and fondness for tranquillity.

216. Perfect valor is to behave, without witnesses, as one would act were all the world watching.

218. Hypocrisy is the tribute that vice pays to virtue.

230. Nothing is as contagious as example, and we never perform an outstandingly good or evil action without its producing others of its sort. We copy goodness in the spirit of emulation, and wickedness owing to the malignity of our nature which shame holds in check until example sets it free.

237. No man should be praised for his goodness if he lacks the strength to be bad: in such cases goodness is usually only the effect of indolence or impotence of will.

259. The pleasure of love is in loving: and there is more joy in the passion one feels than in that which one inspires.

264. Pity is often only the sentiment of our own misfortunes felt in the ills of others. It is a clever pre-science of the evil times upon which we may fall. We help others in order to ensure their help in similar circumstances; and the kindnesses we do them are, if the truth were told, only acts of charity towards ourselves invested against the future.

276. Absence diminishes small loves and increases great ones, as the wind blows out the candle and blows up the bonfire.

277. Women frequently believe themselves to be in love even when they are not: the pursuit of an intrigue, the stimulus of gallantry, the natural inclination towards the joys of being loved, and the difficulty of refusal, all these combine to tell them that their passions are aroused when in fact it is but their coquetry at play.

375. It is the habit of mediocre minds to condemn all that is beyond their grasp.

376. True friendship destroys envy, as true love puts an end to coquetry.

378. We give advice but we do not inspire behavior.

392. One should treat one's fate as one does one's health; enjoy it when it is good, be patient with it when it is poorly, and never attempt any drastic cure save as an ultimate resort.

399. There is a form of eminence which is quite independent of our fate; it is an air which distinguishes us from our fellow men and makes us appear destined for great things; it is the value which we imperceptibly attach to ourselves; it is the quality which wins us the deference of others; more than birth, honours or even merit, it gives us ascendancy.

417. In love, the person who recovers first recovers best.

423. Few people know how to be old.

467. Vanity leads us to act against our inclinations more often than does reason.

479. Only people who are strong can be truly gentle: what normally passes for gentleness is mere weakness, which quickly turns sour.

483. Vanity, rather than malice, is the usual source of slander.

540. Hope and fear are inseparable. There is no hope without fear, nor any fear without hope.

576. We always discover, in the misfortunes of our dearest friends, something not altogether displeasing.

597. No man can be sure of his own courage until he has stared danger in the face.

617. How can we expect another to keep our secret, if we cannot keep it ourself?

History

Henry David Thoreau

THE BATTLE OF THE ANTS

One day when I went out to my wood-pile, or rather my pile of stumps, I observed two large ants, the one red, the other much larger, nearly half an inch long, and black, fiercely contending with one another. Having once got hold they never let go, but struggled and wrestled and rolled on the chips incessantly. Looking farther, I was surprised to find that the chips were covered with such combatants, that it was not a *duellum*, but a *bellum*, a war between two races of ants, the red always pitted against the black, and frequently two red ones to one black. The legions of these Myrmidons[1] covered all the hills and vales in my wood-yard, and the ground was already strewn with the dead and dying, both red and black. It was the only battle which I have ever witnessed, the only battle-field I ever trod while the battle was raging; internecine war; the red republicans on the one hand, and the black imperialists on the other. On every side they were engaged in deadly combat, yet without any noise that I could hear, and human soldiers never fought so resolutely. I watched a couple that were fast locked in each other's embraces, in a little sunny valley amid the chips, now at noonday prepared to fight till the sun went down, or life went out. The smaller red champion had fastened himself like a vice to his adversary's front, and through all the tumblings on that field never for an instant ceased to gnaw at one of his feelers near the root, having already caused the other to go by the board; while the stronger black one dashed him from side to side, and, as I saw on looking nearer, had already divested him of several of his members. They fought with more pertinacity than bulldogs. Neither manifested the least disposition to retreat. It was evident that their battle-cry was "Conquer or

From *Walden* (1854).

1. The reference is to the powerful soldiers of Achilles in Homer's *Iliad*.

die." In the meanwhile there came along a single red ant on the hill-side of this valley, evidently full of excitement, who either had des-patched his foe, or had not yet taken part in the battle; probably the latter, for he had lost none of his limbs; whose mother had charged him to return with his shield or upon it. Or perchance he was some Achilles, who had nourished his wrath apart, and had now come to avenge or rescue his Patroclus.[2] He saw this unequal combat from afar—for the blacks were nearly twice the size of the red—he drew near with rapid pace till he stood on his guard within half an inch of the combatants; then, watching his opportunity, he sprang upon the black warrior, and commenced his operations near the root of his right fore leg, leaving the foe to select among his own members; and so there were three united for life, as if a new kind of attraction had been invented which put all other locks and cements to shame. I should not have wondered by this time to find that they had their respective musical bands stationed on some eminent chip, and playing their na-tional airs the while, to excite the slow and cheer the dying combat-ants. I was myself excited somewhat even as if they had been men. The more you think of it, the less the difference. And certainly there is not the fight recorded in Concord history, at least, if in the history of America, that will bear a moment's comparison with this, whether for the numbers engaged in it, or for the patriotism and heroism dis-played. For numbers and for carnage it was an Austerlitz or Dresden.[3] Concord Fight! Two killed on the patriots' side, and Luther Blanchard wounded! Why here every ant was a Buttrick—"Fire! for God's sake fire!"—and thousands shared the fate of Davis and Hosmer. There was not one hireling there. I have no doubt that it was a principle they fought for, as much as our ancestors, and not to avoid a three-penny tax on their tea; and the results of this battle will be as important and memorable to those whom it concerns as those of the battle of Bunker Hill, at least.

I took up the chip on which the three I have particularly described were struggling, carried into my house, and placed it under a tumbler on my window-sill, in order to see the issue. Holding a microscope to the first-mentioned red ant, I saw that, though he was assiduously gnawing at the near fore leg of his enemy, having severed his remaining feeler, his own breast was all torn away, exposing what vitals he had there to the jaws of the black warrior, whose breastplate was apparently too thick for him to pierce; and the dark carbuncles of the sufferer's eyes shone with ferocity such as war only could excite. They struggled half

2. A Greek warrior in the *Iliad*, whose   3. Bloody Napoleonic victories.
death Achilles avenges.

an hour longer under the tumbler, and when I looked again the black soldier had severed the heads of his foes from their bodies, and the still living heads were hanging on either side of him like ghastly trophies at his saddle-bow, still apparently as firmly fastened as ever, and he was endeavoring with feeble struggles, being without feelers, and with only the remnant of a leg, and I know not how many other wounds, to divest himself of them; which at length, after half an hour more, he accomplished. I raised the glass, and he went off over the window-sill in that crippled state. Whether he finally survived that combat, and spent the remainder of his days in some Hôtel des Invalides,[4] I do not know; but I thought that his industry would not be worth much thereafter. I never learned which party was victorious, nor the cause of the war, but I felt for the rest of that day as if I had my feelings excited and harrowed by witnessing the struggle, the ferocity and carnage, of a human battle before my door.

Kirby and Spence tell us that the battles of ants have long been celebrated and the date of them recorded, though they say that Huber[5] is the only modern author who appears to have witnessed them. "Aeneas Sylvius," say they, "after giving a very circumstantial account of one contested with great obstinacy by a great and small species on the trunk of a pear tree," adds that " 'this action was fought in the pontificate of Eugenius the Fourth, in the presence of Nicholas Pistoriensis, an eminent lawyer, who related the whole history of the battle with the greatest fidelity.' A similar engagement between great and small ants is recorded by Olaus Magnus, in which the small ones, being victorious, are said to have buried the bodies of their own soldiers, but left those of their giant enemies a prey to the birds. This event happened previous to the expulsion of the tyrant Christiern the Second from Sweden." The battle which I witnessed took place in the Presidency of Polk, five years before the passage of Webster's Fugitive-Slave Bill.[6]

4. The famous French hospital for wounded soldiers and sailors.
5. Kirby and Spence were nineteenth-cen-

tury American entomologists; Huber was a great Swiss entomologist.
6. Passed in 1851.

THE READER

1. *Thoreau uses the Latin word* bellum *to describe the battle of the ants, and he quickly follows this with a reference to the Myrmidons of Achilles. What comparison is implicit here? Find further examples of it.*

2. *This passage comes from a chapter in Thoreau's* Walden *titled "Brute Neighbors." How does the comparison alluded to in the previous question amplify the meaning of that title?*

THE WRITER

1. How might a strictly scientific account of the behavior of ants differ from Thoreau's?
2. Why does Thoreau end his account the way he does?
3. Describe the life, or part of the life, of an animal so that, while remaining faithful to the facts as you understand them, your description opens outward, as does Thoreau's, and speaks not only of the animal but also of man, society, or nature.

Herbert Butterfield

THE ORIGINALITY OF THE OLD TESTAMENT

The Old Testament sometimes seems very ancient, but the earliest considerable body of historical literature that we possess was being produced through a period of a thousand years and more before that. It consisted of what we call "annals," written in the first person singular by the heads of great empires which had their centre in Egypt or Mesopotamia or Asia Minor. These monarchs, often year by year, would produce accounts—quite detailed accounts sometimes—of their military campaigns. It is clear from what they say that one of their objects in life was to put their own personal achievements on record—their building feats, their prowess in the hunt, but also their victories in war. They show no sign of having had any interest in the past, but, among other things, they betray a great anxiety about the reputation they would have after they were dead. They did not look behind them to previous generations, but instead they produced what we should call the history of their own times, in a way rather like Winston Churchill producing his account of his wars against Germany in the twentieth century.

After this, however, a great surprise occurs. There emerges from nowhere a people passionately interested in the past, dominated by an historical memory. It is clear that this is due to the fact that there is a bygone event that they really cannot get over; it takes command over their whole mentality. This people were the ancient Hebrews. They had been semi-nomads, moving a great deal in the desert, but having also certain periods in rather better areas where they could grow a bit of something. Like semi-nomads in general, they had longed to have land of their own, a settled land which they could properly cultivate. This is what they expected their God to provide for them, and what he prom-

From *Writings on Christianity and History,* edited by C. T. McIntire (1979).

ised to provide. Indeed the semi-nomads would tend to judge his effectiveness as a god by his ability to carry out his promise. The ancient Hebrews, the Children of Israel, had to wait a long time for their due reward, and perhaps this was the reason why they were so tremendously impressed when ultimately the Promise was actually fulfilled.

The earliest thing that we know from sheer historical evidence about these people is that as soon as they appear in the light of day they are already dominated by this historical memory. In some of the earliest books of the Bible there are embedded patches of text far earlier still, far earlier than the Old Testament itself, and repeatedly they are passages about this very thing. Fresh references go on perpetually being made to the same matter throughout the many centuries during which the Old Testament was being produced, indeed also in the Jewish literature that was written for a few centuries after that. We are more sure that the memory of this historical event was the predominating thing among them than we are of the reality, the actual historicity, of the event itself.

What they commemorated in this tremendous way, of course, was the fact that God had brought them up out of the land of Egypt and into the Promised Land. In reality it seems pretty clear that some of the tribes of Israel did not come into the land of Palestine from Egypt at all. Nevertheless I think it would be a central view among scholars that some of the ancient Hebrews came to the Promised Land from Egypt, and the impression of this was so powerful that it became the common memory of the whole group of tribes which settled in the land of Canaan; it became the accepted tradition even among the tribes that had never been in Egypt. Moreover the common tradition was the very thing that became the effective bond between the tribes of Israel, helping to weld them together as a people. This sense of a common history is always a powerful factor in fusing a group of tribes into a nation, just as Homer made the various bodies of Greeks feel that they had had a common experience in the past, a consciousness that they were all Hellenes. All this was so powerful with the Children of Israel because they felt such a fabulous gratitude for what had happened. I know of no other case in history where gratitude was carried so far, no other case where gratitude proved to be such a generative thing. Their God had stepped into history and kept his ancient Promise, bringing them to freedom and the Promised Land, and they simply could not get over it.

This was not the first time in history that gratitude had been a factor in religion, for at a date earlier still there are signs amongst the Hittites that the very sincerity of their feeling of indebtedness added an attractive kind of devotion to their worship of their pagan deities. But this gratitude was such a signal thing amongst the Israelitish people that it

5

altered the whole development of religion in that quarter of the globe; it altered the character of religion in the area from which our Western civilization sprang. It gave the Children of Israel a historical event that they could not get over, could not help remembering, and in the first place it made them historians—historians in a way that nobody had ever been before. The ancient Hebrews worshiped the God who brought them up out of the land of Egypt more than they worshipped God as the Creator of the World. By all the rules of the game, when once they had settled down in the land of Canaan and become an agricultural people, they ought to have turned to the gods of nature, the gods of fertility, and this is what some of their number wanted to do. But their historical memory was too strong. Even when they borrowed rites and ceremonies from neighboring peoples—pieces of ritual based on the cycle of nature, the succession of the seasons—they turned these into celebrations of historical events, just as I suppose Christianity may have turned the rites of Spring into a celebration of the Resurrection. The Hebrews took over circumcision, which existed among their neighbors, but they turned even this into the celebration of a historical event. A Harvest Festival is an occasion on which even among Christians today we call attention to the cycle of the seasons and the bounty of nature. But among the Children of Israel at this ceremony you handed your thankoffering to the priest and then, if you please, you did not speak of the corn or the vine—you recited your national history, you narrated the story of the Exodus. It was set down in writing that if the younger generation started asking why they were expected to obey God's commandments they should be told that it was because God had brought their forefathers out of the house of bondage. Everything was based on their gratitude for what God had done for the nation. And it is remarkable to see to what a degree the other religious ideas of the Old Testament always remained historical in character—the Promise, the Covenant, the Judgment, the Messiah, the remnant of Israel, etc.

Yet this Promised Land to which God had brought them and on which they based a religion of extravagant gratitude was itself no great catch, and if they called it a land flowing with milk and honey, this was only because it looked rich when compared to the life that they had hitherto led. In the twentieth century Palestine has demanded a tremendous wrestling with nature, and if one looks back to the state of that region in Old Testament times one cannot help feeling that Providence endowed this people with one of the riskiest bits of territory that existed in that part of the globe. They were placed in an area which had already been encircled by vast empires, based on Egypt and on Mesopotamia and on a Hittite realm in Asia Minor. And, for all their gratitude, they were one of the most unlucky peoples of history. Other great empires soon arose again in the same regions, and they were so placed that they

could not be expected to keep their freedom—their independence as a
state only lasted for a few centuries, something like the period between
Tudor England and the present day.[1] The one stroke of luck that they
did have was that for just a space at the crucial period those surrounding
empires had come into decline, and this gave the Hebrews the chance
of forming an independent state for a while. They virtually stood in the
cockpit in that part of the world, just as Belgium stood in the cockpit
in Western Europe and Poland in Eastern Europe. The fact that the
Hebrews became, along with the Greeks, one of the main contributors
to the formation of Western civilization is a triumph of mind over
matter, of the human spirit over misfortune and disaster. They almost
built their religion on gratitude for their good fortune in having a
country at all, a country that they could call their own.

Because of the great act of God which had brought them to Palestine
they devoted themselves to the God of History rather than to the gods
of nature. Here is their great originality, the thing that in a way enabled
them to change the very nature of religion. Because they turned their
intellect to the actions of God in history, they were drawn into an ethical
view of God. They were continually wrestling with him about ethical
questions, continually debating with him as to whether he was playing
fair with them. Religion became intimately connected with morality
because this was a God who was always in personal relations with human
beings in the ordinary historical realm, and in any case you find that it
was the worshipers of the gods of nature who ran to orgies and cruelties
and immoralities. In fact, the ancient Hebrews developed their thought
about God, about personality, and about ethics all together, all rolled
into one. Because these things all involved what we call problems of
personal relations they developed their thought about history step by
step along with the rest. For a student of history, one of the interesting
features of the Old Testament is that it gives us evidence of religious
development from very early stages, from most primitive ideas about
God, some of these ideas being quite shocking to the modern mind.
Indeed, in some of the early books of the Bible there are still embedded
certain ancient things that make it look as though, here as in no other
parts of Western Asia, the God of History may at one stage have been
really the God of War.

So far as I have been able to discover—approaching the matter as a
modern historian, and rather an outsider, and using only what is available in Western languages—the Children of Israel, while still a comparatively primitive society, are the first people who showed a really significant interest in the past, the first to produce anything like a history of
their nation, the first to lay out what we call a universal history, doing

1. Queen Elizabeth I, the last of the Tudor monarchs, died in 1603.

it with the help of some Babylonian legends but attempting to see the whole story of the human race. Because what we possess in the Old Testament is history as envisaged by the priests, or at least by the religious people, it is also a history very critical of the rulers—not like the mass of previous historical writing, a case of monarchs blowing their own trumpets. The history they wrote is a history of the people and not just of the kings, and it is very critical even of the people. So far as I know here is the only case of a nation producing a national history and making it an exposure of its national sins. In a technical sense this ancient Hebrew people became very remarkable as writers of history, some of their narratives (for example, the death of King David and the question of the succession to his throne) being quite wonderful according to modern standards of judgment. It was to be of momentous importance for the development of Western civilization, that, growing up in Europe (with Christianity presiding over its creative stages), it was influenced by the Old Testament, by this ancient Jewish passion for history. For century after century over periods of nearly 2000 years, the European could not even learn about his religion without studying the Bible, including the Old Testament—essentially a history-book, a book of very ancient history. Our civilization, unlike many others, became historically-minded, therefore, one that was interested in the past, and we owe that in a great part to the Old Testament.

THE READER

1. *What difference does Butterfield find between the writings of the ancient Hebrews and writings made in the empires of the Near East? What caused the difference?*

2. *What was the effect of historical memory on the formation of the ancient nation of Israel?*

3. *How did the sense of history in Israel make Hebrew religion different from the religions around Israel?*

THE WRITER

1. *What value does Butterfield attach to being "historically minded"? In what specific ways does his essay imply that being so minded is beneficial?*

2. *Butterfield believes that one of the key factors in the development of our civilization is that we "became historically minded." Write a brief essay discussing to what degree we are still "historically minded" today.*

John Livingston Lowes

TIME IN THE MIDDLE AGES

We live in terms of *time*. And so pervasive is that element of our
consciousness that we have to stand, as it were, outside it for a moment
to realize how completely it controls our lives. For we think and act
perpetually, we mortals who look before and after, in relation to hours
and days and weeks and months and years. Yesterday and tomorrow,
next week, a month from now, a year ago, in twenty minutes—those are
the terms in which, wittingly or automatically, we act and plan and
think. And to orient ourselves at any moment in that streaming continuum we carry watches on our wrists, and put clocks about our houses
and on our public towers, and somewhere in our eye keep calendars, and
scan time-tables when we would go abroad. And all this is so utterly
familiar that it has ceased to be a matter of conscious thought or
inference at all. And—to come to the heart of the business—unless we
are mariners or woodsmen or astronomers or simple folk in lonely places,
we never any longer reckon with the *sky*. Except for its bearing on the
weather or upon our moods, or for contemplation of its depths of blue
or fleets of white, or of the nightly splendor of its stars, we are oblivious
of its influence. And therein lies the great gulf fixed between Chaucer's
century [1] and ours.

For Chaucer and his contemporaries, being likewise human, also lived
in terms of time. But their calendar and time-piece was that sky through
which moved immutably along predestined tracks the planets and the
constellations. And no change, perhaps, wrought by the five centuries
between us is more revealing of material differences than that shift of
attitude toward "this brave o'erhanging firmament," the sky. And it is
that change, first of all, that I wish, if I can, to make clear.

There could be, I suspect, no sharper contrast than that between the
"mysterious universe" of modern science, as interpreters like Eddington
and Jeans have made even laymen dimly perceive it, and the nest of
closed, concentric spheres in terms of which Chaucer and his coevals
thought. The structure of that universe may be stated simply enough.
Its intricacies need not concern us here. About the earth, as the fixed
center, revolved the spheres of the seven then known planets, of which
the sun and the moon were two. Beyond these seven planetary spheres
lay the sphere of the fixed stars. Beyond that in turn, and carrying along

From Chapter I, "Backgrounds and Horizons," of *Geoffrey Chaucer*, 1934.

1. The fourteenth; the reference is to the great Middle English poet Geoffrey Chaucer.

with it in its "diurnal sway" the eight spheres which lay within it, moved the *primum mobile,* a ninth sphere with which, to account for certain planetary eccentricities, the Middle Ages had supplemented the Ptolemaic system. We must think, in a word, of Chaucer's universe as geocentric—the "litel erthe," encompassed by "thilke speres thryes three."[2] As an interesting fact which we have learned, we know it; to conceive it as reality demands an exercise of the imagination. And only with that mental *volte-face* accomplished can we realize the cosmos as Chaucer thought of it.

Now the order of succession of the planetary spheres had far-reaching implications. Starting from the earth, which was their center, that succession was as follows: Moon, Mercury, Venus, Sun, Mars, Jupiter, Saturn. And implicit in that order were two fundamental consequences—the astrological status of the successive hours of the day, and the sequence of the days of the week. The two phenomena stood in intimate relation, and some apprehension of each is fundamental to an understanding of the framework of conceptions within which Chaucer thought, and in terms of which he often wrote.

5   There were, then, in the first place—and this is strange to us—two sorts of *hours,* with both of which everybody reckoned. There were the hours from midnight to midnight, which constituted the "day natural"—the hours, that is, with which we are familiar—and these, in Chaucer's phrase, were "hours equal," or "hours of the *clock.*" But there were also the hours which were reckoned from sunrise to sunset (which made up "day artificial"), and on from sunset to sunrise again. And these, which will most concern us, were termed "hours inequal," or "hours of the *planets.*" And they were the hours of peculiar significance, bound up far more closely with human affairs than the "hours of the clock." It is worth, then, a moment's time to get them clear.

They were termed "inequal" for an obvious reason. For the periods between sunrise and sunset, and sunset and sunrise, respectively, change in length with the annual course of the sun, and the length of their twelfths, or hours, must of necessity change too, Between the equinoxes, then, it is clear that the inequal hours will now be longer by day than by night, now longer by night than by day. And only twice in the year, at the equinoxes, will the equal hours and the inequal hours—the hours of the clock and the hours of the planets—be identical. Moreover, each of the inequal hours (and this is of the first importance) was "ruled" by one of the seven planets, and it was as "hours of the planets" that the "hours inequal" touched most intimately human life. And that brings us at once to the days of the week, and their now almost forgotten implications. Why, to be explicit, is today Saturday? And why tomorrow

---

2. "Those spheres thrice three" [Lowes' note].

Sunday? To answer those two questions is to arrive at one of the determining concepts of Chaucer's world.

Let me first arrange the seven planets in their order, starting (to
simplify what follows) with the outermost. Their succession will then be
this: Saturn, Jupiter, Mars, Sun, Venus, Mercury, Moon. Now Saturn will
rule the first hour of the day which, for that reason, bears his name, and
which we still call *Saturday*. Of that day Jupiter will rule the second hour,
Mars the third, the Sun the fourth, Venus the fifth, Mercury the sixth,
the Moon the seventh, and Saturn again, in due order, the eighth.
Without carrying the computation farther around the clock it is obvious
that Saturn will also rule the fifteenth and the twenty-second hours of the
twenty-four which belong to his day. The twenty-third hour will then be
ruled by Jupiter, the twenty-fourth by Mars, and the twenty-fifth by the
Sun. But the twenty-fifth hour of one day is the first hour of the next, and
accordingly the day after Saturn's day will be the sun's day. And so,
through starry compulsion, the next day after Saturday *must* be Sunday.
In precisely the same fashion—accomplished most quickly by remembering that each planet must rule the twenty-second hour of its own day—
the ruling planet of the first hour of each of the succeeding days may
readily be found. And their order, so found, including Saturn and the Sun,
is this: Saturn, Sun, Moon, Mars, Mercury, Jupiter, Venus—then Saturn
again, and so on *ad libitum*. And the days of the week will accordingly be
the days of the seven planets in that fixed order.

Now Saturn's day, the Sun's day, and the Moon's day are clearly
recognizable in their English names of Saturday, Sunday, and Monday.
But what of the remaining four—to wit, the days of Mars, Mercury,
Jupiter, and Venus, which we call Tuesday, Wednesday, Thursday, and
Friday? French has preserved, as also in Lundi, the planetary designa-
tions: Mardi (*Martis dies*), Mercredi (*Mercurii dies*), Jeudi (*Jovis dies*),
and Vendredi (*Veneris dies*). The shift of the names in English is due
to the ousting, in those four instances, of the Roman pantheon by the
Germanic. Tiw, Woden, Thor, and Frig (or Freya) have usurped the
seats of Mars, Mercury, Jupiter, and Venus, and given their barbarous
names to the days. And in France a fourth, even more significant
substitution has taken place. For the sun's day is in French *dimanche*,
and dimanche is *dominica dies*, the Lord's day. And so between Saturn's
planet and Diana's moon is memorialized, along with Mercury and
Jupiter and Venus and Mars, the second Person of the Christian Trinity.
The ancient world has crumbled, and its detritus has been remoulded
into almost unrecognizable shapes. But half the history of Europe and
of its early formative ideas is written in the nomenclature of the week.
And that nomenclature depends in turn upon the succession of the
planetary hours. And it was in terms of those hours that Chaucer and
his contemporaries thought. * * *

Moreover, as the day and week were conceived in terms of planetary sequence, so the year stood in intricate relation to the *stars*. The sun, with the other planets, moved annually along the vast starry track across the sky which then, as now, was called the zodiac—so called, as Chaucer lucidly explains to "litel Lowis" in the *Treatise on the Astrolabe,* because (and his etymology is sound) *"zodia* in langage of Greek sowneth [signifies] 'bestes' . . . and in the zodiak ben the twelve signes that han names of bestes." These twelve signs, as everybody knows, are Aries, Taurus, Gemini, Cancer, Leo, Virgo, Libra, Scorpio, Sagittarius, Capricornus, Aquarius, Pisces—or, to follow Chaucer's praiseworthy example and translate, Ram, Bull, Twins, Crab, Lion, Virgin, Scales, Scorpion, Archer, Goat, Water-carrier, Fishes. There they were, "eyrish bestes," as Chaucer calls them in a delightful passage that will meet us later, and along their celestial highway passed, from one sign to another, and from house to house, the seven eternal wanderers. To us who read this— though not to countless thousands even yet—the twelve constellations of the zodiac are accidental groupings, to the eye, of infinitely distant suns. To Chaucer's century they were strangely living potencies, and the earth, in the words of a greater than Chaucer, was "this huge stage . . . whereon the stars in secret influence comment." Each sign, with its constellation, had its own individual efficacy or quality—Aries, "the colerik hote signe"; Taurus, cold and dry; and so on through the other ten. Each planet likewise had its own peculiar nature—Mars, like Aries, hot and dry; Venus hot and moist; and so on through the other five. And as each planet passed from sign to sign, through the agency of the successive constellations its character and influence underwent change. Chaucer in the *Astrolabe* put the matter in its simplest terms: "Whan an hot planete cometh in-to an hot signe, then encresseth his hete; and yif a planete be cold, thanne amenuseth [diminishes] his coldnesse, by cause of the hote signe." But there was far more to it than that. For these complex planetary changes exercised a determining influence upon human beings and their affairs. Arcite behind prison bars cries out:

> Som wikke aspect or disposicioun
> Of Saturne, *by sum constellacioun,*
> Hath yeven us this.

And "the olde colde Saturnus" names the constellation.

> Myn is the prison in the derke cote. . .
> *Whyl I dwelle in the signe of the Leoun.*

10   The tragedy of Constance, as the Man of Law conceived it, comes about because Mars, at the crucial moment, was in his "derkest hous."

Mars gave, on the other hand, the Wife of Bath,[3] as she avers, her "sturdy hardinesse," because Mars, at her birth, was in the constellation Taurus, which was, in astrological terminology, her own "ascendent." And since the constellation Taurus was also the "night house" of Venus, certain other propensities which the wife displayed had been thrust upon her, as she cheerfully averred, by the temporary sojourn of Mars in Venus's house, when she was born.

But the march of the signs along the zodiac touched human life in yet another way. "Everich of thise twelve signes," Chaucer wrote again to his little Lewis, "hath respecte to a certein parcelle of the body of a man and hath it in governance; as Aries hath thyn heved, and Taurus thy nekke and thy throte. Gemini thyn armholes and thyn armes, and so forth." And at once one recalls Sir Toby Belch and Sir Andrew Aguecheek in *Twelfth Night*. "Shall we not set about some revels?" asks Sir Andrew. "What shall we do else?" replies Sir Toby. "Were we not born under Taurus?" "Taurus!" exclaims Sir Andrew, "that's sides and heart." "No, sir," retorts Sir Toby, "it is legs and thighs." And you may still pick up, in the shops of apothecaries here and there, cheaply printed almanacs, designed to advertise quack remedies, in which the naked human figure is displayed with lines drawn from each of the pictured zodiacal signs—Ram, Bull, Crab, Scorpion—to the limbs or organs, legs, thighs, sides, or heart, which that particular sign (in Chaucerian phrase) "hath in governance." It is not only in worn stone and faded parchments that strange fragments of the elder world survive.

3. The forthright and lusty teller of "The Wife of Bath's Tale" in Chaucer's *Canterbury Tales.*

THE READER

1. *Explain the difference between the two kinds of hours that Lowes talks about.*

2. *Explain why "through starry compulsion, the next day after Saturday must be Sunday" (p. 751).*

3. *What does Lowes mean by the difference between* knowing *something as a* fact *and* conceiving *it as* reality?

4. *Explain Lowes' statement that "half the history of Europe and of its early formative ideas is written in the nomenclature of the week" (p. 751).*

THE WRITER

1. *Arrange the steps of Lowes' explanation of medieval time in a different order. What are the relative merits of your arrangement and Lowes' arrangement?*

2. *Write a short essay explaining why the advertising man or the engineer*

from the electronics laboratory may have to reckon with the sky and neglect their watches and calendars when they become suburban gardeners.

3. *List some ways in which the abstractions of watch, calendar, and timetable "rule" our lives. Then look at this list of particulars from daily life and write an essay developing one or more generalizations about our society that these particulars might justify.*

Barbara Tuchman

"THIS IS THE END OF THE WORLD": THE BLACK DEATH

In October 1347, two months after the fall of Calais,[1] Genoese trading ships put into the harbor of Messina in Sicily with dead and dying men at the oars. The ships had come from the Black Sea port of Caffa (now Feodosiya) in the Crimea, where the Genoese maintained a trading post. The diseased sailors showed strange black swellings about the size of an egg or an apple in the armpits and groin. The swellings oozed blood and pus and were followed by spreading boils and black blotches on the skin from internal bleeding. The sick suffered severe pain and died quickly within five days of the first symptoms. As the disease spread, other symptoms of continuous fever and spitting of blood appeared instead of the swellings or buboes. These victims coughed and sweated heavily and died even more quickly, within three days or less, sometimes in 24 hours. In both types everything that issued from the body—breath, sweat, blood from the buboes and lungs, bloody urine, and blood-blackened excrement—smelled foul. Depression and despair accompanied the physical symptoms, and before the end "death is seen seated on the face."

The disease was bubonic plague, present in two forms: one that infected the bloodstream, causing the buboes and internal bleeding, and was spread by contact; and a second, more virulent pneumonic type that infected the lungs and was spread by respiratory infection. The presence of both at once cause the high mortality and speed of contagion. So lethal was the disease that cases were known of persons going to bed well and dying before they woke, of doctors catching the illness at a bedside

From *A Distant Mirror: The Calamitous Fourteenth Century* (1978).

1. After a yearlong siege, the French citizens of Calais surrendered to Edward III, king of England and self-declared king of France.

and dying before the patient. So rapidly did it spread from one to another that to a French physician, Simon de Covino, it seemed as if one sick person "could infect the whole world." The malignity of the pestilence appeared more terrible because its victims knew no prevention and no remedy.

The physical suffering of the disease and its aspect of evil mystery were expressed in a strange Welsh lament which saw "death coming into our midst like black smoke, a plague which cuts off the young, a rootless phantom which has no mercy for fair countenance. Woe is me of the shilling in the armpit! It is seething, terrible . . . a head that gives pain and causes a loud cry . . . a painful angry knob . . . Great is its seething like a burning cinder . . . a grievous thing of ashy color." Its eruption is ugly like the "seeds of black peas, broken fragments of brittle sea-coal . . . the early ornaments of black death, cinders of the peelings of the cockle weed, a mixed multitude, a black plague like halfpence, like berries. . . ."

Rumors of a terrible plague supposedly arising in China and spreading through Tartary (Central Asia) to India and Persia, Mesopotamia, Syria, Egypt, and all of Asia Minor had reached Europe in 1346. They told of a death toll so devastating that all of India was said to be depopulated, whole territories covered by dead bodies, other areas with no one left alive. As added up by Pope Clement VI at Avignon, the total of reported dead reached 23,840,000. In the absence of a concept of contagion, no serious alarm was felt in Europe until the trading ships brought their black burden of pestilence into Messina while other infected ships from the Levant carried it to Genoa and Venice.

By January 1348 it penetrated France via Marseille, and North Africa via Tunis. Shipborne along coasts and navigable rivers, it spread westward from Marseille through the ports of Languedoc to Spain and northward up the Rhône to Avignon, where it arrived in March. It reached Narbonne, Montpellier, Carcassonne, and Toulouse between February and May, and at the same time in Italy spread to Rome and Florence and their hinterlands. Between June and August it reached Bordeaux, Lyon, and Paris, spread to Burgundy and Normandy, and crossed the Channel from Normandy into southern England. From Italy during the same summer it crossed the Alps into Switzerland and reached eastward to Hungary.

In a given area the plague accomplished its kill within four to six months and then faded, except in the larger cities, where, rooting into the close-quartered population, it abated during the winter, only to reappear in spring and rage for another six months.

In 1349 it resumed in Paris, spread to Picardy, Flanders, and the Low Countries, and from England to Scotland and Ireland as well as to Norway, where a ghost ship with a cargo of wool and a dead crew drifted

5

offshore until it ran aground near Bergen. From there the plague passed into Sweden, Denmark, Prussia, Iceland, and as far as Greenland. Leaving a strange pocket of immunity in Bohemia, and Russia unattacked until 1351, it had passed from most of Europe by mid-1350. Although the mortality rate was erratic, ranging from one fifth in some places to nine tenths or almost total elimination in others, the overall estimate of modern demographers has settled—for the area extending from India to Iceland—around the same figure expressed in Froissart's casual words: "a third of the world died." His estimate, the common one at the time, was not an inspired guess but a borrowing of St. John's figure for mortality from plague in Revelation, the favorite guide to human affairs of the Middle Ages.

A third of Europe would have meant about 20 million deaths. No one knows in truth how many died. Contemporary reports were an awed impression, not an accurate count. In crowded Avignon, it was said, 400 died daily; 7,000 houses emptied by death were shut up; a single graveyard received 11,000 corpses in six weeks; half the city's inhabitants reportedly died, including 9 cardinals or one third of the total, and 70 lesser prelates. Watching the endlessly passing death carts, chroniclers let normal exaggeration take wings and put the Avignon death toll at 62,000 and even at 120,000, although the city's total population was probably less than 50,000.

When graveyards filled up, bodies at Avignon were thrown into the Rhône until mass burial pits were dug for dumping the corpses. In London in such pits corpses piled up in layers until they overflowed. Everywhere reports speak of the sick dying too fast for the living to bury. Corpses were dragged out of homes and left in front of doorways. Morning light revealed new piles of bodies. In Florence the dead were gathered up by the Compagnia della Misericordia—founded in 1244 to care for the sick—whose members wore red robes and hoods masking the face except for the eyes. When their efforts failed, the dead lay putrid in the streets for days at a time. When no coffins were to be had, the bodies were laid on boards, two or three at once, to be carried to graveyards or common pits. Families dumped their own relatives into the pits, or buried them so hastily and thinly "that dogs dragged them forth and devoured their bodies."

Amid accumulating death and fear of contagion, people died without last rites and were buried without prayers, a prospect that terrified the last hours of the stricken. A bishop in England gave permission to laymen to make confession to each other as was done by the Apostles, "or if no man is present then even to a woman," and if no priest could be found to administer extreme unction, "then faith must suffice." Clement VI found it necessary to grant remissions of sin to all who died of the plague because so many were unattended by priests. "And no bells tolled," wrote a chronicler of Siena, "and nobody wept no matter what his loss because almost everyone expected death. . . . And people said and believed, 'This is the end of the world.'"

In Paris, where the plague lasted through 1349, the reported death rate was 800 a day, in Pisa 500, in Vienna 500 to 600. The total dead in Paris numbered 50,000 or half the population. Florence, weakened by the famine of 1347, lost three to four fifths of its citizens, Venice two thirds, Hamburg and Bremen, though smaller in size, about the same proportion. Cities, as centers of transportation, were more likely to be affected than villages, although once a village was infected, its death rate was equally high. At Givry, a prosperous village in Burgundy of 1,200 to 1,500 people, the parish register records 615 deaths in the space of fourteen weeks, compared to an average of thirty deaths a year in the previous decade. In three villages of Cambridgeshire, manorial records show a death rate of 47 percent, 57 percent, and in one case 70 percent. When the last survivors, too few to carry on, moved away, a deserted village sank back into the wilderness and disappeared from the map altogether, leaving only a grass-covered ghostly outline to show where mortals once had lived.

In enclosed places such as monasteries and prisons, the infection of one person usually meant that of all, as happened in the Franciscan convents of Carcassonne and Marseille, where every inmate without exception died. Of the 140 Dominicans at Montpellier only seven survived. Petrarch's[2] brother Gherardo, member of a Carthusian monastery, buried the prior and 34 fellow monks one by one, sometimes three a day, until he was left alone with his dog and fled to look for a place that would take him in. Watching every comrade die, men in such places could not but wonder whether the strange peril that filled the air had not been sent to exterminate the human race. In Kilkenny, Ireland, Brother John Clyn of the Friars Minor, another monk left alone among dead men, kept a record of what had happened lest "things which should be remembered perish with time and vanish from the memory of those who come after us." Sensing "the whole world, as it were, placed within the grasp of the Evil One," and waiting for death to visit him too, he wrote, "I leave parchment to continue this work, if perchance any man survive and any of the race of Adam escape this pestilence and carry on the work which I have begun." Brother John, as noted by another hand, died of the pestilence, but he foiled oblivion.

The largest cities of Europe, with populations of about 100,000, were Paris and Florence, Venice and Genoa. At the next level, with more than 50,000, were Ghent and Bruges in Flanders, Milan, Bologna,

---

2. Francesco Petrarch (1304–74), Italian writer whose sonnets to "my lady Laura" influenced a tradition of European love poetry for centuries afterward.

Rome, Naples, and Palermo, and Cologne. London hovered below 50,000, the only city in England except York with more than 10,000. At the level of 20,000 to 50,000 were Bordeaux, Toulouse, Montpellier, Marseille, and Lyon in France, Barcelona, Seville, and Toledo in Spain, Siena, Pisa, and other secondary cities in Italy, and the Hanseatic trading cities of the Empire. The plague raged through them all, killing anywhere from one third to two thirds of their inhabitants. Italy, with a total population of 10 to 11 million, probably suffered the heaviest toll. Following the Florentine bankruptcies, the crop failures and workers' riots of 1346–47, the revolt of Cola di Rienzi that plunged Rome into anarchy, the plague came as the peak of successive calamities. As if the world were indeed in the grasp of the Evil One, its first appearance on the European mainland in January 1348 coincided with a fearsome earthquake that carved a path of wreckage from Naples up to Venice. Houses collapsed, church towers toppled, villages were crushed, and the destruction reached as far as Germany and Greece. Emotional response, dulled by horrors, underwent a kind of atrophy epitomized by the chronicler who wrote, "And in these days was burying without sorrowe and wedding without friendschippe."

In Siena, where more than half the inhabitants died of the plague, work was abandoned on the great cathedral, planned to be the largest in the world, and never resumed, owing to loss of workers and master masons and "the melancholy and grief" of the survivors. The cathedral's truncated transept still stands in permanent witness to the sweep of death's scythe. Agnolo di Tura, a chronicler of Siena, recorded the fear of contagion that froze every other instinct. "Father abandoned child, wife husband, one brother another," he wrote, "for this plague seemed to strike through the breath and sight. And so they died. And no one could be found to bury the dead for money or friendship. . . . And I, Agnolo di Tura, called the Fat, buried my five children with my own hands, and so did many others likewise."

15 There were many to echo his account of inhumanity and few to balance it, for the plague was not the kind of calamity that inspired mutual help. Its loathsomeness and deadliness did not herd people together in mutual distress, but only prompted their desire to escape each other. "Magistrates and notaries refused to come and make the wills of the dying," reported a Franciscan friar of Piazza in Sicily; what was worse, "even the priests did not come to hear their confessions." A clerk of the Archbishop of Canterbury reported the same of English priests who "turned away from the care of their benefices from fear of death." Cases of parents deserting children and children their parents were reported across Europe from Scotland to Russia. The calamity chilled the hearts of men, wrote Boccaccio[3] in his famous account of the plague in Florence that serves as introduction to the *Decameron*.

"One man shunned another . . . kinsfolk held aloof, brother was forsaken by brother, oftentimes husband by wife; nay, what is more, and scarcely to be believed, fathers and mothers were found to abandon their own children to their fate, untended, unvisited as if they had been strangers." Exaggeration and literary pessimism were common in the 14th century, but the Pope's physician, Guy de Chauliac, was a sober, careful observer who reported the same phenomenon: "A father did not visit his son, nor the son his father. Charity was dead."

Yet not entirely. In Paris, according to the chronicler Jean de Venette, the nuns of the Hôtel Dieu or municipal hospital, "having no fear of death, tended the sick with all sweetness and humility." New nuns repeatedly took the places of those who died, until the majority "many times renewed by death now rest in peace with Christ as we may piously believe."

When the plague entered northern France in July 1348, it settled first in Normandy and, checked by winter, gave Picardy a deceptive interim until the next summer. Either in mourning or warning, black flags were flown from church towers of the worst-stricken villages of Normandy. "And in that time," wrote a monk of the abbey of Fourcarment, "the mortality was so great among the people of Normandy that those of Picardy mocked them." The same unneighborly reaction was reported of the Scots, separated by a winter's immunity from the English. Delighted to hear of the disease that was scourging the "southrons," they gathered forces for an invasion, "laughing at their enemies." Before they could move, the savage mortality fell upon them too, scattering some in death and the rest in panic to spread the infection as they fled.

In Picardy in the summer of 1349 the pestilence penetrated the castle of Coucy to kill Enguerrand's[4] mother, Catherine, and her new husband. Whether her nine-year-old son escaped by chance or was perhaps living elsewhere with one of his guardians is unrecorded. In nearby Amiens, tannery workers, responding quickly to losses in the labor force, combined to bargain for higher wages. In another place villagers were seen dancing to drums and trumpets, and on being asked the reason, answered that, seeing their neighbors die day by day while their village remained immune, they believed they could keep the plague from entering "by the jollity that is in us. That is why we dance." Further north in Tournai on the border of Flanders, Gilles li Muisis, Abbot of St. Martin's, kept one of the epidemic's most vivid accounts. The passing bells rang all day and all night, he recorded, because sextons were anxious

3. Giovanni Boccaccio (1313–75), Italian writer best known for his collection of stories, *The Decameron,* in which seven young ladies and three young men flee from Florence to escape the Black Death and tell stories for ten days to while away the time.
4. Enguerrand de Coucy, a French nobleman, is the historical figure around whom Tuchman constructs her account of the fourteenth century.

to obtain their fees while they could. Filled with the sound of mourning, the city became oppressed by fear, so that the authorities forbade the tolling of bells and the wearing of black and restricted funeral services to two mourners. The silencing of funeral bells and of criers' announcements of deaths was ordained by most cities. Siena imposed a fine on the wearing of mourning clothes by all except widows.

Flight was the chief recourse of those who could afford it or arrange it. The rich fled to their country places like Boccaccio's young patricians of Florence, who settled in a pastoral palace "removed on every side from the roads" with "wells of cool water and vaults of rare wines." The urban poor died in their burrows, "and only the stench of their bodies informed neighbors of their death." That the poor were more heavily afflicted than the rich was clearly remarked at the time, in the north as in the south. A Scottish chronicler, John of Fordun, stated flatly that the pest "attacked especially the meaner sort and common people— seldom the magnates." Simon de Covino of Montpellier made the same observation. He ascribed it to the misery and want and hard lives that made the poor more susceptible, which was half the truth. Close contact and lack of sanitation was the unrecognized other half. It was noticed too that the young died in greater proportion than the old; Simon de Covino compared the disappearance of youth to the withering of flowers in the fields.

20   In the countryside peasants dropped dead on the roads, in the fields, in their houses. Survivors in growing helplessness fell into apathy, leaving ripe wheat uncut and livestock untended. Oxen and asses, sheep and goats, pigs and chickens ran wild and they too, according to local reports, succumbed to the pest. English sheep, bearers of the precious wool, died throughout the country. The chronicler Henry Knighton, canon of Leicester Abbey, reported 5,000 dead in one field alone, "their bodies so corrupted by the plague that neither beast nor bird would touch them," and spreading an appalling stench. In the Austrian Alps wolves came down to prey upon sheep and then, "as if alarmed by some invisible warning, turned and fled back into the wilderness." In remote Dalmatia bolder wolves descended upon a plague-stricken city and attacked human survivors. For want of herdsmen, cattle strayed from place to place and died in hedgerows and ditches. Dogs and cats fell like the rest.

The dearth of labor held a fearful prospect because the 14th century lived close to the annual harvest both for food and for next year's seed. "So few servants and laborers were left," wrote Knighton, "that no one knew where to turn for help." The sense of a vanishing future created a kind of dementia of despair. A Bavarian chronicler of Neuberg on the Danube recorded that "Men and women . . . wandered around as if mad" and let their cattle stray "because no one had any inclination to concern themselves about the future." Fields went uncultivated, spring seed unsown. Second growth with nature's awful energy crept back over cleared land, dikes crumbled, salt water reinvaded and soured the low-lands. With so few hands remaining to restore the work of centuries, people felt, in Walsingham's words, that "the world could never again regain its former prosperity."

Though the death rate was higher among the anonymous poor, the known and the great died too. King Alfonso XI of Castile was the only reigning monarch killed by the pest, but his neighbor King Pedro of Aragon lost his wife, Queen Leonora, his daughter Marie, and a niece in the space of six months. John Cantacuzene, Emperor of Byzantium, lost his son. In France the lame Queen Jeanne and her daughter-in-law Bonne de Luxemburg, wife of the Dauphin, both died in 1349 in the same phase that took the life of Enguerrand's mother. Jeanne, Queen of Navarre, daughter of Louis X, was another victim. Edward III's second daughter, Joanna, who was on her way to marry Pedro, the heir of Castile, died in Bordeaux. Women appear to have been more vulnera-ble than men, perhaps because, being more housebound, they were more exposed to fleas. Boccaccio's mistress Fiammetta, illegitimate daughter of the King of Naples, died, as did Laura, the beloved—whether real or fictional—of Petrarch. Reaching out to us in the future, Petrarch cried, "Oh happy posterity who will not experience such abysmal woe and will look upon our testimony as a fable."

In Florence Giovanni Villani, the great historian of his time, died at 68 in the midst of an unfinished sentence: ". . . e dure questo pistolenza fino a . . . (in the midst of this pestilence there came to an end . . .)." Siena's master painters, the brothers Ambrogio and Pietro Lorenzetti, whose names never appear after 1348, presumably perished in the plague, as did Andrea Pisano, architect and sculptor of Florence. Wil-liam of Ockham and the English mystic Richard Rolle of Hampole both disappear from mention after 1349. Francisco Datini, merchant of Prato, lost both his parents and two siblings. Curious sweeps of mortality afflicted certain bodies of merchants in London. All eight wardens of the Company of Cutters, all six wardens of the Hatters, and four wardens of the Goldsmiths died before July 1350. Sir John Pulteney, master draper and four times Mayor of London, was a victim, likewise Sir John Montgomery, Governor of Calais.

Among the clergy and doctors the mortality was naturally high be-cause of the nature of their professions. Out of 24 physicians in Venice, 20 were said to have lost their lives in the plague, although, according to another account, some were believed to have fled or to have shut themselves up in their houses. At Montpellier, site of the leading medie-val medical school, the physician Simon de Covino reported that, de-spite the great number of doctors, "hardly one of them escaped." In

Avignon, Guy de Chauliac confessed that he performed his medical visits only because he dared not stay away for fear of infamy, but "I was in continual fear." He claimed to have contracted the disease but to have cured himself by his own treatment; if so, he was one of the few who recovered.

25   Clerical mortality varied with rank. Although the one-third toll of cardinals reflects the same proportion as the whole, this was probably due to their concentration in Avignon. In England, in strange and almost sinister procession, the Archbishop of Canterbury, John Stratford, died in August 1348, his appointed successor died in May 1349, and the next appointee three months later, all three within a year. Despite such weird vagaries, prelates in general managed to sustain a higher survival rate than the lesser clergy. Among bishops the deaths have been estimated at about one in twenty. The loss of priests, even if many avoided their fearful duty of attending the dying, was about the same as among the population as a whole.

Government officials, whose loss contributed to the general chaos, found, on the whole, no special shelter. In Siena four of the nine members of the governing oligarchy died, in France one third of the royal notaries, in Bristol 15 out of the 52 members of the Town Council or almost one third. Tax-collecting obviously suffered, with the result that Philip VI was unable to collect more than a fraction of the subsidy granted him by the Estates in the winter of 1347–48.

Lawlessness and debauchery accompanied the plague as they had during the great plague of Athens of 430 B.C., when according to Thucydides, men grew bold in the indulgence of pleasure: "For seeing how the rich died in a moment and those who had nothing immediately inherited their property, they reflected that life and riches were alike transitory and they resolved to enjoy themselves while they could." Human behavior is timeless. When St. John had his vision of plague in Revelation, he knew from some experience or race memory that those who survived "repented not of the work of their hands. . . . Neither repented they of their murders, nor of their sorceries, nor of their fornication, nor of their thefts."

Ignorance of the cause augmented the sense of horror. Of the real carriers, rats and fleas, the 14th century had no suspicion, perhaps because they were so familiar. Fleas, though a common household nuisance, are not once mentioned in contemporary plague writings, and rats only incidentally, although folklore commonly associated them with pestilence. The legend of the Pied Piper arose from an outbreak of 1284. The actual plague bacillus, *Pasturella pestis,* remained undiscovered for another 500 years. Living alternately in the stomach of the flea and the bloodstream of the rat who was the flea's host, the bacillus in its bubonic form was transferred to humans and animals by the bite of either rat or flea. It traveled by virtue of *Rattus rattus*, the small medieval black rat that lived on ships, as well as by the heavier brown or sewer rat. What precipitated the turn of the bacillus from innocuous to virulent form is unknown, but the occurrence is now believed to have taken place not in China but somewhere in central Asia and to have spread along the caravan routes. Chinese origin was a mistaken notion of the 14th century based on real but belated reports of huge death tolls in China from drought, famine, and pestilence which have since been traced to the 1330s, too soon to be responsible for the plague that appeared in India in 1346.

The phantom enemy had no name. Called the Black Death only in later recurrences, it was known during the first epidemic simply as the Pestilence or Great Mortality. Reports from the East, swollen by fearful imaginings, told of strange tempests and "sheets of fire" mingled with huge hailstones that "slew almost all," or a "vast rain of fire" that burned up men, beasts, stones, trees, villages, and cities. In another version, "foul blasts of wind" from the fires carried the infection to Europe "and now as some suspect it cometh round the seacoast." Accurate observation in this case could not make the mental jump to ships and rats because no idea of animal- or insect-borne contagion existed.

The earthquake was blamed for releasing sulfurous and foul fumes from the earth's interior, or as evidence of a titanic struggle of planets and oceans causing waters to rise and vaporize until fish died in masses and corrupted the air. All these explanations had in common a factor of poisoned air, of miasmas and thick, stinking mists traced to every kind of natural or imagined agency from stagnant lakes to malign conjunction of the planets, from the hand of the Evil One to the wrath of God. Medical thinking, trapped in the theory of astral influences, stressed air as the communicator of disease, ignoring sanitation or visible carriers. The existence of two carriers confused the trail, the more so because the flea could live and travel independently of the rat for as long as a month and, if infected by the particularly virulent septicemic form of the bacillus, could infect humans without reinfecting itself from the rat. The simultaneous presence of the pneumonic form of the disease, which was indeed communicated through the air, blurred the problem further.

The mystery of the contagion was "the most terrible of all the terrors," as an anonymous Flemish cleric in Avignon wrote to a correspondent in Bruges. Plagues had been known before, from the plague of Athens (believed to have been typhus) to the prolonged epidemic of the 6th century A.D., to the recurrence of sporadic outbreaks in the 12th and 13th centuries, but they had left no accumulated store of understanding. That the infection came from contact with the sick or with their houses, clothes, or corpses was quickly observed but not comprehended. Gentile

30

da Foligno, renowned physician of Perugia and doctor of medicine at the universities of Bologna and Padua, came close to respiratory infection when he surmised that poisonous material was "communicated by means of air breathed out and in." Having no idea of microscopic carriers, he had to assume that the air was corrupted by planetary influences. Planets, however, could not explain the ongoing contagion. The agonized search for an answer gave rise to such theories as transference by sight. People fell ill, wrote Guy de Chauliac, not only by remaining with the sick but "even by looking at them." Three hundred years later Joshua Barnes, the 17th century biographer of Edward III, could write that the power of infection had entered into beams of light and "darted death from the eyes."

Doctors struggling with the evidence could not break away from the terms of astrology, to which they believed all human physiology was subject. Medicine was the one aspect of medieval life, perhaps because of its links with the Arabs, not shaped by Christian doctrine. Clerics detested astrology, but could not dislodge its influence. Guy de Chauliac, physician to three popes in succession, practiced in obedience to the zodiac. While his *Cirurgia* was the major treatise on surgery of its time, while he understood the use of anesthesia made from the juice of opium, mandrake, or hemlock, he nevertheless prescribed bleeding and purgatives by the planets and divided chronic from acute diseases on the basis of one being under the rule of the sun and the other of the moon.

In October 1348 Philip VI asked the medical faculty of the University of Paris for a report on the affliction that seemed to threaten human survival. With careful thesis, antithesis, and proofs, the doctors ascribed it to a triple conjunction of Saturn, Jupiter, and Mars in the 40th degree of Aquarius said to have occurred on March 20, 1345. They acknowledged, however, effects "whose cause is hidden from even the most highly trained intellects." The verdict of the masters of Paris became the official version. Borrowed, copied by scribes, carried abroad, translated from Latin into various vernaculars, it was everywhere accepted, even by the Arab physicians of Cordova and Granada, as the scientific if not the popular answer. Because of the terrible interest of the subject, the translations of the plague tracts stimulated use of national languages. In that one respect, life came from death.

To the people at large there could be but one explanation—the wrath of God. Planets might satisfy the learned doctors, but God was closer to the average man. A scourge so sweeping and unsparing without any visible cause could only be seen as Divine punishment upon mankind for its sins. It might even be God's terminal disappointment in his creature. Matteo Villani compared the plague to the Flood in ultimate purpose and believed he was recording "the extermination of mankind."

Efforts to appease Divine wrath took many forms, as when the city of Rouen ordered that everything that could anger God, such as gambling, cursing, and drinking, must be stopped. More general were the penitent processions authorized at first by the Pope, some lasting as long as three days, some attended by as many as 2,000, which everywhere accompanied the plague and helped to spread it.

Barefoot in sackcloth, sprinkled with ashes, weeping, praying, tearing their hair, carrying candles and relics, sometimes with ropes around their necks or beating themselves with whips, the penitents wound through the streets, imploring the mercy of the Virgin and saints at their shrines. In a vivid illustration for the *Très Riches Heures* of the Duc de Berry, the Pope is shown in a penitent procession attended by four cardinals in scarlet from hat to hem. He raises both arms in supplication to the angel on top of the Castel Sant'Angelo, while white-robed priests bearing banners and relics in golden cases turn to look as one of their number, stricken by the plague, falls to the ground, his face contorted with anxiety. In the rear, a gray-clad monk falls beside another victim already on the ground as the townspeople gaze in horror. (Nominally the illustration represents a 6th century plague in the time of Pope Gregory the Great, but as medieval artists made no distinction between past and present, the scene is shown as the artist would have seen it in the 14th century.) When it became evident that these processions were sources of infection, Clement VI had to prohibit them.

In Messina, where the plague first appeared, the people begged the Archbishop of neighboring Catania to lend them the relics of St. Agatha. When the Catanians refused to let the relics go, the Archbishop dipped them in holy water and took the water himself to Messina, where he carried it in a procession with prayers and litanies through the streets. The demonic, which shared the medieval cosmos with God, appeared as "demons in the shape of dogs" to terrify the people. "A black dog with a drawn sword in his paws appeared among them, gnashing his teeth and rushing upon them and breaking all the silver vessels and lamps and candlesticks on the altars and casting them hither and thither. . . . So the people of Messina, terrified by this prodigious vision, were all strangely overcome by fear."

The apparent absence of earthly cause gave the plague a supernatural and sinister quality. Scandinavians believed that a Pest Maiden emerged from the mouth of the dead in the form of a blue flame and flew through the air to infect the next house. In Lithuania the Maiden was said to wave a red scarf through the door or window to let in the pest. One brave man, according to legend, deliberately waited at his open window with drawn sword and, at the fluttering of the scarf, chopped off the hand. He died of his deed, but his village was spared and the scarf long preserved as a relic in the local church.

35

Beyond demons and superstition the final hand was God's. The Pope acknowledged it in a Bull of September 1348, speaking of the "pestilence with which God is afflicting the Christian people." To the Emperor John Cantacuzene it was manifest that a malady of such horrors, stenches, and agonies, and especially one bringing the dismal despair that settled upon its victims before they died, was not a plague "natural" to mankind but "a chastisement from Heaven." To Piers Plowman "these pestilences were for pure sin."

The general acceptance of this view created an expanded sense of guilt, for if the plague were punishment there had to be terrible sin to have occasioned it. What sins were on the 14th century conscience? Primarily greed, the sin of avarice, followed by usury, worldliness, adultery, blasphemy, falsehood, luxury, irreligion. Giovanni Villani, attempting to account for the cascade of calamity that had fallen upon Florence, concluded that it was retribution for the sins of avarice and usury that oppressed the poor. Pity and anger about the condition of the poor, especially victimization of the peasantry in war, was often expressed by writers of the time and was certainly on the conscience of the century. Beneath it all was the daily condition of medieval life, in which hardly an act or thought, sexual, mercantile, or military, did not contravene the dictates of the Church. Mere failure to fast or attend mass was sin. The result was an underground lake of guilt in the soul that the plague now tapped.

40   That the mortality was accepted as God's punishment may explain in part the vacuum of comment that followed the Black Death. An investigator has noticed that in the archives of Périgord references to the war are innumerable, to the plague few. Froissart mentions the great death but once, Chaucer gives it barely a glance. Divine anger so great that it contemplated the extermination of man did not bear close examination.

THE READER

1. *Why does Tuchman begin with the account of the Genoese trading ships?*

2. *What ways does Tuchman find to group related facts together—in other words, what categories does she develop?*

3. *Read Stephen Jay Gould's "The Terrifying Normalcy of AIDS" (p. 702). In what ways is our reaction to this twentieth-century plague similar to the fourteenth-century response to the Black Death? In what ways is it different? What are the differences in purpose between Tuchman and Gould, and how have these differences helped to determine what kind of material each includes?*

THE WRITER

1. *In her introduction to* A Distant Mirror: The Calamitous Fourteenth Century, *the book from which this selection is taken, Tuchman talks about major problems or obstacles for the medieval historian: (1) "uncertain and contradictory data with regard to dates, numbers, and hard facts," (2) the changing prejudices and points of view of past historians, (3) lack of information, (4) the "disproportionate survival of the bad side," producing an "overload of the negative," and (5) the "difficulty of empathy, of genuinely entering into the mental and emotional values of the Middle Ages." Would you encounter similar problems in writing a research paper in another subject area or time period? Which of these problems seem most serious? How successful do you think Tuchman is in meeting these problems? Explain.*

2. *Suggest other categories that Tuchman might have used in arranging her facts. What would she have gained or lost by using other categories?*

3. *Can you determine the basis for Tuchman's decision sometimes to quote a source, sometimes to recount it in her own words? Explain whether you think she is operating under a general principle in making these choices.*

4. *Write a brief account of a disaster in our own time, first doing research from several sources.*

Leo McNamara

THE STATE OF IRELAND

> *I am of Ireland*
> *And of the holy land of Ireland:*
> *Come, out of charity,*
> *Come and dance with me*
> *In Ireland.*

So runs the old refrain, a fragment of the earliest English verse composed in Ireland, a dancing measure appropriate to that green and pleasant, tuneful land. The modern Irish poet William Butler Yeats makes fine use of it in his sequence *Words for Music Perhaps.* Those who have responded to the lilting plea know that it is a true and perduring characterization of the island.

An island lying between Spain and the Scandinavian north, according

From *LSA Magazine* (Spring 1988).

to the medieval cartographers and commentators: however queer that
way of situating Ireland might seem, a glance at a medieval map will
show the validity of the point. Ireland did not begin to lie off the coast
of Great Britain until England, Wales, and Scotland became Great
Britain, not a long time ago.

The emergence of England as a powerful nation state in the sixteenth
century transformed the geography and cartography of western Europe:
it was necessary, for "national security," for England to break out of the
encircling perimeter that bound her in an inland sea, from the Scandinavian north down through Scotland and Ireland to the Iberian peninsula.
Once the circle was broken, Ireland became England's Cuba, and that
specter has determined England's political and military policy toward
Ireland down to the present day. Not of any consequence in itself,
Ireland must not be allowed to fall within the sphere of influence of
England's great antagonists: first Spain, then France, then Germany.

For four hundred years this has been a remarkably consistent and
tenacious policy, perhaps one of the most firmly held verities amid a
bewilderment of geopolitical changes. Whether England's need will
continue to dictate Ireland's fortune to such a large degree is an open
question; there are signs (the Anglo-Irish Agreement of 1986 among
them) that the old policy is no longer in tune with today's political
realities.

Meanwhile, the most visible legacy of the policy is the fact that
Ireland is composed of (decomposed into?) two political states: the
Republic of Ireland and Northern Ireland. While it is quite erroneous
to suppose that the partition of Ireland exists only at England's bidding
(and a very pernicious error, indeed, to suppose that the troubles in
Northern Ireland are caused by its being "occupied" by Britain) it is
nevertheless true that the intertwining of British and Irish history has
resulted in the present political entities.

The History

Before 1800, the kingdom of Ireland was not at all homogeneous in
culture. The great mass of the people was Catholic in religion and Gaelic
in language, a people into which earlier invaders of Norse and Norman
and English stock had been largely assimilated. These people were
dominated through economic power and punitive legislation by a class
that was Protestant in religion and English in provenance. It is one of
the strange ironies of Irish history that it was this dominant and domi-
neering class—the Anglo-Irish, as they were now conceiving themselves
to be, descendants of the Tudor conquerors and the colonists, settlers,
planters of the seventeenth century—this people, that rebelled against
its dependency upon England. By creating its version of the idea of Irish

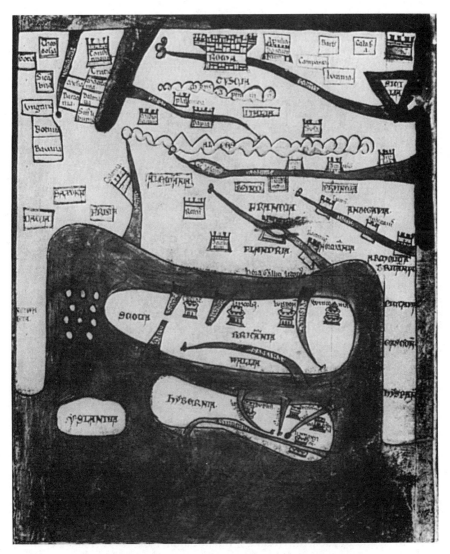

Map of Europe from the Giraldus MS. 700, National Library, Dublin.
Looking at Europe from the west, the spectator sees Hybernia at bottom
center, Iceland (Yslandia) at left, and Spain (Hyspania) at right. Above are
England (Brittania) and Scotland (Scotia), with the Orkney Islands. Beyond
them, Flanders (Flandria), France, the Rhone, the Alps, Italy, and Rome
(Roma, top center). At left are Norway, Bavaria, and Greece.

nationalism, it was this people that made the governance of Ireland so troublesome from England's point of view.

At the time of the American Revolution, political and economic relations between Britain and Ireland were strained—for much the same set of reasons that relations were strained between Britain and her North American colonies. The Anglo-Irish Rebellion of 1798 was answered by the Act of Union, which in 1800 united Great Britain and Ireland. While the outcome of the American rebellion was independence and the United States of America, the outcome for Ireland (an independent kingdom, but treated by the English Parliament much more like a colony) was assimilation into the United Kingdom: a union of States equal in theory but, in fact, far from equal in power.

The uniting of the two islands in 1800 was meant to be a solution to persistent problems in the governance of the hitherto independent kingdom of Ireland, a kingdom with its own parliament and judiciary but having in common with Great Britain the same monarch—the crown of Great Britain, itself having been formed by a union of the kingdoms of England (with its principality, Wales) and Scotland. Throughout the nineteenth century, a unified Ireland was a constituent part of the United Kingdom of Great Britain and Ireland. Today the six counties of Northern Ireland constitute the portion of the island that is still part of the United Kingdom.

The Republic of Ireland has its foundation in the Anglo-Irish War of 1919–21, consequent upon the insurrection of Easter Week 1916. Irish nationalists had become impatient with the promise of a moderate and often-postponed measure of home rule (control over domestic affairs). This measure had previously been sought by a majority in Ireland but was bitterly resisted by an alliance between the Conservative Party in England and Irish Unionists. The treaty that brought an end to the Anglo-Irish War provided for the establishment in Ireland of a Free State, but excluded the six counties in the north where Unionist sentiment was strongest, and decisive. The Free State of that day successively dissolved its remaining ties to Great Britain and to the Commonwealth until, after a quarter-century (in 1949), it rather casually declared itself to be the Republic of Ireland, a totally autonomous, sovereign state.

10   The continuation of the six counties of Northern Ireland as part of the United Kingdom is an arrangement commanding the allegiance, the loyalty, of about one million Irish people, citizens of that state. The ineluctable fact that about one-quarter of the total population of the island sincerely, wholeheartedly, fiercely desires not to be included in a unified Ireland is the most basic reason that the political reunification of Ireland simply is not going to happen, at least in the foreseeable future. Another reason is the fact that the overwhelming majority of the citizens of the Republic of Ireland really don't care much one way or

the other whether the north is included. They would mostly prefer it to be—but not at the cost of imagining a polity, much different from the Republic at present, that would accommodate the North.

While it is official policy in the Republic to deplore the loss of one of the "four fair fields," and to seek an end to partition, the average citizen in the Republic takes about as much interest in the North as a citizen of Ontario takes in Quebec, perhaps less. The consequence is that actively seeking an end to partition does not rank very high on the government's list of priorities. In the circumstances, and given the odds, that is perhaps just as well.

The Conflict

The Irish are not, northern or southern, an especially pugnacious or violent people. A phrase such as "the fighting Irish" is about as just a stereotype as would be "the obese American" (the notion that Americans are characteristically obese and naive being a prejudice entertained by a surprisingly large number of intelligent Irish persons). Of course they sometimes do fight, and of course there is plenty of violence in Ireland today: the annual homicide rate in Northern Ireland over the past twenty years, while not nearly as high as that in the city of Detroit, say, has been high enough. Because television magnifies the sensational and flatters us by making us impervious to any but distant alarms, Belfast seems to us a more hazardous city than Detroit, which it certainly is not.

Most people know that the conflict in Ireland today is not warfare between Northern Ireland and the Republic, but many are puzzled by the apparent inability of Catholics and Protestants within Northern Ireland to live together in peace.

They have a right to be puzzled: "Catholic" and "Protestant" are not, as elsewhere, terms designating religious profession, but code words used (sometimes carelessly, and sometimes by deliberate design) to signify realities more economic, social, and cultural than theological. Sectarian divisions do matter in Ireland, and they do play a part in the conflict, but not to the extent it pleases outsiders to imagine (or interested parties, again by design, to pretend). The basic conflict has been much less exotic, much more familiar. It has been a struggle between those who held and have long been accustomed to hold money and power, and those who had been denied money and power, between haves and have-nots. The first category included by no means all Protestants, but very few Catholics; and excluded Protestants did not need live in dread of permanent consignment, with Catholics, to the second category.

We may use the past tense to characterize the basic conflict as it existed up to twenty years ago, at the inception of the Civil Rights Movement in Northern Ireland, not because the basic issue is now

15

utterly other, but because developments in the past two decades have introduced new elements, some of them of very great importance. The most salient of these most publicized, has been the summoning back into a ghastly form of life of the then-defunct Irish Republican Army, which pretends to represent the cause of the Catholic minority, and its inevitable partner in assassination, the paramilitary thuggery practiced by the most psychotic Loyalists, who see themselves as defending a Protestant state for a Protestant people. Then, too, one must take into account the killings and maimings resultant from extortion and protection rackets, bank robberies, shoot-outs, settling of old scores, the general rise in criminality spawned by economic and political unrest.

The basic issue was for long manifest in the nature of the Northern Ireland polity, in the fact that it was, and was meant to be, a radically unjust state. For to ensure that the two-thirds Unionist majority sustaining the continued inclusion of the Six Counties in the United Kingdom never be displaced by the one-third minority (Catholic, and therefore likely to increase in number), the minority was systematically and blithely discriminated against: in employment, in housing, in voting. By this means the Unionist Party maintained itself in power for over a half-century: while the Third Reich rose and fell, while diadems dropped, and dynasties disappeared, while the Empire vanished, the Unionist Party soldiered on.

And indeed there was a kind of glazed logic to it: what, after all, was the alternative, but to call into question the whole existence of, the whole rationale for, the state? There really could be no loyal opposition. The Unionist Party remained in power longer than any party in western Europe because its sole principle and entire platform was maintenance of the Union, by any means needful—and it had the means to hand.

The Civil Rights Movement of the late sixties, taking its strategy and tactics from that in the United States, began by repudiating the frozen politics of nationalist opposition to Loyalist rule. It began by accepting the actual existence of the state, by taking it as a real fact rather than a temporary aberration, and by exposing its radical injustice for the world to see. In one short year, from the autumn of 1967 to the autumn of 1968, it recapitulated, like a speeded-up film, a decade of American experience: from sit-ins and squat-ins to peaceful protests to passive resistance to rallies and marches and demonstrations.

Then violence came in October 1968, when the Reverend Ian Paisley's Loyalist goons set upon and beat members of a protest march on its way to Derry, and baton-wielding police joined in, clubbing the marchers, not their attackers. Street violence in Derry and Belfast took place in the months that followed; British troops were summoned to protect the minority; the chronic malaise of the North entered into the acute phase evident from that time to the present. The Civil Rights

Movement, having achieved gains thought too modest by some and far too frighteningly excessive by others, gave way to a return to the old futile battle-cries of "Up the Republic!" and "No surrender."

It should be borne in mind that the republic sought by the IRA is the "real" one, the heart's ideal, not the spurious usurpation, as it is considered, seated in Dublin. That is why the usual journalistic account of the IRA objective, "unification with the South," is so inadequate and misleading. What the Loyalists will not surrender is also an affair of the heart: an ethnic pride of place and domination.

However irreconcilable these cherished ideals (explaining as they do the tragic heroism of hunger strikes unto death and the baffled opposition to power-sharing), it is clear that much has changed in the North. There can be no return to the Unionist state of old, unlikely as is territorial unification with the Republic. Perhaps the best hope for the future of both states of Ireland lies in the further development of the EEC (the Common Market to which both North and South belong) along political lines. In something like a United States of Europe, both states of Ireland might have a secure place. In these states Irish men and women might acknowledge the reality common to them all, as do the fictive Irish from Shakespeare and Joyce, in the closing sequence of Seamus Heaney's poem "Traditions":

> *MacMorris, gallivanting*
> *round the Globe, whinged*
> *to courtier and groundling*
> *who had heard tell of us*
> *as going very bare*
> *of learning, as wild hares,*
> *as anatomies of death:*
> *'What ish my nation?'*
>
> *And sensibly, though so much*
> *later, the wandering Bloom*
> *replied, 'Ireland,' said Bloom,*
> *'I was born in Ireland.'*

Barry Lopez

THE STONE HORSE

1

The deserts of southern California, the high, relatively cooler and wetter Mojave and the hotter, dryer Sonoran to the south of it, carry the signatures of many cultures. Prehistoric rock drawings in the Mojave's Coso Range, probably the greatest concentration of petroglyphs in North America, are at least three thousand years old. Big-game-hunting cultures that flourished six or seven thousand years before that are known from broken spear tips, choppers, and burins left scattered along the shores of great Pleistocene[1] lakes, long since evaporated. Weapons and tools discovered at China Lake may be thirty thousand years old; and worked stone from a quarry in the Calico Mountains is, some argue, evidence that human beings were here more than 200,000 years ago.

Because of the long-term stability of such arid environments, much of this prehistoric stone evidence still lies exposed on the ground, accessible to anyone who passes by—the studious, the acquisitive, the indifferent, the merely curious. Archaeologists do not agree on the sequence of cultural history beyond about twelve thousand years ago, but it is clear that these broken bits of chalcedony, chert, and obsidian, like the animal drawings and geometric designs etched on walls of basalt throughout the desert, anchor the earliest threads of human history, the first record of human endeavor here.

Western man did not enter the California desert until the end of the eighteenth century, 250 years after Coronado brought his soldiers into the Zuni pueblos in a bewildered search for the cities of Cibola.[2] The earliest appraisals of the land were cursory, hurried. People traveled *through* it, en route to Santa Fe or the California coastal settlements. Only miners tarried. In 1823 what had been Spain's became Mexico's, and in 1848 what had been Mexico's became America's;[3] but the bare,

From *Antaeus* (Autumn 1986), "On Nature" issue.

1. A geological epoch lasting from 1 million to 20,000 years ago, during which primitive man first appeared on earth.
2. Francisco Vasquez de Coronado (1510–54), Spanish explorer of the region that is now the southwestern United States, searched for the seven cities of Cibola, fa-

bled for their wealth.
3. Mexico acquired much of the present U.S. Southwest after the Mexicans won their independence from Spain, but lost this territory to the United States in the Treaty of Guadalupe Hidalgo in 1848 at the conclusion of the Mexican War.

jagged mountains and dry lake beds, the vast and uniform plains of creosote bush and yucca plants, remained as obscure as the northern Sudan until the end of the nineteenth century.

Before 1940 the tangible evidence of twentieth-century man's passage here consisted of very little—the hard tracery of travel corridors; the widely scattered, relatively insignificant evidence of mining operations; and the fair expanse of irrigated fields at the desert's periphery. In the space of a hundred years or so the wagon roads were paved, railroads were laid down, and canals and high-tension lines were built to bring water and electricity across the desert to Los Angeles from the Colorado River. The dark mouths of gold, talc, and tin mines yawned from the bony flanks of desert ranges. Dust-encrusted chemical plants stood at work on the lonely edges of dry lake beds. And crops of grapes, lettuce, dates, alfalfa, and cotton covered the Coachella and Imperial valleys, north and south of the Salton Sea, and the Palo Verde Valley along the Colorado.

These developments proceeded with little or no awareness of earlier   5
human occupations by cultures that preceded those of the historic Indians—the Mohave, the Chemehuevi, the Quechan. (Extensive irrigation began actually to change the climate of the Sonoran Desert, and human settlements, the railroads, and farming introduced many new, successful plants into the region.)

During World War II, the American military moved into the desert in great force, to train troops and to test equipment. They found the clear weather conducive to year-round flying, the dry air and isolation very attractive. After the war, a complex of training grounds, storage facilities, and gunnery and test ranges was permanently settled on more than three million acres of military reservations. Few perceived the extent or significance of the destruction of the aboriginal sites that took place during tank maneuvers and bombing runs or in the laying out of highways, railroads, mining districts, and irrigated fields. The few who intuited that something like an American Dordogne Valley[4] lay exposed here were (only) amateur archaeologists; even they reasoned that the desert was too vast for any of this to matter.

After World War II, people began moving out of the crowded Los Angeles basin into homes in Lucerne, Apple, and Antelope valleys in the western Mojave. They emigrated as well to a stretch of resort land at the foot of the San Jacinto Mountains that included Palm Springs, and farther out to old railroad and military towns like Twentynine Palms and Barstow. People also began exploring the desert, at first in military-surplus jeeps and then with a variety of all-terrain and off-road vehicles that became available in the 1960s. By the mid-1970s, the number of

4. A region in southwestern France, site of numerous prehistoric caves.

people using such vehicles for desert recreation had increased exponentially. Most came and went in innocent curiosity; the few who didn't wreaked a havoc all out of proportion to their numbers. The disturbance of previously isolated archaeological sites increased by an order of magnitude. Many sites were vandalized before archaeologists, themselves late to the desert, had any firm grasp of the bounds of human history in the desert. It was as though in the same moment an Aztec[5] library had been discovered intact various lacunae[6] had begun to appear.

The vandalism was of three sorts: the general disturbance usually caused by souvenir hunters and by the curious and the oblivious; the wholesale stripping of a place by professional thieves for black-market sale and trade; and outright destruction, in which vehicles were actually used to ram and trench an area. By 1980, the Bureau of Land Management estimated that probably 35 percent of the archaeological sites in the desert had been vandalized. The destruction at some places by rifles and shotguns, or by power winches mounted on vehicles, was, if one cared for history, demoralizing to behold.

In spite of public education, land closures, and stricter law enforcement in recent years, the BLM estimates that, annually, about 1 percent of the archaeological record in the desert continues to be destroyed or stolen.

2

10   A BLM archaeologist told me, with understandable reluctance, where to find the intaglio. I spread my Automobile Club of Southern California map of Imperial County out on his desk, and he traced the route with a pink felt-tip pen. The line crossed Interstate 8 and then turned west along the Mexican border.

"You can't drive any farther than about here," he said, marking a small X. "There's boulders in the wash. You walk up past them."

On a separate piece of paper he drew a route in a smaller scale that would take me up the arroyo to a certain point where I was to cross back east, to another arroyo. At its head, on higher ground just to the north, I would find the horse.

"It's tough to spot unless you know it's there. Once you pick it up . . ." He shook his head slowly, in a gesture of wonder at its existence.

I waited until I held his eye. I assured him I would not tell anyone else how to get there. He looked at me with stoical despair, like a man

5. A Nahuatl-speaking people who in the fifteenth and early sixteenth centuries ruled a large empire in what is now central and southern Mexico.

6. In this sense, spaces where something has been omitted or has come out; a gap, a hiatus.

who had been robbed twice, whose belief in human beings was offered without conviction.

I did not go until the following day because I wanted to see it at dawn. I ate breakfast at four A.M. in El Centro and then drove south. The route was easy to follow, though the last section of road proved difficult, broken and drifted over with sand in some spots. I came to the barricade of boulders and parked. It was light enough by then to find my way over the ground with little trouble. The contours of the landscape were stark, without any masking vegetation. I worried only about rattlesnakes.

I traversed the stone plain as directed, but, in spite of the frankness of the land, I came on the horse unawares. In the first moment of recognition I was without feeling. I recalled later being startled, and that I held my breath. It was laid out on the ground with its head to the east, three times life size. As I took in its outline I felt a growing concentration of all my senses, as though my attentiveness to the pale rose color of the morning sky and other peripheral images had now ceased to be important. I was aware that I was straining for sound in the windless air, and I felt the uneven pressure of the earth hard against my feet. The horse, outlined in a standing profile on the dark ground, was as vivid before me as a bed of tulips.

I've come upon animals suddenly before, and felt a similar tension, a precipitate heightening of the senses. And I have felt the inexplicable but sharply boosted intensity of a wild moment in the bush, where it is not until some minutes later that you discover the source of electricity—the warm remains of a grizzly bear kill, or the still moist tracks of a wolverine.

But this was slightly different. I felt I had stepped into an unoccupied corridor. I had no familiar sense of history, the temporal structure in which to think: this horse was made by Quechan people three hundred years ago. I felt instead a headlong rush of images: people hunting wild horses with spears on the Pleistocene veld of southern California; Cortés riding across the causeway into Montezuma's Tenochtitlán;[7] a short-legged Comanche, astride his horse like some sort of ferret, slashing through cavalry lines of young men who rode like farmers;[8] a hoof exploding past my face one morning in a corral in Wyoming. These images had the weight and silence of stone.

When I released my breath, the images softened. My initial feeling,

7. Hernando Cortés (c.1485–1547), Spanish conqueror of Mexico, conquered in 1521 the Aztec capital city of Tenochtitlán, which was located on an island in Lake Texoco, where Mexico City stands today. Montezuma II, ruler of the Aztecs, had welcomed Cortés to his capital on November 8, 1519, and the Spanish stayed there, holding him hostage.

8. The Comanches, who often attacked settlers on the southern U.S. plains until the last of them were settled on a reservation in 1875, were known as the finest native American horsemen of the West.

of facing a wild animal in a remote region, was replaced with a calm sense of antiquity. It was then that I became conscious, like an ordinary tourist, of what was before me, and thought: this horse was probably laid out by Quechan people. But when? I wondered. The first horses they saw, I knew, might have been those that came north from Mexico in 1692 with Father Eusebio Kino. [9] But Cocopa people, I recalled, also came this far north on occasion, to fight with their neighbors, the Quechan. And *they* could have seen horses with Melchior Díaz, [1] at the mouth of the Colorado River in the fall of 1540. So, it could be four hundred years old. (No one in fact knows.)

20   I still had not moved. I took my eyes off the horse for a moment to look south over the desert plain into Mexico, to look east past its head at the brightening sunrise, to situate myself. Then, finally, I brought my trailing foot slowly forward and stood erect. Sunlight was running like a thin sheet of water over the stony ground and it threw the horse into relief. It looked as though no hand had ever disturbed the stones that gave it its form.

The horse had been brought to life on ground called desert pavement, a tight, flat matrix of small cobbles blasted smooth by sand-laden winds. The uniform, monochromatic blackness of the stones, a patina of iron and magnesium oxides called desert varnish, is caused by long-term exposure to the sun. To make this type of low-relief ground glyph, or intaglio, the artist either selectively turns individual stones over to their lighter side or removes areas of stone to expose the lighter soil underneath, creating a negative image. This horse, about eighteen feet from brow to rump and eight feet from withers to hoof, had been made in the latter way, and its outline was bermed at certain points with low ridges of stone a few inches high to enhance its three-dimensional qualities. (The left side of the horse was in full profile; each leg was extended at 90 degrees to the body and fully visible, as though seen in three-quarter profile.)

I was not eager to move. The moment I did I would be back in the flow of time, the horse no longer quivering in the same way before me. I did not want to feel again the sequence of quotidian events—to be drawn off into deliberation and analysis. A human being, a four-footed animal, the open land. That was all that was present—and a "thoughtless" understanding of the very old desires bearing on this particular animal: to hunt it, to render it, to fathom it, to subjugate it, to honor it, to take it as a companion.

What finally made me move was the light. The sun now filled the

9. Kino (1644–1711) was the most famous of the seventeenth-century Spanish explorers and Jesuit missionaries in what became the U.S. Southwest.

1. Díaz, one of Coronado's officers, explored the Sonoran Desert and the delta of the Colorado River in 1540.

shallow basin of the horse's body. The weighted line of the stone berm created the illusion of a mane and the distinctive roundness of an equine belly. The change in definition impelled me. I moved to the left, circling past its rump, to see how the light might flesh the horse out from various points of view. I circled it completely before squatting on my haunches. Ten or fifteen minutes later I chose another view. The third time I moved, to a point near the rear hooves, I spotted a stone tool at my feet. I stared at it a long while, more in awe than disbelief, before reaching out to pick it up. I turned it over in my left palm and took it between my fingers to feel its cutting edge. It is always difficult, especially with something so portable, to rechannel the desire to steal.

I spent several hours with the horse. As I changed positions and as the angle of the light continued to change I noticed a number of things. The angle at which the pastern carried the hoof away from the ankle was perfect. Also, stones had been placed within the image to suggest at precisely the right spot the left shoulder above the foreleg. The line that joined thigh and hock was similarly accurate. The muzzle alone seemed distorted—but perhaps these stones had been moved by a later hand. It was an admirably accurate representation, but not what a breeder would call perfect conformation. There was the suggestion of a bowed neck and an undershot jaw, and the tail, as full as a winter coyote's did not appear to be precisely to scale.

The more I thought about it, the more I felt I was looking at an individual horse, a unique combination of generic and specific detail. It was easy to imagine one of Kino's horses as a model, or a horse that ran off from one of Coronado's columns. What kind of horses would these have been? I wondered. In the sixteenth century the most sought-after horses in Europe were Spanish, the offspring of Arabian stock and Barbary horses that the Moors brought to Iberia and bred to the older, eastern European strains brought in by the Romans. The model for this horse, I speculated, could easily have been a palomino, or a descendant of horses trained for lion hunting in North Africa.

A few generations ago, cowboys, cavalry quartermasters, and draymen would have taken this horse before me under consideration and not let up their scrutiny until they had its heritage fixed to their satisfaction. Today, the distinction between draft and harness horses is arcane knowledge, and no image may come to mind for a blue roan or a claybank horse. The loss of such refinement in everyday conversation leaves me unsettled. People praise the Eskimo's ability to distinguish among forty types of snow but forget the skill of others who routinely differentiate between overo and tobiano pintos.[2] Such distinctions are made for the

2. The two color patterns for this breed of horse. The overo have white spreading irregularly up from the belly, mixed with a darker color, and the tobiano have white spreading down from the back in clear-cut patterns.

same reason. You have to do it to be able to talk clearly about the world.

For parts of two years I worked as a horse wrangler and packer in Wyoming. It is dim knowledge now; I would have to think to remember if a buckskin was a kind of dun horse. And I couldn't throw a double-diamond hitch over a set of panniers—the packer's basic tie-down—without guidance. As I squatted there in the desert, however, these more personal memories seemed tenuous in comparison with the sweep of this animal in human time. My memories had no depth. I thought of the Hittite cavalry riding against the Syrians 3,500 years ago. And the first of the Chinese emperors, Ch'in Shih Huang, buried in Shensi Province in 210 B.C. with thousands of life-size horses and soldiers, a terra-cotta guardian army. What could I know of what was in the mind of whoever made this horse? Was there some racial memory of it as an animal that had once fed the artist's ancestors and then disappeared from North America? And then returned in this strange alliance with another race of men?

Certainly, whoever it was, the artist had observed the animal very closely. Certainly the animal's speed had impressed him. Among the first things the Quechan would have learned from an encounter with Kino's horses was that their own long-distance runners—men who could run down mule deer—were no match for this animal.

From where I squatted I could look far out over the Mexican plain. Juan Bautista de Anza[3] passed this way in 1774, extending El Camino Real into Alta California from Sinaloa. He was followed by others, all of them astride the magical horse; *gente de razón,* the people of reason, coming into the country of *los primitivos.* The horse, like the stone animals of Egypt, urged these memories upon me. And as I drew them up from some forgotten corner of my mind—huge horses carved in the white chalk downs of southern England by an Iron Age people; Spanish horses rearing and wheeling in fear before alligators in Florida—the images seemed tethered before me. With this sense of proportion, a memory of my own—the morning I almost lost my face to a horse's hoof—now had somewhere to fit.

30   I rose up and began to walk slowly around the horse again. I had taken the first long measure of it and was now looking for a way to depart, a new angle of light, a fading of the image itself before the rising sun, that would break its hold on me. As I circled, feeling both heady and serene at the encounter, I realized again how strangely vivid it was. It had been created on a barren bajada[4] between two arroyos, as nondescript a place as one could imagine. The only plant life here was a few wands of ocotillo cactus. The ground beneath my shoes was so hard it wouldn't take the

3. De Anza (1735–88), later governor of New Mexico, explored the route to California, founding San Francisco in 1775.

4. A broad slope of debris of rocks and gravel.

print of a heavy animal even after a rain. The only sounds I heard here were the voices of quail.

The archaeologist had been correct. For all its forcefulness, the horse is inconspicuous. If you don't care to see it you can walk right past it. That pleases him, I think. Unmarked on this bleak shoulder of the plain, the site signals to no one; so he wants no protective fences here, no informative plaque, to act as beacons. He would rather take a chance that no motorcyclist, no aimless wanderer with a flair for violence and a depth of ignorance, will ever find his way here.

The archaeologist had given me something before I left his office that now seemed peculiar—an aerial photograph of the horse. It is widely believed that an aerial view of an intaglio provides a fair and accurate depiction. It does not. In the photograph the horse looks somewhat crudely constructed; from the ground it appears far more deftly rendered. The photograph is of a single moment, and in that split second the horse seems vaguely impotent. I watched light pool in the intaglio at dawn; I imagine you could watch it withdraw at dusk and sense the same animation I did. In those prolonged moments its shape and so, too, its general character changed—noticeably. The living quality of the image, its immediacy to the eye, was brought out by the light-in-time, not, at least here, in the camera's frozen instant.

Intaglios, I thought, were never meant to be seen by gods in the sky above. They were meant to be seen by people on the ground, over a long period of shifting light. This could even be true of the huge figures on the Plain of Nazca in Peru, where people could walk for the length of a day beside them.[5] It is our own impatience that leads us to think otherwise.

This process of abstraction, almost unintentional, drew me gradually away from the horse. I came to a position of attention at the edge of the sphere of its influence. With a slight bow I paid my respects to the horse, its maker, and the history of us all, and departed.

3

A short distance away I stopped the car in the middle of the road to make a few notes. I could not write down what I was thinking when I was with the horse. It would have seemed disrespectful, and it would have required another kind of attention. So now I patiently drained my memory of the details it had fastened itself upon. The road I'd stopped on was adjacent to the All American Canal, the major source of water for the Imperial and Coachella valleys. The water flowed west placidly. 35

5. Gigantic lines from an unknown civilization are laid out geometrically on the thirty-seven-mile-long Plain of Nazca in southern Peru.

A disjointed flock of coots, small, dark birds with white bills, was paddling against the current, foraging in the rushes.

I was peripherally aware of the birds as I wrote, the only movement in the desert, and of a series of sounds from a village a half-mile away. The first sounds from this collection of ramshackle houses in a grove of cottonwoods were the distracted dawn voices of dogs. I heard them intermingled with the cries of a rooster. Later, the high-pitched voices of children calling out to each other came disembodied through the dry desert air. Now, a little after seven, I could hear someone practicing on the trumpet, the same rough phrases played over and over. I suddenly remembered how as children we had tried to get the rhythm of a galloping horse with hands against our thighs, or by fluttering our tongues against the roofs of our mouths.

After the trumpet, the impatient calls of adults summoning children. Sunday morning. Wood smoke hung like a lens in the trees. The first car starts—a cold eight-cylinder engine, of Chrysler extraction perhaps, goosed to life, then throttled back to murmur through dual mufflers, the obbligato music of a shade-tree mechanic. The rote bark of mongrel dogs at dawn, the jagged outcries of men and women, an engine coming to life. Like a thousand villages from West Virginia to Guadalajara.

I finished my notes—where was I going to find a description of the horses that came north with the conquistadors? Did their manes come forward prominently over the brow, like this one's, like the forelocks of Blackfeet and Assiniboin men in nineteenth-century paintings? I set the notes on the seat beside me.

The road followed the canal for a while and then arced north, toward Interstate 8. It was slow driving and I fell to thinking how the desert had changed since Anza had come through. New plants and animals— the MacDougall cottonwood, the English house sparrow, the chukar from India[6]—have about them now the air of the native born. Of the native species, some—no one knows how many—are extinct. The populations of many others, especially the animals, have been sharply reduced. The idea of a desert impoverished by agricultural poisons and varmint hunters, by off-road vehicles and military operations, did not seem as disturbing to me, however, as this other horror, now that I had been those hours with the horse. The vandals, the few who crowbar rock art off the desert's walls, who dig up graves, who punish the ground that holds intaglios, are people who devour history. Their self-centered scorn, their disrespect for ideas and images beyond their ken, create the awful atmosphere of loose ends in which totalitarianism thrives, in which the past is merely curious or wrong.

6. A gray-and-black partridge introduced into dry parts of the western United States from India.

I thought about the horse sitting out there on the unprotected plain.   40
I enumerated its qualities in my mind until a sense of its vulnerability
receded and it became an anchor for something else. I remembered that
history, a history like this one, which ran deeper than Mexico, deeper
than the Spanish, was a kind of medicine. It permitted the great breadth
of human expression to reverberate, and it did not urge you to locate
its apotheosis in the present.

Each of us, individuals and civilizations, has been held upside down
like Achilles in the River Styx.[7] The artist mixing his colors in the dim
light of Altamira;[8] an Egyptian ruler lying still now, wrapped in his
byssus, stored against time in a pyramid; the faded Dorset culture of the
Arctic;[9] the Hmong and Samburu and Walbiri of historic time;[1] the
modern nations. This great, imperfect stretch of human expression is the
clarification and encouragement, the urging and the reminder, we call
history. And it is inscribed everywhere in the face of the land, from the
mountain passes of the Himalayas to a nameless bajada in the California
desert.

Small birds rose up in the road ahead, startled, and flew off. I prayed
no infidel would ever find that horse.

7. Achilles' mother dipped him in the
River Styx, holding him upside down by
the heels, to make him invulnerable and
hence immortal.
8. A cave in northern Spain with Old Stone
Age drawings of animals.
·9. A culture in Greenland and the Canadian eastern Arctic that flourished between
approximately 800 B.C. and A.D. 1300; it is
not certain exactly when or why Dorset
culture disappeared, although the artifacts
that remain give an idea of its nature and
its daily life.
1. The Hmong, also called Miao or Meo,
are mountain-dwelling peoples of China
and Southeast Asia; the Samburu are a
tribe in Kenya; the Walbiri are aborigines
of the desert in central Australia.

Chief Seattle
ADDRESS

The Governor made a fine speech, but he was outranged and out-
classed that day. Chief Seattle, who answered on behalf of the Indians,
towered a foot above the Governor. He wore his blanket like the toga
of a Roman senator, and he did not have to strain his famous voice,

In 1854, Governor Isaac Stevens, Commissioner of Indian Affairs for the Washington
Territory, proffered a treaty to the Indians providing for the sale of two million acres of
their land to the federal government. This address is the reply of Chief Seattle of the
Duwampo tribe. The translator was Henry A. Smith.

which everyone agreed was audible and distinct at a distance of half a mile.

Seattle's oration was in Duwamish. Doctor Smith, who had learned the language, wrote it down; under the flowery garlands of his translation the speech rolls like an articulate iron engine, grim with meanings that outlasted his generation and may outlast all the generations of men. As the amiable follies of the white race become less amiable, the iron rumble of old Seattle's speech sounds louder and more ominous.

Standing in front of Doctor Maynard's office in the stumpy clearing, with his hand on the little Governor's head, the white invaders about him and his people before him, Chief Seattle said:

"Yonder sky that has wept tears of compassion upon my people for centuries untold, and which to us appears changeless and eternal, may change. Today is fair. Tomorrow may be overcast with clouds. My words are like the stars that never change. Whatever Seattle says the great chief at Washington can rely upon with as much certainty as he can upon the return of the sun or the seasons. The White Chief says that Big Chief at Washington sends us greetings of friendship and goodwill. That is kind of him for we know he has little need of our friendship in return. His people are many. They are like the grass that covers vast prairies. My people are few. They resemble the scattering trees of a storm-swept plain. The great, and—I presume—good, White Chief sends us word that he wishes to buy our lands but is willing to allow us enough to live comfortably. This indeed appears just, even generous, for the Red Man no longer has rights that he need respect, and the offer may be wise also, as we are no longer in need of an extensive country. . . . I will not dwell on, nor mourn over, our untimely decay, nor reproach our paleface brothers with hastening it, as we too may have been somewhat to blame.

"Youth is impulsive. When our young men grow angry at some real or imaginary wrong, and disfigure their faces with black paint, it denotes that their hearts are black, and then they are often cruel and relentless, and our old men and old women are unable to restrain them. Thus it has ever been. Thus it was when the white men first began to push our forefathers further westward. But let us hope that the hostilities between us may never return. We would have everything to lose and nothing to gain. Revenge by young men is considered gain, even at the cost of their own lives, but old men who stay at home in times of war, and mothers who have sons to lose, know better.

"Our good father at Washington—for I presume he is now our father as well as yours, since King George has moved his boundaries further north—our great good father, I say, sends us word that if we do as he desires he will protect us. His brave warriors will be to us a bristling wall of strength, and his wonderful ships of war will fill our harbors so that our ancient enemies far to the northward—the Hydas and Tsimpsians—will cease to frighten our women, children, and old men. Then in reality will he be our father and we his children. But can that ever be? Your God is not our God! Your God loves your people and hates mine. He folds his strong and protecting arms lovingly about the paleface and leads him by the hand as a father leads his infant son—but He has forsaken His red children—if they really are his. Our God, the Great Spirit, seems also to have forsaken us. Your God makes your people wax strong every day. Soon they will fill the land. Our people are ebbing away like a rapidly receding tide that will never return. The white man's God cannot love our people or He would protect them. They seem to be orphans who can look nowhere for help. How then can we be brothers? How can your God become our God and renew our prosperity and awaken in us dreams of returning greatness? If we have a common heavenly father He must be partial—for He came to his paleface children. We never saw Him. He gave you laws but He had no word for His red children whose teeming multitudes once filled this vast continent as stars fill the firmament. No; we are two distinct races with separate origins and separate destinies. There is little in common between us.

"To us the ashes of our ancestors are sacred and their resting place is hallowed ground. You wander far from the graves of your ancestors and seemingly without regret. Your religion was written upon tables of stone by the iron finger of your God so that you could not forget. The Red Man could never comprehend nor remember it. Our religion is the traditions of our ancestors—the dreams of our old men, given them in solemn hours of night by the Great Spirit; and the visions of our sachems; and it is written in the hearts of our people.

"Your dead cease to love you and the land of their nativity as soon as they pass the portals of the tomb and wander way beyond the stars. They are soon forgotten and never return. Our dead never forget the beautiful world that gave them being.

"Day and night cannot dwell together. The Red Man has ever fled the approach of the White Man, as the morning mist flees before the morning sun. However, your proposition seems fair and I think that my people will accept it and will retire to the reservation you offer them. Then we will dwell apart in peace, for the words of the Great White Chief seem to be the words of nature speaking to my people out of dense darkness.

"It matters little where we pass the remnant of our days. They will not be many. A few more moons; a few more winters—and not one of the descendants of the mighty hosts that once moved over this broad land or lived in happy homes, protected by the Great Spirit, will remain to mourn over the graves of a people once more powerful and hopeful than yours. But why should I mourn at the untimely fate of my people? Tribe follows tribe, and nation follows nation, like the waves of the sea. It is the order of nature, and regret is useless. Your time of decay may be distant, but it will surely come, for even the White Man whose God walked and talked with him as friend with friend, cannot be exempt from the common destiny. We may be brothers after all. We will see.

10   "We will ponder your proposition, and when we decide we will let you know. But should we accept it, I here and now make this condition that we will not be denied the privilege without molestation of visiting at any time the tombs of our ancestors, friends and children. Every part of this soil is sacred in the estimation of my people. Every hillside, every valley, every plain and grove, has been hallowed by some sad or happy event in days long vanished. . . . The very dust upon which you now stand responds more lovingly to their footsteps than to yours, because it is rich with the blood of our ancestors and our bare feet are conscious of the sympathetic touch. . . . Even the little children who lived here and rejoiced here for a brief season will love these somber solitudes and at eventide they greet shadowy returning spirits. And when the last Red Man shall have perished, and the memory of my tribe shall have become a myth among the White Men, these shores will swarm with the invisible dead of my tribe, and when your children's children think themselves alone in the field, the store, the shop, upon the highway, or in the silence of the pathless woods, they will not be alone. . . . At night when the streets of your cities and villages are silent and you think them deserted, they will throng with the returning hosts that once filled and still love this beautiful land. The White Man will never be alone.

"Let him be just and deal kindly with my people, for the dead are not powerless. Dead, did I say? There is no death, only a change of worlds."

Walt Whitman

DEATH OF ABRAHAM LINCOLN

I shall not easily forget the first time I ever saw Abraham Lincoln. It must have been about the 18th or 19th of February, 1861. It was rather a pleasant afternoon, in New York city, as he arrived there from the West, to remain a few hours, and then pass on to Washington, to prepare for his inauguration. I saw him in Broadway, near the site of the present Post-office. He came down, I think from Canal street, to stop

From *Specimen Days* (1882).

at the Astor House. The broad spaces, sidewalks, and streets in the neighborhood, and for some distance, were crowded with solid masses of people, many thousands. The omnibuses and other vehicles had all been turn'd off, leaving an unusual hush in that busy part of the city. Presently two or three shabby hack barouches made their way with some difficulty through the crowd, and drew up at the Astor House entrance. A tall figure stepp'd out of the centre of these barouches, paus'd leisurely on the sidewalk, look'd up at the granite walls and looming architecture of the grand old hotel—then, after a relieving stretch of arms and legs, turn'd round for over a minute to slowly and good-humoredly scan the appearance of the vast and silent crowds. There were no speeches—no compliments—no welcome—as far as I could hear, not a word said. Still much anxiety was conceal'd in the quiet. Cautious persons had fear'd some mark'd insult or indignity to the President-elect—for he possess'd no personal popularity at all in New York City, and very little political. But it was evidently tacitly agreed that if the few political supporters of Mr. Lincoln present would entirely abstain from any demonstration on their side, the immense majority, who were anything but supporters, would abstain on their sides also. The result was a sulky, unbroken silence, such as certainly never before characterized so great a New York crowd.

Almost in the same neighborhood I distinctly remember'd seeing Lafayette on his visit to America in 1825. I had also personally seen and heard, various years afterward, how Andrew Jackson, Clay, Webster, Hungarian Kossuth, Filibuster Walker, the Prince of Wales on his visit, and other *célèbres,* native and foreign, had been welcom'd there—all that indescribable human roar and magnetism, unlike any other sound in the universe—the glad exulting thunder-shouts of countless unloos'd throats of men! But on this occasion, not a voice—not a sound. From the top of an omnibus, (driven up one side, close by, and block'd by the curbstone and the crowds), I had, I say, a capital view of it all, and especially of Mr. Lincoln, his look and gait—his perfect composure and coolness—his unusual and uncouth height, his dress of complete black, stovepipe hat push'd back on the head, dark-brown complexion, seam'd and wrinkled yet canny-looking face, black, bushy head of hair, dispro-portionately long neck, and his hands held behind as he stood observing the people. He look'd with curiosity upon that immense sea of faces, and the sea of faces return'd the look with similar curiosity. In both there was a dash of comedy, almost farce, such as Shakspere puts in his blackest tragedies. The crowd that hemm'd around consisted I should think of thirty to forty thousand men, not a single one his personal friend—while I have no doubt, (so frenzied were the ferments of the time,) many an assassin's knife and pistol lurk'd in hip or breast-pocket there, ready, soon as break and riot came.

But no break or riot came. The tall figure gave another relieving stretch or two of arms and legs; then with moderate pace, and accompanied by a few unknown-looking persons, ascended the portico-steps of the Astor House, disappear'd through its broad entrance—and the dumb-show ended.

I saw Abraham Lincoln often the four years following that date. He changed rapidly and much during his Presidency—but this scene, and him in it, are indelibly stamp'd upon my recollection. As I sat on the top of my omnibus, and had a good view of him, the thought, dim and inchoate then, has since come out clear enough, that four sorts of genius, four mighty and primal hands, will be needed to the complete limning of this man's future portrait—the eyes and brains and finger-touch of Plutarch and Eschylus and Michel Angelo, assisted now by Rabelais.

5   And now—(Mr. Lincoln passing on from this scene to Washington, where he was inaugurated, amid armed cavalry, and sharpshooters at every point—the first instance of the kind in our history—and I hope it will be the last)—now the rapid succession of well-known events, (too well-known—I believe, these days, we almost hate to hear them mention'd)—the national flag fired on at Sumter—the uprising of the North, in paroxysms of astonishment and rage—the chaos of divided councils—the call for troops—the first Bull Run—the stunning cast-down, shock, and dismay of the North—and so in full flood the Secession war. Four years of lurid, bleeding, murky, murderous war. Who paint those years, with all their scenes?—the hard-fought engagements—the defeats, plans, failures—the gloomy hours, days, when our Nationality seem'd hung in pall of doubt, perhaps death—the Mephistophelean sneers of foreign lands and attachés—the dreaded Scylla of European interference, and the Charybdis of the tremendously dangerous latent strata of seccession sympathizers throughout the free States, (far more numerous than is supposed)—the long marches in summer—the hot sweat, and many a sunstroke, as on the rush to Gettysburg in '63—the night battles in the woods, as under Hooker at Chancellorsville—the camps in winter—the military prisons—the hospitals—(alas! alas! the hospitals.)

The Secession war? Nay, let me call it the Union war. Though whatever call'd, it is even yet too near us—too vast and too closely overshadowing—its branches unform'd yet, (but certain,) shooting too far into the future—and the most indicative and mightiest of them yet ungrown. A great literature will yet arise out of the era of those four years, those scenes—era compressing centuries of native passion, first-class pictures, tempests of life and death—an inexhaustible mine for the histories, drama, romance, and even philosophy, of peoples to come—indeed the verteber[1] of poetry and art, (of personal character too,) for

---

1. Vertebra.

all future America—far more grand, in my opinion, to the hands capable of it, than Homer's siege of Troy, or the French wars to Shakspere.

But I must leave these speculations, and come to the theme I have assign'd and limited myself to. Of the actual murder of President Lincoln, though so much has been written, probably the facts are yet very indefinite in most persons' minds. I read from my memoranda, written at the time, and revised frequently and finally since.

The day, April 14, 1865, seems to have been a pleasant one throughout the whole land—the moral atmosphere pleasant too—the long storm, so dark, so fratricidal, full of blood and doubt and gloom, over and ended at last by the sunrise of such an absolute National victory, and utter break-down of Secessionism—we almost doubted our own senses! Lee had capitulated beneath the apple-tree of Appomattox. The other armies, the flanges of the revolt, swiftly follow'd. And could it really be, then? Out of all the affairs of this world of woe and failure and disorder, was there really come the confirm'd, unerring sign of plan, like a shaft of pure light—of rightful rule—of God? So the day, as I say, was propitious. Early herbage, early flowers, were out. (I remember where I was stopping at the time, the season being advanced, there were many lilacs in full bloom. By one of those caprices that enter and give tinge to events without being at all a part of them, I find myself always reminded of the great tragedy of that day by the sight and odor of these blossoms.[2] It never fails.)

But I must not dwell on accessories. The deed hastens. The popular afternoon paper of Washington, the little *Evening Star*, has spatter'd all over its third page, divided among the advertisements in a sensational manner, in a hundred different places, *"The President and his Lady will be at the Theatre this evening. . . ."* (Lincoln was fond of the theatre. I have myself seen him there several times. I remember thinking how funny it was that he, in some respects the leading actor in the stormiest drama known to real history's stage through centuries, should sit there and be so completely interested and absorb'd in those human jackstraws, moving about with their silly little gestures, foreign spirit, and flatulent text.)

On this occasion the theatre was crowded, many ladies in rich and gay costumes, officers in their uniforms, many well-known citizens, young folks, the usual clusters of gas-lights, the usual magnetism of so many people, cheerful, with perfumes, music of violins and flutes—(and over all, and saturating all, that vast, vague wonder, *Victory,* the nation's victory, the triumph of the Union, filling the air, the thought, the sense, with exhilaration more than all music and perfumes.)

10

2. Cf. Whitman's elegy on Lincoln, "When Lilacs Last in the Dooryard Bloom'd" (1865–66).

The President came betimes, and, with his wife, witness'd the play from the large stage-boxes of the second tier, two thrown into one, and profusely drap'd with the national flag. The acts and scenes of the piece—one of those singularly written compositions which have at least the merit of giving entire relief to an audience engaged in mental action or business excitements and cares during the day, as it makes not the slightest call on either the moral, emotional, esthetic, or spiritual nature—a piece, (*Our American Cousin,*) in which, among other characters so call'd, a Yankee, certainly such a one as was never seen, or the least like it ever seen, in North America, is introduced in England, with a varied fol-de-rol of talk, plot, scenery, and such phantasmagoria as goes to make up a modern popular drama—had progress'd through perhaps a couple of its acts, when in the midst of this comedy, or non-such, or whatever it is to be call'd, and to offset it, or finish it out, as if in Nature's and the great Muse's mockery of those poor mimes, came interpolated that scene, not really or exactly to be described at all, (for on the many hundreds who were there it seems to this hour to have left a passing blur, a dream, a blotch)—and yet partially to be described as I now proceed to give it. There is a scene in the play representing a modern parlor, in which two unprecedented English ladies are inform'd by the impossible Yankee that he is not a man of fortune, and therefore undesirable for marriage-catching purposes; after which, the comments being finish'd, the dramatic trio make exit, leaving the stage clear for a moment. At this period came the murder of Abraham Lincoln. Great as all its manifold train, circling round it, and stretching into the future for many a century, in the politics, history, art &c., of the New World, in point of fact the main thing, the actual murder, transpired with the quiet and simplicity of any commonest occurrence—the bursting of a bud or pod in the growth of vegetation, for instance. Through the general hum following the stage pause, with the change of positions, came the muffled sound of a pistol-shot, which not one-hundredth part of the audience heard at the time—and yet a moment's hush—somehow, surely, a vague startled thrill—and then, through the ornamented, draperied, starr'd and striped space-way of the President's box, a sudden figure, a man, raises himself with hands and feet, stands a moment on the railing, leaps below to the stage, (a distance of perhaps fourteen or fifteen feet), falls out of position, catching his boot-heel in the copious drapery, (the American flag,) falls on one knee, quickly recovers himself, rises as if nothing had happen'd, (he really sprains his ankle, but unfelt then)— and so the figure, Booth, the murderer, dress'd in plain black broadcloth, bare-headed, with full, glossy, raven hair, and his eyes like some mad animal's flashing with light and resolution, yet with a certain strange calmness, holds aloft in one hand a large knife—walks along not much back from the footlights—turns fully toward the audience his face of statuesque beauty, lit by those basilisk eyes, flashing with desperation, perhaps insanity—launches out in a firm and steady voice the words *Sic semper tyrannis* [3]—and then walks with neither slow nor very rapid pace diagonally across to the back of the stage, and disappears. (Had not all this terrible scene—making the mimic ones preposterous—had it not all been rehears'd, in blank, by Booth, beforehand?)

A moment's hush—a scream—the cry of *"murder"*—Mrs. Lincoln leaning out of the box, with ashy cheeks and lips, with involuntary cry, pointing to the retreating figure, *"He has kill'd the President."* And still a moment's strange, incredulous suspense—and then the deluge! then that mixture of horror, noises, uncertainty—(the sound, somewhere back, of a horse's hoofs clattering with speed)—the people burst through chairs and railings, and break them up—there is inextricable confusion and terror—women faint—quite feeble persons fall, and are trampl'd on—many cries of agony are heard—the broad stage suddenly fills to suffocation with a dense and motley crowd, like some horrible carnival— the audience rush generally upon it, at least the strong men do—the actors and actresses are all there in their play-costumes and painted faces, with mortal fright showing through the rouge—the screams and calls, confused talk—redoubled, trebled—two or three manage to pass up water from the stage to the President's box—others try to clamber up—&c., &c.

In the midst of all this, the soldiers of the President's guard, with others, suddenly drawn to the scene, burst in—(some two hundred altogether)—they storm the house, through all the tiers, especially the upper ones, inflam'd with fury, literally charging the audience with fix'd bayonets, muskets, and pistols, shouting *"Clear out! clear out! you sons of — — —"*. . . . Such a wild scene, or a suggestion of it rather, inside the play-house that night.

Outside, too, in the atmosphere of shock and craze, crowds of people, fill'd with frenzy, ready to seize any outlet for it, come near committing murder several times on innocent individuals. One such case was especially exciting. The infuriated crowd, through some chance, got started against one man, either for words he utter'd, or perhaps without any cause at all, and were proceeding at once to actually hang him on a neighboring lamp-post, when he was rescued by a few heroic policemen, who placed him in their midst, and fought their way slowly and amid great peril toward the station-house. It was a fitting episode of the whole affair. The crowd rushing and eddying to and fro—the night, the yells, the pale faces, many frighten'd people trying in vain to extricate themselves—the attack'd man, not yet freed from the jaws of death, looking like a corpse—the silent, resolute, half-dozen policemen, with no weap-

---

3. "Thus always to tyrants."

ons but their little clubs, yet stern and steady through all those eddying swarms—made a fitting side-scene to the grand tragedy of the murder. They gain'd the station house with the protected man, whom they placed in security for the night, and discharged him in the morning.

15   And in the midst of that pandemonium, infuriated soldiers, the audience and the crowd, the stage, and all its actors and actresses, its paint-pots, spangles, and gas-lights—the life blood from those veins, the best and sweetest of the land, drips slowly down, and death's ooze already begins its little bubbles on the lips.

Thus the visible incidents and surroundings of Abraham Lincoln's murder, as they really occur'd. Thus ended the attempted secession of these States: thus the four years' war. But the main things come subtly and invisibly afterward, perhaps long afterward—neither military, political, nor (great as those are,) historical. I say, certain secondary and indirect results, out of the tragedy of this death, are, in my opinion, greatest. Not the event of the murder itself. Not that Mr. Lincoln strings the principal points and personages of the period, like beads, upon the single string of his career. Not that his idiosyncrasy, in its sudden appearance and disappearance, stamps this Republic with a stamp more mark'd and enduring than any yet given by any one man— (more even than Washington's;)—but, join'd with these, the immeasurable value and meaning of that whole tragedy lies, to me, in senses finally dearest to a nation, (and here all our own)—the imaginative and artistic senses—the literary and dramatic ones. Not in any common or low meaning of those terms, but a meaning precious to the race, and to every age. A long and varied series of contradictory events arrives at last at its highest poetic, single, central, pictorial *dénouement*. The whole involved, baffling, multiform whirl of the secession period comes to a head, and is gather'd in one brief flash of lightning-illumination—one simple, fierce deed. Its sharp culmination, and as it were solution, of so many bloody and angry problems, illustrates those climax-moments on the stage of universal Time, where the historic Muse at one entrance, and the tragic Muse at the other, suddenly ringing down the curtain, close an immense act in the long drama of creative thought, and give it radiation, tableau, stranger than fiction. Fit radiation—fit close! How the imagination—how the student loves these things! America, too, is to have them. For not in all great deaths, not far or near—not Caesar in the Roman senate-house, or Napoleon passing away in the wild night-storm at St. Helena—not Paleologus,[4] falling, desperately fighting, piled over dozens deep with Grecian corpses—not calm old Socrates, drinking the hemlock—outvies that terminus of the secession war, in one man's life, here in our midst, in our time—that seal of the emancipation of three million slaves—that parturition and delivery of

4. Emperor Constantine XI, who yielded Constantinople to the Turks in 1453.

our at last really free Republic, born again, henceforth to commence its career of genuine homogeneous Union, compact, consistent with itself.

Nor will ever future American Patriots and Unionists, indifferently over the whole land, or North or South, find a better moral to their lesson. The final use of the greatest men of a Nation is, after all, not with reference to their deeds in themselves, or their direct bearing on their times or lands. The final use of a heroic-eminent life—especially of a heroic-eminent death—is its indirect filtering into the nation and the race, and to give, often at many removes, but unerringly, age after age, color and fibre to the personalism of the youth and maturity of that age, and of mankind. Then, there is a cement to the whole people, subtler, more underlying, than any thing in written constitution, or courts or armies—namely, the cement of a death identified thoroughly with that people, at its head, and for its sake. Strange, (is it not?) that battles, martyrs, agonies, blood, even assassination, should so condense—perhaps only really, lastingly condense—a Nationality.

I repeat it—the grand deaths of the race—the dramatic deaths of every nationality—are its most important inheritance-value—in some respects beyond its literature and art—(as the hero is beyond his finest portrait, and the battle itself beyond its choicest song or epic.) Is not here indeed the point underlying all tragedy? the famous pieces of the Grecian masters—and all masters? Why, if the old Greeks had had this man, what trilogies of plays—what epics—would have been made out of him! How the rhapsodes would have recited him! How quickly that quaint tall form would have enter'd into the region where men vitalize gods, and gods divinify men! But Lincoln, his times, his death—great as any, any age—belong altogether to our own, and are autochthonic.[5] (Sometimes indeed I think our American days, our own stage—the actors we know and have shaken hands, or talk'd with—more fateful than any thing in Eschylus[6]—more heroic than the fighters around Troy—afford kings of men for our Democracy prouder than Agamemnon—models of character cute and hardy as Ulysses—deaths more pitiful than Priam's.)

When centuries hence, (as it must, in my opinion, be centuries hence before the life of these States, or of Democracy, can be really written and illustrated,) the leading historians and dramatists seek for some personage, some special event, incisive enough to mark with deepest cut, and mnemonize, this turbulent nineteenth century of ours, (not only these States, but all over the political and social world)—something, perhaps, to close that gorgeous procession of European feudalism, with all its pomp and caste-prejudices, (of whose long train we in America are

5. Aboriginal, indigenous.
6. Eschylus (i.e., Aeschylus): Greek tragic dramatist (525–456 B.C.) whose plays, like Homer's epics, dealt with such figures of the Trojan War as Agamemnon, leader of the Greek forces; Ulysses, whose return to Ithaca after the war took ten years; and Priam, slaughtered king of Troy.

yet so inextricably the heirs)—something to identify with terrible identification, by far the greatest revolutionary step in the history of the United States, (perhaps the greatest of the world, our century)—the absolute extirpation and erasure of slavery from the States—those historians will seek in vain for any point to serve more thoroughly their purpose, than Abraham Lincoln's death.

20   Dear to the Muse—thrice dear to Nationality—to the whole human race—precious to this Union—precious to Democracy—unspeakably and forever precious—their first great Martyr Chief.

THE READER

1. Whitman says that "four sorts of genius" would be needed to give a complete portrait of Lincoln. What does he mean by this? Look up more about each of the four people he mentions, and determine what each might contribute to a complete picture of Lincoln.
2. Whitman says that the murder of Lincoln "transpired with the quiet and simplicity of any commonest occurrence—the bursting of a bud or pod in the growth of vegetation, for instance." What meaning and effect does this metaphor convey?
3. At the end, Whitman speaks grandly of Lincoln's significance for far more than the citizens of the still United States. As he sees it, what do all these people have in common that would allow for this more-than-national significance?

THE WRITER

1. Whitman delivered this piece as a lecture. How might it have differed if he had composed it as an essay to be read rather than a lecture to be heard?
2. The events of the assassination lead Whitman to mention his perception of Lincoln's fondness for the theater. What does he do to make this particular observation serve a larger purpose?
3. How does Whitman convey the sense of horror and confusion in the scene when Lincoln is shot? Using some of Whitman's techniques, write an account of a similar scene which produces a strong emotional effect.
4. Using a dictionary if you like, explain the different meanings of the different names for the war. Be sure to consider our own name, which Whitman does not use—the Civil War. Does this difference about names imply a difference about attitudes toward the war? Toward Lincoln?
5. Using the details Whitman provides, write a movie or TV script for one of the scenes he describes. What things will the camera "see" and focus on?

Kildare Dobbs

GALLIPOLI

Most visitors to the First World War battlefields and cemeteries of
Gallipoli are Australians or New Zealanders who want to see the place
where their countrymen died in such numbers. And perhaps the Australian movie *Gallipoli* has given them the idea that this catastrophic
campaign in 1915 was entirely an ANZAC (Australia New Zealand
Army Corps) affair. But the spearhead of the operation was the British
29th Division, made up of regular army units, among them a number
of famous Irish regiments. It was because of one young officer in the 1st
Battalion, the Royal Dublin Fusiliers, that I came to Gallipoli that gray
morning in early spring.

My middle names, Robert and Eric, commemorate two uncles killed
in the First World War before I was born. Lieutenant Robert Bernard
of the Dublins was one of them. He fell on the second day of the assault
on the Gallipoli peninsula in one of its most desperate battles.

I could recall little of the facts when I arrived.

Next morning I visited the office of the Commonwealth War Graves
Commission, where a pleasant Turkish assistant had just arrived. Soft-
spoken, plump, of fiery complexion, he gave me a glass of tea and a stack
of tattered printed lists of the fallen—about a hundred thousand names.
I did not succeed in finding that of Robert Bernard. Nor could the
Englishman in charge help me when he arrived.

I found an agency called Troyanzac and asked the proprietor to   5
arrange a taxi to the Helles monument at the entrance to the Dardanelles on the Gallipoli peninsula. I would not need a guide. Two young
couples, Australian and New Zealander, were also taking a Gallipoli
tour, but they were going to Anzac cove, a different area from the one
I sought. I would have to go alone and it would cost about thirty
American dollars. Mr. Husseyin, the proprietor, made a little speech
before we set out. The British, he said, had undertaken the Gallipoli
campaign in 1915 in an attempt to force a passage through the Dardanelles, capture Constantinople and open a new front against the
Central Powers. British and Commonwealth troops had fought gallantly
for many months, but the fierce resistance of the Turks under Mustafa
Kemal had in the end defeated them. At least 36,000 men on each side
had been killed.

Mr. Husseyin, a small, tweedy gentleman with a fine mustache,

From *Anatolian Suite* (1989).

looked suitably melancholy as he said this. I noticed his gleaming shoes, perhaps a tribute to men who had died with their boots clean. "Their name," he added sombrely, "liveth for evermore." And I thought that was one of the lies of history, that the dead would be remembered, a lie to comfort the next-of-kin. I would be the first of Robbie Bernard's kin to come to this remote place.

After a pause Husseyin Bey told us that we would cross the Dardanelles in a private launch. We were to follow his assistant now to the wharf.

The launch turned out to be an ancient, private-enterprise ferry. The official one went to Eceabat. Ours crossed directly to Kilitbahir, a medieval Ottoman fortress built by Mehmet II, the conqueror of Constantinople. From the upper deck I could see a Turkish war memorial scarring a hillside opposite. Akin to those prehistoric images cut into the turf of the British downs, this was a white figure on a gray ground, a soldier with one arm thrown out toward a poem in Turkish. The words were translated in my guidebook, no doubt losing something in the process: "Stop O Passer By . . ." and then something to the effect that this soil was where the heart of a nation throbbed. The poet's unlucky name was Onan, though verse so publicly exposed on a hillside could hardly be called a solitary vice.

On the wharf my yellow taxi was waiting. The driver spoke a few words of English. He had carefully carpeted the floor of his car with pieces of clean cardboard, to protect it from muddy feet.

10   As we headed toward open sea along the Gallipoli shore I saw many ships passing through the Dardanelles, to and from Istanbul and the Black Sea. The sky was gray and overcast. My spirits were raised by the sight of a large school of dolphins leaping through the waves near the shore. I remembered Yeats's[1] line in the poem "Byzantium":

> That dolphin-torn, that gong-tormented sea.

Symbols of rebirth, I recalled, dolphins were among the earliest images in Christian art, ferrying spirits over death's river. Yeats had never been in these waters except in imagination. He got his gongs and dolphins from books. Yet, such is the power of genius, here they were in this haunted channel. On the far side, the land was flat along the Asian shore, easier country for an attacker to capture, reason enough why the strategic city of Troy, buried for centuries a few miles from the Hellespont, had fallen at least seven times. The Turks' German advisors had expected the British to make their assault over there; and in fact

1. William Butler Yeats (1865–1939), Irish poet and dramatist whose Irish nationalism was one of the central elements of his work.

a French contingent did attack Kumkale, as diversion from the main thrust, suffering heavy casualties before they withdrew.

Soon we turned inland where the ground was high. Orchards and broom were in blossom. There were olive groves and stands of pine and myrtle, and a few patches of green wheat or barley. This was April, the same month in which the campaign had begun. The grass was green, spring was reawakening the land with daisies, poppies and anemones. We passed shepherds with flocks of shivering sheep and goats, a village, two or three small cemeteries. At last we came to the Helles Memorial, at the south western point of the Gallipoli peninsula.

This rough stone obelisk, designed by Sir John Burnet, commemorates the Gallipoli campaign itself, together with the names of some twenty thousand dead whose bodies were never found and a roll call of the ships and regiments that took part. Among the latter I found the 6th Royal Irish Rifles, the 5th Connaught Rangers, the 6th Leinster Regiment, the 6th and 7th Royal Munster Fusiliers, the 6th and 7th Royal Dublin Fusiliers, the 5th and 6th Inniskilling Fusiliers, the 5th and 6th Royal Irish Fusiliers. Ireland itself had forgotten the military virtue of these soldiers and regiments, whose battle honors were part of the imperial myth. The official Irish myth had eclipsed them. Gallipoli, 1915, was overshadowed by the Easter Rising of 1916.[2]

A little to my right there was a lighthouse, slightly to the left the ruins of a redoubt where a couple of big guns had been blown off their mountings, and farther off along the beach the wreck of a fortress and a village, clustered around its minaret.

"What is the name of that village?" I asked the driver.   15

After some shouting and gesticulating I made myself understood. He told me the place was called Sedd-el-Bahr.

Vaguely I recalled having been told that that was the place where Uncle Robbie had been killed. Was there another cemetery down there? I asked. The driver led me to the edge of a bluff and pointed. There it was, below us, just inshore from the beach. This was V Beach Cemetery.

Telling the driver to wait for me, I walked down a rough, dirt road, passing a shepherd and some very dirty sheep on the way. *"Merhaba!"* I said. The man gave a grunt.

The cemetery was beautifully kept, with trim lawn and flowering judas trees. Some instinct led me straight to the marker. "Believed to be buried in this cemetery," I read. "Lieutenant Robert Bernard, Royal Dublin Fusiliers. 26 April 1915. Age 23. Dearly loved son of Most Rev. J. H. Bernard D.D. and Maud his wife."

2. Republican insurrection in Ireland against the British government there, which began on Easter Monday, April 24, 1916, in Dublin.

20   At his son's death, Dr. Bernard was bishop of Ossory, residing in
Kilkenny, thus Right Rev. Later that year he became archbishop of
Dublin, distinguished as Most Rev.

I stared for a while at the beach, at the cliffs on the left, the hill behind
it and the fortress on the right, fixing them in my memory. I took
photographs despite the uninteresting light.

So that now, weeks later, I am able to see in my mind the desperate
fighting and the horror that took place here in April 1915. I can do so
because Dr. Bernard in his grief brought all the weight of his meticulous
scholarship to bear on the problem of finding out how his son died. And
he used his access to the inner councils of empire to collect the evidence.
It is all here, in a thick album in my possession, along with every letter
Robbie Bernard wrote to his parents in the entire course of his short life.
Only three letters are withheld, Dr. Bernard notes, and those contain
nothing dishonorable.

Men in the front line, at the cutting edge of battle, are not aware of
the big picture. They know only what confronts them. They know their
own unit's objectives, and as much of the general plan as their commanders think they need to understand. Robbie Bernard did not live to
see the failure of the whole campaign, but the staff had not deceived
the fighting units about what faced them. Historians see that the whole
thing was a muddle, a project backed by young Winston Churchill (then
first lord of the admiralty) that was never adequately thought through
by the admiralty or the war office. The Royal Navy had failed to blast
a passage through the Dardanelles on March 18. All they had achieved,
apart from the loss of three capital ships, was to put the enemy on notice
that they would be attacked again, so that the Turks, guided by their
German advisers, were able to fortify the beaches and dig in.

The Royal Dublin Fusiliers were to be shock troops of the Covering
Force, that is, among the units detailed to capture the beaches at Cape
Helles and their defences, and hold them while the main body of the
army came ashore. The Dublins were an elite regiment of Irishmen. The
1st Battalion, until its disbandment in 1922, was one of the oldest units
in the British army, raised in 1646 and assigned to the East India
Company as the Madras Fusiliers; the 2nd Battalion, raised in 1662,
became the Bombay Fusiliers when the port was ceded to the Company.

25   "Clive[3] led you to Arcot and Plassey," King George V told them as
he received their colors at disbandment; "Eyre Coote to Wandewash;
Forde to Condore. Your history is the history of the early British dominance in India. . . ."

As the spearhead of the 29th Division the 1st Dublins and 1st Mun-

---

3. Robert Clive (1725–74), the celebrated British general and statesman whose victories
in India helped achieve Great Britain's control of India.

sters were to attack V Beach at dawn, April 25, after heavy bombardment of the defences by the big guns of the Royal Navy. They were to
seize the beach, capture and hold the hill behind it and the village of
Sedd-el-Bahr with its fortress. An Englishman who met them before the
attack described them as "typical paddies," long-service professionals for
whom war was a big joke. Certainly they were a cheerful lot, officers no
less than the men.

On April 12, Robbie Bernard wrote a note in pencil to his parents.
He was annoyed with the Senior Service (the navy): "They seem to have
done absolutely nothing and if they were not so infernally jealous of our
Service they would have called us in long ago and finished things off.
Now, when our adversaries have had time to get things together we
come in." Yet on April 22 he wrote in his diary—the last entry: "Hurrah!
Off today. At least we have left the harbour."

Robbie had joined the regiment in March 1912, after passing out of
Sandhurst Royal Military College. A photograph shows him in full dress
uniform, scarlet tunic with gold bullion epaulets, blue facings and
trews,[4] a magenta sash, sword and heavy bearskin hat. Six feet in height,
athletic in build, he had blue eyes, reddish mustache and hair parted in
the middle. His letters reveal an affectionate character, without intellectual leanings, perhaps somewhat oppressed by the desire to please his
scholarly father. His father's brief sketch supports this view.

"He was a very small baby," Dr. Bernard wrote, "but grew into a
powerfully built man of six feet high. He was a jolly, cheerful child—
much fonder of games than of books, as he continued to be throughout
his life. But he would work hard, as he proved when he read for the army.
He was always a good trier (as his teachers said) and 'did his best.' " One
of the boy's earliest letters begins, "Dear father How are you I doing my
best to please you."

After schooling at Arnold House in Wales (where Evelyn Waugh was   30
to teach) and at Marlborough, Robbie took three tries at the army
examination before he succeeded. He had served in Ludlow, Shropshire,
where he fell in love with a girl called Eva Macaulay; and then in India
and Egypt. His father hoped to get him transferred to the Indian army,
which offered better pay than the imperial service, and where his uncle
Colonel Herbert Bernard had kept a place for him in the 45th (Rat-
tray's) Sikhs, the illustrious regiment he commanded. These plans were
derailed by the world war, in which not only poor Robbie fell, but Uncle
Herbie as well, leading his men, Irish this time, at the Somme.

Back in England, in January 1915, he found that Eva was tired of
waiting for him. "She won't climb down and I won't so there's an end

---

4. From an old Gaelic word, *trews* means "trousers," more specifically close-fitting ones
still sometimes worn by some Scottish regiments.

of the matter," he told his parents, "—sickening I call it." He left her
his diaries, watches and a small camera. There is no picture of her in
the album.

Two friends of Robbie's survived to tell the story of the landing on
Sunday, April 25, at V Beach, described by Lieutenant Desmond O'-
Hara as "a small sandy bay about 200 yards long, very like the Silver Sand
at Wicklow; it was commanded by high ground all round, and into this
the ships poured such shellfire, that you would never believe a living
thing could survive it for a minute."

O'Hara's company was in a tramp steamer, the *River Clyde*, which
had had doors cut in her sides through which the troops could disembark
when she ran aground on the beach. The rest of the 1st Dublins, in pith
helmets and khaki, and loaded down with heavy packs, ammunition and
iron rations, were in cutters towed by pinnaces. Dawn was breaking as
the thunder of the naval guns suddenly stopped. There was an ominous
silence as the tows neared the beach. Some of the men must have hoped
that the bombardment had knocked out all resistance.

They were within a few yards of the shore when a hurricane of fire
from rifles, maxim-guns and pom-poms[5] tore into the crowded boats.
Within seconds about half of the first wave of Dublins was killed or
wounded. In a letter to his mother O'Hara wrote, "The whole of the
high ground round was honeycombed with the enemy's trenches, and
they waited till the boats which were crammed full got about five yards
from the shore when they let drive at them. . . . Numbers of men were
killed in the boats, others as they waded ashore, and more on the sand
before they could take cover behind a sandbank some twelve or fifteen
yards from the shore."

Today the sandbank is simply a low scarp marking the highest point
of spring tides.

Lieutenant-Colonel R. A. Rooth, commanding the battalion, was
killed as he stepped ashore with his men. His second-in-command,
Major E. Fetherstonhaugh, was mortally wounded before he could leave
his boat. Captain G. M. Dunlop "just managed to crawl into the sand
and died there. Poor young [Lieutenant R. V. C.] Corbet was horribly
wounded in the boat, and died an hour later, in awful pain, I am afraid.
[Captain and Adjutant W. F.] Higginson was able to get under cover,
but put his head up and was killed. . . . [Captain D. V. F.] Anderson
was shot through the body and killed almost instantly. "Second Lieutenants Maffet and Walters were wounded, as was Lieutenant Lanigan
O'Keeffe, a particular friend of Robbie's who had only just rejoined his
unit after recovering from serious wounds suffered in France.

---

5. Maxim-guns and pom-poms are names of quick-firing, water-cooled machine guns
invented by Sir Hiram S. Maxim.

O'Keeffe described his ordeal to his sister in a letter written from a hospital ship May 3, 1915: "Well, here I am on my back again, having been whacked in both legs almost as soon as the show started. . . . We had to land from open boats on the shore of a small bay under fierce fire from either side and in front.

"Tremendous numbers of our fellows were killed or wounded even before the boats grounded, and then it was another 50 yards or so to the shore.

"They got me twice between the boat and the shore, but I was able to struggle ashore and into a more or less safe spot where I remained all that day and night and half the next day before being taken off by the ambulance people. No fault of theirs at all as we didn't drive the enemy from the cliffs just over my head until the next morning, and they couldn't do much by day, as our friends have a happy knack of firing at stretcher parties. I don't feel strong enough to describe that 30 hours minutely just yet. Suffice it to say it was extremely unpleasant.

"Poor old Robbie Bernard was killed on the morning of the 2nd day (Monday), I believe and hope instantaneously. Poor old lad—there were few better in every way on this earth."

40

Somehow Robbie Bernard had survived the carnage of the first, terrible day. The men in the tramp steamer were so cut up as they tried to sally from the doors into boats that the attempt to land them was postponed till dark. O'Hara wrote: "I got our company ashore about 12 o'clock that night. Next morning we attacked a small village [Sedd-el-Bahr] to clear the snipers out of it. Bernard was killed by a hand grenade." But O'Hara had not witnessed this, and it was to be corrected by Sergeant-Major George Baker of Robbie's company, who saw what actually happened. In the horror of battle men were none too sure of what was going on.

Among the soldiers Dr. Bernard wrote to in his quest for information was a private in the Dublins who had been wounded. His letter gives some idea of the confusion: "1st-6-1915. Dear Sir in answer to your letter as regards the death of your son I could not tell you what he was doeing when he got shot for the last time I seen him was on the night of the 25 that is the day before he got shot but I think he was in charge of his company or the 26 as his capation got wounded the first day but on the 26 we made a bayonet charge on the front and great number of officers fell in the charge as they where all in front of there companies. Dear Sir I am very sorry I can not give you very much information about the brave officer. Pte. R. McGillin 1st Royal Dublin Fusiliers Clarendon House Keneton."

The bayonet charge referred to was carried out by the shattered remnant of the Dublins and the Munsters. They captured the hill inland from the beach, a desperate exploit that more than one commentator called glorious. "One of the most magnificent deeds of the whole war," said the French General Gouraud, who witnessed it. War correspondents took pride in it as a feat of "British" arms.

The Dublins lost twenty-one officers in the two days of fighting, and more than two-thirds of the rank and file. Sergeant-Major Baker reported the death of Robbie Bernard: "Lieutenant Bernard fell too bravely leading a charge through the village." That was how Baker recalled it from a military hospital on May 30. On June 3 he wrote in more detail: "Y company was ordered to go through the village of Seddul Bahr which was rather strongly held, but it had to be cleared and we were getting weaker and the men dubious of doing it, when Lieut. Bernard led the rush to their positions which cleared them out, but both he and Lieut. Andrews were shot dead at point-blank range by rifle fire, for he led the rush right up to the house without trying to take cover."

Dr. Bernard's inquiries would continue. On May 1 a blizzard of telegrams had descended on Dublin and the southern Irish counties, each with its shocking bulletin. One of them was delivered around nine A.M. to the Palace, Kilkenny, the gray mansion that stands next to St. Canice's Cathedral and its ancient round tower. Robbie's mother dashed off a note to her sister Alice: "I know how you will grieve with us when I tell you our darling Robbie was killed on the 25th—The cruel wire has just come, it seems quite unbearable, your loving Nan." Addressed to the Bishop of Ossory, the wire, scribbled in pencil, said, "Deeply regret to inform you that Lieutenant R. Bernard R Dublin Fusiliers is reported from Alexandria to have been killed in action 25th April Lord Kitchener expresses his sympathy. Secy War Office." It is noticeable that the date of death is wrong in this official notification, an error that was repeated in newspaper notices, and even in a regimental history.

Early in December 1915 Dr. Bernard was able to interview Baker in person about his son: "He saw him killed. It was quite instantaneous. Baker says that Robert was not in any way foolhardy. What gave rise to this suggestion probably was this: Robert, being in command, should (in theory) have kept behind and not exposed himself. But the thing was very dangerous, and the men were doubtful. If Robert had said 'Go on' and not 'Come on,' the men might have hesitated. He had crept up to the corner of the village street with his men, and was peering about with his revolver out. He saw a Turk and fired at him. But the Turk had already fired, and that was the end. No pain, for the Sergeant saw him hours afterwards and there were no signs of struggle or movement at all. He was hit twice—in the shoulder and behind the ear . . . I am thankful. It could not have been more merciful, or more gallant."

Lieutenant O'Hara, who was killed in August of that year, was awarded the Distinguished Service Order for his courage and competence. After Robbie's death the Turks were driven out of Sedd-el-Bahr, and in the afternoon the "Dubsters" carried their other objective, the hill behind the village. "When the Turks had been driven off," O'Hara wrote, "we entrenched for the night, and had a few hours rest next day. Then, on the following day, we had a tremendous battle, and gained four miles of land, and next morning attacked again with disastrous results. The French gave way on the right, and the whole division retired in disorder—a very little more, and it would have been a rout. It was an awful time, and at the end I was the only officer left in the regiment. The Turks made no attempt to follow up their advantage, and we were able to dig in. We remained there for two nights, and on the third the Turks advanced, 20,000 strong, and tried to break through the line. The fight went on from 10.30 at night till 5 o'c next morning—a desperate fight the whole time. My regiment alone got through 150,000 rounds, and they were only 360 strong. The Turks were simply driven on to the barbed wire in front of the trenches by the German officers, and shot down by the score. They must have lost thousands. The fighting is of the most desperate kind—very little quarter on either side. One wounded German officer was found just in front of our trenches when day broke, and was instantly riddled by bullets. The men are absolutely mad to get at them, as they mutilate our wounded when they catch them. For the first three nights I did not have a wink of sleep, and actually fell asleep once during the big night attack. We had no food for about 36 hours after landing, as we were fighting incessantly. There were only 1600 left in the brigade out of 4000. I have only had my boots off once since landing." It was now May 1.

Thanks to the tenacity of the Dublins and the Munsters, and of the Royal Lancashire Fusiliers on an adjacent beach, the invading army was ashore by the next day. The failure to break out of the beachhead was in the end fatal to the enterprise. Ignorance of topography, even of geography, seems to have been a failing of Churchill's. In the Second World War, he would speak of "the soft underbelly of Europe," referring to an area that presents an almost unbroken barrier of mountains.

According to a letter from Captain A. W. Molony, Bernard's company commander, who was wounded the first day, "The Turks fought extremely well, and hung on with the greatest tenacity. They made very clever use of their machine guns, which were very well concealed and did a lot of damage. Our losses were terribly heavy."

Eventual victory at Gallipoli gave the Turks, under Mustafa Kemal, a new confidence. For them it was the first of many ordeals on the blood-soaked road to a new nation. The virus of nationalism which had eaten away the Ottoman Empire was to create the Republic of Turkey, and to make Kemal the first of the twentieth-century dictators and the founding hero of his country.

50

And now, some seventy-three springs later, I see in my mind, not the quiet and remote beach where the Aegean enters the Dardanelles and the judas blossom trembles in the breeze, but the inferno of 1915 where Irishmen died gallantly in a vain cause with friends and countrymen.

Under Robbie Bernard's photo, his father has written: *"Qui ante diem periit sed miles, sed pro patria."*[6]

Gallipoli is today a national park, but Turkish country people live there. In spring and winter when visitors come there is a little money to be made selling souvenirs or driving taxis. One enterprising villager has even built a tiny motel on V Beach.

The day I went to Cape Helles I was the only visitor, not only at the British memorial but also at the colossal Turkish one, whose principal merit is sheer magnitude and visibility from far off. And the small group from down under at Anzac cove was there largely because it was the scene of a famous movie. The world of shadows is more real than that of memory or history.

55 And in the afternoon I would take a minibus to the site of ancient Troy, surely because it was the scene of a famous poem called the *Iliad.* [7]

6. "Who died before his time, but as a soldier, and for his country," part of a line taken from Sir Henry Newbolt (1862–1938), *The Island Race, Clifton Chapel.*

7. Greek epic poem (eighth century B.C.?) attributed to Homer that in twenty-four books of dactylic hexameter verse, details the events of the few days near the end of the Trojan War.

Hannah Arendt

DENMARK AND THE JEWS

At the Wannsee Conference,[1] Martin Luther, of the Foreign Office, warned of great difficulties in the Scandinavian countries, notably in Norway and Denmark. (Sweden was never occupied, and Finland, though in the war on the side of the Axis, was one country the Nazis never even approached on the Jewish question. This surprising exception of Finland, with some two thousand Jews, may have been due to Hitler's great esteem for the Finns, whom perhaps he did not want to subject to threats and humiliating blackmail.) Luther proposed postponing evacuations from Scandinavia for the time being, and as far as Denmark was concerned, this really went without saying, since the country re-

From *Eichmann in Jerusalem: A Report on the Banality of Evil* (1963). Originally appeared in *The New Yorker* in a slightly different form.

1. A meeting of German officials on "the Jewish question."

tained its independent government, and was respected as a neutral state, until the fall of 1943, although it, along with Norway, had been invaded by the German Army in April, 1940. There existed no Fascist or Nazi movement in Denmark worth mentioning, and therefore no collaborators. In Norway, however, the Germans had been able to find enthusiastic supporters; indeed, Vidkun Quisling, leader of the pro-Nazi and anti-Semitic Norwegian party, gave his name to what later became known as a "quisling government." The bulk of Norway's seventeen hundred Jews were stateless, refugees from Germany; they were seized and interned in a few lightning operations in October and November, 1942. When Eichmann's office ordered their deportation to Auschwitz, some of Quisling's own men resigned their government posts. This may not have come as a surprise to Mr. Luther and the Foreign Office, but what was much more serious, and certainly totally unexpected, was that Sweden immediately offered asylum, and even Swedish nationality, to all who were persecuted. Dr. Ernst von Weizsäcker, Undersecretary of State of the Foreign Office, who received the proposal, refused to discuss it, but the offer helped nevertheless. It is always relatively easy to get out of a country illegally, whereas it is nearly impossible to enter the place of refuge without permission and to dodge the immigration authorities. Hence, about nine hundred people, slightly more than half of the small Norwegian community, could be smuggled into Sweden.

It was in Denmark, however, that the Germans found out how fully justified the Foreign Office's apprehensions had been. The story of the Danish Jews is *sui generis,* and the behavior of the Danish people and their government was unique among all the countries in Europe— whether occupied, or a partner of the Axis, or neutral and truly independent. One is tempted to recommend the story as required reading in political science for all students who wish to learn something about the enormous power potential inherent in non-violent action and in resistance to an opponent possessing vastly superior means of violence. To be sure, a few other countries in Europe lacked proper "understanding of the Jewish question," and actually a majority of them were opposed to "radical" and "final" solutions. Like Denmark, Sweden, Italy, and Bulgaria proved to be nearly immune to anti-Semitism, but of the three that were in the German sphere of influence, only the Danes dared speak out on the subject to their German masters. Italy and Bulgaria sabotaged German orders and indulged in a complicated game of double-dealing and double-crossing, saving their Jews by a tour de force of sheer ingenuity, but they never contested the policy as such. That was totally different from what the Danes did. When the Germans approached them rather cautiously about introducing the yellow badge, they were simply told that the King would be the first to wear it, and the Danish government officials were careful to point out that anti-Jewish measures of any sort would cause their own immediate resignation. It was decisive in this whole matter that the Germans did not even succeed in introducing the vitally impor⁺ant distinction between native Danes of Jewish origin, of whom there were about sixty-four hundred, and the fourteen hundred German Jewish refugees who had found asylum in the country prior to the war and who now had been declared stateless by the German government. This refusal must have surprised the Germans no end, since it appeared so "illogical" for a government to protect people to whom it had categorically denied naturalization and even permission to work. (Legally, the prewar situation of refugees in Denmark was not unlike that in France, except that the general corruption in the Third Republic's civil services enabled a few of them to obtain naturalization papers, through bribes or "connections," and most refugees in France could work illegally, without a permit. But Denmark, like Switzerland, was no country *pour se débrouiller.* ²) The Danes, however, explained to the German officials that because the stateless refugees were no longer German citizens, the Nazis could not claim them without Danish assent. This was one of the few cases in which statelessness turned out to be an asset, although it was of course not statelessness per se that saved the Jews but, on the contrary, the fact that the Danish government had decided to protect them. Thus, none of the preparatory moves, so important for the bureaucracy of murder, could be carried out, and operations were postponed until the fall of 1943.

What happened then was truly amazing; compared with what took place in other European countries, everything went topsy-turvy. In August, 1943—after the German offensive in Russia had failed, the Afrika Korps had surrendered in Tunisia, and the Allies had invaded Italy—the Swedish government canceled its 1940 agreement with Germany which had permitted German troops the right to pass through the country. Thereupon, the Danish workers decided that they could help a bit in hurrying things up; riots broke out in Danish shipyards, where the dock workers refused to repair German ships and then went on strike. The German military commander proclaimed a state of emergency and imposed martial law, and Himmler thought this was the right moment to tackle the Jewish question, whose "solution" was long overdue. What he did not reckon with was that—quite apart from Danish resistance—the German officials who had been living in the country for years were no longer the same. Not only did General von Hannecken, the military commander, refuse to put troops at the disposal of the Reich plenipotentiary, Dr. Werner Best; the special S.S. units (*Einsatz-kommandos*) employed in Denmark very frequently objected to "the measures they were ordered to carry out by the central agencies"—according

2. For wangling—using bribery to circumvent bureaucratic regulations.

to Best's testimony of Nuremberg. And Best himself, an old Gestapo man and former legal adviser to Heydrich, author of a then famous book on the police, who had worked for the military government in Paris to the entire satisfaction of his superiors, could not longer be trusted, although it is doubtful that Berlin ever learned the extent of his unreliability. Still, it was clear from the beginning that things were not going well, and Eichmann's office sent one of its best men to Denmark—Rolf Günther, whom no one had ever accused of not possessing the required "ruthless toughness." Günther made no impression on his colleagues in Copenhagen, and now von Hannecken refused even to issue a decree requiring all Jews to report for work.

Best went to Berlin and obtained a promise that all Jews from Denmark would be sent to Theresienstadt[3] regardless of their category—a very important concession, from the Nazis' point of view. The night of October 1 was set for their seizure and immediate departure—ships were ready in the harbor—and since neither the Danes nor the Jews nor the German troops stationed in Denmark could be relied on to help, police units arrived from Germany for a door-to-door search. At the last moment, Best told them that they were not permitted to break into apartments, because the Danish police might then interfere, and they were not supposed to fight it out with the Danes. Hence they could seize only those Jews who voluntarily opened their doors. They found exactly 477 people, out of a total of more then 7,800, at home and willing to let them in. A few days before the date of doom, a German shipping agent, Georg F. Duckwitz, having probably been tipped off by Best himself, had revealed the whole plan to Danish government officials, who, in turn, had hurriedly informed the heads of the Jewish community. They, in marked contrast to Jewish leaders in other countries, had then communicated the news openly in the synagogues on the occasion of the New Year services. The Jews had just time enough to leave their apartments and go into hiding, which was very easy in Denmark, because, in the words of the judgment, "all sections of the Danish people, from the King down to simple citizens," stood ready to receive them.

They might have remained in hiding until the end of the war if the Danes had not been blessed with Sweden as a neighbor. It seemed reasonable to ship the Jews to Sweden, and this was done with the help of the Danish fishing fleet. The cost of transportation for people without means—about a hundred dollars per person—was paid largely by wealthy Danish citizens, and that was perhaps the most astounding feat of all, since this was a time when Jews were paying for their own deportation, when the rich among them were paying fortunes for exit permits (in Holland, Slovakia, and, later, in Hungary) either by bribing

5

---

3. A camp for certain classes of prisoners who were to receive special treatment.

the local authorities or by negotiating "legally" with the S.S., who accepted only hard currency and sold exit permits, in Holland, to the tune of five or ten thousand dollars per person. Even in places where Jews met with genuine sympathy and a sincere willingness to help, they had to pay for it, and the chances poor people had of escaping were nil.

It took the better part of October to ferry all the Jews across the five to fifteen miles of water that separates Denmark from Sweden. The Swedes received 5,919 refugees, of whom at least 1,000 were of German origin, 1,310 were half-Jews, and 686 were non-Jews married to Jews. (Almost half the Danish Jews seem to have remained in the country and survived the war in hiding.) The non-Danish Jews were better off than ever before, they all received permission to work. The few hundred Jews whom the German police had been able to arrest were shipped to Theresienstadt. They were old or poor people, who either had not received the news in time or had not been able to comprehend its meaning. In the ghetto, they enjoyed greater privileges than any other group because of the never-ending "fuss" made about them by Danish institutions and private persons. Forty-eight persons died, a figure that was not particularly high, in view of the average age of the group. When everything was over, it was the considered opinion of Eichmann that "for various reasons the action against the Jews in Denmark has been a failure," whereas the curious Dr. Best declared that "the objective of the operation was not to seize a great number of Jews but to clean Denmark of Jews, and this objective has now been achieved."

Politically and psychologically, the most interesting aspect of this incident is perhaps the role played by the German authorities in Denmark, their obvious sabotage of orders from Berlin. It is the only case we know of in which the Nazis met with *open* native resistance, and the result seems to have been that those exposed to it changed their minds. They themselves apparently no longer looked upon the extermination of a whole people as a matter of course. They had met resistance based on principle, and their "toughness" had melted like butter in the sun, they had even been able to show a few timid beginnings of genuine courage. That the ideal of "toughness," except, perhaps, for a few half-demented brutes, was nothing but a myth of self-deception, concealing a ruthless desire for conformity at any price, was clearly revealed at the Nuremberg Trials, where the defendants accused and betrayed each other and assured the world that they "had always been against it" or claimed, as Eichmann was to do, that their best qualities had been "abused" by their superiors. (In Jerusalem, he accused "those in power" of having abused his "obedience." "The subject of a good government is lucky, the subject of a bad government is unlucky. I had no luck.") The atmosphere had changed, and although most of them must have known that they were doomed, not a single one of them had the guts to defend the Nazi ideology. Werner Best claimed at Nuremberg that he had played a complicated double role and that it was thanks to him that the Danish officials had been warned of the impending catastrophe; documentary evidence showed, on the contrary, that he himself had proposed the Danish operation in Berlin, but he explained that this was all part of the game. He was extradited to Denmark and there condemned to death, but he appealed the sentence, with surprising results; because of "new evidence," his sentence was commuted to five years in prison, from which he was released soon afterward. He must have been able to prove to the satisfaction of the Danish court that he really had done his best.

Edward Jay Epstein

THE SELECTION OF REALITY

The daily agenda of reports produced by the media and called "news" is not the inevitable product of chance events; it is the result of decisions made within a news organization. Many of these decisions are made prior to the event itself. For example, deadlines determine in advance the point at which happenings will no longer be considered viable news. The crucial decisions as to definition of news—what will and what will not be covered—are made not by the journalist on the spot but by executives of the news organization. Such decisions include the selection, advancement, and deployment of reporters (and editors), the expenditure of time and resources for news gathering, and the allocation of space for the presentation of the news.

In making such basic decisions, news organizations must consider their own requirements for surviving in a competitive environment. A news organization obviously cannot spend more on news than it earns in revenues for a sustained period of time without going bankrupt. Similarly, a news organization cannot advance the career of journalists who undermine its basic values. Eventually, it may be assumed, the key decision-makers in an organization will identify with the needs of the organization and they will make decisions consistent with its overriding interests. These decisions will in turn shape its product—the news. If these premises are accepted, news must be viewed as the by-product of three factors: events, the journalist's perceptions of them, and the requisites of news organizations.

From *What's News: The Media in American Society* (1981), edited by Elie Abel.

THE ORGANIZATION CONTROLS THE NEWS

The most predictable part of this equation is the news organization which provides the machinery—including the journalist—for processing reality. News organizations perform in much the same way as does an intelligence service. They collect information concerning a set of targets, analyze the data according to some rules of relevance, and then present it to a particular audience. And, as is the case with intelligence services, news organizations generally operate in an environment of competition that requires secrecy (protection of sources), speed, and precision. Such an admittedly simplified model of the news business provides little room for idiosyncratic or biased reporting.

Consider, for example, the following operation of the Reuters news service.[1] Reporters in twenty key cities around the world are asked each day to call a list of food warehouses and request the temperature at a given hour. This list of warehouse temperatures is then compiled into a table by an editor and made available to a special audience of food shippers who pay for the service; presumably, the service is valuable because it allows them to consign their cargo to the warehouse with the lowest temperature. This news operation is not trivial. Along with similar data compilations on currencies and commodities, it now provides Reuters with more than half its income.

Nor is such "scorekeeping" journalism confined to Reuters. Most afternoon newspapers in the United States depend for their audience maintenance on such computer-delivered scores as the closing prices of stocks on Wall Street, racetrack results (which also determine illegal lottery payoffs in many cities), and weather services. "News," in such cases, is merely reporting the numerical score of some event of interest to a special audience.

In this form of reporting, there is no analysis or journalistic bias. The "targets" are selected by the news organization on the calculus of profitability; the space is allocated to the scores for which audiences will presumably pay the most money—or which will attract the greatest number of readers. Such reporting involves only the decision by the news organization as to the time and place of data collection; it involves no discretion on the part of the journalist.

The news organization may also preselect targets which are necessary to cover to maintain its credibility. The television networks, for example, have a policy of covering presidential announcements and press conferences. If the White House press officer announces there will be a presidential statement, television coverage is automatic. Neither the White House correspondent, the Washington bureau chief, nor the news

1. British cooperative news agency, one of the leading news wire services in the world, established in 1851 by Paul Julius Reuter.

producer has the discretion to decide *not* to record the president's word. Like warehouse temperature reporting, televising presidential press conferences is merely an exercise in data collection. While different news organizations maintain different policies on such mandatory coverage— and these, of course, change from time to time—a considerable portion of the events covered are preselected by the news organization.

Journalist Discretion

To be sure, not all coverage targets are chosen in advance by the news organization. Journalists, and especially the more established journalists in print media, have the discretion to select their own news targets. Even here, however, the organization generally imposes constraints. The journalist may be restricted to a "beat," or to a certain prescribed set of conceptual targets (such as arrests reported at police stations); he may be restricted geographically to targets in a certain bailiwick, or he may be restricted by deadlines to a certain time period. And ultimately, whatever the discretion a journalist may have in assigning himself targets of opportunity, his story must be approved at a higher level before it is printed or broadcast.

The perceptions and biases of journalists assume a far more influential role in the intermediary stage of the news process: the analysis of events. Journalistic analysis involves choosing and ordering the significant aspects of the data collected about an assigned target. Surrounding almost any happening is a confusing, confounding blur of information. The journalist—who seldom, if ever, witnesses the entire event—must reconstruct it from a welter of conflicting assertions, fragments of evidence, and possibly some eyewitness accounts. (The only events that journalists can count on witnessing in their entirety are those staged especially for the media, such as press conferences and interviews.) In sifting through the data surrounding an event, the journalist must have some overall view of reality to help him put together a coherent picture. Some statements might be emphasized and highlighted; others, played down or omitted entirely. Indeed, the journalist often organizes the material to coincide with what he believes is the true meaning of the happening. For instance, television reporters covering a political rally commonly find that from the same audience they can choose a picture either of a participant cheering with enthusiasm or of one yawning with boredom. If they select the former, they provide a visual cue indicating approval; if they select the latter, they signal disapproval.

It is precisely because journalists appear to have this power to reconstruct reality according to their preferences and biases that they have come under increasing attack by politicians and critics. In 1969, it will be recalled, then Vice-President Spiro T. Agnew directed his fury at

10

newsmen's "instant analysis" of presidential statements and suggested that this analysis distorted issues of vital importance to the nation.

Even in analyzing events, however, journalists must conform to the rules and values of the news organization that employs them. They can, of course, assert an idiosyncratic opinion or version of reality in an isolated news report; but if they are to succeed, the analysis they provide must, over the long run, reflect the organization's view of reality. During the Vietnam war in 1965, for example, Morley Safer narrated a dramatic television story that showed U.S. Marines using cigarette lighters to set fire to Vietnamese huts. This report was attacked by the Johnson administration as "unpatriotic" and defended by CBS executives as "the single most famous bit of reporting in South Vietnam." Despite the attention given to this incident, it turned out to be a decided aberration in the reporting of the war in Vietnam. An analysis of network news between 1962 and 1968 revealed few other examples of televised reports depicting the wanton destruction of civilian homes by American soldiers.[2] During this period American television journalists undoubtedly had countless opportunities to film burning huts and other atrocities; the fact that few such reports other than Safer's were ever broadcast indicates that the values of the news organizations themselves prevailed over the preferences of journalists to depict American soldiers as foes rather than friends of Vietnamese civilians. In this case, television networks had no doubt what the organizational interest was: the Johnson administration, on which television stations depended for license renewals, had declared the Safer report "unpatriotic."[3]

News Presentation

It is in the final stage of journalism—the presentation of news—that the news organization exerts ultimate control over the product. Before a news story is published or broadcast, it is read—or screened, edited, and okayed—by a responsible executive of the news organization. Until relatively recently, most newspapers had rewrite desks which actually wrote some stories at the central office; reporters telephoned in facts and editors rewrote them into stories. This system permitted centralized control of news writing. As reporters increasingly tended to write their own stories in the field, it became more difficult to enforce the organizational rules. Editors had to gradually inculcate values through conferences, reediting and "spiking" stories that failed to fit the mold. The introduction of word processors and electronic editing of news will again

2. The analysis was by Lawrence Litchy of the University of Wisconsin. Quoted in Edward Jay Epstein, *Between Fact and Fiction* (New York: Vintage Press, 1975), 214

[Epstein's note].

3. Epstein, *Between Fact and Fiction*, 214 [Epstein's note].

facilitate centralized editing by giving the organization's editors instant access to the reporter's story, previous drafts, and even research.

On television, the presentation process provides the organization with even tighter control over the news. Most reports are filmed days or hours in advance and sent to an editing room in the central office. Producers thus have the opportunity to review the story, and to instruct the editors and reporters how to construct, "play," and narrate it. And if the editing fails to conform to organizational values, the producer can kill the story with ease. Under these circumstances, there is little opportunity for a report to be aired that contradicts a value of the news organization.

There is a legitimate concern with bias in news reporting. Unfortunately, critical audiences tend to assume that the bias they detect is the personal bias of the reporter whom they see on television or whose by-line is at the top of the article. This reduces the issue to one of personal fairness (or ignorance), and the remedy most often suggested is to replace or educate the newsman. This focus on personal bias tends to distract attention from the far more important issue of organizational bias. Indeed, if the organization is "tilted" in its preferences in one direction, news will tend to be distorted regardless of the fairness—or unfairness—of the individual newsman. Just as a roulette wheel mounted on a tilted table tends to favor some numbers over other numbers no matter how fair the croupier might be,[4] a news organization that is tilted in a certain direction because of the way it is structured will also tend to favor certain types of stories over others. When confronted with such a biased wheel, it would obviously be unprofitable to attempt to explain its outcomes by studying the biases of the croupier. To understand the criteria by which the media decide what is news, it is necessary first to describe the interests and values of the news organizations.

PROCESSING NETWORK NEWS

Television news provides perhaps the clearest case of the process by which reality is systematically reconstructed by news organizations. To begin with, network news organizations have, unlike some newspapers and magazines, absolute control over their product. Av Westin, vice-president of ABC News, described the process of control candidly in a memorandum:

> The senior producers decide if the story has been adequately covered and they also estimate how long the report should run. In most cases, corre-

4. Roulette (from French, "small wheel"), gambling game in which players bet on which numbered slot of a revolving wheel a small plastic or ivory ball, spun in the opposite direction, will come to rest within. The croupier calls for players to make their bets and spins the wheel and ball.

15

spondents deliberately overwrite their scripts giving the producers at home the option of editing it down: selecting which portions of the interviews are to be used and which are to be discarded. . . . In some cases, the senior producer "salvages" a report by assigning the correspondent to redo his narration or by sending a cameraman to refilm a sequence. [5]

Under such a regime, a correspondent has little opportunity to insert in a news story personal values that run counter to the network's objectives. Nor does the description in the Westin memorandum quoted above apply only to ABC. During the year I spent observing NBC's and CBS's news operations, I saw even more rigorous controls maintained on news stories—including constant review by network executives.

In controlling the news product, the network organizations attempt to satisfy certain basic requirements that will allow them to continue as viable businesses. They must maintain a national audience for their advertisers, a need which, in turn, requires that the news programs be accepted by the affiliated (but independently owned) stations around the country. They must satisfy the ground rules laid down by the Federal Communications Commission (FCC), which licenses and monitors television stations. They also must maintain credibility as news media. And they must conform to budgetary and time restrictions to maintain profitability.

The Pressure of Time

Out of these basic requisites flow the rules and logic that shape network news. The most obvious constraint is time. The networks allocate only thirty minutes each night for their network news programs. From this time budget, approximately seven minutes must be deducted for commercials and non-news items. This leaves only twenty-three minutes for the presentation of between five to eight filmed news stories and the narration of other news events. Confronted with this reality, the producers of network news programs have no choice but to limit most of the news stories to a duration of two to four minutes. This enforced brevity leaves little room for presenting complex explanations or multi-faceted arguments. In practical terms, two to four minutes is not sufficient for providing the historical context or detailed geographic situations of most events. To make news stories understandable to a national audience in this brief slice of time, producers find that they have to be reported almost entirely in the present/future tense. The focus is on what is happening, not why it is happening or what the root causes are. This time requisite ineluctably leads to a picture of society as unstable. If great events happen without cause or historic context, then it appears—at least, to constant viewers of network news—that any institu-

5. Epstein, *Between Fact and Fiction,* 200 [Epstein's note].

tion is capable of foundering, collapsing, or being overthrown without evident cause.

The Audience and the Advertiser

A second requisite that shapes television news is audience maintenance. It is assumed by network executives that if the stories on a news program are unclear, confusing, or visually uninteresting, a portion of the audience will switch the channel to another network. Such a loss of audience would not only lessen the advertising revenues from the news program, it would—even more important—lessen the revenues from all the network programs that follow, since the news program is regarded as a "lead-in" for the network's evening of entertainment programs. Network executives therefore insist that news stories have both visual interest and visual clarity. In attempting to satisfy this requisite, news producers have come up with a common formula for audience maintenance.

The first assumption made by news executives and producers is that viewers' interest is most likely to be maintained through easily recognizable and palpable images; conversely, it is most likely to be distracted by unfamiliar or confusing images. This has special force in the case of dinnertime news when, according to studies, the audience has fewer years of formal education than the population at large—and when a large proportion of the viewers are children. In practice, therefore, cameramen, correspondents, and editors are instructed to seek and select pictures that have an almost universal meaning. Stories thus tend to fit into a limited repertory of images, which explains why so often shabbily dressed children stand for poverty, why fire—symbolically— stands for destruction, and so forth. Since television is regarded as a medium for the "transmission of experience" rather than for "information," complex issues are represented in terms of human experience; inflation, for example, is pictured as a man unable to afford dinner in a restaurant. The repertory, of course, changes. But at any given time, images—especially emotional ones, which are presumed to have the broadest possible recognition—are used to illustrate news events.

A second assumption in this logic of audience maintenance is that scenes of potential conflict are more interesting to the audience than scenes of placidity. Virtually all executives and producers share this view. Network news thus seeks situations in which there is a high potential for violence but a low potential for audience confusion. News events showing a violent confrontation between two easily recognizable sides in conflict—for example, blacks versus whites, uniformed police versus demonstrators, or military versus civilians—are preferable to those in which the issues are less easily identifiable. Even when the conflict

20

involves confusing elements, however, it usually can be reconstructed in the form of a two-sided conflict. Network news therefore tends to present the news in terms of highly dramatic conflicts between clearly defined sides.

A third, closely related, assumption is that the viewers' span of attention—which is presumed to be limited—is prolonged by action or by subjects in motion, and is sharply reduced by static subjects such as "talking heads." As has been previously discussed, the high value placed on action footage by executives leads to a three-step distillation of news happenings by correspondents, cameramen, and editors, all of whom seek the moment of highest action. Through this process, the action in a news event, which in fact may account for only a fraction of the time, is concentrated and becomes the central feature of the happening. This helps to explain why news on television tends willy-nilly to focus on activity.

A fourth assumption made by news producers is that stories are more likely to hold viewers' attention if they are cast in the form of the fictive story, with a discernible beginning, middle, and end. One NBC vice-president suggested to news producers that all stories should have rising action, a climax, then a falling action, and a seeming resolution. According to analyses done by NBC's audience research experts,[6] this form would "lock" the audience into the news story. Since the film is generally reedited by the producers, it is relatively simple to cast most happenings in this fictive form. The net effect, however, is that reality is reconstructed into a series of events that never actually happened in the form in which the audience witnesses them. Events do not necessarily begin, build, and resolve themselves in terms of the visual data that are available to a television news team. Yet all the behind-the-scenes oscillations, twists, and contingencies of reality are neatly ironed out.

Networks and the Local Stations

Another basic requisite flows from the demand of affiliated stations that network news be differentiated from their own local news programs. It must appear to be national news. The problem is, of course, that all news is local in the sense that it occurs in some locality. Network producers resolve this tension by combining a series of local reports into a single national story. For example, the opening of a new subway line in Washington, D.C., may be considered a local story; it can be converted, however, into a national story by commissioning and fusing stories about subways in two or three other cities and then subsuming them all under a nationwide theme such as "Can the Cities Survive?"

6. See Edward Jay Epstein, *News from Nowhere* (New York: Random House, 1973), 263 [Epstein's note].

This process of nationalizing the news yields a constant agenda of national crises in place of local happenings.

Finally, governmental regulation of television imposes another basic requisite on producers: they must appear to be fair on controversial issues by presenting opposing views. This requisite is satisfied by soliciting views from spokesmen of two opposing sides in a dispute—and then editing these conflicting views into a "dialogue." To avoid obvious disparities, the producers usually seek the most articulate spokesman for each side. Not only does this treatment tend to reduce complicated issues to a mere debate, point/counterpoint style, but it also gives presumptive legitimacy to both sides.

MEDIA RESTRICTIONS AND REALITY

Organizational requisites cannot by any means explain all the outputs of television news. The personal quirks of producers, editors, and reporters contribute to news programs. There are also indisputable fashions and trends that change the level of consciousness of news reporting. The organizational requisites do explain, however, many of the built-in tilts that influence television news.   25

Print media have a different set of organizational requisities. Most afternoon newspapers, for example, face the problem of delivery: the news must be reported, written, printed, and delivered to newsstands spread over a metropolitan area before commuters have returned home from their jobs. They also must find news that has occurred after the deadlines of the morning newspapers. This severe restriction on time, coupled with union regulations that restrict periods in which the paper can be printed, have led the afternoon newspapers to focus their coverage on sports, horse racing, and stock markets. Morning newspapers, news magazines, and monthly magazines face different sets of organizational problems.

One question finally must be asked: Given these constraints, do the media present a picture of reality upon which rational men may make decisions? In spending over a year watching the three television networks collect, analyze, and present data in the form of news stories, I concluded that these pictures of reality were systematically distorted by organizational requirements. Dealing with such distortions involves the same problem as dealing with systematic distortions in a map. No map presents a perfect picture of reality. However, if one understands that such areas as Australia and Greenland are reduced in size, it is feasible to use a map to understand the geography of the world. Similarly, news itself requires some adjustments to compensate for systematic distortions.

If news media clearly and honestly stated the constraints and limits under which they operate, the adjustment would be far easier to make. Unfortunately, they tend to hide rather than to explain these constraints. News magazines, for example, print a false publishing date on each issue (usually a week after publication). This deception makes it difficult for the reader to ascertain the point when news had to be cut off because of the deadline. The value of news to the public would be greatly enhanced if news organizations revealed, rather than obscured, the methods by which they select and process reality.

Frances FitzGerald

REWRITING AMERICAN HISTORY

Those of us who grew up in the fifties believed in the permanence of our American-history textbooks. To us as children, those texts were the truth of things: they were American history. It was not just that we read them before we understood that not everything that is printed is the truth, or the whole truth. It was that they, much more than other books, had the demeanor and trappings of authority. They were weighty volumes. They spoke in measured cadences: imperturbable, humorless, and as distant as Chinese emperors. Our teachers treated them with respect, and we paid them abject homage by memorizing a chapter a week. But now the textbook histories have changed, some of them to such an extent that an adult would find them unrecognizable.

One current junior-high-school American history begins with a story about a Negro cowboy called George McJunkin. It appears that when McJunkin was riding down a lonely trail in New Mexico one cold spring morning in 1925 he discovered a mound containing bones and stone implements, which scientists later proved belonged to an Indian civilization ten thousand years old. The book goes on to say that scientists now believe there were people in the Americas at least twenty thousand years ago. It discusses the Aztec, Mayan, and Incan civilizations and the meaning of the word "culture" before introducing the European explorers.

Another history text—this one for the fifth grade—begins with the story of how Henry B. Gonzalez, who is a member of Congress from Texas, learned about his own nationality. When he was ten years old, his teacher told him he was an American because he was born in the United States. His grandmother, however, said, "The cat was born in

From *America Revised: History Schoolbooks in the Twentieth Century* (1979). Originally appeared as Part I of "Rewriting American History," in *The New Yorker* (Feb. 26, 1979).

the oven. Does that make him bread?" After reporting that Mr. Gonzalez eventually went to college and law school, the book explains that "the melting pot idea hasn't worked out as some thought it would," and that now "some people say that the people of the United States are more like a salad bowl than a melting pot."

Poor Columbus! He is a minor character now, a walk-on in the middle of American history. Even those books that have not replaced his picture with a Mayan temple or an Iroquois mask do not credit him with discovering America—even for the Europeans. The Vikings, they say, preceded him to the New World, and after that the Europeans, having lost or forgotten their maps, simply neglected to cross the ocean again for five hundred years. Columbus is far from being the only personage to have suffered from time and revision. Captain John Smith, Daniel Boone, and Wild Bill Hickok—the great self-promoters of American history—have all but disappeared, taking with them a good deal of the romance of the American frontier. General Custer has given way to Chief Crazy Horse; General Eisenhower no longer liberates Europe single-handed; and, indeed, most generals, even to Washington and Lee, have faded away, as old soldiers do, giving place to social reformers such as William Lloyd Garrison and Jacob Riis. A number of black Americans have risen to prominence: not only George Washington Carver but Frederick Douglass and Martin Luther King, Jr. W. E. B. Du Bois now invariably accompanies Booker T. Washington. In addition, there is a mystery man called Crispus Attucks, a fugitive slave about whom nothing seems to be known for certain except that he was a victim of the Boston Massacre and thus became one of the first casualties of the American Revolution. Thaddeus Stevens has been reconstructed—his character changed, as it were, from black to white, from cruel and vindictive to persistent and sincere. As for Teddy Roosevelt, he now champions the issue of conservation instead of charging up San Juan Hill. No single President really stands out as a hero, but all Presidents— except certain unmentionables in the second half of the nineteenth century—seem to have done as well as could be expected, given difficult circumstances.

Of course, when one thinks about it, it is hardly surprising that modern scholarship and modern perspectives have found their way into children's books. Yet the changes remain shocking. Those who in the sixties complained of the bland optimism, the chauvinism, and the materialism of their old civics text did so in the belief that, for all their protests, the texts would never change. The thought must have had something reassuring about it, for that generation never noticed when its complaints began to take effect and the songs about radioactive rainfall and houses made of ticky-tacky began to appear in the textbooks. But this is what happened.

The history texts now hint at a certain level of unpleasantness in American history. Several books, for instance, tell the story of Ishi, the last "wild" Indian in the continental United States, who, captured in 1911 after the massacre of his tribe, spent the final four and a half years of his life in the University of California's museum of anthropology, in San Francisco. At least three books show the same stunning picture of the breaker boys, the child coal miners of Pennsylvania—ancient children with deformed bodies and blackened faces who stare stupidly out from the entrance to a mine. One book quotes a soldier on the use of torture in the American campaign to pacify the Philippines at the beginning of the century. A number of books say that during the American Revolution the patriots tarred and feathered those who did not support them, and drove many of the loyalists from the country. Almost all the present-day history books note that the United States interned Japanese-Americans in detention camps during the Second World War.

Ideologically speaking, the histories of the fifties were implacable, seamless. Inside their covers, America was perfect: the greatest nation in the world, and the embodiment of democracy, freedom, and technological progress. For them, the country never changed in any important way: its values and its political institutions remained constant from the time of the American Revolution. To my generation—the children of the fifties—these texts appeared permanent just because they were so self-contained. Their orthodoxy, it seemed, left no handholds for attack, no lodging for decay. Who, after all, would dispute the wonders of technology or the superiority of the English colonists over the Spanish? Who would find fault with the pastorale of the West or the Old South? Who would question the anti-Communist crusade? There was, it seemed, no point in comparing these visions with reality, since they were the public truth and were thus quite irrelevant to what existed and to what anyone privately believed. They were—or so it seemed—the permanent expression of mass culture in America.

But now the texts have changed, and with them the country that American children are growing up into. The society that was once uniform is now a patchwork of rich and poor, old and young, men and women, blacks, whites, Hispanics, and Indians. The system that ran so smoothly by means of the Constitution under the guidance of benevolent conductor Presidents is now a rattletrap affair. The past is no highway to the present; it is a collection of issues and events that do not fit together and that lead in no single direction. The word "progress" has been replaced by the word "change": children, the modern texts insist, should learn history so that they can adapt to the rapid changes taking place around them. History is proceeding in spite of us. The present, which was once portrayed in the concluding chapters as a peaceful haven of scientific advances and Presidential inaugurations, is now a tangle of problems: race problems, urban problems, foreign-policy problems, problems of pollution, poverty, energy depletion, youthful rebellion, assassination, and drugs. Some books illustrate these problems dramatically. One, for instance, contains a picture of a doll half buried in a mass of untreated sewage; the caption reads, "Are we in danger of being overwhelmed by the products of our society and wastage created by their production? Would you agree with this photographer's interpretation?" Two books show the same picture of an old black woman sitting in a straight chair in a dingy room, her hands folded in graceful resignation; the surrounding text discusses the problems faced by the urban poor and by the aged who depend on Social Security. Other books present current problems less starkly. One of the texts concludes sagely:

> Problems are part of life. Nations face them, just as people face them, and try to solve them. And today's Americans have one great advantage over past generations. Never before have Americans been so well equipped to solve their problems. They have today the means to conquer poverty, disease, and ignorance. The technetronic age has put that power into their hands.

Such passages have a familiar ring. Amid all the problems, the deus ex machina[1] of science still dodders around in the gloaming of pious hope.

Even more surprising than the emergence of problems is the discovery that the great unity of the texts has broken. Whereas in the fifties all texts represented the same political view, current texts follow no pattern of orthodoxy. Some books, for instance, portray civil-rights legislation as a series of actions taken by a wise, paternal government; others convey some suggestion of the social upheaval involved and make mention of such people as Stokely Carmichael and Malcolm X.[2] In some books, the Cold War has ended; in others, it continues, with Communism threatening the free nations of the earth.

The political diversity in the books is matched by a diversity of pedagogical approach. In addition to the traditional narrative histories, with their endless streams of facts, there are so-called "discovery," or "inquiry," texts, which deal with a limited number of specific issues in American history. These texts do not pretend to cover the past; they focus on particular topics, such as "stratification in Colonial society" or "slavery and the American Revolution," and illustrate them with documents from primary and secondary sources. The chapters in these books amount to something like case studies, in that they include testimony from people with different perspectives or conflicting views on a single subject. In addition, the chapters provide background information, ex-

1. God from a machine. A reference to early plays in which a god, lowered to the stage by mechanical means, solved the drama's problems; thus, an artificial solution to a difficulty.

2. Radical black leaders of the 1960s.

planatory notes, and a series of questions for the student. The questions are the heart of the matter, for when they are carefully selected they force students to think much as historians think: to define the point of view of the speaker, analyze the ideas presented, question the relationship between events, and so on. One text, for example, quotes Washington, Jefferson, and John Adams on the question of foreign alliances and then asks, "What did John Adams assume that the international situation would be after the American Revolution? What did Washington's attitude toward the French alliance seem to be? How do you account for his attitude?" Finally, it asks, "Should a nation adopt a policy toward alliances and cling to it consistently, or should it vary its policies toward other countries as circumstances change?" In these books, history is clearly not a list of agreed-upon facts or a sermon on politics but a babble of voices and a welter of events which must be ordered by the historian.

In matters of pedagogy, as in matters of politics, there are not two sharply differentiated categories of books; rather, there is a spectrum. Politically, the books run from moderate left to moderate right; pedagogically, they run from the traditional history sermons, through a middle ground of narrative texts with inquiry-style questions and of inquiry texts with long stretches of narrative, to the most rigorous of case-study books. What is common to the current texts—and makes all of them different from those of the fifties—is their engagement with the social sciences. In eighth-grade histories, the "concepts" of social sciences make fleeting appearances. But these "concepts" are the very foundation stones of various elementary-school social-studies series. The 1970 Harcourt Brace Jovanovich[3] series, for example, boasts in its preface of "a horizontal base or ordering of conceptual schemes" to match its "vertical arm of behavioral themes." What this means is not entirely clear, but the books do proceed from easy questions to hard ones, such as—in the sixth-grade book—"How was interaction between merchants and citizens different in the Athenian and Spartan social systems?" Virtually all the American-history texts for older children include discussions of "role," "status," and "culture." Some of them stage debates between eminent social scientists in roped-off sections of the text; some include essays on economics or sociology; some contain pictures and short biographies of social scientists of both sexes and of diverse races. Many books seem to accord social scientists a higher status than American Presidents.

Quite as striking as these political and pedagogical alterations is the change in the physical appearance of the texts. The schoolbooks of the fifties showed some effort in the matter of design: they had maps, charts, cartoons, photographs, and an occasional four-color picture to break up the columns of print. But beside the current texts they look as naïve as

3. Major textbook publisher.

Soviet fashion magazines. The print in the fifties books is heavy and far too black, the colors muddy. The photographs are conventional news shots—portraits of Presidents in three-quarters profile, posed "action" shots of soldiers. The other illustrations tend to be Socialist-realist-style[4] drawings (there are a lot of hefty farmers with hoes in the Colonial-period chapters) or incredibly vulgar made-for-children paintings of patriotic events. One painting shows Columbus standing in full court dress on a beach in the New World from a perspective that could have belonged only to the Arawaks.[5] By contrast, the current texts are paragons of sophisticated modern design. They look not like *People* or *Family Circle* but, rather, like *Architectural Digest* or *Vogue.* * * * The amount of space given to illustrations is far greater than it was in the fifties; in fact, in certain "slow-learner" books the pictures far outweigh the text in importance. However, the illustrations have a much greater historical value. Instead of made-up paintings or anachronistic sketches, there are cartoons, photographs, and paintings drawn from the periods being treated. The chapters on the Colonial period will show, for instance, a ship's carved prow, a Revere bowl, a Copley[6] painting—a whole gallery of Early Americana. The nineteenth century is illustrated with nineteenth-century cartoons and photographs—and the photographs are all of high artistic quality. As for the twentieth-century chapters, they are adorned with the contents of a modern-art museum.

The use of all this art and high-quality design contains some irony. The nineteenth-century photographs of child laborers or urban slum apartments are so beautiful that they transcend their subjects. To look at them, or at the Victor Gatto painting of the Triangle shirtwaist-factory fire, is to see not misery or ugliness but an art object. In the modern chapters, the contrast between style and content is just as great: the color photographs of junk yards or polluted rivers look as enticing as *Gourmet's* photographs of food. The book that is perhaps the most stark in its description of modern problems illustrates the horrors of nuclear testing with a pretty Ben Shahn picture of the Bikini explosion,[7] and the potential for global ecological disaster with a color photograph of the planet swirling its mantle of white clouds. Whereas in the nineteen-fifties the texts were childish in the sense that they were naïve and clumsy, they are now childish in the sense that they are polymorphous-

4. Socialist realism, which originated in the Soviet Union, is a style of art in which the communal labor of farmers and industrial workers is glorified in works of poster-like crudity.
5. Native Americans, then inhabiting the Caribbean area.
6. The reference is to John Singleton Copley (1738–1815), greatest of the American old masters; he specialized in portraits and historical paintings.
7. The Bikini atoll, part of the Marshall Islands in the Pacific, was the site of American nuclear-bomb testing from 1946 to 1958. Ben Shahn (1898–1969) was an American painter and graphic artist with strong social and political concerns.

perverse. American history is not dull any longer; it is a sensuous experience.

The surprise that adults feel in seeing the changes in history texts must come from the lingering hope that there is, somewhere out there, an objective truth. The hope is, of course, foolish. All of us children of the twentieth century know, or should know, that there are no absolutes in human affairs, and thus there can be no such thing as perfect objectivity. We know that each historian in some degree creates the world anew and that all history is in some degree contemporary history. But beyond this knowledge there is still a hope for some reliable authority, for some fixed stars in the universe. We may know that journalists cannot be wholly unbiased and that "balance" is an imaginary point between two extremes, and yet we hope that Walter Cronkite will tell us the truth of things. In the same way, we hope that our history will not change—that we learned the truth of things as children. The texts, with their impersonal voices, encourage this hope, and therefore it is particularly disturbing to see how they change, and how fast.

15   Slippery history! Not every generation but every few years the content of American-history books for children changes appreciably. Schoolbooks are not, like trade books,[8] written and left to their fate. To stay in step with the cycles of "adoption"[9] in school districts across the country, the publishers revise most of their old texts or substitute new ones every three or four years. In the process of revision, they not only bring history up to date but make changes—often substantial changes—in the body of the work. History books for children are thus more contemporary than any other form of history. How should it be otherwise? Should students read histories written ten, fifteen, thirty years ago? In theory, the system is reasonable—except that each generation of children reads only one generation of schoolbooks. The transient history is those children's history forever—their particular version of America.

8. Books written for a general audience, as   9. Choice of required textbooks.
opposed to textbooks.

THE READER

1. *What sorts of difference does FitzGerald find between the history textbooks of the 1950s and those of today? In what ways—according to what she states or implies—have the texts been improved? Does she see any changes for the worse?*

2. *On p. 820, FitzGerald says that in the new texts "the word 'progress' has been replaced by the word 'change.'" What is the difference between these two words? What does the replacement imply?*

3. *Is FitzGerald showing that the new textbooks give a truer account of American history?*

THE WRITER

1. By "rewriting," does FitzGerald mean changing the facts of history? What is the relationship between the facts of history and history textbooks?
2. Why does FitzGerald give the story about George McJunkin (p. 818)? Was his discovery important?
3. Write a brief account of the revisions you would like to see in some textbook you have used.

Daniel J. Boorstin

THE HISTORIAN: 'A WRESTLER WITH THE ANGEL'

The historian is both discoverer and creator. To the uniqueness of his role we have a clue in the very word "history," which means both the course of the past and the legible account of the past. The historian is always trying to reduce, or remove, that ambiguity. If he is successful, he leads his readers to take—or mistake—his account for what was really there.

The historian sets himself a dangerous, even an impossible, task. In the phrase of the great Dutch historian J. H. Huizinga,[1] he is "a wrestler with the angel." It is the angel of death who makes his work necessary yet destined never to be definitive. If man were not mortal, we would not be deprived of the living testimony of the actors, and so required to give new form to the receding infinity. From my own work I will describe the historian's quest. And I will suggest both the universal obstacles to recovery of the past and some special resources, opportunities and temptations for the historian in our own time.

Historians can rediscover the past only by the relics it has left for the present. They try to convince us that the relics they have examined and interpreted in their narrative are a reliable sample of the experience people really had. But how reliable are the remains of the past as clues to what was really there?

My life as a historian has brought me vivid reminders of how partial is the remaining evidence of the whole human past, how casual and how

From the *New York Times Book Review* (Sept. 20, 1987). Adapted from an essay in *Hidden History: Exploring Our Secret Past* (1987).

1. Huizinga (1872–1945), internationally recognized for his *Herfsttij der middeleeuwen* (1919) (*The Waning of the Middle Ages*, 1924).

accidental is the survival of its relics. One of my first shocks came while exploring the American experience in colonial times, in my effort to recapture the meaning of religion to the settlers of New England. Their basic vehicle of religious instruction was "The New England Primer." This, the chief text of compulsory education in early Massachusetts, carried a full rhymed alphabet—from "Adam" ("In Adam's Fall we sinned all") to "Zaccheus"—along with moral aphorisms, fragments of the Old Testament and the text of prayers, including the familiar "Now I lay me down to sleep." This influential work, which first appeared about 1690, became the best-selling New England schoolbook and had sold some three million copies within the next century. Benjamin Franklin, who knew a commercial opportunity when he saw one, made a tidy profit publishing his own secularized version.

5   For the flavor of New England religion, I went in search of original copies of the "Primer," but they were hard to find. By contrast I found it easy to consult the heavy tomes of Puritan theology. These volumes, kept in the rare-book rooms of university libraries, were often in mint condition, sometimes even with uncut pages. Modern scholars pore over such works in plush bibliophilic comfort to discover what the early Puritans were "really thinking" about religion.

This set me thinking about the limits of historical discovery. I had a similar experience when I came to the early 19th century, trying to learn about American heroes of the age and what people thought of them. I turned at once to the popular Crockett Almanacs. These were pamphlets of wide appeal published in the name of Davy Crockett (1786–1836), the man of little education and little respect for book learning, who said the rules of spelling were "contrary to nature." Besides recipes and useful everyday hints for health and crops, they recounted Crockett's astonishing feats wrestling men and alligators, along with legends of other frontier prodigies like Mike Fink, Daniel Boone and Kit Carson.[2] The earliest of these almanacs in 1835 offered an "autobiography," which Crockett supposedly wrote soon before his death.

Between 1835 and 1856 some 50 such almanacs poured out of Nashville, New York, Boston, Philadelphia and elsewhere by the tens of thousands, in the name of Davy Crockett or his "heirs." Embellished by crude woodcuts on cheap paper, these almanacs were carried in saddlebags, slipped into hip pockets, handed about Western inns and bars and around campfires as Americans moved west. But by the mid-20th century they had become rare and costly collector's items.

2. American folk heroes: Mike Fink (1770?–1823), notorious Mississippi riverman, "the king of the keelboatmen"; Daniel Boone (1734–1820), legendary Kentucky frontiersman, celebrated for Cumberland Gap trailblazing in the Appalachian Mountains; Kit (Christopher) Carson (1809–68), trapper, soldier, and Indian agent famous for his contributions to U.S. westward expansion.

A dramatic contrast for the historian of American hero worship was the monumental official life of George Washington, authorized by his nephew Bushrod Washington and written by Chief Justice John Marshall.[3] The work came to five volumes, sold by subscription at the then considerable price of $3 a volume. Even the flamboyant Parson Weems,[4] who put his best efforts into it, could not make it sell. And when the first volume of the much-touted project reached subscribers in 1804, it quickly established itself as the publishing catastrophe of the age. John Adams charitably characterized this as not a book at all but rather "a Mausoleum, 100 feet square at the base and 200 feet high." History justified Adams's description, because the volumes survived, as unread as they were unreadable. Today, of course, it is much more convenient for the scholar to mine the elegant bound volumes of Marshall than to handle the ragged half-legible fragments of Davy Crockett. These two episodes of my own research led me to a rather troubling hypothesis:

The Law of the Survival of the Unread—the more widely used a document, the more likely it is to have disappeared or been destroyed. Is the historian, then, the victim of a diabolical solipsism? Is there an inverse relation between the probability of a document's surviving and its value as evidence of the daily life of the age from which it survives?

To this troublesome "law" of historical evidence there are countless exceptions. But the exceptions themselves are also reminders of the casual and accidental causes of preservation, survival and accessibility. These only confirm our doubts that there is any positive correlation between survival and importance as clues to the past. Survival is chancy, whimsical and unpredictable. Yet it is not impossible to list some of the "biases of survival." They apply not only to documents and printed matter but to all kinds of relics.

Survival of the Durable, and That Which Is Not Removed or Displaced. While this has the sound of tautology, its consequences are not always noticed—the tendency toward emphasis on the monumental, on experience recorded in writing or in books. Since religions are a deliberate effort to transcend the transience of the individual human life, monuments of religion are often more durable than other monuments. Tombs, burial objects, mummies, temples, churches and pyramids tend to skew our view of the past. They give a prominence to religion in the relics of the past that it may not actually have had in the lives people lived. A contrast with monumental houses of religion are the simple

10

3. *Life of George Washington* (1804–07).
4. Parson (Mason Locke) Weems (1759–1825), American clergyman, biographer, and bookseller, remembered for what he called his masterpiece—*The Life and*

Memorable Actions of George Washington (ca. 1800)—in whose fifth edition Washington's cherry-tree incident first appeared in book form.

dwellings of the people who did (or did not) worship there. Chartres Cathedral[5] survives in its solid 13th-century glory, but the mud and wattle and wood houses of the citizens of Chartres surrounding it have been many times replaced.

In the United States this bias obscures some of the peculiar achievements of a mobile and technologically progressive civilization. One of the most characteristic architectural innovations in the United States is the balloon frame house. This American invention, which appeared in Chicago about 1833, was notable not for its durability but for its ease and speed of construction. Houses built by nailing together light timbers (instead of by the mortise and tenon of heavy beams) were put up quickly by people without the carpenter's skill. Such houses were taken down, and their frames transported by wagon or riverboat to the next stopping place in the transient, booming West. While the country mansions of the Dutch patroons of New York and plantation mansions of Virginia and Maryland survive, where are the balloon frames? This momentous American invention, whose 20th-century products surround us today, has hardly entered the historical record.

Survival of the Collected and the Protected: What Goes in Government Files. We emphasize political history and government in the life of the past partly because governments keep records, while families and other informal groups seldom do. Yet informal groups—for example, the anonymous wagon trains that crossed the continent—were among the most remarkable and most characteristic of American communities. Much of the peculiarly American experience, which has had this voluntary, spontaneous character, has eluded historians. The volunteer enthusiasms of ministers and their congregations and the haphazard philanthropy of wealthy citizens leave few official records. A democratic society like ours, a community of voluntary mobile communities, leaves a random report of its past.

Survival of Objects That Are Not Used or That Have a High Intrinsic Value. It is not only in printed matter that rarity and scarcity induce survival. European palaces, churches and now their museums display the jeweled and filigreed clocks and watches of early modern times. But the special timekeeping triumph of 19th-century America was the inexpensive household clock and then the "dollar watch," the wonder of European visitors. These dollar watches were not made for ease of repair and seemed not worth repairing. They seldom find their way into museums. Similarly, the elegantly engraved muskets with which European princes and their hunting companions enjoyed their leisure can be admired in many European museums. But the plain Kentucky rifle, which was the

---

5. Located in northwestern France, it is noted for its thirteenth-century stained-glass windows and Renaissance choir screen.

early westward-moving pioneer's weapon of defense and staff of life, was not preserved as an object of beauty.

Survival of the Academically Classifiable and the Dignified. Teachers teach the subjects in which they have been instructed. The trivium (grammar, logic and rhetoric) and quadrivium (arithmetic, geometry, astronomy and music) which composed the seven liberal arts of the medieval universities were an exhaustive catalogue of what students were expected to learn. Geography, for example, had no place in the medieval scheme. We must piece together their notions of the earth, its shapes and its dimensions, from works of theology, along with the ephemeral maps, portolans and planispheres used by navigators, traders, pirates, and empire builders. When geographic knowledge was valuable merchandise, the cartographic secrets of shorter, safer passages to remote treasure-troves of pepper, spice and precious gems were classified information. Now they are hidden from us as well. In the field of literature, this academic conservatism has perpetuated the study of familiar classics but left much of what many people read stigmatized as "subliterature" beneath the interest of serious students.

Survival of Printed and Other Materials Surrounding Controversies. What has passed for the study of the history of religion in America should more accurately be described as the history of religious controversies. The silent or spoken prayers of the devout leave few records behind. But the disputations of theologians, the acrimony of the religious academies and the resolutions of church councils pour out print. Then it is these disputes that command the interest and the ingenuity of historians of religion while the passions of the heart and the yearnings of the God-struck spirit, however constant and universal, remain private and invisible. Similarly, if we go in quest of the daily eating and drinking habits of early Americans, it is not easy to find records. Yet the history of the temperance movement and the prohibition of alcoholic beverages has left an abundant literature to arrest the attention of historians. The daily sexual habits of those who conform to the prevalent mores are seldom recorded and have rarely been chronicled. The history of sexual conduct has tended to become a record of deviants, of contraception and abortion, of polygamy and homosexuality. The history of law enforcement and obedience to law eludes us, while our shelves are filled with detective stories and the chronicles of crime.

Survival of the Self-Serving: The Psychopathology of Diarists and Letter Writers. Historians in professional training are urged to seek records by participants in events, preferably those made at the time or soon after. So there is a natural tendency to rely on diaries and letters. The quirks and quiddities of the obsessive diarist Samuel Pepys (1633–1703) loom in the foreground of the social history of England in the 17th century. In America we inevitably lean heavily on the diaries and letters of William Byrd (1674–1744), a witty but atypical planter-politician, and on the memoirs of the articulate plantation tutor Phillip Vickers Fithian. And we make much of the copious 19th-century diary written in the barely legible, minuscule hand of the observant New Yorker George Templeton Strong, or the gargantuan "confessions" of the eccentric Arthur Inman.[6] Of course intimate feelings interest the historian. But does not our hunger for the recorded word exaggerate the unusual point of view of those who happened to be diarists and letter writers? Are we victims, willingly or not, of a Casanova syndrome[7] that puts us at the mercy of the most articulate boasters of the past?

How will the rise of the telephone and the decline of letter writing "correct" or newly distort our recorded past? When President Thomas Jefferson wanted to instruct his Secretary of State James Madison, he would commonly write him a note, which remains for us. But when President Lyndon Johnson wanted to instruct Secretary of State Dean Rusk, he would more often have used the telephone. Consequently, when historians find a memorandum from President Johnson to Secretary Rusk, they will wonder whether the record was made not to guide action but to convey a desired impression to future historians. President Nixon's notorious effort to use the new electronic technology to provide a taped chronicle of his work in the Oval Office reveals the new biases, opportunities and risks—and reminds us of how much we lack of the earlier historical record. Meanwhile, the flood of press releases and pseudo-events, expressly created to be reported, further dilutes and confuses the record.

Survival of the Victorious Point of View: The Success Bias. The history of inventions we read today seems to have become the story of successful inventors. Eli Whitney, Isaac Merritt Singer, Henry Ford, Thomas A. Edison[8] and other lucky ones leave a vivid record. But the countless anonymous experimenters, the frustrated tinkerers who nearly made it, disappear. How many of their efforts ought to be part of the story?

6. Philip Vickers Fithian (1747–76); Arthur Crew Inman (1895–1963).

7. Giovanni Giacomo (Jean-Jacques, Chevalier de Seingalt, 1725–98), ecclesiastic, writer, soldier, spy, and diplomatist, chiefly remembered as the prince of Italian adventurers. He wrote an exaggerated, vivid autobiography, which was published after his death as *Memoires de J. Casanova de Seingalt,* 12 vols. (1826–38).

8. American inventors: Eli Whitney (1765–1825), designed the cotton gin; Isaac Merritt Singer (1811–75) developed the first practical domestic sewing machine; Henry Ford (1863–1947), revolutionized factory production with the assembly-line method that was implemented in automobile manufacturing; Thomas A. Edison (1847–1931), patented more than 1,300 inventions, including the phonograph and kinetoscope (peep-show device).

A dominant theme in the writing of American history has been the 20
filling of the continent, the consolidating of a great nation. But the
desire to secede, to move away from the larger political community,
might have become the leitmotif. Just as the Puritans came to America
as seceders from Britain, so the westward movers in the 19th century
were seceders from the heavily settled, increasingly urban Atlantic
coastal nation. If the South had won the Civil War, if the Republic of
Texas had remained independent, the earlier American settlers too
would have continued to shine not as nation builders but as courageous
seceders.

Survival of the Epiphenomenal. Often people write books and read
them because they cannot personally experience what is described. We
often remain uncertain whether writers were recording their experience
or escaping it. In my own efforts to describe American manners and
household customs I have been tantalized by this ambiguity. Emily
Post's "Etiquette," first published in 1922 and frequently revised thereafter, was so popular that her name became a synonym for proper
behavior. The style of private entertaining she prescribed during the
Great Depression in the lean 1930's still resembled what Scott Fitzgerald depicted in the luxuriant age of "The Great Gatsby" (1925). And
her books remained popular. Was this because people expected to follow
her economically obsolete, impractical advice or because they enjoyed
fantasizing about how they never could, or could no longer, afford to
entertain? The answers to these inward, private questions may be
beyond the historian's ken.

Knowledge Survives and Accumulates, but Ignorance Disappears. A
medieval folk tale reports that a young alchemist was once told that
if he recited a certain formula he could transform lead into silver
and copper into gold. The only condition was that while reciting his
formula, he must never be thinking of a white elephant. He learned
the formula and tried reciting it. Unfortunately, he could never make
it work—for all the while he was earnestly trying not to think of a
white elephant. The problem of latter day historians is much like
that of the young alchemist. For our minds are furnished with all the
accumulated knowledge and experience of the ages since the period
of the past we are trying to recapture. The modern globe of the earth
is so firmly fixed in our vision we find it hard to imagine the three-
continent planet with a surface only one-seventh water, on which
Columbus thought he was sailing. As we try to relive the experience
of Americans hastening across the continent in the early 19th century, we see them traversing the fertile Great Plains, destined to be
the granary of a great nation. But they thought they were crossing
what on their maps was the Great American Desert. Some even
sought camels to help their passage. How can we recapture their ig-

norance? Yet if we do not, we cannot really share their fears and their courage.

It is the sheerest folly to believe that we can ever know the extent or the boundaries of our ignorance. Or that we can conquer the biases of survival by some new technology. We transfer inflammable, self-destructive nitrate motion picture films of the years before 1950 to acetate film and so avoid the immediate catastrophes of combustion. But how long will the acetate film survive? We have less than a century of use to guide us.

We should be chastened in our hope to master the whole real past by the ironic comprehensiveness of the oldest records of civilization. We know more about some aspects of daily life in the Babylon of 3000 B.C. than we do about daily life in parts of Europe or America 100 years ago. By a happy accident, ancient Babylonians wrote not on paper but on the clay they found underfoot. Our grand dividend is thousands of tablets recording everything from codes of laws and religious texts to teachers' copybooks, the notes of schoolchildren, the records of war booty, recipes, scientific works and receipts for the sale of slaves and cattle. The messages we receive from that remote past were neither intended for us nor chosen by us, but are the casual relics of climate, geography and human activity. They, too, remind us of the whimsical dimensions of our knowledge and the limits of our powers of discovery.

25   The historian-creator refuses to be defeated by the biases of survival. For he chooses, defines and shapes his subject to provide a reasonably truthful account from miscellaneous remains. Of course he must use the social sciences, but he must transcend dogmas and theories. Like other literary artists and unlike the advancing social scientist, he is not engaged merely in revising his predecessors. He adds to our inheritance. At his best he is not accumulating knowledge that becomes obsolete, but creating a work with a life of its own. While Adam Smith survives in the reflected light of Ricardo and Marx and Keynes, Gibbon shines with a light all his own.[9] The truth the historian in any age finds in the past becomes part of our literary treasure. Inevitably the historian is torn between his efforts to create anew what he sees was really there and the urgent, shifting demands of the living audience. His motto could be St.

9. Adam Smith (1723–90), Scottish moral philosopher and political economist whose *Wealth of Nations* (1776)—advocating self-interest and a laissez-faire economy—was the first systematic formulation of classic English economics; David Ricardo (1772–1823), English economist influenced primarily by Adam Smith; Karl Marx (1818–83), German socialist who, with Friedrich Engels, formulated the principles of dialectical materialism (economic determinism); John Maynard Keynes (1883–1946), English economist, originator of the so-called New Economics and advocate of deficit spending; Edward Gibbon (1737–94), English historian, noted for his masterpiece *The History of the Decline and Fall of the Roman Empire* (1776).

Augustine's[1] *"Credo quia impossibilia"*—"I believe because it is impossible." At his best he remains a wrestler with the angel.

1. St. Augustine ("Aurelius Augustinus," A.D. 354–430), early Christian church father and philosopher.

Edward Hallett Carr

THE HISTORIAN AND HIS FACTS

What is history? Lest anyone think the question meaningless or superfluous, I will take as my text two passages relating respectively to the first and second incarnations of *The Cambridge Modern History.* Here is Acton in his report of October 1896 to the Syndics of the Cambridge University Press on the work which he had undertaken to edit:

> It is a unique opportunity of recording, in the way most useful to the greatest number, the fullness of the knowledge which the nineteenth century is about to bequeath. . . . By the judicious division of labor we should be able to do it, and to bring home to every man the last document, and the ripest conclusions of international research.
>
> Ultimate history we cannot have in this generation; but we can dispose of conventional history, and show the point we have reached on the road from one to the other, now that all information is within reach, and every problem has become capable of solution.

And almost exactly sixty years later Professor Sir George Clark, in his general introduction to the second *Cambridge Modern History,* commented on this belief of Acton and his collaborators that it would one day be possible to produce "ultimate history," and went on:

> Historians of a later generation do not look forward to any such prospect. They expect their work to be superseded again and again. They consider that knowledge of the past has come down through one or more human minds, has been "processed" by them, and therefore cannot consist of elemental and impersonal atoms which nothing can alter. . . . The exploration seems to be endless, and some impatient scholars take refuge in scepticism, or at least in the doctrine that, since all historical judgments involve persons and points of view, one is as good as another and there is no "objective" historical truth.

Where the pundits contradict each other so flagrantly the field is open to enquiry. I hope that I am sufficiently up-to-date to recognize that

From *What is History?* (1961).

anything written in the 1890's must be nonsense. But I am not yet advanced enough to be committed to the view that anything written in the 1950's necessarily makes sense. Indeed, it may already have occurred to you that this enquiry is liable to stray into something even broader than the nature of history. The clash between Acton and Sir George Clark is a reflection of the change in our total outlook on society over the interval between these two pronouncements. Acton speaks out of the positive belief, the clear-eyed self-confidence of the later Victorian age; Sir George Clark echoes the bewilderment and distracted scepticism of the beat generation. When we attempt to answer the question, What is history?, our answer, consciously or unconsciously, reflects our own position in time, and forms part of our answer to the broader question, what view we take of the society in which we live. I have no fear that my subject may, on closer inspection, seem trivial. I am afraid only that I may seem presumptuous to have broached a question so vast and so important.

The nineteenth century was a great age for facts. "What I want," said Mr. Gradgrind in *Hard Times*, "is Facts. . . . Facts alone are wanted in life." Nineteenth-century historians on the whole agreed with him. When Ranke in the 1830's, in legitimate protest against moralizing history, remarked that the task of the historian was "simply to show how it really was [*wie es eigentlich gewesen*]" this not very profound aphorism had an astonishing success. Three generations of German, British, and even French historians marched into battle intoning the magic words, "*Wie es eigentlich gewesen*" like an incantation—designed, like most incantations, to save them from the tiresome obligation to think for themselves. The Positivists, anxious to stake out their claim for history as a science, contributed the weight of their influence to this cult of facts. First ascertain the facts, said the positivists, then draw your conclusions from them. In Great Britain, this view of history fitted in perfectly with the empiricist tradition which was the dominant strain in British philosophy from Locke to Bertrand Russell. The empirical theory of knowledge presupposes a complete separation between subject and object. Facts, like sense-impressions, impinge on the observer from outside, and are independent of his consciousness. The process of reception is passive: having received the data, he then acts on them. *The Shorter Oxford English Dictionary,* a useful but tendentious work of the empirical school, clearly marks the separateness of the two processes by defining a fact as "a datum of experience as distinct from conclusions." This is what may be called the common-sense view of history. History consists of a corpus of ascertained facts. The facts are available to the historian in documents, inscriptions, and so on, like fish on the fishmonger's slab. The historian collects them, takes them home, and cooks and serves them in whatever style appeals to him. Acton, whose culinary

tastes were austere, wanted them served plain. In his letter of instructions to contributors to the first *Cambridge Modern History* he announced the requirement "that our Waterloo must be one that satisfies
French and English, German and Dutch alike; that nobody can tell,
without examining the list of authors where the Bishop of Oxford laid
down the pen, and whether Fairbairn or Gasquet, Liebermann or Harrison took it up." Even Sir George Clark, critical as he was of Acton's
attitude, himself contrasted the "hard core of facts" in history with the
"surrounding pulp of disputable interpretation"—forgetting perhaps
that the pulpy part of the fruit is more rewarding than the hard core.
First get your facts straight, then plunge at your peril into the shifting
sands of interpretation—that is the ultimate wisdom of the empirical,
common-sense school of history. It recalls the favorite dictum of the
great liberal journalist C. P. Scott: "Facts are sacred, opinion is free."

Now this clearly will not do. I shall not embark on a philosophical
discussion of the nature of our knowledge of the past. Let us assume for
present purposes that the fact that Caesar crossed the Rubicon and the
fact that there is a table in the middle of the room are facts of the same
or of a comparable order, that both these facts enter our consciousness
in the same or in a comparable manner, and that both have the same
objective character in relation to the person who knows them. But, even
on this bold and not very plausible assumption, our argument at once
runs into the difficulty that not all facts about the past are historical
facts, or are treated as such by the historian. What is the criterion which
distinguishes the facts of history from other facts about the past?

What is a historical fact? This is a crucial question into which we must
look a little more closely. According to the common-sense view, there
are certain basic facts which are the same for all historians and which
form, so to speak, the backbone of history—the fact, for example, that
the Battle of Hastings was fought in 1066. But this view calls for two
observations. In the first place, it is not with facts like these that the
historian is primarily concerned. It is no doubt important to know that
the great battle was fought in 1066 and not in 1065 or 1067, and that
it was fought at Hastings and not at Eastbourne or Brighton. The
historian must not get these things wrong. But when points of this kind
are raised, I am reminded of Housman's remark[1] that "accuracy is a
duty, not a virtue." To praise a historian for his accuracy is like praising
an architect for using well-seasoned timber or properly mixed concrete
in his building. It is a necessary condition of his work, but not his
essential function. It is precisely for matters of this kind that the historian is entitled to rely on what have been called the "auxiliary sciences"
of history—archaeology, epigraphy, numismatics, chronology, and so

1. In the preface to his critical edition of Manilius, *Astronomicon*, an obscure Latin work.

forth. The historian is not required to have the special skills which enable the expert to determine the origin and period of a fragment of pottery or marble, or decipher an obscure inscription, or to make the elaborate astronomical calculations necessary to establish a precise date. These so-called basic facts which are the same for all historians commonly belong to the category of the raw materials of the historian rather than of history itself. The second observation is that the necessity to establish these basic facts rests not on any quality in the facts themselves, but on an *a priori* decision of the historian. In spite of C. P. Scott's motto, every journalist knows today that the most effective way to influence opinion is by the selection and arrangement of the appropriate facts. It used to be said that facts speak for themselves. This is, of course, untrue. The facts speak only when the historian calls on them: It is he who decides to which facts to give the floor, and in what order or context. It was, I think, one of Pirandello's characters who said that a fact is like a sack—it won't stand up till you've put something in it. The only reason why we are interested to know that the battle was fought at Hastings in 1066 is that historians regard it as a major historical event. It is the historian who has decided for his own reasons that Caesar's crossing of that petty stream, the Rubicon, is a fact of history, whereas the crossing of the Rubicon by millions of other people before or since interests nobody at all. The fact that you arrived in this building half an hour ago on foot, or on a bicycle, or in a car, is just as much a fact about the past as the fact that Caesar crossed the Rubicon. But it will probably be ignored by historians. Professor Talcott Parsons once called science "a selective system of cognitive orientations to reality." It might perhaps have been put more simply. But history is, among other things, that. The historian is necessarily selective. The belief in a hard core of historical facts existing objectively and independently of the interpretation of the historian is a preposterous fallacy, but one which it is very hard to eradicate.

5   Let us take a look at the process by which a mere fact about the past is transformed into a fact of history. At Stalybridge Wakes in 1850, a vendor of gingerbread, as the result of some petty dispute, was deliberately kicked to death by an angry mob. Is this a fact of history? A year ago I should unhesitatingly have said "no." It was recorded by an eyewitness in some little-known memoirs;[2] but I had never seen it judged worthy of mention by any historian. A year ago Dr. Kitson Clark cited it in his Ford lectures in Oxford. Does this make it into a historical fact? Not, I think, yet. Its present status, I suggest, is that it has been proposed for membership of the select club of historical facts. It now

2. Lord George Sanger: *Seventy Years a Showman* (London: J. M. Dent & Sons, 1926), pp. 188–9 [Carr's note].

awaits a seconder and sponsors. It may be that in the course of the next few years we shall see this fact appearing first in footnotes, then in the text, of articles and books about nineteenth-century England, and that in twenty or thirty years' time it may be a well established historical fact. Alternatively, nobody may take it up, in which case it will relapse into the limbo of unhistorical facts about the past from which Dr. Kitson Clark has gallantly attempted to rescue it. What will decide which of these two things will happen? It will depend, I think, on whether the thesis or interpretation in support of which Dr. Kitson Clark cited this incident is accepted by other historians as valid and significant. Its status as a historical fact will turn on a question of interpretation. This element of interpretation enters into every fact of history.

May I be allowed a personal reminiscence? When I studied ancient history in this university many years ago, I had as a special subject "Greece in the period of the Persian Wars." I collected fifteen or twenty volumes on my shelves and took it for granted that there, recorded in these volumes, I had all the facts relating to my subject. Let us assume— it was very nearly true—that those volumes contained all the facts about it that were then known, or could be known. It never occurred to me to enquire by what accident or process of attrition that minute selection of facts, out of all the myriad facts that must have once been known to somebody, had survived to become *the* facts of history. I suspect that even today one of the fascinations of ancient and mediaeval history is that it gives us the illusion of having all the facts at our disposal within a manageable compass: the nagging distinction between the facts of history and other facts about the past vanishes because the few known facts are all facts of history. As Bury, who had worked in both periods, said, "the records of ancient and mediaeval history are starred with lacunae." History has been called an enormous jig-saw with a lot of missing parts. But the main trouble does not consist of the lacunae. Our picture of Greece in the fifth century *b.c.* is defective not primarily because so many of the bits have been accidentally lost, but because it is, by and large, the picture formed by a tiny group of people in the city of Athens. We know a lot about what fifth-century Greece looked like to an Athenian citizen; but hardly anything about what it looked like to a Spartan, a Corinthian, or a Theban—not to mention a Persian, or a slave or other non-citizen resident in Athens. Our picture has been preselected and predetermined for us, not so much by accident as by people who were consciously or unconsciously imbued with a particular view and thought the facts which supported that view worth preserving. In the same way, when I read in a modern history of the Middle Ages that the people of the Middle Ages were deeply concerned with religion, I wonder how we know this, and whether it is true. What we know as the facts of mediaeval history have almost all been selected for us by generations of chroniclers who were professionally occupied in the theory and practice of religion, and who therefore thought it supremely important, and recorded everything relating to it, and not much else. The picture of the Russian peasant as devoutly religious was destroyed by the revolution of 1917. The picture of mediaeval man as devoutly religious, whether true or not, is indestructible, because nearly all the known facts about him were preselected for us by people who believed it, and wanted others to believe it, and a mass of other facts, in which we might possibly have found evidence to the contrary, has been lost beyond recall. The dead hand of vanished generations of historians, scribes, and chroniclers has determined beyond the possibility of appeal the pattern of the past. "The history we read," writes Professor Barraclough, himself trained as a mediaevalist, "though based on facts, is, strictly speaking, not factual at all, but a series of accepted judgments."

But let us turn to the different, but equally grave, plight of the modern historian. The ancient or mediaeval historian may be grateful for the vast winnowing process which, over the years, has put at his disposal a manageable corpus of historical facts. As Lytton Strachey said in his mischievous way, "ignorance is the first requisite of the historian, ignorance which simplifies and clarifies, which selects and omits." When I am tempted, as I sometimes am, to envy the extreme competence of colleagues engaged in writing ancient or mediaeval history, I find consolation in the reflection that they are so competent mainly because they are so ignorant of their subject. The modern historian enjoys none of the advantages of this built-in ignorance. He must cultivate this necessary ignorance for himself—the more so the nearer he comes to his own times. He has the dual task of discovering the few significant facts and turning them into facts of history, and of discarding the many insignificant facts as unhistorical. But this is the very converse of the nineteenth-century heresy that history consists of the compilation of a maximum number of irrefutable and objective facts. Anyone who succumbs to this heresy will either have to give up history as a bad job, and take to stamp-collecting or some other form of antiquarianism, or end in a madhouse. It is this heresy, which during the past hundred years has had such devastating effects on the modern historian, producing in Germany, in Great Britain, and in the United States a vast and growing mass of dry-as-dust factual histories, of minutely specialized monographs, of would-be historians knowing more and more about less and less, sunk without trace in an ocean of facts. It was, I suspect, this heresy—rather than the alleged conflict between liberal and Catholic loyalties—which frustrated Acton as a historian. In an early essay he said of his teacher Döllinger: "He would not write with imperfect materials, and to him the materials were always imperfect."[3] Acton was surely here pronouncing an anticipatory verdict on himself, on that strange phenomenon of a historian whom many would regard as the most distinguished occupant the Regius Chair of Modern History in this university has ever had—but who wrote no history. And Acton wrote his own epitaph in the introductory note to the first volume of the *Cambridge Modern History,* published just after his death, when he lamented that the requirements pressing on the historian "threaten to turn him from a man of letters into the compiler of an encyclopedia." Something had gone wrong. What had gone wrong was the belief in this untiring and unending accumulation of hard facts as the foundation of history, the belief that facts speak for themselves and that we cannot have too many facts, a belief at that time so unquestioning that few historians then thought it necessary—and some still think it unnecessary today—to ask themselves the question: What is history?

The nineteenth-century fetishism of facts was completed and justified by a fetishism of documents. The documents were the Ark of the Covenant in the temple of facts. The reverent historian approached them with bowed head and spoke of them in awed tones. If you find it in the documents, it is so. But what, when we get down to it, do these documents—the decrees, the treaties, the rent-rolls, the blue books, the official correspondence, the private letters and diaries—tell us? No document can tell us more than what the author of the document thought—what he thought had happened, what he thought ought to happen or would happen, or perhaps only what he wanted others to think he thought, or even only what he himself thought he thought. None of this means anything until the historian has got to work on it and deciphered it. The facts, whether found in documents or not, have still to be processed by the historian before he can make any use of them: the use he makes of them is, if I may put it that way, the processing process.

Let me illustrate what I am trying to say by an example which I happen to know well. When Gustav Stresemann, the Foreign Minister of the Weimar Republic, died in 1929, he left behind him an enormous mass—300 boxes full—of papers, official, semiofficial, and private, nearly all relating to the six years of his tenure of office as Foreign Minister. His friends and relatives naturally thought that a monument should be raised to the memory of so great a man. His faithful secretary Bernhardt got to work; and within three years there appeared three massive volumes, of some 600 pages each, of selected documents from the 300 boxes, with the impressive title *Stresemanns Vermächtnis.*[4] In the ordinary way the documents themselves would have moldered away in some cellar or attic and disappeared for ever; or perhaps in a hundred years or so some curious scholar would have come upon them and set

3. Later Acton said of Döllinger that "it was given him to form his philosophy of history on the largest induction ever availa- ble to man" [Carr's note].
4. *Stresemann's Legacy.*

out to compare them with Bernhardt's text. What happened was far more dramatic. In 1945 the documents fell into the hands of the British and the American governments, who photographed the lot and put the photostats at the disposal of scholars in the Public Record Office in London and in the National Archives in Washington, so that, if we have sufficient patience and curiosity, we can discover exactly what Bernhardt did. What he did was neither very unusual nor very shocking. When Stresemann died, his Western policy seemed to have been crowned with a series of brilliant successes—Locarno, the admission of Germany to the League of Nations, the Dawes and Young plans and the American loans, the withdrawal of allied occupation armies from the Rhineland. This seemed the important and rewarding part of Stresemann's foreign policy; and it was not unnatural that it should have been over-represented in Bernhardt's selection of documents. Stresemann's Eastern policy, on the other hand, his relations with the Soviet Union, seemed to have led nowhere in particular; and, since masses of documents about negotiations which yielded only trivial results were not very interesting and added nothing to Stresemann's reputation, the process of selection could be more rigorous. Stresemann in fact devoted a far more constant and anxious attention to relations with the Soviet Union, and they played a far larger part in his foreign policy as a whole, than the reader of the Bernhardt selection would surmise. But the Bernhardt volumes compare favorably, I suspect, with many published collections of documents on which the ordinary historian implicitly relies.

10   This is not the end of my story. Shortly after the publication of Bernhardt's volumes, Hitler came into power. Stresemann's name was consigned to oblivion in Germany, and the volumes disappeared from circulation: many, perhaps most, of the copies must have been destroyed. Today *Stresemanns Vermächtnis* is a rather rare book. But in the West Stresemann's reputation stood high. In 1935 an English publisher brought out an abbreviated translation of Bernhardt's work—a selection from Bernhardt's selection; perhaps one third of the original was omitted. Sutton, a well-known translator from the German, did his job competently and well. The English version, he explained in the preface, was "slightly condensed, but only by the omission of a certain amount of what, it was felt, was more ephemeral matter . . . of little interest to English readers or students." This again is natural enough. But the result is that Stresemann's Eastern policy, already under-represented in Bernhardt, recedes still further from view, and the Soviet Union appears in Sutton's volumes merely as an occasional and rather unwelcome intruder in Stresemann's predominantly Western foreign policy. Yet it is safe to say that, for all except a few specialists, Sutton and not Bernhardt—and still less the documents themselves—represents for the Western world the authentic voice of Stresemann. Had the

documents perished in 1945 in the bombing, and had the remaining Bernhardt volumes disappeared, the authenticity and authority of Sutton would never have been questioned. Many printed collections of documents gratefully accepted by historians in default of the originals rest on no securer basis than this.

But I want to carry the story one step further. Let us forget about Bernhardt and Sutton, and be thankful that we can, if we choose, consult the authentic papers of a leading participant in some important events in recent European history. What do the papers tell us? Among other things they contain records of some hundreds of Stresemann's conversations with the Soviet ambassador in Berlin and of a score or so with Chicherin.[5] These records have one feature in common. They depict Stresemann as having the lion's share of the conversations and reveal his arguments as invariably well put and cogent, while those of his partner are for the most part scanty, confused, and unconvincing. This is a familiar characteristic of all records of diplomatic conversations. The documents do not tell us what happened, but only what Stresemann thought had happened. It was not Sutton or Bernhardt, but Stresemann himself, who started the process of selection. And, if we had, say Chicherin's records of these same conversations, we should still learn from them only what Chicherin thought, and what really happened would still have to be reconstructed in the mind of the historian. Of course, facts and documents are essential to the historian. But do not make a fetish of them. They do not by themselves constitute history; they provide in themselves no ready-made answer to this tiresome question: What is history?

At this point I should like to say a few words on the question of why nineteenth-century historians were generally indifferent to the philosophy of history. The term was invented by Voltaire, and has since been used in different senses; but I shall take it to mean, if I use it at all, our answer to the question: What is history? The nineteenth century was, for the intellectuals of Western Europe, a comfortable period exuding confidence and optimism. The facts were on the whole satisfactory; and the inclination to ask and answer awkward questions about them was correspondingly weak. Ranke piously believed that divine providence would take care of the meaning of history if he took care of the facts; and Burckhardt with a more modern touch of cynicism observed that "we are not initiated into the purposes of the eternal wisdom." Professor Butterfield as late as 1931 noted with apparent satisfaction that "historians have reflected little upon the nature of things and even the nature of their own subject." But my predecessor in these lectures, Dr. A. L. Rowse, more justly critical, wrote of Sir Winston Churchill's *The World*

5. Soviet foreign minister from 1918 to 1928.

Crisis—his book about the First World War—that, while it matched Trotsky's *History of the Russian Revolution* in personality, vividness, and vitality, it was inferior in one respect: it had "no philosophy of history behind it." British historians refused to be drawn, not because they believed that history had no meaning, but because they believed that its meaning was implicit and self-evident. The liberal nineteenth-century view of history had a close affinity with the economic doctrine of *laissez-faire*—also the product of a serene and self-confident outlook on the world. Let everyone get on with his particular job, and the hidden hand would take care of the universal harmony. The facts of history were themselves a demonstration of the supreme fact of a beneficent and apparently infinite progress towards higher things. This was the age of innocence, and historians walked in the Garden of Eden, without a scrap of philosophy to cover them, naked and unashamed before the god of history. Since then, we have known Sin and experienced a Fall; and those historians who today pretend to dispense with a philosophy of history are merely trying, vainly and self-consciously, like members of a nudist colony, to recreate the Garden of Eden in their garden suburb. Today the awkward question can no longer be evaded. * * *

During the past fifty years a good deal of serious work has been done on the question: What is history? It was from Germany, the country which was to do so much to upset the comfortable reign of nineteenth-century liberalism, that the first challenge came in the 1880's and 1890's to the doctrine of the primacy and autonomy of facts in history. The philosophers who made the challenge are now little more than names: Dilthey is the only one of them who has recently received some belated recognition in Great Britain. Before the turn of the century, prosperity and confidence were still too great in this country for any attention to be paid to heretics who attacked the cult of facts. But early in the new century, the torch passed to Italy, where Croce began to propound a philosophy of history which obviously owed much to German masters. All history is "contemporary history," declared Croce,[6] meaning that history consists essentially in seeing the past through the eyes of the present and in the light of its problems, and that the main work of the historian is not to record, but to evaluate; for, if he does not evaluate, how can he know what is worth recording? In 1910 the American philosopher, Carl Becker, argued in deliberately provocative language that "the facts of history do not exist for any historian till he creates

6. The context of this celebrated aphorism is as follows: "The practical requirements which underlie every historical judgment give to all history the character of 'contemporary history,' because, however remote in time events thus recounted may seem to be, the history in reality refers to present needs and present situations wherein those events vibrate" [Carr's note].

them." These challenges were for the moment little noticed. It was only after 1920 that Croce began to have a considerable vogue in France and Great Britain. This was not perhaps because Croce was a subtler thinker or a better stylist than his German predecessors, but because, after the First World War, the facts seemed to smile on us less propitiously than in the years before 1914, and we were therefore more accessible to a philosophy which sought to diminish their prestige. Croce was an important influence on the Oxford philosopher and historian Collingwood, the only British thinker in the present century who has made a serious contribution to the philosophy of history. He did not live to write the systematic treatise he had planned; but his published and unpublished papers on the subject were collected after his death in a volume entitled *The Idea of History,* which appeared in 1945.

The views of Collingwood can be summarized as follows. The philosophy of history is concerned neither with "the past by itself" nor with "the historian's thought about it by itself," but with "the two things in their mutual relations." (This dictum reflects the two current meanings of the word "history"—the enquiry conducted by the historian and the series of past events into which he enquires.) "The past which a historian studies is not a dead past, but a past which in some sense is still living in the present." But a past act is dead, *i.e.* meaningless to the historian, unless he can understand the thought that lay behind it. Hence "all history is the history of thought," and "history is the re-enactment in the historian's mind of the thought whose history he is studying." The reconstitution of the past in the historian's mind is dependent on empirical evidence. But it is not in itself an empirical process, and cannot consist in a mere recital of facts. On the contrary, the process of reconstitution governs the selection and interpretation of the facts: this, indeed, is what makes them historical facts. "History," says Professor Oakeshott, who on this point stands near to Collingwood, "is the historian's experience. It is 'made' by nobody save the historian: to write history is the only way of making it."

This searching critique, though it may call for some serious reservations, brings to light certain neglected truths.

In the first place, the facts of history never come to us "pure," since they do not and cannot exist in a pure form: they are always refracted through the mind of the recorder. It follows that when we take up a work of history, our first concern should be not with the facts which it contains but with the historian who wrote it. Let me take as an example the great historian in whose honor and in whose name these lectures were founded. Trevelyan, as he tells us in his autobiography, was "brought up at home on a somewhat exuberantly Whig tradition"; and he would not, I hope, disclaim the title if I described him as the last and not the least of the great English liberal historians of the Whig tradition.

15

It is not for nothing that he traces back his family tree, through the great Whig historian George Otto Trevelyan, to Macaulay, incomparably the greatest of the Whig historians. Dr. Trevelyan's finest and maturest work *England under Queen Anne* was written against that background, and will yield its full meaning and significance to the reader only when read against that background. The author, indeed, leaves the reader with no excuse for failing to do so. For if, following the technique of connoisseurs of detective novels. you read the end first, you will find on the last few pages of the third volume the best summary known to me of what is nowadays called the Whig interpretation of history; and you will see that what Trevelyan is trying to do is to investigate the origin and development of the Whig tradition, and to root it fairly and squarely in the years after the death of its founder, William III. Though this is not, perhaps, the only conceivable interpretation of the events of Queen Anne's reign, it is a valid and, in Trevelyan's hands, a fruitful interpretation. But, in order to appreciate it at its full value, you have to understand what the historian is doing. For if, as Collingwood says, the historian must re-enact in thought what has gone on in the mind of his *dramatis personae,* so the reader in his turn must re-enact what goes on in the mind of the historian. Study the historian before you begin to study the facts. This is, after all, not very abstruse. It is what is already done by the intelligent undergraduate who, when recommended to read a work by that great scholar Jones of St. Jude's, goes round to a friend at St. Jude's to ask what sort of chap Jones is, and what bees he has in his bonnet. When you read a work of history, always listen out for the buzzing. If you can detect none, either you are tone deaf or your historian is a dull dog. The facts are really not at all like fish on the fishmonger's slab. They are like fish swimming about in a vast and sometimes inaccessible ocean; and what the historian catches will depend partly on chance, but mainly on what part of the ocean he chooses to fish in and what tackle he chooses to use—these two factors being, of course, determined by the kind of fish he wants to catch. By and large, the historian will get the kind of facts he wants. History means interpretation. Indeed, if, standing Sir George Clark on his head, I were to call history "a hard core of interpretation surrounded by a pulp of disputable facts," my statement would, no doubt, be one-sided and misleading, but no more so, I venture to think, than the original dictum.

The second point is the more familiar one of the historian's need of imaginative understanding for the minds of the people with whom he is dealing, for the thought behind their acts: I say "imaginative understanding," not "sympathy," lest sympathy should be supposed to imply agreement. The nineteenth century was weak in mediaeval history, because it was too much repelled by the superstitious beliefs of the Middle Ages and by the barbarities which they inspired, to have any imaginative understanding of mediaeval people. Or take Burckhardt's censorious remark about the Thirty Years' War: "It is scandalous for a creed, no matter whether it is Catholic or Protestant, to place its salvation above the integrity of the nation." It was extremely difficult for a nineteenth-century liberal historian, brought up to believe that it is right and praiseworthy to kill in defense of one's country, but wicked and wrongheaded to kill in defense of one's religion, to enter into the state of mind of those who fought the Thirty Years' War. This difficulty is particularly acute in the field in which I am now working. Much of what has been written in English-speaking countries in the last ten years about the Soviet Union, and in the Soviet Union about the English-speaking countries, has been vitiated by this inability to achieve even the most elementary measure of imaginative understanding of what goes on in the mind of the other party, so that the words and actions of the other are always made to appear malign, senseless, or hypocritical. History cannot be written unless the historian can achieve some kind of contact with the mind of those about whom he is writing.

The third point is that we can view the past, and achieve our understanding of the past, only through the eyes of the present. The historian is of his own age, and is bound to it by the conditions of human existence. The very words which he uses—words like democracy, empire, war, revolution—have current connotations from which he cannot divorce them. Ancient historians have taken to using words like *polis* and *plebs* in the original, just in order to show that they have not fallen into this trap. This does not help them. They, too, live in the present, and cannot cheat themselves into the past by using unfamiliar or obsolete words, any more than they would become better Greek or Roman historians if they delivered their lectures in a *chlamys* or a *toga*. The names by which successive French historians have described the Parisian crowds which played so prominent a role in the French revolution—*les sansculottes, le peuple, la canaille, les bras-nus*—are all, for those who know the rules of the game, manifestos of a political affiliation and of a particular interpretation. Yet the historian is obliged to choose: the use of language forbids him to be neutral. Nor is it a matter of words alone. Over the past hundred years the changed balance of power in Europe has reversed the attitude of British historians to Frederick the Great. The changed balance of power within the Christian churches between Catholicism and Protestantism has profoundly altered their attitude to such figures as Loyola, Luther, and Cromwell. It requires only a superficial knowledge of the work of French historians of the last forty years on the French revolution to recognize how deeply it has been affected by the Russian revolution of 1917. The historian belongs not to the past but to the present. Professor Trevor-Roper tells us that the historian "ought to love the past." This is a dubious injunction. To love the past may easily be an expression of the nostalgic romanticism of old men and old societies, a symptom of loss of faith and interest in the present or future.[7] *Cliché* for *cliché*, I should prefer the one about freeing oneself from "the dead hand of the past." The function of the historian is neither to love the past nor to emancipate himself from the past, but to master and understand it as the key to the understanding of the present.

If, however, these are some of the sights of what I may call the Collingwood view of history, it is time to consider some of the dangers. The emphasis on the role of the historian in the making of history tends, if pressed to its logical conclusion, to rule out any objective history at all: history is what the historian makes. Collingwood seems indeed, at one moment, in an unpublished note quoted by his editor, to have reached this conclusion:

> St. Augustine looked at history from the point of view of the early Christian; Tillemont, from that of a seventeenth-century Frenchman; Gibbon, from that of an eighteenth-century Englishman; Mommsen, from that of a nineteenth-century German. There is no point in asking which was the right point of view. Each was the only one possible for the man who adopted it.

This amounts to total scepticism, like Froude's remark that history is "a child's box of letters with which we can spell any word we please." Collingwood, in his reaction against "scissors-and-paste history," against the view of history as a mere compilation of facts, comes perilously near to treating history as something spun out of the human brain, and leads back to the conclusion referred to by Sir George Clark in the passage which I quoted earlier, that "there is no 'objective' historical truth." In place of the theory that history has no meaning, we are offered here the theory of an infinity of meanings, none any more right than any other— which comes to much the same thing. The second theory is surely as untenable as the first. It does not follow that, because a mountain appears to take on different shapes from different angles of vision, it has objectively either no shape at all or an infinity of shapes. It does not follow that, because interpretation plays a necessary part in establishing the facts of history, and because no existing interpretation is wholly objective, one interpretation is as good as another, and the facts of history are in principle not amenable to objective interpretation. I shall have to consider at a later stage what exactly is meant by objectivity in history.

20　　But a still greater danger lurks in the Collingwood hypothesis. If the

---

7. Compare Nietzsche's view of history: "To old age belongs the old man's business of looking back and casting up his ac- counts, of seeking consolation in the memories of the past, in historical culture" [Carr's note].

historian necessarily looks at his period of history through the eyes of his own time, and studies the problems of the past as a key to those of the present, will he not fall into a purely pragmatic view of the facts, and maintain that the criterion of a right interpretation is its suitability to some present purpose? On this hypothesis, the facts of history are nothing, interpretation is everything. Nietzsche had already enunciated the principle: "The falseness of an opinion is not for us any objection to it. . . . The question is how far it is life-furthering, life-preserving, species-preserving, perhaps species-creating." The American pragmatists moved, less explicitly and less wholeheartedly, along the same line. Knowledge is knowledge for some purpose. The validity of the knowledge depends on the validity of the purpose. But, even where no such theory has been professed, the practice has often been no less disquieting. In my own field of study, I have seen too many examples of extravagant interpretation riding roughshod over facts, not to be impressed with the reality of this danger. It is not surprising that perusal of some of the more extreme products of Soviet and anti-Soviet schools of historiography should sometimes breed a certain nostalgia for that illusory nineteenth-century heaven of purely factual history.

How then, in the middle of the twentieth century, are we to define the obligation of the historian to his facts? I trust that I have spent a sufficient number of hours in recent years chasing and perusing documents, and stuffing my historical narrative with properly footnoted facts, to escape the imputation of treating facts and documents too cavalierly. The duty of the historian to respect his facts is not exhausted by the obligation to see that his facts are accurate. He must seek to bring into the picture all known or knowable facts relevant, in one sense or another, to the theme on which he is engaged and to the interpretation proposed. If he seeks to depict the Victorian Englishman as a moral and rational being, he must not forget what happened at Stalybridge Wakes in 1850. But this, in turn, does not mean that he can eliminate interpretation, which is the life-blood of history. Laymen—that is to say, non-academic friends or friends from other academic disciplines—sometimes ask me how the historian goes to work when he writes history. The commonest assumption appears to be that the historian divides his work into two sharply distinguishable phases or periods. First, he spends a long preliminary period reading his source and filling his notebooks with facts: then, when this is over, he puts away his sources, takes out his notebooks, and writes his book from beginning to end. This is to me an unconvincing and unplausible picture. For myself, as soon as I have got going on a few of what I take to be the capital sources, the itch becomes too strong and I begin to write—not necessarily at the beginning, but somewhere, anywhere. Thereafter, reading and writing go on simultaneously. The writing is added to, subtracted from, re-shaped, cancelled, as I go on reading. The reading is guided and directed and made fruitful by the writing: the more I write, the more I know what I am looking for, the better I understand the significance and relevance of what I find. Some historians probably do all this preliminary writing in their head without using pen, paper, or typewriter, just as some people play chess in their heads without recourse to board and chess-men: this is a talent which I envy, but cannot emulate. But I am convinced that, for any historian worth the name, the two processes of what economists call "input" and "output" go on simultaneously and are, in practice, parts of a single process. If you try to separate them, or to give one priority over the other, you fall into one of two heresies. Either you write scissors-and-paste history without meaning or significance; or you write propaganda or historical fiction, and merely use facts of the past to embroider a kind of writing which has nothing to do with history.

Our examination of the relation of the historian to the facts of history finds us, therefore, in an apparently precarious situation, navigating delicately between the Scylla of an untenable theory of history as an objective compilation of facts, of the unqualified primacy of fact over interpretation, and the Charybdis of an equally untenable theory of history as the subjective product of the mind of the historian who establishes the facts of history and masters them through the process of interpretation, between a view of history having the center of gravity in the past and the view having the center of gravity in the present. But our situation is less precarious than it seems. We shall encounter the same dichotomy of fact and interpretation again in these lectures in other guises—the particular and the general, the empirical and the theoretical, the objective and the subjective. The predicament of the historian is a reflection of the nature of man. Man, except perhaps in earliest infancy and in extreme old age, is not totally involved in his environment and unconditionally subject to it. On the other hand, he is never totally independent of it and its unconditional master. The relation of man to his environment is the relation of the historian to his theme. The historian is neither the humble slave, nor the tyrannical master, of his facts. The relation between the historian and his facts is one of equality, of give-and-take. As any working historian knows, if he stops to reflect on what he is doing as he thinks and writes, the historian is engaged in a continuous process of molding his facts to his interpretation and his interpretation to his facts. It is impossible to assign primacy to one over the other.

The historian starts with the provisional selection of facts and a provisional interpretation in the light of which that selection has been made—by others as well as by himself. As he works, both the interpretation and the selection and ordering of facts undergo subtle and perhaps partly unconscious changes through the reciprocal action of one or the other. And this reciprocal action also involves reciprocity between present and past, since the historian is part of the present and the facts belong to the past. The historian and the facts of history are necessary to one another. The historian without his facts is rootless and futile; the facts without their historian are dead and meaningless. My first answer therefore to the question, What is history?, is that it is a continuous process of interaction between the historian and his facts, an unending dialogue between the present and the past.

THE READER

1. *In his discussion of the facts of history, Carr distinguishes between "a mere fact about the past" and "a fact of history." Into which category should Bettelheim's encounter with the infirmary guard go (p. 29)?*
2. *If you were commissioned to write a history of the semester or of a particular group during the semester, what would be your most important "facts of history"?*

THE WRITER

1. *Carr begins with a question but does not answer it until the last sentence. What are the main steps of the discussion leading to his answer? The answer takes the form of a definition. Which is the most important of the defining words?*
2. *Carr says that the historian's "facts are really not at all like fish on the fishmonger's slab. They are like fish swimming about in a vast and sometimes inaccessible ocean; and what the historian catches will depend partly on chance, but mainly on what part of the ocean he chooses to fish in and what tackle he chooses to use—these two factors being, of course, determined by the kind of fish he wants to catch (p. 844)." How appropriate a description is this of the way other kinds of writers use facts—for example, the scientist, the psychologist, the novelist, the familiar essayist?*
3. *Write a brief "history" of an event, keeping in mind what Carr says about what the historian does.*

Politics and Government

George Orwell

SHOOTING AN ELEPHANT

In Moulmein, in Lower Burma, I was hated by large numbers of people—the only time in my life that I have been important enough for this to happen to me. I was sub-divisional police officer of the town, and in an aimless, petty kind of way anti-European feeling was very bitter. No one had the guts to raise a riot, but if a European woman went through the bazaars alone somebody would probably spit betel juice over her dress. As a police officer I was an obvious target and was baited whenever it seemed safe to do so. When a nimble Burman tripped me up on the football field and the referee (another Burman) looked the other way, the crowd yelled with hideous laughter. This happened more than once. In the end the sneering yellow faces of young men that met me everywhere, the insults hooted after me when I was at a safe distance, got badly on my nerves. The young Buddhist priests were the worst of all. There were several thousands of them in the town and none of them seemed to have anything to do except stand on street corners and jeer at Europeans.

All this was perplexing and upsetting. For at that time I had already made up my mind that imperialism was an evil thing and the sooner I chucked up my job and got out of it the better. Theoretically—and secretly, of course—I was all for the Burmese and all against their oppressors, the British. As for the job I was doing, I hated it more bitterly than I can perhaps make clear. In a job like that you see the dirty work of Empire at close quarters. The wretched prisoners huddling in the stinking cages of the lock-ups, the grey, cowed faces of the long-term convicts, the scarred buttocks of the men who had been flogged with

First published in *New Writing* (Autumn 1936).

bamboos—all these oppressed me with an intolerable sense of guilt. But I could get nothing into perspective. I was young and ill-educated and I had had to think out my problems in the utter silence that is imposed on every Englishman in the East. I did not even know that the British Empire is dying, still less did I know that it is a great deal better than the younger empires that are going to supplant it. All I knew was that I was stuck between my hatred of the empire I served and my rage against the evil-spirited little beasts who tried to make my job impossible. With one part of my mind I thought of the British Raj[1] as an unbreakable tyranny, as something clamped down, in *saecula saeculorum*,[2] upon the will of prostrate peoples; with another part I thought that the greatest joy in the world would be to drive a bayonet into a Buddhist priest's guts. Feelings like these are the normal by-products of imperialism; ask any Anglo-Indian official, if you can catch him off duty.

One day something happened which in a roundabout way was enlightening. It was a tiny incident in itself, but it gave me a better glimpse than I had had before of the real nature of imperialism—the real motives for which despotic governments act. Early one morning the sub-inspector at a police station the other end of the town rang me up on the 'phone and said that an elephant was ravaging the bazaar. Would I please come and do something about it? I did not know what I could do, but I wanted to see what was happening and I got on to a pony and started out. I took my rifle, an old .44 Winchester and much too small to kill an elephant, but I thought the noise might be useful *in terrorem.* Various Burmans stopped me on the way and told me about the elephant's doings. It was not, of course, a wild elephant, but a tame one which had gone "must."[3] It had been chained up, as tame elephants always are when their attack of "must" is due, but on the previous night it had broken its chain and escaped. Its mahout, the only person who could manage it when it was in that state, had set out in pursuit, but had taken the wrong direction and was now twelve hours' journey away, and in the morning the elephant had suddenly reappeared in the town. The Burmese population had no weapons and were quite helpless against it. It had already destroyed somebody's bamboo hut, killed a cow and raided some fruit-stalls and devoured the stock; also it had met the municipal rubbish van and, when the driver jumped out and took to his heels, had turned the van over and inflicted violences upon it.

The Burmese sub-inspector and some Indian constables were waiting for me in the quarter where the elephant had been seen. It was a very poor quarter, a labyrinth of squalid bamboo huts, thatched with palm-

1. The imperial government of British India and Burma.   2. Forever and ever.   3. Gone into sexual heat.

leaf, winding all over a steep hillside. I remember that it was a cloudy, stuffy morning at the beginning of the rains. We began questioning the people as to where the elephant had gone and, as usual, failed to get any definite information. That is invariably the case in the East; a story always sounds clear enough at a distance, but the nearer you get to the scene of events the vaguer it becomes. Some of the people said that the elephant had gone in one direction, some said that he had gone in another, some professed not even to have heard of any elephant. I had almost made up my mind that the whole story was a pack of lies, when we heard yells a little distance away. There was a loud, scandalized cry of "Go away, child! Go away this instant!" and an old woman with a switch in her hand came round the corner of a hut, violently shooing away a crowd of naked children. Some more women followed, clicking their tongues and exclaiming; evidently there was something that the children ought not to have seen. I rounded the hut and saw a man's dead body sprawling in the mud. He was an Indian, a black Dravidian coolie, almost naked, and he could not have been dead many minutes. The people said that the elephant had come suddenly upon him round the corner of the hut, caught him with its trunk, put its foot on his back and ground him into the earth. This was the rainy season and the ground was soft, and his face had scored a trench a foot deep and a couple of yards long. He was lying on his belly with arms crucified and head sharply twisted to one side. His face was coated with mud, the eyes wide open, the teeth bared and grinning with an expression of unendurable agony. (Never tell me, by the way, that the dead look peaceful. Most of the corpses I have seen looked devilish.) The friction of the great beast's foot had stripped the skin from his back as neatly as one skins a rabbit. As soon as I saw the dead man I sent an orderly to a friend's house nearby to borrow an elephant rifle. I had already sent back the pony, not wanting it to go mad with fright and throw me if it smelt the elephant.

5   The orderly came back in a few minutes with a rifle and five cartridges, and meanwhile some Burmans had arrived and told us that the elephant was in the paddy fields below, only a few hundred yards away. As I started forward practically the whole population of the quarter flocked out of the houses and followed me. They had seen the rifle and were all shouting excitedly that I was going to shoot the elephant. They had not shown much interest in the elephant when he was merely ravaging their homes, but it was different now that he was going to be shot. It was a bit of fun to them, as it would be to an English crowd; besides they wanted the meat. It made me vaguely uneasy. I had no intention of shooting the elephant—I had merely sent for the rifle to defend myself if necessary—and it is always unnerving to have a crowd following you. I marched down the hill, looking and feeling a fool, with

the rifle over my shoulder and an ever-growing army of people jostling at my heels. At the bottom, when you got away from the huts, there was a metalled road and beyond that a miry waste of paddy fields a thousand yards across, not yet ploughed but soggy from the first rains and dotted with coarse grass. The elephant was standing eight yards from the road, his left side towards us. He took not the slightest notice of the crowd's approach. He was tearing up bunches of grass, beating them against his knees to clean them and stuffing them into his mouth.

I had halted on the road. As soon as I saw the elephant I knew with perfect certainty that I ought not to shoot him. It is a serious matter to shoot a working elephant—it is comparable to destroying a huge and costly piece of machinery—and obviously one ought not to do it if it can possibly be avoided. And at that distance, peacefully eating, the elephant looked no more dangerous than a cow. I thought then and I think now that his attack of "must" was already passing off; in which case he would merely wander harmlessly about until the mahout came back and caught him. Moreover, I did not in the least want to shoot him. I decided that I would watch him for a little while to make sure that he did not turn savage again, and then go home.

But at that moment I glanced round at the crowd that had followed me. It was an immense crowd, two thousand at the least and growing every minute. It blocked the road for a long distance on either side. I looked at the sea of yellow faces above the garish clothes—faces all happy and excited over this bit of fun, all certain that the elephant was going to be shot. They were watching me as they would watch a conjurer about to perform a trick. They did not like me, but with the magical rifle in my hands I was momentarily worth watching. And suddenly I realized that I should have to shoot the elephant after all. The people expected it of me and I had got to do it; I could feel their two thousand wills pressing me forward, irresistibly. And it was at this moment, as I stood there with the rifle in my hands, that I first grasped the hollowness, the futility of the white man's dominion in the East. Here was I, the white man with his gun, standing in front of the unarmed native crowd—seemingly the leading actor of the piece; but in reality I was only an absurd puppet pushed to and fro by the will of those yellow faces behind. I perceived in this moment that when the white man turns tyrant it is his own freedom that he destroys. He becomes a sort of hollow, posing dummy, the conventionalized figure of a sahib. For it is the condition of his rule that he shall spend his life in trying to impress the "natives," and so in every crisis he has got to do what the "natives" expect of him. He wears a mask, and his face grows to fit it. I had got to shoot the elephant. I had committed myself to doing it when I sent for the rifle. A sahib has got to act like a sahib; he has got to appear resolute, to know his own mind and do definite things. To come all that way, rifle in hand, with two thousand people marching at my heels, and then to trail feebly away, having done nothing—no, that was impossible. The crowd would laugh at me. And my whole life, every white man's life in the East, was one long struggle not to be laughed at.

But I did not want to shoot the elephant. I watched him beating his bunch of grass against his knees, with that preoccupied grandmotherly air that elephants have. It seemed to me that it would be murder to shoot him. At that age I was not squeamish about killing animals, but I had never shot an elephant and never wanted to. (Somehow it always seems worse to kill a *large* animal.) Besides, there was the beast's owner to be considered. Alive, the elephant was worth at least a hundred pounds; dead, he would only be worth the value of his tusks, five pounds, possibly. But I had got to act quickly. I turned to some experienced-looking Burmans who had been there when we arrived, and asked them how the elephant had been behaving. They all said the same thing: he took no notice of you if you left him alone, but he might charge if you went too close to him.

It was perfectly clear to me what I ought to do. I ought to walk up to within, say, twenty-five yards of the elephant and test his behavior. If he charged, I could shoot; if he took no notice of me, it would be safe to leave him until the mahout came back. But also I knew that I was going to do no such thing. I was a poor shot with a rifle and the ground was soft mud into which one would sink at every step. If the elephant charged and I missed him, I should have about as much chance as a toad under a steam-roller. But even then I was not thinking particularly of my own skin, only of the watchful yellow faces behind. For at that moment, with the crowd watching me, I was not afraid in the ordinary sense, as I would have been if I had been alone. A white man mustn't be frightened in front of "natives"; and so, in general, he isn't frightened. The sole thought in my mind was that if anything went wrong those two thousand Burmans would see me pursued, caught, trampled on and reduced to a grinning corpse like that Indian up the hill. And if that happened it was quite probable that some of them would laugh. That would never do. There was only one alternative. I shoved the cartridges into the magazine and lay down on the road to get a better aim.

10　　　　The crowd grew very still, and a deep, low, happy sigh, as of people who see the theatre curtain go up at last, breathed from innumerable throats. They were going to have their bit of fun after all. The rifle was a beautiful German thing with cross-hair sights. I did not then know that in shooting an elephant one would shoot to cut an imaginary bar running from ear-hole to ear-hole. I ought, therefore, as the elephant was sideways on, to have aimed straight at his ear-hole; actually I aimed several inches in front of this, thinking the brain would be further forward.

When I pulled the trigger I did not hear the bang or feel the kick—one never does when a shot goes home—but I heard the devilish roar of glee that went up from the crowd. In that instant, in too short a time, one would have thought, even for the bullet to get there, a mysterious, terrible change had come over the elephant. He neither stirred nor fell, but every line of his body had altered. He looked suddenly stricken, shrunken, immensely old, as though the frightful impact of the bullet had paralysed him without knocking him down. At last, after what seemed a long time—it might have been five seconds, I dare say—he sagged flabbily to his knees. His mouth slobbered. An enormous senility seemed to have settled upon him. One could have imagined him thousands of years old. I fired again into the same spot. At the second shot he did not collapse but climbed with desperate slowness to his feet and stood weakly upright, with legs sagging and head drooping. I fired a third time. That was the shot that did for him. You could see the agony of it jolt his whole body and knock the last remnant of strength from his legs. But in falling he seemed for a moment to rise, for as his hind legs collapsed beneath him he seemed to tower upward like a huge rock toppling, his trunk reaching skywards like a tree. He trumpeted, for the first and only time. And then down he came, his belly towards me, with a crash that seemed to shake the ground even where I lay.

I got up. The Burmans were already racing past me across the mud. It was obvious that the elephant would never rise again, but he was not dead. He was breathing very rhythmically with long rattling gasps, his great mound of a side painfully rising and falling. His mouth was wide open—I could see far down into caverns of pale pink throat. I waited a long time for him to die, but his breathing did not weaken. Finally I fired my two remaining shots into the spot where I thought his heart must be. The thick blood welled out of him like red velvet, but still he did not die. His body did not even jerk when the shots hit him, the tortured breathing continued without a pause. He was dying, very slowly and in great agony, but in some world remote from me where not even a bullet could damage him further. I felt that I had got to put an end to that dreadful noise. It seemed dreadful to see the great beast lying there, powerless to move and yet powerless to die, and not even to be able to finish him. I sent back for my small rifle and poured shot after shot into his heart and down his throat. They seemed to make no impression. The tortured gasps continued as steadily as the ticking of a clock.

In the end I could not stand it any longer and went away. I heard later that it took him half an hour to die. Burmans were bringing dahs[4] and

4. Butcher knives.

baskets even before I left, and I was told they had stripped his body almost to the bones by the afternoon.

Afterwards, of course, there were endless discussions about the shooting of the elephant. The owner was furious, but he was only an Indian and could do nothing. Besides, legally I had done the right thing, for a mad elephant has to be killed, like a mad dog, if its owner fails to control it. Among the Europeans opinion was divided. The older men said I was right, the younger men said it was a damn shame to shoot an elephant for killing a coolie, because an elephant was worth more than any damn Coringhee coolie. And afterwards I was very glad that the coolie had been killed; it put me legally in the right and it gave me a sufficient pretext for shooting the elephant. I often wondered whether any of the others grasped that I had done it solely to avoid looking a fool.

THE READER

1. *What issue does Orwell address, and what kind of evidence is proper to it? Does he actually prove anything?*
2. *Does Robley (see question 2, "The Writer," below) show any sign that he recognizes what Orwell calls "the futility of the white man's dominion in the East" (p. 853)? Could it be that this dominion was not futile for Robley, or in his day?*

THE WRITER

1. *The proportion of this essay devoted to narrative is relatively high. What effect(s) does Orwell aim at? How does he organize his essay? Where does he state his thesis? Would he have done better to argue his thesis directly rather than mainly by example? Why, or why not?*
2. *The following is a sketch from* The Graphic *(London) of January 21, 1888, written by a Major-General H. G. Robley:*

SHOOTING A MAN-EATING CROCODILE

It is tedious work waiting for the man-eater to come out of the water, but a fat native child as a lure will make the monster speedily walk out of his aqueous lair. Contracting the loan of a chubby infant, however, is a matter of some negotiation, and it is perhaps not to be wondered at that mammas occasionally object to their offspring being pegged down as food for a great crocodile; but there are always some parents to be found whose confidence in the skill of the British sportsman is unlimited. My sketch [omitted here] gives a view of the collapse of the man-eater, who, after viewing the tempting morsel tethered carefully to a bamboo near the water's edge, makes a rush through the sedges. The sportsman, hidden behind a bed of reeds, then fires, the bullet penetrates the heart, and the monster is dead in a moment. The little bait, whose only alarm has been caused by the report of the rifle, is now taken home by its doting mother for its matutinal banana. The natives wait to get the musky flesh of the animal, and the sportsman secures the scaly skin and the massive head of porous bone as a trophy.

There are probably educational and social similarities between Robley and Orwell, and, of course, both were imperial Englishmen in a colonial setting. However, the differences between the two men are far more striking. Briefly and basically, what are they? How are these similarities and differences reflected in the essays' styles?

3. *Compare Robley's sketch with Swift's "A Modest Proposal" (p. 878). How can you tell that Robley is not ironic and that Swift is? If you can't tell, what does your uncertainty suggest about the nature of irony?*

4. *Adapt Robley's sketch to meet an ironic purpose like Swift's.*

Stephen Hume

THE SPIRIT WEEPS

In anticipation of the high international profile Canada would achieve during the 1988 winter Olympics in Calgary, organizing officials planned a dazzling constellation of parallel events intended to showcase the richness and diversity of our national culture. Writers, poets, musicians and painters were to celebrate the Greek ideal of mind and body with demonstrations of their creative prowess to match the physical performances of athletes. As part of this program, Alberta's Glenbow Institute, backed by the major corporate sponsorship of an oil industry giant, Shell Canada Limited, began preparations for what was to be the most complex and complete display of the art of Canadian aboriginal peoples in world history.

For five years before the Olympic Games began, a committee of six distinguished scholars, each bringing specialized knowledge from one of the six cultural regions of aboriginal Canada, began planning the exhibition. The Glenbow is itself a world class museum and archive, particularly with reference to the culture and ethnology of plains Indians. But it was clear from the beginning that the scope and magnitude of the exhibition planned could not be mounted with the resources of the Glenbow alone. Starting with a commitment of $600,000 in seed money from the Olympic Organizing Committee and $1,100,000 from Shell, the curatorial scholars began taking inventory of where Canadian aboriginal artifacts might be located outside Canada and subsequently borrowed for exhibition before national and international audiences. By the

First appeared in the *Edmonton Journal* (Feb. 1988).

time they were finished, the committee had scoured more than 150 museums and private collections across 20 foreign countries and arranged the display of more than 600 artifacts. The show was staged in two segments. The first took place at the Glenbow itself, preceding and coinciding with the Olympic Games; the second, in association with the new National Museum of Civilization, was mounted three months later in Ottawa, using the former premises of Canada's national art gallery for the eastern venue.

The Spirit Sings proved a curator's tour de force. The committee had mounted a show of stunning power and intensity. All the displays resonated with aesthetic genius and a deep sense of spiritual place. Yet this exhibition of the artistic traditions of Canada's first people, so wonderful in the hermetic context of ethnological display, was also an act of national hypocrisy so shocking as to border on the obscene. It triggered deep anger and hurt among the very native peoples it purported to celebrate and raised profound questions regarding the integrity of Canada's social and intellectual conscience.

Art cannot be detached from the social and historical matrix in which it originates, however much museum curators might desire to do so in the interests of neat classification and compartmentalized analysis, and however much the state might seize upon it as an opportunity for shameless propagandizing and outright lying. And that was the great irony of The Spirit Sings. Mounted in celebration of our first peoples, it used their art to tell the world a fundamental lie about our national concern for their rights and well-being. The exhibits displayed in The Spirit Sings and the powerful controversy surrounding them were testimony not only to the richness and diversity of native culture, but also to the rapacious and destructive force of European settlement in North America and the continued brutality of Canadian institutions toward native social and political aspirations.

5   If much of the early destruction of aboriginal culture was caused by people who were not Canadians, but the worst of European adventurers—the ancestors of those who now piously seek to deprive remote and impoverished native communities of their traditional economic base in hunting and trapping—Canadians later had the opportunity to chart a different course. The Spirit Sings exhibited damning evidence of our choice not to do so.

While the relics displayed were the beautiful works of sensitive and intelligent artists, they also represented the debris that we robbed from the rubble of cultures whose traditions we first demolished, then sought to extinguish.

Indiscriminate bombardments of Indian villages by naval flotillas, massacres of women and children by punitive fur traders, tolerance of the ravages of disease and economic impoverishment, denial of universal access in the law, selective official segregation, the corporal punishment of children for speaking their own language in federal schools, the legal banning of ritual, ceremony and religion, denial of the vote—these are phenomena not of some barbarous Dark Age, but of recent Canadian history.

It was significant that while the officials and curators were congratulating themselves on the commercial success and aesthetic quality of their show, Georges Erasmus of the Assembly of First Nations was warning Canadians that a new generation of young native "warriors" may be contemplating armed violence instead of talk, having learned that negotiation in good faith with Canada's political institutions appears to be a failure. Indeed, as Alberta officials basked in the Olympic limelight, the Sioux nation was announcing the appointment of its first formal war chief since Sitting Bull[1] crossed the Medicine Line not far from Calgary, carrying the scalps of Custer's Seventh Cavalry. The Sioux had called back Philip Stevens, the 59-year-old great grandson of Chief Standing Bear. Stevens, head of a multi-million-dollar engineering firm, was charged with responsibility for recovering the Black Hills, a sacred spiritual center for the Sioux nation which was never surrendered by treaty.

In Alberta, while The Spirit Sings talked about the importance of art, no less than a dozen outstanding aboriginal claims awaited formal adjudication in the courts. Some of them, like the question of title to the lands of the dispossessed—and now conveniently dispersed—Papaschase band, are the matters of historic and legal curiosity. The Papaschase lands, now occupied by the University of Alberta and most of the south side of Edmonton, may have been surrendered to land speculators under manipulated, defective and highly questionable procedures. But with no survivors of the band, who could legally reopen the issue? Other aboriginal claims are more immediate, from the Peigan of southern Alberta who object that the Oldman River dam constructed by the provincial government destroys their ancestral spiritual centers, to the Lubicons of the north who simply want a settlement after half a century of moral dithering, legalistic equivocating and political indecision by federal and provincial authorities.

The tiny and isolated Lubicon band, 20% of which had just tested positive for tuberculosis—a disease long banished from the general population—went so far as to attempt political action, demonstrating outside the Glenbow in Calgary and seeking public support for a boycott of The Spirit Sings during the Olympics. The 350 Lubicons were joined in protest by the Mohawks, who went to court in an unsuccessful

10

1. Sitting Bull (1834?–90) was at the battle of the Little Big Horn (1876), where General George Armstrong Custer (1839–76) and his troops were annihilated by Sioux warriors under Crazy Horse.

attempt to block the showing of a sacred ceremonial mask, public display of which amounted to a religious desecration. As the simple, rural Lubicons made their small public protest outside the Glenbow, the racist and abusive remarks of Calgarians entering the exhibition shocked even the worldly correspondent from *The Chicago Tribune,* assigned to cover the show and no stranger to racism. The attitude of the public towards the Indians, of course, marred the Olympic spirit in a far more fundamental way than the Lubicons' protest had. It also revealed the true nature of The Spirit Sings exhibition: not so much a celebration of native culture as self-congratulatory propaganda regarding the importance of such peoples to the Canadian state.

In this context, passing through the opening gallery at The Spirit Sings exhibition and gazing upon the 30 or so pathetic little artifacts that represented Canada's extinguished Beothuk nation in Newfoundland, what manner of person could not feel appalled and shamed that the memory of an exterminated nation should be so evoked in the service of our national pride? What perverted manner of pride could be taken from this? It was as though the Berlin Olympics had put on a display of Jewish religious objects to celebrate the diversity, pluralism and tolerance of Nazi culture.

Staring at the tiny pair of baby's moccasins, or near them, the little effigy taken from the grave of a four-year-old child, I could think only of the story of Demasduwit. She had given birth only two days earlier when she was seized by John Peyton's party in 1819. Her husband pleaded fruitlessly for his wife's return. When he struggled to free her, he was killed before her eyes like a troublesome cur. Demasduwit's baby was abandoned to die. The mother was taken off to be "civilized." A month later, in an act of unusual generosity, her corpse was returned to her dwindling people in a coffin—a gesture intended, no doubt, to emphasize her captor's civilized concern with appearances. Ten years later, the last of her people had died in captivity and the Beothuk nation was extinct.

Demasduwit had not even the dignity of a quiet grave. In 1827, in the interests of preserving for posterity something of the vanished Beothuk culture, William Cormack robbed the grave of the woman, her husband and the little baby, taking two skulls and the collection of burial offerings. To witness the murdered woman's modest possessions—for murder it most certainly was—displayed in honor of a sports event and Canadian self-aggrandizement, is to sense the trivialization of a tragedy of enormous proportions.

Elaborate apologies have been written regarding the fate of the Beothuk in Canadian history, dismissing as mere legend the popular accounts of bounties paid for ears and 18th Century "hunting" expeditions by European settlers. In many cases the demise of the Beothuk is blamed upon incursions by warlike neighbors from the mainland. Denial, prevarication and casting of blame upon the victims are typical of the consistent Canadian refusal to take ownership of the ugly parts of our past, although this approach fails to address the simple fact that the Beothuk were a coastal people when the European settlers arrived, then suddenly fled to a bitter and inhospitable interior that remains largely uninhabited even today. It was there, as far from the settlers as they could get, that they finally perished in poverty, starvation and disease.

The magnificent artifacts of the Beothuk's neighbors in the Maritime provinces, also displayed by The Spirit Sings, are equally poignant in forcing our attention to the brutality of European conquest and occupation. Think of their fate this way: when the most bloodthirsty Roman despots set out to terrorize dissident elements, they would order a "decimation" in which every tenth person was executed. Between 1600 and 1700, not one out of every 10 but nine out of every 10 people of the Micmac and Maliseet nations died or were killed—a number which makes Caligula[2] seem moderate by comparison. Or one might admire the lovely decoration of deerskin dresses by Huron women. The Huron population declined by 65%, from 25,000 to 9,000 people, in little over a decade. A similar rate of decline in contemporary Canada would see the disappearance of every person living outside Quebec. The Huron's major mistake was in becoming an ally of the French, who lost to the English. By the time the winners were finished, the Huron were in diaspora, some fleeing as far as the present state of Oklahoma. This pattern is characteristic of the Canadian experience. It is estimated by some scholars that the total native population of the Canadian landmass might have been as high as 1,000,000 people at the time of first European contact. At the turn of the century it had declined to about 100,000. This is a cultural destruction that approaches genocidal proportions.

The Spirit Sings exhibition dealt with these unpleasant realities in an oblique and less than forthright way. It was, after all, an "ethnological" display rather than an expression of historical context. On reflection, it is clear, the show was actually intended to tell the world and ourselves what a generous and tolerant country we live in; how quick we are to recognize and honor the way in which the culture of native peoples has enriched our broader society. In fact, the social, ethical, political, spiritual and philosophical values of native culture have been almost universally rejected by the dominant society. On the other hand, native culture has certainly enriched museums, even if we consistently exclude it from

2. Caligula (Gaius Caesar, A.D. 12–41), Roman emperor from A.D. 37–41, first revered by the people but who, after a serious illness, became increasingly depraved and eventually notorious for his extortion and plunder.

contributing to the mainstream. And many of the museums that have been enriched are not even Canadian. Douglas Cole, a historian at Simon Fraser University in Vancouver, exhaustively documents the patterns of theft and acquisition in his important book *Captured Heritage*. An estimated 300,000 artifacts from the Northwest Pacific coastal cultures are now held by international collections—this is looting on the scale of the Visigoths.[3]

The cataloging and administration of such collections have made fine careers for curators, who by some extraordinary ethical gymnastics find easy praise for the value of native art while remaining strangely ineffectual regarding the social value of the human beings who produced it. But instead of debating the collective responsibility of the collectors, we might consider instead the social context of a selection of wonderful Assiniboine drawings, kindly loaned by their European owner to The Spirit Sings organizers for display in Canada.

The Assiniboines, numbering about 9,000 and among the great traders of the plains tribes, ranged across the central Canadian prairies. In 1833, the winter counts of the Teton Sioux, Kiowa and Blackfeet record unusual numbers of shooting stars, generally considered a harbinger of some natural catastrophe. Major Alexander Culbertson at Fort McKenzie confirms the sightings. The native people did not have long to wait. By 1837, horrified European travelers were reporting the whole prairie region littered with the rotting corpses of men, women and children, abandoned equipment, straying horse herds, and the encampments that brought a new term to plains Indian language—the Ghost Camp, where the lodges are occupied only by the dead.

The pestilence and infection of smallpox reduced the Assiniboines from the most powerful nation on the great plains to a pitiful, ragged remnant, begging for food. They had been, in the reports of appalled observers, virtually exterminated. While the cycle of plagues which ravaged the plains cultures in 1837 and again in 1864, 1868 and 1883 could hardly be attributed to federal policy, they did offer a convenient clearing of the landscape for unencumbered settlement by the huge influx of farmers that was deliberate policy in Ottawa.

Shortly thereafter, the strategic elimination of the plains Indians' primary food source occurred. In 1875, the Baker Company of Fort Benton, Montana, shipped 75,000 buffalo hides to the east. Most of them had been taken from the hunting grounds of Canada's Blackfeet, Blood, Peigan and Sarcee tribes, the carcasses left to rot in the summer sun, the bones later collected and shipped for fertilizer production. Four years later, the buffalo were gone forever from the southern Alberta

3. A Germanic people who separated from the Ostrogoths in the fourth century, raided Roman territories repeatedly, and established great kingdoms in Gaul and Spain.

grasslands and Canadian society marched its native people into the concentration camp.

Today we call them Indian reserves, sharing our love of the euphemism with the South Africans, who call them "homelands," but let us not deceive ourselves about their original function. The rationalization for reserves, of course, was that they were created to save the few aboriginals who managed to survive the dismantling of their economy and the wrecking of their political structure, social organization, religion and family units. Indian reserves were invented by bureaucrats to control the movements of free-ranging people and to "concentrate" them in one place and bring them under the power of the dominant society.

Indian reserves were designed with the specific purpose of destroying plains Indian culture, which was predicated upon movement and freedom, so that the land might be carved up by newcomers who could get more productive use out of it by farming. As the topsoil of Palliser's Triangle, the arid region of southeastern Alberta and southwestern Saskatchewan, blows away on the dry winds of drought, demanding more and more dams and irrigation districts, with the attendant hazards of salinization—not to mention the overall tax burden—the definitions of what constitutes productivity require a new evaluation.

The most intense element of The Spirit Sings was its remarkable and moving celebration of the deep and complex spiritual nature of Indian life. In this, too, the exhibition brings shame upon us. Consider all those missionaries, acting in the name of a compassionate Christ, whose objective was the displacement of all the spiritual beliefs the exhibition purports to celebrate. To this day the church has difficulty bringing itself to acknowledge its role as an agent of cultural destruction. Yet with all the best of intentions, missionaries representing the two mainstreams of Christian religion waged an active campaign to displace traditional religious belief and value systems among native peoples. At a time when aboriginal societies faced enormous upheaval and change, their societies threatened by the growing military, economic and commercial pressure from the European invaders, church missionaries set about sucking out the glue which held native communities together. By devaluing the moral force of traditional spiritual leaders and co-opting the belief and value systems of native people, the church served as an active agent in fomenting confusion and increasing vulnerability—always there with compassion, of course, to help pick up the pieces and shape them into a Christian and essentially European framework.

Evocative examples of the disruptive influence of Christian missionaries can be found almost everywhere. The Inuit settlement of Igloolik, high in Canada's central arctic, provides one good example. It was the site of a shameless "war for souls" which raged between Anglicans and Roman Catholics, as though the numbers of converted were pieces in a chess game. Fifty years later, a visitor from outside could still witness the scars of deep division in a community that had been homogeneous and secure. The Tsartlip Indian Reserve of Vancouver Island is another example. It had the early distinction of having all its residents formally converted by itinerant priests, first to Roman Catholicism, then Anglicanism and then Methodism—all in the same year.

The state certainly concurred with this approach, seeing the church as a powerful instrument of assimilation. Missionaries like William Duncan, who established a mission to the Tsimshian at Metlakatla, off the coast of what is now the Alaska Panhandle, saw traditional native rites as an obstacle to Christian conversion and lobbied for their prohibition. Duncan was particularly offended by the ancient puberty rites that accompanied potlatch ceremonials. By 1885, with the wholehearted backing of the various churches, Canada's Parliament had passed legislation which prohibited the practice of native religious and spiritual ceremonies.

The Canadian state took suppression of native ceremonies seriously indeed. In 1922, following a traditional potlatch at Alert Bay, a prosperous Kwakiutl community located just off the northeast coast of Vancouver Island, a large number of men and women (the Indians say 45, the official records say 29) were arrested for the offences of making speeches, singing, dancing, arranging and distributing gifts. The police action followed complaints from the federal Indian agent, William Halliday, who, in a gross conflict of interest, conveniently doubled as magistrate for the trial. The arresting officer, an RCMP sergeant, took the role of prosecutor. In this perversion of justice, 20 of the men and women arrested were sentenced to prison terms of two and three months. Fines were levied in the form of their ancestral ceremonial regalia, which were seized by the federal government. Halliday reported more than 450 items filling 300 cubic feet of space. Some, according to Cole, he sold off to a foreign collector for $291, the rest went to the curators at the National Museum in Ottawa, the forerunner of the same Museum of Civilization which hosted The Spirit Sings.

These officials salved their conscience in the matter by assigning arbitrary commercial values to the items and sending cheques to the Indian agent for distribution. Cole points out in *Captured Heritage* that some Indians claim never to have received a penny's compensation for the priceless material—one item of which was believed by the Indians themselves to have a value of 18,250 Hudson's Bay Company blankets. Ultimately, part of the stolen property was returned after 66 years and a legal battle, but much of it has been lost to the owners and, in any event, as Cole points out: "The charges and convictions, the surrenders and imprisonments, were a severe blow even to so resilient a culture as that of the Kwakiutl. . . . But the forced cessation of the public potlatch, the feasts, and the dances was a more severe blow."

This essential contempt by the collectors of artifacts for the validity of traditional cultural values which the material items represent continues today. At the Calgary segment of The Spirit Sings, the curators insisted on displaying sacred objects in bald defiance of the wishes of those who consider them sacred. Sacred objects, it seems, are merely property, and in Canadian society ownership is nine-tenths of the law. Would the Pope and the Archbishop of Canterbury feel that way about the sacraments and holy relics of their faith, one wonders. At the Ottawa segment of the exhibition, at least, the authorities reportedly decided not to include the false-face mask of the Mohawk nation, public display of which the Indians had fruitlessly sought to block by court action. One wonders, however, whether this decision had more to do with the proximity of angry Iroquois to Ottawa than with real understanding or compassion for the ethical issue.

At the Glenbow exhibit in Calgary, which is surrounded by the Blood, Peigan, Sarcee, Blackfeet and Stoney reserves, cards were provided for observers to record their feelings. "Sometimes our spirit has wept," wrote one viewer. "Sadness for my people who lost so much of their spirit when their ceremonial objects were laid down or taken away"—an interesting irony considered in the context of the consistent robbing of native cultural items in order that museums might provide evidence of the "preservation" of native culture. This juxtaposition of the aboriginal view and the official view says much about Canadian values. It confirms what has long been clear—that we actually prefer our native culture in museums. We certainly do not prefer it running the Department of Indian Affairs or the Department of Fisheries. Nor do we prefer native culture announcing the news on national television or determining its own political destiny.

"Where are the natives whose heritage this is?" asked another observer in Calgary. "Couldn't you find ANY to guide us through THEIR history . . . the spirits must be crying." This, too, draws attention to the wretched lie at the heart of The Spirit Sings. We prefer native culture that we may put on display when it conveniences us, called out for ceremonies that make us appear magnanimous—whether the creators of the artifacts like it or not.

"Why get upset, it's all in the past," one young white observer said to me after hearing my feelings about the show. "We didn't do it, somebody else did. Don't expect me to feel guilty for my great-grandfather." This view I did not find surprising. It is the constant bleat of Canadian society with respect to native peoples. It was somebody else's fault. It is somebody else's responsibility. This familiar refrain lies at the

30

very heart of northern Alberta's Lubicon band dispute, still festering after 50 years of political buck-passing and evasion of moral responsibility by the federal and provincial governments.

"It's all in the past . . ."

Tell that to the people of Peerless Lake, where on 10 March 1986, six young people died after drinking methyl hydrate—children erasing their futures with school duplicating fluid.

Tell it to Donald Marshall, imprisoned for 11 years for a crime he did not commit because of what is now the obviously entrenched racism of the justice system.

35 Tell it to the relatives of Helen Betty Osborne in The Pas, Man. She was abducted, raped, stabbed 50 times with a screwdriver and left dying in the snow by four white teenagers. For 16 years the murderers were sheltered from the law by their community. Testimony at the trial made it clear that the identities of Helen's abductors were no secret in The Pas—but then, the victim was only an Indian.

Try telling the Lubicons that the injustice is all in the past. They who struggle to defend themselves against the encroachments of the very same oil industry that so sanctimoniously sponsored The Spirit Sings exhibition in honor of native culture.

All of this adds up to the old story. Native culture is nice, but not if it gets in our way. Native culture is important, but not in terms of the people in whom it resides, only in the artifacts—the things we can collect and display in museum cases.

In the context of what The Spirit Sings claimed to say about the importance and value of native culture, Canadians need to ask some pointed questions of ourselves and our governing authorities. We need to ask why, in a province as wealthy as Alberta, we permit continuation of the conditions which lead to a death rate among Indian infants that is more than twice what it is for the general population. Why, in a country prepared to spend millions of dollars telling the world how much we value native culture, we tolerate conditions in which native people are four times as likely as the rest of us to die before reaching their life expectancy and three times as likely to die by violence.

We need to ask how we can accept the conditions under which native people are 10 times as likely to be diagnosed as alcoholics. Why it was possible, for nearly a decade, for the suicide rate for native people in northern Saskatchewan to remain 15 times greater than the national average. What landscape of sorrow and despair do such people inhabit?

40 Why do 75% of native students in the Northwest Territories abandon school between Grade 7 and Grade 12—is this a failure to be blamed on the victims, or is the failure in the structure of a system which can neither visualize nor address their needs? How can it be that only 2% of the Canadian population provides 10% of the prison inmates—

perhaps because the unemployment rate for native people consistently runs about 800% higher than that deemed acceptable for mainstream society?

These statistics provide the reality behind the self-serving lies of exhibitions like The Spirit Sings. They reveal far more about the hypocrisy of the dominant culture than they do about the propensities of native people. They tell us, in fact, that far from honoring native culture, Canadian society dismisses it in its living forms.

Made invisible by our denial of the worth of their own cultural values; excluded from economic participation in the dominant culture and squeezed into ghettos at the least productive margins of society; cheated of their promised patrimony; cheated of an equal opportunity at life itself and fully cognizant of our hypocrisy, aboriginal Canadians are far from the honored participants in our society that The Spirit Sings would have the world believe. They remain deeply estranged from the social and political process of this nation. How long before, as Georges Erasmus warns, the sorrow and despair becomes rage and vengeance? The tragedy, unfortunately, is not all in the past. It is all in the present. It is not somebody else's responsibility. It is Canadians' responsibility. If The Spirit Sings served one purpose, it was to remind thinking Canadians that the pathetic remnants of the Beothuk should be on display all right. They should be on display in a national shrine of shame and humility. The first act of every prime minister should be to kneel before them and pray to the God that we invoke in our national anthem—both for national forgiveness and that what was done to the Beothuk, the Huron, the Assinboines, may never be done to Canada.

Oscar Lewis

THE CULTURE OF POVERTY

Throughout recorded history, in literature, in proverbs, and in popular sayings, we find two opposite evaluations of the nature of the poor. Some characterize the poor as blessed, virtuous, upright, serene, independent, honest, kind, and happy. Others characterize them as evil, mean, violent, sordid, and criminal. These contradictory and confusing evaluations are also reflected in the in-fighting that is going on in the current war against poverty. Some stress the great potential of the poor for self-help, leadership, and community organization, while others point to the sometimes irreversible destructive effect of poverty upon individual

From *Anthropological Essays* (1946).

character, and therefore emphasize the need for guidance and control to remain in the hands of the middle class, which presumably has better mental health.

These opposing views reflect a political power struggle between competing groups. However, some of the confusion results from the failure to distinguish between poverty *per se* and the culture of poverty, and from the tendency to focus upon the individual personality rather than upon the group—that is, the family and the slum community.

As an anthropologist I have tried to understand poverty and its associated traits as a culture or, more accurately, as a subculture[1] with its own structure and rationale, as a way of life which is passed down from generation to generation along family lines. This view directs attention to the fact that the culture of poverty in modern nations is not only a matter of economic deprivation, of disorganization, or of the absence of something. It is also something positive and provides some rewards without which the poor could hardly carry on.

Elsewhere I have suggested that the culture of poverty transcends regional, rural-urban, and national differences and shows remarkable similarities in family structure, interpersonal relations, time orientation, value systems, and spending patterns.[2] These cross-national similarities are examples of independent invention and convergence. They are common adaptations to common problems.

The culture of poverty can come into being in a variety of historical contexts. However, it tends to grow and flourish in societies with the following set of conditions: (1) a cash economy, wage labor, and production for profit; (2) a persistently high rate of unemployment and underemployment for unskilled labor; (3) low wages; (4) the failure to provide social, political, and economic organization, either on a voluntary basis or by government imposition, for the low-income population; (5) the existence of a bilateral kinship system rather than a unilateral one; and finally, (6) the existence of a set of values in the dominant class which stresses the accumulation of wealth and property, the possibility of upward mobility, and thrift, and explains low economic status as the result of personal inadequacy or inferiority.

The way of life which develops among some of the poor under these conditions is the culture of poverty. It * * * is both an adaptation and a reaction of the poor to their marginal position in a class-stratified, highly individuated, capitalistic society. It represents an effort to cope with feelings of hopelessness and despair which develop from the realization of the improbability of achieving success in terms of the values and

---

1. Although the term "subculture of poverty" is technically more accurate, I sometimes use "culture of poverty" as a shorter form [Lewis' note].

2. Oscar Lewis, *Five Families: Mexican Case Studies in the Culture of Poverty* (New York: Basic Books, 1959) [Lewis' note].

goals of the larger society. Indeed, many of the traits of the culture of poverty can be viewed as attempts at local solutions for problems not met by existing institutions and agencies because the people are not eligible for them, cannot afford them, or are ignorant or suspicious of them. For example, unable to obtain credit from banks, they are thrown upon their own resources and organize informal credit devices without interest.

The culture of poverty, however, is not only an adaptation to a set of objective conditions of the larger society. Once it comes into existence, it tends to perpetuate itself from generation to generation because of its effect on the children. By the time slum children are six or seven years old, they usually have absorbed the basic values and attitudes of their subculture and are not psychologically geared to take full advantage of changing conditions or increased opportunities which may occur in their lifetime.

Most frequently the culture of poverty develops when a stratified social and economic system is breaking down or is being replaced by another as in the case of the transition from feudalism to capitalism or during periods of rapid technological change. Often it results from imperial conquest in which the native social and economic structure is smashed and the natives are maintained in a servile colonial status, sometimes for many generations. It can also occur in the process of detribalization such as that now going on in Africa.

The most likely candidates for the culture of poverty are the people who come from the lower strata of a rapidly changing society and are already partially alienated from it. Thus, landless rural workers who migrate to the cities can be expected to develop a culture of poverty much more readily than migrants from stable peasant villages with a well-organized traditional culture. In this connection there is a striking contrast between Latin America, where the rural population long ago made the transition from a tribal to a peasant society, and Africa, which is still close to its tribal heritage. The more corporate nature of many of the African tribal societies, in contrast to Latin American rural communities, and the persistence of village ties tend to inhibit or delay the formation of a full-blown culture of poverty in many of the African towns and cities. * * *

The culture of poverty can be studied from various points of view: the relationship between the subculture and the larger society; the nature of the slum community; the nature of the family; and the attitudes, values, and character structure of the individual.

1. The lack of effective participation and integration of the poor in the major institutions of the larger society is one of the crucial characteristics of the culture of poverty. This is a complex matter and results from

a variety of factors which may include lack of economic resources, segregation and discrimination, fear, suspicion, or apathy, and the development of local solutions for problems. However, participation in some of the institutions of the larger society—for example, in the jails, the army, and the public relief system—does not *per se* eliminate the traits of the culture of poverty. In the case of a relief system which barely keeps people alive, both the basic poverty and the sense of hopelessness are perpetuated rather than eliminated.

Low wages, chronic unemployment, and underemployment lead to low income, lack of property ownership, absence of savings, absence of food reserves in the home, and a chronic shortage of cash. These conditions reduce the possibility of effective participation in the larger economic system. And as a response to these conditions, we find in the culture of poverty a high incidence of pawning of personal goods, borrowing from local money lenders at usurious rates of interest, spontaneous informal credit devices organized by neighbors, the use of second-hand clothing and furniture, and the pattern of frequent buying of small quantities of food many times a day as the need arises.

People with a culture of poverty produce very little wealth and receive very little in return. They have a low level of literacy and education, do not belong to labor unions, are not members of political parties, generally do not participate in the national welfare agencies, and make very little use of banks, hospitals, department stores, museums, or art galleries. They have a critical attitude toward some of the basic institutions of the dominant classes, hatred of the police, mistrust of government and those in high position, and a cynicism which extends even to the church. This gives the culture of poverty a high potential for protest and for being used in political movements aimed against the existing social order.

People with a culture of poverty are aware of middle-class values, talk about them, and even claim some of them as their own; but on the whole, they do not live by them.[3] Thus it is important to distinguish between what they say and what they do. For example, many will tell you that marriage by law, by the church, or by both, is the ideal form of marriage; but few will marry. For men who have no steady jobs or other source of income, who do not own property and have no wealth to pass on to their children, who are present-time oriented and who want to avoid the expense and legal difficulties involved in formal marriage and divorce, free union or consensual marriage makes a lot of sense. Women will often turn down offers of marriage because they feel that

3. In terms of Hyman Rodman's concept of "The Lower-Class Value Stretch" (*Social Forces*, Vol. 42, No. 2 [December, 1963], pp. 205–15), I would say that the culture of poverty exists where this value stretch is at a minimum, that is, where the belief in middle-class values is at a minimum [Lewis' note].

marriage ties them down to men who are immature, punishing, and generally unreliable. Women feel that consensual union gives them a better break; it gives them some of the freedom and flexibility that men have. By not giving the fathers of their children legal status as husbands, the women have a stronger claim on their children if they decide to leave their men. It also gives women exclusive rights to a house or any other property they may own.

2. In describing the culture of poverty on the local community level, we find poor housing conditions, crowding, gregariousness, but above all, a minimum of organization beyond the level of the nuclear and extended family. Occasionally there are informal temporary groupings or voluntary associations within slums. The existence of neighborhood gangs which cut across slum settlements represents a considerable advance beyond the zero point of the continuum that I have in mind. Indeed, it is the low level of organization which gives the culture of poverty its marginal and anachronistic quality in our highly complex, specialized, organized society. Most primitive peoples have achieved a higher level of socio-cultural organization than our modern urban slum dwellers.

In spite of the generally low level of organization, there may be a sense of community and *esprit de corps* [4] in urban slums and in slum neighborhoods. This can vary within a single city, or from region to region or country to country. The major factors which influence this variation are the size of the slum, its location and physical characteristics, length of residence, incidence of home and landownership (versus squatter rights), rentals, ethnicity, kinship ties, and freedom or lack of freedom of movement. When slums are separated from the surrounding area by enclosing walls or other physical barriers, when rents are low and fixed and stability of residence is great (twenty or thirty years), when the population constitutes a distinct ethnic, racial, or language group, is bound by ties of kinship or *compadrazgo*, [5] and when there are some internal voluntary associations, then the sense of local community approaches that of a village community. In many cases this combination of favorable conditions does not exist. However, even where internal organization and esprit de corps are at a bare minimum and people move around a great deal, a sense of territoriality develops which sets off the slum neighborhoods from the rest of the city. * * *

3. On the family level the major traits of the culture of poverty are the absence of childhood as a specially prolonged and protected stage in the life cycle, early initiation into sex, free unions or consensual marriages, a relatively high incidence of the abandonment of wives and children, a trend toward female- or mother-centered families and conse-

4. French, regard for honor and interests of the body one belongs to; team spirit.   5. Spanish, conspiracy.

quently a much greater knowledge of maternal relatives, a strong predisposition to authoritarianism, lack of privacy, verbal emphasis upon family solidarity, which is only rarely achieved because of sibling rivalry, and competition for limited goods and maternal affection.

4. On the level of the individual, the major characteristics are a strong feeling of marginality, of helplessness, of dependence, and of inferiority. I found this to be true of slum dwellers in Mexico City and San Juan among families that do not constitute a distinct ethnic or racial group and that do not suffer from racial discrimination. In the United States, of course, the culture of poverty of the Negroes has the additional disadvantage of racial discrimination; but as I have already suggested, this additional disadvantage contains a great potential for revolutionary protest and organization which seems to be absent in the slums of Mexico City or among the poor whites in the South.

Other traits include a high incidence of maternal deprivation, orality, weak ego structure, confusion of sexual identification, a lack of impulse control, a strong present-time orientation with relatively little ability to defer gratification and to plan for the future, a sense of resignation and fatalism, a widespread belief in male superiority, and a high tolerance for psychological pathology of all sorts.

20   People with a culture of poverty are provincial and locally oriented and have very little sense of history. They know only their own troubles, their own local conditions, their own neighborhood, their own way of life. Usually they do not have the knowledge, the vision, or the ideology to see the similarities between their problems and those of their counterparts elsewhere in the world. They are not class conscious although they are very sensitive indeed to status distinctions.

In considering the traits discussed above, the following propositions must be kept in mind. (1) The traits fall into a number of clusters and are functionally related within each cluster. (2) Many, but not all, of the traits of different clusters are also functionally related. For example, men who have low wages and suffer chronic unemployment develop a poor self-image, become irresponsible, abandon their wives and children, and take up with other women more frequently than do men with high incomes and steady jobs. (3) None of the traits, taken individually, is distinctive *per se* of the subculture of poverty. It is their conjunction, their function, and their patterning that define the subculture. (4) The subculture of poverty, as defined by these traits, is a statistical profile; that is, the frequency of distribution of the traits both singly and in clusters will be greater than in the rest of the population. In other words, more of the traits will occur in combination in families with a subculture of poverty than in stable working-class, middle-class, or upper-class families. Even within a single slum there will probably be a gradient from culture of poverty families to families without a culture of poverty. (5)

The profiles of the subculture of poverty will probably differ in systematic ways with the difference in the national cultural contexts of which they are a part. It is expected that some new traits will become apparent with research in different nations.

I have not yet worked out a system of weighing each of the traits, but this could probably be done and a scale could be set up for many of the traits. Traits that reflect lack of participation in the institutions of the larger society or an outright rejection—in practice, if not in theory—would be the crucial traits; for example, illiteracy, provincialism, free unions, abandonment of women and children, lack of membership in voluntary associations beyond the extended family.

When the poor become class conscious or active members of trade-union organizations or when they adopt an internationalist outlook on the world, they are no longer part of the culture of poverty although they may still be desperately poor. Any movement, be it religious, pacifist, or revolutionary, which organizes and gives hope to the poor and which effectively promotes solidarity and a sense of identification with larger groups, destroys the psychological and social core of the culture of poverty. In this connection, I suspect that the civil-rights movement among the Negroes in the United States has done more to improve their self-image and self-respect than have their economic advances although, without doubt, the two are mutually reinforcing.

The distinction between poverty and the culture of poverty is basic to the model described here. There are degrees of poverty and many kinds of poor people. The culture of poverty refers to one way of life shared by poor people in given historical and social contexts. The economic traits which I have listed for the culture of poverty are necessary but not sufficient to define the phenomena I have in mind. There are a number of historical examples of very poor segments of the population which do not have a way of life that I would describe as a subculture of poverty. Here I should like to give four examples:

a) Many of the primitive or preliterate peoples studied by anthropologists suffer from dire poverty which is the result of poor technology and/or poor natural resources or both, but they do not have the traits of the subculture of poverty. Indeed, they do not constitute a subculture because their societies are not highly stratified. In spite of their poverty, they have a relatively integrated, satisfying, and self-sufficient culture. Even the simplest food-gathering and hunting tribes have a considerable amount of organization—bands and band chiefs, tribal councils, and local self-government—elements which are not found in the culture of poverty.

b) In India the lower castes (the *Camars* or leatherworkers, and the *Bhangis* or sweepers) may be desperately poor both in the villages and in the cities, but most of them are integrated into the larger society and

have their own *panchayat* organizations[6] which cut across village lines
and give them a considerable amount of power.[7] In addition to the caste
system, which gives individuals a sense of identity and belonging, there
is still another factor, the clan system. Wherever there are unilateral
kinship systems or clans, one would not expect to find the culture of
poverty because a clan system gives people a sense of belonging to a
corporate body which has a history and a life of its own and therefore
provides a sense of continuity, a sense of a past and of a future.

c) The Jews of Eastern Europe were very poor but they did not have
many of the traits of the culture of poverty because of their tradition
of literacy, the great value placed upon learning, the organization of
the community around the rabbi, the proliferation of local voluntary associations, and their religion, which taught that they were the chosen
people.

d) My fourth example is speculative and relates to socialism. On the
basis of my limited experience in one socialist country—Cuba—and on
the basis of my reading, I am inclined to believe that the culture of
poverty does not exist in the socialist countries. I first went to Cuba in
1947 as a visiting professor for the State Department. At that time I
began a study of a sugar plantation in Melena del Sur and of a slum in
Havana. After the Castro Revolution[8] I made my second trip to Cuba
as a correspondent for a major magazine, and I revisited the same slum
and some of the same families. The physical aspect of the slum had
changed very little, except for a beautiful new nursery school. It was clear
that the people were still desperately poor, but I found much less of the
feelings of despair, apathy, and hopelessness which are so diagnostic of
urban slums in the culture of poverty. They expressed great confidence
in their leaders and hope for a better life in the future. The slum itself
was now highly organized, with block committees, educational committees, party committees. The people had a new sense of power and
importance. They were armed and were given a doctrine which glorified
the lower class as the hope of humanity. (I was told by one Cuban official
that they had practically eliminated delinquency by giving arms to the
delinquents!) * * *

In effect, we find that in primitive societies, and in caste societies, the
culture of poverty does not develop. In socialist, fascist, and highly
developed capitalist societies with a welfare state, the culture of poverty
tends to decline. I suspect that the culture of poverty flourishes in, and

6. East Indian, a council of five (or more)
persons, assembled as a jury or as a committee to decide on matters affecting a village,
community, or body.
7. It may be that in the slums of Calcutta
and Bombay an incipient culture of poverty
is developing. It would be highly desirable

to do family studies there as a crucial test
of the culture-of-poverty hypothesis [Lewis'
note].
8. Overthrow of the Cuban government of
President General Fulgencio Batista in
1958, organized and led by Communist
revolutionary Fidel Castro (1926–   ).

is generic to, the early free enterprise stage of capitalism and that it is also endemic in colonialism.

It is important to distinguish between different profiles in the subculture of poverty depending upon the national context in which these subcultures are found. If we think of the culture of poverty primarily in terms of the factor of integration in the larger society and a sense of identification with the great tradition of that society, or with a new emerging revolutionary tradition, then we will not be surprised that some slum dwellers with a lower per capita income may have moved farther away from the core characteristics of the culture of poverty than others with a higher per capita income. * * *

I have listed fatalism and a low level of aspiration as among the key traits for the subculture of poverty. Here too, however, the national context makes a big difference. Certainly the level of aspiration of even the poorest sector of the population in a country like the United States, with its traditional ideology of upward mobility and democracy, is much higher than in more backward countries like Ecuador and Peru, where both the ideology and the actual possibilities of upward mobility are extremely limited and where authoritarian values still persist in both the urban and rural milieu.

Because of the advanced technology, the high level of literacy, the development of mass media, and the relatively high aspiration level of all sectors of the population, especially when compared with underdeveloped nations, I believe that although there is still a great deal of poverty in the United States (estimates range between thirty and fifty million people) there is relatively little of what I would call the culture of poverty. My rough guess would be that only about 20 per cent of the population below the poverty line (between six and ten million people) in the United States have characteristics which would justify classifying their way of life as that of a culture of poverty. Probably the largest sector within this group would consist of very low-income Negroes, Mexicans, Puerto Ricans, American Indians, and southern poor whites. The relatively small number of people in the United States with a culture of poverty is a positive factor because it is much more difficult to eliminate the culture of poverty than to eliminate poverty *per se*.

Middle-class people, and this would certainly include most social scientists, tend to concentrate on the negative aspects of the culture of poverty. They tend to associate negative values with such traits as present-time orientation and concrete versus abstract orientation. I do not intend to idealize or romanticize the culture of poverty. As someone has said, "It is easier to praise poverty than to live in it"[9]: yet some of the

9. Proverbial, possibly from the Latin *Nemo paupertatem commendaret nisi pauper* ("No man should commend poverty but one who is poor"), St Bernard, *Sermons* (c. 1153).

positive aspects of these traits must not be overlooked. Living in the present may develop a capacity for spontaneity, for the enjoyment of the sensual, the indulgence of impulse, which is often blunted in the middle-class, future-oriented man. Perhaps it is this reality of the moment which the existentialist writers are so desperately trying to recapture but which the culture of poverty experiences as a natural, everyday phenomenon. The frequent use of violence certainly provides a ready outlet for hostility so that people in the culture of poverty suffer less from repression than does the middle class.

In the traditional view of culture, anthropologists have said that it provides human beings with a design for living, with a ready-made set of solutions for human problems so that individuals don't have to begin all over again from scratch each generation. That is, the core of culture is its positive adaptive function. I, too, have called attention to some of the adaptive mechanisms in the culture of poverty—for example, low aspiration level helps to reduce frustration; legitimization of short-range hedonism makes possible spontaneity and enjoyment. However, on the whole it seems to me that it is a thin, relatively superficial culture. There is a great deal of pathos, suffering, and emptiness among those who live in the culture of poverty. It does not provide much support or satisfaction and its encouragement of mistrust tends to magnify helplessness and isolation. Indeed, the poverty of culture is one of the crucial aspects of the culture of poverty.

35   The concept of the culture of poverty provides a high level of generalization which, hopefully, will unify and explain a number of phenomena which have been viewed as distinctive characteristics of racial, national, or regional groups. For example, matrifocality, a high incidence of consensual unions, and a high percentage of households headed by women, which have been thought to be distinctive of Caribbean family organization or of Negro family life in the U.S.A., turn out to be traits of the culture of poverty and are found among diverse peoples in many parts of the world and among peoples who have had no history of slavery.

The concept of a cross-societal subculture of poverty enables us to see that many of the problems we think of as distinctively our own or distinctively Negro problems (or that of any other special racial or ethnic group) also exist in countries where there are no distinct ethnic minority groups. It suggests, too, that the elimination of physical poverty *per se* may not be enough to eliminate the culture of poverty which is a whole way of life.

What is the future of the culture of poverty? In considering this question, one must distinguish between those countries in which it represents a relatively small segment of the population and those in which it constitutes a very large one. Obviously the solutions will differ in these two situations. In the United States, the major solution proposed by planners and social workers in dealing with multiple-problem families and the so-called "hard core" of poverty has been to attempt slowly to raise their level of living and to incorporate them into the middle class. Wherever possible, there has been some reliance upon psychiatric treatment.

In the underdeveloped countries, however, where great masses of people live in the culture of poverty, a social-work solution does not seem feasible. Because of the magnitude of the problem, psychiatrists can hardly begin to cope with it. They have all they can do to care for their own growing middle class. In these countries the people with a culture of poverty may seek a more revolutionary solution. By creating basic structural changes in society, by redistributing wealth, by organizing the poor and giving them a sense of belonging, of power, and of leadership, revolutions frequently succeed in abolishing some of the basic characteristics of the culture of poverty even when they do not succeed in abolishing poverty itself.

Some of my readers have misunderstood the subculture of poverty model and have failed to grasp the importance of the distinction between poverty and the subculture of poverty. In making this distinction I have tried to document a broader generalization; namely, that it is a serious mistake to lump all poor people together, because the causes, the meaning, and the consequences of poverty vary considerably in different socio-cultural contexts. There is nothing in the concept that puts the onus of poverty on the character of the poor. Nor does the concept in any way play down the exploitation and neglect suffered by the poor. Indeed, the subculture of poverty is part of the larger culture of capitalism, whose social and economic system channels wealth into the hands of a relatively small group and thereby makes for the growth of sharp class distinctions.

I would agree that the main reasons for the persistence of the subculture are no doubt the pressures that the larger society exerts over its members and the structure of the larger society itself. However, this is not the only reason. The subculture develops mechanisms that tend to perpetuate it, especially because of what happens to the world view, aspirations, and character of the children who grow up in it. For this reason, improved economic opportunities, though absolutely essential and of the highest priority, are not sufficient to alter basically or eliminate the subculture of poverty. Moreover, elimination is a process that will take more than a single generation, even under the best of circumstances, including a socialist revolution. 40

Some readers have thought that I was saying, "Being poor is terrible, but having a culture of poverty is not so bad." On the contrary, I am saying that it is easier to eliminate poverty than the culture of poverty. I am also suggesting that the poor in a precapitalistic caste-ridden society like India had some advantages over modern urban slum dwellers because the people were organized in castes and *panchayats* and this organization gave them some sense of identity and some strength and power. Perhaps Gandhi[1] had the urban slums of the West in mind when he wrote that the caste system was one of the greatest inventions of mankind. Similarly, I have argued that the poor Jews of Eastern Europe, with their strong tradition of literacy and community organization, were better off than people with the culture of poverty. On the other hand, I would argue that people with the culture of poverty, with their strong sense of resignation and fatalism, are less driven and less anxious than the striving lower middle class, who are still trying to make it in the face of the greatest odds.

1. Gandhi Mohandas Karamchand; Mahatma ("Great Souled") (1869–1948), leader of the Indian nationalist movement against British rule, considered to be the father of his country. Internationally esteemed for his doctrine of nonviolent protest to achieve political and social progress.

Jonathan Swift

A MODEST PROPOSAL

For Preventing the Children of Poor People in Ireland from Being a Burden to Their Parents or Country, and for Making Them Beneficial to the Public

It is a melancholy object to those who walk through this great town[1] or travel in the country, when they see the streets, the roads, and cabin doors, crowded with beggars of the female-sex, followed by three, four, or six children, all in rags and importuning every passenger for an alms. These mothers, instead of being able to work for their honest livelihood, are forced to employ all their time in strolling to beg sustenance for their helpless infants, who, as they grow up, either turn thieves for want of work, or leave their dear native country to fight for the Pretender in Spain, or sell themselves to the Barbadoes.[2]

A pamphlet printed in 1729.

1. Dublin.
2. Many poor Irish sought to escape poverty by emigrating to the Barbadoes and other western English colonies, paying for transport by binding themselves to work for a landowner there for a period of years. The Pretender, claimant to the English throne, was barred from succession after his father, King James II, was deposed in a Protestant revolution; thereafter, many Irish Catholics joined the Pretender in his exile in France and Spain, and in his unsuccessful attempts at counterrevolution.

I think it is agreed by all parties that this prodigious number of children in the arms, or on the backs, or at the heels of their mothers, and frequently of their fathers, is in the present deplorable state of the kingdom a very great additional grievance; and therefore whoever could find out a fair, cheap, and easy method of making these children sound, useful members of the commonwealth would deserve so well of the public as to have his statue set up for a preserver of the nation.

But my intention is very far from being confined to provide only for the children of professed beggars; it is of a much greater extent, and shall take in the whole number of infants at a certain age who are born of parents in effect as little able to support them as those who demand our charity in the streets.

As to my own part, having turned my thoughts for many years upon this important subject, and maturely weighed the several schemes of other projectors,[3] I have always found them grossly mistaken in their computation. It is true, a child just dropped from its dam may be supported by her milk for a solar year, with little other nourishment; at most not above the value of two shillings,[4] which the mother may certainly get, or the value in scraps, by her lawful occupation of begging; and it is exactly at one year old that I propose to provide for them in such a manner as instead of being a charge upon their parents or the parish, or wanting food and raiment for the rest of their lives, they shall on the contrary contribute to the feeding, and partly to the clothing, of many thousands.

There is likewise another great advantage in my scheme, that it will prevent those voluntary abortions, and that horrid practice of women murdering their bastard children, alas, too frequent among us, sacrificing the poor innocent babes, I doubt, more to avoid the expense than the shame, which would move tears and pity in the most savage and inhuman breast.

The number of souls in this kingdom being usually reckoned one million and a half, of these I calculate there may be about two hundred thousand couple whose wives are breeders; from which number I subtract thirty thousand couples who are able to maintain their own children, although I apprehend there cannot be so many under the present distresses of the kingdom; but this being granted, there will remain an hundred and seventy thousand breeders. I again subtract fifty thousand for those women who miscarry, or whose children die by accident or disease within the year. There only remain an hundred and twenty thousand children of poor parents annually born. The question therefore is, how this number shall be reared and provided for, which, as I have

5

---

3. People with projects; schemers.

4. A shilling used to be worth about twenty-five cents.

already said, under the present situation of affairs, is utterly impossible by all the methods hitherto proposed. For we can neither employ them in handicraft or agriculture; we neither build houses (I mean in the country) nor cultivate land. They can very seldom pick up a livelihood by stealing till they arrive at six years old, except where they are of towardly parts;[5] although I confess they learn the rudiments much earlier, during which time they can however be looked upon only as probationers, as I have been informed by a principal gentleman in the county of Cavan, who protested to me that he never knew above one or two instances under the age of six, even in a part of the kingdom so renowned for the quickest proficiency in that art.

I am assured by our merchants that a boy or a girl before twelve years old is no salable commodity; and even when they come to this age they will not yield above three pounds, or three pounds and half a crown[6] at most on the Exchange; which cannot turn to account either to the parents or the kingdom, the charge of nutriment and rags having been at least four times that value.

I shall now therefore humbly propose my own thoughts, which I hope will not be liable to the least objection.

I have been assured by a very knowing American of my acquaintance in London, that a young healthy child well nursed is at a year old a most delicious, nourishing, and wholesome food, whether stewed, roasted, baked, or boiled; and I make no doubt that it will equally serve in a fricassee or a ragout.

I do therefore humbly offer it to public consideration that of the hundred and twenty thousand children, already computed, twenty thousand may be reserved for breed, whereof only one fourth part to be males, which is more than we allow to sheep, black cattle, or swine; and my reason is that these children are seldom the fruits of marriage, a circumstance not much regarded by our savages, therefore one male will be sufficient to serve four females. That the remaining hundred thousand may at a year old be offered in sale to the persons of quality and fortune through the kingdom, always advising the mother to let them suck plentifully in the last month, so as to render them plump and fat for a good table. A child will make two dishes at an entertainment for friends; and when the family dines alone, the fore or hind quarter will make a reasonable dish, and seasoned with a little pepper or salt will be very good boiled on the fourth day, especially in winter.

I have reckoned upon a medium that a child just born will weigh twelve pounds, and in a solar year if tolerably nursed increaseth to twenty-eight pounds.

---

5. Promising abilities.

6. A pound was twenty shillings; a crown, five shillings.

I grant this food will be somewhat dear, and therefore very proper for landlords, who, as they have already devoured most of the parents, seem to have the best title to the children.

Infant's flesh will be in season throughout the year, but more plentiful in March, and a little before and after. For we are told by a grave author, an eminent French physician,[7] that fish being a prolific diet, there are more children born in Roman Catholic countries about nine months after Lent than at any other season; therefore, reckoning a year after Lent, the markets will be more glutted than usual, because the number of popish infants is at least three to one in this kingdom; and therefore it will have one other collateral advantage, by lessening the number of Papists among us.[8]

I have already computed the charge of nursing a beggar's child (in which list I reckon all cottagers, laborers, and four fifths of the farmers) to be about two shillings per annum, rags included; and I believe no gentleman would repine to give ten shillings for the carcass of a good fat child, which, as I have said, will make four dishes of excellent nutritive meat, when he hath only some particular friend or his own family to dine with him. Thus the squire will learn to be a good landlord, and grow popular among the tenants; the mother will have eight shillings net profit, and be fit for work till she produces another child.

Those who are more thrifty (as I must confess the times require) may flay the carcass; the skin of which artificially[9] dressed will make admirable gloves for ladies, and summer boots for fine gentlemen. 15

As to our city of Dublin, shambles[1] may be appointed for this purpose in the most convenient parts of it, and butchers we may be assured will not be wanting; although I rather recommend buying the children alive, and dressing them hot from the knife as we do roasting pigs.

A very worthy person, a true lover of his country, and whose virtues I highly esteem, was lately pleased in discoursing on this matter to offer a refinement upon my scheme. He said that many gentlemen of this kingdom, having of late destroyed their deer, he conceived that the want of venison might be well supplied by the bodies of young lads and maidens, not exceeding fourteen years of age nor under twelve, so great a number of both sexes in every county being now ready to starve for want of work and service; and these to be disposed of by their parents, if alive, or otherwise by their nearest relations. But with due deference to so excellent a friend and so deserving a patriot, I cannot be altogether in his sentiments; for as to the males, my American acquaintance assured me from frequent experience that their flesh was generally tough and

7. The sixteenth-century comic writer François Rabelais.
8. The speaker is addressing Protestant Anglo-Irish, who were the chief landown-

ers and administrators, and his views of Catholicism in Ireland and abroad echo theirs.
9. Skillfully.
1. Slaughterhouses.

lean, like that of our schoolboys, by continual exercise, and their taste disagreeable; and to fatten them would not answer the charge. Then as to the females, it would, I think with humble submission, be a loss to the public, because they soon would become breeders themselves: and besides, it is not improbable that some scrupulous people might be apt to censure such a practice (although indeed very unjustly) as a little bordering upon cruelty; which, I confess, hath always been with me the strongest objection against any project, how well soever intended.

But in order to justify my friend, he confessed that this expedient was put into his head by the famous Psalmanazar,[2] a native of the island Formosa,[2] who came from thence to London above twenty years ago, and in conversation told my friend that in his country when any young person happened to be put to death, the executioner sold the carcass to persons of quality as a prime dainty; and that in his time the body of a plump girl of fifteen, who was crucified for an attempt to poison the emperor, was sold to his Imperial Majesty's prime minister of state, and other great mandarins of the court, in joints from the gibbet, at four hundred crowns. Neither indeed can I deny that if the same use were made of several plump young girls in this town, who without one single groat[3] to their fortunes cannot stir abroad without a chair,[4] and appear at the playhouse and assemblies in foreign fineries which they never will pay for, the kingdom would not be the worse.

Some persons of a desponding spirit are in great concern about that vast number of poor people who are aged, diseased, or maimed, and I have been desired to employ my thoughts what course may be taken to ease the nation of so grievous an encumbrance. But I am not in the least pain upon that matter, because it is very well known that they are every day dying and rotting by cold and famine, and filth and vermin, as fast as can be reasonably expected. And as to the younger laborers, they are now in almost as hopeful a condition. They cannot get work, and consequently pine away for want of nourishment to a degree that if at any time they are accidentally hired to common labor, they have not strength to perform it; and thus the country and themselves are happily delivered from the evils to come.

20   I have too long digressed, and therefore shall return to my subject. I think the advantages by the proposal which I have made are obvious and many, as well as of the highest importance.

For first, as I have already observed, it would greatly lessen the number of Papists, with whom we are yearly overrun, being the principal

2. Actually a Frenchman, George Psalmanazar had passed himself off as from Formosa (now Taiwan) and had written a fictitious book about his "homeland," with descriptions of human sacrifice and cannibalism.
3. An English coin worth about four pennies.
4. A sedan chair.

breeders of the nation as well as our most dangerous enemies; and who stay at home on purpose to deliver the kingdom to the Pretender, hoping to take their advantage by the absence of so many good Protestants, who have chosen rather to leave their country than to stay at home and pay tithes against their conscience to an Episcopal curate.

Secondly, the poorer tenants will have something valuable of their own, which by law may be made liable to distress,[5] and help to pay their landlord's rent, their corn and cattle being already seized and money a thing unknown.

Thirdly, whereas the maintenance of an hundred thousand children, from two years old and upwards, cannot be computed at less than ten shillings a piece per annum, the nation's stock will be thereby increased fifty thousand pounds per annum, besides the profit of a new dish introduced to the tables of all gentlemen of fortune in the kingdom who have any refinement in taste. And the money will circulate among ourselves, the goods being entirely of our own growth and manufacture.

Fourthly, the constant breeders, besides the gain of eight shillings sterling per annum by the sale of their children, will be rid of the charge of maintaining them after the first year.

Fifthly, this food would likewise bring great custom to taverns, where the vintners will certainly be so prudent as to procure the best receipts for dressing it to perfection, and consequently have their houses frequented by all the fine gentlemen, who justly value themselves upon their knowledge in good eating; and a skillful cook, who understands how to oblige his guests, will contrive to make it as expensive as they please.

Sixthly, this would be a great inducement to marriage, which all wise nations have either encouraged by rewards or enforced by laws and penalties. It would increase the care and tenderness of mothers toward their children, when they were sure of a settlement for life to the poor babes, provided in some sort by the public, to their annual profit instead of expense. We should see an honest emulation among the married women, which of them could bring the fattest child to the market. Men would become as fond of their wives during the time of their pregnancy as they are now of their mares in foal, their cows in calf, or sows when they are ready to farrow; nor offer to beat or kick them (as is too frequent a practice) for fear of a miscarriage.

Many other advantages might be enumerated. For instance, the addition of some thousand carcasses in our exportation of barreled beef, the propagation of swine's flesh, and improvement in the art of making good bacon, so much wanted among us by the great destruction of pigs, too frequent at our tables, which are no way comparable in taste or magnifi-

25

5. Seizure for the payment of debts.

cence to a well-grown, fat, yearling child, which roasted whole will make a considerable figure at a lord mayor's feast or any other public entertainment. But this and many others I omit, being studious of brevity.

Supposing that one thousand families in this city would be constant customers for infants' flesh, besides others who might have it at merry meetings, particularly weddings and christenings, I compute that Dublin would take off annually about twenty thousand carcasses, and the rest of the kingdom (where probably they will be sold somewhat cheaper) the remaining eighty thousand.

I can think of no one objection that will possibly be raised against this proposal, unless it should be urged that the number of people will be thereby much lessened in the kingdom. This I freely own, and it was indeed one principal design in offering it to the world. I desire the reader will observe, that I calculate my remedy for this one individual kingdom of Ireland and for no other that ever was, is, or I think ever can be upon earth. Therefore let no man talk to me of other expedients: of taxing our absentees at five shillings a pound: of using neither clothes nor household furniture except what is of our own growth and manufacture: of utterly rejecting the materials and instruments that promote foreign luxury: of curing the expensiveness of pride, vanity, idleness, and gaming in our women: of introducing a vein of parsimony, prudence, and temperance: of learning to love our country, in the want of which we differ even from Laplanders and the inhabitants of Topinamboo[6]: of quitting our animosities and factions, nor acting any longer like the Jews, who were murdering one another at the very moment their city was taken: of being a little cautious not to sell our country and conscience for nothing: of teaching landlords to have at least one degree of mercy toward their tenants: lastly, of putting a spirit of honesty, industry, and skill into our shopkeepers; who, if a resolution could now be taken to buy only our native goods, would immediately unite to cheat and exact upon us in the price, the measure, and the goodness, nor could ever yet be brought to make one fair proposal of just dealing, though often and earnestly invited to it.[7]

30   Therefore I repeat, let no man talk to me of these and the like expedients, till he hath at least some glimpse of hope that there will ever be some hearty and sincere attempt to put them in practice.

But as to myself, having been wearied out for many years with offering vain, idle, visionary thoughts, and at length utterly despairing of success, I fortunately fell upon this proposal, which, as it is wholly new, so it hath something solid and real, of no expense and little trouble, full in our own power, and whereby we can incur no danger in disobliging England. For

6. A district in Brazil.   7. Swift himself had made these proposals
                                            seriously in various previous works.

this kind of commodity will not bear exportation, the flesh being of too tender a consistence to admit a long continuance in salt, although perhaps I could name a country[8] which would be glad to eat up our whole nation without it.

After all, I am not so violently bent upon my own opinion as to reject any offer proposed by wise men, which shall be found equally innocent, cheap, easy, and effectual. But before something of that kind shall be advanced in contradiction to my scheme, and offering a better, I desire the author or authors will be pleased maturely to consider two points. First, as things now stand, how they will be able to find food and raiment for an hundred thousand useless mouths and backs. And secondly, there being a round million of creatures in human figure throughout this kingdom, whose sole subsistence put into a common stock would leave them in debt two millions of pounds sterling, adding those who are beggars by profession to the bulk of farmers, cottagers, and laborers, with their wives and children who are beggars in effect; I desire those politicians who dislike my overture, and may perhaps be so bold to attempt an answer, that they will first ask the parents of these mortals whether they would not at this day think it a great happiness to have been sold for food at a year old in the manner I prescribe, and thereby have avoided such a perpetual scene of misfortunes as they have since gone through by the oppression of landlords, the impossibility of paying rent without money or trade, the want of common sustenance, with neither house nor clothes to cover them from the inclemencies of the weather, and the most inevitable prospect of entailing the like or greater miseries upon their breed forever.

I profess, in the sincerity of my heart, that I have not the least personal interest in endeavoring to promote this necessary work, having no other motive than the public good of my country, by advancing our trade, providing for infants, relieving the poor, and giving some pleasure to the rich. I have no children by which I can propose to get a single penny; the youngest being nine years old, and my wife past childbearing.

8. England.

THE READER

1. At what point do you begin to suspect that Swift is using irony? What further evidence accumulates to make you certain that Swift is being ironic?
2. Does the essay shock you? Was it Swift's purpose to shock you?
3. What is the main target of Swift's attack? What subsidiary targets are there? Does Swift offer any serious solutions for the problems and conditions he is describing?

THE WRITER

1. *This essay has been called one of the best examples of sustained irony in the English language. Irony is difficult to handle because there is always the danger that the reader will miss the irony and take what is said literally. What does Swift do to try to prevent this?*

2. *Why does Swift use such phrases as "just dropped from its dam," "whose wives are breeders," "one fourth part to be males"?*

3. *What devices of argument, apart from the use of irony, does Swift use that could be successfully applied to other subjects?*

4. *In the study questions for Orwell's "Shooting an Elephant" (p. 856), there is a brief sketch from* The Graphic *of 1888, "Shooting a Man-eating Crocodile." How can you tell that this sketch is not ironic and that "A Modest Proposal" is? If you can't tell, what does your uncertainty suggest about the nature of irony?*

5. *Write your own modest proposal for something, keeping in mind Swift's technique.*

Martin Luther King, Jr.

LETTER FROM BIRMINGHAM JAIL[1]

MY DEAR FELLOW CLERGYMEN:

While confined here in the Birmingham city jail, I came across your recent statement calling my present activities "unwise and untimely." Seldom do I pause to answer criticism of my work and ideas. If I sought to answer all the criticisms that cross my desk, my secretaries would have little time for anything other than such correspondence in the course of the day, and I would have no time for constructive work. But since I feel that you are men of genuine good will and that your criticisms are

Written April 16, 1963; published in *Why We Can't Wait* (1964).

1. This response to a published statement by eight fellow clergymen from Alabama (Bishop C. C. J. Carpenter, Bishop Joseph A. Durick, Rabbi Milton L. Grafman, Bishop Paul Hardin, Bishop Holan B. Harmon, the Reverend George M. Murray, the Reverend Edward V. Ramage and the Reverend Earl Stallings) was composed under somewhat constricting circumstances. Begun on the margins of the newspaper in which the statement appeared while I was in jail, the letter was continued on scraps of writing paper supplied by a friendly Negro trusty, and concluded on a pad my attorneys were eventually permitted to leave me. Although the text remains in substance unaltered, I have indulged in the author's prerogative of polishing it for publication [King's note].

sincerely set forth, I want to try to answer your statement in what I hope will be patient and reasonable terms.

I think I should indicate why I am here in Birmingham, since you have been influenced by the view which argues against "outsiders coming in." I have the honor of serving as president of the Southern Christian Leadership Conference, an organization operating in every southern state, with headquarters in Atlanta, Georgia. We have some eighty-five affiliated organizations across the South, and one of them is the Alabama Christian Movement for Human Rights. Frequently we share staff, educational, and financial resources with our affiliates. Several months ago the affiliate here in Birmingham asked us to be on call to engage in a nonviolent direct-action program if such were deemed necessary. We readily consented, and when the hour came we lived up to our promise. So I, along with several members of my staff, am here because I was invited here. I am here because I have organizational ties here.

But more basically, I am in Birmingham because injustice is here. Just as the prophets of the eighth century B.C. left their villages and carried their "thus saith the Lord" far beyond the boundaries of their home towns, and just as the Apostle Paul left his village of Tarsus and carried the gospel of Jesus Christ to the far corners of the Greco-Roman world, so am I compelled to carry the gospel of freedom beyond my own home town. Like Paul, I must constantly respond to the Macedonian call for aid.

Moreover, I am cognizant of the interrelatedness of all communities and states. I cannot sit idly by in Atlanta and not be concerned about what happens in Birmingham. Injustice anywhere is a threat to justice everywhere. We are caught in an inescapable network of mutuality, tied in a single garment of destiny. Whatever affects one directly, affects all indirectly. Never again can we afford to live with the narrow, provincial "outside agitator" idea. Anyone who lives inside the United States can never be considered an outsider anywhere within its bounds.

You deplore the demonstrations taking place in Birmingham. But your statement, I am sorry to say, fails to express a similar concern for the conditions that brought about the demonstrations. I am sure that none of you would want to rest content with the superficial kind of social analysis that deals merely with effects and does not grapple with underlying causes. It is unfortunate that demonstrations are taking place in Birmingham, but it is even more unfortunate that the city's white power structure left the Negro community with no alternative.

In any nonviolent campaign there are four basic steps: collection of the facts to determine whether injustices exist; negotiation; self-purification; and direct action. We have gone through all these steps in Birmingham. There can be no gainsaying the fact that racial injustice engulfs this community. Birmingham is probably the most thoroughly segregated city in the United States. Its ugly record of brutality is widely known. Negroes have experienced grossly unjust treatment in the courts. There have been more unsolved bombings of Negro homes and churches in Birmingham than in any other city in the nation. These are the hard, brutal facts of the case. On the basis of these conditions, Negro leaders sought to negotiate with the city fathers. But the latter consistently refused to engage in good-faith negotiation.

Then, last September, came the opportunity to talk with leaders of Birmingham's economic community. In the course of the negotiations, certain promises were made by the merchants—for example, to remove the stores' humiliating racial signs. On the basis of these promises, the Reverend Fred Shuttlesworth and the leaders of the Alabama Christian Movement for Human Rights agreed to a moratorium on all demonstrations. As the weeks and months went by, we realized that we were the victims of a broken promise. A few signs, briefly removed, returned; the others remained.

As in so many past experiences, our hopes had been blasted, and the shadow of deep disappointment settled upon us. We had no alternative except to prepare for direct action, whereby we would present our very bodies as a means of laying our case before the conscience of the local and the national community. Mindful of the difficulties involved, we decided to undertake a process of self-purification. We began a series of workshops on nonviolence, and we repeatedly asked ourselves: "Are you able to accept blows without retaliating?" "Are you able to endure the ordeal of jail?" We decided to schedule our direct-action program for the Easter season, realizing that except for Christmas, this is the main shopping period of the year. Knowing that a strong economic-withdrawal program would be the by-product of direct action, we felt that this would be the best time to bring pressure to bear on the merchants for the needed change.

Then it occurred to us that Birmingham's mayoral election was coming up in March, and we speedily decided to postpone action until after election day. When we discovered that the Commissioner of Public Safety, Eugene "Bull" Connor, had piled up enough votes to be in the run-off, we decided again to postpone action until the day after the run-off so that the demonstrations could not be used to cloud the issues. Like many others, we wanted to see Mr. Connor defeated, and to this end we endured postponement after postponement. Having aided in this community need, we felt that our direct-action program could be delayed no longer.

10   You may well ask, "Why direct action? Why sit-ins, marches, and so forth? Isn't negotiation a better path?" You are quite right in calling for negotiation. Indeed, this is the very purpose of direct action. Nonviolent

direct action seeks to create such a crisis and foster such a tension that a community which has constantly refused to negotiate is forced to confront the issue. It seeks so to dramatize the issue that it can no longer be ignored. My citing the creation of tension as part of the work of the nonviolent-resister may sound rather shocking. But I must confess that I am not afraid of the word "tension." I have earnestly opposed violent tension, but there is a type of constructive, nonviolent tension which is necessary for growth. Just as Socrates felt that it was necessary to create a tension in the mind so that individuals could rise from the bondage of myths and half-truths to the unfettered realm of creative analysis and objective appraisal, so must we see the need for nonviolent gadflies to create the kind of tension in society that will help men rise from the dark depths of prejudice and racism to the majestic heights of understanding and brotherhood.

The purpose of our direct-action program is to create a situation so crisis-packed that it will inevitably open the door to negotiation. I therefore concur with you in your call for negotiation. Too long has our beloved Southland been bogged down in a tragic effort to live in monologue rather than dialogue.

One of the basic points in your statement is that the action that I and my associates have taken in Birmingham is untimely. Some have asked: "Why didn't you give the new city administration time to act?" The only answer that I can give to this query is that the new Birmingham administration must be prodded about as much as the outgoing one, before it will act. We are sadly mistaken if we feel that the election of Albert Boutwell as mayor will bring the millennium to Birmingham. While Mr. Boutwell is a much more gentle person than Mr. Connor, they are both segregationists, dedicated to maintenance of the status quo. I have hoped that Mr. Boutwell will be reasonable enough to see the futility of massive resistance to desegregation. But he will not see this without pressure from devotees of civil rights. My friends, I must say to you that we have not made a single gain in civil rights without determined legal and nonviolent pressure. Lamentably, it is an historical fact that privileged groups seldom give up their privileges voluntarily. Individuals may see the moral light and voluntarily give up their unjust posture; but, as Reinhold Niebuhr has reminded us, groups tend to be more immoral than individuals.

We know through painful experience that freedom is never voluntarily given by the oppressor; it must be demanded by the oppressed. Frankly, I have yet to engage in a direct-action campaign that was "well timed" in the view of those who have not suffered unduly from the disease of segregation. For years now I have heard the word "Wait!" It rings in the ear of every Negro with piercing familiarity. This "Wait" has almost always meant "Never." We must come to see, with one of our distinguished jurists, that "justice too long delayed is justice denied."

We have waited for more than 340 years for our constitutional and God-given rights. The nations of Asia and Africa are moving with jetlike speed toward gaining political independence, but we still creep at horse-and-buggy pace toward gaining a cup of coffee at a lunch counter. Perhaps it is easy for those who have never felt the stinging darts of segregation to say, "Wait." But when you have seen vicious mobs lynch your mothers and fathers at will and drown your sisters and brothers at whim; when you have seen hate-filled policemen curse, kick, and even kill your black brothers and sisters; when you see the vast majority of your twenty million Negro brothers smothering in an airtight cage of poverty in the midst of an affluent society; when you suddenly find your tongue twisted and your speech stammering as you seek to explain to your six-year-old daughter why she can't go to the public amusement park that has just been advertised on television, and see tears welling up in her eyes when she is told that Funtown is closed to colored children, and see ominous clouds of inferiority beginning to form in her little mental sky, and see her beginning to distort her personality by develop-ing an unconscious bitterness toward white people; when you have to concoct an answer for a five-year-old son who is asking, "Daddy, why do white people treat colored people so mean?"; when you take a cross-country drive and find it necessary to sleep night after night in the uncomfortable corners of your automobile because no motel will accept you; when you are humiliated day in and day out by nagging signs reading "white" and "colored"; when your first name becomes "nigger," your middle name becomes "boy" (however old you are) and your last name becomes "John," and your wife and mother are never given the respected title "Mrs."; when you are harried by day and haunted by night by the fact that you are a Negro, living constantly at tiptoe stance, never quite knowing what to expect next, and are plagued with inner fears and outer resentments; when you are forever fighting a degenerat-ing sense of "nobodiness"—then you will understand why we find it difficult to wait. There comes a time when the cup of endurance runs over, and men are no longer willing to be plunged into the abyss of despair. I hope, sirs, you can understand our legitimate and unavoidable impatience.

15   You express a great deal of anxiety over our willingness to break laws. This is certainly a legitimate concern. Since we so diligently urge people to obey the Supreme Court's decision of 1954 outlawing segregation in the public schools, at first glance it may seem rather paradoxical for us consciously to break laws. One may well ask: "How can you advocate breaking some laws and obeying others?" The answer lies in the fact that there are two types of laws: just and unjust. I would be the first to advocate obeying just laws. One has not only a legal but a moral responsi-

bility to obey just laws. Conversely, one has a moral responsibility to disobey unjust laws. I would agree with St. Augustine that "an unjust law is no law at all."

Now, what is the difference between the two? How does one determine whether a law is just or unjust? A just law is a man-made code that squares with the moral law or the law of God. An unjust law is a code that is out of harmony with the moral law. To put it in the terms of St. Thomas Aquinas: An unjust law is a human law that is not rooted in eternal law and natural law. Any law that uplifts human personality is just. Any law that degrades human personality is unjust. All segregation statutes are unjust because segregation distorts the soul and damages the personality. It gives the segregator a false sense of superiority and the segregated a false sense of inferiority. Segregation, to use the terminology of the Jewish philosopher Martin Buber, substitutes an "I-it" relationship for an "I-thou" relationship and ends up relegating persons to the status of things. Hence segregation is not only politically, economically, and sociologically unsound, it is morally wrong and sinful. Paul Tillich has said that sin is separation. Is not segregation an existential expression of man's tragic separation, his awful estrangement, his terrible sinfulness? Thus it is that I can urge men to obey the 1954 decision of the Supreme Court, for it is morally right; and I can urge them to disobey segregation ordinances, for they are morally wrong.

Let us consider a more concrete example of just and unjust laws. An unjust law is a code that a numerical or power majority group compels a minority group to obey but does not make binding on itself. This is *difference* made legal. By the same token, a just law is a code that a majority compels a minority to follow and that it is willing to follow itself. This is *sameness* made legal.

Let me give another explanation. A law is unjust if it is inflicted on a minority that, as a result of being denied the right to vote, had no part in enacting or devising the law. Who can say that the legislature of Alabama which set up that state's segregation laws was democratically elected? Throughout Alabama all sorts of devious methods are used to prevent Negroes from becoming registered voters, and there are some counties in which, even though Negroes constitute a majority of the population, not a single Negro is registered. Can any law enacted under such circumstances be considered democratically structured?

Sometimes a law is just on its face and unjust in its application. For instance, I have been arrested on a charge of parading without a permit. Now, there is nothing wrong in having an ordinance which requires a permit for a parade. But such an ordinance becomes unjust when it is used to maintain segregation and to deny citizens the First-Amendment privilege of peaceful assembly and protest.

I hope you are able to see the distinction I am trying to point out.   20

In no sense do I advocate evading or defying the law, as would the rabid segregationist. That would lead to anarchy. One who breaks an unjust law must do so openly, lovingly, and with a willingness to accept the penalty. I submit that an individual who breaks a law that conscience tells him is unjust, and who willingly accepts the penalty of imprisonment in order to arouse the conscience of the community over its injustice, is in reality expressing the highest respect for law.

Of course, there is nothing new about this kind of civil disobedience. It was evidenced sublimely in the refusal of Shadrach, Meshach, and Abednego to obey the laws of Nebuchadnezzar, on the ground that a higher moral law was at stake. It was practiced superbly by the early Christians, who were willing to face hungry lions and the excruciating pain of chopping blocks rather than submit to certain unjust laws of the Roman Empire. To a degree, academic freedom is a reality today because Socrates practiced civil disobedience.[2] In our own nation, the Boston Tea Party represented a massive act of civil disobedience.

We should never forget that everything Adolf Hitler did in Germany was "legal" and everything the Hungarian freedom fighters[3] did in Hungary was "illegal." It was "illegal" to aid and comfort a Jew in Hitler's Germany. Even so, I am sure that, had I lived in Germany at the time, I would have aided and comforted my Jewish brothers. If today I lived in a Communist country where certain principles dear to the Christian faith are suppressed, I would openly advocate disobeying that country's anti-religious laws.

I must make two honest confessions to you, my Christian and Jewish brothers. First, I must confess that over the past few years I have been gravely disappointed with the white moderate. I have almost reached the regrettable conclusion that the Negro's great stumbling block in his stride toward freedom is not the White Citizen's Counciler or the Ku Klux Klanner, but the white moderate, who is more devoted to "order" than to justice; who prefers a negative peace which is the absence of tension to a positive peace which is the presence of justice; who constantly says, "I agree with you in the goal you seek, but I cannot agree with your methods of direct action"; who paternalistically believes he can set the timetable for another man's freedom; who lives by a mythical concept of time and who constantly advises the Negro to wait for a "more convenient season." Shallow understanding from people of good will is more frustrating than absolute misunderstanding from people of

2. The ancient Greek philosopher Socrates was tried by the Athenians for corrupting their youth through his skeptical, questioning manner of teaching. He refused to change his ways, and was condemned to death.

3. In the anti-Communist revolution of 1956, which was quickly put down by the Russian army.

ill will. Lukewarm acceptance is much more bewildering than outright rejection.

I had hoped that the white moderate would understand that law and order exist for the purpose of establishing justice and that when they fail in this purpose they become the dangerously structured dams that block the flow of social progress. I had hoped that the white moderate would understand that the present tension in the South is a necessary phase of the transition from an obnoxious negative peace, in which the Negro passively accepted his unjust plight, to a substantive and positive peace, in which all men will respect the dignity and worth of human personality. Actually, we who engage in nonviolent direct action are not the creators of tension. We merely bring to the surface the hidden tension that is already alive. We bring it out in the open, where it can be seen and dealt with. Like a boil that can never be cured so long as it is covered up but must be opened with all its ugliness to the natural medicines of air and light, injustice must be exposed, with all the tension its exposure creates, to the light of human conscience and the air of national opinion, before it can be cured.

In your statement you assert that our actions, even though peaceful,   25
must be condemned because they precipitate violence. But is this a logical assertion? Isn't this like condemning a robbed man because his possession of money precipitated the evil act of robbery? Isn't this like condemning Socrates because his unswerving commitment to truth and his philosophical inquiries precipitated the act by the misguided populace in which they made him drink hemlock? Isn't this like condemning Jesus because his unique God-consciousness and never-ceasing devotion to God's will precipitated the evil act of crucifixion? We must come to see that, as the federal courts have consistently affirmed, it is wrong to urge an individual to cease his efforts to gain his basic constitutional rights because the quest may precipitate violence. Society must protect the robbed and punish the robber.

I had also hoped that the white moderate would reject the myth concerning time in relation to the struggle for freedom. I have just received a letter from a white brother in Texas. He writes: "All Christians know that the colored people will receive equal rights eventually, but it is possible that you are in too great a religious hurry. It has taken Christianity almost two thousand years to accomplish what it has. The teachings of Christ take time to come to earth." Such an attitude stems from a tragic misconception of time, from the strangely irrational notion that there is something in the very flow of time that will inevitably cure all ills. Actually, time itself is neutral; it can be used either destructively or constructively. More and more I feel that the people of ill will have used time much more effectively than have the people of good will. We will have to repent in this generation not merely for the hateful words and actions of the bad people, but for the appalling silence of the good people. Human progress never rolls in on wheels of inevitability; it comes through the tireless efforts of men willing to be co-workers with God, and without this hard work, time itself becomes an ally of the forces of social stagnation. We must use time creatively, in the knowledge that the time is always ripe to do right. Now is the time to make real the promise of democracy and transform our pending national elegy into a creative psalm of brotherhood. Now is the time to lift our national policy from the quicksand of racial injustice to the solid rock of human dignity.

You speak of our activity in Birmingham as extreme. At first I was rather disappointed that fellow clergymen would see my nonviolent efforts as those of an extremist. I began thinking about the fact that I stand in the middle of two opposing forces in the Negro community. One is a force of complacency, made up in part of Negroes who, as a result of long years of oppression, are so drained of self-respect and a sense of "somebodiness" that they have adjusted to segregation; and in part of a few middle-class Negroes who, because of a degree of academic and economic security and because in some ways they profit by segregation, have become insensitive to the problems of the masses. The other force is one of bitterness and hatred, and it comes perilously close to advocating violence. It is expressed in the various black nationalist groups that are springing up across the nation, the largest and best-known being Elijah Muhammad's Muslim movement. Nourished by the Negro's frustration over the continued existence of racial discrimination, this movement is made up of people who have lost faith in America, who have absolutely repudiated Christianity, and who have concluded that the white man is an incorrigible "devil."

I have tried to stand between these two forces, saying that we need emulate neither the "do-nothingism" of the complacent nor the hatred and despair of the black nationalist. For there is the more excellent way of love and nonviolent protest. I am grateful to God that, through the influence of the Negro church, the way of nonviolence became an integral part of our struggle.

If this philosophy had not emerged, by now many streets of the South would, I am convinced, be flowing with blood. And I am further convinced that if our white brothers dismiss as "rabblerousers" and "outside agitators" those of us who employ nonviolent direct action, and if they refuse to support our nonviolent efforts, millions of Negroes will, out of frustration and despair, seek solace and security in black-nationalist ideologies—a development that would inevitably lead to a frightening racial nightmare.

30   Oppressed people cannot remain oppressed forever. The yearning for freedom eventually manifests itself, and that is what has happened to

the American Negro. Something within has reminded him of his birth-right of freedom, and something without has reminded him that it can be gained. Consciously or unconsciously, he has been caught up by the *Zeitgeist,*[4] and with his black brothers of Africa and his brown and yellow brothers of Asia, South America, and the Caribbean, the United States Negro is moving with a sense of great urgency toward the prom-ised land of racial justice. If one recognizes this vital urge that has engulfed the Negro community, one should readily understand why public demonstrations are taking place. The Negro has many pent-up resentments and latent frustrations, and he must release them. So let him march; let him make prayer pilgrimages to the city hall; let him go on freedom rides—and try to understand why he must do so. If his repressed emotions are not released in nonviolent ways, they will seek expression through violence; this is not a threat but a fact of history. So I have not said to my people, "Get rid of your discontent." Rather, I have tried to say that this normal and healthy discontent can be chan-neled into the creative outlet of nonviolent direct action. And now this approach is being termed extremist.

But though I was initially disappointed at being categorized as an extremist, as I continued to think about the matter I gradually gained a measure of satisfaction from the label. Was not Jesus an extremist for love: "Love your enemies, bless them that curse you, do good to them that hate you, and pray for them which despitefully use you, and perse-cute you." Was not Amos an extremist for justice: "Let justice roll down like waters and righteousness like an ever-flowing stream." Was not Paul an extremist for the Christian gospel: "I bear in my body the marks of the Lord Jesus." Was not Martin Luther an extremist: "Here I stand; I cannot do otherwise, so help me God." And John Bunyan: "I will stay in jail to the end of my days before I make a butchery of my conscience." And Abraham Lincoln: "This nation cannot survive half slave and half free." And Thomas Jefferson: "We hold these truths to be self-evident, that all men are created equal. . . ." So the question is not whether we will be extremists, but what kind of extremists we will be. Will we be extremists for hate or for love? Will we be extremists for the preservation of injustice or for the extension of justice? In that dramatic scene on Calvary's hill three men were crucified. We must never forget that all three were crucified for the same crime—the crime of extremism. Two were extremists for immorality, and thus fell below their environment. The other, Jesus Christ, was an extremist for love, truth, and goodness, and thereby rose above his environment. Perhaps the South, the nation, and the world are in dire need of creative extremists.

I had hoped that the white moderate would see this need. Perhaps

4. The spirit of the times.

I was too optimistic; perhaps I expected too much. I suppose I should have realized that few members of the oppressor race can understand the deep groans and passionate yearnings of the oppressed race, and still fewer have the vision to see that injustice must be rooted out by strong, persistent, and determined action. I am thankful, however, that some of our white brothers in the South have grasped the meaning of this social revolution and committed themselves to it. They are still all too few in quantity, but they are big in quality. Some—such as Ralph McGill, Lillian Smith, Harry Golden, James McBridge Dabbs, Ann Braden, and Sarah Patton Boyle—have written about our struggle in eloquent and prophetic terms. Others have marched with us down nameless streets of the South. They have languished in filthy, roach-infested jails, suffering the abuse and brutality of policemen who view them as "dirty nigger-lovers." Unlike so many of their moderate brothers and sisters, they have recognized the urgency of the moment and sensed the need for powerful "action" antidotes to combat the disease of segregation.

Let me take note of my other major disappointment. I have been so greatly disappointed with the white church and its leadership. Of course, there are some notable exceptions. I am not unmindful of the fact that each of you has taken some significant stands on this issue. I commend you, Reverend Stallings, for your Christian stand on this past Sunday, in welcoming Negroes to your worship service on a nonsegregated basis. I commend the Catholic leaders of this state for integrating Spring Hill College several years ago.

But despite these notable exceptions, I must honestly reiterate that I have been disappointed with the church. I do not say this as one of those negative critics who can always find something wrong with the church. I say this as a minister of the gospel, who loves the church; who was nurtured in its bosom; who has been sustained by its spiritual blessings and who will remain true to it as long as the cord of life shall lengthen.

When I was suddenly catapulted into the leadership of the bus protest in Montgomery, Alabama, a few years ago, I felt we would be supported by the white church. I felt that the white ministers, priests, and rabbis of the South would be among our strongest allies. Instead, some have been outright opponents, refusing to understand the freedom movement and misrepresenting its leaders; all too many others have been more cautious than courageous and have remained silent behind the anesthetizing security of stainedglass windows.

In spite of my shattered dreams, I came to Birmingham with the hope that the white religious leadership of this community would see the justice of our cause and, with deep moral concern, would serve as the channel through which our just grievances could reach the power structure. I had hoped that each of you would understand. But again I have been disappointed.

I have heard numerous southern religious leaders admonish their worshipers to comply with a desegregation decision because it is the law, but I have longed to hear white ministers declare: "Follow this decree because integration is morally right and because the Negro is your brother." In the midst of blatant injustices inflicted upon the Negro, I have watched white churchmen stand on the sideline and mouth pious irrelevancies and sanctimonious trivialities. In the midst of a mighty struggle to rid our nation of racial and economic injustice, I have heard many ministers say: "Those are social issues, with which the gospel has no real concern." And I have watched many churches commit themselves to a completely otherworldly religion which makes a strange, un-Biblical distinction between body and soul, between the sacred and the secular.

I have traveled the length and breadth of Alabama, Mississippi, and all the other southern states. On sweltering summer days and crisp autumn mornings I have looked at the South's beautiful churches with their lofty spires pointing heavenward. I have beheld the impressive outlines of her massive religious-education buildings. Over and over I have found myself asking: "What kind of people worship here? Who is their God? Where were their voices when the lips of Governor Barnett dripped with words of interposition and nullification? Where were they when Governor Wallace gave a clarion call for defiance and hatred? Where were their voices of support when bruised and weary Negro men and women decided to rise from the dark dungeons of complacency to the bright hills of creative protest?"

Yes, these questions are still in my mind. In deep disappointment I have wept over the laxity of the church. But be assured that my tears have been tears of love. There can be no deep disappointment where there is not deep love. Yes, I love the church. How could I do otherwise? I am in the rather unique position of being the son, the grandson, and the great-grandson of preachers. Yes, I see the church as the body of Christ. But, oh! How we have blemished and scarred that body through social neglect and through fear of being nonconformists.

There was a time when the church was very powerful—in the time when the early Christians rejoiced at being deemed worthy to suffer for what they believed. In those days the church was not merely a thermometer that recorded the ideas and principles of popular opinion; it was a thermostat that transformed the mores of society. Whenever the early Christians entered a town, the people in power became disturbed and immediately sought to convict the Christians for being "disturbers of the peace" and "outside agitators." But the Christians pressed on, in the conviction that they were "a colony of heaven," called to obey God rather than man. Small in number, they were big in commitment. They were too God-intoxicated to be "astronomically intimidated." By their effort and example they brought an end to such ancient evils as infanticide and gladiatorial contests.

Things are different now. So often the contemporary church is a weak, ineffectual voice with an uncertain sound. So often it is an arch-defender of the status quo. Far from being disturbed by the presence of the church, the power structure of the average community is consoled by the church's silent—and often even vocal—sanction of things as they are.

But the judgment of God is upon the church as never before. If today's church does not recapture the sacrificial spirit of the early church, it will lose its authenticity, forfeit the loyalty of millions, and be dismissed as an irrelevant social club with no meaning for the twentieth century. Every day I meet young people whose disappointment with the church has turned into outright disgust.

Perhaps I have once again been too optimistic. Is organized religion too inextricably bound to the status quo to save our nation and the world? Perhaps I must turn my faith to the inner spiritual church, the church within the church, as the true *ekklesia* [5] and the hope of the world. But again I am thankful to God that some noble souls from the ranks of organized religion have broken loose from the paralyzing chains of conformity and joined us as active partners in the struggle for freedom. They have left their secure congregations and walked the streets of Albany, Georgia, with us. They have gone down the highways of the South on tortuous rides for freedom. Yes, they have gone to jail with us. Some have been dismissed from their churches, have lost the support of their bishops and fellow ministers. But they have acted in the faith that right defeated is stronger than evil triumphant. Their witness has been the spiritual salt that has preserved the true meaning of the gospel in these troubled times. They have carved a tunnel of hope through the dark mountain of disappointment.

I hope the church as a whole will meet the challenge of this decisive hour. But even if the church does not come to the aid of justice, I have no despair about the future. I have no fear about the outcome of our struggle in Birmingham, even if our motives are at present misunderstood. We will reach the goal of freedom in Birmingham and all over the nation, because the goal of America is freedom. Abused and scorned though we may be, our destiny is tied up with America's destiny. Before the pilgrims landed at Plymouth, we were here. Before the pen of Jefferson etched the majestic words of the Declaration of Independence across the pages of history, we were here. For more than two centuries

5. The Greek New Testament word for the early Christian church.

our forebears labored in this country without wages; they made cotton king; they built the homes of their masters while suffering gross injustice and shameful humiliation—and yet out of a bottomless vitality they continued to thrive and develop. If the inexpressible cruelties of slavery could not stop us, the opposition we now face will surely fail. We will win our freedom because the sacred heritage of our nation and the eternal will of God are embodied in our echoing demands.

Before closing I feel impelled to mention one other point in your statement that has troubled me profoundly. You warmly commended the Birmingham police force for keeping "order" and "preventing violence." I doubt that you would have so warmly commended the police force if you had seen its dogs sinking their teeth into unarmed, nonviolent Negroes. I doubt that you would so quickly commend the policemen if you were to observe their ugly and inhumane treatment of Negroes here in the city jail; if you were to watch them push and curse old Negro women and young Negro girls; if you were to see them slap and kick old Negro men and young boys; if you were to observe them, as they did on two occasions, refuse to give us food because we wanted to sing our grace together. I cannot join you in your praise of the Birmingham police department. 45

It is true that the police have exercised a degree of discipline in handling the demonstrators. In this sense they have conducted themselves rather "nonviolently" in public. But for what purpose? To preserve the evil system of segregation. Over the past few years I have consistently preached that nonviolence demands that the means we use must be as pure as the ends we seek. I have tried to make clear that it is wrong to use immoral means to attain moral ends. But now I must affirm that it is just as wrong, or perhaps even more so, to use moral means to preserve immoral ends. Perhaps Mr. Connor and his policemen have been rather nonviolent in public, as was Chief Pritchett in Albany, Georgia, but they have used the moral means of nonviolence to maintain the immoral end of racial injustice. As T. S. Eliot has said, "The last temptation is the greatest treason: To do the right deed for the wrong reason."

I wish you had commended the Negro sit-inners and demonstrators of Birmingham for their sublime courage, their willingness to suffer, and their amazing discipline in the midst of great provocation. One day the South will recognize its real heroes. They will be the James Merediths, [6] with the noble sense of purpose that enables them to face jeering and hostile mobs, and with the agonizing loneliness that characterizes the life of the pioneer. They will be old, oppressed, battered Negro women, symbolized in a seventy-two-year-old woman in Montgomery, Alabama,

---

6. Meredith was the first black to enroll at the University of Mississippi.

who rose up with a sense of dignity and with her people decided not to ride segregated buses, and who responded with ungrammatical profundity to one who inquired about her weariness: "My feets is tired, but my soul is at rest." They will be the young high school and college students, the young ministers of the gospel and a host of their elders, courageously and nonviolently sitting in at lunch counters and willingly going to jail for conscience' sake. One day the South will know that when these disinherited children of God sat down at lunch counters, they were in reality standing up for what is best in the American dream and for the most sacred values in our Judaeo-Christian heritage, thereby bringing our nation back to those great wells of democracy which were dug deep by the founding fathers in their formulation of the Constitution and the Declaration of Independence.

Never before have I written so long a letter. I'm afraid it is much too long to take your precious time. I can assure you that it would have been much shorter if I had been writing from a comfortable desk, but what else can one do when he is alone in a narrow jail cell, other than write long letters, think long thoughts, and pray long prayers?

If I have said anything in this letter that overstates the truth and indicates an unreasonable impatience, I beg you to forgive me. If I have said anything that understates the truth and indicates my having a patience that allows me to settle for anything less than brotherhood, I beg God to forgive me.

50   I hope this letter finds you strong in the faith. I also hope that circumstances will soon make it possible for me to meet each of you, not as an integrationist or a civil-rights leader but as a fellow clergyman and a Christian brother. Let us all hope that the dark clouds of racial prejudice will soon pass away and the deep fog of misunderstanding will be lifted from our fear-drenched communities, and in some not too distant tomorrow the radiant stars of love and brotherhood will shine over our great nation with all their scintillating beauty.

Yours for the cause of Peace and Brotherhood,
MARTIN LUTHER KING, JR.

Niccolò Machiavelli

THE MORALS OF THE PRINCE

On the Reasons Why Men Are Praised or Blamed—Especially Princes

It remains now to be seen what style and principles a prince ought to adopt in dealing with his subjects and friends. I know the subject has been treated frequently before, and I'm afraid people will think me rash for trying to do so again, especially since I intend to differ in this discussion from what others have said. But since I intend to write something useful to an understanding reader, it seemed better to go after the real truth of the matter than to repeat what people have imagined. A great many men have imagined states and princedoms such as nobody ever saw or knew in the real world, for there's such a difference between the way we really live and the way we ought to live that the man who neglects the real to study the ideal will learn how to accomplish his ruin, not his salvation. Any man who tries to be good all the time is bound to come to ruin among the great number who are not good. Hence a prince who wants to keep his post must learn how not to be good, and use that knowledge, or refrain from using it, as necessity requires.

Putting aside, then, all the imaginary things that are said about princes, and getting down to the truth, let me say that whenever men are discussed (and especially princes because they are prominent), there are certain qualities that bring them either praise or blame. Thus some are considered generous, others stingy (I use a Tuscan term, since "greedy" in our speech means a man who wants to take other people's goods. We call a man "stingy" who clings to his own); some are givers, others grabbers; some cruel, others merciful; one man is treacherous, another faithful; one is feeble and effeminate, another fierce and spirited; one humane, another proud; one lustful, another chaste; one straightforward, another sly; one harsh, another gentle; one serious, another playful; one religious, another skeptical, and so on. I know everyone will agree that among these many qualities a prince certainly ought to have all those that are considered good. But since it is impossible to have and exercise them all, because the conditions of human life simply do not allow it, a prince must be shrewd enough to avoid the public disgrace of those vices that would lose him his state. If he possibly can, he should also guard against vices that will not lose him his state;

From *The Prince* (1513), a book on statecraft written for Giuliano de' Medici (1479–1516), a member of one of the most famous and powerful families of Renaissance Italy. Excerpted from an edition translated and edited by Robert M. Adams (1977).

but if he cannot prevent them, he should not be too worried about indulging them. And furthermore, he should not be too worried about incurring blame for any vice without which he would find it hard to save his state. For if you look at matters carefully, you will see that something resembling virtue, if you follow it, may be your ruin, while something else resembling vice will lead, if you follow it, to your security and well-being.

On Liberality and Stinginess

Let me begin, then, with the first of the qualities mentioned above, by saying that a reputation for liberality is doubtless very fine; but the generosity that earns you that reputation can do you great harm. For if you exercise your generosity in a really virtuous way, as you should, nobody will know of it, and you cannot escape the odium of the opposite vice. Hence if you wish to be widely known as a generous man, you must seize every opportunity to make a big display of your giving. A prince of this character is bound to use up his entire revenue in works of ostentation. Thus, in the end, if he wants to keep a name for generosity, he will have to load his people with exorbitant taxes and squeeze money out of them in every way he can. This is the first step in making him odious to his subjects; for when he is poor, nobody will respect him. Then, when his generosity has angered many and brought rewards to a few, the slightest difficulty will trouble him, and at the first approach of danger, down he goes. If by chance he foresees this, and tries to change his ways, he will immediately be labeled a miser.

Since a prince cannot use this virtue of liberality in such a way as to become known for it unless he harms his own security, he won't mind, if he judges prudently of things, being known as a miser. In due course he will be thought the more liberal man, when people see that his parsimony enables him to live on his income, to defend himself against his enemies, and to undertake major projects without burdening his people with taxes. Thus he will be acting liberally toward all those people from whom he takes nothing (and there are an immense number of them), and in a stingy way toward those people on whom he bestows nothing (and they are very few). In our times, we have seen great things being accomplished only by men who have had the name of misers; all the others have gone under. Pope Julius II, though he used his reputation as a generous man to gain the papacy, sacrificed it in order to be able to make war; the present king of France has waged many wars without levying a single extra tax on his people, simply because he could take care of the extra expenses out of the savings from his long parsimony. If the present king of Spain had a reputation for generosity, he would never have been able to undertake so many campaigns, or win so many of them.

Hence a prince who prefers not to rob his subjects, who wants to be   5
able to defend himself, who wants to avoid poverty and contempt, and
who doesn't want to become a plunderer, should not mind in the least
if people consider him a miser; this is simply one of the vices that enable
him to reign. Someone may object that Caesar used a reputation for
generosity to become emperor, and many other people have also risen
in the world, because they were generous or were supposed to be so.
Well, I answer, either you are a prince already, or you are in the process
of becoming one; in the first case, this reputation for generosity is
harmful to you, in the second case it is very necessary. Caesar was one
of those who wanted to become ruler in Rome; but after he had reached
his goal, if he had lived, and had not cut down on his expenses, he would
have ruined the empire itself. Someone may say: there have been plenty
of princes, very successful in warfare, who have had a reputation for
generosity. But I answer: either the prince is spending his own money
and that of his subjects, or he is spending someone else's. In the first
case, he ought to be sparing; in the second case, he ought to spend
money like water. Any prince at the head of his army, which lives on
loot, extortion, and plunder, disposes of other people's property, and is
bound to be very generous; otherwise, his soldiers would desert him. You
can always be a more generous giver when what you give is not yours
or your subjects'; Cyrus, Caesar, and Alexander[1] were generous in this
way. Spending what belongs to other people does no harm to your
reputation, rather it enhances it; only spending your own substance
harms you. And there is nothing that wears out faster than generosity;
even as you practice it, you lose the means of practicing it, and you
become either poor and contemptible or (in the course of escaping
poverty) rapacious and hateful. The thing above all against which a
prince must protect himself is being contemptible and hateful; generosity leads to both. Thus, it's much wiser to put up with the reputation
of being a miser, which brings you shame without hate, than to be
forced—just because you want to appear generous—into a reputation for
rapacity, which brings shame on you and hate along with it.

On Cruelty and Clemency: Whether It Is Better to Be Loved or Feared

Continuing now with our list of qualities, let me say that every prince
should prefer to be considered merciful rather than cruel, yet he should
be careful not to mismanage this clemency of his. People thought Cesare
Borgia[2] was cruel, but that cruelty of his reorganized the Romagna,

1. Persian, Roman, and Macedonian con-   to later) and duke of Romagna, which he
querors and rulers in ancient times.   subjugated in 1499–1502.
2. The son of Pope Alexander VI (referred

united it, and established it in peace and loyalty. Anyone who views the
matter realistically will see that this prince was much more merciful than
the people of Florence, who, to avoid the reputation of cruelty, allowed
Pistoia to be destroyed.[3] Thus, no prince should mind being called cruel
for what he does to keep his subjects united and loyal; he may make
examples of a very few, but he will be more merciful in reality than those
who, in their tenderheartedness, allow disorders to occur, with their
attendant murders and lootings. Such turbulence brings harm to an
entire community, while the executions ordered by a prince affect only
one individual at a time. A new prince, above all others, cannot possibly
avoid a name for cruelty, since new states are always in danger. And
Virgil, speaking through the mouth of Dido,[4] says:

> My cruel fate
> And doubts attending an unsettled state
> Force me to guard my coast from foreign foes.

Yet a prince should be slow to believe rumors and to commit himself
to action on the basis of them. He should not be afraid of his own
thoughts; he ought to proceed cautiously, moderating his conduct with
prudence and humanity, allowing neither overconfidence to make him
careless, nor overtimidity to make him intolerable.

Here the question arises: is it better to be loved than feared, or vice
versa? I don't doubt that every prince would like to be both; but since
it is hard to accommodate these qualities, if you have to make a choice,
to be feared is much safer than to be loved. For it is a good general rule
about men, that they are ungrateful, fickle, liars and deceivers, fearful
of danger and greedy for gain. While you serve their welfare, they are
all yours, offering their blood, their belongings, their lives, and their
children's lives, as we noted above—so long as the danger is remote. But
when the danger is close at hand, they turn against you. Then, any
prince who has relied on their words and has made no other preparations
will come to grief; because friendships that are bought at a price, and
not with greatness and nobility of soul, may be paid for but they are not
acquired, and they cannot be used in time of need. People are less
concerned with offending a man who makes himself loved than one who
makes himself feared: the reason is that love is a link of obligation which
men, because they are rotten, will break any time they think doing so
serves their advantage; but fear involves dread of punishment, from
which they can never escape.

Still, a prince should make himself feared in such a way that, even if
he gets no love, he gets no hate either; because it is perfectly possible
to be feared and not hated, and this will be the result if only the prince

3. By unchecked rioting between opposing   4. Queen of Carthage and tragic heroine of
factions (1502).   Virgil's epic, *The Aeneid*.

will keep his hands off the property of his subjects or citizens, and off their women. When he does have to shed blood, he should be sure to have a strong justification and manifest cause; but above all, he should not confiscate people's property, because men are quicker to forget the death of a father than the loss of a patrimony. Besides, pretexts for confiscation are always plentiful, it never fails that a prince who starts living by plunder can find reasons to rob someone else. Excuses for proceeding against someone's life are much rarer and more quickly exhausted.

But a prince at the head of his armies and commanding a multitude of soldiers should not care a bit if he is considered cruel; without such a reputation, he could never hold his army together and ready for action. Among the marvelous deeds of Hannibal,[5] this was prime: that, having an immense army, which included men of many different races and nations, and which he led to battle in distant countries, he never allowed them to fight among themselves or to rise against him, whether his fortune was good or bad. The reason for this could only be his inhuman cruelty, which, along with his countless other talents, made him an object of awe and terror to his soldiers; and without the cruelty, his other qualities would never have sufficed. The historians who pass snap judgments on these matters admire his accomplishments and at the same time condemn the cruelty which was their main cause.

When I say, "His other qualities would never have sufficed," we can see that this is true from the example of Scipio,[6] an outstanding man not only among those of his own time, but in all recorded history; yet his armies revolted in Spain, for no other reason than his excessive leniency in allowing his soldiers more freedom than military discipline permits. Fabius Maximus rebuked him in the senate for this failing, calling him the corrupter of the Roman armies. When a lieutenant of Scipio's plundered the Locrians,[7] he took no action in behalf of the people, and did nothing to discipline that insolent lieutenant; again, this was the result of his easygoing nature. Indeed, when someone in the senate wanted to excuse him on this occasion, he said there are many men who knew better how to avoid error themselves than how to correct error in others. Such a soft temper would in time have tarnished the fame and glory of Scipio, had he brought it to the office of emperor; but as he lived under the control of the senate, this harmful quality of his not only remained hidden but was considered creditable.

10

5. Carthaginian general who led a massive but unsuccessful invasion of Rome in 218–03 B.C.
6. The Roman general whose successful invasion of Carthage in 203 B.C. caused Hannibal's army to be recalled from Rome. The

episode described here occurred in 206 B.C.
7. A people of Sicily, defeated by Scipio in 205 B.C. and placed under Q. Pleminius; *Fabius Maximus:* not only a senator but a high public official and general who had fought against Hannibal in Italy.

Returning to the question of being feared or loved, I conclude that since men love at their own inclination but can be made to fear at the inclination of the prince, a shrewd prince will lay his foundations on what is under his own control, not on what is controlled by others. He should simply take pains not to be hated, as I said.

The Way Princes Should Keep Their Word

How praiseworthy it is for a prince to keep his word and live with integrity rather than by craftiness, everyone understands; yet we see from recent experience that those princes have accomplished most who paid little heed to keeping their promises, but who knew how craftily to manipulate the minds of men. In the end, they won out over those who tried to act honestly.

You should consider then, that there are two ways of fighting, one with laws and the other with force. The first is properly a human method, the second belongs to beasts. But as the first method does not always suffice, you sometimes have to turn to the second. Thus a prince must know how to make good use of both the beast and the man. Ancient writers made subtle note of this fact when they wrote that Achilles and many other princes of antiquity were sent to be reared by Chiron the centaur,[8] who trained them in his discipline. Having a teacher who is half man and half beast can only mean that a prince must know how to use both these two natures, and that one without the other has no lasting effect.

Since a prince must know how to use the character of beasts, he should pick for imitation the fox and the lion. As the lion cannot protect himself from traps, and the fox cannot defend himself from wolves, you have to be a fox in order to be wary of traps, and a lion to overawe the wolves. Those who try to live by the lion alone are badly mistaken. Thus a prudent prince cannot and should not keep his word when to do so would go against his interest, or when the reasons that made him pledge it no longer apply. Doubtless if all men were good, this rule would be bad; but since they are a sad lot, and keep no faith with you, you in your turn are under no obligation to keep it with them.

Besides, a prince will never lack for legitimate excuses to explain away his breaches of faith. Modern history will furnish innumerable examples of this behavior, showing how many treaties and promises have been made null and void by the faithlessness of princes, and how the man succeeded best who knew best how to play the fox. But it is a necessary part of this nature that you must conceal it carefully; you must be a great

15

8. Half man and half horse, the mythical Chiron was said to have taught the arts of war and peace, including hunting, medi- cine, music, and prophecy; *Achilles:* fore- most among the Greek heroes in the Tro- jan War.

liar and hypocrite. Men are so simple of mind, and so much dominated by their immediate needs, that a deceitful man will always find plenty who are ready to be deceived. One of many recent examples calls for mention. Alexander VI[9] never did anything else, never had another thought, except to deceive men, and he always found fresh material to work on. Never was there a man more convincing in his assertions, who sealed his promises with more solemn oaths, and who observed them less. Yet his deceptions were always successful, because he knew exactly how to manage this sort of business.

In actual fact, a prince may not have all the admirable qualities we listed, but it is very necessary that he should seem to have them. Indeed, I will venture to say that when you have them and exercise them all the time, they are harmful to you; when you just seem to have them, they are useful. It is good to appear merciful, truthful, humane, sincere, and religious; it is good to be so in reality. But you must keep your mind so disposed that, in case of need, you can turn to the exact contrary. This has to be understood: a prince, and especially a new prince, cannot possibly exercise all those virtues for which men are called "good." To preserve the state, he often has to do things against his word, against charity, against humanity, against religion. Thus he has to have a mind ready to shift as the winds of fortune and the varying circumstances of life may dictate. And as I said above, he should not depart from the good if he can hold to it, but he should be ready to enter on evil if he has to.

Hence a prince should take great care never to drop a word that does not seem imbued with the five good qualities noted above; to anyone who sees or hears him, he should appear all compassion, all honor, all humanity, all integrity, all religion. Nothing is more necessary than to seem to have this last virtue. Men in general judge more by the sense of sight than by the sense of touch, because everyone can see but only a few can test by feeling. Everyone sees what you seem to be, few know what you really are; and those few do not dare take a stand against the general opinion, supported by the majesty of the government. In the actions of all men, and especially of princes who are not subject to a court of appeal, we must always look to the end. Let a prince, therefore, win victories and uphold his state; his methods will always be considered worthy, and everyone will praise them, because the masses are always impressed by the superficial appearance of things, and by the outcome of an enterprise. And the world consists of nothing but the masses; the few who have no influence when the many feel secure. A certain prince of our own time, whom it's just as well not to name,[1] preaches nothing

---

9. Pope from 1492 to 1503.   1. Probably Ferdinand of Spain, then allied with the house of Medici.

but peace and mutual trust, yet he is the determined enemy of both; and if on several different occasions he had observed either, he would have lost both his reputation and his throne.

THE READER

1. *Toward the end of the first paragraph, Machiavelli says, "The man who neglects the real to study the ideal will learn how to accomplish his ruin." Explain the logical relation between that statement and the statements of the last two sentences of that paragraph.*
2. *Speaking of a prince, Machiavelli uses a moral, personal vocabulary: "liberality"/"stinginess," "cruelty"/"clemency," "loved"/"feared," etc. Other vocabularies are possible. For example, the stinginess of a miser (p. 902) might be fiscal responsibility. Provide alternatives for some of the other terms in his moral, personal vocabulary.*
3. *Machiavelli speaks about government by a prince. To what degree do his observations and advice apply to a democracy?*

THE WRITER

1. *On p. 907, the author speaks of five admirable qualities: compassion, honor, humanity, integrity, and religion. How admirable do you think he believes those qualities to be? Base your answer on your sense of what matters to him in this essay. What would you say he admires most?*
2. *Machiavelli clearly says a prince should seem to be virtuous. Write a one-page strategy paper for Machiavelli as if you were the media consultant to a prince, or for yourself as if you were the media consultant to a candidate.*
3. *Machiavelli sees men as "a sad lot" and has a generally bleak view of human behavior. What would be the best logical strategy for an argument in refutation? Can you get any help from King (p. 886) or Lincoln (p. 922) or the Declaration of Independence (p. 928)?*

James Thurber

THE RABBITS WHO CAUSED ALL THE TROUBLE

Within the memory of the youngest child there was a family of rabbits who lived near a pack of wolves. The wolves announced that they

From *Fables for Our Time* (1940).

did not like the way the rabbits were living. (The wolves were crazy about the way they themselves were living, because it was the only way to live.) One night several wolves were killed in an earthquake and this was blamed on the rabbits, for it is well known that rabbits pound on the ground with their hind legs and cause earthquakes. On another night one of the wolves was killed by a bolt of lightning and this was also blamed on the rabbits, for it is well known that lettuce-eaters cause lightning. The wolves threatened to civilize the rabbits if they didn't behave, and the rabbits decided to run away to a desert island. But the other animals, who lived at a great distance, shamed them, saying, "You must stay where you are and be brave. This is no world for escapists. If the wolves attack you, we will come to your aid, in all probability." So the rabbits continued to live near the wolves and one day there was a terrible flood which drowned a great many wolves. This was blamed on the rabbits, for it is well known that carrot-nibblers with long ears cause floods. The wolves descended on the rabbits, for their own good, and imprisoned them in a dark cave, for their own protection.

When nothing was heard about the rabbits for some weeks, the other animals demanded to know what had happened to them. The wolves replied that the rabbits had been eaten and since they had been eaten the affair was a purely internal matter. But the other animals warned that they might possibly unite against the wolves unless some reason was given for the destruction of the rabbits. So the wolves gave them one. "They were trying to escape," said the wolves, "and, as you know, this is no world for escapists."

Moral: Run, don't walk, to the nearest desert island.

Edith Hamilton

XENOPHON

To turn from Thucydides to Xenophon is a pleasant, but surprising, experience. The lives of the two men overlapped, although Xenophon was much the younger. Both were Athenians and soldiers; both lived through the war and saw the defeat of Athens.[1] Yet they inhabited

---

Chapter 10 in the expanded version of *The Greek Way* (1930), published in 1942, first under the title *The Great Age of Greek Literature*. In the preceding chapter Hamilton gives an account of Thucydides and his picture of the corruption of the Athenian ideals of democracy and fair play by "the desire for power which greed and ambition inspire." Chapter 10 had the subtitle "The Ordinary Athenian Gentleman."

different worlds; worlds so different, they seem to have no connection with each other. Thucydides' world was a place racked and ruined and disintegrated by war, where hope was gone and happiness was unimaginable. Xenophon's was a cheerful place with many nice people in it and many agreeable ways of passing the time. There was hunting, for instance. He writes a charming essay about it: of the delights of the early start, in winter over the snow, to track the hare with hounds as keen for the chase as their masters; in spring "when the fields are so full of wildflowers, the scent for the dogs is poor"; or a deer may be the quarry, first-rate sport; or a wild boar, dangerous, but delightfully exciting. Such rewards, too, as the hunter has: he keeps strong and young far longer than other men; he is braver, and even more trustworthy—although why that should be our author does not trouble to explain. A hunting man just is better than one who does not hunt and that is all there is to it. Ask any fox-hunting squire in English literature. Hunting is a good, healthy, honest pleasure, and a young man is lucky if he takes to it. It will save him from city vices and incline him to love virtue.

At what period in Thucydides' history were the Athenians going a hunting, one wonders. Did that man of tragic vision ever watch a hunt? Did he ever listen to stories about the size of the boar that had been killed? Was he ever at a dinner party where any stories were told over the wine? The imagination fails before the attempt to put him there, even if Socrates[2] had been a guest as he was at a dinner Xenophon went to and reported. It followed more closely, we must suppose, the fashion of the day for such parties than did Plato's famous supper at Agathon's house,[3] where conversation was the only entertainment. Agathon's guests were the elite of Athens and wanted lofty discourse for their diversion. The guests at Xenophon's dinner, except for himself and Socrates, were ordinary people who would quickly have been bored by the speeches in the *Symposium*. But no one could possibly have been bored at the party Xenophon describes. It was from first to last a most enjoyable occasion. There was some good talk at the table, of course— Socrates would see to that; and now and then the discourse turned to matters sober enough to have engaged even Thucydides' attention. But for the most part, it was lighthearted as befitted a good dinner. There was a great deal of laughter when, for instance, Socrates defended his flat nose as being preferable to a straight one, and when a man newly

1. Sparta conquered Athens in 404 B.C., after twenty-seven years of war. Thucydides lived from about 471 to about 400 B.C., Xenophon from about 435 to about 355 B.C.
2. Socrates (c.470–399 B.C.), ancient Greek philosopher who led philosophy toward analyses of the character and conduct of human life. He is remembered for his admonition to "know thyself."
3. The philosopher Plato's (c.428–348/47 B.C.) dialogue *Symposium* takes place at a banquet celebrating the victory of Agathon (c.445–400 B.C.), an Athenian tragic poet, in the festival of the Great Dionysia in which plays were presented and judged.

married refused the onions. There was music, too, and Socrates obliged with a song, to the delighted amusement of the others. A pleasant interlude was afforded by a happy boy, and Xenophon's description reveals his power of keen observation and quick sympathy. The lad had been invited to come with his father, a great honor, but he had just won the chief contest for boys at the principal Athenian festival. He sat beside his father, regarded very kindly by the company. They tried to draw him out, but he was too shy to speak a word until someone asked him what he was most proud of, and someone else cried, "Oh, his victory, of course." At this he blushed and blurted out, "No—I'm not." All were delighted to have him finally say something and they encouraged him. "No? Of what are you proudest, then?" "Of my father," he said, and pressed closer to him. It is an attractive picture of Athenian boyhood in the brilliant, corrupt city where Thucydides could find nothing good.

As was usual, entertainment had been provided for the guests. A girl did some diverting and surprising feats. The best turn was when she danced and kept twelve hoops whirling in the air, catching and throwing them in perfect time with the music. Watching her with great attention Socrates declared that he was forced to conclude, "Not only from this girl, my friends, but from other things, too, that a woman's talent is not at all inferior to a man's." A pleasant thing to know, he added, if any of them wanted to teach something to his wife. A murmur passed around the table: "Xanthippe"; and one of the company ventured, "Why do not you, then, teach good temper to yours?" "Because," Socrates retorted, "my great aim in life is to get on well with people, and I chose Xanthippe because I knew if I could get on with her I could with anyone." The explanation was unanimously voted satisfactory.

A little desultory talk followed that finally turned upon exercise, and Socrates said, to the intense delight of all, that he danced every morning in order to reduce. "It's true," one of the others broke in. "I found him doing it and I thought he'd gone mad. But he talked to me and I tell you he convinced me. When I went home—will you believe it? I did not dance; I don't know how; but I waved my arms about." There was a general outcry, "O, Socrates, let us see you, too."

By this time the dancing girl was turning somersaults and leaping headfirst into a circle formed by swords. This displeased Socrates. "No doubt it is a wonderful performance," he conceded. "But pleasure? In watching a lovely young creature exposing herself to danger like that? I don't find it agreeable." The others agreed, and a pantomime between the girl and her partner, a graceful boy, was quickly substituted: "The Rescue of the Forsaken Ariadne by Bacchus." It was performed to admiration. Not a word was spoken by the two actors, but such was their skill that by gestures and dancing they expressed all the events and

5

emotions of the story with perfect clarity to the spectators. "They seemed not actors who had learned their parts, but veritable lovers." With that the party broke up, Socrates walking home with the nice boy and his father. Of himself Xenophon says nothing throughout the essay except at the very beginning when he explains that he was one of the guests and decided to give an account of the dinner because he thought what honorable and virtuous men did in their hours of amusement had its importance. One can only regret that so few Greek writers agreed with him.

Another pleasant picture he gives of domestic Athens has an interest not only as a period piece but because it shows a glimpse of that person so elusive in all periods, the woman of ancient Greece. A man lately married talks about his wife. She was not yet fifteen, he says, and had been admirably brought up "to see as little, and hear as little, and ask as few questions as possible." The young husband had the delightful prospect of inscribing on this blank page whatever he chose. There was no doubt in his mind what he should start with. "Of course," Xenophon reports him as saying, "I had to give her time to grow used to me; but when we had reached a point where we could talk easily together, I told her she had great responsibilities. I took up with her what I expected of her as a housekeeper. She said wonderingly, 'But my mother told me I was of no consequence, only you. All I had to do, she said, was to be sensible and careful.' " Her husband was quick to seize the cue. Kindly but weightily he explained to the young thing that her life henceforth was to be a perpetual exercise in carefulness and good sense. She would have to keep stock of everything brought into the house; oversee all the work that went on; superintend the spinning, the weaving, the making of clothes; train the new servants and nurse the sick. At this point the girl's spirits seem to have risen a little for she murmured that she thought she would like to take care of sick people. But her husband kept steadily on. Of course she would stay indoors. He himself enjoyed starting the day with a long ride into the country—very healthful as well as very pleasant. But for a woman to be roaming abroad was most discreditable. However, she could get plenty of exercise, at the loom, or making beds, or supervising the maids. Kneading bread was said to be as good exercise as one could find. All that sort of thing would improve her health and help her complexion—very important in keeping herself attractive to her husband. Artificial substitutes were no good: husbands always knew when their wives painted, and they never liked it; white and red stuff on the face was disgusting when a man was aware of it, as a husband must be. The essay ends happily with the declaration, "Ever since, my wife has done in all respects just as I taught her."

It is as hard to fit the dutiful young wife and the happily important husband and their immaculate household into Thucydides' Athens as it is to put Thucydides himself at the table beside Socrates watching the girl with the hoops. There is no use trying to make a composite picture out of Xenophon and Thucydides. The only result would be to lose the truth on each side. Thucydides' truth was immeasurably more profound. In life's uneasy panorama he could discover unchanging verities. He could probe to the depths in the never varying evils of human nature. In Sparta's victory over Athens he saw what the decision of war was worth as a test of values, and that war would forever decide matters of highest importance to the world if men continued to be governed by greed and the passion for power. What he knew was truth indeed, with no shadow of turning and inexpressibly sad.

But Xenophon's truths were true, too. There were pleasant parties and well-ordered homes and nice lads and jolly hunters in war-wracked Greece. History never takes account of such pleasantries, but they have their importance. The Greek world would have gone insane if Thucydides' picture had been all-inclusive. Of course, Xenophon's mind was on an altogether lower level. Eternal truths were not in his line. The average man in Periclean Athens can be seen through Xenophon's eyes as he cannot be through Thucydides' or Plato's. In Xenophon there are no dark, greed-ridden schemers such as Thucydides saw in Athens; neither are there any Platonic idealists. The people in his books are ordinary, pleasant folk, not given to extremes in any direction and convincingly real, just as Xenophon himself is. Here is a picture he draws of one of them:

> He said that he had long realized that "unless we know what we ought to do and try our best to do it God has decided that we have no right to be prosperous. If we are wise and do take pains he makes some of us prosperous, although not all. So to start with, I reverence him and then do all I can to be worthy when I pray to be given health and strength of body and the respect of the Athenians and the affection of my friends and an increase of wealth—with honor, and safety in war—with honor."

These eminently sensible aspirations strike a true Greek note. The man who uttered them and the man who recorded them were typical Athenian gentlemen. What Xenophon was comes through clearly in his writings—a man of good will and good sense, kindly, honest, pious; intelligent, too, interested in ideas, not the purely speculative kind, rather those that could be made to work toward some rational, practical good. His friends were like him, they were representative Athenians of the better sort.

In another way, too, Xenophon represented his times. His life shows the widely separated interests and varied occupations which made the Periclean Athenians different from other men. As a young man he came to Athens from his father's estate in Attica, to be educated out of country ways; he joined the circle around Socrates, where young and old alike were, as Plato puts it, "possessed and maddened with the passion for knowledge," or, as he himself states, "wanting to become good and fine men and learn their duty to their family, their servants, their friends and their country." The Socrates he listened to did not, like Plato's Socrates, discourse upon "the glorious sights of justice and wisdom and truth the enraptured soul beholds, shining in pure light," or anything like that. This Socrates was a soberly thinking man, distinguished for common sense, and in Xenophon's record of him, the *Memorabilia*, what he chiefly does for his young friends is to give them practical advice on how to manage their affairs. A budding officer is told the way to make his men efficient soldiers; a conscientious lad, burdened with many female relatives, is shown how they can be taught to support themselves, and so on, while Xenophon listens entranced by such serviceable wisdom. How long Xenophon lived this delightful life of conversation is not known, but he was still young when he left it for the very opposite kind of life, that of a soldier. He was truly a man of his times, when poets and dramatists and historians were soldiers and generals and explorers.

In his campaigns he traveled far and saw the great world. He also got enough money to live on for the rest of his days by capturing and holding for ransom a rich Persian noble. Then he went back to Greece—but to Sparta, not Athens. Curiously, although he has left in his *Anabasis* an unsurpassed picture of what the democratic ideal can accomplish, he was himself no democrat. He came of a noble family and all his life kept the convictions of his class. He always loved Sparta and distrusted Athens. Even so, in the great crisis of his life, when he and his companions faced imminent destruction, he acted like a true Athenian, who knew what freedom was and what free men could achieve. When the Ten Thousand elected him general in order to get them out of their terrible predicament, he never tried out any Spartan ideas on them. He became as democratic a leader as there could possibly be of the freest democracy conceivable. The fact that the astonishing success which resulted had no permanent effect upon his point of view should not be surprising; a converted aristocrat is a rare figure in history. Xenophon never went back to Athens; indeed, a few years after his return to Greece he was fighting on the Spartan side against her and was declared an exile. The Spartans gave him an estate in the pleasant country near Olympia, where he lived for many years, riding and hunting and farming, a model country gentleman. Here he wrote a great many books on subjects as far apart as the dinner Socrates attended and the proper management of the Athenian revenues. With two or three exceptions the writings are quite pedestrian; sensible, straightforward, clearly written, but no more. There are a few sentences, however, scattered through them which show a surprising power of thought and far-reaching vision. Although, or perhaps because, he had fought much, he believed that peace should be the aim of all states. Diplomacy, he says, is the way to settle disputes, not war. He urges Athens to use her influence to maintain peace, and he suggests making Delphi a meeting place for the nations, where they can talk out their differences. "He who conquers by force," he says, "may fancy that he can continue to do so, but the only conquests that last are when men willingly submit to those who are better than themselves. The only way really to conquer a country is through generosity." The world has not yet caught up with Xenophon.

His best book, however, the book he really lives by, is on war. It is, of course, the *Anabasis*, the "Retreat of the Ten Thousand," a great story, and of great importance for our knowledge of the Greeks. No other piece of writing gives so clear a picture of Greek individualism, that instinct which was supremely characteristic of ancient Greece and decided the course of the Greek achievement. It was the cause, or the result, as one chooses to look at it, of the Greek love for freedom. A Greek had a passion for being left free to live his life in his own way. He wanted to act by himself and think for himself. It did not come natural to him to turn to others for direction; he depended upon his own sense of what was right and true. Indeed, there was no generally acknowledged source of direction anywhere in Greece except the oracles, difficult to reach and still more difficult to understand. Athens had no authoritarian church, or state either, to formulate what a man should believe and to regulate the details of how he should live. There was no agency or institution to oppose his thinking in any way he chose on anything whatsoever. As for the state, it never entered an Athenian's head that it could interfere with his private life: that it could see, for instance, that his children were taught to be patriotic, or limit the amount of liquor he could buy, or compel him to save for his old age. Everything like that a citizen of Athens had to decide himself and take full responsibility for.

The basis of the Athenian democracy was the conviction of all democracies—that the average man can be depended upon to do his duty and to use good sense in doing it. *Trust the individual* was the avowed doctrine in Athens, and expressed or unexpressed it was common to Greece. Sparta we know as the exception, and there must have been other backwaters; nevertheless, the most reactionary Greek might at any time revert to type. It is on record that Spartan soldiers abroad shouted down an unpopular officer; threw stones at a general whose orders they did not approve; in an emergency, put down incompetent leaders and acted for themselves. Even the iron discipline of Sparta could not completely eradicate the primary Greek passion for independence. "A people ruling," says Herodotus, "—the very name of it is so beautiful." In Aeschylus' play about the defeat of the Persians at Salamis, the Persian queen asks, "Who is set over the Greeks as despots?" and the proud answer is, "They are the slaves and vassals of no man." Therefore, all Greeks believed, they conquered the slave-subjects of the Persian tyrant. Free men, independent men, were always worth inexpressibly more than men submissive and controlled.

Military authorities have never advocated this point of view, but how applicable it is to soldiers, too, is shown for all time by the *Anabasis*. The Ten Thousand got back safely after one of the most perilous marches ever undertaken just because they were not a model, disciplined army but a band of enterprising individuals.

15   The epic of the Retreat begins in a camp beside a little town in Asia not far from Babylon. There, more than ten thousand Greeks were gathered. They had come from different places: one of the leaders was from Thessaly; another from Boeotia; the commander-in-chief was a Spartan; on his staff was a young civilian from Athens named Xenophon. They were soldiers of fortune, a typical army of mercenaries who had gone abroad because there was no hope of employment at home. Greece was not at war for the moment. A Spartan peace was over the land. It was the summer of 401, three years after the fall of Athens.

Persia, however, was a hotbed of plots and counterplots that were bringing a revolution near. The late king's two sons were enemies, and the younger planned to take the throne from his brother. This young man was Cyrus, named for the great Cyrus, the conqueror of Babylon a hundred and fifty years earlier. His namesake is famous for one reason only: because when he marched into Persia Xenophon joined his army. If that had not happened he would be lost in the endless list of little Asiatic royalties forever fighting for no purpose of the slightest importance to the world. As it is, he lives in Xenophon's pages, gay and gallant and generous; careful for his soldiers' welfare; sharing their hardships; always first in the fighting; a great leader.

The Ten Thousand had enlisted under his banner with no clear idea of what they were to do beyond the matter of real importance, get regular pay and enough food. They earned their share of both in the next few months. They marched from the Mediterranean through sandy deserts far into Asia Minor living on the country, which generally meant a minimum of food and occasionally none at all. There was a large Asiatic contingent, a hundred thousand strong at the least, but they play very little part in the *Anabasis*. The Greeks are the real army Cyrus depends upon. As Xenophon tells the story they won the day for him when he met the king's forces. The battle of Cunaxa was a decisive victory for Cyrus. Only, he himself was dead, killed in the fighting as he struck at his brother and wounded him. With his death the reason for the expedition ceased to exist. The Asiatic forces melted away. The little Greek army was alone in the heart of Asia, in an unknown country swarming with hostile troops, with no food, no ammunition, and no notion how to get back. Soon there were no leaders either. The chief officers went to a conference with the Persians under a safe-conduct. Their return, eagerly awaited, was alarmingly delayed; and all eyes were watching for them when in the distance a man, one man all alone, was seen advancing very slowly, a Greek by his dress. They ran to meet him and caught him as he fell dying, terribly wounded. He could just gasp out that all the others were dead, assassinated by the Persians.

That was a terrible night. The Persian plan was clear. In their experience leaderless men were helpless. Kill the officers and the army would be a lot of sheep waiting to be slaughtered. The only thing wrong with the idea was that this was a Greek army.

Xenophon, all his friends dead, wandered away from the horrified camp, found a quiet spot and fell asleep. He dreamed a dream. He saw the thunderbolt of Zeus fall on his home and a great light shine forth, and he awoke with the absolute conviction that Zeus had chosen him to save the army. On fire with enthusiasm, he called a council of the under officers who had not gone to the conference. There, young and a civilian, he stood up and addressed them, hardened veterans all. He told them to throw off despair and "show some superiority to misfortune." He reminded them that they were Greeks, not to be cowed by mere Asiatics. Something of his own fire was communicated to them. He even got them laughing. One man who stubbornly objected to everything and would talk only of their desperate case, Xenophon advised reducing to the ranks and using to carry baggage; he would make an excellent mule, he told his appreciative audience. They elected him unanimously to lead the rear, and then had the general assembly sounded so that he could address the soldiers. He gave them a rousing talk. Things were black and might seem hopeless to others, but they were Greeks, free men, living in free states, born of free ancestors. The enemy they had to face were slaves, ruled by despots, ignorant of the very idea of freedom. "They think we are defeated because our officers are dead and our good old general Clearchus. But we will show them that they have turned us all into generals. Instead of one Clearchus they have ten thousand Clearchuses against them." He won them over and that very morning the ten thousand generals started the march back.

They had only enemies around them, not one man they could trust as a guide, and there were no maps in those days and no compasses. One thing only they were sure of: they could not go back by the way they had come. Wherever they had passed the food was exhausted. They were forced to turn northward and follow the course of the rivers up to the mountains where the Tigris and the Euphrates rise, through what is to-day the wilds of Kurdistan and the highlands of Georgia and Armenia, all inhabited by savage mountain tribes. These were their only

20

source of provisions. If they could not conquer their strongholds and get at their stores they would starve. Mountain warfare of the most desperate character awaited them, waged by an enemy who knew every foot of the country, who watched for them on the heights above narrow valleys and rolled masses of rocks down on them, whose sharpshooters attacked them hidden in thickets on the opposite bank of some torrential icy river while the Greeks searched desperately for a ford. As they advanced ever higher into the hills, they found bitter cold and deep snow, and their equipment was designed for the Arabian desert.

Probably anyone to-day considering their plight would conclude that their only chance of safety would lie in maintaining strict discipline, abiding by their excellent military tradition, and obeying their leaders implicitly. The chief leaders, however, were dead; mountain fighting against savages was not a part of their military tradition; above all, being Greeks, they did not incline to blind obedience in desperate circumstances. In point of fact, the situation which confronted them could be met only by throwing away the rules and regulations that had been drilled into them. What they needed was to draw upon all the intelligence and power of initiative every man of them possessed.

They were merely a band of mercenaries, but they were Greek mercenaries and the average of intelligence was high. The question of discipline among ten thousand generals would otherwise certainly have been serious and might well have proved fatal, but, no less than our westward-faring pioneer ancestors who resembled them, they understood the necessity of acting together. Not a soldier but knew what it would mean to have disorder added to the perils they faced. Their discipline was a voluntary product, but it worked. When the covered wagons made their way across America any leader that arose did so by virtue of superior ability, which men in danger always follow willingly. The leaders of the Ten Thousand got their posts in the same way. The army was keen to perceive a man's quality and before long the young civilian Xenophon was practically in command.

Each man, however, had a share in the responsibility. Once when Xenophon sent out a reconnoitering force to find a pass through the mountains, he told them, "Every one of you is the leader." At any crisis an assembly was held, the situation explained and full discussion invited. "Whoever has a better plan, let him speak. Our aim is the safety of all and that is the concern of all." The case was argued back and forth, then put to the vote and the majority decided. Incompetent leaders were brought to trial. The whole army sat as judges and acquitted or punished. It reads like a caricature, but there has never been a better vindication of the average man when he is up against it. The ten thousand judges, which the ten thousand generals turned into on occasion, never, so far as Xenophon's record goes, passed an unjust sentence. On one occasion

Xenophon was called to account for striking a soldier. " 'I own that I did so,' he said. 'I told him to carry to camp a wounded man, but I found him burying him still alive. I have struck others, too, half-frozen men who were sinking down in the snow to die, worn-out men lagging behind where the enemy might catch them. A blow would often make them get up and hasten. Those I have given offense to now accuse me. But those I have helped, in battle, on the march, in cold, in sickness, none of them speak up. They do not remember. And yet surely it is better— and happier, too—to remember a man's good deeds than his evil deeds.' Upon this," the narrative goes on, "the assembly, calling the past to mind, rose up and Xenophon was acquitted."

This completely disarming speech for the defense shows how well Xenophon knew the way to manage men. There is wounded feeling in his words, but no anger, no resentment, above all, no self-righteousness. Those listening were convinced by his frankness of his honesty; re- minded, without a suggestion of boasting, how great his services had been; and given to understand that far from claiming to be faultless, he appealed to them only to remember his deserts as well as his mistakes. He understood his audience and the qualities a leader must have, at least any leader who would lead Greeks. In a book he wrote on the education of the great Cyrus he draws a picture of the ideal general which, absurd as it is when applied to an Oriental monarch, shows to perfection the Greek idea of the one method that will make men who are worth anything independent, self-reliant men, willing to follow another man. "The leader," he writes, "must himself believe that willing obedience always beats forced obedience, and that he can get this only by really knowing what should be done. Thus he can secure obedience from his men because he can convince them that he knows best, precisely as a good doctor makes his patients obey him. Also he must be ready to suffer more hardships than he asks of his soldiers, more fatigue, greater ex- tremes of heat and cold. 'No one,' Cyrus always said, 'can be a good officer who does not undergo more than those he commands.' " How- ever that may be, it is certain that the inexperienced civilian Xenophon was could have won over the Ten Thousand in no other way. He was able to convince them that he knew best and they gave up their own ideas and followed him willingly.

He showed them too that even if they made him their leader, it was share and share alike between him and the army. On one occasion when he was riding up from his post in the rear to consult with the van, and the snow was deep and the marching hard, a soldier cried to him, "Oh, it's easy enough for you on horseback." Xenophon leaped from his horse, flung the man aside and marched in his place.

Always, no matter how desperate things seemed, the initiative which only free men can be counted on to develop got them through. They

25

abandoned their baggage by common consent and threw away their loot. "We will make the enemy carry our baggage for us," they said. "When we have conquered them we can take what we want." Early in the march they were terribly harassed by the Persian cavalry because they had none of their own. The men of Rhodes could throw with their slings twice as far as the Persians. They set them on baggage mules, directed them to aim at the riders, but spare their mounts and bring them back, and from that time on the Persians kept them in horses. If they needed ammunition they sent bowmen who could shoot farther than the foe to draw down showers of arrows that fell short and could be easily collected. One way or another they forced the Persians into service. When they got to the hills they discarded the tactics they had been trained in. They gave up the solid line, the only formation they knew, and the army advanced by columns, sometimes far apart. It was merely common sense in the rough broken country, but that virtue belongs peculiarly to men acting for themselves. The disciplined military mind has never been distinguished for it.

So, always cold and sometimes freezing, always hungry and sometimes starving, and always, always fighting, they held their own. No one by now had any clear idea where in the world they were. One day, Xenophon, riding in the rear, putting his horse up a steep hill, heard a great noise in front. A tumult was carried back to him by the wind, loud cries and shouting. An ambush, he thought, and calling to the others to follow at full speed, he drove his horse forward. No enemy was on the hilltop; only the Greeks. They were standing, all faced the same way, with tears running down their faces, their arms stretched out to what they saw before them. The shouting swelled into a great roar, "The sea! The sea!"

They were home at last. The sea was home to a Greek. It was the middle of January. They had left Cunaxa on the seventh of September. In four months they had marched well on to two thousand miles in circumstances never surpassed before or since for hardship and danger.

The *Anabasis* is the story of the Greeks in miniature. Ten thousand men, fiercely independent by nature, in a situation where they were a law unto themselves, showed that they were pre-eminently able to work together and proved what miracles of achievement willing co-operation can bring to pass. The Greek state, at any rate the Athenian state, which we know best, showed the same. What brought the Greeks safely back from Asia was precisely what made Athens great. The Athenian was a law unto himself, but his dominant instinct to stand alone was counterbalanced by his sense of overwhelming obligation to serve the state. This was his own spontaneous reaction to the facts of his life, nothing imposed upon him from outside. The city was his defense in a hostile world, his security, his pride, too, the guarantee to all of his worth as an Athenian.

Plato said that men could find their true moral development only in service to the city. The Athenian was saved from looking at his life as a private affair. Our word "idiot" comes from the Greek name for the man who took no share in public matters. Pericles in the funeral oration reported by Thucydides says:

> We are a free democracy, but we are obedient. We obey the laws, more especially those which protect the oppressed, and the unwritten laws whose transgression brings acknowledged shame. We do not allow absorption in our own affairs to interfere with participation in the city's. We differ from other states in regarding the man who holds aloof from public life as useless, yet we yield to none in independence of spirit and complete self-reliance.

This happy balance was maintained for a very brief period. No doubt at its best it was as imperfect as the working out of every lofty idea in human terms is bound to be. Even so, it was the foundation of the Greek achievement. The creed of democracy, spiritual and political liberty for all, and each man a willing servant of the state, was the conception which underlay the highest reach of Greek genius. It was fatally weakened by the race for money and power in the Periclean age; the Peloponnesian War destroyed it and Greece lost it forever. Nevertheless, the ideal of free individuals unified by a spontaneous service to the common life was left as a possession to the world, never to be forgotten.

THE READER

1. Hamilton says that Thucydides and Xenophon inhabited "worlds so different they seem to have no connection with each other." What are some of the major differences between these worlds and how does Hamilton illustrate them? Can you account for these differences by differences in the experience of each man or in their personalities or in both?

2. What implications for the writing and study of history do you find in the contrasts between Xenophon and Thucydides? Compare your conclusions with Edward Hallett Carr's discussion of the nature of historical fact ("The Historian and His Facts," p. 833).

3. Characterize the different kinds of "truth" that Thucydides and Xenophon wrote about. What does the kind of truth each chose to write about suggest about each man?

4. What does Xenophon's description of the dinner party indicate of the life of ancient Greece? Which details seem peculiar to that time and place? Which appear perennial, details that might be matched in accounts of comparable dinner parties at any time or place?

5. Does the account Xenophon gives of Socrates accord with that given by Plato? To what extent can the two accounts be reconciled? What

does each account show about its author (rather than about its subject)?

6. *In what ways is Xenophon's* Anabasis *"the story of the Greeks in miniature" (p. 920)?*

THE WRITER

1. *Hamilton's account of Xenophon has two main parts, a description of his life and writings in Greece and an account of his conduct during the Persian campaign. How does the characterization of Xenophon in Greece prepare for or illuminate his actions as commander of the Ten Thousand? What details does Hamilton choose to reveal each side of his experience? Explain whether the overall portrayal of Xenophon's character seems consistent.*

2. *Recount an incident in your experience (comparable to Xenophon's dinner party) as if you were going to include it in a history of your own time. Take into consideration the results of your thinking about questions 2 and 4, "The Reader" (above).*

3. *Xenophon's account of the newly married man's advice to his wife says something about the role of women in Greek life. Write a short essay giving advice, either from a wife to a husband or a husband to a wife, which reflects something about the role of women or men in our time.*

4. *Hamilton shows something about the theory and practice of Greek democracy. Write an essay comparing Greek democracy with our present-day theory and practice of democracy. You might find it useful to first read E. B. White's short piece on democracy (p. 934).*

Abraham Lincoln
SECOND INAUGURAL ADDRESS

At this second appearing to take the oath of the presidential office, there is less occasion for an extended address than there was at the first. Then a statement, somewhat in detail, of a course to be pursued, seemed fitting and proper. Now, at the expiration of four years, during which public declarations have been constantly called forth on every point and phase of the great contest which still absorbs the attention, and engrosses the energies of the nation, little that is new could be presented. The progress of our arms, upon which all else chiefly depends, is as well known to the public as to myself; and it is, I trust, reasonably satisfactory

Delivered March 4, 1865.

and encouraging to all. With high hope for the future, no prediction in regard to it is ventured.

On the occasion corresponding to this four years ago, all thoughts were anxiously directed to an impending civil war. All dreaded it—all sought to avert it. While the inaugural address was being delivered from this place, devoted altogether to *saving* the Union without war, insurgent agents were in the city seeking to *destroy* it without war—seeking to dissolve the Union, and divide effects, by negotiation. Both parties deprecated war; but one of them would *make* war rather than let the nation survive; and the other would *accept* war rather than let it perish. And the war came.

One-eighth of the whole population were colored slaves, not distributed generally over the Union, but localized in the Southern part of it. These slaves constituted a peculiar and powerful interest. All knew that this interest was, somehow, the cause of the war. To strengthen, perpetuate, and extend this interest was the object for which the insurgents would rend the Union, even by war; while the government claimed no right to do more than to restrict the territorial enlargement of it. Neither party expected for the war, the magnitude, or the duration, which it has already attained. Neither anticipated that the *cause* of the conflict might cease with, or even before, the conflict itself should cease. Each looked for an easier triumph, and a result less fundamental and astounding. Both read the same Bible, and pray to the same God; and each invokes His aid against the other. It may seem strange that any men should dare to ask a just God's assistance in wringing their bread from the sweat of other men's faces; but let us judge not that we be not judged.[1] The prayers of both could not be answered; that of neither has been answered fully. The Almighty has His own purposes. "Woe unto the world because of offenses! for it must needs be that offenses come; but woe to that man by whom the offense cometh!"[2] If we shall suppose that American slavery is one of those offenses which, in the providence of God, must needs come, but which, having continued through His appointed time, He now wills to remove, and that He gives to both North and South, this terrible war, as the woe due to those by whom the offense came, shall we discern therein any departure from those divine attributes which the believers in a Living God always ascribe to Him? Fondly do we hope—fervently do we pray—that this mightly scourge of war may speedily pass away. Yet, if God wills that it continue, until all the wealth piled by the bondman's two hundred and fifty years of unrequited toil shall be sunk, and until every drop of blood drawn with

1. Lincoln alludes to Jesus' statement in the Sermon on the Mount—"Judge not, that ye be not judged" (Matthew vii.1)—and to God's curse on Adam—"In the sweat of thy face shalt thou eat bread, till thou return unto the ground" (Genesis iii.19).
2. From Jesus' speech to his disciples (Matthew xviii.7).

the lash, shall be paid by another drawn with the sword, as was said three thousand years ago, so still it must be said "the judgments of the Lord are true and righteous altogether."[3]

With malice toward none; with charity for all; with firmness in the right, as God gives us to see the right, let us strive on to finish the work we are in; to bind up the nation's wounds; to care for him who shall have borne the battle, and for his widow, and his orphan—to do all which may achieve and cherish a just, and a lasting peace, among ourselves, and with all nations.

3. Psalms xix.9.

Thomas Jefferson

ORIGINAL DRAFT OF THE DECLARATION OF INDEPENDENCE

A DECLARATION OF THE REPRESENTATIVES OF THE UNITED STATES OF AMERICA, IN GENERAL CONGRESS ASSEMBLED.

When in the course of human events it becomes necessary for a people to advance from that subordination in which they have hitherto remained, & to assume among the powers of the earth the equal & independant station to which the laws of nature & of nature's god entitle them, a decent respect to the opinions of mankind requires that they should declare the causes which impel them to the change.

We hold these truths to be sacred & undeniable; that all men are created equal & independant, that from that equal creation they derive rights inherent & inalienable, among which are the preservation of life, & liberty, & the spirit of happiness; that to secure these ends, governments are instituted among men, deriving their just powers from the consent of the governed; that whenever any form of government shall become destructive of these ends, it is the right of the people to alter or to abolish it, & to institute new government, laying it's foundation on such principles & organising it's powers in such form, as to them shall seem most likely to effect their safety & happiness. prudence indeed will dictate that governments long established should not be changed for light & transient causes: and accordingly all experience hath shewn that

On June 11, 1776, Jefferson was elected by the Second Continental Congress to join John Adams, Benjamin Franklin, Roger Sherman, and Robert Livingston in drafting a declaration of independence. The draft presented to Congress on June 28 was primarily the work of Jefferson.

mankind are more disposed to suffer while evils are sufferable, than to right themselves by abolishing the forms to which they are accustomed. but when a long train of abuses & usurpations, begun at a distinguished period, & pursuing invariably the same object, evinces a design to subject them to arbitrary power, it is their right, it is their duty, to throw off such government & to provide new guards for their future security. such has been the patient sufferance of these colonies; & such is now the necessity which constrains them to expunge their former systems of government. The history of his present majesty, is a history of unremitting injuries and usurpations, among which no one fact stands single or solitary to contradict the uniform tenor of the rest, all of which have in direct object the establishment of an absolute tyranny over these states. to prove this, let facts be submitted to a candid world, for the truth of which we pledge a faith yet unsullied by falsehood.

he has refused his assent to laws the most wholesome and necessary for the public good:

he has forbidden his governors to pass laws of immediate & pressing importance, unless suspended in their operation till his assent should be obtained; and when so suspended, he has neglected utterly to attend to them.

he has refused to pass other laws for the accommodation of large districts of people unless those people would relinquish the right of representation, a right inestimable to them, & formidable to tyrants alone: [1]

he has dissolved Representative houses repeatedly & continually, for opposing with manly firmness his invasions on the rights of the people:

he has refused for a long space of time to cause others to be elected, whereby the legislative powers, incapable of annihilation, have returned to the people at large for their exercise, the state remaining in the mean time exposed to all the dangers of invasion from without, &, convulsions within:

he has suffered the administration of justice totally to cease in some of these colonies, refusing his assent to laws for establishing judiciary powers:

he has made our judges dependant on his will alone, for the tenure of their offices, and amount of their salaries:

1. At this point in the manuscript a strip containing the following clause is inserted: "He called together legislative bodies at places unusual, unco[mfortable, & distant from] the depository of their public records for the sole purpose of fatiguing [them into compliance] with his measures:" Missing parts in the Library of Congress text are supplied from the copy made by Jefferson for George Wythe. This copy is in the New York Public Library. The fact that this passage was omitted from John Adams's transcript suggests that it was not a part of Jefferson's original rough draft.

he has erected a multitude of new offices by a self-assumed power, &
sent hither swarms of officers to harrass our people & eat out their
substance:

he has kept among us in times of peace standing armies & ships of
war:

he has affected[2] to render the military, independent of & superior to
the civil power:

he has combined with others to subject us to a jurisdiction foreign to
our constitutions and unacknowledged by our laws; giving his assent
to their pretended acts of legislation, for quartering large bodies of
armed troops among us;

for protecting them by a mock-trial from punishment for any murders they should commit on the inhabitants of these states;

for cutting off our trade with all parts of the world;

for imposing taxes on us without our consent;

for depriving us of the benefits of trial by jury

he has endeavored to prevent the population of these states; for
that purpose obstructing the laws for naturalization of foreigners;
refusing to pass others to encourage their migrations hither; &
raising the conditions of new appropriations of lands;

for transporting us beyond seas to be tried for pretended offences:

for taking away our charters & altering fundamentally the forms of
our governments;

for suspending our own legislatures & declaring themselves invested with power to legislate for us in all cases whatsoever:

he has abdicated government here, withdrawing his governors, &
declaring us out of his allegiance & protection:

he has plundered our seas, ravaged our coasts, burnt our towns &
destroyed the lives of our people:

he is at this time transporting large armies of foreign mercenaries
to compleat the works of death, desolation & tyranny, already
begun with circumstances of cruelty & perfidy unworthy the head
of a civilized nation:

he has endeavored to bring on the inhabitants of our frontiers the
merciless Indian savages, whose known rule of warfare is an undistinguished destruction of all ages, sexes, & conditions of existence:

he has incited treasonable insurrections of our fellow-citizens, with
the allurements of forfeiture & confiscation of our property:

he has waged cruel war against human nature itself, violating it's
most sacred rights of life & liberty in the persons of a distant people
who never offended him, captivating & carrying them into slavery
in another hemisphere, or to incur miserable death in their trans-

2. Tried.

portation thither. this piratical warfare, the opprobrium of *infidel* powers, is the warfare of the CHRISTIAN king of Great Britain. determined to keep open a market where MEN should be bought & sold; he has prostituted his negative for suppressing every legislative attempt to prohibit or to restrain this execrable commerce: and that this assemblage of horrors might want no fact of distinguished die, he is now exciting those very people to rise in arms among us, and to purchase that liberty of which *he* has deprived them, by murdering the people upon whom *he* also obtruded them; thus paying off former crimes committed against the *liberties* of one people, with crimes which he urges them to commit against the *lives* of another.

in every stage of these oppressions we have petitioned for redress in the most humble terms; our repeated petitions have been answered by repeated injury. a prince whose character is thus marked by every act which may define a tyrant, is unfit to be the ruler of a people who mean to be free. future ages will scarce believe that the hardiness of one man, adventured within the short compass of twelve years only, on so many acts of tyranny without a mask, over a people fostered & fixed in principles of liberty.

Nor have we been wanting in attentions to our British brethren. we have warned them from time to time of attempts by their legislature to extend a jurisdiction over these our states. we have reminded them of the circumstances of our emigration & settlement here, no one of which could warrant so strange a pretension: that these were effected at the expence of our own blood & treasure, unassisted by the wealth or the strength of Great Britain: that in constituting indeed our several forms of government, we had adopted one common king, thereby laying a foundation for perpetual league & amity with them; but that submission to their [Parliament, was no Part of our Constitution, nor ever in Idea, if History may be] [3] credited: and we appealed to their native justice & magnanimity, as to the ties of our common kindred to disavow these usurpations which were likely to interrupt our correspondence & connection. they too have been deaf to the voice of justice & of consanguinity, & when occasions have been given them, by the regular course of their laws, of removing from their councils the disturbers of our harmony, they have by their free election re-established them in power. at this very time too they are permitting their chief magistrate to send over not only soldiers of our common blood, but Scotch & foreign mercenaries to invade & deluge us in blood. these facts have given the last stab to agonizing affection, and manly spirit bids us to renounce for ever these unfeeling brethren. we must endeavor to forget our former love

3. An illegible passage is supplied from John Adams' transcription.

for them, and to hold them as we hold the rest of mankind, enemies in war, in peace friends. we might have been a free & a great people together; but a communication of grandeur & of freedom it seems is below their dignity. be it so, since they will have it: the road to glory & happiness is open to us too; we will climb it in a separate state, and acquiesce in the necessity which pronounces our everlasting Adieu!

We therefore the representatives of the United States of America in General Congress assembled do, in the name & by authority of the good people of these states, reject and renounce all allegiance & subjection to the kings of Great Britain & all others who may hereafter claim by, through, or under them; we utterly dissolve & break off all political connection which may have heretofore subsisted between us & the people or parliament of Great Britain; and finally we do assert and declare these colonies to be free and independant states, and that as free & independant states they shall hereafter have power to levy war, conclude peace, contract alliances, establish commerce, & to do all other acts and things which independant states may of right do. And for the support of this declaration we mutually pledge to each other our lives, our fortunes, & our sacred honour.

Thomas Jefferson and Others
THE DECLARATION OF INDEPENDENCE

IN CONGRESS, JULY 4, 1776
THE UNANIMOUS DECLARATION OF THE
THIRTEEN UNITED STATES OF AMERICA

When in the Course of human events it becomes necessary for one people to dissolve the political bands which have connected them with another, and to assume among the powers of the earth, the separate and equal station to which the Laws of Nature and of Nature's God entitle them, a decent respect to the opinions of mankind requires that they should declare the causes which impel them to the separation.

We hold these truths to be self-evident, that all men are created equal, that they are endowed by their Creator with certain unalienable Rights, that among these are Life, Liberty and the pursuit of Happiness. That to secure these rights, Governments are instituted among Men, deriving their just powers from the consent of the governed. That whenever any Form of Government becomes destructive of these ends, it is the Right of the People to alter or to abolish it, and to institute new Government, laying its foundation on such principles and organizing its powers in such form, as to them shall seem most likely to affect their Safety and Happiness. Prudence, indeed, will dictate that Governments long established should not be changed for light and transient causes; and accordingly all experience hath shewn that mankind are more disposed to suffer, while evils are sufferable, than to right themselves by abolishing the forms to which they are accustomed. But when a long train of abuses and usurpations, pursuing invariably the same Object evinces a design to reduce them under absolute Despotism, it is their right, it is their duty, to throw off such Government, and to provide new Guards for their future security. Such has been the patient sufferance of these Colonies; and such is now the necessity which constrains them to alter their former Systems of Government. The history of the present King of Great Britain is a history of repeated injuries and usurpations, all having in direct object the establishment of an absolute Tyranny over these States. To prove this, let Facts be submitted to a candid world.

He has refused his Assent to Laws, the most wholesome and necessary for the public good.

He has forbidden his Government to pass laws of immediate and pressing importance, unless suspended in their operation till his Assent should be obtained; and when so suspended, he has utterly neglected to attend to them.

He has refused to pass other Laws for the accommodation of large districts of people, unless those people would relinquish the right of Representation in the Legislature, a right inestimable to them and formidable to tyrants only.

He has called together legislative bodies at places unusual, uncomfortable, and distant from the depository of their Public Records, for the sole purpose of fatiguing them into compliance with his measures.

He has dissolved Representative Houses repeatedly, for opposing with manly firmness his invasions on the rights of the people.

He has refused for a long time, after such dissolutions, to cause others to be elected; whereby the Legislative Powers, incapable of Annihilation, have returned to the People at large for their exercise; the State remaining in the mean time exposed to all the dangers of invasion from without, and convulsions within.

He has endeavored to prevent the population of these States; for that purpose obstructing the Laws for Naturalization of Foreigners; refusing to pass others to encourage their migration hither, and raising the conditions of new Appropriations of Lands.

He has obstructed the Administration of Justice, by refusing his Assent to Laws for establishing Judiciary Powers.

He has made Judges dependent on his Will alone, for the tenure of their offices, and the amount and payment of their salaries.

He has erected a multitude of New Offices, and sent hither swarms of Officers to harass our people, and eat out their substance.

He has kept among us, in times of peace, Standing Armies without the Consent of our legislatures.

He has affected to render the Military independent of and superior to the Civil Power.

He has combined with others to subject us to a jurisdiction foreign to our constitution, and unacknowledged by our laws; giving his Assent to their Acts of pretended Legislation: For quartering large bodies of armed troops among us: For protecting them, by a mock Trial, from punishment for any Murders which they should commit on the Inhabitants of these States: For cutting off our Trade with all parts of the world: For imposing Taxes on us without our Consent: For depriving us in many cases, of the benefits of Trial by Jury; For transporting us beyond Seas to be tried for pretended offenses: for abolishing the free System of English Laws in a neighboring Province, establishing therein an Arbitrary government, and enlarging its Boundaries so as to render it at once an example and fit instrument for introducing the same absolute rule into these Colonies: For taking away our Charters, abolishing our most valuable Laws and altering fundamentally the Forms of our Governments: For suspending our own Legislatures, and declaring themselves invested with power to legislate for us in all cases whatsoever.

He has abdicated Government here, by declaring us out of his Protection and waging War against us.

He has plundered our seas, ravaged our Coasts, burnt our towns, and destroyed the lives of our people.

He is at this time transporting large Armies of foreign Mercenaries to complete the works of death, desolation and tyranny, already begun with circumstances of Cruelty & Perfidy scarcely paralleled in the most barbarous ages, and totally unworthy the Head of a civilized nation.

He has constrained our fellow Citizens taken Captive on the high Seas to bear Arms against their Country, to become the executioners of their friends and Brethren, or to fall themselves by their Hands.

He has excited domestic insurrections amongst us, and has endeavored to bring on the inhabitants of our frontiers, the merciless Indian Savages, whose known rule of warfare, is an undistinguished destruction of all ages, sexes, and conditions.

In every stage of these Oppressions We have Petitioned for Redress in the most humble terms: Our repeated Petitions have been answered only by repeated injury. A Prince, whose character is thus marked by every act which may define a Tyrant, is unfit to be the ruler of a free people.

Nor have We been wanting in attention to our British brethren. We have warned them from time to time of attempts by their legislature to extend an unwarrantable jurisdiction over us. We have reminded them of the circumstances of our emigration and settlement here. We have appealed to their native justice and magnanimity, and we have conjured them by the ties of our common kindred to disavow these usurpations, which would inevitably interrupt our connections and correspondence. They too have been deaf to the voice of justice and of consanguinity. We must, therefore, acquiesce in the necessity, which denounces our Separation, and hold them, as we hold the rest of mankind, Enemies in War, in Peace Friends.

We, THEREFORE the Representatives of the UNITED STATES OF AMERICA, in General Congress, Assembled, appealing to the Supreme Judge of the world for the rectitude of our intentions, do, in the Name, and by Authority of the good People of these Colonies, solemnly publish and declare, That these United Colonies are, and of Right ought to be FREE AND INDEPENDENT STATES; that they are Absolved from all Allegiance to the British Crown, and that all political connection between them and the State of Great Britain, is and ought to be totally dissolved; and that as Free and Independent States, they have full Power to levy War, conclude Peace, contract Alliances, establish Commerce, and to do all other Acts and Things which Independent States may of right do. And for the support of this Declaration, with a firm reliance on the protection of Divine Providence, we mutually pledge to each other our Lives, our Fortunes, and our sacred Honor.

THE READER

1. Find the key terms and phrases of the Declaration (such as "these truths . . . self-evident," "created equal," "unalienable Rights," and so on), and determine how fully they are defined by the contexts in which they occur. Why are no formal definitions given for them?
2. The signers of the Declaration appeal both to general principles and to factual evidence in presenting their case. Which of the appeals to principle could still legitimately be made today by a nation eager to achieve independence? In other words, how far does the Declaration reflect unique events of history, and how far does it reflect universal aspirations and ideals?

THE WRITER

1. The Declaration of Independence was addressed to several audiences: the king of Great Britain, the people of Great Britain, the people of America, and the world at large. Show ways in which the final draft was adapted for its several audiences.
2. Closely examine the second paragraph of both the original draft and

the final version of the Declaration. How have the revisions of the final
version increased its effectiveness over the first draft?

3. The Declaration has often been called a classic example of deductive
   argument: setting up general statements, relating particular cases to
   them, and drawing conclusions. Trace this pattern through the document, noting the way each part is developed. Would the document
   have been as effective if the long middle part had either come first or
   been left out entirely? Explain.

4. Using only what is implied in the Declaration, write a brief definition
   for one of the key terms referred to in question 1, "The Reader"
   (above).

5. Burgess refers to the "dangerous naiveté" of the Declaration (p. 446).
   Read Burgess' remark in its context, and then write a paragraph or two
   supporting or opposing his view.

Carl Becker

DEMOCRACY

Democracy, like liberty or science or progress, is a word with which
we are all so familiar that we rarely take the trouble to ask what we mean
by it. It is a term, as the devotees of semantics say, which has no
"referent"—there is no precise or palpable thing or object which we all
think of when the word is pronounced. On the contrary, it is a word
which connotes different things to different people, a kind of conceptual
Gladstone bag which, with a little manipulation, can be made to accommodate almost any collection of social facts we may wish to carry about
in it. In it we can as easily pack a dictatorship as any other form of
government. We have only to stretch the concept to include any form
of government supported by a majority of the people, for whatever
reasons and by whatever means of expressing assent, and before we know
it the empire of Napoleon, the Soviet regime of Stalin, and the Fascist
systems of Mussolini and Hitler are all safely in the bag. But if this is
what we mean by democracy, then virtually all forms of government are
democratic, since virtually all governments, except in times of revolution, rest upon the explicit or implicit consent of the people. In order
to discuss democracy intelligently it will be necessary, therefore, to
define it, to attach to the word a sufficiently precise meaning to avoid
the confusion which is not infrequently the chief result of such discussions.

From *Modern Democracy* (1941).

All human institutions, we are told, have their ideal forms laid away in heaven, and we do not need to be told that the actual institutions conform but indifferently to these ideal counterparts. It would be possible then to define democracy either in terms of the ideal or in terms of the real form—to define it as government of the people, by the people, for the people; or to define it as government of the people, by the politicians, for whatever pressure groups can get their interests taken care of. But as a historian I am naturally disposed to be satisfied with the meaning which, in the history of politics, men have commonly attributed to the word—a meaning, needless to say, which derives partly from the experience and partly from the aspirations of mankind. So regarded, the term democracy refers primarily to a form of government, and it has always meant government by the many as opposed to government by the one—government by the people as opposed to government by a tyrant, a dictator, or an absolute monarch. This is the most general meaning of the word as men have commonly understood it.

In this antithesis there are, however, certain implications, always tacitly understood, which give a more precise meaning to the term. Peisistratus, for example, was supported by a majority of the people, but his government was never regarded as a democracy for all that. Caesar's power derived from a popular mandate, conveyed through established republican forms, but that did not make his government any the less a dictatorship. Napoleon called his government a democratic empire, but no one, least of all Napoleon himself, doubted that he had destroyed the last vestiges of the democratic republic. Since the Greeks first used the term, the essential test of democratic government has always been this: the source of political authority must be and remain in the people and not in the ruler. A democratic government has always meant one in which the citizens, or a sufficient number of them to represent more or less effectively the common will, freely act from time to time, and according to established forms, to appoint or recall the magistrates and to enact or revoke the laws by which the community is governed. This I take to be the meaning which history has impressed upon the term democracy as a form of government.

E. B. White

DEMOCRACY

We received a letter from the Writers' War Board the other day asking for a statement on "The Meaning of Democracy." It presumably is our duty to comply with such a request, and it is certainly our pleasure.

Surely the Board knows what democracy is. It is the line that forms on the right. It is the don't in don't shove. It is the hole in the stuffed shirt through which the sawdust slowly trickles; it is the dent in the high hat. Democracy is the recurrent suspicion that more than half of the people are right more than half of the time. It is the feeling of privacy in the voting booths, the feeling of communion in the libraries, the feeling of vitality everywhere. Democracy is a letter to the editor. Democracy is the score at the beginning of the ninth. It is an idea which hasn't been disproved yet, a song the words of which have not gone bad. It's the mustard on the hot dog and the cream in the rationed coffee. Democracy is a request from a War Board, in the middle of a morning in the middle of a war, wanting to know what democracy is.

First appeared in *The New Yorker* (July 3, 1943); later reprinted in *The Wild Flag* (1946).

THE READER

1. *Look up* democracy *in a standard desk dictionary. Of the several meanings given, which one best applies to White's definition? Does more than one apply?*
2. *If White were writing this piece today, which of his examples might he change and which would he probably retain?*
3. *Compare White's definition of* democracy *with Becker's (p. 932).*

THE WRITER

1. *White's piece is dated July 3, 1943, the middle of World War II. How did the occasion shape what White says about democracy?*
2. *Translate White's definition into nonmetaphorical language. (For example, "It is the line that forms on the right" might be translated by "It has no special privileges.") Determine what is lost in the translation or, in other words, what White has gained by using figurative language.*
3. *If you didn't know that White was the author of "Some Remarks on Humor" (p. 1132), what specific features of his use of metaphor in that piece might enable you to guess that he was?*

4. Using White's technique for definition, write a definition of an abstraction such as love, justice, or beauty.

Walter Lippmann

THE INDISPENSABLE OPPOSITION

Were they pressed hard enough, most men would probably confess that political freedom—that is to say, the right to speak freely and to act in opposition—is a noble ideal rather than a practical necessity. As the case for freedom is generally put today, the argument lends itself to this feeling. It is made to appear that, whereas each man claims his freedom as a matter of right, the freedom he accords to other men is a matter of toleration. Thus, the defense of freedom of opinion tends to rest not on its substantial, beneficial, and indispensable consequences, but on a somewhat eccentric, a rather vaguely benevolent, attachment to an abstraction.

It is all very well to say with Voltaire, "I wholly disapprove of what you say, but will defend to the death your right to say it," but as a matter of fact most men will not defend to the death the rights of other men: if they disapprove sufficiently what other men say, they will somehow suppress those men if they can.

So, if this is the best that can be said for liberty of opinion, that a man must tolerate his opponents because everyone has a "right" to say what he pleases, then we shall find that liberty of opinion is a luxury, safe only in pleasant times when men can be tolerant because they are not deeply and vitally concerned.

Yet actually, as a matter of historic fact, there is a much stronger foundation for the great constitutional right of freedom of speech, and as a matter of practical human experience there is a much more compelling reason for cultivating the habits of free men. We take, it seems to me, a naïvely self-righteous view when we argue as if the right of our opponents to speak were something that we protect because we are magnanimous, noble, and unselfish. The compelling reason why, if liberty of opinion did not exist, we should have to invent it, why it will eventually have to be restored in all civilized countries where it is now suppressed, is that we must protect the right of our opponents to speak because we must hear what they have to say.

We miss the whole point when we imagine that we tolerate the freedom of our political opponents as we tolerate a howling baby next

First published in the *Atlantic Monthly* (Aug. 1939).

door, as we put up with the blasts from our neighbor's radio because we are too peaceable to heave a brick through the window. If this were all there is to freedom of opinion, that we are too goodnatured or too timid to do anything about our opponents and our critics except to let them talk, it would be difficult to say whether we are tolerant because we are magnanimous or because we are lazy, because we have strong principles or because we lack serious convictions, whether we have the hospitality of an inquiring mind or the indifference of an empty mind. And so, if we truly wish to understand why freedom is necessary in a civilized society, we must begin by realizing that, because freedom of discussion improves our own opinions, the liberties of other men are our own vital necessity.

We are much closer to the essence of the matter, not when we quote Voltaire, but when we go to the doctor and pay him to ask us the most embarrassing questions and to prescribe the most disagreeable diet. When we pay the doctor to exercise complete freedom of speech about the cause and cure of our stomachache, we do not look upon ourselves as tolerant and magnanimous, and worthy to be admired by ourselves. We have enough common sense to know that if we threaten to put the doctor in jail because we do not like the diagnosis and the prescription it will be unpleasant for the doctor, to be sure, but equally unpleasant for our own stomachache. That is why even the most ferocious dictator would rather be treated by a doctor who was free to think and speak the truth than by his own Minister of Propaganda. For there is a point, the point at which things really matter, where the freedom of others is no longer a question of their right but of our own need.

The point at which we recognize this need is much higher in some men than in others. The totalitarian rulers think they do not need the freedom of an opposition: they exile, imprison, or shoot their opponents. We have concluded on the basis of practical experience, which goes back to Magna Carta and beyond, that we need the opposition. We pay the opposition salaries out of the public treasury.

In so far as the usual apology for freedom of speech ignores this experience, it becomes abstract and eccentric rather than concrete and human. The emphasis is generally put on the right to speak, as if all that mattered were that the doctor should be free to go out into the park and explain to the vacant air why I have a stomachache. Surely that is a miserable caricature of the great civic right which men have bled and died for. What really matters is that the doctor should tell *me* what ails me, that I should listen to him; that if I do not like what he says I should be free to call in another doctor; and that then the first doctor should have to listen to the second doctor; and that out of all the speaking and listening, the give-and-take of opinions, the truth should be arrived at.

This is the creative principle of freedom of speech, not that it is a system for the tolerating of error, but that it is a system for finding the truth. It may not produce the truth, or the whole truth all the time, or often, or in some cases ever. But if the truth can be found, there is no other system which will normally and habitually find so much truth. Until we have thoroughly understood this principle, we shall not know why we must value our liberty, or how we can protect and develop it.

Let us apply this principle to the system of public speech in a totalitarian state. We may, without any serious falsification, picture a condition of affairs in which the mass of the people are being addressed through one broadcasting system by one man and his chosen subordinates. The orators speak. The audience listens but cannot and dare not speak back. It is a system of one-way communication; the opinions of the rulers are broadcast outwardly to the mass of the people. But nothing comes back to the rulers from the people except the cheers; nothing returns in the way of knowledge of forgotten facts, hidden feelings, neglected truths, and practical suggestions.

But even a dictator cannot govern by his own one-way inspiration alone. In practice, therefore, the totalitarian rulers get back the reports of the secret police and of their party henchmen down among the crowd. If these reports are competent, the rulers may manage to remain in touch with public sentiment. Yet that is not enough to know what the audience feels. The rulers have also to make great decisions that have enormous consequences, and here their system provides virtually no help from the give-and-take of opinion in the nation. So they must either rely on their own intuition, which cannot be permanently and continually inspired, or, if they are intelligent despots, encourage their trusted advisers and their technicians to speak and debate freely in their presence.

On the walls of the houses of Italian peasants one may see inscribed in large letters the legend, "Mussolini is always right." But if that legend is taken seriously by Italian ambassadors, by the Italian General Staff, and by the Ministry of Finance, then all one can say is heaven help Mussolini, heaven help Italy, and the new Emperor of Ethiopia.[1]

For at some point, even in a totalitarian state, it is indispensable that there should exist the freedom of opinion which causes opposing opinions to be debated. As time goes on, that is less and less easy under a despotism; critical discussion disappears as the internal opposition is liquidated in favor of men who think and feel alike. That is why the early successes of despots, of Napoleon I and of Napoleon III, have usually been followed by an irreparable mistake. For in listening only to his yes men—the others being in exile or in concentration camps, or terri-

1. Benito Mussolini was then dictator of Italy, which he led into World War II; after Italy's conquest of Ethiopia in 1936, he had the Italian king, Victor Emanuel III, proclaimed its emperor.

fied—the despot shuts himself off from the truth that no man can dispense with.

We know all this well enough when we contemplate the dictatorships. But when we try to picture our own system, by way of contrast, what picture do we have in our minds? It is, is it not, that anyone may stand up on his own soapbox and say anything he pleases, like the individuals in Kipling's poem [2] who sit each in his separate star and draw the Thing as they see it for the God of Things as they are. Kipling, perhaps, could do this, since he was a poet. But the ordinary mortal isolated on his separate star will have an hallucination, and a citizenry declaiming from separate soapboxes will poison the air with hot and nonsensical confusion.

15   If the democratic alternative to the totalitarian one-way broadcasts is a row of separate soapboxes, than I submit that the alternative is unworkable, is unreasonable, and is humanly unattractive. It is above all a false alternative. It is not true that liberty has developed among civilized men when anyone is free to set up a soapbox, is free to hire a hall where he may expound his opinions to those who are willing to listen. On the contrary, freedom of speech is established to achieve its essential purpose only when different opinions are expounded in the same hall to the same audience.

For, while the right to talk may be the beginning of freedom, the necessity of listening is what makes the right important. Even in Russia and Germany [3] a man may still stand in an open field and speak his mind. What matters is not the utterance of opinions. What matters is the confrontation of opinions in debate. No man can care profoundly that every fool should say what he likes. Nothing has been accomplished if the wisest man proclaims his wisdom in the middle of the Sahara Desert. This is the shadow. We have the substance of liberty when the fool is compelled to listen to the wise man and learn; when the wise man is compelled to take account of the fool, and to instruct him; when the wise man can increase his wisdom by hearing the judgment of his peers.

That is why civilized men must cherish liberty—as a means of promoting the discovery of truth. So we must not fix our whole attention on the right of anyone to hire his own hall, to rent his own broadcasting station, to distribute his own pamphlets. These rights are incidental; and though they must be preserved, they can be preserved only by regarding them as incidental, as auxiliary to the substance of liberty that must be cherished and cultivated.

Freedom of speech is best conceived, therefore, by having in mind the picture of a place like the American Congress, an assembly where

2. "L'Envoi."
3. Lippmann is referring to the totalitarian   regimes of the Soviet Union under Stalin and Nazi Germany under Hitler.

opposing views are represented, where ideas are not merely uttered but debated, or the British Parliament, where men who are free to speak are also compelled to answer. We may picture the true condition of freedom as existing in a place like a court of law, where witnesses testify and are cross-examined, where the lawyer argues against the opposing lawyer before the same judge and in the presence of one jury. We may picture freedom as existing in a forum where the speaker must respond to questions; in a gathering of scientists where the data, the hypothesis, and the conclusion are submitted to men competent to judge them; in a reputable newspaper which not only will publish the opinions of those who disagree but will re-examine its own opinion in the light of what they say.

Thus the essence of freedom of opinion is not in mere toleration as such, but in the debate which toleration provides: it is not in the venting of opinion, but in the confrontation of opinion. That this is the practical substance can readily be understood when we remember how differently we feel and act about the censorship and regulation of opinion purveyed by different media of communication. We find then that, in so far as the medium makes difficult the confrontation of opinion in debate, we are driven towards censorship and regulation.

There is, for example, the whispering campaign, the circulation of anonymous rumors by men who cannot be compelled to prove what they say. They put the utmost strain on our tolerance, and there are few who do not rejoice when the anonymous slanderer is caught, exposed, and punished. At a higher level there is the moving picture, a most powerful medium for conveying ideas, but a medium which does not permit debate. A moving picture cannot be answered effectively by another moving picture; in all free countries there is some censorship of the movies, and there would be more if the producers did not recognize their limitations by avoiding political controversy. There is then the radio. Here debate is difficult: it is not easy to make sure that the speaker is being answered in the presence of the same audience. Inevitably, there is some regulation of the radio.

When we reach the newspaper press, the opportunity for debate is so considerable that discontent cannot grow to the point where under normal conditions there is any disposition to regulate the press. But when newspapers abuse their power by injuring people who have no means of replying, a disposition to regulate the press appears. When we arrive at Congress we find that, because the membership of the House is so large, full debate is impracticable. So there are restrictive rules. On the other hand, in the Senate, where the conditions of full debate exist, there is almost absolute freedom of speech.

This shows us that the preservation and development of freedom of opinion are not only a matter of adhering to abstract legal rights, but

20

also, and very urgently, a matter of organizing and arranging sufficient debate. Once we have a firm hold on the central principle, there are many practical conclusions to be drawn. We then realize that the defense of freedom of opinion consists primarily in perfecting the opportunity for an adequate give-and-take of opinion; it consists also in regulating the freedom of those revolutionists who cannot or will not permit or maintain debate when it does not suit their purposes.

We must insist that free oratory is only the beginning of free speech; it is not the end, but a means to an end. The end is to find the truth. The practical justification of civil liberty is not that self-expression is one of the rights of man. It is that the examination of opinion is one of the necessities of man. For experience tells us that it is only when freedom of opinion becomes the compulsion to debate that the seed which our fathers planted has produced its fruit. When that is understood, freedom will be cherished not because it is a vent for our opinions but because it is the surest method of correcting them.

The unexamined life, said Socrates, is unfit to be lived by man. This is the virtue of liberty, and the ground on which we may best justify our belief in it, that it tolerates error in order to serve the truth. When men are brought face to face with their opponents, forced to listen and learn and mend their ideas, they cease to be children and savages and begin to live like civilized men. Then only is freedom a reality, when men may voice their opinions because they must examine their opinions.

25   The only reason for dwelling on all this is that if we are to preserve democracy we must understand its principles. And the principle which distinguishes it from all other forms of government is that in a democracy the opposition not only is tolerated as constitutional but must be maintained because it is in fact indispensable.

The democratic system cannot be operated without effective opposition. For, in making the great experiment of governing people by consent rather than by coercion, it is not sufficient that the party in power should have a majority. It is just as necessary that the party in power should never outrage the minority. That means that it must listen to the minority and be moved by the criticisms of the minority. That means that its measures must take account of the minority's objections, and that in administering measures it must remember that the minority may become the majority.

The opposition is indispensable. A good statesman, like any other sensible human being, always learns more from his opponents than from his fervent supporters. For his supporters will push him to disaster unless his opponents show him where the dangers are. So if he is wise he will often pray to be delivered from his friends, because they will ruin him. But, though it hurts, he ought also to pray never to be left without opponents; for they keep him on the path of reason and good sense.

The national unity of a free people depends upon a sufficiently even balance of political power to make it impracticable for the administration to be arbitrary and for the opposition to be revolutionary and irreconcilable. Where that balance no longer exists, democracy perishes. For unless all the citizens of a state are forced by circumstances to compromise, unless they feel that they can affect policy but that no one can wholly dominate it, unless by habit and necessity they have to give and take, freedom cannot be maintained.

THE READER

1. What is the importance of Lippmann's distinction between "free oratory" and "free speech" (p. 940)?
2. What does Lippmann mean when he says that the point at which we recognize the need for the freedom of others "is much higher in some men than in others" (p. 936)? Does this assertion in any way weaken his argument?
3. Thurber's rabbits (p. 908) listened to their opposition—that is, "the other animals, who lived at a great distance"—and were annihilated. Does Thurber's fable suggest any necessary qualification for Lippmann's thesis concerning the value of the opposition? Explain.
4. Lippmann's essay was written before the term brainwashing was in common use. If he were writing the essay today, how might he take account of this term?

THE WRITER

1. What is Lippmann's reason for dividing the essay into three parts? What is the purpose of the third part?
2. Why has Lippmann discussed motion pictures but not literature (p. 939)? How sound is his view that the motion picture is "a medium which does not permit debate"? Does literature permit debate?
3. What does Lippmann mean by his statement that "the usual apology for freedom of speech . . . becomes abstract and eccentric rather than concrete and human" (p. 941)? Why has he chosen these particular words to contrast the "usual apology" with his own view? Is his argument "concrete and human"?
4. Write a brief essay in which you test whether opposition is necessary to democracy in the way that Becker (p. 932) or White (p. 934) defines it.

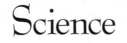

Science

Horace Freeland Judson
THE RAGE TO KNOW

Certain moments of the mind have a special quality of well-being. A mathematician friend of mine remarked the other day that his daughter, aged eight, had just stumbled without his teaching onto the fact that some numbers are prime numbers—those, like 11 or 19 or 83 or 1023, that cannot be divided by any other integer (except, trivially, by 1). "She called them 'unfair' numbers," he said. "And when I asked her why they were unfair, she told me, 'Because there's no way to share them out evenly.'" What delighted him most was not her charming turn of phrase nor her equitable turn of mind (seventeen peppermints to give to her friends?) but—as a mathematician—the knowledge that the child had experienced a moment of pure scientific perception. She had discovered for herself something of the way things are.

The satisfaction of such a moment at its most intense—and this is what ought to be meant, after all, by the tarnished phrase "the moment of truth"—is not easy to describe. It partakes at once of exhilaration and tranquillity. It is luminously clear. It is beautiful. The clarity of the moment of discovery, the beauty of what in that moment is seen to be true about the world, is the fundamental attraction that draws scientists on.

Science is enormously disparate—easily the most varied and diverse of human pursuits. The scientific endeavor ranges from the study of animal behavior all the way to particle physics, and from the purest of mathematics back again to the most practical problems of shelter and hunger, sickness and war. Nobody has succeeded in catching all this in one net. And yet the conviction persists—scientists themselves believe, at heart—that behind the diversity lies a unity. In those luminous moments of discovery, in the various approaches and the painful tension required to arrive at them, and then in the community of science,

From the *Atlantic* (Apr. 1980). Adapted from *The Search for Solutions* (1980).

organized worldwide to doubt and criticize, test and exploit discoveries—somewhere in that constellation, to begin with, there are surely constants. Deeper is the lure that in the bewildering variety of the world as it is there may be found some astonishing simplicities.

Philosophers, and some of the greatest among them, have offered descriptions of what they claim is the method of science. These make most scientists acutely uncomfortable. The descriptions don't seem to fit what goes on in the doing of science. They seem at once too abstract and too limited. Scientists don't believe that they think in ways that are wildly different from the way most people think at least in some areas of their lives. "We'd be in real trouble—we could get nowhere—if ordinary methods of inference did not apply," Philip Morrison said in a conversation a while ago. (Morrison is a theoretical physicist at the Massachusetts Institute of Technology.) The wild difference, he went on to say, is that scientists apply these everyday methods to areas that most people never think about seriously and carefully. The philosophers' descriptions don't prepare one for either this ordinariness or this extreme diversity of the scientific enterprise—the variety of things to think about, the variety of obstacles and traps to understanding, the variety of approaches to solutions. They hardly acknowledge the fact that a scientist ought often to find himself stretching to the tiptoe of available technique and apparatus, out beyond the frontier of the art, attempting to do something whose difficulty is measured most significantly by the fact that it has never been done before. Science is carried on—this, too, is obvious—in the field, in the observatory, in the laboratory. But historians leave out the arts of the chef and the watchmaker, the development at the bench of a new procedure or a new instrument. "And *making it work*," Morrison said. "This is terribly important." Indeed, biochemists talk about "the cookbook." Many a Nobel Prize has been awarded, not for a discovery, as such, but for a new technique or a new tool that opened up a whole field of discovery. "I am a theoretician," Morrison said. "And yet the most important problem for me is to be in touch with the people who are making new instruments or finding new ways of observing, and to try to get them to do the right experiments." And then, in a burst of annoyance, "I feel very reluctant to give any support to descriptions of 'scientific method.' The scientific enterprise is very difficult to model. You have to look at what scientists of all kinds *actually do*."

It's true that by contrast philosophers and historians seem bookbound—or paper-blindered, depending chiefly on what has been published as scientific research for their understanding of the process of discovery. In this century, anyway, published papers are no guide to the way scientists get the results they report. We have testimony of the highest authenticity for that. Sir Peter Medawar has both done fine science and written well about how it is done: he won his Nobel Prize

5

for investigations of immunological tolerance, which explained, among other things, why foreign tissue, like a kidney or a heart, is rejected by the body into which it is transplanted, and he has described the methods of science in essays of grace and distinction. A while ago, Medawar wrote, "What scientists *do* has never been the subject of a scientific . . . inquiry. It is no use looking to scientific 'papers,' for they not merely conceal but actively misrepresent the reasoning that goes into the work they describe." The observation has become famous, its truth acknowledged by other scientists. Medawar wrote further, "Scientists are building explanatory structures, *telling stories* which are scrupulously tested to see if they are stories about real life."

Scientists do science for a variety of reasons, of course, and most of them are familiar to the sculptor, or to the surgeon or the athlete or the builder of bridges: the professional's pride in skill; the swelling gratification that comes with recognition accorded by colleagues and peers; perhaps the competitor's fierce appetite; perhaps ambition for a kind of fame more durable than most. At the beginning is curiosity, and with curiosity the delight in mastery—the joy of figuring it out that is the birthright of every child. I once asked Murray Gell-Mann, a theoretical physicist, how he got started in science. His answer was to point to the summer sky: "When I was a boy, I used to ask all sorts of simple questions—like, 'What holds the clouds up?' " Rosalind Franklin, the crystallographer whose early death deprived her of a share in the Nobel Prize for the discovery of the structure of DNA,[1] one day was helping a young collaborator draft an application for research money, when she looked up at him and said, "What we can't tell them is that it's so much *fun!*" He still remembers her glint of mischief. The play of the mind, in an almost childlike innocence, is a pleasure that appears again and again in scientists' reflections on their work. The geneticist Barbara McClintock, as a woman in American science in the 1930s, had no chance at the academic posts open to her male colleagues, but that hardly mattered to her. "I did it because it was *fun!*" she said forty years later. "I couldn't wait to get up in the morning! I never thought of it as 'science.' "

The exuberant innocence can be poignant. François Jacob,[2] who won his share of a Nobel Prize as one of the small group of molecular biologists in the fifties who brought sense and order into the interactions by which bacteria regulate their life processes, recently read an account I had written of that work, and said to me with surprise and an evident

1. The structure of DNA was discovered by James Watson and Francis Crick.
2. Jacob (1920–   ), French biologist who, with André Lwoff and Jacques Monod, won the 1965 Nobel Prize for Physiology or Medicine in recognition for discoveries concerning regulatory activities in bacteria.

pang of regret, "We were like children playing!" He meant the fun of it—but also the simplicity of the problems they had encountered and the innocence of mind they had brought to them. Two hundred and fifty years before—although Jacob did not consciously intend the parallel—Isaac Newton,[3] shortly before his death, said:

> I do not know what I may appear to the world, but to myself I seem to have been only like a boy playing on the sea shore, and diverting myself in now and then finding a smoother pebble or a prettier shell than ordinary, whilst the great ocean of truth lay all undiscovered before me.

For some, curiosity and the delight of putting the world together deepen into a life's passion. Sheldon Glashow, a fundamental-particle physicist at Harvard, also got started in science by asking simple questions. "In eighth grade, we were learning about how the earth goes around the sun, and the moon around the earth, and so on," he said. "And I thought about that, and realized that the Man in the Moon is always looking at us"—that the moon as it circles always turns the same face to the earth. "And I asked the teacher, 'Why is the Man in the Moon always looking at us?' She was pleased with the question—but said it was hard to answer. And it turns out that it's not until you're in college-level physics courses that one really learns the answers," Glashow said. "But the *difference* is that most people would look at the moon and wonder for a moment and say, 'That's interesting'—and then forget it. But some people can't let go."

Curiosity is not enough. The word is too mild by far, a word for infants. Passion is indispensable for creation, no less in the sciences than in the arts. Medawar once described it in a talk addressed to young scientists. "You must feel in yourself an exploratory impulse—an *acute discomfort* at incomprehension." This is the rage to know. The other side of the fun of science, as of art, is pain. A problem worth solving will surely require weeks and months of lack of progress, whipsawed between hope and the blackest sense of despair. The marathon runner or the young swimmer who would be a champion knows at least that the pain may be a symptom of progress. But here the artist and the scientist part company with the athlete—to join the mystic for a while. The pain of creation, though not of the body, is in one way worse. It must be not only endured but reflected back on itself to increase the agility, variety, inventiveness of the play of the mind. Some problems in science have demanded such devotion, such willingness to bear repeated rebuffs, not just for years but for decades. There are times in the

3. (1642–1727), English mathematician and natural philosopher whose scientific discoveries include the method of fluxions, which forms the basis of modern calculus; the law of the composition of light; and the law of universal gravitation.

practice of the arts, we're told, of abysmal self-doubt. There are like passages in the doing of science.

Albert Einstein[4] took eleven years of unremitting concentration to produce the general theory of relativity; long afterward, he wrote, "In the light of knowledge attained, the happy achievement seems almost a matter of course, and any intelligent student can grasp it without too much trouble. But the years of anxious searching in the dark, with their intense longing, their alternations of confidence and exhaustion, and the final emergence into the light—only those who have experienced it can understand it." Einstein confronting Einstein's problems: the achievement, to be sure, is matched only by Newton's and perhaps Darwin's[5] —but the experience is not rare. It is all but inseparable from high accomplishment. In the black cave of unknowing, when one is groping for the contours of the rock and the slope of the floor, tossing a pebble and listening for its fall, brushing away false clues as insistent as cobwebs, a touch of fresh air on the cheek can make hope leap up, an unexpected scurrying whisper can induce the mood of the brink of terror. "Afterward it can be told—trivialized—like a *roman policier*, a detective story," François Jacob once said. "While you're there, it is the sound and the fury." But it was the poet and adept of mysticism St. John of the Cross who gave to this passionate wrestling with bafflement the name by which, ever since, it has been known: "the dark night of the soul."

Enlightenment may not appear, or not in time; the mystic at least need not fear forestalling. Enlightenment may dawn in ways as varied as the individual approaches of scientists at work—and, in defiance of stereotypes, the sciences far outrun the arts in variety of personal styles and in the crucial influence of style on the creative process. During a conversation with a co-worker—and he just as baffled—a fact quietly shifts from the insignificant background to the foreground; a trivial anomaly becomes a central piece of evidence, the entire pattern swims into focus, and at least one sees. "How obvious! We knew it all along!" Or a rival may publish first but yet be wrong—and in the crashing wave of fear that he's got it right, followed and engulfed by the wave of realization that it must be wrong, the whole view of the problem skews, the tension of one's concentration twists abruptly higher, and at last one sees. "Not that way, *this* way!"

One path to enlightenment, though, has been reported so widely, by writers and artists, by scientists, and especially by mathematicians, that it has become established as a discipline for courting inspiration. The

4. Einstein (1879–1955), German-born, Swiss-educated American physicist.
5. Charles Darwin (1809–82), English nat- uralist and original expounder of the theory of evolution by natural selection, since known as Darwinism.

first stage, the reports agree, is prolonged contemplation of the problem, days of saturation in the data, weeks of incessant struggle—the torment of the unknown. The aim is to set in motion the unconscious processes of the mind, to prepare for the intuitive leap. William Lipscomb, a physical chemist at Harvard who won a Nobel Prize for finding the unexpected structures of some unusual molecules, the boranes, said recently that, for him, "The unconscious mind pieces together random impressions into a continuous story. If I really want to work on a problem, I do a good deal of the work at night—because then I worry about it as I go to sleep." The worry must be about the problem intensely and exclusively. Thought must be free of distraction or competing anxieties. Identification with the problem grows so intimate that the scientist has the experience of the detective who begins to think like the terrorist, of the hunter who feels, as though directly, the silken ripple of the tiger's instincts. One great physical chemist was credited by his peers, who watched him awestruck, with the ability to think about chemical structures directly in quantum terms—so that if a proposed molecular model was too tightly packed he felt uncomfortable, as though his shoes pinched. Joshua Lederberg, president of the Rockefeller University, who won his Nobel for discoveries that established the genetics of microorganisms, said recently, "One needs the ability to strip to the essential attributes of some actor in a process, the ability to imagine oneself *inside* a biological situation; I literally had to be able to think, for example, 'What would it be like if I were one of the chemical pieces in a bacterial chromosome?'—and to try to understand what my environment was, try to know *where* I was, try to know when I was supposed to function in a certain way, and so forth." Total preoccupation to the point of absentmindedness is no eccentricity—just as the monstrous egoism and contentiousness of some scientists, like that of some artists, are the overflow of the strength and reserves of sureness they must find how they can.

Sometimes out of that saturation the answer arises, spontaneous and entire, as though of its own volition. In a famous story, Friedrich Kekulé, a German chemist of the mid-nineteenth century, described how a series of discoveries came to him in the course of hypnagogic reveries—waking dreams. His account, though far from typical, is charming. Kekulé was immersed in one of the most perplexing problems of his day, to find the structural basis of organic chemistry—that is, of the chemistry of compounds that contain carbon atoms. Enormous numbers of such compounds were coming to be known, but their makeup—from atoms of carbon, hydrogen, oxygen, and a few other elements—seemed to follow no rules. Kekulé had dwelt on the compounds' behavior so intensely that the atoms on occasion seemed to appear to him and dance. In the dusk of a summer evening, he was going home by horse-drawn omnibus, sitting outside and alone. "I fell into a reverie, and lo! The atoms were gamboling before my eyes," he later wrote. "I saw how, frequently, two smaller atoms united to form a pair; how a larger one embraced two smaller ones; how still larger ones kept hold of three or even four of the smaller; whilst the whole kept whirling in a giddy dance. I saw how the larger ones formed a chain." He spent hours that night sketching the forms he had envisioned. Another time, when Kekulé was nodding in his chair before the fire, the atoms danced for him again—but only the larger ones, this time, in long rows, "all twining and twisting in snakelike motion. But look! What was that? One of the snakes had seized hold of its own tail, and the form whirled mockingly before my eyes." The chains and rings that carbon atoms form with each other are indeed the fundamental structures of organic chemistry.

Several other scientists have told me that the fringes of sleep set the problem-sodden mind free to make uninhibited, bizarre, even random connections that may throw up the unexpected answer. One said that the technical trick that led to one of his most admired discoveries—it was about the fundamental molecular nature of genetic mutations—had sprung to mind while he was lying insomniac at three in the morning. Another said he was startled from a deep sleep one night by the fully worked-out answer to a puzzle that had blocked him for weeks—though at breakfast he was no longer able to remember any detail except the jubilant certainty. So the next night he went to sleep with paper and pencil on the bedside table; and when, once again, he awoke with the answer, he was able to seize it.

15   More usually, however, in the classic strategy for achieving enlightenment the weeks of saturation must be followed by a second stage that begins when the problem is deliberately set aside. After several days of silence, the solution wells up. The mathematician Henri Poincaré was unusually introspective about the process of discovery. (He also came nearer than anyone else to beating Einstein to the theory of relativity, except that in that case, though he had the pieces of the problem, inspiration did not strike.) In 1908, Poincaré gave a lecture, before the Psychological Society of Paris, about the psychology of mathematical invention, and there he described how he made some of his youthful discoveries. He reassured his audience, few of them mathematical: "I will tell you that I found the proof of a certain theorem in certain circumstances. The theorem will have a barbarous name, which many of you will never have heard of. But that's of no importance, for what is interesting to the psychologist is not the theorem—it's the circumstances."

The youthful discovery was about a class of mathematical functions which he named in honor of another mathematician, Lazarus Fuchs— but, as he said, the mathematical content is not important here. The young Poincaré believed, and for fifteen days he strove to prove, that no functions of the type he was pondering could exist in mathematics. He struggled with the disproof for hours every day. One evening, he happened to drink some black coffee, and couldn't sleep. Like Kekulé with his carbon atoms, Poincaré found mathematical expressions arising before him in crowds, combining and recombining. By the next morning, he had established a class of the functions that he had begun by denying. Then, a short time later, he left town to go on a geological excursion for several days. "The changes of travel made me forget my mathematical work." One day during the excursion, though, he was carrying on a conversation as he was about to board a bus. "At the moment when I put my foot on the step, the idea came to me, without anything in my former thoughts seeming to have paved the way for it, that the transformations I had used to define the Fuchsian functions were identical with those of non-Euclidian geometry." He did not try to prove the idea, but went right on with his conversation. "But I felt a perfect certainty," he wrote. When he got home, "for conscience's sake I verified the result at my leisure."

The quality of such moments of the mind has not often been described successfully; Charles P. Snow was a scientist as well as a novelist, and whenever his experience of science comes together with his writer's imagination his witness is authentic. In *The Search*, a novel about scientists at work, the protagonist makes a discovery for which he had long been striving.

> Then I was carried beyond pleasure. . . . My own triumph and delight and success were there, but they seemed insignificant beside this tranquil ecstasy. It was as though I had looked for a truth outside myself, and finding it had become for a moment a part of the truth I sought; as though all the world, the atoms and the stars, were wonderfully clear and close to me, and I to them, so that we were part of a lucidity more tremendous than any mystery.
>
> I had never known that such a moment could exist. . . . Since then I have never quite regained it. But one effect will stay with me as long as I live; once, when I was young, I used to sneer at the mystics who have described the experience of being at one with God and part of the unity of things. After that afternoon, I did not want to laugh again; for though I should have interpreted the experience differently, I thought I knew what they meant.

This experience beyond pleasure, like the dark night of the soul, has a name: the novelist Romain Rolland, in a letter to Sigmund Freud, called it "the oceanic sense of well-being."

Science is our century's art. Nearly 400 years ago, when modern science was just beginning, Francis Bacon wrote that "knowledge is power." Yet Bacon was not a scientist. He wrote as a bureaucrat in retirement. His slogan was actually the first clear statement of the promise by which, ever since, bureaucrats justify to each other and to king or taxpayer the spending of money on science. Knowledge is power: today we would say, less grandly, that science is essential to technology. Bacon's promise has been fulfilled abundantly, magnificently. The rage to know has been matched by the rage to make. Therefore—with the proviso, abundantly demonstrated, that it's rarely possible to predict which program of fundamental research will produce just what technology and when—the promise has brought scientists in the Western world unprecedented freedom of inquiry. Nonetheless, Bacon's promise hardly penetrates to the thing that moves most scientists. Science has several rewards, but the greatest is that it is the most interesting, difficult, pitiless, exciting, and beautiful pursuit that we have yet found. Science is our century's art.

The takeover can be dated more precisely than the beginning of most eras: Friday, June 30, 1905, will do, the day when Albert Einstein, a clerk in the Swiss patent office in Bern, submitted a thirty-one-page paper, "On the Electrodynamics of Moving Bodies," to the journal *Annalen der Physik*. No poem, no play, no piece of music written since then comes near the theory of relativity in its power, as one strains to apprehend it, to make the mind tremble with delight. Whereas fifty years ago it was often said that hardly two score people understood the theory of relativity, today its essential vision, as Einstein himself said, is within reach of any reasonably bright high school student—and that, too, is characteristic of the speed of assimilation of the new in the arts.

20   Consider also the molecular structure of that stuff of the gene, the celebrated double helix of deoxyribonucleic acid. This is two repetitive strands, one winding up, the other down, but hooked together, across the tube of space between them, by a sequence of pairs of chemical entities—just four sorts of these entities, making just two kinds of pairs, with exactly ten pairs to a full turn of the helix. It's a piece of sculpture. But observe how form and function are one. That sequence possesses a unique duality: one way, it allows the strands to part and each to assemble on itself, by the pairing rules, a duplicate of the complementary strand; the other way, the sequence enciphers, in a four-letter alphabet, the entire specification for the substance of the organism. The structure thus encompasses both heredity and embryological growth, the passing-on of potential and its expression. The structure's elucidation, in March of 1953, was an event of such surpassing explanatory power that it will reverberate through whatever time mankind has remaining. The structure is also perfectly economical and splendidly elegant. There is no sculpture made in this century that is so entrancing.

If to compare science to art seems—in the last quarter of this century—to undervalue what science does, that must be, at least partly, because we now expect art to do so little. Before our century, everyone naturally supposed that the artist imitates nature. Aristotle had said so; the idea was obvious, it had flourished and evolved for 2000 years; those who thought about it added that the artist imitates not just nature as it accidentally happens but as it has to be. Yet today that describes the scientist. "Scientific reasoning," Medawar also said, "is a constant interplay or interaction between hypotheses and the logical expectations they give rise to: there is a restless to-and-fro motion of thought, the formulation and reformulation of hypotheses, until we arrive at a hypothesis which, to the best of our prevailing knowledge, will satisfactorily meet the case." Thus far, change only the term "hypothesis" and Medawar described well the experience the painter or the poet has of his own work. "Scientific reasoning is a kind of dialogue between the possible and the actual, between what might be and what is in fact the case," he went on—and there the difference lies. The scientist enjoys the harsher discipline of what is and is not the case. It is he, rather than the painter or the poet in this century, who pursues in its stringent form the imitation of nature.

Many scientists—mathematicians and physicists especially—hold that beauty in a theory is itself almost a form of proof. They speak, for example, of "elegance." Paul Dirac predicted the existence of antimatter (what would science fiction be without him?) several years before any form of it was observed. He won a share in the Nobel Prize in physics in 1933 for the work that included that prediction. "It is more important to have beauty in one's equations than to have them fit experiment," Dirac wrote many years later. "It seems that if one is working from the point of view of getting beauty in one's equations, and if one has really a sound insight, one is on a sure line of progress."

Here the scientist parts company with the artist. The insight must be sound. The dialogue is between what might be and what is in fact the case. The scientist is trying to get the thing right. The world is there.

And so are other scientists. The social system of science begins with the apprenticeship of the graduate student with a group of his peers and elders in the laboratory of a senior scientist; it continues to collaboration at the bench or the blackboard, and on to formal publication—which is a formal invitation to criticism. The most fundamental function of the social system of science is to enlarge the interplay between imagination and judgment from a private into a public activity. The oceanic feeling of well-being, the true touchstone of the artist, is for the scientist, even the most fortunate and gifted, only the midpoint of the process of doing science.

THE READER

1. In the third paragraph Judson asserts, "Science is enormously disparate—easily the most varied and diverse of human pursuits." Does this view of science correspond with what you have been taught or have experienced (about science, and about diversity)? How does Judson support his assertion?
2. What do you take "the scientific method" to mean? To what extent does that notion correspond with Judson's description of how science is done?
3. At several points Judson asserts a connection between doing science and experiencing pleasure. Is this connection important to his essay? Indicate the several links he asserts between science and pleasure.

THE WRITER

1. Judson begins paragraph 18 with the sentence "Science is our century's art" and closes it with the same sentence. What purpose is served by this repetition? Is it effective?
2. Compare Judson's account of how science is done with the views of Bronowski in "The Nature of Scientific Reasoning" (p. 1008) and "The Reach of Imagination" (p. 196), and the views of Asimov in "The Eureka Phenomenon" (p. 208). Do these essays have any important ideas in common? Do they differ in any important respects?
3. Judson implies that there may be a considerable difference between the way a piece of scientific work is presented (in a scientific journal, for example) and what actually happened in the course of that work. Look at John Henry Sloan et al.'s "Handgun Regulations" (p. 966) and imagine the actual process of research that preceded its writing. If you are taking a science course, compare the official report you turned in after an experiment with your narrative of what actually happened. Alternatively, interview one of your science professors about a research project that he or she published. Write up your interview and compare it with the published research. What are the differences?

Niko Tinbergen

THE BEE-HUNTERS OF HULSHORST [1]

On a sunny day in the summer of 1929 I was walking rather aimlessly over the sands, brooding and a little worried. I had just done my finals, had got a half-time job, and was hoping to start on research for a doctor's thesis. I wanted very much to work on some problem of animal behaviour and had for that reason rejected some suggestions of my well-meaning supervisor. But rejecting sound advice and taking one's own decisions are two very different things, and so far I had been unable to make up my mind.

While walking about, my eye was caught by a bright orange-yellow wasp the size of the ordinary jam-loving *Vespa*. It was busying itself in a strange way on the bare sand. With brisk, jerky movements it was walking slowly backwards, kicking the sand behind it as it proceeded. The sand flew away with every jerk. I was sure that this was a digger wasp. The only kind of that size I knew was *Bembex*, the large fly-killer. But this was no *Bembex*. I stopped to watch it, and soon saw that it was shovelling sand out of a burrow. After ten minutes of this, it turned round, and now, facing away from the entrance, began to rake loose sand over it. In a minute the entrance was completely covered. Then the wasp flew up, circled a few times round the spot, describing wider and wider loops in the air, and finally flew off. Knowing something of the way of digger wasps, I expected it to return with a prey within a reasonable time, and decided to wait.

Sitting down on the sand, I looked round and saw that I had blundered into what seemed to be a veritable wasp town. Within ten yards I saw more than twenty wasps occupied at their burrows. Each burrow had a patch of yellow sand round it the size of a hand, and to judge from the number of these sand patches there must have been hundreds of burrows.

I had not to wait long before I saw a wasp coming home. It descended slowly from the sky, alighting after the manner of a helicopter on a sand patch. Then I saw that it was carrying a load, a dark object about its own size. Without losing hold of it, the wasp made a few raking movements with its front legs, the entrance became visible and, dragging its load after it, the wasp slipped into the hole.

From *Curious Naturalists* (1958).

1. Hulshorst is the sparsely populated region in Holland where Tinbergen's observations and experiments were carried out.

At the next opportunity I robbed a wasp of its prey, by scaring it on its arrival, so that it dropped its burden. Then I saw that the prey was a Honey Bee.

I watched these wasps at work all through that afternoon, and soon became absorbed in finding out exactly what was happening in this busy insect town. It seemed that the wasps were spending part of their time working at their burrows. Judging from the amount of sand excavated these must have been quite deep. Now and then a wasp would fly out and, after half an hour or longer, return with a load, which was then dragged in. Every time I examined the prey, it was a Honey Bee. No doubt they captured all these bees on the heath for all to and fro traffic was in the direction of the south-east, where I knew the nearest heath to be. A rough calculation showed that something was going on here that would not please the owners of the bee-hives on the heath; on a sunny day like this several thousand bees fell victims to this large colony of killers.

As I was watching the wasps, I began to realize that here was a wonderful opportunity for doing exactly the kind of field work I would like to do. Here were many hundreds of digger wasps—exactly which species I did not know yet, but that would not be difficult to find out. I had little doubt that each wasp was returning regularly to its own burrow, which showed that they must have excellent powers of homing. How did they manage to find their way back to their own burrow? * * *

Settling down to work, I started spending the wasps' working days (which lasted from about 8 a.m. till 6 p.m. and so did not put too much of a strain on me) on the 'Philanthus plains', as we called this part of the sands as soon as we had found out that *Philanthus triangulum Fabr.* was the official name of this bee-killing digger wasp. Its vernacular name was 'Bee-Wolf'.

An old chair, field glasses, note-books, and food and water for the day were my equipment. The local climate of the open sands was quite amazing, considering that ours is a temperate climate. Surface temperatures of 110° F were not rare. * * *

My first job was to find out whether each wasp was really limited to one burrow, as I suspected from the unhesitating way in which the home-coming wasps alighted on the sand patches in front of the burrows. I installed myself in a densely populated quarter of the colony, five yeards or so from a group of about twenty-five nests. Each borrow was marked and mapped. Whenever I saw a wasp at work at a burrow, I caught it and, after a short unequal struggle, adorned its back with one or two colour dots (using quickly drying enamel paint) and released it. Such wasps soon returned to work, and after a few hours I had ten wasps, each marked with a different combination of colours, working right in front of me. It was remarkable how this simple trick of marking my wasps changed my whole attitude to them. From members of the species *Philanthus triangulum* they were transformed into personal acquaintances, whose lives from that very moment became affairs of the most personal interest and concern to me.

While waiting for events to develop, I spent my time having a close look at the wasps. A pair of lenses mounted on a frame that could be worn as spectacles enabled me, by crawling up slowly to a working wasp, to observe it, much enlarged, from a few inches away. When seen under such circumstances most insects reveal a marvellous beauty, totally unexpected as long as you observe them with the unaided eye. Through my lenses I could look at my *Philanthus* right into their huge compound eyes; I saw their enormous, claw-like jaws which they used for crumbling up the sandy crust; I saw their agile black antennae in continuous, restless movement; I watched their yellow, bristled legs rake away the loose sand with such vigour that it flew through the air in rhythmic puffs, landing several inches behind them.

Soon several of my marked wasps stopped working at their burrows, raked loose sand back over the entrance, and flew off. The take-off was often spectacular. Before leaving they circled a little while over the burrow, at first low above the ground, soon higher, describing ever widening loops; then flew away, but returned to cruise once more low over the nest. Finally, they would set out in a bee-line, fifteen to thirty feet above the ground, a rapidly vanishing speck against the blue sky. All the wasps disappeared towards the south-east. Half a mile away in that direction the bare sands bordered upon an extensive heath area, buzzing with bees. This, as I was to see later, was the wasps' hunting area.

The curious loops my wasps described in the air before leaving their home area had been described by other observers of many other digger wasps. Philip Rau had given them the name of 'locality studies'. Yet so far nobody proved that they deserved that name; that the wasps actually took in the features of the burrow's surroundings while circling above them. To check this if possible was one of my aims—I thought that it was most probable that the wasps would use landmarks, and that this locality study was what the name implied. First, however, I had to make sure that my marked wasps would return to their own holes. * * *

Before the first day was over, each of them had returned with a bee; some had returned twice or even three times. At the end of that day it was clear that each of them had its own nest, to which it returned regularly.

On subsequent days I extended these observations and found out some more facts about the wasps' daily life. As in other species, the digging of the large burrows and the capturing of prey that served as

15

food for the larvae was exclusively the task of the females. And a formidable task it was. The wasps spent hours digging the long shafts, and throwing the sand out. Often they stayed down for a long time and, waiting for them to reappear, my patience was often put to a hard test. Eventually, however, there would be some almost imperceptible movement in the sand, and a small mound of damp soil was gradually lifted up, little by little, as if a miniature Mole were at work. Soon the wasp emerged, tail first, and all covered with sand. One quick shake, accompanied by a sharp staccato buzz, and the wasp was clean. Then it began to mop up, working as if possessed, shovelling the sand several inches away from the entrance.

I often tried to dig up the burrows to see their inner structure. Usually the sand crumbled and I lost track of the passage before I was ten inches down, but sometimes, by gently probing with a grass shoot first, and then digging down along it, I succeeded in getting down to the cells. These were found opening into the far end of the shaft, which itself was a narrow tube, often more than 2 ft. long. Each cell contained an egg or a larva with a couple of Honey Bees, its food store. A burrow contained from one to five cells. Each larva had its own living room-cum-larder in the house, provided by the hard-working female. From the varying nunber of cells I found in the nests, and the varying ages of the larvae in one burrow, I concluded that the female usually filled each cell with bees before she started to dig a new cell, and I assumed that it was the tunnelling out of a new cell that made her stay down for such long spells.

I did not spend much time digging up the burrows, for I wanted to observe the wasps while they were undisturbed. Now that I was certain that each wasp returned regularly to her own burrow, I was faced with the problem of her orientation. The entire valley was littered with the yellow sand patches; how could a wasp, after a hunting trip of about a mile in all, find exactly her own burrow?

Having seen the wasps make their 'locality studies', I naturally believed that each female actually did what this term implied: take her bearings. A simple test suggested that this was correct. While a wasp was away I brushed over the ground surrounding the nest entrance, moving all possible landmarks such as pebbles, twigs, tufts of grass, Pine cones, etc, so that over an area of 3–4 square metres none of them remained in exactly the same place as before. The burrow itself, however, I left intact. Then I awaited the wasp's return. When she came, slowly descending from the skies, carrying her bee, her behaviour was striking. All went well until she was about 4ft. above the ground. There she suddenly stopped, dashed back and forth as if in panic, hung motionless in the air for a while, then flew back and up in a wide loop, came slowly down again in the same way, and again shied at the same distance from the nest. Obviously she was severely disturbed. Since I had left the nest itself, its entrance, and the sand patch in front of it untouched, this showed that the wasp was affected by the change in the surroundings.

Gradually she calmed down, and began to search low over the disturbed area. But she seemed to be unable to find the nest. She alighted now here, now there, and began to dig tentatively at a variety of places at the approximate site of the nest entrance. After a while she dropped her bee and started a thorough trial-and-error search. After twenty-five minutes or so she stumbled on the nest entrance as if by accident, and only then did she take up her bee and drag it in. A few minutes later she came out again, closed the entrance, and set off. And now she had a nice surprise in store for me: upon leaving she made an excessively long 'locality study': for fully two minutes she circled and circled, coming back again and again to fly over the disturbed area before she finally zoomed off.

I waited for another hour and a half, and had the satisfaction of seeing her return once more. And what I had hoped for actually happened: there was scarcely a trace of hesitation this time. Not only had the wasp lost her shyness of the disturbed soil, but she now knew her way home perfectly well.

I repeated this test with a number of wasps, and their reactions to my interference were roughly the same each time. It seemed probable, therefore, that the wasps found their way home by using something like landmarks in the environment, and not by responding to some stimulus (visual or otherwise) sent out by the nest itself. I had now to test more critically whether this was actually the case.

The test I did next was again quite simple. If a wasp used landmarks it should be possible to do more than merely disturb her by throwing her beacons all over the place; I ought to be able to mislead her, to make her go to the wrong place, by moving the whole constellation of her landmarks over a certain distance. I did this at a few nests that were situated on bare sandy soil and that had only a few, but conspicuous, objects nearby, such as twigs, or tufts of grass. After the owner of such a nest was gone, I moved these two or three objects a foot to the south-west, roughly at right angles to the expected line of approach. The result was as I had hoped for and expected, and yet I could not help being surprised as well as delighted: each wasp missed her own nest, and alighted at exactly the spot where the nest 'ought' to be according to the landmarks' new positions! I could vary my tests by very cautiously shooing the wasp away, then moving the beacons a foot in another direction, and allowing the wasp to alight again. In whatever position I put the beacons, the wasp would follow them. At the end of such a series of tests I replaced the landmarks in their original position, and this finally enabled the wasp to return to her home. Thus the tests always had a happy ending—for both of us. This was no pure altruism on my part—I could now use the wasp for another test if I wished.

When engaged in such work, it is always worth observing oneself as well as the animals, and to do it as critically and as detachedly as possible—which, of course, is a tall order. I have often wondered why the outcome of such a test delighted me so much. A rationalist would probably like to assume that it was the increased predictability resulting from the test. This was a factor of considerable importance, I am sure. But a more important factor still (not only to me, but to many other people I have watched in this situation) is of a less dignified type: people enjoy, they relish the satisfaction of their desire for power. The truth of this was obvious, for instance, in people who enjoyed seeing the wasps being misled without caring much for the intellectual question whether they used landmarks or not. I am further convinced that even the joy of gaining insight was not often very pure either; it was mixed with pride at having had success with the tests.

To return to the wasps: next I tried to make the wasps use landmarks which I provided. This was not only for the purpose of satisfying my lust for power, but also for nobler purposes, as I hope to show later. Since changing the environment while the wasp was away disturbed her upon her return and even might prevent her from finding her nest altogether, I waited until a wasp had gone down into her nest, and then put my own landmarks round the entrance—sixteen Pine cones arranged in a circle of about eight inches diameter.

25   The first wasp to emerge was a little upset, and made a rather long locality study. On her return home, she hesitated for some time, but eventually alighted at the nest. When next she went out she made a really thorough locality study, and from then on everything went smoothly. Other wasps behaved in much the same way, and next day regular work was going on at five burrows so treated. I now subjected all five wasps, one by one, to a displacement test similar to those already described. The results, however, were not clearcut. Some wasps, upon returning, followed the cones; but others were not fooled, and went straight home, completely ignoring my beacons. Others again seemed to be unable to make up their minds, and oscillated between the real nest and the ring of cones. This half-hearted behaviour did not disturb me, however, for if my idea was correct—that the wasps use land-marks—one would rather expect that my tests put the wasps in a kind of conflict situation: the natural landmarks which they must have been using before I gave them the Pine cones were still in their original position; only the cones had been moved. And while the cones were very conspicuous landmarks, they had been there for no more than one day. I therefore put all the cone-rings back and waited for two more days before testing the wasps again. And sure enough, this time the tests gave

a hundred per cent preference for the Pine cones; I had made the wasps train themselves to my landmarks.

The rest of this first summer I spent mainly in consolidating this result in various ways. There was not much time to do this, for the season lasts only two months; by the end of August the wasps became sluggish, and soon after they died, leaving the destiny of their race in the hands of the pupae deep down in the sand, which were to lie there dormant until next July. And even in this short summer season the wasps could not work steadily, but were active on dry sunny days only—and of these a Dutch summer rarely supplies more than about twenty in all.

However, I had time to make sure that the wasps relied for their homing mainly on vision. First, I could cut off their antennae—the bearers of delicate organs of smell, of touch and of other sense organs—without at all disturbing the orientation. Second, when, in other tests, I covered the eyes of intact wasps with black paint, the wasps could not fly at all. Removing the cover of paint restored their eyesight, and with it their normal behaviour. Furthermore, when I trained a wasp to accept a circle of Pine cones together with two small squares of cardboard drenched in Pine oil, which gave off a strong scent, displacement of the cones would mislead the wasps in the usual way, but moving the scented squares had not the slightest effect. Finally, when wasps used to rings of cones were given, instead of cones, a ring of grey pebbles a foot from the nest, they followed these pebbles. This can only have been due to the pebbles being visually similar to the cones.

* * *

We began by investigating the wasp's 'locality study' a little more closely. As I mentioned before, we had already quite suggestive indications that it really deserved this name, but clear-cut proof was still lacking. The otherwise annoying vagaries of the Atlantic climate provided us with a wonderful opportunity to get this proof. Long spells of cold rainy weather are not uncommon in a Dutch summer—in fact they are more common than periods of sunny weather, which alone could tempt the wasps to 'work'. Rainy weather put a strain on morale in our camp, but the first sign of improvement usually started an outburst of feverish activity, all of us doing our utmost to be ready for the wasps before they could resume their flights.

We had previously noticed that many (though not all) wasps spent cold and wet periods in their burrows. Rain and wind often played havoc with their landmarks and perhaps the wasps also forgot their exact position while sitting indoors. At any rate, with the return of good weather, all the wasps made prolonged 'locality studies' when setting out on their first trip. Could it be that they had to learn anew the lie of the land?

On one such morning, while the ground was still wet but the

30

weather sunny and promising, we were at the colony at 7.30 a.m. Each of us took up a position near a group of nests and watched for the first signs of emerging wasps. We had not to wait long before we saw the sand covering one of the entrances move—a sure sign of a wasp trying to make her way into the open. Quickly we put a circle of Pine cones round the burrow. When the wasp came out, she started digging and working at her nest, then raked sand over the entrance and left. In the course of the morning many wasps emerged and each received pine cones round her entrance before she had 'opened the door'. Some of these wasps did not bother to work at the nest, but left at once after coming out. These latter wasps we were going to use for our tests. As expected, they made elaborate locality studies, describing many loops of increasing range and altitude before finally departing. We timed these flights carefully. As soon as one of these wasps had definitely gone, we took the Pine cones away. This was done in order to make absolutely sure that, if the wasp should return unobserved, she could not see cones round her nest. If then, when we saw her return with a bee, a displacement test in which the circle of Pine cones was laid out some distance away from the nest would give positive results (i.e., the wasp would choose these cones), we would have proved that she must have learnt them during her locality study, for at no other time could she have seen them.

Not all such wasps returned on the same day. Their prolonged stay and their fast down in the burrows probably forced them to feed themselves in the Heather first. Some, however, returned with a bee and with these we succeeded in doing some exciting tests. In all we tested 13 wasps. They were observed to choose 93 times between the true nest and a 'sham nest' surrounded by the Pine cones. Seventy-three choices fell on the sham nests, against only 20 on the real nests. In control tests taken after the experiments, when the cones were put back round the real nest, of a total of 39 only 3 choices were now in favour of the sham nests, the other 36 being in favour of the real nests. There was no doubt then that these wasps had learnt the nature and the position of the new landmarks during the locality study.

The most impressive achievement was that of wasp No. 179. She had made one locality study of a mere six seconds and had left without returning, let alone alighting. When she was tested upon her return more than an hour later she chose the cones 12 times and never came near the nest. When the original situation was restored she alighted at once on her burrow and slipped in. Nos. 174 and 177 almost equalled this record; both were perfectly trained after uninterrupted locality studies of 13 seconds. All the other wasps either made longer locality studies or interrupted them by alighting on the nest one or more times before leaving again. Such wasps might have learnt during alighting rather than while performing the locality study, so their results were less convincing.

This result, while not at all unexpected, nevertheless impressed us very much. It not only revealed an amazing capacity in these little insects to learn so quickly, but we were struck even more by the fact that a wasp, when not fully oriented, would set out to perform such a locality study, as if it knew what the effect of this specialized type of behaviour would be.

I have already described that a wasp, which has made a number of flights to and from a burrow, makes no, or almost no, locality study, but that it will make an elaborate one after the surroundings have been disturbed. Further tests threw light on the question what exactly made her do this. We studied the effect on locality studies of two types of disturbances. In tests of type A we either added or removed a conspicuous landmark before the wasp returned and then restored the original situation while she was inside. Such wasps, although finding the old, familiar situation upon emerging again, made long locality studies. In tests of type B the wasps were not disturbed at all when entering, but changes similar to those of the A-tests were made just before they left. None of these wasps made locality studies. Wasps used for A-tests always hesitated before alighting. Therefore, disturbances of the familiar surroundings perceived upon returning make the wasps perform a locality study when next departing, while the same disturbances actually present at the time of departure have no influence!

Some further, rather incomplete and preliminary tests pointed to another interesting aspect. Conspicuous new landmarks given before the return of the wasp and left standing until after her departure influenced the form of the locality study as well as its duration: the wasp would repeatedly circle round this particular landmark. If, however, such a landmark was left for some time, so that the wasp passed it several times on her way out and back, and then moved to a new place, the wasp would make a longer locality study than before, yet she would not describe extra loops round the beacon. She obviously recognized the object and had merely to learn its new position. These tests were too few and not fully conclusive, but they did suggest that there is more to this locality study than we had at first suspected. The whole phenomenon is remarkable and certainly deserves further study.

We next turned our attention to the exact nature of the landmarks that were used by the wasps. What exactly did they learn? We spent several seasons examining this and the more striking of our tests are worth describing.

First of all we found that not all objects round the nest were of equal value to the wasps. The first indication of this was found when we tried to train them to use sheets of coloured paper about 3 x 4 inches, which we put out near the nests, as a preparation to study colour vision. It proved to be almost impossible to make the wasps use even a set of three of them; even after leaving them out for days on end we rarely succeeded with the same simple displacement tests that worked so well with the Pine cones. Most wasps just ignored them. Yet the bright blue, yellow and red papers were very conspicuous to us. For some reason, the Pine cones were meeting the wasps' requirements for landmarks better than the flat sheets. [We] worked out a method to test this. We provided two types of objects round a nest—for instance, flat discs and Pine cones—arranged in a circle in alternation. After a day or so, we moved the whole circle and checked whether the wasps used it. If so, we then provided two sham nests at equal distances, one on each side of the real nest, and put all objects of one type round one of these sham nests, all of the other type round the other. If then the wasp had trained herself to one type of landmark rather than to the other, it should prefer one of the two sham nests. Such a preferential choice could not be due to anything but the difference in the wasps' attitude towards the two classes of objects, for all could have been seen by the wasp equally often, their distance to the nest entrance had been the same, they had been offered all round the nest, etc.—in short, they had had absolutely equal chances.

In this way we compared flat objects with solid, dark with light, those contrasting with the colour of the background with those matching it, larger with smaller, nearer with more distant ones, and so on. Each test had, of course, to be done with many wasps and each wasp had to make a number of choices for us to be sure that there was consistency in her preference. This programme kept us busy for a long time, but the results were worth the trouble. The wasps actually showed for landmarks a preference which was different from ours.

When we offered flat circular discs and hemispheres of the same diameter, the wasps always followed the hemispheres (43 against 2 choices). This was not due to the larger surface area of the hemispheres, for when we did similar tests with flat discs of much larger size (of 10 cm. diameter, whereas the hemispheres had a diameter of only 4 cm.), the choices were still 73 in favour of the hemispheres against 19 for the discs.

40

In other tests we found out that the hemispheres were not preferred because of their shading, nor because they showed contrasts between highlights and deep blacks, nor because they were three-dimensional, but because of the fact that they stood out above the ground. The critical test for this was to offer hollow cones, half of them standing up on top of the soil on their bases, half sunk upside down into the ground. Both were three dimensional, but one extended above the ground while the others formed pits in the ground. The standing cones were almost always chosen (108 against 21).

The preference for objects that projected above the ground was one of the reasons why Pine cones were preferred. Another reason was that Pine cones offered a chequered pattern of light and dark, while yet another reason was the fact that they had a broken instead of a smooth surface—i.e., dented objects were more stimulating than smooth ones. Similar facts had been found about Honey Bees by other students and much of this has probably to do with the organization of the compound eyes of insects.

We further found that large objects were better than small objects; near objects better than the same objects further away from the nest, objects that contrasted in tone with the background better than those matching the background, objects presented during critical periods (such as at the start of digging a new nest or immediately after a rainy period) better than objects offered once a wasp had acquired a knowledge of its surroundings.

It often amazed us, when doing these tests, that the wasps frequently chose a sham nest so readily although the circle offered contained only half the objects to which they had been trained. This would not be so strange if the wasps had just ignored the weaker 'beacons', but this was not the case. If, in our original test with flat discs and hemispheres, we would offer the discs alone, the wasps, confronted with a choice between the discs and the original nest without either discs or hemispheres, often chose the discs. These, therefore, had not been entirely ignored; they were potential beacons, but were less valued than the hemispheres. Once we knew this, we found that with a little perseverance we could train the wasps to our flat coloured papers. But it took time.

The fact that the wasps accepted these circles, with half the number of objects they used to see, suggested that they responded to the circular arrangement as a whole as well as to the properties of the individual beacon. This raised the interesting issue of 'configurational' stimuli and it seemed to offer good opportunities for experiment. This work was taken up by Van Beusekom who, in a number of ingenious tests, showed that the wasps responded to a very complicated stimulus situation indeed.

First of all, he made sure that wasps could recognize beacons such as Pine cones fairly well. He trained wasps to the usual circle of Pine cones and then gave them the choice between these and a similar arrangement of smooth blocks of Pine cone size. The wasps decided predominantly in favour of the Pine cones, which showed that they were responding to details which distinguished the two types of beacons.

He next trained a number of wasps to a circle of 16 Pine cones and subjected them to two types of tests. In Type A the wasp had to choose between two sets of 16 cones, one arranged in a circle, the other in a figure of another shape, such as a square, a triangle, or an ellipse. He

45

found that, unless the figure was very similar to the circle, the wasps could distinguish between the two figures and alighted in the circle. In those tests the individual cones did not count; he could either use the original cones for constructing the circle or use them for the square or triangle. It was the circular figure the wasps chose, not the Pine cones used during training.

In tests of type B, after the usual training to a circle of 16, he offered the 16 cones in a non-circular arrangement against 8 or even fewer cones in a (loose) circle—and found that the wasps chose the circle in spite of the smaller number of cones. He could even go further and offer a circle of quite different elements, such as square blocks (which the wasps could distinguish from cones, as other tests had shown). If such a circle was offered against cones in a noncircular arrangement, it was the circle that won. Thus it was shown in a variety of ways that the wasps responded not only to the individual beacons (as the preference tests * * * had shown), but also to the circle as a whole.

However, all these experiments, while giving us valuable information about the way our wasps perceived their environment, had one limitation in common—they showed us only how the wasps behaved at the last stage of their journey home. We had many indications that the Pine cones were not seen until the wasps were within a few yards from the nest. How did they find their way previous to this?

Although we were aware of these limitations, it was extremely difficult to extend our tests. However, we did a little about this. More than once we displaced small Pine trees growing at a distance of several yards from nests under observation. In many cases wasps were misled by this and tried to find their nests in the correct position in relation to the displaced tree. The precision of their orientation to such relatively distant marks was truly amazing.

Such large landmarks were used in a slightly different way from the Pine cones. Firstly, they were used even when relatively far from the nest. Secondly, they could be moved over far greater distances than the Pine cones. A circle of Pine cones would fail to draw the wasp with it if it was moved over more than about 7 ft., but a Pine tree, or even a branch of about 4 ft. high, could lure the wasps away even if moved over 8 metres. We further observed in many of our earlier tests that wasps, upon finding the immediate surroundings of the nest disturbed, flew back, circled round a Pine tree or a large sandhill perhaps 70 yards away, and then again approached the nest. This looked very much as though they were taking their bearings upon these larger landmarks.

Van der Linde and others also spent a great deal of time and energy in transporting individual wasps in light-proof cloth over distances up to 1,000 metres in all directions. Since good hunting grounds were to the south and south-east of the colony, whereas in other directions bare sand flats or dense Pine plantations bordered upon the *Philanthus* plains, we could assume that our wasps knew the country to the south and south-east better than in other directions—an assumption which was confirmed by the fact that our wasps always flew out in a south or south-east direction and returned with bees from there. The transported wasps, whose return to their nests was watched, did indeed much better from the south and south-east than from any other direction. From the northwest, for instance, half the wasps never returned as long as our observations lasted. This did indeed suggest that return from unknown country was difficult if not impossible and, therefore, that learning of some kind was essential, but it could not tell us more.

THE READER

1. *Which of Tinbergen's activities, as described in this account of his research, are the kind you expect of a scientist? Do any of them surprise you?*
2. *How did Tinbergen find the question he decided to study?*

THE WRITER

1. *In the paragraph beginning "When engaged in such work . . . " (p. 958), Tinbergen suggests that it is desirable for the scientific observer to observe himself as well as the object of study. Why? In his own case, did this attention to himself interfere with his objective study of the facts? What did Tinbergen observe in this particular instance?*
2. *Before Tinbergen started his research, what was known of the "locality studies" made by the wasps? What steps did he go through to find out more about this matter? To what degree and in what ways was his study a matter of observation? What arrangements did he make to change the conditions for observing? Write a description of scientific method as exemplified by Tinbergen's study.*
3. *Write a brief comparison of Tinbergen's account of his research and that of Lorenz in "The Taming of the Shrew" (p. 588). If these authors convey to you a sense of excitement about their work, show some of the specific ways in which their writing does this.*

John Henry Sloan et al.*
HANDGUN REGULATIONS, CRIME, ASSAULTS, AND HOMICIDE:
A Tale of Two Cities**

Abstract To investigate the associations among handgun regulations, assault and other crimes, and homicide, we studied robberies, burglaries, assaults, and homicides in Seattle, Washington, and Vancouver, British Columbia, from 1980 through 1986.

Although similar to Seattle in many ways, Vancouver has adopted a more restrictive approach to the regulation of handguns. During the study period, both cities had similar rates of burglary and robbery. In Seattle, the annual rate of assault was modestly higher than that in Vancouver (simple assault: relative risk, 1.18; 95 percent confidence interval, 1.15 to 1.20; aggravated assault: relative risk, 1.16; 95 percent confidence interval, 1.12 to 1.19).*** However, the rate of assaults involving firearms was seven times higher in Seattle than in Vancouver. Despite similar overall rates of criminal activity and assault, the relative risk of death from homicide, adjusted for age and sex, was significantly higher in Seattle than in Vancouver (relative risk, 1.63; 95 percent confidence interval, 1.28 to 2.08). Virtually all of this excess risk was explained by a 4.8-fold higher risk of being murdered with a handgun in Seattle as compared with Vancouver. Rates of homicide by means other than guns were not substantially different in the two study communities.

We conclude that restricting access to handguns may reduce the rate of homicide in a community (*N. Engl. J. Med.* 1988; 319:1256–62).

Approximately 20,000 persons are murdered in the United States each year, making homicide the 11th leading cause of death and the 6th leading cause of the loss of potential years of life before age 65.[1-3] In the United States between 1960 and 1980, the death rate from homicide by means other than firearms increased by 85 percent. In contrast, the

From the *New England Journal of Medicine* (Nov. 10, 1988).

*John Henry Sloan, M.D., M.P.H., Arthur L. Kellermann, M.D., M.P.H., Donald T. Reay, M.D., James A. Ferris, M.D., Thomas Koepsell, M.D., M.P.H., Frederick P. Rivara, M.D., M.P.H., Charles Rice, M.D., Laurel Gray, M.D., and James LoGerfo, M.D., M.P.H.
**The authors' notes are collected at the end as "References," as in the style of *N.*

Engl. J. Med. The editors' explanatory footnotes are marked by asterisks (*).
***A statistical method for expressing the likelihood of error; that is, in this instance there is a 95 percent chance that the risk of simple assault in Seattle relative to that in Vancouver, which the authors calculate to be 1.18, will fall between 1.15 and 1.2.

death rate from homicide by firearms during this same period increased by 160 percent.[3]

Approximately 60 percent of homicides each year involve firearms. Handguns alone account for three fourths of all gun-related homicides.[4] Most homicides occur as a result of assaults during arguments or altercations; a minority occur during the commission of a robbery or other felony.[2,4] Baker has noted that in cases of assault, people tend to reach for weapons that are readily available.[5] Since attacks with guns more often end in death than attacks with knives, and since handguns are disproportionately involved in intentional shootings, some have argued that restricting access to handguns could substantially reduce our annual rate of homicide.[5-7]

To support this view, advocates of handgun control frequently cite data from countries like Great Britain and Japan, where the rates of both handgun ownership and homicide are substantially lower than those in the United States.[8] Rates of injury due to assault in Denmark are comparable to those in northeastern Ohio, but the Danish rate of homicide is only one fifth as high as Ohio's.[5,6] In Denmark, the private ownership of guns is permitted only for hunting, and access to handguns is tightly restricted.[6]

Opponents of gun control counter with statistics from Israel and Switzerland, where the rates of gun ownership are high but homicides are relatively uncommon.[9] However, the value of comparing data from different countries to support or refute the effectiveness of gun control is severely compromised by the large number of potentially confounding social, behavioral, and economic factors that characterize large national groups. To date, no study has been able to separate the effects of handgun control from differences among populations in terms of socioeconomic status, aggressive behavior, violent crime, and other factors.[7] To clarify the relation between firearm regulations and community rates of homicide, we studied two large cities in the Pacific Northwest: Seattle, Washington, and Vancouver, British Columbia. Although similar in many ways, these two cities have taken decidedly different approaches to handgun control.

METHODS

Study Sites

Seattle and Vancouver are large port cities in the Pacific Northwest. Although on opposite sides of an international border, they are only 140 miles apart, a three-hour drive by freeway. They share a common geography, climate, and history. Citizens in both cities have attained comparable levels of schooling and have almost identical rates of unemployment.

When adjusted to U.S. dollars, the median annual income of a household in Vancouver exceeds that in Seattle by less than $500. Similar percentages of households in both cities have incomes of less than $10,000 (U.S.) annually. Both cities have large white majorities. However, Vancouver has a larger Asian population, whereas Seattle has larger black and Hispanic minorities (Table 1).[10,11] The two communities also share many cultural values and interests. Six of the top nine network television programs in Seattle are among the nine most watched programs in Vancouver.[12,13]

Firearm Regulations

Although similar in many ways, Seattle and Vancouver differ markedly in their approaches to the regulation of firearms (Table 2). In Seattle, handguns may be purchased legally for self-defense in the street or at home. After a 30-day waiting period, a permit can be obtained to carry a handgun as a concealed weapon. The recreational use of handguns is minimally restricted.[15]

In Vancouver, self-defense is not considered a valid or legal reason to purchase a handgun. Concealed weapons are not permitted. Recreational uses of handguns (such as target shooting and collecting) are regulated by the province, and the purchase of a handgun requires a restricted-weapons permit. A permit to carry a weapon must also be obtained in order to transport a handgun, and these weapons can be

TABLE 1

Socioeconomic Characteristics and Racial and Ethnic Composition of the Populations in Seattle and Vancouver

Index	Seattle	Vancouver
1980 Population	493,846	415,220
1985–1986 Population estimate	491,400	430,826
Unemployment rate (%)	5.8	6.0
High-school graduates (%)	79.0	66.0
Median household income (U.S. dollars)	16,254	16,681
Households with incomes ≤$10,000 (U.S.) (%)	30.6	28.9
Ethnic and racial groups (%)		
White (non-Hispanic)	79.2	75.6
Asian	7.4	22.1
Black	9.5	0.3
Hispanic	2.6	0.5
Native North American	1.3	1.5

TABLE 2

REGULATION AND OWNERSHIP OF FIREARMS AND LAW-ENFORCEMENT ACTIVITY IN SEATTLE AND VANCOUVER

	Seattle	Vancouver
Regulations		
Handguns	Concealed-weapons permit is required to carry a gun for self-defense on the street; none is required for self-defense in the home. Registration of handguns is not mandatory for private sales.	Restricted-weapons permit is required for sporting and collecting purposes. Self-defense in the home or street is not legally recognized as a reason for possession of a handgun. Handguns must be registered.
Long guns (rifles, shotguns)	Long guns are not registered.	Firearm-acquisition certificate is required for purchase. Long guns are not registered.
Law enforcement and sentencing		
Additional sentence for commission of a class A felony with a firearm	Minimum of 2 extra years.	1 to 14 extra years.
Percent of firearm-related homicides that result in police charges (police estimate)	80 to 90%	80 to 90%
Minimum jail sentence for first-degree murder	20 years in prison.	25 years in prison (parole is possible after 15 years).
Status of capital punishment	Legal, though no one has been executed since 1963.	Abolished.
Prevalence of weapons		
Total concealed-weapons permits issued (March 1984 to March 1988)	15,289	—
Total restricted-weapons permits issued (March 1984 to March 1988)	—	4137
Cook's gun prevalence index[14]	41%	12%

discharged only at a licensed shooting club. Handguns can be transported by car, but only if they are stored in the trunk in a locked box. [16,17]

Although they differ in their approach to firearm regulations, both cities aggressively enforce existing gun laws and regulations, and convictions for gun-related offenses carry similar penalties. For example, the commission of a class A felony (such as murder or robbery) with a firearm in Washington State adds a minimum of two years of confinement to the sentence for the felony. [18] In the Province of British Columbia, the same offense generally results in 1 to 14 years of imprisonment in addition to the felony sentence. [16] Similar percentages of homicides in both communities eventually lead to arrest and police charges. In Washington, under the Sentencing Reform Act of 1981, murder in the first degree carries a minimum sentence of 20 years of confinement. [19] In British Columbia, first-degree murder carries a minimum sentence of 25 years, with a possible judicial parole review after 15 years. [20] Capital punishment was abolished in Canada during the 1970s. [21] In Washington State, the death penalty may be invoked in cases of aggravated first-degree murder, but no one has been executed since 1963.

Rates of Gun Ownership

Because direct surveys of firearm ownership in Seattle and Vancouver have never been conducted, we assessed the rates of gun ownership indirectly by two independent methods. First, we obtained from the Firearm Permit Office of the Vancouver police department a count of the restricted-weapons permits issued in Vancouver between March 1984 and March 1988 and compared this figure with the total number of concealed-weapons permits issued in Seattle during the same period, obtained from the Office of Business and Profession Administration, Department of Licensing, State of Washington. Second, we used Cook's gun prevalence index, a previously validated measure of intercity differences in the prevalence of gun ownership. [14] This index is based on data from 49 cities in the United States and correlates each city's rates of suicide and assaultive homicide involving firearms with survey-based estimates of gun ownership in each city. Both methods indicate that firearms are far more commonly owned in Seattle than in Vancouver (Table 2).

Identification and Definition of Cases

From police records, we identified all the cases of robbery, burglary, and assault (both simple and aggravated) and all the homicides that occurred in Seattle or Vancouver between January 1, 1980, and December 31, 1986. In defining cases, we followed the guidelines of the U.S.

Federal Bureau of Investigation's uniform crime reports (UCR).[22] The UCR guidelines define aggravated assault as an unlawful attack by one person on another for the purpose of inflicting severe or aggravated bodily harm. Usually this type of assault involves the actual or threatened use of a deadly weapon. Simple assault is any case of assault that does not involve the threat or use of a deadly weapon or result in serious or aggravated injuries.

A homicide was defined as the willful killing of one human being by another. This category included cases of premeditated murder, intentional killing, and aggravated assault resulting in death. "Justifiable homicide," as defined by the UCR guidelines, was limited to cases of the killing of a felon by a law-enforcement officer in the line of duty or the killing of a felon by a private citizen during the commission of a felony.[22] Homicides that the police, the prosecuting attorney, or both thought were committed in self-defense were also identified and noted separately.

Statistical Analysis

From both Seattle and Vancouver, we obtained annual and cumulative data on the rates of aggravated assault, simple assault, robbery, and burglary. Cases of aggravated assault were categorized according to the weapon used. Data on homicides were obtained from the files of the medical examiner or coroner in each community and were supplemented by police case files. Each homicide was further categorized according to the age, sex, and race or ethnic group of the victim, as well as the weapon used.

Population-based rates of simple assault, aggravated assault, robbery, burglary, and homicide were then calculated and compared. These rates are expressed as the number per 100,000 persons per year and, when possible, are further adjusted for any differences in the age and sex of the victims. Unadjusted estimates of relative risk and 95 percent confidence intervals were calculated with use of the maximum-likelihood method and are based on Seattle's rate relative to Vancouver's.[23] Age-adjusted relative risks were estimated with use of the Mantel-Haenszel summary odds ratio.[24]

RESULTS

During the seven-year study period, the annual rate of robbery in Seattle was found to be only slightly higher than that in Vancouver (relative risk, 1.09; 95 percent confidence interval, 1.08 to 1.12). Burglaries, on the other hand, occurred at nearly identical rates in the two communities (relative risk, 0.99; 95 percent confidence interval, 0.98 to 1.00). During the study period, 18,925 cases of aggravated assault were reported in Seattle, as compared with 12,034 cases in Vancouver. When the annual rates of assault in the two cities were compared for each year of the study, we found that the two communities had similar rates of assault during the first four years of the study. In 1984, however, reported rates of simple and aggravated assault began to climb sharply in Seattle, whereas the rates of simple and aggravated assault remained relatively constant in Vancouver (Fig. 1). This change coincided with the enactment that year of the Domestic Violence Protection Act by the Washington State legislature. Among other provisions, this law required changes in reporting and arrests in cases of domestic violence.[25] It is widely believed that this law and the considerable media attention that followed its passage resulted in dramatic increases in the number of incidents reported and in related enforcement costs in Seattle.[26] Because in Vancouver there was no similar legislative initiative requiring police to change their reporting methods, we restricted our comparison of the data on assaults to the first four years of our study (1980 through 1983) (Fig. 1).

During this four-year period, the risk of being a victim of simple assault in Seattle was found to be only slightly higher than that in Vancouver (relative risk, 1.18; 95 percent confidence interval, 1.15 to

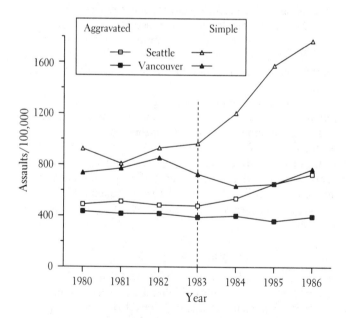

Figure 1. Rates of aggravated and simple assault in Seattle and Vancouver, 1980 through 1986. The dotted line indicates the passage of the Domestic Violence Protection Act in Washington State in 1984.

1.20). The risk of aggravated assault in Seattle was also only slightly higher than in Vancouver (relative risk, 1.16; 95 percent confidence interval, 1.12 to 1.19). However, when aggravated assaults were subdivided by the type of weapon used and the mechanism of assault, a striking pattern emerged. Although both cities reported almost identical rates of aggravated assault involving knives, other dangerous weapons, or hands, fists, and feet, firearms were far more likely to have been used in cases of assault in Seattle than in Vancouver (Table 3). In fact, all the difference in the relative risk of aggravated assault between these two communities was due to Seattle's 7.7-fold higher rate of assaults involving firearms (Fig. 2).

Over the whole seven-year study period, 388 homicides occurred in Seattle (11.3 per 100,000 person-years). In Vancouver, 204 homicides occurred during the same period (6.9 per 100,000 person-years). After adjustment for differences in age and sex between the populations, the relative risk of being a victim of homicide in Seattle, as compared with Vancouver, was found to be 1.63 (95 percent confidence interval, 1.28 to 2.08). This difference is highly unlikely to have occurred by chance.

When homicides were subdivided by the mechanism of death, the rate of homicide by knives and other weapons (excluding firearms) in Seattle was found to be almost identical to that in Vancouver (relative

20

TABLE 3

ANNUAL CRUDE RATES AND RELATIVE RISKS OF AGGRAVATED ASSAULT, SIMPLE ASSAULT, ROBBERY, BURGLARY, AND HOMICIDE IN SEATTLE AND VANCOUVER, 1980 THROUGH 1986[a]

Crime	Period	Seattle	Vancouver	Relative Risk	95% CI
		no./100,000			
Robbery	1980–1986	492.2	450.9	1.09	1.08–1.12
Burglary	1980–1986	2952.7	2985.7	0.99	0.98–1.00
Simple assault	1980–1983	902	767.7	1.18	1.15–1.20
Aggravated assault	1980–1983	486.5	420.5	1.16	1.12–1.19
Firearms		87.9	11.4	7.70	6.70–8.70
Knives		78.1	78.9	0.99	0.92–1.07
Other		320.6	330.2	0.97	0.94–1.01
Homicides	1980–1986	11.3	6.9	1.63	1.38–1.93
Firearms		4.8	1.0	5.08	3.54–7.27
Knives		3.1	3.5	0.90	0.69–1.18
Other		3.4	2.5	1.33	0.99–1.78

[a]CI denotes confidence interval. The "crude rate" for these crimes is the number of events occurring in a given population over a given time period. The relative risks shown are for Seattle in relation to Vancouver.

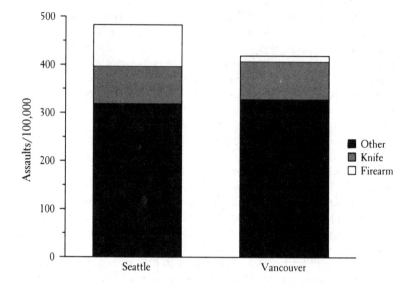

Figure 2. Annual rates of aggravated assault in Seattle and Vancouver, 1980 through 1983, according to the Weapon Used. "Other" includes blunt instruments, other dangerous weapons, and hands, fists, and feet.

risk, 1.08; 95 percent confidence interval, 0.89 to 1.32) (Fig. 3). Virtually all of the increased risk of death from homicide in Seattle was due to a more than fivefold higher rate of homicide by firearms (Table 3). Handguns, which accounted for roughly 85 percent of the homicides involving firearms in both communities, were 4.8 times more likely to be used in homicides in Seattle than in Vancouver.

To test the hypothesis that the higher rates of homicide in Seattle might be due to more frequent use of firearms for self-protection, we examined all the homicides in both cities that were ruled "legally justifiable" or were determined to have been committed in self-defense. Thirty-two such homicides occurred during the study period, 11 of which involved police intervention. After the exclusion of justifiable homicide by police, 21 cases of homicide by civilians acting in self-defense or in other legally justifiable ways remained, 17 of which occurred in Seattle and 4 of which occurred in Vancouver (relative risk, 3.64; 95 percent confidence interval, 1.32 to 10.06). Thirteen of these cases (all of which occurred in Seattle) involved firearms. The exclusion of all 21 cases (which accounted for less than 4 percent of the homicides during the study interval) had little overall effect on the relative risk of homicide in the two communities (age-

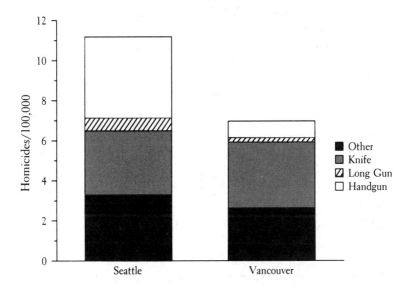

Figure 3. Annual rates of homicide in Seattle and Vancouver, 1980 through 1986, according to the Weapon Used. "Other" includes blunt instruments, other dangerous weapons, and hands, fists, and feet.

and sex-adjusted relative risk, 1.57; 95 percent confidence interval, 1.22 to 2.01).

When homicides were stratified by the race or ethnic group of the victim, a complex picture emerged (Table 4). The homicide rates in Table 4 were adjusted for age to match the 1980 U.S. population. This technique permits fairer comparisons among racial and ethnic groups with differing age compositions in each city. The relative risk for each racial or ethnic group, however, was estimated with use of the Mantel-Haenszel summary odds ratio.[24] This method, in effect, uses a different set of weights for the various age strata, depending on the distribution of persons among the age strata for that racial or ethnic group only. Hence, these estimates of relative risk differ slightly from a simple quotient of the age-adjusted rates.

Whereas similar rates of death by homicide were noted for whites in both cities, Asians in Seattle had higher rates of death by homicide than their counterparts in Vancouver. This difference persisted even after the exclusion of the 13 persons who died in the Wah Mee gambling club massacre in Seattle in 1983. Blacks and Hispanics in Seattle had higher relative risks of death by homicide than blacks and Hispanics in Vancouver, but the confidence intervals were very wide, given the relatively

TABLE 4
ANNUAL AGE-ADJUSTED HOMICIDE RATES AND RELATIVE
RISKS OF DEATH BY HOMICIDE IN SEATTLE AND VANCOUVER,
1980 THROUGH 1986, ACCORDING TO THE RACE OR
ETHNIC GROUP OF THE VICTIM[a]

Race or Ethnic Group	Seattle	Vancouver	Relative Risk	95% CI
	no./100,000			
White (non-Hispanic)	6.2	6.4	1	0.8–1.2
Asian	15.0	4.1	3.5	2.1–5.7
Excluding Wah Mee murders	9.5	—	2.3	1.4–4.0
Black	36.6	9.5	2.8	0.4–20.4
Hispanic	26.9	7.9	5	0.7–34.3
Native American	64.9	71.3	0.9	0.5–1.5

[a]CI denotes confidence interval. The relative risks shown are for Seattle in relation to Vancouver.

small size of both minorities in Vancouver. Only one black and one Hispanic were killed in Vancouver during the study period. Native Americans had the highest rates of death by homicide in both cities.

DISCUSSION

Previous studies of the effectiveness of gun control have generally compared rates of homicide in nations with different approaches to the regulation of firearms.[7] Unfortunately, the validity of these studies has been compromised by the large number of confounding factors that characterize national groups. We sought to circumvent this limitation by focusing our analysis on two demographically comparable and physically proximate cities with markedly different approaches to handgun control. In many ways, these two cities have more in common with each other than they do with other major cities in their respective countries. For example, Seattle's homicide rate is consistently half to two thirds that reported in cities such as Chicago, Los Angeles, New York, and Houston,[4] whereas Vancouver experiences annual rates of homicide two to three times higher than those reported in Ottawa, Toronto, and Calgary (Canadian Centre for Justice Statistics, Homicide Program, Ottawa: unpublished data).

In order to exclude the possibility that Seattle's higher homicide rate may be explained by higher levels of criminal activity or aggressiveness in its population, we compared the rates of burglary, robbery, simple assault, and aggravated assault in the two communities. Although we observed a slightly higher rate of simple and aggravated assault in Seattle, these differences were relatively small—the rates in Seattle were 16 to 18 percent higher than those reported in Vancouver during a period of comparable case reporting. Virtually all of the excess risk of aggravated assault in Seattle was explained by a sevenfold higher rate of assaults involving firearms. Despite similar rates of robbery and burglary and only small differences in the rates of simple and aggravated assault, we found that Seattle had substantially higher rates of homicide than Vancouver. Most of the excess mortality was due to an almost fivefold higher rate of murders with handguns in Seattle.

Critics of handgun control have long claimed that limiting access to guns will have little effect on the rates of homicide, because persons who are intent on killing others will only work harder to acquire a gun or will kill by other means.[7,27] If the rate of homicide in a community were influenced more by the strength of intent than by the availability of weapons, we might have expected the rate of homicides with weapons other than guns to have been higher in Vancouver than in Seattle, in direct proportion to any decrease in Vancouver's rate of firearm homicides. This was not the case. During the study interval, Vancouver's rate of homicides with weapons other than guns was not significantly higher than that in Seattle, suggesting that few would-be assailants switched to homicide by other methods.

Ready access to handguns has been advocated by some as an important way to provide law-abiding citizens with an effective means to defend themselves.[27–29] Were this true, we might have expected that much of Seattle's excess rate of homicides, as compared with Vancouver's, would have been explained by a higher rate of justifiable homicides and killings in self-defense by civilians. Although such homicides did occur at a significantly higher rate in Seattle than in Vancouver, these cases accounted for less than 4 percent of the homicides in both cities during the study period. When we excluded cases of justifiable homicide or killings in self-defense by civilians from our calculation of relative risk, our results were almost the same.

It also appears unlikely that differences in law-enforcement activity accounted for the lower homicide rate in Vancouver. Suspected offenders are arrested and cases are cleared at similar rates in both cities. After arrest and conviction, similar crimes carry similar penalties in the courts in Seattle and Vancouver.

We found substantial differences in the risk of death by homicide according to race and ethnic group in both cities. In the United States, blacks and Hispanics are murdered at substantially higher rates than whites.[2] Although the great majority of homicides in the United States involve assailants of the same race or ethnic group, current evidence suggests that socioeconomic status plays a much greater role in explaining racial and ethnic differences in the rate of homicide than any intrinsic tendency toward violence.[2,30,31] For example, Centerwall has shown that when household crowding is taken into account, the rate of domestic homicide among blacks in Atlanta, Georgia, is no higher than that of whites living in similar conditions.[32] Likewise, a recent study of childhood homicide in Ohio found that once cases were stratified by socioeconomic status, there was little difference in race-specific rates of homicide involving children 5 to 14 years of age.[33]

30

Since low-income populations have higher rates of homicide, socioeconomic status is probably an important confounding factor in our comparison of the rates of homicide for racial and ethnic groups. Although the median income and the overall distribution of household incomes in Seattle and Vancouver are similar, the distribution of household incomes by racial and ethnic group may not be the same in Vancouver as in Seattle. For example, blacks in Vancouver had a slightly higher mean income in 1981 than the rest of Vancouver's population (Statistics Canada, 1981 Census Custom Tabulation: unpublished data). In contrast, blacks in Seattle have a substantially lower median income than the rest of Seattle's population.[34] Thus, much of the excess risk of homicide among blacks in Seattle, as compared with blacks in Vancouver, may be explained by their lower socioeconomic status. If, on the other hand, more whites in Vancouver have low incomes than whites in Seattle, the higher risk of homicide expected in this low-income subset may push the rate of homicide among whites in Vancouver higher than that for whites in Seattle. Unfortunately, neither hypothesis can be tested in a quantitative fashion, since detailed information about household incomes according to race is not available for Vancouver.

Three limitations of our study warrant comment. First, our measures of the prevalence of firearm ownership may not precisely reflect the availability of guns in the two communities. Although the two measures we used were derived independently and are consistent with the expected effects of gun control, their validity as indicators of community rates of gun ownership has not been conclusively established. Cook's gun prevalence index has been shown to correlate with data derived from national surveys, but it has not been tested for accuracy in cities outside the United States. Comparisons of concealed-weapons permits in Seattle with restricted-weapons permits in Vancouver are probably of limited validity, since these counts do not include handguns obtained illegally. In fact, the comparison of permit data of this sort probably substantially underestimates the differences between the communities in the rate of handgun ownership, since only a fraction of the handguns in Seattle are purchased for use as concealed weapons, whereas all legal handgun purchases in Vancouver require a restricted-weapons permit. Still, these indirect estimates of gun ownership are consistent with one another, and both agree with prior reports that estimate the rate of handgun ownership in Canada to be about one fourth that in the United States.[35]

Second, although similar in many ways, Seattle and Vancouver may well differ in other aspects that could affect their rates of homicide. For example, differences in the degree of illegal drug-related activity, differences in the rate of illicit gun sales, or other, less readily apparent differences may confound the relation between firearm regulations and the rate of homicide. Although such differences may exist, striking socioeconomic similarities between the cities and the fact that they had similar rates of burglary, robbery, and both simple and aggravated assault during comparable reporting periods make such confounding less likely. Unfortunately, changes in the rules for reporting assault cases in Seattle, mandated by the State of Washington in 1984, precluded a valid comparison of the rates of simple and aggravated assault over the entire seven-year period.

Third, conclusions based on a comparison of two cities in the Pacific Northwest may not be generalizable to other urban areas in North America. Given the complex interaction of individual behavior, environment, and community factors in the pathogenesis of violent death, we cannot predict the precise impact that Canadian-style gun control might have in the United States. Even if such a major change in public policy were to take place, the current high rates of handgun ownership might blunt any effects of tougher handgun regulations for years to come.

Our analysis of the rates of homicide in these two largely similar cities suggests that the modest restriction of citizens' access to firearms (especially handguns) is associated with lower rates of homicide. This association does not appear to be explained by differences between the communities in aggressiveness, criminal behavior, or response to crime. Although our findings should be corroborated in other settings, our results suggest that a more restrictive approach to handgun control may decrease national homicide rates.

References

1. Homicide surveillance: 1970–78. Atlanta: Centers for Disease Control, September, 1983.
2. Homicide surveillance: high risk racial and ethnic groups—blacks and Hispanics, 1970 to 1983. Atlanta: Centers for Disease Control, November, 1986.
3. Baker SP, O'Neill B, Karpf RS. The injury fact book. Lexington, Mass.: Lexington Books, 1984.
4. Department of Justice, Federal Bureau of Investigation. Crime in the United States (Uniform Crime Reports). Washington, D.C.: Government Printing Office, 1986.
5. Baker SP. Without guns, do people kill people? Am J Public Health 1985; 75:587–8.
6. Hedeboe J, Charles AV, Nielsen J, et al. Interpersonal violence: patterns in a Danish community. Am J Public Health 1985; 75:651–3.
7. Wright J, Rossi P, Daly K, Weber-Burdin E. Weapons, crime and violence in

America: a literature review and research agenda. Washington, D.C.: Department of Justice, National Institute of Justice, 1981.

8. Weiss JMA. Gun control: a question of public/mental health? J Oper Psychiatr 1981; 12:86–8.

9. Bruce-Briggs B. The great American gun war. Public Interest 1976; 45:37–62.

10. Bureau of Census. 1980 Census of population, Washington. Washington, D.C.: Government Printing Office, 1981.

11. Statistics Canada: 1981 census of Canada, Vancouver, British Columbia. Ottawa, Ont.: Minister of Supply and Services, 1983.

12. Seattle local market T.V. ratings, 1985–86. (Based on Arbitron television ratings.) Provided by KING TV, Seattle, Washington.

13. Vancouver local market T.V. ratings, 1985–86. Provided by Bureau of Broadcast Measurement, Toronto.

14. Cook PJ. The role of firearms in violent crime. In: Wolfgang M, ed. Criminal violence. Beverly Hills, Calif.: Sage, 1982:236–90.

15. Revised Code of State of Washington. RCW chapter 9.41.090, 9.41.095, 9.41.070, 1986.

16. Criminal Code of Canada. Firearms and other offensive weapons. Martin's Criminal Code of Canada, 1982. Part II.1 (Sections 81–016.9, 1982).

17. *Idem.* Restricted Weapons and Firearm Control Regulations Sec. 106.2 (11); Amendment Act, July 18, 1977, 1982.

18. Revised Code of State of Washington, Sentence Reform Act Chapter 9 94A.125.1980.

19. Revised Code of State of Washington. Murder I, 9A.32.040.1984.

20. Criminal Code of Canada. Application for judicial review sentence of life imprisonment, 1988 Part XX 669–67, 1(1).

21. *Idem.* Act to Amend Criminal Code B.11 C84, 1976.

22. Department of Justice, Federal Bureau of Investigation. Uniform crime reporting handbook. Washington, D.C.: Government Printing Office, 1984.

23. Rothman KJ, Boice JD Jr. Epidemiologic analysis with a programmable calculator. Boston: Epidemiology Resources, 1982.

24. Armitage P, Berry G. Statistical methods in medical research. 2nd ed. Oxford: Blackwell, 1987.

25. Revised Code of State of Washington. RCW Chapter 10.99.010–.100, 1984.

26. Seattle Police Department. Inspectional service division report, domestic violence arrest costs: 1984–87, Seattle, 1986.

27. Drooz RB. Handguns and hokum: a methodological problem. JAMA 1977; 238:43–5.

28. Copeland AR. The right to keep and bear arms—a study of civilian homicides committed against those involved in criminal acts in metropolitan Dade County from 1957 to 1982. J Forensic Sci 1984; 29:584–90.

29. Kleck G. Crime control through the private use of armed force. Soc Probl 1988; 35:1–21.

30. Loftin C, Hill RH. Regional subculture and homicide: an examination of the Gastil-Hackney thesis. Am Sociol Rev 1974; 39:714–24.

31. Williams KR. Economic sources of homicide: reestimating the effects of poverty and inequality. Am Sociol Rev 1984; 49:283–9.

32. Centerwall BS. Race, socioeconomic status, and domestic homicide, Atlanta, 1971–72. Am J Public Health 1984; 74:813–5.

33. Muscat JE. Characteristics of childhood homicide in Ohio, 1974–84. Am J Public Health 1988; 78:822–4.

34. Seattle City Government. General social and economic characteristics, city of Seattle: 1970–1980. Planning research bulletin no. 45. Seattle: Department of Community Development, 1983.

35. Newton G, Zimring F. Firearms and violence in American life: a staff report to the National Commission on the Causes and Prevention of Violence. Washington, D.C.: Government Printing Office, 1969.

Jeremy Bernstein

SN–1987 A

On the evening of February 23, 1987, Albert Jones of Nelson, New Zealand, as was his custom, went out after dinner to the driveway near his home. In the driveway, he had set up a large astronomical telescope of his own construction. Jones, who is now sixty-seven, retired not long ago after working in the repair division of an automobile company in Nelson. But, since 1944, he has spent much of his free time as an amateur astronomer, studying "variable stars"—stars whose brightness varies in the course of time. It is estimated that he has made about 350,000 variable star observations. He has been called the world's greatest amateur observational astronomer, and, in the summer of 1987, he was awarded the Order of the British Empire for his work. On February 23, he began his star scan by examining a relatively nearby galaxy known as the Large Magellanic Cloud, which, at about nine-thirty local time (the time he was looking at it), was quite high in the sky. He noticed nothing unusual.

In view of what was about to happen, it is instructive to quantify Jones's non-observation. His home-constructed telescope is what is known as a 12.5-inch "Newtonian reflector." This means that in essence it is a long tube into which light enters, where it is then collected and focused by a mirror—in this case, 12.5 inches in diameter. The mirror is one of the few things Jones actually bought that was designed for a telescope. The light is reflected out the side of the telescope by a second mirror and can be examined through an eyepiece. In Jones's case, the eyepiece was a Second World War bombsight. The telescope was powerful enough to detect stars up to what astronomers call the $+13.5$ magnitude. Astronomers have traditionally utilized a magnitude scale that, perversely, is adjusted so that the larger the number, the *weaker* the apparent brightness. Negative numbers are assigned to strong sources. Thus on a logarithmic scale the Sun has an apparent magnitude of -26.6, the Moon -12.6, and the planet Venus, at its brightest, -4.4. Jones could have detected any peculiar star with a magnitude less

From *The American Scholar* (Spring 1988).

than $+7.5$, and he saw none in the Large Magellanic Cloud that evening.

The next morning, as he often did, Jones set his alarm clock for a pre-dawn hour so that he could continue his observations. By this time, the Large Magellanic Cloud was setting, and, as he already had studied it that evening, he passed it by. This, as it turned out, was a pity. If someone had continued to watch for an hour or so after Jones had turned his attention elsewhere, they would have seen the most spectacular astronomical event to occur in our vicinity in the last 383 years. The unprepossessing blue star Sk–69° 202, so designated in a catalog by Nicholas Sanduleak of Case Western Reserve University, had suddenly become a supernova—SN–1987 A—so bright that it would have been visible with the naked eye. While many supernovas are observed each year, this was the first one in nearly four centuries seen to explode in our own or a neighboring galaxy.

The next evening Jones was back at his telescope. Now, to sort out the sequence of events, it is useful to describe things in what astronomers call "Universal Time." (This is also known as Greenwich mean time.) The advantage of doing so is that the effect of the longitude gets subtracted out, and one can see at a glance what event is earlier and what is later. In these units, Jones's initial non-observation was recorded at 9:22 UT (Universal Time) on February 23. It was now 8:52 UT the following evening. When Jones pointed his telescope at the Large Magellanic Cloud, the supernova, in his words, "popped out" at him. By this time it was $+4.4$ magnitude, which is to say, it was as bright as a star visible to the naked eye. He at once called Frank Bateson in nearby Touranga.

Bateson has been, for sixty years, the director of the Variable Star Section of the Royal Astronomical Society of New Zealand. Jones said to Bateson, "Frank, there is a star in the Large Magellanic Cloud where there was no star before." Bateson would have telexed this remarkable news to the International Astronomical Union in the United States, but, as it happens, no commercial telexes can be sent from New Zealand at night. He did, however, get word immediately by telephone to astronomers in Australia. Meanwhile, a Canadian observer—a professional astronomer, Ian Shelton of the University of Toronto, working at the Las Campanas station in Chile—happened to develop a photographic plate at 5:31 UT, some three and a half hours earlier. The photographic plate was of the Large Magellanic Cloud, and in it was an image of what appeared to be a very bright star. At first Shelton thought it was a flaw in the plate. He went outside to look and, sure enough, the new supernova was visible to the naked eye. Thus Shelton became the second person to discover SN–1987 A, with Jones a close third.

The first person actually to see the supernova, an hour and a half earlier, was another Las Campanas observer named Oscar Duhelde, who did not tell anyone until Shelton brought the matter up. Because Jones did not see the supernova the night before, he was able to narrow down the instant of the explosion. Unknown to anyone at the time, remnants of the supernova first made their appearance here at 7:35:41 UT on February 23, nearly two hours prior to Jones's non-observation. These remnants were in the form of ghostly, elusive particles called neutrinos.

At the Fairport mine in Painesville, Ohio, some twenty miles from Cleveland, miners and other employees of the Morton Salt Company— "When it rains, it pours"—tend to wear patches on their overalls and miner's helmets that read "Think Snow!" This is not because these people have an affinity to skiing. Rather, it is because they mine rock salt, which is sprinkled on icy roads—when it pours, they reign. The Fairport mine is very much a working commercial mine. Visiting it is a serious matter. The increasingly uneasy visitor is given a safety lecture that includes an interlude on using a rather heavy catalytic converter worn on a thick leather belt at all times when one is underground. The converter transforms, in the case of a mine fire, carbon monoxide, which is poisonous, into carbon dioxide, which isn't. It also gets very hot when it is working and, one is told, despite that, one had better keep it in one's mouth in order to survive. One is then given a pair of high-top shoes with iron toes (in case one trips on some lumps of salt), a pair of blue coveralls, and a hard plastic helmet with a miner's lamp attached to it. One is then ready to go underground.

The mine shaft is two thousand feet deep—nearly two Empire State buildings down. There are two elevators that connect the bottom to the surface: a freight elevator—a sort of bucket—that brings up the salt and can be used in emergencies for people, and a passenger elevator that is big enough to hold ten miners on each of its decks (about forty at a time are at work in the mine) and, if necessary, various kinds of material. It is a comfortable, if austere, steel cage.

The ride down takes about four minutes and feels, to a newcomer, as if it takes an eternity. The temperature increases as one goes down. The walls of the working face of the mine are at a temperature of about eighty-five degrees Fahrenheit. There is a good deal of humidity at the bottom of the shaft. Murky tunnels seem to lead in all directions. One passes a huge noisy fan and is led down a dark tunnel, with one's miner's lamp illuminating the way. One has to be careful not to slip on the humid salt. After walking for what seems like another small eternity, one is confronted by what looks like an impassable steel wall. There are warning signs about electrical equipment, but with a proper key the iron barrier can be opened and passed. At first, one is startled by the bright sodium vapor lights and the air-conditioning. One is in another world, the world of a high-energy physics laboratory.

10   The laboratory is devoted to a single enterprise: the care and feeding
of an entity known as the "IMB detector." The initials *IMB* stand for
Irvine, Michigan, and Brookhaven—that is, the University of California
at Irvine, the University of Michigan at Ann Arbor, and the Brookhaven
National Laboratory at Upton, Long Island, New York. These three
institutions built the detector and maintain and run it. What is the
detector? In November of 1979, work was started on the currently
occupied chamber, which is separate from the rest of the mining operation (though close enough that blasting can be felt in it), and the
evacuation was completed on August 20, 1980. It has been partitioned
into four separate areas.

As one enters the chamber, one passes through a large room filled with
what looks like, and is, a very complex water filtration system (the reason
for which will become evident shortly). In the next room, there is a kind
of laboratory bench area with, among other things, a microwave oven
suitable for making coffee. In the next area there is a maze of computer
equipment, and, finally, one comes to the heart and soul of the detector:
a gigantic pool of translucent and highly purified water. The tank is
rectangular in shape: sixty feet wide by eighty feet long. It is sixty-five
feet deep and holds a total of eight thousand metric tons of water. The
water is so clear that, when the divers from the University of Michigan
who service the tank about every three weeks first went into it, they got
vertigo. It was like falling through thin air. Looking into this water, one
sees an array of 2,048 photo-multiplier tubes. These very large—eight
inches in diameter—hemispherical tubes were recently developed for
this kind of detection of weak light signals. Each one costs about a
thousand dollars. A couple of them probably cost about as much as Mr.
Jones's entire telescope.

As one might gather from the name, the purpose of the photo-
multiplier tubes is to detect light. Therein lies a tale. The light (more
generally, electromagnetic radiation) to be detected is emitted by rapidly
moving electrons. If the electrons are moving more rapidly than the
effective speed of light in water—nothing can move more rapidly than
the speed of light in a vacuum, but a material medium slows the light
up—then they can emit a form of radiation known as "Čerenkov radiation," named after the Russian scientist Pavel Aleksejevic Čerenkov,
who shared the 1958 Nobel Prize in physics for proposing it. This
radiation is emitted in a narrow cone—something like a sonic boom—
with its axis in the direction of the electron's motion, a detail that is
crucial to using it in a detector. By detecting the Čerenkov radiation,
it is possible to reconstruct the trajectory of the particle that emitted
it—in this case, an electron.

The electrons that the detector was built to detect had, in the first
instance, nothing to do with supernovas. In the middle of the 1970s,

several theoretical physicists proposed theories that unified previously disparate parts of elementary particle physics (of this, more later). An inevitable consequence of this unification program, it appeared, was that matter had to be somewhat unstable. The proton, which had usually been taken as the stable building block of matter, would, it was thought, actually decay but with a very long lifetime—some 10^{31} years, much longer than the age of the universe, which is about 10^{10} years. As a result, not very many protons in an average sample of matter were predicted to decay in, say, a year.

Most of the theories predicted a proton decay mode in which a very energetic positive electron would be emitted. Hence one needed a detector that could detect a very rare event involving the emission of the very energetic electron by a decaying proton—ergo, the tank. The 8,000 tons of water in the tank contain about 2×10^{33} protons. If each proton lived even as long as 10^{31} years, in such a mass of protons there could still be about two hundred decays in a year—an event every couple of days, or enough to work with.

Now, one may well ask, once one sees the reason to build the tank, why do so in a mine chamber two thousand feet below the surface of the earth—a mine chamber that, incidentally, cost $200,000 to dig? (The physicists got a very good price because Morton Salt wanted to try out a new piece of digging equipment.) The reason for the mine chamber is what the physicists call "background." The earth's atmosphere is constantly bombarded by cosmic rays, and these can produce energetic positive electrons that can look just like the ones from proton decay. The mine shaft is located under two thousand feet of absorber, which screens out most of the background. The odd neutrino does get through but only produces events that mock up what one is looking for every two or three years. The proposal to dig the tunnel was supported financially by the Department of Energy in 1979, and the digging was completed in the summer of 1980. The tank was filled completely with ultra-pure water by July 30, 1982, and the experimenters began to wait for proton decay events. They are still waiting. In the words of Maurice Goldhaber, one of the senior experimenters from Brookhaven, "We had some candidates, but they weren't elected." At this writing, the conclusion is that the proton must live at least 3.5×10^{32} years—a disappointingly long time for some of the theorists who championed simple models of unification that predicted shorter times.

In order to understand what happened on February 23, we must return once again to the tank. Occasionally, very occasionally, high energy neutrinos that course through the tank because of cosmic ray phenomena hit one of the electrons in the water molecules that make up the content of the tank and knock it for a loop. Neutrinos can also interact with protons and produce positive electrons—positrons. The

15

velocity of light in water is about three-quarters of the velocity of light in a vacuum, which is, in turn, about three hundred million meters a second. If the electron recoils from its collision with the neutrino with enough energy so as to be moving faster than the velocity of light in water, which is about 70 percent of its speed in a vacuum, it will "Čerenkov radiate." The greater its energy, the more intense will be this radiation, and if it has enough energy, it will trigger enough of the 2,048 photo-multiplier tubes to be detectable. The signals from these tubes are carried over wires into the neighboring room, where they are fed into computers that make a preliminary analysis of them. This process takes place automatically and goes on night and day, so long as the detector is in service, whether or not anyone is actually down in the mine to observe it.

It was going on during the early hours, Cleveland time, of the morning of February 23, which happened to be a Monday. That is why no one was there to notice that a power supply had tripped off, shutting down a quarter of the phototubes. In the meantime, it was late in the afternoon in Kamioka, Japan, where there is another detector—the Kamiokanda II, a modified version of the IMB, in a zinc mine—this one with a tank of 3,000 tons of water, but with phototubes that cover a larger fraction of the surface, meaning that electrons, and hence neutrinos, of lower energy can be detected. At precisely 7:35:35 UT—within an error of fifty milliseconds—both detectors recorded bursts of energetic neutrinos. The Kamiokanda II detector recorded eleven neutrinos in 12.439 seconds while the IMB detector recorded eight in 5.59 seconds.

One should understand that all of this was realized only several days after the fact. That it was realized at all is a tribute to the interplay between theory and experiment. In the first place, over the past two decades a picture has evolved of how a supernova develops. For a star to become a supernova, it must be more massive than what is known as the "Chandrasekhar limit"—after the Indian-born American astrophysicist Subrahmanyan Chandrasekhar who won the 1983 Nobel Prize in physics for this and other fundamental contributions to theoretical astronomy. The "classical" Chandrasekhar limit is 1.456 times the mass of the Sun, but subtle corrections can make it as low as about 1.2 times the mass of the Sun or as high as about 2 times the mass of the Sun. Fortunately for us, or our descendants, it is always larger than the mass of the Sun, because a star that has a mass that exceeds this limit at the end of its evolution is doomed to collapse and, in the case of a supernova, to explode. Before the explosion, such a star consists of a dense iron core—iron because the fusion reactions that power a star cannot produce elements heavier than iron—surrounded by onion skins of lighter elements, typically, moving outwards, silicon, oxygen, carbon, helium, and hydrogen. Once the iron core becomes sufficiently massive and sufficiently hot, it simply collapses in a fraction of a second—milliseconds.

At first, the outer layers do not know that the inner core has collapsed. Then they are hit by a stupendous shock wave. The final destination of the inner core is to become a neutron star—a crystalline mass of neutrons, denser than an atomic nucleus, weighing about the mass of the Sun, and only about ten kilometers across. To accomplish this, and still conserve energy, a mind-boggling amount of energy must be released— about 3×10^{53} ergs in about a second. To have some perspective on this number, note that the Sun (no mean radiator) emits energy at a rate of only 3.9×10^{33} ergs per second. The emission rate in supernova formation is, therefore, equivalent to 10^{20} Suns. The general belief of the scientists who study such matters is that most of this energy is released in the form of neutrinos, not in the first explosion but in the resultant shock wave. The supernova turns into a sort of neutrino star. These neutrinos, in the case of SN–1987 A, took about 163,000 years to reach our planet, where they arrived on February 23, some three hours before the associated visible light, also produced by the shock wave. About, it is thought, 10^{58} neutrinos were emitted in the explosion. About 30 million billion of these passed through the IMB detector in six seconds, of which eight made suitable collisions and were detected, though after the fact. Nothing in the IMB circuitry, as it was then (the software has since been modified) would have instantaneously signaled to an experimenter that such a neutrino burst had taken place. Now a computer readout will say, "Possible neutrino burst detected at time . . ." if there is one.

Both the IMB people and the physicists at the Kamiokanda II were alerted to the possibility that neutrino events could be found retrospectively in their data by the discovery of Duhelde, Shelton, and then Jones of visible supernova. As it happens, we were lucky to have found these neutrinos at all. The IMB, as I noted, had a power surge that shut off a quarter of its phototubes, while, as it turned out, the Kamiokanda II suffered a complete power outage on February 25, which made it impossible to make an absolute calibration of the time the neutrinos arrived there. It was, then, in this serendipitous way, that the subject of extragalactic observational neutrino astronomy was founded.

20

THE READER

1. Bernstein's narrative explores the interplay between theory and experiment in science. What events, exactly, were observed? Which elements in the story are theoretical explanations for the observed facts?

2. What do you understand by scientific method? Was extragalactic observational neutrino astronomy founded by scientific method?

THE WRITER

1. *What does the title of the essay signify? Is the language of the essay similar to the language of the title?*
2. *Is Bernstein describing a cooperative or a competitive endeavor? What features of the language and organization of the essay help you to answer that question?*
3. *In his concluding sentence Bernstein calls the process by which this branch of astronomy was established "serendipitous." Serendipity is an often-noted feature of everyday life. Write an account of how you, by serendipity, have come on new knowledge or a new absorbing interest.*

Arthur Koestler

GRAVITY AND THE HOLY GHOST

"If I have been able to see farther than others," said Newton, "it was because I stood on the shoulders of giants." One of the giants was Johannes Kepler (1571–1630) whose three laws of planetary motion provided the foundation on which the Newtonian universe was built. They were the first "natural laws" in the modern sense: precise, verifiable statements expressed in mathematical terms; at the same time, they represent the first attempt at a synthesis of astronomy and physics which, during the preceding two thousand years, had developed on separate lines.

Astronomy before Kepler had been a purely descriptive geometry of the skies. The motion of stars and planets had been represented by the device of epicycles and eccentrics—an imaginary clockwork of circles turning on circles turning on circles. Copernicus, for instance, had used forty-eight wheels to represent the motion of the five known planets around the sun. These wheels were purely fictitious, and meant as such—they enabled astronomers to make more or less precise predictions, but, above all, they satisfied the dogma that all heavenly motion must be uniform and in perfect circles. Though the planets moved neither uniformly nor in perfect circles, the imaginary cogwheels did, and thereby "saved the appearances."

Kepler's discoveries put an end to this state of affairs. He reconciled astronomy with physics, and substituted for the fictitious clockwork a universe of material bodies not unlike the earth, freely floating and

From *The Act of Creation* (1964).

turning in space, moved by forces acting on them. His most important book bears the provocative title: *A New Astronomy Based on Causation, or Physics of the Sky* (1609). It contains the first and second of Kepler's three laws. The first says that the planets move around the sun not in circles but in elliptic orbits; the second says that a planet moves in its orbit not at uniform speed but at a speed that varies according to its position, and is defined by a simple and beautiful law: the line connecting planet and sun sweeps over equal areas in equal times. The third law establishes an equally elegant mathematical correlation between the length of a planet's year and its mean distance from the sun.

Kepler did not start his career as an astronomer, but as a student of theology (at the Lutheran University of Thuebingen); yet already as a student he was attracted by the Copernican idea of a sun-centered universe. Now Canon Copernicus's book, *On the Revolutions of the Heavenly Spheres,* had been published in the year of his death, 1543; that is, fifty years before Kepler first heard of him; and during that half century it had attracted very little attention. One of the reasons was its supreme unreadability, which made it into an all-time worst-seller: its first edition of a thousand copies was never sold out. Kepler was the first Continental astronomer to embrace the Copernican theory. His *Mysterium Cosmographicum,* published in 1597 (fifty-four years after Copernicus's death) started the great controversy—Galileo entered the scene fifteen years later.

The reason why the idea of a sun-centered universe appealed to   5
Kepler was repeatedly stated by himself: "I often defended the opinions of Copernicus in the disputations of the candidates and I composed a careful disputation on the first motion which consists in the rotation of the earth; then I was adding to this the motion of the earth around the sun *for physical or, if you prefer, metaphysical reasons.* " I have emphasized the last words because they contain the leitmotif of Kepler's quest, and because he used the same expression in various passages in his works. Now what were those "physical or, if you prefer, metaphysical reasons" which made Kepler prefer to put the sun into the center of the universe instead of the earth?

> My ceaseless search concerned primarily three problems, namely, the number, size, and motion of the planets—why they are just as they are and not otherwise arranged. I was encouraged in my daring inquiry by that beautiful analogy between the stationary objects, namely, the sun, the fixed stars, and the space between them, with God the Father, the Son, and the Holy Ghost. I shall pursue this analogy in my future cosmographical work.

Twenty-five years later, when he was over fifty, Kepler repeated his credo: "It is by no means permissible to treat this analogy as an empty comparison; it must be considered by its Platonic form and archetypal quality as one of the primary causes."

He believed in this to the end of his life. Yet gradually the analogy underwent a significant change:

> The sun in the middle of the *moving* stars, himself at rest and yet the source of motion, carries the image of God the Father and Creator. He distributes his motive force through a medium which contains the moving bodies, even as the Father creates through the Holy Ghost.

Thus the "moving bodies"—that is, the planets—are now brought into the analogy. The Holy Ghost no longer merely fills the space between the motionless sun and the motionless fixed stars. It has become an active force, a *vis motrix,* which *drives* the planets. Nobody before Kepler had postulated, or even suspected, the existence of a physical force acting between the sun and the planets. Astronomy was not concerned with physical forces, nor with the causes of the heavenly motions, merely with their description. The passages which I have just quoted are the first intimation of the forthcoming marriage between physics and astronomy—the act of betrothal, as it were. By looking at the sky, not through the eyes of the geometrician only, but of the physicist concerned with natural causes, he hit upon a question which nobody had asked before. The question was: "Why do the planets closer to the sun move faster than those which are far away? What is the mathematical relation between a planet's distance from the sun and the length of its year?"

These questions could only occur to one who had conceived the revolutionary hypothesis that the motion of the planet—and therefore its velocity and the duration of its year—was governed by a physical force emanating from the sun. Every astronomer knew, of course, that the greater their distance from the sun the slower the planets moved. But this phenomenon was taken for granted, just as it was taken for granted that boys will be boys and girls will be girls, as an irreducible fact of creation. Nobody asked the cause of it because physical causes were not assumed to enter into the motion of heavenly bodies. The greatness of the philosophers of the scientific revolution consisted not so much in finding the right answers but in asking the right questions; in seeing a problem where nobody saw one before; in substituting a "why" for a "how."

10   Kepler's answer to the question why the outer planets move slower than the inner ones, and how the speed of their motion is related to their distance from the sun, was as follows:

> There exists only one moving soul in the center of all the orbits that is the sun which drives the planets the more vigorously the closer the planet is, but whose force is quasi-exhausted when acting on the outer planets because of the long distance and the weakening of the force which it entails.

Later on he commented: "If we substitute for the word 'soul' the word 'force,' then we get just the principle which underlies my 'Physics of the Skies.' As I reflected that this cause of motion *diminishes in proportion to distance* just as the light of the sun diminishes in proportion to distance from the sun, I came to the conclusion that this force must be substantial—'substantial' not in the literal sense but . . . in the same manner as we say that light is something substantial, meaning by this an unsubstantial entity emanating from a substantial body."

We notice that Kepler's answer came *before* the question—that it was the answer that begot the question. The answer, the starting point, was the analogy between God the Father and the sun—the former acting through the Holy Ghost, the latter through a physical force. The planets must obey the law of the sun—the law of God—the mathematical law of nature; and the Holy Ghost's action through empty space diminishes, as the light emanating from the sun does, with distance. The degenerate, purely descriptive astronomy which originated in the period of the Greek decline, and continued through the Dark and Middle Ages until Kepler, did not ask for meaning and causes. But Kepler was convinced that physical causes operate between heavenly, just as between earthly, bodies, and more specifically that the sun exerts a physical force on the planets. It was this conviction which enabled him to formulate his laws. Physics became the auxiliary matrix which secured his escape from the blocked situation into which astronomy had maneuvered itself.

The blockage—to cut a very long story short—was due to the fact that Tycho de Brahe[1] had improved the instruments and methods of stargazing, and produced observational data of a hitherto unequaled abundance and precision; and the new data did not fit into the traditional schemes. Kepler, who served his apprenticeship under Tycho, was given the task of working out the orbit of Mars. He spent six years on the task and covered nine thousand foliosheets with calculations in his small handwriting without getting anywhere. When at last he believed he had succeeded he found to his dismay that certain observed positions of Mars differed from those which his theory demanded by magnitudes up to eight minutes arc. Eight minutes arc is approximately one-quarter of the apparent diameter of the moon.

This was a catastrophe. Ptolemy, and even Copernicus, could afford to neglect a difference of eight minutes, because their observations were accurate only within a margin of ten minutes, anyway. "But," Kepler wrote in the *New Astronomy*, "but for us, who by divine kindness were given an accurate observer such as Tycho Brahe, for us it is fitting that we should acknowledge this divine gift and put it to use. . . . Henceforth I shall lead the way toward that goal according to my ideas. For if I had

1. Danish astronomer (1546–1601).

believed that we could ignore these eight minutes, I would have patched up my hypothesis accordingly. But since it was not permissible to ignore them, those eight minutes point the road to a complete reformation of astronomy. . . ."

15   Thus a theory, built on years of labor and torment, was instantly thrown away because of a discord of eight miserable minutes arc. Instead of cursing those eight minutes as a stumbling block, he transformed them into the cornerstone of a new science. For those eight minutes arc had at last made him realize that the field of astronomy in its traditional framework was well and truly blocked.

One of the recurrent frustrations and tragedies in the history of thought is caused by the uncertainty whether it is possible to solve a given problem by traditional methods previously applied to problems which seem to be of the same nature. Who can say how many lives were wasted and good minds destroyed in futile attempts to square the circle, or to construct a *perpetuum mobile?* [2] The proof that these problems are *insoluble* was in each case an original discovery in itself (such as Maxwell's second law of thermodynamics);[3] and such proofs could only be found by looking at the problem from a point of view outside its traditional matrix. On the other hand, the mere knowledge that a problem is soluble means that half the game is already won.

The episode of the eight minutes arc had convinced Kepler that his problem—the orbit of Mars—was insoluble so long as he felt bound by the traditional rules of sky-geometry. Implied in those rules was the dogma of "uniform motion in perfect circles." *Uniform* motion he had already discarded before the crisis; now he felt that the even more sacred one of *circular* motion must also go. The impossibility of constructing a circular orbit which would satisfy all existing observations suggested to him that the circle must be replaced by some other curve.

> The conclusion is quite simply that the planet's path is not a circle—it curves inward on both sides and outward again at opposite ends. Such a curve is called an oval. The orbit is not a circle but an oval figure.

This oval orbit was a wild, frightening new departure for him. To be fed up with cycles and epicycles, to mock the slavish imitators of Aristotle was one thing; to assign an entirely new, lopsided, implausible path for the heavenly bodies was quite another. Why indeed an oval? There is something in the perfect symmetry of spheres and circles which has a deep, reassuring appeal to the unconscious mind—otherwise it could

2. A hypothetical machine that, once set in motion, would continue in motion forever unless stopped by some external force or by its own wearing out.
3. The second law of thermodynamics, put forward not by James Clerk Maxwell, but by Rudolf Julius Emmanuel Clausius (1822–88), provides an explanation of why a perpetual-motion machine cannot exist.

not have survived two millennia. The oval lacks that archetypal appeal. It has an arbitrary, distorted form. It destroyed the dream of the "harmony of the spheres," which lay at the origin of the whole quest. At times he felt like a criminal, or worse: a fool. All he had to say in his own defense was: "I have cleared the Augean stables of astronomy of cycles and spirals, and left behind me only a single cartful of dung."

That cartful of dung—nonuniform motion in noncircular orbits—could only be justified and explained by arguments derived not from geometry, but from physics. A phrase kept humming in his ear like a catchy tune, and crops up in his writings over and again: there is a force in the sun which moves the planets, there is a force in the sun. . . . And since there is a force in the sun, there must exist some simple relationship between the planet's distance from the sun, and its speed. A light shines the brighter the nearer one is to its source, and the same must apply to the force of the sun: the closer the planet to it, the quicker it will move. This had been his instinctive conviction; but now he thought that he had found the proof of it. "Ye physicists, prick your ears, for now we are going to invade your territory." The next six chapters in the *Astronomia Nova* are a report on that invasion into celestial physics, which had been out of bounds for astronomy since Plato. He had found the second matrix which would unblock his problem.

That excursion was something of a comedy of errors—which nevertheless ended with finding the truth. Since he had no notion of the principle of inertia, which makes a planet persist in its tangential motion under its own momentum, and had only a vague intuition of gravity, he had to invent a force which, emanating from the sun, sweeps the planet round its path like a broom. In the second place, to account for the eccentricity of the orbits he had to postulate that the planets were "huge round magnets" whose poles pointed always in the same direction so that they would alternately be drawn closer to and be repelled by the sun. But although today the whole thing seems cockeyed, his intuition that there are *two antagonistic forces* acting on the planets, guided him in the right direction. A single force, as previously assumed—the divine Prime Mover and its allied hierarchy of angels—would never produce elliptic orbits and periodic changes of speed. These could only be the result of some dynamic tug of war going on in the sky—as indeed there is. The concept of two antagonistic forces provided rules for a new game in which elliptic orbits and velocities depending on solar distance have their legitimate place.

He made many mistakes during that wild flight of thought; but "as if by miracle"—as he himself remarked—the mistakes canceled out. It looks as if at times his conscious critical faculties had been anesthetized by the creative impulse, by the impatience to get to grips with the physical forces in the solar system. The problem of the planetary orbits had been hopelessly bogged down in its purely geometrical frame of reference, and when he realized that he could not get it unstuck he tore it out of that frame and removed it into the field of physics. That there were inconsistencies and impurities in his method did not matter to him in the heat of the moment, hoping that somehow they would right themselves later on—as they did. This inspired cheating—or, rather, borrowing on credit—is a characteristic and recurrent feature in the history of science. The latest example is subatomic physics, which may be said to live on credit—in the pious hope that one day its inner contradictions and paradoxes will somehow resolve themselves.

Kepler's determination of the orbit of Mars became the unifying link between the two formerly separate realisms of physics and astronomy. His was the first serious attempt at explaining the mechanism of the solar system in terms of physical forces; and once the example was set, physics and cosmology could never again be divorced.

THE READER

1. *Why, according to Koestler, was it so difficult for Kepler to discard the notion of circular movement for the heavenly bodies, and why was it difficult to conceive of physical forces acting between the heavenly bodies? Are there any ideas in your own way of thinking that might be similarly difficult to discard or to accept? Perhaps Bronowski's "The Reach of Imagination" (p. 196) and "The Nature of Scientific Reasoning" (p. 1008) may help you in thinking or writing about these questions.*

2. *What was the role of Tycho Brahe's observations, fact finding, and data gathering in the formulation of Kepler's thought? Did the facts speak for themselves and make a true conception of the solar system evident at once? Explain the reasons for your answer.*

3. *On p. 992, Koestler says of Kepler, "Instead of cursing those eight minutes as a stumbling block, he transformed them into the cornerstone of a new science." What does this statement mean? Is a difference of such small scale between theory and observation necessarily significant in itself? If so, of what? Do you know of similar differences between expectation and actual behavior in your own personal relationships? How have you handled such discrepancies?*

THE WRITER

1. *What effect is produced by the essay's title, "Gravity and the Holy Ghost"? What relationship between the two terms in the title does the essay explore? Which of the two terms is more familiar to you? Which do you think you know more about? Write an account of your understanding of them.*

2. *Koestler says that "the greatness of the philosophers of the scientific revolution consisted not so much in finding the right answers but in asking the right questions." On the basis of your reading of "Humanities and Science" (p. 329), do you think Thomas would agree or disagree? Put your answer in the form of a brief essay.*

Richard S. Westfall

THE CAREER OF ISAAC NEWTON: A SCIENTIFIC LIFE IN THE SEVENTEENTH CENTURY

If anyone has had a good press among the scientific community, surely it is Isaac Newton. He has appeared as the archetype of the modern empirical scientist, the example on which the majority of contemporary scientists would happily model themselves. It is not surprising that Newton should have assumed this role. In his *Principia* he produced the paradigm of the scientific world view. The law of universal gravitation was almost the least of its contents. Its three laws of motion, still presented today at the beginning of any introduction to physics, provided the foundation of a general science of mechanics. The work also presented the ideal of science as exact mathematical description, not confined to ideal situations as mathematical descriptions had been in earlier works such as those of Galileo, but exact descriptions of the extent to which physical reality fails to embody the ideal. In his other great work, *Opticks*, Newton produced one of the earliest exemplars of experimental procedure. Finally, he capped the whole performance with the invention of calculus, the basic instrument of physical science. It was, all in all, an achievement without equal—one indeed without serious rival. More than any other single man, Newton defined what modern science would be.

The case for Newton as the archetype of the empirical scientist extends beyond his achievement in science. Throughout his career he consistently expressed a methodological point of view to which most contemporary scientists would readily subscribe. The first occasion for such utterance came soon after he burst upon the scientific scene, in 1672, with his paper on colors. The paper contained an experimental investigation that established the heterogeneity of light. It was laid before a community convinced by a tradition some two thousand years

From *The American Scholar* (Vol. 50, No. 3, Summer 1981).

old, which common sense supported, that primary light—the light of the sun—is homogeneous and that colors appear in certain circumstances, such as rainbows, when media modify primary light. Influenced as well by the mechanical philosophy of nature, the audience who read his paper looked for mechanistic explanations that would explain both the modification light undergoes and the nature of colors.

Not surprisingly, they misunderstood Newton's paper. In reply to their criticism, he took a methodological stand. In science, he insisted, experimental investigations must take precedence over explanatory hypotheses devised to explain phenomena. "For if the possibility of hypotheses is to be the test of the truth and reality of things, I see not how certainty can be obtained in any science; since numerous hypotheses may be devised, which shall seem to overcome new difficulties." "The proper Method for inquiring after the properties of things," he added, in another letter, "is to deduce them from Experiments. And I told you that the Theory wch I propounded was evinced by me, *not by inferring tis thus because not otherwise,* that is not by deducing it onely from the confutation of contrary suppositions, but *by deriving it from Experiments concluding positively & directly.* The way therefore to examin it is by considering whether the experiments wch I propound do prove those parts of the Theory to wch they are applyed, or by prosecuting other experiments wch the Theory may suggest for its examination."

More than forty years later, when he was well past his seventieth year, Newton asserted the same position to distinguish himself from Leibniz. "The Philosophy which Mr. Newton in his *Principles* and *Optiques* has pursued is Experimental," he stated, referring to himself in the third person; "and it is not the Business of Experimental Philosophy to teach the Causes of things any further than they can be proved by Experiments. We are not to fill this Philosophy with Opinions which cannot be proved by Phaenomena. In this Philosophy Hypotheses have no place, unless as Conjectures or Questions proposed to be examined by Experiments. . . . And . . . one would wonder that Mr. Newton should be reflected upon for not explaining the Causes of Gravity and other Attractions by Hypotheses; as if it were a crime to content himself with Certainties and let Uncertainties alone." In his own age, this was a stance that differed from the prevailing one. It is, in general terms, the one modern science has adopted, and it is small wonder that Newton is seen by contemporary scientists as the archetype of the experimental, empirical scientist.

How familiar he looks, from a distance. Up close and examined in detail, how completely strange Newton's career appears—a career so unlike what we now take for granted that we would hardly recognize it as a career in science were we not convinced a priori that it must have been. "The past is like a foreign country," a character in the movie *The*

Go-Between remarked, "they do things differently there." Certainly they pursued science differently in the seventeenth century. Three features of Newton's career—three important features which differ profoundly from the normal career of a twentieth-century scientist who sees Newton as his model—illustrate how foreign the past indeed was.

Physical isolation is the first feature distinguishing past from present. People familiar with Newton's life are apt to object to such a characterization. He was, after all, President of the Royal Society for the final twenty-three years of his life and a fellow of the Society for nearly thirty-two years before that. Newton's relationship to the Royal Society can be misleading if it is not closely inspected. When he assumed its presidency, he had passed well beyond his age of scientific creativity; and during the earlier period when he was a fellow, he lived far away, separated from its activities and its members by sixty miles of impossible roads. With only the smallest exceptions, all of Newton's creative work, all of what we remember him for today, stemmed from his Cambridge years. Physical isolation characterized him in his Cambridge setting; it is necessary to understand him in that context.

Of Newton's isolation, it is hard to distinguish between factors that were purely personal and factors that were general and, therefore, offer some insight into scientific life in his day. Newton was a born recluse if ever one existed. As early as grammar school he found it difficult to get along with fellow students. It did not become any easier at the university, and his isolation only increased when he proceeded to a fellowship in Trinity College. It is striking that only one personal letter from Newton to one of his peers in Trinity exists, and there is some doubt that it was ever mailed. No letter at all from one of them to him is known. He was hardly mentioned by those who reflected on college life during the period when he was a fellow—this despite the fact that he had become the leading intellectual of the land by the time the reflections were set down.

Newton's strange and bizarre habits were the lone characteristics recorded about him. When he set out for dinner in the Hall, he would sometimes take the wrong turn, go out through the gate into the town, and then, when he realized something was wrong, return to his room rather than the Hall. When he did make it to dinner, he was apt to show up disheveled, dressed in the wrong gown, and then to sit there silently, lost in thought, while the meal remained on his plate uneaten. This last habit—about which a number of stories have come down—appeared an excessive peculiarity to the age. Cambridge was at that time going through a disastrous decline. Its dons, who no longer believed in the mission of the university and treated their fellowships as freeholds to be exploited for their personal benefit, happily surrendered to the attractions of the plate and the bottle, becoming, in the splendid phrase of

Roger North, wet epicures. They found Newton quite impossible to comprehend. He lived in Trinity College thirty-five years from the time of his admission as an undergraduate. During that time he did not form any close friendships except with his chamber fellow Wickins, and that relationship ended with a breach. After he left, Newton did not exchange a single personal letter with anyone he had known there, and he never returned to Cambridge for any purpose other than electioneering for a university seat in Parliament.

Even though all of the above is true, we can still not ignore the intellectual dimension of Newton's isolation. As an undergraduate he deliberately cut himself off from the established curriculum in order to pursue his own interests: mathematics, as he found it in the writings of Wallis, Viète, and Descartes; and the new natural philosophy, as he found it in Descartes, Galileo, Gassendi, and others. In following this course, Newton very nearly destroyed his prospects. If he wished to remain in the university, where alone he could have pursued the intellectual life from which his achievement sprang, he had to be elected to a scholarship in Trinity College. A scholarship was the necessary preliminary to a fellowship, and since he was a student in Trinity, a Trinity fellowship was the only one to which he could aspire. Even under the best of circumstances, the odds against a sizar (a student who supported himself by performing menial tasks in the college) were enormous. Every year approximately half the scholarships were reserved for a privileged clique of students from Westminster School. The younger sons and clients of powerful men secured most of the rest. The possibilities for Newton, a strange young man without evident connections and from a remote village in Lincolnshire, were hardly great.

10   Nevertheless, sometime less than a year before the election of 1664, the only one at which he would be eligible, Newton chose to throw over the established curriculum in order to pursue his own line of interests. There is a story, told by Newton in his old age, that he was sent to be examined in mathematics by Isaac Barrow. At this time Newton had mastered Descartes' geometry and was beginning to move beyond it toward his own discoveries. Barrow examined him on Euclid, however, and formed, as Newton recalled it, a tepid opinion of his knowledge of mathematics. Nevertheless, luck was on Newton's side. He was, in fact, not entirely without connections. Among the most senior fellows in the college was one Humphrey Babington, who not only hailed from Newton's corner of Lincolnshire but was the brother of the woman with whom he had boarded in Grantham. It appears likely that Babington was instrumental in his election. Although his early studies did not finally exclude him from a fellowship, his continuing interest in such things always formed a barrier that separated him from the rest of the college. One of Newton's strange habits, as they were later remembered,

was a tendency to draw geometric diagrams in the walks of the fellows' garden. The other fellows were awed as much as they were amused by their strange compatriot, and they carefully walked around the diagrams in order not to disturb them. It is not known if another fellow ever stopped to study them.

Within a year and a half of taking his bachelor's degree, Newton had invented calculus and recorded it in a definitive tract in the notebook that he called his Waste Book. By every indication we have, Newton carried out his education in mathematics and his program of research entirely on his own. At the time, as far as we know, no one at all was aware of his achievement. It was his isolation that set the stage for the destructive conflict with Leibniz half a century later, for initially Newton's accomplishments were not known to anyone, and during the following two decades they were known only within a small circle gathered around John Collins, the London mathematical enthusiast.

By the late 1660s, one man, Isaac Barrow, the Lucasian Professor of Mathematics at Cambridge, had become acquainted with Newton's work. As it happened, Barrow was then preparing to vacate the mathematics chair, and he secured Newton's nomination to succeed him. For his initial lectures, Newton chose the subject of optics, and the lectures served to emphasize his isolation anew. He had discovered a new property of one of the major phenomena of nature: the heterogeneity of light. Not only was the discovery unknown to anyone, but when he presented it in three series of lectures, they were as unknown as the discovery itself. There is no testimony of any kind that a single listener heard and understood what the new Lucasian Professor was presenting.

Optics did bring Newton's complete isolation to an end, however. His theory of colors had led him to the idea of a reflecting telescope to eliminate chromatic aberration, and he was proud enough of the telescope to show it around. Eventually the Royal Society in London heard about it and asked to see it, and ultimately Newton sent them a paper on his theory of colors early in 1672.

The moment Newton ended his isolation, he discovered how much he preferred it. His paper stimulated a modest number of questions and objections which he found it necessary to answer, and he quickly came to resent the intrusion on his time. Thus Newton was no sooner brought into communication with the scientific community, both of Britain and of Europe, than he wanted to sever the connection. He did finally succeed in doing so to a considerable degree and lived mostly in renewed isolation during the decade from the mid-1670s to the mid-1680s. He reinforced his isolation by turning almost entirely away from his studies in mathematics and physics to devote himself to alchemy and theology.

Newton's extraordinary intellectual capacity had become known, however, and letters intermittently intruded upon his isolation. In Au-

15

gust 1684, he received a visit from Edmund Halley. We must not overestimate the personal contact that resulted from the visit. Halley put one question to Newton: What would be the shape of the orbit followed by a planet moving in an inverse square force field? That question and all that it implied grasped Newton's attention and refused to let it go. It stimulated the process from which, two and a half years later, the *Principia* emerged. Once more the composition was carried out in isolation. Halley retired to London after he posed his question, made only two brief visits to Cambridge during the following thirty months, and refrained from imposing a burden of correspondence on Newton. The period between his visit and the completion of the manuscript constitutes the largest gap in our knowledge of Newton's adult life, for he had cut himself off from every contact in order to work out the consequences of his ideas alone. The investigation culminated in the book that, by its impact on the scientific world, ended his isolation once and for all. By 1687, however, Newton stood only a few years from the end of his creative intellectual activity, and nearly everything which has made his name immortal had already been accomplished.

Significant personal elements figured in Newton's isolation. He was reclusive by nature. In the early 1670s, after Barrow made Collins aware of Newton's mathematical abilities, Newton consented to Collins's publication of a solution to the annuity problem that he had written only if his, Newton's, name was left off. "It would perhaps increase my acquaintance," he told Collins, "ye thing wch I cheifly study to decline." Nevertheless, the issue stretches far beyond the limits of a personal idiosyncracy. With whom could he have communicated had he not been a recluse? In Britain there were perhaps four men: John Wallis of the previous generation; James Gregory and Christopher Wren of his own; and Edmund Halley of the following. All, for various reasons, would have been less than ideal collaborators. In the rest of Europe, Newton had indeed two scientific peers, Christiaan Huygens and Gottfried Wilhelm Leibniz. Obviously, as such a list implies, we deal here in part with the problem of genius, which is in short supply everywhere always. The short supply of genius does not exhaust the issue, however. The brevity of the list serves to remind us of what we too readily forget, that modern science was created in the seventeenth century by the philosophic rebellion of a tiny handful of men.

By the second half of the seventeenth century, these men were becoming numerous enough to form the first scientific societies. We need to remember how small those societies were. The *Académie Royale des Sciences* in Paris was created in 1666 with sixteen members to cover the entire range of scientific endeavor. The Royal Society in London was a popular organization instead of an exclusive one, and it became for a time a fad in London society, so that its membership swelled to around two hundred. While even two hundred is not an imposing number, it is still misleading as a guide to the size of the English scientific community. It is instructive to listen in briefly on a typical meeting of the Royal Society in the 1690s. John Van de Bembde solemnly informed the society that "cows piss drank to about a pint, will either purge or vomit with great Ease." You may think that he was summarily ejected, whether for indelicacy or irrelevancy. Not at all. The membership seized on the remark as the opportunity for a general discussion of bovine elixir, which was clearly the most stimulating part of the meeting. If we focus, not on the total membership of the Royal Society, but on the number of working scientists in its ranks, we find fewer than the sixteen that made up the Royal Academy. Relative isolation was an unavoidable aspect of the scientific revolution. Newton's reclusive habits only reinforced what would have been his lot in any case.

Physical isolation was of course not equivalent to intellectual isolation. Through the printed page, kindred spirits of more than one locale and more than one age could communicate with one another. Unencumbered as he was with endless committees, colloquia, and consultations, the seventeenth-century scientist had the opportunity to attend carefully to the printed page and to wrestle earnestly with what it presented. It may have been a more effective form of communication than the plethora of immediate contacts in which contemporary scientists of all sorts struggle desperately to preserve some sense of sustained endeavor.

A second distinctive feature of Newton's career was its philosophic breadth. By that phrase I mean to indicate the constant concern in his scientific work more with the total philosophy of nature than with the specific results of immediate investigations. Once again, those familiar with Newton are likely to object. *Opticks,* an experimental investigation of the heterogeneity of light and of the periodicity of some phenomena, especially appears to belie such a characterization. But, in response to the objection, let me call attention first of all to the *Principia.* The *Principia* presented more than the law of universal gravitation, and more than a new science of dynamics which entailed universal gravitation. What it presented, and consciously so, was a new philosophy of nature based on the principle of forces. "I wish we could derive the rest of the phenomena of Nature by the same kind of reasoning from mechanical principles," Newton stated in the preface, with reference to his explanation of the solar system from the concept of gravitational attraction, "for I am induced by many reasons to suspect that they may all depend upon certain forces by which the particles of bodies, by some causes hitherto unknown, are either mutually impelled towards one another, and cohere in regular figures, or are repelled and recede from one another. These forces being unknown, philosophers have hitherto attempted the search of Nature in vain; but

I hope the principles here laid down will afford some light either to this or some truer method of philosophy."

During the years that immediately followed the publication of the *Principia*, when Newton first put the *Opticks* together, he treated the work primarily as an exposition of the new philosophy in which he used optical phenomena further to demonstrate the existence of forces in nature. True, in the end, apparently to avoid controversy, he eliminated most of these features, so that the work he eventually published confined such matters mostly, though not entirely, to the Queries at the work's close. Nevertheless, he always saw his scientific work as so many aspects of a new natural philosophy, and the considerable number of followers who wrote popular versions of it in the early eighteenth century all presented it in such terms.

To appreciate this facet of Newton, it is necessary to comprehend his historical situation. When Newton enrolled in Cambridge in 1661, he was educated in a natural philosophy that was more than two thousand years old. The universities of medieval Europe had built themselves in the Aristotelian system. It was still being taught, and not only in Cambridge, when Newton began his university education. In England the Parliamentary statutes that prescribed the curricula of the universities required the study of Aristotle. Newton's first step in natural science was to rebel against the established Aristotelian philosophy and to embrace a new one. The rebellion coincided with his rejection of the standard curriculum, which I mentioned earlier. He was still an undergraduate. Somehow he had found the writings of the men of the previous generation who had offered a radical new approach to nature—among them, Descartes, Gassendi, and Hobbes. Historians call their philosophy (for they agreed on a common core of principles despite their differences on many details) the mechanical philosophy. It provided the intellectual framework of the scientific revolution. Although he did not date his notes, it was apparently in 1664 that Newton embraced the mechanical philosophy and in doing so inaugurated his scientific career.

He did not embrace it for long, however, for he quickly became dissatisfied with aspects of the mechanical philosophy. His dissatisfaction rested partly on religious grounds. Mechanical philosophers proposed, or appeared to propose, the autonomy of the material realm, and Newton decided that such was a program for atheism. In his revulsion, he found in alchemy a concept of nature more in harmony with the demands of religion, and alchemy was one of Newton's major enterprises during the years of silence before the *Principia*.

Alchemy is not a popular topic in many circles. Even to bring it up is to raise doubts in some minds that one is competent to talk about science at all. Newton's alchemical manuscripts are nevertheless authentic. There can be no doubt that he did devote himself to alchemy, and quite extensively. If the goal of history, including the history of science, is to present the past in its own terms to the best of our ability, and not merely to present it as a pale anticipation of the twentieth century, we cannot afford to ignore Newton's immersion in alchemy. We especially cannot afford to ignore its influence on his philosophy of nature, for it appears to have been primarily alchemy that led Newton toward the concept of forces.

The idea of forces was not a single, limited concept; it turned out in the end to involve the entire philosophy of nature. From the beginning, Newton's disenchantment with standard mechanical philosophy had not been solely religious. Mechanical philosophies generated an abundance of talk about the invisible mechanisms by which nature produces phenomena, but their mechanical models proved incapable of yielding exact quantitative results. The great advantage of forces in Newton's eyes was exactly their capacity to generate such results. As he contemplated their import, they promised to revise every corner of natural philosophy. Descartes had argued that nature is a plenum; although atomists rejected the plenum, they nevertheless thought of a universe well filled with matter mixed with dispersed voids. Newton depopulated the universe of matter as he filled it with forces. As he finally conceived of it, nature was an infinite void seasoned with the merest suggestion of solid matter. For example, he paid careful attention to the implications of relative densities. Gold, he argued, cannot be absolutely dense since thin leaves of gold are translucent. He assumed for the moment that gold is made up half of solid matter and half of voids. Gold is nineteen times denser than water; water therefore can contain only one-thirty-eighth part of solid matter. In fact, he continued, water must contain far less solid matter than that, for water readily transmits rays of light in straight lines at every angle. Water in turn cannot be compressed. Newton ended up with a picture of matter in the form of tenuous nets composed of punctiform particles held together by forces, and eighteenth-century Newtonians would argue that all of the solid matter in the universe could fit inside a nutshell.

Method was involved in the change as much as in the system of nature; the statement on method quoted above comes from a passage on his natural philosophy. Most general of all, his position embodied a new ideal of science as the exact mathematical description both of ideal patterns in nature and of the extent to which material embodiments deviate from the ideal. Even his conception of the relation of God to the physical universe was involved. The dispute with Leibniz over priority in the discovery of calculus, a dispute which reached its climax during the second decade of the eighteenth century, was equally a debate about the philosophy of nature in which all of the above issues were enmeshed.

Moreover, philosophic breadth was not a characteristic unique to

25

Newton. Its greatest interest lies in the fact that it was not. To be sure, Newton may have been of a more contemplative spirit than the average scientist of his time. Despite his reputation as an empirical scientist, he was perhaps the greatest speculator of the age. His meditations on the nature of things, ruminations that extended throughout the length of his career, furnished the warp on which he wove the fabric of his career in science. His concept of forces was only the most fruitful of a long series of speculations. Nevertheless, every member of the scientific community of the age, of necessity, also concerned himself with the philosophy of nature. Virtually without exception, they had been educated like Newton in the Aristotelian philosophy, and like him they had all gone through their own personal rebellions against it. Such was the very meaning of the mechanical philosophy—a new beginning, a determination to reshape natural philosophy according to new principles. In the early eighteenth century, in turn, no one could stand aloof from the controversy that separated Newtonian natural philosophy from the prevailing forms of the mechanical philosophy. It was precisely in this feature that Newton most diverged from the image of the archetype of the modern empirical scientist. It is indeed a distortion of language to call him a scientist at all. In his own eyes, he was a natural philosopher.

A third prominent feature of Newton's career was his theological depth. No one familiar with Newton is likely to protest against this, for Newton's religious concerns are well known. The General Scholium to the *Principia*, to cite only one example, hymns a rhapsody to God. "This most beautiful system of the sun, planets, and comets, could only proceed from the counsel and dominion of an intelligent and powerful Being. . . . This Being governs all things, not as the soul of the world, but as Lord over all; and on account of his dominion He is wont to be called *Lord God*, *pantokrator*, or *Universal Ruler*. . . . We know him only by his most wise and excellent contrivances of things, and final causes; we admire him for his perfections; but we reverence and adore him on account of his dominion. . . ." "When I wrote my treatise about our Systeme," he wrote to Richard Bentley, "I had an eye upon such Principles as might work wth considering men for the beleife of a Deity. . . ."

These passages and similar ones are well known. They do not, however, constitute Newton's theological depth. They are evidence, rather, of his personal piety. To find the theological depth we must turn to his private papers instead of his published works, to papers fully opened to public scrutiny only within the last decade. They reveal that Newton plunged into serious and sustained theological study in the early 1670s—not in his old age as is usually assumed, but during the full flower of his early manhood, when he was approaching the age of thirty. Together with alchemy, theology constituted the primary substance of his intellectual life from that time until the composition of the *Principia*. The Bible supplied part of his reading; Newton's extensive knowledge of it, which John Locke said was equaled by few whom he knew, undoubtedly derived from the intense study of this period. The Bible was by no means the only object of his attention. He took up the early fathers of the church and read and digested the writings of every father of any significance. He turned to the prophecies and invested immense energy in an interpretation of them. To be sure that he had the correct text of the Book of Revelation, he collated more than twenty versions of the Greek text. Since he regarded the prophecies as the core of the Bible and the key to the rest, he combed the Scriptures for supporting passages; and since he insisted on an exact correlation between prophecy and history, he devoted equal zeal to the history of the early Christian centuries. The prophecies took him into the study of Judaism. As part of that study he became interested in the plan of the Jewish temple. Newton was never interested in things only in a general way. He wanted to know the exact plan of the temple, and for that purpose he reconstructed four chapters of Ezekiel while he drew a detailed plan of the temple to accompany the text.

In such activities one may begin to sense the measure of Newton's theological depth. They do not yet indicate the full depth, however. Behind all his study of theology was a fundamental goal—an anguished reassessment of the whole Christian tradition. The initial stimulus to his theological reading was probably the requirement that bore upon Fellows of Trinity College to be ordained to the Anglican clergy within seven years of taking their M.A. degrees. Almost the first result of Newton's study was an impassable obstacle to ordination, for he quickly convinced himself that the dominant Christian tradition, Trinitarianism, was false. The doctrine of the Trinity, he believed, was more than false; it was a deliberate fraud foisted onto the church in the fourth century by deceitful and evil men pursuing their own selfish interests. Newton adopted the ancient belief of Arianism as his own theological position, a position that denied the full divinity of Christ. Trinitarianism stood at the center of his interpretation of the prophecies. It was the Great Apostasy foretold by God when men would fall away from the true worship into idolatry; the plagues and vials of wrath of the Apocalypse, corresponding to the barbarian invasions of the empire, were God's punishment on a stiff-necked people who had gone whoring after false gods. In a word, Newton was one of the more advanced heretics of his day. His constant concern to conceal opinions which would have led to ostracism, first from the university, and later from the government's service, furnished a basic theme throughout his life. The piety of the General Scholium was sincere. No one should question it. Nevertheless it concealed a reality more complicated than has generally been realized.

30   This feature of Newton's career was also a general characteristic of
the age. The constant references to God and to Christianity in the
writings of scientists, like those of Newton, are usually taken as testimonies to the piety of the age. They derived rather from the fact that
traditional piety had been called into question. Basil Willey has referred
to the seventeenth century's "touch of cold philosophy." It had dissipated the enchanted world of medieval Christianity before the very
eyes of scientists like Newton. They were unable to ignore this fact of
their existence, as unsettling a piece of reality as one can readily imagine.
Not many followed Newton into heterodoxy, but the endless refutations
of atheism and proofs of the existence of God with which they filled
their books adequately testify that they were aware of the same motives
that animated Newton's lifelong inquiry into the true religion. When
Robert Boyle died in 1691, after soundly refuting atheism at least fifty
times, he left part of his fortune to endow a series of lectures. What were
the lectures to do? Refute atheism still more. When during the previous
thousand years of Western history had anyone thought that was necessary? Thinkers of the late seventeenth century knew only too well that
the ground on which Christianity stood was shifting. In one way or
another, most of them took account of the new circumstances. Many
things contributed to Willey's touch of cold philosophy, but the birth
of modern science was not the least among its sources. No wonder
theological depth was a common feature of scientists (or natural philosophers) such as Newton.

          Let us now turn the three chief characteristics of Newton's career
back on ourselves and use them as a yardstick to measure the contemporary scientific community. No one, I suspect, would suggest that physical
isolation is a normal feature of a twentieth-century scientist. Every year
throughout the Western and Communist worlds there are meetings,
such as those of the AAAS,[1] where thousands of scientists come together; increasingly they are spreading into the third world as well. I
teach at Indiana University, a distinguished institution but not, in the
opinion of any informed judge, a leading center of contemporary science. Nevertheless, the scientific community at Indiana University is
larger than the whole of Europe could have mustered at any time during
the seventeenth century. There are several other groups of equal size in
the state of Indiana and well over fifty centers in the state where
scientists can be and are in immediate contact with trained and interested colleagues. This situation is also normal throughout the Western
and Communist worlds. When one adds to the scientists the considerable army of technical experts called into being by modern science—an
army which had no counterpart in the seventeenth century—the scientific community emerges as a significant portion of the working popula-

1. American Association for the Advancement of Science.

tion. The small handful of natural philosophers who created the scientific revolution has burgeoned into a sociological phenomenon of immense scope.

As for philosophic breadth, it is no longer required. It is true of some contemporary scientists; it is not required of any one—that is, it is no longer necessary for every scientist constantly to consider the fundamental issues of natural philosophy. Although our century has witnessed a profound revision of the conception of nature, virtually no one in the scientific community considers that the system as a whole is in serious question, and it is perfectly proper for scientists to ignore the problems that occupied Newton in order to work at clarifying details of the system. Thus a typical issue of the *Physical Review* contains articles on "Three-body Lippmann-Schwinger Equations," "Influence of Vibrations of Gas Molecules on Neutron Reaction Cross Sections," "Core Coupled States in ^{145}Eu," and "Decays of Mass-separated ^{139}Xe and ^{139}Cs," together with many more in a similar vein. The articles all assume the existence of a coherent philosophy of nature. Without bothering themselves about such questions, their authors devote themselves, without manifest anxiety, to getting on with the work of science.

Theological depth has become for most scientists irrelevant. There are of course a number of scientists as pious as any in the seventeenth century; a like number are equally committed to articulate atheism. For most scientists, however, the issue has ceased to have any meaning. In the three centuries that have passed since Newton published the *Principia,* Christianity and science have exchanged roles, and natural science today occupies the position in Western civilization that Christianity once held. Theologians are now the small handful. Once theology was queen of all the sciences. We have redefined what the word *science* means, and every other intellectual discipline now measures itself against the enterprise that carries the word in its new meaning as its name.

Thus the scientific career of Isaac Newton enables us to appreciate the full extent to which natural science has been the most successful and significant endeavor of the modern world, reshaping first the intellectual structure of the West, then the economic system, and finally society itself. There is no way to avoid the conclusion: the scientists have inherited the earth. The rest of us are waiting breathlessly to see what they will do with it.

THE READER

1. *Westfall states that Isaac Newton's career had three distinguishing characteristics. What are they? How does Newton's career differ from a typical career in science today, as given in Westfall's concluding paragraphs? Is this difference good or bad, in the view of the author? In your view?*

2. How did the three distinguishing features of Newton's career contribute to or detract from the work he did in science? What, by the way, does science owe to Newton?

3. What view of science does the author propose in his closing paragraph? Do you subscribe to that view? Why, or why not?

THE WRITER

1. What role do the three distinguishing characteristics of Newton's career play in the essay's organization?

2. Does the author succeed in making Newton come alive as a person? If so, by what particular means does he accomplish this? If not, what might he have done to bring out Newton as a person?

3. Write a brief character sketch of Newton, based on the information in this essay. What additional information might it have been useful to have?

Jacob Bronowski

THE NATURE OF SCIENTIFIC REASONING

What is the insight in which the scientist tries to see into nature? Can it indeed be called either imaginative or creative? To the literary man the question may seem merely silly. He has been taught that science is a large collection of facts; and if this is true, then the only seeing which scientists need to do is, he supposes, seeing the facts. He pictures them, the colorless professionals of science, going off to work in the morning into the universe in a neutral, unexposed state. They then expose themselves like a photographic plate. And then in the darkroom or laboratory they develop the image, so that suddenly and startlingly it appears, printed in capital letters, as a new formula for atomic energy.

Men who have read Balzac and Zola[1] are not deceived by the claims of these writers that they do no more than record the facts. The readers of Christopher Isherwood[2] do not take him literally when he writes "I am a camera." Yet the same readers solemnly carry with them from their schooldays this foolish picture of the scientist fixing by some mechanical process the facts of nature. I have had of all people a historian tell me

First delivered as a lecture at the Massachusetts Institute of Technology in 1953; reprinted as part of Chapter One of *Science and Human Values* (1956).

1. Honoré de Balzac and Émile Zola, nineteenth-century French novelists.   2. Modern English novelist and playwright.

that science is a collection of facts, and his voice had not even the ironic rasp of one filing cabinet reproving another.

It seems impossible that this historian had ever studied the beginnings of a scientific discovery. The Scientific Revolution can be held to begin in the year 1543 when there was brought to Copernicus, perhaps on his deathbed, the first printed copy of the book he had finished about a dozen years earlier. The thesis of this book is that the earth moves around the sun. When did Copernicus go out and record this fact with his camera? What appearance in nature prompted his outrageous guess? And in what odd sense is this guess to be called a neutral record of fact?

Less than a hundred years after Copernicus, Kepler published (between 1609 and 1619) the three laws which describe the paths of the planets. The work of Newton and with it most of our mechanics spring from these laws. They have a solid, matter-of-fact sound. For example, Kepler says that if one squares the year of a planet, one gets a number which is proportional to the cube of its average distance from the sun. Does anyone think that such a law is found by taking enough readings and then squaring and cubing everything in sight? If he does, then, as a scientist, he is doomed to a wasted life; he has as little prospect of making a scientific discovery as an electronic brain has.

It was not this way that Copernicus and Kepler thought, or that scientists think today. Copernicus found that the orbits of the planets would look simpler if they were looked at from the sun and not from the earth. But he did not in the first place find this by routine calculation. His first step was a leap of imagination—to lift himself from the earth, and put himself wildly, speculatively into the sun. "The earth conceives from the sun," he wrote; and "the sun rules the family of stars." We catch in his mind an image, the gesture of the virile man standing in the sun, with arms outstretched, overlooking the planets. Perhaps Copernicus took the picture from the drawings of the youth with outstretched arms which the Renaissance teachers put into their books on the proportions of the body. Perhaps he had seen Leonardo's drawings of his loved pupil Salai. I do not know. To me, the gesture of Copernicus, the shining youth looking outward from the sun, is still vivid in a drawing which William Blake in 1780 based on all these: the drawing which is usually called *Glad Day*.

Kepler's mind, we know, was filled with just such fanciful analogies; and we know what they were. Kepler wanted to relate the speeds of the planets to the musical intervals. He tried to fit the five regular solids into their orbits. None of these likenesses worked, and they have been forgotten; yet they have been and they remain the stepping stones of every creative mind. Kepler felt for his laws by way of metaphors, he searched mystically for likenesses with what he knew in every strange corner of nature. And when among these guesses he hit upon his laws, he did not

5

think of their numbers as the balancing of a cosmic bank account, but as a revelation of the unity in all nature. To us, the analogies by which Kepler listened for the movement of the planets in the music of the spheres are farfetched. Yet are they more so than the wild leap by which Rutherford and Bohr in our own century found a model for the atom in, of all places, the planetary system?

No scientific theory is a collection of facts. It will not even do to call a theory true or false in the simple sense in which every fact is either so or not so. The Epicureans held that matter is made of atoms two thousand years ago and we are now tempted to say that their theory was true. But if we do so we confuse their notion of matter with our own. John Dalton in 1808 first saw the structure of matter as we do today, and what he took from the ancients was not their theory but something richer, their image: the atom. Much of what was in Dalton's mind was as vague as the Greek notion, and quite as mistaken. But he suddenly gave life to the new facts of chemistry and the ancient theory together, by fusing them to give what neither had: a coherent picture of how matter is linked and built up from different kinds of atoms. The act of fusion is the creative act.

All science is the search for unity in hidden likenesses. The search may be on a grand scale, as in the modern theories which try to link the fields of gravitation and electromagnetism. But we do not need to be browbeaten by the scale of science. There are discoveries to be made by snatching a small likeness from the air too, if it is bold enough. In 1935 the Japanese physicist Hideki Yukawa wrote a paper which can still give heart to a young scientist. He took as his starting point the known fact that waves of light can sometimes behave as if they were separate pellets. From this he reasoned that the forces which hold the nucleus of an atom together might sometimes also be observed as if they were solid pellets. A schoolboy can see how thin Yukawa's analogy is, and his teacher would be severe with it. Yet Yukawa without a blush calculated the mass of the pellet he expected to see, and waited. He was right; his meson was found, and a range of other mesons, neither the existence nor the nature of which had been suspected before. The likeness had borne fruit.

The scientist looks for order in the appearances of nature by exploring such likenesses. For order does not display itself of itself; if it can be said to be there at all, it is not there for the mere looking. There is no way of pointing a finger or camera at it; order must be discovered and, in a deep sense, it must be created. What we see, as we see it, is mere disorder.

This point has been put trenchantly in a fable by Karl Popper. Suppose that someone wished to give his whole life to science. Suppose that he therefore sat down, pencil in hand, and for the next twenty, thirty, forty years recorded in notebook after notebook everything that he could observe. He may be supposed to leave out nothing: today's humidity, the racing results, the level of cosmic radiation and the stockmarket prices and the look of Mars, all would be there. He would have compiled the most careful record of nature that has ever been made; and, dying in the calm certainty of a life well spent, he would of course leave his notebooks to the Royal Society. Would the Royal Society thank him for the treasure of a lifetime of observation? It would not. The Royal Society would treat his notebooks exactly as the English bishops have treated Joanna Southcott's box.[3] It would refuse to open them at all, because it would know without looking that the notebooks contain only a jumble of disorderly and meaningless items.

Science finds order and meaning in our experience, and sets about this in quite a different way. It sets about it as Newton did in the story which he himself told in his old age, and of which the schoolbooks give only a caricature. In the year 1665, when Newton was twenty-two, the plague broke out in southern England, and the University of Cambridge was closed. Newton therefore spent the next eighteen months at home, removed from traditional learning, at a time when he was impatient for knowledge and, in his own phrase, "I was in the prime of my age for invention." In this eager, boyish mood, sitting one day in the garden of his widowed mother, he saw an apple fall. So far the books have the story right; we think we even know the kind of apple; tradition has it that it was a Flower of Kent. But now they miss the crux of the story. For what struck the young Newton at the sight was not the thought that the apple must be drawn to the earth by gravity; that conception was older than Newton. What struck him was the conjecture that the same force of gravity, which reaches to the top of the tree, might go on reaching out beyond the earth and its air, endlessly into space. Gravity might reach the moon: this was Newton's new thought; and it might be gravity which holds the moon in her orbit. There and then he calculated what force from the earth (falling off as the square of the distance) would hold the moon, and compared it with the known force of gravity at tree height. The forces agreed; Newton says laconically, "I found them answer pretty nearly." Yet they agreed only nearly: the likeness and the approximation go together, for no likeness is exact. In Newton's science modern science is full grown.

It grows from a comparison. It has seized a likeness between two unlike appearances; for the apple in the summer garden and the grave

3. Southcott was a nineteenth-century English farm servant who claimed to be a prophetess. She left behind a box which was to be opened in a time of national emergency in the presence of all the English bishops. In 1927, a bishop agreed to officiate; when the box was opened, it was found to contain only some odds and ends.

1012 JACOB BRONOWSKI

moon overhead are surely as unlike in their movements as two things can be. Newton traced in them two expressions of a single concept, gravitation: and the concept (and the unity) are in that sense his free creation. The progress of science is the discovery at each step of a new order which gives unity to what had long seemed unlike.

* * *

THE READER

1. In his opening paragraph, Bronowski pictures what the "literary man," or perhaps the ordinary nonscientist, thinks of as the nature of science. Is this a fair representation of the layman's view? What features of science or of the presentation of science might contribute to the development of that view? How does the process depicted in that paragraph compare with the actual activity of a scientist, as described in the account of his own work given by Lorenz in "The Taming of the Shrew" (p. 588) or in the account of Kepler given by Koestler in "Gravity and the Holy Ghost" (p. 988)?
2. Bronowski recounts the famous story of Newton and the apple. What general principle about science is the author exemplifying in this story?
3. In "The Reach of Imagination" (p. 196), Bronowski shows the work of imagination in Newton's thinking of the moon as a huge ball, thrown hard, and in Galileo's imaginary experiment with unequal weights. In what particular ways do these examples relate to and supplement Bronowski's remarks on science in "The Nature of Scientific Reasoning"?

THE WRITER

1. On pp. 1008–1009, Bronowski says: "I have had of all people a historian tell me that science is a collection of facts, and his voice had not even the ironic rasp of one filing cabinet reproving another." Is that image appropriate to the point he wants to make? Can you find other such uses of language in the selection?
2. In his fourth paragraph, Bronowski indicates that an electronic brain has little or no chance of making a scientific discovery. Do you agree? Why, or why not? Develop your answer in a brief essay.
3. Write an essay comparing Bronowski's description of the process of science with that given by Kuhn in "The Route to Normal Science" (p. 1033). In what respects are the views of these authors similar? Do they differ in any important ways? What sorts of language does each of them use to convey his thoughts? How would you account for differences in tone and usage?

Stephen Jay Gould
DARWIN'S MIDDLE ROAD

"We began to sail up the narrow strait lamenting," narrates Odysseus. "For on the one hand lay Scylla, with twelve feet all dangling down; and six necks exceeding long, and on each a hideous head, and therein three rows of teeth set thick and close, full of black death. And on the other mighty Charybdis sucked down the salt sea water. As often as she belched it forth, like a cauldron on a great fire she would seethe up through all her troubled deeps." Odysseus managed to swerve around Charybdis, but Scylla grabbed six of his finest men and devoured them in his sight—"the most pitiful thing mine eyes have seen of all my travail in searching out the paths of the sea."

False lures and dangers often come in pairs in our legends and metaphors—consider the frying pan and the fire, or the devil and the deep blue sea. Prescriptions for avoidance either emphasize a dogged steadiness—the straight and narrow of Christian evangelists—or an averaging between unpleasant alternatives—the golden mean of Aristotle. The idea of steering a course between undesirable extremes emerges as a central prescription for a sensible life.

The nature of scientific creativity is both a perennial topic of discussion and a prime candidate for seeking a golden mean. The two extreme positions have not been directly competing for allegiance of the unwary. They have, rather, replaced each other sequentially, with one now in the ascendency, the other eclipsed.

The first—inductivism—held that great scientists are primarily great observers and patient accumulators of information. For new and significant theory, the inductivists claimed, can only arise from a firm foundation of facts. In this architectural view, each fact is a brick in a structure built without blueprints. Any talk or thought about theory (the completed building) is fatuous and premature before the bricks are set. Inductivism once commanded great prestige within science, and even represented an "official" position of sorts, for it touted, however falsely, the utter honesty, complete objectivity, and almost automatic nature of scientific progress towards final and incontrovertible truth.

Yet, as its critics so rightly claimed, inductivism also depicted science as a heartless, almost inhuman discipline offering no legitimate place to quirkiness, intuition, and all the other subjective attributes adhering to our vernacular notion of genius. Great scientists, the critics claimed, are

5

From *The Panda's Thumb* (1980). First appeared in *Natural History* (Aug.–Sept. 1977).

distinguished more by their powers of hunch and synthesis, than their skill in experiment or observation. The criticisms of inductivism are certainly valid and I welcome its dethroning during the past thirty years as a necessary prelude to better understanding. Yet, in attacking it so strongly, some critics have tried to substitute an alternative equally extreme and unproductive in its emphasis on the essential subjectivity of creative thought. In this "eureka" view, creativity is an ineffable something, accessible only to persons of genius. It arises like a bolt of lightning, unanticipated, unpredictable and unanalyzable—but the bolts strike only a few special people. We ordinary mortals must stand in awe and thanks. (The name refers, of course, to the legendary story of Archimedes running naked through the streets of Syracuse shouting eureka [I have discovered it] when water displaced by his bathing body washed the scales abruptly from his eyes and suggested a method for measuring volumes.)

I am equally disenchanted by both these opposing extremes. Inductivism reduces genius to dull, rote operations; eurekaism grants it an inaccessible status more in the domain of intrinsic mystery than in a realm where we might understand and learn from it. Might we not marry the good features of each view, and abandon both the elitism of eurekaism and the pedestrian qualities of inductivism? May we not acknowledge the personal and subjective character of creativity, but still comprehend it as a mode of thinking that emphasizes or exaggerates capacities sufficiently common to all of us that we may at least understand if not hope to imitate?

In the hagiography of science, a few men hold such high positions that all arguments must apply to them if they are to have any validity. Charles Darwin, as the principal saint of evolutionary biology, has therefore been presented both as an inductivist and as a primary example of eurekaism. I will attempt to show that these interpretations are equally inadequate, and that recent scholarship on Darwin's own odyssey towards the theory of natural selection supports an intermediate position.

So great was the prestige of inductivism in his own day, that Darwin himself fell under its sway and, as an old man, falsely depicted his youthful accomplishments in its light. In an autobiography, written as a lesson in morality for his children and not intended for publication, he penned some famous lines that misled historians for nearly a hundred years. Describing his path to the theory of natural selection, he claimed: "I worked on true Baconian principles, and without any theory collected facts on a wholesale scale."[1]

The inductivist interpretation focuses on Darwin's five years aboard

---

1. Francis Bacon (1561–1626), English philosopher, statesman, and essayist, and the first apostle of inductivism.

the *Beagle* and explains his transition from a student for the ministry to the nemesis of preachers as the result of his keen powers of observation applied to the whole world. Thus, the traditional story goes, Darwin's eyes opened wider and wider as he saw, in sequence, the bones of giant South American fossil mammals, the turtles and finches of the Galapagos, and the marsupial fauna of Australia. The truth of evolution and its mechanism of natural selection crept up gradually upon him as he sifted facts in a sieve of utter objectivity.

The inadequacies of this tale are best illustrated by the falsity of its conventional premier example—the so-called Darwin's finches of the Galapagos. We now know that although these birds share a recent and common ancestry on the South American mainland, they have radiated into an impressive array of species on the outlying Galapagos. Few terrestrial species manage to cross the wide oceanic barrier between South America and the Galapagos. But the fortunate migrants often find a sparsely inhabited world devoid of the competitors that limit their opportunities on the crowded mainland. Hence, the finches evolved into roles normally occupied by other birds and developed their famous set of adaptations for feeding—seed crushing, insect eating, even grasping and manipulating a cactus needle to dislodge insects from plants. Isolation—both of the islands from the mainland and among the islands themselves—provided an opportunity for separation, independent adaptation, and speciation.

According to the traditional view, Darwin discovered these finches, correctly inferred their history, and wrote the famous lines in his notebook: "If there is the slightest foundation for these remarks the zoology of Archipelagoes will be worth examining; for such facts would undermine the stability of Species." But, as with so many heroic tales from Washington's cherry tree to the piety of Crusaders, hope rather than truth motivates the common reading. Darwin found the finches to be sure. But he didn't recognize them as variants of a common stock. In fact, he didn't even record the island of discovery for many of them—some of his labels just read "Galapagos Islands." So much for his immediate recognition of the role of isolation in the formation of new species. He reconstructed the evolutionary tale only after his return to London, when a British Museum ornithologist correctly identified all the birds as finches.

The famous quotation from his notebook refers to Galapagos tortoises and to the claim of native inhabitants that they can "at once pronounce from which Island any Tortoise may have been brought" from subtle differences in size and shape of body and scales. This is a statement of different, and much reduced, order from the traditional tale of finches. For the finches are true and separate species—a living example of evolution. The subtle differences among tortoises represent minor geographic

10

variation within a species. It is a jump in reasoning, albeit a valid one as we now know, to argue that such small differences can be amplified to produce a new species. All creationists, after all, acknowledged geographic variation (consider human races), but argued that it could not proceed beyond the rigid limits of a created archetype.

I don't wish to downplay the pivotal influence of the *Beagle* voyage on Darwin's career. It gave him space, freedom and endless time to think in his favored mode of independent self-stimulation. (His ambivalence towards university life, and his middling performance there by conventional standards, reflected his unhappiness with a curriculum of received wisdom.) He writes from South America in 1834: "I have not one clear idea about cleavage, stratification, lines of upheaval. I have no books, which tell me much and what they do I cannot apply to what I see. In consequence I draw my own conclusions, and most gloriously ridiculous ones they are." The rocks and plants and animals that he saw did provoke him to the crucial attitude of doubt—midwife of all creativity. Sydney, Australia—1836. Darwin wonders why a rational God would create so many marsupials on Australia since nothing about its climate or geography suggests any superiority for pouches: "I had been lying on a sunny bank and was reflecting on the strange character of the animals of this country as compared to the rest of the World. An unbeliever in everything beyond his own reason might exclaim, 'Surely two distinct Creators must have been at work.' "

Nonetheless, Darwin returned to London without an evolutionary theory. He suspected the truth of evolution, but had no mechanism to explain it. Natural selection did not arise from any direct reading of the *Beagle's* facts, but from two subsequent years of thought and struggle as reflected in a series of remarkable notebooks that have been unearthed and published during the past twenty years. In these notebooks, we see Darwin testing and abandoning a number of theories and pursuing a multitude of false leads—so much for his later claim about recording facts with an empty mind. He read philosophers, poets, and economists, always searching for meaning and insight—so much for the notion that natural selection arose inductively from the *Beagle's* facts. Later, he labelled one notebook as "full of metaphysics on morals."

15   Yet if this tortuous path belies the Scylla of inductivism, it has engendered an equally simplistic myth—the Charybdis of eurekaism. In his maddeningly misleading autobiography, Darwin does record a eureka and suggests that natural selection struck him as a sudden, serendipitous flash after more than a year of groping frustration:

> In October 1838, that is, fifteen months after I had begun my systematic inquiry, I happened to read for amusement Malthus on Population,[2] and

2. Thomas Malthus, whose work on population was published under several titles between 1798 and 1817.

being well prepared to appreciate the struggle for existence which every-where goes on from long-continued observation of the habits of animals and plants, it at once struck me that under these circumstances favorable variations would tend to be preserved, and unfavorable ones to be de-stroyed. The result of this would be the formation of new species. Here, then, I had at last got a theory by which to work.

Yet, again, the notebooks belie Darwin's later recollections—in this case by their utter failure to record, at the time it happened, any special exultation over his Malthusian insight. He inscribes it as a fairly short and sober entry without a single exclamation point, though he habitually used two or three in moments of excitement. He did not drop everything and reinterpret a confusing world in its light. On the very next day, he wrote an even longer passage on the sexual curiosity of primates.

The theory of natural selection arose neither as a workmanlike induc-tion from nature's facts, nor as a mysterious bolt from Darwin's sub-conscious, triggered by an accidental reading of Malthus. It emerged instead as the result of a conscious and productive search, proceeding in a ramifying but ordered manner, and utilizing both the facts of natural history and an astonishingly broad range of insights from dispar-ate disciplines far from his own. Darwin trod the middle path between inductivism and eurekaism. His genius is neither pedestrian nor inacces-sible.

Darwinian scholarship has exploded since the centennial of the *Ori-gin* [3] in 1959. The publication of Darwin's notebooks and the attention devoted by several scholars to the two crucial years between the *Beagle's* docking and the demoted Malthusian insight has clinched the argument for a "middle path" theory of Darwin's creativity. Two particularly important works focus on the broadest and narrowest scales. Howard E. Gruber's masterful intellectual and psychological biography of this phase in Darwin's life, *Darwin on Man,* traces all the false leads and turning points in Darwin's search. Gruber shows that Darwin was continually proposing, testing, and abandoning hypotheses, and that he never sim-ply collected facts in a blind way. He began with a fanciful theory involving the idea that new species arise with a prefixed life span, and worked his way gradually, if fitfully, towards an idea of extinction by competition in a world of struggle. He recorded no exultation upon reading Malthus, because the jigsaw puzzle was only missing a piece or two at the time.

Silvan S. Schweber has reconstructed, in detail as minute as the record will allow, Darwin's activities during the few weeks before Malthus (The Origin of the *Origin* Revisited, *Journal of the History of Biology,* 1977). He argues that the final pieces arose not from new facts in natural history, but from Darwin's intellectual wanderings in distant fields. In

3. *The Origin of Species* (1859).

particular, he read a long review of social scientist and philosopher Auguste Comte's most famous work, the *Cours de philosophie positive.* [4] He was particularly struck by Comte's insistence that a proper theory be predictive and at least potentially quantitative. He then turned to Dugald Stewart's *On the Life and Writing of Adam Smith,* and imbibed the basic belief of the Scottish economists that theories of overall social structure must begin by analyzing the unconstrained actions of individuals. (Natural selection is, above all, a theory about the struggle of individual organisms for success in reproduction.) Then, searching for quantification, he read a lengthy analysis of work by the most famous statistician of his time—the Belgian Adolphe Quetelet. In the review of Quetelet, he found, among other things, a forceful statement of Malthus's quantitative claim—that population would grow geometrically and food supplies only arithmetically, thus guaranteeing an intense struggle for existence. In fact, Darwin had read the Malthusian statement several times before; but only now was he prepared to appreciate its significance. Thus, he did not turn to Malthus by accident, and he already knew what it contained. His "amusement," we must assume, consisted only in a desire to read in its original formulation the familiar statement that had so impressed him in Quetelet's secondary account.

20   In reading Schweber's detailed account of the moments preceding Darwin's formulation of natural selection, I was particularly struck by the absence of deciding influence from his own field of biology. The immediate precipitators were a social scientist, an economist, and a statistician. If genius has any common denominator, I would propose breadth of interest and the ability to construct fruitful analogies between fields.

In fact, I believe that the theory of natural selection should be viewed as an extended analogy—whether conscious or unconscious on Darwin's part I do not know—to the laissez faire economics of Adam Smith. The essence of Smith's argument is a paradox of sorts: if you want an ordered economy providing maximal benefits to all, then let individuals compete and struggle for their own advantages. The result, after appropriate sorting and elimination of the inefficient, will be a stable and harmonious polity. Apparent order arises naturally from the struggle among individuals, not from predestined principles or higher control. Dugald Stewart epitomized Smith's system in the book Darwin read:

> The most effective plan for advancing a people . . . is by allowing every man, as long as he observes the rules of justice, to pursue his own interest in his own way, and to bring both his industry and his capital into the freest competition with those of his fellow citizens. Every system of policy which endeavors . . . to draw towards a particular species of industry a greater

4. *Course in Positivist Philosophy* (1830–42).

share of the capital of the society than would naturally go to it . . . is, in reality, subversive of the great purpose which it means to promote.

As Schweber states: "The Scottish analysis of society contends that the combined effect of individual actions results in the institutions upon which society is based, and that such a society is a stable and evolving one and functions without a designing and directing mind."

We know that Darwin's uniqueness does not reside in his support for the idea of evolution—scores of scientists had preceded him in this. His special contribution rests upon his documentation and upon the novel character of his theory about how evolution operates. Previous evolutionists had proposed unworkable schemes based on internal perfecting tendencies and inherent directions. Darwin advocated a natural and testable theory based on immediate interaction among individuals (his opponents considered it heartlessly mechanistic). The theory of natural selection is a creative transfer to biology of Adam Smith's basic argument for a rational economy: the balance and order of nature does not arise from a higher, external (divine) control, or from the existence of laws operating directly upon the whole, but from struggle among individuals for their own benefits (in modern terms, for the transmission of their genes to future generations through differential success in reproduction).

Many people are distressed to hear such an argument. Does it not compromise the integrity of science if some of its primary conclusions originate by analogy from contemporary politics and culture rather than from data of the discipline itself? In a famous letter to Engels, Karl Marx identified the similarities between natural selection and the English social scene:

> It is remarkable how Darwin recognizes among beasts and plants his English society with its division of labor, competition, opening up of new markets, 'invention,' and the Malthusian 'struggle for existence.' It is Hobbes' *bellum omnium contra omnes* (the war of all against all).[5]

Yet Marx was a great admirer of Darwin—and in this apparent paradox lies resolution. For reasons involving all the themes I have emphasized here—that inductivism is inadequate, that creativity demands breadth, and that analogy is a profound source of insight—great thinkers cannot be divorced from their social background. But the source of an idea is one thing; its truth or fruitfulness is another. The psychology and utility of discovery are very different subjects indeed. Darwin may have cribbed the idea of natural selection from economics, but it may still be right. As the German socialist Karl Kautsky wrote in 1902: "The fact that an idea emanates from a particular class, or accords with their interests, of

5. From the English philosopher Thomas Hobbes' *Leviathan* (1651).

course proves nothing as to its truth or falsity." In this case, it is ironic that Adam Smith's system of laissez faire does not work in his own domain of economics, for it leads to oligopoly and revolution, rather than to order and harmony. Struggle among individuals does, however, seem to be the law of nature.

Many people use such arguments about social context to ascribe great insights primarily to the indefinable phenomenon of good luck. Thus, Darwin was lucky to be born rich, lucky to be on the *Beagle,* lucky to live amidst the ideas of his age, lucky to trip over Parson Malthus— essentially little more than a man in the right place at the right time. Yet, when we read of his personal struggle to understand, the breadth of his concerns and study, and the directedness of his search for a mechanism of evolution, we understand why Pasteur made his famous quip that fortune favors the prepared mind. [6]

6. Louis Pasteur (1822–95): French chemist.

Evelyn Fox Keller

WOMEN IN SCIENCE: A SOCIAL ANALYSIS

Are women's minds different from men's minds? In spite of the women's movement, the age-old debate centering around this question continues. We are surrounded by evidence of *de facto* differences between men's and women's intellects—in the problems that interest them, in the ways they try to solve those problems, and in the professions they choose. Even though it has become fashionable to view such differences as environmental in origin, the temptation to seek an explanation in terms of innate differences remains a powerful one.

Perhaps the area in which this temptation is strongest is in science. Even those of us who would like to argue for intellectual equality are hard pressed to explain the extraordinarily meager representation of women in science, particularly in the upper echelons. Some would argue that the near absence of great women scientists demonstrates that women don't have the minds for true scientific creativity. While most of us would recognize the patent fallacies of this argument, it nevertheless causes us considerable discomfort. After all, the doors of the scientific establishment appear to have been open to women for some time now—shouldn't we begin to see more women excelling?

In the last fifty years the institutional barriers against women in science have been falling. During most of that time, the percentage of

First appeared in *Harvard Magazine* (Oct. 1974).

women scientists has declined, although recent years have begun to show an upswing (Table 1). Of those women who do become scientists, few are represented in the higher academic ranks (Table 2). In order to have a proper understanding of these data, it is necessary to review the many influences that operate. I would like to argue that the convenient explanation that men's minds are intrinsically different from women's is not only unwarranted by the evidence, but in fact reflects a mythology that is in itself a major contribution to the phenomena observed.

As a woman scientist, I have often pondered these questions, particularly at those times when my commitment to science seemed most precarious. Noticing that almost every other woman I had known in science had experienced similar crises of commitment, I sought to explain my ambivalence by concluding that science as a profession is not as gratifying for women as it is for men, and that the reasons for this are to be found in the intrinsic nature of women and science. Several years ago, I endeavored to find out how general my own experiences were. In studying the statistics of success and failure for women in the professions, I indeed found that women fared less well in science than in other professions, although the picture that emerged seemed fairly bleak for all of us.

I collected these data during a leave of absence I had taken to accom-

5

TABLE 1

PERCENTAGE OF PH.D.'S EARNED BY WOMEN,
1920–1970

	1920–29	1940–49	1950–59	1960–69
Physics and Astronomy	5.9	4.2	2.0	2.2
Biological Sciences	19.5	15.7	11.8	15.1
Mathematics	14.5	10.7	5.0	5.7
Psychology	29.4	24.1	14.8	20.7

Source: National Research Council.

TABLE 2

PERCENTAGE REPRESENTATION OF WOMEN, BY RANK,
IN 20 LEADING UNIVERSITIES
(1962)

	Instructor	Assistant Professor	Associate Professor	Professor
Physics	5.6	1.2	1.3	0.9
Biological Sciences	16.3	7.1	6.7	1.3
Mathematics	16.7	10.1	7.3	0.4
Psychology	8.3	10.4	11.1	2.7

Source: J. B. Parrish. A. A. U. W. Journal, 55, 99.

pany my husband to California. At the same time, I was also engaged in completing work I had begun the year before with a (male) colleague—work that seemed less and less compelling as the year wore on. Each week I would receive an enthusiastic telephone call from my colleague, reporting new information and responses he had received from workers he had met while delivering invited lectures on this work. At some point it occurred to me that perhaps there was a relation between my declining interest and isolation on the one hand, and his growing enthusiasm and public recognition on the other. Over the course of the year, he had received a score or more invitations to speak about this work, while I had received none. It began to dawn on me that there were far simpler explanations for both the observations I had made privately and the data I was collecting than that of intrinsic differences between the sexes.

I began to realize, for example, that had I been less isolated and more rewarded, my enthusiasm would have been correspondingly greater—a recognition that has been amply corroborated by my subsequent experience. Upon further reflection, I became aware of how much my own, and other similar, attitudes are influenced by a complex interplay of subtle factors affecting us from birth on. The ways in which we rear our children, train our students, and interact with our colleagues are all so deeply imbued with our expectations and beliefs as to virtually guarantee a fulfillment of these beliefs.

How do men and women develop the characteristics we attribute to them? There are clear differences between the sexes at birth, and there is even some evidence that these differences extend to the brain. Primate studies reveal marked differences in behavior between males and females—differences determined by the prenatal hormonal environment. It seems therefore quite possible that there are even intellectual differences determined prior to birth. For those inclined to believe in such predetermination, such a possibility may appear attractive. It is important to say, however, that there is to date no evidence for biologically determined differences in intelligence or cognitive styles, and that this remains true in spite of a rather considerable desire among many people to find such evidence.

An example of this interest is provided by the great enthusiasm with which a recent study was met. This study purported to show that prenatal injection of progestin, a synthetic male hormone, leads to higher than average I.Q.'s in adolescent girls. Although this result was refuted by the original authors shortly after its original announcement, it nevertheless found its way into a rash of textbooks, where it remains. Similarly, there has been a great deal of interest in the measurement of differences in perceptual modes between girls and boys. Tests designed to measure the degree to which one's perception of a figure is independent of its background, or field, show that girls, by the time they enter school, are more field-dependent than boys. Field independence is positively correlated with mathematical and analytic abilities. While the results of these tests are remarkably culturally invariant (the Eskimos are a notable exception), it is important to point out both that the disparities observed are extremely small (of the order of 2 percent) and that they cannot be discerned before the age of five. While the possibility that these disparities are the result of innate differences between the sexes cannot be excluded, there is evidence relating performance on such tests to the individual's environment. What are the environmental differences that could account for such results?

We treat our sons and daughters differently from birth onward, although the magnitude of our distinction is largely unconscious. A rude awakening to the extent of our differential treatment can come in those rare instances when a fallacious sex assignment is made at birth, usually as a result of ambiguous genitalia, and must be subsequently corrected. The impact of these early cues can be assessed by the fact that such reassignments are considered unduly traumatic to make after the child is eighteen months old, in spite of the fact that failure to do so dooms the child to an apparent sexual identity at odds with his or her genotype. Sex reassignments made before that time result in apparently normal development. From this and related evidence, workers in this area have concluded that gender identity appears to be established, primarily on the basis of parental treatment, by the age of eighteen months.

Children acquire the meaning of their sex identity from the models before them. Their concept of female is based largely on the women they see, as their concept of male is based on the men they see. Their immediate perceptions are later expanded by the images they perceive on TV, and in children's literature. It hardly need be pointed out that both of the latter present to our children extraordinarily rigid stereotypes.

It is not surprising, then, that children, even before they enter school, have acquired the belief that certain activities are male and others female. Science is a male activity.

The tenacity of this early view is such as to resist easy change. When my daughter was in nursery school, her class was asked one day about the occupation of their fathers. I objected to this, and, as a result, the next day the teacher asked, "Sarah, what does your mother do?" She replied, "My mother cooks, she sews, she cleans, and she takes care of us." "But Sarah, isn't your mother a scientist?" "Oh, yes," said Sarah—clearly implying that this was not a very relevant piece of information.

The explanation of her response lies not only in her need to define a conventional image of her mother, but also in the reality of her direct perceptions. Indeed it is true that, like many professional women, I do cook, sew, clean, and take care of my children. My professional identity is not brought into my home, although my husband's is. My daughter, therefore, like my son, continues to view mathematics and science as male, in spite of their information to the contrary.

While a child may be concerned with assigning sex labels only to external attributes, such as clothes, mannerisms, and occupations, the adolescent has already begun to designate internal states as male and female. Thus, in particular, clear thinking is characterized as hard thinking (a male image), and fuzzy thinking as soft thinking (a female image). A girl who thinks clearly and well is told she thinks "like a man." What are the implications of such associations for the girl who (for whatever reasons) does transcend social expectation and finds herself interested in science? Confusion in sexual identity is the inevitable concomitant of a self-definition at variance with the surrounding definitions of sexual norm. The girl who can take pride in "thinking like a man" without cost to her integrity as a girl is rare indeed.

Nevertheless, a considerable number of women, for whatever reasons, experience enough motivation and have demonstrated enough ability to embark on professional training for a scientific career. Graduate school is a time to prove that one is, in spite of one's aspirations, a woman, and—at one and the same time, because of one's aspirations—"more than" a woman. Social acceptability requires the former, and is considerably facilitated by the acquisition of a husband, while professional respectability requires the latter. The more exclusively male the definition of the profession, the more difficult it is to accomplish these conflicting goals.

My own experience as a graduate student of theoretical physics at Harvard was extreme, but possibly illustrative. I was surrounded by incessant prophecies of failure, independent of my performance. I knew of no counter-examples to draw confidence from, and was led to believe that none existed. (Later, however, I learned that some women in theoretical physics have survived, even at Harvard.) Warned that I would ultimately despair as I came to learn how impossible my ambitions were, I did, though not for the reasons that were then implied. Having denied myself rage, depression was in fact one of the few reasonable responses to the isolation, mockery, and suspicion that I experienced, both within and without my department. Ultimately I did earn my Ph.D. from the Harvard physics department, but only after having adapted my interests and thereby removed myself from the most critical pressures—a course many women have taken before and since.

Hostility, however, was not the only response I received, and not necessarily the usual response experienced by professionally ambitious young women. The necessity of proving one's femininity leaves some women particularly susceptible to another danger—that of accepting, and even seeking, sexual approbation for intellectual and academic performance. There are enough men willing, if not eager, to provide such translated affirmation as to make this a serious problem. The relation between sexuality and intellectuality is an enormously complex subject. I raise it only to point out one perhaps obvious consequence of this confusion for women. Because, unlike men, they are often dependent on sexual and intellectual affirmation from one and the same individual or group, they can never be entirely confident of what is being affirmed. Is it an "A for a Lay" or a "Lay for an A"?

Finally, the female scientist is launched. What are her prospects? Many women choose this point to withdraw for a time in order to have children. Although there is a logic to this choice, it reflects a lack of awareness of the dynamics of normal professional growth. For the male scientist, the period immediately following acquisition of the Ph.D. is perhaps the most critical in his professional development. It is the time that he has, free of all the responsibilities that will later come to plague him, to accomplish enough work to establish his reputation. Often it is a time to affiliate himself with a school of thought, to prove his own independent worth. Although this may have been the original function of the graduate training period, it has in recent times been displaced to the postgraduate years. Awareness of this displacement, of the critical importance of these years, has not permeated to the general public, or even, for the most part, to the science student. Many women therefore take this sometimes fatal step in ignorance. After having been out of a field for a few years, they usually find it next to impossible to return to their field except in the lowest-level positions. Only when it is too late do they learn that it would have been better to have their children first, before completing the Ph.D.

I need hardly enumerate the additional practical difficulties involved in combining a scientific (or any other) career with the raising of children. While the practical drains on one's time and energy are generally recognized, perhaps it is worth pointing out that the drains on one's intellectual energy are not generally recognized by men. Only those men who have spent full time, for an extended period, caring for their children are aware of the extraordinary amount of mental space occupied by the thousand and one details and concerns that mothers routinely juggle. Many have come to the conclusion—beginning with Engels,[1] and more recently including the Swedish government—that equality of the sexes in the work and professional force is not a realistic

1. Friedrich Engels (1820–95), German Socialist and, with Karl Marx, author of *The Communist Manifesto.*

possibility until the sex roles in the family are radically redefined. Equality must begin at home.

20   Well, one might ask, what about those women in science who have no children, who never marry? Surely they are freed from all of these difficulties. Why don't they perform better?

First of all, to be freed of responsibilities towards others is not equivalent to having your own responsibilities assumed by others. Nowhere among women is to be found the counterpart of the male scientist who has a wife at home to look after his daily needs. The question, however, deserves a more serious answer, although the answer is almost painfully obvious. Our society does not have a place for unmarried women. They are among the most isolated, ostracized groups of our culture. When one thinks about the daily social and psychological pressures on the unmarried professional woman, one can hardly be surprised to discover that the data reveal that indeed, on the average, married women in science—even with children—publish more and perform better than unmarried women.

The enumeration of obstacles or handicaps faced by women in science would hardly be complete without at least a reference to the inequalities of reward and approval awarded to work done by men and women. The personal anecdote I began with is more than an anecdote—it is evidence of a rather ubiquitous tendency, neither malicious nor necessarily even conscious, to give more public recognition to a man's accomplishments than to a woman's accomplishments. There are many different reasons for this—not least of which includes the habitually lesser inclination of many women to put themselves forward. There is also a simple, although documented, difference in evaluation of the actual work done by men and women.

While all of the above difficulties are hardly exclusive problems of women in science, the question of identity in what has been defined as an almost exclusively male profession is more serious for women in science than in other fields. Not only is the field defined as male by virtue of its membership, it is also defined as male in relation to its methodology, style of thought, indeed its goals. To the extent that analytic thought is conceived as male thought, to the extent that we characterize the natural sciences as the "hard" sciences, to the extent that the procedure of science is to "attack" problems, and its goal, since Bacon,[2] has been to "conquer" or "master" nature, a woman in science *must* in some way feel alien.

Traditionally, as in other similar situations, women who have suc-

2. Francis Bacon (1561–1626), English thinker who argued for a scientific methodology based on experimentation.

ceeded in scientific careers have dealt with this conflict by identifying with the "aggressor"—incorporating its values and ideals, at the cost, inevitably, of separating themselves from their own sex. An alternative resolution, one opted for frequently in other professions, is to attempt to redefine one's subject so as to permit a more comfortable identification with it. It is in this way, and for this reason, that so many professional women root themselves in subjects that are viewed by the profession as peripheral. In science this is not easy to do, but perhaps not impossible. There is another tradition within science that is as replete with female images as the tradition that dominates today is replete with male images. We all know that the most creative science requires, in addition to a hardness of mind, also fertility and receptivity. The best scientists are those who have combined the two sets of images. It may be that a certain degree of intellectual security is necessary in order to permit the expression of both "male" and "female" thought in science. If women have first to prove their "male" qualifications for admission into the profession, they may never achieve the necessary confidence to allow themselves to use their "female" abilities. What is to be done?

The central theme of my discussion is that the differential performance of men and women in science, the apparent differences between conceptual styles of men and women everywhere, are the result, not so much of innate differences between the sexes, but rather of the myth that prevails throughout our culture identifying certain kinds of thinking as male and others as female. The consequent compartmentalization of our minds is as effective as if it had been biologically, and not socially, induced.   25

People conform to the expectations imposed upon them in the evolution of their definition of sexual identity, thus confirming the very myth upon which these expectations are based. Such a process is not easy to change. Myths as deeply rooted and as self-affirming as this one can neither be wished nor willed away. The only hope is to chip away at it everywhere, to make enough small inroads so that future generations may ultimately grow up less hampered. Counter-measures can be effected at every stage of the process. Each may be of only limited effectiveness, but cumulatively they may permit enough women to emerge with intact, fully developed mental capacities—women who can serve as role models for future generations of students.

Specifically, we can begin by exerting a conscious effort to raise our children to less rigid stereotypes. Although the full extent to which we differentiate our treatment of our sons and daughters is hidden from us, being largely unconscious, we can, by attending to what we do, raise our consciousness of our own behavior.

We can specifically encourage and reward interests and abilities that survive social pressures. As teachers, men can consciously refrain from mixing academic with sexual approval. More generally, we can inform women students interested in science about the realities of the external difficulties they will face. It is all too easy for an individual experiencing such obstacles to internalize the responsibility for these obstacles. Specific advice can be given—for instance, to avoid interrupting a career immediately after the Ph.D. High-quality work by professional women can be sought out for recognition and encouragement in order to counteract the normal tendency to grant them less recognition. (The physicist Ernest Courant, a very wise man, responded to the news that one of his most talented students was pregnant by giving her a raise—thus enabling her to hire competent help, and, simultaneously, obligating her to continue. After four such raises, she indeed did go on to become one of the country's better mathematicians.)

Extra care can be taken not to exclude women from professional interaction on any level. Finally, hiring policies must take into account the human and political realities. Women students need role models if they are to mature properly. Providing such a model is an important part of the function of a faculty member and should be considered along with scholarly performance in hiring deliberations. Similarly, marriage is a social reality, and women scientists who marry male scientists need jobs in the same area. Anti-nepotism hiring policies discriminate against women scientists, and even a neutral policy effectively does so as well. Universities might well consider pro-nepotism policies that would recognize the limitations of humans and geographical reality.

30   Most of the recommendations I have made require the cooperation of the male scientific community to implement. Why should they? Further, one may ask, why should women even be encouraged to become scientists when the list of odds against them is so overwhelming? Is a career in science intrinsically of so much greater value than other options more available to women?

I don't believe it is. Nevertheless, our society has become more and more technologically oriented. As we continue to move in this direction, as we come to attach increasing importance to scientific and technological know-how, women are threatened with a disenfranchisement possibly greater than ever before. The traditional role of the woman becomes increasingly eroded with technology and overpopulation, while the disparity between the more humanly oriented kinds of knowledge thought to be hers and the more technical kinds of knowledge operating in the real world grows larger. This disparity operates not only at the expense of the women who are thus barred from meaningful roles in society, but also at the expense of the society that has been content to relegate to women those more humanistic values we all claim to support.

Finally, myths that compartmentalize our minds by defining certain mental attributes as "male" and others as "female" leave us all functioning with only part of our minds. Though there may well be some innate biological differences between the sexes, there is hardly room for doubt that our preconceptions serve to exaggerate and rigidify any distinctions that might exist. These preconceptions operate as straitjackets for men and women alike. I believe that the best, most creative science, like the most creative human efforts of any kind, can only be achieved with a full, unhampered mind—if you like, an androgynous mind. Therefore, the giving up of the central myth that science is a product of male thought may well lead to a more creative, more imaginative, and, who knows, possibly even a more humanistic science.

THE READER

1. *To what causes does Keller trace the relative disproportion of women in the sciences? Do you find the evidence for her arguments compelling? Can you think of other causes that she does not mention?*
2. *Keller speaks of a "myth that prevails throughout our culture identifying certain kinds of thinking as male and others as female" (p. 1027). What does she mean by "our culture"? What myth is she referring to, and how prevalent do you estimate it to be?*
3. *With respect to Table 1 (p. 1021), Keller writes: "during most of that time [i.e., 1920–69], the percentage of women scientists has declined, although recent years have begun to show an upswing." Does she account for the decline? That is, does her essay account for why the percentage in physics and astronomy and that in mathematics was more than twice as high in the 1920s as it was in the 1960s? Consider that, as she has written, "in the last fifty years the institutional barriers against women in science have been falling" (p. 1020). Is that fact reflected in Table 1?*

THE WRITER

1. *Keller's essay combines a personal and an impersonal approach to her subject. Why does she do so? Indicate where you think this approach strengthens her argument.*
2. *Write an essay combining your personal perceptions with an examination of facts relating to a topic that falls within your experience.*

Stephen Jay Gould

SCIENTIFIC ERROR

We all learned that Galileo[1] discovered some of the moons of Jupiter and the phases of Venus. Few people realize, however, that he made a gigantic goof about Saturn. His telescope, scarcely better than a modern toy, did not resolve the rings well—and rings, in any case, were then so far beyond the conceptual bounds of permissible features for a planet that even a clear view might not have produced a good mental resolution. In any case, Galileo thought that he saw a central sphere tightly surrounded by two smaller spheres too big and too close to be ordinary moons.

Following the custom of his day, and in order to establish priority without revealing his results, Galileo sent a complex Latin anagram to Johannes Kepler,[2] announcing his discovery in code.

Kepler never resolved the message (and actually misscrambled the anagram as a statement about Mars). Galileo later revealed his true intent: *Altissimum planetam tergeminum observavi*—I have observed that the most distant planet is threefold (the planets beyond Saturn, invisible to the naked eye, had not yet been discovered).

Under Arrest

We also all learned that Galileo was later convicted of heresy for defending and teaching the Copernican system, and that he spent the rest of his life under house arrest. We continue to deplore Galileo's fate and rank him first in the noble army of scientific martyrs. And yet, in the light of recent developments in Washington, I'm not so sure that Galileo might not be in more trouble today. Several Congressional committees have been investigating scientific misconduct and some seem ready to view error as a cause for investigation into the misuse of Federal funds. On this model, the Medicis of Florence might consider prosecuting Galileo for his misreading of Saturn.

"Scientific misconduct" is the subject under scrutiny by Representative John D. Dingell, Democrat of Michigan, and his Oversight and Investigations Subcommittee. The cause célèbre, a paper written by

First appeared in the *New York Times* (July 30, 1989).

1. Galileo Galilei (1564–1642), Italian astronomer and physicist who defended the new astronomy of Copernicus and its heliocentric model of the universe against the older geocentric model.

2. Kepler (1571–1603), German astronomer and physicist.

David Baltimore and colleagues, has been placed under the forensic equivalent of an electron microscope. [3] The paper contains some errors, and some evidence of poor record keeping. The more public charge of fraud cannot be sustained.

Fraud and error are as different as arsenic and apple pie. The first is a pathology and a poison, the second an unavoidable consequence of any complex human activity.

(Of course, not all error is blameless as an epiphenomenon of creativity. Some errors may arise from serious carelessness; others from precipitous grandstanding prompted by the allure of fame or fortune. But most errors, a great majority by far, are honorable. They belong in the category of honest effort, not in the domain of duplicity.)

Taxonomy, or the study of classification, is generally accorded low status among the sciences—as an exercise in mere ordering, fit only for bookkeepers, and roughly equivalent to pasting stamps in prearranged spaces in nature's album. This attitude is both arrogant and false. Nature is full of facts, but any "album" for their arrangement must record human decisions about order and cause. Thus, taxonomies represent the height of human creativity, and embody our most fundamental ideas about the causes of natural order.

Taxonomies also channel our thinking into fruitful paths when a classification properly captures causes of order, but often into ludicrous or vicious error (older racial taxonomies, for example) when we mistake thoughtless prejudice for objective truth.

False taxonomies are most dangerous when we mistake them for an obvious "right way" and don't even question their underlying theory of order. The implied taxonomy of "scientific misconduct" falls into this category of worst cases.

Legislators and journalists seem to acknowledge that true fraud, as the worst expression of misconduct, must be rare and therefore difficult to study. They therefore envisage a continuum shading away from fraud toward less severe forms in the same category of misconduct—finagling, coverup, sloppiness and error, for example. Since types of misconduct become more common as their severity decreases, error may be the most practical subject for study. Two aspects of this conceptual scheme are desperately wrong.

First, while we all accept that any beneficiary of Federal funds must be subject to the scrutiny of benefactors, what could possibly be more chilling to creativity than an office of censorship (it would have another

3. The paper in question carried the name of David Baltimore as one of its six authors, although he was not immediately engaged in the research and writing. Another of its authors had been accused of misreporting observations, of error, that is, rather than fraud. Prior to Gould's essay, Baltimore, a Nobel Prize winner, defended the paper to the Dingell committee; later (in 1991) he agreed to its retraction.

name, but the effect is what counts) trying to impose the impossible and the inhuman—freedom from error in thought and deed? We might as well rule that any orchestra receiving a penny in state funds must employ an umpire to tap the conductor on the shoulder every time the principal French horn plays a sour note.

Second, the implied taxonomy of "scientific misconduct" is wrong in the worst way. The supposed continuum, shading away from fraud to less serious but more common forms of the same phenomenon, is backwards. Fraud and error belong on opposite sides of any proper dichotomy.

A Matter of Trust

Fraud is a pathology. I doubt that nonscientists realize how concerned all scientists are to purge any detected incident. The reason for our loathing is not widely understood, and its basis is not abstractly moral. Science must be based on trust. We cannot easily identify most cases of fraud; only the careless, the unbalanced and the foolishly daring leave palpable tracks. We cannot hover over all our colleagues at their workbenches, any more than the Internal Revenue Service can monitor every trip to the bank or call to a stockbroker.

15   We must believe that the publications of our colleagues are presented in good faith, for only then can we analyze their work to discover errors. Fraud is the worst of all offenses—a violation of community standards that must be respected and internalized, lest the community die.

Fallibility and Creativity

Error, on the other hand, falls into the category of unavoidable side consequences to commendable activity—like a pitcher's sore arm after a shut-out. Lord knows we try our damnedest to cut down and eliminate these consequences, for they are embarrassing and personally harmful (just as pitchers have been trying various nostrums from prayers to whirlpool baths to changes of delivery, from time immemorial in the field of dreams).

But we cannot completely eliminate the consequences without compromising the main activity. (I could pitch batting practice all day, but I'd never make the bigs.) In any proper taxonomy of scientific activity, error belongs in the category of proper procedure—for three major reasons:

1. People work this way. We are fallible creatures. Ambiguity defines the richness of our intellectual lives. Computers frustrate us because they display the inhuman property of shutting down when faced with any error or ambiguity; we have had to establish an entire profession—debugging—to mediate between our two opposing styles.

2. Work of intellectual daring carries the danger of increased error, in both frequency and consequence. If they wished to avoid all possibility of error, Galileo would have trained his telescope on the next building, and Darwin would have stuck with pigeons.[4] Intrusive regulation by nonscientists is most frightening for this reason; innovation and chanciness will die. Error is the flipside of great discovery. Together they form one coin, and their common currency is brilliance.

3. Error is a spur to correction. Errors promote good science, if only because one-up-manship seems as intrinsically human as error itself. "False views, if supported by some evidence, do little harm, for every one takes a salutary pleasure in proving their falseness," Darwin wrote, in one of his most famous lines.

Great intellectuals have always understood this principle, and have been accepting of honorable error and fiercely intolerant of fraud.

The economist Vilfredo Pareto[5] wrote of Kepler, who contributed a thing or two to human knowledge, though he never unscrambled Galileo's anagram: "Give me a fruitful error any time, full of seeds, bursting with its own corrections. You can keep your sterile truth for yourself."

4. Darwin did not observe pigeons; such an activity, unlike his observations in the Galapagos Islands (in the Pacific Ocean off the coast of Ecuador) and his theory build-

ing, would have carried little risk of error.
5. Pareto (1848–1923), Italian economist and sociologist.

Thomas S. Kuhn

THE ROUTE TO NORMAL SCIENCE

In this essay, 'normal science' means research firmly based upon one or more past scientific achievements, achievements that some particular scientific community acknowledges for a time as supplying the foundation for its further practice. Today such achievements are recounted, though seldom in their original form, by science textbooks, elementary and advanced. These textbooks expound the body of accepted theory, illustrate many or all of its successful applications, and compare these applications with exemplary observations and experiments. Before such books became popular early in the nineteenth century (and until even more recently in the newly matured sciences), many of the famous classics of science fulfilled a similar function. Aristotle's *Physica*, Ptolemy's *Almagest*, Newton's *Principia* and *Opticks*, Franklin's *Electricity*,

From *The Structure of Scientific Revolutions* (1962).

Lavoisier's *Chemistry,* and Lyell's *Geology*—these and many other works served for a time implicitly to define the legitimate problems and methods of a research field for succeeding generations of practitioners. They were able to do so because they shared two essential characteristics. Their achievement was sufficiently unprecedented to attract an enduring group of adherents away from competing modes of scientific activity. Simultaneously, it was sufficiently open-ended to leave all sorts of problems for the redefined group of practitioners to resolve.

Achievements that share these two characteristics I shall henceforth refer to as 'paradigms,' a term that relates closely to 'normal science.' By choosing it, I mean to suggest that some accepted examples of actual scientific practice—examples which include law, theory, application, and instrumentation together—provide models from which spring particular coherent traditions of scientific research. These are the traditions which the historian describes under such rubrics as 'Ptolemaic astronomy' (or 'Copernican'), 'Aristotelian dynamics' (or 'Newtonian'), 'corpuscular optics' (or 'wave optics'), and so on. The study of paradigms, including many that are far more specialized than those named illustratively above, is what mainly prepares the student for membership in the particular scientific community with which he will later practice. Because he there joins men who learned the bases of their field from the same concrete models, his subsequent practice will seldom evoke overt disagreement over fundamentals. Men whose research is based on shared paradigms are committed to the same rules and standards for scientific practice. That commitment and the apparent consensus it produces are prerequisites for normal science, i.e., for the genesis and continuation of a particular research tradition.

Because in this essay the concept of a paradigm will often substitute for a variety of familiar notions, more will need to be said about the reasons for its introduction. Why is the concrete scientific achievement, as a locus of professional commitment, prior to the various concepts, laws, theories, and points of view that may be abstracted from it? In what sense is the shared paradigm a fundamental unit for the student of scientific development, a unit that cannot be fully reduced to logically atomic components which might function in its stead? There can be a sort of scientific research without paradigms, or at least without any so unequivocal and so binding as the ones named above. Acquisition of a paradigm and of the more esoteric type of research it permits is a sign of maturity in the development of any given scientific field.

If the historian traces the scientific knowledge of any selected group of related phenomena backward in time, he is likely to encounter some minor variant of a pattern here illustrated from the history of physical optics. Today's physics textbooks tell the student that light is photons, i.e., quantum-mechanical entities that exhibit some characteristics of waves and some of particles. Research proceeds accordingly, or rather according to the more elaborate and mathematical characterization from which this usual verbalization is derived. That characterization of light is, however, scarcely half a century old. Before it was developed by Planck, Einstein, and others early in this century, physics texts taught that light was transverse wave motion, a conception rooted in a paradigm that derived ultimately from the optical writings of Young and Fresnel in the early nineteenth century. Nor was the wave theory the first to be embraced by almost all practitioners of optical science. During the eighteenth century the paradigm for this field was provided by Newton's *Opticks*, which taught that light was material corpuscles. At that time physicists sought evidence, as the early wave theorists had not, of the pressure exerted by light particles impinging on solid bodies.

These transformations of the paradigms of physical optics are scientific revolutions, and the successive transition from one paradigm to another via revolution is the usual developmental pattern of mature science. It is not, however, the pattern characteristic of the period before Newton's work, and that is the contrast that concerns us here. No period between remote antiquity and the end of the seventeenth century exhibited a single generally accepted view about the nature of light. Instead there were a number of competing schools and sub-schools, most of them espousing one variant or another of Epicurean, Aristotelian, or Platonic theory.[1] One group took light to be particles emanating from material bodies; for another it was a modification of the medium that intervened between the body and the eye; still another explained light in terms of an interaction of the medium with an emanation from the eye; and there were other combinations and modifications besides. Each of the corresponding schools derives strength from its relation to some particular metaphysic, and each emphasized, as paradigmatic observations, the particular cluster of optical phenomena that its own theory could do most to explain. Other observations were dealt with by *ad hoc* elaborations, or they remained as outstanding problems for further research.

At various times all these schools made significant contributions to the body of concepts, phenomena, and techniques from which Newton drew the first nearly uniformly accepted paradigm for physical optics. Any definition of the scientist that excludes at least the more creative members of these various schools will exclude their modern successors as well. Those men were scientists. Yet anyone examining a survey of physical optics before Newton may well conclude that, though the field's practitioners were scientists, the net result of their activity was something less than science. Being able to take no common body of belief

1. The reference is to the three principal world views of ancient Greek philosophy.

for granted, each writer on physical optics felt forced to build his field anew from its foundations. In doing so, his choice of supporting observation and experiment was relatively free, for there was no standard set of methods or of phenomena that every optical writer felt forced to employ and explain. Under these circumstances, the dialogue of the resulting books was often directed as much to the members of other schools as it was to nature. That pattern is not unfamiliar in a number of creative fields today, nor is it incompatible with significant discovery and invention. It is not, however, the pattern of development that physical optics acquired after Newton and that other natural sciences make familiar today.

The history of electrical research in the first half of the eighteenth century provides a more concrete and better known example of the way a science develops before it acquires its first universally received paradigm. During that period there were almost as many views about the nature of electricity as there were important electrical experimenters, men like Haukshee, Gray, Desaguliers, Du Fay, Nollett, Watson, Franklin, and others. All their numerous concepts of electricity had something in common—they were partially derived from one or another version of the mechanico-corpuscular philosophy that guided all scientific research of the day. In addition, all were components of real scientific theories, of theories that had been drawn in part from experiment and observation and that partially determined the choice and interpretation of additional problems undertaken in research. Yet though all the experiments were electrical and though most of the experimenters read each other's works, their theories had no more than a family resemblance.

One early group of theories, following seventeenth-century practice, regarded attraction and frictional generation as the fundamental electrical phenomena. This group tended to treat repulsion as a secondary effect due to some sort of mechanical rebounding and also to postpone for as long as possible both discussion and systematic research on Gray's newly discovered effect, electrical conduction. Other "electricians" (the term is their own) took attraction and repulsion to be equally elementary manifestations of electricity and modified their theories and research accordingly. (Actually, this group is remarkably small—even Franklin's theory never quite accounted for the mutual repulsion of two negatively charged bodies.) But they had as much difficulty as the first group in accounting simultaneously for any but the simplest conduction effects. Those effects, however, provided the starting point for still a third group, one which tended to speak of electricity as a "fluid" that could run through conductors rather than as an "effluvium" that emanated from non-conductors. This group, in its turn, had difficulty reconciling its theory with a number of attractive and repulsive effects. Only through the work of Franklin and his immediate successors did a theory arise that could account with something like equal facility for very nearly all these effects and that therefore could and did provide a subsequent generation of "electricians" with a common paradigm for its research.

Excluding those fields, like mathematics and astronomy, in which the first firm paradigms date from prehistory and also those, like biochemistry, that arose by division and recombination of specialties already matured, the situations outlined above are historically typical. Though it involves my continuing to employ the unfortunate simplification that tags an extended historical episode with a single and somewhat arbitrarily chosen name (e.g., Newton or Franklin), I suggest that similar fundamental disagreements characterized, for example, the study of motion before Aristotle and of statics before Archimedes, the study of heat before Black, of chemistry before Boyle and Boerhaave, and of historical geology before Hutton. In parts of biology—the study of heredity, for example—the first universally received paradigms are still more recent; and it remains an open question what parts of social science have yet acquired such paradigms at all. History suggests that the road to a firm research consensus is extraordinarily arduous.

History also suggests, however, some reasons for the difficulties encountered on the road. In the absence of a paradigm or some candidate for paradigm, all of the facts that could possibly pertain to the development of a given science are likely to seem equally relevant. As a result, early fact-gathering is a far more nearly random activity than the one that subsequent scientific development makes familiar. Futhermore, in the absence of a reason for seeking some particular form of more recondite information, early fact-gathering is usually restricted to the wealth of data that lie ready to hand. The resulting pool of facts contains those accessible to casual observation and experiment together with some of the more esoteric data retrievable from established crafts medicine, calendar making, and metallurgy. Because the crafts are one readily accessible source of facts that could not have been casually discovered, technology has often played a vital role in the emergence of new sciences. 10

But though this sort of fact-collecting has been essential to the origin of many significant sciences, anyone who examines, for example, Pliny's encyclopedic writings or the Baconian natural histories of the seventeenth century will discover that it produces a morass. One somehow hesitates to call the literature that results scientific. The Baconian "histories" of heat, color, wind, mining, and so on, are filled with information, some of it recondite. But they juxtapose facts that will later prove revealing (e.g., heating by mixture) with others (e.g., the warmth of dung heaps) that will for some time remain too complex to be integrated with theory at all. In addition, since any description must be partial, the typical natural history often omits from its immensely circumstantial accounts just those details that later scientists will find sources of important illumination. Almost none of the early "histories" of electricity, for example, mention that chaff, attracted to a rubbed glass rod, bounces off again. That effect seemed mechanical, not electrical. Moreover, since the casual fact-gatherer seldom possesses the time or the tools to be critical, the natural histories often juxtapose descriptions like the above with others, say, heating by antiperistasis (or by cooling), that we are now quite unable to confirm.[2] Only very occasionally, as in the cases of ancient statics, dynamics, and geometrical optics, do facts collected with so little guidance from pre-established theory speak with sufficient clarity to permit the emergence of a first paradigm.

This is the situation that creates the schools characteristic of the early stages of a science's development. No natural history can be interpreted in the absence of at least some implicit body of intertwined theoretical and methodological belief that permits selection, evaluation, and criticism. If that body of belief is not already implicit in the collection of facts—in which case more than "mere facts" are at hand—it must be externally supplied, perhaps by a current metaphysic, by another science, or by personal and historical accident. No wonder, then, that in the early stages of the development of any science different men confronting the same range of phenomena, but not usually all the same particular phenomena, describe and interpret them in different ways. What is surprising, and perhaps also unique in its degree to the fields we call science, is that such initial divergences should ever largely disappear.

For they do disappear to a very considerable extent and then apparently once and for all. Furthermore, their disappearance is usually caused by the triumph of one of the pre-paradigm schools, which, because of its own characteristic beliefs and pre-conceptions, emphasized only some special part of the too sizable and inchoate pool of information. Those electricians who thought electricity a fluid and therefore gave particular emphasis to conduction provide an excellent case in point. Led by this belief, which could scarcely cope with the known multiplicity of attractive and repulsive effects, several of them conceived the idea of bottling the electrical fluid. The immediate fruit of their efforts was the Leyden jar, a device which might never have been discovered by a man exploring nature casually or at random, but which was in fact independently developed by at least two investigators in the early 1740's. Almost from the start of his electrical researches, Franklin was particularly concerned to explain that strange and, in the event, particularly revealing piece of special apparatus. His success in doing so provided the

2. Bacon [in the *Novum Organum*] says, "Water slightly warm is more easily frozen than quite cold" [Kuhn's note]; *antiperistasis:* an old word meaning a reaction caused by the action of an opposite quality or principle—here, heating through cooling.

most effective of the arguments that made his theory a paradigm, though one that was still unable to account for quite all the known cases of electrical repulsion.[3] To be accepted as a paradigm, a theory must seem better than its competitors, but it need not, and in fact never does, explain all the facts with which it can be confronted.

What the fluid theory of electricity did for the subgroup that held it, the Franklinian paradigm later did for the entire group of electricians. It suggested which experiments would be worth performing and which, because directed to secondary or to overly complex manifestations of electricity, would not. Only the paradigm did the job far more effectively, partly because the end of interschool debate ended the constant reiteration of fundamentals and partly because the confidence that they were on the right track encouraged scientists to undertake more precise, esoteric, and consuming sorts of work.[4] Freed from the concern with any and all electrical phenomena, the united group of electricians could pursue selected phenomena in far more detail, designing much special equipment for the task and employing it more stubbornly and systematically than electricians had ever done before. Both fact collection and theory articulation became highly directed activities. The effectiveness and efficiency of electrical research increased accordingly, providing evidence for a societal version of Francis Bacon's acute methodological dictum: "Truth emerges more readily from error than from confusion."

We shall be examining the nature of this highly directed or paradigm-based research in the next section, but must first note briefly how the emergence of a paradigm affects the structure of the group that practices the field. When, in the development of a natural science, an individual or group first produces a synthesis able to attract most of the next generation's practitioners, the older schools gradually disappear. In part their disappearance is caused by their members' conversion to the new paradigm. But there are always some men who cling to one or another of the older views, and they are simply read out of the profession, which thereafter ignores their work. The new paradigm implies a new and more rigid definition of the field. Those unwilling or unable to accommodate their work to it must proceed in isolation or attach themselves to some

15

3. The troublesome case was the mutual repulsion of negatively charged bodies [Kuhn's note].
4. It should be noted that the acceptance of Franklin's theory did not end quite all debate. In 1759 Robert Symmer proposed a two-fluid version of that theory, and for many years thereafter electricians were divided about whether electricity was a single fluid or two. But the debates on this subject only confirm what has been said above about the manner in which a universally recognized achievement unites the profession. Electricians, though they continued divided on this point, rapidly concluded that no experimental tests could distinguish the two versions of the theory and that they were therefore equivalent. After that, both schools could and did exploit all the benefits that the Franklinian theory provided [Kuhn's note].

other group.[5] Historically, they have often simply stayed in the departments of philosophy from which so many of the special sciences have been spawned. As these indications hint, it is sometimes just its reception of a paradigm that transforms a group previously interested merely in the study of nature into a profession or, at least, a discipline. In the sciences (though not in fields like medicine, technology, and law, of which the principal *raison d'être* is an external social need), the formation of specialized journals, the foundation of specialists' societies, and the claim for a special place in the curriculum have usually been associated with a group's first reception of a single paradigm. At least this was the case between the time, a century and a half ago, when the institutional pattern of scientific specialization first developed and the very recent time when the paraphernalia of specialization acquired a prestige of their own.

The more rigid definition of the scientific group has other consequences. When the individual scientist can take a paradigm for granted, he need no longer, in his major works, attempt to build his field anew, starting from first principles and justifying the use of each concept introduced. That can be left to the writer of textbooks. Given a textbook, however, the creative scientist can begin his research where it leaves off and thus concentrate exclusively upon the subtlest and most esoteric aspects of the natural phenomena that concern his group. And as he does this, his research communiqués will begin to change in ways whose evolution has been too little studied but whose modern end products are obvious to all and oppressive to many. No longer will his researches usually be embodied in books addressed, like Franklin's *Experiments . . . on Electricity* or Darwin's *Origin of Species,* to anyone who might be interested in the subject matter of the field. Instead they will usually appear as brief articles addressed only to professional colleagues, the men whose knowledge of a shared paradigm can be assumed and who prove to be the only ones able to read the papers addressed to them.

Today in the sciences, books are usually either texts or retrospective reflections upon one aspect or another of the scientific life. The scientist who writes one is more likely to find his professional reputation impaired than enhanced. Only in the earlier, pre-paradigm, stages of the develop-

5. The history of electricity provides an excellent example which could be duplicated from the careers of Priestley, Kelvin, and others. Franklin reports that Nollet, who at mid-century was the most influential of the Continental electricians, "lived to see himself the last of his Sect, except Mr. B.—his *Eleve* [pupil] and immediate Disciple." More interesting, however, is the endurance of whole schools in increasing isolation from professional science. Consider, for example, the case of astrology, which was once an integral part of astronomy. Or consider the continuation in the late eighteenth, and early nineteenth centuries of a previously respected tradition of "romantic" chemistry [Kuhn's note].

ment of the various sciences did the book ordinarily possess the same relation to professional achievement that it still retains in other creative fields. And only in those fields that still retain the book, with or without the article, as a vehicle for research communication are the lines of professionalization still so loosely drawn that the layman may hope to follow progress by reading the practitioners' original reports. Both in mathematics and astronomy, research reports had ceased already in antiquity to be intelligible to a generally educated audience. In dynamics, research became similarly esoteric in the latter Middle Ages, and it recaptured general intelligibility only briefly during the early seventeenth century when a new paradigm replaced the one that had guided medieval research. Electrical research began to require translation for the layman before the end of the eighteenth century, and most other fields of physical science ceased to be generally accessible in the nineteenth. During the same two centuries similar transitions can be isolated in the various parts of the biological sciences. In parts of the social sciences they may well be occurring today. Although it has become customary, and is surely proper, to deplore the widening gulf that separates the professional scientist from his collegues in other fields, too little attention is paid to the essential relationship between that gulf and the mechanisms intrinsic to scientific advance.

Ever since prehistoric antiquity one field of study after another has crossed the divide between what the historian might call its prehistory as a science and its history proper. These transitions to maturity have seldom been so sudden or so unequivocal as my necessarily schematic discussion may have implied. But neither have they been historically gradual, coextensive, that is to say, with the entire development of the fields within which they occurred. Writers on electricity during the first four decades of the eighteenth century possessed far more information about electrical phenomena than had their sixteenth-century predecessors. During the half-century after 1740, few new sorts of electrical phenomena were added to their lists. Nevertheless, in important respects, the electrical writings of Cavendish, Coulomb, and Volta in the last third of the eighteenth century seem further removed from those of Gray, Du Fay, and even Franklin than are the writings of these early eighteenth-century electrical discoverers from those of the sixteenth century.[6] Sometime between 1740 and 1780, electricians were for the first time enabled to take the foundations of their field for granted. From that point they pushed on to more concrete and recondite problems, and

6. The post-Franklinian developments include an immense increase in the sensitivity of charge detectors, the first reliable and generally diffused techniques for measuring charge, the evolution of the concept of capacity and its relation to a newly refined notion of electric tension, and the quantification of electrostatic force [Kuhn's note].

increasingly they then reported their results in articles addressed to other electricians rather than in books addressed to the learned world at large. As a group they achieved what had been gained by astronomers in antiquity and by students of motion in the Middle Ages, of physical optics in the late seventeenth century, and of historical geology in the early nineteenth. They had, that is, achieved a paradigm that proved able to guide the whole group's research. Except with the advantage of hindsight, it is hard to find another criterion that so clearly proclaims a field a science.

THE READER

1. *What does Kuhn mean by a "paradigm" in science, and what advantages for science does he ascribe to it? Can you state the prevailing paradigm in sciences other than those he uses for illustration (for example, chemistry, biology, psychology)? Does the search for or the finding of the paradigms help you to understand what these sciences are about?*

2. *What is the relationship, by Kuhn's account, of the science textbook to the nature and practice of science? Examine a textbook in your course in one of the natural or social sciences. Does it have the character Kuhn ascribes to textbooks? Does regarding the textbook in this light help you in your study of the subject?*

THE WRITER

1. *What is Kuhn's thesis? How is the essay organized to develop that thesis?*

2. *What does Kuhn's essay suggest about the nature of a scientific fact or the place of fact in science? By and large, does this conclusion agree or disagree with Bronowski's statement of the matter in "The Reach of Imagination" (p. 196)? Is it not the business of a science to observe and record the facts? Is this not what Tinbergen, for instance, does in "The Bee-Hunters of Hulshorst" (p. 953)? What more should science do? Put your answer to one or more of these questions into a brief essay.*

Literature and the Arts

Eudora Welty

ONE WRITER'S BEGINNINGS

I learned from the age of two or three that any room in our house, at any time of day, was there to read in, or to be read to. My mother read to me. She'd read to me in the big bedroom in the mornings, when we were in her rocker together, which ticked in rhythm as we rocked, as though we had a cricket accompanying the story. She'd read to me in the diningroom on winter afternoons in front of the coal fire, with our cuckoo clock ending the story with "Cuckoo," and at night when I'd got in my own bed. I must have given her no peace. Sometimes she read to me in the kitchen while she sat churning, and the churning sobbed along with *any* story. It was my ambition to have her read to me while *I* churned; once she granted my wish, but she read off my story before I brought her butter. She was an expressive reader. When she was reading "Puss in Boots,"[1] for instance, it was impossible not to know that she distrusted *all* cats.

It had been startling and disappointing to me to find out that story books had been written by *people*, that books were not natural wonders, coming up of themselves like grass. Yet regardless of where they came from, I cannot remember a time when I was not in love with them— with the books themselves, cover and binding and the paper they were printed on, with their smell and their weight and with their possession in my arms, captured and carried off to myself. Still illiterate, I was ready for them, committed to all the reading I could give them.

From a set of three lectures delivered at Harvard University in April 1983, to inaugurate the William E. Massey lecture series; later published as *One Writer's Beginnings* (1984).

1. A fairy tale.

Neither of my parents had come from homes that could afford to buy many books, but though it must have been something of a strain on his salary, as the youngest officer in a young insurance company, my father was all the while carefully selecting and ordering away for what he and Mother thought we children should grow up with. They bought first for the future.

Besides the bookcase in the livingroom, which was always called "the library," there were the encyclopedia tables and dictionary stand under windows in our diningroom. Here to help us grow up arguing around the diningroom table were the Unabridged Webster, the Columbia Encyclopedia, Compton's Pictured Encyclopedia, the Lincoln Library of Information, and later the Book of Knowledge. And the year we moved into our new house, there was room to celebrate it with the new 1925 edition of the Britannica, which my father, his face always deliberately turned toward the future, was of course disposed to think better than any previous edition.

5   In "the library," inside the mission-style bookcase with its three diamond-latticed glass doors, with my father's Morris chair and the glass-shaded lamp on its table beside it, were books I could soon begin on—and I did, reading them all alike and as they came, straight down their rows, top shelf to bottom. There was the set of Stoddard's Lectures, in all its late nineteenth-century vocabulary and vignettes of peasant life and quaint beliefs and customs, with matching halftone illustrations: Vesuvius erupting, Venice by moonlight, gypsies glimpsed by their campfires. I didn't know then the clue they were to my father's longing to see the rest of the world. I read straight through his other love-from-afar: the Victrola Book of the Opera, with opera after opera in synopsis, with portraits in costume of Melba, Caruso, Galli-Curci, and Geraldine Farrar,[2] some of whose voices we could listen to on our Red Seal records.

My mother read secondarily for information; she sank as a hedonist into novels. She read Dickens in the spirit in which she would have eloped with him. The novels of her girlhood that had stayed on in her imagination, besides those of Dickens and Scott and Robert Louis Stevenson,[3] were *Jane Eyre, Trilby, The Woman in White, Green Mansions, King Solomon's Mines.*[4] Marie Corelli's[5] name would crop up but I understood she had gone out of favor with my mother, who had

2. Nellie Melba (1861–1931), Enrico Caruso (1837–1921), Amelita Galli-Curci (1889–1964), Geraldine Farrar (1882–1967).
3. Charles Dickens (1812–70), Sir Walter Scott (1771–1832), Robert Louis Stevenson (1850–94). The first was English, the others Scottish.

4. Respectively by Charlotte Brontë (1816–55), George Du Maurier (1834–96), Wilkie Collins (1824–89), William Henry Hudson (1841–1922), Sir H. Rider Haggard (1856–1925). All were English.
5. The pen name of Mary Mackay (1855–1924), a popular and prolific English novelist.

only kept *Ardath* out of loyalty. In time she absorbed herself in Galsworthy, Edith Wharton, above all in Thomas Mann of the *Joseph* volumes.[6]

St. Elmo was not in our house; I saw it often in other houses. This wildly popular Southern novel is where all the Edna Earles in our population started coming from. They're all named for the heroine, who succeeded in bringing a dissolute, sinning roué and atheist of a lover (St. Elmo) to his knees. My mother was able to forgo it. But she remembered the classic advice given to rose growers on how to water their bushes long enough: "Take a chair and *St. Elmo.*"[7]

To both my parents I owe my early acquaintance with a beloved Mark Twain. There was a full set of Mark Twain and a short set of Ring Lardner in our bookcase,[8] and those were the volumes that in time united us all, parents and children.

Reading everything that stood before me was how I came upon a worn old book without a back that had belonged to my father as a child. It was called *Sanford and Merton.* Is there anyone left who recognizes it, I wonder? It is the famous moral tale written by Thomas Day in the 1780s, but of him no mention is made on the title page of *this* book; here it is *Sanford and Merton in Words of One Syllable* by Mary Godolphin. Here are the rich boy and the poor boy and Mr. Barlow, their teacher and interlocutor, in long discourses alternating with dramatic scenes—danger and rescue allotted to the rich and the poor respectively. It may have only words of one syllable, but one of them is "quoth." It ends with not one but two morals, both engraved on rings: "Do what you ought, come what may," and "If we would be great, we must first learn to be good."

This book was lacking its front cover, the back held on by strips of pasted paper, now turned golden, in several layers, and the pages stained, flecked, and tattered around the edges; its garish illustrations had come unattached but were preserved, laid in. I had the feeling even in my heedless childhood that this was the only book my father as a little boy had had of his own. He had held onto it, and might have gone to sleep on its coverless face: he had lost his mother when he was seven. My father had never made any mention to his own children of the book, but he had brought it along with him from Ohio to our house and shelved it in our bookcase.

My mother had brought from West Virginia that set of Dickens; those books looked sad, too—they had been through fire and water

10

6. John Galsworthy (1867–1933), English; Edith Wharton (1862–1937), American; Thomas Mann (1875–1955), German, whose *Joseph* novels appeared in four parts, from 1933 to 1943.

7. By Augusta Jane Evans (1835–1909).
8. Mark Twain: the pen name of Samuel Langhorne Clemens (1835–1910), Ring (Ringgold Wilmer) Lardner (1885–1933). Both were American.

before I was born, she told me, and there they were, lined up—as I later realized, waiting for *me*.

I was presented, from as early as I can remember, with books of my own, which appeared on my birthday and Christmas morning. Indeed, my parents could not give me books enough. They must have sacrificed to give me on my sixth or seventh birthday—it was after I became a reader for myself—the ten-volume set of Our Wonder World. These were beautifully made, heavy books I would lie down with on the floor in front of the diningroom hearth, and more often than the rest volume 5, *Every Child's Story Book*, was under my eyes. There were the fairy tales— Grimm, Andersen, the English, the French, "Ali Baba and the Forty Thieves"; and there was Aesop and Reynard the Fox; there were the myths and legends, Robin Hood, King Arthur, and St. George and the Dragon, even the history of Joan of Arc; a whack of *Pilgrim's Progress* and a long piece of *Gulliver*. [9] They all carried their classic illustrations. I located myself in these pages and could go straight to the stories and pictures I loved; very often "The Yellow Dwarf" was first choice, with Walter Crane's Yellow Dwarf in full color making his terrifying appearance flanked by turkeys. [1] Now that volume is as worn and backless and hanging apart as my father's poor *Sanford and Merton*. The precious page with Edward Lear's "Jumblies" [2] on it has been in danger of slipping out for all these years. One measure of my love for Our Wonder World was that for a long time I wondered if I would go through fire and water for it as my mother had done for Charles Dickens; and the only comfort was to think I could ask my mother to do it for me.

I believe I'm the only child I know of who grew up with this treasure in the house. I used to ask others, "Did you have Our Wonder World?" I'd have to tell them The Book of Knowledge could not hold a candle to it.

I live in gratitude to my parents for initiating me—and as early as I begged for it, without keeping me waiting—into knowledge of the word, into reading and spelling, by way of the alphabet. They taught it to me at home in time for me to begin to read before starting to school. I believe the alphabet is no longer considered an essential piece of equipment for traveling through life. In my day it was the keystone to knowledge. You learned the alphabet as you learned to count to ten, as you learned "Now I lay me" and the Lord's Prayer and your father's and mother's name and address and telephone number, all in case you were lost.

15   My love for the alphabet, which endures, grew out of reciting it but, before that, out of seeing the letters on the page. In my own story books,

9. Respectively by John Bunyan (1628–88) and Jonathan Swift (1667–1745). Both were English.

1. A fairy tale illustrated by Walter Crane (1845–1915), popular illustrator of chil-

dren's books.

2. A narrative poem about creatures called Jumblies who went to sea in a sieve. Edward Lear (1812–88), English, wrote nonsense poems for children.

before I could read them for myself, I fell in love with various winding, enchanting-looking initials drawn by Walter Crane at the heads of fairy tales. In "Once upon a time," an "O" had a rabbit running it as a treadmill, his feet upon flowers. When the day came, years later, for me to see the Book of Kells,[3] all the wizardry of letter, initial, and word swept over me a thousand times over, and the illumination, the gold, seemed a part of the word's beauty and holiness that had been there from the start.

Learning stamps you with its moments. Childhood's learning is made up of moments. It isn't steady. It's a pulse.

In a children's art class, we sat in a ring on kindergarten chairs and drew three daffodils that had just been picked out of the yard; and while I was drawing, my sharpened pencil and the cup of the yellow daffodil gave off whiffs just alike. That the pencil doing the drawing should give off the same smell as the flower it drew seemed a part of the art lesson—as shouldn't it be? Children, like animals, use all their senses to discover the world. Then artists come along and discover it the same way, all over again. Here and there, it's the same world. Or now and then we'll hear from an artist who's never lost it.

In my sensory education I include my physical awareness of the *word*. Of a certain word, that is; the connection it has with what it stands for. At around age six, perhaps, I was standing by myself in our front yard waiting for supper, just at that hour in a late summer day when the sun is already below the horizon and the risen full moon in the visible sky stops being chalky and begins to take on light. There comes the moment, and I saw it then, when the moon goes from flat to round. For the first time it met my eyes as a globe. The word "moon" came into my mouth as though fed to me out of a silver spoon. Held in my mouth the moon became a word. It had the roundness of a Concord grape Grandpa took off his vine and gave me to suck out of its skin and swallow whole, in Ohio.

This love did not prevent me from living for years in foolish error about the moon. The new moon just appearing in the west was the rising moon to me. The new should be rising. And in early childhood the sun and moon, those opposite reigning powers, I just as easily assumed rose in east and west respectively in their opposite sides of the sky, and like partners in a reel they advanced, sun from the east, moon from the west, crossed over (when I wasn't looking) and went down on the other side. My father couldn't have known I believed that when, bending behind me and guiding my shoulder, he positioned me at our telescope in the front yard and, with careful adjustment of the focus, brought the moon close to me.

---

3. An illustrated Irish manuscript of the four Gospels from the eighth or ninth century.

20   The night sky over my childhood Jackson[4] was velvety black. I could
see the full constellations in it and call their names; when I could read,
I knew their myths. Though I was always waked for eclipses, and indeed
carried to the window as an infant in arms and shown Halley's Comet[5]
in my sleep, and though I'd been taught at our diningroom table about
the solar system and knew the earth revolved around the sun, and our
moon around us, I never found out the moon didn't come up in the west
until I was a writer and Herschel Brickell, the literary critic, told me after
I misplaced it in a story. He said valuable words to me about my new
profession: "Always be sure you get your moon in the right part of the
sky."

My mother always sang to her children. Her voice came out just a
little bit in the minor key. "Wee Willie Winkie's" song was wonderfully
sad when she sang the lullabies.

"Oh, but now there's a record. She could have her own record to listen
to," my father would have said. For there came a Victrola record of
"Bobby Shafftoe" and "Rock-a-Bye Baby,"[6] all of Mother's lullabies,
which could be played to take her place. Soon I was able to play her my
own lullabies all day long.

Our Victrola stood in the diningroom. I was allowed to climb onto
the seat of a diningroom chair to wind it, start the record turning, and
set the needle playing. In a second I'd jumped to the floor, to spin or
march around the table as the music called for—now there were all the
other records I could play too. I skinned back onto the chair just in time
to lift the needle at the end, stop the record and turn it over, then
change the needle. That brass receptable with a hole in the lid gave off
a metallic smell like human sweat, from all the hot needles that were
fed it. Winding up, dancing, being cocked to start and stop the record,
was of course all in one the act of *listening*—to "Overture to *Daughter
of the Regiment*," "Selections from *The Fortune Teller*," "Kiss Me
Again," "Gypsy Dance from *Carmen*," "Stars and Stripes Forever,"
"When the Midnight Choo-Choo Leaves for Alabam," or whatever
came next.[7] Movement must be at the very heart of listening.

4. Jackson, Mississippi, where Welty grew up.
5. A comet named after Edmund Halley (1656–1742), English astronomer.
6. "Wee Willie Winkie," a nursery rhyme of 1841 in which sleep is personified; "Bobby Shafftoe," a traditional sea chantey dating from about 1750; "Rock-a-Bye Baby," words from *Mother Goose's Melodies* (1765) set to music in 1884.
7. *Daughter of the Regiment*, an opera (1840) by the Italian composer Gaetano Donizetti; *The Fortune Teller*, an operetta (1898) by the American Victor Herbert; "Kiss Me Again," a song from Herbert's *Mlle. Modiste* (1905); *Carmen*, an opera (1875) by the French composer Georges Bizet; "Stars and Stripes Forever," a march (1897) by the American John Philip Sousa (the "March King"); "When the Midnight Choo-Choo Leaves for Alabam," a popular song (1912) by the American Irving Berlin.

Ever since I was first read to, then started reading to myself, there has never been a line read that I didn't *hear*. As my eyes followed the sentence, a voice was saying it silently to me. It isn't my mother's voice, or the voice of any person I can identify, certainly not my own. It is human, but inward, and it is inwardly that I listen to it. It is to me the voice of the story or the poem itself. The cadence, whatever it is that asks you to believe, the feeling that resides in the printed word, reaches me through the reader-voice. I have supposed, but never found out, that this is the case with all readers—to read as listeners—and with all writers, to write as listeners. It may be part of the desire to write. The sound of what falls on the page begins the process of testing it for truth, for me. Whether I am right to trust so far I don't know. By now I don't know whether I could do either one, reading or writing, without the other.

My own words, when I am at work on a story, I hear too as they go, in the same voice that I hear when I read in books. When I write and the sound of it comes back to my ears, then I act to make my changes. I have always trusted this voice.

25

THE READER

1. *On p. 1047, Welty devotes a paragraph to drawing a daffodil in children's art class. What is the relation of that paragraph to the one about the initial "O" just before and to the one about the full moon just after?*
2. *Welty concludes by talking of* trust *and* truth. *What meaning does she give to these words?*
3. *When she speaks of her father's belief about the 1925 edition of the* Britannica *or puts quotation marks around "the library," Welty suggests that her mature judgment differs from her parents' judgment. How significant is her mature judgment on these matters? How does the answer to this question relate to the meaning she gives to* trust *and* truth *(see question 2, above)?*

THE WRITER

1. *Welty speaks of her "sensory education." What does she mean?*
2. *Welty got her sensory education before television. Suppose she had watched children's television as a child. Write a couple of sentences in her voice explaining its function in her sensory education. Write a paragraph in your own voice explaining its function in your sensory education.*

Vladimir Nabokov

GOOD READERS AND GOOD WRITERS

"How to be a Good Reader" or "Kindness to Authors"—something of that sort might serve to provide a subtitle for these various discussions of various authors, for my plan is to deal lovingly, in loving and lingering detail, with several European masterpieces. A hundred years ago, Flaubert in a letter to his mistress made the following remark: *Comme l'on serait savant si l'on connaissait bien seulement cinq à six livres:* "What a scholar one might be if one knew well only some half a dozen books."

In reading, one should notice and fondle details. There is nothing wrong about the moonshine of generalization when it comes *after* the sunny trifles of the book have been lovingly collected. If one begins with a ready-made generalization, one begins at the wrong end and travels away from the book before one has started to understand it. Nothing is more boring or more unfair to the author than starting to read, say, *Madame Bovary,* with the preconceived notion that it is a denunciation of the bourgeoisie. We should always remember that the work of art is invariably the creation of a new world, so that the first thing we should do is to study that new world as closely as possible, approaching it as something brand new, having no obvious connection with the worlds we already know. When this new world has been closely studied, then and only then let us examine its links with other worlds, other branches of knowledge.

Another question: Can we expect to glean information about places and times from a novel? Can anybody be so naive as to think he or she can learn anything about the past from those buxom best-sellers that are hawked around by book clubs under the heading of historical novels? But what about the masterpieces? Can we rely on Jane Austen's picture of landowning England with baronets and landscaped grounds when all she knew was a clergyman's parlor? And *Bleak House,* that fantastic romance within a fantastic London, can we call it a study of London a hundred years ago? Certainly not. And the same holds for other such novels in this series. The truth is that great novels are great fairy tales— and the novels in this series are supreme fairy tales.

Time and space, the colors of the seasons, the movements of muscles and minds, all these are for writers of genius (as far as we can guess and I trust we guess right) not traditional notions which may be borrowed from the circulating library of public truths but a series of unique

From *Lectures on Literature* (1980).

surprises which master artists have learned to express in their own unique way. To minor authors is left the ornamentation of the commonplace: these do not bother about any reinventing of the world; they merely try to squeeze the best they can out of a given order of things, out of traditional patterns of fiction. The various combinations these minor authors are able to produce within these set limits may be quite amusing in a mild ephemeral way because minor readers like to recognize their own ideas in a pleasing disguise. But the real writer, the fellow who sends planets spinning and models a man asleep and eagerly tampers with the sleeper's rib, that kind of author has no given values at his disposal: he must create them himself. The art of writing is a very futile business if it does not imply first of all the art of seeing the world as the potentiality of fiction. The material of this world may be real enough (as far as reality goes) but does not exist at all as an accepted entirety: it is chaos, and to this chaos the author says "go!" allowing the world to flicker and to fuse. It is now recombined in its very atoms, not merely in its visible and superficial parts. The writer is the first man to map it and to name the natural objects it contains. Those berries there are edible. That speckled creature that bolted across my path might be tamed. That lake between those trees will be called Lake Opal or, more artistically, Dishwater Lake. That mist is a mountain—and that mountain must be conquered. Up a trackless slope climbs the master artist, and at the top, on a windy ridge, whom do you think he meets? The panting and happy reader, and there they spontaneously embrace and are linked forever if the book lasts forever.

One evening at a remote provincial college through which I happened to be jogging on a protracted lecture tour, I suggested a little quiz—ten definitions of a reader, and from these ten the students had to choose four definitions that would combine to make a good reader. I have mislaid the list, but as far as I remember the definitions went something like this. Select four answers to the question what should a reader be to be a good reader:

1. The reader should belong to a book club.
2. The reader should identify himself or herself with the hero or heroine.
3. The reader should concentrate on the social-economic angle.
4. The reader should prefer a story with action and dialogue to one with none.
5. The reader should have seen the book in a movie.
6. The reader should be a budding author.
7. The reader should have imagination.
8. The reader should have memory.
9. The reader should have a dictionary.
10. The reader should have some artistic sense.

The students leaned heavily on emotional identification, action, and the social-economic or historical angle. Of course, as you have guessed, the good reader is one who has imagination, memory, a dictionary, and some artistic sense—which sense I propose to develop in myself and in others whenever I have the chance.

Incidentally, I use the word *reader* very loosely. Curiously enough, one cannot *read* a book: one can only reread it. A good reader, a major reader, an active and creative reader is a rereader. And I shall tell you why. When we read a book for the first time the very process of laboriously moving our eyes from left to right, line after line, page after page, this complicated physical work upon the book, the very process of learning in terms of space and time what the book is about, this stands between us and artistic appreciation. When we look at a painting we do not have to move our eyes in a special way even if, as in a book, the picture contains elements of depth and development. The element of time does not really enter in a first contact with a painting. In reading a book, we must have time to acquaint ourselves with it. We have no physical organ (as we have the eye in regard to a painting) that takes in the whole picture and then can enjoy its details. But at a second, or third, or fourth reading we do, in a sense, behave towards a book as we do towards a painting. However, let us not confuse the physical eye, that monstrous masterpiece of evolution, with the mind, an even more monstrous achievement. A book, no matter what it is—a work of fiction or a work of science (the boundary line between the two is not as clear as is generally believed)—a book of fiction appeals first of all to the mind. The mind, the brain, the top of the tingling spine, is, or should be, the only instrument used upon a book.

Now, this being so, we should ponder the question how does the mind work when the sullen reader is confronted by the sunny book. First, the sullen mood melts away, and for better or worse the reader enters into the spirit of the game. The effort to begin a book, especially if it is praised by people whom the young reader secretly deems to be too old-fashioned or too serious, this effort is often difficult to make; but once it is made, rewards are various and abundant. Since the master artist used his imagination in creating his book, it is natural and fair that the consumer of a book should use his imagination too.

There are, however, at least two varieties of imagination in the reader's case. So let us see which one of the two is the right one to use in reading a book. First, there is the comparatively lowly kind which turns for support to the simple emotions and is of a definitely personal nature. (There are various subvarieties here, in this first section of emotional reading.) A situation in a book is intensely felt because it reminds us of something that happened to us or to someone we know or knew. Or, again, a reader treasures a book mainly because it evokes a country, a landscape, a mode of living which he nostalgically recalls as part of his own past. Or, and this is the worst thing a reader can do, he identifies himself with a character in the book. This lowly variety is not the kind of imagination I would like readers to use.

So what is the authentic instrument to be used by the reader? It is impersonal imagination and artistic delight. What should be established, I think, is an artistic harmonious balance between the reader's mind and the author's mind. We ought to remain a little aloof and take pleasure in this aloofness while at the same time we keenly enjoy— passionately enjoy, enjoy with tears and shivers—the inner weave of a given masterpiece. To be quite objective in these matters is of course impossible. Everything that is worthwhile is to some extent subjective. For instance, you sitting there may be merely my dream, and I may be your nightmare. But what I mean is that the reader must know when and where to curb his imagination and this he does by trying to get clear the specific world the author places at his disposal. We must see things and hear things, we must visualize the rooms, the clothes, the manners of an author's people. The color of Fanny Price's eyes in *Mansfield Park* and the furnishing of her cold little room are important.

We all have different temperaments, and I can tell you right now that   10
the best temperament for a reader to have, or to develop, is a combination of the artistic and the scientific one. The enthusiastic artist alone is apt to be too subjective in his attitude towards a book, and so a scientific coolness of judgment will temper the intuitive heat. If, however, a would-be reader is utterly devoid of passion and patience—of an artist's passion and a scientist's patience—he will hardly enjoy great literature.

Literature was born not the day when a boy crying wolf, wolf came running out of the Neanderthal valley with a big gray wolf at his heels: literature was born on the day when a boy came crying wolf, wolf and there was no wolf behind him. That the poor little fellow because he lied too often was finally eaten up by a real beast is quite incidental. But here is what is important. Between the wolf in the tall grass and the wolf in the tall story there is a shimmering go-between. That go-between, that prism, is the art of literature.

Literature is invention. Fiction is fiction. To call a story a true story is an insult to both art and truth. Every great writer is a great deceiver, but so is that arch-cheat Nature. Nature always deceives. From the simple deception of propagation to the prodigiously sophisticated illusion of protective colors in butterflies or birds, there is in Nature a marvelous system of spells and wiles. The writer of fiction only follows Nature's lead.

Going back for a moment to our wolf-crying woodland little woolly fellow, we may put it this way: the magic of art was in the shadow of the wolf that he deliberately invented, his dream of the wolf; then the story of his tricks made a good story. When he perished at last, the story told about him acquired a good lesson in the dark around the camp fire. But he was the little magician. He was the inventor.

There are three points of view from which a writer can be considered: he may be considered as a storyteller, as a teacher, and as an enchanter. A major writer combines these three—storyteller, teacher, enchanter—but it is the enchanter in him that predominates and makes him a major writer.

To the storyteller we turn for entertainment, for mental excitement of the simplest kind, for emotional participation, for the pleasure of traveling in some remote region in space or time. A slightly different though not necessarily higher mind looks for the teacher in the writer. Propagandist, moralist, prophet—this is the rising sequence. We may go to the teacher not only for moral education but also for direct knowledge, for simple facts. Alas, I have known people whose purpose in reading the French and Russian novelists was to learn something about life in gay Paree or in sad Russia. Finally, and above all, a great writer is always a great enchanter, and it is here that we come to the really exciting part when we try to grasp the individual magic of his genius and to study the style, the imagery, the pattern of his novels or poems.

The three facets of the great writer—magic, story, lesson—are prone to blend in one impression of unified and unique radiance, since the magic of art may be present in the very bones of the story, in the very marrow of thought. There are masterpieces of dry, limpid, organized thought which provoke in us an artistic quiver quite as strongly as a novel like *Mansfield Park* does or as any rich flow of Dickensian sensual imagery. It seems to me that a good formula to test the quality of a novel is, in the long run, a merging of the precision of poetry and the intuition of science. In order to bask in that magic a wise reader reads the book of genius not with his heart, not so much with his brain, but with his spine. It is there that occurs the telltale tingle even though we must keep a little aloof, a little detached when reading. Then with a pleasure which is both sensual and intellectual we shall watch the artist build his castle of cards and watch the castle of cards become a castle of beautiful steel and glass.

Northrop Frye

THE MOTIVE FOR METAPHOR

For the past twenty-five years I have been teaching and studying English literature in a university. As in any other job, certain questions stick in one's mind, not because people keep asking them, but because they're the questions inspired by the very fact of being in such a place. What good is the study of literature? Does it help us to think more clearly, or feel more sensitively, or live a better life than we could without it? What is the function of the teacher and scholar, or of the person who calls himself, as I do, a literary critic? What difference does the study of literature make in our social or political or religious attitude? In my early days I thought very little about such questions, not because I had any of the answers, but because I assumed that anybody who asked them was naïve. I think now that the simplest questions are not only the hardest to answer, but the most important to ask, so I'm going to raise them and try to suggest what my present answers are. I say try to suggest, because there are only more or less inadequate answers to such questions—there aren't any right answers. The kind of problem that literature raises is not the kind that you ever "solve." Whether my answers are any good or not, they represent a fair amount of thinking about the questions. As I can't see my audience, I have to choose my rhetorical style in the dark, and I'm taking the classroom style, because an audience of students is the one I feel easiest with.

There are two things in particular that I want to discuss with you. In school, and in university, there's a subject called "English" in English-speaking countries. English means, in the first place, the mother tongue. As that, it's the most practical subject in the world: you can't understand anything or take any part in your society without it. Wherever illiteracy is a problem, it's as fundamental a problem as getting enough to eat or a place to sleep. The native language takes precedence over every other subject of study: nothing else can compare with it in its usefulness. But then you find that every mother tongue, in any developed or civilized society, turns into something called literature. If you keep on studying "English," you find yourself trying to read Shakespeare and Milton. Literature, we're told, is one of the arts, along with painting and music, and, after you've looked up all the hard words and the Classical allusions and learned what words like imagery and diction are supposed to mean, what you use in understanding it, or so you're told, is your imagination.

From *The Educated Imagination* (1964).

Here you don't seem to be in quite the same practical and useful area: Shakespeare and Milton, whatever their merits, are not the kind of thing you must know to hold any place in society at all. A person who knows nothing about literature may be an ignoramus, but many people don't mind being that. Every child realizes that literature is taking him in a different direction from the immediately useful, and a good many children complain loudly about this. Two questions I want to deal with, then, are, first: what is the relation of English as the mother tongue to English as a literature? Second: What is the social value of the study of literature, and what is the place of the imagination that literature addresses itself to, in the learning process?

Let's start with the different ways there are of dealing with the world we're living in. Suppose you're shipwrecked on an uninhabited island in the South Seas. The first thing you do is to take a long look at the world around you, a world of sky and sea and earth and stars and trees and hills. You see this world as objective, as something set over against you and not yourself or related to you in any way. And you notice two things about this objective world. In the first place, it doesn't have any conversation. It's full of animals and plants and insects going on with their own business, but there's nothing that responds to you: it has no morals and no intelligence, or at least none that you can grasp. It may have a shape and a meaning, but it doesn't seem to be a human shape or a human meaning. Even if there's enough to eat and no dangerous animals, you feel lonely and frightened and unwanted in such a world.

In the second place, you find that looking at the world, as something set over against you, splits your mind in two. You have an intellect that feels curious about it and wants to study it, and you have feelings or emotions that see it as beautiful or austere or terrible. You know that both these attitudes have some reality, at least for you. If the ship you were wrecked in was a Western ship, you'd probably feel that your intellect tells you more about what's really there in the outer world, and that your emotions tell you more about what's going on inside you. If your background were Oriental, you'd be more likely to reverse this and say that the beauty or terror was what was really there, and that your instinct to count and classify and measure and pull to pieces was what was inside your mind. But whether your point of view is Western or Eastern, intellect and emotion never get together in your mind as long as you're simply looking at the world. They alternate, and keep you divided between them.

5   The language you use on this level of the mind is the language of consciousness or awareness. It's largely a language of nouns and adjectives. You have to have names for things, and you need qualities like "wet" or "green" or "beautiful" to describe how things seem to you. This is the speculative or contemplative position of the mind, the posi-

tion in which the arts and sciences begin, although they don't stay there very long. The sciences begin by accepting the facts and the evidence about an outside world without trying to alter them. Science proceeds by accurate measurement and description, and follows the demands of the reason rather than the emotions. What it deals with is there, whether we like it or not. The emotions are unreasonable: for them it's what they like and don't like that comes first. We'd be naturally inclined to think that the arts follow the path of emotion, in contrast to the sciences. Up to a point they do, but there's a complicating factor.

That complicating factor is the contrast between "I like this" and "I don't like this." In this Robinson Crusoe life I've assigned you, you may have moods of complete peacefulness and joy, moods when you accept your island and everything around you. You wouldn't have such moods very often, and when you had them, they'd be moods of identification, when you felt that the island was a part of you and you a part of it. That is not the feeling of consciousness or awareness, where you feel split off from everything that's not your perceiving self. Your habitual state of mind is the feeling of separation which goes with being conscious, and the feeling "this is not a part of me" soon becomes "this is not what I want." Notice the word "want": we'll be coming back to it.

So you soon realize that there's a difference between the world you're living in and the world you want to live in. The world you want to live in is a human world, not an objective one: it's not an environment but a home; it's not the world you see but the world you build out of what you see. You go to work to build a shelter or plant a garden, and as soon as you start to work you've moved into a different level of human life. You're not separating only yourself from nature now, but constructing a human world and separating it from the rest of the world. Your intellect and emotions are now both engaged in the same activity, so there's no longer any real distinction between them. As soon as you plant a garden or a crop, you develop the conception of a "weed," the plant you don't want in there. But you can't say that "weed" is either an intellectual or an emotional conception, because it's both at once. Further, you go to work because you feel you have to, and because you want something at the end of the work. That means that the important categories of your life are no longer the subject and the object, the watcher and the things being watched: the important categories are what you have to do and what you want to do—in other words, necessity and freedom.

One person by himself is not a complete human being, so I'll provide you with another shipwrecked refugee of the opposite sex and an eventual family. Now you're a member of a human society. This human society after a while will transform the island into something with a human shape. What that human shape is, is revealed in the shape of the work you do: the buildings, such as they are, the paths through the woods, the planted crops fenced off against whatever animals want to eat them. These things, these rudiments of city, highway, garden, and farm, are the human form of nature, or the form of human nature, whichever you like. This is the area of the applied arts and sciences, and it appears in our society as engineering and agriculture and medicine and architecture. In this area we can never say clearly where the art stops and the science begins, or vice versa.

The language you use on this level is the language of practical sense, a language of verbs or words of action and movement. The practical world, however, is a world where actions speak louder than words. In some way it's a higher level of existence than the speculative level, because it's doing something about the world instead of just looking at it, but in itself it's a much more primitive level. It's the process of adapting to the environment, or rather of transforming the environment in the interests of one species, that goes on among animals and plants as well as human beings. The animals have a good many of our practical skills: some insects make pretty fair architects, and beavers know quite a lot about engineering. In this island, probably, and certainly if you were alone, you'd have about the ranking of a second-rate animal. What makes our practical life really human is a third level of the mind, a level where consciousness and practical skill come together.

10   This third level is a vision or model in your mind of what you want to construct. There's that word "want" again. The actions of man are prompted by desire, and some of these desires are needs, like food and warmth and shelter. One of these needs is sexual, the desire to reproduce and bring more human beings into existence. But there's also a desire to bring a social human form into existence: the form of cities and gardens and farms that we call civilization. Many animals and insects have this social form too, but man knows that he has it: he can compare what he does with what he can imagine being done. So we begin to see where the imagination belongs in the scheme of human affairs. It's the power of constructing possible models of human experience. In the world of the imagination, anything goes that's imaginatively possible, but nothing really happens. If it did happen, it would move out of the world of imagination into the world of action.

We have three levels of the mind now, and a language for each of them, which in English-speaking societies means an English for each of them. There's the level of consciousness and awareness, where the most important thing is the difference between me and everything else. The English of this level is the English of ordinary conversation, which is mostly monologue, as you'll soon realize if you do a bit of eavesdropping, or listening to yourself. We can call it the language of self-expression. Then there's the level of social participation, the working or technological language of teachers and preachers and politicians and advertisers and lawyers and journalists and scientists. We've already called this the language of practical sense. Then there's the level of imagination, which produces the literary language of poems and plays and novels. They're not really different languages, of course, but three different reasons for using words.

On this basis, perhaps, we can distinguish the arts from the sciences. Science begins with the world we have to live in, accepting its data and trying to explain its laws. From there, it moves towards the imagination: it becomes a mental construct, a model of a possible way of interpreting experience. The further it goes in this direction, the more it tends to speak the language of mathematics, which is really one of the languages of the imagination, along with literature and music. Art, on the other hand, begins with the world we construct, not with the world we see. It starts with the imagination, and then works towards ordinary experience: that is, it tries to make itself as convincing and recognizable as it can. You can see why we tend to think of the sciences as intellectual and the arts as emotional: one starts with the world as it is, the other with the world we want to have. Up to a point it is true that science gives an intellectual view of reality, and that the arts try to make the emotions as precise and disciplined as sciences do the intellect. But of course it's nonsense to think of the scientist as a cold unemotional reasoner and the artist as somebody who's in a perpetual emotional tizzy. You can't distinguish the arts from the sciences by the mental processes the people in them use: they both operate on a mixture of hunch and common sense. A highly developed science and and a highly developed art are very close together, psychologically and otherwise.

Still, the fact that they start from opposite ends, even if they do meet in the middle, makes for one important difference between them. Science learns more and more about the world as it goes on: it evolves and improves. A physicist today knows more physics than Newton did, even if he's not as great a scientist. But literature begins with the possible model of experience, and what it produces is the literary model we call the classic. Literature doesn't evolve or improve or progress. We may have dramatists in the future who will write plays as good as *King Lear*, though they'll be very different ones, but drama as a whole will never get better than *King Lear*. *King Lear* is it, as far as drama is concerned; so is *Oedipus Rex*, written two thousand years earlier than that, and both will be models of dramatic writing as long as the human race endures. Social conditions may improve: most of us would rather live in nineteenth-century United States than in thirteenth-century Italy, and for most of us Whitman's celebration of democracy makes a lot more sense than Dante's Inferno. But it doesn't follow that Whitman is a better poet than Dante: literature won't line up with that kind of improvement.

So we find that everything that does improve, including science, leaves the literary artist out in the cold. Writers don't seem to benefit much by the advance of science, although they thrive on superstitions of all kinds. And you certainly wouldn't turn to contemporary poets for guidance or leadership in the twentieth-century world. You'd hardly go to Ezra Pound, with his fascism and social credit and Confucianism and anti-semitism. Or to Yeats, with his spiritualism and fairies and astrology. Or to D. H. Lawrence, who'll tell you that it's a good thing for servants to be flogged because that restores the precious current of blood-reciprocity between servant and master. Or to T. S. Eliot, who'll tell you that to have a flourishing culture we should educate an élite, keep most people living in the same spot, and never disestablish the Church of England. The novelists seem to be a little closer to the world they're living in, but not much. When Communists talk about the decadence of bourgeois culture, this is the kind of thing they always bring up. Their own writers don't seem to be any better, though; just duller. So the real question is a bigger one. Is it possible that literature, especially poetry, is something that a scientific civilization like ours will eventually outgrow? Man has always wanted to fly, and thousands of years ago he was making sculptures of winged bulls and telling stories about people who flew so high on artificial wings that the sun melted them off. In an Indian play fifteen hundred years old, *Sakuntala,* there's a god who flies around in a chariot that to a modern reader sounds very much like a private aeroplane. Interesting that the writer had so much imagination, but do we need such stories now that we have private aeroplanes?

15   This is not a new question: it was raised a hundred and fifty years ago by Thomas Love Peacock, who was a poet and novelist himself, and a very brilliant one. He wrote an essay called *Four Ages of Poetry,* with his tongue of course in his cheek, in which he said that poetry was the mental rattle that awakened the imagination of mankind in its infancy, but that now, in an age of science and technology, the poet has outlived his social function. "A poet in our times," said Peacock, "is a semi-barbarian in a civilized community. He lives in the days that are past. His ideas, thoughts, feelings, associations, are all with barbarous manners, obsolete customs, and exploded superstitions. The march of his intellect is like that of a crab, backwards." Peacock's essay annoyed his friend Shelley, who wrote another essay called *A Defence of Poetry* to refute it. Shelley's essay is a wonderful piece of writing, but it's not likely to convince anyone who needs convincing. I shall be spending a good deal of my time on this question of the relevance of literature in the world of today, and I can only indicate the general lines my answer will take. There are two points I can make now, one simple, the other more difficult.

The simple point is that literature belongs to the world man constructs, not to the world he sees; to his home, not his environment. Literature's world is a concrete human world of immediate experience. The poet uses images and objects and sensations much more than he uses abstract ideas; the novelist is concerned with telling stories, not with working out arguments. The world of literature is human in shape, a world where the sun rises in the east and sets in the west over the edge of a flat earth in three dimensions, where the primary realities are not atoms or electrons but bodies, and the primary forces not energy or gravitation but love and death and passion and joy. It's not surprising if writers are often rather simple people, not always what we think of as intellectuals, and certainly not always any freer of silliness or perversity than anyone else. What concerns us is what they produce, not what they are, and poetry, according to Milton, who ought to have known, is "more simple, sensuous and passionate" than philosophy or science.

The more difficult point takes us back to what we said when we were on that South Sea island. Our emotional reaction to the world varies from "I like this" to "I don't like this." The first, we said, was a state of identity, a feeling that everything around us was part of us, and the second is the ordinary state of consciousness, or separation, where art and science begin. Art begins as soon as "I don't like this" turns into "this is not the way I could imagine it." We notice in passing that the creative and the neurotic minds have a lot in common. They're both dissatisfied with what they see; they both believe that something else ought to be there, and they try to pretend it is there or to make it be there. The differences are more important, but we're not ready for them yet.

At the level of ordinary consciousness the individual man is the centre of everything, surrounded on all sides by what he isn't. At the level of practical sense, or civilization, there's a human circumference, a little cultivated world with a human shape, fenced off from the jungle and inside the sea and the sky. But in the imagination anything goes that can be imagined, and the limit of the imagination is a totally human world. Here we recapture, in full consciousness, that original lost sense of identity with our surroundings, where there is nothing outside the mind of man, or something identical with the mind of man. Religions present us with visions of eternal and infinite heavens or paradises which have the form of the cities and gardens of human civilization, like the Jerusalem and Eden of the Bible, completely separated from the state of frustration and misery that bulks so large in ordinary life. We're not concerned with these visions as religion, but they indicate what the limits of the imagination are. They indicate too that in the human world the imagination has no limits, if you follow me. We said that the desire to fly produced the aeroplane. But people don't get into planes because they want to fly; they get into planes because they want to get somewhere else faster. What's produced the aeroplane is not so much a desire to fly as a rebellion against the tyranny of time and space. And that's a process that can never stop, no matter how high our Titovs[1] and Glenns[2] may go.

For each of these six talks I've taken a title from some work of literature, and my title for this one is "The Motive for Metaphor," from a poem of Wallace Stevens. Here's the poem:

> You like it under the trees in autumn,
> Because everything is half dead.
> The wind moves like a cripple among the leaves
> And repeats words without meaning.
>
> In the same way, you were happy in spring,
> With the half colors of quarter-things,
> The slightly brighter sky, the melting clouds,
> The single bird, the obscure moon—
>
> The obscure moon lighting an obscure world
> Of things that would never be quite expressed,
> Where you yourself were never quite yourself
> And did not want nor have to be,
>
> Desiring the exhilarations of changes:
> The motive for metaphor, shrinking from
> The weight of primary noon,
> The A B C of being,
>
> The ruddy temper, the hammer
> Of red and blue, the hard sound—
> Steel against intimation—the sharp flash,
> The vital, arrogant, fatal, dominant X.

What Stevens calls the weight of primary noon, the A B C of being, and the dominant X is the objective world, the world set over against us. Outside literature, the main motive for writing is to describe this world. But literature itself uses language in a way which associates our minds with it. As soon as you use associative language, you begin using figures of speech. If you say this talk is dry and dull, you're using figures associating it with bread and breadknives. There are two main kinds of association, analogy and identity, two things that are like each other and two things that are each other. You can say with Burns, "My love's like a red, red rose," or you can say with Shakespeare:

> Thou that art now the world's fresh ornament
> And only herald to the gaudy spring.

1. Gherman S. Titov, Russian astronaut and first man to make a multi-orbital flight (Aug. 1961).   2. John H. Glenn, astronaut and first American to make an orbital flight (Feb. 1962).

One produces the figure of speech called the simile; the other produces the figure called metaphor.

In descriptive writing you have to be careful of associative language. You'll find that analogy, or likeness to something else, is very tricky to handle in description, because the differences are as important as the resemblances. As for metaphor, where you're really saying "this *is* that," you're turning your back on logic and reason completely, because logically two things can never be the same thing and still remain two things. The poet, however, uses these two crude, primitive, archaic forms of thought in the most uninhibited way, because his job is not to describe nature, but to show you a world completely absorbed and possessed by the human mind. So he produces what Baudelaire called a "suggestive magic including at the same time object and subject, the world outside the artist and the artist himself." The motive for metaphor, according to Wallace Stevens, is a desire to associate, and finally to identify, the human mind with what goes on outside it, because the only genuine joy you can have is in those rare moments when you feel that although we may know in part, as Paul says, we are also a part of what we know.

THE READER

1. At what point in his essay does Frye come to the meaning of his title? What does this essay say the motive for metaphor is? Does it seem to you to be a satisfactory motive?

2. How far does Frye go in this essay toward responding to the simple, big questions he starts out with? Has he clarified for you or answered any of these questions? Is there indication in the essay that this is a beginning of the discussion, with more to follow?

3. What are the three kinds of English Frye talks about in his essay? Do we really need three kinds—isn't one enough?

4. Why do you have to take so much English in school when you already know how to use English even before you start school?

THE WRITER

1. Why does Frye ask his reader to imagine him- or herself a castaway on a South Sea island? Are you ever likely to be in that position, or is it a bit far-fetched? Is it just a colorful way to get his point across? If so, what is his point?

2. Does Frye anticipate a possible objection that metaphor distorts the truth and misleads us as to the way things really are? Why, or why not?

3. Why doesn't literature get any better, the way science does? Can literature be any good, seeing that it doesn't improve? Given the fact that it doesn't improve, shouldn't much of it be outdated? Cast your answer to these questions in the form of two brief essays, one addressed

to an English teacher, one addressed to a fellow student majoring in science. How do your two essays differ?

Annie Dillard

ABOUT SYMBOL

Fiction does interpret the world at large. It traffics in understanding. Does it also traffic in knowledge? Do its interpretations have the status of hard data? Does art know?

Knowledge and understanding meet where science meets theology, where substance and idea mingle their parts. This juncture is the apex of the pyramid of abstractions. It is the apogee of all our researches; it is the vanishing point where all lines of thought converge. Here eternity gives birth to time. I wish to assert that art is especially competent to penetrate these regions, and others as well.

Zola, according to Charles Child Walcutt,[1] said that fiction "had been an art but would henceforth be an instrument for the scientific study of man and society." Now, no one is going to attack Zola, who is not so much a sacred cow as a dead horse. Let me just use these notions. Zola makes a false distinction when he says that fiction was formerly an art but was now an instrument for scientific study—an instrument, I infer, like a lens or a sextant. Because the truth is that only by being art is fiction an instrument at all. Art itself is an instrument, a cognitive instrument, and with religion the only instrument, for probing certain materials and questions. Art and religion probe the mysteries in those difficult areas where blurred and powerful symbols are the only possible speech and their arrangement into coherent religions and works of art the only possible grammar.

All art may be said to be symbolic in this sense: it is a material mock-up of bright idea. Any work of art symbolizes the process by which spirit generates matter, or materials generate idea. Any work of art symbolizes juncture itself, the socketing of eternity into time and energy into form. Of course, all that man makes is similar in this respect: a bowl,

From *Living by Fiction* (1982), originally published in *The Massachussetts Review* (Spring 1982).

1. Émile Zola (1840–1902), French novelist and founder of Naturalism in literature; Walcutt (1908–   ): American literary critic, novelist, textbook author.

a highway, and a triangle are also material mock-ups of mental orders. But this is *all* that art is, in essence and by intent. A highway intends something quite other. Any art object is essentially a model in which the creative process is frozen with its product in its arms.

Any art object as a whole is symbolic, then. But more pertinent to my point is the familiar level at which an art object is symbolic because its parts are. These things warrant a brief restatement.

An allegorical symbol is precise and bounded. When fair-haired Virtue shatters the opium pipe of Indolence, we may conclude that moral virtue in the abstract, which the author finds as attractive as he finds blondes, rejects indolence, strongly. Nonallegorical symbols, which are the topic at hand, are not precise. It is when these symbols break their allegorical boundaries, their commitment to reference, that they start stepping out on us. The laxity of their bonds permits them to enter unsuspected relationships. They become suggestive. These artistic symbols do not represent things in the great world directly, as the opium pipe represents indolence. Instead, these symbols, like art objects themselves, are semi-enclosed worlds of meaning the essence of whose referential substance we may approximate, but whose boundaries and total possibilities for significance we can never locate precisely or exhaust.

Of the "stately pleasure dome" of "Kubla Khan," shall we say it is an ordered, pleasing, and aloof work of art ("A stately pleasure dome"); or any conscious product of active power ("decree"); or the passive receptacle of the wellspring of the creative imagination itself ("Where Alph, the sacred river, ran"); or a formal ordering of subconscious materials ("Through caverns measureless to man"); or the civilization from which instruments of cognition are launched which discover and illuminate that civilization's sources in chaos, or its fated destiny, or its brute environment ("Down to a sunless sea") ? Of course, these are just opening suggestions; the other parts of the poem shed much light on the pleasure dome, clarifying some interpretations and suggesting others. Complete readings of the poem are available. If we even begin to investigate "Kubla Khan," do we not hazard into realms where paraphrase is inadequate? Of course. That is truism. Well, then, does this not mean that the pleasure dome, and other symbolic parts of the poem, and the poem itself, are vehicles of understanding? They are not the express products of past knowledge and understanding, such as the expression $2 + 3 = 5$, or the statement that virtue rejects indolence; instead, they are new objects wherein new understanding may be sought and found. They are objects set beyond the limits of the already known.

We may find symbolized in "Kubla Khan"—by the dome, by Kubla Khan, the river and its fountain, the forests, the caverns, the sea, the ice, and the Abyssinian maid and her song—something of the relationship between order and chaos, and between spirit and matter, between the artist and his materials, and the artist and society ("Ancestral voices prophesying war!"), and the romantic imagination and its sources and values ("A savage place! as holy and enchanted"), and the dangerously close relationship in the art object and perhaps in the artist between inspirational sources and the appalling chaos of the abyss ("the mingled measure / From the fountain and the caves"). We are interested in these relationships. The poem presents them. The poem is a form of knowledge. [2]

But what is knowledge if we cannot state it? If art objects quit the bounds of the known and make blurry feints at the unknown, can they truly add to knowledge or understanding? I think they can; for although we may never exhaust or locate precisely the phenomena they signify, we may nevertheless approximate them—and this, of course, is our position in relation to all knowledge and understanding. All our knowledge is partial and approximate; if we are to know electrons and chimpanzees less than perfectly, and call it good enough, we may as well understand phenomena like love and death, or art and freedom, imperfectly also.

10   Artistic symbol, in other words, instead of merely imitating the flux and mystery of the great world, actually penetrates them on its own. That is, if a document like *The New York Times* or Pepys' *Diary* [3] is a kind of island miniature of our planet, an island which we may explore on foot, then a symbol or a structure of related symbols (including myth, religion, and innumerable works of art, like *Moby Dick* and "Kubla Khan") is, by contrast, a kind of exploratory craft. It is a space probe. Although it is constructed of the planet's materials, it nevertheless leaves the planet altogether. It is a rocket ship; it opens new and hitherto inaccessible regions.

This is the unique cognitive property of symbol: there is no boundary, and probably no difference, between symbol and the realm it comes to mean. An art object, say, and a myth are each the agent and the object of cognition. Each is a lens focused on itself. Say that the story of Christ is a symbol. Say that generations of thinkers have enlarged and enriched the symbol. What then? What is the difference between this narrative, or this artifact, and what it symbolizes? It is it, itself. You cannot address this question (or any other) in depth without using its own terms, which

2. Incidentally, "Kubla Khan" also raises the question of its own beauty. Why is it so beautiful? Why do otherwise rational people—sober, grouchy, skeptical people—turn soft in the head about "Kubla Khan" ? Why is this creepy-crawly, misty, overland-scaped, striving-after-beautiful-effect, water-colorish little portentous poem one of the most beautiful and powerful poems in English [Dillard's note]?

3. Pepys' *Diary*, January 1, 1660–May 31, 1669, written by Samuel Pepys (1633–1703), gives an honest presentation of the ways of court and everyday life in seventeenth-century England.

are symbolic at every level: cup, manger, and cross, or grace, incarnation, and sacrifice—and so on, either "up" or "down" the levels of abstraction. You must either learn to use these terms, and like them, or relinquish this field of knowledge altogether.

Similarly, to speak of "Kubla Khan" at any useful level is to speak of the pleasure dome and of Alph the sacred river, and the caverns measureless to man, and the Abyssinian maid. You learn the poem as you learn Italian. You cease to translate its bits in your mind, and instead let them speak for themselves. All our knowledge is of course in one sense symbolic, and to go deeply into any field—physics, say, or art—is to learn faith in its symbols. At first you notice that these tools and objects of thought are symbols; you translate them, as you go, into your own familiar idiom. Later you learn faith and release them. You learn to let them relate on their own terms, hadron[4] to hadron, paint surface to paint surface—and only then do you begin to make progress. (In this sense, faith is the requisite of knowledge.)

One interesting, well-known, yet elusive thing about true symbols is something unmanageable about the way they are formed. Since their regions of meaning are blurred, and since there is no clear difference between symbols and the realms they come to mean, and since they act at the level where the scarcely understood fades into the unknown, the hapless artist who sets one of these things in motion shortly finds himself out of control. Symbols, and the many works of art that contain them, "assume a life of their own," as the cliché goes; they outreach the span of their maker's arm; they guide their creator's hand; they illuminate a wider area than that which their maker ever intended. * * * The art object is always passive in relation to its audience. It is alarmingly active, however, in relation to its creator. Far from being like a receptacle in which you, the artist, drop your ideas, and far from being like a lump of clay which you pummel until it fits your notion of an ashtray, the art object is more like an enthusiastic and ill-trained Labrador retriever which yanks you into traffic. I do not intend to wax mystical or sentimental at this juncture; nevertheless, this familiar notion—that the art object drags its maker into deep waters—is worth mentioning again, matter-of-factly, as one evidence that art, especially insofar as it is symbolic art, is not only an object of past knowledge but an instrument of new knowledge. For if you already understood all the relationships among phenomena to which the parts of your art referred, you could control them easily from the start—and you cannot. It is the artist's business, then, to learn from his art and to order formally his new understanding. Confused art is merely confusing. When in the art object the artist has mastered his own confusion, he has gained new ground; and if he is

4. A subatomic particle.

mature enough and educated enough to have begun at the far edge of his own culture's knowledge, then he has won new ground not only for himself but for his culture as well.

Symbol does not only refer; it acts. There is no such thing as a *mere* symbol. When you climb to the higher levels of abstraction, symbols, those enormous, translucent planets, are all there is. They are at once your only tools of knowledge and that knowledge's only object. It is no leap to say that space-time is itself a symbol. If the material world is a symbol, it is the symbol of mind, or of God. Which is more or less meaningless—as you choose. But is not *mere.* In the last analysis, symbols and art objects do not stand for things; they manifest them, in their fullness. You begin by using symbols, and end by contemplating them.

THE READER

1. *What does Dillard mean when she says a poem "is a form of knowledge"?*
2. *Is Dillard right in asserting that "there is no boundary, and probably no difference, between symbol and the realm it comes to mean"?*
3. *Dillard says that "to go deeply into any field—physics, say, or art—is to learn faith in its symbols." Why does she believe this is necessary?*
4. *Dillard says that "the art object . . . is alarmingly active . . . in its relation to its creator. Far from being like a receptacle in which you, the artist, drop your ideas, and far from being like a lump of clay which you pummel until it fits your notion of an ashtray, the art object is more like an enthusiastic and ill-trained Labrador retriever which yanks you into traffic." Rewrite this passage, translating the metaphors into non-metaphorical statements. Have you lost any of the meaning?*

THE WRITER

1. *Dillard discusses "Kubla Khan" (printed below) at some length. How does discussing the poem allow her to make some of her key points?*

KUBLA KHAN

OR A VISION IN A DREAM. A FRAGMENT

The following fragment is here published at the request of a poet of great and deserved celebrity,[1] and, as far as the author's own opinions are concerned, rather as a psychological curiosity, than on the ground of any supposed *poetic* merits.

In the summer of the year 1797, the author, then in ill health, had retired to a lonely farmhouse between Porlock and Linton, on the Exmoor

1. Lord Byron.

confines of Somerset and Devonshire. In consequence of a slight indisposition, an anodyne had been prescribed, from the effects of which he fell asleep in his chair at the moment that he was reading the following sentence, or words of the same substance, in *Purchas's Pilgrimage:* "Here the Khan Kubla commanded a palace to be built, and a stately garden thereunto. And thus ten miles of fertile ground were inclosed with a wall.[2] The author continued for about three hours in a profound sleep, at least of the external senses,[3] during which time he has the most vivid confidence that he could not have composed less than from two to three hundred lines; if that indeed can be called composition in which all the images rose up before him as *things,* with a parallel production of the correspondent expressions, without any sensation or consciousness of effort. On awaking he appeared to himself to have a distinct recollection of the whole, and taking his pen, ink, and paper, instantly and eagerly wrote down the lines that are here preserved. At this moment he was unfortunately called out by a person on business from Porlock, and detained by him above an hour, and on his return to his room, found, to his no small surprise and mortification, that though he still retained some vague and dim recollection of the general purport of his vision, yet, with the exception of some eight or ten scattered lines and images, all the rest had passed away like the images on the surface of a stream into which a stone has been cast, but, alas! without the after restoration of the latter!

> Then all the charm
> Is broken—all that phantom world so fair
> Vanishes, and a thousand circlets spread,
> And each misshape[s] the other. Stay awhile,
> Poor youth! who scarcely dar'st lift up thine eyes—
> The stream will soon renew its smoothness, soon
> The visions will return! And lo, he stays,
> And soon the fragments dim of lovely forms
> Come trembling back, unite, and now once more
> The pool becomes a mirror.

> [From Coleridge's *The Picture;
> or, the Lover's Resolution,* lines 91–100]

Yet from the still surviving recollections in his mind, the author has frequently purposed to finish for himself what had been originally, as it

2. "In Xamadu did Cublai Can build a stately Palace, encompassing sixteene miles of plaine ground with a wall, wherein fertile Meddowes, pleasant springs, delightfull Streames, and all softs of beasts of chase and game, and in the middest thereof a sumptuous house of pleasure, which may be removed from place to place." From Samuel Purchas, *Purchas his Pilgrimage* (1613). The historical Kublai Khan founded the Mongol dynasty in China in the thirteenth century.

3. In a note on a manuscript copy of *Kubla Khan,* Coleridge gave a more precise account of the nature of this "sleep": "This fragment with a good deal more, not recoverable, composed, in a sort of reverie brought on by two grains of opium, taken to check a dysentery, at a farmhouse between Porlock and Linton, a quarter of a mile from Culbone Church, in the fall of the year, 1797."

were, given to him. Σαμερον αδιον ασω:[4] but the tomorrow is yet to come.

> In Xanadu did Kubla Khan
> A stately pleasure dome decree:
> Where Alph, the sacred river, ran
> Through caverns measureless to man
> > Down to a sunless sea.
> So twice five miles of fertile ground
> With walls and towers were girdled round:
> And there were gardens bright with sinuous rills,
> Where blossomed many an incense-bearing tree;
> And here were forests ancient as the hills,
> Enfolding sunny spots of greenery.
>
> But oh! that deep romantic chasm which slanted
> Down the green hill athwart a cedarn cover!
> A savage place! as holy and enchanted
> As e'er beneath a waning moon was haunted
> By woman wailing for her demon lover!
> And from this chasm, with ceaseless turmoil seething,
> As if this earth in fast thick pants were breathing,
> A mighty fountain momently was forced:
> Amid whose swift half-intermitted burst
> Huge fragments vaulted like rebounding hail,
> Or chaffy grain beneath the thresher's flail:
> And 'mid these dancing rocks at once and ever
> It flung up momently the sacred river.
> Five miles meandering with a mazy motion
> Through wood and dale the sacred river ran,
> Then reached the caverns measureless to man,
> And sank in tumult to a lifeless ocean:
> And 'mid this tumult Kubla heard from far
> Ancestral voices prophesying war!
> > The shadow of the dome of pleasure
> > Floated midway on the waves;
> > Where was heard the mingled measure
> > From the fountain and the caves.
> It was a miracle of rare device,
> A sunny pleasure dome with caves of ice!
>
> > A damsel with a dulcimer
> > In a vision once I saw:
> > It was an Abyssinian maid,
> > And on her dulcimer she played,
> > Singing of Mount Abora.

---

4. "I shall sing a sweeter song today." In the edition of 1834, Σαμερον ("today") was changed to αυριον ("tomorrow"). Coleridge had in mind Theocritus, *Idyls* I.145: εφ υστερον αδιον ασω ("I shall sing a sweeter song on a later day").

Could I revive within me
Her symphony and song,
To such a deep delight 'twould win me,
That with music loud and long,
I would build that dome in air,
That sunny dome! those caves of ice!
And all who heard should see them there,
And all should cry, Beware! Beware!
His flashing eyes, his floating hair!
Weave a circle round him thrice,
And close your eyes with holy dread,
For he on honeydew hath fed,
And drunk the milk of Paradise.

c. 1797–98   1816

2. *In a footnote, Dillard calls "Kubla Khan" "one of the most beautiful and powerful poems in English" and a "creepy-crawly, misty, over-landscaped, striving-after-beautiful-effect, water-colorish little portentous poem" (p. 1066). Is there a contradiction here? Embody your answer in a brief essay.*
3. *Dillard calls a work of art "a space probe . . . [that] opens new and hitherto inaccessible regions" (p. 1066). What other metaphors might she have used to convey this idea? Try out one or two, and compare their effectiveness with Dillard's.*

Alice Munro

WHAT IS REAL?

Whenever people get an opportunity to ask me questions about my writing, I can be sure that some of the questions asked will be these:

"Do you write about real people?"

"Did those things really happen?"

"When you write about a small town are you really writing about Wingham?" (Wingham is the small town in Ontario where I was born and grew up, and it has often been assumed, by people who should know better, that I have simply "fictionalized" this place in my work. Indeed, the local newspaper has taken me to task for making it the "butt of a soured and cruel introspection.")

Originally appeared in *Making It New: Contemporary Canadian Stories* (1982) edited by John Metcalf.

5   The usual thing, for writers, is to regard these either as very naive questions, asked by people who really don't understand the difference between autobiography and fiction, who can't recognize the device of the first-person narrator, or else as catch-you-out questions posed by journalists who hope to stir up exactly the sort of dreary (and to outsiders, slightly comic) indignation voiced by my home-town paper. Writers answer such questions patiently or crossly according to temperament and the mood they're in. They say, no, you must understand, my characters are composites; no, those things didn't happen the way I wrote about them; no, of course not, that isn't Wingham (or whatever other place it may be that has had the queer unsought-after distinction of hatching a writer). Or the writer may, riskily, ask the questioners what is real, anyway? None of this seems to be very satisfactory. People go on asking these same questions because the subject really does interest and bewilder them. It would seem to be quite true that they don't know what fiction is.

And how could they know, when what it is, is changing all the time, and we differ among ourselves, and we don't really try to explain because it is too difficult?

What I would like to do here is what I can't do in two or three sentences at the end of a reading. I won't try to explain what fiction is, and what short stories are (assuming, which we can't, that there is any fixed thing that it is and they are), but what short stories are to me, and how I write them, and how I use things that are "real." I will start by explaining how I read stories written by other people. For one thing, I can start reading them anywhere; from beginning to end, from end to beginning, from any point in between in either direction. So obviously I don't take up a story and follow it as if it were a road, taking me somewhere, with views and neat diversions along the way. I go into it, and move back and forth and settle here and there, and stay in it for a while. It's more like a house. Everybody knows what a house does, how it encloses space and makes connections between one enclosed space and another and presents what is outside in a new way. This is the nearest I can come to explaining what a story does for me, and what I want my stories to do for other people.

So when I write a story I want to make a certain kind of structure, and I know the feeling I want to get from being inside that structure. This is the hard part of the explanation, where I have to use a word like "feeling," which is not very precise, because if I attempt to be more intellectually respectable I will have to be dishonest. "Feeling" will have to do.

There is no blueprint for the structure. It's not a question of, "I'll make this kind of house because if I do it right it will have this effect." I've got to make, I've got to build up, a house, a story, to fit around the indescribable "feeling" that is like the soul of the story, and which I must insist upon in a dogged, embarrassed way, as being no more definable than that. And I don't know where it comes from. It seems to be already there, and some unlikely clue, such as a shop window or a bit of conversation, makes me aware of it. Then I start accumulating the material and putting it together. Some of the material I may have lying around already, in memories and observations, and some I invent, and some I have to go diligently looking for (factual details), while some is dumped in my lap (anecdotes, bits of speech). I see how this material might go together to make the shape I need, and I try it. I keep trying and seeing where I went wrong and trying again.

I suppose this is the place where I should talk about technical problems and how I solve them. The main reason I can't is that I'm never sure I do solve anything. Even when I say that I see where I went wrong, I'm being misleading. I never figure out how I'm going to change things, I never say to myself, "That page is heavy going, that paragraph's clumsy, I need some dialogue and shorter sentences." I feel a part that's wrong, like a soggy weight; then I pay attention to the story, as if it were really happening somewhere, not just in my head, and in its own way, not mine. As a result, the sentences may indeed get shorter, there may be more dialogue, and so on. But though I've tried to pay attention to the story, I may not have got it right; those shorter sentences may be an evasion, a mistake. Every final draft, every published story, is still only an attempt, an approach, to the story.

I did promise to talk about using reality. "Why, if Jubilee isn't Wingham, has it got Shuter Street in it?" people want to know. Why have I described somebody's real ceramic elephant sitting on the mantelpiece? I could say I get momentum from doing things like this. The fictional room, town, world, needs a bit of starter dough from the real world. It's a device to help the writer—at least it helps me—but it arouses a certain baulked fury in the people who really do live on Shuter Street and the lady who owns the ceramic elephant. "Why do you put in something true and then go on and tell lies?" they say, and anybody who has been on the receiving end of this kind of thing knows how they feel.

"I do it for the sake of my art and to make this structure which encloses the soul of my story, that I've been telling you about," says the writer. "That is more important than anything."

Not to everybody, it isn't.

So I can see there might be a case, once you've written the story and got the momentum, for going back and changing the elephant to a camel (though there's always a chance the lady might complain that you made a nasty camel out of a beautiful elephant), and changing Shuter Street to Blank Street. But what about the big chunks of reality, without which your story can't exist? In the story *Royal Beatings*, I use a big chunk of reality: the story of the butcher, and of the young men who may have been egged on to "get" him. This is a story out of an old newspaper; it really did happen in a town I know. There is no legal difficulty about using it because it has been printed in a newspaper, and besides, the people who figure in it are all long dead. But there is a difficulty about offending people in that town who would feel that use of this story is a deliberate exposure, taunt and insult. Other people who have no connection with the real happening would say, "Why write about anything so hideous?" And lest you think that such an objection could only be raised by simple folk who read nothing but Harlequin Romances, let me tell you that one of the questions most frequently asked at universities is, "Why do you write about things that are so depressing?" People can accept almost any amount of ugliness if it is contained in a familiar formula, as it is on television, but when they come closer to their own place, their own lives, they are much offended by a lack of editing.

15	There are ways I can defend myself against such objections. I can say, "I do it in the interests of historical reality. That is what the old days were really like." Or, "I do it to show the dark side of human nature, the beast let loose, the evil we can run up against in communities and families." In certain countries I could say, "I do it to show how bad things were under the old system when there were prosperous butchers and young fellows hanging around livery stables and nobody thought about building a new society." But the fact is, the minute I say *to show* I am telling a lie. I don't do it to show anything. I put this story at the heart of my story because I need it there and it belongs there. It is the black room at the centre of the house with all other rooms leading to and away from it. That is all. A strange defence. Who told me to write this story? Who feels any need of it before it is written? I do. I do, so that I might grab off this piece of horrid reality and install it where I see fit, even if Hat Nettleton and his friends[1] were still around to make me sorry.

The answer seems to be as confusing as ever. Lots of true answers are. Yes and no. Yes, I use bits of what is real, in the sense of being really there and really happening, in the world, as most people see it, and I transform it into something that is really there and really happening, in my story. No, I am not concerned with using what is real to make any sort of record or prove any sort of point, and I am not concerned with any methods of selection but my own, which I can't fully explain. This is quite presumptuous, and if writers are not allowed to be so—and quite often, in many places, they are not—I see no point in the writing of fiction.

1. Three thuggish youths in Munro's short story "Royal Beatings."

Susanne K. Langer

EXPRESSIVENESS

When we talk about "Art" with a capital "A"—that is, about any or all of the arts: painting, sculpture, architecture, the potter's and goldsmith's and other designers' arts, music, dance, poetry, and prose fiction, drama and film—it is a constant temptation to say things about "Art" in this general sense that are true only in one special domain, or to assume that what holds for one art must hold for another. For instance, the fact that music is made for performance, for presentation to the ear, and is simply not the same thing when it is given only to the tonal imagination of a reader silently perusing the score, has made some aestheticians pass straight to the conclusion that literature, too, must be physically heard to be fully experienced, because words are originally spoken, not written; an obvious parallel, but a careless and, I think, invalid one. It is dangerous to set up principles by analogy, and generalize from a single consideration.

But it is natural, and safe enough, to ask analogous questions:

"What is the function of sound in music? What is the function of sound in poetry? What is the function of sound in prose composition? What is the function of sound in drama?" The answers may be quite heterogeneous; and that is itself an important fact, a guide to something more than a simple and sweeping theory. Such findings guide us to exact relations and abstract, variously exemplified basic principles.

At present, however, we are dealing with principles that have proven to be the same in all the arts, when each kind of art—plastic, musical, balletic, poetic, and each major mode, such as literary and dramatic writing, or painting, sculpturing, building plastic shapes—has been studied in its own terms. Such candid study is more rewarding than the usual passionate declaration that all the arts are alike, only their materials differ, their principles are all the same, their techniques all analogous, etc. That is not only unsafe, but untrue. It is in pursuing the differences among them that one arrives, finally, at a point where no more differences appears; then one has found, not postulated, their unity. At that deep level there is only one concept exemplified in all the different arts, and that is the concept of Art.

The principles that obtain wholly and fundamentally in every kind of art are few, but decisive; they determine what is art, and what is not. Expressiveness, in one definite and appropriate sense, is the same in all art works of any kind. What is created is not the same in any two distinct

5

From *Problems in Art* (1957).

arts—this is, in fact, what makes them distinct—but the principle of creation is the same. And "living form" means the same in all of them.

A work of art is an expressive form created for our perception through sense or imagination, and what it expresses is human feeling. The word "feeling" must be taken here in its broadest sense, meaning *everything that can be felt*, from physical sensation, pain and comfort, excitement and repose, to the most complex emotions, intellectual tensions, or the steady feeling-tones of a conscious human life. In stating what a work of art is, I have just used the words "form," "expressive," and "created"; these are key words. One at a time, they will keep us engaged.

Let us consider first what is meant, in this context, by a *form*. The word has many meanings, all equally legitimate for various purposes; even in connection with art it has several. It may, for instance—and often does—denote the familiar, characteristic structures known as the sonnet form, the sestina, or the ballad form in poetry, the sonata form, the madrigal, or the symphony in music, the contredance or the classical ballet in choreography, and so on. This is not what I mean; or rather, it is only a very small part of what I mean. There is another sense in which artists speak of "form" when they say, for instance, "form follows function," or declare that the one quality shared by all good works of art is "significant form," or entitle a book *The Life of Forms in Art*, or *Search for Form*. They are using "form" in a wider sense, which on the one hand is close to the commonest, popular meaning, namely just the *shape* of a thing, and on the other hand to the quite unpopular meaning it has in science and philosophy, where it designates something more abstract; "form" in its most abstract sense means structure, articulation, a whole resulting from the relation of mutually dependent factors, or more precisely, the way that whole is put together.

The abstract sense, which is sometimes called "logical form," is involved in the notion of expression, at least the kind of expression that characterizes art. That is why artists, when they speak of achieving "form," use the word with something of an abstract connotation, even when they are talking about a visible and tangible art object in which that form is embodied.

The more recondite concept of form is derived, of course, from the naive one, that is, material shape. Perhaps the easiest way to grasp the idea of "logical form" is to trace its derivation.

Let us consider the most obvious sort of form, the shape of an object, say a lampshade. In any department store you will find a wide choice of lampshades, mostly monstrosities, and what is monstrous is usually their shape. You select the least offensive one, maybe even a good one, but realize that the color, say violet, will not fit into your room; so you look about for another shade of the same shape but a different color, perhaps green. In recognizing this same shape in another object, possibly of another material as well as another color, you have quite naturally and easily abstracted the concept of this shape from your actual impression of the first lampshade. Presently it may occur to you that this shade is too big for your lamp; you ask whether they have *this same shade* (meaning another one of this shape) in a smaller size. The clerk understands you.

But what is *the same* in the big violet shade and the little green one? Nothing but the interrelations among their respective various dimensions. They are not "the same" even in their spatial properties, for none of their actual measures are alike; but their shapes are congruent. Their respective spatial factors are put together in the same way, so they exemplify the same form.

It is really astounding what complicated abstractions we make in our ordinary dealing with forms—that is to say, through what twists and transformations we recognize the same logical form. Consider the similarity of your two hands. Put one on the table, palm down, superimpose the other, palm down, as you may have superimposed cut-out geometric shapes in school—they are not alike at all. But their shapes are *exact opposites*. Their respective shapes fit the same description, provided that the description is modified by a principle of application whereby the measures are read one way for one hand and the other way for the other—like a timetable in which the list of stations is marked: "Eastbound, read down; Westbound, read up."

As the two hands exemplify the same form with a principle of reversal understood, so the list of stations describes two ways of moving, indicated by the advice to "read down" for one and "read up" for the other. We can all abstract the common element in these two respective trips, which is called the *route*. With a return ticket we may return only by the same route. The same principle relates a mold to the form of the thing that is cast in it, and establishes their formal correspondence, or common logical form.

So far we have considered only objects—lampshades, hands, or regions of the earth—as having forms. These have fixed shapes; their parts remain in fairly stable relations to each other. But there are also substances that have no definite shapes, such as gases, mist, and water, which take the shape of any bounded space that contains them. The interesting thing about such amorphous fluids is that when they are put into violent motion they do exhibit visible forms, not bounded by any container. Think of the momentary efflorescence of a bursting rocket, the mushroom cloud of an atomic bomb, the funnel of water or dust screwing upward in a whirlwind. The instant the motion stops, or even slows beyond a certain degree, those shapes collapse and the apparent "thing" disappears. They are not shapes of things at all, but forms of motions, or dynamic forms.

15   Some dynamic forms, however, have more permanent manifestations, because the stuff that moves and makes them visible is constantly replenished. A waterfall seems to hang from the cliff, waving streamers of foam. Actually, of course, nothing stays there in midair; the water is always passing; but there is more and more water taking the same paths, so we have a lasting shape made and maintained by its passage—a permanent dynamic form. A quiet river, too, has dynamic form; if it stopped flowing it would either go dry or become a lake. Some twenty-five hundred years ago, Heracleitos was struck by the fact that you cannot step twice into the same river at the same place—at least, if the river means the water, not its dynamic form, the flow.

When a river ceases to flow because the water is deflected or dried up, there remains the river bed, sometimes cut deeply in solid stone. That bed is shaped by the flow, and records as graven lines the currents that have ceased to exist. Its shape is static, but it *expresses* the dynamic form of the river. Again, we have two congruent forms, like a cast and its mold, but this time the congruence is more remarkable because it holds between a dynamic form and a static one. That relation is important; we shall be dealing with it again when we come to consider the meaning of "living form" in art.

The congruence of two given perceptible forms is not always evident upon simple inspection. The common *logical* form they both exhibit may become apparent only when you know the principle whereby to relate them, as you compare the shapes of your hands not by direct correspondence, but by correspondence of opposite parts. Where the two exemplifications of the single logical form are unlike in most other respects one needs a rule for matching up the relevant factors of one with the relevant factors of the other; that is to say, a *rule of translation,* whereby one instance of the logical form is shown to correspond formally to the other.

The logical form itself is not another thing, but an abstract concept, or better an *abstractable* concept. We usually don't abstract it deliberately, but only use it, as we use our vocal cords in speech without first learning all about their operation and then applying our knowledge. Most people perceive intuitively the similarity of their two hands without thinking of them as conversely related; they can guess at the shape of the hollow inside a wooden shoe from the shape of a human foot, without any abstract study of topology. But the first time they see a map in the Mercator projection—with parallel lines of longitude, not meeting at the poles—they find it hard to believe that this corresponds logically to the circular map they used in school, where the meridians bulged apart toward the equator and met at both poles. The visible shapes of the continents are different on the two maps, and it takes abstract thinking to match up the two representations of the same earth.

If, however, they have grown up with both maps, they will probably see the geographical relationships either way with equal ease, because these relationships are not *copied* by either map, but *expressed,* and expressed equally well by both; for the two maps are different *projections* of the same logical form, which the spherical earth exhibits in still another—that is, a spherical—projection.

An expressive form is any perceptible or imaginable whole that exhibits relationships of parts, or points, or even qualities or aspects within the whole, so that it may be taken to represent some other whole whose elements have analogous relations. The reason for using such a form as a symbol is usually that the thing it represents is not perceivable or readily imaginable. We cannot see the earth as an object. We let a map or a little globe express the relationships of places on the earth, and think about the earth by means of it. The understanding of one thing through another seems to be a deeply intuitive process in the human brain; it is so natural that we often have difficulty in distinguishing the symbolic expressive form from what it conveys. The symbol seems to be the thing itself, or contain it, or be contained in it. A child interested in a globe will not say: "This means the earth," but: "Look, this is the earth." A similar identification of symbol and meaning underlies the widespread conception of holy names, of the physical efficacy of rites, and many other primitive but culturally persistent phenomena. It has a bearing on our perception of artistic import; that is why I mention it here.

The most astounding and developed symbolic device humanity has evolved is language. By means of language we can conceive the intangible, incorporeal things we call our *ideas,* and the equally inostensible elements of our perceptual world that we call *facts.* It is by virtue of language that we can think, remember, imagine, and finally conceive a universe of facts. We can describe things and represent their relations, express rules of their interactions, speculate and predict and carry on a long symbolizing process known as reasoning. And above all, we can communicate, by producing a serried array of audible or visible words, in a pattern commonly known, and readily understood to reflect our multifarious concepts and percepts and their interconnections. This use of language is *discourse;* and the pattern of discourse is known as *discursive* form. It is a highly versatile, amazingly powerful pattern. It has impressed itself on our tacit thinking, so that we call all systematic reflection "discursive thought." It has made, far more than most people know, the very frame of our sensory experience—the frame of objective facts in which we carry on the practical business of life.

Yet even the discursive pattern has its limits of usefulness. An expressive form can express any complex of conceptions that, via some rule of projection, appears congruent with it, that is, appears to be of that form. Whatever there is in experience that will not take the impress—directly

20

or indirectly—of discursive form, is not discursively communicable or, in the strictest sense, logically thinkable. It is unspeakable, ineffable; according to practically all serious philosophical theories today, it is unknowable.

Yet there is a great deal of experience that is knowable, not only as immediate, formless, meaningless impact, but as one aspect of the intricate web of life, yet defies discursive formulation, and therefore verbal expression: that is what we sometimes call the *subjective aspect* of experience, the direct feeling of it—what it is like to be waking and moving, to be drowsy, slowing down, or to be sociable, or to feel self-sufficient but alone; what it feels like to pursue an elusive thought or to have a big idea. All such directly felt experiences usually have no names—they are named, if at all, for the outward conditions that normally accompany their occurrence. Only the most striking ones have names like "anger," "hate," "love," "fear," and are collectively called "emotion." But we feel many things that never develop into any designable emotion. The ways we are moved are as various as the lights in a forest; and they may intersect, sometimes without cancelling each other, take shape and dissolve, conflict, explode into passion, or be transfigured. All these inseparable elements of subjective reality compose what we call the "inward life" of human beings. The usual factoring of that life-stream into mental, emotional, and sensory units is an arbitrary scheme of simplification that makes scientific treatment possible to a considerable extent; but we may already be close to the limit of its usefulness, that is, close to the point where its simplicity becomes an obstacle to further questioning and discovery instead of the revealing, ever-suitable logical projection it was expected to be.

Whatever resists projection into the discursive form of language is, indeed, hard to hold in conception, and perhaps impossible to communicate, in the proper and strict sense of the word "communicate." But fortunately our logical intuition, or form-perception, is really much more powerful than we commonly believe, and our knowledge—genuine knowledge, understanding—is considerably wider than our discourse. Even in the use of language, if we want to name something that is too new to have a name (e.g., a newly invented gadget or a newly discovered creature), or want to express a relationship for which there is no verb or other connective word, we resort to metaphor; we mention it or describe it as something else, something analogous. The principle of metaphor is simply the principle of saying one thing and meaning another, and expecting to be understood to mean the other. A metaphor is not language, it is an idea expressed by language, an idea that in its turn functions as a symbol to express something. It is not discursive and therefore does not really make a statement of the idea it conveys; but it formulates a new conception for our direct imaginative grasp.

Sometimes our comprehension of a total experience is mediated by a metaphorical symbol because the experience is new, and language has words and phrases only for familiar notions. Then an extension of language will gradually follow the wordless insight, and discursive expression will supersede the non-discursive pristine symbol. This is, I think, the normal advance of human thought and language in that whole realm of knowledge where discourse is possible at all.

But the symbolic presentation of subjective reality for contemplation is not only tentatively beyond the reach of language—that is, not merely beyond the words we have; it is impossible in the essential frame of language. That is why those semanticists who recognize only discourse as a symbolic form must regard the whole life of feeling as formless, chaotic, capable only of symptomatic expression, typified in exclamations like "Ah!" "Ouch!" "My sainted aunt!" They usually do believe that art is an expression of feeling, but that "expression" in art is of this sort, indicating that the speaker has an emotion, a pain, or other personal experience, perhaps also giving us a clue to the general kind of experience it is—pleasant or unpleasant, violent or mild—but not setting that piece of inward life objectively before us so we may understand its intricacy, its rhythms and shifts of total appearance. The differences in feeling-tones or other elements of subjective experience are regarded as differences in quality, which must be felt to be appreciated. Furthermore, since we have no intellectual access to pure subjectivity, the only way to study it is to study the symptoms of the person who is having subjective experiences. This leads to physiological psychology—a very important and interesting field. But it tells us nothing about the phenomena of subjective life, and sometimes simplifies the problem by saying they don't exist.

Now, I believe the expression of feeling in a work of art—the function that makes the work an expressive form—is not symptomatic at all. An artist working on a tragedy need not be in personal despair or violent upheaval; nobody, indeed, could work in such a state of mind. His mind would be occupied with the causes of his emotional upset. Self-expression does not require composition and lucidity; a screaming baby gives his feeling far more release than any musician, but we don't go into a concert hall to hear a baby scream; in fact, if that baby is brought in we are likely to go out. We don't want self-expression.

A work of art presents feeling (in the broad sense I mentioned before, as everything that can be felt) for our contemplation, making it visible or audible or in some way perceivable through a symbol, not inferable from a symptom. Artistic form is congruent with the dynamic forms of our direct sensuous, mental, and emotional life; works of art are projections of "felt life," as Henry James called it, into spatial, temporal, and poetic structures. They are images of feeling, that formulate it for our cognition. What is artistically good is whatever articulates and presents feeling to our understanding.

Artistic forms are more complex than any other symbolic forms we know. They are, indeed, not abstractable from the works that exhibit them. We may abstract a shape from an object that has this shape, by disregarding color, weight and texture, even size; but to the total effect that is an artistic form, the color matters, the thickness of lines matters, and the appearance of texture and weight. A given triangle is the same in any position, but to an artistic form its location, balance, and surroundings are not indifferent. Form, in the sense in which artists speak of "significant form" or "expressive form," is not an abstracted structure, but an apparition; and the vital processes of sense and emotion that a good work of art expresses seem to the beholder to be directly contained in it, not symbolized but really presented. The congruence is so striking that symbol and meaning appear as one reality. Actually, as one psychologist who is also a musician has written, "Music sounds as feelings feel." And likewise, in good painting, sculpture, or building, balanced shapes and colors, lines and masses look as emotions, vital tensions and their resolutions feel.

An artist, then, expresses feeling, but not in the way a politician blows off steam or a baby laughs and cries. He formulates that elusive aspect of reality that is commonly taken to be amorphous and chaotic; that is, he objectifies the subjective realm. What he expresses is, therefore, not his own actual feelings, but what he knows about human feeling. Once he is in possession of a rich symbolism, that knowledge may actually exceed his entire personal experience. A work of art expresses a conception of life, emotion, inward reality. But it is neither a confessional nor a frozen tantrum; it is a developed metaphor, a non-discursive symbol that articulates what is verbally ineffable—the logic of consciousness itself.

Lance Morrow

IMPRISONING TIME IN A RECTANGLE

Balzac[1] had a "vague dread" of being photographed. Like some primitive peoples, he thought the camera steals something of the soul—that, as he told a friend "every body in its natural state is made up of

First printed in a special issue of *Time* magazine on photojournalism (Fall 1989).

1. Honoré de Balzac (born Honoré Balssa, 1799–1850), French writer, best known for the novels and short stories that comprise

La Comédie Humaine (*The Human Comedy*).

a series of ghostly images superimposed in layers to infinity, wrapped in infinitesimal films." Each time a photograph was made, he believed, another thin layer of the subject's being would be stripped off to become not life as before but a membrane of memory in a sort of translucent antiworld.

If that is what photography is up to, then the onion of the world is being peeled away, layer by layer—lenses like black holes gobbling up life's emanations. Mere images proliferate, while history pares down to a phosphorescence of itself.

The idea catches something of the superstition (sometimes justified, if you think about it) and the spooky metaphysics that go ghosting around photography. Taking pictures is a transaction that snatches instants away from time and imprisons them in rectangles. These rectangles become a collective public memory and an image-world that is located usually on the verge of tears, often on the edge of a moral mess.

It is possible to be entranced by photography and at the same time disquieted by its powerful capacity to bypass thought. Photography, as the critic Susan Sontag has pointed out, is an elegiac, nostalgic phenomenon. No one photographs the future. The instants that the photographer freezes are ever the past, ever receding. They have about them the brilliance or instancy of their moment but also the cello sound of loss that life makes when going irrecoverably away and lodging at last in the dreamworks.

The pictures made by photojournalists have the legitimacy of being   5
news, fresh information. They slice along the hard edge of the present. Photojournalism is not self-conscious, since it first enters the room (the brain) as a battle report from the far-flung Now. It is only later that the artifacts of photojournalism sink into the textures of the civilization and tincture its memory: Jack Ruby shooting Lee Harvey Oswald,[2] an image so raw and shocking, subsides at last into the ecology of memory where we also find thousands of other oddments from the time—John John saluting at the funeral, Jack and Jackie on Cape Cod, who knows?—bright shards that stimulate old feelings (ghost pangs, ghost tendernesses, wistfulness) but not thought really. The shocks turn into dreams. The memory of such pictures, flipped through like a disordered Rolodex, makes at last a cultural tapestry, an inventory of the kind that brothers and sisters and distant cousins may rummage through at family reunions, except that the greatest photojournalism has given certain memories the emotional prestige of icons.

If journalism—the kind done with words—is the first draft of history,

2. Jack L. Ruby (1911–67) shot and killed Lee Harvey Oswald (1939–63), the accused assassin of President John F. Kennedy, on November 24, 1963, two days after Kennedy was shot, in the Dallas County Jail where Oswald was being held under arrest. A national television audience witnessed the event.

what is photojournalism? Is it the first impression of history, the first graphic flash? Yes, but it is also (and this is the disturbing thing) history's lasting visual impression. The service that the pictures perform is splendid, and so powerful as to seem preternatural. But sometimes the power they possess is more than they deserve.

Call up Eddie Adams' 1968 photo of General Nguyen Ngoc Loan, the police chief of Saigon, firing his snub-nosed revolver into the temple of a Viet Cong officer. Bright sunlight, Saigon: the scrawny police chief's arm, outstretched, goes by extension through the trigger finger into the V.C.'s brain. That photograph, and another in 1972 showing a naked young Vietnamese girl running in arms-outstretched terror up a road away from American napalm, outmanned the force of three U.S. Presidents and the most powerful Army in the world. The photographs were considered, quite ridiculously, to be a portrait of America's moral disgrace. Freudians spend years trying to call up the primal image-memories, turned to trauma, that distort a neurotic patient's psyche. Photographs sometimes have a way of installing the image and legitimizing the trauma: the very vividness of the image, the greatness of the photograph as journalism or even as art, forestalls examination.

Adams has always felt uncomfortable about his picture of Loan executing the Viet Cong officer. What the picture does not show is that a few moments earlier the Viet Cong had slaughtered the family of Loan's best friend in a house just up the road. All this occurred during the Tet offensive, a state of general mayhem all over South Viet Nam. The Communists in similar circumstances would not have had qualms about summary execution.

But Loan shot the man; Adams took the picture. The image went firing around the world and lodged in the conscience. Photography is the very dream of the Heisenberg uncertainty principle, which holds that the act of observing a physical event inevitably changes it. War is merciless, bloody, and by definition it occurs outside the orbit of due process. Loan's Viet Cong did not have a trial. He did have a photographer. The photographer's picture took on a life of its own and changed history.

All great photographs have lives of their own, but they can be as false as dreams. Somehow the mind knows that and sorts out the matter, and permits itself to enjoy the pictures without getting sunk in the really mysterious business that they involve.

Still, a puritan conscience recoils a little from the sheer power of photographs. They have lingering about them the ghost of the golden calf—the bright object too much admired, without God's abstract difficulties. Great photographs bring the mind alive. Photographs are magic things that traffic in mystery. They float on the surface, and they have a strange life in the depths of the mind. They bear watching.

THE READER

1. What relationship does Morrow suggest between photography and time? Between photojournalism and truth?
2. Examine each of these propositions in light of Morrow's essay: "One picture is worth a thousand words" and "The camera doesn't lie."
3. Morrow suggests that certain photographs taken during the war in Vietnam affected the course of history. By what means does he imply that?

THE WRITER

1. Morrow makes frequent use of verbal images, metaphors, and symbols. How are these uses of language relevant to his topic? Which of them express his central thesis? Are they effective?
2. Morrow concludes his essay about photographs by saying that they "bear watching." In light of his essay, what meanings may be discerned in that single phrase? Is the phrase an appropriate one for the idea and language of this essay?
3. Examine a photograph from the newspaper, either a photo famous in history such as Morrow writes of (for example, the shooting at Kent State) or a photo you select from a contemporary news journal. Write a paragraph describing what the photo shows or suggests.

Carl Gustav Jung

THE POET

Creativeness, like the freedom of the will, contains a secret. The psychologist can describe both these manifestations as processes, but he can find no solution of the philosophical problems they offer. Creative man is a riddle that we may try to answer in various ways, but always in vain, a truth that has not prevented modern psychology from turning now and again to the question of the artist and his art. Freud thought that he had found a key in his procedure of deriving the work of art from the personal experiences of the artist. It is true that certain possibilities lay in this direction, for it was conceivable that a work of art, no less than a neurosis, might be traced back to those knots in psychic life that we call the complexes. It was Freud's great discovery that neuroses have a causal origin in the psychic realm—that they take their rise from emotional states and from real or imagined childhood experiences. Certain

From *Modern Man in Search of a Soul* (1933).

of his followers, like Rank and Stekel, have taken up related lines of enquiry and have achieved important results. It is undeniable that the poet's psychic disposition permeates his work root and branch. Nor is there anything new in the statement that personal factors largely influence the poet's choice and use of his materials. Credit, however, must certainly be given to the Freudian school for showing how far-reaching this influence is and in what curious ways it comes to expression.

Freud takes the neurosis as a substitute for a direct means of gratification. He therefore regards it as something inappropriate—a mistake, a dodge, an excuse, a voluntary blindness. To him it is essentially a shortcoming that should never have been. Since a neurosis, to all appearances, is nothing but a disturbance that is all the more irritating because it is without sense or meaning, few people will venture to say a good word for it. And a work of art is brought into questionable proximity with the neurosis when it is taken as something which can be analysed in terms of the poet's repressions. In a sense it finds itself in good company, for religion and philosophy are regarded in the same light by Freudian psychology. No objection can be raised if it is admitted that this approach amounts to nothing more than the elucidation of those personal determinants without which a work of art is unthinkable. But should the claim be made that such an analysis accounts for the work of art itself, then a categorical denial is called for. The personal idiosyncrasies that creep into a work of art are not essential; in fact, the more we have to cope with these peculiarities, the less is it a question of art. What is essential in a work of art is that it should rise far above the realm of personal life and speak from the spirit and heart of the poet as man to the spirit and heart of mankind. The personal aspect is a limitation—and even a sin—in the realm of art. When a form of "art" is primarily personal it deserves to be treated as if it were a neurosis. There may be some validity in the idea held by the Freudian school that artists without exception are narcissistic—by which is meant that they are undeveloped persons with infantile and autoerotic traits. The statement is only valid, however, for the artist as a person, and has nothing to do with the man as an artist. In his capacity of artist he is neither auto-erotic, nor hetero-erotic, nor erotic in any sense. He is objective and impersonal—even inhuman—for as an artist he is his work, and not a human being.

Every creative person is a duality or a synthesis of contradictory aptitudes. On the one side he is a human being with a personal life, while on the other side he is an impersonal, creative process. Since as a human being he may be sound or morbid, we must look at his psychic make-up to find the determinants of his personality. But we can only understand him in his capacity of artist by looking at his creative achievement. We should make a sad mistake if we tried to explain the mode of life of an English gentleman, a Prussian officer, or a cardinal in terms of personal factors. The gentleman, the officer and the cleric function as such in an impersonal role, and their psychic make-up is qualified by a peculiar objectivity. We must grant that the artist does not function in an official capacity—the very opposite is nearer the truth. He nevertheless resembles the types I have named in one respect, for the specifically artistic disposition involves an overweight of collective psychic life as against the personal. Art is a kind of innate drive that seizes a human being and makes him its instrument. The artist is not a person endowed with free will who seeks his own ends, but one who allows art to realize its purposes through him. As a human being he may have moods and a will and personal aims, but as an artist he is "man" in a higher sense—he is "collective man"—one who carries and shapes the unconscious, psychic life of mankind. To perform this difficult office it is sometimes necessary for him to sacrifice happiness and everything that makes life worth living for the ordinary human being.

All this being so, it is not strange that the artist is an especially interesting case for the psychologist who uses an analytical method. The artist's life cannot be otherwise than full of conflicts, for two forces are at war within him—on the one hand the common human longing for happiness, satisfaction and security in life, and on the other a ruthless passion for creation which may go so far as to override every personal desire. The lives of artists are as a rule so highly unsatisfactory—not to say tragic—because of their inferiority on the human and personal side, and not because of a sinister dispensation. There are hardly any exceptions to the rule that a person must pay dearly for the divine gift of the creative fire. It is as though each of us were endowed at birth with a certain capital of energy. The strongest force in our make-up will seize and all but monopolize this energy, leaving so little over that nothing of value can come of it. In this way the creative force can drain the human impulses to such a degree that the personal ego must develop all sorts of bad qualities—ruthlessness, selfishness and vanity (so-called "auto-erotism")—and even every kind of vice, in order to maintain the spark of life and to keep itself from being wholly bereft. The auto-erotism of artists resembles that of illegitimate or neglected children who from their tenderest years must protect themselves from the destructive influence of people who have no love to give them—who develop bad qualities for that very purpose and later maintain an invincible egocentrism by remaining all their lives infantile and helpless or by actively offending against the moral code or the law. How can we doubt that it is his art that explains the artist, and not the insufficiencies and conflicts of his personal life? These are nothing but the regrettable results of the fact that he is an artist—that is to say, a man who from his very birth has been called to a greater task than the ordinary mortal. A special ability means a heavy expenditure of energy in a particular direction, with a consequent drain from some other side of life.

5   It makes no difference whether the poet knows that his work is begotten, grows and matures with him, or whether he supposes that by taking thought he produces it out of the void. His opinion of the matter does not change the fact that his own work outgrows him as a child its mother. The creative process has feminine quality, and the creative work arises from unconscious depths—we might say, from the realm of the mothers. Whenever the creative force predominates, human life is ruled and moulded by the unconscious as against the active will, and the conscious ego is swept along on a subterranean current, being nothing more than a helpless observer of events. The work in process becomes the poet's fate and determines his psychic development. It is not Goethe who creates *Faust*, but *Faust* which creates Goethe. And what is *Faust* but a symbol? By this I do not mean an allegory that points to something all too familiar, but an expression that stands for something not clearly known and yet profoundly alive. Here it is something that lives in the soul of every German, and that Goethe has helped to bring to birth. Could we conceive of anyone but a German writing *Faust* or *Also sprach Zarathustra?* Both play upon something that reverberates in the German soul—a "primordial image," as Jacob Burckhardt once called it— the figure of a physician or teacher of mankind. The archetypal image of the wise man, the saviour or redeemer, lies buried and dormant in man's unconscious since the dawn of culture; it is awakened whenever the times are out of joint and a human society is committed to a serious error. When people go astray they feel the need of a guide or teacher or even of the physician. These primordial images are numerous, but do not appear in the dreams of individuals or in works of art until they are called into being by the waywardness of the general outlook. When conscious life is characterized by one-sidedness and by a false attitude, then they are activated—one might say, "instinctively"—and come to light in the dreams of individuals and the visions of artists and seers, thus restoring the psychic equilibrium of the epoch.

In this way the work of the poet comes to meet the spiritual need of the society in which he lives, and for this reason his work means more to him than his personal fate, whether he is aware of this or not. Being essentially the instrument for his work, he is subordinate to it, and we have no reason for expecting him to interpret it for us. He has done the best that in him lies in giving it form, and he must leave the interpretation to others and to the future. A great work of art is like a dream; for all its apparent obviousness it does not explain itself and is never unequivocal. A dream never says: "You ought," or: "This is the truth." It presents an image in much the same way as nature allows a plant to grow, and we must draw our own conclusions. If a person has a nightmare, it means either that he is too much given to fear, or else that he is too exempt from it; and if he dreams of the old wise man it may mean that he is too pedagogical, as also that he stands in need of a teacher. In a subtle way both meanings come to the same thing, as we perceive when we are able to let the work of art act upon us as it acted upon the artist. To grasp its meaning, we must allow it to shape us as it once shaped him. Then we understand the nature of his experience. We see that he has drawn upon the healing and redeeming forces of the collective psyche that underlies consciousness with its isolation and its painful errors; that he has penetrated to that matrix of life in which all men are embedded, which imparts a common rhythm to all human existence, and allows the individual to communicate his feeling and his striving to mankind as a whole.

The secret of artistic creation and of the effectiveness of art is to be found in a return to the state of *participation mystique*—to that level of experience at which it is man who lives, and not the individual, and at which the weal or woe of the single human being does not count, but only human existence. This is why every great work of art is objective and impersonal, but none the less profoundly moves us each and all. And this is also why the personal life of the poet cannot be held essential to his art—but at most a help or a hindrance to his creative task. He may go the way of a Philistine, a good citizen, a neurotic, a fool or a criminal. His personal career may be inevitable and interesting, but it does not explain the poet.

THE READER

1. *Jung makes a distinction between the "human being with a personal life" and the "impersonal, creative process." What is the importance of this distinction? How does it help to shape the rest of Jung's argument?*
2. *Consider the following stanzas (69–72) from Byron's "Childe Harold's Pilgrimage." To what extent would Jung feel that psychological considerations were helpful in analyzing these lines?*

> To fly from, need not be to hate, mankind:
> All are not fit with them to stir and toil,
> Nor is it discontent to keep the mind
> Deep in its fountain, lest it overboil
> In the hot throng, where we become the spoil
> Of our infection, till too late and long
> We may deplore and struggle with the coil,
> In wretched interchange of wrong for wrong
> Midst a contentious world, striving where none are strong.

There, in a moment we may plunge our years
In fatal penitence, and in the blight
Of our own Soul turn all our blood to tears,
And colour things to come with hues of Night;
The race of life becomes a hopeless flight
To those that walk in darkness: on the sea
The boldest steer but where their ports invite—
But there are wanderers o'er Eternity
Whose bark drives on and on, and anchored ne'er shall be.

Is it not better, then, to be alone,
And love Earth only for its earthly sake?
By the blue rushing of the arrowy Rhone,
Or the pure bosom of its nursing Lake,
Which feeds it as a mother who doth make
A fair but froward infant her own care,
Kissing its cries away as these awake;—
Is it not better thus our lives to wear,
Than join the rushing crowd, doomed to inflict or bear?

I live not in myself, but I become
Portion of that around me; and to me
High mountains are a feeling, but the hum
Of human cities torture: I can see
Nothing to loathe in Nature, save to be
A link reluctant in a fleshly chain,
Classed among creatures, when the soul can flee,
And with the sky—the peak—the heaving plain
Of ocean, or the stars, mingle—and not in vain.

THE WRITER

1. Jung says that the "personal idiosyncracies that creep into a work of art are not essential," since art "should rise far above the realm of personal life and speak from the spirit and heart of the poet as man to the spirit and heart of mankind" (p. 1086). Is a contradiction involved here? Can a poet speak from the heart without being personal? Are "personal idiosyncracies" desirable in a work to give it the flavor of a distinctive style?
2. In a brief essay, compare Jung's view of creativity with that of Bronowski in "The Reach of Imagination" (p. 196).

Robert Frost

EDUCATION BY POETRY:
A MEDITATIVE MONOLOGUE

I am going to urge nothing in my talk. I am not an advocate. I am going to consider a matter, and commit a description. And I am going to describe other colleges than Amherst. Or, rather say all that is good can be taken as about Amherst; all that is bad will be about other colleges.

I know whole colleges where all American poetry is barred—whole colleges. I know whole colleges where all contemporary poetry is barred.

I once heard of a minister who turned his daughter—his poetry-writing daughter—out on the street to earn a living, because he said there should be no more books written; God wrote one book, and that was enough. (My friend George Russell, "Æ", has read no literature, he protests, since just before Chaucer.)

That all seems sufficiently safe, and you can say one thing for it. It takes the onus off the poetry of having to be used to teach children anything. It comes pretty hard on poetry, I sometimes think, what it has to bear in the teaching process.

Then I know whole colleges where, though they let in older poetry, they manage to bar all that is poetical in it by treating it as something other than poetry. It is not so hard to do that. Their reason I have often hunted for. It may be that these people act from a kind of modesty. Who are professors that they should attempt to deal with a thing as high and as fine as poetry? Who are *they*? There is a certain manly modesty in that.

That is the best general way of settling the problem; treat all poetry as if it were something else than poetry, as if it were syntax, language, science. Then you can even come down into the American and into the contemporary without any special risk.

There is another reason they have, and that is that they are, first and foremost in life, markers. They have the marking problem to consider. Now, I stand here a teacher of many years' experience and I have never complained of having had to mark. I had rather mark anyone for anything—for his looks, carriage, his ideas, his correctness, his exactness, anything you please—I would rather give him a mark in terms of letters, A, B, C, D, than have to use adjectives on him. We are all being marked by each other all the time, classified, ranked, put in our place, and I see

5

An address given at Amherst College in 1930.

1091

no escape from that. I am no sentimentalist. You have got to mark, and you have got to mark, first of all, for accuracy, for correctness. But if I am going to give a mark, that is the least part of my marking. The hard part is the part beyond that, the part where the adventure begins.

One other way to rid the curriculum of the poetry nuisance has been considered. More merciful than the others it would neither abolish nor denature the poetry, but only turn it out to disport itself, with the plays and games—in no wise discredited, though given no credit for. Any one who liked to teach poetically could take his subject, whether English, Latin, Greek or French, out into the nowhere along with the poetry. One side of a sharp line would be left to the rigorous and righteous; the other side would be assigned to the flowery where they would know what could be expected of them. Grade marks were more easily given, of course, in the courses concentrating on correctness and exactness as the only forms of honesty recognized by plain people; a general indefinite mark of X in the courses that scatter brains over taste and opinion. On inquiry I have found no teacher willing to take position on either side of the line, either among the rigors or among the flowers. No one is willing to admit that his discipline is not partly in exactness. No one is willing to admit that his discipline is not partly in taste and enthusiasm.

How shall a man go through college without having been marked for taste and judgment? What will become of him? What will his end be? He will have to take continuation courses for college graduates. He will have to go to night schools. They are having night schools now, you know, for college graduates. Why? Because they have not been educated enough to find their way around in contemporary literature. They don't know what they may safely like in the libraries and galleries. They don't know how to judge an editorial when they see one. They don't know how to judge a political campaign. They don't know when they are being fooled by a metaphor, an analogy, a parable. And metaphor is, of course, what we are talking about. Education by poetry is education by metaphor.

Suppose we stop short of imagination, initiative, enthusiasm, inspiration and originality—dread words. Suppose we don't mark in such things at all. There are still two minimal things, that we have got to take care of, taste and judgment. Americans are supposed to have more judgment than taste, but taste is there to be dealt with. That is what poetry, the only art in the colleges of arts, is there for. I for my part would not be afraid to go in for enthusiasm. There is the enthusiasm like a blinding light, or the enthusiasm of the deafening shout, the crude enthusiasm that you get uneducated by poetry, outside of poetry. It is exemplified in what I might call "sunset raving." You look westward toward the sunset, or if you get up early enough, eastward toward the sunrise, and you rave. It is oh's and ah's with you and no more.

But the enthusiasm I mean is taken through the prism of the intellect and spread on the screen in a color, all the way from hyperbole at one end—or overstatement, at one end—to understatement at the other end. It is a long strip of dark lines and many colors. Such enthusiasm is one object of all teaching in poetry. I heard wonderful things said about Virgil yesterday, and many of them seemed to me crude enthusiasm, more like a deafening shout, many of them. But one speech had range, something of overstatement, something of statement, and something of understatement. It had all the colors of an enthusiasm passed through an idea.

I would be willing to throw away everything else but that: enthusiasm tamed by metaphor. Let me rest the case there. Enthusiasm tamed to metaphor, tamed to that much of it. I do not think anybody ever knows the discreet use of metaphor, his own and other people's, the discreet handling of metaphor, unless he has been properly educated in poetry.

Poetry begins in trivial metaphors, petty metaphors, "grace" metaphors, and goes on to the profoundest thinking that we have. Poetry provides the one permissible way of saying one thing and meaning another. People say, "Why don't you say what you mean?" We never do that, do we, being all of us too much poets. We like to talk in parables and in hints and in indirections—whether from diffidence or some other instinct.

I have wanted in late years to go further and further in making metaphor the whole of thinking. I find some one now and then to agree with me that all thinking, except mathematical thinking, is metaphorical, or all thinking except scientific thinking. The mathematical might be difficult for me to bring in, but the scientific is easy enough.

Once on a time all the Greeks were busy telling each other what the All was—or was like unto. All was three elements, air, earth, and water (we once thought it was ninety elements; now we think it is only one). All was substance, said another. All was change, said a third. But best and most fruitful was Pythagoras' comparison of the universe with number. Number of what? Number of feet, pounds, and seconds was the answer, and we had science and all that has followed in science. The metaphor has held and held, breaking down only when it came to the spiritual and psychological or the out of the way places of the physical.

The other day we had a visitor here, a noted scientist, whose latest word to the world has been that the more accurately you know where a thing is, the less accurately you are able to state how fast it is moving. You can see why that would be so, without going back to Zeno's problem of the arrow's flight. In carrying numbers into the realm of space and at the same time into the realm of time you are mixing metaphors, that is all, and you are in trouble. They won't mix. The two don't go together.

Let's take two or three more of the metaphors now in use to live by.

I have just spoken of one of the new ones, a charming mixed metaphor right in the realm of higher mathematics and higher physics: that the more accurately you state where a thing is, the less accurately you will be able to tell how fast it is moving. And, of course everything is moving. Everything is an event now. Another metaphor. A thing, they say, is an event. Do you believe it is? Not quite. I believe it is almost an event. But I like the comparison of a thing with an event.

I notice another from the same quarter. "In the neighborhood of matter space is something like curved." Isn't that a good one! It seems to me that that is simply and utterly charming—to say that space is something like curved in the neighborhood of matter. "Something like."

Another amusing one is from—what is the book?—I can't say it now; but here is the metaphor. Its aim is to restore you to your ideas of free will. It wants to give you back your freedom of will. All right, here it is on a platter. You know that you can't tell by name what persons in a certain class will be dead ten years after graduation, but you can tell actuarially how many will be dead. Now, just so this scientist says of the particles of matter flying at a screen, striking a screen; you can't tell what individual particles will come, but you can say in general that a certain number will strike in a given time. It shows, you see, that the individual particle can come freely. I asked Bohr about that particularly, and he said, "Yes, it is so. It can come when it wills and as it wills; and the action of the individual particle is unpredictable. But it is not so of the action of the mass. There you can predict." He says, "That gives the individual atom its freedom, but the mass its necessity."

20   Another metaphor that has interested us in our time and has done all our thinking for us is the metaphor of evolution. Never mind going into the Latin word. The metaphor is simply the metaphor of the growing plant or of the growing thing. And somebody very brilliantly, quite a while ago, said that the whole universe, the whole of everything, was like unto a growing thing. That is all. I know the metaphor will break down at some point, but it has not failed everywhere. It is a very brilliant metaphor, I acknowledge, though I myself get too tired of the kind of essay that talks about the evolution of candy, we will say, or the evolution of elevators—the evolution of this, that, and the other. Everything is evolution. I emancipate myself by simply saying that I didn't get up the metaphor and so am not much interested in it.

What I am pointing out is that unless you are at home in the metaphor, unless you have had your proper poetical education in the metaphor, you are not safe anywhere. Because you are not at ease with figurative values: you don't know the metaphor in its strength and its weakness. You don't know how far you may expect to ride it and when it may break down with you. You are not safe in science; you are not safe in history. In history, for instance—to show that is the same in history as elsewhere—I heard somebody say yesterday that Aeneas was to be likened unto (those words, "likened unto"!) George Washington. He was that type of national hero, the middle-class man, not thinking of being a hero at all, bent on building the future, bent on his children, his descendants. A good metaphor, as far as it goes, and you must know how far. And then he added that Odysseus should be likened unto Theodore Roosevelt. I don't think that is so good. Someone visiting Gibbon at the point of death, said he was the same Gibbon as of old; still at his parallels.

Take the way we have been led into our present position morally, the world over. It is by a sort of metaphorical gradient. There is a kind of thinking—to speak metaphorically—there is a kind of thinking you might say was endemic in the brothel. It is always there. And every now and then in some mysterious way it becomes epidemic in the world. And how does it do so? By using all the good words that virtue has invented to maintain virtue. It uses honesty, first—frankness, sincerity—those words; picks them up, uses them. "In the name of honesty, let us see what we are." You know. And then it picks up the word joy. "Let us in the name of joy, which is the enemy of our ancestors, the Puritans . . . Let us in the name of joy, which is the enemy of the kill-joy Puritan . . ." You see. "Let us," and so on. And then, "In the name of health . . ." Health is another good word. And that is the metaphor Freudianism trades on, mental health. And the first thing we know, it has us all in up to the top knot. I suppose we may blame the artists a good deal, because they are great people to spread by metaphor. The stage too—the stage is always a good intermediary between the two worlds, the under and the upper, if I may say so without personal prejudice to the stage.

In all this, I have only been saying that the devil can quote Scripture, which simply means that the good words you have lying around the devil can use for his purposes as well as anybody else. Never mind about my morality. I am not here to urge anything. I don't care whether the world is good or bad—not on any particular day.

Let me ask you to watch a metaphor breaking down here before you.

Somebody said to me a little while ago, "It is easy enough for me to think of the universe as a machine, as a mechanism."

I said, "You mean the universe is like a machine?"

He said, "No. I think it is one . . . Well, it is like . . ."

"I think you mean the universe is like a machine."

"All right. Let it go at that."

I asked him, "Did you ever see a machine without a pedal for the foot, or a lever for the hand, or a button for the finger?"

He said "No—no."

I said, "All right. Is the universe like that?"

And he said, "No. I mean it is like a machine, only . . ."

". . . it is different from a machine," I said.

He wanted to go just that far with that metaphor and no further. And so do we all. All metaphor breaks down somewhere. That is the beauty of it. It is touch and go with the metaphor, and until you have lived with it long enough you don't know when it is going. You don't know how much you can get out of it and when it will cease to yield. It is a very living thing. It is as life itself.

I have heard this ever since I can remember, and ever since I have taught: the teacher must teach the pupil to think. I saw a teacher once going around in a great school and snapping pupils' heads with thumb and finger and saying, "Think." That was when thinking was becoming the fashion. The fashion hasn't yet quite gone out.

We still ask boys in college to think, as in the nineties, but we seldom tell them what thinking means; we seldom tell them it is just putting this and that together; it is saying one thing in terms of another. To tell them is to set their feet on the first rung of a ladder the top of which sticks through the sky.

Greatest of all attempts to say one thing in terms of another is the philosophical attempt to say matter in terms of spirit, or spirit in terms of matter, to make the final unity. That is the greatest attempt that ever failed. We stop just short there. But it is the height of poetry, the height of all thinking, the height of all poetic thinking, that attempt to say matter in terms of spirit and spirit in terms of matter. It is wrong to call anybody a materialist simply because he tries to say spirit in terms of matter, as if that were a sin. Materialism is not the attempt to say all in terms of matter. The only materialist—be he poet, teacher, scientist, politician, or statesman—is the man who gets lost in his material without a gathering metaphor to throw it into shape and order. He is the lost soul.

We ask people to think, and we don't show them what thinking is. Somebody says we don't need to show them how to think; bye and bye they will think. We will give them the forms of sentences and, if they have any ideas, then they will know how to write them. But that is preposterous. All there is to writing is having ideas. To learn to write is to learn to have ideas.

The first little metaphor . . . Take some of the trivial ones. I would rather have trivial ones of my own to live by than the big ones of other people.

I remember a boy saying, "He is the kind of person that wounds with his shield." That may be a slender one, of course. It goes a good way in character description. It has poetic grace. "He is the kind that wounds with his shield."

The shield reminds me—just to linger a minute—the shield reminds me of the inverted shield spoken of in one of the books of the *Odyssey*, the book that tells about the longest swim on record. I forget how long it lasted—several days, was it?—but at last as Odysseus came near the coast of Phoenicia, he saw it on the horizon "like an inverted shield."

There is a better metaphor in the same book. In the end Odysseus comes ashore and crawls up the beach to spend the night under a double olive tree, and it says, as in a lonely farmhouse where it is hard to get fire—I am not quoting exactly—where it is hard to start the fire again if it goes out, they cover the seeds of fire with ashes to preserve it for the night, so Odysseus covered himself with the leaves around him and went to sleep. There you have something that gives you character, something of Odysseus himself. "Seeds of fire." So Odysseus covered the seeds of fire in himself. You get the greatness of his nature.

But these are slighter metaphors than the ones we live by. They have their charm, their passing charm. They are as it were the first steps toward the great thoughts, grave thoughts, thoughts lasting to the end.

The metaphor whose manage we are best taught in poetry—that is all there is of thinking. It may not seem far for the mind to go but it is the mind's furthest. The richest accumulation of the ages is the noble metaphors we have rolled up.

I want to add one thing more that the experience of poetry is to anyone who comes close to poetry. There are two ways of coming close to poetry. One is by writing poetry. And some people think I want people to write poetry, but I don't; that is, I don't necessarily. I only want people to write poetry if they want to write poetry. I have never encouraged anybody to write poetry that did not want to write it, and I have not always encouraged those who did want to write it. That ought to be one's own funeral. It is a hard, hard life, as they say.

(I have just been to a city in the West, a city full of poets, a city they have made safe for poets. The whole city is so lovely that you do not have to write it up to make it poetry; it is ready-made for you. But, I don't know—the poetry written in that city might not seem like poetry if read outside of the city. It would be like the jokes made when you were drunk; you have to get drunk again to appreciate them.)

But as I say, there is another way to come close to poetry, fortunately, and that is in the reading of it, not as linguistics, not as history, not as anything but poetry. It is one of the hard things for a teacher to know how close a man has come in reading poetry. How do I know whether a man has come close to Keats in reading Keats? It is hard for me to know. I have lived with some boys a whole year over some of the poets and I have not felt sure whether they have come near what it was all about. One remark sometimes told me. One remark was their mark for the year; had to be—it was all I got that told me what I wanted to know. And that is enough, if it was the right remark, if it came close enough.

45

I think a man might make twenty fool remarks if he made one good one some time in the year. His mark would depend on that good remark.

The closeness—everything depends on the closeness with which you come, and you ought to be marked for the closeness, for nothing else. And that will have to be estimated by chance remarks, not by question and answer. It is only by accident that you know some day how near a person has come.

The person who gets close enough to poetry, he is going to know more about the word *belief* than anybody else knows, even in religion nowadays. There are two or three places where we know belief outside of religion. One of them is at the age of fifteen to twenty, in our self-belief. A young man knows more about himself than he is able to prove to anybody. He has no knowledge that anybody else will accept as knowledge. In his foreknowledge he has something that is going to believe itself into fulfilment, into acceptance.

50　There is another belief like that, the belief in someone else, a relationship of two that is going to be believed into fulfillment. That is what we are talking about in our novels, the belief of love. And disillusionment that the novels are full of is simply the disillusionment from disappointment in that belief. That belief can fail, of course.

Then there is a literary belief. Every time a poem is written, every time a short story is written, it is written not by cunning, but by belief. The beauty, the something, the little charm of the thing to be, is more felt than known. There is a common jest, one that always annoys me, on the writers, that they write the last end first, and then work up to it; that they lay a train toward one sentence that they think is pretty nice and have all fixed up to set like a trap to close with. No, it should not be that way at all. No one who has ever come close to the arts has failed to see the difference between things written that way, with cunning and device, and the kind that are believed into existence, that begin in something more felt than known. This you can realize quite as well—not quite as well, perhaps, but nearly as well—in reading as you can in writing. I would undertake to separate short stories on that principle; stories that have been believed into existence and stories that have been cunningly devised. And I could separate the poems still more easily.

Now I think—I happen to think—that those three beliefs that I speak of, the self-belief, the love-belief, and the art-belief, are all closely related to the God-belief, that the belief in God is a relationship you enter into with Him to bring about the future.

There is a national belief like that, too. One feels it. I have been where I came near getting up and walking out on the people who thought that they had to talk against nations, against nationalism, in order to curry favor with internationalism. Their metaphors are all mixed up. They think that because a Frenchman and an American and an Englishman can all sit down on the same platform and receive honors together, it must be that there is no such thing as nations. That kind of bad thinking springs from a source we all know. I should want to say to anyone like that: "Look! First I want to be a person. And I want you to be a person, and then we can be as interpersonal as you please. We can pull each other's noses—do all sorts of things. But, first of all, you have got to have the personality. First of all, you have got to have the nations and then they can be as international as they please with each other."

I should like to use another metaphor on them. I want my palette, if I am a painter, I want my palette on my thumb or on my chair, all clean, pure, separate colors. Then I will do the mixing on the canvas. The canvas is where the work of art is, where we make the conquest. But we want the nations all separate, pure, distinct, things as separate as we can make them; and then in our thoughts, in our arts, and so on, we can do what we please about it.

But I go back. There are four beliefs that I know more about from having lived with poetry. One is the personal belief, which is a knowledge that you don't want to tell other people about because you cannot prove that you know. You are saying nothing about it till you see. The love belief, just the same, has that same shyness. It knows it cannot tell; only the outcome can tell. And the national belief we enter into socially with each other, all together, party of the first part, party of the second part, we enter into that to bring the future of the country. We cannot tell some people what it is we believe, partly, because they are too stupid to understand and partly because we are too proudly vague to explain. And anyway it has got to be fulfilled, and we are not talking until we know more, until we have something to show. And then the literary one in every work of art, not of cunning and craft, mind you, but of real art; that believing the thing into existence, saying as you go more than you even hoped you were going to be able to say, and coming with surprise to an end that you foreknew only with some sort of emotion. And then finally the relationship we enter into with God to believe the future in—to believe the hereafter in.

55

THE READER

1. *How can the "poetry nuisance" be gotten out of the curriculum? Does Frost think it ought to stay in? Why?*

2. *What is meant by "enthusiasm passed through an idea" and "enthusiasm tamed to metaphor" (p. 1093)? What sort of metaphors does Frost use in those phrases, and what do they imply?*

3. *What does Frost mean when he says "unless you have had your proper poetical education in the metaphor, you are not safe anywhere" (p. 1094)? Indicate some of the metaphors Frost examines in this essay.*

From what fields are they drawn? What does he say about each?
Nominate some further metaphors—from politics, science, sociology,
or anything else—and analyze them. To what extent are they useful?
Do they have a breaking point? How might they mislead beyond the
breaking point?

THE WRITER

1. *In what way does the subtitle describe this essay? Is it rambling? Is it*
   unified?
2. *Frost admires a speech that has "range, something of overstatement,*
   something of statement, and something of understatement" (p. 1093).
   Is this spectrum visible in Frost's own speech? Show where and how.
3. *Choose two metaphors from different fields (like literature and science,*
   politics and biology, etc.), and write a brief essay comparing the use
   and usefulness of the metaphors in each field.

Scott Russell Sanders
THE SINGULAR FIRST PERSON

The first soapbox orator I ever saw was haranguing a crowd beside the
Greyhound Station in Providence about the evils of fluoridated water.
What the man stood on was actually an upturned milk crate, all the
genuine soapboxes presumably having been snapped up by antique deal-
ers. He wore an orange plaid sportscoat and matching bow tie and held
aloft a bottle filled with mossy green liquid. I don't remember the details
of his spiel, except his warning that fluoride was an invention of the
communists designed to weaken our bones and thereby make us push-
overs for a Red invasion. What amazed me, as a tongue-tied kid of
seventeen newly arrived in the city from the boondocks, was not his
message but his courage in delivering it to a mob of strangers. I figured
it would have been easier for me to jump straight over the Greyhound
Station than to stand there on that milk crate and utter my thoughts.

To this day, when I read or when I compose one of those curious
monologues we call the personal essay, I often think of that soapbox
orator. Nobody had asked him for his two cents' worth, but there he was
declaring it with all the eloquence he could muster. The essay, although
enacted in private, is no less arrogant a performance. Unlike novelists
and playwrights, who lurk behind the scenes while distracting our atten-

First appeared in the *Sewanee Review* (Fall 1988).

tion with the puppet show of imaginary characters, unlike scholars and
journalists, who quote the opinions of others and shelter behind the
hedges of neutrality, the essayist has nowhere to hide. While the poet
can lean back on a several-thousand-year-old legacy of ecstatic speech,
the essayist inherits a much briefer and skimpier tradition. The poet is
allowed to quit in less than a page, but the essayist must generally hold
forth over several thousand words. It is an arrogant and foolhardy form,
this one-man or one-woman circus, which relies on the tricks of anecdote, memory, conjecture, and wit to hold our attention.

Addressing a monologue to the world seems all the more brazen or
preposterous an act when you consider what a tiny fraction of the human
chorus any single voice is. At the Boston Museum of Science an electronic meter records with flashing lights the population of the United
States. Figuring in the rate of births, deaths, emigrants leaving the
country and immigrants arriving, the meter calculates that we add one
fellow citizen every twenty-one seconds. When I looked at it recently,
the count stood at 242,958,483. As I wrote that figure in my notebook,
the final number jumped from three to four. Another mouth, another
set of ears and eyes, another brain. A counter for the earth's population
would stand somewhere past five billion at the moment, and would be
rising in a blur of digits. Amid this avalanche of selves it is a wonder that
anyone finds the gumption to sit down and write one of those naked,
lonely, quixotic letters-to-the-world.

A surprising number do find the gumption. In fact I have the impression there are more essayists at work in America today, and more gifted
ones, than at any time in recent decades. Whom do I have in mind?
Here is a sampler: Edward Abbey, James Baldwin, Wendell Berry, Carol
Bly, Joan Didion, Annie Dillard, Stephen Jay Gould, Elizabeth Hard-
wick, Edward Hoagland, Barry Lopez, Peter Matthiessen, John
McPhee, Cynthia Ozick, Paul Theroux, Lewis Thomas, Tom Wolfe.
No doubt you could make up a wiser list of your own—with a greater
ethnic range, say, or fewer nature enthusiasts—a list that would provide
even more convincing support for my view that we are blessed right now
with an abundance of essayists. We do not have anyone to rival Emerson
or Thoreau,[1] but in sheer quantity of first-rate work our time stands
comparison with any period since the heyday of the form in the mid-
nineteenth century.

In the manner of a soapbox orator I now turn my hunch into a fact
and state boldly that in America these days the personal essay is flourishing. Why are so many writers taking up this risky form, and why are so

1. Ralph Waldo Emerson (1803–82),
American lecturer, poet, and essayist; he
was the leading exponent of New England
transcendentalism; Henry David Thoreau
(1817–62), American essayist, poet, and
philosopher, renowned for having lived the
doctrines of transcendentalism, as recorded
in *Walden* (1854).

many readers—to judge by the statistics of book and magazine publication—seeking it out?

In this era of prepackaged thought the essay is the closest thing we
have, on paper, to a record of the individual mind at work and play. It
is an amateur's raid in a world of specialists. Feeling overwhelmed by
data, random information, the flotsam and jetsam of mass culture, we
relish the spectacle of a single consciousness making sense of a part of
the chaos. We are grateful to Lewis Thomas for shining his light into
the dark corners of biology, to John McPhee for laying bare the geology
beneath our landscape, to Annie Dillard for showing us the universal fire
blazing in the branches of a cedar, to Peter Matthiessen for chasing after
snow leopards and mystical insights in the Himalayas. No matter if they
are sketchy—these maps of meaning are still welcome. As Joan Didion
observes in *The White Album*, "We live entirely, especially if we are
writers, by the imposition of a narrative line upon disparate images, by
the 'ideas' with which we have learned to freeze the shifting phantasmagoria which is our actual experience." Dizzy from a dance that seems
to accelerate hour by hour, we cling to the narrative line, even though
it may be as pure an invention as the shapes drawn by Greeks to identify
the constellations.

The essay is a haven for the private idiosyncratic voice in an era of
anonymous babble. Like the blandburgers served in their millions along
our highways, most language served up in public these days is textureless
tasteless mush. On television, over the phone, in the newspaper, wherever human beings bandy words, we encounter more and more abstractions, more empty formulas. Think of the pablum ladled out by politicians. Think of the fluffy white bread of advertising. Think, lord help
us, of committee reports. By contrast the essay remains stubbornly
concrete and particular: it confronts you with an oil-smeared toilet at the
Sunoco station, a red vinyl purse shaped like a valentine heart, a bow-
legged dentist hunting deer with an elephant gun. As Orwell forcefully
argued, and as dictators seem to agree, such a bypassing of abstractions,
such an insistence on the concrete, is a politically subversive act. Clinging to this door, that child, this grief, following the zigzag motions of
an inquisitive mind, the essay renews language and clears trash from the
springs of thought. A century and a half ago Emerson called on a new
generation of writers to cast off the hand-me-down rhetoric of the day,
to "pierce this rotten diction and fasten words again to visible things."
The essayist aspires to do just that.

As if all these virtues were not enough to account for a renaissance
of this protean genre, the essay has also taken over some of the territory
abdicated by contemporary fiction. Pared down to the brittle bones of
plot, camouflaged with irony, muttering in brief sentences and grade-
school vocabulary, today's fashionable fiction avoids disclosing where the

author stands on anything. Most of the trends in the novel and short story over the past twenty years have led away from candor—toward satire, artsy jokes, close-lipped coyness, metafictional hocus-pocus, anything but a direct statement of what the author thinks and feels. If you hide behind enough screens, no one will ever hold you to an opinion or demand from you a coherent vision or take you for a charlatan.

The essay is not fenced round by these literary inhibitions. You may speak without disguise of what moves and worries and excites you. In fact you had better speak from a region pretty close to the heart or the reader will detect the wind of phoniness whistling through your hollow phrases. In the essay you may be caught with your pants down, your ignorance and sentimentality showing, while you trot recklessly about on one of our hobbyhorses. You cannot stand back from the action, as Joyce instructed us to do, and pare your fingernails. You cannot palm off your cockamamy notions on some hapless character. If the words you put down are foolish, everyone knows precisely who the fool is.

To our list of the essay's contemporary attractions we should add the perennial ones of verbal play, mental adventure, and sheer anarchic high spirits. The writing of an essay is like finding one's way through a forest without being quite sure what game you are chasing, what landmark you are seeking. You sniff down one path until some heady smell tugs you in a new direction, and then off you go, dodging and circling, lured on by the songs of unfamiliar birds, puzzled by the tracks of strange beasts, leaping from stone to stone across rivers, barking up one tree after another. Much of the pleasure in writing an essay—and, when the writing is any good, the pleasure in reading it—comes from this dodging and leaping, this movement of the mind. It must not be idle movement, however, if the essay is to hold up; it must be driven by deep concerns. The surface of a river is alive with lights and reflections, the breaking of foam over rocks, but underneath that dazzle it is going somewhere. We should expect as much from an essay: the shimmer and play of mind on the surface and in the depths a strong current.

To see how the capricious mind can be led astray, consider my last paragraph, in which the making of essays is likened first to the romping of a dog and then to the surge of a river. That is bad enough, but it could have been worse. For example I began to draft a sentence in that paragraph with the following words: "More than once, in sitting down to beaver away at a narrative, felling trees of memory and dragging brush to build a dam that might slow down the waters of time. . . ." I had set out to make some innocent remark, and here I was gnawing down trees and building dams, all because I had let that *beaver* slip in. On this occasion I had the good sense to throw out the unruly word. I don't always, as no doubt you will have noticed. I might as well drag in another metaphor—and another unoffending animal—by saying that each doggy sentence, as it noses forward into the underbrush of thought, scatters a bunch of rabbits that go rushing off in all directions. The essayist can afford to chase more of those rabbits than the fiction writer can, but fewer than the poet. If you refuse to chase any of them, and keep plodding along in a straight line, you and your reader will have a dull outing. If you chase too many, you will soon wind up lost in a thicket of confusion with your tongue hanging out.

The pursuit of mental rabbits was strictly forbidden by the teachers who instructed me in English composition. For that matter nearly all the qualities of the personal essay, as I have been sketching them, violate the rules that many of us were taught in school. You recall we were supposed to begin with an outline and stick by it faithfully, like a train riding its rails, avoiding sidetracks. Each paragraph was to have a topic sentence pasted near the front, and these orderly paragraphs were to be coupled end-to-end like so many boxcars. Every item in those boxcars was to bear the stamp of some external authority, preferably a footnote referring to a thick book, although appeals to magazines and newspapers would do in a pinch. Our diction was to be formal, dignified, shunning the vernacular. Polysyllabic words derived from Latin were preferable to the blunt lingo of the streets. Metaphors were to be used only in emergencies, and no two of them were to be mixed. And even in emergencies we could not speak in the first-person singular.

Already, as a schoolboy, I chafed against those rules. Now I break them shamelessly—in particular the taboo against using the lonely capital *I.* Just look at what I'm doing right now. My speculations about the state of the essay arise, needless to say, from my own practice as reader and writer, and they reflect my own tastes, no matter how I may pretend to gaze dispassionately down on the question from a hot-air balloon. As Thoreau declares in his brash manner on the opening page of *Walden:* "In most books the *I,* or first person, is omitted; in this it will be retained; that, in respect to egotism, is the main difference. We commonly do not remember that it is, after all, always the first person that is speaking. I should not talk so much about myself if there were anybody else whom I knew as well." True for the personal essay, it is doubly true for an essay about the essay: one speaks always and inescapably in the first-person singular.

We could sort out essays along a spectrum according to the degree to which the writer's ego is on display—with John McPhee, perhaps, at the extreme of self-effacement, and Norman Mailer at the opposite extreme of self-dramatization. Brassy or shy, stage-center or hanging back in the wings, the author's persona commands our attention. For the length of an essay, or a book of essays, we respond to that persona as we would to a friend caught up in a rapturous monologue. When the monologue is finished, we may not be able to say precisely what it was about, any more than we can draw conclusions from a piece of music. "Essays don't usually boil down to a summary, as articles do," notes Edward Hoagland, one of the least summarizable of companions, "and the style of the writer has a 'nap' to it, a combination of personality and originality and energetic loose ends that stand up like the nap of a piece of wool and can't be brushed flat." We make assumptions about that speaking voice, assumptions we cannot validly make about the narrators in fiction. Only a sophomore is permitted to ask how many children had Huckleberry Finn. But even literary sophisticates wonder in print about Thoreau's love life, Montaigne's domestic arrangements, De Quincey's opium habit, Virginia Woolf's[2] depression.

Montaigne, who not only invented the form but perfected it as well, announced from the start that his true subject was himself. In his note "To the Reader," he slyly proclaimed:

> I want to be seen here in my simple, natural, ordinary fashion, without straining or artifice; for it is myself that I portray. My defects will here be read to the life, and also my natural form, as far as respect for the public has allowed. Had I been placed among those nations which are said to live still in the sweet freedom of nature's first laws, I assure you I should very gladly have portrayed myself here entire and wholly naked.

A few pages after this disarming introduction we are told of the Emperor Maximilian, who was so prudish about displaying his private parts that he would not let a servant dress him or see him in the bath. The emperor went so far as to give orders that he be buried in his underdrawers. Having let us in on this intimacy about Maximilian, Montaigne then confessed that he himself, although "bold-mouthed," was equally prudish, and that "except under great stress of necessity or voluptuousness," he never allowed anyone to see him naked. Such modesty, he feared, was unbecoming in a soldier. But such honesty is quite becoming in an essayist. The very confession of his prudery is a far more revealing gesture than any doffing of clothes.

Every English major knows that the word *essay*, as adapted by Montaigne, means a trial or attempt. The Latin root carries the more vivid sense of a weighing out. In the days when that root was alive and green, merchants discovered the value of goods and alchemists discovered the composition of unknown metals by the use of scales. Just so the essay, as Montaigne was the first to show, is a weighing out, an inquiry into the value, meaning, and true nature of experience; it is a private experi-

15

2. Michel (Eyquem) de Montaigne (1533– 92), French moralist and author of the *Es- sais* (*Essays*), which established the literary form of the personal essay; Thomas De Quincey (1785–1859), English essayist and critic, best known for his *Confessions of an English Opium-Eater* (1821); Virginia Woolf (1882–1941), English novelist, critic, and essayist.

ment carried out in public. In each of three successive editions Montaigne inserted new material into his essays without revising the old material. Often the new statements contradicted the original ones, but Montaigne let them stand, since he believed that the only consistent fact about human beings is their inconsistency. Lewis Thomas has remarked of him that he was "fond of his mind, and affectionately entertained by everything in his head." Whatever Montaigne wrote about (and he wrote about everything under the sun—fears, smells, growing old, the pleasures of scratching) he weighed on the scales of his own character.

It is the *singularity* of the first person—its warts and crotchets and turn of voice—that lures many of us into reading essays, and that lingers with us after we finish. Consider the lonely melancholy persona of Loren Eiseley, forever wandering, forever brooding on our dim and bestial past, his lips frosty with the chill of the Ice Age. Consider the volatile dionysian persona of D. H. Lawrence, with his incandescent gaze, his habit of turning peasants into gods and trees into flames, his quick hatred and quicker love. Consider that philosophical farmer Wendell Berry, who speaks with a countryman's knowledge and a deacon's severity. Consider E. B. White, with his cheery affection for brown eggs and dachshunds, his unflappable way of herding geese while the radio warns of an approaching hurricane.

White, that engaging master of the genre, a champion of idiosyncrasy, introduced one of his own collections by admitting the danger of narcissism:

> I think some people find the essay the last resort of the egoist, a much too self-conscious and self-serving form for their taste; they feel that it is presumptuous of a writer to assume that his little excursions or his small observations will interest the reader. There is some justice in their complaint. I have always been aware that I am by nature self-absorbed and egoistical; to write of myself to the extent I have done indicates a too great attention to my own life, not enough to the lives of others.

Yet the self-absorbed Mr. White was in fact a delighted observer of the world, and shared that delight with us. Thus, after describing memorably how a circus girl practiced her bareback riding in the leisure moments between shows ("The Ring of Time"), he confessed: "As a writing man, or secretary, I have always felt charged with the safekeeping of all unexpected items of worldly or unworldly enchantment, as though I might be held personally responsible if even a small one were to be lost." That may still be presumptuous, but it is presumption turned outward on the world.

This looking outward on the world helps distinguish the essay from pure autobiography, which dwells more complacently on the self. Mass murderers, movie stars, sports heroes, Wall Street crooks, and defrocked politicians may blather on about whatever high jinks or low jinks made them temporarily famous, may chronicle their exploits, their diets, their hobbies, in perfect confidence that the public is eager to gobble up every last gossipy scrap. And the public, according to sales figures, generally is. On the other hand I assume the public does not give a hoot about my private life (an assumption also borne out by sales figures). If I write of hiking up a mountain with my one-year-old boy riding like a papoose on my back, and of what he babbled to me while we gazed down from the summit onto the scudding clouds, it is not because I am deluded into believing that my baby, like the offspring of Prince Charles, matters to the great world. It is because I know the great world produces babies of its own and watches them change cloud-fast before its doting eyes. To make that climb up the mountain vividly present for readers is harder work than the climb itself. I choose to write about my experience not because it is mine, but because it seems to me a door through which others might pass.

On that cocky first page of *Walden* Thoreau justified his own seeming   20
self-absorption by saying that he wrote the book for the sake of his fellow citizens, who kept asking him to account for his peculiar experiment by the pond. There is at least a sliver of truth to this, since Thoreau, a town character, had been invited more than once to speak his mind at the public lectern. Most of us, however, cannot honestly say the townspeople have been clamoring for our words. I suspect that all writers of the essay, even Norman Mailer and Gore Vidal, must occasionally wonder if they are egomaniacs. For the essayist, in other words, the problem of authority is inescapable. By what right does one speak? Why should anyone listen? The traditional sources of authority no longer serve. You cannot justify your words by appealing to the Bible or some other holy text, you cannot merely stitch together a patchwork of quotations from classical authors, you cannot lean on a podium at the Atheneum and deliver your wisdom to a rapt audience.

In searching for your own soapbox, a sturdy platform from which to deliver your opinionated monologues, it helps if you have already distinguished yourself at making some other, less fishy form. When Yeats[3] describes his longing for Maud Gonne or muses on Ireland's misty lore, everything he says is charged with the prior strength of his poetry. When Virginia Woolf, in *A Room of One's Own*, reflects on the status of women and the conditions necessary for making art, she speaks as the author of *Mrs. Dalloway* and *To the Lighthouse*. The essayist may also claim our attention by having lived through events or traveled through terrains that already bear a richness of meaning. When James Baldwin

---

3. William Butler Yeats (1865–1939), Irish poet and dramatist.

writes his *Notes of a Native Son,* he does not have to convince us that racism is a troubling reality. When Barry Lopez takes us on a meditative tour of the far north in *Arctic Dreams,* he can rely on our curiosity about that fabled and forbidding place. When Paul Theroux climbs aboard a train and invites us on a journey to some exotic destination, he can count on the romance of railroads and the allure of remote cities to bear us along.

Most essayists, however, cannot draw on any source of authority from beyond the page to lend force to the page itself. They can only use language to put themselves on display and to gesture at the world. When Annie Dillard tells us in the opening lines of *Pilgrim at Tinker Creek* about the tomcat with bloody paws who jumps through the window onto her chest, why should we listen? Well, because of the voice that goes on to say: "And some mornings I'd wake in daylight to find my body covered with paw prints in blood; I looked as though I'd been painted with roses." Listen to her explaining a few pages later what she is up to in this book, this broody zestful record of her stay in the Roanoke Valley: "I propose to keep here what Thoreau called 'a meteorological journal of the mind,' telling some tales and describing some of the sights of this rather tamed valley, and exploring, in fear and trembling, some of the unmapped dim reaches and unholy fastnesses to which those tales and sights so dizzingly lead." The sentence not only describes the method of her literary search, but also displays the breathless, often giddy, always eloquent and spiritually hungry soul who will do the searching. If you enjoy her company, you will relish Annie Dillard's essays; if you don't, you won't.

Listen to another voice which readers tend to find either captivating or insufferable:

> That summer I began to see, however dimly, that one of my ambitions, perhaps my governing ambition, was to belong fully to this place, to belong as the thrushes and the herons and the muskrats belonged, to be altogether at home here. That is still my ambition. But now I have come to see that it proposes an enormous labor. It is a spiritual ambition, like goodness. The wild creatures belong to the place by nature, but as a man I can belong to it only by understanding and by virtue. It is an ambition I cannot hope to succeed in wholly, but I have come to believe that it is the most worthy of all.

That is Wendell Berry writing about his patch of Kentucky. Once you have heard that stately, moralizing, cherishing voice, laced through with references to the land, you will not mistake it for anyone else's. Berry's themes are profound and arresting ones. But it is his voice, more than anything he speaks about, that either seizes us or drives us away.

Even so distinct a persona as Wendell Berry's or Annie Dillard's is still only a literary fabrication, of course. The first-person singular is too narrow a gate for the whole writer to pass through. What we meet on the page is not the flesh-and-blood author, but a simulacrum, a character who wears the label *I*. Introducing the lectures that became *A Room of One's Own*, Virginia Woolf reminded her listeners that " 'I' is only a convenient term for somebody who has no real being. Lies will flow from my lips, but there may perhaps be some truth mixed up with them; it is for you to seek out this truth and to decide whether any part of it is worth keeping." Here is a part I consider worth keeping: "Women have served all these centuries as looking-glasses possessing the magic and delicious power of reflecting the figure of man at twice its natural size." From such elegant revelatory sentences we build up our notion of the "I" who speaks to us under the name of Virginia Woolf.

What the essay tells us may not be true in any sense that would satisfy a court of law. As an example think of Orwell's brief narrative "A Hanging," which describes an execution in Burma. Anyone who has read it remembers how the condemned man as he walked to the gallows stepped aside to avoid a puddle. That is the sort of haunting detail only an eyewitness should be able to report. Alas, biographers, those zealous debunkers, have recently claimed that Orwell never saw such a hanging; that he reconstructed it from hearsay. What then do we make of his essay? Or has it become the sort of barefaced lie we prefer to call a story?

I don't much care what label we put on "A Hanging"—fiction or nonfiction: it is a powerful statement either way; but Orwell might have cared a great deal. I say this because not long ago I found one of my own essays treated in a scholarly article as a work of fiction, and when I got over the shock of finding any reference to my work at all, I was outraged. Here was my earnest report about growing up on a military base, my heartfelt rendering of indelible memories, being confused with the airy figments of novelists! To be sure, in writing the piece I had used dialogue, scenes, settings, character descriptions, the whole fictional bag of tricks; sure, I picked and chose among a thousand beckoning details; sure, I downplayed some facts and highlighted others; but I was writing about the actual, not the invented. I shaped the matter, but I did not make it up.

To explain my outrage I must break another taboo, which is to speak of the author's intention. My teachers warned me strenuously to avoid the intentional fallacy. They told me to regard poems and plays and stories as objects washed up on the page from some unknown and unknowable shores. Now that I am on the other side of the page, so to speak, I think quite recklessly of intention all the time. I believe that if we allow the question of intent in the case of murder, we should allow it in literature. The essay is distinguished from the short story not by the presence or absence of literary devices, not by tone or theme or

25

subject, but by the writer's stance toward the material. In composing an essay about what it was like to grow up on that military base, I *meant* something quite different from what I mean when concocting a story. I meant to preserve and record and help give voice to a reality that existed independently of me. I meant to pay my respects to a minor passage of history in an out-of-the-way place. I felt responsible to the truth as known by other people. I wanted to speak directly out of my own life into the lives of others.

You can see I am teetering on the brink of metaphysics. One step farther and I will plunge into the void, wondering as I fall how to prove there is any external truth for the essayist to pay homage to. I draw back from the brink and simply declare that I believe one writes, in essays, with a regard for the actual world, with a respect for the shared substance of history, the autonomy of other lives, the being of nature, the mystery and majesty of a creation we have not made.

When it comes to speculating about the creation, I feel more at ease with physics than with metaphysics. According to certain bold and lyrical cosmologists, there is at the center of black holes a geometrical point, the tiniest conceivable speck, where all the matter of a collapsed star has been concentrated, and where everyday notions of time, space, and force break down. That point is called a singularity. The boldest and most poetic theories suggest that anything sucked into a singularity might be flung back out again, utterly changed, somewhere else in the universe. The lonely first person, the essayist's microcosmic "I," may be thought of as a verbal singularity at the center of the mind's black hole. The raw matter of experience, torn away from the axes of time and space, falls in constantly from all sides, undergoes the mind's inscrutable alchemy, and reemerges in the quirky unprecedented shape of an essay.

30   Now it is time for me to step down, before another metaphor seizes hold of me, before you notice that I am standing, not on a soapbox, but on the purest air.

THE READER

1. *Sanders begins a paragraph with the statement, "The pursuit of mental rabbits was strictly forbidden by the teachers who instructed me in English composition" (p. 1104). What does he mean by "mental rabbits"? Why was the pursuit of these strictly forbidden?*
2. *Sanders goes on to list the rules of English composition taught him, and the ones he now violates. Which of these rules have you been taught? Should you ever violate them?*
3. *Which rules of composition does Sanders violate in his essay "Looking at Women" (p. 222), and to what effect?*
4. *What is the main point of "The Singular First Person?"*

THE WRITER

1. *Why does Sanders call his essay "The Singular First Person" instead of, say, "The First Person Singular"?*
2. *Sanders begins and ends his essay with reference to a soapbox. What has happened in the interval to make the soapbox vanish at the end into "the purest air"?*
3. *What evidence is there that Sanders is fond of words, likes playing and fooling around with them? Give some examples and describe the effect produced by his choice of words.*
4. *Sanders in his essay treats the subject of "authority." In what ways might authority be established in an essay? Does Sanders establish his authority for you? If so, in what ways?*
5. *Write a brief essay on any subject, violating (to good purpose) as many rules of composition as you can.*

Virginia Woolf

IN SEARCH OF A ROOM OF ONE'S OWN

It was disappointing not to have brought back in the evening some important statement, some authentic fact. Women are poorer than men because—this or that. Perhaps now it would be better to give up seeking for the truth, and receiving on one's head an avalanche of opinion hot as lava, discoloured as dish-water. It would be better to draw the curtains; to shut out distractions; to light the lamp; to narrow the enquiry and to ask the historian, who records not opinions but facts, to describe under what conditions women lived, not throughout the ages, but in England, say in the time of Elizabeth.

For it is a perennial puzzle why no woman wrote a word of that extraordinary literature when every other man, it seemed, was capable of song or sonnet. What were the conditions in which women lived, I asked myself; for fiction, imaginative work that is, is not dropped like a pebble upon the ground, as science may be; fiction is like a spider's

This selection is Chapter 3 of Woolf's *A Room of One's Own*, a long essay published in 1929 that began as two lectures on women and fiction given at Newnham College and Girton College, women's colleges at Cambridge University, in 1928. In Chapter 1, Woolf advances the proposition that "a woman must have money and a room of her own if she is to write fiction." In Chapter 2, she describes a day spent at the British Museum (now the British Library) looking for information about the lives of women.

web, attached ever so lightly perhaps, but still attached to life at all four corners. Often the attachment is scarcely perceptible; Shakespeare's plays, for instance, seem to hang there complete by themselves. But when the web is pulled askew, hooked up at the edge, torn in the middle, one remembers that these webs are not spun in midair by incorporeal creatures, but are the work of suffering human beings, and are attached to grossly material things, like health and money and the houses we live in.

I went, therefore, to the shelf where the histories stand and took down one of the latest, Professor Trevelyan's *History of England.* Once more I looked up Women, found "position of," and turned to the pages indicated. "Wife-beating," I read, "was a recognised right of man, and was practised without shame by high as well as low. . . . Similarly," the historian goes on, "the daughter who refused to marry the gentleman of her parents' choice was liable to be locked up, beaten and flung about the room, without any shock being inflicted on public opinion. Marriage was not an affair of personal affection, but of family avarice, particularly in the 'chivalrous' upper classes. . . . Betrothal often took place while one or both of the parties was in the cradle, and marriage when they were scarcely out of the nurses' charge." That was about 1470, soon after Chaucer's time. The next reference to the position of women is some two hundred years later, in the time of the Stuarts. "It was still the exception for women of the upper and middle class to choose their own husbands, and when the husband had been assigned, he was lord and master, so far at least as law and custom could make him. Yet even so," Professor Trevelyan concludes, "neither Shakespeare's women nor those of authentic seventeenth-century memoirs, like the Verneys and the Hutchinsons, seem wanting in personality and character." Certainly, if we consider it, Cleopatra must have had a way with her; Lady Macbeth, one would suppose, had a will of her own; Rosalind, one might conclude, was an attractive girl. Professor Trevelyan is speaking no more than the truth when he remarks that Shakespeare's women do not seem wanting in personality and character. Not being a historian, one might go even further and say that women have burnt like beacons in all the works of all the poets from the beginning of time—Clytemnestra, Antigone, Cleopatra, Lady Macbeth, Phèdre, Cressida, Rosalind, Desdemona, the Duchess of Malfi, among the dramatists; then among the prose writers: Millamant, Clarissa, Becky Sharp, Anna Karenina, Emma Bovary, Madame de Guermantes—the names flock to mind, nor do they recall women "lacking in personality and character." Indeed, if woman had no existence save in the fiction written by men, one would imagine her a person of the utmost importance; very various; heroic and mean; splendid and sordid; infinitely beautiful and hideous in the extreme; as great as a man, some think even greater.[1] But this is woman in fiction. In fact, as Professor Trevelyan points out, she was locked up, beaten and flung about the room.

A very queer, composite being thus emerges. Imaginatively she is of the highest importance; practically she is completely insignificant. She pervades poetry from cover to cover; she is all but absent from history. She dominates the lives of kings and conquerors in fiction; in fact she was the slave of any boy whose parents forced a ring upon her finger. Some of the most inspired words, some of the most profound thoughts in literature fall from her lips; in real life she could hardly read, could scarcely spell, and was the property of her husband.

It was certainly an odd monster that one made up by reading the   5
historians first and the poets afterwards—a worm winged like an eagle; the spirit of life and beauty in a kitchen chopping up suet. But these monsters, however amusing to the imagination, have no existence in fact. What one must do to bring her to life was to think poetically and prosaically at one and the same moment, thus keeping in touch with fact—that she is Mrs. Martin, aged thirty-six, dressed in blue, wearing a black hat and brown shoes; but not losing sight of fiction either—that she is a vessel in which all sorts of spirits and forces are coursing and flashing perpetually. The moment, however, that one tries this method with the Elizabethan woman, one branch of illumination fails; one is held up by the scarcity of facts. One knows nothing detailed, nothing perfectly true and substantial about her. History scarcely mentions her. And I turned to Professor Trevelyan again to see what history meant to him. I found by looking at his chapter headings that it meant—

"The Manor Court and the Methods of Open-field Agriculture . . . The Cistercians and Sheep-farming . . . The Crusades . . . The University . . . The House of Commons . . . The Hundred Years' War . . . The Wars of the Roses . . . The Renaissance Scholars . . . The

---

1. "It remains a strange and almost inexplicable fact that in Athena's city, where women were kept in almost Oriental suppression as odalisques or drudges, the stage should yet have produced figures like Clytemnestra and Cassandra, Atossa and Antigone, Phèdre and Medea, and all the other heroines who dominate play after play of the 'misogynist' Euripides. But the paradox of this world where in real life a respectable woman could hardly show her face alone in the street, and yet on the stage woman equals or surpasses man, has never been satisfactorily explained. In modern tragedy the same predominance exists. At all events, a very cursory survey of Shakespeare's work (similarly with Webster, though not with Marlowe or Jonson) suffices to reveal how this dominance, this initiative of women, persists from Rosalind to Lady Macbeth. So too in Racine; six of his tragedies bear their heroines' names; and what male characters of his shall we set against Hermione and Andromaque, Bérénice and Roxane, Phèdre and Athalie? So again with Ibsen; what men shall we match with Solveig and Nora, Hedda and Hilda Wangel and Rebecca West?"—F. L. LUCAS, Tragedy, pp. 114–15 [Woolf's note].

Dissolution of the Monasteries . . . Agrarian and Religious Strife . . . The Origin of English Sea-power . . . The Armada . . ." and so on. Occasionally an individual woman is mentioned, an Elizabeth, or a Mary; a queen or a great lady. But by no possible means could middle-class women with nothing but brains and character at their command have taken part in any one of the great movements which, brought together, constitute the historian's view of the past. Nor shall we find her in any collection of anecdotes. Aubrey[2] hardly mentions her. She never writes her own life and scarcely keeps a diary; there are only a handful of her letters in existence. She left no plays or poems by which we can judge her. What one wants, I thought—and why does not some brilliant student at Newnham or Girton supply it?—is a mass of information; at what age did she marry; how many children had she as a rule; what was her house like; had she a room to herself; did she do the cooking; would she be likely to have a servant? All these facts lie somewhere, presumably, in parish registers and account books; the life of the average Elizabethan woman must be scattered about somewhere, could one collect it and make a book of it. It would be ambitious beyond my daring, I thought, looking about the shelves for books that were not there, to suggest to the students of those famous colleges that they should re-write history, though I own that it often seems a little queer as it is, unreal, lop-sided; but why should they not add a supplement to history? calling it, of course, by some inconspicuous name so that women might figure there without impropriety? For one often catches a glimpse of them in the lives of the great, whisking away into the background, concealing, I sometimes think, a wink, a laugh, perhaps a tear. And, after all, we have lives enough of Jane Austen; it scarcely seems necessary to consider again the influence of the tragedies of Joanna Baillie upon the poetry of Edgar Allan Poe; as for myself, I should not mind if the homes and haunts of Mary Russell Mitford were closed to the public for a century at least.[3] But what I find deplorable, I continued, looking about the bookshelves again, is that nothing is known about women before the eighteenth century. I have no model in my mind to turn about this way and that. Here am I asking why women did not write poetry in the Elizabethan age, and I am not sure how they were educated; whether they were taught to write; whether they had sitting-rooms to themselves; how many women had children before they were twenty-one; what, in short, they did from eight in the morning till eight at night. They had no money evidently; according to Professor Trevelyan they were married

---

2. John Aubrey (1626–97), whose biographical writings were published posthumously as *Brief Lives*.
3. Jane Austen (1775–1817), English novelist; Joanna Baillie (1762–1851), Scottish dramatist and poet; Mary Russell Mitford (1787–1855), English novelist and dramatist.

whether they liked it or not before they were out of the nursery, at fifteen or sixteen very likely. It would have been extremely odd, even upon this showing, had one of them suddenly written the plays of Shakespeare, I concluded, and I thought of that old gentleman, who is dead now, but was a bishop, I think, who declared that it was impossible for any woman, past, present, or to come, to have the genius of Shakespeare. He wrote to the papers about it. He also told a lady who applied to him for information that cats do not as a matter of fact go to heaven, though they have, he added, souls of a sort. How much thinking those old gentlemen used to save one! How the borders of ignorance shrank back at their approach! Cats do not go to heaven. Women cannot write the plays of Shakespeare.

Be that as it may, I could not help thinking, as I looked at the works of Shakespeare on the shelf, that the bishop was right at least in this; it would have been impossible, completely and entirely, for any woman to have written the plays of Shakespeare in the age of Shakespeare. Let me imagine, since facts are so hard to come by, what would have happened had Shakespeare had a wonderfully gifted sister, called Judith, let us say. Shakespeare himself went, very probably—his mother was an heiress—to the grammar school, where he may have learnt Latin— Ovid, Virgil and Horace—and the elements of grammar and logic. He was, it is well known, a wild boy who poached rabbits, perhaps shot a deer, and had, rather sooner than he should have done, to marry a woman in the neighbourhood, who bore him a child rather quicker than was right. That escapade sent him to seek his fortune in London. He had, it seemed, a taste for the theatre; he began by holding horses at the stage door. Very soon he got work in the theatre, became a successful actor, and lived at the hub of the universe, meeting everybody, knowing everybody, practising his art on the boards, exercising his wits in the streets, and even getting access to the palace of the queen. Meanwhile his extraordinarily gifted sister, let us suppose, remained at home. She was as adventurous, as imaginative, as agog to see the world as he was. But she was not sent to school. She had no chance of learning grammar and logic, let alone of reading Horace and Virgil. She picked up a book now and then, one of her brother's perhaps, and read a few pages. But then her parents came in and told her to mend the stockings or mind the stew and not moon about with books and papers. They would have spoken sharply but kindly, for they were substantial people who knew the conditions of life for a woman and loved their daughter—indeed, more likely than not she was the apple of her father's eye. Perhaps she scribbled some pages up in an apple loft on the sly, but was careful to hide them or set fire to them. Soon, however, before she was out of her teens, she was to be betrothed to the son of a neighbouring wool-stapler.

She cried out that marriage was hateful to her, and for that she was severely beaten by her father. Then he ceased to scold her. He begged her instead not to hurt him, not to shame him in this matter of her marriage. He would give her a chain of beads or a fine petticoat, he said; and there were tears in his eyes. How could she disobey him? How could she break his heart? The force of her own gift alone drove her to it. She made up a small parcel of her belongings, let herself down by a rope one summer's night and took the road to London. She was not seventeen. The birds that sang in the hedge were not more musical than she was. She had the quickest fancy, a gift like her brother's, for the tune of words. Like him, she had a taste for the theatre. She stood at the stage door; she wanted to act, she said. Men laughed in her face. The manager—a fat, loose-lipped man—guffawed. He bellowed something about poodles dancing and women acting—no woman, he said, could possibly be an actress. [4] He hinted—you can imagine what. She could get no training in her craft. Could she even seek her dinner in a tavern or roam the streets at midnight? Yet her genius was for fiction and lusted to feed abundantly upon the lives of men and women and the study of their ways. At last—for she was very young, oddly like Shakespeare the poet in her face, with the same grey eyes and rounded brows—at last Nick Greene the actor-manager took pity on her; she found herself with child by that gentleman and so—who shall measure the heat and violence of the poet's heart when caught and tangled in a woman's body?—killed herself one winter's night and lies buried at some cross-roads where the omnibuses now stop outside the Elephant and Castle.

That, more or less, is how the story would run, I think, if a woman in Shakespeare's day had had Shakespeare's genius. But for my part, I agree with the deceased bishop, if such he was—it is unthinkable that any woman in Shakespeare's day should have had Shakespeare's genius. For genius like Shakespeare's is not born among labouring, uneducated, servile people. It was not born in England among the Saxons and the Britons. It is not born today among the working classes. How, then, could it have been born among women whose work began, according to Professor Trevelyan, almost before they were out of the nursery, who were forced to it by their parents and held to it by all the power of law and custom? Yet genius of a sort must have existed among women as it must have existed among the working classes. Now and again an Emily Brontë or a Robert Burns blazes out and proves its presence. [5] But certainly it never got itself on to paper. When, however, one reads of a witch being ducked, of a woman possessed by devils, of a wise woman selling herbs, or even of a very remarkable man who had a mother, then

4. In the Elizabethan theater boys played women's parts.
5. Woolf's examples are Emily Brontë (1818–48), the English novelist, and Robert Burns (1759–96), the Scottish poet.

I think we are on the track of a lost novelist, a suppressed poet, of some mute and inglorious Jane Austen,[6] some Emily Brontë who dashed her brains out on the moor or mopped and mowed about the highways crazed with the torture that her gift had put her to. Indeed, I would venture to guess that Anon, who wrote so many poems without signing them, was often a woman. It was a woman Edward Fitzgerald,[7] I think, suggested who made the ballads and the folk-songs, crooning them to her children, beguiling her spinning with them, or the length of the winter's night.

This may be true or it may be false—who can say?—but what is true in it, so it seemed to me, reviewing the story of Shakespeare's sister as I had made it, is that any woman born with a great gift in the sixteenth century would certainly have gone crazed, shot herself, or ended her days in some lonely cottage outside the village, half witch, half wizard, feared and mocked at. For it needs little skill in psychology to be sure that a highly gifted girl who had tried to use her gift for poetry would have been so thwarted and hindered by other people, so tortured and pulled asunder by her own contrary instincts, that she must have lost her health and sanity to a certainty. No girl could have walked to London and stood at a stage door and forced her way into the presence of actor-managers without doing herself a violence and suffering an anguish which may have been irrational—for chastity may be a fetish invented by certain societies for unknown reasons—but were none the less inevitable. Chastity had then, it has even now, a religious importance in a woman's life, and has so wrapped itself round with nerves and instincts that to cut it free and bring it to the light of day demands courage of the rarest. To have lived a free life in London in the sixteenth century would have meant for a woman who was poet and playwright a nervous stress and dilemma which might well have killed her. Had she survived, whatever she had written would have been twisted and deformed, issuing from a strained and morbid imagination. And undoubtedly, I thought, looking at the shelf where there are no plays by women, her work would have gone unsigned. That refuge she would have sought certainly. It was the relic of the sense of chastity that dictated anonymity to women even so late as the nineteenth century. Currer Bell, George Eliot, George Sand, all the victims of inner strife as their writings prove, sought ineffectively to veil themselves by using the name of a man.[8] Thus they did homage to the convention, which if not implanted by the other sex was liberally

6. Woolf alludes to Thomas Gray's "Elegy Written in a Country Churchyard": "Some mute inglorious Milton here may rest."
7. Edward Fitzgerald (1809–83), poet and translator.

8. The pseudonyms of Charlotte Brontë (1816–55), English novelist; Mary Ann Evans (1819–80), English novelist; and Amandine Aurore Lucie Dupin, Baronne Dudevant (1804–76), French novelist.

encouraged by them (the chief glory of a woman is not to be talked of, said Pericles,[9] himself a much-talked-of man), that publicity in women is detestable. Anonymity runs in their blood. The desire to be veiled still possesses them. They are not even now as concerned about the health of their fame as men are, and, speaking generally, will pass a tombstone or a signpost without feeling an irresistible desire to cut their names on it, as Alf, Bert or Chas. must do in obedience to their instinct, which murmurs if it sees a fine woman go by, or even a dog, Ce chien est à moi.[1] And, of course, it may not be a dog, I thought, remembering Parliament Square, the Sieges Allee and other avenues; it may be a piece of land or a man with curly black hair. It is one of the great advantages of being a woman that one can pass even a very fine negress without wishing to make an Englishwoman of her.

10   That woman, then, who was born with a gift of poetry in the sixteenth century, was an unhappy woman, a woman at strife against herself. All the conditions of her life, all her own instincts, were hostile to the state of mind which is needed to set free whatever is in the brain. But what is the state of mind that is most propitious to the act of creation, I asked. Can one come by any notion of the state that furthers and makes possible that strange activity? Here I opened the volume containing the Tragedies of Shakespeare. What was Shakespeare's state of mind, for instance, when he wrote *Lear* and *Antony and Cleopatra*? It was certainly the state of mind most favourable to poetry that there has ever existed. But Shakespeare himself said nothing about it. We only know casually and by chance that he "never blotted a line."[2] Nothing indeed was ever said by the artist himself about his state of mind until the eighteenth century perhaps. Rousseau perhaps began it.[3] At any rate, by the nineteenth century self-consciousness had developed so far that it was the habit for men of letters to describe their minds in confessions and autobiographies. Their lives also were written, and their letters were printed after their deaths. Thus, though we do not know what Shakespeare went through when he wrote *Lear,* we do know what Carlyle went through when he wrote the *French Revolution*; what Flaubert went through when he wrote *Madame Bovary*; what Keats was going through when he tried to write poetry against the coming of death and the indifference of the world.

And one gathers from this enormous modern literature of confession and self-analysis that to write a work of genius is almost always a feat of prodigious difficulty. Everything is against the likelihood that it will

9. Pericles (d. 429 B.C.), Athenian statesman.
1. That dog is mine.
2. As recorded by his contemporary Ben Jonson (*Timber: Or Discoveries Made Upon Men and Matter.*)
3. Jean-Jacques Rousseau (1712–78), whose *Confessions* were published posthumously.

come from the writer's mind whole and entire. Generally material circumstances are against it. Dogs will bark; people will interrupt; money must be made; health will break down. Further, accentuating all these difficulties and making them harder to bear is the world's notorious indifference. It does not ask people to write poems and novels and histories; it does not need them. It does not care whether Flaubert finds the right word or whether Carlyle scrupulously verifies this or that fact. Naturally, it will not pay for what it does not want. And so the writer, Keats, Flaubert, Carlyle, suffers, especially in the creative years of youth, every form of distraction and discouragement. A curse, a cry of agony, rises from those books of analysis and confession. "Mighty poets in their misery dead"[4]—that is the burden of their song. If anything comes through in spite of all this, it is a miracle, and probably no book is born entire and uncrippled as it was conceived.

But for women, I thought, looking at the empty shelves, these difficulties were infinitely more formidable. In the first place, to have a room of her own, let alone a quiet room or a sound-proof room, was out of the question, unless her parents were exceptionally rich or very noble, even up to the beginning of the nineteenth century. Since her pin money, which depended on the good will of her father, was only enough to keep her clothed, she was debarred from such alleviations as came even to Keats or Tennyson or Carlyle, all poor men, from a walking tour, a little journey to France, from the separate lodging which, even if it were miserable enough, sheltered them from the claims and tyrannies of their families. Such material difficulties were formidable; but much worse were the immaterial. The indifference of the world which Keats and Flaubert and other men of genius have found so hard to bear was in her case not indifference but hostility. The world did not say to her as it said to them, Write if you choose; it makes no difference to me. The world said with a guffaw, Write? What's the good of your writing? Here the psychologists of Newnham and Girton might come to our help, I thought, looking again at the blank spaces on the shelves. For surely it is time that the effect of discouragement upon the mind of the artist should be measured, as I have seen a dairy company measure the effect of ordinary milk and Grade A milk upon the body of the rat. They set two rats in cages side by side, and of the two one was furtive, timid and small, and the other was glossy, bold and big. Now what food do we feed women as artists upon? I asked, remembering, I suppose, that dinner of prunes and custard.[5] To answer that question I had only to open the evening paper and to read that Lord Birkenhead is of opinion—but

4. From William Wordsworth's poem "Resolution and Independence."
5. In Chapter 1, Woolf contrasts the lavish dinner—partridge and wine—she ate as a guest in a men's college at Cambridge University with the plain fare—prunes and custard—served in a women's college.

really I am not going to trouble to copy out Lord Birkenhead's opinion upon the writing of women. What Dean Inge says I will leave in peace. The Harley Street specialist may be allowed to rouse the echoes of Harley Street with his vociferations without raising a hair on my head. I will quote, however, Mr. Oscar Browning, because Mr. Oscar Browning was a great figure in Cambridge at one time, and used to examine the students at Girton and Newnham.[6] Mr. Oscar Browning was wont to declare "that the impression left on his mind, after looking over any set of examination papers, was that, irrespective of the marks he might give, the best woman was intellectually the inferior of the worst man." After saying that Mr. Browning went back to his rooms—and it is this sequel that endears him and makes him a human figure of some bulk and majesty—he went back to his rooms and found a stable-boy lying on the sofa—"a mere skeleton, his cheeks were cavernous and sallow, his teeth were black, and he did not appear to have the full use of his limbs. . . . 'That's Arthur' [said Mr. Browning]. 'He's a dear boy really and most high-minded.' " The two pictures always seem to me to complete each other. And happily in this age of biography the two pictures often do complete each other, so that we are able to interpret the opinions of great men not only by what they say, but by what they do.

But though this is possible now, such opinions coming from the lips of important people must have been formidable enough even fifty years ago. Let us suppose that a father from the highest motives did not wish his daughter to leave home and become writer, painter or scholar. "See what Mr. Oscar Browning says," he would say; and there was not only Mr. Oscar Browning; there was the *Saturday Review*; there was Mr. Greg[7]—the "essentials of a woman's being," said Mr. Greg emphatically, "are that *they are supported by, and they minister to, men*"—there was an enormous body of masculine opinion to the effect that nothing could be expected of women intellectually. Even if her father did not read out loud these opinions, any girl could read them for herself; and the reading, even in the nineteenth century, must have lowered her vitality, and told profoundly upon her work. There would always have been that assertion—you cannot do this, you are incapable of doing that—to protest against, to overcome. Probably for a novelist this germ is no longer of much effect; for there have been women novelists of merit. But for painters it must still have some sting in it; and for musicians, I imagine, is even now active and poisonous in the extreme. The women composer stands where the actress stood in the time of

---

6. In Chapter 2, Woolf lists the fruits of her day's research on the lives of women, which include Lord Birkenhead's, Dean Inge's, and Mr. Oscar Browning's opinions of women; she does not, however, quote them. Harley Street is where fashionable medical doctors in London have their offices.

7. Mr. Greg does not appear on Woolf's list (see preceding note).

Shakespeare. Nick Greene, I thought, remembering the story I had made about Shakespeare's sister, said that a woman acting put him in mind of a dog dancing. Johnson repeated the phrase two hundred years later of women preaching.[8] And here, I said, opening a book about music, we have the very words used again in this year of grace, 1928, of women who try to write music. "Of Mlle. Germaine Tailleferre one can only repeat Dr. Johnson's dictum concerning a woman preacher, transposed into terms of music. 'Sir, a woman's composing is like a dog's walking on his hind legs. It is not done well, but you are surprised to find it done at all.' "[9] So accurately does history repeat itself.

Thus, I concluded, shutting Mr. Oscar Browning's life and pushing away the rest, it is fairly evident that even in the nineteenth century a woman was not encouraged to be an artist. On the contrary, she was snubbed, slapped, lectured and exhorted. Her mind must have been strained and her vitality lowered by the need of opposing this, of disproving that. For here again we come within range of that very interesting and obscure masculine complex which has had so much influence upon the woman's movement; that deep-seated desire, not so much that *she* shall be inferior as that *he* shall be superior, which plants him wherever one looks, not only in front of the arts, but barring the way to politics too, even when the risk to himself seems infinitesimal and the suppliant humble and devoted. Even Lady Bessborough, I remembered, with all her passion for politics, must humbly bow herself and write to Lord Granville Leveson-Gower[1]: ". . . notwithstanding all my violence in politics and talking so much on that subject, I perfectly agree with you that no woman has any business to meddle with that or any other serious business, farther than giving her opinion (if she is ask'd)." And so she goes on to spend her enthusiasm where it meets with no obstacle whatsoever upon that immensely important subject, Lord Granville's maiden speech in the House of Commons. The spectacle is certainly a strange one, I thought. The history of men's opposition to women's emancipation is more interesting perhaps than the story of that emancipation itself. An amusing book might be made of it if some young student at Girton or Newnham would collect examples and deduce a theory—but she would need thick gloves on her hands, and bars to protect her of solid gold.

But what is amusing now, I recollected, shutting Lady Bessborough,

8. The quotation is from James Boswell's *The Life of Samuel Johnson, L.L.D.* Woolf, in her tale of Judith Shakespeare, imagines the manager bellowing "something about poodles dancing and women acting."
9. *A Survey of Contemporary Music*, Cecil Gray, p. 246 [Woolf's note].

1. Henrietta, Countess of Bessborough (1761–1821) and Lord Granville Leveson Gower, first Earl Granville (1773–1846). Their correspondence, edited by Castalia Countess Granville, was published as his *Private Correspondence, 1781 to 1821*, in 1916.

had to be taken in desperate earnest once. Opinions that one now pastes in a book labelled cock-a-doodle-dum and keeps for reading to select audiences on summer nights once drew tears, I can assure you. Among your grandmothers and great-grandmothers there were many that wept their eyes out. Florence Nightingale[2] shrieked aloud in her agony.[3] Moreover, it is all very well for you, who have got yourselves to college and enjoy sitting-rooms—or is it only bed-sitting-rooms?—of your own to say that genius should disregard such opinions; that genius should be above caring what is said of it. Unfortunately, it is precisely the men or women of genius who mind most what is said of them. Remember Keats. Remember the words he had cut on his tombstone. Think of Tennyson;[4] think—but I need hardly multiply instances of the undeniable, if very unfortunate, fact that it is the nature of the artist to mind excessively what is said about him. Literature is strewn with the wreckage of men who have minded beyond reason the opinions of others.

And this susceptibility of theirs is doubly unfortunate, I thought, returning again to my original enquiry into what state of mind is most propitious for creative work, because the mind of an artist, in order to achieve the prodigious effort of freeing whole and entire the work that is in him, must be incandescent, like Shakespeare's mind, I conjectured, looking at the book which lay open at *Antony and Cleopatra.* There must be no obstacle in it, no foreign matter unconsumed.

For though we say that we know nothing about Shakespeare's state of mind, even as we say that, we are saying something about Shakespeare's state of mind. The reason perhaps why we know so little of Shakespeare—compared with Donne or Ben Jonson or Milton—is that his grudges and spites and antipathies are hidden from us. We are not held up by some "revelation" which reminds us of the writer. All desire to protest, to preach, to proclaim an injury, to pay off a score, to make the world the witness of some hardship or grievance was fired out of him and consumed. Therefore his poetry flows from him free and unimpeded. If ever a human being got his work expressed completely, it was Shakespeare. If ever a mind was incandescent, unimpeded, I thought, turning again to the bookcase, it was Shakespeare's mind.

2. Florence Nightingale (1820–1910), English nurse and philanthropist.
3. See *Cassandra,* by Florence Nightingale, printed in *The Cause,* by R. Strachey [Woolf's note].

4. Keats's epitaph reads "Here lies one whose name was writ in water." Tennyson was notably sensitive to reviews of his poetry.

S. I. Hayakawa

SEX IS NOT A SPECTATOR SPORT

In current discussions of pornography and obscenity, there is widespread confusion about two matters. First there is sexual behavior and what it means to the participants. Secondly there is the outside observer of sexual behavior and what it means to him. When a man and a woman make love, enjoying themselves and each other unself-consciously, a rich relationship is reaffirmed and made richer by their lovemaking. However beautiful or sacred that love relationship may be to that man and woman, it would have an entirely different significance to a Peeping Tom, secretly watching the proceedings from outside the window. The sexual behavior is not itself obscene. Obscenity is peculiarly the evaluation of the outside observer. Theoretically the actors may themselves be made the observers. If, for example, unknown to the man and woman, a movie were to be made of their lovemaking, and that movie were to be shown to them later, that lovemaking might take on an entirely different significance. What was performed unself-consciously and spontaneously might be viewed later by the actors themselves with giggling or shame or shock. They might even insist that the film be destroyed—which is entirely different from saying that they would stop making love.

What I am saying is that obscenity and pornography can happen only when sexual events are seen from the outside, from a spectator's point of view. This is the crux of the pornography problem. Pornography is sexual behvior made public through symbolization—by representation in literature, by simulation or enactment in a nightclub act or on stage, by arts such as painting, photography, or the movies. To object to pornographic movies or art is not, as some would have us believe, a result of hang-ups about sex. One may be completely healthy and still object to many of the current representations of sexual acts in the movies and on the stage.

Standards of morality are one thing. Standards of decorum are another. There is nothing immoral about changing one's clothes or evacuating one's bowels. But in our culture people as a rule do not change their clothing in the presence of the other sex, excepting their spouses. Men and women have separate public lavatories, and within them each toilet is in a separate compartment for privacy. Love too needs privacy. Human beings normally make love in private, whether that love is socially sanctioned, as in marriage, or unsanctioned, as in a house of prostitution.

From *Through the Communication Barrier* (1979).

The trouble with sexual intercourse as an object of artistic or literary representation is that its meaning is not apparent in the behavior. Hence serious writers have historically been reticent in their description of sex. In Dante's *Divine Comedy* Francesca tells of her tragic love for Paolo. They were reading an ancient romance, and as they read, their passions suddenly overcame them. What happened? Dante simply has Francesca say, "That day we read no further." The rest is left to the reader's imagination—and the reader cannot help feeling the power of that onrushing, fatal passion.

5   Men and women couple with each other for a wide variety of reasons. Sometimes the sexual encounter is the fulfillment of true love and respect for each other. Sometimes one of the partners is using sex as an instrument of exploitation or aggression against the other. Sometimes sex is a commercial transaction, with either party being the prostitute. Sometimes sex is the expression of neurosis. Sometimes it is evidence of people getting over their neuroses. However, to the movie camera, as to a Peeping Tom, they are all "doing the same thing." To concentrate on the mechanics of sex is to ignore altogether its human significance.

Today movies do not stop at exhibiting copulation. Every kind of aberrant sexual behavior and sadomasochistic perversion is being shown. The advertisements in the newspaper before me announce such titles as *Nude Encounter, Too Hot to Handle, Deep Throat, The Devil in Miss Jones, The Passion Parlor, Hot Kitten,* and *Honeymoon Suite,* as well as "16 hours of hard-core male stag." The only purpose of movies such as these, from all I can tell from advertisements and reviews, is, as D. H. Lawrence expressed it, "to do dirt on sex." Let the American Civil Liberties Union fight for the right of these movies to be shown. I will not.

THE READER

1. *This is a short essay. What is the functional relation of its six paragraphs?*
2. *What is the function of Hayakawa's idea of decorum? How does he establish it?*
3. *What is the argumentative function of Hayakawa's distinction between meaning and behavior? Would behavior be obscene if it didn't have the right meaning?*

THE WRITER

1. *Is Hayakawa refuting an argument directed against the opponents of pornography, or is he asserting an argument opposing pornography? Does it matter? What is the position he takes at the end?*

2. *Rewrite Hayakawa's conclusion so that it asserts a stronger position.
Can you do this without changing his argument?*

Robertson Davies

HAM AND TONGUE

There are, I believe, something like three hundred millions of people
on this continent at this moment. I have added a few additional millions,
to include visitors from abroad who are here for the express purpose of
making speeches. I estimate very roughly that of those three hundred
millions, at least three hundred thousand are on their feet at this moment, talking to various groups drawn from the others. Speech-making
is one of the principal pursuits of the Western World, but although
everybody does it, nobody seems to talk about how it is done. We have
keen critics of the techniques of all sports and pastimes, but who criticizes the technique of the speaker? Every art—drama, music, painting—
comes under the reducing lens of the critic, except the art of making
speeches. Literature, even on the lowest levels, is the fodder for thousands of critics, and the subject of countless graduate-school theses, but
the body of a public speech is rarely examined as if it were a literary
creation. The content of a speech is frequently chewed over, but the
manner in which it is delivered, and the circumstances of its delivery go
undiscussed. One wonders why.

In part, I think, it is because there is a widespread belief that a public
speaker is a more or less inspired creature, who is making up what he
says as he goes along, and that he should not be held accountable for
his grammatical muddles, his inaccurate facts, and his uncouth delivery.
In my lifetime I have seen the growth of what might be called The
North American Myth of Sincerity, a myth which suggests that anything that is done skillfully, or with accomplishment, is of less worth
than what is botched. This Myth applies very strongly to the public
speaker; the botcher is thought to be a worthy fellow, who is searching
his soul for every word that falls maimed and bleeding from his lips. The
reality is otherwise; sincerity can be as much of a mannerism as anything
else, and I am always suspicious of speakers who appear to be struggling
for every sentence. They are frequently crooks, who have mastered their
barbarous style just as, in an earlier day, they would have mastered the
elements of rhetoric.

In my boyhood I heard many speakers of that earlier day, who prided

Adapted from a speech given on April 6, 1977, at the Cosmos Club, Washington, D.C.

themselves upon being spell-binders and silver-tongued orators. I have heard speakers of whom it was said—the remark was by no means original, but it never failed to give pleasure—that when they were infants the bees had clustered round their cradles, to sip the honey from their lips. In retrospect, I wonder if any bee ever came back for a second sip. They were very strong on manner, those spell-binders, but they were no better stocked with matter than their less gaudy contemporaries. At the time I heard them, their day was passing. The Age of Sincerity was dawning; I hope that I may live to see the sun set on the Sincere Speaker. There is only one way to make a speech, and that is to have something to say, and to say it as clearly as you can, in a fashion that does not insult or patronize your hearers. Easy to say: not in the least easy to do. Nor is the fault all with the speakers. The passion for public speaking that possesses us on this continent, the unquenchable thirst for everything from full-scale oratory to what is misleadingly called "a few words," makes public speakers of thousands who would do better to remain silent, and drives those who have some knack for speaking to speak altogether too much.

Consider the situation in which we find ourselves. I am greatly complimented to have been asked to speak to you; I am delighted to be here. But common decency compels me to recognize that you would be far better off if you were being entertained by a first-rate conjuror, or a talented clown, or perhaps even by a ventriloquist. There was a time when this fact was given due consideration. When I was a boy I used often to go with my parents to political rallies, where candidates for Parliament appealed for votes. Those men were no fools. They included in their entourage an entertainer, who put the audience in a good mood. After the entertainer had delighted us with his comic songs and his imitation of a Red Indian reciting *The Charge of the Light Brigade*, [1] we were softened up for the political address. As a boy, I had no vote; if I had been enfranchised, I should unhesitatingly have voted for the entertainer. I learned a lesson at those meetings, and it was this: if you haven't got a professional entertainer on your side, you should do your best to be entertaining in your own person.

5   I put this lesson into practice at an early age. At my school many prizes were offered, and two I regarded as my personal property; they were the prize for reading aloud, and the prize for public speaking. I sought them, not for glory, but for money. Each contest carried a prize of a finely bound book but, in addition, the right to buy twenty-five dollars' worth of books. Fifty dollars! It was the riches of Ali Baba in a day when a very good book could be bought for three dollars and fifty

1. I.e., a burlesque rendition of Alfred Lord Tennyson's lengthy war poem.

cents. The unappeasable lust for books which has been one of the glories and the nuisances of my life made it absolutely obligatory for me to get that money. How? Other boys had similar ambitions. But I had a degree of low cunning that was beyond my years, and I reduced the arts of reading and speaking to a formula drawn from the world of the sand-wich-maker. It was, very simply, Ham and Tongue.

How well I remember those school contests! My rivals, who were fine boys and have since grown up to be fine men, went in very heavily for Sincerity. They knew where the wellspring of sincerity was; it resided in their fathers. They would admit, though of course not to the judges of the contest, that they had received some help from their fathers in preparing their speeches. In consequence the physician's son was apt to harass the audience with addresses on Man's Struggle Against the Com-mon Cold, and the chartered accountant's son pontificated on Munici-pal Taxation—Whither? They shouted and waved their fists; the cords in their necks stood out with strain. But I was not a fine boy; looking back, I think I must have been a rather horrid boy, because I adopted a conversational manner, cracked a lot of jokes, and sometimes—I blush to recall—made fun of the other speakers. These were very probably the promptings of the Evil One, but the Evil One was a good friend to me, and I always got the fifty dollars.

I think that the Evil One must have whispered something to the Headmaster of the school as well, because during my time he changed the rules, and demanded that the speeches be extemporary, on subjects drawn from a list he prepared himself. The experts on the Common Cold and Municipal Taxation were flummoxed. But Ham and Tongue carried me through. My affectation of naturalness was precisely that—an affectation; my apparently conversational delivery was in fact quite a loud, carefully articulated yell; I could make myself heard over a brass band.

The Headmaster's purpose in changing the rules was to give us some experience of thinking on our feet. And so it did. It could not, however, do much for a boy who never by any chance thought in any other posture. Personally, I mistrust the notion of thinking on one's feet; I have known many speakers who prided themselves on that ability, and I am sorry to say that many of them were blatherers; they did not know when to stop. This took me some time to realize, because my father was a great admirer of these extemporary speakers; it was the fashion of his day to value length of oratory, and he exulted over political figures who could hold forth for two hours, without a note. My father particularly stressed this: "Without a note!" he would cry, fixing me with a glowing eye. So when my turn came, I naturally tried to speak without notes, but I soon found that it was not for me. Not merely notes, but a prepared script was what I liked. Of course I did not know it, but I was part of a movement toward the prepared speech, with a typescript for the assistance of reporters who cannot write shorthand.

The prepared script also has its dangers. Politicians were probably the first to discover that the script might as well be prepared by somebody else. But no—I wrong them; credit for that discovery belongs to the clergy. Politicians—slapdash fellows with a boundless faith in the gullibility of mankind—all too often gave speeches which were as new to them as to the audience, and not infrequently they came upon words that were unfamiliar to them and ideas that surprised them.

I know all about that. My own political career was a very quiet one: I was a back-room literary hack. I recall writing a series of broadcast speeches for a political aspirant whose fame had been gained as a professional hockey-player. Nothing could persuade him to look at his speech before going on the air, and although I did my level best to write in his own style and vocabulary, such as it was, every now and then he would gag over something—a subordinate clause, or a crumb of unfamiliar punctuation—and reveal himself in all his pitiable insufficiency. Once I gave him a joke, and that was a very great miscalculation, because the cast of his mind was not jocular. Having uttered the joke, and being dimly aware that something untoward had happened, he tried—if I may so express it—to suck the joke back out of the microphone. His committee were displeased with me, but as they were not paying me anything and I was writing simply out of political loyalty, I could afford to ignore their huffing and puffing.

Another experience as a political ghost-writer found me preparing speeches for a man who had been, thirty years earlier, a modest success as a baseball player. He was convinced that his small fame was still resounding in the minds of the youth of the day, and he kept urging me to get it into the speeches. "Tell them I'm a straight shooter," he would say. So I did, but without conviction, for he was so plainly not a shooter at all; he was a magazine of blanks, and he lost the election. He seemed to think that I was a contributing cause. You cannot make a Demosthenes[2] out of an old ball-player; you cannot even cloak him in the grey mantle of Phoney Sincerity. If he has no conception of Ham and Tongue, you are beaten, and so is he.

When I speak of Ham, I hope you do not think I recommend a grossly histrionic style of delivery. That used to be popular. There were speakers who wept, speakers who were immense in their indignation, speakers who were hugely sarcastic. At the very bottom of the list came the speakers who told funny stories.

A funny story is, in itself, a good thing, but we have not the appetite

2. Demosthenes (383?–322 B.C.), Athenian orator and statesman.

for them that existed in our grandfathers. Their taste now seems to us to be gross; their delight in stories involving dialect or racial characteristics is out of fashion. But there was a day when a speaker who rose to his feet and declared that the situation in which he found himself reminded him of the Scotchman, the Irishman, and the Jew who went to a funeral could hold an audience in the palm of his hand. Scotchmen, Irishmen, and Jews were all, by definition, funny, but the real gold of the story lay in the funeral. In Canada forty years ago funerals were surefire.

Let me recall one of these rib-binders. A Scotchman was attending the funeral of his wife, and when the ceremony was concluded, and everyone had left the graveyard, he was to be seen standing by the grave, looking into it with a countenance set in what might have been taken for deep grief. A friend approached him, and said gently: "Well, Jock, so Margaret's gone." "Aye," said the bereaved husband. "She was always a good wife to you," said the friend. "Aye, so she was for fifty years and more," said the widower, and then, after a moment's reflection, "but ye ken I never really likit the wumman."

I have seen that joke throw an audience into paroxysms. Scotchmen   15
and their wives nudged one another in ecstasy and slapped one another's thighs as they laughed at it. Irishmen and Jews laughed, at the same time wondering how they could adapt the story to their own races. But of course that was out of the question; there was something resolutely Scotch about it, and you could no more change it than you could hope to bleach a piece of tartan.

All of these modes of oratory depended heavily on Ham, that quality of histrionism without which a public speech is as piffle before the wind. Ham is out of favor in our age of sincerity, except for the assumption of fake modesty of which I have already spoken. When I left the world of journalism to become a university professor I quickly discovered that Ham was nowhere so deplored as in the academic world. The professor who calls upon the arts of rhetoric and oratory to make his students pay attention quickly wins a name as a charlatan. I have always been glad of my twenty years in the newspaper world, because it taught me many useful things, and one of them is that the public has no particular objection to a charlatan if he does not overstep the bounds of modesty and artistic restraint. Better the charlatan you can hear than the sincere scholar who lulls you to sleep with a sound like the moan of doves in immemorial elms. My own education was prolonged and various, and my best professors were all hams.

I recall with particular affection a Scotsman who was lecturing about the Romantic Poets; he was trying to give us some understanding of the stress of soul and intolerable pressure of imagination that made those men great, and I suppose we looked uncomprehending. He paused, and walked to the window, and looked out at the snowy landscape for perhaps a full minute, and then he said, in a sorrowful voice: "I don't suppose there is one of you mutts who has the slightest idea what I'm talking about." What happened? Did we rise in indignation? Did we rush to his office and burn his library, and demand that he apologize on his knees before we would consent to hear another word? No; we sat up straight and listened very hard and loved him forever after. About two weeks ago I sent a contribution to a fund to create a scholarship in his name. Greater love hath no student than this; that he lay out hard cash to memorialize a dead professor.

That was Ham. What about Tongue?

To me, it is almost wholly a matter of vocabulary. We have all met those excitable, exuberant people who assure us that they just love words. People who just love words too often delight in the showy siftings of the dictionary. I would rather listen to somebody who loved meanings better than words themselves, a speaker who would remain silent rather than use a word he did not truly know. People who just love words are all too often people who talk about "meaningful interface," and spend a lot of time on "marginal variables" whenever they set out upon an "in-depth overview." Doubtless these expressions have some original meaning, but as the people who just love words use them they are gaudy toys, bearing the same relationship to a perceptible meaning that a Christmas tree ornament bears to a fine jewel.

20   The true word-lover must be constantly on the alert to changes in language. When I was a young man at Oxford I took heed of the fate that befell an American friend of mine, who was reprimanded on his oral examination because he dearly loved the word "motivate" and used it often. The examiner who rebuked him was an old man who explained courteously and patiently—but oh, the courtesy and patience at Oxford can burn like a refiner's fire!—that the word had no respectable ancestry, that it could not be derived from Latin and had sneaked into the language from France and Germany; it was a low word which my friend would do well to scrub from his tongue with acid. I took warning by my friend's experience, and I shrink from "motivate" still. But much time has passed; "motivate" is now in the *Oxford English Dictionary* and I have become a fossil, in this respect at least. My recollection of this incident makes me cautious about rebuking my own pupils when they say "prestigious" when they mean "distinguished." To me "prestigious" means, and always will mean, juggling tricks, because it derives from *praestigiae,* and when it is used in the modern way I feel as though a rusty sword had been thrust into my—well, not perhaps into my heart, but into some sensitive part of my body. But I do not want to parade as a conservator of endangered species in the world of words. Let the

unlettered yahoos ravish the language; what do I care? But I refuse to join in the gang-bang.

I refuse for what I consider a good reason. I am not one of those tedious people who writes to the papers correcting other correspondents about English usage. No, my concern is that of a writer, and on occasion a formal speaker, who wants to be as careful and even pernickety about meanings as he can. Without precision of meaning we damage not simply language, but thought. The language we share is beautiful and alarmingly complex. Try as we may, we are all likely to make mistakes, and very few among us can claim to know the English language in perfection. But we can try.

A humbling lessom for me came about a few years ago when I had an Oriental student of great promise who was terribly worried about English idiom. Blithely I undertook to help him, and we set to work to go right through Fowler's *Modern English Usage,* I to explain and he to learn. It was not long before I was over my head in difficulties and my Japanese friend was in gales of laughter. I was embarrassed because of my ignorance and he was embarrassed because it was wholly against his code to laugh at a professor. What do you say when someone asks: "Why do they say 'Let's drink toast,' when they are drinking wine? What does it mean, 'By hook or by crook'?" But we managed to laugh our way through from A to Z with great benefit to us both; the difference is that he has remembered most of what we learned, whereas I have lapsed into my old bad habits. To this day I cannot be sure when I should use "that" and when I should use "which," but my secretary knows, and between us we keep up some sort of pretense.

It is the idioms that ensnare us, and never so fatally as when we have learned them by ear rather than by the eye. Some years ago I was being introduced at a dinner where I was to make a speech, and the man who had undertaken this dangerous work had the easy fluency of a politician. Having told his hearers my age—which is something about which all audiences feel an unseemly curiosity—and all the jobs I had held, he announced solemnly; "Mr. Davies is a man of many faucets." There was a little coarse laughter, but most of the audience looked at me with new respect.

Ham and Tongue are the essentials of public speaking, and ideally they should be balanced in roughly equal quantity. Shakespeare supplied a splendid object lesson in the Forum Scene in *Julius Caesar.* The first speaker is Marcus Brutus, and he is a skilled rhetorician; schoolmasters and professors delight in demonstrating how finely balanced is his address to the mob. But Brutus was wholly a patrician; he was too much a gentleman to stoop to emotional appeals. The second speaker of the day, as you recall, was Mark Antony. He was no mean rhetorician, but in addition to Tongue he had a splendid endowment of Ham, and we all know what happened. Brutus won respect, but Antony started a riot.

E. B. White

SOME REMARKS ON HUMOR

Analysts have had their go at humor, and I have read some of this interpretative literature, but without being greatly instructed. Humor can be dissected, as a frog can, but the thing dies in the process and the innards are discouraging to any but the pure scientific mind.

In a newsreel theatre the other day I saw a picture of a man who had developed the soap bubble to a higher point than it had ever before reached. He had become the ace soap bubble blower of America, had perfected the business of blowing bubbles, refined it, doubled it, squared it, and had even worked himself up into a convenient lather. The effect was not pretty. Some of the bubbles were too big to be beautiful, and the blower was always jumping into them or out of them, or playing some sort of unattractive trick with them. It was, if anything, a rather repulsive sight. Humor is a little like that: it won't stand much blowing up, and it won't stand much poking. It has a certain fragility, an evasiveness, which one had best respect. Essentially, it is a complete mystery. A human frame convulsed with laughter, and the laughter becoming hysterical and uncontrollable, is as far out of balance as one shaken with the hiccoughs or in the throes of a sneezing fit.

One of the things commonly said about humorists is that they are really very sad people—clowns with a breaking heart. There is some truth in it, but it is badly stated. It would be more accurate, I think, to say that there is a deep vein of melancholy running through everyone's life and that the humorist, perhaps more sensible of it than some others, compensates for it actively and positively. Humorists fatten on trouble. They have always made trouble pay. They struggle along with a good will and endure pain cheerfully, knowing how well it will serve them in the sweet by and by. You find them wrestling with foreign languages, fighting folding ironing boards and swollen drainpipes, suffering the terrible discomfort of tight boots (or as Josh Billings[1] wittily called

Adapted from the preface to *A Subtreasury of American Humor* (1941), edited by Katharine S. White and E. B. White.

1. Pseudonym of Henry Wheeler Shaw, nineteenth-century American humorist whose sketches often depended on an exaggerated imitation of the dialect of rural New England or New York.

them, "tite" boots). They pour out their sorrows profitably, in a form that is not quite fiction nor quite fact either. Beneath the sparkling surface of these dilemmas flows the strong tide of human woe.

Practically everyone is a manic depressive of sorts, with his up moments and his down moments, and you certainly don't have to be a humorist to taste the sadness of situation and mood. But there is often a rather fine line between laughing and crying, and if a humorous piece of writing brings a person to the point where his emotional responses are untrustworthy and seem likely to break over into the opposite realm, it is because humor, like poetry, has an extra content. It plays close to the big hot fire which is Truth, and sometimes the reader feels the heat.

THE READER

1. White uses a number of concrete details: dissected frog, soap bubbles and bubble blower, clowns with a breaking heart, fighting folding ironing boards and swollen drain pipes, suffering the terrible discomfort of tight boots, big hot fire which is Truth. Which of these are metaphors or analogies (comparisons with a different kind of thing), and which are concrete examples of general statements? Why does White use so many metaphors or analogies in his definition?

THE WRITER

1. Compare White's definition of humor with his definition of democracy (p. 934). Is there a recognizable similarity in language or style? In devices used?
2. Rewrite White's definition in abstract or general language, leaving out the analogies or metaphors and the concrete examples. Then compare the rewritten version with the original. Which is clearer? Which is more interesting to read?

Aaron Copland

HOW WE LISTEN

We all listen to music according to our separate capacities. But, for the sake of analysis, the whole listening process may become clearer if we break it up into its component parts, so to speak. In a certain sense we all listen to music on three separate planes. For lack of a better terminology, one might name these: (1) the sensuous plane, (2) the

From *What to Listen for in Music* (1957).

expressive plane, (3) the sheerly musical plane. The only advantage to be gained from mechanically splitting up the listening process into these hypothetical planes is the clearer view to be had of the way in which we listen.

The simplest way of listening to music is to listen for the sheer pleasure of the musical sound itself. That is the sensuous plane. It is the plane on which we hear music without thinking, without considering it in any way. One turns on the radio while doing something else and absentmindedly bathes in the sound. A kind of brainless but attractive state of mind is engendered by the mere sound appeal of the music.

You may be sitting in a room reading this book. Imagine one note struck on the piano. Immediately that one note is enough to change the atmosphere of the room—proving that the sound element in music is a powerful and mysterious agent, which it would be foolish to deride or belittle.

The surprising thing is that many people who consider themselves qualified music lovers abuse that plane in listening. They go to concerts in order to lose themselves. They use music as a consolation or an escape. They enter an ideal world where one doesn't have to think of the realities of everyday life. Of course they aren't thinking about the music either. Music allows them to leave it, and they go off to a place to dream, dreaming because of and apropos of the music yet never quite listening to it.

5   Yes, the sound appeal of music is a potent and primitive force, but you must not allow it to usurp a disproportionate share of your interest. The sensuous plane is an important one in music, a very important one, but it does not constitute the whole story.

There is no need to digress further on the sensuous plane. Its appeal to every normal human being is self-evident. There is, however, such a thing as becoming more sensitive to the different kinds of sound stuff as used by various composers. For all composers do not use that sound stuff in the same way. Don't get the idea that the value of music is commensurate with its sensuous appeal or that the loveliest sounding music is made by the greatest composer. If that were so, Ravel would be a greater creator than Beethoven. The point is that the sound element varies with each composer, that his usage of sound forms an integral part of his style and must be taken into account when listening. The reader can see, therefore, that a more conscious approach is valuable even on this primary plane of music listening.

The second plane on which music exists is what I have called the expressive one. Here, immediately, we tread on controversial ground. Composers have a way of shying away from any discussion of music's expressive side. Did not Stravinsky himself proclaim that his music was an "object," a "thing," with a life of its own, and with no other meaning than its own purely musical existence? This intransigent attitude of Stravinsky's may be due to the fact that so many people have tried to read different meanings into so many pieces. Heaven knows it is difficult enough to say precisely what it is that a piece of music means, to say it definitely, to say it finally so that everyone is satisfied with your explanation. But that should not lead one to the other extreme of denying to music the right to be "expressive."

My own belief is that all music has an expressive power, some more and some less, but that all music has a certain meaning behind the notes and that that meaning behind the note constitutes, after all, what the piece is saying, what the piece is about. This whole problem can be stated quite simply by asking, "Is there a meaning to music?" My answer to that would be. "Yes." And "Can you state in so many words what the meaning is?" My answer to that would be, "No." Therein lies the difficulty.

Simple-minded souls will never be satisfied with the answer to the second of these questions. They always want music to have a meaning, and the more concrete it is the better they like it. The more the music reminds them of a train, a storm, a funeral, or any other familiar conception the more expressive it appears to be to them. This popular idea of music's meaning—stimulated and abetted by the usual run of musical commentator—should be discouraged wherever and whenever it is met. One timid lady once confessed to me that she suspected something seriously lacking in her appreciation of music because of her inability to connect it with anything definite. That is getting the whole thing backward, of course.

Still, the question remains, How close should the intelligent music lover wish to come to pinning a definite meaning to any particular work? No closer than a general concept, I should say. Music expresses, at different moments, serenity or exuberance, regret or triumph, fury or delight. It expresses each of these moods, and many others, in a numberless variety of subtle shadings and differences. It may even express a state of meaning for which there exists no adequate word in any language. In that case, musicians often like to say that it has only a purely musical meaning. They sometimes go farther and say that *all* music has only a purely musical meaning. What they really mean is that no appropriate word can be found to express the music's meaning and that, even if it could, they do not feel the need of finding it.

But whatever the professional musician may hold, most musical novices still search for specific words with which to pin down their musical reactions. That is why they always find Tchaikovsky easier to "understand" than Beethoven. In the first place, it is easier to pin a meaning-word on a Tchaikovsky piece than on a Beethoven one. Much easier. Moreover, with the Russian composer, every time you come back to a piece of his it almost always says the same thing to you, whereas with Beethoven it is often quite difficult to put your finger right on what he is saying. And any musician will tell you that that is why Beethoven is the greater composer. Because music which always says the same thing to you will necessarily soon become dull music, but music whose meaning is slightly different with each hearing has a greater chance of remaining alive.

Listen, if you can, to the forty-eight fugue themes of Bach's *Well Tempered Clavichord.* Listen to each theme, one after another. You will soon realize that each theme mirrors a different world of feeling. You will also soon realize that the more beautiful a theme seems to you the harder it is to find any word that will describe it to your complete satisfaction. Yes, you will certainly know whether it is a gay theme or a sad one. You will be able, in other words, in your own mind, to draw a frame of emotional feeling around your theme. Now study the sad one a little closer. Try to pin down the exact quality of its sadness. Is it pessimistically sad or resignedly sad; is it fatefully sad or smilingly sad?

Let us suppose that you are fortunate and can describe to your own satisfaction in so many words the exact meaning of your chosen theme. There is still no guarantee that anyone else will be satisfied. Nor need they be. The important thing is that each one feel for himself the specific expressive quality of a theme or, similarly, an entire piece of music. And if it is a great work of art, don't expect it to mean exactly the same thing to you each time you return to it.

Themes or pieces need not express only one emotion, of course. Take such a theme as the first main one of the *Ninth Symphony,* for example. It is clearly made up of different elements. It does not say only one thing. Yet anyone hearing it immediately gets a feeling of strength, a feeling of power. It isn't a power that comes simply because the theme is played loudly. It is a power inherent in the theme itself. The extraordinary strength and vigor of the theme results in the listener's receiving an impression that a forceful statement has been made. But one should never try to boil it down to "the fateful hammer of life," etc. That is where the trouble begins. The musician, in his exasperation, says it means nothing but the notes themselves, whereas the nonprofessional is only too anxious to hang on to any explanation that gives him the illusion of getting closer to the music's meaning.

Now, perhaps, the reader will know better what I mean when I say that music does have an expressive meaning but that we cannot say in so many words what that meaning is.

The third plane on which music exists is the sheerly musical plane. Besides the pleasurable sound of music and the expressive feeling that it gives off, music does exist in terms of the notes themselves and of their manipulation. Most listeners are not sufficiently conscious of this third plane. . . .

Professional musicians, on the other hand, are, if anything, too conscious of the mere notes themselves. They often fall into the error of becoming so engrossed with their arpeggios and staccatos that they forget the deeper aspects of the music they are performing. But from the layman's standpoint, it is not so much a matter of getting over bad habits on the sheerly musical plane as of increasing one's awareness of what is going on, in so far as the notes are concerned.

When the man in the street listens to the "notes themselves" with any degree of concentration, he is most likely to make some mention of the melody. Either he hears a pretty melody or he does not, and he generally lets it go at that. Rhythm is likely to gain his attention next, particularly if it seems exciting. But harmony and tone color are generally taken for granted, if they are thought of consciously at all. As for music's having a definite form of some kind, that idea seems never to have occurred to him.

It is very important for all of us to become more alive to music on its sheerly musical plane. After all, an actual musical material is being used. The intelligent listener must be prepared to increase his awareness of the musical material and what happens to it. He must hear the melodies, the rhythms, the harmonies, the tone colors in a more conscious fashion. But above all he must, in order to follow the line of the composer's thought, know something of the principles of musical form. Listening to all of these elements is listening on the sheerly musical plane.

Let me repeat that I have split up mechanically the three separate planes on which we listen merely for the sake of greater clarity. Actually, we never listen on one or the other of these planes. What we do is to correlate them—listening in all three ways at the same time. It takes no mental effort, for we do it instinctively. 20

Perhaps an analogy with what happens to us when we visit the theater will make this instinctive correlation clearer. In the theater, you are aware of the actors and actresses, costumes and sets, sounds and movements. All these give one the sense that the theater is a pleasant place to be in. They constitute the sensuous plane in our theatrical reactions.

The expressive plane in the theater would be derived from the feeling that you get from what is happening on the stage. You are moved to pity, excitement, or gayety. It is this general feeling, generated aside from the particular words being spoken, a certain emotional something which exists on the stage, that is analogous to the expressive quality in music.

The plot and plot development is equivalent to our sheerly musical plane. The playwright creates and develops a character in just the same way that a composer creates and develops a theme. According to the degree of your awareness of the way in which the artist in either field handles his material will you become a more intelligent listener.

It is easy enough to see that the theatergoer never is conscious of any of these elements separately. He is aware of them all at the same time. The same is true of music listening. We simultaneously and without thinking listen on all three planes.

25   In a sense, the ideal listener is both inside and outside the music at the same moment, judging it and enjoying it, wishing it would go one way and watching it go another—almost like the composer at the moment he composes it; because in order to write his music, the composer must also be inside and outside his music, carried away by it and yet coldly critical of it. A subjective and objective attitude is implied in both creating and listening to music.

What the reader should strive for, then, is a more *active* kind of listening. Whether you listen to Mozart or Duke Ellington, you can deepen your understanding of music only by being a more conscious and aware listener—not someone who is just listening, but someone who is listening *for* something.

Joyce Carol Oates

ON BOXING

They are young welterweight boxers so evenly matched they might be twins—though one has a redhead's pallor and the other is a dusky-skinned Hispanic. Circling each other in the ring, they try jabs, tentative left hooks, right crosses that dissolve in midair or turn into harmless slaps. The Madison Square Garden crowd is derisive, impatient. "Those two! What'd they do, wake up this morning and decide they were boxers?" a man behind me says contemptuously. (He's dark, nattily dressed, with a neatly trimmed mustache and tinted glasses. A sophisticated fight fan. Two hours later he will be crying, "Tommy! Tommy! Tommy!" over and over in a paroxysm of grief as, on the giant closed-circuit television screen, middleweight champion Marvelous Marvin Hagler batters his challenger, Thomas Hearns, into insensibility.)

The young boxers must be conscious of the jeers and boos in this great cavernous space reaching up into the $20 seats in the balconies amid the constant milling of people in the aisles, the smells of hotdogs, beer,

From the *New York Times Magazine* (June 16, 1985).

cigarette and cigar smoke, hair oil. But they are locked desperately together, circling, jabbing, slapping, clinching, now a flurry of light blows, clumsy footwork, another sweaty stumbling despairing clinch into the ropes that provokes a fresh wave of derision. Why are they here in the Garden of all places, each fighting what looks like his first professional fight? What are they doing? Neither is angry at the other. When the bell sounds at the end of the sixth and final round, the crowd boos a little louder. The Hispanic boy, silky yellow shorts, damp, frizzy, floating hair, strides about his corner of the ring with his gloved hand aloft—not in defiance of the boos, which increase in response to his gesture, or even in acknowledgment of them. It's just something he has seen older boxers do. He seems to be saying "I'm here, I made it, I did it." When the decision is announced as a draw, the crowd's derision increases in volume. "Get out of the ring!" "Go home!" Contemptuous male laughter follows the boys in their robes, towels about their heads, sweating, breathless. Why had they thought they were boxers?

How can you enjoy so brutal a sport, people ask. Or don't ask.

And it's too complicated to answer. In any case, I don't "enjoy" boxing, and never have; it isn't invariably "brutal"; I don't think of it as a sport.

Nor do I think of it in writerly terms as a metaphor for something else. (For *what* else?) No one whose interest in boxing began in childhood—as mine did as an offshoot of my father's interest—is likely to suppose it is a symbol of something beyond itself, though I can entertain the proposition that life is a metaphor for boxing—for one of those bouts that go on and on, round following round, small victories, small defeats, nothing determined, again the bell and again the bell and you and your opponent so evenly matched it's clear your opponent *is* you and why are the two of you jabbing and punching at each other on an elevated platform enclosed by ropes as in a pen beneath hot crude all-exposing lights in the presence of an indifferent crowd: that sort of writerly metaphor. But if you have seen five hundred boxing matches, you have seen five hundred boxing matches, and their common denominator, which surely exists, is not of primary interest to you. "If the Host[1] is only a symbol," the Catholic writer Flannery O'Connor said, "I'd say the hell with it." 5

Each boxing match is a story, a highly condensed, highly dramatic story—even when nothing much happens: then failure is the story. There are two principal characters in the story, overseen by a shadowy third. When the bell rings no one knows what will happen. Much is

1. The bread or wafer of the Communion service or Eucharist.

speculated, nothing known. The boxers bring to the fight everything
that is themselves, and everything will be exposed: including secrets
about themselves they never knew. There are boxers possessed of such
remarkable intuition, such prescience, one would think they had fought
this particular fight before. There are boxers who perform brilliantly, but
mechanically, who cannot improvise in midfight; there are boxers performing at the height of their skill who cannot quite comprehend that
it won't be enough; to my knowledge there was only one boxer who
possessed an extraordinary and disquieting awareness, not only of his
opponent's every move or anticipated move, but of the audience's keen-
est shifts in mood as well—Muhammad Ali, of course.

In the ring, death is always a possibility, which is why I prefer to see
films or tapes of fights already past—already crystallized into art. In fact,
death is a statistically rare possibility of which no one likes to think—like
your possible death tomorrow morning in an automobile crash, or in next
month's airplane crash, or in a freak accident involving a fall on the
stairs—a skull fracture, subarachnoid hemorrhage.[2]

A boxing match is a play without words, which doesn't mean that it
has no text or no language, only that the text is improvised in action,
the language a dialogue between the boxers in a joint response to the
mysterious will of the crowd, which is always that the fight be a worthy
one so that the crude paraphernalia of the setting—the ring, the lights,
the onlookers themselves—be obliterated. To go from an ordinary preliminary match to a "Fight of the Century"—like those between Joe
Louis and Billy Conn, Muhammad Ali and Joe Frazier, most recently
Marvin Hagler and Thomas Hearns—is to go from listening or half-
listening to a guitar being idly plucked to hearing Bach's "Well-Tempered Clavier"[3] being perfectly played, and that too is part of the story.
So much is happening so swiftly and so subtly you cannot absorb it
except to know that something memorable is happening and it is happening in a place beyond words.

The fighters in the ring are time-bound—is anything so excruciatingly
long as a fiercely contested three-minute round?—but the fight itself is
timeless. By way of films and tapes, it has become history, art. If boxing
is a sport, it is the most tragic of all sports because, more than any human
activity, it consumes the very excellence it displays: Its very drama is this
consumption. To expend oneself in fighting the greatest fight of one's
life is to begin immediately the downward turn that next time may be
a plunge, a sudden incomprehensible fall. *I am the greatest,* Muhammad
Ali says. *I am the greatest,* Marvin Hagler says. You always think you're

---

2. Under the membrane enveloping the
brain.
3. Johann Sebastian Bach (1685–1750),
composer and most renowned member of a
large family of North German musicians.
The Well-Tempered Clavier (Book I, 1722;
Book II, 1744) contains a set of preludes
and fugues for the harpsichord.

going to win, Jack Dempsey wryly observed in his old age, otherwise you can't fight at all. The punishment—to the body, the brain, the spirit—a man must endure to become a great boxer is inconceivable to most of us whose idea of personal risk is largely ego related or emotional. But the punishment, as it begins to show in even a young and vigorous boxer, is closely assessed by his rivals. After junior-welterweight champion Aaron Pryor won a lackluster fight on points a few months ago, a younger boxer in his weight division, interviewed at ringside, said: "My mouth is watering."

So the experience of seeing great fighters of the past—and great sporting events are always *past*—is radically different from having seen them when they were reigning champions. Jack Johnson, Jack Dempsey, Joe Louis, Sugar Ray Robinson, Willie Pep, Rocky Marciano, Muhammad Ali—as spectators we know not only how a fight ends but how a career ends. Boxing is always particulars, second by incalculable second, but in the abstract it suggests these haunting lines by Yeats:

> Everything that man esteems
> Endures a moment or a day.
> Love's pleasure drives his love away,
> The painter's brush consumes his dreams;
> The herald's cry, the soldier's tread
> Exhaust his glory and his might:
> Whatever flames upon the night
> Man's own resinous heart has fed.

—from "The Resurrection"

The referee, the third character in the story, usually appears to be a mere observer, even an intruder, a near-ghostly presence as fluid in motion and quick-footed as the boxers themselves (he is frequently a former boxer). But so central to the drama of boxing is the referee that the spectacle of two men fighting each other unsupervised in an elevated ring would appear hellish, obscene—life rather than art. The referee is our intermediary in the fight. He is our moral conscience, extracted from us as spectators so that, for the duration of the fight, "conscience" is not a factor in our experience; nor is it a factor in the boxers' behavior.

Though the referee's role is a highly demanding one, and it has been estimated that there are perhaps no more than a dozen really skilled referees in the world, it seems to be necessary in the intense dramatic action of the fight that the referee have no dramatic identity. Referees' names are quickly forgotten, even as they are announced over the microphone preceding a fight. Yet, paradoxically, the referee's position is one of crucial significance. The referee cannot control what happens in the ring, but he can frequently control, to a degree, *that* it happens: he is responsible for the fight, if not for the individual fighter's performance.

It is the referee solely who holds the power of life and death at certain times; whose decision to terminate a fight, or to allow it to continue, determines a man's fate. (One should recall that a well-aimed punch with a boxer's full weight behind it can have an astonishing impact—a blow that must be absorbed by the brain in its jelly sac.)

In a recent heavyweight fight in Buffalo, 220-pound Tim Witherspoon repeatedly struck his 260-pound opponent, James Broad, caught in the ropes, while the referee looked on without acting—though a number of spectators called for the fight to be stopped. In the infamous Benny Paret–Emile Griffith fight of March 24, 1962, the referee Ruby Goldstein was said to have stood paralyzed as Paret, trapped in the ropes, suffered as many as 18 powerful blows to the head before he fell. (He died ten days later.) Boxers are trained not to quit; if they are knocked down they will try to get up to continue the fight, even if they can hardly defend themselves. The primary rule of the ring—to defend oneself at all times—is both a parody and a distillation of life.

Boxing is a purely masculine world. (Though there are female boxers—the most famous is the black champion Lady Tyger Trimiar with her shaved head and tiger-striped attire—women's role in the sport is extremely marginal.) The vocabulary of boxing is attuned to a quintessentially masculine sensibility in which the role of patriarch/protector can only be assured if there is physical strength underlying it. First comes this strength—"primitive," perhaps; then comes civilization. It should be kept in mind that "boxing" and "fighting," though always combined in the greatest of boxers, can be entirely different and even unrelated activities. If boxing can be, in the lighter weights especially, a highly complex and refined skill belonging solely to civilization, fighting seems to belong to something predating civilization, the instinct not merely to defend oneself—for when has the masculine ego ever been assuaged by so minimal a gesture?—but to attack another and to force him into absolute submission. Hence the electrifying effect upon a typical fight crowd when fighting emerges suddenly out of boxing—the excitement when a boxer's face begins to bleed. The flash of red is the visible sign of the fight's authenticity in the eyes of many spectators, and boxers are right to be proud—if they are—of their facial scars.

To the untrained eye, boxers in the ring usually appear to be angry. But, of course, this is "work" to them; emotion has no part in it, or should not. Yet in an important sense—in a symbolic sense—the boxers *are* angry, and boxing is fundamentally about anger. It is the only sport in which anger is accommodated, ennobled. Why are boxers angry? Because, for the most part, they belong to the disenfranchised of our society, to impoverished ghetto neighborhoods in which anger is an appropriate response. ("It's hard being black. You ever been black? I was black once—when I was poor," Larry Holmes has said.) Today, when most boxers—most good boxers—are black or Hispanic, white men begin to look anemic in the ring. Yet after decades of remarkable black boxers—from Jack Johnson to Joe Louis to Muhammad Ali—heavyweight champion Larry Holmes was the object of racist slurs and insults when he defended his title against the over-promoted white challenger Gerry Cooney a few years ago.

Liberals who have no personal or class reason to feel anger tend to disparage, if not condemn, such anger in others. Liberalism is also unfairly harsh in its criticism of all that predates civilization—or "liberalism" itself—without comprehending that civilization is a concept, an idea, perhaps at times hardly more than a fiction, attendant upon, and always subordinate to, physical strength: missiles, nuclear warheads. The terrible and tragic silence dramatized in the boxing ring is the silence of nature before language, when the physical *was* language, a means of communication swift and unmistakable. 15

The phrase "killer instinct" is said to have been coined in reference to Jack Dempsey in his famous early fights against Jess Willard, Georges Carpentier, Luis Firpo ("The Wild Bull of the Pampas"), and any number of other boxers, less renowned, whom he savagely beat. The ninth of eleven children born to an impoverished Mormon sharecropper and itinerant railroad worker, Dempsey seems to have been, as a young boxer in his prime, the very embodiment of angry hunger; and if he remains the most spectacular heavyweight champion in history, it is partly because he fought when rules governing boxing were somewhat casual by present-day standards. Where aggression must be learned, even cultivated, in some champion boxers (Tunney, Louis, Marciano, Patterson, for example), Dempsey's aggression was direct and natural: Once in the ring he seems to have wanted to kill his opponent.

Dempsey's first title fight in 1919, against the aging champion Jess Willard, was called "pugilistic murder" by some sportswriters and is said to have been one of boxing's all-time blood baths. Today, this famous fight—which brought the nearly unknown twenty-four-year-old Dempsey to national prominence—would certainly have been stopped in the first minute of the first round. Badly out of condition, heavier than Dempsey by almost sixty pounds, the thirty-seven-year-old Willard had virtually no defense against the challenger. By the end of the fight, Willard's jaw was broken, his cheekbone split, nose smashed, six teeth broken off at the gum, an eye was battered shut, much further damage was done to his body. Both boxers were covered in Willard's blood. Years later Dempsey's estranged manager Kearns confessed—perhaps falsely—that he had "loaded" Dempsey's gloves—treated his hand tape with a talcum substance that turned concrete-hard when wet.

For the most part, boxing matches today are scrupulously monitored

by referees and ring physicians. The devastating knockout blow is frequently the one never thrown. In a recent televised junior-middleweight
bout between Don Curry and James Green, the referee stopped the fight
because Green seemed momentarily disabled: His logic was that Green
had dropped his gloves and was therefore in a position to be hurt. (Green
and his furious trainer protested the decision but the referee's word is
final: No fight, stopped, can be resumed.) The drama of the ring begins
to shift subtly as more and more frequently one sees a referee intervene
to embrace a weakened or defenseless man in a gesture of paternal
solicitude that in itself carries much theatrical power—a gesture not so
dramatic as the killing blow but one that suggests that the ethics of the
ring are moving toward those that prevail beyond it. As if fighter-
brothers whose mysterious animosity has somehow brought them to
battle are saved by their father. . . .

In the final moment of the Hagler-Hearns fight, the dazed Hearns—
on his feet but clearly not fully conscious, gamely prepared to take
Hagler's next assault—was saved by the referee from what might well
have been serious injury, if not death, considering the ferocity of Hagler's fighting and the personal anger he seems to have brought to it that
night. This eight-minute fight, generally believed to be one of the great
fights in boxing history, ends with Hearns in the referee's protective
embrace—an image that is haunting, in itself profoundly mysterious, as
if an indefinable human drama had been spontaneously created for us,
brilliantly improvised, performed one time and one time only, yet permanently ingrained upon our consciousness.

20   Years ago in the early 1950s, when my father first took me to a Golden
Gloves boxing tournament in Buffalo, I asked him why the boys wanted
to fight one another, why they were willing to get hurt. My father said,
"Boxers don't feel pain quite the way we do."

Gene Tunney's single defeat in an eleven-year career was to a flamboyant and dangerous fighter named Harry Greb ("The Human Wind-
mill"), who seems to have been, judging from boxing literature, the
dirtiest fighter in history. Low blows, butting, fouls, holding and hitting,
using his laces on an opponent's eyes—Greb was famous for his lack of
interest in the rules. He was world middleweight champion for three
years but a presence in the boxing world for a long time. After the first
of his several fights with Greb, the twenty-four-year-old Tunney had to
spend a week in bed, he was so badly hurt; he'd lost two quarts of blood
during the fifteen-round fight. But as Tunney said years afterward:
"Greb gave me a terrible whipping. He broke my nose, maybe with a
butt. He cut my eyes and ears, perhaps with his laces. . . . My jaw was
swollen from the right temple down the cheek, along under the chin and

part way up the other side. The referee, the ring itself, was full of blood. . . . But it was in that first fight, in which I lost my American light-heavyweight title, that I knew I had found a way to beat Harry eventually. I was fortunate, really. If boxing in those days had been afflicted with the commission doctors we have today—who are always poking their noses into the ring and examining superficial wounds—the first fight with Greb would have been stopped before I learned how to beat him. It's possible, even probable, that if this had happened I would never have been heard of again."

Tommy Loughran, the light-heavyweight champion from 1927 to 1929, was a master boxer greatly admired by other boxers. He approached boxing literally as a science—as Tunney did—studying his opponents' styles and mapping out ring strategy for each fight. He rigged up mirrors in his basement so that he could see himself as he worked out—for, as Loughran realized, no boxer ever sees himself quite as he appears to his opponent. But the secret of Loughran's career was that he had a right hand that broke so easily he could use it only once in each fight: It had to be the knockout punch or nothing. "I'd get one shot, then the agony of the thing would hurt me if the guy got up. Anybody I ever hit with a left hook, I knocked flat on his face, but I would never take a chance for fear if my left hand goes, I'm done for."

Both Tunney and Loughran, it is instructive to note, retired from boxing before they were forced to retire. Tunney was a highly successful businessman and Loughran a successful sugar broker on the Wall Street commodities market—just to suggest that boxers are not invariably illiterate, stupid, or punch-drunk.

One of the perhaps not entirely acknowledged reasons for the attraction of serious writers to boxing (from Swift, Pope, Johnson to Hazlitt, Lord Byron, Hemingway, and our own Norman Mailer, George Plimpton, Wilfrid Sheed, Daniel Halpern et al.) is the sport's systematic cultivation of pain in the interests of a project, a life-goal: the willed transposing of the sensation called "pain" (whether physical or psychological) into its opposite. If this is masochism—and I doubt that it is, or that it is simply—it is also intelligence, cunning, strategy. It is the active welcoming of that which most living beings try to avoid and to flee. It is the active subsuming of the present moment in terms of the future. Pain now but control (and therefore pleasure) later.

Still, it is the rigorous training period leading up to the public appearance that demands the most discipline. In this, too, the writer senses some kinship, however oblique and one-sided, with the professional boxer. The brief public spectacle of the boxing match (which could last as little as sixty seconds), like the publication of the writer's book, is but the final, visible stage in a long, arduous, fanatic, and sometimes quixotic, subordination of the self. It was Rocky Marciano who seems to have trained with the most monastic devotion, secluding himself from his wife and family for as long as three months before a fight. Quite apart from the grueling physical training of this period and the constant preoccupation with diet and weight, Marciano concentrated on only the upcoming fight, the opening bell, his opponent. Every minute of the boxer's life was planned for one purpose. In the training camp the name of the opponent was never mentioned and Marciano's associates were careful about conversation in his presence: They talked very little about boxing.

In the final month, Marciano would not write a letter. The last ten days before a fight he saw no mail, took no telephone calls, met no new acquaintances. The week before the fight he would not shake hands with anyone. Or go for a ride in a car. No new foods! No envisioning the morning after the fight! All that was not *the fight* was taboo: when Marciano worked out punching the bag he saw his opponent before him, when he jogged early in the morning he saw his opponent close beside him. What could be a more powerful image of discipline—madness?— than this absolute subordination of the self, this celibacy of the fighter-in-training? Instead of focusing his energies and fantasies upon Woman, the boxer focuses them upon the Opponent.

No sport is more physical, more direct, than boxing. No sport appears more powerfully homoerotic: the confrontation in the ring—the disrobing—the sweaty, heated combat that is part dance, courtship, coupling—the frequent urgent pursuit by one boxer of the other in the fight's natural and violent movement toward the "knockout." Surely boxing derives much of its appeal from this mimicry of a species of erotic love in which one man overcomes the other in an exhibition of superior strength.

Most fights, however fought, lead to an embrace between the boxers after the final bell—a gesture of mutual respect and apparent affection that appears to the onlooker to be more than perfunctory. Rocky Graziano, often derided for being a slugger rather than a "classic" boxer, sometimes kissed his opponents out of gratitude for the fight. Does the boxing match, one almost wonders, lead irresistibly to this moment: the public embrace of two men who otherwise, in public or in private, could not approach each other with such passion. Are men privileged to embrace with love only after having fought? A woman is struck by the tenderness men will express for boxers who have been hurt, even if it is only by way of commentary on photographs: the startling picture of Ray (Boom Boom) Mancini after his second losing fight with Livingstone Bramble, for instance, when Mancini's face was hideously battered (photographs in *Sports Illustrated* and elsewhere were gory, near-pornographic); the much-reprinted photograph of the defeated Thomas

Hearns being carried to his corner in the arms of an enormous black man in formal attire—the "Hit Man" from Detroit now helpless, only semi-conscious, looking precisely like a black Christ taken from the cross. These are powerful, haunting, unsettling images, cruelly beautiful, very much bound up with the primitive appeal of the sport.

Yet to suggest that men might love one another directly without the violent ritual of combat is to misread man's greatest passion—for war, not peace. Love, if there is to be love, comes second.

Boxing is, after all, about lying. It is about cultivating a double person- 30
ality. As José Torres, the ex-light-heavyweight champion who is now the New York State Boxing Commissioner, says: "We fighters understand lies. What's a feint? What's a left hook off the jab? What's an opening? What's thinking one thing and doing another . . . ?"

There is nothing fundamentally playful about boxing, nothing that seems to belong to daylight, to pleasure. At its moments of greatest intensity it seems to contain so complete and so powerful an image of life—life's beauty, vulnerability, despair, incalculable and often reckless courage—that boxing *is* life, and hardly a mere game. During a superior boxing match we are deeply moved by the body's communion with itself by way of another's flesh. The body's dialogue with its shadow-self—or Death. Baseball, football, basketball—these quintessentially American pastimes are recognizably sports because they involve play: They are games. One *plays* football; one doesn't *play* boxing.

Observing team sports, teams of adult men, one sees how men are children in the most felicitous sense of the word. But boxing in its elemental ferocity cannot be assimilated into childhood—though very young men box, even professionally, and numerous world champions began boxing when they were hardly more than children. Spectators at public games derive much of their pleasure from reliving the communal emotions of childhood, but spectators at boxing matches relive the murderous infancy of the race. Hence the notorious cruelty of boxing crowds and the excitement when a man begins to bleed. ("When I see blood," says Marvin Hagler, "I become a bull." He means his own.)

The boxing ring comes to seem an altar of sorts, one of those legend-ary magical spaces where the laws of a nation are suspended: Inside the ropes, during an officially regulated three-minute round, a man may be killed at his opponent's hands but he cannot be legally murdered. Boxing inhabits a sacred space predating civilization; or, to use D. H. Law-rence's phrase, before God was love. If it suggests a savage ceremony or a rite of atonement, it also suggests the futility of such rites. For what atonement is the fight waged, if it must shortly be waged again . . . ?

All this is to speak of the paradox of boxing—its obsessive appeal for many who find in it not only a spectacle involving sensational feats of physical skill but an emotional experience impossible to convey in words; an art form, as I have suggested, with no natural analogue in the arts. And of course this accounts, too, for the extreme revulsion it arouses in many people. ("Brutal," "disgusting," "barbaric," "inhuman," "a terrible, terrible sport"—typical comments on the subject.)

In December 1984, the American Medical Association passed a resolution calling for the abolition of boxing on the principle that it is the only sport in which the *objective* is to cause injury. This is not surprising. Humanitarians have always wanted to reform boxing—or abolish it altogether. The 1896 heavyweight title match between Ruby Robert Fitzsimmons and Peter Maher was outlawed in many parts of the United States, so canny promoters staged it across the Mexican border four hundred miles from El Paso. (Some three hundred people made the arduous journey to see what must have been one of the most disappointing bouts in boxing history—Fitzsimmons knocked out his opponent in a mere ninety-five seconds.)

During the prime of Jack Dempsey's career in the 1920s, boxing was illegal in many states, like alcohol, and like alcohol, seems to have aroused a hysterical public enthusiasm. Photographs of jammed outdoor arenas taken in the 1920s with boxing rings like postage-sized altars at their centers, the boxers themselves scarcely visible, testify to the extraordinary emotional appeal boxing had at that time, even as reform movements were lobbying against it. When Jack Johnson won the heavyweight title in 1908 (he had to pursue the white champion Tommy Burns all the way to Australia to confront him), the special "danger" of boxing was also that it might expose and humiliate white men in the ring. After Johnson's victory over the "White Hope" contender Jim Jeffries, there were race riots and lynchings throughout the United States; even films of some of Johnson's fights were outlawed in many states. And because boxing has become a sport in which black and Hispanic men have lately excelled, it is particularly vulnerable to attack by white middle-class reformers, who seem uninterested in lobbying against equally dangerous but "establishment" sports like football, auto racing, and thoroughbred horse racing.

There is something peculiarly American in the fact that, while boxing is our most controversial sport, it is also the sport that pays its top athletes the most money. In spite of the controversy, boxing has never been healthier financially. The three highest paid athletes in the world in both 1983 and 1984 were boxers; a boxer with a long career like heavyweight champion Larry Holmes—forty-eight fights in thirteen years as a professional—can expect to earn somewhere beyond $50 million. (Holmes said that after retirement what he would miss most about boxing is his million-dollar checks.) Dempsey, who said that a man fights for one thing only—money—made somewhere beyond $3,500,000 in the ring in his long and varied career. Now $1.5 million is a fairly common figure for a single fight. Thomas Hearns made at least $7 million in his fight with Hagler while Hagler made at least $7.5 million. For the first of his highly publicized matches with Roberto Duran in 1980—which he lost on a decision—the popular black welterweight champion Sugar Ray Leonard received a staggering $10 million to Duran's $1.3 million. And none of these figures takes into account various subsidiary earnings (from television commercials, for instance) which in Leonard's case are probably as high as his income was from boxing.

Money has drawn any number of retired boxers back into the ring, very often with tragic results. The most notorious example is perhaps Joe Louis, who, owing huge sums in back taxes, continued boxing well beyond the point at which he could perform capably. After a career of seventeen years he was stopped by Rocky Marciano—who was said to have felt as upset by his victory as Louis by the defeat. (Louis then went on to a degrading second career as a professional wrestler. This, too, ended abruptly when 300-pound Rocky Lee stepped on the forty-two-year-old Louis's chest and damaged his heart.) Ezzard Charles, Jersey Joe Walcott, Joe Frazier, Muhammad Ali—each continued fighting when he was no longer in condition to defend himself against young heavyweight boxers on the way up. Of all heavyweight champions, only Rocky Marciano, to whom fame and money were not of paramount significance, was prudent enough to retire before he was defeated. In any case, the prodigious sums of money a few boxers earn do not account for the sums the public is willing to pay them.

Though boxing has long been popular in many countries and under many forms of government, its popularity in the United States since the days of John I. Sullivan has a good deal to do with what is felt as the spirit of the individual—his "physical" spirit—in conflict with the constrictions of the state. The rise of boxing in the 1920s in particular might well be seen as a consequence of the diminution of the individual vis-à-vis society; the gradual attrition of personal freedom, will, and strength—whether "masculine" or otherwise. In the Eastern bloc of nations, totalitarianism is a function of the state; in the Western bloc it has come to seem a function of technology, or history—"fate." The individual exists in his physical supremacy, but does the individual matter?

In the magical space of the boxing ring so disquieting a question has no claim. There, as in no other public arena, the individual as a unique physical being asserts himself; there, for a dramatic if fleeting period of time, the great world with its moral and political complexities, its terrifying impersonality, simply ceases to exist. Men fighting one another with only their fists and their cunning are all contemporaries, all brothers,

40

belonging to no historical time. "He can run, but he can't hide"—so said Joe Louis before his famous fight with young Billy Conn in 1941. In the brightly lighted ring, man is *in extremis,* performing an atavistic rite or agon for the mysterious solace of those who can participate only vicariously in such drama: the drama of life in the flesh. Boxing has become America's tragic theater.

Prose Forms: Parables

When we read a short story or a novel, we are less interested in the working out of ideas than in the working out of characters and their destinies. In Dickens' Great Expectations, for example, Pip, the hero, undergoes many triumphs and defeats in his pursuit of success, only to learn finally that he has expected the wrong things, or the right things for the wrong reasons; that the great values in life are not always to be found in what the world calls success. In realizing this meaning we entertain, with Dickens, certain concepts or ideas that organize and evaluate the life in the novel, and that ultimately we apply to life generally. Ideas are there not to be exploited discursively, but to be understood as the perspective which shapes the direction of the novel and our view of its relation to life.

When ideas in their own reality are no longer the primary interest in writing, we have obviously moved from expository to other forms of prose. The shift need not be abrupt and complete, however; there is an area where the discursive interest in ideas and the narrative interest in characters and events blend. In allegory, for example, abstract ideas are personified. "Good Will" or "Peace" may be shown as a young woman, strong, confident, and benevolent in her bearing but vulnerable, through her sweet reasonableness, to the single-minded, fierce woman who is "Dissension." Our immediate interest is in their behavior as characters, but our ultimate interest is in the working out, through them, of the ideas they represent. We do not ask that the characters and events be entirely plausible in relation to actual life, as we do for the novel; we are satisfied if they are consistent with the nature of the ideas that define their vitality.

Ideas themselves have vitality, a mobile and dynamic life with a behavior of its own. The title of the familiar Negro spiritual "Sometimes I Feel Like a Motherless Child," to choose a random instance, has several kinds of "motion" as an idea. The qualitative identity of an adult's feelings and those of a child; the whole burgeoning possibility of all that the phrase "motherless child" can mean; the subtle differences in meaning—the power of context—that occur when it is a black who feels this and when it is a white; the speculative possibilities of the title as social commentary or psychological analysis—these suggest something of the "life" going on in and around the idea.

Definition, analogy, assumption, implication, context, illustration *are some of the familiar terms we use to describe this kind of life.*

There is, of course, another and more obvious kind of vitality that an idea has: its applicability to the affairs of people in everyday life. Both the kind and extent of an idea's relevance are measures of this vitality. When an essayist wishes to exploit both the life in an idea and the life it comprehends, he or she often turns to narration, because there one sees the advantage of lifelike characters and events, and of showing through them the liveliness of ideas in both the senses we have noted. Ideas about life can be illustrated in life. And, besides, people like stories. The writer's care must be to keep the reader's interest focused on the ideas, rather than on the life itself; otherwise, he or she has ceased being essentially the essayist and has become the short-story writer or novelist.

The parable and the moral fable are ideal forms for this purpose. In both, the idea is the heart of the composition; in both the ideas usually assume the form of a lesson about life, some moral truth of general consequence; and in both there are characters and actions. Jesus often depended on parables in his teaching. Simple, economical, pointed, the parables developed a "story," but more importantly, applied a moral truth to experience. Peter asked Jesus how often he must forgive the brother who sins against him, and Jesus answered with the parable of the king and his servants, one of whom asked and got forgiveness of the king for his debts but who would not in turn forgive a fellow servant his debt. The king, on hearing of this harshness, retracted his own benevolence and punished the unfeeling servant. Jesus concluded to Peter, "So likewise shall my heavenly Father do also unto you, if ye from your hearts forgive not every one his brother their trespasses." But before this direct drawing of the parallel, the lesson was clear in the outline of the narrative.

Parables usually have human characters; fables often achieve a special liveliness with animals or insects. Swift, in "The Spider and the Bee," narrates the confrontation of a comically humanized spider and bee who debate the merits of their natures and their usefulness in the world of experience. The exchange between the two creatures is brilliantly and characteristically set out, but by its end, the reader realizes that extraordinary implications about the nature of art, of education, of human psychological and intellectual potential have been the governing idea all along.

The writer will be verging continually on strict prose narrative in writing the parable or fable, but through skill and tact he or she can preserve the essayist's essential commitment to the definition and development of ideas in relation to experience.

Aesop: THE FROGS DESIRING A KING

The frogs always had lived a happy life in the marshes. They had jumped and splashed about with never a care in the world. Yet some of them were not satisfied with their easygoing life. They thought they should have a king to rule over them and to watch over their morals. So they decided to send a petition to Jupiter[1] asking him to appoint a king.

Jupiter was amused by the frogs' plea. Good-naturedly he threw down a log into the lake, which landed with such a splash that it sent all the frogs scampering for safety. But after a while, when one venturesome frog saw that the log lay still, he encouraged his friends to approach the fallen monster. In no time at all the frogs, growing bolder and bolder, swarmed over the log Jupiter had sent and treated it with the greatest contempt.

Dissatisfied with so tame a ruler, they petitioned Jupiter a second time, saying: "We want a real king, a king who will really rule over us." Jupiter, by this time, had lost some of his good nature and was tired of the frogs' complaining.

So he sent them a stork, who proceeded to gobble up the frogs right and left. After a few days the survivors sent Mercury[2] with a private message to Jupiter, beseeching him to take pity on them once more.

"Tell them," said Jupiter coldly, "that this is their own doing. They wanted a king. Now they will have to make the best of what they asked for."

Moral: Let well enough alone!

3rd century A.D.

1. The king of the gods.   2. The messenger of the gods.

Plato: THE ALLEGORY OF THE CAVE

And now, I said, let me show in a figure how far our nature is enlightened or unenlightened: Behold! human beings living in an underground den, which has a mouth open towards the light and reaching all along the den; here they have been from their childhood, and have their

4th century B.C.

legs and necks chained so that they cannot move, and can only see before them, being prevented by the chains from turning round their heads. Above and behind them a fire is blazing at a distance, and between the fire and the prisoners there is a raised way; and you will see, if you look, a low wall built along the way, like the screen which marionette players have in front of them, over which they show the puppets.

I see.

And do you see, I said, men passing along the wall carrying all sorts of vessels, and statues and figures of animals made of wood and stone and various materials, which appear over the wall? Some of them are talking, others silent.

You have shown me a strange image, and they are strange prisoners.

Like ourselves, I replied; and they see only their own shadows, or the shadows of one another, which the fire throws on the opposite wall of the cave?

True, he said; how could they see anything but the shadows if they were never allowed to move their heads?

And of the objects which are being carried in like manner they would only see the shadows?

Yes, he said.

And if they were able to converse with one another, would they not suppose that they were naming what was actually before them?

Very true.

And suppose further that the prison had an echo which came from the other side, would they not be sure to fancy when one of the passers-by spoke that the voice which they heard came from the passing shadow?

No question, he replied.

To them, I said, the truth would be literally nothing but the shadows of the images.

That is certain.

And now look again, and see what will naturally follow if the prisoners are released and disabused of their error. At first, when any of them is liberated and compelled suddenly to stand up and turn his neck round and walk and look towards the light, he will suffer sharp pains; the glare will distress him and he will be unable to see the realities of which in his former state he had seen the shadows; and then conceive some one saying to him, that what he saw before was an illusion, but that now, when he is approaching nearer to being and his eye is turned towards more real existence, he has a clearer vision—what will be his reply? And you may further imagine that his instructor is pointing to the objects as they pass and requiring him to name them—will he not be perplexed? Will he not fancy that the shadows which he formerly saw are truer than the objects which are now shown to him?

Far truer.

And if he is compelled to look straight at the light, will he not have a pain in his eyes which will make him turn away to take refuge in the objects of vision which he can see, and which he will conceive to be in reality clearer than the things which are now being shown to him?

True, he said.

And suppose once more, that he is reluctantly dragged up a steep and rugged ascent, and held fast until he is forced into the presence of the sun himself, is he not likely to be pained and irritated? When he approaches the light his eyes will be dazzled and he will not be able to see anything at all of what are now called realities.

Not all in a moment, he said.   20

He will require to grow accustomed to the sight of the upper world. And first he will see the shadows best, next the reflections of men and other objects in the water, and then the objects themselves; then he will gaze upon the light of the moon and the stars and the spangled heaven; and he will see the sky and the stars by night better than the sun or the light of the sun by day?

Certainly.

Last of all he will be able to see the sun, and not mere reflections of him in the water, but he will see him in his own proper place, and not in another; and he will contemplate him as he is.

Certainly.

He will then proceed to argue that this is he who gives the season and   25
the years, and is the guardian of all that is in the visible world, and in a certain way the cause of all things which he and his fellows have been accustomed to behold?

Clearly, he said, he would first see the sun and then reason about him.

And when he remembered his old habitation, and the wisdom of the den and his fellow-prisoners, do you not suppose that he would felicitate himself on the change, and pity them?

Certainly, he would.

And if they were in the habit of conferring honors among themselves on those who were quickest to observe the passing shadows and to remark which of them went before, and which followed after, and which were together; and who were therefore best able to draw conclusions as to the future, do you think that he would care for such honors and glories, or envy the possessors of them? Would he not say with Homer,

> Better to be the poor servant of a poor master,

and to endure anything, rather than think as they do and live after their manner?

Yes, he said, I think that he would rather suffer anything than enter-   30
tain these false notions and live in this miserable manner.

Imagine once more, I said, such an one coming suddenly out of the sun to be replaced in his old situation; would he not be certain to have his eyes full of darkness?

To be sure, he said.

And if there were a contest, and he had to compete in measuring the shadows with the prisoners who had never moved out of the den, while his sight was still weak, and before his eyes had become steady (and the time which would be needed to acquire this new habit of sight might be very considerable) would he not be ridiculous? Men would say of him that up he went and down he came without his eyes; and that it was better not even to think of ascending; and if any one tried to loose another and lead him up to the light, let them only catch the offender, and they would put him to death.

No question, he said.

35   This entire allegory, I said, you may now append, dear Glaucon, to the previous argument; the prison-house is the world of sight, the light of the fire is the sun, and you will not misapprehend me if you interpret the journey upwards to be the ascent of the soul into the intellectual world according to my poor belief, which, at your desire, I have expressed—whether rightly or wrongly God knows. But, whether true or false, my opinion is that in the world of knowledge the idea of good appears last of all, and is seen only with an effort; and, when seen, is also inferred to be the universal author of all things beautiful and right, parent of light and of the lord of light in this visible world, and the immediate source of reason and truth in the intellectual; and that this is the power upon which he who would act rationally either in public or private life must have his eye fixed.

I agree, he said, as far as I am able to understand you.

Moreover, I said, you must not wonder that those who attain to this beatific vision are unwilling to descend to human affairs; for their souls are ever hastening into the upper world where they desire to dwell; which desire of theirs is very natural, if our allegory may be trusted.

Yes, very natural.

And is there anything surprising in one who passes from divine contemplations to the evil state of man, misbehaving himself in a ridiculous manner; if, while his eyes are blinking and before he has become accustomed to the surrounding darkness, he is compelled to fight in courts of law, or in other places, about the images or the shadows of images of justice, and is endeavouring to meet the conceptions of those who have never yet seen absolute justice?

Anything but surprising, he replied.

40   Any one who has common sense will remember that the bewilderments of the eyes are of two kinds, and arise from two causes, either from coming out of the light or from going into the light, which is true of the mind's eye, quite as much as of the bodily eye; and he who remem-

bers this when he sees any one whose vision is perplexed and weak, will
not be too ready to laugh; he will first ask whether that soul of man has
come out of the brighter life, and is unable to see because unaccustomed
to the dark, or having turned from darkness to the day is dazzled by
excess of light. And he will count the one happy in his condition and
state of being, and he will pity the other; or, if he have a mind to laugh
at the soul which comes from below into the light, there will be more
reason in this than in the laugh which greets him who returns from
above out of the light into the den.

That, he said, is a very just distinction.   40

Jesus: Parables of the Kingdom

Then shall the kingdom of heaven be likened unto ten virgins, which
took their lamps, and went forth to meet the bridegroom.

And five of them were wise, and five *were* foolish.

They that *were* foolish took their lamps, and took no oil with them:
But the wise took oil in their vessels with their lamps.

While the bridegroom tarried, they all slumbered and slept.   5

And at midnight there was a cry made, Behold, the bridegroom
cometh; go ye out to meet him.

Then all those virgins arose, and trimmed their lamps.

And the foolish said unto the wise, Give us of your oil; for our lamps
are gone out.

But the wise answered, saying *Not so;* lest there be not enough for
us and you: but go ye rather to them that sell, and buy for yourselves.

And while they went to buy, the bridgroom came; and they that were   10
ready went in with him to the marriage: and the door was shut.

Afterward came also the other virgins, saying, Lord, Lord, open to us.

But he answered and said, Verily I say unto you, I know you not.

Watch therefore, for ye know neither the day nor the hour wherein
the Son of man cometh.

For *the kingdom of heaven is* as a man travelling into a far country,
who called his own servants, and delivered unto them his goods.

And unto one he gave five talents, to another two, and to another one; 15
to every man according to his several ability; and straightway took his
journey.

From Jesus' teachings to his disciples on the Mount of Olives, as written in Matthew xxv;
from the King James Bible (1611).

Then he that had received the five talents went and traded with the same, and made *them* other five talents.

And likewise he that *had received* two, he also gained other two.

But he that had received one went and digged in the earth, and hid his lord's money.

After a long time the lord of those servants cometh, and reckoneth with them.

20 And so he that had received five talents came and brought other five talents, saying, Lord, thou deliveredst unto me five talents: behold, I have gained beside them five talents more.

His lord said unto him, Well done, *thou* good and faithful servant: thou hast been faithful over a few things, I will make thee ruler over many things: enter thou into the joy of thy lord.

He also that had received two talents came and said, Lord, thou deliverdst unto me two talents: behold, I have gained two other talents beside them.

His lord said unto him, Well done, good and faithful servant; thou hast been faithful over a few things, I will make thee ruler over many things: enter thou into the joy of thy lord.

Then he which had received the one talent came and said, Lord, I knew thee that thou art an hard man, reaping where thou hast not sown, and gathering where thou hast not strawed:

25 And I was afraid, and went and hid thy talent in the earth: lo, *there* thou hast *that is* thine.

His lord answered and said unto him, *Thou* wicked and slothful servant, thou knewest that I reap where I sowed not, and gather where I have not strawed:

Thou oughtest therefore to have put my money to the exchanges, and *then* at my coming I should have received mine own with usury.

Take therefore the talent from him, and give *it* unto him which hath ten talents.

For unto every one that hath shall be given, and he shall have abundance: but from him that hath not shall be taken away even that which he hath.

30 And cast ye the unprofitable servant into outer darkness: there shall be weeping and gnashing of teeth.

When the Son of man shall come in his glory, and all the holy angels with him, then shall he sit upon the throne of his glory:

And before him shall be gathered all nations: and he shall separate them one from another, as a shepherd divideth *his* sheep from the goats:

And he shall set the sheep on his right hand, but the goats on the left.

Then shall the King say unto them on his right hand, Come, ye blessed of my Father, inherit the kingdom prepared for you from the foundation of the world:

For I was an hungred, and ye gave me meat: I was thirsty, and ye gave   35
me drink: I was a stranger, and ye took me in:

Naked, and ye clothed me: I was sick, and ye visited me: I was in
prison, and ye came unto me.

Then shall the righteous answer him, saying, Lord, when saw we thee
an hungred, and fed *thee?* or thirsty, and gave *thee* drink?

When saw we thee a stranger, and took *thee* in? or naked, and clothed
thee?

Or when saw we thee sick, or in prison, and came unto thee?

And the King shall answer and say unto them, Verily I say unto you,   40
Inasmuch as ye have done *it* unto one of the least of these my brethren,
ye have done *it* unto me.

Then shall he say also unto them on the left hand, Depart from me,
ye cursed, into everlasting fire, prepared for the devil and his angels:

For I was an hungred, and ye gave me no meat: I was thirsty, and ye
gave me no drink.

I was a stranger, and ye took me not in: naked, and ye clothed me
not: sick, and in prison, and ye visited me not.

Then shall they also answer him, saying, Lord, when saw we thee an
hungred, or athirst, or a stranger, or naked, or sick, or in prison, and did
not minister unto thee?

Then shall he answer them, saying, Verily I say unto you, Inasmuch   45
as ye did *it* not to one of the least of these, ye did *it* not to me.

And these shall go away into everlasting punishment: but the righteous into life eternal.

ZEN PARABLES

Muddy Road

Tanzan and Ekido were once traveling together down a muddy road.
A heavy rain was still falling.

Coming around a bend, they met a lovely girl in a silk kimono and
sash, unable to cross the intersection.

"Come on, girl," said Tanzan at once. Lifting her in his arms, he
carried her over the mud.

Ekido did not speak again until that night when they reached a
lodging temple. Then he no longer could restrain himself. "We monks

From *Zen Flesh, Zen Bones* (1957).

don't go near females," he told Tanzan, "especially not young and lovely ones. It is dangerous. Why did you do that?"

5   "I left the girl there," said Tanzan. "Are you still carrying her?"

A Parable

Buddha told a parable in a sutra:

A man traveling across a field encountered a tiger. He fled, the tiger after him. Coming to a precipice, he caught hold of the root of a wild vine and swung himself down over the edge. The tiger sniffed at him from above. Trembling, the man looked down to where, far below, another tiger was waiting to eat him. Only the vine sustained him.

Two mice, one white and one black, little by little started to gnaw away the vine. The man saw a luscious strawberry near him. Grasping the vine with one hand, he plucked the strawberry with the other. How sweet it tasted!

Learning to Be Silent

The pupils of the Tendai school used to study meditation before Zen entered Japan. Four of them who were intimate friends promised one another to observe seven days of silence.

10   On the first day all were silent. Their meditation had begun auspiciously, but when night came and the oil lamps were growing dim one of the pupils could not help exclaiming to a servant: "Fix those lamps."

The second pupil was surprised to hear the first one talk. "We are not supposed to say a word," he remarked.

"You two are stupid. Why did you talk?" asked the third.

"I am the only one who has not talked," concluded the fourth pupil.

Jonathan Swift: THE SPIDER AND THE BEE

Things were at this crisis, when a material accident fell out. For, upon the highest corner of a large window, there dwelt a certain spider, swollen up to the first magnitude by the destruction of infinite numbers of flies, whose spoils lay scattered before the gates of his palace, like human bones before the cave of some giant. The avenues of his castle were guarded with turnpikes and palisadoes, all after the modern way of fortification. After you had passed several courts, you came to the

From *The Battle of the Books* (1704).

center, wherein you might behold the constable himself in his own lodgings, which had windows fronting to each avenue, and ports to sally out upon all occasions of prey or defense. In this mansion he had for some time dwelt in peace and plenty, without danger to his person by swallows from above, or to his palace by brooms from below, when it was the pleasure of fortune to conduct thither a wandering bee, to whose curiosity a broken pane in the glass had discovered itself, and in he went; where expatiating a while, he at last happened to alight upon one of the outward walls of the spider's citadel; which, yielding to the unequal weight, sunk down to the very foundation. Thrice he endeavored to force his passage, and thrice the center shook. The spider within, feeling the terrible convulsion, supposed at first that nature was approaching to her final dissolution; or else that Beelzebub,[1] with all his legions, was come to revenge the death of many thousands of his subjects, whom his enemy had slain and devoured. However, he at length valiantly resolved to issue forth, and meet his fate. Meanwhile the bee had acquitted himself of his toils, and posted securely at some distance, was employed in cleansing his wings, and disengaging them from the ragged remnants of the cobweb. By this time the spider was adventured out, when beholding the chasms, and ruins, and dilapidations of his fortress, he was very near at his wit's end; he stormed and swore like a madman, and swelled till he was ready to burst. At length, casting his eye upon the bee, and wisely gathering causes from events (for they knew each other by sight), "A plague split you," said he, "for a giddy son of a whore. Is it you, with a vengeance, that have made this litter here? Could you not look before you, and be d—nd? Do you think I have nothing else to do (in the devil's name) but to mend and repair after your arse?" "Good words, friend," said the bee (having pruned himself, and being disposed to droll) "I'll give you my hand and word to come near your kennel no more; I was never in such a confounded pickle since I was born." "Sirrah," replied the spider, "if it were not for breaking an old custom in our family, never to stir abroad against an enemy, I should come and teach you better manners." "I pray have patience," said the bee, "or you will spend your substance, and for aught I see, you may stand in need of it all, towards the repair of your house." "Rogue, rogue," replied the spider, "yet methinks you should have more respect to a person, whom all the world allows to be so much your betters." "By my troth," said the bee, "the comparison will amount to a very good jest, and you will do me a favor to let me know the reasons that all the world is pleased to use in so hopeful a dispute." At this the spider, having swelled himself into the size and posture of a disputant, began his argument in the true spirit of controversy, with a resolution to be heartily scurrilous and angry,

1. The Hebrew god of flies.

to urge on his own reasons, without the least regard to the answers or objections of his opposite, and fully predetermined in his mind against all conviction.

"Not to disparage myself," said he, "by the comparison with such a rascal, what art thou but a vagabond without house or home, without stock or inheritance, born to no possession of your own, but a pair of wings and a drone-pipe? Your livelihood is an universal plunder upon nature; a freebooter over fields and gardens; and for the sake of stealing will rob a nettle as easily as a violet. Whereas I am a domestic animal, furnished with a native stock within myself. This large castle (to show my improvements in the mathematics) is all built with my own hands, and the materials extracted altogether out of my own person."

"I am glad," answered the bee, "to hear you grant at least that I am come honestly by my wings and my voice; for then, it seems, I am obliged to Heaven alone for my flights and my music; and Providence would never have bestowed on me two such gifts, without designing them for the noblest ends. I visit indeed all the flowers and blossoms of the field and the garden; but whatever I collect from thence enriches myself, without the least injury to their beauty, their smell, or their taste. Now, for you and your skill in architecture and other mathematics, I have little to say: in that building of yours there might, for aught I know, have been labor and method enough, but by woful experience for us both, 'tis too plain, the materials are naught, and I hope you will henceforth take warning, and consider duration and matter as well as method and art. You boast, indeed, of being obliged to no other creature, but of drawing and spinning out all from yourself; that is to say, if we may judge of the liquor in the vessel by what issues out, you possess a good plentiful store of dirt and poison in your breast; and, tho' I would by no means lessen or disparage your genuine stock of either, yet I doubt you are somewhat obliged for an increase of both, to a little foreign assistance. Your inherent portion of dirt does not fail of acquisitions, by sweepings exhaled from below; and one insert furnishes you with a share of poison to destroy another. So that in short, the question comes all to this—which is the nobler being of the two, that which by a lazy contemplation of four inches round, by an overweening pride, feeding and engendering on itself, turns all into excrement and venom, produces nothing at last, but flybane and a cobweb; or that which, by an universal range, with long search, much study, true judgment, and distinction of things, brings home honey and wax."

Samuel L. Clemens: THE WAR PRAYER

It was a time of great and exalting excitement. The country was up in arms, the war was on, in every breast burned the holy fire of patriotism; the drums were beating, the bands playing, the toy pistols popping, the bunched firecrackers hissing and spluttering; on every hand and far down the receding and fading spread of roofs and balconies a fluttering wilderness of flags flashed in the sun; daily the young volunteers marched down the wide avenue gay and fine in their new uniforms, the proud fathers and mothers and sisters and sweethearts cheering them with voices choked with happy emotion as they swung by; nightly the packed mass meetings listened, panting, to patriot oratory which stirred the deepest deeps of their hearts and which they interrupted at briefest intervals with cyclones of applause, the tears running down their cheeks the while; in the churches the pastors preached devotion to flag and country and invoked the God of Battles, beseeching His aid in our good cause in outpouring of fervid eloquence which moved every listener. It was indeed a glad and gracious time, and the half-dozen rash spirits that ventured to disapprove of the war and cast a doubt upon its righteousness straightway got such a stern and angry warning that for their personal safety's sake they quickly shrank out of sight and offended no more in that way.

Sunday morning came—next day the battalions would leave for the front; the church was filled; the volunteers were there, their young faces alight with martial dreams—visions of the stern advance, the gathering momentum, the rushing charge, the flashing sabers, the flight of the foe, the tumult, the enveloping smoke, the fierce pursuit, the surrender!— then home from the war, bronzed heroes, welcomed, adored, submerged in golden seas of glory! With the volunteers sat their dear ones, proud, happy, and envied by the neighbors and friends who had no sons and brothers to send forth to the field of honor, there to win for the flag or, failing die the noblest of noble deaths. The service proceeded; a war chapter from the Old Testament was read; the first prayer was said; it was followed by an organ burst that shook the building, and with one impulse the house rose, with glowing eyes and beating hearts, and poured out that tremendous invocation—

> "God the all-terrible! Thou who ordainest,
> Thunder thy clarion and lightning thy sword!"

Then came the "long" prayer. None could remember the like of it for passionate pleading and moving and beautiful language. The burden of

Dictated in 1904 or 1905; published in *Europe and Elsewhere* (1923).

its supplication was that an ever-merciful and benignant Father of us all
would watch over our noble young soldiers and aid, comfort, and encourage them in their patriotic work; bless them, shield them in the day of
battle and the hour of peril, bear them in His mighty hand, make them
strong and confident, invincible in the bloody onset; help them to crush
the foe, grant to them and to their flag and country imperishable honor
and glory—

An aged stranger entered and moved with slow and noiseless step up
the main aisle, his eyes fixed upon the minister, his long body clothed
in a robe that reached to his feet, his head bare, his white hair descending in a frothy cataract to his shoulders, his seamy face unnaturally pale,
pale even to ghastliness. With all eyes following him and wondering, he
made his silent way; without pausing, he ascended to the preacher's side
and stood there, waiting. With shut lids the preacher, unconscious of
his presence, continued his moving prayer, and at last finished it with
the words, uttered in fervent appeal, "Bless our arms, grant us the
victory, O Lord our God, Father and Protector of our land and flag!"

The stranger touched his arm, motioned him to step aside—which
the startled minister did—and took his place. During some moments he
surveyed the spellbound audience with solemn eyes in which burned an
uncanny light; then in a deep voice he said:

"I come from the Throne—bearing a message from Almighty God!"
The words smote the house with a shock; if the stranger perceived it he
gave no attention. "He has heard the prayer of His servant your shepherd and will grant it if such shall be your desire after I, His Messenger,
shall have explained to you its import—that is to say, its full import. For
it is like unto many of the prayers of men, in that it asks for more than
he who utters it is aware of—except he pause and think.

"God's servant and yours has prayed his prayer. Has he paused and
taken thought? Is it one prayer? No, it is two—one uttered, the other
not. Both have reached the ear of Him Who heareth all supplications,
the spoken and the unspoken. Ponder this—keep it in mind. If you
would beseech a blessing upon yourself, beware! lest without intent you
invoke a curse upon a neighbor at the same time. If you pray for the
blessing of rain upon your crop which needs it, by that act you are
possibly praying for a curse upon some neighbor's crop which may not
need rain and can be injured by it.

"You have heard your servant's prayer—the uttered part of it. I am
commissioned of God to put into words the other part of it—that part
which the pastor, and also you in your hearts, fervently prayed silently.
And ignorantly and unthinkingly? God grant that it was so! You heard
these words: 'Grant us the victory, O Lord our God!' That is sufficient.
The *whole* of the uttered prayer is compact into those pregnant words.
Elaborations were not necessary. When you have prayed for victory you

have prayed for many unmentioned results which follow victory—*must* follow it, cannot help but follow it. Upon the listening spirit of God the Father fell also the unspoken part of the prayer. He commandeth me to put it into words. Listen!

"O Lord our Father, our young patriots, idols of our hearts, go forth to battle—be Thou near them! With them, in spirit, we also go forth from the sweet peace of our beloved firesides to smite the foe. O Lord our God, help us to tear their soldiers to bloody shreds with our shells; help us to cover their smiling fields with the pale forms of their patriot dead; help us to drown the thunder of the guns with the shrieks of their wounded, writhing in pain; help us to lay waste their humble homes with a hurricane of fire; help us to wring the hearts of their unoffending widows with unavailing grief; help us to turn them out roofless with their little children to wander unfriended the wastes of their desolated land in rags and hunger and thirst, sports of the sun flames of summer and the icy winds of winter, broken in spirit, worn with travail, imploring Thee for the refuge of the grave and denied it—for our sakes who adore Thee, Lord, blast their hopes, blight their lives, protract their bitter pilgrimage, make heavy their steps, water their way with their tears, stain the white snow with the blood of their wounded feet! We ask it, in the spirit of love, of Him Who is the Source of Love, and Who is the ever-faithful refuge and friend of all that are sore beset and seek His aid with humble and contrite hearts. Amen.

(*After a pause*) "Ye have prayed it: if ye still desire it, speak! The messenger of the Most High waits."

It was believed afterward that the man was a lunatic, because there was no sense in what he said.

10

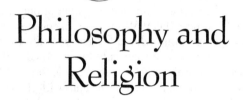

Philosophy and Religion

Arthur M. Schlesinger, Jr.
THE OPENING OF THE AMERICAN MIND

Little is more surprising these days than the revival of blasphemy as a crime. A secular age had presumably relegated blasphemy—irreverence toward things sacred—to the realm of obsolete offenses. No American has been convicted for blasphemy since Abner Kneeland in Massachusetts a century and a half ago (for what was deemed a "scandalous, impious, obscene, blasphemous and profane libel of and concerning God"); and the last prosecution, in Maryland 20 years ago, was dismissed by an appellate court as a violation of the First Amendment.

But a secular age, when it creates its own absolutes, may well secularize blasphemy too. Consider the deplorable role the Pledge of Allegiance to the flag played in a recent Presidential campaign; or the cries of outrage provoked by the Supreme Court decision in Texas v. Johnson, holding that punishment for the political burning of an American flag breached the Constitution; or the demonstrations protesting the "desecration" of the flag at the Art Institute of Chicago.

The very word "desecration" implies that the American flag is sanctified, an object of worship. We are witnessing the rise of what Charles Fried, Ronald Reagan's Solicitor General, calls the "doctrine of civil blasphemy." Whether religious or secular in guise, all forms of blasphemy have in common that there are things so sacred that they must be protected by the arm of the state from irreverence and challenge—that absolutes of truth and virtue exist and that those who scoff are to be punished.

It is this belief in absolutes, I would hazard, that is the great enemy

Adapted from a lecture given at Brown University on the occasion of Vartan Gregorian's inauguration as president. From the *New York Times Book Review* (July 23, 1989).

today of the life of the mind. This may seem a rash proposition. The fashion of the time is to denounce relativism as the root of all evil. But history suggests that the damage done to humanity by the relativist is far less than the damage done by the absolutist—by the fellow who, as Mr. Dooley[1] once put it, "does what he thinks th' Lord wud do if He only knew th' facts in th' case."

Let me not be misunderstood lest I be taken for a blasphemer myself and thereby subject to the usual dire penalties. I hold religion in high regard. As Chesterton[2] once said, the trouble when people stop believing in God is not that they thereafter believe in nothing; it is that they thereafter believe in anything. I agree with Tocqueville[3] that religion has an indispensable social function: "How is it possible that society should escape destruction if the moral tie is not strengthened in proportion as the political tie is relaxed?" I also sympathize with Tocqueville who, André Jardin, his most recent biographer, tells us, went to his death an unbeliever.

It would hardly seem necessary to insist on the perils of moral absolutism in our own tawdry age. By their fruits ye shall know them. It is as illogical to indict organized religion because of Jimmy Swaggart and the Bakkers as Paul Johnson is to indict the intelligentsia because of the messy private lives of selected intellectuals; but the moral absolutists who are presently applauding Paul Johnson's cheap book *Intellectuals* might well be invited to apply the same methodology to their own trade. As the great theologian Reinhold Niebuhr[4] said, "The worst corruption is a corrupt religion"—and organized religion, like all powerful institutions, lends itself to corruption. Absolutism, whether in religious or secular form, becomes a haven for racketeers.

As a historian, I confess to a certain amusement when I hear the Judeo-Christian tradition praised as the source of our concern for human rights. In fact, the great religious ages were notable for their indifference to human rights in the contemporary sense. They were notorious not only for acquiescence in poverty, inequality, exploitation and oppression but for enthusiastic justifications of slavery, persecution, abandonment of small children, torture, genocide.

Religion enshrined and vindicated hierarchy, authority and inequality

1. Martin Dooley, an imaginary Irishman who presided over a small saloon on Chicago's West Side, created by Finley Peter Dunne (1867–1936), American journalist and humorist. Dunne wrote his first "Mr. Dooley" essays for the *Evening Post*.
2. G. K. Chesterton (1874–1936), English essayist, novelist, and journalist who became a vigorous polemicist for his Catholicism and conservative political views.
3. Count Alexis (Charles Henri Maurice Clérel) de Tocqueville (1805–59), French historian known for his studies in the nature and operation of democracy.
4. Niebuhr (1892–1971), American theologian and social and political critic widely influential in midtwentieth-century intellectual life.

and had no compunction about murdering heretics and blasphemers. Till the end of the 18th century, torture was normal investigative procedure in the Roman Catholic church as well as in most European states. In Protestant America in the early 19th century, as Larry Tise points out in his book *Pro-Slavery: A History of the Defense of Slavery in America, 1701–1840,* men of the cloth "wrote almost half of all the defenses of slavery published in America"; an appendix lists 275 ministers of the Gospel who piously proclaimed the Christian virtue of a system in which one man owned another as private property to be used as he pleased.

Human rights is not a religious idea. It is a secular idea, the product of the last four centuries of Western history.

10   It was the age of equality that brought about the disappearance of such religious appurtenances as the auto-da-fé and burning at the stake, the abolition of torture and of public executions, the emancipation of the slaves. Only later, as religion itself began to succumb to the humanitarian ethic and to view the Kingdom of God as attainable within history, could the claim be made that the Judeo-Christian tradition commanded the pursuit of happiness in this world. The basic human rights documents—the American Declaration of Independence and the French Declaration of the Rights of Man—were written by political, not by religious, leaders. And the revival of absolutism in the 20th century, whether in ecclesiastical or secular form, has brought with it the revival of torture, of slaughter and of other monstrous violations of human rights.

Take a look at the world around us today. Most of the organized killing now going on is the consequence of absolutism: Protestants and Catholics killing each other in Ireland; Muslims and Jews killing each other in the Middle East; Sunnites and Shiites killing each other in the Persian Gulf; Buddhists and Hindus killing each other in Ceylon; Hindus and Sikhs killing each other in India; Christians and Muslims killing each other in Armenia and Azerbaijan; Buddhists and Communists killing each other in Tibet. "We have," as Swift[5] said, "just enough religion to make us hate, but not enough to make us love." The Santa Barbara Peace Resource Center, reporting on the 32 wars in progress around the planet in 1988, found that 25 had "a significant ethnic, racial or religious dimension." And when religious religion is not the cause, then the totalitarian social religions of our age inspire mass slaughter.

It is natural enough, I suppose, if you believe you have privileged access to absolute truth, to want to rid the world of those who insist on divergent truths of their own. But I am not sure that it is a useful principle on which to build a society. Yet, as I noted earlier, the prevail-

5. Jonathan Swift (1667–1745), English satirist, poet, political writer, and clergyman.

ing fashion is, or was a year or two ago, to hold relativism responsible for the ills of our age. A key document, of course, is Allan Bloom's best seller of a couple of years back, *The Closing of the American Mind.* Indeed, one cannot but regard the very popularity of that murky and pretentious book as the best evidence for Mr. Bloom's argument about the degradation of American culture. It is another of those half-read best sellers, like Charles Reich's murky and pretentious *Greening of America* 17 years before, that plucks a momentary nerve, materializes fashionably on coffee tables, is rarely read all the way through and is soon forgotten.

Now one may easily share Mr. Bloom's impatience with many features of higher education in the United States. I too lament the incoherence in the curriculums, the proliferation of idiotic courses, the shameful capitulation to factional demands and requisitions, the decay of intellectual standards. For better or for worse, in my view, we inherit an American experience, as America inherits a Western experience; and solid learning must begin with our own origins and traditions. The bonds of cohesion in our society are sufficiently fragile, or so it seems to me, that we should not strain them by excessive worship at artificial shrines of ethnicity, bilingualism, global cultural base-touching and the like. Let us take pride in our own distinctive inheritance as other countries take pride in their distinctive inheritances; and let us understand that no culture can hope to ingest other cultures all at once, certainly not before it ingests its own.

But a belief in solid learning, rigorous standards, intellectual coherence, the virtue of elites is a different thing from a faith in absolutes. It is odd that Professor Bloom spends 400 pages laying down the law about the American mind and never once mentions the two greatest and most characteristic American thinkers, Emerson[6] and William James.[7] One can see why he declined the confrontation: it is because he would have had to concede the fact that the American mind is by nature and tradition skeptical, irreverent, pluralistic and relativistic.

Nor does relativism necessarily regard all claims to truth as equal or believe that judgment is no more than the expression of personal preference. For our relative values are not matters of whim and happenstance. History has given them to us. They are anchored in our national experience, in our great national documents, in our national heroes, in our folkways, traditions, standards. Some of these values seem to us so self-evident that even relativists think they have, or ought to have,

15

---

6. Ralph Waldo Emerson (1803–82), American poet, essayist, and philosopher who became the chief spokesman for transcendentalism, characterized by its reliance on intuition as the only way to comprehend reality.

7. William James (1842–1910), American philosopher, psychologist, and teacher usually identified with the school of pragmatist philosophy.

universal application: the right to life, liberty and the pursuit of happiness, for example; the duty to treat persons as ends in themselves; the prohibition of slavery, torture, genocide. People with a different history will have different values. But we believe that our own are better for us. They work for us; and, for that reason, we live and die by them.

At least this is what great Americans have always believed. "Deepseated preferences," as Justice Holmes put it, "cannot be argued about . . . and therefore, when differences are sufficiently far-reaching, we try to kill the other man rather than let him have his way. But that is perfectly consistent with admitting that, so far as it appears, his grounds are just as good as ours."

Once Justice Holmes and Judge Learned Hand[8] discussed these questions on a long train ride. Learned Hand gave as his view that "opinions are at best provisional hypotheses, incompletely tested. The more they are tested . . . the more assurance we may assume, but they are never absolutes. So we must be tolerant of opposite opinions." Holmes wondered whether Hand might not be carrying his tolerance to dangerous lengths. "You say," Hand wrote Holmes later, "that I strike at the sacred right to kill the other fellow when he disagrees. The horrible possibility silenced me when you said it. Now, I say, 'Not at all, kill him for the love of Christ and in the name of God, but always remember that he may be the saint and you the devil.' "

These "deep-seated preferences" are what Holmes called his "Can't Helps"—"When I say that a thing is true, I mean that I cannot help believing it. . . . But . . . I do not venture to assume that my inabilities in the way of thought are inabilities of the universe. I therefore define truth as the system of my limitations, and leave absolute truth for those who are better equipped." He adds: "Certitude is not the test of certainty. We have been cock-sure of many things that were not so."

Absolutism is abstract, monistic, deductive, ahistorical, solemn, and it is intimately bound up with deference to authority. Relativism is concrete, pluralistic, inductive, historical, skeptical and intimately bound up with deference to experience. Absolutism teaches by rote; relativism by experiment. "I respect faith," that forgotten wit Wilson Mizener once said, "but doubt is what gets you an education."

20   I would even hazard the proposition that relativism comports far more than absolutism with the deepest and darkest teachings of religion. For

8. Oliver Wendell Holmes, Jr. (1841–1935), American jurist, son of the celebrated physician and author of the same name. His vigorous and eloquent dissents on the First- and Fourteenth-Amendment cases earned his reputation as "The Great Dissenter"; Learned Hand (1872–1961), American jurist and federal judge for fifty-two years who, although he never served as a U.S. Supreme Court justice, was generally considered to be the greatest judge of his day.

what we have learned from Augustine, from Calvin, from Jonathan Edwards[9] is not man's capacity to grasp the absolute but quite the contrary: the frailty of man, the estrangement of man from God, the absolute distance between mortals and divinity—and the arrogance of those who suppose they are doing what the Lord would do if He only knew the facts in the case. That is why Reinhold Niebuhr acknowledged such an affinity with William James—far more, I would warrant, than he would have found with Allan Bloom.

When it came to worldly affairs, Niebuhr was a relativist, not because he disbelieved in the absolute, but precisely because he believed in the absoluteness of the absolute—because he recognized that for finite mortals the infinite thinker was inaccessible, unfathomable, unattainable. Nothing was more dangerous, in Niebuhr's view, than for frail and erring humans to forget the inevitable "contradiction between divine and human purposes." "Religion," he wrote, "is so frequently a source of confusion in political life, and so frequently dangerous to democracy, precisely because it introduces absolutes into the realm of relative values." He particularly detested "the fanaticism of all good men, who do not know that they are not as good as they esteem themselves," and he warned against "the depth of evil to which individuals and communities may sink . . . when they try to play the role of God to history."

Niebuhr accepted, as James did, "the limits of all human striving, the fragmentariness of all human wisdom, the precariousness of all historic configurations of power, and the mixture of good and evil in all human virtue." His outlook is as far away from Mr. Bloom's simple-minded absolutism as one can imagine. It represents, in my view, the real power of religious insight as well as the far more faithful expression of the American mind.

I would summon one more American, the greatest of them all, as a last witness in the case for relativism against absolutes. In his Second Inaugural, Lincoln noted that both sides in the Civil War "read the same Bible, and pray to the same God; and each invokes His aid against the other. . . . The prayers of both could not be answered; that of neither has been answered fully. The Almighty has His own purposes." Replying thereafter to a congratulatory letter from Thurlow Weed, Lincoln doubted that such sentiments would be "immediately popular. Men are not flattered by being shown that there has been a difference of purpose between the Almighty and them. To deny it, however, in this case, is to deny that there is a God governing the world."

The Almighty has His own purposes: this is the reverberant answer to those who tell us that we must live by absolutes. Relativism is the

9. St. Augustine (354–430), early Christian church father and philosopher; John Calvin (1509–64), French Protestant refor-mer; Jonathan Edwards (1703–58), American theologian and philosopher.

American way. As that most quintessential of American historians, George Bancroft, wrote in another connection, "The feud between the capitalist and laborer, the house of Have and the house of Want, is as old as social union, and can never be entirely quieted; but he who will act with moderation, prefer fact to theory, and remember that every thing in this world is relative and not absolute, will see that the violence of the contest may be stilled."

25   The mystic prophets of the absolute cannot save us. Sustained by our history and traditions, we must save ourselves, at whatever risk of heresy or blasphemy. We can find solace in the memorable representation of the human struggle against the absolute in the finest scene in the greatest of American novels. I refer of course to the scene when Huckleberry Finn decides that the "plain hand of Providence" requires him to tell Miss Watson where her runaway slave Jim is to be found. Huck writes his letter of betrayal to Miss Watson and feels "all washed clean of sin for the first time I had ever felt so in my life, and I knowed I could pray now." He sits there for a while thinking "how good it was all this happened so, and how near I come to being lost and going to hell."

Then Huck begins to think about Jim and the rush of the great river and the talking and the singing and the laughing and friendship. "Then I happened to look around and see that paper. . . . I took it up, and held it in my hand. I was a-trembling because I'd got to decide, forever, betwixt two things, and I knowed it. I studied a minute, sort of holding my breath, and then says to myself: 'All right, then, I'll go to hell'—and tore it up."

That, if I may say so, is what America is all about.

Letters in Response

To the Editor:

In its wealth of quotations and anecdotes drawn from his long experience as an Americanist, Arthur Schlesinger Jr.'s defense of relativism against absolutism is a delight to read ("The Opening of the American Mind," July 23). But his treatment of religion seems to me fundamentally contradictory. Mr. Schlesinger, who holds "religion in high regard," agrees with Tocqueville, an atheist, that religion has "an indispensable social function" where morality is concerned. As a historian, however, he rejects the idea that the Judeo-Christian tradition is the source of our concern for human rights. On the contrary, the great ages of faith were

From the *New York Times Book Review* (Aug. 13, 1988).

notorious for "enthusiastic justifications of slavery, persecution, abandonment of small children, torture, genocide." Religion "had no compunction about murdering heretics and blasphemers."

But how can the religious morality supposedly necessary for a free
democracy derive from such cruelty and injustice? Is it conveyed
through the Bible, which Mr. Schlesinger, though favoring religion, does
not even mention? The Bible is notoriously inconsistent where moral
behavior is concerned, from the Sermon on the Mount, which Christians generally ignore as impractical, to the Ten Commandments, which
the patriarchs, Moses and the early leaders of Israel could so flagrantly
violate and yet retain God's favor.

Though our political leaders routinely mention God in the last paragraph of campaign speeches, they never, when discussing policy toward
other nations, ask seriously how the purposes of a God of Love are being
served, whether the Prince of Peace who preached the Sermon on the
Mount approves of all those warheads set to explode at the touch of a
button. Quoting Reinhold Niebuhr and Abraham Lincoln, Mr. Schlesinger says it would be wrong to claim that we know God's will. This
would encourage the absolutism that he fears. "Relativism is the American way."

We can agree. But if our God is a God who never speaks to us, whose
will we can never know, how is this different from not having any God
at all? And how does it provide the basis for a specific morality "indispensable" to a democracy?

Robert Gorham Davis
Cambridge, Mass.

To the Editor:

As usual, Arthur Schlesinger Jr. is so lubricious in making his points   5
that it is very difficult to take hold of anything to refute him. Yet he
is speaking nonsense. Mr. Schlesinger's argument, in essence: Whatever
promotes authority, hierarchy, torture and wars is wrong and un-Ameri-
can and therefore should not be followed. Absolutism does these things.
Therefore, etc.

First, not all of Mr. Schlesinger's evils are on a par. It is typical of the
man that he shudders as much in saying that religion has justified
authority as in saying that it has justified torture. Second, on his own
premises, Mr. Schlesinger has no right to speak authoritatively on what
is right and best for America. He does have the right to make a logical
argument, which he does not do. Third, "absolutism" means many
things. Mr. Schlesinger writes as if anyone who believes in God or any
other absolute goes about murdering his neighbors.

Robert B. Nordberg
Fox Point, Wis.

To the Editor:

Though not without merits of its own, Arthur Schlesinger Jr.'s rebuttal to Allan Bloom's *Closing of the American Mind* is exceedingly strange. Nowhere in the book does Mr. Bloom contrast the "relativism" he deplores with religious absolutism; nowhere does he propose a return to any such absolutism. Instead, he goes to great lengths to describe an intellectual groundwork prepared by such secular thinkers as Locke and Rousseau,[1] on which the academic world built solid structures until the ravages of the 1960's.

Howard Kissel
New York

To the Editor:

Arthur Schlesinger Jr.'s call for a more tolerant, pluralistic America is undermined by the author's own intolerance toward those who would disagree with him. Even as Mr. Schlesinger decries the notion of "privileged access to absolute truth," he presents his relativism as a truth in itself: "Relativism is concrete, pluralistic, inductive, historical, skeptical and intimately bound up with deference to experience." The *truth* of relativism is presented as superior to that of absolutism. Mr. Schlesinger's essay does not oppose all absolute standards of social behavior, only those that contradict his own. For instance, the Constitution is not attacked for granting citizens the absolute right to burn their flag if they wish.

Joseph R. Bardin
New York

To the Editor:

Arthur Schlesinger Jr.'s essay is a study in near misses and subtle qualifications that lead to testimony he is not entitled to. To say that today's local wars are a "consequence" of absolutism is the summary technique of the propagandist, not the scholar. To say that human rights are a secular idea is to ignore the efforts of the church through the centuries to advance them. Mr. Schlesinger's offensive effort to portray religion as a willing partner in poverty and cruelty ignores the progress that (at least) Western man has made; equally important, it ignores the influence of time, place and circumstance on these matters, unpardonable for a historian. Mr. Schlesinger fails to mention directly the most unforgiving of all of man's experiences in cruelty, the Nazi and Communist horrors in Europe, and when he does allude to them he identifies them as products of absolutism! Is he embarrassed that these nearly total

1. John Locke (1632–1704), English philosopher; Jean Jacques Rousseau (1712–78), Swiss-born French philosopher, author, political theorist, and composer.

desecrations of man's essential worth came in an enlightened century almost free of all those God-centered absolutes that he chastises?

G. Roger Cahaney
Cold Spring Harbor, L.I.

To the Editor:

I must comment on Arthur Schlesinger Jr.'s muddled and startlingly wrongheaded essay. This urge is fueled by a diametrically opposed view: *ignoring* absolutes has brought us to the sorry state Mr. Schlesinger describes. For instance:

"Thou shalt not kill." That's about as absolute as you can get. It's only when you add exceptions making it a relative prohibition that the slaughter begins.

F. Paul Wilson
Brick, N.J.

To the Editor:

I agree that revealed, dogmatic absolutes such as those that inform modern conservatism and the recent crusade against flag burning do have disastrous consequences. But relativism, the rejection of *any* absolute standards, rational or irrational, is not the answer to dogmatic absolutes. Religion is a rejection of reason, but so is relativism with its spurning of certainty as a legitimate goal of inquiry and its view that any ethics is inherently subjective and undemonstrable or culturally "relative." Can't we be certain that assassinating Salman Rushdie[2] would be evil, even if his assassin were not to agree? In fact, there are universal truths, and we can be certain of them.

David M. Brown
Trenton

2. (Ahmed) Salman Rushdie (1947–   ), Indian novelist and critic who lives in England. His novel *The Satanic Verses* pro- voked threats of assassination from the powerful and influential Iranian Shiite cleric Ruhollah Khomeini (1900?–89).

James Thurber

THE OWL WHO WAS GOD

Once upon a starless midnight there was on owl who sat on the branch of an oak tree. Two ground moles tried to slip quietly by, unnoticed. "You!" said the owl. "Who?" they quavered, in fear and astonishment, for they could not believe it was possible for anyone to see them in that thick darkness. "You two!" said the owl. The moles hurried away and told the other creatures of the field and forest that the owl was the greatest and wisest of all animals because he could see in the dark and because he could answer any question. "I'll see about that," said a secretary bird, and he called on the owl one night when it was again very dark. "How many claws am I holding up?" said the secretary bird, "Two," said the owl, and that was right. "Can you give me another expression for 'that is to say' or 'namely'?" asked the secretary bird. "To wit," said the owl. "Why does a lover call on his love?" asked the secretary bird. "To woo," said the owl.

The secretary bird hastened back to the other creatures and reported that the owl was indeed the greatest and wisest animal in the world because he could see in the dark and because he could answer any question. "Can he see in the daytime, too?" asked a red fox. "Yes," echoed a dormouse and a French poodle. "Can he see in the daytime, too?" All the other creatures laughed loudly at this silly question, and they set upon the red fox and his friends and drove them out of the region. Then they sent a messenger to the owl and asked him to be their leader.

When the owl appeared among the animals it was high noon and the sun was shining brightly. He walked very slowly, which gave him an appearance of great dignity, and he peered about him with large, staring eyes, which gave him an air of tremendous importance. "He's God!" screamed a Plymouth Rock hen. And the others took up the cry "He's God!" So they followed him wherever he went and when he began to bump into things they began to bump into things, too. Finally he came to a concrete highway and he started up the middle of it and all the other creatures followed him. Presently a hawk, who was acting as outrider, observed a truck coming toward them at fifty miles an hour, and he reported to the secretary bird and the secretary bird reported to the owl. "There's danger ahead," said the secretary bird. "To wit?" said the owl. The secretary bird told him. "Aren't you afraid?" He asked. "Who?"

From *Fables for Our Time* (1940).

said the owl calmly, for he could not see the truck. "He's God!" cried all the creatures again, and they were still crying "He's God!" when the truck hit them and ran them down. Some of the animals were merely injured, but most of them, including the owl, were killed.

Moral: You can fool too many of the people too much of the time.

Robert Graves

MYTHOLOGY

Mythology is the study of whatever religious or heroic legends are so foreign to a student's experience that he cannot believe them to be true. Hence the English adjective "mythical," meaning "incredible"; and hence the omission from standard European mythologies of all Biblical narratives even when closely paralleled by myths from Persia, Babylonia, Egypt, and Greece, and of all hagiological legends. * * *

Myth has two main functions. The first is to answer the sort of awkward questions that children ask, such as: "Who made the world? How will it end? Who was the first man? Where do souls go after death?" The answers, necessarily graphic and positive, confer enormous power on the various deities credited with the creation and care of souls—and incidentally on their priesthoods.

The second function of myth is to justify an existing social system and account for traditional rites and customs. The Erechtheid clan of Athens, who used a snake as an amulet, preserved myths of their descent from King Erichthonius, a man-serpent, son of the Smith-god Hephaestus and foster-son of the Goddess Athene. The Ioxids of Caria explained their veneration for rushes and wild asparagus by a story of their ancestress Perigune, whom Theseus the Erechtheid courted in a thicket of these plants; thus incidentally claiming cousinship with the Attic royal house. The real reason may have been that wild asparagus stalks and rushes were woven into sacred baskets, and therefore taboo.

Myths of origin and eventual extinction vary according to the climate. In the cold North, the first human beings were said to have sprung from the licking of frozen stones by a divine cow named Audumla; and the Northern afterworld was a bare, misty, featureless plain where ghosts wandered hungry and shivering. According to a myth from the kinder climate of Greece, a Titan named Prometheus, kneading mud on a

Originally appeared as the introduction to the *Larousse Encyclopedia of Mythology* (1959).

flowery riverbank, made human statuettes which Athene—who was once the Libyan Moon-goddess Neith—brought to life, and Greek ghosts went to a sunless, flowerless underground cavern. These after-worlds were destined for serfs or commoners; deserving nobles could count on warm, celestial mead halls in the North, and Elysian Fields in Greece.

5   Primitive peoples remodel old myths to conform with changes produced by revolutions, or invasions and, as a rule, politely disguise their violence: thus a treacherous usurper will figure as a lost heir to the throne who killed a destructive dragon or other monster and, after marrying the king's daughter, duly succeeded him. Even myths of origin get altered or discarded. Prometheus' creation of men from clay superseded the hatching of all nature from a world-egg laid by the ancient Mediterranean Dove-goddess Eurynome—a myth common also in Polynesia, where the Goddess is called Tangaroa.

A typical case-history of how myths develop as culture spreads: Among the Akan of Ghana, the original social system was a number of queendoms, each containing three or more clans and ruled by a Queen-mother with her council of elder women, descent being reckoned in the female line, and each clan having its own animal deity. The Akan believed that the world was born from the all-powerful Moon-goddess Ngame, who gave human beings souls, as soon as born, by shooting lunar rays into them. At some time or other, perhaps in the early Middle Ages, patriarchal nomads from the Sudan forced the Akans to accept a male Creator, a Sky-god named Odomankoma, but failed to destroy Ngame's dispensation. A compromise myth was agreed upon: Odomankoma created the world with hammer and chisel from inert matter, after which Ngame brought it to life. These Sudanese invaders also worshipped the seven planetary powers ruling the week—a system originating in Babylonia. (It had spread to Northern Euope, bypassing Greece and Rome, which is why the names of pagan deities—Tuisto, Woden, Thor, and Frigg—are still attached to Tuesday, Wednesday, Thursday, and Friday.) This extra cult provided the Akan with seven new deities, and the compromise myth made both them and the clan gods bisexual. Towards the end of the fourteenth century A.D., a social revolution deposed Odomankoma in favor of a Universal Sun-god, and altered the myth accordingly. While Odomankoma ruled, a queendom was still a queendom, the king acting merely as a consort and male representative of the sovereign Queen-mother, and being styled "Son of the Moon": a yearly dying, yearly resurrected, fertility godling. But the gradual welding of small queendoms into city-states, and of city-states into a rich and populous nation, encouraged the High King—the king of the dominant city-state—to borrow a foreign custom. He styled himself "Son of the Sun," as well as "Son of the Moon," and claimed limitless authority. The

Sun, which, according to the myth, had hitherto been reborn every morning from Ngame, was now worshipped as an eternal god altogether independent of the Moon's life-giving function. New myths appeared when the Akan accepted the patriarchal principle, which Sun-worship brought in; they began tracing succession through the father, and mothers ceased to be the spiritual heads of households.

This case-history throws light on the complex Egyptian corpus of myth. Egypt, it seems, developed from small matriarchal Moonqueendoms to Pharaonic patriarchal Sun-monarchy. Grotesque animal deities of leading clans in the Delta became city-gods, and the cities were federated under the sovereignty of a High King (once a "Son of the Moon"), who claimed to be the Son of Ra the Sun-god. Opposition by independent-minded city-rulers to the Pharaoh's autocratic sway appears in the undated myth of how Ra grew so old and feeble that he could not even control his spittle; the Moon-goddess Isis plotted against him and Ra retaliated by casting his baleful eye on mankind—they perished in their thousands. Ra nevertheless decided to quit the ungrateful land of Egypt, whereupon Hathor, a loyal Cow-goddess, flew him up to the vault of Heaven. The myth doubtless records a compromise that consigned the High King's absolutist pretensions, supported by his wife, to the vague realm of philosophic theory. He kept the throne, but once more became, for all practical purposes, an incarnation of Osiris, consort of the Moon-goddess Isis—a yearly dying, yearly resurrected fertility godling.

Indian myth is highly complex, and swings from gross physical abandon to rigorous asceticism and fantastic visions of the spirit world. Yet it has much in common with European myth, since Aryan invasions in the second millennium B.C. changed the religious system of both continents. The invaders were nomad herdsmen, and the peoples on whom they imposed themselves as a military aristocracy were peasants. Hesiod, an early Greek poet, preserves a myth of pre-Aryan "Silver Age" heroes: "divinely created eaters of bread, utterly subject to their mothers however long they lived, who never sacrificed to the gods, but at least did not make war against one another." Hesiod put the case well: in primitive agricultural communities, recourse to war is rare, and goddessworship the rule. Herdsmen, on the contrary, tend to make fighting a profession and, perhaps because bulls dominate their herds, as rams do flocks, worship a male Sky-god typified by a bull or a ram. He sends down rain for the pastures, and they take omens from the entrails of the victims sacrificed to him.

When an invading Aryan chieftain, a tribal rainmaker, married the Moon-priestess and Queen of a conquered people, a new myth inevitably celebrated the marriage of the Sky-god and the Moon. But since the Moon-goddess was everywhere worshipped as a triad, in honor of the

Moon's three phases—waxing, full, and waning—the god split up into a complementary triad. This accounts for three-bodied Geryon, the first king of Spain; three-headed Cernunnos, the Gallic god; the Irish triad, Brian, Iuchar, and Iucharba, who married the three queenly owners of Ireland; and the invading Greek brothers Zeus, Poseidon, and Hades, who, despite great opposition, married the pre-Greek Moon-goddess in her three aspects, respectively as Queen of Heaven, Queen of the Sea, and Queen of the Underworld.

The Queen-mother's decline in religious power, and the goddesses' continual struggle to preserve their royal prerogatives, appears in the Homeric myth of how Zeus ill-treated and bullied Hera, and how she continually plotted against him. Zeus remained a Thunder-god, because Greek national sentiment forbad his becoming a Sun-god in Oriental style. But his Irish counterpart, a thunder-god named The Dagda, grew senile at last and surrendered the throne to his son Bodb the Red, a war-god—in Ireland, the magic of rainmaking was not so important as in Greece.

One constant rule of mythology is that whatever happens among the gods above reflects events on earth. Thus a father-god named "The Ancient One of the Jade" (Yu-ti) ruled the pre-revolutionary Chinese Heaven: like Prometheus, he had created human beings from clay. His wife was the Queen-mother, and their court an exact replica of the old Imperial Court at Pekin, with precisely the same functionaries: ministers, soldiers, and a numerous family of the gods' sisters, daughters, and nephews. The two annual sacrifices paid by the Emperor to the August One of the Jade—at the winter solstice when the days first lengthen and at the Spring equinox when they become longer than the nights—show him to have once been a solar god. And the theological value to the number 72 suggests that the cult started as a compromise between Moongoddess worship and Sun-god worship. 72 means three-times-three, the Moon's mystical number, multipled by two-times-two-times-two, the Sun's mystical number, and occurs in solar-lunar divine unions throughout Europe, Asia, and Africa. Chinese conservatism, by the way, kept these gods dressed in ancient court-dress, making no concessions to the new fashions which the invading dynasty from Manchuria had introduced.

In West Africa, whenever the Queen-mother, or King, appointed a new functionary at Court, the same thing happened in Heaven, by royal decree. Presumably this was also the case in China; and if we apply the principle to Greek myth, it seems reasonably certain that the account of Tirynthian Heracles' marriage to Hera's daughter Hebe, and his appointment as Celestial Porter to Zeus, commemorates the appointment of a Tirynthian prince as vizier at the court of the Mycenaean

High King, after marriage to a daughter of his Queen, the High Priestess of Argos. Probably the appointment of Ganymede, son of an early Trojan king, as cup-bearer to Zeus, had much the same significance: Zeus, in this context, would be more likely the Hittite king resident at Hattusas.

Myth, then, is a dramatic shorthand record of such matters as invasions, migrations, dynastic changes, admission of foreign cults, and social reforms. When bread was first introduced into Greece—where only beans, poppyseeds, acorns, and asphodel roots had hitherto been known—the myth of Demeter and Triptolemus sanctified its use; the same event in Wales produced a myth of "The Old White One," a Sow-goddess who went around the country with gifts of grain, bees, and her own young; for agriculture, pig breeding and beekeeping were taught to the aborigines by the same wave of neolithic invaders. Other myths sanctified the invention of wine.

A proper study of myth demands a great store of abstruse geographical, historical, and anthropological knowledge, also familiarity with the properties of plants and trees, and the habits of wild birds and beasts. Thus a Central American stone sculpture, a Toad-god sitting beneath a mushroom, means little to mythologists who have not considered the worldwide association of toads with toxic mushrooms or heard of a Mexican Mushroom-god, patron of an oracular cult; for the toxic agent is a drug, similar to that secreted in the sweat glands of frightened toads, which provides magnificent hallucinations of a heavenly kingdom.

Myths are fascinating and easily misread. Readers may smile at the picture of Queen Maya and her prenatal dream of the Buddha descending upon her disguised as a charming white baby elephant—he looks as though he would crush her to pulp—when "at once all nature rejoiced, trees burst into bloom, and musical instruments played of their own accord." In English-speaking countries, "white elephant" denotes something not only useless and unwanted, but expensive to maintain; and the picture could be misread there as indicating the Queen's grave embarrassment at the prospect of bearing a child. In India, however, the elephant symbolizes royalty—the supreme God Indra rides one—and white elephants (which are not albinos, but animals suffering from a vitiliginous skin disease) are sacred to the Sun, as white horses were for the ancient Greeks, and white oxen for the British druids. The elephant, moreover, symbolizes intelligence, and Indian writers traditionally acknowledge the Elephant-god Ganesa as their patron; he is supposed to have dictated the *Mahabharata*. [1]

Again, in English, a scallop shell is associated either with cookery or

15

1. A vast Indian epic of 200,000 lines, written before A.D. 500

with medieval pilgrims returning from a visit to the Holy Sepulcher; but Aphrodite the Greek Love-goddess employed a scallop shell for her voyages across the sea, because its two parts were so tightly hinged together as to provide a symbol of passionate sexual love—the hinge of the scallop being a principal ingredient in ancient love-philters. The lotus-flower sacred to Buddha and Osiris has five petals, which symbolize the four limbs and the head; the five senses; the five digits; and, like the pyramid, the four points of the compass and the zenith. Other esoteric meanings abound, for myths are seldom simple, and never irresponsible.

Ronald A. Knox

THE NATURE OF ENTHUSIASM

I have called this book *Enthusiasm,* not meaning thereby to name (for name it has none) the elusive thing that is its subject. I have only used a cant term, pejorative, and commonly misapplied, as a label for a tendency. And, lest I should be accused of setting out to mystify the reader, I must proceed to map out, as best I may, the course of this inquiry. There is, I would say, a recurrent situation in Church history— using the word "church" in the widest sense—where an excess of charity threatens unity. You have a clique, an *élite,* of Christian men and (more importantly) women, who are trying to live a less worldly life than their neighbors; to be more attentive to the guidance (directly felt, they would tell you) of the Holy Spirit. More and more, by a kind of fatality, you see them draw apart from their co-religionists, a hive ready to swarm. There is provocation on both sides; on the one part, cheap jokes at the expense of over-godliness, acts of stupid repression by unsympathetic authorities; on the other, contempt of the half-Christian, ominous references to old wine and new bottles,[1] to the kernel and the husk. Then, while you hold your breath and turn away your eyes in fear, the break comes; condemnation or secession, what difference does it make? A fresh name has been added to the list of Christianities.

The pattern is always repeating itself, not in outline merely but in detail. Almost always the enthusiastic movement is denounced as an innovation, yet claims to be preserving, or to be restoring, the primitive discipline of the Church. Almost always the opposition is twofold; good Christian people who do not relish an eccentric spirituality find them-

From Chapter 1 of *Enthusiasm* (1950).

1. See Matthew ix. 17.

selves in unwelcome alliance with worldlings who do not relish any spirituality at all. Almost always schism begets schism; once the instinct of discipline is lost, the movement breeds rival prophets and rival coteries, at the peril of its internal unity. Always the first fervors evaporate; prophecy dies out, and the charismatic is merged in the institutional. "The high that proved too high, the heroic for earth too hard" [2]—it is a fugal melody that runs through the centuries.

If I could have been certain of the reader's goodwill, I would have called my tendency "ultrasupernaturalism." For that is the real character of the enthusiast; he expects more evident results from the grace of God than we others. He sees what effects religion can have, does sometimes have, in transforming a man's whole life and outlook; these exceptional cases (so we are content to think them) are for him the average standard of religious achievement. He will have no "almost-Christians," no weaker brethren who plod and stumble, who (if the truth must be told) would like to have a foot in either world, whose ambition is to qualify, not to excel. He has before his eyes a picture of the early Church, visibly penetrated with supernatural influences; and nothing less will serve him for a model. Extenuate, accommodate, interpret, and he will part company with you.

Quoting a hundred texts—we also use them but with more of embarrassment—he insists that the members of his society, saved members of a perishing world, should live a life of angelic purity, of apostolic simplicity; worldly amusements, the artifices of a polite society, are not for them. Poor human nature! Every lapse that follows is marked by pitiless watchers outside the fold, creates a harvest of scandal within. Worse still, if the devout circle has cultivated a legend of its own impeccability; we shall be told, in that case, that actions which bring damnation to the worldling may be inculpable in the children of light. We must be prepared for strange alternations of rigorism and antinomianism [3] as our history unfolds itself.

Meanwhile, it must not be supposed that the new birth which the enthusiast preaches can be limited to a mere reformation of manners. It involves a new approach to religion; hitherto this has been a matter of outward forms and ordinances, now it is an affair of the heart. Sacraments are not necessarily dispensed with; but the emphasis lies on a direct personal access to the Author of our salvation, with little of intellectual background or of liturgical expression. The appeal of art and music, hitherto conceived as a ladder which carried human thought

5

2. Browning, "Abt Vogler," stanza 10.
3. Opposing theological doctrines; rigorism holds that when doubts arise as to whether a Roman Catholic law is binding, the law must always be obeyed; antinomianism holds that faith and grace exempt Christians from Old Testament law and from law and standards of morality within a culture.

upwards, is frowned upon as a barrier which interferes with the simplicity of true heart-worship. An inward experience of peace and joy is both the assurance which the soul craves for and its characteristic prayer-attitude. The strength of this personal approach is that it dominates the imagination, and presents a future world in all the colours of reality. Its weakness—but we are not concerned here to criticize—is an anthropocentric bias; not God's glory but your own salvation preoccupies the mind, with some risk of scruples, and even of despair.

But the implications of enthusiasm go deeper than this; at the root of it lies a different theology of grace. Our traditional doctrine is that grace perfects nature, elevates it to a higher pitch, so that it can bear its part in the music of eternity, but leaves it nature still. The assumption of the enthusiast is bolder and simpler; for him, grace has destroyed nature, and replaced it. The saved man has come out into a new order of being, with a new set of faculties which are proper to his state; David must not wear the panoply of Saul.[4] Especially, he decries the use of human reason as a guide to any sort of religious truth. A direct indication of the Divine will is communicated to him at every turn, if only he will consent to abandon the "arm of flesh"—Man's miserable intellect, fatally obscured by the Fall. If no oracle from heaven is forthcoming, he will take refuge in sortilege;[5] anything, to make sure that he is leaving the decision in God's hands. That God speaks to us through the intellect is a notion which he may accept on paper, but fears, in practice, to apply.

A new set of faculties, and also a new status; man saved becomes, at last, fully man. It follows that "the seed of grace," God's elect people, although they must perforce live cheek by jowl with the sons of perdition, claim another citizenship and own another allegiance. For the sake of peace and charity, they will submit themselves to every ordinance of man, but always under protest; worldly governments, being of purely human institution, have no real mandate to exercise authority, and sinful folk have no real rights, although, out of courtesy, their fancied rights must be respected. Always the enthusiast hankers after a theocracy, in which the anomalies of the present situation will be done away, and the righteous bear rule openly. Disappointed of this hope, a group of sectaries will sometimes go out into the wilderness, and set up a little theocracy of their own, like Cato's senate at Utica.[6] The American continent has more than once been the scene of such an adventure; in these days, it is the last refuge of the enthusiast.

4. David declined the armor of Saul before going out to meet Goliath, preferring as weapons only his familiar stick and sling. See I Samuel xvii. 38–40.
5. Divination, sorcery.
6. Marius Porcius Cato (95–46 B.C.), champion of the Roman republican ideal and foe of Julias Caesar, separated himself from the main body of the republicans after Caesar's decisive victory at Pharsala and withdrew with a small group of followers to Utica in north Africa.

THE READER

1. *Why does Knox start his definition of* enthusiasm *by implying that it really can't be defined?*
2. *Explain what Knox means by the expression "an excess of charity threatens unity" (p. 1182).*
3. *What kind of texts is Knox referring to at the beginning of his fourth paragraph?*
4. *Knox says he is "not concerned here to criticize" the weaknesses of enthusiasm. Explain why you think this is or isn't true.*
5. *Is Knox sympathetic to enthusiasm? How can you tell?*

THE WRITER

1. *Knox refers to enthusiasts about to form a new movement as "a hive ready to swarm." Discuss the effectiveness of this and other metaphors that Knox uses.*
2. *How would you characterize Knox's tone in such phrases as "the list of Christianities," "pitiless watchers outside the fold," "hankers after a theocracy"? How does this tone contribute to his definition of enthusiasm?*
3. *Why does Knox say he could have called* enthusiasm *"ultrasupernaturalism" if he "could have been certain of the reader's goodwill"? Is he really worried about losing the reader's goodwill?*
4. *Knox is both writing a definition and conveying his attitude toward the thing he is defining. Write two brief definitions of a similar subject, one objective, one conveying your attitude. How did the process of writing differ in each case?*

E. F. Schumacher

LEVELS OF BEING

Our task is to look at the world and see it whole.

We see what our ancestors have always seen: a great Chain of Being which seems to divide naturally into four sections—four "kingdoms," as they used to be called: mineral, plant, animal, and human. This "was, in fact, until not much more than a century ago, probably the most widely familiar conception of the general *scheme* of things, of the

Chapter 2 from *A Guide for the Perplexed* (1977).

constitutive pattern of the universe." [1] The Chain of Being can be seen as extending downward from the Highest to the lowest, or it can be seen as extending upward from the lowest to the Highest. The ancient view begins with the Divine and sees the downward Chain of Being as moving an ever-increasing distance from the Center, with a progressive loss of qualities. The modern view, largely influenced by the doctrine of evolution, tends to start with inanimate matter and to consider man the last link of the chain, as having evolved the widest range of useful qualities. For our purposes here, the direction of looking—upward or downward—is unimportant, and, in line with modern habits of thought, we shall start at the lowest level, the mineral kingdom, and consider the successive gain of qualities or *powers* as we move to the higher levels.

No one has any difficulty recognizing the astonishing and mysterious difference between a living plant and one that has died and has thus fallen to the lowest Level of Being, inanimate matter. What is this *power* that has been lost? We call it "life." Scientists tell us that we must not talk of a "life force" because no such force has ever been found to exist. Yet the *difference* between alive and dead exists. We could call it "x," to indicate something that is there to be noticed and studied but that cannot be explained. If we call the mineral level "m," we can call the plant level $m + x$. This factor x is obviously worthy of our closest attention, particularly since we are able to destroy it, although it is completely outside our ability to create it. Even if somebody could provide us with a recipe, a set of instructions, for creating life out of lifeless matter, the mysterious character of x would remain, and we would never cease to marvel that something that could do nothing is now able to extract nourishment from its environment, grow, and repro- duce itself, "true to form," as it were. There is nothing in the laws, concepts, and formulae of physics and chemistry to explain or even to describe such powers. X is something quite new and additional, and the more deeply we contemplate it, the clearer it becomes that we are faced here with what might be called an *ontological discontinuity* or, more simply, a jump in the Level of Being.

From plant to animal, there is a similar jump, a similar addition of powers, which enable the typical, fully developed animal to do things that are totally outside the range of possibilities of the typical, fully developed plant. These powers, again, are mysterious and, strictly speak- ing, nameless. We can refer to them by the letter "y," which will be the safest course, because any word label we might attach to them could lead people to think that such a designation was not merely a hint as to their nature but an adequate description. However, since we cannot talk without words, I shall attach to these mysterious powers the label

1. Arthur O. Lovejoy, *The Great Chain of Being* (New York, 1960) [Schumacher's note].

consciousness. It is easy to recognize consciousness in a dog, a cat, or a horse, if only because they can be knocked unconscious: the processes of life continue as in a plant, although the animal has lost its peculiar powers.

If the plant, in our terminology, can be called $m + x$, the animal has to be described as $m + x + y$. Again, the new factor $"y"$ is worthy of our closest attention; we are able to destroy but not to create it. Anything that we can destroy but are unable to make is, in a sense, sacred, and all our "explanations" of it do not really explain anything. Again we can say that y is something quite new and additional when compared with the level "plant"—another *ontological discontinuity,* another jump in the Level of Being.

Moving from the animal to the human level, who would seriously deny the addition, again, of new powers? What precisely they are has become a matter of controversy in modern times, but the fact that man is able to do—and is doing—innumerable things which lie totally outside the range of possibilities of even the most highly developed animals cannot be disputed and has never been denied. Man has powers of life like the plant, powers of consciousness like the animal, and evidently something more: the mysterious power $"z."$ What is it? How can it be defined? What can it be called? This power z has undoubtedly a great deal to do with the fact that man is not only able to think but is also *able to be aware of his thinking.* Consciousness and intelligence, as it were, recoil upon themselves. There is not merely a conscious being, but a being capable of being conscious of its consciousness; not merely a thinker, but a thinker capable of watching and studying his own thinking. There is something able to say "I" and *to direct consciousness* in accordance with its own purposes, a master or controller, a power at a higher level than consciousness itself. This power z, consciousness recoiling upon itself, opens up unlimited possibilities of purposeful learning, investigating, exploring, and of formulating and accumulating knowledge. What shall we call it? As it is necessary to have word labels, I shall call it *self-awareness.* We must, however, take great care always to remember that such a word label is merely (to use a Buddhist phrase) "a finger pointing to the moon." The "moon" itself remains highly mysterious and needs to be studied with the greatest patience and perseverance if we want to understand anything about man's position in the Universe.

Our initial review of the four great Levels of Being can be summed up as follows:

Man can be written $m + x + y + z$
Animal can be written $m + x + y$
Plant can be written $m + x$
Mineral can be written m

Only m is visible; x, y, and z are invisible, and they are extremely difficult to grasp, although their effects are matters of everyday experience.

If, instead of taking "minerals" as our base line and reaching the higher Levels of Being by the addition of powers, we start with the highest level directly known to us—man—we can reach the lower Levels of Being by the progressive subtraction of powers. We can then say:

Man can be written   M
Animal can be written $M - z$
Plant can be written $M - z - y$
Mineral can be written $M - z - y - x$

Such a downward scheme is easier for us to understand than the upward one, simply because it is closer to our practical experience. We know that all three factors—x, y, and z—can weaken and die away; we can in fact deliberately destroy them. Self-awareness can disappear while consciousness continues; consciousness can disappear while life continues; and life can disappear leaving an inanimate body behind. We can observe, and in a sense *feel*, the process of diminution to the point of the apparently total disappearance of self-awareness, consciousness, and life. But it is outside our power to give life to inanimate matter, to give consciousness to living matter, and finally to add the power of self-awareness to conscious beings.

What we can do ourselves, we can, in a sense, understand; what we cannot do at all, we cannot understand—not even "in a sense." Evolution as a process of the spontaneous, accidental emergence of the powers of life, consciousness, and self-awareness, out of inanimate matter, is totally incomprehensible.

For our purposes, however, there is no need to enter into such speculations at this stage. We hold fast to what we can see and experience: the Universe is as a great hierarchic structure of four markedly different Levels of Being. Each level is obviously a broad band, allowing for higher and lower beings within each band, and the precise determination of where a lower band ends and a higher band begins may sometimes be a matter of difficulty and dispute. The existence of the four kingdoms, however, is not put into question by the fact that some of the frontiers are occasionally disputed.

Physics and chemistry deal with the lowest level, "minerals." At this level, x, y, and z—life, consciousness, and self-awareness—do not exist, (or, in any case, are totally inoperative and therefore cannot be noticed). Physics and chemistry can tell us nothing, *absolutely nothing*, about them. These sciences possess no concepts relating to such powers and are incapable of describing their effects. Where there is life, there is form, *Gestalt*, which reproduces itself over and over again from seed or similar beginnings which do not possess this *Gestalt* but develop it in the process of growth. Nothing comparable is to be found in physics or chemistry.

To say that life is nothing but a property of certain peculiar combinations of atoms is like saying that Shakespeare's *Hamlet* is nothing but a property of a peculiar combination of letters. The truth is that the peculiar combination of letters is nothing but a property of Shakespeare's *Hamlet.* The French or German versions of the play "own" different combinations of letters.

The extraordinary thing about the modern "life sciences" is that they hardly ever deal with *life as such,* the factor *x,* but devote infinite attention to the study and analysis of the physicochemical body that is life's carrier. It may well be that modern science has no method for coming to grips with *life as such.* If this is so, let it be frankly admitted; there is no excuse for the pretense that life is nothing but physics and chemistry.

Nor is there any excuse for the pretense that consciousness is nothing but a property of life. To describe an animal as a physicochemical system of extreme complexity is no doubt perfectly correct, except that it misses out on the "animalness" of the animal. Some zoologists, at least, have advanced beyond this level of erudite absurdity and have developed an ability to see in animals more than complex machines. Their influence, however, is as yet deplorably small, and with the increasing "rationalization" of the modern life-style, more and more animals are being treated as if they really were nothing but "animal machines." (This is a very telling example of how philosophical theories, no matter how absurd and offensive to common sense, tend to become, after a while, "normal practice" in everyday life.)

All the "humanities," as distinct from the natural sciences, deal in one way or another with factor *y*—consciousness. But a distinction between consciousness (*y*) and self-awareness (*z*) is seldom drawn. As a result, modern thinking has become increasingly uncertain whether or not there is any "real" difference between animal and man. A great deal of study of the behavior of animals is being undertaken for the purpose of understanding the nature of man. This is analogous to studying physics with the hope of learning something about life (*x*). Naturally, since man, as it were, *contains* the three lower Levels of Being, certain things about him can be elucidated by studying minerals, plants, and animals—in fact, everything can be learned about him *except that which makes him human.* All the four constituent elements of the human person—*m, x, y,* and *z*—deserve study, but there can be little doubt about their relative importance in terms of *knowledge for the conduct of our lives.*

This importance increases in the order given above, and so do the

15

difficulty and uncertainty experienced by modern humanity. Is there really anything beyond the world of matter, of molecules and atoms and electrons and innumerable other small particles, the ever more complex combinations of which allegedly account for simply everything, from the crudest to the most sublime? Why talk about fundamental differences, "jumps" in the Chain of Being, or "ontological discontinuities" when all we can be really sure of are *differences in degree?* It is not necessary for us to battle over the question whether the palpable and overwhelmingly obvious differences between the four great Levels of Being are better seen as differences in kind or differences in degree. What has to be fully understood is that there are differences in kind, and not simply in degree, between the *powers* of life, consciousness, and self-awareness. Traces of these powers may already exist at the lower levels, although not noticeable (or not yet noticed) by man. Or maybe they are infused, so to speak, on appropriate occasions from "another world." It is not essential for us to have theories about their origin, provided we recognize their quality and, in so doing, never fail to remember that they are beyond anything our own intelligence enables us to create.

It is not unduly difficult to appreciate the difference between what is alive and what is lifeless; it is more difficult to distinguish consciousness from life; and to realize, experience, and appreciate the difference between self-awareness and consciousness (that is, between z and y) is hard indeed. The reason for the difficulty is not far to seek: While the higher comprises and therefore in a sense understands the lower, no being can understand anything higher than itself. A human being can indeed strain and stretch toward the higher and induce a process of growth through adoration, awe, wonder, admiration, and imitation, and by attaining a higher level expand its understanding * * *. But people within whom the power of self-awareness (z) is poorly developed cannot grasp it as a separate power and tend to take it as *nothing but* a slight extension of consciousness (y). Hence we are given a large number of definitions of man which make him out to be *nothing but* an exceptionally intelligent animal with a measurably larger brain, or a tool-making animal, or a political animal, or an unfinished animal, or simply a naked ape.

No doubt, people who use these terms cheerfully include themselves in their definitions—and may have some reason for doing so. For others, they sound merely inane, like defining a dog as a barking plant or a running cabbage. Nothing is more conducive to the brutalization of the modern world than the launching, in the name of science, of wrongful and degrading definitions of man, such as "the naked ape." What could one expect of such a creature, of other "naked apes," or, indeed, of oneself? When people speak of animals as "animal machines," they soon start treating them accordingly, and when they think of people as naked apes, all doors are opened to the free entry of bestiality.

"What a piece of work is a man! how noble in reason! how infinite in faculty!"[2] Because of the power of self-awareness (z), his faculties are indeed infinite; they are not narrowly determined, confined, or "programmed" as one says today. Werner Jaeger[3] expressed a profound truth in the statement that once a human potentiality is realized, it exists. It is the greatest human achievements that define man, not any average behavior or performance, and certainly not anything that can be derived from the observation of animals. "All men cannot be outstanding," says Catherine Roberts. "Yet all men, through knowledge of superior humanness, could know what it means to be a human being and that, as such, they too have a contribution to make. It is magnificent to become as human as one is able. And it requires no help from science. In addition, the very act of realising one's potentialities might constitute an advance over what has gone before."[4]

This "open-endedness" is the wonderful result of the specifically human powers of self-awareness (z), which, as distinct from the powers of life and consciousness, have nothing automatic or mechanical about them. The powers of self-awareness are *essentially* a limitless potentiality rather than an actuality. They have to be developed and "realized" by each human individual if he is to become truly human, that is to say, a *person*.

I said earlier on that man can be written

$$m + x + y + z.$$

These four elements form a sequence of increasing rarity and vulnerability. Matter (m) cannot be destroyed; to kill a body means to deprive it of x, y, and z, and the inanimate matter remains; it "returns" to the earth. Compared with inanimate matter, life is rare and precarious; in turn, compared with the ubiquitousness and tenacity of life, consciousness is even rarer and more vulnerable. Self-awareness is the rarest power of all, precious and vulnerable to the highest degree, the supreme and generally fleeting achievement of a person, present one moment and all too easily gone the next. The study of this factor z has in all ages— except the present—been the primary concern of mankind. How is it possible to study something so vulnerable and fleeting? How is it possible to study that which does the studying? How, indeed, can I study the "I" that employs the very consciousness needed for the study? * * *. Before we can turn to [these questions] directly, we shall do well to take a closer

20

2. *Hamlet* II.ii.303–304.
3. Jaeger (1888–1961): German-born scholar of literature, theology, and philosophy.
4. Catherine Roberts, *The Scientific Conscience* (Fontwell, Sussex, 1974) [Schumacher's note].

look at the four great Levels of Being: how the intervention of additional powers introduces *essential* changes, even though similarities and "correspondences" remain.

Matter (m), life (x), consciousness (y), self-awareness (z)—these four elements are ontologically—that is, in their fundamental nature—different, incomparable, incommensurable, and discontinuous. Only one of them is directly accessible to objective, scientific observation by means of our five senses. The other three are none the less known to us because we ourselves, every one of us, can verify their existence from our own inner experience.

We never find life except as living matter; we never find consciousness except as conscious living matter; and we never find self-awareness except as self-aware, conscious, living matter. The ontological differences between these four elements are analogous to the discontinuity of dimensions. A line is one-dimensional, and no elaboration of a line, no subtlety in its construction, and no complexity can ever turn it into a surface. Equally, no elaboration of a two-dimensional surface, no increase in complexity, subtlety, or size, can ever turn it into a solid. Existence in the physical world we know is attained only by three-dimensional beings. One- or two-dimensional things exist only in our minds. Analogically speaking, it might be said that only man has "real" existence in this world insofar as he alone possesses the "three dimensions" of life, consciousness, and self-awareness. In this sense, animals, with only two dimensions—life and consciousness—have but a shadowy existence, and plants, lacking the dimensions of self-awareness and consciousness, relate to a human being as a line relates to a solid. In terms of this analogy, matter, lacking the three "invisible dimensions," has no more reality than a geometrical point.

This analogy, which may seem farfetched from a logical point of view, points to an inescapable *existential* truth: The most "real" world we live in is that of our fellow human beings. Without them we should experience a sense of enormous emptiness; we could hardly be human ourselves, for we are made or marred by our relations with other people. The company of animals could console us only because, and to the extent to which, they were reminders, even caricatures, of human beings. A world without fellow human beings would be an eerie and unreal place of banishment; with neither fellow humans nor animals the world would be a dreadful wasteland, no matter how luscious its vegetation. To call it one-dimensional would not seem to be an exaggeration. Human existence in a totally inanimate environment, if it were possible, would be total emptiness, total despair. It may seem absurd to pursue such a line of thought, but it is surely not so absurd as a view which counts as "real" only inanimate matter and treats as "unreal," "subjective," and there-

fore scientifically nonexistent the invisible dimensions of life, consciousness, and self-awareness.

A simple inspection of the four great Levels of Being has led us to   25
the recognition of their four "elements"—matter, life, consciousness,
and self-awareness. It is this recognition that matters, not the precise
association of the four elements with the four Levels of Being. If the
natural scientists should come and tell us that there are some beings they
call animals in whom no trace of consciousness can be detected, it would
not be for us to argue with them. Recognition is one thing; identification
quite another. For us, only recognition is important, and we are entitled
to choose for our purpose typical and fully developed specimens from
each Level of Being. If they manifest and demonstrate most clearly the
"invisible dimensions" of life, consciousness, and self-awareness, this
demonstration is not nullified or invalidated by any difficulty of classification in other cases.

Once we have recognized the ontological gaps and discontinuities
that separate the four "elements"—m,x,y,z— from one another, we
know also that there can exist no "links" or "transitional forms": Life
is either present or absent; there cannot be a half-presence; and the same
goes for consciousness and self-awareness. Difficulties of identification
are often increased by the fact that the lower level appears to present
a kind of mimicry or counterfeit of the higher, just as an animated
puppet can at times be mistaken for a living person, or a two-dimensional picture can look like three-dimensional reality. But neither difficulties of identification and demarcation nor possibilities of deception
and error can be used as arguments against the existence of the four
great Levels of Being, exhibiting the four "elements" we have called
Matter, Life, Consciousness, and Self-awareness. These four "elements"
are four irreducible mysteries, which need to be most carefully observed
and studied, but which cannot be explained, let alone "explained away."

In a hierarchic structure, the higher does not merely possess powers
that are additional to and exceed those possessed by the lower; it also
has power *over* the lower: it has the power to organize the lower and use
it for its own purposes. Living beings can organize and utilize inanimate
matter, conscious beings can utilize life, and self-aware beings can utilize
consciousness. Are there powers that are higher than self-awareness? Are
there Levels of Being above the human? At this stage in our investigation we need do no more than register the fact that the great majority
of mankind throughout its known history, until very recently, has been
unshakenly convinced that the Chain of Being extends upward beyond
man. This universal conviction of mankind is impressive for both its
duration and its intensity. Those individuals of the past whom we still
consider the wisest and greatest not only shared this belief but considered it of all truths the most important and the most profound.

John Donne

LET ME WITHER

Let me wither and wear out mine age in a discomfortable, in an unwholesome, in a penurious prison, and so pay my debts with my bones and recompense the wastefulness of my youth with the beggary of mine age. Let me wither in a spital[1] under sharp and foul and infamous diseases, and so recompense the wantonness of my youth with that loathsomeness in mine age. Yet if God withdraw not his spiritual blessings, his grace, his patience; if I can call my suffering his doing, my passion[2] his action; all this that is temporal is but a caterpillar got into one corner of my garden, but a mildew fallen upon one acre of my corn. The body of all, the substance of all, is safe as long as the soul is safe.

But when I shall trust to that which we call a good spirit and God shall deject[3] and impoverish and evacuate[4] that spirit; when I shall rely upon a moral constancy and God shall shake and enfeeble and enervate, destroy and demolish that constancy; when I shall think to refresh myself in the serenity and sweet air of a good conscience and God shall call up the damps and vapors of hell itself and spread a cloud of diffidence[5] and an impenetrable crust of desperation upon my conscience; when health shall fly from me, and I shall lay hold upon riches to succor me and comfort me in my sickness, and riches shall fly from me and I shall snatch after favor and good opinion to comfort me in my poverty; when even this good opinion shall leave me and calumnies and misinformations shall prevail against me; when I shall need peace because there is none but thou, O Lord, that should stand for me, and then shall find that all the wounds that I have come from thy hand, all the arrows that stick in me from thy quiver; when I shall see that because I have given myself to my corrupt nature thou hast changed thine, and because I am all evil towards thee, therefore thou hast given over being good towards me: when it comes to this height, that the fever is not in the humors but in the spirits,[6] that mine enemy is not an imaginary enemy, Fortune, nor a transitory enemy, Malice in great persons, but a real and an irresistible and an inexorable and an everlasting enemy, the Lord of

From a sermon delivered 1625–40.

1. Hospital.
2. State of being acted upon.
3. Cast down.
4. Make empty.
5. Distrust.

6. Not merely in the physical fluids of the body but even in those more refined vapors thought to permeate the blood and organs and to serve as a link between body and soul.

Hosts himself, the Almighty God himself—the Almighty God himself only knows the weight of this affliction, and except[7] he put in that *pondus gloriae,* that exceeding weight of an eternal glory, with his own hand into the other scale, we are weighed down, we are swallowed up irreparably, irrevocably, irrecoverably, irremediably.

7. Unless.

THE READER

1. *Donne is perhaps more famous as a poet than as a preacher, yet all that any author writes will in one way or another bear the stamp of his thought and personality. Read the following passage from a poem by Donne, and compare it with the sermon. Does the conception of God suggested in the poem resemble that in the sermon? Does the poem accomplish any of the same purposes as the sermon? Is the sermon "poetic" in any way? What differences arise from the fact that in the sermon Donne is speaking to a congregation, in the poem he is addressing God?*

> Batter my heart, three person'd God; for, you
> As yet but knocke, breathe, shine, and seeke to mend.
> That I may rise, and stand, o'erthrow mee, and bend
> Your force, to breake, blowe, burn and make me new.
> I, like an usurpt towne, to another due,
> Labour to admit you, but Oh, to no end,
> Reason your viceroy in mee, mee should defend,
> But is captiv'd, and proves weake or untrue.

2. *How far is Donne's sermon intelligible to a reader or hearer who is not a Christian?*

THE WRITER

1. *Rewrite Donne's first paragraph, substituting direct statements for all the metaphors. Compare your revision with Donne's original.*
2. *Write a brief essay comparing Donne's sermon to the above poem (see question 1, "The Reader," above).*

Langston Hughes

SALVATION

I was saved from sin when I was going on thirteen. But not really saved. It happened like this. There was a big revival at my Auntie Reed's church. Every night for weeks there had been much preaching, singing, praying, and shouting, and some very hardened sinners had been brought to Christ, and the membership of the church had grown by leaps and bounds. Then just before the revival ended, they held a special meeting for children, "to bring the young lambs to the fold." My aunt spoke of it for days ahead. That night I was escorted to the front row and placed on the mourners' bench with all the other young sinners, who had not yet been brought to Jesus.

My aunt told me that when you were saved you saw a light, and something happened to you inside! And Jesus came into your life! And God was with you from then on! She said you could see and hear and feel Jesus in your soul. I believed her. I had heard a great many old people say the same thing and it seemed to me they ought to know. So I sat there calmly in the hot, crowded church, waiting for Jesus to come to me.

The preacher preached a wonderful rhythmical sermon, all moans and shouts and lonely cries and dire pictures of hell, and then he sang a song about the ninety and nine safe in the fold, but one little lamb was left out in the cold. Then he said: "Won't you come? Won't you come to Jesus? Young lambs, won't you come?" And he held out his arms to all us young sinners there on the mourners' bench. And the little girls cried. And some of them jumped up and went to Jesus right away. But most of us just sat there.

A great many old people came and knelt around us and prayed, old women with jet-black faces and braided hair, old men with work-gnarled hands. And the church sang a song about the lower lights are burning, some poor sinners to be saved. And the whole building rocked with prayer and song.

Still I kept waiting to *see* Jesus.

Finally all the young people had gone to the altar and were saved, but one boy and me. He was a rounder's[1] son named Westley. Westley and I were surrounded by sisters and deacons praying. It was very hot in the

From *The Big Sea* (1940).

1. Loafer's, bum's.

church, and getting late now. Finally Westley said to me in a whisper: "God damn! I'm tired o' sitting here. Let's get up and be saved." So he got up and was saved.

Then I was left all alone on the mourners' bench. My aunt came and knelt at my knees and cried, while prayers and songs swirled all around me in the little church. The whole congregation prayed for me alone, in a mightly wail of moans and voices. And I kept waiting serenely for Jesus, waiting, waiting—but he didn't come. I wanted to see him, but nothing happened to me. Nothing! I wanted something to happen to me, but nothing happened.

I heard the songs and the minister saying: "Why don't you come? My dear child, why don't you come to Jesus? Jesus is waiting for you. He wants you. Why don't you come? Sister Reed, what is this child's name?"

"Langston," my aunt sobbed.

"Langston, why don't you come? Why don't you come and be saved?   10
Oh, Lamb of God! Why don't you come?"

Now it was really getting late. I began to be ashamed of myself, holding everything up so long. I began to wonder what God thought about Westley, who certainly hadn't seen Jesus either, but who was now sitting proudly on the platform, swinging his knickerbockered legs and grinning down at me, surrounded by deacons and old women on their knees praying. God had not struck Westley dead for taking his name in vain or for lying in the temple. So I decided that maybe to save further trouble, I'd better lie, too, and say that Jesus had come, and get up and be saved.

So I got up.

Suddenly the whole room broke into a sea of shouting, as they saw me rise. Waves of rejoicing swept the place. Women leaped in the air. My aunt threw her arms around me. The minister took me by the hand and led me to the platform.

When things quieted down, in a hushed silence, punctuated by a few ecstatic "Amens," all the new young lambs were blessed in the name of God. Then joyous singing filled the room.

That night, for the last time in my life but one—for I was a big   15
boy twelve years old—I cried. I cried, in bed alone, and couldn't stop. I buried my head under the quilts, but my aunt heard me. She woke up and told my uncle I was crying because the Holy Ghost had come into my life, and because I had seen Jesus. But I was really crying because I couldn't bear to tell her that I had lied, that I had deceived everybody in the church, and I hadn't seen Jesus, and that now I didn't believe there was a Jesus any more, since he didn't come to help me.

THE READER

1. *When the preacher held out his arms to the young sinners, Hughes says, the little girls cried and some of them jumped up and went to Jesus right away. Is this a sexist observation? Does the fact that this was published in 1940 affect your answer?*
2. *Hughes obviously does not accept his Auntie Reed's explanation for his behavior. It is pretty hard to get around his explanation of why he cried, but when it comes to his salvation at the meeting, can her explanation be disproved?*

THE WRITER

1. *What are the signs in the first two paragraphs that point to the outcome?*
2. *What is Hughes' attitude toward Westley? Toward Auntie Reed?*
3. *This essay is written simply, with a careful regard for the facts. Replace Hughes' last paragraph with a plausible alternative that presents a different conclusion.*

Paul Tillich

THE RIDDLE OF INEQUALITY

For to him who has will more be given; and from him
who has not, even what he has will be taken away.

—MARK iv. 25

One day a learned colleague called me up and said to me with angry excitement: "There is a saying in the New Testament which I consider to be one of the most immoral and unjust statements ever made!" And then he started quoting our text: "To him who has will more be given," and his anger increased when he continued: "and from him who has not, even what he has will be taken away." We all, I think, feel offended with him. And we cannot easily ignore the offense by suggesting what *he* suggested—that the words may be due to a misunderstanding of the disciples. It appears at least four times in the gospels with great emphasis. And even more, we can clearly see that the writers of the gospels felt exactly as we do. For them it was a stumbling block, which they tried to interpret in different ways. Probably none of these explanations satisfied them fully, for with this saying of Jesus, we are confronted immediately with the greatest and perhaps most painful riddle of life, that of

From *The Eternal Now* (1963).

the inequality of all beings. We certainly cannot hope to solve it when neither the Bible nor any other of the great religions and philosophies was able to do so. But we can do two things: We can show the breadth and the depth of the riddle of inequality and we can try to find a way to live with it, even if it is unsolved.

I

If we hear the words, "to him who has will more be given," we ask ourselves: What *do* we have? And then we may find that much is given to us in terms of external goods, of friends, of intellectual gifts and even of a comparatively high moral level of action. So we can expect that more will be given to us, while we must expect that those who are lacking in all that will lose the little they already have. Even further, according to Jesus' parable, the one talent[1] they have will be given to us who have five or ten talents. We shall be richer because they will be poorer. We may cry out against such an injustice. But we cannot deny that life confirms it abundantly. We cannot deny it, but we can ask the question, do we *really* have what we believe we have so that it cannot be taken from us? It is a question full of anxiety, confirmed by a version of our text rendered by Luke. "From him who has not, even what he *thinks* that he has will be taken away." Perhaps our having of those many things is not the kind of having which is increased. Perhaps the having of few things by the poor ones is the kind of having which makes them grow. In the parable of the talents, Jesus confirms this. Those talents which are used, even with a risk of losing them, are those which we really have; those which we try to preserve without using them for growth are those which we do not really have and which are being taken away from us. They slowly disappear, and suddenly we feel that we have lost these talents, perhaps forever.

Let us apply this to our own life, whether it is long or short. In the memory of all of us many things appear which we had without having them and which were taken away from us. Some of them became lost because of the tragic limitations of life; we had to sacrifice them in order to make other things grow. We all were given childish innocence; but innocence cannot be used and increased. The growth of our lives is possible only because we have sacrificed the original gift of innocence. Nevertheless, sometimes there arises in us a melancholy longing for a purity which has been taken from us. We all were given youthful enthusiasm for many things and aims. But this also cannot be used and increased. Most of the objects of our early enthusiasm must be sacrificed for a few, and the few must be approached with soberness. No maturity is possible without this sacrifice. Yet often a melancholy longing for the

1. A Middle Eastern coin at the time of Christ (see p. 1157).

lost possibilities and enthusiasm takes hold of us. Innocence and youthful enthusiasm: we had them and had them not. Life itself demanded
that they were taken from us.

But there are other things which we had and which were taken from
us, because we let them go through our own guilt. Some of us had a deep
sensitivity for the wonder of life as it is revealed in nature. Slowly under
the pressure of work and social life and the lure of cheap pleasures, we
lose the wonder of our earlier years when we felt intense joy and the
presence of the mystery of life through the freshness of the young day
or the glory of the dying day, the majesty of the mountains or the infinity
of the sea, a flower breaking through the soil or a young animal in the
perfection of its movements. Perhaps we try to produce such feelings
again, but we are empty and do not succeed. We had it and had it not,
and it has been taken from us.

Others had the same experience with music, poetry, the great novels
and plays. One wanted to devour all of them, one lived in them and
created for oneself a life above the daily life. We *had* all this and did
not have it; we did not let it grow; our love towards it was not strong
enough and so it was taken from us.

Many, especially in this group, remember a time in which the desire
to learn to solve the riddles of the universe, to find truth has been the
driving force in their lives. They came to college and university, not in
order to buy their entrance ticket into the upper middle classes or in
order to provide for the preconditions of social and economic success,
but they came, driven by the desire for knowledge. They had something
and more could have been given to them. But in reality they did not
have it. They did not make it grow and so it was taken from them and
they finished their academic work in terms of expediency and indifference towards truth. Their love for truth has left them and in some
moments they are sick in their hearts because they realize that what they
have lost they may never get back.

We all know that any deeper relation to a human being needs watchfulness and growth, otherwise it is taken away from us. And we cannot
get it back. This is a form of having and not having which is the root
of innumerable human tragedies. We all know about them. And there
is another, the most fundamental kind of having and not having—our
having and losing God. Perhaps we were rich towards God in our
childhood and beyond it. We may remember the moments in which we
felt his ultimate presence. We may remember prayers with an overflowing heart, the encounter with the holy in word and music and holy
places. We had communication with God; but it was taken from us
because we had it and had it not. We did not let it grow, and so it slowly
disappeared leaving an empty space. We became unconcerned, cynical,
indifferent, not because we doubted about our religious traditions—such

doubt belongs to being rich towards God—but because we turned away from that which once concerned us infinitely.

Such thoughts are a first step in approaching the riddle of inequality. Those who have, receive more if they really have it, if they use it and make it grow. And those who have not, lose what they have because they never had it really.

II

But the question of inequality is not yet answered. For one now asks: Why do some receive more than others in the very beginning, before there is even the possibility of using or wasting our talents? Why does the one servant receive five talents and the other two and the third one? Why is the one born in the slums and the other in a well-to-do suburban family? It does not help to answer that of those to whom much is given much is demanded and little of those to whom little is given. For it is just this inequality of original gifts, internal and external, which arouses our question. Why is it given to one human being to gain so much more out of his being human than to another one? Why is so much given to the one that much *can* be asked of him, while to the other one little is given and little *can* be asked? If this question is asked, not only about individual men but also about classes, races and nations, the everlasting question of political inequality arises, and with it the many ways appear in which men have tried to abolish inequality. In every revolution and in every war, the will to solve the riddle of inequality is a driving force. But neither war nor revolution can remove it. Even if we imagine that in an indefinite future most social inequalities are conquered, three things remain: the inequality of talents in body and mind, the inequality created by freedom and destiny, and the fact that all generations before the time of such equality would be excluded from its blessings. This would be the greatest possible inequality! No! In face of one of the deepest and most torturing problems of life, it is unpermittably shallow and foolish to escape into a social dreamland. We have to live now; we have to live this our life, and we must face today the riddle of inequality.

Let us not confuse the riddle of inequality with the fact that each of us is a unique incomparable self. Certainly our being individuals belongs to our dignity as men. It is given to us and must be used and intensified and not drowned in the gray waters of conformity which threaten us today. One should defend every individuality and the uniqueness of every human self. But one should not believe that this is a way of solving the riddle of inequality. Unfortunately, there are social and political reactionaries who use this confusion in order to justify social injustice. They are at least as foolish as the dreamers of a future removal of inequality. Whoever has seen hospitals, prisons, sweatshops, battlefields, houses for the insane, starvation, family tragedies, moral aberrations should be cured from any confusion of the gift of individuality with the riddle of inequality. He should be cured from any feelings of easy consolation.

III

And now we must make the third step in our attempt to penetrate the riddle of inequality and ask: Why do some use and increase what was given to them, while others do not, so that it is taken from them? Why does God say to the prophet in our Old Testament lesson that the ears and eyes of a nation are made insensible for the divine message?

Is it enough to answer: Because some use their freedom responsibly and do what they ought to do while others fail through their own guilt? Is this answer, which seems so obvious, sufficient? Now let me first say that it *is* sufficient if we apply it to ourselves. Each of us must consider the increase or the loss of what is given to him as a matter of his own responsibility. Our conscience tells us that we cannot put the blame for our losses on anybody or anything else than ourselves.

But if we look at others, this answer is not sufficient. On the contrary: If we applied the judgment which we *must* apply to anyone else we would be like the Pharisee in Jesus' parable.[2] You cannot tell somebody who comes to you in distress about himself: Use what has been given to you; for he may come to you just because he is unable to do so! And you cannot tell those who are in despair about what they are: Be something else; for this is just what despair means—the inability of getting rid of oneself. You cannot tell those who did not conquer the destructive influences of their surroundings and were driven into crime and misery that they should have been stronger; for it was just of this strength they had been deprived by heritage or environment. Certainly they all are men, and to all of them freedom is given; but they all are also subject to destiny. It is not up to us to condemn them because they were free, as it is not up to us to excuse them because they were under their destiny. We cannot judge them. And when we judge ourselves, we must be conscious that even this is not the last word, but that we like them are under an ultimate judgment. In it the riddle of inequality is eternally answered. But this answer is not ours. It is our predicament that we must ask. And we ask with an uneasy conscience. Why are they in misery, why not we? Thinking of some who are near to us, we can ask: Are we partly responsible? But even if we are, it does not solve the riddle of inequality. The uneasy conscience asks about the farthest as well as about the nearest: Why they, why not we?

2. Praying in the temple, the Pharisee said, "God, I thank thee, that I am not as other men are, extortioners, unjust, adulterers" (Luke xviii.11).

Why has my child, or any of millions and millions of children, died before even having a chance to grow out of infancy? Why is my child, or any child, born feeble-minded or crippled? Why has my friend or relative, or anybody's friend or relative, disintegrated in his mind and lost both his freedom and his destiny? Why has my son or daughter, gifted as I believe with many talents, wasted them and been deprived of them? And why does this happen to any parent at all? Why have this boy's or this girl's creative powers been broken by a tyrannical father or by a possessive mother?

In all these questions it is not the question of our own misery which   15
we ask. It is not the question: Why has this happened to *me?*

It is not the question of Job which God answers by humiliating him and then by elevating him into communion with him.[3] It is not the old and urgent question: Where is the divine justice, where is the divine love towards me? But it is almost the opposite question: Why has this *not* happened to me, why has it happened to the other one, to the innumerable other ones to whom not even the power of Job is given to accept the divine answer? Why—and Jesus has asked the same question—are many called and few elected?

He does not answer; he only states that this is the human predicament. Shall we therefore cease to ask and humbly accept the fact of a divine judgment which condemns most human beings away from the community with him into despair and self-destruction? Can we accept the eternal victory of judgment over love? We cannot; and nobody ever could, even if he preached and threatened in these terms. As long as he could not see himself with complete certainty as eternally rejected, his preaching and threatening would be self-deceiving. And who could see himself eternally rejected?

But if this is not the solution of the riddle of inequality at its deepest level, can we trespass the boundaries of the Christian tradition and listen to those who tell us that this life does not decide about our eternal destiny? There will be occasions in other lives, as our present life is determined by previous ones and what we have achieved or wasted in them. It is a serious doctrine and not completely strange to Christianity. But if we don't know and never will know what each of us has been in the previous or future lives, then it is not really *our* destiny which develops from life to life, but in each life it is the destiny of someone else. This answer also does not solve the riddle of inequality.

There is no answer at all if we ask about the temporal and eternal destiny of the single being separated from the destiny of the whole. Only

3. Job, one of God's favored servants, was stricken with afflictions. His question, very briefly, was "Why?" God's answer was to remind Job of how powerless man was in comparison with God, and to refuse to explain His actions. After accepting this pronouncement, Job was elevated again into God's favor.

in the unity of all beings in time and eternity can a humanly possible answer to the riddle of inequality be found. *Humanly* possible does not mean an answer which removes the riddle of inequality, but an answer with which we can live.

There is an ultimate unity of all beings, rooted in the divine life from which they come and to which they go. All beings, nonhuman as well as human, participate in it. And therefore they all participate in each other. We participate in each other's having and we participate in each other's not-having. If we become aware of this unity of all beings, something happens. The fact that others have-not changes in every moment the character of my having: It undercuts its security, it drives me beyond myself, to understand, to give, to share, to help. The fact that others fall into sin, crime and misery changes the character of the grace which is given to me: It makes me realize my own hidden guilt, it shows to me that those who suffer for their sin and crime, suffer also for me; for I am guilty of their guilt—at least in the desire of my heart—and ought to suffer as they do. The awareness that others who *could* have become fully developed human beings and never *have*, changes my state of full humanity. Their early death, their early or late disintegration, makes my life and my health a continuous risk, a dying which is not yet death, a disintegration which is not yet destruction. In every death which we encounter, something of us dies; in every disease which we encounter, something of us tends to disintegrate.

Can we live with this answer? We can to the degree in which we are liberated from the seclusion within ourselves. But nobody can be liberated from himself unless he is grasped by the power of that which is present in everyone and everything—the eternal from which we come and to which we go, which gives us to ourselves and which liberates us *from* ourselves. It is the greatness and the heart of the Christian message that God—as manifest in the Cross of the Christ—participates totally in the dying child, in the condemned criminal, in the disintegrating mind, in the starving one and in him who rejects him. There is no extreme human condition into which the divine presence would not reach. This is what the Cross, the most extreme of all human conditions, tells us. The riddle of inequality cannot be solved on the level of our separation from each other. It is eternally solved in the divine participation in all of us and every being. The certainty of the divine participation gives us the courage to stand the riddle of inequality, though finite minds cannot solve it. Amen.

Gilbert Highet

THE MYSTERY OF ZEN

The mind need never stop growing. Indeed, one of the few experiences which never pall is the experience of watching one's own mind, and observing how it produces new interests, responds to new stimuli, and develops new thoughts, apparently without effort and almost independently of one's own conscious control. I have seen this happen to myself a hundred times; and every time it happens again, I am equally fascinated and astonished.

Some years ago a publisher sent me a little book for review. I read it, and decided it was too remote from my main interests and too highly specialized. It was a brief account of how a young German philosopher living in Japan had learned how to shoot with a bow and arrow, and how this training had made it possible for him to understand the esoteric doctrines of the Zen sect of Buddhism. Really, what could be more alien to my own life, and to that of everyone I knew, than Zen Buddhism and Japanese archery? So I thought, and put the book away.

Yet I did not forget it. It was well written, and translated into good English. It was delightfully short, and implied much more than it said. Although its theme was extremely odd, it was at least highly individual; I had never read anything like it before or since. It remained in my mind. Its name was *Zen in the Art of Archery,* its author Eugen Herrigel, its publisher Pantheon of New York. One day I took it off the shelf and read it again; this time it seemed even stranger than before and even more unforgettable. Now it began to cohere with other interests of mine. Something I had read of the Japanese art of flower arrangement seemed to connect with it; and then, when I wrote an essay on the peculiar Japanese poems called *haiku,* other links began to grow. Finally I had to read the book once more with care, and to go through some other works which illuminated the same subject. I am still grappling with the theme; I have not got anywhere near understanding it fully; but I have learned a good deal, and I am grateful to the little book which refused to be forgotten.

The author, a German philosopher, got a job teaching philosophy at the University of Tokyo (apparently between the wars), and he did what Germans in foreign countries do not usually do: he determined to adapt himself and to learn from his hosts. In particular, he had always been interested in mysticism—which, for every earnest philosopher, poses a

From *Talent and Geniuses* (1957).

problem that is all the more inescapable because it is virtually insoluble. Zen Buddhism is not the only mystical doctrine to be found in the East, but it is one of the most highly developed and certainly one of the most difficult to approach. Herrigel knew that there were scarcely any books which did more than skirt edge of the subject, and that the best of all books on Zen (those by the philosopher D. T. Suzuki) constantly emphasize that Zen can never be learned from books, can never be studied as we can study other disciplines such as logic or mathematics. Therefore he began to look for a Japanese thinker who could teach him directly.

5   At once he met with embarrassed refusals. His Japanese friends explained that he would gain nothing from trying to discuss Zen as a philosopher, that its theories could not be spread out for analysis by a detached mind, and in fact that the normal relationship of teacher and pupil simply did not exist within the sect, because the Zen masters felt it useless to explain things stage by stage and to argue about the various possible interpretations of their doctrine. Herrigel had read enough to be prepared for this. He replied that he did not want to dissect the teachings of the school, because he knew that would be useless. He wanted to become a Zen mystic himself. (This was highly intelligent of him. No one could really penetrate into Christian mysticism without being a devout Christian; no one could appreciate Hindu mystical doctrine without accepting the Hindu view of the universe.) At this, Herrigel's Japanese friends were more forthcoming. They told him that the best way, indeed the only way, for a European to approach Zen mysticism was to learn one of the arts which exemplified it. He was a fairly good rifle shot, so he determined to learn archery; and his wife cooperated with him by taking lessons in painting and flower arrangement. How any philosopher could investigate a mystical doctrine by learning to shoot with a bow and arrow and watching his wife arrange flowers, Herrigel did not ask. He had good sense.

A Zen master who was a teacher of archery agreed to take him as a pupil. The lessons lasted six years, during which he practiced every single day. There are many difficult courses of instruction in the world: the Jesuits, violin virtuosi, Talmudic scholars, all have long and hard training, which in one sense never comes to an end; but Herrigel's training in archery equaled them all in intensity. If I were trying to learn archery, I should expect to begin by looking at a target and shooting arrows at it. He was not even allowed to aim at a target for the first four years. He had to begin by learning how to hold the bow and arrow, and then how to release the arrow; this took ages. The Japanese bow is not like our sporting bow, and the stance of the archer in Japan is different from ours. We hold the bow at shoulder level, stretch our left arm out ahead, pull the string and the nocked arrow to a point either below the chin or sometimes past the right ear, and then shoot. The Japanese hold the bow above the head, and then pull the hands apart to left and right until the left hand comes down to eye level and the right hand comes to rest above the right shoulder; then there is a pause, during which the bow is held at full stretch, with the tip of the three-foot arrow projecting only a few inches beyond the bow; after that, the arrow is loosed. When Herrigel tried this, even without aiming, he found it was almost impossible. His hands trembled. His legs stiffened and grew cramped. His breathing became labored. And of course he could not possibly aim. Week after week he practiced this, with the Master watching him carefully and correcting his strained attitude; week after week he made no progress whatever. Finally he gave up and told his teacher that he could not learn: it was absolutely impossible for him to draw the bow and loose the arrow.

To his astonishment, the Master agreed. He said, "Certainly you cannot. It is because you are not breathing correctly. You must learn to breathe in a steady rhythm, keeping your lungs full most of the time, and drawing in one rapid inspiration with each stage of the process, as you grasp the bow, fit the arrow, raise the bow, draw, pause, and loose the shot. If you do, you will both grow stronger and be able to relax." To prove this, he himself drew his massive bow and told his pupil to feel the muscles of his arms: they were perfectly relaxed, as though he were doing no work whatever.

Herrigel now started breathing exercises; after some time he combined the new rhythm of breathing with the actions of drawing and shooting; and, much to his astonishment, he found that the whole thing, after this complicated process, had become much easier. Or rather, not easier, but different. At times it became quite unconscious. He says himself that he felt he was not breathing, but being breathed; and in time he felt that the occasional shot was not being dispatched by him, but shooting itself. The bow and arrow were in charge; he had become merely a part of them.

All this time, of course, Herrigel did not even attempt to discuss Zen doctrine with his Master. No doubt he knew that he was approaching it, but he concentrated solely on learning how to shoot. Every stage which he surmounted appeared to lead to another stage even more difficult. It took him months to learn how to loosen the bowstring. The problem was this. If he gripped the string and arrowhead tightly, either he froze, so that his hands were slowly pulled together and the shot was wasted, or else he jerked, so that the arrow flew up into the air or down into the ground; and if he was relaxed, then the bowstring and arrow simply *leaked* out of his grasp before he could reach full stretch, and the arrow went nowhere. He explained this problem to the Master. The Master understood perfectly well. He replied, "You must hold the drawn bowstring like a child holding a grownup's finger. You know how firmly a child grips; and yet when it lets go, there is not the slightest jerk— because the child does not think of itself, it is not self-conscious, it does not say, 'I will now let go and do something else,' it merely acts instinctively. That is what you must learn to do. Practice, practice, and practice, and then the string will loose itself at the right moment. The shot will come as effortlessly as snow slipping from a leaf." Day after day, week after week, month after month, Herrigel practiced this; and then, after one shot, the Master suddenly bowed and broke off the lesson. He said "Just then it shot. Not you, but *it.*" And gradually thereafter more and more right shots achieved themselves; the young philosopher forgot himself, forgot that he was learning archery for some other purpose, forgot even that he was practicing archery, and became part of that unconsciously active complex, the bow, the string, the arrow, and the man.

10   Next came the target. After four years, Herrigel was allowed to shoot at the target. But he was strictly forbidden to aim at it. The Master explained that even he himself did not aim; and indeed, when he shot, he was so absorbed in the act, so selfless and unanxious, that his eyes were almost closed. It was difficult, almost impossible, for Herrigel to believe that such shooting could ever be effective; and he risked insulting the Master by suggesting that he ought to be able to hit the target blindfolded. But the Master accepted the challenge. That night, after a cup of tea and long meditation, he went into the archery hall, put on the lights at one end and left the target perfectly dark, with only a thin taper burning in front of it. Then, with habitual grace and precision, and with that strange, almost sleepwalking, selfless confidence that is the heart of Zen, he shot two arrows into the darkness. Herrigel went out to collect them. He found that the first had gone to the heart of the bull's eye, and that the second had actually hit the first arrow and splintered it. The Master showed no pride. He said, "Perhaps, with unconscious memory of the position of the target, *I* shot the first arrow; but the second arrow? *It* shot the second arrow, and *it* brought it to the center of the target."

At last Herrigel began to understand. His progress became faster and faster; easier, too. Perfect shots (perfect because perfectly unconscious) occurred at almost every lesson; and finally, after six years of incessant training, in a public display he was awarded the diploma. He needed no further instruction: he had himself become a Master. His wife meanwhile had become expert both in painting and in the arrangement of flowers—two of the finest of Japanese arts. (I wish she could be persuaded to write a companion volume, called *Zen in the Art of Flower Arrangement;* it would have a wider general appeal than her husband's work.) I gather also from a hint or two in his book that she had taken part in the archery lessons. During one of the most difficult periods in Herrigel's training, when his Master had practically refused to continue teaching him—because Herrigel had tried to cheat by *consciously* opening his hand at the moment of loosing the arrow— his wife had advised him against that solution, and sympathized with him when it was rejected. She in her own way had learned more quickly than he, and reached the final point together with him. All their effort had not been in vain: Herrigel and his wife had really acquired a new and valuable kind of wisdom. Only at this point, when he was about to abandon his lessons forever, did his Master treat him almost as an equal and hint at the innermost doctrines of Zen Buddhism. Only hints he gave; and yet, for the young philosopher who had now become a mystic, they were enough. Herrigel understood the doctrine, not with his logical mind, but with his entire being. He at any rate had solved the mystery of Zen.

Without going through a course of training as absorbing and as complete as Herrigel's, we can probably never penetrate the mystery. The doctrine of Zen cannot be analyzed from without: it must be lived.

But although it cannot be analyzed, it can be hinted at. All the hints that the adherents of this creed give us are interesting. Many are fantastic; some are practically incomprehensible, and yet unforgettable. Put together, they take us toward a way of life which is utterly impossible for westerners living in a western world, and nevertheless has a deep fascination and contains some values which we must respect.

The word Zen means "meditation." (It is the Japanese word, corresponding to the Chinese Ch'an and the Hindu Dhyana.) It is the central idea of a special sect of Buddhism which flourished in China during the Sung period (between *a.d.* 1000 and 1300) and entered Japan in the twelfth century. Without knowing much about it, we might be certain that the Zen sect was a worthy and noble one, because it produced a quantity of highly distinguished art, specifically painting. And if we knew anything about Buddhism itself, we might say that Zen goes closer than other sects to the heart of Buddha's teaching: because Buddha was trying to found, not a religion with temples and rituals, but a way of life based on meditation. However, there is something eccentric about the Zen life which is hard to trace in Buddha's teaching; there is an active energy which he did not admire, there is a rough grasp on reality which he himself eschewed, there is something like a sense of humor, which he rarely displayed. The gravity and serenity of the Indian preacher are transformed, in Zen, to the earthy liveliness of Chinese and Japanese sages. The lotus brooding calmly on the water has turned into a knotted tree covered with spring blossoms.

15   In this sense, "meditation" does not mean what we usually think of when we say a philosopher meditates: analysis of reality, a long-sustained effort to solve problems of religion and ethics, the logical dissection of the universe. It means something not divisive, but whole; not schematic, but organic; not long-drawn-out, but immediate. It means something more like our words "intuition" and "realization." It means a way of life in which there is no division between thought and action; none of the painful gulf, so well known to all of us, between the unconscious and the conscious mind; and no absolute distinction between the self and the external world, even between the various parts of the external world and the whole.

     When the German philosopher took six years of lessons in archery in order to approach the mystical significance of Zen, he was not given direct philosophical instruction. He was merely shown how to breathe, how to hold and loose the bowstring, and finally how to shoot in such a way that the bow and arrow used him as an instrument. There are many such stories about Zen teachers. The strangest I know is one about a fencing master who undertook to train a young man in the art of the sword. The relationship of teacher and pupil is very important, almost sacred, in the Far East; and the pupil hardly ever thinks of leaving a master or objecting to his methods, however extraordinary they may seem. Therefore this young fellow did not at first object when he was made to act as a servant, drawing water, sweeping floors, gathering wood for the fire, and cooking. But after some time he asked for more direct instruction. The master agreed to give it, but produced no swords. The routine went on just as before, except that every now and then the master would strike the young man with a stick. No matter what he was doing, sweeping the floor or weeding in the garden, a blow would descend on him apparently out of nowhere; he had always to be on the alert, and yet he was constantly receiving unexpected cracks on the head or shoulders. After some months of this, he saw his master stooping over a boiling pot full of vegetables; and he thought he would have his revenge. Silently he lifted a stick and brought it down; but without any effort, without even a glance in his direction, his master parried the blow with the lid of the cooking pot. At last, the pupil began to understand the instinctive alertness, the effortless perception and avoidance of danger, in which his master had been training him. As soon as he had achieved it, it was child's play for him to learn the management of the sword: he could parry every cut and turn every slash without anxiety, until his opponent, exhausted, left an opening for his counterattack. (The same principle was used by the elderly samurai for selecting his comrades in the Japanese motion picture *The Magnificent Seven.*)

     These stories show that Zen meditation does not mean sitting and thinking. On the contrary, it means acting with as little thought as possible. The fencing master trained his pupil to guard against every attack with the same immediate, instinctive rapidity with which our eyelid closes over our eye when something threatens it. His work was aimed at breaking down the wall between thought and act, at completely fusing body and senses and mind so that they might all work together rapidly and effortlessly. When a Zen artist draws a picture, he does it in a rhythm almost the exact reverse of that which is followed by a Western artist. We begin by blocking out the design and then filling in the details, usually working more and more slowly as we approach the completion of the picture. The Zen artist sits down very calmly; examines his brush carefully; prepares his own ink; smooths out the paper on which he will work; falls into a profound silent ecstasy of contemplation—during which he does not think anxiously of various details, composition, brushwork, shades of tone, but rather attempts to become the vehicle through which the subject can express itself in painting; and then, very quickly and almost unconsciously, with sure effortless strokes, draws a picture containing the fewest and most effective lines. Most of the paper is left blank; only the essential is depicted, and that not completely. One long curving line will be enough to show a mountainside; seven streaks will become a group of bamboos bending in the wind; and yet, though technically incomplete, such pictures are unforgettably clear. They show the heart of reality.

All this we can sympathize with, because we can see the results. The young swordsman learns how to fence. The intuitional painter produces a fine picture. But the hardest thing for us to appreciate is that the Zen masters refuse to teach philosophy or religion directly, and deny logic. In fact, they despise logic as an artificial distortion of reality. Many philosophical teachers are difficult to understand because they analyze profound problems with subtle intricacy: such is Aristotle in his *Metaphysics*. Many mystical writers are difficult to understand because, as they themselves admit, they are attempting to use words to describe experiences which are too abstruse for words, so that they have to fall back on imagery and analogy, which they themselves recognize to be poor media, far coarser than the realities with which they have been in contact. But the Zen teachers seem to deny the power of language and thought altogether. For example, if you ask a Zen master what is the ultimate reality, he will answer, without the slightest hesitation, "The bamboo grove at the foot of the hill" or "A branch of plum blossom." Apparently he means that these things, which we can see instantly without effort, or imagine in the flash of a second, are real with the ultimate reality; that nothing is more real than these; and that we ought to grasp ultimates as we grasp simple immediates. A Chinese master was once asked the central question, "What is the Buddha?" He said nothing whatever, but held out his index finger. What did he mean? It is hard to explain; but apparently he meant "Here. Now. Look and realize with the effortlessness of seeing. Do not try to use words. Do not think. Make no efforts toward withdrawal from the world. Expect no sublime ecstasies. Live. All *that* is the ultimate reality, and it can be understood from the motion of a finger as well as from the execution of any complex ritual, from any subtle argument, or from the circling of the starry universe."

In making that gesture, the master was copying the Buddha himself, who once delivered a sermon which is famous, but was hardly understood by his pupils at the time. Without saying a word, he held up a flower and showed it to the gathering. One man, one alone, knew what he meant. The gesture became renowned as the Flower Sermon.

20

In the annals of Zen there are many cryptic answers to the final question, "What is the Buddha?"—which in our terms means "What is the meaning of life? What is truly real?" For example, one master, when asked "What is the Buddha?" replied, "Your name is Yecho." Another said, "Even the finest artist cannot paint him." Another said, "No nonsense here." And another answered, "The mouth is the gate of woe." My favorite story is about the monk who said to a Master, "Has a dog Buddha-nature too?" The Master replied, "Wu"—which is what the dog himself would have said.

Now, some critics might attack Zen by saying that this is the creed of a savage or an animal. The adherents of Zen would deny that—or more probably they would ignore the criticism, or make some cryptic remark which meant that it was pointless. Their position—if they could ever be persuaded to put in into words—would be this. An animal is instinctively in touch with reality, and so far is living rightly, but it has never had a mind and so cannot perceive the Whole, only that part with which it is in touch. The philosopher sees both the Whole and the parts, and enjoys them all. As for the savage, he exists only through the group; he feels himself as part of a war party or a ceremonial dance team or a ploughing-and-sowing group or the Snake clan; he is not truly an individual at all, and therefore is less than fully human. Zen has at its heart an inner solitude; its aim is to teach us to live, as in the last resort we do all have to live, alone.

A more dangerous criticism of Zen would be that it is nihilism, that its purpose is to abolish thought altogether. (This criticism is handled, but not fully met, by the great Zen authority Suzuki in his *Introduction to Zen Buddhism.*) It can hardly be completely confuted, for after all the central doctrine of Buddhism is—Nothingness. And many of the sayings of Zen masters are truly nihilistic. The first patriarch of the sect in China was asked by the emperor what was the ultimate and holiest principle of Buddhism. He replied, "Vast emptiness, and nothing holy in it." Another who was asked the searching question "Where is the abiding-place for the mind?" answered, "Not in this dualism of good and evil, being and non-being, thought and matter." In fact, thought is an activity which divides. It analyzes, it makes distinctions, it criticizes, it judges, it breaks reality into groups and classes and individuals. The aim of Zen is to abolish that kind of thinking, and to substitute—not unconsciousness, which would be death, but a consciousness that does not analyze but experiences life directly. Although it has no prescribed prayers, no sacred scriptures, no ceremonial rites, no personal god, and no interest in the soul's future destination, Zen is a religion rather than a philosophy. Jung points out that its aim is to produce a religious conversion, a "transformation": and he adds, "The transformation process is incommensurable with intellect." Thought is always interesting, but often painful; Zen is calm and painless. Thought is incomplete; Zen enlightenment brings a sense of completeness. Thought is a process; Zen illumination is a state. But it is a state which cannot be defined. In the Buddhist scriptures there is a dialogue between a master and a pupil in which the pupil tries to discover the exact meaning of such a state. The master says to him, 'If a fire were blazing in front of you, would you know that it was blazing?'

"Yes, master."

"And would you know the reason for its blazing?"

"Yes, because it had a supply of grass and sticks."   25

"And would you know if it were to go out?"

"Yes, master."

"And on its going out, would you know where the fire had gone? To the east, to the west, to the north, or to the south?"

"The question does not apply, master. For the fire blazed because it had a supply of grass and sticks. When it had consumed this and had no other fuel, then it went out."

"In the same way," replies the master, "no question will apply to the   30
meaning of Nirvana, and no statement will explain it."

Such, then, neither happy nor unhappy but beyond all divisive description, is the condition which students of Zen strive to attain. Small wonder that they can scarcely explain it to us, the unilluminated.

THE READER

1. On p. 1213, Highet says that "Zen is a religion rather than a philosophy." How has he led up to this conclusion? What definitions of religion and philosophy does he imply?
2. To what extent is Zen "the creed of a savage or an animal"? How does Highet go about refuting this charge?

THE WRITER

1. *What difficulties does Highet face in discussing Zen? How does he manage to give a definition in spite of his statement that Zen "cannot be analyzed"?*
2. *Why does Highet describe the training in archery in such detail?*
3. *By what means does Highet define* meditation? *Would other means have worked as well? Explain. Write a brief definition of a similar term (perhaps* intuition *or* realization*), using an approach similar to Highet's.*

Virginia Woolf

THE DEATH OF THE MOTH

Moths that fly by day are not properly to be called moths; they do not excite that pleasant sense of dark autumn nights and ivy-blossom which the commonest yellow-underwing asleep in the shadow of the curtain never fails to rouse in us. They are hybrid creatures, neither gay like butterflies nor sombre like their own species. Nevertheless the present specimen, with his narrow hay-coloured wings, fringed with a tassel of the same colour, seemed to be content with life. It was a pleasant morning, mid-September, mild, benignant, yet with a keener breath than that of the summer months. The plough was already scoring the field opposite the window, and where the share had been, the earth was pressed flat and gleamed with moisture. Such vigour came rolling in from the fields and the down beyond that it was difficult to keep the eyes strictly turned upon the book. The rooks too were keeping one of their annual festivities; soaring round the tree tops until it looked as if a vast net with thousands of black knots in it had been cast up into the air; which, after a few moments sank slowly down upon the trees until every twig seemed to have a knot at the end of it. Then, suddenly, the net would be thrown into the air again in a wider circle this time, with the utmost clamour and vociferation, as though to be thrown into the air and settle slowly down upon the tree tops were a tremendously exciting experience.

The same energy which inspired the rooks, the ploughmen, the horses, and even, it seemed, the lean bare-backed downs, sent the moth fluttering from side to side of his square of the window-pane. One could not help watching him. One was, indeed, conscious of a queer feeling

From *The Death of the Moth and Other Essays* (1942).

of pity for him. The possibilities of pleasure seemed that morning so enormous and so various that to have only a moth's part in life, and a day moth's at that, appeared a hard fate, and his zest in enjoying his meagre opportunities to the full, pathetic. He flew vigorously to one corner of his compartment, and, after waiting there a second, flew across to the other. What remained for him but to fly to a third corner and then to a fourth? That was all he could do, in spite of the size of the downs, the width of the sky, the far-off smoke of houses, and the romantic voice, now and then, of a steamer out at sea. What he could do he did. Watching him, it seemed as if a fibre, very thin but pure, of the enormous energy of the world had been thrust into his frail and diminutive body. As often as he crossed the pane, I could fancy that a thread of vital light became visible. He was little or nothing but life.

Yet, because he was so small, and so simple a form of the energy that was rolling in at the open window and driving its way through so many narrow and intricate corridors in my own brain and in those of other human beings, there was something marvellous as well as pathetic about him. It was as if someone had taken a tiny bead of pure life and decking it as lightly as possible with down and feathers, had set it dancing and zig-zagging to show us the true nature of life. Thus displayed one could not get over the strangeness of it. One is apt to forget all about life, seeing it humped and bossed and garnished and cumbered so that it has to move with the greatest circumspection and dignity. Again, the thought of all that life might have been had he been born in any other shape caused one to view his simple activities with a kind of pity.

After a time, tired by his dancing apparently, he settled on the window ledge in the sun, and, the queer spectacle being at an end, I forgot about him. Then, looking up, my eye was caught by him. He was trying to resume his dancing, but seemed either so stiff or so awkward that he could only flutter to the bottom of the window-pane; and when he tried to fly across it he failed. Being intent on other matters I watched these futile attempts for a time without thinking, unconsciously waiting for him to resume his flight, as one waits for a machine, that has stopped momentarily, to start again without considering the reason of its failure. After perhaps a seventh attempt he slipped from the wooden ledge and fell, fluttering his wings, on to his back on the window sill. The helplessness of his attitude roused me. It flashed upon me that he was in difficulties; he could no longer raise himself; his legs struggled vainly. But, as I stretched out a pencil, meaning to help him to right himself, it came over me that the failure and awkwardness were the approach of death. I laid the pencil down again.

The legs agitated themselves once more. I looked as if for the enemy against which he struggled. I looked out of doors. What had happened there? Presumably it was midday, and work in the fields had stopped.

5

Stillness and quiet had replaced the previous animation. The birds had taken themselves off to feed in the brooks. The horses stood still. Yet the power was there all the same, massed outside indifferent, impersonal, not attending to anything in particular. Somehow it was opposed to the little hay-coloured moth. It was useless to try to do anything. One could only watch the extraordinary efforts made by those tiny legs against an oncoming doom which could, had it chosen, have submerged an entire city, not merely a city, but masses of human beings; nothing, I knew, had any chance against death. Nevertheless after a pause of exhaustion the legs fluttered again. It was superb this last protest, and so frantic that he succeeded at last in righting himself. One's sympathies, of course, were all on the side of life. Also, when there was nobody to care or to know, this gigantic effort on the part of an insignificant little moth, against a power of such magnitude, to retain what no one else valued or desired to keep, moved one strangely. Again, somehow, one saw life, a pure bead. I lifted the pencil again, useless though I knew it to be. But even as I did so, the unmistakable tokens of death showed themselves. The body relaxed, and instantly grew stiff. The struggle was over. The insignificant little creature now knew death. As I looked at the dead moth, this minute wayside triumph of so great a force over so mean an antagonist filled me with wonder. Just as life had been strange a few minutes before, so death was now as strange. The moth having righted himself now lay most decently and uncomplainingly composed. O yes, he seemed to say, death is stronger than I am.

THE READER

1. *Why does Woolf describe the rooks in some detail, but not the ploughmen?*
2. *Does Woolf see any resemblances between the moth and human beings? How do you know?*
3. *Are there any devices of fiction in "The Death of the Moth"? Could Woolf be said to have written a biography of the moth?*

THE WRITER

1. *Observe an insect, and describe it from two points of view—one objective and one subjective, or as a scientist might describe it and as a poet or a novelist might describe it.*
2. *Read Frost's poem "To a Moth Seen in Winter," printed below. Does Frost feel the same way about his moth that Woolf does about hers? Does one author identify with the moth more than the other? Woolf's piece takes place in the fall, Frost's in winter. What is the significance of the difference in seasons? Embody some of your conclusions in a brief essay of comparison.*

To a Moth Seen in Winter

Here's first a gloveless hand warm from my pocket,
A perch and resting place 'twixt wood and wood,
Bright-black-eyed silvery creature, brushed with brown,
The wings not folded in repose, but spread.
(Who would you be, I wonder, by those marks
If I had moths to friend as I have flowers?)
And now pray tell what lured you with false hope
To make the venture of eternity
And seek the love of kind in wintertime?
But stay and hear me out. I surely think
You make a labor of flight for one so airy
Spending yourself too much in self-support.
Nor will you find love either nor love you.
And what I pity in you is something human,
The old incurable untimeliness,
Only begetter of all ills that are.
But go. You are right. My pity cannot help.
Go till you wet your pinions and are quenched.
You must be made more simply wise than I
To know the hand I stretch impulsively
Across the gulf of well nigh everything
May reach to you, but cannot touch your fate.
I cannot touch your life, much less can save,
Who am tasked to save my own a little while.

3. *Explain whether you think another person looking over Woolf's shoulder would have described the moth differently. How might Petrunkevitch (see "The Spider and the Wasp," p. 601) or Thoreau (see "The
   Battle of the Ants," p. 741) have described it?*

Annie Dillard

SIGHT INTO INSIGHT

When I was six or seven years old, growing up in Pittsburgh, I used
to take a penny of my own and hide it for someone else to find. It was
a curious compulsion; sadly, I've never been seized by it since. For some
reason I always "hid" the penny along the same stretch of sidewalk up
the street. I'd cradle it at the roots of a maple, say, or in a hole left by
a chipped-off piece of sidewalk. Then I'd take a piece of chalk and,
starting at either end of the block, draw huge arrows leading up to the

From *Harper's* magazine (Feb. 1974).

penny from both directions. After I learned to write I labeled the arrows "SURPRISE AHEAD" or "MONEY THIS WAY." I was greatly excited, during all this arrowdrawing, at the thought of the first lucky passerby who would receive in this way, regardless of merit, a free gift from the universe. But I never lurked about. I'd go straight home and not give the matter another thought, until, some months later, I would be gripped by the impulse to hide another penny.

There are lots of things to see, unwrapped gifts and free surprises. The world is fairly studded and strewn with pennies cast broadside from a generous hand. But—and this is the point—who gets excited by a mere penny? If you follow one arrow, if you crouch motionless on a bank to watch a tremulous ripple thrill on the water, and are rewarded by the sight of a muskrat kit paddling from its den, will you count that sight a chip of copper only, and go your rueful way? It is very dire poverty indeed for a man to be so malnourished and fatigued that he won't stoop to pick up a penny. But if you cultivate a healthy poverty and simplicity, so that finding a penny will make your day, then, since the world is in fact planted in pennies, you have with your poverty bought a lifetime of days. What you see is what you get.

Unfortunately, nature is very much a now-you-see-it, now-you-don't affair. A fish flashes, then dissolves in the water before my eyes like so much salt. Deer apparently ascend bodily into heaven; the brightest oriole fades into leaves. These disappearances stun me into stillness and concentration; they say of nature that it conceals with a grand nonchalance, and they say of vision that it is a deliberate gift, the revelation of a dancer who for my eyes only flings away her seven veils.

For nature does reveal as well as conceal: now-you-don't-see-it, now-you-do. For a week this September migrating red-winged blackbirds were feeding heavily down by Tinker Creek at the back of the house. One day I went out to investigate the racket; I walked up to a tree, an Osage orange, and a hundred birds flew away. They simply materialized out of the tree. I saw a tree, then a whisk of color, then a tree again. I walked closer and another hundred blackbirds took flight. Not a branch, not a twig budged: the birds were apparently weightless as well as invisible. Or, it was as if the leaves of the Osage orange had been freed from a spell in the form of redwinged blackbirds; they flew from the tree, caught my eye in the sky, and vanished. When I looked again at the tree, the leaves had reassembled as if nothing had happened. Finally I walked directly to the trunk of the tree and a final hundred, the real diehards, appeared, spread, and vanished. How could so many hide in the tree without my seeing them? The Osage orange, unruffled, looked just as it had looked from the house, when three hundred red-winged blackbirds cried from its crown. I looked upstream where they flew, and they were gone. Searching, I couldn't spot one. I wandered upstream to force them to play their hand, but they'd crossed the creek and scattered. One show to a customer. These appearances catch at my throat; they are the free gifts, the bright coppers at the roots of trees.

It's all a matter of keeping my eyes open. Nature is like one of those line drawings that are puzzles for children: Can you find hidden in the tree a duck, a house, a boy, a bucket, a giraffe, and a boot? Specialists can find the most incredibly hidden things. A book I read when I was young recommended an easy way to find caterpillars: you simply find some fresh caterpillar droppings, look up, and there's your caterpillar. More recently an author advised me to set my mind at ease about those piles of cut stems on the ground in grassy fields. Field mice make them; they cut the grass down by degrees to reach the seeds at the head. It seems that when the grass is tightly packed, as in a field of ripe grain, the blade won't topple at a single cut through the stem; instead, the cut stem simply drops vertically, held in the crush of grain. The mouse severs the bottom again and again, the stem keeps dropping an inch at a time, and finally the head is low enough for the mouse to reach the seeds. Meanwhile the mouse is positively littering the field with its little piles of cut stems into which, presumably, the author is constantly stumbling.

If I can't see these minutiae, I still try to keep my eyes open. I'm always on the lookout for ant lion traps in sandy soil, monarch pupae near milkweed, skipper larvae in locust leaves. These things are utterly common, and I've not seen one. I bang on hollow trees near water, but so far no flying squirrels have appeared. In flat country I watch every sunset in hopes of seeing the green ray. The green ray is a seldom-seen streak of light that rises from the sun like a spurting fountain at the moment of sunset; it throbs into the sky for two seconds and disappears. One more reason to keep my eyes open. A photography professor at the University of Florida just happened to see a bird die in midflight; it jerked, died, dropped, and smashed on the ground.

I squint at the wind because I read Stewart Edward White: "I have always maintained that if you looked closely enough you could *see* the wind—the dim, hardly-made-out, fine débris fleeing high in the air." White was an excellent observer, and devoted an entire chapter of *The Mountains* to the subject of seeing deer: "As soon as you can forget the naturally obvious and construct an artificial obvious, then you too will see deer."

But the artificial obvious is hard to see. My eyes account for less than 1 percent of the weight of my head; I'm bony and dense; I see what I expect. I once spent a full three minuites looking at a bullfrog that was so unexpectedly large I couldn't see it even though a dozen enthusiastic campers were shouting directions. Finally I asked, "What color am I

5

looking for?" and a fellow said, "Green." When at last I picked out the frog, I saw what painters are up against: the thing wasn't green at all, but the color of wet hickory bark.

The lover can see, and the knowledgeable. I visited an aunt and uncle at a quarter-horse ranch in Cody, Wyoming. I couldn't do much of anything useful, but I could, I thought, draw. So, as we all sat around the kitchen table after supper, I produced a sheet of paper and drew a horse. "That's one lame horse," my aunt volunteered. The rest of the family joined in: "Only place to saddle that one is his neck"; "Looks like we better shoot the poor thing, on account of those terrible growths." Meekly, I slid the pencil and paper down the table. Everyone in that family, including my three young cousins, could draw a horse. Beautifully. When the paper came back it looked as though five shining, real quarter horses had been corraled by mistake with a papier-mâché moose; the real horses seemed to gaze at the monster with a steady, puzzled air. I stay away from horses now, but I can do a creditable goldfish. The point is that I just don't know what the lover knows; I just can't see the artificial obvious that those in the know construct. The herpetologist asks the native, "Are there snakes in that ravine?" "Nosir." And the herpetologist comes home with, yessir, three bags full. Are there butterflies on that mountain? Are the bluets in bloom, are there arrowheads here, or fossil shells in the shale?

10   Peeping through my keyhole I see within the range of only about 30 percent of the light that comes from the sun; the rest is infrared and some little ultraviolet, perfectly apparent to many animals, but invisible to me. A nightmare network of ganglia, charged and firing without my knowledge, cuts and splices what I do see, editing it for my brain. Donald E. Carr points out that the sense impressions of one-celled animals are *not* edited for the brain: "This is philosophically interesting in a rather mournful way, since it means that only the simplest animals perceive the universe as it is."

A fog that won't burn away drifts and flows across my field of vision. When you see fog move against a backdrop of deep pines, you don't see the fog itself, but streaks of clearness floating across the air in dark shreds. So I see only tatters of clearness through a pervading obscurity. I can't distinguish the fog from the overcast sky; I can't be sure if the light is direct or reflected. Everywhere darkness and the presence of the unseen appalls. We estimate now that only one atom dances alone in every cubic meter of intergalactic space. I blink and squint. What planet or power yanks Halley's Comet out of orbit? We haven't seen it yet; it's a question of distance, density, and the pallor of reflected light. We rock, cradled in the swaddling band of darkness. Even the simple darkness of night whispers suggestions to the mind. This summer, in August, I stayed at the creek too late.

Where Tinker Creek flows under the sycamore log bridge to the tear-shaped island, it is slow and shallow, fringed thinly in cattail marsh. At this spot an astonishing bloom of life supports vast breeding populations of insects, fish, reptiles, birds, and mammals. On windless summer evenings I stalk along the creek bank or straddle the sycamore log in absolute stillness, watching for muskrats. The night I stayed too late I was hunched on the log staring spellbound at spreading, reflected stains of lilac on the water. A cloud in the sky suddenly lighted as if turned on by a switch; its reflection just as suddenly materialized on the water upstream, flat and floating, so that I couldn't see the creek bottom, or life in the water under the cloud. Downstream, away from the cloud on the water, water turtles smooth as beans were gliding down with the current in a series of easy, weightless push-offs, as men bound on the moon. I didn't know whether to trace the progress of one turtle I was sure of, risking sticking my face in one of the bridge's spider webs made invisible by the gathering dark, or take a chance on seeing the carp, or scan the mudbank in hope of seeing a muskrat, or follow the last of the swallows who caught at my heart and trailed it after them like streamers as they appeared from directly below, under the log, flying upstream with their tails forked, so fast.

But shadows spread and deepened and stayed. After thousands of years we're still strangers to darkness, fearful aliens in an enemy camp with our arms crossed over our chests. I stirred. A land turtle on the bank, startled, hissed the air from its lungs and withdrew to its shell. An uneasy pink here, an unfathomable blue there, gave great suggestion of lurking beings. Things were going on. I couldn't see whether that rustle I heard was a distant rattle-snake, slit-eyed, or a nearby sparrow kicking in the dry flood debris slung at the foot of a willow. Tremendous action roiled the water everywhere I looked, big action, inexplicable. A tremor welled up beside a gaping muskrat burrow in the bank and I caught my breath, but no muskrat appeared. The ripples continued to fan upstream with a steady, powerful thrust. Night was knitting an eyeless mask over my face, and I still sat transfixed. A distant airplane, a delta wing out of nightmare, made a gliding shadow on the creek's bottom that looked like a stingray cruising upstream. At once a black fin slit the pink cloud on the water, shearing it in two. The two halves merged together and seemed to dissolve before my eyes. Darkness pooled in the cleft of the creek and rose, as water collects in a well. Untamed, dreaming lights flickered over the sky. I saw hints of hulking underwater shadows, two pale splashes out of the water, and round ripples rolling close together from a blackened center.

At last I stared upstream where only the deepest violet remained of the cloud, a cloud so high its underbelly still glowed, its feeble color reflected from a hidden sky lighted in turn by a sun halfway to China.

And out of that violet, a sudden enormous black body arced over the water. Head and tail, if there was a head and tail, were both submerged in cloud. I saw only one ebony fling, a headlong dive to darkness; then the waters closed, and the lights went out.

15   I walked home in a shivering daze, up hill and down. Later I lay openmouthed in bed, my arms flung wide at my sides to steady the whirling darkness. At this latitude I'm spinning 836 miles an hour round the earth's axis; I feel my sweeping fall as a breakneck arc like the dive of dolphins, and the hollow rushing of wind raises the hairs on my neck and the side of my face. In orbit around the sun I'm moving 64,800 miles an hour. The solar system as a whole, like a merry-go-round unhinged, spins, bobs, and blinks at the speed of 43,-200 miles an hour along a course set east of Hercules. Someone has piped, and we are dancing a tarantella until the sweat pours. I open my eyes and I see dark, muscled forms curl out of water, with flapping gills and flattened eyes. I close my eyes and I see stars, deep stars giving way to deeper stars, deeper stars bowing to deepest stars at the crown of an infinite cone.

"Still," wrote Van Gogh in a letter, "a great deal of light falls on everything." If we are blinded by darkness, we are also blinded by light. Sometimes here in Virginia at sunset low clouds on the southern or northern horizon are completely invisible in the lighted sky. I only know one is there because I can see its reflection in still water. The first time I discovered this mystery I looked from cloud to no-cloud in bewilderment, checking my bearings over and over, thinking maybe the ark of the covenant was just passing by south of Dead Man Mountain. Only much later did I learn the explanation: polarized light from the sky is very much weakened by reflection, but the light in clouds isn't polarized. So invisible clouds pass among visible clouds, till all slide over the mountains; so a greater light extinguishes a lesser as though it didn't exist.

In the great meteor shower of August, the Perseid, I wail all day for the shooting stars I miss. They're out there showering down committing hara-kiri in a flame of fatal attraction, and hissing perhaps at last into the ocean. But at dawn what looks like a blue dome clamps down over me like a lid on a pot. The stars and planets could smash and I'd never know. Only a piece of ashen moon occasionally climbs up or down the inside of the dome, and our local star without surcease explodes on our heads. We have really only that one light, one source for all power, and yet we must turn away from it by universal decree. Nobody here on the planet seems aware of this strange, powerful taboo, that we all walk about carefully averting our faces, this way and that, lest our eyes be blasted forever.

Darkness appalls and light dazzles; the scrap of visible light that doesn't hurt my eyes hurts my brain. What I see sets me swaying. Size and distance and the sudden swelling of meanings confuse me, bowl me over. I straddle the sycamore log bridge over Tinker Creek in the summer. I look at the lighted creek bottom: snail tracks tunnel the mud in quavering curves. A crayfish jerks, but by the time I absorb what has happened, he's gone in a billowing smoke screen of silt. I look at the water; minnows and shiners. If I'm thinking minnows, a carp will fill my brain till I scream. I look at the water's surface: skaters, bubbles, and leaves sliding down. Suddenly, my own face, reflected, startles me wit-less. Those snails have been tracking my face! Finally, with a shuddering wrench of the will, I see clouds, cirrus clouds. I'm dizzy, I fall in.

This looking business is risky. Once I stood on a humped rock on nearby Purgatory Mountain, watching through binoculars the great autumn hawk migration below, until I discovered that I was in danger of joining the hawks on a vertical migration of my own. I was used to binoculars, but not, apparently, to balancing on humped rocks while looking through them. I reeled. Everything advanced and receded by turns; the world was full of unexplained foreshortenings and depths. A distant huge object, a hawk the size of an elephant, turned out to be the browned bough of a nearby loblolly pine. I followed a sharp-shinned hawk against a featureless sky, rotating my head unawares as it flew, and when I lowered the glass a glimpse of my own looming shoulder sent me staggering. What prevents the men at Palomar[1] from falling, voice-less and blinded, from their tiny, vaulted chairs?

I reel in confusion: I don't understand what I see. With the naked   20
eye I can see two million light-years to the Andromeda galaxy. Often I slop some creek water in a jar, and when I get home I dump it in a white china bowl. After the silt settles I return and see tracings of minute snails on the bottom, a planarian or two winding round the rim of water, roundworms shimmying, frantically, and finally, when my eyes have adjusted to these dimensions, amoebae. At first the amoebae look like *muscae volitantes,* those curled moving spots you seem to see in your eyes when you stare at a distant wall. Then I see the amoebae as drops of water congealed, bluish, translucent, like chips of sky in the bowl. At length I choose one individual and give myself over to its idea of an evening. I see it dribble a grainy foot before it on its wet, unfathomable way. Do its unedited sense impressions include the fierce focus of my eyes? Shall I take it outside and show it Andromeda, and blow its little endoplasm? I stir the water with a finger, in case it's running out of oxygen. Maybe I should get a tropical aquarium with motorized bubblers and lights, and keep this one for a pet. Yes, it would tell its fissioned

1. An astronomical observatory in California.

descendants, the universe is two feet by five, and if you listen closely you can hear the buzzing music of the spheres.

Oh, it's mysterious, lamplit evenings here in the galaxy, one after the other. It's one of those nights when I wander from window to window, looking for a sign. But I can't see. Terror and a beauty insoluble are a riband of blue woven into the fringe of garments of things both great and small. No culture explains, no bivouac offers real haven or rest. But it could be that we are not seeing something. Galileo thought comets were an optical illusion. This is fertile ground: since we are certain that they're not, we can look at what our scientists have been saying with fresh hope. What if there are *really* gleaming, castellated cities hung up-side-down over the desert sand? What limpid lakes and cool date palms have our caravans always passed untried? Until, one by one, by the blindest of leaps, we light on the road to these places, we must stumble in darkness and hunger. I turn from the window. I'm blind as a bat, sensing only from every direction the echo of my own thin cries.

I chanced on a wonderful book called *Space and Sight*, by Marius Von Senden. When Western surgeons discovered how to perform safe cataract operations, they ranged across Europe and America operating on dozens of men and women of all ages who had been blinded by cataracts since birth. Von Senden collected accounts of such cases; the histories are fascinating. Many doctors had tested their patients' sense perceptions and ideas of space both before and after the operations. The vast majority of patients, of both sexes and all ages, had, in Von Senden's opinion, no idea of space whatsoever. Form, distance, and size were so many meaningless syllables. A patient "had no idea of depth, confusing it with roundness." Before the operation a doctor would give a blind patient a cube and a sphere; the patient would tongue it or feel it with his hands, and name it correctly. After the operation the doctor would show the same objects to the patient without letting him touch them; now he had no clue whatsoever to what he was seeing. One patient called lemonade "square" because it pricked on his tongue as a square shape pricked on the touch of his hands. Of another post-operative patient the doctor writes, "I have found in her no notion of size, for example, not even within the narrow limits which she might have encompassed with the aid of touch. Thus when I asked her to show me how big her mother was, she did not stretch out her hands, but set her two index fingers a few inches apart."

For the newly sighted, vision is pure sensation unencumbered by meaning. When a newly sighted girl saw photographs and paintings, she asked, "'Why do they put those dark marks all over them?' 'Those aren't dark marks,' her mother explained, 'those are shadows. That is one of the ways the eye knows that things have shape. If it were not for shadows, many things would look flat.' 'Well, that's how things do look,' Joan answered. 'Everything looks flat with dark patches.' "

In general the newly sighted see the world as a dazzle of "colorpatches." They are pleased by the sensation of color, and learn quickly to name the colors, but the rest of seeing is tormentingly difficult. Soon after his operation a patient "generally bumps into one of these colourpatches and observes them to be substantial, since they resist him as tactual objects do. In walking about it also strikes him—or can if he pays attention—that he is continually passing in between the colours he sees, that he can go past a visual object, that a part of it then steadily disappears from view; and that in spite of this, however he twists and turns—whether entering the room from the door, for example, or returning back to it—he always has a visual space in front of him. Thus he gradually comes to realize that there is also a space behind him, which he does not see."

The mental effort involved in these reasonings proves overwhelming for many patients. It oppresses them to realize that they have been visible to people all along, perhaps unattractively so, without their knowledge or consent. A disheartening number of them refuse to use their new vision, continuing to go over objects with their tongues, and lapsing into apathy and despair.   25

On the other hand, many newly sighted people speak well of the world, and teach us how dull our own vision is. To one patient, a human hand, unrecognized, is "something bright and then holes." Shown a bunch of grapes, a boy calls out, "It is dark, blue and shiny. . . . It isn't smooth, it has bumps and hollows." A little girl visits a garden. "She is greatly astonished, and can scarcely be persuaded to answer, stands speechless in front of the tree, which she only names on taking hold of it, and then as 'the tree with the lights in it.' " Another patient, a twenty-two-year-old girl, was dazzled by the world's brightness and kept her eyes shut for two weeks. When at the end of that time she opened her eyes again, she did not recognize any objects, but "the more she now directed her gaze upon everything about her, the more it could be seen how an expression of gratification and astonishment overspread her features; she repeatedly exclaimed: 'Oh God! How beautiful!' "

I saw color-patches for weeks after I read this wonderful book. It was summer; the peaches were ripe in the valley orchards. When I woke in the morning, color-patches wrapped round my eyes, intricately, leaving not one unfilled spot. All day long I walked among shifting color-patches that parted before me like the Red Sea and closed again in silence, transfigured, wherever I looked back. Some patches swelled and loomed, while others vanished utterly, and dark marks flitted at random over the whole dazzling sweep. But I couldn't sustain the illusion of flatness. I've been around for too long. Form is condemned to an eternal danse macabre with meaning: I couldn't unpeach the peaches. Nor can I remember ever having seen without understanding; the color-patches of infancy are lost. My brain then must have been smooth as any balloon. I'm told I reached for the moon; many babies do. But the color-patches of infancy swelled as meaning filled them; they arrayed themselves in solemn ranks down distance which unrolled and stretched before me like a plain. The moon rocketed away. I live now in a world of shadows that shape and distance color, a world where space makes a kind of terrible sense. What Gnosticism [2] is this, and what physics? The fluttering patch I saw in my nursery window—silver and green and shape-shifting blue— is gone; a row of Lombardy poplars takes its place, mute, across the distant lawn. That humming oblong creature pale as light that stole along the walls of my room at night, stretching exhilaratingly around the corners, is gone, too, gone the night I ate of the bittersweet fruit, put two and two together and puckered forever my brain. Martin Buber tells this tale: "Rabbi Mendel once boasted to his teacher Rabbi Elimelekh that evenings he saw the angel who rolls away the light before the darkness, and mornings the angel who rolls away the darkness before the light. 'Yes,' said Rabbi Elimelekh, 'in my youth I saw that too. Later on you don't see these things anymore.' "

Why didn't someone hand those newly sighted people paints and brushes from the start, when they still didn't know what anything was? Then maybe we all could see color-patches too, the world unraveled from reason, Eden before Adam gave names. The scales would drop from my eyes; I'd see trees like men walking; I'd run down the road against all orders, hallooing and leaping.

Seeing is of course very much a matter of verbalization. Unless I call my attention to what passes before my eyes, I simply won't see it. If Tinker Mountain erupted, I'd be likely to notice. But if I want to notice the lesser cataclysms of valley life, I have to maintain in my head a running description of the present. It's not that I'm observant; it's just that I talk too much. Otherwise, especially in a strange place, I'll never know what's happening. Like a blind man at the ball game, I need a radio.

30   When I see this way I analyze and pry. I hurl over logs and roll away stones; I study the bank a square foot at a time, probing and tilting my head. Some days when a mist covers the mountains, when the muskrats won't show and the microscope's mirror shatters, I want to climb up the blank blue dome as a man would storm the inside of a circus tent, wildly, dangling, and with a steel knife claw a rent in the top, peep, and, if I must, fall.

2. Pretension to esoteric spiritual knowledge.

But there is another kind of seeing that involves a letting go. When I see this way I sway transfixed and emptied. The difference between the two ways of seeing is the difference between walking with and without a camera. When I walk with a camera I walk from shot to shot, reading the light on a calibrated meter. When I walk without a camera, my own shutter opens, and the moment's light prints on my own silver gut. When I see this second way I am above all an unscrupulous observer.

It was sunny one evening last summer at Tinker Creek; the sun was low in the sky, upstream. I was sitting on the sycamore log bridge with the sunset at my back, watching the shiners the size of minnows who were feeding over the muddy sand in skittery schools. Again and again, one fish, then another, turned for a split second across the current and flash! the sun shot out from its silver side. I couldn't watch for it. It was always just happening somewhere else, and it drew my vision just as it disappeared: flash! like a sudden dazzle of the thinnest blade, a sparking over a dun and olive ground at chance intervals from every direction. Then I noticed white specks, some sort of pale petals, small, floating from under my feet on the creek's surface, very slow and steady. So I blurred my eyes and gazed toward the brim of my hat and saw a new world. I saw the pale white circles roll up, roll up, like the world's turning, mute and perfect, and I saw the linear flashes, gleaming silver, like stars being born at random down a rolling scroll of time. Something broke and something opened. I filled up like a new wineskin. I breathed an air like light; I saw a light like water. I was the lip of a fountain the creek filled forever; I was ether, the leaf in the zephyr; I was flesh-flake, feather, bone.

When I see this way I see truly. As Thoreau says, I return to my senses. I am the man who watches the baseball game in silence in an empty stadium. I see the game purely; I'm abstracted and dazed. When it's all over and the white-suited players lope off the green field to their shadowed dugouts, I leap to my feet, I cheer and cheer.

But I can't go out and try to see this way. I'll fail, I'll go mad. All I can do is try to gag the commentator, to hush the noise of useless interior babble that keeps me from seeing just as surely as a newspaper dangled before my eyes. The effort is really a discipline requiring a lifetime of dedicated struggle; it marks the literature of saints and monks of every order east and west, under every rule and no rule, discalced and shod. The world's spiritual geniuses seem to discover universally that the mind's muddy river, this ceaseless flow of trivia and trash, cannot be dammed, and that trying to dam it is a waste of effort that might lead to madness. Instead you must allow the muddy river to flow unheeded in the dim channels of consciousness; you raise your sights; you look along it, mildly, acknowledging its presence without interest and gazing beyond it into the realm of the real where subjects and objects act and rest purely, without utterance. "Launch into the deep," says Jacques Ellul, "and you shall see."

35   The secret of seeing, then, is the pearl of great price. If I thought he could teach me to find it and keep it forever I would stagger barefoot across a hundred deserts after any lunatic at all. But although the pearl may be found, it may not be sought. The literature of illumination reveals this above all: although it comes to those who wait for it, it is always, even to the most practiced and adept, a gift and a total surprise. I return from one walk knowing where the killdeer nests in the field by the creek and the hour the laurel blooms. I return from the same walk a day later scarcely knowing my own name. Litanies hum in my ears; my tongue flaps in my mouth, *Alim non,* alleluia! I cannot cause light; the most I can do is try to put myself in the path of its beam. It is possible, in deep space, to sail on solar wind. Light, be it particle or wave, has force: you rig a giant sail and go. The secret of seeing is to sail on solar wind. Hone and spread your spirit till you yourself are a sail, whetted, translucent, broadside to the merest puff.

When her doctor took her bandages off and led her into the garden, the girl who was no longer blind saw "the tree with the lights in it." It was for this tree I searched through the peach orchards of summer, in the forests of fall and down winter and spring for years. Then one day I was walking along Tinker Creek thinking of nothing at all and I saw the tree with the lights in it. I saw the backyard cedar where the mourning doves roost charged and transfigured, each cell buzzing with flame. I stood on the grass with the lights in it, grass that was wholly fire, utterly focused and utterly dreamed. It was less like seeing than like being for the first time seen, knocked breathless by a powerful glance. The flood of fire abated, but I'm still spending the power. Gradually the lights went out in the cedar, the colors died, the cells unflamed and disappeared. I was still ringing. I had been my whole life a bell, and never knew it until at that moment I was lifted and struck. I have since only very rarely seen the tree with the lights in it. The vision comes and goes, mostly goes, but I live for it, for the moment when the mountains open and a new light roars in spate through the crack, and the mountains slam.

THE READER

1. *Is the kind of seeing Dillard talks about at the end of her essay the same as the one she talks about at the beginning?*
2. *Why is verbalization so important to seeing (p. 1226)?*

THE WRITER

1. What accounts for the intensity of Dillard's description of staying at the creek too late (p. 1221)?
2. How does Dillard establish her authority during the course of her argument?
3. Dillard says, "I see what I expect." Look at an object or a scene briefly, and jot down what you see. Then look at it longer and more intensely, and jot down the additional things you see. Write a brief comparison of your first view and your later view of the object or scene.

Jean-Paul Sartre

EXISTENTIALISM

Man is nothing else but what he makes of himself. Such is the first principle of existentialism. It is also what is called subjectivity, the name we are labeled with when charges are brought against us. But what do we mean by this, if not that man has a greater dignity than a stone or table? For we mean that man first exists, that is, that man first of all is the being who hurls himself toward a future and who is conscious of imagining himself as being in the future. Man is at the start a plan which is aware of itself, rather than a patch of moss, a piece of garbage, or a cauliflower; nothing exists prior to this plan; there is nothing in heaven; man will be what he will have planned to be. Not what he will want to be. Because by the word "will" we generally mean a conscious decision, which is subsequent to what we have already made of ourselves. I may want to belong to a political party, write a book, get married; but all that is only a manifestation of an earlier, more spontaneous choice that is called "will." But if existence really does precede essence, man is responsible for what he is. Thus, existentialism's first move is to make every man aware of what he is and to make the full responsibility of his existence rest on him. And when we say that a man is responsible for himself, we do not only mean that he is responsible for his own individuality, but that he is responsible for all men.

The word "subjectivism" has two meanings, and our opponents play on the two. Subjectivism means, on the one hand, that an individual chooses and makes himself; and, on the other, that it is impossible for man to transcend human subjectivity. The second of these is the essen-

From *Existentialism* (1947).

tial meaning of existentialism. When we say that man chooses his own self, we mean that every one of us does likewise; but we also mean by that that in making this choice he also chooses all men. In fact, in creating the man that we want to be, there is not a single one of our acts which does not at the same time create an image of man as we think he ought to be. To choose to be this or that is to affirm at the same time the value of what we choose, because we can never choose evil. We always choose the good, and nothing can be good for us without being good for all.

If, on the other hand, existence precedes essence, and if we grant that we exist and fashion our image at one and the same time, the image is valid for everybody and for our whole age. Thus, our responsibility is much greater than we might have supposed, because it involves all mankind. If I am a workingman and choose to join a Christian trade union rather than be a Communist, and if by being a member, I want to show that the best thing for man is resignation, that the kingdom of man is not of this world, I am not only involving my own case—I want to be resigned for everyone. As a result, my action has involved all humanity. To take a more individual matter, if I want to marry, to have children, even if this marriage depends solely on my own circumstances or passion or wish, I am involving all humanity in monogamy and not merely myself. Therefore, I am responsible for myself and for everyone else. I am creating a certain image of man of my own choosing. In choosing myself, I choose man.

This helps us understand what the actual content is of such rather grandiloquent words as anguish, forlornness, despair. As you will see, it's all quite simple.

First, what is meant by anguish? The existentialists say at once that man is anguish. What that means is this: the man who involves himself and who realizes that he is not only the person he chooses to be, but also a lawmaker who is, at the same time, choosing all mankind as well as himself, cannot help escape the feeling of his total and deep responsibility. Of course, there are many people who are not anxious; but we claim that they are hiding their anxiety, that they are fleeing from it. Certainly, many people believe that when they do something, they themselves are the only ones involved, and when someone says to them, "What if everyone acted that way?" they shrug their shoulders and answer, "Everyone doesn't act that way." But really, one should always ask himself, "What would happen if everybody looked at things that way?" There is no escaping this disturbing thought except by a kind of double-dealing. A man who lies and makes excuses for himself by saying "not everybody does that," is someone with an uneasy conscience, because the act of lying implies that a universal value is conferred upon the lie.

Anguish is evident even when it conceals itself. This is the anguish that Kierkegaard called the anguish of Abraham. You know the story: an angel has ordered Abraham to sacrifice his son; if it really were an angel who has come and said, "You are Abraham, you shall sacrifice your son," everything would be all right. But everyone might first wonder, "Is it really an angel, and am I really Abraham? What proof do I have?"

There was a madwoman who had hallucinations; someone used to speak to her on the telephone and give her orders. Her doctor asked her, "Who is it who talks to you?" She answered, "He says it's God." What proof did she really have that it was God? If an angel comes to me, what proof is there that it's an angel? And if I hear voices, what proof is there that they come from heaven and not from hell, or from the sub-conscious, or a pathological condition? What proves that they are ad-dressed to me? What proof is there that I have been appointed to impose my choice and my conception of man on humanity? I'll never find any proof or sign to convince me of that. If a voice addresses me, it is always for me to decide that this is the angel's voice; if I consider that such an act is a good one, it is I who will choose to say that it is good rather than bad.

Now, I'm not being singled out as an Abraham, and yet at every moment I'm obliged to perform exemplary acts. For every man, every-thing happens as if all mankind had its eyes fixed on him and were guiding itself by what he does. And every man ought to say to himself, "Am I really the kind of man who has the right to act in such a way that humanity might guide itself by my actions?" And if he does not say that to himself, he is masking his anguish.

There is no question here of the kind of anguish which would lead to quietism, to inaction. It is a matter of a simple sort of anguish that anybody who has had responsibilities is familiar with. For example, when a military officer takes the responsibility for an attack and sends a certain number of men to death, he chooses to do so, and in the main he alone makes the choice. Doubtless, orders come from above, but they are too broad; he interprets them, and on this interpretation depend the lives of ten or fourteen or twenty men. In making a decision he cannot help having a certain anguish. All leaders know this anguish. That doesn't keep them from acting; on the contrary, it is the very condition of their action. For it implies that they envisage a number of possibilities, and when they choose one, they realize that it has value only because it is chosen. We shall see that this kind of anguish, which is the kind that existentialism describes, is explained, in addition, by a direct responsibil-ity to the other men whom it involves. It is not a curtain separating us from action, but is part of action itself.

When we speak of forlornness, a term Heidegger was fond of, we mean only that God does not exist and that we have to face all the consequences of this. This existentialist is strongly opposed to a certain kind of secular ethics which would like to abolish God with the least possible expense. About 1880, some French teachers tried to set up a secular ethics which went something like this: God is a useless and costly hypothesis; we are discarding it; but, meanwhile, in order for there to be an ethics, a society, a civilization, it is essential that certain values be taken seriously and that they be considered as having an *a priori* existence. It must be obligatory, *a priori,* to be honest, not to lie, not to beat your wife, to have children, etc., etc. So we're going to try a little device which will make it possible to show that values exist all the same, inscribed in a heaven of ideas, though otherwise God does not exist. In other words—and this, I believe, is the tendency of everything called reformism in France—nothing will be changed if God does not exist. We shall find ourselves with the same norms of honesty, progress, and humanism, and we shall have made of God an outdated hypothesis which will peacefully die off by itself.

The existentialist, on the contrary, thinks it very distressing that God does not exist, because all possibility of finding values in a heaven of ideas disappears along with Him; there can no longer be an *a priori* Good, since there is no infinite and perfect consciousness to think it. Nowhere is it written that the Good exists, that we must be honest, that we must not lie; because the fact is we are on a plane where there are only men. Dostoievsky said, "If God didn't exist, everything would be possible." That is the very starting point of existentialism. Indeed, everything is permissible if God does not exist, and as a result man is forlorn, because neither within him nor without does he find anything to cling to. He can't start making excuses for himself.

If existence really does precede essence, there is no explaining things away by reference to a fixed and given human nature. In other words, there is no determinism, man is free, man is freedom. On the other hand, if God does not exist, we find no values or commands to turn to which legitimize our conduct. So, in the bright realm of values, we have no excuse behind us, nor justification before us. We are alone, with no excuses.

That is the idea I shall try to convey when I say that man is condemned to be free. Condemned, because he did not create himself, yet, in other respects is free; because, once thrown into the world, he is responsible for everything he does. The existentialist does not believe in the power of passion. He will never agree that a sweeping passion is a ravaging torrent which fatally leads a man to certain acts and is therefore an excuse. He thinks that man is responsible for his passion.

The existentialist does not think that man is going to help himself by finding in the world some omen by which to orient himself. Because he thinks that man will interpret the omen to suit himself. Therefore, he thinks that man, with no support and no aid, is condemned every moment to invent man. Ponge, in a very fine article, has said, "Man is the future of man." That's exactly it. But if it is taken to mean that this future is recorded in heaven, that God sees it, then it is false, because it would really no longer be a future. If it is taken to mean that, whatever a man may be, there is a future to be forged, a virgin future before him, then this remark is sound. But then we are forlorn.

To give you an example which will enable you to understand forlorn- ness better, I shall cite the case of one of my students who came to see me under the following circumstances: his father was on bad terms with his mother, and, moreover, was inclined to be a collaborationist,[1] his older brother had been killed in the German offensive of 1940, and the young man, with somewhat immature but generous feelings, wanted to avenge him. His mother lived alone with him, very much upset by the half-treason of her husband and the death of her older son; the boy was her only consolation.

The boy was faced with the choice of leaving for England and joining the Free French forces—that is, leaving his mother behind—or remain- ing with his mother and helping her to carry on. He was fully aware that the woman lived only for him and that his going off—and perhaps his death—would plunge her into despair. He was also aware that every act that he did for his mother's sake was a sure thing, in the sense that it was helping her to carry on, whereas every effort he made toward going off and fighting was an uncertain move which might run aground and prove completely useless; for example, on his way to England he might, while passing through Spain, be detained indefinitely in a Spanish camp; he might reach England or Algiers and be stuck in an office at a desk job. As a result, he was faced with two very different kinds of action: one, concrete, immediate, but concerning only one individual; the other concerned an incomparably vaster group, a national collectivity, but for that very reason was dubious, and might be interrupted en route. And, at the same time, he was wavering between two kinds of ethics. On the one hand, an ethics of sympathy, of personal devotion; on the other, a broader ethics, but one whose efficacy was more dubious. He had to choose between the two.

Who could help him choose? Christian doctrine? No. Christian doc- trine says, "Be charitable, love your neighbor, take the more rugged path, etc., etc." But which is the more rugged path? Whom should he love as a brother? The fighting man or his mother? Which does the greater good, the vague act of fighting in a group, or the concrete one of helping a particular human being to go on living? Who can decide *a priori?* Nobody. No book of ethics can tell him. The Kantian ethics

---

1. With the occupying German army, or its puppet government in Vichy.

says, "Never treat any person as a means, but as an end." Very well, if I stay with my mother, I'll treat her as an end and not as a means; but by virtue of this very fact, I'm running the risk of treating the people around me who are fighting, as means; and, conversely, if I go to join those who are fighting, I'll be treating them as an end, and, by doing that, I run the risk of treating my mother as a means.

If values are vague, and if they are always too broad for the concrete and specific case that we are considering, the only thing left for us is to trust our instincts. That's what this young man tried to do; and when I saw him, he said, "In the end, feeling is what counts. I ought to choose whichever pushes me in one direction. If I feel that I love my mother enough to sacrifice everything else for her—my desire for vengeance, for action, for adventure—then I'll stay with her. If, on the contrary, I feel that my love for my mother isn't enough, I'll leave."

But how is the value of a feeling determined? What gives his feeling for his mother value? Precisely the fact that he remained with her. I may say that I like so-and-so well enough to sacrifice a certain amount of money for him, but I may say so only if I've done it. I may say "I love my mother well enough to remain with her" if I have remained with her. The only way to determine the value of this affection is, precisely, to perform an act which confirms and defines it. But, since I require this affection to justify my act, I find myself caught in a vicious circle.

On the other hand, Gide has well said that a mock feeling and a true feeling are almost indistinguishable; to decide that I love my mother and will remain with her, or to remain with her by putting on an act, amount somewhat to the same thing. In other words, the feeling is formed by the acts one performs; so, I cannot refer to it in order to act upon it. Which means that I can neither seek within myself the true condition which will impel me to act, nor apply to a system of ethics for concepts which will permit me to act. You will say, "At least, he did go to a teacher for advice." But if you seek advice from a priest, for example, you have chosen this priest; you already knew, more or less, just about what advice he was going to give you. In other words, choosing your adviser is involving yourself. The proof of this is that if you are a Christian, you will say, "Consult a priest." But some priests are collaborating, some are just marking time, some are resisting. Which to choose? If the young man chooses a priest who is resisting or collaborating, he has already decided on the kind of advice he's going to get. Therefore, in coming to see me he knew the answer I was going to give him, and I had only one answer to give: "You're free, choose, that is, invent." No general ethics can show you what is to be done; there are no omens in the world. The Catholics will reply, "But there are." Granted—but, in any case, I myself choose the meaning they have.

When I was a prisoner, I knew a rather remarkable young man who was a Jesuit. He had entered the Jesuit order in the following way: he had had a number of very bad breaks; in childhood, his father died, leaving him in poverty, and he was a scholarship student at a religious institution where he was constantly made to feel that he was being kept out of charity; then, he failed to get any of the honors and distinctions that children like; later on, at about eighteen, he bungled a love affair; finally, at twenty-two, he failed in military training, a childish enough matter, but it was the last straw.

This young fellow might well have felt that he had botched everything. It was a sign of something, but of what? He might have taken refuge in bitterness or despair. But he very wisely looked upon all this as a sign that he was not made for secular triumphs, and that only the triumphs of religion, holiness, and faith were open to him. He saw the hand of God in all this, and so he entered the order. Who can help seeing that he alone decided what the sign meant?

Some other interpretation might have been drawn from this series of setbacks; for example, that he might have done better to turn carpenter or revolutionist. Therefore, he is fully responsible for the interpretation. Forlornness implies that we ourselves choose our being. Forlornness and anguish go together.

As for despair, the term has a very simple meaning. It means that we shall confine ourselves to reckoning only with what depends upon our will, or on the ensemble of probabilities which make our action possible. When we want something, we always have to reckon with probabilities. I may be counting on the arrival of a friend. The friend is coming by rail or streetcar; this supposes that the train will arrive on schedule, or that the streetcar will not jump the track. I am left in the realm of possibility; but possibilities are to be reckoned with only to the point where my action comports with the ensemble of these possibilities, and no further. The moment the possibilities I am considering are not rigorously involved by my action, I ought to disengage myself from them, because no God, no scheme, can adapt the world and its possibilities to my will. When Descartes said, "Conquer yourself rather than the world," he meant essentially the same thing.

The Marxists to whom I have spoken reply, "You can rely on the support of others in your action, which obviously has certain limits because you're not going to live forever. That means: rely on both what others are doing elsewhere to help you, in China, in Russia, and what they will do later on, after your death, to carry on the action and lead it to its fulfillment, which will be the revolution. You even *have* to rely upon that, otherwise you're immoral." I reply at once that I will always rely on fellow-fighters insofar as these comrades are involved with me in a common struggle, in the unity of a party or a group in which I can more or less make my weight felt; that is, one whose ranks I am in as

25

a fighter and whose movements I am aware of at every moment. In such a situation, relying on the unity and will of the party is exactly like counting on the fact that the train will arrive on time or that the car won't jump the track. But, given that man is free and that there is no human nature for me to depend on, I cannot count on men whom I do not know by relying on human goodness or man's concern for the good of society. I don't know what will become of the Russian revolution; I may make an example of it to the extent that at the present time it is apparent that the proletariat plays a part in Russia that it plays in no other nation. But I can't swear that this will inevitably lead to a triumph of the proletariat. I've got to limit myself to what I see.

Given that men are free and that tomorrow they will freely decide what man will be, I cannot be sure that, after my death, fellow-fighters will carry on my work to bring it to its maximum perfection. Tomorrow, after my death, some men may decide to set up Fascism, and the others may be cowardly and muddled enough to let them do it. Fascism will then be the human reality, so much the worse for us.

Actually, things will be as man will have decided they are to be. Does that mean that I should abandon myself to quietism? No. First, I should involve myself; then, act on the old saw, "Nothing ventured, nothing gained." Nor does it mean that I shouldn't belong to a party, but rather that I shall have no illusions and shall do what I can. For example, suppose I ask myself, "Will socialization, as such, ever come about?" I know nothing about it. All I know is that I'm going to do everything in my power to bring it about. Beyond that, I can't count on anything. Quietism is the attitude of people who say, "Let others do what I can't do." The doctrine I am presenting is the very opposite of quietism, since it declares, "There is no reality except in action." Moreover, it goes further, since it adds, "Man is nothing else than his plan; he exists only to the extent that he fulfills himself; he is therefore nothing else than the ensemble of his acts, nothing else than his life."

According to this, we can understand why our doctrine horrifies certain people. Because often the only way they can bear their wretchedness is to think, "Circumstances have been against me. What I've been and done doesn't show my true worth. To be sure, I've had no great love, no great friendship, but that's because I haven't met a man or woman who was worthy. The books I've written haven't been very good because I haven't had the proper leisure. I haven't had children to devote myself to because I didn't find a man with whom I could have spent my life. So there remains within me, unused and quite viable, a host of propensities, inclinations, possibilities, that one wouldn't guess from the mere series of things I've done."

Now, for the existentialist there is really no love other than one which manifests itself in a person's being in love. There is no genius other than one which is expressed in works of art; the genius of Proust is the sum of Proust's works; the genius of Racine is his series of tragedies. Outside of that, there is nothing. Why say that Racine could have written another tragedy, when he didn't write it? A man is involved in life, leaves his impress on it, and outside of that there is nothing. To be sure, this may seem a harsh thought to someone whose life hasn't been a success. But, on the other hand, it prompts people to understand that reality alone is what counts, that dreams, expectations, and hopes warrant no more than to define a man as a disappointed dream, as miscarried hopes, as vain expectations. In other words, to define him negatively and not positively. However, when we say, "You are nothing else than your life," that does not imply that the artist will be judged solely on the basis of his works of art; a thousand other things will contribute toward summing him up. What we mean is that a man is nothing else than a series of undertakings, that he is the sum, the organization, the ensemble of the relationships which make up these undertakings.

When all is said and done, what we are accused of, at bottom, is not our pessimism, but an optimistic toughness. If people throw up to us our works of fiction in which we write about people who are soft, weak, cowardly, and sometimes even downright bad, it's not because these people are soft, weak, cowardly, or bad; because if we were to say, as Zola did, that they are that way because of heredity, the workings of environment, society, because of biological or psychological determinism, people would be reassured. They would say, "Well, that's what we're like, no one can do anything about it." But when the existentialist writes about a coward, he says that this coward is responsible for his cowardice. He's not like that because he has a cowardly heart or lung or brain; he's not like that on account of his physiological make-up; but he's like that because he has made himself a coward by his acts. There's no such thing as a cowardly constitution; there are nervous constitutions; there is poor blood, as the common people say, or strong constitutions. But the man whose blood is poor is not a coward on that account, for what makes cowardice is the act of renouncing or yielding. A constitution is not an act; the coward is defined on the basis of the acts he performs. People feel, in a vague sort of way, that this coward we're talking about is guilty of being a coward, and the thought frightens them. What people would like is that a coward or a hero be born that way. . . .

From these few reflections it is evident that nothing is more unjust than the objections that have been raised against us. Existentialism is nothing else than an attempt to draw all the consequences of a coherent atheistic position. It isn't trying to plunge man into despair at all. But if one calls every attitude of unbelief despair, like the Christians, then the word is not being used in its original sense. Existentialism isn't so atheistic that it wears itself out showing that God doesn't exist. Rather,

30

it declares that even if God did exist, that would change nothing. There you've got our point of view. Not that we believe that God exists, but we think that the problem of His existence is not the issue. In this sense existentialism is optimistic, a doctrine of action, and it is plain dishonesty for Christians to make no distinction between their own despair and ours and then to call us despairing.

THE READER

1. What is the significance of the words "if existence really does precede essence" (p. 1229)? What does this mean? What is the force of if? Why does Sartre repeat the words later in the essay?
2. Why does Sartre use three separate terms—anguish, forlornness, despair? What, if any, are the differences among them?
3. Sartre makes a distinction between treating "any person as a means . . . [and] as an end" (p. 1234). What are the implications of this distinction?

THE WRITER

1. What are some of the methods or devices Sartre uses to define existentialism? Why does he use more than one method or device? Compare the techniques that Sartre uses with those that Highet uses in defining Zen (p. 1205).
2. Sartre says that "when we say that a man is responsible for himself, we do not only mean that he is responsible for his own individuality, but that he is responsible for all men" (p. 1229). Write a brief essay explaining how, in the existentialist view, this is possible.

Richard B. Sewall

A SENSE OF THE ENDING

The last time I appeared on this stage[1] was in a minor part in a Cap and Bells production of *Much Ado About Nothing*. I was Friar Francis. I had nine speeches—six one-liners and two big juicy ones. The two big ones were full of wisdom and sound advice, as befits a friar—or, indeed, a convocation speaker. I read the Friar's part through the other day, to get myself in the spirit of this platform again and perhaps to recall a little bit of the old undergraduate glory. As a matter of fact, for me, it was

Adapted for the *Williams Alumni Review* (Fall 1975). From a convocation address delivered at Williams College, Williamstown, Massachusetts.

1. As an undergraduate at Williams College.

anything but glorious. My timing was bad on the one-liners, and the big speeches fell curiously flat. Frankly, I don't think I understood them then. But I know more about Shakespeare (and a few other things) now; and, as I read those lines over, they hit me at 67 as they never did at 17. Listen to Friar Francis trying to get his listeners to accept something he feels deeply—in this case, his belief in the innocence of a slandered young lady. One can feel his frustration in every word:

> Call me a fool;
> Trust not my reading nor my observations,
> Which with experimental seal doth warrant
> The tenour of my book; trust not my age,
> My reverence, calling, nor divinity,
> If this sweet lady lie not guiltless here
> Under some biting error.

Fifty years (between 17 and 67) make a lot of difference, and now at last I know what the Friar felt: the frustration of trying to convey something you feel deeply to an audience that is either skeptical or uninvolved. The Friar put my difficulty plainly, even if it is not quite the same as his. I want to talk to you today about matters which cannot be to you as intensely personal as they are to me; I'm involved as you cannot be, and I cannot bridge the gap by the triumphant march of logic, by statistics, by hard evidence. I want to share with you, simply, a bit of experience I've picked up on the way.

Oh, there are lots of "biting errors" I could expose, were my mood so inclined: educational fallacies rampant in my own beloved New Haven and right here in Williamstown; the sinister drift of our national culture and politics and economy; the global threats to our environment and our peace. I could scare you to death! Or, changing the tune, as appropriate to this day, I could talk about the library as the beating heart of this or any other educational institution. I could talk about Jack Sawyer and all he did for this college. But although all these possibilities are close to my mind and heart, they are not closest, and I decided I must talk about what is closest or I'd better not talk at all. What is closest? Just two things, intimately bound, almost inseparable: love and death.

Shortly after I came to this decision, I ran across a remark by William Butler Yeats. [2] "I am still of the opinion," he wrote, "that only two topics can be of the least interest to a serious and studious mind—sex and death." My first thought was: What a stuffy way to put it! And my second was: Why be so glandular? Why sex and death? I prefer my way of putting it, and Woody Allen's: love and death. [3] I don't intend to be clinical about either, and I am not addressing the "serious and studious

---

2. Yeats (1865–1939): Irish poet and playwright.

3. *Love and Death* was the title of a 1975 film by Woody Allen.

mind." I am talking to you as fellow pilgrims—old, middle-aged and young—in this vale of tears and laughter. And I want to share with you a little of what I've learned this past year—I would say the most educational year of my life, the high-water mark of my experience as a human being.

5   I guess you'll have to know the facts: My wife, Mathilde, died of cancer of the pancreas last November, and my brother John (Williams '28) was killed in a car accident last March. With all the tragedy in the world, you may wonder at my bringing up these two personal losses. It may seem a little impudent of me, even a little embarrassing. "They talk of hallowed things aloud," said Emily Dickinson, trying to explain her aversion to society, "and embarrass my dog." But she was young when she said that. She clammed up, and she was wrong. She was too easily embarrassed.

So here's the first and perhaps simplest thing I've learned this past year: Never be embarrassed to talk about hallowed things, like love and death. We Americans are a little finicky about both. We reduce love to sex and talk about it clinically as in Kinsey[4] and the sex books, or grossly as in *Playboy* and *Penthouse,* or sentimentally as in the popular songs. There's very little talk about the tragic side of love, the comic side of love, love as a discipline, love as a means of education, love as the end and aim of education, the very reason we're here today.

And as for death, we hide from it, pretty it up, pack it away in hospitals, spend millions every year on lavish funerals, or get so glutted with it over the media that we hear or read, with hardly a tremor, about hundreds of thousands dying in Vietnam, or Africa, or Bangladesh. The result is that death is hardly real at all to us. It's a forbidden subject except at funerals and in sermons that aim to take away its sting. I think we'd be better able to cope with it if we talked about it more, if we shared our experience of it more frankly. And so I'm facing you with it—ironically, on this festive occasion, this day of a new beginning when the last thing you want to hear about is the old, old ending.

Which leads me to the second thing I've learned this past year: It's a sense of the ending that makes the beginning, and all that follows therefrom, so much more meaningful. Why deny a reality that, paradoxically, can be so life-giving, so enriching?

I heard the other day of a great-great-grandmother who—this was generations ago—amazed her family by announcing one morning: "I want to die in that rocking chair, and I'm going to close my own eyes." She did both. Her name was Experience Bardwell Lyman. The young

---

4. Alfred Charles Kinsey (1894–1956), American zoologist and student of human sexual behavior whose findings, published in two volumes as *Sexual Behavior in the* *Human Male* (1948) and *Sexual Behavior in the Human Female* (1953), constitute what is popularly known as the Kinsey Report.

people called her "Aunt Speedie," and a hundred years later her descendants are still talking and laughing about her and living a little more fully because of her. I wonder if this is what Wallace Stevens[5] had in mind when he wrote, "Death is the mother of beauty."

Her great-grandchildren still point to that rocker. Aunt Speedie knew   10
how to die and how to talk about it. She had a sense of her ending—clear-eyed, frank, unabashed, humorous. My friend Emily Dickinson knew how to talk about it, too—in her poetry:

> By a departing light
> We see acuter, quite,
> Than by a wick that stays.
> There's something in the flight
> That clarifies the sight
> And decks the rays.

"There's something in the flight / That clarifies the sight . . ." or, in the words of the old hymn, takes "The dimness of our souls away." Why do things get so dim and unclear? Going along in the old routine, we get in a kind of acquiescent numbness, we get used to things, we don't see sharply or hear clearly or feel intensely.

I had a teacher of creative writing once who told our class, "You must look at things not only as if you were seeing them for the first time but as if you were seeing them for the last time, as if you were never to see them again and had to take them all in and remember them forever." Keep that in mind the next time you look around at these hills. Never, never get used to them!

We need to be jolted out of our numbness, often not so gently as my teacher did it. "Such men as I," cried Dmitri Karamazov,[6] "need a blow . . ." and he spoke for the whole human race. Sometimes nothing but death will remind us that we are alive. That's a terrible thing to say, but it's true.

Love and death . . . What has tortured me these past ten months since Mathilde died are the things I didn't say, the love I didn't express. Why was I so dim, so finicky, so inhibited, so embarrassed? Or were the look in the eyes enough, the squeeze of the hand, the kiss on the brow? I hope to God they were. Heaven knows she was up to anything. She had nerve for both of us. She and Aunt Speedie would have gotten along fine. A week before she died, I came in her room wearing a new dark-green shirt under an old greenish tweed jacket. "They were made for each other," she said. "You could wear them anywhere—even my funeral." Which I did.

The evening of the night she died, she was hilarious, never wittier,

5. Stevens (1879–1955), American poet.   6. A character in Feodor Dostoyevsky's
                                               novel *The Brothers Karamazov* (1879–80).

and (as always) a bit of a rascal. She ribbed her doctor about what a lousy skier he was. When a friend asked her why she couldn't eat a bit of the lovely cheese cake she'd brought her, she replied, "Because, my dear, I have a touch of cancer."

It was at the time those three doctors went to examine Nixon in San Clemente to see if he was well enough to testify.[7] In my then state of compassion, I averred as how it was tough on the poor man to have to go through all that examination again. Our cheese-cake friend, a veteran Nixon-hater, said, "Nonsense! Nothing is bad enough for that man," etc., etc. "No," said Mathilde, looking quite saintly on her sickbed, "you're wrong. I'm so full of love I can't wish harm on any one." And with a twinkle she added, "You know, if I should get well, I think I'd be rather nice." ("Death is the mother of beauty.")

Then another friend said, "Tillie, when you get well, I want you to make me one of those saints." (Til was a potter, I should tell you, and did ceramic sculpture. One of her favorite themes was St. Francis[8] and the birds.) "Evaline," she answered, "if I get well, I'll make nothing but saints." Six hours later she was dead. Aunt Speedie was one up on her: Mathilde didn't close her own eyes. Will it shock you—it shouldn't by now—when I tell you that I closed them? It was very simple, very sad and very beautiful.

Love and death . . . It's clear to me that the closer she came to death, the more she learned to love and the more she learned *about* love—and the more she taught us both *to love* and *about love.* The departing light clarified the sight—in all of us. She knew where she was going, and she knew what she was learning, and she talked about it. "These last three months," she told her doctor a few weeks before the end, "have been the best of my life. I wouldn't have missed them for anything."

To understand more fully this remarkable statement, you must hear the last letter she ever wrote. It was to a friend, Holly Tuttle of New Haven, who lost her husband some years ago. The letter says more about love and death than I could in a week of convocation addresses. It's more than just a letter; it's a document. And I read it to you with no embarrassment at all. Remember: "There's something in the flight / That clarifies the sight." All things—individual lives, colleges, libraries, college educations—take on new meaning in the light of their endings—or

7. Richard Milhous Nixon, whose resignation from the presidency, the first in American history, became official on August 9, 1974. While en route to his retirement home in San Clemente, California, Nixon was pardoned by his successor, Gerald R. Ford, for all offenses committed during his administration, thus saving Nixon from the possibility of criminal indictment and trial for his involvement in the Watergate scandal.

8. St. Francis of Assisi (1181 or 1182–1226), Italian monk who founded the Franciscan order of men and women. His faith was characterized by its joyousness and love of nature, and his preaching to the birds has become a popular subject for artists.

when they end for you, as they must. *Love them while you can,* and never, never be embarrassed.

And now here's the letter, and I'm done:

> DEAR HOLLY—You sent me such a good letter—I do want to answer— The problem of dealing with this fellow Death has been interesting (funny—what would woman's lib. say to my making Death masculine— surely I can't think of myself being swept up by a lady). In the first place—when I saw him come striding up to my house—garbed in all his strange garments that we humans have wished on him—I wasn't in the least spooked. I opened the door and we had a nice little chat. Subsequent chats have been reassuring and I know he's my good friend. I'm sure you too have a nodding acquaintance with him so you have the same feelings.
>
> Then there's LOVE. I feel I'd never have known its endless horizons had I lived out my full span. Somehow in a smooth life we take each other for granted and now even with someone like Richard new little vistas open up—and with casual acquaintances—whole worlds. My plumber— Tommy Citerella—stopped in to see me after he'd attended to my drips and leaks—sat down and looked out at the view I have from my bed—a valley—a mill house—a waterfall—a lake—all hung in the most sensational color—
>
> "Missus" he said—"you have to have faith. You have to pray. God's never failed me. He's saved me three times."
>
> "Tommy," I said, "I don't know where to aim my prayers. God is such a mystery."
>
> "Missus," he said, "don't worry. I'll take over all the praying"—and he took my two hands and leaned down and kissed me on the brow.
>
> So now—what do I have to worry about?
>
>   LOVE, TIL

Death is the mother of beauty . . . a sense of the ending. Do you see   20
what I mean?

Authors

Edward Abbey (b. 1926)
American writer, essayist, and self-described "agrarian anarchist." Born in Pennsylvania, Abbey has lived in the Southwest since 1948, when he arrived there to study at the University of New Mexico. A former ranger for the National Park Service, he takes as his most pervasive theme the beauty of that region and the ways it has been despoiled by government, business interests, and tourism. Abbey's books include the novels *Fire on the Mountain* (1963), *The Monkey Wrench Gang* (1975), and *Good News* (1980). He has also published several essay collections, among them *Desert Solitaire: A Season in the Wilderness* (1968), in which "The Serpents of Paradise" appears; *Abbey's Road* (1979); *Beyond the Wall: Essays from the Outside* (1984); and *One Life at a Time, Please* (1988).

Diane Ackerman (b. 1948)
American poet, playwright, and nonfiction writer. Born in Waukegan, Illinois, Ackerman attended Boston, Pennsylvania State, and Cornell universities. Driven perhaps by what she calls "an intense, nomadic curiosity," she has held a variety of jobs, including social worker, government researcher, and editorial assistant, before settling on teaching. In addition to her poetry collections, which include *Wife of Light* (1978), *Lady Faustus* (1983), and *Jaguar of Sweet Laughter* (1991), Ackerman has written plays and nonfiction books, including her most recent *A Natural History of the Senses* (1990). "Mass Meeting on the Coast" originally appeared in *Life* magazine (May 1987).

Aesop (ca. 620–560 B.C.)
Legendary Greek storyteller. A collection of Greek fables, orally composed and transmitted, was ascribed to Aesop, a Phrygian slave, sometime in the third century A.D., but many are far older,

being found on Egyptian papyri of 800 to 1,000 years earlier. Preserved and copied during the Middle Ages, the fables probably made their way into English through the work of the Dutch scholar Erasmus, who translated them into Latin; Erasmus's Latin text was later rendered into English. The fable has proved to be an enduring literary form, practiced in this century by writers as different as Orwell, Golding, and Nabokov.

Woody Allen (b. 1935)
Popular name of Heywood Allen, born Allen Stewart Konigsberg, American comedian, writer, playwright, actor, and film director. Allen began his career as a television comedy writer in the late 1950s. Eventually he became a comedian himself, then a screenwriter, playwright (*Don't Drink the Water*, 1966; *Play It Again, Sam*, 1969), and film director. His films include *Annie Hall* (1977), which won Allen the Academy Award for best director; *Manhattan* (1979); *The Purple Rose of Cairo* (1985); *Hannah and Her Sisters* (1986); *Crimes and Misdemeanors* (1989); and *Alice* (1991). Allen's books include *Getting Even* (1971), *Without Feathers* (1975), and *Side Effects* (1980). "Selections from the Allen Notebooks" first appeared in *Without Feathers* (1975).

Maya Angelou (b. 1928)
American author, playwright, actress, poet, and singer. Born in St. Louis, Angelou attended public schools in Arkansas and California before studying music and dance. In a richly varied career, she has been a cook, streetcar conductor, singer, actress, dancer, and teacher. Author of several volumes of poetry and ten plays (stage, screen, and television), Angelou may be best known for her autobiography, a work-in-progress of which five volumes have been published so far. "Graduation" originally appeared in *I Know Why the Caged Bird Sings*

(1970), the first volume of that autobiography and one of the fullest accounts of the African-American woman's experience in contemporary literature.

Hannah Arendt (1906–1975)
German-American political scientist and philosopher. Born in Hanover, Germany, and educated at the University of Heidelberg, Arendt began her academic career in Germany but was forced to leave when Hitler came to power. Arriving in the United States in 1940, she became chief editor for a major publisher and a frequent lecturer on college campuses. Arendt taught at a number of American colleges and universities, finishing her career at the New School for Social Research in New York City. Of the dozen or so major books she wrote, three received greatest attention: *Eichmann in Jerusalem: A Report on the Banality of Evil* (1963); *On Revolution* (1963); and *The Origins of Totalitarianism* (1968). "Denmark and the Jews" comes from *Eichmann in Jerusalem;* in slightly different form, it first appeared in *The New Yorker.*

Matthew Arnold (1822–1888)
English poet, literary critic, and social critic. Son of distinguished educator Thomas Arnold, Matthew Arnold studied at Balliol College, Oxford, before beginning work as an inspector of schools, a position he held for thirty-five years. Arnold wrote poetry early in his literary career, establishing his reputation with poems like "Stanzas from the Grand Chartreuse" (1855) and "Dover Beach" (1867). The publication of his *Essays in Criticism,* First Series (1867) marked a shift to writing prose. The recurrent topic in Arnold's writing is the problem of living a full and an enjoyable life in a modern industrial society. "Culture" comes from *Culture and Anarchy* (1869), a collection of critical essays considered central to Arnold's thought. Another important collection is *Literature and Dogma* (1873).

Isaac Asimov (1920–1992)
American biochemist, science writer, and novelist. Born in Russia, Asimov was educated in the United States and received a Ph.D. in biochemistry from Columbia Unversity. He became a member of the faculty at the School of Medicine, Boston University, in 1949 and he is currently professor of biochemistry there. An extraordinarily prolific author, Asimov has published more than 250 books

on topics as diverse as mathematics, astronomy, physics, chemistry, biology, mythology, Shakespeare, the Bible, and geography; his science fiction works include some of the most famous and influential in that genre. Among his books: *The Stars, Like the Dust* (1951), *Science, Numbers and I* (1968), *ABC's of the Earth* (1971), *The Road to Infinity* (1979), *The Exploding Suns: The Secrets of Supernovas* (1985), and *The Tyrannosaurus Prescription* (1989). "The Eureka Phenomenon" comes from *The Left Hand of the Electron* (1972).

W. H. Auden (1907–1973)
Wystan Hugh Auden, English poet, playwright, librettist, and essayist. Called "the foremost poet of his generation," Auden was born in York, England, and educated at Christ Church College, Oxford. After Oxford, Auden supported himself as a schoolmaster (1930–35), making his literary debut in 1930 with the publication of *Poems.* During the 1930s, he and Christopher Isherwood collaborated on three plays: *The Dog Beneath the Skin* (1935); *The Ascent of F6* (1936); and *On the Frontier* (1938). In 1939, he settled in the United States, became an American citizen in 1946, and, with the exception of the period from 1956 to 1961, when he was professor of poetry at Oxford, made his home there until 1972. Among the more important collections of his poems are *Another Time* (1940) and *The Shield of Achilles* (1955). He also wrote opera libretti as well as scores of reviews and introductions for books of poetry. Some of these were collected in *The Dyer's Hand* (1962), from which "Apothegms" comes.

Francis Bacon (1561–1626)
English civil servant, politician, statesman, and philosopher. Trained as a lawyer, Bacon served as a member of Parliament during the reign of Queen Elizabeth I. After her death, he found favor with King James I and advanced in government service to the position of lord chancellor. His career was cut short in 1621 when he was convicted of accepting bribes. Retired, he married and devoted the rest of his life to study and writing philosophical works. Bacon's only predecessor in the field of the essay was Michel de Montaigne. His books include *The Advancement of Learning* (1605), *Novum Organum* (1620), which contains "Of Simulation and Dissimulation," and *Essays* (various editions,

1597–1625), from which "Of Revenge" comes.

Russell Baker (b. 1925)
American journalist, humorist, and social commentator. A Pulitzer Prize–winning author, Baker began his career as a journalist with the *Baltimore Sun* and has written "The Observer" and "The Sunday Observer" columns for the *New York Times* since 1962. His humor runs from broad, sometimes allegorical satires on American politics and taste to witty criticisms of current jargon and slang. Baker's columns have been collected in such books as *An American in Washington* (1961), *Poor Russell's Almanac* (1972), and *The Rescue of Miss Yaskell and Other Pipe Dreams* (1983). He has also written an autobiography, *Growing Up* (1982), and edited *The Norton Book of Light Verse* (1986). "Surely Not Cigar-Shaped!" appeared in the *New York Times* (Aug. 8, 1987).

James Baldwin (1924–1987)
American essayist, novelist, and social activist. Baldwin was born in Harlem, became a minister at fourteen, and grew to maturity in an America disfigured by racism and prejudice. Only after moving to Paris in 1948 did he begin to write. Both his first novel, *Go Tell It on the Mountain* (1953), and his first play, *The Amen Corner* (1955), are autobiographical explorations. Although he would write other plays—*Blues for Mister Charlie* (1964) was one of his best—Baldwin concentrated his energies on novels such as *Giovanni's Room* (1956), *Another Country* (1962), and *If Beale Street Could Talk* (1974) as well as on essays. His stories are collected in *Going to Meet the Man* (1965); his essay collections, including *Notes of a Native Son* (1955), from which "Stranger in the Village" comes, *Nobody Knows My Name* (1961), *The Fire Next Time* (1963), and *No Name in the Street* (1972), demonstrate Baldwin's skills as a social critic of insight and passion. A number of his most important essays and reviews have been gathered in *The Price of the Ticket* (1985).

Carl Becker (1873–1945)
American historian and teacher. Educated at the University of Wisconsin, Becker held several teaching appointments (Dartmouth, University of Kansas, University of Minnesota) before joining the faculty of Cornell Univeristy, where he taught from 1917 until 1941.

The author of fifteen books, Becker wrote "Democracy" for his most important book, the text *Modern Democracy* (1941).

William Bennett (b. 1943)
American educator and federal official. Born in Brooklyn, New York, Bennett earned a B.A. at Williams College before attending the University of Texas and Harvard Law School. He began his wide-ranging public career as assistant to the president of Boston University, and continued as executive director of the National Humanities Center, professor at North Carolina State University and the University of North Carolina, chairperson of the National Endowment for the Humanities, secretary of education, and, most recently, director of the President's Office of Drug Control Policy. Bennett's publications include *Schools without Drugs* (1986). His "Address," delivered at Harvard on the 350th anniversary of Harvard College, was first reprinted in the *Chronicle of Higher Education* (Oct. 15, 1986).

Jeremy Bernstein (b. 1929)
American physicist and science writer. Although his earliest ambition was to be a jazz trumpeter, Bernstein became a physicist instead, earning an M.A. and Ph.D. in physics at Harvard. He spent several years at the Institute for Advanced Study at Princeton and the National Science Foundation, later teaching physics, first at New York University and then at the Stevens Institute of Technology, where he has remained since 1967. He is also a staff writer for *The New Yorker* magazine, where he contributes articles on scientific topics. Bernstein's books include *A Comprehensible World: On Modern Science and Its Origins* (1967), *Einstein* (1973), and *Science Observed: Essays Out of My Mind* (1982). "SN–1987A" first appeared in *The American Scholar* (Spring 1988).

Bruno Bettelheim (1903–1990)
American child psychologist, teacher, and writer. Born and educated in Vienna, Bettelheim came to the United States in 1939 and joined the faculty of the University of Chicago in 1944, beginning a long and distinguished teaching career there (1944–73). He wrote several dozen books, including *Love Is Not Enough: The Treatment of Emotionally Disturbed Children* (1950), *The Informed Heart: Autonomy in a Mass*

Age (1960), *The Children of the Dream* (1969), *The Uses of Enchantment: The Meaning and Importance of Fairy Tales* (1976), and *A Good Enough Parent* (1987). "A Victim" originally appeared in *The Informed Heart.*

Ambrose Bierce (1842–1914?)
American journalist, poet, and writer. Bierce was born the tenth child of a poor Ohio family. After serving in the Civil War and working as a journalist in San Francisco, he went to England, where he wrote comic and satiric sketches for several publications. In 1876, he returned to San Francisco as a reporter for William Randolph Hearst's *Examiner.* The death of his two sons, along with a divorce, might well have led him to Mexico, where he reportedly rode with Pancho Villa's revolutionaries; he disappeared and is presumed to have died there. Bierce's twelve-volume *Collected Works* (1909–12) include a generous sampling of his tales, essays, verses, and fables. Today, Bierce may be best known for *The Devil's Dictionary* (1906), a collection of ironic definitions compiled while he was a Hearst correspondent in Washington, D.C. Selections included in "Prose Forms: Apothegms" come from *The Devil's Dictionary.*

Caroline Bird (b. 1915)
American journalist, public-relations specialist, and writer. Bird attended Vassar College, graduated from the University of Toledo, and received her master's from the University of Wisconsin (1939). She worked as a researcher at *Newsweek* and *Fortune* in the 1940s, then moved into public relations, which she left after twenty years to pursue writing full time. Bird is the author of a number of books focussing on feminist concerns: *Born Female: The High Cost of Keeping Women Down* (1968), *Everything a Woman Needs to Know to Get Paid What She's Worth* (1973; revised edition, 1982), *The Two-Paycheck Marriage* (1979), and *The Good Years: Your Life in the Twenty-first Century* (1983). "College Is a Waste of Time and Money" comes from *The Case Against College* (1975).

William Blake (1757–1827)
English poet, artist, and writer. The son of a London haberdasher, Blake studied drawing at ten and became an engraver and illustrator by trade; he established a printing shop in London, where he engraved and printed his second volume

of poems, *Songs of Innocence* (1789). Blake's poems and illuminations, reflecting an independent spirit seeking freedom from repression, take their inspiration from nature and religion, both being transformed into a deeply personal and unorthodox vision. His major works include the *Songs of Experience* (1794), *The Four Zoas* (1803), *Milton* (1804), and *Jerusalem* (1809). "Proverbs of Hell" comes from *The Marriage of Heaven and Hell* (1793), Blake's principal prose work.

Carol Bly (b. 1930)
American short-story writer, poet, and teacher. Born Carol McLean, Bly grew up in Minnesota and Virginia, went to boarding school in New England, and attended Wellesley College and the University of Minnesota. After graduate work there she married and raised four children in a small mining town on the western edge of Minnesota. Out of this time came a book *Letters from the Country* (1981), a collection of essays originally written for the *Minnesota Monthly.* Bly is a lecturer, teacher, and in 1971 was the co-founder of the Prairie Arts Center. She has also written *Backbone* (1985), a collection of stories. "Bruno Bettelheim: Three Ideas to Try in Madison, Minnesota" is taken from *Letters from the Country.* It first appeared in *Minnesota Monthly* (Jan. 1974).

Daniel J. Boorstin (b. 1914)
American historian. A graduate of Harvard and a Rhodes scholar with two degrees from Oxford University, Boorstin is a lawyer by training and brings to the study of history an interest in subjects— particularly the effects of mass media, social behavior, and popular culture— that traditional historians have tended to ignore. Perhaps his best-known works are *The Decline of Radicalism: Reflections of America Today* (1969), *The Americans: The Democratic Experience* (1974; Pulitzer Prize), and *The Republic of Technology* (1978). The Historian: 'A Wrestler with an Angel' " originally appeared in the *New York Times Book Review* (Sept. 20, 1987).

Wayne C. Booth (b. 1921)
American writer, literary critic, and teacher. After receiving a Ph.D. from the University of Chicago in 1950, Booth began a teaching career that has taken him to Haverford College, Earlham College, and back to the University

of Chicago, where he is now professor of English. Among Booth's books are *The Rhetoric of Fiction* (1961; revised edition, 1983), *Now Don't Try to Reason with Me* (1970), *A Rhetoric of Irony* (1974), *Modern Dogma and the Rhetoric of Assent* (1974), *Critical Understanding: The Powers and Limits of Pluralism* (1979), and *The Company We Keep: An Ethics of Fiction* (1988). "Is There Any Knowledge That a Man *Must* Have?" originally appeared in *The Knowledge Most Worth Having* (1967); "Boring from Within: The Art of the Freshman Essay" was an address given to the Illinois Council of College Teachers (1963).

Jacob Bronowski (1908–1974)
English mathematician, scientist, and writer. Born in Poland and educated in England, where he received a Ph.D. in mathematics from Cambridge in 1933, Bronowski served as a university lecturer before entering government service during World War II. From 1950 until 1963, he was head of research for Britain's National Coal Board; from 1964 until his death, he was a resident fellow at the Salk Institute, La Jolla, California. The author of many books, among them *Science and Human Values* (1956; 1965), *Nature and Knowledge* (1969), *Magic, Science, and Civilization* (published posthumously, 1978), Bronowski is best known for the thirteen-part television series, "The Ascent of Man" (1973–74). "The Nature of Scientific Reasoning" comes from *Science and Human Values*. "The Reach of Imagination" from *Proceedings of the American Academy of Arts and Letters and National Institute of Arts and Letters*, 2nd ser., No. 17 (1967).

Anatole Broyard (1920–1990)
American literary critic and essayist. Born in New Orleans, Broyard attended Brooklyn College and the New School for Social Research, afterward staying on at the New School as a lecturer in sociology and literature for twenty-one years. In 1971 he began working as a book reviewer and feature writer for the *New York Times*, becoming an influential voice in the literary and publishing worlds. Broyard's two books, *Aroused by Books* (1974) and *Men, Women and Other Anticlimaxes* (1980), are both collections of book reviews and essays that originally appeared in the *Times*. "Intoxicated by My Illness" is from the *New York Times Magazine* (Nov. 12, 1989).

Jerome S. Bruner (b. 1915)
American psychologist and teacher. Educated at Duke and Harvard, Bruner has made major contributions to understanding how human beings process information. At Harvard from 1945 to 1981, he founded the Center for Cognitive Studies, an interdisciplinary research center devoted to analyzing the learning process. Bruner has concentrated his research on the development of learning capacities in children. In 1981, he accepted an appointment at the New School for Social Research and currently teaches at New York University. Among Bruner's most important books are *A Study of Thinking* (1956), *The Process of Education* (1960), *The Relevance of Education* (1971), *In Search of Mind*, an autobiography (1983), *Actual Minds, Possible Worlds* (1986); and *Making Sense* (1987). "Freud and the Image of Man" originally appeared in the *Partisan Review* (Summer 1956).

Anthony Burgess (b. 1917)
[John] Anthony Burgess [Wilson], English novelist, playwright, editor, and writer. Born in Manchester, England, and a graduate of Manchester University, Burgess was a lecturer and teacher of English until 1954, when he became an education officer in the Colonial Service, stationed in Malaya. His writing career began there. In 1959, when he was told that he had a year to live, Burgess returned to England and wrote five novels in one year. Since then he has written several dozen more, including *A Clockwork Orange* (1962), *Enderby Outside* (1968), *Earthly Powers* (1980), *The End of the World News: An Entertainment* (1984), and *Any Old Iron* (1989). In addition, Burgess has written critical studies, giving special attention to James Joyce and D. H. Lawrence. "Is America Falling Apart?" originally appeared in the *New York Times* in 1971.

Herbert Butterfield (1900–1979)
British educator and writer. He was educated at Cambridge and has spent his career there, serving in a variety of capacities including professor of modern history (1944–63), vice-chancellor (1959–61), and Regius Professor. A specialist in eighteenth-century English and French history, Butterfield wrote a classic study, *The Whig Interpretation of History* (1931), as well as *Lord North and the People* (1949) and *George III*

and the Historians (1957). "The Originality of the Old Testament" originally
appeared in *Writings on Christianity
and History* (1979), a collection of Butterfield's essays edited by C. T. McIntire.

Edward Hallett Carr (1892–1982)
English historian, journalist, and statesman. After studying classics at Trinity
College, Cambridge, Carr spent twenty
years in the diplomatic service. In 1936,
he became professor of international relations at University College in Wales
and began to write about diplomatic history. In 1941, he became assistant editor
of the *Times* (London). In 1946, he left
teaching and journalism to begin work
on his major opus, a fourteen-volume
study titled *A History of Russia,* which
he completed in 1978. "The Historian
and His Facts" comes from Carr's *What
Is History?* (1961).

Lord Chesterfield (1694–1773)
Philip Dormer Stanhope, fourth earl of
Chesterfield, English statesman, diplomat, and writer. Although attracted to
the literary world as a youth, Chesterfield entered diplomatic service and held
important posts in Holland and Ireland.
His literary reputation rests on his *Letters.* Addressed to his son Philip and
written with near-daily frequency beginning in 1737, they became a handbook
of gentlemanly conduct when they were
published in 1774. In a now-famous episode, Samuel Johnson sent the *Plan* for
his *Dictionary* to Chesterfield but received no response. Even though Chesterfield published two favorable reviews
when the *Dictionary* was printed, Johnson, always sensitive to slights, wrote his
"Letter to Lord Chesterfield," scorning
the nobleman's praise.

Samuel L. Clemens (1835–1910)
American novelist, journalist, humorist,
and writer. First apprenticed as a
printer, Clemens was by turns a river-
boat pilot, gold prospector, and journalist. Under the pen name Mark Twain,
he became famous when his short story
"The Celebrated Jumping Frog of
Calaveras County" was published in
1867. Clemens wrote a good deal and
lectured widely after that. At least two of
his novels, *The Adventures of Tom Sawyer* (1876) and *The Adventures of Huckleberry Finn* (1885), rank as American
classics. "Advice to Youth" is the text of
a lecture delivered by Clemens in 1882.
He dictated "The War Prayer" in 1904

or 1905, but it was not published until
1923 in *Europe and Elsewhere.*

Carl Cohen (b. 1931)
American philosopher and teacher.
After taking a Ph.D. in philosophy at the
Univeristy of California, Los Angeles
(1955), Cohen became a member of the
Department of Philosophy at the Uni-
versity of Michigan, Ann Arbor, where
he has been professor of philosophy since
1960. With special interests in political
philosophy and the philosophy of law,
Cohen has published widely in a number
of journals. His books include *Civil Dis-
obedience: Conscience, Tactics, and the
Law* (1971) and *Democracy* (1973).
"The Case for the Use of Animals in
Biomedical Research" originally appeared in the *New England Journal of
Medicine* (Oct. 2, 1986).

(Alfred) Alistair Cooke (b. 1908)
English journalist, broadcaster, and
writer. Born in Manchester, England,
Cooke attended Cambridge University
and spent a year each at Yale and Harvard Universities before beginning work
for the BBC in London, first as a film
critic and later as a commentator on
American affairs. In the course of a wide-
ranging career in print and broadcast
journalism, he as worked as a correspondent for *NBC News, The London Times,
The London Daily Herald,* and *The
Manchester Guardian;* has hosted Public
Television's "Masterpiece Theatre" for
many years; and has written and narrated a major television series, "American: A Personal History of the U.S."
(1972–73). Cooke's books include *A
Generation on Trial* (1950); *Talk About
America* (1968); *Alistair Cooke's America* (1973); *The Patient Has the Floor*
(1986), from which "Doctor and Patient: Face to Face" is taken; and *America Observed* (1988).

Aaron Copland (1900–1990)
American composer, conductor, and
writer. Born in New York City, Copland
studied music theory and practice in
Paris (1921–24), then returned to New
York to write, organize concert series,
publish American scores, and further the
cause of the American composer. After
some experimentation with adapting
jazz to classical composition, Copland
developed a distinctly American style,
incorporating American folk songs and
legends into three ballet scores: *Billy the
Kid* (1938), *Rodeo* (1942), and *Appalachian Spring* (1944; Pulitzer Prize); po-

etry into *Twelve Poems of Emily Dickinson*, songs for voice and piano (1950); and historical material into *Lincoln Portrait* (1942), for narrator and orchestra. Copland also wrote *about* music; "How We Listen" comes from a collection of his essays, *What to Listen for in Music* (1957).

Malcolm Cowley (1898–1989)
American critic, poet, editor, and literary historian. Cowley grew up in Pittsburgh, began his college career—twice interrupted by World War I—at Harvard in 1915, graduated in 1920, and thereafter supported himself as a professional writer. Although he wrote poetry (*Blue Juniata*, 1929; *The Dry Season*, 1941; *Blue Juniata: Collected Poems*, 1968), he earned a more important place for himself as a literary historian and memoirist. In *Exile's Return* (1934), *The Literary Situation* (1954), *Think Back on Us: A Contemporary Chronicle of the 1930s* (1967), *A Many-windowed House* (1970), and *A Second Flowering* (1973), Cowley recorded vital chapters in American literary life. His memoirs, *And I Worked at the Writer's Trade* (1978) and *The Dream of the Golden Mountains* (1980), amplified and further personalized those chronicles. "The View from 80" comes from a collection of essays with the same title, published in 1980.

Robertson Davies (b. 1913)
Canadian novelist, playwright, and critic. Educated in Canada and at Balliol College, Oxford, Davies' first job out of college was as an actor for two seasons with England's prestigious Old Vic Company. From 1940 to 1962, he worked as a critic and book reviewer while keeping a hand in theater by writing and directing plays. He returned to Canada and taught at the University of Toronto until 1981. Davies is best known for his novels, among them *The Salterton Trilogy* (1951–58), *The Deptford Trilogy* (1970–75) and more recently, *What's Bred in the Bone* (1985) and *The Lyre of Orpheus* (1989). "Ham and Tongue" comes from *One Half of Robertson Davies* (1978), a collection of essays. It is an abridged version of a speech given on April 6, 1977, for the Cosmos Club of Washington, D.C.

Joan Didion (b. 1934)
American novelist, essayist, and screenwriter. A native Californian, Didion studied at the University of California,

Berkeley. After winning *Vogue* magazine's Prix de Paris contest for excellence in writing, she went to work for the magazine. Didion rose from promotional copywriter to associate feature editor before leaving *Vogue* in 1963, the year her first novel, *Run River*, was published. Since then, she has written three more novels (*Play It as It Lays*, 1971; *A Book of Common Prayer*, 1977; *Democracy*, 1984). A frequent contributor to magazines such as *Vogue* and *Harper's Bazaar*, Didion's essay collections include *Slouching towards Bethlehem* (1969) and *The White Album* (1979). *Salvador*, a work of reportage based on her visit to El Salvador in 1983, marked Didion's growing concern with politics. *Miami* (1987), another book of reportage, is an attempt to come to terms with the complexities of an American city. "On Going Home" and "On Keeping a Notebook" originally appeared in *Slouching towards Bethlehem*.

Annie Dillard (b. 1945)
American naturalist, poet, critic, and editor. Dillard received a B.A. and an M.A. from Hollins College. A keen observer of the natural world, Dillard published her first collection of poems, *Tickets for a Prayer Wheel*, and a Pulitzer Prize–winning volume of essays, *Pilgrim at Tinker Creek*, in 1974. Since then, she has written ten books on a range of subjects, including *Holy the Firm* (1977); *Living by Fiction* (1982), from which "About Symbol" comes; *Encounters with Chinese Writers* (1984); and *An American Childhood* (1987), a collection of nonfiction pieces, from which "Terwilliger Bunts One" is taken. Dillard is a contributing editor for *Harper's* magazine, where "Sight into Insight" originally appeared (Feb. 1974).

Kildare Dobbs (b. 1923)
Canadian writer. Born in India and educated at Cambridge, Dobbs spent time in the British foreign service before becoming a journalist and an editor; he is now a free-lance writer. He has written autobiographical sketches (*Running to Paradise*, 1962), short stories (*Pride and Fall*, 1981), and essays, which have been collected in *Reading the Time* (1968), in which "The Shatterer of Worlds" appears; and *Anatolian Suite* (1989), in which "Gallipoli" appears.

John Donne (1572–1631)
English poet, essayist, and cleric. Born into an old Roman Catholic family,

Donne attended Oxford and Cambridge, but could not receive a degree because of his religion. He studied, although never practiced, law and, after quietly abandoning Catholicism some time during the 1590s, entered government service. In 1615, he was received into the Anglican Church. One of the greatest religious orators of his age, Donne became dean of St. Paul's Cathedral in 1621. Donne's literary reputation rests on his poetry as well as on his sermons, among them "Let Me Wither," and devotions. "No Man Is an Island" is excerpted from *Meditation 17* of *Devotions upon Emergent Occasions*, written in the aftermath of a serious illness in 1623.

Gretel Ehrlich (b. 1946)
American poet, essayist, journalist, and filmmaker. Born in Santa Barbara, California, Ehrlich studied at Bennington College in Vermont, at the UCLA Film School, and at the New School for Social Research in New York before working as a documentary filmmaker. Arriving in Wyoming to film a documentary on sheep herding for the American Public Broadcasting Service, she fell in love with the place and stayed. In addition to her poetry, Ehrlich has published two collections of essays—*The Solace of Open Spaces* (1985), from which "The Solace of Open Spaces" is taken, and *Islands, the Universe, Home* (1987)—as well as a novel, *Heart Mountain* (1988). Her work has appeared in the *New York Times, Harper's, The Atlantic,* and the annual collections *Antaeus.* "Spring" was first published in *Antaeus* (1986).

Loren Eiseley (1907–1977)
American anthropologist, sociologist, archaeologist, historian of science, and poet. Educated at the University of Nebraska and the University of Pennsylvania, Eiseley taught at the University of Kansas, Oberlin, and finally back at the University of Pennsylvania, where he remained for thirty years. A humanist concerned with the whole spectrum of life on earth and our place in it, he established a national reputation with his writings: *The Immense Journey* (1957); *Darwin's Century: Evolution and the Men Who Discovered It* (1958); *The Firmament of Time* (revised edition, 1960); *The Mind as Nature* (1962); *The Night Country* (1971), in which "The Brown Wasps" originally appeared; and *The Unexpected Universe* (1972). A collection of Eiseley's poems, *Another Kind of*

Autumn, was published posthumously in 1977.

Ralph Waldo Emerson (1803–1882)
American poet, philosopher, and essayist. One of the most influential writers in the American tradition, Emerson entered Harvard at the age of fourteen. After graduation in 1821, he taught school for several years before beginning theological studies in 1825. In 1829, he was ordained a Unitarian minister. In 1832, he resigned his pastorate, retiring to Concord, Massachusetts, to a life of study and reflection. With the publication of his first book, *Nature* in 1836, Emerson became an important force in the development of American transcendentalism. Emerson's occasional lectures at Harvard and the publication of his *Essays* (1841) enhanced his reputation. The selections included under "Journals" are from *The Journals and Miscellaneous Notebooks of Ralph Waldo Emerson,* edited by George Clark and others (1960–78).

Daniel Mark Epstein (b. 1948)
American poet, playwright, and essayist. Educated at Kenyon College, Epstein is the author of several books of poetry (including *No Vacancies in Hell,* 1973; *The Follies,* 1977; *Young Men's Gold,* 1978; *The Book of Fortune,* (1982), two plays (*Jenny and the Phoenix,* 1977; *The Gayety Burlesque,* 1978), and a collection of essays (*Star of Wonder,* 1986). He is much concerned with myth and ritual, both political and religious, and with the American character. Epstein is a frequent contributor to *The Atlantic, The New Yorker,* and *The New Criterion,* where "The Case of Harry Houdini" originally appeared (Oct. 1986).

Edward Jay Epstein (b. 1935)
American journalist and political critic. Born in New York City, Epstein received his B.A. and M.A. from Cornell University, his Ph.D. in political science from Harvard University, and has taught political science at Harvard and M.I.T. He has written a number of articles for *The New Yorker* on journalism and subjects of political interest. Epstein's books include *Inquest: The Warren Commission and the Establishment of Truth* (1966), *News from Nowhere: Television and the News* (1973), *Between Fact and Fiction: The Problem of Journalism* (1975), and *Deception: The Invisible War Between the KGB and the CIA*

(1989). "The Selection of Reality" is taken from the essay collection *What's News: The Media and American Society* (1981).

William Faulkner (1897–1962)

American novelist. A native of Mississippi, Faulkner lived his whole life there, with the exception of a short time in military service and a period spent in Hollywood as a screenwriter. He attended the University of Mississippi in the town of Oxford. With the help of the author Sherwood Anderson, he published his first novel, *Soldier's Pay*, in 1926. His work, which won him a Nobel Prize in 1949, often depicts life in fictional Yoknapatawpha County, an imaginative reconstruction of the area near Oxford. Faulkner's major novels include *The Sound and the Fury* (1929), *As I Lay Dying* (1930), *Sanctuary* (1931), *Light in August* (1932), and *Absalom! Absalom!* (1936). His short stories are included in the collections *These Thirteen* (1931), *Go Down, Moses and Other Stories* (1942), and *The Collected Stories of William Faulkner* (1950).

Robert Finch (b. 1943)

American writer. Finch combines a keen interest in the world of the naturalist with a concern for the craft of writing. He has published three books—*Common Ground: A Naturalist's Cape Cod* (1981), *The Primal Place* (1983), and *Outlands: Journeys to the Outer Edges of Cape Cod* (1986)—and co-edited, with John Elder, *The Norton Book of Nature Writing* (1990). Publicity director for the Cape Cod Museum of Natural History, he also serves on the staff of the Bread Loaf Writers' Conference at Middlebury College. "Being at Two with Nature" was first published in *The Georgia Review* (Mar. 1991).

M. F. K. Fisher (b. 1908)

American memoirist, food and travel writer. Born in Albion, Michigan, Fisher grew up in the Quaker town of Whittier, California, married at the age of twenty-one, and spent three years in France with her husband. Returning to California, she worked as a front in a store that sold pornography and began doing research on food and gastronomy at the Los Angeles Public Library. The resulting essays, written largely for her own pleasure, were eventually published in 1937 as *Serve It Forth*. A number of books followed, including her renowned translation of Brillat-Savarin's *The Physi-*

ology of Taste (1949); *How to Cook a Wolf* (1942); *The Art of Eating* (1954); *The Cooking of Provincial France* (1968); and more recently, *A Considerable Town* (1978), about Marseille, and the memoirs *As They Were* (1982) and *Sister Age* (1983), from which "Moment of Wisdom" is taken.

Frances FitzGerald (b. 1940)

American journalist and writer. Coming from a family with a strong interest in politics and international affairs (her father was a deputy director of the CIA, her mother an ambassador to the United Nations), FitzGerald has worked as a free-lance journalist since her graduation from Radcliffe in 1962. She went to Vietnam in 1966 and achieved critical success with her first book, *Fire in the Lake: The Vietnamese and Americans in Vietnam* (1972); it won four major awards, including a Pulitzer Prize and a National Book Award. Her other books include *America Revised: History Schoolbooks in the Twentieth Century* (1979) and *Cities on a Hill: Journeys through American Cultures* (1986). Although FitzGerald regularly contributes to several American periodicals, she is most closely associated with *The New Yorker*, where "Rewriting American History" appeared before being published in *America Revised*.

Benjamin Franklin (1706–1790)

American statesman, inventor, writer, and diplomat. Apprenticed at the age of twelve to his brother, a Philadelphia printer, Franklin learned all aspects of the trade, from setting type to writing editorials. At the age of twenty-four, he was editor and publisher of the *Pennsylvania Gazette*. In 1733, he began writing *Poor Richard's Almanack*, a collection of aphorisms and advice. He retired from business at the age of forty-two to devote himself to study and research but soon found himself involved in colonial politics. From 1757 until 1763, he was diplomatic representative for the colonies in England. He served as a member of the committee appointed to draft the Declaration of Independence and later as minister to France and delegate to the Paris peace conference that officially concluded the Revolutionary War. "The Convenience of Being 'Reasonable'" comes from Franklin's *Autobiography*, written between 1771 and 1788; the selections from *Poor Richard's Almanack* are from the editions noted in the text.

Erich Fromm (1900–1980)
German-American psychoanalyst and social philosopher. Born in Frankfurt, he received a Ph.D. in philosophy from the University of Heidelberg, then trained at the Psychoanalytic Institute in Berlin. He immigrated to the United States in 1934, where he held a succession of academic appointments at Columbia University, Bennington College, Yale University, Michigan State University, and New York University. In establishing a reputation as a gifted and innovative psychoanalyst, Fromm wrote twenty books, among them *Escape from Freedom* (1941), *The Forgotten Language* (1951), *The Sane Society* (1955), and *The Art of Loving* (1956). "The Nature of Symbolic Language" comes from *The Forgotten Language*.

Robert Frost (1874–1963)
American poet, teacher, and lecturer. This quintessential "New England" poet was born in California and spent his childhood there. He studied briefly at Dartmouth and Harvard, married, and tried farming for a while. In 1912, he moved to England, where his first book of poems, *A Boy's Will*, was published. In 1914, his second collection, *North of Boston*, received favorable reviews, and the poet returned to the United States. For the next fifty years, Frost was a respected and successful poet, writing about the people and landscape of New England in a voice sometimes lyric, sometimes humorous, sometimes desolate. During the last part of his life, Frost held a number of teaching appointments and lectured widely on poetry and the role of the poet. "Education by Poetry: A Meditative Monologue," an address delivered at Amherst College in 1930, comes from *Selected Prose of Robert Frost*, edited by Hyde Cox and Edward Connery Latham (1966).

Northrop Frye (b. 1912)
Canadian literary critic and teacher. Educated at the University of Toronto and at Merton College, Oxford, he has been a member of the faculty at Victoria College, University of Toronto, since 1939. Although Frye specializes in Renaissance and Romantic literature, he has also written on Milton, the Bible, and Canadian literature. He has published more than forty books, including *Fearful Symmetry: A Study of William Blake* (1947); *Anatomy of Criticism* (1957); *The Educated Imagination* (1964), from which "The Motive for Metaphor"

comes; *The Secular Scripture: A Study of the Structure of Romance* (1976); *The Great Code: The Bible and Literature* (1982); and *A Natural Perspective: The Development of Shakespearean Comedy and Romance* (1988).

Paul Fussell (b. 1924)
American writer and teacher. After distinguished military service in World War II, Fussell earned a Ph.D. at Harvard and became an instructor of English at Connecticut College. In 1955, he was hired by the University of Pennsylvania, where he is professor of English today. Fussell's early books deal with poetic theory (*Poetic Meter and Poetic Form*, 1965) and eighteenth-century literature (*Samuel Johnson and the Life of Writing*, 1971). With the publication of *The Great War and Modern Memory* (1975) and *Abroad: British Literary Traveling between the Wars* (1980), his attention shifted to the twentieth century. In 1983, he published *Class: A Guide through the American Status System*. Two recent essay collections are *The Boy Scout Handbook and Other Observations* (1982) and *Thank God for the Atom Bomb and Other Essays*, from which "Thank God for the Atom Bomb" is taken. Fussell has also edited *The Norton Book of Travel* (1987) and *The Norton Book of Modern War* (1990).

Willard Gaylin (b. 1925)
American psychiatrist and psychoanalyst. After receiving an M.D. degree from Case Western Reserve University, Gaylin did advanced work in psychoanalytic medicine at Columbia and opened a private practice in psychiatry. In 1970, he co-founded the Hastings Center, Institute of Society, Ethics and the Life Sciences at Hastings-on-Hudson, New York. His writings reflect a broad range of interests: *In the Service of Their Country: War Resisters in Prison* (1970), *Partial Justice: A Study of Bias in Sentencing* (1974), *Feelings: Our Vital Signs* (1979), and *Rediscovering Love* (1986). Gaylin's study of the use of the insanity defense, *The Killing of Bonnie Garland: A Question of Justice* (1982), received considerable attention. "What You See Is the Real You" originally appeared in the *New York Times* (Oct. 7, 1977).

Herb Goldberg (b. 1937)
American psychologist and nonfiction writer. Born in Berlin, Germany, Goldberg studied at City College (now City College of the City University of New

York) and at Adelphi University; since then he has taught psychology at California State university in Los Angeles. Goldberg's books, which interpret and explain for the lay reader the phenomena he deals with as a professional, include *Creative Aggression* (1974); *The Hazards of Being Male* (1976), from which "In Harness: The Male Condition" is taken; *The New Male: From Self-Destruction to Self-Care* (1979); and *The New Male-Female Relationship* (1983).

William Golding (b. 1911)
English novelist. Educated at Marlborough Grammar School and Oxford (from which "Thinking as a Hobby" draws its settings), Golding was a schoolmaster at Bishop Wordsworth's School, Salisbury, before becoming a novelist at the age of forty-three. His novels are characterized by their darkly poetic tone, dense symbolism, and rejection of societal norms. His most famous work is *Lord of the Flies* (1954), a story of schoolboys marooned on an island who revert to savagery. Other novels include *Pincher Martin* (1956), *The Spire* (1964), *The Pyramid* (1967), *Rites of Passage* (1980), *Close Quarters* (1987), and *Fire Down Below* (1989). In 1983, Golding received the Nobel Prize for literature. "Thinking as a Hobby" originally appeared in *Holiday Magazine* (Aug. 1961).

Stephen Jay Gould (b. 1941)
American paleontologist, writer, and teacher. Gould grew up in New York City, graduated from Antioch College, and received his Ph.D. from Columbia in 1967, joining Harvard the same year. Now professor of geology and zoology at Harvard, Gould teaches paleontology, biology, and history of science. Witty and fluent, Gould demystifies science for lay readers in essays written for a regular column in *Natural History* magazine and collected in *Ever since Darwin* (1977); *The Panda's Thumb* (1980); *Hen's Teeth and Horse's Toes* (1983); and *The Flamingo's Smile* (1985). His books include *Ontogeny and Phylogeny* (1977), *Time's Arrow, Time's Cycle: Myth and Metaphor in the Discovery of Geological Time* (1987), and *Wonderful Life* (1989). "Our Allotted Lifetimes" originally appeared in *Natural History* (Vol. 86, No. 7, 1977); "Darwin's Middle Road" comes from *The Panda's Thumb*; "The Terrifying Normalcy of AIDS" first appeared in the *New York Times Magazine* (Apr. 19, 1987); "Scientific

Error" first appeared in the *New York Times* (July 30, 1989).

Robert Graves (1895–1985)
British poet, novelist, and classical scholar. After private education, distinguished service in World War I, and study at St. John's College, Oxford, Graves held a brief appointment at the University of Cairo before becoming a professional writer. In a long and prolific career, he published 130 volumes, ranging from poetry and novels to essays, lectures, and criticism. He is perhaps best known for his classic memoir, *Goodbye to All That* (1929); his historical novels, *I, Claudius* (1934) and *King Jesus* (1946); his work on writing, *The Reader over Your Shoulder* (1943); and his study of poetic myth, *The White Goddess* (1948). Graves' classical scholarship provided much of the material for his fiction and poetry. "Mythology" originally appeared as the Introduction to the *Larousse Encyclopedia of Mythology* (1959).

Edith Hamilton (1867–1963)
American classicist, historian, and teacher. Hamilton's writing career began only after her retirement, at the age of sixty-three, from her job as headmistress of a private school. In her eighties, she began giving public addresses and lectures on ancient Greek culture and society, and at the age of ninety she visited Athens and was made an honorary citizen. Hamilton's books include *The Greek Way* (1930, 1942), in which "Xenophon" appears; *The Roman Way* (1932); *The Prophets of Israel* (1936); *Mythology* (1942); *Witness to Truth: Christ and His Interpreters* (1948); and *The Ever-Present Past* (1964).

Nathaniel Hawthorne (1804–1864)
American novelist, short-story writer, and essayist. Educated at Bowdoin College, Hawthorne returned to his home in Salem, Massachusetts, and devoted himself to writing tales. In 1837, *Twice-told Tales* appeared, and Hawthorne became a public literary figure. After his marriage in 1842, he and his wife moved to Concord, where they lived for three years. In 1846, Hawthorne was appointed surveyor of the Port of Salem, the first of a number of political positions that would culminate in his appointment as American consul in Liverpool, England (1853). Although he may be best known for his short stories or novels—*The Scarlet Letter* (1850) and

The House of the Seven Gables (1851) in particular—Hawthorne also wrote a series of valuable sketches for the *Atlantic Monthly.* "Abraham Lincoln" (1862) is one of these.

S. I. Hayakawa (b. 1906)
Samuel Ichize Hayakawa, Japanese-American writer, educator, and politician. Before becoming president of San Francisco State College, Hayakawa established himself as a scholar and pioneer in language and semantics with books such as *Language in Action* (1941; revised as *Language in Thought and Action,* 1949), *Our Language and Our World* (1959), and *Symbol, Status and Personality* (1963). His tenure as college president (1969–73) was marked by student demonstrations and protests. Throughout, Hayakawa asserted a firm belief in authority, traditional values, and the rule of law and order. With the same ideas as a campaign platform, he was elected to the United States Senate, where he served from 1977 until 1982. "Sex Is Not a Spectator Sport" comes from a collection of Hayakawa's essays, *Through the Communication Barrier* (1979).

Ernest Hemingway (1899–1961)
American novelist and short-story writer. Hemingway began his professional writing career as a journalist, reporting for newspapers in Kansas City and Toronto. In the 1920s, he lived in Paris, a part of the American expatriate community that included Gertrude Stein and Ezra Pound. Hemingway's literary reputation rests on his short stories, collected in volumes like *In Our Time* (1925) and *Men without Women* (1927), and his novels, including *The Sun Also Rises* (1926), *A Farewell to Arms* (1929), and *For Whom the Bell Tolls* (1940). *The Old Man and the Sea* (1952) was the last work published during his lifetime. Hemingway received the Nobel Prize for literature in 1954.

Gilbert Highet (1906–1978)
American scholar of classical literature, poet, writer, and teacher. Born in Glasgow, Scotland, Highet was educated at the University of Glasgow and Oxford University. From 1932 until 1936, he taught at St. John's College, Oxford, then accepted an appointment at Columbia University, where he taught Greek and Latin literature for thirty years. Considered a master teacher, Highet communicated his enthusiasm for classical literature not only in the classroom, but also in a number of books. Of the fourteen books he wrote, perhaps the most famous are *The Classical Tradition* (1949), *The Art of Teaching* (1950), and *The Anatomy of Satire* (1962). "The Mystery of Zen" comes from *Talents and Geniuses* (1957), a collection of essays by Highet.

Andrew Holleran (b. 1943?)
American novelist, nonfiction writer, and critic. A Harvard graduate, a well-known journalist, and a frequent contributor to major gay publications, Holleran writes pseudonymously. His first two novels, *Dancer from the Dance* (1978) and *Nights in Aruba* (1983) explore psychological and social aspects of gay life. Holleran's most recent book, *Ground Zero* (1988), from which "The Names of Flowers" is taken, examines the personal and social effects of the AIDS crisis on the gay community.

John Holt (1923–1985)
American education theorist. Born in New York City, Holt taught for many years at high schools in Colorado and Massachusetts and at Harvard University and the University of California at Berkeley. His numerous books, based on his teaching experience and all centrally concerned with learning and education, include *How Children Fail* (1964); *How Children Learn* (1967); *The Under-Achieving School* (1967), in which "How Teachers Make Children Hate Reading" appears; *Freedom and Beyond* (1972); and *Escape from Childhood* (1984).

Langston Hughes (1902–1967)
American poet, playwright, and writer. An extraordinarily prolific writer, Hughes published in his lifetime seventeen volumes of poetry, two novels, seven collections of short stories, and twenty-six plays. He emerged as a key figure in the Harlem Renaissance of the 1920s and 1930s, an awakening of black artists centered in New York City. Encouraged by his fellow artists, Hughes published his first collection of poems, *The Weary Blues* (1926). Although critical response was mixed, the degree of public acceptance achieved by Hughes with this and subsequent works enabled him to become the first black American writer to support himself from his writing and lecturing. "Salvation" is a chapter from Hughes's autobiography *The Big Sea* (1940).

Stephen Hume (b. 1947)
Canadian poet, essayist, and editor. Hume's family moved to Canada a year after his birth in Blackpool, England. While attending the university of Victoria, he worked as a reporter for the *Victoria Times* and later served as Arctic correspondent, city editor, weekend editor, and general manager for the *Edmonton Journal*. More recently, he has worked as columnist-at-large for the *Vancouver Sun*. Hume's books include *Signs against an Empty Sky* (1980), *And the House Sank Like a Ship in the Long Prairie Grass* (1987), and *Ghost Camps: Memory and Myth on Canada's Frontier* (1989). "The Spirit Weeps" first appeared in the *Edmonton Journal* between February and June 1988 and was later anthologized in the 1989 edition of *Best Canadian Essays*.

Zora Neale Hurston (1891–1960)
American writer and folklorist. A central figure of the Harlem Renaissance of the 1920s and 1930s, Hurston was born in Eatonville, Florida, daughter of a Baptist preacher and a seamstress. She attended Howard University and received a B.A. from Barnard in 1928, where she studied anthropology and developed an interest in black folk traditions and in oral history. Hurston's writing, pulled from her knowledge of folklore, reveals a vigorous, rhythmical, direct prose style that has influenced later writers. Rediscovered by the women's movement, Hurston's works include plays (*e.g.*, *Mule Bone: A Comedy of Negro Life in Three Acts*, 1931, with Langston Hughes) as well as novels (*Their Eyes Were Watching God*, 1937; *Moses, Man of the Mountain*, 1939; *Seraph on the Suwanee*, 1948). "How It Feels to Be Colored Me" was originally published in *The World Tomorrow*, vol. 11 (May 1928), and was reprinted in *I Love Myself When I'm Laughing* (1975), a collection of Hurston's writings edited by Alice Walker.

Ada Louise Huxtable (b. 1921)
American architecture critic and social commentator. Born in New York City, Huxtable studied at Hunter College and New York University before working as curator for architecture and design at the Museum of Modern Art. Later, she studied architecture in Italy, worked as a free-lance writer, and was architecture critic for the *New York Times* from 1963 to 1973. Huxtable won the Pulitzer Prize for distinguished criticism in 1970; she recently received the prestigious MacAr-

thur Foundation Award. Her books include *Pier Luigi Nervi* (1960), *Classic New York* (1964), *Will They Ever Finish Bruckner Boulevard?* (1970), and *Kicked a Building Lately?* (1976). "Modern-Life Battle: Conquering Clutter" originally appeared in the "Design Notebook" column of the *New York Times* (Feb. 5, 1981).

Thomas Jefferson (1743–1826)
Third president of the United States, lawyer, architect, and writer. An educated man of significant accomplishments in many fields, Jefferson entered politics in his native state of Virginia, serving in the House of Burgesses and eventually becoming governor (1779–81). He founded the University of Virginia (1809) and designed both the buildings and curriculum. Jefferson served as secretary of state to Washington (1789–93), vice-president to John Adams (1797–1801), and president (1801–09). A fluent stylist, Jefferson wrote books on science, religion, architecture, even Anglo-Saxon grammar, but is probably best known for writing the final draft of the Declaration of Independence. Preliminary drafts were done by committee, but it was to Jefferson that the members turned for the last revision. "George Washington" is taken from a letter written in 1814 to a Dr. Jones.

Jesus (c. 6 B.C.–c. A.D. 30)
Jesus of Nazareth, first-century Jewish religious teacher. Acknowledged by Christians as the Son of God, Jesus spent his short public career in Palestine, preaching a message of conversion and repentance. One of his favorite teaching devices was the parable, a literary form with a long history and used extensively in rabbinic tradition.

Samuel Johnson (1709–1784)
English lexicographer, critic, moralist, and journalist. In spite of childhood poverty, poor eyesight, and scant advanced education, Johnson achieved renown in his day as wit, conversationalist, and astute observer of the human experience. In 1737, having failed as a schoolmaster, he sought his fortune in London, where he soon found work contributing essays and poems to *The Gentleman's Magazine*. Johnson's literary career prospered as he wrote and published poems, plays, and essays. In 1750, he founded *The Rambler*, a popular periodical containing essays, fables, and criticism: "On Self-Love and Indolence" appeared in

The Rambler (1751). One of the greatest prose stylists of the English language, Johnson prepared the monumental *Dictionary* (1755) that bears his name, wrote *Rasselas* (1759), a novel from which "The Pyramids" comes, and *Lives of the Poets* (1779–81).

Horace Freeland Judson (b. 1931)
American historian and teacher. Born in New York City, Judson studied at the University of Chicago and later worked for the Office of the Military Government in Berlin after World War II. Since then he has held various teaching and editing positions, and has worked as a staff writer and book reviewer for *Time* magazine, a free-lance writer in Cambridge, England, a professor of writing and history of science at Johns Hopkins University, and a contributing editor to *The Sciences.* Judson's books include *The Techniques of Reading* (1954, 1971); *The Eighth Day of Creation* (1979); and *The Search for Solutions* (1980), from which "The Rage to Know" is adapted.

Carl Gustav Jung (1875–1961)
Swiss psychiatrist and founder of analytic psychology. Jung was educated at the University of Basel and began practice in 1900 at a mental hospital in Zürich. From 1907 to 1913, he and Sigmund Freud collaborated in research on psychiatry and psychoanalysis. In 1914, after the two had severed connections, Jung devoted himself to private practice and writing. A prolific writer, whose *Collected Works* consist of eighteen volumes, Jung did pioneering work on schizophrenia and related personality disorders, and, in the process of classifying personality types, introduced terms like "extrovert," "complex," and "introvert" into the vocabulary of psychiatry. Jung's interest in human creativity led him to posit the existence of a "collective unconscious," a part of the human mind to which human beings relegate unpleasant experiences and from which creativity springs. Among Jung's major books are *The Psychology of Dementia* (1906), *The Psychology of the Unconscious* (1912), and *Psychological Types* (1921). "The Poet" comes from his *Modern Man in Search of a Soul* (1933).

Evelyn Fox Keller (b. 1936)
American research scientist, teacher, and social critic. Keller wrote on her experience of demoralization and neglect as a graduate student in theoretical phys-

ics at Harvard in the late 1950s in "The Anomaly of Women in Physics." Her response was an active commitment to equality for women scientists throughout her professional life. Despite persistent discrimination, Keller earned her Ph.D. in physics from Harvard in 1963 and worked in New York as a research scientist in molecular biology before becoming a professor of mathematics at the State University of New York at Purchase in 1972. She currently teaches at the University of California at Berkeley. Keller's recent books include *A Feeling for the Organism: The Life and Work of Barbara McClintock* (1984) and *Reflections on Gender and Science* (1985). "Women in Science: A Social Analysis" originally appeared in *Harvard Magazine* (Oct. 1974).

Martin Luther King, Jr. (1929–1968)
American clergyman and civil rights leader. By the age of twenty-six, King had completed his undergraduate education, finished divinity school, and received a Ph.D. in religion from Boston University. The Montgomery bus boycott (1956) marked King's entry into public politics; blacks in Montgomery, Alabama, boycotted segregated buses, and King took a public stand in their support. Drawing on the New Testament teachings of Jesus and the principles of passive resistance of Mahatma Gandhi, King advocated nonviolent protest to effect significant social change. In the years following the boycott, he became a major figure in the civil rights movement, uniting disparate groups in their struggle. In 1963, Birmingham, Alabama, the most segregated city in the South, became the focal point for violent confrontations between blacks and whites; 2,400 civil rights workers, King among them, went to jail. It was then that he wrote his now-famous "Letter from Birmingham Jail." In 1964, at the age of thirty-five, Martin Luther King, Jr., became the youngest person ever to receive the Nobel Peace Prize. He was assassinated on April 14, 1968, in Memphis, Tennessee.

Maxine Hong Kingston (b. 1940)
American memoirist and novelist. Born in California, the eldest of six children in a Chinese immigrant family, Kingston grew up in a world where English was a distant second language and friends and relatives regularly gathered at her family's laundry to tell stories and reminisce about their native country. Graduating

from the University of California at Berkeley, she taught school in California and Hawaii, and began publishing poetry, stories, and articles in a number of magazines, including *The New Yorker*, *New West*, the *New York Times Magazine*, *Ms*, and *Iowa Review*. Her two acclaimed books of reminiscence are *The Woman Warrior: Memoirs of a Girlhood among Ghosts* (1976), from which "Tongue-Tied" is taken, and *China Men* (1980); her most recent work is a novel, *Tripmaster Monkey* (1989).

Ronald A. Knox (1888–1957)
British clergyman, translator, and religious thinker. Born in Leicestershire, England, Knox was an Anglican chaplain at Trinity College, Oxford, but in 1937 converted to Roman Catholicism and two years later was ordained as a priest. In 1939 he began work on his translation of the Bible into modern English. His account of preparing the work is presented in a collection of essays titled *The Trials of a Translator* (1949). In addition to his writings on religious matters, Knox published numerous suspense novels. "The Nature of Enthusiasm" is taken from his book *Enthusiasm* (1950).

Arthur Koestler (1905–1983)
British writer. Born in Hungary and educated at the University of Vienna, Koestler worked as an editor of a Cairo newspaper, then as foreign correspondent for several other papers before settling in England in 1941, when his novel, *Darkness at Noon*, appeared. That novel, an indictment of the Communist party, mapped the territory for Koestler's next ten years of work. In the 1950s, however, he turned to writing about a wide range of topics: psychology, religion, philosophy, evolution, among others. Koestler wrote over forty books, among them *The God That Failed* (1950), *The Ghost in the Machine* (1967), and *The Lion and the Ostrich* (1973). "Gravity and the Holy Ghost" originally appeared in *The Act of Creation* (1964).

Joseph Wood Krutch (1893–1970)
American naturalist, journalist, theater and literary critic. Born in Knoxville, Krutch studied science at the University of Tennessee before sharply changing direction to take a Ph.D. in English at Columbia University; he later remarked that he knew "more about botany than any other New York critic, and more about the theatre than any other botanist." A significant essayist and frequent

contributor to such periodicals as *The Atlantic Monthly*, *Harper's*, *The Saturday Review*, and *Natural History*, Krutch is best known for two widely read and influential books, *The Desert Year* (1952) and *The Modern Temper* (1956). "The Most Dangerous Predator" is taken from *The Best Nature Writing of Joseph Wood Krutch* (1969).

Elisabeth Kübler-Ross (b. 1926)
Swiss-American psychologist. Born and educated in Switzerland, Kübler-Ross has come to prominence in the United States, where she has lived since 1958. Her work is largely a response to what she calls "the horrifying experience of the [postwar European] concentration camps." She has given seminars and written about death and dying not only in order to understand the process better, but also to learn how to care for the terminally ill. "On the Fear of Death" comes from Kübler-Ross' best-selling book *On Death and Dying* (1969). Other books on the subject have followed, including *On Children and Death* (1983) and *AIDS: The Ultimate Challenge* (1987).

Thomas S. Kuhn (b. 1922)
American philosopher and historian. Educated at Harvard, where he earned a Ph.D. in physics, Kuhn is a specialist in the history and philosophy of science. The author of *The Copernican Revolution* (1957) and *The Essential Tension: Selected Studies in Scientific Tradition and Change* (1977), he is perhaps best known for *The Structure of Scientific Revolutions* (1962, 1970), from which "The Route to Normal Science" is taken. Kuhn is currently Laurance S. Rockefeller Professor of Philosophy at MIT.

La Rochefoucauld (1613–1680)
François, duc de La Rochefoucauld, French nobleman, soldier, and writer. La Rochefoucauld's literary fame rests on his *Réflexions ou sentences et maximes morales* (1665), better known as *Maxims*. This collection of witty observations about human behavior established him as a moralist of decidedly pragmatic persuasion.

Charles Lamb (1775–1834)
English essayist and poet. A contemporary and colleague of Coleridge and Wordsworth—although not himself a romantic—Lamb was born in London, left school before he was fifteen, and

soon thereafter became a clerk in the accounting department of the huge commercial house, the East India Company, where he remained for thirty-three years. To supplement his salary there, he had early turned to writing in a variety of forms. In 1818, at the age of forty-three, he published his *Works*, consisting of a good deal of minor verse, a sentimental novel, a blank verse tragedy in the Elizabethan style, and, in collaboration with his sister Mary, the famous children's book, *Tales from Shakespeare*. At the time he apparently thought his major writing had already been accomplished, yet not until two years after the *Works* appeared did Lamb begin to contribute, to the *London Magazine*, the *Essays of Elia* (1820–23), among them, "The Two Races of Men," work which elevated him to the rank of a major writer.

Susanne K. Langer (1895–1985)
American philosopher and teacher. After studying at Radcliffe, and the University of Vienna, Langer became a tutor in philosophy at Radcliffe, beginning a teaching career that would last more than fifty years. She was particularly interested in esthetics, that branch of philosophy concerned with beauty; her book *Feeling and Form* (1953) is a classic in the field. She also wrote *Problems of Art* (1957), from which "Expressiveness" comes, and a three-volume study, *Mind: An Essay on Human Feeling* (1967–82).

Margaret Laurence (1926–1987)
Canadian novelist, short-story writer, and essayist. Born in Neepawa, Manitoba, and educated at United College, University of Manitoba, Laurence began her professional writing career as a translator. She soon established a reputation as a novelist with *The Stone Angel* (1964) and *A Jest of God* (1966). Between 1964 and 1975, Laurence tried her hand at writing essays and articles, mostly for Canadian periodicals. Laurence, whose life took her across Canada and to Africa, displays a strong sense of geography in her prose. Her work often deals with the search for personal identity in the midst of the conflict between tradition and modernization. "Where the World Began" first appeared in *Maclean's*, a Canadian magazine (Dec. 1972); it was reprinted in *Heart of a Stranger* (1976), a collection of occasional and autobiographical essays by Laurence.

Aldo Leopold (1887–1948)
American conservationist. Born in Burlington, Iowa, and educated at Yale University, Leopold was a forester who early understood the value of wilderness and a professor of wildlife management at the University of Wisconsin who became a champion of the predator's role within a healthy ecosystem. He was one of the founders of the Wilderness Society in the 1930s, but his most important contribution to both the environmental movement and to literature is *A Sand County Almanac*, published in 1949, shortly after he had died while helping to fight a forest fire on a neighbor's land. "Thinking Like a Mountain" is from *A Sand County Almanac*.

Doris Lessing (b. 1919)
British novelist and political activist. Lessing was born in Persia but grew up in Southern Rhodesia, where she was largely responsible for her own education. She married and divorced twice before leaving Africa for London in 1949. There, her career as a writer of more than thirty books began with the publication of her first novel, *The Grass Is Singing* (1950). The central theme of Lessing's work has been women's quest for identity in a world fragmented by prejudice, ideology, and violence (the *Children of Violence* Series, 1952–69; *The Golden Notebook*, 1962). In the *Canopus in Argos: Archives* Series (1979–1983), she has turned to science fiction. Her latest work includes two novels about the stages of women's lives (*The Diary of a Good Neighbor*, 1983; *If the Old Could . . .* , 1984) and three political novels (*The Good Terrorist*, 1985; *African Tale*, 1987; *The Wind Blows Away Our Words*, 1987). "My Father" first appeared in the London *Sunday Telegraph* (Sept. 1, 1963); it was reprinted in the collection of essays, reviews, and interviews entitled *A Small Personal Voice* (1975).

Michael Levin (b. 1943)
American philosopher. Educated at Michigan State University and Columbia, Levin was a member of the Department of Philosophy at Columbia from 1968 until 1980. He is currently professor of philosophy at City College of the City University of New York. His research interests include ethics, philosophy, and the mind. The author of a number of scholarly articles, Levin has published *Metaphysics and the Mind-Body Problem* (1979). "The Case for Tor-

ture" originally appeared in *Newsweek* (June 7, 1982).

Oscar Lewis (1914–1970)
American anthropologist. Born in New York City, Lewis grew up on a small farm in upstate New York. He received his Ph.D. in anthropology from Columbia University and taught at Brooklyn College, Washington University, and the University of Illinois. His active engagement in the study of other cultures took him from the Blackfoot tribe of Canada to Texas farmers, from a Cuban sugar plantation to Guadalupe, Spain, and from a Mexican village to a village in northern India, and resulted in such books as *Anthropological Essays* (1946), in which "The Culture of Poverty" appears; *Life in a Mexican Village* (1951); *Five Families: Mexican Case Studies in the Culture of Poverty* (1959); and *Pedro Martinez: A Mexican Peasant and His Family* (1964).

Abraham Lincoln (1809–1865)
Lawyer, orator, and sixteenth president of the United States (1861–65). Born in Kentucky, Lincoln was a self-made and self-taught man. His family moved to Illinois in 1830, where Lincoln prepared himself for a career in law. In 1834, he was elected to the first of four terms in the Illinois state legislature and in 1847, to the U.S. Congress. Elected president in 1860, Lincoln sought to preserve the Union amid the strife of the Civil War while he worked for the passage of the Thirteenth Amendment, which would outlaw slavery everywhere and forever in the United States. Lincoln was assassinated by actor John Wilkes Booth on April 15, 1865. During his first term, Lincoln delivered the "Gettysburg Address" (1863) at the site of one of the Civil War's bloodiest battles. Reelected in 1864, he gave his Second Inaugural Address, an eloquent appeal for reconciliation and peace.

Walter Lippmann (1889–1974)
American journalist and political commentator. Esteemed as the dean of American political columnists, Lippmann published twenty books and over 4,000 columns in a career that extended from the presidency of Woodrow Wilson to that of Richard Nixon. Noted for his ability to bring reason to bear in political matters and distinguished by his crisp style, Lippmann was a powerful voice in the American political forum. He began his famous column "Today

and Tomorrow" in the *New York Herald Tribune* in 1931. He also wrote for *The New Republic*, *Newsweek*, and the *Atlantic Monthly*, where "The Indispensable Opposition" originally appeared (Aug. 1939).

Barry Lopez (b. 1945)
American nature writer and novelist. Born in New York State, Lopez grew up largely in California's San Fernando Valley and studied at the University of Notre Dame and the University of Oregon. Since the early 1970s he has lived on the McKenzie River in the Cascade Mountains of western Oregon; there he writes full time, when he isn't gathering material in the Arctic Circle or a California desert. Lopez's books include *Desert Notes* (1976), *Of Wolves and Men* (1978), *River Notes* (1979), *Winter Count* (1981), and *Arctic Dreams* (1986). Some of his best essays and short fiction are collected in *Crossing Open Ground* (1988). "The Stone Horse" originally appeared in *Antaeus* (1986)

Konrad Z. Lorenz (1903–1989)
Austrian-German scientist; the founder of ethology, the scientific study of patterns in animal behavior. Although he studied medicine at the University of Vienna, Lorenz's early interests lay in the field of animal behavior. *King Solomon's Ring* (1952), from which "The Taming of the Shrew" comes, deals with the behavior of jackdaws, geese, and other animals. *On Aggression* (1963) and *Civilized Man's Eight Deadly Sins* (1974) detail Lorenz's beliefs about humankind's behavior and civilization's harmful effects on people and the environment. With Niko Tinbergen and Karl von Frisch, Lorenz won the Nobel Prize for Physiology or Medicine in 1973.

John Livingston Lowes (1867–1945)
American scholar of medieval literature and theosophy. A student of mathematics and theosophy, Lowes earned degrees from Washington and Jefferson College and Presbyterian Western Theological Seminary at Pittsburgh. Ordained in 1893, Lowes became McKee Professor of Ethics and Christian Evidences and Professor of English at Haverford College. He received a Ph.D. from Harvard in 1905, where he later taught. In his articles and books, Lowe explored the role of medieval mythology, cosmology, and alchemy in the work of Chaucer and his contemporaries. Among Lowe's

books are *Convention and Revolution in Poetry* (1919), *The Road to Xanadu: A Study in the Ways of the Imagination* (1927), and *Geoffrey Chaucer* (1934), a volume of Lowe's lectures given at Haverford, from which "Time in the Middle Ages" is taken.

David McCullough (b. 1933)
American historian, teacher, and broadcaster. Born in Pittsburgh, McCullough received his B.A. from Yale University before going to work as a writer and editor, first for *Time* and later for the U.S. Information Agency and *American Heritage* magazine. Since 1970 he has worked as a free-lance writer, punctuating his work with stints as professor and writer-in-residence at various universities, and as host of two major television series, *Smithsonian World* (1984–88) and *The American Experience* (1988–   ). McCullough's books include *The Great Bridge* (1972), *The Path Between the Seas* (1977), and *Mornings on Horseback* (1981). "The Unexpected Mrs. Stowe" is taken from *A Sense of History: The Best Writing from the Pages of* American Heritage (1985).

Dorothy Gies McGuigan (1914–1982)
American essayist, social critic, and teacher. Born in Ann Arbor, Michigan, McGuigan studied at the University of Michigan, Columbia University, and King's College, London, after which she worked for five years at a publishing company. After another thirteen years as a free-lance writer for various magazines, she joined the staff of the University of Michigan, first as an instructor in English and later as program director and editor at the Center for the Continuing Education of Women. McGuigan's work includes the books *The Hapsburgs* (1966), *A Dangerous Experiment* (1970), and *Metternich and the Duchess* (1975); she also edited *The Role of Women in Conflict and Peace: Papers* (1977) and *Changing Family, Changing Workplace: New Research* (1980).

Niccolò Machiavelli (1469–1527)
Florentine statesman and political philosopher. An aristocrat who held office while Florence was a republic, Machiavelli fell from favor when the Medicis returned to power in 1512. Briefly imprisoned, he was restored to an office of some influence, but he never regained his former importance. Machiavelli's most famous work, *The Prince* (1513), from which "The Morals of the Prince" comes, has exerted considerable literary and political influence within the Western tradition.

John McMurtry (b. 1939)
Canadian athlete, writer, and teacher. Educated at the University of Toronto, McMurtry became a professional football player before earning his Ph.D. in philosophy at the University of London. A member of the Department of Philosophy at the University of Guelph since 1970, he has written two books: *The Dimensions of English: A Concise Compendium* (1970) and *The Structure of Marx's World View* (1978). "Kill 'Em! Crush 'Em! Eat 'Em Raw!" originally appeared in the October 1971 issue of the Canadian news magazine *Macleans*.

Leo F. McNamara (b. 1933)
American educator. A graduate of Harvard College, McNamara was a research associate in clinical psychology at Harvard until 1959; since then he has taught at the University of Michigan, in both the departments of English and history. In 1955 he was Fulbright Scholar in Celtic Studies at the Queen's University, Belfast, Northern Ireland, and in 1969 he was Fulbright Lecturer in American Literature and Anglo-Irish Literature, Trinity College, Dublin. A frequent visitor to Ireland, he has written numerous scholarly articles on Irish history, literature, and culture, and in his teaching specializes in these subjects. He has been an editor of *The Norton Reader* through eight editions. "The State of Ireland" appeared in *LSA Magazine* (Spring 1988).

Nancy Mairs (b. 1943)
American nonfiction writer and essayist. Married at nineteen, Mairs finished college, bore a child, and earned an M.F.A. and a Ph.D. from the University of Arizona. The personal difficulties that inform her writing include six months spent in a state mental hospital, suffering from a near-suicidal mixture of agoraphobia and anorexia, and the later discovery that she suffered from multiple sclerosis. She found a dual salvation in writing and in Roman Catholicism, to which she converted in her thirties. Mairs' major works, *Plaintext* (1986) and *Remembering the Bone House* (1989), are both autobiographical. "Who Are You?" originally appeared in the *New York Times* (Aug. 13, 1987).

D. Keith Mano (b. 1942)

American novelist and essayist. Born in New York City, Mano graduated from Columbia University and went on to do postgraduate work at Cambridge University. Since then he has worked as vice-president of a building maintenance company, contributing editor and columnist for the *National Review*, *Playboy*, and *Oui*, part-time film critic, and scriptwriter for the television series "St. Elsewhere"; he also finds time to write novels. Mano's books include *Bishop's Progress* (1968), *War in Heaven* (1970), *The Proselytizer* (1972), *Take Five* (1982), and *Topless* (1991). "How to Keep from Getting Mugged" originally appeared in *Playboy* magazine (July 1982).

Fredelle Maynard (1922–1989)

Canadian child psychologist and teacher. Born in Foam Lake, Saskatchewan, Maynard studied at the University of Manitoba, the University of Toronto, and Harvard University before taking teaching positions at Wellesley College and the University of New Hampshire. Maynard's interest in education, child care and development, and family relationships led to *Raisins and Almonds* (1964), which, because of its humor, sensitivity, and vivid personal insight, earned deserved recognition as one of Canada's major works of nonfiction. Its sequel *Tree of Life*, from which "And Therefore I Have Sailed the Seas . . ." is taken, was published in 1989.

Joyce Maynard (b. 1953)

Canadian-American journalist and novelist. As an eighteen-year-old Yale freshman, Maynard created a literary sensation when she published a critical appraisal of the jaded youth of the 1960s in the *New York Times*. That essay was expanded into book-length form in *Looking Back: A Chronicle of Growing Old in the Sixties* (1973). Her books, generally about American life and particularly about the lives of women and the generation of the 1970s, include the story collections *Baby Love* (1981) and *New House* (1987). "Four Generations" originally appeared in the *New York Times Magazine* (Apr. 12, 1979).

Margaret Mead (1901–1978)

American anthropologist. Mead's graduate work in anthropology developed into her first major work, *Coming of Age in Samoa* (1928), an investigation of culture, sexual behavior, and self-image in Samoa. This highly influential book was followed by *Growing Up in New Guinea* (1930) and *Sex and Temperament in Three Primitive Societies* (1935). In the latter part of her life, Mead increasingly turned her anthropological techniques on American society, analyzing a number of American behavioral and societal problems, among them racism, sexual biases, and violence. "Home and Travel" is taken from *Blackberry Winter* (1972).

H. L. Mencken (1880–1956)

Henry Louis Mencken, American journalist, editor, writer, and social critic. Until the Great Depression, Mencken was a successful writer, popular for his scathing attacks on pretense and organized activities of all kinds, from religion to politics. Most of his material was published either in *The Smart Set*, a magazine of which he was literary editor and then co-editor (1908–23), or in the *American Mercury*, which he founded in 1924 and edited until 1933. When reading tastes shifted, Mencken turned his talents to revising his *American Language*, first published in 1919, and to adding two supplements to it, as well as to writing a three-volume autobiography (*Happy Days*, 1940; *Newspaper Days*, 1941; *Heathen Days*, 1943). "Gamalielese" originally appeared in the *Baltimore Sun* (Mar. 7, 1921).

Mary Midgley (b. 1919)

British philosopher. Born in London, Midgley studied at Oxford University and immediately after graduation began work first as a civil servant, then as a high-school teacher, as a lecturer in philosophy at a number of British universities, and as a broadcaster. Midgley is perhaps best known for her books that delve into the relationship between humans and animals, including *Beast and Man: The Roots of Human Nature* (1978). Other books include *Heart and Mind: The Varieties of Moral Experience* (1981), in which "Trying Out One's New Sword" appears; *Wickedness: A Philosophical Essay* (1984); and *Wisdom, Information, and Wonder: What Is Knowledge For?* (1989).

Casey Miller (b. 1919) and **Kate Swift** (b. 1923)

American essayists and editors. Miller and Swift have written numerous articles together on sexism and language for national newspapers and magazines. Born in Toledo, Ohio, Miller graduated from Smith College, studied graphic arts at

Yale, and was for ten years an editor at Seabury Press. Swift was born in Yonkers, New York, studied journalism at the University of North Carolina, and later worked as a science writer and editor with the American Museum of Natural History and the Yale School of Medicine. As free-lance partners since 1970, they have explored sexual prejudice and language in such books as *Words and Women: New Language in New Times* (1976) and *The Handbook of Nonsexist Writing* (1980). "Who's in Charge of the English Language?" originally appeared in *The Exchange* (Fall 1990).

Richard Mitchell (b. 1929)
American teacher and nonfiction writer. Born in New York City, Mitchell attended the University of the South and Syracuse University before embarking on a teaching career, first at Defiance College in Ohio and later at Glassboro State College in New Jersey. He has also served as editor of the *Underground Grammarian* and contributed numerous articles, essays, and reviews to academic journals. Mitchell's books include *Less than Words Can Say* (1979), from which "The Voice of Sisera" is taken; *The Leaning Tower of Babel* (1984); and *The Gift of Fire* (1987).

Jessica Mitford (b. 1917)
Anglo-American writer and social critic. Born into one of England's most famous aristocratic families, Mitford left for the United States shortly after completing her education (1936). A naturalized American citizen (1944), she has established herself as an investigative reporter with a talent for pungent social criticism. Her study of the American funeral industry, *The American Way of Death* (1963), was followed by *The Trial of Dr. Spock* (1969) and *Kind and Unusual Punishment: The Prison Business* (1973). Her most recent work is autobiographical: *Faces of Philip* (1984) and *Grace Had an English Heart* (1989). "Behind the Formaldehyde Curtain" comes from *The American Way of Death*.

N. Scott Momaday (b. 1934)
Native American poet, writer, and artist. Momaday grew up on reservations in the Southwest, deeply influenced by the example and traditions of the Kiowa people. He studied at the University of New Mexico and Stanford University before beginning a teaching career. Currently, Momaday teaches at Stanford University. He has published several volumes of poetry, including *Angle of Geese and Other Poems* (1973) and *The Gourd Dancer* (1976); a Pulitzer Prize-winning novel, *House Made of Dawn* (1968); an autobiography, *The Names: A Memoir* (1976); and a collection of Kiowa folktales, *The Way to Rainy Mountain* (1969), from which "The Way to Rainy Mountain" comes. His most recent book is *The Ancient Child* (1989).

Desmond Morris (b. 1928)
British zoologist and writer on human and animal behavior. After receiving a Ph.D. in zoology from Oxford, Morris remained there to do research. In 1959, he became curator of mammals at the London Zoo. During the next eight years, he wrote five books on animals. In 1968, he returned to research at Oxford and began writing books on human and animal behavior: *The Naked Ape* (1967), *The Human Zoo* (1969), *Intimate Behavior* (1971), *Manwatching* (1977), *Bodywatching* (1985), *Catwatching* (1987), *Dogwatching* (1987), and *Horsewatching* (1989). "Territorial Behavior" comes from *Manwatching*.

Lance Morrow (b. 1939)
American journalist and nonfiction writer. Born in Philadelphia, Morrow attended Harvard University, from which he graduated in 1963. Shortly thereafter he joined the staff of *Time* and has been one of the magazine's regular contributors since 1965, writing on a wide range of topics of current interest. Morrow's recent books include *The Chief: A Memoir of Fathers and Sons* (1985), *America: A Rediscovery* (1987), and *Fishing in the Tiber* (1989). The article "Imprisoning Time in a Rectangle" originally appeared in a special issue of *Time* on photojournalism (Fall 1989).

Alice Munro (b. 1931)
Canadian novelist and short-story writer. Munro was born in Wingham, Ontario, and was educated at the University of Western Ontario. Her first collection of stories, *Dance of the Happy Shades* (1968), won the Governor General's literary award, and her novel *Lives of Girls and Women* (1971) won the Canadian Bookseller's award. In 1978 she again won the Governor General's award with a story collection published in Canada as *Who Do You Think You Are?* and in the United States as *The Beggar Maid*. Her books include *A Place for Everything* (1970), *Something I've Been Meaning to*

Tell You (1974), *The Moons of Jupiter* (1982), *The Progress of Love* (1986), and *Friend of My Youth* (1990). "What Is Real?" is taken from *Making It New: Contemporary Canadian Stories* (1982).

Vladimir Nabokov (1899–1977)
American fiction writer and teacher. Born in Russia and educated at Trinity College, Cambridge, Nabokov came to the United States in 1940 to lecture at Stanford University and stayed for twenty years. While teaching at Wellesley and Cornell, he wrote dozens of novels and contributed essays, stories, and poems to several American magazines. Although he was well known in literary circles, Nabokov did not achieve fame until 1958, when his controversial and explicit novel *Lolita* was published. *Lolita* earned Nabokov enough money so that he could retire to Switzerland and write fiction full time. "Good Readers and Good Writers" comes from *Lectures on Literature* (1980), a collection of Nabokov's essays and classroom presentations.

Gloria Naylor (b. 1950)
American fiction writer and essayist. Naylor received her B.A. from Brooklyn College, and an M.A. in Afro-American studies from Yale. She has been a writer-in-residence at George Washington University. Naylor has written three books: *The Women of Brewster Place* (1982), *Linden Hills* (1985), and *Mama Day* (1989). " 'Mommy, What Does "Nigger" Mean?' " originally appeared as a "Hers" column in the *New York Times* (Feb. 20, 1986).

John Henry Newman (1801–1890)
English Roman Catholic prelate, poet, novelist, and religious thinker. Educated at Trinity College, Oxford, Newman became a priest in the Anglican Church. He was a major force in the Oxford movement, an effort to reestablish the authority and traditions of the Church of England. In 1845, Newman became Roman Catholic; in 1846, he was ordained in Rome and then returned to England. From 1852 on, he delivered not only sermons but also a number of influential lectures on education. The latter culminated in one of Newman's finest works, *The Idea of a University Defined and Illustrated* (1852), which ranks with his treatise *An Essay in Aid of a Grammar of Assent* (1870) as a classic statement of belief. Newman wrote two novels (*Loss and Gain*, 1848; *Cal-*

lista, 1856), an explanation of his conversion (*Apologia Pro Vita Sua*, 1864), and a visionary poem ("The Dream of Gerontius," 1865). In 1879, he became a cardinal in the Roman Catholic Church. "Knowledge and Virtue" comes from *The Idea of a University*.

Joyce Carol Oates (b. 1938)
American fiction writer, playwright, and essayist. Born in a small town in Upstate New York, Oates published her first story while still an undergraduate at Syracuse University. She received an M.A. from the University of Wisconsin and taught at the universities of Detroit and Windsor (Ontario) while she began to write and publish in earnest. Despite her work teaching at Princeton University and editing a magazine, Oates is an extraordinarily prolific writer; she generally publishes more than a book a year. Her third novel, *Them* (1970) won a National Book Award. Her more recent work includes *The Profane Art* (1983), *Last Days: Stories* (1984), *You Must Remember This* (1987), *American Appetites* (1989), and *Because It Is Bitter, and Because It Is My Heart* (1990). "On Boxing" appeared in the *New York Times Magazine* (June 16, 1985).

George Orwell (1903–1950)
Pen name of Eric Blair, English journalist, essayist, novelist, and critic. Born in India and educated in England, Orwell became an officer in the Indian Imperial Police in Burma (1922–27), a part of his life that he later recounted in a novel, *Burmese Days* (1934). In 1927, he went to Europe to develop his writing talents. His first book, *Down and Out in Paris and London* (1933), depicts his years of poverty and struggle while working as a dishwasher and day laborer. Orwell's experiences fighting in the Spanish Civil War are the subject of his memoir, *Homage to Catalonia* (1938). Of his seven novels, *Animal Farm* (1945) and *Nineteen Eighty-Four* (1949), satires directed at totalitarian government, have become twentieth-century classics. Orwell published five collections of essays, including *Shooting an Elephant* (1950), from which both "Politics and the English Language" and "Shooting an Elephant" come.

Walter Pater (1839–1894)
English novelist, art and literary critic, and essayist. Educated at King's School, Canterbury, and Queen's College, Oxford, Pater devoted his life to study, re-

flection, and writing. As a prose stylist, he has few equals in the English language. Pater's first book, *Studies in the History of the Renaissance,* appeared in 1873. *Marius the Epicurean* (1885), a novel set in Rome, *Imaginary Portraits* (1887), a collection of fictional sketches, and *Appreciations: With an Essay on Style* (1889) followed. "The Mona Lisa" comes from Pater's essay on Leonardo da Vinci in *Studies in the History of the Renaissance.*

William G. Perry, Jr. (b. 1913)

American educator. Born in Paris and educated at Harvard, Perry taught at Williams College from 1941 to 1945 before moving to Harvard, where he has been director of the Bureau of Study Counsel since 1948 and professor of education since 1964. With C. P. Whitelock, he wrote the *Harvard Reading Course* (1948). His *Forms of Intellectual and Ethical Development in the College Years: A Scheme* was published in 1968. "Examsmanship and the Liberal Arts: A Study in Educational Epistemology" originally appeared in *Examining in Harvard College: A Collection of Essays,* by members of the Harvard faculty (1964).

Alexander Petrunkevitch (1875–1964)

Russian-born zoologist and teacher. Petrunkevitch was educated in Russia and Germany before coming to the United States as a lecturer at Harvard in 1904. In 1910, he joined the Department of Zoology at Yale, where he became professor in 1917, and served until 1944. Petrunkevitch was an expert on the behavior of American spiders; his *Index Catalogue of Spiders of North, Central, and South America* (1911) and *An Inquiry into the Natural Classification of Spiders* (1933) are classic studies. Petrunkevitch's essay "The Spider and the Wasp" originally appeared in *Scientific American* (Aug. 1952).

Robert Pirsig (b. 1928)

American fiction writer and teacher. After receiving a bachelor's and a master's from the University of Minnesota, Pirsig became a college teacher of composition and rhetoric (1959–62). He then worked as a technical writer (1963–73). With the publication of his novel/meditation *Zen and the Art of Motorcycle Maintenance* (1974), from which "Concrete, Brick, and Neon" comes, Pirsig became a full-time professional writer.

Plato (c. 428–c. 348 B.C.)

Greek philosopher and teacher. When Socrates died in 339 B.C., Plato went into exile. He returned in the 380s and founded a school, the Academy. He adopted the Socratic method of teaching, a technique of asking, rather than answering, questions. Although many of Plato's writings take the form of dialogues, he does occasionally, as in the case of "The Allegory of the Cave," use the parable.

Letty Cottin Pogrebin (b. 1939)

American editor, columnist, and social critic. Born in New York City, Pogrebin studied at Brandeis University before going to work in a publishing company and rising to vice-president. Since then she has written many strong articles on feminism and social issues as columnist for the *Ladies Home Journal,* as columnist and contributing editor for *Ms.* as writer for the *New York Times,* and as editor for *Newsday.* Pogrebin's books include *How to Make the System Work for the Working Woman* (1975), *Stories for Free Children* (1982), *Among Friends* (1986), and *Debra, Golda, and Me: A Jewish Feminist Memoir* (1991). "It Still Takes a Bride and Groom" appeared in the *New York Times Magazine* (July 12, 1989).

Tom Regan (b. 1938)

American philosopher and teacher. After receiving a Ph.D. in philosophy from the University of Virginia, Regan taught at Sweet Briar College before joining the Department of Philosophy at North Carolina State University. He does research in theoretical and applied ethics. "The Case for Animal Rights" originally appeared in *In Defense of Animals* (1985), edited by Peter Singer.

Adrienne Rich (b. 1929)

American poet. While she was an undergraduate at Radcliffe, Rich's first book of poetry, *A Change of World,* was chosen by W. H. Auden for the Yale Younger Poet's Prize (1951). Since then, Rich has published thirteen books of poetry and several collections of provocative essays. Much of her poetry and prose speak with power and clarity to issues in women's lives. She has recently published *An Atlas of the Difficult World: Poems 1988–1991, Time's Power: Poems 1985–1988* (1989), and *Bread, Blood, and Poetry* (1986), a volume of prose pieces. "Taking Women Students Seriously" was an address given for the New Jersey

College and University Coalition on Women's Education, May 9, 1978. "When We Dead Awaken: Writing as Re-Vision," written in 1971 for the forum "The Woman Writer in the Twentieth Century," was first published in 1972; it later appeared in Rich's collection of essays and lectures *On Lies, Secrets, and Silence: Selected Prose: 1966–1978* (1979).

Richard Rodriguez (b. 1944)
American essayist and teacher. The son of Mexican-American immigrants, Rodriguez learned to speak English in a Catholic grammar school. A proficient student, he received a B.A. from Stanford and an M.A. from Columbia. Enrolled in the doctoral program in English literature at the University of California, Berkeley, Rodriguez won a Fulbright and attended the Warburg Institute in London (1972–73). He now works as a lecturer and educational consultant as well as a free-lance writer. In *Hunger of Memory: The Education of Richard Rodriguez* (1982), from which "Aria" comes, Rodriguez recounts his assimilation into mainstream American society.

Betty Rollin (b. 1936)
American journalist, television reporter, and nonfiction writer. Rollin spent several years as a stage and television actress before beginning a career in journalism, first at *Vogue* (1964), then at *Look* (1965–71). Since 1971, she has worked as a network correspondent, chiefly for NBC. Rollin is the author of several books, including *First, You Cry* (1976); *Am I Getting Paid for This?: A Romance about Work* (1982); and *Last Wish* (1985). "Motherhood: Who Needs It?" originally appeared in *Look* (Sept. 22, 1970).

Ned Rorem (b. 1923)
American composer, nonfiction writer, and memoirist. Born in Richmond, Indiana, Rorem studied music at Northwestern University, the Curtis Institute, and the Julliard School before taking up teaching positions at Buffalo University, the University of Utah, and the Curtis Institute. His musical gift is matched by his powers of description; in addition to symphonic and chamber music, operas and song cycles, he has written a number of books, which include *The Paris Diary of Ned Rorem* (1966), *The New York Diary* (1967), *Critical Affairs* (1970), *Pure Contraption* (1973), *An Absolute Gift* (1978), *Setting the Tone* (1983),

and *The Nantucket Diary* (1987), from which "30 August (1981)" is taken.

Oliver Sacks (b. 1933)
Anglo-American physician and nonfiction writer. Son of parents who were medical doctors, Sacks and his three older brothers all became physicians. Educated at Queen's College, Oxford, Sacks earned his M.D. from Middlesex Hospital, London (1960), and then came to the United States for five years' advanced study at UCLA. A practicing neurologist, he has written five books: *Migraine: The Evolution of a Common Disorder* (1970; revised edition, 1985), an exploration of the mind-body connection in illness; *Awakenings* (1973), a study of Sack's controversial treatment of patients afflicted with sleeping sickness; *A Leg to Stand On* (1984), the story of his own serious injury and recovery; *The Man Who Mistook His Wife for a Hat and Other Clinical Tales* (1985), a collection of short works from which "Rebecca" comes; and *Seeing Voices: A Journey into the World of the Deaf* (1989).

Carl Sagan (b. 1934)
American astronomer, science writer, and novelist. Sagan received a Ph.D. in astronomy and astrophysics from the University of Chicago in 1960. He taught at the University of California, Berkeley, and at Harvard before joining the faculty of Cornell, where he is currently professor of astronomy and director of the Laboratory for Planetary Studies. While Sagan's early writing concerns his work as an astronomer, *The Dragons of Eden* (1977) delves into the subject of human intelligence. Like *Broca's Brain* (1979) and his television series "Cosmos," it extended Sagan's audience considerably. His novel *Contact* (1985) became a best seller. Sagan's most recent book is *A Path Where No Man Thought: Nuclear Winter and the End of the Arms Race* (1991), written with Richard Turco. "The Abstractions of Beasts" originally appeared in his Pulitzer Prize–winning book *The Dragons of Eden.*

Scott Russell Sanders (b. 1945)
American writer and teacher. Born in Tennessee and educated at Brown and Cambridge, Sanders has spent his entire teaching career in the Department of English at Indiana University, where he is now professor of English. He has written scholarly works on literature (*D. H. Lawrence: The World of the Major Nov-*

els, 1974), science fiction (*Fetching the Dead: Stories*, 1984), and studies of American places and people (*Wilderness Plots: Tales about the Settlement of the American Land*, 1983; *Audubon's Early Years*, 1984). Another work is *The Paradise of Bombs* (1987), a collection of essays on violence in the United States. "Looking at Women" originally appeared in *Georgia Review* (Spring 1989); "The Singular First Person" appeared in *Sewanee Review* (Fall 1988).

May Sarton (b. 1912)

American novelist, poet, and essayist. Born in Belgium, Sarton came to the United States as a child. The daughter of a Harvard professor, she did not attend college. Instead, she pursued a career in the theater, which she left to become a scriptwriter, then an instructor in writing. She now lives on the coast of Maine. Sarton is the author of seventeen novels, among them *The Bridge of Years* (1946), *Kinds of Love* (1970), and *A Reckoning* (1978), as well as fourteen books of poetry, including *Encounter in April* (1937), *The Land of Silence* (1953), and *A Durable Fire* (1972). She has also published several nonfiction works. The selection here comes from *Journal of a Solitude* (1973).

Jean-Paul Sartre (1905–1980)

French playwright, novelist, critic, philosopher, and political activist. After earning an advanced degree in philosophy, Sartre became a provincial schoolmaster, then a playwright and writer of philosophical essays. Described by the *New York Times* as "a rebel of a thousand causes, a modern Don Quixote," Sartre was a major force in the intellectual life of post–World War II France. His philosophy of existentialism influenced generations of artists and thinkers. Steadfastly independent, Sartre refused both the Noble Prize for Literature (1964) and the Legion of Honor. He died having completed only three volumes of a four-volume study of Gustave Flaubert. A sampling of his major works includes *The Flies* (1943), *Being and Nothingness* (1943), *No Exit* (1944), and *Life Situations* (1977). "Existentialism" is taken from *Existentialism* (1947).

Arthur M. Schlesinger, Jr. (b. 1917)

American historian, teacher, and social critic. Born in Columbus, Ohio, Schlesinger studied at Harvard University and did postgraduate work at Cambridge University. Returning to Harvard in 1946 as a professor of history, he remained there until asked to serve as special assistant to presidents Kennedy and Johnson. Since 1966 he has taught at the City University of New York as Schweitzer Professor of the Humanities. In addition to his nonacademic activities, Schlesinger has written such influential books as *The Age of Jackson* (1945; Pulitzer Prize), *The Crisis of the Old Order* (1957), *A Thousand Days* (1965; Pulitzer Prize and National Book Award), *The Imperial Presidency* (1973), and *The Cycles of American History* (1986). He has contributed many articles to magazines, newspapers, and scholarly journals. "The Opening of the American Mind" appeared in the *New York Times Book Review* (July 23, 1989).

E. F. Schumacher (1911–1977)

British economist and writer. Born in Bonn, Schumacher studied abroad in the 1930s and returned to Germany under Hitler only to flee to England in 1937. Schumacher worked for the British government during World War II, drafting theories for a welfare state. After the war, he became economic adviser to Britain's National Coal Board (1950–70). His *Small Is Beautiful* (1973), an economic study that advocates small-scale use of technology, became an international best-seller. "Levels of Being" is the second chapter in Schumacher's last book, *A Guide for the Perplexed* (1977).

Chief Seattle (c. 1786–1866)

Native American leader. A fierce young warrior, Seattle (also Seathl or Sealth) was chief of the Suquamish, Duwamish, and allied Salish-speaking tribes of the Northwest. In the 1830s, he was converted to Christianity and became an advocate of peace. Local settlers honored him and his work by naming their town Seattle. When the Port Ellicott Treaty of 1855 established reservations for native Americans, Seattle signed it and lived the rest of his life at the Port Madison Reservation. Because of his example, his people did not become involved in the bloody warfare that marked the history of the territory from 1855 until 1870. His "Address" is the reply to a treaty proffered in 1854 by Governor Isaac Stevens, commissioner of Indian Affairs for the Washington Territory. Chief Seattle died on June 7, 1866 and was buried at the Suquamish cemetery near Seattle.

Richard B. Sewall (b. 1908)

American scholar and biographer. Sewall graduated from Williams College in 1929 and, in 1933, received a Ph.D. in English from Yale University, where he taught for forty-two years. His first book, a comparative study of cultural views on tragedy, *The Vision of Tragedy*, was published in 1959. In 1974, his comprehensive *Life of Emily Dickinson* won the National Book Award for biography and the Poetry Society of America Award. Among his other works are *The Lyman Letters: New Light on Emily Dickinson and Her Family, Tragedy: Twentieth-Century Views*, and *Emily Dickinson: Twentieth-Century Views*. "A Sense of the Ending" is adapted from a convocation address delivered at Williams College; it first appeared in the *Williams Alumni Review* (Fall 1975).

Gary Soto (b. 1952)

American poet and memoirist. Born in Fresno, California, Soto studied at California State University at Fresno and the University of California at Irvine. His first two books—*The Element of San Joaquin* (1977) and *The Tale of Sunlight* (1978)—comprise a journey from urban poverty in Fresno and the dreary toil of farm work in the San Joaquin Valley, a life Soto himself has experienced. He has won a number of awards for his vital and expressive rendering of the Chicano experience in the United States, including a Guggenheim Fellowship, the Academy of American Poets Award, Discovery–The Nation Prize, and, in 1985, the American Book Award for his first volume of recollections, *Living Up the Street*. "The Pie" is taken from another book of recollections, *A Summer Life* (1990).

Brent Staples (b. 1951)

American journalist and writer. Born in Chester, Pennsylvania, Staples holds a Ph.D. in psychology from the University of Chicago. He is assistant metropolitan editor of the *New York Times*. His essay "Just Walk on By" appeared in *Ms.* magazine (Sept. 1986). An excerpt, titled "Black Men and Public Space," was published in *Harper's* (Dec. 1986).

Shelby Steele (b. 1946)

American essayist and nonfiction writer. Currently a professor of English at San Jose State University in California, Steele won a National Magazine Award in 1989, and one of his essays on race was chosen for the 1989 edition of *Best American Essays*. He is recipient, as well, of the 1991 National Book Critics Circle Award for General Nonfiction. His work has appeared in such diverse publications as *Harper's*, *The American Scholar*, the *Washington Post*, *The New Republic*, and the *New York Times Book Review*. Steele's first book, *The Content of Our Character: A New Vision of Race in America* (1990), in which "The Recoloring of Campus Life" appears, received wide critical acclaim.

Wallace Stegner (b. 1909)

American essayist, novelist, and teacher. Influenced by Twain, Cather, and Conrad, Stegner writes of the development of individuals within particular landscapes. Stegner's landscapes are often those of the American West, for he is a serious naturalist with special interest in that area. In a long career, he has written and edited more than forty books, among them the novels *Remembering Laughter* (1937), *The Big Rock Candy Mountain* (1943), and *Recapitulation* (1979), as well as historical narratives like *Mormon Country* (1941) and *The Gathering of Zion: The Story of the Mormon Trail* (1964). Stegner is a member of the Department of English at Stanford University. "The Town Dump" originally appeared in *Wolf Willow: A History, a Story, and a Memory of the Last Plains Frontier* (1963, 1980).

Gloria Steinem (b. 1934)

American essayist, journalist, and editor. After receiving a B.A. from Smith College, Steinem spent two years studying in India. On her return, she held several positions in publishing and worked as a writer for television, film, and political campaigns until 1968, when she and others founded *New York Magazine*. Founding editor of *Ms.* magazine (1971), Steinem is an influential spokesperson for the women's movement. "The Good News Is: These Are Not the Best Years of Your Life" first appeared in *Ms.* with the title "Why Young Women Are More Conservative" (Sept. 1979). It was reprinted in *Outrageous Acts and Everyday Rebellions* (1983), a collection of Steinem's essays and articles.

Jonathan Swift (1667–1745)

Anglo-Irish poet, satirist, and cleric. Born to English parents who resided in

Ireland, Swift studied at Trinity College, Dublin, then departed for London (1689). There he became part of the literary and political worlds, beginning his career by writing political pamphlets in support of the Tory cause. Ordained in the Church of Ireland (1695), Swift was appointed dean of St. Patrick's Cathedral, Dublin, in 1713 and held the post until his death. One of the master satirists of the English language, he wrote several scathing attacks on extremism, including *The Tale of a Tub* (1704), *The Battle of the Books* (1704), and *A Modest Proposal* (1729), as well as poetry, but he is probably best known for his novel *Gulliver's Travels* (1726). "The Spider and the Bee" comes from *The Battle of the Books.*

Paul Theroux (b. 1941)

American novelist, essayist, and travel writer. Born in Medford, Massachusetts, Theroux took his B.A. at the University of Massachusetts and later taught in Africa and Asia. For some time he has lived in London, at least when he has not been traveling all over the world—by railway whenever possible. Theroux's novels include *The Family Arsenal* (1976), *The Mosquito Coast* (1982), and *O-Zone* (1986). His best-known travel books are *The Great Railway Bazaar: By Train Through Asia* (1975) and *The Old Patagonian Express: By Train Through the Americas* (1979). His essays are collected in *Sunrise with Seamonsters* (1985), from which "Being a Man" is taken.

Dylan Thomas (1914–1953)

Welsh poet and writer. Born and raised in the coal-mining district of Wales, Thomas lived a turbulent life marked by chronic alcoholism that helped bring about his early death. His writing, though, particularly his recollections of childhood, reveals an awareness of the sweetness of living that is expressed in bold, inventive, often playful language. Although he is perhaps best known for his poetry, particularly the verse drama *Under Milk Wood* (1954), Thomas also wrote short stories, plays, and film scripts. *Quite Early One Morning* (1954), a collection of his reminiscences of a Welsh childhood, and especially *A Child's Christmas in Wales* (1954) have become classics. "Memories of Christmas" first appeared in *The Listener* (Dec. 20, 1945). It was later reprinted in *Quite Early One Morning.*

Lewis Thomas (b. 1913)

American physician, teacher, science writer, and humanist. Educated at Princeton and Harvard Medical School, Thomas has specialized in pediatrics, public health, and cancer research. From 1973 until 1980, he served as president of Memorial Sloan-Kettering Cancer Center in New York City; he is currently emeritus president there. In 1970, Thomas began writing occasional essays for the *New England Journal of Medicine.* A number of these, gathered in *The Lives of a Cell* (1974), established Thomas's reputation as a writer. Other collections are *The Medusa and the Snail* (1979), *The Youngest Science* (1983), *Late Night Thoughts on Listening to Mahler's Ninth Symphony* (1983), and *Et Cetera, Et Cetera* (1991). His most recent work, *The Lasker Awards: Four Decades of Scientific Medical Progress* (1986), traces developments in cancer research. "Humanities and Science" was first published in *Late Night Thoughts*; "Notes on Punctuation" and "On Magic in Medicine" originally appeared in the *New England Journal of Medicine* before publication in *The Medusa and the Snail*; "The Long Habit" appeared in *The Lives of a Cell* after having been published in the *New England Journal of Medicine.*

Henry David Thoreau (1817–1862)

American philosopher, essayist, naturalist, and poet. A graduate of Harvard, Thoreau worked at a number of jobs—schoolmaster, house painter, employee in his father's pencil factory—before becoming a writer and political activist. He became a friend of Emerson's and a member of the Transcendental Club, contributing frequently to its journal *The Dial.* Drawn to the world of nature, he wrote his first book, *A Week on the Concord and Merrimac Rivers* (1849), about his impressions. Thoreau's strong stance against slavery led to his arrest for refusing to pay the Massachusetts poll tax (an act of protest against government sanction of the Mexican War, which he viewed as serving the interests of slaveholders). His eloquent essay defending this act, "Civil Disobedience" (1849), his probing meditation on the solitary life, *Walden* (1854), and his speech, "A Plea for Captain John Brown" (1859), are classic literary documents in the history of American life and thought. "The Battle of the Ants" comes from *Walden*; "Observation" and selections printed here in "Prose Forms:

Journals" come from Thoreau's *Journal.*

James Thurber (1894–1961)
American humorist, cartoonist, essayist, and fiction writer. Born in Columbus, Ohio, Thurber attended Ohio State University. He began his career as a professional writer working for the *Columbus Dispatch* (1920–24), then moved on to the *Chicago Tribune* and the *New York Evening Post.* In 1927, encouraged by E. B. White, he became managing editor of and staff writer for *The New Yorker.* Throughout his career he contributed stories, essays, and cartoons to the magazine. Thurber wrote more than thirty books, including *The Owl in the Attic and Other Perplexities* (1931), *The Beast in Me and Other Animals* (1948), and *The Secret Life of Walter Mitty* (1939). "University Days" comes from Thurber's *My Life and Hard Times* (1933); "A Dog's Eye View of Man" comes from his *Thurber's Dogs* (1955); "The Bear Who Let It Alone," "The Rabbits Who Caused All the Trouble," and "The Owl Who Was God" come from his *Fables for Our Time* (1940).

Paul Tillich (1886–1965)
German-American philosopher and theologian. Born into a German Lutheran family and educated at several German universities, Tillich served as an army chaplain in World War I. Afterward, he joined the theology faculty of the University of Berlin. When Hitler came to power, Tillich was dismissed from the Chair of Philosophy at Frankfurt University. He fled to the United States, where he spent over twenty years on the faculty of the Union Theological Seminary in New York City. Upon retirement, he became University Professor at Harvard. Tillich's most important work, the three-volume *Systematic Theology,* was published in 1963. Among other important works are *The Eternal Now* (1963) and *A History of Christian Thought* (revised edition 1968). "The Riddle of Inequality" comes from *The Eternal Now,* a collection of Tillich's sermons.

Niko Tinbergen (b. 1907)
British zoologist. Born in the Netherlands, Tinbergen studied at the State University of Leyden, receiving his Ph.D. in zoology in 1932. Fascinated since childhood by animals, he spent fourteen months in Greenland observing arctic life. He then joined the faculty at

Leyden, conducting research on the homing habits of sand wasps, the mating rituals of butterflies, and the behavior of falcons. In 1949, he became a lecturer at Oxford. His research there on communication systems among gulls led him to the study of autistic children. In 1973, he was one of three scientists to share the Nobel Prize for Physiology or Medicine. Tinbergen's work *The Animal in Its World: Explorations of an Ethologist, 1932–1972* is widely respected. "The Bee-Hunters of Hulshorst," an essay drawn from his experiences at his parents' vacation cottage in the Netherlands, comes from a collection of Tinbergen's essays, *Curious Naturalists* (1958).

Barbara Tuchman (1912–1989)
American historian. After graduating from Radcliffe College in 1933, Tuchman worked as a research assistant for the Institute of Pacific Relations (an experience that later found expression in *Stilwell and the American Experience in China,* which won a Pulitzer Prize in 1971). During the late 1930s she wrote on politics for *The Nation,* covered the Spanish Civil War as a journalist in London, and after Pearl Harbor took a job with the Office of War Information in Washington. Critical and public acclaim followed the publication of *The Zimmerman Telegram* (1958) and *The Guns of August,* both on the origins of World War I. Her later books include *The Proud Tower* (1966) and *The March of Folly* (1984); *Practicing History* (1981) is a collection of articles, reviews, and talks. " 'This is the End of the World': The Black Death" comes from *A Distant Mirror: The Calamitous Fourteenth Century* (1978).

John Updike (b. 1932)
American poet, fiction writer, and critic. After attending Harvard and Oxford, Updike joined the staff of *The New Yorker,* beginning an association that continues today. He has written over thirty books, including collections of poetry (*The Carpentered Hen and Other Tame Creatures,* 1958; *Seventy Poems,* 1972), short stories (some collected in *The Music School,* 1966; *Trust Me,* 1987), and novels (*The Centaur,* 1963; *The Witches of Eastwick,* 1984; *Roger's Version,* 1986; and his quartet of "Rabbit" novels, the most recent *Rabbit at Rest,* 1990). Today, Updike writes occasional essays, short stories, and poems for *The New Yorker,* while serving as a regu-

lar book reviewer for that magazine. "Beer Can" originally appeared in the "Talk of the Town" section of *The New Yorker* (Jan. 18, 1964).

David Rains Wallace (b. 1945)
American essayist and environmental writer. Born in Charlottesville, Virginia, Wallace studied at Wesleyan University, Columbia University, and Mills College, shortly afterward embarking on a career as a free-lance writer specializing in ecological and environmental issues. His writing, he says, "arises from a fascination with this planet—its climate, waters, rocks, soils, plants, and animals. I want to awaken readers to the fact that we remain a part of the biosphere, that we cannot destroy it without destroying ourselves." Wallace's books include *The Dark Range: A Naturalist's Night Notebook* (1978); *Idle Weeds: The Life of a Sandstone Ridge* (1980); *The Klamath Knot: Explorations of Myth and Evolution* (1984); *The Turquoise Dragon* (1985); and *The Untamed Garden and Other Personal Essays* (1986), from which "The Mind of the Beaver" is taken.

Eudora Welty (b. 1909)
American writer, critic, amateur painter, and photographer. Born and brought up in Jackson, Mississippi, Welty has retained her deep attachment to the people and places of the South. After graduating from the University of Wisconsin in 1929 and a year's study at Columbia University's School of Business, she returned to Jackson and eventually found work as a publicity agent for the Works Progress Administration, a New Deal social agency. With the help of Robert Penn Warren and Cleanth Brooks, she had several short stories published, and her literary career was launched. Welty has published several collections of short stories, including a *Collected Stories* (1980); novellas, and novels, including *Delta Wedding* (1946), *Losing Battles* (1970), and *The Optimist's Daughter* (Pulitzer Prize, 1972); two volumes of photographs; and an acclaimed collection of critical essays, *The Eye of the Story* (1978). "Clamorous to Learn" and "One Writer's Beginnings" are excerpts from a set of three lectures delivered at Harvard in April 1983, and published as *One Writer's Beginnings* (1984).

Richard S. Westfall (b. 1924)
American professor of history and philosophy of science. Educated at Yale,

Westfall has taught at the State University of Iowa, Grinnell, and Indiana State University, where, since 1976, he has been Distinguished Professor of History. A specialist in the work of Isaac Newton, Westfall has published three books on the subject: *Development of Newton's Philosophy of Color* (1962), *Force in Newton's Physics* (1971), and *Never at Rest: A Biography of Isaac Newton* (1980). "The Career of Isaac Newton: A Scientific Life in the Seventeenth Century" originally appeared in *The American Scholar* (Summer 1981).

E. B. White (1899–1985)
American poet, journalist, editor, and essayist. After graduating from Cornell in 1921, White became a reporter, then an advertising copywriter before beginning a sixty-year career on the staff of *The New Yorker*. With Harold Ross, the magazine's founding editor, and Katharine Angell, its literary editor, White made *The New Yorker* the most important publication of its kind in the United States. He wrote poems and articles for the magazine and served as a discreet and helpful editor. Among his many books, three written for children earned him lasting fame: *Stuart Little* (1945), *Charlotte's Web* (1952), and *The Trumpet of the Swan* (1970). White revised and edited William Strunk's text *The Elements of Style,* a classic guide. "Once More to the Lake" originally appeared in "One Man's Meat," White's column for *Harper's* magazine (Oct. 1941); it was reprinted in *The Essays of E. B. White* (1977). "Progress and Change" also appeared in "One Man's Meat" (Dec. 1938); it was reprinted in a collection of the same title (1942). "Democracy" first appeared in *The New Yorker* (July 3, 1944); it was reprinted in *The Wild Flag* (1946). "Four Letters on Freedom of Expression" originally appeared as indicated in the text; these and other letters were gathered in a volume, *Letters of E. B. White,* edited by Dorothy Lobrano Guth (1976). "Some Remarks on Humor" is adapted from the preface to *A Subtreasury of American Humor,* edited by Katharine S. White and E. B. White (1941).

Walt Whitman (1819–1892)
American poet and writer. Born on Long Island and raised in Brooklyn, New York, Whitman received scant formal education before going to work at age

eleven in a newspaper office. Even though he taught school from 1835 to 1840 and worked at several government posts during his lifetime, Whitman considered himself a writer, publishing poetry, stories, and newspaper articles from the age of nineteen. In 1855, he published *Leaves of Grass*, a series of twelve poems that most scholars consider his finest work. As it evolved through a number of editions, *Leaves of Grass* came to include well over 100 poems, including "Calamus," "Crossing Brooklyn Ferry," and "Out of the Cradle Endlessly Rocking." In his poetry and prose, Whitman celebrates the landscape and people of the United States. Although he was an ardent Democrat, he supported Lincoln; indeed, Lincoln was one of the subjects of Whitman's moving elegy "When Lilacs Last in the Dooryard Bloom'd" (1865). "Abraham Lincoln" comes from Whitman's *Specimen Days* (1882), which partly consists of diary entries and newspaper articles written during the previous two decades.

Terry Tempest Williams (b. 1955)
American naturalist and nonfiction writer. Williams, currently naturalist-in-residence at the Utah Museum of Natural History in Salt Lake City, grew up surrounded by the vast desert landscape of her native Utah. She says that she writes "through my biases of gender, geography, and culture, that I am a woman whose ideas have been shaped by the Colorado Plateau and the Great Basin, that these ideas are then sorted out through the prism of my culture—and my culture is Mormon." Her first book, *Pieces of White Shell: A Journey to Navajoland* (1984), is a personal retelling and exploration of native American myths. *Coyote's Canyon* (1989) combines personal narratives of southern Utah's desert canyons with photographs by John Telford. "The Clan of One-Breasted Women" originally appeared in *Witness* (Winter 1989).

Tom Wolfe (b. 1931)
American journalist, essayist, novelist, and social commentator. After receiving a Ph.D. from Yale, Wolfe began a career in journalism that has taken him from newspapers like the *Washington Post* and *New York Herald Tribune* to magazines like *New York, Esquire,* and *Vanity Fair.* Several of Wolfe's books have established his reputation as a witty social critic and historian of popular culture:

The Kandykolored Tangerine-Flake Streamline Baby (1965), *Radical Chic and Mau-Mauing the Flak Catchers* (1970), *From Bauhaus to Our House* (1981), and *Bonfire of the Vanities* (1987), his scathing satirical novel. Wolfe's chronicle of the American space program, *The Right Stuff* (1979), became a successful film. "Land of Wizards" appeared in *Best American Essays* (1987).

Virginia Woolf (1882–1941)
English novelist, critic, and essayist. The daughter of respected philosopher and writer Sir Leslie Stephen, Woolf educated herself by unrestricted reading in her father's library. She lived at the center of the "Bloomsbury Group," a celebrated gathering of artists, scholars, and writers. Woolf, together with her husband socialist writer Leonard Woolf, founded the Hogarth Press. Her work, whether it be nonfiction or fiction, is marked by a resonant autobiographical voice. *A Room of One's Own* (1929), an historical investigation of women and creativity; *Mrs. Dalloway* (1925), *To the Lighthouse* (1927), and *The Waves* (1931), novels about artistic consciousness and the development of personality; *The Common Reader* (1925, 1932), collections of essays on topics as diverse as literature and automobiles, reveal penetrating intelligence as well as innovations in narrative technique. "My Father: Leslie Stephen," originally titled "Leslie Stephen, the Philosopher at Home: A Daughter's Memories," was first published in the London *Times* (Nov. 28, 1932), the centenary of his birth; it was later reprinted in *Atlantic Monthly* (Mar. 1950) and in a collection of Woolf's essays, *The Captain's Death Bed* (1950). "The Death of the Moth" first appeared in a collection of essays bearing that title (1942). "What the Novelist Gives Us" comes from the essay "How Should One Read a Book?" in *The Second Common Reader* (1932). "In Search of a Room of One's Own" comes from *A Room of One's Own.*

William Zinsser (b. 1922)
American journalist, writer, and teacher. After graduating from Princeton in 1944 and serving in the army for two years, Zinsser joined the staff of the *New York Herald Tribune* (1946–59), first as a features editor, then as a drama editor and film critic, and finally as an editorial writer. In 1959, he became a free-lance

writer, joining the English faculty at Yale University from 1971 until 1979. Zinsser is the author of more than a dozen books, among them the well-known *On Writing Well: An Informal Guide to Writing Non-Fiction* (1976; revised edition, 1980), and *Writing with a Word-Processor* (1983). "College Pressures" originally appeared in *Blair and Ketchum's Country Journal* (Apr. 1979).

Acknowledgments

Abbey: "The Serpents of Paradise" from *Desert Solitaire* by Edward Abbey. Reprinted by permission of Don Congdon Associates, Inc. Copyright © 1988 by Edward Abbey.

Ackerman: "Mass Meeting on the Coast" by Diane Ackerman. Originally appeared in *Life*, May 1987. Copyright © 1987 by Diane Ackerman. Reprinted by permission of the author.

Aesop: "The Frogs Desiring a King" reprinted by permission of Prestige Books Inc.

Allen: "Selections from the Allen Notebooks" from *Without Feathers* by Woody Allen. Copyright © 1973 by Woody Allen. Reprinted by permission of Random House, Inc.

Angelou: "Graduation" from *I Know Why the Caged Bird Sings* by Maya Angelou. Copyright © 1969 by Maya Angelou. Reprinted by permission of Random House, Inc.

Arendt: "Denmark and the Jews" from *Eichmann in Jerusalem* by Hannah Arendt. Copyright © 1963, 1964 by Hannah Arendt. Used by permission of Viking Penguin, a division of Penguin Books USA Inc.

Asimov: "The Eureka Phenomenon," Copyright © 1971 by Mercury Press, Inc. from *The Left Hand of the Electron* by Isaac Asimov. Used by permission of Doubleday, a division of Bantam Doubleday Dell Publishing Group, Inc.

Auden: "Apothegms" plus 3 paragraphs from *The Dyer's Hand* by W. H. Auden. Copyright 1948, 1950, 1952, 1953, 1954, 1956, 1960, 1962 by W. H. Auden. Reprinted by permission of Random House, Inc.

Baker: "Surely Not Cigar-Shaped!" from the *New York Times*, Aug. 8, 1987. Copyright © 1987 by The New York Times Company. Reprinted by permission.

Baldwin: "Stranger in the Village" from *Notes of a Native Son* by James Baldwin. Copyright © 1955, renewed 1983, by James Baldwin. Reprinted by permission of Beacon Press.

Becker: "Democracy" from *Modern Democracy* by Carl L. Becker. Copyright © 1941 by Yale University Press. Reprinted by permission of Yale University Press.

Bennett: "Address" by William Bennett. Reprinted by permission of the author.

Bernstein: "SN–1987 A" by Jeremy Bernstein. Reprinted from *The American Scholar*, Vol. 57, No. 2, Spring 1988. Copyright © 1988 by the author.

Bettelheim: "A Victim" from *The Informed Heart* by Bruno Bettelheim. Copyright © 1960 by The Free Press, renewed 1988 by Bruno Bettelheim. Reprinted with permission of The Free Press, a division of Macmillan, Inc.

Bird: "College Is a Waste of Time and Money" from *The Case Against College* by Caroline Bird. Reprinted by permission of the author.

Bly: "Bruno Bettelheim" from *Letters from the Country* by Carol Bly. Copyright © 1981 by Carol Bly. Reprinted by permission of HarperCollins Publishers.

Boorstin: "The Historian: 'A Wrestler with an Angel' " from *Hidden History* by Daniel J. Boorstin. Copyright © 1987 by Daniel J. Boorstin. Reprinted by permission of the author.

Booth: "Is There Any Knowledge That a Man *Must* Have" from *The Knowledge Most Worth Having* by Wayne C. Booth. Copyright © by the University of Chicago Press. Reprinted by permission of the University of Chicago Press. "Boring from Within: The Art of the Freshman Essay" from an address to the Illinois Council of College Teachers in 1963. Copyright © Wayne C. Booth. Reprinted by permission of the author.

Bronowski: "The Nature of Scientific Reasoning" from *Science and Human Values* by Jacob Bronowski. Copyright © 1956, 1965 by Jacob Bronowski; renewed 1984 by Rita Bronowski. Reprinted by permission of Julian Messner Books, a division of Simon & Schuster, Inc. "The Reach of Imagination," delivered as the Blashfield Address, May 1966. Reprinted by permission from the *Proceedings of the American Academy of Arts and Letters and National Institute of Arts and Letters*, 2nd Ser., No. 17, 1967.

1275

Broyard: "Intoxicated by My Illness" from the *New York Times Magazine*, Nov. 12, 1989. Copyright © 1989 by The New York Times Company. Reprinted by permission.

Bruner: "Freud and the Image of Man" by Jerome S. Bruner. Originally appeared in *Partisan Review*, Vol. 23, No. 3, 1956. Reprinted by permission of the author.

Burgess: "Is America Falling Apart?" from the *New York Times Magazine*, Nov. 7, 1971. Copyright © 1971 by The New York Times Company. Reprinted by permission.

Butterfield: "The Originality of the Old Testament" from *Writings on Christianity and History* edited by C. T. MacIntire. Copyright © 1979 by Oxford University Press, Inc. Reprinted by permission.

Carr: "The Historian and His Facts" from *What Is History?* by Edward Hallett Carr. Copyright © 1961 by Edward Hallett Carr. Reprinted by permission of Alfred A. Knopf, Inc.

Cohen: "The Case for the Use of Animals in Biomedical Research," No. 315, Oct. 1986. Reprinted by permission of the *New England Journal of Medicine.*

Cooke: "Doctor and Patient: Face to Face" from *The Patient Has the Floor* by Alistair Cooke. Copyright © 1986 by Alistair Cooke. Reprinted by permission of Alfred A. Knopf, Inc.

Copland: "How We Listen" from *What to Listen for in Music* by Aaron Copland. Copyright © 1957. Reprinted by permission of McGraw-Hill Book Company.

Cowley: "The View from 80" is reprinted from *The View from 80* by Malcolm Cowley. Copyright © 1976, 1978, 1980 by Malcolm Cowley. Reprinted by permission of Viking Penguin, a division of Penguin Books USA Inc.

Cummings: "the first president to be loved by his" from *ViVa* by E. E. Cummings, edited by George James Firmage. Copyright © 1931, 1959 by E.E. Cummings. Copyright © 1979, 1973 by the trustees of the E.E. Cummings Trust. Copyright © 1979, 1973 by George James Firmage. Reprinted by permission of Liveright Publishing Corporation.

Davies: "Ham and Tongue" from *One Half of Robertson Davies.* Copyright © 1977 by Robertson Davies. Used by permission of Viking Penguin, a division of Penguin Books USA Inc.

Didion: "On Keeping a Notebook" and "On Going Home" from *Slouching Towards Bethlehem* by Joan Didion. Copyright © 1966, 1967, 1968 by Joan Didion. Reprinted by permission of Farrar, Straus & Giroux, Inc.

Dillard: "Sight into Insight" from *Harper's* magazine, Feb. 1974. Copyright © 1974 by Annie Dillard. Reprinted by permission of the author and her agent Blanche C. Gregory, Inc. "About Symbol" excerpted from *Living by Fiction.* Copyright © 1982 by Annie Dillard. Reprinted by permission of HarperCollins Publishers, Inc. "Terwilliger Bunts One" excerpt from *An American Childhood.* Copyright © 1987 by Annie Dillard. Reprinted by permission of HarperCollins Publishers Inc.

Dobbs: "The Shatterer of Worlds" from *Reading the Time* by Kildare Dobbs. Copyright © Kildare Dobbs 1968. Reprinted with permission of Kildare Dobbs.

Dobbs: "Gallipoli" by Kildare Dobbs. Reprinted by permission of the author.

Ehrlich: "The Solace of Open Spaces" from *The Solace of Open Spaces* by Gretel Ehrlich. Copyright © 1985 by Gretel Ehrlich. Used by permission of Viking Penguin, a division of Penguin Books USA Inc. "Spring" originally appeared in *Antaeus* 1986. Copyright © 1986 by Gretel Ehrlich. Reprinted by permission of the author.

Eiseley: "The Brown Wasps" from *The White Country* by Loren Eiseley. Copyright © 1971 by Loren Eiseley. Reprinted with permission of Charles Scribner's Sons, an imprint of Macmillan Publishing Company

Daniel Mark Epstein: "The Case of Harry Houdini" from *The Star of Wonder* by Daniel Mark Epstein. Copyright © 1986 by Daniel Mark Epstein. Published by the Overlook Press, Lewis Hollow Road, Woodstock, New York 12498. Reprinted by permission of the Overlook Press.

Edward Jay Epstein: "The Selection of Reality" from *What's News: The Media on American Society* by Edward Jay Epstein. Reprinted by permission of the Institute for Contemporary Studies.

Faulkner: "Nobel Prize Award Speech." From *Essays, Speeches and Public Letters by William Faulkner* by William Faulkner, ed. by James Meriwether. Copyright © 1965 Random House, Inc. Reprinted by permission of Random House, Inc.

Finch: "Being at Two with Nature" by Robert Finch. Originally appeared in *The Georgia Review*, March 1991. Reprinted by permission of the author.

Fisher: "Moment of Wisdom" from *Sister Age* by M. F. K. Fisher. Copyright © 1983 by M. F. K. Fisher. Reprinted by permission of Alfred A. Knopf, Inc.

FitzGerald: "Rewriting American History" from *America Revised: History Schoolbooks in the Twentieth Century* by Frances FitzGerald. Copyright © 1979 by Frances FitzGerald. First appeared in *The New Yorker.*

Fromm: "The Nature of Symbolic Language" from *The Forgotten Language* by Erich Fromm.

Jung: "The Poet" from *Modern Man in Search of a Soul* by C. G. Jung. Published by Routledge & Kegan Paul Ltd., London 1933. Reprinted by permission.

Keller: "Women in Science: A Social Analysis." Copyright © 1974 *Harvard Magazine*. Reprinted with permission.

King: "Letter from Birmingham Jail" from *Why We Can't Wait* by Martin Luther King, Jr. Copyright © 1963, 1964 by Martin Luther King, Jr.; copyright © renewed 1991 by Coretta Scott King. Reprinted by permission of HarperCollins Publishers Inc.

Kingston: "Tongue-Tied" from *The Woman Warrior* by Maxine Hong Kingston. Copyright © 1975, 1976, by Maxine Hong Kingston. Reprinted by permission of Alfred A. Knopf, Inc.

Knox: "The Nature of Enthusiasm" from *Enthusiasm* by Ronald A. Knox. Reprinted by permission of A P Watt Limited on behalf of The Earl of Oxford & Asquith.

Koestler: "Gravity and the Holy Ghost" from *The Act of Creation* by Arthur Koestler. Reprinted with permission of Peters Fraser & Dunlop Limited.

Krutch: "The Most Dangerous Predator" from *The Best Nature Writing of Joseph Wood Krutch*. Copyright © 1961 by Joseph Wood Krutch. Reprinted by permission of William Morrow & Company, Inc. Publishers, New York.

Kübler-Ross: "On the Fear of Death" from *On Death and Dying* by Elisabeth Kübler-Ross. Copyright © 1969 by Elisabeth Kübler-Ross. Reprinted by permission from Macmillan Publishing Company.

Kuhn: "The Route to Normal Science" from *The Structure of Scientific Revolutions* by Thomas S. Kuhn. Reprinted by permission of the University of Chicago Press.

Langer: "Expressiveness" Copyright © 1957 by Susanne K. Langer; copyright renewed © 1985 by Leonard Langer. Reprinted by permission of Macmillan Publishing Company from *Problems of Art* by Susanne K. Langer.

Laurence: "Where the World Began." Copyright © 1976 by Margaret Laurence. Reprinted with the permission of the Estate of Margaret Laurence.

Leopold: "Thinking Like a Mountain" from *A Sand County Almanac: And Sketches Here and There* by Aldo Leopold. Copyright © 1949, 1977 by Oxford University Press, Inc. Reprinted by permission.

Lessing: "My Father" from *A Small Personal Voice* by Doris Lessing. Copyright © 1963 by Doris Lessing. Reprinted by permission of Curtis Brown Group Ltd.

Levin: "The Case for Torture" from *Newsweek*, June 7, 1982. Copyright © 1982 by Michael Levin. Reprinted by permission of the author.

Lewis: "The Culture of Poverty" originally appeared in *Scientific American*, October 1966. Copyright © 1966 by Oscar Lewis. Reprinted by permission of Harold Ober Associates Incorporated.

Lippmann: "The Indispensable Opposition" from *The Atlantic Monthly*, Aug. 1939. Copyright © 1939 ® 1967 The Atlantic Monthly Company, Boston, Mass. Reprinted with permission of the President and Fellows of Harvard Collage.

Lopez: "The Stone Horse" by Barry Lopez. Originally appeared in *Antaeus*, Autumn 1986. Copyright © 1986 by Barry Lopez. Reprinted by permission of Sterling Lord Literistic, Inc.

Lorenz: "The Taming of the Shrew" from *King Solomon's Ring* by Konrad Lorenz, translated by Marjorie Kerr Wilson. Copyright © 1952 by Harper & Row Publishers, Inc. Reprinted by permission of Methuen & Co.

Lowes: "Time in the Middle Ages" from *Geoffrey Chaucer* by John Livingston Lowes. Copyright © 1934 by John Livingston Lowes. Copyright © renewed 1955 by John Wilbur Lowes. Reprinted by permission of Houghton Mifflin Company.

Machiavelli: "The Morals of the Prince" reprinted from *The Prince* by Niccolò Machiavelli, translated by Robert M. Adams. A Norton Critical Edition. Copyright © 1977 by W. W. Norton & Company, Inc. Reprinted by permission of W. W. Norton & Company, Inc.

Mairs: "Who Are You?" from the *New York Times Magazine*, Aug. 13, 1989. Copyright © 1989 by The New York Times Company. Reprinted by permission.

Mano: "How to Keep from Getting Mugged" from *Street Smarts* by D. Keith Mano. Originally appeared in *Playboy Magazine*, July 1982. Reprinted by permission of the author. D. Keith Mano's most recent novel is *Topless* (Random House, August 1991).

Maynard: "And Therefore I Have Sailed the Seas . . ." from *The Tree of Life* by Fredelle Bruser Maynard. Copyright © 1988 by Fredelle Bruser Maynard. Reproduced by permission of Rona and Joyce Maynard.

Maynard, Joyce: "Four Generations" from the *New York Times*, Apr. 12, 1979. Copyright © 1979 by The New York Times Company. Reprinted by permission.

McCullough: "The Unexpected Mrs. Stowe" from *American Heritage* Vol. 24, No. 5. Copyright © 1973 by American Heriage, a Division of Forbes, Inc. Reprinted by permission.

McGuigan: "To Be a Woman and a Scholar" from *LSA Magazine*, Fall 1978. Reprinted with permission.

McMurtry: "Kill 'Em! Crush 'Em! Eat 'Em Raw!" from *Macleans*, Oct. 1971. Copyright © 1971 John McMurtry. Reprinted by permission.

McNamara: "The State of Ireland" originally appeared in *LSA Magazine*, Spring 1988. Reprinted with permission from *LSA Magazine*.

Mead: "Home and Travel" from *Blackberry Winter* by Margaret Mead. Copyright © 1972 by Margaret Mead. Reprinted by permission of William Morrow & Company, Inc. Publishers, New York.

Mencken: "Gamalielese" from *The Baltimore Sun*, Mar. 7, 1921. Courtesy of Enoch Pratt Free Library, in accordance with the terms of the will of H. L. Mencken.

Midgley: "Trying Out One's New Sword" from *Heart and Mind* (1981) by Mary Midgley. Reprinted by permission of St. Martin's Press Inc.

Miller and Swift: "Who Is in Charge of the English Language?" first appeared in *The Exchange*, No. 62. Reprinted by permission of the authors.

Mitchell: "The Voice of Sisera" from *Less Than Words Can Say* (1981) by Richard Mitchell. Copyright © 1979 by Richard Mitchell. By permission of Little, Brown & Company.

Mitford: "Behind the Formaldehyde Curtain" from *The American Way of Death* by Jessica Mitford. Copyright © 1963 by Jessica Mitford. Reprinted by permission of Jessica Mitford. All rights reserved.

Momaday: "The Way to Rainy Mountain" from *The Way to Rainy Mountain* by N. Scott Momaday. Copyright © 1969 by The University of New Mexico Press. First published in the *Reporter*, Jan. 26, 1967.

Morris: "Territorial Behavior" from *Manwatching: A Field Guide to Human Behavior* (1977) by Desmond Morris. Text copyright © 1977 by Desmond Morris. Published by Harry N. Abrams, Inc. All rights reserved.

Morrow: "Imprisoning Time in a Rectangle" from *Time*, Fall 1989 issue. Copyright © 1989 The Time Inc. Magazine Company. Reprinted by permission.

Munro: "What Is Real?" by Alice Munro. Originally appeared in *Making it New: Contemporary Canadian Stories* edited by John Metcalf. Copyright © 1982 by Alice Munro. Reprinted by permission of Methuen Books.

Nabokov: "Good Readers and Good Writers" from *Lectures on Literature*. Copyright © 1980 by the Estate of Vladimir Nabokov. Reprinted by permission of Harcourt Brace Jovanovich, Inc.

Naylor: "Mommy, What does 'Nigger' Mean?" from the *New York Times Magazine*, Feb. 20, 1986. Copyright © 1986 by Gloria Naylor. Reprinted by permission of Sterling Lord Literistic, Inc.

Oates: "On Boxing" from the *New York Times Magazine*, June 16, 1985. Copyright © 1985 by The New York Times Company. Reprinted by permission.

Orwell: "Politics and the English Language" copyright © 1946 by Sonia Brownell Orwell, renewed 1974 by Sonia Orwell. "Shooting an Elephant" copyright © 1950 by Sonia Brownell Orwell, renewed 1978 by Sonia Pitt-Rivers. Both selections reprinted from *Shooting an Elephant and Other Essays* by George Orwell. Both selections reprinted by permission of Harcourt, Brace, Jovanovich, Inc. and the estate of the late Sonia Brownall Orwell and Martin Seckter & Warburg, Ltd.

Perry: "Examsmanship and the Liberal Arts: A Study in Educational Epistemology" from *Examining in Harvard College: A Collection of Essays*, by members of the Harvard Faculty. Copyright © 1963. Reprinted by permission of Harvard University Press.

Petrunkevitch: "The Spider and the Wasp" from *Scientific American*, Aug. 1952. Copyright © 1952 by Scientific American, Inc. Reprinted by permission of the publisher. All rights reserved.

Pirsig: "Concrete, Brick, and Neon" from *Zen and the Art of Motorcycle Maintenance* by Robert M. Pirsig. Copyright © 1974 by Robert M. Pirsig. Reprinted by permission of William Morrow & Company.

Pogrebin: "It Still Takes a Bride and Groom" from the *New York Times Magazine*, July 2, 1989. Copyright © 1989 by The New York Times Company. Reprinted by permission.

Regan: "The Case for Animal Rights" from *In Defense of Animals* by Tom Regan. Copyright © 1985 by Tom Regan. Reprinted by permission of Basil Blackwell Inc.

Rich: "Taking Women Students Seriously" and "When We Dead Awaken: Writing as Revision" from *On Lies, Secrets, and Silence: Selected Prose, 1966–1978* by Adrienne Rich. Copyright © 1979 by W. W. Norton & Company, Inc. Reprinted by permission of W. W. Norton & Company Inc.

Rodriguez: "Aria" from *Hunger of Memory* by Richard Rodriguez. Copyright © 1982 by Richard Rodriguez. Reprinted by permission of David R. Godine, Publisher.

Rollin: "Motherhood: Who Needs It?" from *Look* magazine, Sept. 22, 1970. Copyright © 1970 by WESH-TV Broadcasting Company.

Rorem: "The Nantucket Diary of Ned Rorem, 1973–1985." Copyright © 1987 by Ned Rorem. Reprinted by permission of Georges Borchardt, Inc. for Ned Rorem.

Sacks: "Rebecca" from *The Man Who Mistook His Wife for a Hat* by Oliver Sacks. Copyright © 1970, 1981, 1983, 1984, 1985 by Oliver Sacks. Reprinted by permission of Summit Books, a division of Simon & Schuster, Inc.

Sagan: "The Abstractions of Beasts" from *The Dragons of Eden* by Carl Sagan. Copyright © 1979 Carl Sagan. Reprinted by permission of the author. All rights reserved.

Sanders: "Looking at Women" from *Secrets of the Universe* by Scott Russell Sanders. Copyright © 1991 by Scott Russell Sanders. Reprinted by permission of Beacon Press. "The Singular First Person" by Scott Russell Sanders first appeared in *The Sewanee Review*, Vol. 96 (Fall 1988). Copyright © 1988 by Scott Russell Sanders. Reprinted by permission of the editor.

Sarton: Excerpts reprinted from *Journal of a Solitude* by May Sarton. Copyright © 1973 by May Sarton. Reprinted by permission of W. W. Norton & Company, Inc.

Sartre: "Existentialism" from *Existentialism* by Jean-Paul Sartre. Reproduced by permission of Philosophical Library Publishers.

Schlesinger: "The Opening of the American Mind" by Arthur M. Schlesinger, Jr. Copyright © 1989 by The New York Times Company. Reprinted by permission. "Letters in Response" appeared in the *New York Times Book Review* August 13, 1989. Copyright © 1989 by The New York Times Company. Reprinted with permission of the respondents.

Schumacher: "Levels of Being" excerpt from *Guide for the Perplexed* by E. F. Schumacher. Copyright © 1977 by E. F. Schumacher. Reprinted by permission of HarperCollins Publishers Inc.

Sewall: "A Sense of the Ending." Reprinted by permission of the author.

Sloan: "Handgun Regulations, Crime, Assaults, and Homicide: A Tale of Two Cities" from the *New England Journal of Medicine*, Vol. 319, pp. 1256–1262, 1988. Copyright © 1988 Massachusetts Medical Society.

Soto: "The Pie" from *A Summer Life* by Gary Soto. Copyright © 1990 by Gary Soto. Reprinted by permission of University Press of New England.

Staples: "Black Men and Public Space" first appeared as "Just Walk on By," in *Ms.* magazine, Sept. 1986. Copyright © 1986 by Brent Staples. Reprinted by permission.

Steele: "The Recoloring of Campus Life." Copyright © 1989 by Harper's Magazine. Reprinted from the February issue by special permission. All rights reserved.

Stegner: "The Town Dump" from *Wolf Willow* by Wallace Stegner. Copyright © 1955, 1957, 1958, 1959, 1962 by Wallace Stegner. Reprinted by permission of Brandt & Brandt Literary Agents, Inc.

Steinem: "The Good News Is: These Are Not the Best Years of Your Life" from *Ms.* magazine, Sept. 1979. Copyright © Gloria Steinem. Reprinted by permission.

Stevens: "The Motive for Metaphor" from *The Collected Poems of Wallace Stevens* by Wallace Stevens. Copyright © 1947 by Wallace Stevens. Reprinted by permission of Alfred A. Knopf, Inc.

Theroux: "Being a Man" from *Sunrises with Seamonsters: Travels and Discoveries* by Paul Theroux. Copyright © 1985 by Cape Cod Scriveners Co. Reprinted by permission of Houghton Mifflin Company. All rights reserved.

Dylan Thomas: "Memories of Christmas" from *Quite Early One Morning* by Dylan Thomas. Copyright © 1954 by New Directions Publishing Corporation. Reprinted by permission of New Directions. Also published by J. M. Dent & Sons Ltd. and reprinted by permission of David Higham Associates Limited.

Lewis Thomas: "Notes on Punctuation" from *The Medusa and the Snail: More Notes of a Biology Watcher* by Lewis Thomas. Copyright © 1979 by Lewis Thomas. Originally published in the *New England Journal of Medicine*. "On Magic in Medicine" from *The Medusa and the Snail* by Lewis Thomas. Copyright © 1978 by Lewis Thomas. "Humanities and Science" from *Late Night Thoughts on Listening to Mahler's Ninth Symphony* by Lewis Thomas. Copyright © 1983 by Lewis Thomas. Reprinted by permission of Viking Penguin, a division of Penguin Books USA Inc. " The Long Habit" from *The Lives of the Cell* by Lewis Thomas. Copyright © 1972 by the Massachusetts Medical Society. Originally published in the *New England Journal of Medicine*.

Thurber: "University Days" from *My life and Hard Times*. Copyright © 1933, 1961 by James Thurber. Reprinted by permission of HarperCollins Publishers Inc. "The Bear Who Let It Alone," "The Rabbits Who Caused All the Trouble," and "The Owl Who Was God" from *Fables of Our Time* by James Thurber. Copyright © 1940 by James Thurber. Copyright © 1968 Helen Thurber. Reprinted by permission of Helen Thurber. "A Dog's Eye View of

Man" from *Thurber's Dogs* by James Thurber. Copyright © 1955 James Thurber. Reprinted by permission of Helen Thurber.

Tillich: "The Riddle of Inequality" from *The Eternal Now* by Paul Tillich. Copyright © 1963 by Paul Tillich. Reprinted with permission of Charles Scribner's Sons, an imprint of Macmillan Publishing Company.

Tinbergen: "The Bee-Hunters of Hulshorst" from *Curious Naturalists* by Nikolaas Tinbergen. Reprinted by permission of the author.

Tuchman: " 'This Is the End of the World': The Black Death" from *A Distant Mirror* by Barbara W. Tuchman. Copyright © 1978 by Barbara W. Tuchman. Reprinted by permission of Alfred A. Knopf, Inc.

Updike: "Beer Can" from *Assorted Prose* by John Updike. Copyright © 1964 by John Updike. Reprinted by permission of Alfred A. Knopf, Inc. Originally appeared in *The New Yorker.*

Wallace: "The Mind of the Beaver" from *The Untamed Garden and Other Personal Essays* (1986) by David Rains Wallace. Reprinted by permission of the author.

Welty: "Clamorous to Learn" from *One Writer's Beginnings* by Eudora Welty. Copyright © 1983, 1984 by Eudora Welty. Reprinted by permission of Harvard University Press.

Westfall: "The Career of Isaac Newton" from *The American Scholar*, Vol. 50, No. 3, Summer 1981. Copyright © 1981 by the author.

White: "Once More to the Lake" from *Essays of E. B. White.* Copyright © 1941 by E. B. White. Reprinted by permission of HarperCollins Publishers. "Progress and Change" from *One Man's Meat* by E. B. White. Copyright © 1938 by E. B. White. Reprinted by permission of HarperCollins Publishers. "Democracy" from *The Wild Flag* by E. B. White. Copyright © 1943, 1971 E. B. White. Published by Houghton Mifflin. Originally appeared in *The New Yorker.* "Some Remarks on Humor" from *The Second Tree from the Corner* by E. B. White. Copyright © 1954 by E. B. White. Reprinted by permission of HarperCollins Publishers.

Williams: "The Clan of One-Breasted Women" first published in *Witness*, Vol. 3, No. 4, Winter 1989, New Nature Writing.

Wolfe: "Land of Wizards" by Tom Wolfe. Reprinted by permission of International Creative Management, Inc. Copyright © 1985 by Tom Wolfe.

Woolf: "Ellen Terry" and "My Father: Leslie Stephen," from *The Captain's Death Bed and Other Essays* by Virginia Woolf. Copyright © 1950, 1978 by Harcourt Brace Jovanovich, Inc. "The Death of the Moth" from *The Death of the Moth and Other Essays* by Virginia Woolf. Copyright © 1942 by Harcourt Brace Jovanovich, Inc., renewed 1970 by Marjorie T. Parsons, Executrix. Reprinted by permission of Harcourt Brace Jovanovich, Inc. All selections reprinted by permission of the Author's Literary Estate and The Hogarth Press.

Zen Parables: Permission for three Zen parables from *Zen Flesh, Zen Bones* granted by the Charles E. Tuttle Publishing Company.

Zinsser: "College Pressures" from *Blair & Ketchum's Country Journal*, Vol. 6, No. 4, Apr. 1979. Copyright © 1979 by William K. Zinsser. Reprinted by permission of the author.

Index